"Not only does Harley Hahn know more about the Intern[e]... actually makes learning fun. If the original yellow pages were this entertaining, I'd spend my spare time reading the phone book."

— *Alan Colmes*
National radio talk show host

"*The Internet* [*Golden Directory*] is an excellent guide to the Internet for Net users of any level. With this book, you will be able to find whatever information you need, quickly and easily. A terrific reference to have sitting beside your desk late at night. The completeness of this book will surprise even the most seasoned Net user."

— *Bill Schwartz*
System Manager, Auggie BBS and BBSLIST
Network Manager, 3M Corporation

"The Internet is the world's largest information appliance, and *The Internet* [*Golden Directory*] is your handbook for the 1990s. Welcome to the largest resource of human knowledge ever accumulated: just be sure to keep the [*Golden Directory*] handy."

— *Iain Lea*
Creator of the tin Usenet newsreader
Engineer and programmer, Siemens AG

"Harley Hahn's *The Internet* [*Golden Directory*] promises indeed to be the book that gets used. It's the best reference list of Internet services we've ever seen."

— *Jack Rickard*
Publisher, Boardwatch *Magazine*

"In the hotel rooms of the near future — in between the Gideon Bible and the modem jack — there will be a copy of *The Internet* [*Golden Directory*]. What a fun book! Harley Hahn is the wizard of the Internet."

— *Jean Armour Polly*
Author of Surfing the Internet
Director of User Services, NYSERNet

"It's amazing how much information is freely available on the Internet. But to make use of it, you have to know where to find what you want. *The Internet* [*Golden Directory*] is just the book to help you. Well organized, comprehensive, and fun to browse — this book will show you how to find everything from obscure song lyrics to Woody Allen jokes to the first million digits of PI."

— *Joe Halpern*
Research Staff Member, IBM Almaden Research Center
Consulting Professor, Stanford University, Computer Science Department

"This book has replaced all the scraps of paper with my notes about the tons of important things I have found around the Net. Now whenever anyone asks me where something is, I just look it up in *The Internet* [*Golden Directory*] (which is always next to my terminal). My advice is to sit down with this book — and about 10 hours of spare time — and start exploring."

— *Lee Brintle*
System Manager, University of Iowa Campus-Wide Information System
Director of Project Panda

"As an information specialist, I pride myself on keeping up with the Internet's vast resources. *The Internet* [*Golden Directory*] contains everything I expected and a whole lot more. This book is unique, comprehensive, indispensable — and funny. I lug it around with me wherever I go, and so will you."

— Mary A. Axford, MLS
Reference Librarian, Georgia Institute of Technology

"Imagine what it would be like if we didn't have the telephone yellow pages and you couldn't find a plumber on Christmas Eve. Having this book is like being handed a wrench when you are knee deep in water. *The Internet* [*Golden Directory*] is a *must-have* for anyone attempting to use the Internet."

— Maureen O'Gara
Publisher, Unigram•X *and* Client Server NEWS

"Once again Harley Hahn has shown himself to be a member of that rare breed: a writer who is at once informative and entertaining. *The Internet* [*Golden Directory*] contains an astonishing amount of Net-related information in a style that is both clear and enjoyable. I recommend this massive directory of resources to anyone who is interested in exploring the Internet in all its curious charm."

— Michael Tucker
Executive Editor, Sun Expert *Magazine*

"This is a great book to skim through while you're downloading files from the Internet, and then you'll find other files you have to download, and faster than you can double grains of wheat on the squares of a checker board you'll have no life, and soon after that you'll have no time to read the stuff you downloaded before you had this goddamn book."

— Penn "informationsuperhighwayhangin'" Jillette
Magician and humorist (the big one of Penn and Teller)

"This trailblazing work has been sorely needed. A truly inspired solution to the vast tangle of information the Internet is becoming. What a COOL book to add to anyone's library!"

— Simona Nass
President, The Society for Electronic Access

"I have introduced countless people to the Internet, and the first thing they ask me is: Where's the cool stuff? I tell them: My personal favorite Net resource is *The Internet* [*Golden Directory*]. This is the place *I* go to when I need to find out where I can talk to people about Spam."

— Stacy Horn
Founder and President of Echo (East Coast Hang Out)
Professor, New York University, Interactive Telecommunications Program

"This book is essential for every Internet user. You need it. Buy it."

—Sara Rushniek
Professor of Computer Information, University of Miami

THE INTERNET GOLDEN DIRECTORY

SECOND EDITION

Harley Hahn
and
Rick Stout

Osborne McGraw-Hill

Berkeley New York St. Louis San Francisco Auckland Bogot   Hamburg London
Madrid Mexico City Milan Montreal New Delhi Panama City Paris São Paulo
Singapore Sydney Tokyo Toronto

THE INTERNET GOLDEN DIRECTORY

SECOND EDITION

OSBORNE MCGRAW-HILL
2600 TENTH STREET
BERKELEY, CALIFORNIA 94710
U.S.A.

For information on translations or book distributors outside of the U.S.A., please write to Osborne **McGraw-Hill** at the above address.

34567890 SEM SEM 9098765

ISBN 0-07-882107-x

To The Little Nipper.

—Harley Hahn

To my lovely wife Dawn, my daughter Jenna, and my new son Alexander.

—Rick Stout

About the Authors . . .

Harley Hahn
is an internationally recognized author, analyst and consultant. He is the author of 15 books, including Osborne's best-selling **The Internet Complete Reference**, and such other titles as **Open Computing Unix Unbound**, **Assembler Inside & Out**, **A Student's Guide to Unix** and the well-known **Peter Norton's Guide to Unix**. Hahn has a degree in mathematics and computer science from the University of Waterloo, Canada, and a graduate degree in computer science from the University of California, at San Diego.

Rick Stout
is a Certified Public Accountant and holds degrees in business administration and accounting. Formerly a consulting manager at the accounting firm of Ernst & Young, Stout is a specialist in business computer and accounting systems. He is the author of several books, including **The Peter Norton Introduction to Computers**, and a coauthor of Osborne's acclaimed **The Internet Complete Reference**.

Table of Contents

Introduction xxx
The Internet and This Book xxxiii
Acknowledgments xxxv

AGRICULTURE 1
Advanced Technology Information
    Network 1
Agricultural Biotechnology Center 1
Agricultural, Flood, Food Supply
    Information 1
Agricultural Genome Resources 1
Agricultural Mailing List 1
Agricultural Software 1
Aquaculture Network Information
    Center 2
Bee Biology 2
Beekeeping 2
Beekeeping Web Page 3
Chinchilla Farming 3
Clemson University Forestry and
    Agriculture Network 3
Commodity Market Reports 3
Cornell Extension Network 3
Farming and Agriculture 4
Florida Agricultural Information
    Retrieval System 4
Forest Tree Genome Mapping
    Database 4
Global Information and Early
    Warning System 4
Global Integrated Pest Management
    Information System 4
Information Resources Management
    Division 4
Iowa State University Scholar
    System 4
Maize Genome Database Project 4
National Cooperative Extension
    Service 5
National Genetic Resources
    Program 5
NetVet — Veterinary Resource Line 5
Not Just Cows 5
Nottingham Arabidopsis Stock
    Centre 5
PENpages 5
RiceGenes 6
Sustainable Agriculture 6
Sustainable Agriculture Information 6
U.S.D.A. Economics and Statistics
    Gopher 6
U.S.D.A. Extension Service 6

ANARCHY 6
Anarchist Resources 6
Anarchy Discussion List 6
Anarchy 'N' Explosives 7
Propaganda 7
The Seed 7
Spunk Press 7

ANIMALS AND PETS 7
Animal Resources 7
Animals in the News 7
Aquaculture Information Center 7
Aquaria Mailing List 7
Aquariums 7
Aquariums and Tropical Fish 8

Bird Keeping 8
Birding 8
Birds 8
Bird-Watching 8
Bird-Watching Archives 8
Bird-Watching Mailing Lists 8
Cats 8
Dog Resources 8
Dogs 9
Equestrian 9
Exotic Pets 9
Ferrets 9
Fish 9
Fish Cam 9
Fleas and Ticks 10
Golden Retrievers 10
Horse Fanciers 10
Kitten Page 10
Pets General Discussion 10
Rabbits 10
Siamese Fighting Fish 10
Specific Domestic Pets 11
Treatment of Animals 11

ANTHROPOLOGY 11
Aboriginal Studies Archive 11
Evolution of Humans and Primates 11

ARCHAEOLOGY 11
Archaeological Computing 11
ArchNet 11
Classics and Mediterranean
    Archaeology 11
Dead Sea Scrolls 12
Egyptian Artifacts 12
National Archaeological Database 12
Research into Artifacts Center for
    Engineering 12
University of Southampton
    Department of Archaeology 13

ARCHITECTURE 13
Alternative Architecture 13
ArchiGopher 13
Architectural Modeling 13
Architectural Visualization 13
Architecture General Discussion 13
Architecture of the Tropics 13
Architronic 14
Association of Collegiate Schools of
    Architecture 14
Classical Architecture of the
    Mediterranean 14
Contemporary Architecture in Hong
    Kong 15
Images of Architecture and
    Sculpture in Turkey 15
Images of Renaissance and Baroque
    Architecture 15
Lighthouses in the Eastern U.S. 15

ART 15
911 Gallery 15
Aart Gallery 16
Access Art 16
African Art 16
The Anecdote 16
Ansel Adams 16
Art Crimes 16

Art Criticism Forum 17
Art Educational Materials 17
Art Exploration 17
Art Gallery 17
Art History Server 17
Art and Images 17
Art Museums and Exhibits 17
Art Network for Integrated Media
    Applications 17
Art News 17
Art Nouveau 18
Art on the Net 18
Art Papers 18
Art Projects on the Internet 18
Art Reviews 18
Artistic Expression 18
Artistic Melange 18
Arts Online 18
ArtSource 18
ArtWorld 19
ASCII Cartoons 19
Basic Design in Art and
    Architecture 19
Beauty for Ashes 19
Book of Kells 19
Brian Eno 19
Cadence Design Systems 19
Carlos Museum of Art 19
Ceramic Arts Discussion List 19
Ceramics Gopher 20
Chesley Bonestell 20
Contemporary Russian Fine Arts
    Gallery 20
CyberNet's Art Gallery 20
Digital Art Archives 20
Digital Journeys 20
Drux Electronic Art Gallery 21
Electric Gallery 21
Electronic Resources for Art
    Historians 21
Enfolding Perspectives 21
Expo Exhibit 21
Fine Art Forum 21
Fine Art Pictures 21
FineArt Forum's Directory of Online
    Resources 21
Graphics 22
Grotesque in Art 22
H.P. Lovecraft Image Gallery 22
Hot Wire 22
International Internet ChainArt
    Project 22
Japanese Animation 22
Kaleidospace 22
Krannert Art Museum 22
Le Louvre 23
Lexia 23
Mona Lisa 23
Museum of New Zealand 23
Nexus 23
Off the Wall Gallery 24
Online Art References 24
OSU Art Gallery 24
OTIS Project 24
Pixel Pushers 25
Playground Gallery 25

Prints Database 25
RoboGopher 25
Rome Reborn 25
Rosen Sculpture Exhibition 25
Roy Lichtenstein Pre-Pop
    1948-1960 25
Sleeping Dog 25
Spectrum 25
Strange Interactions 26
Virtual Art Gallery 26

ASTROLOGY 26
Astrology Collection 26
Astrology Discussion Group 26
Astrology Resources 26
Horoscopes by Yul and Doc X 26
Interactive Astrology Chart 27

ASTRONOMY 27
Amateur Radio Transmissions 27
Astro FTP List 27
Astrometry Science Team 27
Astronomical Internet Resources 27
Astronomical Museum 27
Astronomy General Discussion 27
Astronomy HyperTextbook 28
Astronomy Programs 28
Astronomy Servers 28
Astrophysics Data System 28
Astrotext 28
Earth Views 28
Flexible Image Transport System
    (FITS) 28
HEASARC Astronomical Browser 28
Hubble Telescope 28
Institutes of Astronomy 28
Mars Atlas 29
National Optical Astronomy
    Observatories 29
Observatories 29
Planetariums 29
Planetary Tour Guide 29
Planets 29
Planets and the Solar System 29
Shoemaker-Levy Comet 29
Sloan Digital Sky Survey (SDSS) 30
Space Telescope Science Institute 30
Starlink 30
Star*s Family 30
Strasbourg Astronomical Data
    Center 30
Sunspots 30
Views of the Solar System 30
WebStars: Astrophysics in
    Cyberspace 30

AUTOMOTIVE: CARS 31
Air-Cooled Volkswagens 31
Alfa Romeo Home Page 31
Antique Cars 31
Audi 31
Auto Racing 31
Automobile General Discussion
    Groups 31
Beemer List 31
BMW Information 32
British Cars 32
Camaros and Firebirds 32
Car Audio 32
Corvette 32
Datsun Roadsters 32
Datsun Z Car 32
Dodge Stealth/Mitsubishi 3000GT ... 33
Driving 33
Driving in California 33
Driving Schools 33
Electric Vehicles 33
Exotic Cars 33

Ford Mustangs 33
High Performance Cars 33
Hot Rods 34
Kit Cars 34
Lancia 34
Offroad Driving 34
Porsche 34
Porschephiles Home Page 34
Racing 34
RoverWeb 35
Saturn 35
Solar Cars 35
Solar Vehicles at UC Berkeley 35
Solar Vehicles at the University of
    Michigan 35
Team.Net Automotive Information
    Archives 35
Technical Automotive Discussion 35
Toyota 35
Volkswagen 36
Volkswagen Names 36

AUTOMOTIVE: MOTORCYCLES ... 36
Motorcycle Archive 36
Motorcycle Design 36
Motorcycle Racing 36
Motorcycle Reviews 36
Motorcycles 36

AVIATION 37
Aerospace Engineering 37
Aircraft Discussion Forum 37
Aircraft Group Ownership 37
Aircraft Images 37
Airline and Airliner Discussion List .. 37
Airline Travel 37
Airport Codes 37
Aviation Archives 38
Aviation Enthusiast Corner 38
Aviation General Discussion 38
Aviation Gopher 38
Aviation Technology 38
Canadian Airlines International 38
Dryden Photo Archive 39
DUAT 39
Flight Planning 39
Flying 39
Flying and Aviation 39
Gliding 39
Hang Gliding Server 39
Instrument Flight Rules 39
Learning to Fly 39
McDonnell Douglas Aerospace 40
Military Aircraft 40
MIT Soaring Association 40
NASA Aviation Server 40
News About the Aviation and
    Aerospace Industries 40
Owning Airplanes 40
Piloting 40
Products for Pilots 40
Q & A About Aviation 41
Stories about Flying 41
Ultralight Flying 41
Upcoming Aviation Events 41
Xpilot Game 41

BBSS (BULLETIN BOARD SYSTEMS) 42
Auggie BBS 42
BBS Access via Gopher 42
BBS Acronyms 42
BBS General Discussion 42
BBS Information 42
BBS Lists 42
BBS Programs 43
BBSs Around the World 43
Cetys-BBS 43
Citadel 43

Csb/Sju BBS 43
CueCosy 43
Cybernet BBS 43
Doors 44
DUBBS 44
Eagles' Nest BBS 44
Endless Forest BBS 44
European Southern Observatory
    Bulletin Board 44
Foothills Multiuser Chat 44
Government-Sponsored Bulletin
    Boards 44
ISCA BBS 45
Launchpad BBS 45
Monochrome 45
NCTU CIS BBS 45
OuluBox 45
Powertech BBS 45
Prism Hotel BBS 46
Quartz BBS 46
Radford University Computer
    Science Club BBS 46
Skynet BBS 46
Softwords COSY 46
Sunset BBS 46
Sysop Information 46
Unix and BBSs 46
UTBBS 46
Web BBS List 46

BIOLOGY 47
Ageing 47
American Type Culture Collection 47
Animal Behavior 47
Arabidopsis Project 47
BioBox Wonder World 47
Biochemistry 47
Biochemistry Graphics Room at
    Aberdeen University 48
BioData Cyberspace Launching Pad .. 48
Biodiversity 48
Bioethics 48
Bioinformatics Resource Gopher 48
Biological Databases 48
Biological Sciences Conferences 48
Biological Scientist's Network
    Guide 48
Biologist's Guide to Internet
    Resources 49
Biology and Information Theory 49
Biology Announcements 49
Biology General Discussion 49
Biology Information Theory 49
Biology Job Opportunities 49
Biology Journals 49
Biology Newsletter 50
Biology Resources 50
Biology Software and Archives 50
Biology Software Search 50
Biomechanics 50
BioMOO 51
Biosphere and Ecology 51
Biotechnology 51
Bird Studies in the Australian 51
National Botanic Gardens 51
Brazilian Tropical Databases 51
Catalog of Marine Fish and
    Invertebrates 51
Cell Biology 51
Chromosome 22 52
Collaborative Clickable Biology 52
Computers and Mathematics 52
Conservation Biology 52
Drosophila 52
EMBL Nucleic Acid Database 52

Entomology at Colorado State
   University 52
European Molecular Biology Net 52
Evolution of Genes and Proteins 52
Frog Dissection Kit 53
Funding and Grants 53
Fungi 53
G Protein-Coupled Receptor
   Database 53
GenBank Database 53
Genetic Linkage 53
Genetics Resources 53
GenomeNet 54
Genome Research at Harvard
   Biological Laboratories 54
Globin Gene Server 54
Human Genome Project 54
Immunology 54
Jackson Laboratory 54
Japan Animal Genome Database 54
Kinetics and Thermodynamics 54
Mapping Chromosomes 54
Methods and Reagents 54
Microbiology at the Technical
   University of Denmark 55
Molecular Biology Laboratory 55
Molecular Biology Network 55
Molecular Biology of HIV 55
Molecular Modeling 55
Motif BioInformatics Server 55
Mouse Biology 55
Neuroscience 55
Nitrogen Fixation 55
Population Biology 55
Primates 56
Protein 56
Protein Crystallography 56
Protein Databases 56
Randomly Amplified Polymorphic
   DNA 56
Related Sciences 56
Salk Institute for Biological Studies 56
Society for Neuroscience 56
Software 57
Taxacom FTP Server 57
Taxacom Listserv Lists 57
Tropical Biology 57
University of Minnesota Medical
   School 57
Virology 57
Virtual Genome Center 57
Who's Who in Biology 58
Whole Frog Project 58
Women in Biology 58
Yale Peabody Museum of Natural
   History 58
Yeast 58
Zebrafish Information Server 58

BIZARRE **58**
Aleister Crowley 58
Anonymity 58
Arcana Arcanorum 59
biancaTroll's Smut Shack 59
Bigfoot 59
Bizarre General Discussion 59
Bizarre Literature 59
Callahan's Bar 59
Cesium 60
Church of the SubGenius 60
Complaining 60
Cryonics 60
Cult of the Dead Cow 61
Dark Side of the Net 61
Devilbunnies 61
Discord and Destruction 61
Explosions and Blowing Things Up 61

Fiction Therapy Group 61
Furry Animals 62
Future Culture Digest Archives 62
Gateway to Darkness 62
Geeks and Nerds 62
Gross and Disgusting 63
Happy Birthday 63
High Weirdness 63
HyperDiscordia 63
Jihad to Destroy Barney on the
   Web 63
Lemurs 63
Lips 63
Ludvigsen Residence — A Family
   Server 63
Lunch Servers 64
Mkzdk 64
Naked Guy 64
Necromicon 64
Negative Emotions 64
Pantyhose 64
Paving the Earth 64
Porter List 65
Positive Emotions 65
Profanity and Insult Server 65
Roadkill R Us 65
Roommates from Hell 65
Rumors 65
Santa Claus 65
Schizophrenia Nervosa 65
Social Deviants 66
Somerville Stories 66
Stories by RICHH 66
Strange Rantings 66
Strange Tales 66
Swedish Chef 66
Talk.Bizarre Web Page Thing 67
Tapestry 67
Tasteless Tales 67
Tasteless Topics 67
Three-Letter Acronyms 67
Unplastic News 67
Vampire Chat Channel 67

BOATING AND SAILING **67**
Boating Discussion Groups 67
Boating Web Server 67
Decavitator 67
Marine Signal Flags 68
Paddling Web Server 68
River and Rowing Museum 68
Sailing 68
Sailing Laser Boats 68
Sailing Mailing List 68
Sailing Page 68

BOOKS **68**
Alternative History 68
Book FAQs and Info 69
Book and Publishing News 69
Book Reviews 69
Book Stacks Unlimited 69
Books General Discussion 69
Books Online 69
Bookstore Reviews 69
Buying and Selling Books 69
Computer Books 70
Doomsday Brunette 70
Electronic Books at Wiretap 70
Etext Resources 70
Internet Book Information Center 70
Internet Books 71
Internet Books List 71
Microsoft Windows 3.1 Book List 71
O'Reilly & Associates 71
O'Reilly Book Samples 71
Online Book Initiative 71

Online Bookstore 72
Pulp Fiction 72
Rare Books 72
Reviews of Children's Books 72
Roswell Electronic Computer
   Bookstore 72
Science Fiction Reviews 72
Technical Books 73
Travels with Samantha 73
Unix Book Lists 73
Unofficial Internet Book List 73

BOTANY **73**
Agroforestry 73
Australian National Botanic
   Gardens 73
Botanical Gardens at the University
   of Delaware 73
Botany Database 74
Bromeliaceae 74
Carnivorous Plants 74
Chlamydomonas 74
Endangered Australian Flora and
   Fauna 74
International Organization of
   Paleobotany 74
Mammal Database 74
Missouri Botanical Garden 74
Photosynthesis 75
Plant Biology 75
Smithsonian Botany Gopher 75
Smithsonian Vertebrate Zoology
   Gopher 75

BUSINESS AND FINANCE **75**
Advertising and Marketing 75
American Risk and Insurance
   Association 75
Asia Online 75
Asia Pacific Business and Marketing
   Resources 75
Banks and Financial Industries
   News 76
Business and Commerce 76
Business and Industry 76
Business Archives 76
Business Conferences 76
Business Electronic Mail Addresses 76
Business Information Resources 76
Business Information Server 76
Business News 77
Business Statistics 77
Businesses on the Internet 77
BusinessWeb 77
Case Online Information System 77
China Import/Export News 77
Cogeneration 77
Commerce Business Daily 77
Commercial Use of the Internet 77
Commodities 78
Corporate Finance News 78
Currency Converter 78
Earnings and Dividend Reports 78
Eastern Europe Trade Leads 78
Eastern European Business
   Network 78
EBB and Agency Information 78
Economic Indicators 78
Economy 78
EDGAR Mutual Funds 79
Entrepreneurs 79
Entrepreneurs on the Web 79
European Commission Host
   Organization 79
Export Guide 79
Feature Stories 79
Federal Information Exchange 80

FinanceNet 80
Financial Executive Journal 80
Financial Ratios for Manufacturing
    Corporations 80
Goethe Investment Heimatseite 80
Hot News 80
Income Taxation Information 80
Industry Statistics 80
Information Technology Laboratory 80
International Business Practices
    Guide 81
International Market Insight Reports 81
Internet Better Business Bureau 81
Internet Business Center 81
Investments 81
Japanese Business Studies 81
Labor 82
Leasing a Web Server 82
Legal News 82
Libraries 82
Mail Addresses of Ukraine
    Businesses 82
Mergers and Acquisitions 82
Mortgage Calculator 82
Multilevel Marketing 83
Mutual Fund Price Movement Chart 83
National Trade Data Bank 83
NETworth 83
New Products and Services 83
Non-Profit Organizations 83
Office Automation 83
Penn World Trade Tables 84
Personal Finance 84
Personal Investing and Finance
    News 84
Price and Volume Charts 84
QuoteCom 84
RISKWeb 84
Savage Archive 84
Security APL Quote Server 84
Small Business Administration 84
Standard & Poors 500 Index 84
Stock Market 85
Stock Market Data 85
Stock Market Discussion Groups 85
Stock Market Report 85
Stock Market Simulations 85
StrategyWeb 85
Taxing Times 85
Technical Aspects 86
Top News 86
Trademark Act of 1946 86
Trademarks 86
Vienna Stock Exchange 86
World Bank 86
World of Coca-Cola 86

BUYING AND SELLING 86
    Anime 86
    Bicycles 86
    Bootleg Music 87
    Computers 87
    MarketBase Online Catalog 87
    Marketplace, Buy and Sell 87
    Pinball and Video Game Machine
        Auctions 87
    Satellite TV Equipment 87
    Science Fiction 87
    Selling on IRC 87
    Video Games 87

CANADA 88
    British Columbia Regional
        Information 88
    British Columbia Tourism
        Information 88
    British Columbian Web Servers 88

Canadian Business Information 88
Canadian Discussion 88
Canadian Geographical Web Server 88
Canadian Government Documents 88
Canadian Government Gophers 89
Canadian History 89
Canadian Investment 89
Canadian Issues Forum 89
Canadian Music 89
Canadian News 89
Canadian Resource Page 89
Canadian Stock Archives 89
Canadian Web Master Index 90
Censorship and Intellectual Freedom
    in Canada 90
Charlottetown Agreement 90
Culture 90
Halifax Nova Scotia 90
Maritimes Web Servers 90
Official Touring Guide to New
    Brunswick 91
Ottawa 91
Prince Edward Island 91
Statistics Canada Daily Reports 91
Tour Canada Without Leaving Your
    Desk 91
Web Servers in Quebec 91

CHEMISTRY 91
    American Chemical Society 91
    Center for Atmospheric Science 91
    Chemical Engineering 92
    Chemical Engineering List 92
    Chemical Information Sources 92
    Chemical Physics Preprint
        Database 92
    Chemistry Art Gallery 92
    Chemistry in Israel 92
    Chemistry Information 93
    Chemistry Talk 93
    Chemistry Telementoring 93
    College of Chemistry at Berkeley 93
    Computational Chemistry List 94
    Hydrogen Bond Calculation
        Program 94
    Hyperactive Molecules 94
    Institute for Molecular Science 94
    Organometallic Chemistry 94
    Periodic Table of the Elements 94
    Periodic Table of the Elements
        (Online) 94
    Periodic Table in Hypertext Format 95
    Polymer Science and Technology 95
    Ponder Lab Web Server 95
    Short-Lived Reactive Pollutants 95
    Virtual Library of Chemistry 95
    WebElements 95
    World Association of Theoretical
        Organic Chemists 95

COMIC BOOKS 96
    Alternative Comics 96
    Comic Book Mailing List 96
    Comics Archives 96
    Comics Marketplace 96
    Comics Newsgroups 96
    Comics Resource Center 96
    More Comics 96
    Superhero Comic Writing 97
    X-Men 97

COMPUTERS: COMMODORE 98
    Amiga Archives 98
    Amiga Information Resources 98
    Amiga Mosaic 98
    Amiga Pictures 98
    Amiga Sounds 98

Amiga Talk 98
Amiga Telecom 98
Amiga Unix 98
Commodore 64/128 Archive 99
Commodore-64 Chat 99

COMPUTERS: COMPANIES 99
    BTG 99
    Celerity Systems 99
    Digital Equipment Corporation 99
    Hewlett-Packard 99
    Microsoft Archives 99
    Microsoft Gopher Server 99
    Microsoft Research 99
    NEC 100
    Santa Cruz Operation 100
    Sun Microsystems 100

COMPUTERS: CULTURE 100
    Art of Technology Digest 100
    Byte Bandit 100
    Code of the Geeks 100
    Computer Professionals for Social
        Responsibility 101
    Computer Underground Digest 101
    Computer-Generated Writing 101
    Computers and Academic Freedom 102
    Concerning Hackers... 102
    Cyberspace 102
    Ethics 102
    Future Culture 102
    Hackers 103
    IBM Songbook 103
    League for Programming
        Freedom/Free Software
        Foundation 103
    Nerd Page 103
    Social Organization of Computer
        Underground 103
    WebWorld 103
    Women and Computer Science 104

COMPUTERS: GRAPHICS 104
    Acid Warp 104
    Annotated Scientific Visualization
        Weblet Bibliography 104
    Computer Graphics Bibliography 104
    Computer Graphics Information 104
    Cool Demos 105
    Figlet Fonts 105
    Fract Int 105
    Fractal Images 105
    Fractal Movie Archive 105
    Fractals 105
    Fractals and Chaos 105
    Gallery of Images from Silicon
        Graphics 106
    Genetic Movies 106
    Geometry Sender 106
    Hyperbolic Movies 106
    Hyperbolic Tiles 106
    Icon Browser 106
    Image and Audio File Formats 107
    Internet Font Browser 107
    JPEG File Viewer for Macintosh 107
    JPEG File Viewer for Windows 107
    Macintosh Graphics 107
    Mandelbrot Explorer 107
    Mosaic Gizmos 108
    Persistence of Vision 108
    Pixel-Planes Graphics Machine 108
    Radiance 108
    Raytrace Graphics 108
    Rayshade 109
    Rob's Multimedia Lab 109
    Silicon Graphics Gallery 109
    Silicon Graphics Silicon Surf 109
    Text-based Animation 109

Thant's Animations Index 109
Tomservo Raytraced Images 109
Virtual Reality Markup Language 110
VuSystem 110
Web Page Graphics and Icons 110
WebOOGL Home Page 110

COMPUTERS: HARDWARE 110
386BSD Unix Supplements for
    Compaq Computers 110
Apple IIgs 110
Compaq Fixes and Patches 110
Computer Information 110
EPROM Models and Manufacturers
    List 111
Hard Disk Guide 111
Hardware Architectures 111
Hardware News 111
Hardware Technical Material 111
How Computers Work 111
Microprocessor Instruction Set
    Cards 111
Modems 112
Parallel Computing Archive 112
PC and Macintosh Guides 112
PC Hardware 112
Performance Database Server 112
Portable Computer Information 112
Powerful Computer List 113
Sinclair ZX-Spectrum Web server 113
Supercomputer Documentation 113
Transputer Archive 113
Troubleshooting Your PC 113
Ultrasound 113
Vaxbook 113

COMPUTERS: LITERATURE 113
Alice in Unix Land 113
Amateur Computerist 114
Artificial Intelligence Journal 114
BBS Issues 114
Computer Emergency Response
    Team 114
Computer Science Technical Papers
    Archive 115
Computer Science Technical
    Reports 115
Computer Underground 115
Computer Virus Technical
    Information 115
Computing Across America 115
Computing Dictionary 115
Computing Newsletters 116
Desktop Publishing 116
EFF's Guide to the Internet 116
Hacker Crackdown 117
Hacker's Dictionary 117
Hacker's Technical Journals 117
How to Steal Code 117
HPCwire 117
Internet Bibliography 117
Internet Computer Index 118
Internet Overview 118
Introduction to HTML 118
IRC Thesis 118
Kermit Manual 118
LAN Management 118
Logintaka 118
Network Bibliography 119
Network Newsletters 119
Networking Computers 119
PC Downloading 119
PC/MS-DOS: The Essentials 119
Tao of Programming 119
Technical Reports Online 119
Tipsheet 119
Zen and the Art of the Internet 119

COMPUTERS: MACINTOSH 120
Buying and Selling Macs 120
Internet Macintosh Resources 120
Mac Hardware 120
MacinTalk 120
Macintosh Announcements 121
Macintosh General Discussion 121
Macintosh Index 121
Macintosh News 121
Macintosh Resources 121
Macintosh in Science and
    Technology 121
Macintosh User's Group 121
Macintosh User's Group at
    Arkansas College 121
Macintosh User's Group at Johns
    Hopkins 121
Resources for Apple Users 121
Source Code for Macintosh 122
TidBITS 122

COMPUTERS: MULTIMEDIA 122
Audio Slideshow Guide 122
Illustrated Audio Slide Show
    Technology 122
Image Processing with Live Video
    Sources 122
MPEG Animation Shows 122
MPEG Movie Archive 123
MPEG Movies 123
MPEG Movies from JRC 123
Multimedia in Education 123
QuickTime Movies 123
Video Webalog 123

COMPUTERS: NETWORKS 123
Bibliography of Internetworking
    Information 123
Bitnet Network 123
Campus Computing Newsletter
    Editors 124
Cisco Information Archive 124
Computer and Networking Column 124
Cyberspace Communications 124
Data Communications and
    Networking Links 124
Datagram 124
European Academic Research
    Network 124
FORTHnet 125
High Performance Computing
    Gopher 125
Inter-Network Mail Guide 125
Mail Gateway Guide 125
Managing Networked Information 125
Matrix News 125
Microsoft Windows Networking
    Environment 125
National Information Infrastructure
    Agenda 126
Network Hardware Suppliers List 126
Network Maps 126
Network Politics 126
Networking Articles 127
NeuroNet 127
OS/2 Networking Environment 127
Rockwell Network Systems 127
TCP/IP Introduction 127
Vnet Outdial Servers 127
WWPing 127
Z39.50 Resources 127

COMPUTERS: PCs 128
Building PC Hardware 128
IBM News 128
Magazine 128

PC Catalog 128
PC Clones 128
PC General Discussion 128
PC Hardware 128
PC Hardware Introduction 129
PC Index 129
PC Lube and Tune 129
PowerPC News 129

COMPUTERS: PICTURES 129
alt.binaries.pictures Image Server 129
Cartoon Pictures 129
Chinese GIF Collection 129
Clip Art 130
Digital Picture Archive on the 17th
    Floor 130
Fantasy Images 130
Fine Art 130
Fractals 130
GIF Image Files 130
Girls, Girls, Girls 130
Icons 130
Image and Movie Archives 131
Japanese Animation Images 131
JPEG Files 131
Kandinsky Image Archive 131
Lighthouses 131
Mandelbrot Images 132
Miscellaneous Pictures 132
Picture-Related Files FTP Site List 132
Picture Viewing Software 132
Satellite Images of Europe 132
Sex Pictures 132
Shuttle and Satellite Images 133
Smithsonian Photographs 133
Supermodels 133
Tasteless Pictures 133
Washington, D.C. 133

COMPUTERS: PROGRAMMING ... 133
Ada 133
Basic Programming Language 133
C Programs 133
C++ Frequently Asked Questions 134
CCMD Source Code in C 134
CompuServe B File Transfer
    Protocol 134
CPUs and Assembly Language 134
Free Language Tools 134
FSP 134
Gnuplot Tutorial 134
Gopher and Utilities for VMS 135
Hello World! 135
Interactive Fiction Game
    Programming 135
Language FAQs 135
Language List 135
Linear Programming Answers 135
Nonlinear Programming Facts 135
Obfuscated C Code 135
Object-Oriented Programming
    Using C++ 136
OS/2 Programming 136
Parallel Programming Laboratory 136
Pascal to C Translator 136
Programming Examples 136
Programming for Microsoft
    Windows 136
Programming General Discussion 136
Programming in Ada 136
Programming Language Material 137
Programming Languages 137
Ravel 137
TCP/IP Development Tools 137
Turbo Vision 137
Twisted Code 137
X Window Software Index 137

COMPUTERS: SECURITY and
PRIVACY 138
Computer Security Gopher 138
Computer Security Sites 138
Computers and the Law 138
Hacker Sites on the Net 138
Incident Response Teams 138
Internet Security Firewalls 138
Network and Computer Security
   Reference Index 139
PGP Keyservers 139
Privacy and Anonymity Issues 139
Privacy Forum Digest 139
RIPEM Resources 139
RSA Data Security, Inc. 139
Security Resources 139
Security Web 140
Stalking the Wily Hacker 140
Unix Security 140
Unix Security Tutorial 140

COMPUTERS: SOUNDS 140
AsTeR 140
Index of Sounds 140
Macintosh Sounds 140
MIDI Archives 140
Miscellaneous Sounds 141
Movies and Television 141
Music 141
NeXT Sounds 141
Number Synthesizer 141
PC Sounds 141
Rplay 141
Sex Sounds 141
Sound Archives 142
Sound Cards 142
Sound Tools 142
Sound Utility Programs 142
Star Trek Sounds 142
Sun Sound Files 142

COMPUTERS: TECHNOLOGY ... 143
Artificial Life 143
Chinese Computing and Word
   Processing 143
Complex Systems Resources 143
Computer Aided Detector Design 143
Computer Lore 143
Computer Science Conferences 143
Computer Speech 143
Computer Standards 143
Computer Viruses 144
Computers and Technology in the
   Home 144
Cybernetics 144
Hebrew Users Group 144
Human and Computer Interaction 144
Japanese Research 144
National Center for Supercomputing
   Applications 144
New and Trendy Protocols 144
SFI BBS 144
Speech Generator 145
Techne 145
Technology Magazines 145
Upcoming Events in the Computer
   Industry 145
Virtual Reality 145
VuSystem and VuNet
   Demonstrations 145
Wanderers, Robots, and Spiders 146
Wombat Dictionaries 146
Xtoys Gallery 146

CONSUMER INFORMATION 146
California Yellow Pages 146

Computer and Communication
   Companies 146
Consumer Information 146
Consumer Issues 146
Consumer News 146
Credit Information 147
Dell Web Server 147
Downtown Anywhere 147
Electronic Mail Directory of
   Companies 147
Fair Credit Reporting Act 147
FaxGate 147
FaxLinq 147
Faxnet 148
Free Offers 148
Houses 148
Infinite Illusions Home Page 149
Internet Consultants Directory 149
Internet Mall 149
Internet Services Directory 149
Travel Marketplace 149
Xerox Corporation 149
Your Complete Guide to Credit 149

CRAFTS 150
Arts and Crafts Information Service 150
Craft Resources 150
Craft Suppliers 150
Crafting on the Internet 150
Crafts 150
Jewelry 150
Needlework 150
Yarn 151

CRYPTOGRAPHY 151
All About Cryptography 151
Crypto Glossary 151
Cryptography General Discussion 151
Cryptography and the Government 151
Cryptography Sources on the
   Internet 151
Cryptography, PGP, and Your
   Privacy 151
Cypherpunks 152
PGP Encryption/Decryption
   Program 152
PGPShell 152
Public Key Exchange 153
Quadralay Cryptography Archive 153
Stego 153

CYBERPUNK 153
Agrippa: A Book of the Dead 153
Bruce Sterling Articles 153
Cyberculture 154
Cyberkind 154
Cybermind 154
Cyberpunk News 154
Cyberpunk Reading List 154
Future Culture and Cyberpunks
   Mailing List 154

DANCE 155
Ballet and Modern Dance 155
Dance Archives and Discussion 155
Dance General Discussion 155
Dance Resources on the Internet 155
Folk and Traditional Dance Mailing
   List 155
Folk Dancing 155
Scottish Dancing 156
Tango 156
UK-Dance 156
Western Square Dancing 156

DISABILITIES 156
Americans with Disabilities Act 156
Blind News Digest 157

Blind and Visually Impaired
   Computer Usage 157
Deaf Magazine 157
Deaf-Blind Discussion List 157
Deafness 157
Developmentally Disabled and Autism 157
Disability Aid 157
Disability Information 158
Disability Information Archive 159
Disabled Computing 159
Disabled Student Services in Higher
   Education 159
Do-It Disability Program 159
Fathers of Children with Disabilities 159
Handicap BBS Lists 159
Handicap Issues 159
Mentally Retarded Deaf 159
Reading Disabilities 160
SAIDIE: The Intellectual Disability
   Network 160
Software and Information for the
   Handicapped 160

DRAMA 160
Dramatic Exchange 160
Hollyweb Film Guide 160
Musicals 160
Opera Schedule Server 161
Play Scripts 161
Shakespeare Discussion 161
Shakespeare Glossary 161
Stagecraft 161
Theater 161
Theater Plays and Musicals 162
Theatre Home Page 162

DRUGS 162
Anti War-on-Drugs Activist List 162
Blotter Art Collection 162
Caffeine 162
Drug Abuse Education Information
   and Research 162
Drug Chemistry and Synthesis 163
Drug Culture 163
Drug Information Resources on the
   Net 163
Drug News 163
Drug Talk 163
Drug Use History 163
Drug Web Servers 163
Ecstasy 164
General Drug Information 164
Hints for Marijuana Growers 164
Illegal Recreational Drug Information 164
LSD: My Problem Child 164
Marijuana Discussion 164
Marijuana Fiction 164
Marijuana Usage 165
Medical Information About
   Marijuana 165
Neuropharmacological Anarchy 165
News About Drugs 165
Nitrous Oxide FAQ 165
Nitrous Oxide Synthesis 165
Nootropics (Intelligence-Enhancing
   Drugs) 165
Pharmacological Cornucopia 166
PiHKAL 166
Politics and Drugs 166
Politics of Contraband 166
Psychoactive Drugs 166
Recreational Drugs 166

EARTH SCIENCE 167
Earth Observation System 167
Earth Science Data Directory 167

Earth Sciences Resources 167
Planet Earth Images and Movies 167
Polar Research 167
Smithsonian Natural History Gopher 168
xearth Graphics Software 168

ECONOMICS 168
British Economics Research 168
Community Economic Development 168
Computational Economics 169
Directory of Economists 169
Economic Bulletin Board 170
Economic Development 170
Economic Problems in Less
    Developed Countries 170
Economic Resources 171
Economics Discussion 171
Economics Gopher 171
Economics Resources on the Web 171
Economies of the Caribbean Basin 171
Economist Resources 171
Employment Statistics 172
Foreign Trade 172
General Agreement on Tariffs and
    Trade (GATT) 172
Gross State Product Tables 172
Marketing 172
Monetary Statistics 172
Morningstar Spotlight 173
Mutual Fund Market Manager 173
Mutual Fund Quotations 173
Mutual Funds Phone Numbers 173
National Income and Products
    Accounts 173
Press Releases from U.S. Trade
    Representative 173
Price and Productivity Statistics 173
Regional Economic Statistics 173
Russian Economics 174
Securities and Exchange
    Commission's Database 174
Summaries of Current Economic
    Conditions 174
Thoughts on Economics 174
U.S. Economic Statistics 174
Working Paper Archive 174

EDUCATION 174
Academic Technology 174
Adult Education and Literacy 175
Adult Literacy 175
AERA SIG/ENET Discussion 175
Alternative Approaches to Learning 175
Armadillo 175
Association for Experiential
    Education 176
Biology Education 176
Commonwealth of Learning 176
Computer Networking 176
Computers in Education 176
Curriculum Materials and Ideas 176
Daily Report Card 177
Education Mailing Lists 177
Education Policy 177
Educational Listserv Lists 177
Educational Newsgroups 177
Educational Reform 178
EDUPAGE 178
Eisenhower National Clearinghouse 178
Engines for Education 178
Global Schoolhouse Project 178
GNA Virtual Library 179
Grants, Scholarships, and Funding 179
Health Sciences Libraries
    Consortium 180
Home School Discussion 180

Home School Resources 180
IBM Kiosk for Education 180
Incomplete Guide to the Internet 180
Indigenous Peoples 180
Institutional Communications
    Network 180
JANET Network 181
K12 Internet School Sites 181
K12 Resources 181
Latin Language Textbook 181
Math Information Server 181
Media in Education 181
MicroMUSE Learning Community 181
Ministry of Education in Singapore 181
Multilingual Classrooms 181
National Education BBS 182
National Referral Center Master
    File 182
New Patterns in Education 182
Newbie Newz 182
Newton 182
Online Journal of Education and
    Communication 182
Perkins Vocational and Applied
    Technology Education 182
Project Kaleidoscope 182
Quality of Education 182
Scholarly Conferences 183
School Nurse Network 183
Schoolnet 183
Schoolnet Resource Manual 183
Schoolnet's News Flash 183
Schools on the Internet 183
Science Education 183
Shadowy Science Projects 184
Simultaneous Projects 184
Talented and Gifted 184
Teaching and Learning with the
    Web 184
Technet 184
Technology and Information
    Education Services 184
Technology in the Classroom 184
U.S. Department of Education 184
U.S. National K12 Gopher 185
Vocational Education 185

EDUCATION: COLLEGES AND
UNIVERSITIES 185
Academic Electronic Mail
    Addresses 185
Apple Computer Higher Education
    Gopher 185
Brown University Alumni 185
Campus Climate 185
Campus Parking 185
Campus-Wide Information Systems 185
Community Colleges 186
Diversity University 186
Globewide Network Academy 186
Graduate Students 186
Higher Education Resources and
    Opportunities 186
Maricopa Center for Learning and
    Instruction (MCLI) 186
Minority College and University
    Information 186
Research and Advanced Study:
    Canada, Italy 187
Student Financial Aid
    Administration 187
Theta Xi Fraternity 187
Two-Year Colleges 187
U.S. Colleges 187

Ultralab — Learning Technology
    Research Center 188
University and College Education 188
Usenet University 188
Virtual Online University 188

EDUCATION: ELEMENTARY 188
Arbor Heights School 188
Kidcafe 188
Kidlink 188
Plugged In 188

EDUCATION: STUDENTS 189
Academic Advice 189
Academic Magazines 189
Exploratorium 189
Math Problem-Solving Skills 189
Scavenger Hunt 190
School Humor 190
Student Governments 191

EDUCATION: TEACHERS 191
AskERIC 191
Best of K12 191
Business School Faculty 191
Catalyst for College Educators 191
CD-ROM Activities 191
Chronicle of Higher Education 191
College and University Teaching
    Assistants 192
Dead Teacher's Society 192
Discovery Communications Online
    Listings 192
Education Net 192
Educational Administration 192
Educational K12 Resources 192
Effectiveness of Teachers 192
Electronic Book Discussion 192
Explorer 192
Globe and Mail 193
KIDSPHERE 193
Kindergarten to Grade 6 Corner 193
Lesson Plans 193
Neat Educational Tricks 193
Physics Teachers 193
Reading Room 194
Satellite Communications for
    Learning Associated 194
Special Education 194
Teaching English as a Second
    Language 194
Teaching Health and Physical
    Education 195
Worldwide Education Net 195

ELECTRONICS 195
Circuit Analysis Discussion List 195
Computer-Aided Design 195
Electronic Design and Development 195
Electronics Repair 196
English-Chinese Electronics Terms 196
HP Calculator BBS 196
IEEE Gopher 196

EMERGENCY AND DISASTER ... 196
California Emergency Services 196
Disaster Management 197
Disaster Situation and Status
    Reports 197
Earthquakes in Alaska 197
Earthquakes in California 197
Emergency Medical Services 197
Emergency Preparedness
    Information eXchange (EPIX) 198
Fire Safety Tips 198
HungerWeb 198
Newcastle Earthquake 198
ReliefNet 198

ENERGY **198**
- Energy Statistics 198
- National Renewable Energy
  Laboratory (NREL) 198
- Oak Ridge National Laboratory 199
- Renewable Energy 199

ENGINEERING **199**
- Advanced Nuclear Reactor
  Technology 199
- Build a Flying Saucer 199
- CAD Mailing Lists 199
- Civil Engineering 199
- Congress of Canadian Engineering
  Students 199
- Electrical Engineering 200
- Facilities and Services 200
- Fluid Mechanics 200
- Mechanical Engineering 200
- Nuclear Engineering 200
- Optical Engineering 200
- Robotics 201
- Software Engineering 201
- Virtual Library of Engineering 201

ENVIRONMENT **201**
- 2020 News & Views 201
- 40 Tips to Go Green 201
- Air Pollution BBS 201
- Australian Environmental Resources
  Network 202
- Biosphere Mailing List and
  Discussion Group 202
- Biosphere Newsletter 202
- California Rivers Assessment 202
- Canadian Forest Service 202
- Centre for Landscape Research
  (CLR) 202
- Chemical Substance Factsheets 202
- Chernobyl Nuclear Accident 203
- Coalition to Ban Dihydrogen
  Monoxide 203
- Coastal Management and
  Resources 203
- Conservation OnLine 203
- Earth and Environmental Science 203
- Earth Day Bibliography 203
- Earth Negotiations Bulletin 203
- Ecological Economics 203
- EcoNet 204
- EcoWeb 204
- Edwards Aquifer Research and Data
  Center 204
- Electronic Membrane Information
  Library 204
- Endangered Species 204
- Energy and the Environment 204
- EnviroLink Network 204
- Environmental Education Database 205
- Environmental Engineering 205
- Environmental Factsheets 205
- Environmental Issues 205
- Environmental Protection Agency 205
- Environmental Resource Center 205
- Environmental Scorecard 205
- Environmental Services Data
  Directory 205
- EnviroWeb 206
- FireNet 206
- Forest Science 206
- Forests 206
- Global Change and Climate
  History 206
- Global Recycling Network 206
- Global Warming 206
- Great Lakes Information Network 206
- Green Manufacturing 206

- GreenDisk Environmental
  Information 206
- Greenpeace 207
- International Arctic Buoy Program 207
- Joshua Tree National Monument 207
- League of Conservation Voters 207
- Man and the Biosphere 207
- National Environmental Data
  Referral Service 207
- National Wetlands Inventory 207
- National Wildlife Refuges 208
- Natural Environment Research
  Council 208
- Northridge Earthquake Simulation 208
- Ozone Depletion 208
- Paleoenvironmental Records of Past
  Climate Change 208
- Pollution and Groundwater
  Recharge 208
- Pollution Research Group 208
- Sea Level Increase 208
- South African Environmental
  Information Gateway 209
- U.S. Environmental Protection
  Agency 209
- ULS Report 209
- UNESCO World Heritage List 209
- Waste Reduction 209
- Wilderness Society 209

FAMILIES AND PARENTING **210**
- Abortion 210
- Babies 210
- Child Support 210
- Childcare Newsletters 211
- Children General Discussion 211
- Family Childcare Newsletter 211
- Family Discussions 211
- Family Life Newsletter 211
- Family News 211
- Family Web Page 211
- FatherNet 212
- Great Beginnings Newsletter 212
- Missing Children 212
- Missing Children Database 212
- News on Children 212
- News on the Family 212
- Parent Trap 212
- Parents and Teens 212
- Vacationing with Children 212

FASHION AND CLOTHING **213**
- Clothes Moths 213
- General Fashion 213
- Historical Costuming 213
- Historical Costuming Discussion 213
- Lingerie 213
- Sewing Discussions 214
- Textiles Discussion Groups 214
- Textiles Mailing List 214
- Textiles Reference Material 214
- Textiles and Sewing Archives 214
- Vintage Clothing and Costume
  Jewelry 214

FLIGHT SIMULATORS **214**
- Aeronautics Simulation 214
- Air Warrior 215
- Falcon 3.0 Archives 215
- Flight Simulator Utilities and
  Scenery 215
- Flight Simulators 216
- IFR Flight Simulator 216
- Microsoft Flight Simulator 216

FOLKLORE AND MYTHOLOGY **216**
- Bulfinch's Mythology 216
- Greek Mythology 216
- Lore 216

- Mythical Animals 217
- Net Legends 217
- Oral Tradition 218
- Scientific Urban Legends 218
- Urban Folklore 218
- Urban Legends 218

FOOD AND DRINK **218**
- Austrian Beer Guide 218
- Beer 219
- Beer Archive 219
- Beer Judging 219
- Beer Page 219
- Beer Ratings 219
- Big Drink List 219
- Boat Drinks 219
- Booze Cookbook 219
- Cereal 220
- Coca-Cola 220
- Coca-Cola World 220
- Coffee 220
- Coffee Lover's Resourcess 220
- Cola: Make Your Own 221
- College Food 221
- Complete Guide to Guinness Beer 221
- Cookie Recipes 221
- Cooking 221
- Crackers 221
- Diabetic Recipes 221
- Dining Out on the Web 222
- Fat-Free Food 222
- Food and Beverages 222
- Food-related Topics 222
- Good Food 222
- Grapevine 222
- Herbs 222
- History of Food 223
- Homebrew Mailing List 223
- Homebrewing 223
- How to Make Your Own Booze 223
- Ice Cream 223
- Japanese Food and Culture 223
- Jewish Recipes 223
- Ketchup 223
- Kool-Aid 224
- Lowfat Vegetarianism 224
- Malt Whiskey Tour 224
- McDonald's 225
- Mead Maker's Resources 225
- Milwaukee Frozen Custard 225
- MotherCity Coffee — A Guide to
  Seattle Coffee 225
- Pancakes 225
- Recipe Archives 225
- Recipe Assortments 226
- Recipes 226
- Recipes from Slovakia 226
- Restaurant Le Cordon Bleu 226
- Restaurants 226
- Restaurants on the Web 226
- Snapple on the Net 227
- Sourdough 227
- Spam 227
- Sporks 227
- Sugar Cereals 227
- Sushi 227
- Unusual Foods of the World 227
- Vegans 227
- Vegetarian Archives 227
- Vegetarianism 228
- Virtual Pub & Beer Emporium 228
- Wine 228
- Wine Page 228

FREEDOM **228**
- ACLU Reading Room 228
- Banned Computer Material 229

Censored Books and News Stories 229
Civil Rights and Liberties 229
File Room 229
Free Speech 229
Freedom of Information Act 230
Liberty Web 230
Piss List 230

FREQUENTLY ASKED
QUESTIONS 230
IRC Questions 230
Newsgroups 230
Usenet FAQ List Archive 230

FUN 231
Adventures of Cyber Cat 231
Anagrams 231
ASCII Art Bazaar 231
Ask Joe 231
Barney's Page 231
Big Fun Lists 231
Bluedog Can Count 232
Boredom 232
Cartoon Collection 232
Chat 232
Confession Booth 232
Conversational Hypertext Access
    Technology 232
Cool Site of the Day 232
Crosswords 233
CyberNet 233
Cybersight 233
Digital Movies 233
Disney 233
Distractions 233
Druid Science Reading Room 233
Dysfunctional Family Circus 233
Froggy Page 234
Get Hooked on the Internet 234
Happy People 234
Hypermedia Star 234
Internet Candy Dish 234
Internet Hunt 234
IRC Bar 234
Joe's Adventure 235
Juggling 235
Madlibs 235
Marshmallow Peanut Circus Home
    Page 235
Movie of the Week 235
Multiple Choice Quiz 235
NetBoy 235
Nicecafe 235
Nude Beaches 235
Orange Room Toy Box 235
Pawn Shop 235
Penn and Teller 236
Pizza Server 236
Poeticus 236
Puzzles 236
Pyramix 236
QuarkWeb 236
Recreational Arts 236
Roller Coasters 236
Rubik's Cube 236
Rubik's Revenge 236
Silicon Sister's Java Hut 237
Time Wasting 237
Toys 237
Universe of Discourse 237
URouLette 237
Void 237
Walking Man 237
Web Addict's Pop-Culture
    Scavenger Hunt 237
Whole Internet Scavenger
    Hunt 237

GAMES 238
AD&D Discussion 238
Addventure! 238
Advanced Dungeons and Dragons 238
Advanced Dungeons and Dragons
    Character Creator 238
Aerial Combat Simulation 238
Anime Video Games 238
Apogee Games 238
Arcade Video Game Tricks 238
Atari Archive 239
Atari Jaguar Game Archive 239
Atomic Cafe 239
Autospamosaurus 239
Backgammon Server 239
Battleships 239
Bizarre Board Game 239
Blackjack 240
Board Game Rules and Information 240
Boggle 240
Bolo 240
Bolo Tracker 240
Bridge 241
Car Wars 241
Chess Archives 241
Chess Discussion List 241
Chess Discussion and Play 241
Chess News 242
Chess Servers 242
Chinese Chess 242
Civilization Editor 242
Connect-4 242
Conquest 242
Core War 242
Cribbage 243
Crossfire 243
Crossword Servers 243
CyberMUD Web Game 243
Diplomacy 243
Diplomacy Discussion List 243
Doom Discussion and Realtime
    Chat 243
Doom Information and Files 244
DoomWeb Node 244
Drool 245
Empire 245
Fascist 245
Flat Top 245
Game Bytes 245
Game Information Archive 245
Game of Life 245
Game Server 245
Game Solutions 246
Games Domain 246
Games and Recreation 246
GNU Chess 246
GNU Go 246
Go 246
Guess the Animal 246
Guess the Disease 247
Hangman 247
Head to Head Daemon Resources 247
Hexapawn 247
Home Video Games History 247
Howitzer95 247
Hunt the Wumpus 248
Illuminati Online Games 248
Initgame 248
Interactive Fiction 248
Interactive Web Games 248
Internet Modem Players Listing 248
Jeopardy 248
Lynx Cheats 248
Magic Square Puzzle 248
Magic: The Gathering 248

Modem Doomer's Hangout 249
Multi-Trek 249
Multiuser Games 249
Nethack 249
Netrek 249
Othello Home Page 249
Outburst 249
Paintball Server 250
PC Games Frequently Asked
    Question List 250
Pinball Pasture 250
Play-by-Mail Archives 250
Poker 250
Prairie Dog Hunt for Windows 250
Praser Maze 250
Risk 251
Rubik's Cube 251
Sega Game Secrets 251
Sega Hardware 251
Shogi 251
Snackman 252
Sokoban 252
Source Code to Omega 252
Tic Tac Toe 252
Tiddlywinks 252
Top 100 PC Games 252
TradeWars Discussion 252
TrekMUSE Gateway 252
Truth or Dare 252
Vectrex Arcade System 252
Video Game Archive 252
Video Game Collecting 253
Video Game Database Browser 254
Video Game Debates 254
Video Game Discussions 254
Video Game List 254
Video Game Systems 254
Video Games Frequently Asked
    Questions 254
Video Puzzle with Live Video
    Sources 254
Walkthroughs 254
x4war 255
x4war Players 255
xsokoban 255
Zarf's List of Interactive Games on
    the Web 255

GARDENING 255
Annuals, Perennials and Bulbs 255
Bonsai 255
Bonsai Mailing List 256
Chia Pets 256
Children's Gardening 256
Flower Gardens 256
Fruit Growing 256
Garden Encyclopedia 257
Gardener's Assistant 257
Gardening Information 257
Gardens and Plants 257
Growing Herbs 257
Growing Vegetables 257
Herb Information 258
Herb Mailing List 258
Herbal Variations 258
Home Gardening Mailing List 258
Hydroponic Gardening 258
Indoor Plants 259
Landscaping and Lawns 259
Master Gardener 259
Pest Management 259
Pests, Diseases and Weeds 259
Plant Factsheets 260
Trees 260
Vegetable and Herb Growing 260
Woody Plants 260

GAY, LESBIAN, BISEXUAL **260**
Assorted Resources 260
Bear Code 261
Bears 261
Bears in Movies 261
Bible's View of Homosexuality 261
Bisexual Resource List 261
Bisexuality 261
Bisexuality and Gender Issues 261
Brochure on Sexual Orientation 261
Collected Queer Information 262
Coming Out 262
Domestic Partners 262
Don't Ask; Don't Tell 262
Electronic Mailing Lists 262
Faces Quiz 262
Gay FTP Site 262
Gay, Lesbian, and Bisexual
    Resources 262
Gay, Lesbian, and Bisexual Trivia
    Game 263
Gay, Lesbian, and Bisexual White
    Pages 263
Gay Public Officials 263
Gay TV Listings of the Week 263
Gays in Russia 264
Hanky Codes 264
Historical and Celebrity Figures 264
Homosexuality 264
Homosexuality and the Church 264
Homosexuality and Gay Rights 264
Homosexuality in the Middle Ages 264
International Association of Gay
    Square Dance Clubs 264
Lesbian Lexicon 265
Lesbian Love 265
Lesbian Mothers 265
Lesbian, Gay, and Bisexual Mailing
    Lists 265
The Out List 265
Politics and Homosexuality 265
Politics and Sex 265
Queer Resources Directory 266
Queer Zines 266
Queers 'R' Us 266
Stonewall Images 266
Stonewall Riot 266
Twink Code 266
GENEALOGY **266**
Canadian Genealogy Resources 266
CyberRoots 267
Database 267
Family History Research 267
Genealogical Smorgasbord 267
Genealogy Newsgroups and
    Mailing Lists 267
Genealogy Software for the PC 267
Genealogy Web 268
Handy Tips and How-To's 268
Jewish Mailing List 268
LifeLines Database 268
National Archives and Records
    Administration 269
Non-DOS Software 269
State by State 269
United Kingdom 269
Vital Records in New York State 269
What's in a Name? 270
GEOGRAPHY **270**
Antarctica Resource Guide 270
Australian Postal Codes 270
CIA World Factbook 270
Earth 271
European Postal Codes 271
Federal Geographic Data Products 271

Geodetic Survey of Canada 271
Geographic Information and
    Analysis Laboratory 271
Geographic Information System 271
Geographic Resources Analysis
    Support System 272
Geographische Informationssyteme 272
Geography Discussion 272
Geography Education Software 272
Geography Server 272
Global Land Information System 272
International Background
    Information 272
Local Times Around the World 273
Map Related Web Sites 273
Maps 273
The New South Polar Times 273
New York State Statistics 273
Pathfinder Land Data Sets 273
U.S. Geographic Name
    Server 274
U.S. Snow Cover Maps 274
U.S.A. Statistics 274
World City Maps 274
World Map Collection 274
Xerox Map Viewer 274
Zip Codes of the U.S. 274
GEOLOGY **275**
Earthquake Information 275
Geological Time Scale 275
National Geophysical Data Center 275
Oklahoma Geological Survey
    Observatory 275
Seismic Information 276
Smithsonian Gem & Mineral
    Collection 276
U.C. Berkeley Museum of
    Paleontology 276
U.S. Geological Survey Gopher 276
U.S.G.S. Seismology Reports 276
Volcanoes 276
Volcanology 276
World Paleomagnetic Database 277
GOVERNMENT **277**
Bureau of Justice Statistics
    Documents 277
Canadian Government 277
Catalog of Federal Domestic
    Assistance 278
Census Data for Massachusetts 278
Code of the Federal Register 278
Cooperative Extension System 278
Copyright Information 278
Department of Commerce 278
Economic Conversion Information
    Exchange 278
Federal Highway 278
Federal Information Processing
    Standards 278
Federal Register 279
FedWorld 279
GAO (General Accounting Office)
    Reports 279
General Accounting Office
    Transitional Reports 279
Government and Civics Archives 279
Government Corruption 279
Government Information Sources on
    the Internet 280
Government Policy 280
Government Publications Network 280
Japanese Prime Minister's Official
    Residence 281
National Archives and Records
    Administration 281

National Performance Review Web
    Site 281
NetResults 281
North American Free Trade
    Agreement 282
Patent Office Reform Panel Report 282
Pennsylvania Census, Housing
    Information 282
Personalities 282
Social Security Administration 282
Social Security Administration
    Information 282
Social Security Administration
    Online 283
U.S. Census Information for 1990 283
U.S. Census Information Server 283
U.S. Department of Housing and
    Urban Development 283
U.S. Federal Government
    Information 283
U.S. Government BBS List 284
U.S. Government Gophers 284
U.S. Government Today 284
GOVERNMENT: U.S. CONGRESS ... **284**
Bibliography of Senate Hearings 284
Budget of the United States
    Government 284
Congress Members 284
Congressional Committee
    Assignments 285
Congressional Firsts 285
Congressional Legislation 285
Congressional Quarterly 285
Edward Kennedy 285
Legislative Branch Resources 285
GOVERNMENT: U.S. EXECUTIVE
BRANCH **285**
Clinton's Cabinet 285
Clinton's Inaugural Address 286
Executive Branch Information via
    Gopher 286
Executive Branch Resources via the
    Web 286
Impeaching Clinton 286
National Performance Review 286
President's Daily Schedule 286
President's Economic Plan 286
Presidential Documents 287
U.S. Government Reports 287
White House 287
White House Archives 287
White House News 287
White House Papers 287
White House Press Releases 287
White House Press Releases: Daily 287
HEALTH **288**
Addictions 288
AIDS Information 288
AIDS News 288
Attention Deficit Disorder Archive 288
Cancer Mailing List 288
Children with Special Needs 288
Communicable Diseases 288
Computers and Health 288
Dental Poisoning 288
Diabetes 289
Dietary Information 289
Dieting 289
Drug and Alcohol Information 289
Exercise 289
Eye Care 290
Food and Drug Administration BBS 290
Food Labeling Information 290
Headaches 290
Health Care Reform Act 290

Health General Information 291
Health Info-Com Network
   Newsletter 291
Health Issue Discussion 291
Health News 291
Health Newsletters 291
Health Resources 291
Health Science Resources 292
Health Sciences Libraries
   Consortium 292
Healthline 292
HealthNet 293
Massage 293
Material Safety Data Sheets 293
Migraine Headaches 293
Morbidity and Mortality Weekly
   Report 293
National Institute of Allergy and
   Infectious Disease 293
National Institute of Health 293
New York State Department of
   Health 293
Nutrition 294
Physical Sciences Conferences 294
Public Health Information Guide 294
Sexual Health Topics 294
Sleeping Problems 294
Snakebites 294
Surgeon General's Warning on
   AIDS 294
Typing Injuries 295
U.S. Department of Health and
   Human Services 295
Wellness Mailing List 295
World Health Organization 295
Yoga 295

HISTORICAL DOCUMENTS 295

American Historical Documents 295
Constitution of the United States of
   America 296
Declaration of Arms, 1775 296
Declaration of Independence 296
Document Archive 296
Emancipation Proclamation 296
Federalist Papers 297
Gulf War Announcement Speech 297
JFK Conspiracy Documents 297
Source Documents on the
   Holocaust 297
U.N. Resolutions on Desert Storm 297

HISTORY 298

Aegean Palaces 298
American Memory Collection 298
American Studies 298
Anglo-Saxon Mailing List 298
ArthurNet 298
Aztec Studies 298
Camelot 299
Charlotte, The Vermont Whale 299
Civil War 299
Classical Studies 299
D-Day 299
Dinosaur Discussion List 300
Dinosaur Exhibit 300
Feudal Terms 300
Hall of Dinosaurs 300
Hiroshima Accounts 300
Historian's Database and
   Information Server 300
Historian's Newsletter 300
Historic American Speeches 300
Historical Sounds and Speeches 301
History Archives 301
History Discussion 301
History Mailing Lists 301

History of the Ancient
   Mediterranean 301
Holocaust Discussion 301
I Have a Dream 302
Interactive Natural History Museum 302
Internet Timeline 302
Jesuits and the Sciences 302
Marx and Engels' Writings 302
Medieval History 302
North America 302
Palace of Diocletian 302
Prehistoric Flying Creatures 303
Renaissance 303
Sardinia 303
Spanish and Portuguese History 303
U.S. History 303
Vatican Exhibit 303
Vietnam War Information 303
Vietnam War Mailing List 304
Vikings 304
War 304
World War II 304
World War II Documents 304

HOBBIES 305

Amateur Radio 305
Amateur Radio Information by
   Mail 305
Antique Newspaper Column 305
Antiques 305
Archery 305
ArtMetal 305
Audio Experts 305
Beads 305
Clocks and Watches 306
Coins and Money 306
Collecting 306
Collector's Network 306
Comics 306
Doll Houses 306
Drums and Marching 306
Fiber Arts 307
Guns 307
Juggling 307
Juggling Archives 307
Kites and Kiting Resources 307
Lacemaking 307
LEGO 308
Living History 308
Magic 308
Metalworking 308
Models 308
Nudity 308
Origami 309
Postcards 309
Puzzles 309
Quilting 309
Radio-Controlled Models 309
Railroad 309
Railroad Databases 310
Railroad Maps 310
Railroad Modeling 310
Railroad-Related Internet Resources 310
Rock Collection 310
Roller Coasters 310
Scouting Meets 310
Scuba Diving 310
Sewing 311
Sewing Archives 311
Skateboarding 311
Skating 311
Society for Creative Anachronism 311
Stamp Collecting 312
Steam Engines 312
SurfNet 312
Trading Cards 312
Trains and Railways 313

Unicycling 313
Usenet Hobby Groups 313
Woodworking 313
Woodworking Archives 313

HOME MAINTENANCE 313

Controlling Pests 313
Home Repairs 314
Joist Span Calculator 314
Paint Estimator 314
Repairs 314
Spills and Stains 315
Vacuum Cleaners 315

HUMANITIES 315

Aging 315
Cognition 315
Coombspapers Social Sciences Data
   Bank 316
Humanist Mailing List 316
Nobel Prize 316
Proposed Idea Exchange 316
REACH 316
Resource Guides to the Humanities 316

HUMOR 317

Amusing Tests and Quizzies 317
Ask Dr. Bean 317
Barney the Dinosaur 317
Bastard Operator from Hell 317
Best of Usenet 317
Better and Better 317
Bootsie Report 318
British Comedy 318
British Humor 318
Canonical Lists 318
Cathouse Archives 318
Classic Practical Jokes 318
College Humor 318
Comedy 319
Comix 319
Computer Cartoons 319
Computer Nerd Humor 319
Computer-Oriented Humor 319
Contemporary Humor 319
Deep Thoughts 319
Dr. Fun 320
Encheferizer 320
English is Tough Stuff 320
Fabio's Top Ten Pick-Up Lines 320
Firesign Theater 320
Funny News 320
Funny People 320
Funny Texts 321
Giggles 321
Guide to System Administrators 321
Hacker Test 321
How to Confuse Your Roommate 321
Humor Archives 321
Humor Mailing List 322
Jive Server 322
Joke Collections 322
Jokes 322
Jokes and Fun Archive 323
Jokes, Moderated 323
Jokes and Stories 324
Late Night Talk Show Monologues 324
Library Humor 324
Limerick Server 324
Manly Men's Ten Commandments 324
Michael Tucker 324
Miss Netters' Advice Column 325
Monty Python's Flying Circus 325
Nerd Humor 325
Netwit Mailing List 325
Ollie the Ostrich 325
Oracle 326
Political Humor 326

Politically Correct Primer 326
Principia Discordia 326
Project Galactic Guide 326
Puns 326
Selected Cartoons 326
Seminars for Men 326
Shakespearean Insults 326
Song and TV Show Parodies 327
Standard Disclaimer 327
Steven Wright Quote Server 327
Swifties 327
Tag Lines Galore 327
Tasteless (and Dirty) Jokes 327
Ten Commandments for C
   Programmers 328
Ten Commandments for C
   Programmers (Annotated) 328
Tintin 328
Top 10 Signs Your Web Homepage
   is Not Cool 328
Toxic Custard Workshop Network 328
Wall O'Shame 328
Why? 328
YourMom 328

INTERNATIONAL POLITICS 329
African National Congress 329
American/Japanese Economic
   Relations 329
Arms and Disarmament 329
Crisis in Rwanda 329
Fighting Hate 329
Global Topics 329
Irish Politics 329
Israeli Politics 329
Josip Broz Tito 330
NATO 330
NATO Handbook 330
NATO Press Releases 330
NATODATA 330
Radio Free Europe/Liberty Research
   Institute 330
Speech by Philip Agee 330
Treaties 331
United Nations Gopher 331
United Nations Resolutions 331

INTERNET 331
Babbage's Best of the Internet 331
CU-SeeMe 331
CU-SeeMe Reflector Sites 332
Exploring the Internet 332
Freenets 332
GopherMail 332
Graphical Information Map
   Tutorial 332
History and Uses of the Internet 332
Internet Conference Calendar 332
Internet Drafts 333
Internet Engineering 333
Internet General Discussion 333
Internet Growth Statistics 333
Internet Society Gopher 333
Internet Talk Radio Traveling Circus 333
Internet Timeline 333
Internet University 335
Internet Worm 335
InterNIC Information Services 335
InterText Magazine 335
IP Address Resolver 335
IRC (Internet Relay Chat) 336
IRC channel #WWW 336
Loopback Service 336
Mail Robot 336
Media Coverage 336
Mosaic Mail Gateway 336
Net Happenings 336

Network Information Services 336
Networks and Community 336
Nixpub List 337
NSFNET Traffic Analysis 337
Overview of the Internet and World
   Wide Web 337
People on the Internet 337
Political Implications of the Internet 337
Search Engines 337
Uniform Resource Identifiers 338
Web Collaboration Projects 338
Web Mailing Lists 338
Web Tutorial Slides 338
The WebCrawler 338
WebWorld 338
Who's Who Online 338
Yarn Server 338

INTERNET: HELP 339
Accessing the Internet by Mail 339
Beginner's Guide to HTML 339
Composing Good HTML 339
Entering the World Wide Web:
   Guide to Cyberspace 339
Guide to Network Resource Tools 339
Guide to SLIP and PPP 339
How to Find a Mail Address 339
How to Make Movies 339
How-to Collection 340
Hypertext Markup Language 340
Internet Access Providers List 340
Internet Classroom 340
Internet Help 340
Internet Information 341
Internet Newbies 341
IRC Help 341
Jargon File 341
John December's Internet Web Text 341
Let's Go Gopherin' Now 341
Listserv Information Home Page 342
Merit Network Information Center 342
Mining the Internet 342
Newbie's Guide to the Net 342
Real-Life on the Internet 342
Surfing the Internet 342
Tutorial for PC Users 342
Web Introduction 343
Why Are Internet Resources Free? 343

INTERNET: RESOURCES 343
Announcements of Internet Services 343
Anonymous FTP Site List 343
Awesome List 343
Best of the Web '94 Recipients 343
Carnegie Mellon School of
   Computer Science 344
Clearinghouse for Networked
   Information Discovery 344
Clearinghouse for Subject-Oriented
   Internet Resources 344
Computer-Mediated
   Communication 344
Content Router 344
Cybersmith 344
Data Explorer 344
Database via finger 344
Databases via Telnet 345
Denver Freenet 345
Directory Servers 345
Discovering Internet Resources 345
Distance Learning Resources 345
ElNet Galaxy 345
Electronic Cafe 345
FingerInfo 346
Freenets via Gopher 346
FTP by Mail 346
FTP Services for Non-FTP Users 346

Global City 346
Global Electronic Marketing
   Service 346
Global Network Navigator 346
Gopher Resources 347
Graphic Web Analysis Program 347
Home Page Publisher 347
Home Pages 347
IBM Whois Server 347
InfoMatch 347
Internet by E-Mail 347
Internet Computer Index 347
Internet Fax Server 348
Internet Mailing Lists 348
Internet Market Place 348
Internet Resource Guide 348
Internet Resource Guides 348
Internet Resources Metamap 348
Internet Services 348
Internet Services List 348
Internet Services and Resources 349
Internet Tools List 349
InterNIC Directory of Directories 349
InterNIC InfoGuide 349
InterNIC Web Picks 349
InterScape 349
Island Internet 350
JumpStation 350
Knowbot Information Service 350
Listserv User Guide 350
LYCOS Web Searcher 351
MaasInfo Files 351
Mailbase Gopher 351
Mailing List Search 351
MapMaker 351
Mother-of-All BBSs 351
NandO.net (North Carolina Web
   Server) 351
Net-Happenings 352
NetPages 352
New Gophers 352
New Sites 352
New telnet Sites 353
New Wais Sources 353
NICOL 353
Nomad 353
Online Services 353
Planet Earth Home Page 353
Popular FTP Archives 353
Public Internet Encyclopedia 353
RTD Web Server 354
Scout Report 354
Searching the Internet 354
Subject Trees 354
Subway 354
SunSITE 354
SunSITE Classic 354
Surfers Web 355
Swiss Academic and Research
   Network 355
Technical Report Index 355
Thousand Points of Sites 355
Today's Internet Highlights 355
Traveler Memories 355
Trickle Server Documentation 355
Wais Gateways 355
Web fingerinfo 355
Web Power Index 356
Web Search Engines 356
Web of Wonder 356
WebCrawler Top 25 356
webNews 356
What's New with NCSA Mosaic
   and the Web 356
Whole Internet Catalog 356
WIT Interactive Talk Forum 356

World Wide Web Access Point 356
World Wide Web by Electronic Mail 357
World Wide Web Home 357
World Wide Web Worm 357

INTERNET: RFCS 357
RFC Archive 357
Connecting to the Internet 357
Experienced Internet User Questions 357
Glossary of Networking Terms 357
Hitchhiker's Guide to the Internet 358
Internet Users' Glossary 358
New Internet User Questions 358
Responsibilities of Host and Network
    Managers 358
RFC Lists 358
There's Gold in them thar
    Networks! 358

INTRIGUE 359
Conspiracies 359
J.F.K. Conspiracy 359
Lincoln Conspiracies 360
Taylorology 360
Vigilantes 360

JOBS 361
Academic Jobs 361
American Astronomical Society Job
    Register 361
American Indian Work Issues 361
Biological Sciences 361
Career Books 361
Career Events 361
CareerMosaic 361
Chronicle of Higher Education -
    Academe This Week 361
Cinema Workers 362
Contract Labor 362
Education-Related Jobs 362
Employee Search 362
Employer Profiles 362
Employment Opportunities at
    Microsoft 362
Entry Level Jobs Offered 363
Federal Jobs 363
Interactive Employment Network 363
Job Search 363
Job Seeking 363
Jobnet 363
Jobs General Discussion 364
Jobs Offered 364
Major Resource Kit 364
MedSearch America 364
Online Career Center 364
Online Job Services 364
Professional Career Organizations 364
Résumé Database 364
Résumé Server 365
Résumés 365
Scientific Research 365
SPIE Employment Service 365
U.S. Department of Justice Job
    Listings 365
Virtual Library of Employment
    Opportunities 365
VMS Jobs 365
Women in Science and
    Engineering 365
Women's Studies 366

JOURNALISM AND MEDIA 366
Broadcasting 366
Gonzo Journalism 366
Journalism 366
Journalism Criticism 366
Journalism Discussions 366
Mass Media 367
Media List 367

Media Magazines 367
Music Journalism 367
News Media 367
Online Newspapers 368
Play-by-Play Sportscasters 368
Press Photographers 368
Print Media 368
Report on Waco 368
Television News Archive 368

KEYS AND LOCKS 369
Guide to Lock Picking 369
Lock Picking 369
Lock Talk 369
Locksmithing Archives 371

KIDS 371
Children's Discussion 371
Children's Stories, Poems and
    Pictures 371
Cool Things to Try 371
Disney 371
Disney Talk 371
Field of Clovers 371
How to Recycle Paper 372
Kid's Internet Delight 372
KidArt 372
Kidlink 372
Kids and Computers 372
Kids Mailing List 372
MayaQuest 372
Neat Tricks 372
Stories About Children 372

LANGUAGE 373
Acronym Servers and Archives 373
American/British Lexicon 373
Arabic 373
Catalan 373
Chinese Text Viewers 373
Colibri 373
College Slang Dictionary 373
Computation and Language E-Print
    Archive 374
Cyrillic Text 374
Czech Slovak 374
Devil's Dictionary 374
Dictionary of Computing Terms 375
Dictionary Word Lists 375
Dutch 375
Echo Eurodictautom 375
English Language 375
English and Modern Language
    Graduate Students 375
English-German Dictionary 376
English-Slovene Dictionary 376
Esperanto 376
Esperanto HyperCourse 376
Esperanto Introduction 376
Esperanto-English Dictionary 376
European Network in Language and
    Speech 376
Foreign Language Dictionaries 376
French 377
Gaelic and Gaelic Culture 377
Gaelic Mailing List 377
German 377
German-English Dictionary 377
Hawaiian Glossary 377
Hindi 377
History of Languages 377
Iceland 378
Italian Lessons 378
Japanese 378
Language Articles 378
Language IRC Channels 378
Languages of the World 378
Latin Study Guides 378

Learn Spanish in South America! 378
Lessons in Spanish 379
Linguist List 379
Linguistics 379
Lojban 379
Middle English 379
Mnemonics 380
Name Guide 380
Palindromes 380
Parler au Quotidien 380
Pronunciation 380
Quick and Dirty Guide to Japanese 380
Rasta Dictionary 381
Roget's Thesaurus 381
Russian and East European Studies 381
Russian Swear Words 381
Russian Talk 381
Serbian 381
Shorter Oxford Dictionary 381
Slang Dictionary 381
Spoonerisms 382
Technical Japanese Program 382
Traveler's Japanese 382
Urdu Dictionary 382
Word Lists 382
Word-a-Day 382

LAW 383
Ananse - International Trade Law
    Project 383
Artificial Intelligence and the Law 383
Australian Law 383
Bruce Lavois Shooting 384
California Legal Codes 384
Canadian Law 384
Computer Fraud and Abuse Act 384
Computer Laws 384
Constitution in Cyberspace 384
Copyright and Intellectual Property
    Forum 384
Criminal Justice Country Profiles 384
Criminal Justice Discussion Group 385
CU-LawNet 385
EINet Galaxy Law List 385
Electronic and Communications
    Privacy Act of 1986 385
European Law Students Association 385
Federal Communications Law
    Journal 385
Hawaii Legislative Information
    Service 385
Indiana University School of Law
    Web Server 385
Information Law Papers 385
Jerry's Guide to Law 386
Law Discussion 386
Law Resources 386
Law Schools 386
Law Schools and Law Firms on the
    Web 386
Law Server 386
LawTalk 386
League for Programming Freedom 387
Legal and Criminal Articles 387
Legal Domain Network 387
Legal News 387
Net Law 388
Socio-Legal Preprint Archive 388
Steve Jackson Games 388
Supreme Court Rulings 388
Trade Law Library 389
U.S. Patent Database 389
Venable Attorneys at Law 389
Virtual Law Library 389
Washburn School of Law 389
Washington and Lee University Law
    Library 389

LIBRARIES 389
Archives and Archivists List 389
Automated Library Information
   Xchange 389
Billy Barron's Library List 390
Carl System 390
Cataloging 390
Circulation Control 390
College Libraries 390
Current Cites 390
Dental Librarians 390
Electronic Jewish Library 391
Eureka 391
Government Document Issues 391
Hytelnet 391
Image Databases 391
Launchpad 392
Library Catalogs and Databases 392
Library Catalogs via telnet 392
Library of Congress 392
Library and Information Science 393
Library Newsletters 393
Library Policy Archive 393
Library Resources 393
Library Resources on the Internet 393
Library Topic Lists 393
Medianet OnLine Public Catalog Access 393
Public Access Catalogs 393
University of Maryland Information
   Database 394
Using Internet Libraries 394
Washington University Services 394
Web Mailing List for Librarians 394
Wiretap Online Library 394

LITERATURE 395
American Literature Discussion List 395
Bibliographies of Literature 395
Bryn Mawr Classical Review 395
Classics 395
Council of Remirement 395
Cthulhu 395
Dutch Literature 396
Electronic Text Resources 396
English Server 396
Fun Reading 396
Gothic Literature Discussion List 396
Index to Literature Servers 397
Information on Authors 397
Jewish Literature 397
Literature Discussions 397
Literature General Discussion 397
Modern British and Irish Literature 397
Mysteries 397
Mystery Genre 398
Nancy Drew 398
Native American Literature 398
Patchwork Electronic Literature 398
Women's Book List 398
Workshop on Electronic Texts 398
Writer Resource Guide 399

LITERATURE: AUTHORS 399
Jane Austen 399
L. Frank Baum 399
Ambrose Bierce 399
Brontë Sisters 399
Lewis Carroll 399
Geoffrey Chaucer Mailing List 400
Joseph Conrad 400
Ceanne DeRohan 400
Philip K. Dick 400
Charles Dickens 400
Frederick Douglass 401
Sir Arthur Conan Doyle 401
Ernest Hemingway 401
Hermann Hesse 401

Ingar Holst 401
Katherine Kurtz 401
H.P. Lovecraft 402
Katherine Mansfield 402
John Milton 402
Edgar Allan Poe 402
Terry Pratchett 402
Saki 402
William Shakespeare 402
J.R.R. Tolkien 403
J.R.R. Tolkien Discussions 403
Mark Twain 403
Mark Twain Discussions 403
Virgil 404
H.G. Wells 404
P.G. Wodehouse 404
William Butler Yeats 404

LITERATURE: COLLECTIONS 404
Anglo-Saxon Tales 404
Books in Zip Format 405
Chinese Literature 405
Electronic Books 405
Electronic Books in ASCII Text 405
Freethought Web 405
French Literature 405
Gothic Tales 405
Hypertext Fiction 405
InterText Magazine 406
Italian Literature 406
Philippine Literature 406
Poetry About Life 406
Poetry Assortments 406
Project Gutenberg 406
Science Fiction, Fantasy, and
   Horror 407
Short Stories 407
Women and Literature 407

LITERATURE: TITLES 407
Aeneid 407
Aesop's Fables 407
Agrippa 407
Aladdin and the Wonderful Lamp 407
Alice's Adventures in Wonderland 407
Anne of Green Gables 408
As a Man Thinketh 408
The Call of the Wild 408
The Canterbury Tales 408
Cast Upon the Breakers 408
A Christmas Carol 408
City of the Sun 408
Civil Disobedience 409
Communist Manifesto 409
A Connecticut Yankee in King
   Arthur's Court 409
Discourse on Reason 409
The Divine Comedy (La Divina
   Commedia) 409
Dracula 409
Essays in Radical Empiricism 409
Fairy Tales 410
Fanny Hill 410
Far from the Madding Crowd 410
Flatland 410
Frankenstein 410
The Gift of the Magi 410
Harold and Maude 410
Herland 411
Hippocratic Oath and Law 411
The House of the Seven Gables 411
The Hunting of the Snark 411
The Invisible Man 411
Jabberwocky 411
Japan That Can Say No 411
The Jungle Book 411
Just David 412

The Keepsake Stories 412
The Legend of Sleepy Hollow 412
Mac Shrodinger's Cat 412
Moby Dick 412
The New Atlantis 412
O Pioneers! 412
The Oedipus Trilogy 413
On Liberty 413
Our Mr. Wrenn 413
Paradise Lost 413
Parnassus on Wheels 413
Peter Pan 413
The Pit and the Pendulum 413
The Scarlet Letter 413
The Scarlet Pimpernel 414
Scientific Secrets, 1861 414
Sherlock Holmes Novels 414
The Song of Hiawatha 414
The Strange Case of Dr. Jekyll and
   Mr. Hyde 414
Susan Lenox: Her Rise and Fall 415
The Time Machine 415
Through the Looking-Glass 415
Tom Sawyer 415
Umney's Last Case 415
United Nations Declaration of
   Human Rights 416
United We Stand 416
Up from Slavery 416
Voyage of the Beagle 416
The War of the Worlds 416
The Wonderful Wizard of Oz 416
Wuthering Heights 416

MAGAZINES 417
Blink Magazine 417
bOING bOING 417
Byte Magazine 417
Chips Online 417
Computer-Mediated
   Communication 417
CTHEORY 417
Cultronix 417
Culture Magazines 417
Electronic Journals Project 417
Electronic Newspapers and
   Magazines 418
Entertainment Magazines Online 418
Family Times 418
Hacking 418
High Times News 418
Internaut 418
Internet with Attitude 418
Internet Business Journal 418
Internet Talk Radio 419
Magazine Summaries 419
Meta 419
Mother Jones 419
Netweaver 419
Open Systems Today 419
PC Magazine 420
PC Week Labs 420
Phrack 420
Quanta 420
SCO World Magazine 420
Skeptic 420
Soapbox 420
Sound Site Newsletter 421
The Lynx 421
The Tech 421
Unix World 421
Virtual Library of Electronic
   Journals 421
Voices from the Net 421
Wired 421

MAIL TO FAMOUS PEOPLE 422

Douglas Adams 422
Scott Adams 422
John Perry Barlow 422
Stewart Brand 422
Bill Clinton 423
Alan Colmes 423
Adam Curry 423
Bill Gates 423
Al Gore 423
Mike Jittlov 423
Mitch Kapor 424
Edward Kennedy 424
Rush Limbaugh 424
Roger McGuinn 424
Marvin Minsky 424
Terry Pratchett 424
Radio and TV Networks Electronic
    Mail Addresses 424
Howard Rheingold 425
Michael Tucker 425
James Woods 425

MATHEMATICS 425

Algebra Assistance 425
American Mathematical
    Society 425
Calculator 425
Calculus Graphics 426
Center for Geometry Analysis
    Numerics and Graphics 426
Center for Nonlinear Studies 426
Centre for Experimental and
    Constructive Mathematics 426
Chance Server 426
Commutative Algebra 426
Consortium for Ordinary Differential
    Equations Experiments 426
Differential Equations 426
E-Math BBS 427
Electronic Journal of Combinatorics 427
Electronic Journal of Differential
    Equations 427
Electronic Sources for Mathematics 427
Electronic Transactions on
    Numerical Analysis 427
Gallery of Interactive Online
    Geometry 427
Geometry Center 427
Geometry Literature Database 427
GNU Plot 427
Hub Mathematics and Science
    Center 427
Illinois Mathematics and Science
    Academy 428
K-theory Preprint Archives 428
Logic 428
Math Archives Gopher 428
Math Articles 428
Math and Calculus Programs 428
Math Gophers 428
Math and Philosophy 429
Math Programs for the Mac 429
Mathematical Association of
    America 429
Mathematical Publications List 429
Mathematical Research 429
Mathematical Sciences Server 429
Mathematical Topics at the Center
    for Scientific Computing 430
Mathematics City 430
Mathematics General Discussion 430
Mathematics Resource Pointers 430
Mathematics Servers 430
MathWorks 430
NetLib Software Server 431

New York Journal of Mathematics 431
Nonlinear Dynamics 431
Numerical Analysis 431
pi Page 431
pi to 1 Million Digits 431
pi to 1.25 Million Digits 431
Society for Industrial and Applied
    Math 432
Spanky Fractal Database 432
Square Root of 2 432
Statistics 432
Statistics and Operations Research 432
StatLib Archives 432
StatLib Gopher Server 432
Symbolic Algebra 432
Symbolic Mathematical
    Computation Information
    Center 432
Teaching: Elementary and High
    Schools 432
Virtual Library of Math 433
Weights and Measures 433

MEDICINE 433

AIDS 433
AIDS Frequently Asked Questions 433
AIDS Information Newsletter 433
AIDS Information via CHAT
    Database 433
AIDS Mailing List 433
AIDS Statistics 433
AIDS Treatment News and Facts 433
Allergies 434
Anatomy Teaching Modules 434
Anesthesiology 434
Biomedical Engineering 434
Brain Tumors 434
Breast Cancer Information 434
CancerNet 434
Chronic Fatigue Syndrome 435
Croatian Medicine 435
Crohn's Disease and Colitis 435
Cryonics Frequently Asked
    Questions 435
Cystic Fibrosis 435
Dentistry 436
Dermatology List 436
Digital Imaging and
    Communications 436
Diseases Involving the Immune
    System 436
Do Power Lines Cause Cancer? 437
Drugs Information 437
E.T. Net 437
Endometriosis 437
Epilepsy Information via CHAT
    Database 437
Forensic Medicine 437
Genetic Sequence Data Bank 438
Genetics Bank 438
German Cancer Research Center 438
Hippocratic Oath 438
History of Medicine Division 438
Home Test Kits 438
HyperDoc 438
Infertility 439
Life-Threatening Medical
    Emergencies 439
MEDCAL 439
Medical Education Information
    Center 439
Medical and Health Information 439
Medical Libraries 439
Medical Physics 439
Medical Resources 439
Medical Software 439
Medical Software and Data 440

Medical Students 440
Medical Students Forum 440
Medicine General Discussion 440
Mednews 440
Mood Disorders Server 440
Multimedia Textbooks 440
National Cancer Center 440
National Cancer Center Database
    (Japan) 441
National Library of Medicine 441
National Library of Medicine
    Locator 441
Nurses 441
Nursing 441
Nursing Web 441
Occupational Medicine 441
Oncology 442
Organ Transplant 442
Paramedics 442
Pathology and Histology Server 442
Pediatric Oncology Group 442
PET Scan Image Database 442
Pharmacy 442
Politics and Medicine 442
Post-Polio Syndrome 443
Radiology 443
Repetitive Motion Injuries 443
Repetitive Stress Injuries 443
Telemedicine 443
Texas Cancer Data Center 443
Topics In Primary Care 443
Veterinary Medicine 443
Victorian Institute for Forensic
    Pathology 443
VIDIMED Project Image Gallery 443
Virtual Hospital 444
Virtual Library of Medicine 444

MEDICINE: ALTERNATIVE 444

Alternative Medicine 444
Alternative Medicine Home Page 444
Articles on Alternative Methods of
    Healing 444
Ayurvedic Medicine 445
Essiac 445
Good Medicine Magazine 445
Herb Archive 445
Herb Books and Sources 446
Herb Hypercard Stack 446
Herbal Caution 446
Herbal Medicine 446
Holistic Healing 446
Laetrile and Vitamin B17 446
Natural Childbirth Anecdotes 447
Nutritional Healing 447
Oxygen and Ozone Therapy 447

MILITARY 448

Defense Conversion Subcommittee 448
Disarmament Discussion List 448
First World War 448
Military Collections 448
Naval Fighting Ships 448
Navy News Service 449
Navy Policy Book 449
NavyOnLine 449
Siege Warfare 450
Tattoo 450
Technology Insertion 450
U.S. Code of Military Justice 450
U.S. Military News 450
War History 451

MISCHIEF 451

April Fools 451
Big Book of Mischief 451
Hack Gallery 451
Practical Jokes 452

Revenge	452
Terrorist's Handbook	452

MOVIES 453

Asian Movies	453
Blade Runner	453
Blues Brothers	453
Cardiff's Movie Database Browser	453
Cinema Discussion List	453
Cinema Talk	453
CinemaSpace	453
Cult Movies	453
Disney Comics and Cartoons	453
Film Database	454
Film Mailing List	454
Film, Television, and Popular Culture	454
Film and TV Studies	454
Film and Video Resources	454
Filmmakers	454
Filmmaking and Reviews	455
Horror Talk	455
Monster Movies	455
Movie Database Request Server	455
Movie and Film Festivals	455
Movie Folklore	455
Movie Information	456
Movie List	456
Movie Reviews	456
Movies Archives	456
Movies and Filmmaking	456
Movies News	456
Science Fiction Movies	457
Society for the Preservation of Film Music	457
Weird Movie List	457

MUDS: GENERAL INFORMATION 457

Administrating MUDs	457
DikuMUDs	457
German Speakers	458
LPMUDs	458
MUD Announcements	458
MUD Documents	458
MUD Information	459
MUD List	459
MUD as a Psychological Model	459
MUD Usenet Discussion Groups	459
MUDWHO Server	459
MUSH Documents	459
Tiny MUDs	460

MUDS: SPECIFIC TYPES 460

Actuator MUD	460
Actuator MUD Gopher	460
AlexMUD	460
Apocalypse	460
Chupchups	460
Copper Diku	460
Deeper Trouble	460
DikuMud II	461
Dirt	461
Discworld MUD	461
Discworld MUD Gopher	461
htMUD	461
Island	461
LambdaMOO	461
MUD Access via Gopher	462
Nails	462
Nightfall MUD	462
Nightfall MUD Information	462
Nightmare MUD	462
PernMush	462
Regenesis	462
Star Wars	462
Three Kingdoms MUD	463
TrekMuse	463
Zen	463

MUSEUMS 463

Exploratorium	463
Interactive Natural History Museum	463
Missing and Stolen Clearinghouse	463
Museums, Exhibits and Special Collections	463
Museums on the Web	463
Natural History Museum, London	463
U.C. Berkeley Museum of Paleontology	464

MUSIC 464

4AD Eyesore	464
A Cappella	464
Acid Jazz	464
Acoustic and Electric Bass	464
Acoustic Guitar Archive	464
Acoustic Guitar Digest	464
Acoustic Music Server	464
Afro-Caribbean Music	464
Afro-Latin	465
Articles of Music Composition	465
Bagpipes	465
Banjo Tablature Archive	465
Barbershop Quartets	465
Bassoon and Oboe	465
Big Band	466
Bluegrass Music Discussion List	466
Blues	466
Bottom Line Zine	466
Brass Musicians	466
Bulgarian Sounds	467
Buying and Selling Music	467
CDs	467
Celtic Music	467
Christian Music	467
Clarinet Players Mailing List	467
Classical Music	467
Classical Music Mailing List	468
Complex Arrangements	468
Computerized Music	468
Computers in Music Research	468
Concert Information	468
Country and Western	468
Creative Internet Home Page	468
Croatia	468
Discographies	469
Drums and Percussion	469
Early Music	469
Electric Music	469
Electronic Music	469
Electronic Music and Synthesizers	469
Electronic/Industrial Music Zine List	470
Ethnomusicology Research Digest	470
Filk Music	470
Film Music	470
Folk Music Archives	470
Folk Music Calendar	470
Folk Music Concerts	470
Folk Music Digital Tradition	470
Folk Music Discussion	470
Folk Music Information	471
Folk Music Lyrics	471
Funk	471
Gothic Web Pages and Chat	471
Gregorian Chants	471
Grunge	471
Guitar	472
Guitar Archive	472
Guitar Chords for Popular Songs	472
Hard Bop Cafe	472
Harpsichord Exercises	472
Heavy Metal	472
Heavy Thrash Music	472
Impulse	473
Indian Classical Music	473

Institutions of Music	473
Japanese Popular Music	473
Jazz/Blues/Rock and Roll Images	473
Jazz Clubs Around the World	473
Jazz Photography	473
Jazz Server	473
Jewish Music	474
Lute	474
Lyrics Archive	474
Lyrics from Musicals	474
Mammoth Records Internet Center	474
Marching Bands	474
Metaverse	475
MIDI Home Page	475
Music Archives	475
Music and Behavior	475
Music Chat	475
Music Composition	475
Music Database	475
Music Discussion	476
Music Facts	476
Music FAQs	476
Music Festival Information	476
Music Kitchen	476
Music Library Association	476
Music List of Lists	476
Music News	476
Music Performance	476
Music Resources	477
Music Reviews	477
Music Samples	477
Music Server	477
Music and Sound Files	477
Music Underground Archive	477
Music Videos	477
Musical Instrument Construction	478
New Age Music	478
New Music	478
Percussion	478
Performing Classical Music	478
Pipe Organ	478
Progressive	478
Punk Rock	478
Rap	478
Rare Groove	478
Rave	479
Rave Discussion	479
Record Production	479
Reggae	479
Renaissance Instruments	479
Rock and Classical Music	479
Rock and Roll	479
San Francisco Bay Area Concerts	479
Scottish Style Drumming	480
Sheet Music Collection	480
Song Lyrics	480
Sonic	480
Southern Rock Music	480
Strange Sounds	480
Techno/Rave Gopher	480
Top (and Bottom) 100 Lists	480
Underground Music Archive	481
Update Electronic Music Newsletter	481
Vibe Magazine	481
Vibe Recording Studio	481
Violin and Bow Makers	481
Virtual Radio	481
Web Wide World of Music	481
WOMAD — World of Music, Arts, and Dance	481
Woodstock '94 Multimedia Center	481
World Music	481

MUSIC: PERFORMERS 482

Allman Brothers	482
Tori Amos	482

Art of Noise 482
Beastie Boys 482
Jimmy Buffett 482
Kate Bush 482
Christian Death Home Page 482
Cocteau Twins Home Page 482
Concrete Blonde 482
Alice Cooper 483
Elvis Costello 483
Miles Davis 483
The Death of Rock 'n' Roll 483
Depeche Mode 483
Dire Straits 483
Bob Dylan 483
Electric Light Orchestra 483
Enya 483
Melissa Etheridge 483
Favorite Musicians and Music
   Groups 484
Front 242 484
Peter Gabriel 484
Marvin Gaye 485
Debbie Gibson 485
Grateful Dead 485
Jimi Hendrix 486
Allan Holdsworth 486
Indigo Girls 486
Jean Michel Jarre 486
Jazz Performers 486
Billy Joel 486
Kiss 486
John Lennon 487
Paul McCartney 487
Paul McCartney Death Rumor 487
Reba McEntire 487
Nine Inch Nails 487
Sinead O'Connor 487
Pink Floyd 487
The Pogues 488
The Police 488
Elvis Presley 488
Prince 489
Rocker Group Web Pages 489
Rolling Stones 489
Rush 489
Severed Heads 489
Frank Sinatra 489
Sisters of Mercy 490
Bruce Springsteen 490
10,000 Maniacs 490
Vangelis 490
Sid Vicious 490
Doc Watson 490
XTC 490

NEW AGE 491
Afterlife 491
AwareNet 491
Biorhythms 491
Lucid Dreams 491
Magick 492
Magick Galore 492
Masters, Extraterrestrials and
   Archangels 492
Meditation 493
Mysticism 493
New Age Talk 493
Occult and Magick Talk 493
Occult Mailing List 493
Paganism 493
Postmodern Culture 493
Revelations of Awareness 493
Sex and Magick 494
Spirit Web 494
Spiritual Grab Bag 494
Spiritual Healing 494
Sumeria Web Page 494

Tarot 494
Tarot Reading 494
Urantia Book 495
Visions of Jesus and Mary 495
Wicca 495

NEWS: U.S. 495
CBC Radio Trial 495
Clarinet 495
Commercial Online News
   Ventures 495
Current Affairs Magazines 495
Daily Sources of Business and
   Economic News 496
EFFector Online and EFF News 496
Electric Examiner 496
Electronic Newsstand 496
The Gate 497
Headline and Business News 497
Middlesex News 497
NASA Hot Topics 497
National News Stories 497
The News & Observer 497
Newsletters and Journals Available
   via Gopher 497
Newspapers and Journalism
   Schools 497
San Francisco Examiner News
   Wires Page 497
State News 498
Submitting News via the Internet 498
USA Today 498
Washington Post 498

NEWS: WORLD 498
ABC's World News Now 498
Australian News 498
Bosnia 498
Chinese News Digest Server 499
Croatian Ministry of Foreign
   Affairs 499
Croatian News 499
Daily Newspaper Electronic Mail
   Addresses 499
Ecuadoran Daily News Summaries 499
French Daily News Transcripts 499
French Language Press Review 499
French News 499
Gazeta Wyborcza 500
German Language News
   Service 500
Islamic News 500
Israeli News 500
Moscow News 500
Pakistan 500
RTE Radio News 500
World News 500

OCEANOGRAPHY 501
Distributed Ocean Data System 501
Global Ocean Flux Study 501
Icelandic Fisheries Laboratories 501
Index to Web Servers 501
Institute for Remote Sensing
   Applications 501
Oceanic (The Ocean Network
   Information Center) 501
Oceanography Information 501
Scripps Institute of Oceanography 502
SeaWiFS Project 502

OPERATING SYSTEMS: DOS ... 502
4DOS Command Processor 502
Desqview 502
DOS News 502
Mail and Usenet News 503
Miscellaneous DOS Topics 503
uucp for DOS 503

**OPERATING SYSTEMS: GENERAL
   TOPICS** 503
Operating Systems General
   Discussion 503
Research on Operating Systems 503
Root Chatline 503

**OPERATING SYSTEMS:
   MICROSOFT WINDOWS** 503
Announcements About Microsoft
   Windows 503
Applications for Microsoft
   Windows 503
Binaries for Windows 504
Microsoft Web Server 504
Microsoft Windows Developer
   Information 504
Networking 504
Programming 504
Sockets for Microsoft Windows 504
Video 504
Windows General Discussion 504
Windows News 505
Windows Setup 505
WordPerfect 505

**OPERATING SYSTEMS:
   MISCELLANEOUS SYSTEMS** 505
AOS 505
CP/M 505
Geos 505
Geos Binaries 505
Internet Connectivity for PCs 505
Lynx 505
Mach 505
Minix 506
Multics 506
Nachos 506
OS9 506
Parix 506
QNX 506
RSTS 506
V 506
VMS 506
VSE/ESA Mainframe 507
VxWorks 507
Xinu 507

OPERATING SYSTEMS: OS/2 .. 507
Announcements About OS/2 507
Applications for OS/2 507
Binaries for OS/2 507
Games 507
Multimedia OS/2 507
OS/2 Beta Releases 507
OS/2 Bugs and Fixes 507
OS/2 Chat 508
OS/2 General Discussion 508
OS/2 Home Page 508
OS/2 Information 508
OS/2 Networking 508
OS/2 Setup 508
OS/2 Versions 1.x 508
Programming in OS/2 508

OPERATING SYSTEMS: SCO 508
Announcements About SCO Unix 508
Binaries for SCO Unix 509
Enhanced Feature Supplements 509
Games for SCO Unix 509
Hardware Compatibility Handbook 509
Open Desktop 509
SCO General Discussion 509
SCO Magazine 509
SCO Unix Files for Compaq
   Computers 509
SCO Unix Supplements: Compaq
   Computers 509

Source Code for Programs for SCO 510
Support Level Supplements 510
Technical Library Supplements 510
Termcap and Terminfo Updates 510
Widget Server 510
Xenix 510

OPERATING SYSTEMS: UNIX IN GENERAL 510
Dial-Up Site List 510
DOS Under Unix 510
Mainframes and Large Networks 510
News About Unix 510
Open Software Foundation 510
PC and Macintosh Guides 511
Programming 511
Questions and Answers About
    Unix 511
Security 511
Shells 511
Source Code to Unix Programs 511
Standards 511
Text Formatter 512
Unix Administration 512
Unix Chat and Help 512
Unix General Discussion 512
Unix Information Server 512
Unix Internals 512
Unix Manual 512
Unix on PC Architectures 512
Unix Software and Source Code 513
User-Friendliness 513
vi Reference Card 513
vi Tutorial 513

OPERATING SYSTEMS: UNIX SYSTEMS 514
A/UX 514
AIX 514
BSD Unix 514
BSD Unix for PCs 514
BSDI 514
Coherent 514
Cray 514
FreeBSD 515
Linux 515
Linux Chat and Support 515
OSF/1 516
Solaris 516
System V 516
Ultrix 516
Xenix 516

OPERATING SYSTEMS: WINDOWS NT 516
Windows NT General Discussion 516
Windows NT News 516
Windows NT Setup 516

ORGANIZATIONS 517
Amnesty International 517
Association for Computing
    Machinery 517
Center for Civil Society
    International 517
Civil Society: USA 517
Earth First 517
Electronic Frontier Foundation 517
History of Philosophy of Science 518
Hume Society 519
Institute for Global
    Communications 519
Jewish Organizations 519
Mensa 519
National Child Rights Alliance 519
National Institute of Standards and
    Technology 519
Nonprofit Organizations 519

Partnerships Against Violence 519
Peace Corps 519
Peace Watch 520
SEA Gopher 520
Service Organizations 520
Toastmasters 520
World Organizations 520

OUTDOOR ACTIVITIES 520
Backcountry Home Page 520
Ballooning 520
Climbing 520
Climbing Archive 521
Diving Server 521
Fishing 521
Hiking 521
Kayaking 521
Mountain Biking 521
Mountain Biking Areas 521
Orienteering and Rogaining 521
Outdoors Discussion Group 522
Paddling 522
Rowing 522
Scouting 522
Snowmobiles 522
Spelunking 522
Surfing Tutorial 522
Windsurfing 522

PARANORMAL 523
Alien Cultures 523
Astral Projection 523
Channeling 523
Freud's Occult Studies 524
Lightful Images 524
Near-Death Experiences 524
Necronomicon 524
Occult Archives 524
Occult and Mysticism Network 524
Occult and Paranormal 524
Occultist Temple of Set 525
Orvotron Newsletter 525
Out-of-Body Experiences 525
Paranormal Phenomena General
    Discussion 525
Parapsychology 525
Psi Phenomena 525
Scientific Theories behind
    Paranormal Events 525
Skepticism 525
Spaceships 526
Starbuilders 526
UFOs - Discussion Groups 527
UFOs - Incident in Roswell 527
UFOs - Mysterious Abductions 527

PARTIES AND ENTERTAINMENT 527
Drinking Games 527
Mardi Gras 527
Party Ideas 528
Party Time 528
Toasts 528

PEOPLE 528
Albert Einstein 528
Buckminster Fuller 528
Celebrities 529
Elders 529
John Muir Exhibit 529
National Press Club Luncheon
    Addresses 529
Nerd Club 529
Obituary Page 530
Random Portrait Gallery 530
Who's Who in Russia 530

PERSONALS 530
41 Plus 530

Bisexuals 530
Chit-Chat 530
Electronic Matchmaker 531
Fat People 531
Friendly Folk 531
Large People 531
Meeting People 531
Polyamory 531
Spanking 531
Virtual MeetMarket 532

PHILOSOPHY 532
American Philosophical
    Association 532
An Enquiry Concerning Human
    Understanding 532
Ancient Philosophy 532
Buddhist Studies 532
Common Sense 532
Electronic Journal of Analytic
    Philosophy 533
Extropians 533
Hakim Bey 533
I Ching 533
Immanuel Kant 533
Soren Kierkegaard 533
J. Krishnamurti 533
Maximizing Life's Choices 533
Memetics 534
Metaphysics 534
New Ways of Thinking 534
Objectivism 534
Objectivism Mailing List 534
Oceania 535
Personal Idealogies 535
Philosophical Discussions 535
Philosophy at the University of
    Bologna 535
Philosophy of the Middle Ages 535
Plato 535
Principia Cybernetica Web 535
University of Chicago Philosophy
    Project 535
Utopia 536
Zen 536

PHOTOGRAPHY 536
California Museum of Photography 536
Darkroom Photography 536
Photo Database 536
Photography Archives 537
Photography General Discussion 537
Photography Mailing List 537
Photography Questions and
    Answers 537
Pinhole Camera 537
Power Tips and Tricks for
    Photoshop 537
Stereograms and 3-D Images 537

PHYSICS 537
American Institute of Physics 537
Austin Fusion Studies 538
Center for Particle Astrophysics 538
Early Instruments 538
Einstein in 3-D 538
Electromagnetic Fields and
    Microwave Electronics 538
Electromagnetics 538
European Group for Atomic
    Spectroscopy 539
Fermilab 539
Fusion 539
HEP Data Archive 539
High Energy Physics Information
    Center 539
Index of Abstracts 539
Institute of High Energy Physics 539

KVI Research Network 540
National Nuclear Data Center
    Online Service 540
OpticsNet 540
Particles 540
Physics Discussion Groups 540
Physics Gopher 540
Physics Information Service 541
Physics Mailing Lists 541
Physics on the Net 541
Physics Student Discussion List 541
Relativity 541
Sounds from Chaos 541
Stanford Linear Accelerator Center 541
Theoretical Physics Pre-print List 541
WebStars: Astrophysics on the
    Web 542

POETRY 542
William Blake 542
Chinese Poetry 542
Dogwood Blossoms 542
Exquisite Sonnet Project 542
Robert Herrick 542
Internet Poetry Archive 542
John Keats 542
Poems 543
Poems and Prose 543
Poet's Cafe 543
Poetry Archives 543
Poetry Index 543
Poetry Workshop 543
Percy Bysshe Shelley 543
Shiki Internet Haiku Salon 543
Song 543
Algernon Charles Swinburne 544
Terance, This Is Stupid Stuff 544
Alfred Lord Tennyson 544
To His Coy Mistress 544
What the Welsh and Chinese Have
    in Common 544
When Lilacs Last in the Dooryard
    Bloom'd 544
John Greenleaf Whittier 544
William Wordsworth 544
World War I Poetry 544

POLITICS: NATIONAL (U.S.) 544
'60s Left Today 544
21st Century Constitution 545
Animal Defense Network 545
Clinton Jokes 545
Clinton Watch 545
Coalition for Networked
    Information 545
Conservation Action 545
Conservative Discussion Lists 545
Conservative Political News 545
Feminism and Liberty 545
Human Rights 546
Libertarian Manifestos 546
Libertarian Student Network 546
Libertarians 546
Liberty Network 546
National Research and Education
    Network Bill 546
The New Republic Magazine 546
No Treason — The Constitution of
    No Authority 546
Political Discussions 547
Political Forum 547
Political Party Platform Statements 547
Politics and the Network
    Community 547
Position Papers of Senator Harkin 547
Right Side of the Web 547
Rush Limbaugh Archives 547

Rush Limbaugh Political Discussion 548
Scandals of the Clinton
    Administration 548
Vince Foster 548
Vote Smart 548
Weird Politics and Conspiracy 548
Whitewater Scandal 548

POLITICS: STATE AND LOCAL
(U.S.) 549
Bay Area Libertarians 549
California Libertarians 549
Colorado Legislative Information 549
Iowa Political Stock Market 549
Jim Warren Gopher 549

PSYCHOLOGY 549
American Psychological Society 549
Brainwashing 549
Cognitive and Psychological
    Sciences Index 550
Cognitive Science 550
Consciousness 550
Creativity and Creative Problem
    Solving 550
Depression Disorders 550
Family Science 550
Family Violence 550
Intimate Violence 550
Panic Disorders 551
Practical Psychology Magazine 551
Psychological Help 552
Psychology Graduate Student
    Journal 552
Psycoloquy 552
Schizophrenia 553
Stuttering 553
Suicide Prevention 553

PUBLICATIONS 553
Dartmouth College Library Online
    System 553
Journalism 553
Journals with a Difference 553
Newsletters, Electronic Journals,
    Zines 554
Online Publications 554
Publisher's Catalogs 554
Whole Earth Review Articles 554

PUBLISHING 554
Association of American University
    Presses 554
Copy Editors Mailing List 554
Electronic Publishing 555
McGraw-Hill Internet Resource
    Area 555
Publisher's Catalogs 555
Sci-Fi Publishers Newsletters 555
Tor Books 555
Ventana Press Internet Resource
    Area 555

QUOTATIONS 556
Woody Allen 556
Beavis and Butthead Quotables 556
Bible Quotes 556
Lenny Bruce 556
Andrew Dice Clay 556
Cyberspace Quotations 556
Rodney Dangerfield 556
W.C. Fields 557
Fortune Cookie Database 559
Samuel Goldwyn 559
High Culture 559
Humorous Quotations 559
David Letterman 559
loQtus 559

Groucho Marx 559
Norm Peterson from Cheers 560
Quotation Reference Books 560
Quotations Archive 560
Quotes About Religion 560
Random Quotes 560
Ren and Stimpy 561
Seinfeld Quotes 561
Star Trek 561
Mark Twain 561
WebWisdom 561
Oscar Wilde 561
Steven Wright 561

RADIO 562
Amateur Radio 562
Campus Radio Disk Jockeys 562
Canadian Broadcasting
    Corporation 562
Citizens Band Radio 562
Digital Audio Broadcasting 563
FM Broadcasting 563
Ham Radio Archives 563
Ham Radio Callbooks 563
Monitor Radio 563
Radio Broadcasting 563
Shortwave Radio 563
Voice of America 564

REAL ESTATE 564
Commercial Real Estate 564
Global Real Estate Guide 564
Homebuyer's Fair 564
Real Estate Brokers 564
Real Estate Discussion Group 564
Real Estate News 565
Research and Data 565

RELIGION 565
Anglican Christianity 565
Articles on Religion 565
Atheism 565
Atheist Manifesto 565
Baptist Discussion List 565
Bible Browser for Unix 565
Bible Gateway 566
Bible Online 566
Bible Program 566
Bible Promises Macintosh Hypercard
    Stack 567
Bible Quiz Game 567
Bible Retrieval System for Unix 567
Bible Search Program 567
Bible Search Tools 567
Bible Study 567
Bible Text 567
Bible Translations 567
Bible Verses 567
Bible Word, Phrase Counts: King
    James Version 568
Biblical Search and Extraction Tool 568
Biblical Timeline 568
Book of Mormon 568
Buddhism 568
Buddhism Discussion 568
Catholic Christianity 569
Catholic Doctrine 569
Catholic Evangelism 569
Catholicism 569
Chabad Lubavitch Judaism 569
Christia 569
Christian Discussion 569
Christian Leadership Forum 569
Christian Resources 570
Christian Thought and Literature in
    Late Antiquity 570
Christian Visions 570
Christianity 570

Christianity and How It Relates to Society ... 570
Christianity and Literature ... 570
Coptic ... 570
Croatian Christian Information Service ... 570
Different Christianities Dialogue ... 571
Eastern Orthodox Christianity ... 571
Eastern Religions ... 571
Electric Mystic's Guide to the Internet ... 571
Episcopal Beliefs and Practices ... 571
First Century Judaism ... 571
Gabriel's Horn ... 571
Genesis ... 571
Global Christianity Discussion ... 571
Hebrew Quiz ... 571
Hindu Dharma ... 572
Hinduism ... 572
History of American Catholicism ... 572
Islam ... 572
Islam Discussion ... 572
Issues in Religion ... 572
Jainism ... 572
Jewish Culture and Religion ... 572
Jewish Law ... 572
Jewish Mailing List ... 573
Jewish Religious Institutions ... 573
Judaica Collection ... 573
Koran (or Qur'an) ... 573
Mennonites ... 573
Moorish Orthodox Church ... 573
Mormon ... 574
Mysticism Discussion ... 574
Orthodox Christianity ... 574
Period Calendar ... 574
Practical Christian Life ... 574
Religious Denominations ... 574
Religious News ... 574
Religious Studies Publications ... 575
Sexuality and Religion ... 575
Shakers ... 575
Society of Friends ... 575
Soka Gakkai International ... 575
Vedic Civilization ... 575
Zen Buddhist Texts ... 575
Zoroastrianism ... 576

RELIGION: ALTERNATIVE ... 576

Ahmadiyya ... 576
Baha'i Faith ... 576
Brother Jed ... 576
Eckankar ... 576
Generic Religions and Secret Societies ... 576
Gnosticism ... 577
Goddess Spirituality and Feminism ... 577
Kriya Yoga ... 577
Mage's Guide to the Internet ... 577
New Religious Movements ... 577
Pagan Religion and Philosophy ... 577
Pagan Yule Customs ... 578
Sabaean Religious Order ... 578
Satanism ... 578
Scientology ... 578
Secular Web ... 578
Shamanism ... 578
Theosophy ... 578
Unitarianism ... 578

RELIGION: HUMOR ... 579

Atheism Satire ... 579
Bible in Pig Latin ... 579
Religious Humor ... 579

ROLE-PLAYING ... 579

Chill Horror Role-Playing Game ... 579
Dark-Sun ... 579
Fantasy Role-Playing ... 579
Fantasy Role-Playing Games ... 580
Flashlife ... 580
Illuminati Online ... 580
Live-Action Role-Playing ... 580
Miniatures ... 581
Pern Role-Playing ... 581
Role-Playing ... 581
Role-Playing Archives ... 581
Role-Playing Famous Last Words ... 582
Role-Playing Games ... 582
RuneQuest ... 582
ShadowRun ... 582
ShadowRun on the Web ... 582
Star Trek Role-Playing ... 582
Tekumel ... 583
Torg ... 583
Traveller ... 583
Vampire ... 583

ROMANCE ... 583

Couples ... 583
Love ... 583
Men and Women ... 583
Penpals ... 584
Polyamory ... 585
Romance ... 585
Romance Readers Anonymous ... 585
Romantic Whisperings ... 585
Singles ... 585
Soulmates ... 585
Unhappy Romances ... 585
Weddings ... 585

SCIENCE ... 586

Annealing ... 586
Anthropology Mailing List ... 586
Aquaculture Discussion List ... 586
Black Holes ... 586
California Academy of Sciences ... 586
Color Perception ... 586
Color and Vision ... 587
Earth and Sky ... 587
Electromagnetics in Medicine, Science and Communication ... 587
Energy Research in Israel ... 587
Ethology ... 587
Global Positioning System ... 587
Hiroshima ... 587
History of Science and Technology ... 587
International System of Units ... 588
The Mind ... 588
Mini-Journal of Irreproducible Results ... 588
National Institute of Health Projects ... 588
National Science Foundation Publications ... 588
NCSA Digital Gallery CD-ROM Science Theater ... 589
Origin of the Universe ... 589
Radiocarbon Gopher ... 589
Radiocarbon and Radioisotopes Mailing List ... 589
Research Methods ... 589
Resource Guides to Science ... 589
Science Beat ... 589
Science Fraud ... 590
Science Magazines ... 590
Science and Technology Information System ... 590
Scientific Articles ... 590
Scientific Ponderings ... 590
Scientific Skepticism ... 591
The Scientist ... 591
Scientist's Workbench ... 591
Virtual School of Natural Sciences ... 591
Women in Science Hypercard Project ... 591

SCIENCE FICTION ... 591

Alien III Script ... 591
Ansible Newsletter ... 592
Bibliographies of Science Fiction ... 592
Bruce Sterling ... 592
Classic Science Fiction and Fantasy Reviews ... 592
Complete Bibliographies of Major Authors ... 592
Conan the Barbarian ... 592
Dragons and Dragonlance Fantasy ... 593
Dune Home Page ... 593
Fandom ... 593
Fans of Science Fiction Writers ... 593
Fantastic Fantasies ... 593
Fantasy, Science Fiction, Horror Calendar ... 593
Furry Stuff ... 593
Highly Imaginative Technologies ... 593
Hugo Awards of 1990 ... 594
Infinity City ... 594
Mystery Science Theater 3000 ... 594
Red Dwarf ... 594
Sci-Fi Books ... 594
Sci-Fi Lovers ... 594
Science and Science Fiction ... 595
Science Fiction and Fantasy ... 595
Science Fiction and Fantasy Archive ... 595
Science Fiction Announcements ... 595
Science Fiction Forum ... 595
Science Fiction Marketplace ... 595
Science Fiction Movies ... 596
Science Fiction Resource Guide ... 596
Science Fiction Reviews ... 596
Science Fiction Television ... 596
Science Fiction TV Series Guides ... 597
Science Fiction Writing ... 597
Speculative Fiction Clearing House ... 597
Star Wars ... 597
Star Wars Archive ... 597
Transformations ... 597
Xanth Series ... 598

SECRET STUFF ... 598

2600 ... 598
Easter Eggs ... 598
Macintosh Secret Tricks List ... 598
Phreaking ... 599
Questionables ... 599
Warez ... 599

SEX ... 599

Adult Movies ... 599
Bondage ... 600
Bondage Talk ... 600
Clothespins as Toys ... 600
Cross-Dressing Chat ... 600
Diaper Fetish ... 600
Discussion of Sex Stories ... 600
Exhibitionism ... 600
Fat Fetish ... 600
Femmes Femmes Femmes ... 601
Foot Fetish ... 601
Hair Fetish ... 601
How to Use a Condom ... 601
Intergenerational Relationships ... 601
Masturbation ... 601
Masturbation Index ... 601
Oriental Fetish ... 601
Pantyhose and Stockings ... 601
Pick-Up Lines ... 602
Playboy ... 602
Playboy Centerfolds ... 602

Polyamory 602
Pornographic Pictures 602
Prostitute Prices 602
Purity Tests 603
Safe Sex 604
Sex, Censorship, and the Internet 604
Sex Experts 604
Sex Questions and Answers 604
Sex-Related Articles 604
Sex-Related Humor 604
Sex Sounds 605
Sex Talk 605
Sex Wanted 605
Sexual Identity and Gender
    Glossary 605
Spanking 606
Stories 606
Strip Joint Reviews 606
U.K. BDSM Scene 606
Urban Sex Legends 606
Voyeurism 606
Watersports 607

SEXUALITY **607**
Abuse and Recovery 607
Amazons International 607
Cross-Dressing 607
Gender Collection 607
Kinsey Questions and Answers 607
Polyfidelity 608
Sex Addiction Recovery 608
Sex in the News 608
Sexual Assault and Sex Abuse
    Recovery 608
Sexual and Gender Identity
    Glossary 608
Transgender 609

SOCIOLOGY **609**
Alternative Institutions 609
Demography and Population
    Studies 610
Family Times Online 610
Men's Issues 610
Paradigms 610
Social Science Gateway 610
Social Science Information
    Gateway 610
Social Sciences Resource Guides 610
Society and Underwear 610
Sociological Issues 611
Sociology and Science 611

SOFTWARE **611**
Academic Software Development 611
ASK Software Information System 611
BrainWave Systems Users Group 611
Bristol Technology 611
Encryption Archives 612
GNU 612
GNU for PCs 612
Graphics Software Search 612
Info und Softserver 612
Jewish Software 613
K-Sculpt Music Software 613
NASA's Computer Software
    Management and Information
    Center 613
NCSA Telnet 613
Non-English Software 613
Nutshell Code 613
OS/2 Archive 613
PC Software Search 614
Perl Archives 614
Perl Scripts 614
Searching for Software 614
SIMTEL Software Archives 614
Software Archives 614

Software Sites 614
System Software 615
TeX Text Typesetter 615
Thesaurus Construction Program 615
VAX/VMS Software List 615
X-10 Protocol 615
ZIB Electronic Library 615
Zmodem 615

SOFTWARE: ARCHIVES **616**
Apple II Archive 616
Atari 616
CPM Archives 616
DECUS Library 616
Garbo (University of Vaasa,
    Finland) 616
Hebrew Software Archive 616
Macintosh Archives 616
PC Archives 617
PC Game Archives 617
Sinclair Archive 617
TeX Archive 617
Unix C Archive 618

SOFTWARE: INTERNET **618**
AirMosiac 618
Archie 618
Cello 618
DOS Internet Kit 618
Eudora for Macintosh and
    Windows 618
Gopher Clients 618
Gopher Software 619
Harvest Information Discovery and
    Access System 619
HTML Developer's JumpStation 619
HTML Editor for Word for
    Windows 619
HTML Mode for emacs 619
IRC II Client 619
Lynx 620
MacWAIS 620
MacWeb 620
mail2html 620
Majordomo Mailing List Software 620
Mosaic for the Mac, Microsoft
    Windows, and X Window 620
Mosaic Users and Developers List 621
NCSA Web Server for Windows 621
NUPop 621
Sunsite Winsock Archive 621
TCP/IP 621
Willow 621
Wintalk 621
WinWAIS 621
WinWeb 621
WSGopher 622

SOFTWARE: MACINTOSH **622**
Applications for the Mac 622
Binaries for the Mac 622
Hypercard 622
Hypercard Stack Archive 622
Mac FTP List 623
Macintosh Games 623
Macintosh Software Search 623
MacWeb 623
Object-Oriented Programming 623
Programming the Mac 623
Software for Macintosh 623
System Software 624

SOFTWARE: PC **624**
Applications for DOS 624
Archives 624
Binaries for DOS 624
Demo Software 624
DOS Archive 624
Games 625

Higher Education National Software
    Archive 625
InfoPop 625
Unix uudecode for Windows 625
Waffle BBS Software 625
Windows Shareware Archive 626
Windows Utilities 626

SOFTWARE: UNIX **626**
Andrew File System Resources 626
Calendar of Days 626
con 626
Elm 627
Elvis 627
Emacs Editor 627
European X User Group 628
Fax-3 Fax Software 628
FlexFAX 628
gawk 628
Ghostscript 628
GNU Archives 628
GNU C Compiler 628
GNU Emacs FAQ 628
GNU File Compression Utilities 628
GNU Shell Utilities 629
GNU Software Search 629
gnuplot 629
gzip 629
Integrated Computer Solutions
    FAQs 629
Internationalized xgopher 629
joe Editor 629
Kterm 630
less 630
Multiverse 630
nenscript 630
nn 630
Oleo 630
Perl 630
Perl Discussion 630
Perl Tools Development 631
Pine 631
Pine Mailer Demo 631
procmail 631
pty 631
Query Interface to the Linux
    Software Map Broker 632
rn/trn 632
screen 632
Shells: bash 632
Shells: pdksh 632
Shells: rc 632
Shells: tcsh 633
Shells: zsh 633
SLaTeX 633
Smalltalk 633
Tgif Image Drawing
    Software 633
Top 633
Un-CGI 633
Unix Software Archive 633
X Window Image Utilities 634
X Window Source Archives 634
xgrabsc: X Window Utility 634
xv 634
ytalk 634

SOFTWARE: UTILITIES **635**
ARJ Utilities 635
ASCII Table 635
Automatic Login Executor 635
Benchmark Software 635
Chimera 635
Chinese telnet 635
Chinese Text Viewer 635
Compilers and Interpreters 635
Displaying Chinese Documents 636

Displaying Hangul (Korean)
  Documents 636
Displaying Japanese Documents 636
DOS uudecode 636
Druid 636
Eiffel 636
Hangul (Korean) Software Tools 637
Internet Tools List 637
Ispell 637
Kerberos Resources 637
OS/2 Utilities 637
PC Archiving Utilities 637
PC Utilities 637
PC Video Card Drivers 637
Source Code for Unix Utilities 637
VESA Driver 638
Visual Basic Runtime Modules 638
VMS Utilities 638
WinPkt 638
Xtoys 638

SPACE 639

Aeronautics and Space Acronyms 639
Aeronautics and Space Articles 639
Center for Earth and Planetary
  Studies 639
Earth Systems Data Directory 639
EnviroNet 639
European Space Agency 640
European Space Information
  System 640
FIFE Information System 640
Galaxy 640
Goddard Space Flight Center 640
Grand Challenge Cosmology
  Consortium 640
Hiraiso Solar Terrestrial Research
  Center 640
Hubble Space Telescope 641
Icarus 641
Lunar and Planetary Institute 641
Manned U.S. Space Flight Images 641
Mount Wilson Observatory 641
NASA Extragalactic Database
  (NED) 641
NASA News 642
NASA Research Labs 642
NASA Space Sensors and
  Instrument Technology Museum 642
NASA Spacelink 642
NASA Technological Reports 642
NASDA 642
News About Space 643
Planetary Data System 643
Planetary Image Finders 644
Politics of Space 644
SETI 644
Shuttle Payloads 644
Shuttle Snapshots 644
Smithsonian Astrophysical
  Observatory 644
Space Calendar 645
Space Digest 645
Space Environment Effects Branch 645
Space Frequently Asked Questions 645
Space General Discussion 645
Space Missions 645
Space Movie Archive 645
Space Newsletter 646
Space Shuttle 646
Spacecraft Information 646
SpaceNews 646
Starship Design Home Page 646
Students for the Exploration and
  Development of Space 646
United Nations Office for Outer
  Space Affairs 647

SPORTS AND ATHLETICS 647

.44 Magnum 647
Aikido Dojos Around the World 647
American Football 647
Aquanaut 647
ATP Tour Weekly 648
Australian Rules Football 648
Australian Sporting News 648
Baseball Archives 648
Baseball Information Center 648
Baseball Schedule 648
Baseball Scores 649
Baseball Server 649
Baseball Strike 649
Baseball Teams 649
Basketball FAQs 649
Basketball Server 649
Basketball Statistics 649
Bicycle Commuting 650
Bicycle Discussion Lists on the
  Internet 650
Bicycle Mailing List 650
Bicycles FAQS 650
Bicycling 650
Big Eight College Football 650
Bitnet Baseball League 650
Boxing 651
Canadian Football League 651
College Football 651
College Hockey 651
College Hockey Computer Rating 651
Commonwealth Games 651
Cricket 651
Cricket Talk 651
Cricket Web Server 651
Cycling Resources 652
Dead Runners Society 652
Disc Sports 652
Diving Server 652
East Coast Hockey League 652
European Championships in
  Athletics 652
Exercise and Sports Psychology 652
Fantasy Baseball 653
Fencing 653
Figure Skating Home Page 653
Footbag 653
Football Resources 653
Football Stadiums 653
Formula One Motor Racing 653
Goddard Tennis Club 654
Golf 654
Golfers Mailing List 654
Hockey 654
Hockey Discussion 654
Horse Racing Archives 654
Human-Powered Vehicles 654
Karate 655
Korfball 655
Major League Baseball Schedules 655
Martial Arts 655
Minor League Baseball 655
Motorsports 655
NBA Schedule 656
NFL Draft Information 656
NFL Schedules and Scores 656
NFL Server 656
NFL Talk 656
NHL Schedule 656
Olympic Results 656
Olympic Winter Games — 1998 656
PAC-10 College Football Schedule 657
Racing Archive 657
rec.sport.soccer — The Web Page 657
Road Rally 657
Rugby 657

Rugby League 657
Running 657
Scuba Diving FTP Sites 657
Scuba Diving Mailing List 658
Scuba Diving Web Pages 658
Skateboarding 658
Skating 658
Ski Information 658
Skydiving 658
Skydiving Archive 658
Soccer Referees Mailing List 659
Soccer Results 659
Soccer Rules 659
Soccer Web Pages 659
Speed Skating 659
Speedway Home Page 659
Sports Highlights 659
Sports Schedules 660
Sports Servers 660
Sports Statistics 660
Sports Web Page 660
Stadium Sports Articles 660
Sumo Wrestling 660
Swimming 660
Technical Diving 660
Tennis Rankings and FAQs 660
Tennis Server 660
Ultimate Frisbee 661
Ultrarunning 661
Women's Basketball 661
World Skiing 661
World Youth Baseball 661
World Wide Web of Sports 661
Wrestler List 661

STAR TREK 662

Animations and Images 662
Conventions and Memorabilia 662
Future Technologists 662
Klingon Shared Reality 662
Klingons 662
Resources 663
Star Trek Archives 663
Star Trek Fetishes 663
Star Trek Games 663
Star Trek General Discussion 663
Star Trek Information and Trivia 663
Star Trek News 663
Star Trek Reviews 663
Star Trek Stories and Parodies 663
Star Trek Universe 664
Trekker Discussion 664
Video Clips 664

SUPPORT GROUPS 664

30 Plus 664
Birthparents of Adoptees 664
Blindness and Family Life 664
Transplant Answers 664
Usenet Support Groups 664

TECHNOLOGY 665

Artificial Intelligence 665
Audio Technology 665
Blacksburg Electronic Village 665
Canada Department of
  Communications 665
CAVE Virtual Reality Environment 665
Central Virginia's Freenet 665
Centre for Research Information
  Storage Technology 665
Compact Disc Formats 665
Conflict Simulation Games 666
Daresbury Laboratory 666
Distribute Interactive Virtual
  Environment 666
Elettra Synchrotron Radiation
  Facility 666

Expert Systems and Vision 666
Hitachi 666
Hot Off the Tree 666
Human Communication Research
    Centre 667
Institute for Systems Engineering and
    Informatics 667
Journal of Artificial Intelligence
    Research 667
Knowledge Representation and
    Reasoning Laboratory 667
Life in the Year 2020 667
Los Alamos National Laboratory 667
Meta Virtual Environments 667
Mogul Media 668
Multicast Backbone FAQ 668
Musee des Arts et Metiers 668
Museum of Machine-Generated
    Speech and Singing 668
National Institute of Standards and
    Technology 668
Neural Network Home Page 668
Photonics 668
Robotics, Video Gallery 668
Sony Research Laboratory 669
Technology Board of Trade 669
Technology General Discussion 669
Technology Marketing Failures 669
Technomads 669
Video Laserdiscs 669
Virtual Reality Resources 669
X-Ray Web Server 669

TELECOMMUNICATIONS 670
Bell Gopher 670
Cell-Relay Communications 670
Data Communications Servers 670
Distributed Electronic
    Telecommunications Archive 670
Fax Technology 670
International Telecommunications
    Union 670
Internet Business Center
    Telecommunications Definitions 670
Internet Fax Server 671
Internet Protocol 671
ISDN 671
National Telecommunications and
    Information Administration 671
OTPAD Gopher 671
Pacific Bell Digital Communications
    Information 671
PC Communications and Modems 671
Privacy and Technology 672
Telecom Discussions 672
Telecommunication Archives 672
Telecommunications Digest 672
Telecommunications News 672
Telecommunications Organizations 672
Telecommunications Page 672

TELEPHONES 672
Cellular Phones 672
Phone Cards 673
Phone Number to Word Translator 673
Russian Phone Directory 673
Swiss Electronic Telephone Book 673
Technical Discussion 673
Telefax Country Codes 673
Telephone Information Sites 674
Toll-Free Numbers for Computer
    Companies 674
Toll-Free Numbers for Non-Profit
    Organizations 674
U.S. Telephone Area Code Guides 674
U.S. Telephone Area Code
    Program 674

TELEVISION 674
Andy Griffith 674
Animaniacs 675
Babylon 5 Reviews 675
Battlestar Galactica Home Page 675
BBC TV and Radio 675
Beavis and Butthead 675
Beverly Hills 90210 676
The Bold and the Beautiful 676
C-SPAN 676
Cable Regulation Digest 676
Cable TV 676
Cable TV Resources 676
Cartoons 676
Cheers 677
Clarissa Explains 677
Comedies 677
Commercials 677
Dark Shadows 677
David Letterman 677
David Letterman Official Song
    Book 678
The Discovery Channel 678
Doctor Who 678
Dr. Quinn, Medicine Woman 678
Dramas 678
European Satellite Information 678
Game Shows 679
Live Television Images 679
Married with Children 679
Max Headroom 679
Melrose Place 679
Muppet Fest 679
Nielson TV Ratings 679
Northern Exposure 680
Parker Lewis 680
Public Broadcasting Service (PBS) 680
Red Dwarf 680
Ren and Stimpy Show Archives 680
Rush Limbaugh 680
Satellite TV Images 680
Satellite TV Page 681
Science Fiction TV Shows 681
Seinfeld 681
Series and Sitcoms 681
The Simpsons 682
Sitcoms of the U.K. 682
Soap Operas 682
Star Trek Archives 682
Star Trek Reviews and Synopses 682
Television Guide 682
Television Industry Discussion 682
Television News 682
Television Series Guides and Facts 682
Television Show Discussion 683
Thirtysomething 684
Tiny Toons 684
Transformers 684
TV Episode Guides 684
TV Nation 685
TV News Archive 685
TV Schedules 685
The Twilight Zone 685
Twin Peaks 685
Video Files 685
The X-Files 685
The Young and the Restless 685

TRAVEL 686
Alaska 686
Amtrak Trains 686
Arctic Adventours 686
Atlanta 686
Australian Alpine Information
    Service 686
Austrian Restaurant Guide 686

Baja California 686
Barbados 686
Bay Area Places to See 686
Bay Area Restaurant Guide 687
Berlin and Prague 687
Boston Restaurant List 687
California 687
Cambridge Pub Guide 687
Canary Islands 687
Caribbean Connection 687
Complete Guide to Galway 688
Currency 688
Cybertour of the U.S.A. 688
Des Moines 688
Dublin Pub Review 688
Explore New York 688
Exploring Japan with Maps 688
Gateway to Antarctica 688
Guide to Australia 689
Guide to London 689
Hawaii 689
International Travel Health Advice 689
Japan 689
Jerusalem Mosaic 689
Journey North 689
Journeys and Destinations 689
Kenn Nesbitt's Travel Adventures 690
Ljubljana 690
Madawaska-Victoria 690
Money Abroad FAQ 691
Net Travel 691
New York City Guide 691
New York City Information 692
Oslo Tour 692
Promus Hotels 692
Railroad Timetables 692
RailServer 692
Recreational Vehicles 692
Route 66 692
Russian Travelogue 692
Smoky Mountains 693
South Dakota 693
St. Petersburg Pictures Gallery 693
Staunton, Virginia 693
Staying Healthy in Asia, Africa and
    Latin America 693
Subway Navigator 693
Thailand 693
Tips for Travelers 694
Tour de France 694
Tourism Offices 694
Travel and Tourism Web Pages 694
Travel Information 694
Travel Marketplace 694
Travel Matters Newsletter 694
Travel Resources 694
Travelers' Tales 695
Travels with Samantha 695
Trip to Antarctica 695
U.S. State Department Travel
    Information 695
Utah's National Parks 695
Virtual Tourist 695
West Virginia 695

TRIVIA 695
Answer Guys 695
Coffee Machine 695
Coin Toss 696
Coke Servers 696
Hot Tub Server 696
Internet Index 696
Talk to a Cat 696
Today's Date 697
Today's Events in History 697
Trivia Time 697
Trivial Questions and Answers 697

Unofficial Smiley Dictionary 698
Vending Machines 698

USENET 699
Anonymous Posting Service 699
ChooseNews II 699
Creating Alternative Hierarchy
  Newsgroups 699
Creating Standard Newsgroups 699
European Usenet 699
FAQs in HTML Format 699
FAQs Searches and Archives 699
Frequently Asked Questions Master
  List 700
Hangul (Korean) Newsgroups 700
Japanese Usenet 700
Periodic Informational Postings List ... 700
Risks of Posting to Usenet 700
Stanford Netnews Filtering Service 700
Usenet Descriptions 700
Usenet Finger Utility 701
Usenet Groups with a Difference 701
Usenet News via Electronic Mail 701
Usenet News via Gopher 701
Usenet Olympics 701
Usenet Word Statistics 701
Worldwide Usenet 702

USENET CURIOSITIES 702
Cascades 702
Flames 702
Kibo 702
Net Abuse 702
Newsgroup Administration 702
Newsgroup Invasion 702
Newsgroup Questions 702
Shared Realities 703
Usenet Announcements 703
Usenet Junkies 703
Usenet Kooks 703
Usenet Personalities 703
Weird Places to Hang Out on
  Usenet 703

VICES 704
Cigar Smoking 704
Gambling and Oddsmaking 704
Hangovers 704
Horse Racing 704
Laszlo's Lengthy List of Luxury Smokes ... 705
Lies 705
Pipe Smoking 705
Sex Services 706
Smoking Addiction 706
Smoking News 706
Strip Clubs 706

WEATHER 707
Canadian Weather 707
Climate Data Catalog 707
Climate Diagnostics Center 707
Climatic Research Unit 707
Colorado Weather Underground 707
Current Weather Maps and Movies 708
DMSP Data Archive Home Page 708
Earth Images from Weather
  Satellites 708
Flood Damage 708
Gray's Atlantic Seasonal Hurricane
  Forecast 708
Hourly Auroral Activity Status
  Report 709
Hurricane Images 709
Interactive Weather Browser 709
Japanese Weather 709
Meteorology 709
Meteorology Information 709
Monthly Temperature Anomalies 709

National Center for Atmospheric
  Research 709
National Weather Service
  Forecasts 710
NOAA Space Environment Services
  Center 710
Solar and Geophysical Reports 710
Surf Conditions in California 710
Surface Analysis and Weather
  Maps 710
Weather Processor 710
Weather Radar 711
Weather Reports 711
Weather Reports for Australia 711
Weather Reports for Canada 711
Weather World 711

WOMEN 712
Abortion and Reproductive Rights 712
Ada Project 712
Attitudes of Women 712
Bibliographies of Women's Studies 712
Calls for Papers in Women's
  Studies 712
Conferences for Women 713
Electronic Forums for Women 713
Feminism 713
Feminism Internationally 713
Feminism and Science and
  Technology 714
Feminist Theology 714
Gender and Computing 714
Gender and Sexuality 714
Global Fund for Women 714
Health Concerns of Women 715
Issues of Interest to Women 715
Liberty and Feminism 715
Living with a Challenge 715
Menopause 715
Midwifery 715
Notable Women 715
Resources for Women 716
Sexual Assault on Campus 716
Women in Congress 716
Women's News 716
Women's Studies Resources 716
Women's Wire 716

WORLD CULTURES 717
Aboriginal Studies 717
Africa 717
African Forum 717
African Resource List 717
African Studies 717
Arab Press Newsletter 717
Argentina 717
Army Area Handbooks 717
Asia Discussion 718
Asian Studies 718
Australia 718
Baltic Republics Discussion List 718
Batish Institute of Music and Fine
  Arts 718
Berlin 718
Bosnia 719
Brazil 719
Bulgaria 719
Cajun Culture 719
California 719
Central America Discussion List 719
Central Asian Studies Mailing Lists 719
Central European Development 719
Chile 720
China 720
Chinese Scenic Pictures 720
Chinese Scholars and Students
  Discussion List 720

Country Statistics 720
Croatian Foreign Press Bureau 720
Diversity Concerns Exchange 721
Egypt 721
England 721
European Community 721
Expatriates 721
Flags of the World 721
Fourth World Documentation
  Project 721
France 721
French Chat 722
French Timeline 722
Friends and Partners 722
Germany 722
Hellenic News 722
Hindu Names 722
Hungary 722
India 722
Inter-Tribal Network 723
Ireland 723
Irish and Celtic Resources 723
Israel 723
Italy 723
Japan 723
Japanese Information 723
Jerusalem One 724
Jerusalem Tour 724
Jewish Calendar and Events 724
Jewish Communities 724
JewishNet 724
Korea 724
Latin America 724
Lebanon and Levant Cultural
  Multimedia Server 724
Library of Congress Cultural
  Exhibits 725
Little Russia 725
Malaysia 725
Malaysia, Singapore, Islam News 725
Mexico 725
Middle Europe 725
Moscow Kremlin Online
  Excursion 725
National Flags 725
National Pages 726
Native American Mailing Lists 726
Native Americans 726
NativeNet 726
NECTEC Server 726
New Zealand 726
Norwegian Internet Resources 726
Palo Alto, California 726
Paris Tours 726
Poland 727
Portugal 727
Russia 727
San Francisco Bay Area 727
Slovakia 727
Slovenia 727
Southeast Asian Archive 727
Southern U.S. Culture 728
Soviet Archives 728
Sweden Channel 728
Taiwan 728
Thailand 728
Third World Studies 728
United Kingdom 728
U.S.A. Chat 728
Usenet Cultural Groups 728
Venezuela 729
World Constitutions 729
World Heritage List 729
Yiddish 729
Yugoslavian Information 729

WRITING **729**
Athene, the Online Magazine of
  Creative Writing 729
The Continuum Machine 729
Create a Story 729
Creative Writing Pedagogy 730
Cyberpunk 730
Dr. Who 730
Erotica 730
Fiction Writers 730
Manga and Anime 731
Memoirs, Journals and
  Correspondence 731
Prose 731
Star Trek 731
Superhero Mailing List 731
Trincoll Journal 731
Writers 731

X-RATED RESOURCES **732**
Bondage, Discipline, Sadism and
  Masochism Stories 732
Brandy's Babes 732
Clothing 732
Dirty Talk 732
Dominant Women 733
Erotic Pictures 733
Erotic Sounds 733
Fetishes 734
Index of Erotic Stories 734
Kama Sutra 734
Limericks 734
Magazines 735
Net Sex 735
Sex Chat 735
Sex General Discussion 735
Sex Stories 735

Sex Story Archives 736
Sexual Massage 736
Slippery When Wet Magazine 736
Tickling 736
Wild Sex 736
X-Rated Movies 736
X-Rated Page 736

YOUTH **737**
Activities for Kids 737
Boy Scouts of America 737
Christian Youth 737
Explorer Posts 737
Fall Nature Fun 738
Fun with Magazines 738
Gangs 738
Jewish Youth 738
Scouting 739
Scouting Around the World 739
Teen Date 739
Teenagers 739
Young People Talk 739

ZINES **740**
Albert Hofmann's Strange Mistake 740
Arm the Spirit 740
Armadillo Culture 740
Art Com 740
Bad Subjects 741
Bust 741
Capacity — The Webzine 741
Chaos Control 741
Cyberspace Vanguard 741
DargonZine 742
Depth Probe 742
E-Zine List 742
Empire Times 742
FactSheet Five - Electric 742

HyperMedia Zines on the Net 742
Inquisitor 742
International Teletimes 743
Journal of Underground
  Computing 743
Morpo Review 743
Netsurfer Publishing 743
The New Sun 743
OtherRealms 743
Random Zines 743
ScreamBaby 744
Spectra 744
Stream of Consciousness 744
Temptation of St. Anthony 744
Verbiage Magazine 744
Virtual Reality Artificial Intelligence
  Neural Net 744
Webster's Weekly 744
Wimsey's Digital Rag 745
Zine Discussion 745
Zine Lists 745
Zine Reviews 745
Zines 745

ZOOLOGY **745**
Camel Research 745
Census of Australian Vertebrate
  Species 746
Electronic Zoo 746
Florida Wildlife 746
Great White Shark 746
Non-Native Fish Information
  Resources 746
Zoo Atlanta 746
Zoological Resources 746

Introduction

If all this works out that way I hope, you will be reading this back in 1995. That is, I will receive this message from myself, sometime in late 1994, just in time to get it to the printer to be included in the second edition.

Wait a minute. Maybe I should take a moment to explain, because if you haven't heard of the Temporal Gateway — and how could you? — you probably haven't the foggiest idea what I am talking about.

Let me start from the beginning. I sent this message to myself from the year 2021, in order that it be included in the second edition of *The Internet Golden Directory*. No wait, that's not the beginning. I guess the beginning was in 2017, when T. L. Nipper figured out how to build the Temporal Gateway into the past.

No, wait, that's not really the beginning. The real beginning would be in the late 1990s when the Internet broke up into pieces and what came to be called the Net (or more formally, the People's Net) emerged as the organized successor to the free non-commercial information network.

Does that help? No, I guess this is all a hopeless muddle. You see, I did write some Internet books at one time, way back in the mid-1990s, but that was about twenty-five years ago and things have changed a lot. I am not sure how to explain it so that you could understand. So many of the New Words don't even exist in 1995, that I wouldn't even know where to start.

How about this: It happened that in 2017, a genius named T.L. Nipper figured out how to send information into the past. Like most people, I don't understand the details — I think it has something to do with neutrinos and tachyons — but the important thing is that the process is only partially dependable and highly restricted by the MFS. Moreover, it takes an enormous amount of energy just to send a few characters.

Transmitting this introduction, for example, consumed the equivalent of a month's energy allotment for the entire Western Region (what used to be California and parts of Nevada and Oregon). In fact, if it wasn't that the Governor of the Continental Fusion Project agreed to cooperate, I would never have been able to send this message at all.

Anyway, this all has to do with the 50th anniversary of what used to be called the Internet, and some researcher in the Information Division of the MFS discovered the date and thought it would be a good idea to send a message into the past — to celebrate, so to speak.

I don't know how they did it and what strings they had to pull, but somehow they got the CFP to cooperate and they were able to set up a Temporal Gateway just long enough to send a message back to 1994. And since I was the author of some old-time Internet books, they asked me to write the message.

The deal was that I could write anything I wanted, which would then be sent back twenty-five years into the past — November 1994 actually — to myself. And, if it all worked, the message from 2021 would suddenly appear in my electronic mailbox back in 1994. The intention was that I would send a message that would be suitable for the introduction of one of my books.

The trouble is, once you send something, it generates what is called an "alternate reality," so that you don't get to see the results of what you send. Thus, I have no way of knowing whether or not this message got through. But if it did, and you are reading this in 1995, at least you will know that it worked.

So, having explained all of that, what do I want to tell you?

Well, to start, I should tell you that the Net is now considered to be the most significant invention of the 20th Century. However, it wasn't until the early 2000s that it became apparent just how important the Net actually was. Unfortunately, the real nature of the Net had been completely misunderstood until this time, and just about nobody anticipated what would happen. In fact, until the Information Decree of 1998, most of what was on the Net was highly disorganized and left up to individual preference.

Perhaps another thing that I should mention is that what we now call the Net (in 2017) is really nothing like the old Internet, although there are a few similarities. We can access information just about anywhere we go, and the speed is so fast as to be unnoticeable. We can view and transmit with ease, and public access (to the Pubnet portion anyway) is universal.

The trouble is, everything is managed and organized and... well... boring. You see, in the olden days (as you are reading this), the Net was not really run by anyone and was poorly organized. Of course, this meant that there were problems, but there was also an enormous amount of personal freedom. This freedom meant that anyone who knew how could create and broadcast information. As I write this, such facilities are completely unknown.*

The point is: you happen to be living in a time when you have enormous opportunity. The Net as you know it is not going to last all that long but, while it does, you will have a chance to *participate* in ways that never existed until the 1990s and certainly do not exist today.

If I remember correctly, back in 1995 you had just about total freedom to send out whatever information you wanted. I urge you to not lose sight of the importance of this capability. I keep thinking that if things had gone otherwise, we might not have had the Information Decree and that the Microsoft Friendship Society might never have had... well, that's neither here nor there and, as the saying goes, you can't change the past.

I guess what I really want to tell you is that the Net as you perceive it is a temporary resource, and you should enjoy and appreciate it while you can. If this message did get through, and you are really reading this in the second edition of *The Internet Golden Directory*, I urge you to buy the book and spend some time exploring. Nothing lasts forever, and some things end all too soon.

And, oh yes... have fun. Soon you will need a permit.

Harley Hahn
December 21, 2021
Third District, Western Region

INTRODUCTION TO THE FIRST EDITION

This book will change the way that you think about the world.

Even more important, this book will change the way that you think about people and how we exist as a species.

How can this be? After all, this book is really just a large catalog, and what could be so important about a catalog?

Well, take a look at the list of categories on the back cover, and you will see that virtually every important type of human activity is represented. Indeed, this book contains descriptions of thousands of separate items, grouped into 185 different categories.

The importance of all this is not so much in the details, but in the fact that it even exists at all. Not long ago, most of what you see in this book had not yet been cre-

ated. A few years ago, none of it existed. But what does it all mean to *you*?...

Imagine yourself exploring. You walk for days through hot steamy jungles, you climb over rocky hills and through canyons; you drag yourself across an endless arid plain until, one day, you look at the horizon and see what looks like a city. As you approach, you see that it is not really a city but — whatever it is — it is vast beyond description: more buildings, vehicles, works of art, and so on, than you have ever seen or even imagined.

You spend many hours exploring, always finding something new, something challenging, and something delightful. Being a stranger, you feel confused and you spend much of your time wandering haphazardly. Once in a while you see a bit of a pattern and, for an instant, you make some sense out of the immediate neighborhood. But for the most part, you wander from place to place in a cloud of distraction and fascination. What makes it all so frustrating is that you get the feeling that everything you see is part of something very large that you just can't understand.

One day, you happen upon a stranger who looks like he knows his way around; at least he seems familiar with the surroundings.

You ask him, how do you find your way?

He shrugs. You'll get used to it.

But, you ask, why is this all here?

I don't know, he says, and he starts to wander away.

Wait, you call after him, where can I get a map?

No such thing, he answers over his shoulder.

But can't you help me at all?

He turns around and looks at you with a gleam in his eye and a funny half smile on his face. Clearly, he knows something that you don't. Something important.

This place, he gestures widely, is only a few years old. In fact, you could travel for days and almost everything you'd see would be less than a year old. You will see new places almost everywhere you look and, every so often, you will notice that old ones have disappeared. You turn around, and when you turn back it's changed — larger, more complicated, more... well, it's hard to explain. Like I said, you'll get used to it.

But don't be confused, he continues. The meaning in what you see is not about the structures or the vehicles. It's not about the art or the beauty; or pleasure or truth or good or bad. It's about people and what they have created. People working together and by themselves.

You will notice that wherever you go, you will never see another person (I know this to be a fact, and I have been

*On the official Net that is. There are rumors of underground Slicknets but, like most people, I have never seen one.

here as long as anyone). However, you can talk to other people whenever you want, so you will never be lonely. No matter who you are, no matter how individual your desires and your preferences, there are people just like you here somewhere.

So where are you? Nobody really knows. The important thing is that we are all here together. We are all connected. We all share. We all belong, especially those of us who have nowhere else to go. And the best thing is that you can come here whenever you want. No one is ever turned away.

Personally, I don't really understand why this place is so important. Most of us just move around from place to place, doing whatever we feel like. Still, just be glad that you are here at all. As I say, most of this is only a few years old and you are among the first.

But wait, you say. You told me that I would never actually see anyone. What about you? I can see you.

He looks at you for a long moment.

You only *think* you see me. I don't really exist. Anyway, for what it's worth, there is a map of sorts. Don't lose it and you can take it with you wherever you go.

He points behind you to a single piece of paper lying on the ground. You turn around to pick it up, and by the time you turn back he is gone. You look down. In the center of an otherwise blank piece of paper is a big "X" and the words "You are here."

You stuff the paper into your pocket and start walking. After a few minutes, you turn around and gasp. Behind you is a large sign. It must have been there all the time, how could you have missed it? Okay, you say to yourself, I may not know where I am, or why I am here, or what anyone is really doing, but now at least, I know the name of this place. For the sign says:

Welcome to the Internet.

The Internet and This Book

WHAT DO YOU NEED TO KNOW TO USE THIS BOOK?

To use this book, you need to have access to the Internet, and you need to know how to use the Internet. Both these topics are fully explained in another one of our books, *The Internet Complete Reference* (Osborne McGraw-Hill).

If you do not as yet have Internet access, start with that book. Read Chapter 3 ("How to Connect to the Internet") for the basic concepts, and then use Appendix A ("Public Access to the Internet") for advice on how to find and choose an Internet provider. The book contains a long list of such providers, as well as a special offer to new users to let you arrange for one month's free access.

Once you have Internet access, you need to master the skills necessary to use the Internet. In practice, this means learning how to use the various Internet resources, all of which are different. The following table shows the various resources that are in *this* book. The chapter numbers show which part of *The Internet Complete Reference* explains that resource. For a quick introduction to all the resources, see Chapter 2.

Resource	Chapters
Quick tour of the Internet	2
Anonymous FTP	16
Archie	17
Finger	8
Gopher	21
Internet Mailing List	25
Internet Relay Chat (IRC)	20
Listserv Mailing List	25
Mail	5, 6
Telnet	7
Usenet: in general	9, 10, 11
Usenet: newsreaders	12, 13, 14, 15
Wais	23
World Wide Web	24

People often ask, how much do I really need to learn? There are two answers — one bad and one good — to that question. The bad answer is:

> You do not need to know how to use everything. You only need to learn how to use the resources that you are interested in.

The good answer is a lot more realistic:

> You will likely become interested in all the resources, so you really do have to know how to use everything.

IS IT HARD TO LEARN HOW TO USE THE INTERNET?

No, it is not hard at all. It just takes practice.

Don't be put off by people who say that the Internet is hard to use or is not "user friendly." You must be realistic. The Internet is one of the most important and complex inventions of mankind. "Using the Internet" really means learning some basic concepts and then teaching yourself how to use a variety of different programs.

Once you become an experienced user, you will see that — considering all that it offers — the Internet and its programs are remarkably user friendly. The problem is that some people confuse the idea of "easy to use" with "easy to learn." The only way you can make a complex system so easy to learn that you can use it on the first day is by removing (or hiding) most of the power. But then, once you become experienced, you find that the system is too simple and awkward.

Millions of people around the world already use the Internet. You don't need to be a computer expert. To put this in perspective, using the Internet is a lot easier than many things that we all do every day, such as driving a car or shopping for groceries. All you need is some practice and some patience.

Our best advice? Open this book to anywhere and find something interesting. Then, use *The Internet Complete Reference* to teach yourself what you need to know. Experiment. Have fun. Go slow. Enjoy.

CENSORSHIP: OR, WHAT SHOULD I DO WHEN I AM OFFENDED?

I promise you that, sooner or later, something on the Internet will offend you. (Indeed, something in this book may offend you.) Please don't let it bother you.

The Internet is the largest gathering of human beings ever assembled and one of the ground rules is that there is No-One-In-Charge, which means that there is no censorship. This freedom is the prime reason that the Internet has become so important and why there are so many diverse resources.

Still, some people have a little trouble getting used to such license. Eventually, we all come to realize that if we don't like something, we can ignore it. For example, if you are reading the articles in a Usenet newsgroup, and you encounter one that you find particularly offensive, you can skip it. However, at the beginning, the temptation to complain is too strong for some people.

So someone complains... "Yes, I do believe in freedom of expression, but comparing the President of the United States to a retarded Nazi feminist minority member with AIDS is just too much and should not be allowed. After all, we must remember that using the Internet is a privilege and not a right, and that if people like you continue to pollute the network with ignorant, racist, dangerous opinions, the Internet will be taken away and... blah, blah, blah..."

Well now. All that such a diatribe means is that, as an Internet user, the writer is still immature. I assure you that no one, anywhere, will pay the least bit of attention to a self-righteous pronouncement of what is right or wrong. So, should you ever run into such a person, remind them gently that the best part of the Internet is its diversity, and that tolerance of other people's opinions and ways of thinking is a virtue.

Indeed, if there is one Internet Golden Rule, it is:

Censor yourself, not others.

Realistically, we all come to learn that we can't do anything about how other people use the Internet, so there is no point even trying. The idea is to share and enjoy. If you don't like something, forget about it.

HOW TO CONTACT US

This catalog contains thousands of items but still, only a small fraction of what the Internet has to offer. If you would like to add something to the next edition of the catalog, just let us know. The address is

catalog@rain.org.

Similarly, if you have any comments, don't bother the publisher. Send them to us directly and Rick and I will be glad to listen.

BEFORE YOU CONTACT US

To save you a bit of time, here are the answers to a few of the most commonly asked questions that we are asked.

(1) I am new to the Internet and I don't know what to do. How do I access the resources in this book?

This book is a catalog. It will *not* teach you how to use the Internet. If you are a new user, you need to spend a fair amount of time learning about the Internet (sorry, but that's a fact), and the best suggestion we have is to use our book *The Internet Complete Reference*. Unless you already know something about using the Internet, don't expect to be able to start in right away. Still, don't be discouraged. The Internet is a lot of fun and will well repay your effort.

(2) I tried to connect to a resource and it asks me for a password. What should I do?

You are probably connecting with the wrong program. To access a resource, you must use the exact service that is listed in the book. For example, for a gopher resource, you must use a gopher program to connect; for an anonymous ftp service, you must connect with an ftp program; and so on. You can use telnet to log in to a remote computer, but you only do so when you *do* have a valid user name and password. If you need help, the best thing to do is get a good reference book on the Internet.

(3) Within the listing of a particular resource, I see a "*" character. What does this mean?

Many of the resources point to files and directories. (A directory is a collection of files.) Occasionally, you will see a resource whose description ends with a "*" character. This character is a shorthand way of saying "all the files in that particular directory." For example, if you see:

/pub/*

it refers to all the files within the **/pub** directory. If this doesn't make sense to you, you can ask someone for help or you can find yourself a good beginner's book on Unix. (The best such book is *Open Computing Unix Unbound*, by Harley. It is published by Osborne McGraw-Hill and the ISBN is 0-07-882050-2.) Although you don't need to know Unix to use the Internet, many of the computers that you will access are Unix computers and having a basic understanding of Unix is extremely helpful.

(4) How can I advertise in this book?

Everything in this book is free. This is *not* a commercial directory, like a telephone yellow pages book. We do our best to ensure that nothing gets in this book unless it is free to use. Thus, we do not take paid advertisements. All the "advertisements" in this book were written by Harley and are just for fun.

Acknowledgments

A great many people helped Rick and me with the production of this book and, if you don't mind, we'd like to take a few minutes to thank these people by name and acknowledge their help. Of course, you don't really need to read all of this. No one is watching and you could probably just skip this section without being caught. Remember though, the real mark of a person is how he or she behaves when no one is watching.

I don't want to scare you, but we did receive a letter from one person who refused to read the acknowledgments in the first edition of this book. Actually, it was pitiful to even hear about it. This poor soul thought no one would ever notice, but he forgot that when you neglect to do what you know is right, you are only fooling yourself. So, throwing caution to the wind, he completely ignored the acknowledgments and within three days, his entire life was exposed as a shallow, meaningless sham.

Still with me? Okay.

To start, we have Wendy Murdock, our principal research assistant: a multi-talented artist and writer whose skill, patience and hard work contributed greatly to the quality of this book. Just between us, Wendy never stops amazing me; I still can't figure out how she can be so talented and accomplished.

Next, we would like to thank Michael Peirce of Ireland. I suppose that it is possible to write a best-selling computer book without Michael's help but, personally, I can't imagine doing so. This guy is just amazing. Between him and Wendy, there isn't much about the Net that they don't know. In fact, I bet that you could walk into any computer conference and throw a brick and not have to worry about hitting someone who knew more about Internet resources than Wendy and Mike. (Although it might be interesting to try.)

To continue. There are four other researchers who also made important contributions: Scott Yanoff (of Milwaukee, Wisconsin), Carrie Carolin (Wenatchee, Washington), John Navarra (Chicago, Illinois) and Jim Hall (San Diego, California). For excellent proofreading and data entry, we also thank Ronda Stout (San Diego).

Moving right along, we have Lunaea Hougland (our favorite copy editor) who did her usual excellent job on the manuscript. What a gem she is. I have been working with Lunaea for so long that I have come to depend upon her as a pillar of grammar and philology. Moreover, she is the most pleasant person in the entire publishing industry.

And, finally, for work on the first edition, we thank Paola Kathuria (London, England), Brooke Jarrett (San Diego), Peter ten Kley (The Netherlands), and Rick Broadhead (Toronto, Canada).

Now, aside from all these individuals, there are a number of people at various companies who provided help. At Rain (Santa Barbara's Regional Alliance for Information Networking), Marcy Montgomery and Timothy Tyndall provided me with Internet access.

For computing resources, I thank IBM (Ken Bracht of the Consultant Relations department); Sun Microsystems (Laura Lilyquest, Laura Sardina, Ranjini Mehdi, and Wayne Gramlich of the Chief Technical Officer department); and Apple (Keri Walker, Tina Rodriguez, Doedy Hunter).

For other equipment, I thank Telebit for modems (Mark Gallant); Ultra Spec Cables for Sun-compatible cables (Ed Hall); and Cybex for PC extension systems (Sid Falling and Bill Neiland). For PPP software for the Sun workstation, I thank Morning Star Technologies (Jamey Laskey and Ashley Burns).

And for telecommunications assistance, I thank GTE (Rhonda Bushno and Lynn Cook), Pacific Bell (Hal Lenox) and AT&T (Dick Muldoon).

At this point you might be wondering, does this mean that Harley and Rick are recommending these companies? Are they telling me that I should buy Internet service from Rain, computers from IBM, Sun or Apple, modems from Telebit, and so on? The answer is that we did think about suggesting that these are good people for you to do business with, but we decided not to, as we felt that we should not make any endorsements. (However, we would like to mention that we maintain our database with Microsoft Access, which we would be glad to recommend except, of course, we do not make endorsements.)

Next we have our publisher, Osborne McGraw-Hill. By far, the person to whom we owe the most is Scott Rogers, our editor. Technically, Scott's title is "Acquisitions Editor", because his job is to find authors and plan new books. However, he does much more than that: Scott was involved with many aspects of both editions of this book — including content, production, marketing and sales — often on a day-to-day basis. So much so, that at one point we even considered sharing the royalties with him. Fortunately, it took but a moment for cooler heads to prevail and reason to return to her throne. Still, Scott worked hard and he certainly deserves as much credit as is safe to give an editor. (You have to be careful, though. Once

For extra special help, including a lot of details that no one else was capable of handling, we thank Ann Wilson and Kelly Vogel, both Editorial Assistants. Ann, in particular, spent many hours working with the final changes as we closed in on the deadline for this edition.

On the production side of the fence, Rick and I would like to thank the talented artists who created the wonderful drawings that you see throughout this book: Leslee Bassin, Helena Worsley, and Marla Shelasky.

As you can see for yourself, Leslee, Marla, and Helena, have real talent and their contribution to this book was an important one. I, for one, am especially grateful, as I had despaired of ever finding artists who had just the right mixture of skill and whimsy to illustrate my jokes. If I had only had these three artists to illustrate my essays in high school, who knows where I might be today.

The other production miracle workers are the ones who worked on the layout of the book (not an easy job): Roberta Steele, Peter Hancik, Jani Beckwith and Rhys Elliott. In addition, Kendal Andersen (Marketing Manager) produced the front and back covers, as well as the entry in the Osborne book catalog.

Finally, Rick and I give special thanks to Marcela Hancik (Production Manager), who coordinated the overall production of this book, which was a complex task. As Marcela put it, "Everybody who had hands was working on the book."

Of course, these people do not run the whole publishing company by themselves. From time to time, they receive small bits of help from a few other people who deserve a mention: Lisa Kissinger (Public Relations and Advertising); Claudia Ramirez (Foreign Rights); Larry Levitsky (Publisher, the big cheese); and Jeff Pepper (Editor-in-Chief, the medium-sized cheese).

For extra special delivery service (more important than you might think), I would like to thank the folks at the DHL office in Santa Barbara: Danielle Ritchko, Terry Chlentzos-Keramaris, Sheila Burrows, Christine Abate, Kraig Williamson, Kelan Raph and the manager Monty Howard. Finally, for excellent service in his local area, Rick would like to thank Chuck James of the San Diego DHL office.

— Harley Hahn

AGRICULTURE

Advanced Technology Information Network

Agricultural news, daily reports, an event calendar, California Agriculture Teacher's Project, agricultural degrees at California State Universities, job listings, weather, labor, and safety information as well as other items of interest.

Note: The first time you log in, the ATI computer will give you your own login name and password.

Telnet:
> Address: **caticsuf.csufresno.edu**
> Login: **super**

Agricultural Biotechnology Center

The Agricultural Biotechnology Center (ABC) is involved with biotechnology research and development in Hungary. The center researches methods for developing Hungary's agriculture using genetic engineering and cellular techniques. This server contains information about the Center's efforts.

See also: Environment

World Wide Web:
> URL: **http://molmod.abc.hu/**

Agricultural, Flood, Food Supply Information

A gopher interface for all kinds of useful information on floods, food supplies and food safety, agricultural market news, and other topics, including vegetable crops and landscaping.

See also: Emergency and Disaster

Gopher:
> Name: IDEA
> Address: **cesgopher.ag.uiuc.edu**
> Choose: **Flood-Information**

Telnet:
> Address: **idea.ag.uiuc.edu**
> Login: **flood**

Agricultural Genome Resources

A service provided by the U.S. Department of Agriculture, the Agricultural Genome gopher and web page present genome information for agriculturally important organisms. Most information is about plants, but the gopher will get more information about animals, insects, and microorganisms over time.

Gopher:
> Name: Agricultural Genome Gopher
> Address: **probe.nalusda.gov**

World Wide Web:
> URL: **http://probe.nalusda.gov:8000/about.html**

Agricultural Mailing List

Grassland husbandry, crop science, ecological simulation, crop production, tropical forestry, plant physiology, water management, irrigation, and anything else to do with agriculture.

Listserv Mailing List:
> List Address: **agric-l@uga.bitnet**
> Subscription Address: **listserv@uga.bitnet**

Agricultural Software

Check out Texas A&M's software catalog, peruse the U.S. Department of Agriculture Extension Service's collection of computer software, or perform a search of specific software at North Carolina State University.

Gopher:
> Name: Johns Hopkins University
> Address: **gopher.gdb.org**
> Choose: **Search and Retrieve Software**
> **I Search for Agricultural Software**

A B C D E F G H I J K L M N O P Q R S T U V W X Y Z

Are you a know-it-all?
Check in Trivia
for tidbits of useless
information.

Aquaculture Network Information Center

AquaNIC is a gateway to the world's electronic resources in aquaculture, including searchable databases, publications, newsletters, an electronic mail directory, and a calendar of events.

Gopher:
Name: AquaNIC
Address: **thorplus.lib.purdue.edu**
Choose: **Scholarly Databases
| AquaNIC**

Telnet:
Address: **thorplus.lib.purdue.edu**
Login: **cwis**
Password: RETURN

World Wide Web:
URL: **gopher://thorplus.lib.purdue.edu:70/11/
databases/AquaNIC**

Bee Biology

Research and information on the biology of bees, including details on honeybees and bumblebees, pollination, honey, and related material.

Anonymous FTP:
Address: **sunsite.unc.edu**
Path: **/pub/academic/agriculture/
sustainable_agriculture/beekeeping/***

Listserv Mailing List:
List Address: **bee-l@uacsc2.albany.edu**
Subscription Address: **listserv@uacsc2.albany.edu**

Beekeeping

Basic beekeeping information, links to newsletters, information about beekeeping supplies, Africanized bees, and university research on pollination.

Gopher:
Name: Ohio State University
Address: **sun1.oardc.ohio-state.edu**
Choose: **Biological and Agricultural Resources
| Bees and Beekeeping**

Excerpt from the Net...

```
Newsgroup: sci.agriculture.beekeeping
Subject: What bees do when they are not busy?


> I have read that bees actually spend about two out of three hours
> resting.  This surprised me, given the lore about the business of
> bees.  Can anyone tell me what bees do when they rest?

I have an observation hive and have studied the bees quite a bit.  I
find them to be busy doing things even when at rest, conserving energy

that would otherwise be wasted.  The bees conserving energy with full
bellys will develop wax that is secreted from eight wax glands on the
abdomen.  Many times the resting bees will be hanging in chains,
motionless, conserving energy for maximum transfer of their food into
wax.  I also observe other bees going from one motionless bee to
another, collecting the wax from the motionless bee's abdomen and
taking it to form the comb.
```

Beekeeping Web Page

The Beekeeping home page seeks to provide the novice and experienced apiarist alike with all the information relating to the art and science of beekeeping available through the Net. It offers archived articles and newsletters, newsgroups, photos, a quicktime movie, FAQs, articles, links to web entomology servers, and ftp archives.

World Wide Web:
 URL: **http://alfred1.u.washington.edu:8080/ ~jlks/bee.html**

To Bee or Not to Bee?

What could be more inviting than sitting on your front porch, relaxing on your rocking chair, and listening to the steady, comforting drone of your pet bees making you honey? Join the Bee-1 mailing list and keep up with the latest in apiarist circles. Bee there or bee square

Chinchilla Farming

Discuss the cultivation and breeding or anything else related to these cute and furry little animals. Did you ever wonder if the name of these critters is really pronounced "chin-chee-ya"? Tune in to find out if that's right.

Usenet:
 Newsgroup: **alt.chinchilla**

The Internet will set you free.

Clemson University Forestry and Agriculture Network

Information on weather, agri-economics, plants and animals, engineering, food, home, health, family and youth, as well as other items of interest.

Telnet:
 Address: **eureka.clemson.edu**
 Login: **public**

Excerpt from the Net...

```
Newsgroup: alt.agriculture.misc
Subject: Sugar Production

>Can anyone tell me where to find sugar
>production by country?

Look in the yearbooks issued by United
Nations organizations, including the
Food and Agriculture Organization's
"Production Yearbook".

Top sugar producers are usually India,
Brazil, China (rising), Russia, Cuba
(falling), USA, Mexico, Pakistan,
France, Colombia and Australia, in that
order.
```

Commodity Market Reports

This server contains the agricultural commodity market reports compiled by the Agricultural Market News Service of the United States Department of Agriculture. There are over a thousand reports from all over the United States. Most of these reports are updated daily. Try searching for "portland grain."

WAIS:
 Database: **agricultural-market-news**

Cornell Extension Network

CENET is a service provided by Cornell University offering information on various agricultural topics, including crops and agronomy, food and nutrition, fruits and vegetables, horticulture, floriculture, and other similar topics.

Telnet:
 Address: **empire.cce.cornell.edu**
 Login: **guest**

A B C D E F G H I J K L M N O P Q R S T U V W X Y Z

Farming and Agriculture

Discuss the finer points of the proud industry that produces our food and fiber. The **.misc** group is for general discussion, and the **.fruit** group is oriented especially toward fruit farming.

Usenet:
Newsgroup: **alt.agriculture.fruit**
Newsgroup: **alt.agriculture.misc**

Florida Agricultural Information Retrieval System

A comprehensive library of research covering topics such as agriculture, energy, food safety and nutrition, natural resources, pesticides and pesticide safety, turfgrass, water quality, wildlife and many other topics.

World Wide Web:
URL: **http://hammock.ifas.ufl.edu/**

Forest Tree Genome Mapping Database

This site contains a collection of specialized forest tree genome databases and other resources at the Institute of Forest Genetics. These databases incorporate a wide variety of scientific information and data relating to the genetics of forest trees.

Gopher:
Name: Dendrome: Forest Tree Genome Mapping Database
Address: **s27w007.pswfs.gov**

Global Information and Early Warning System

The Global Information and Early Warning System (GIEWS) provides the food supply outlook for the world, including information on food crops and shortages, crop developments, and special reports and alerts.

Gopher:
Name: U.N. Food and Agriculture Organization
Address: **gopher.fao.org**
Port: **2070**
Choose: **Global Information and Early Warning System (GIEWS)**

The Net is mankind's greatest achievement.

Global Integrated Pest Management Information System

A bulletin board system with information about international integrated pest management programs. This resource also provides an interactive communication channel for promoting pest management programs and crop protection.

Telnet:
Address: **cicp.biochem.vt.edu**

Information Resources Management Division

The Information Resources Management Division (IRMD) plans, develops, and otherwise supports Soil Conservation Service systems.

World Wide Web:
URL: **http://peabody.ftc.scs.ag.gov/**

Iowa State University Scholar System

A publication database that contains documents on many topics, including agriculture, applied sciences and technology, biology, and other agriculture-related subjects.

Note: At the DIAL: prompt, log in with the userid **scholar**, press ENTER when prompted for a vt100 terminal or enter another terminal type, then type **scholar** again at the Command: prompt. Type **stop** to leave the Scholar system.

Telnet:
Address: **isn.iastate.edu**
Login: **scholar**

Maize Genome Database Project

The Maize Genome Database Project is yet another genome database project — this one providing genome information on corn. The web page has direct links to the gopher and ftp servers.

Anonymous FTP:
Address: **teosinte.agron.missouri.edu**
Path: **/pub/***

Gopher:
Name: University of Missouri
Address: **teosinte.agron.missouri.edu**

World Wide Web:
URL: **http://teosinte.agron.missouri.edu/more_info.html**

National Cooperative Extension Service

This easy-to-use, menu-driven database is loaded with agricultural information covering a variety of topics such as sustainable agriculture, pesticides and soil problems. Search databases and research papers by typing in keywords and letting the computer do the work for you.

See also: Environment

Gopher:
Name: SunSITE
Address: **calypso-2.oit.unc.edu**
Choose: **Worlds of SunSITE**
  | **Cooperative Extension Service Information**

Yup, we love agriculture. And not just because it's cool and the food is good. We love those old agricultural songs. Our favorite, of course, is "The Farmer in the Dell." In fact, we like it so much that we feel like singing it right now. Feel free to sing right along. Just remember: the cheese stands alone.

National Genetic Resources Program

The USDA's National Genetic Resources Program (NGRP) provides germplasm information about plants, animals, microbes and insects, as well as links to other biological gopher resources around the world.

Gopher:
Name: NGRP
Address: **gopher.ars-grin.gov**

NetVet — Veterinary Resource Line

Archives and information of interest to veterinarians, including newsletters, publications, conference information and proceedings, oncology, and information about specific species of animals.

Gopher:
Name: NETVET Veterinary Resources
Address: **netvet.wustl.edu**
Choose: **NETVET Veterinary Resources**

Man Does Not Live By Cows Alone

There is a lot more to life than cows. True, they can be a lot of fun at birthday parties, and your pet cow does come in handy when you need a fourth for bridge. Still, the needs of the farming community stretch far beyond the bovine.

CHECK OUT **Not Just Cows**

...a comprehensive guide to the Internet's agricultural resources, and make your life happy and complete.

Not Just Cows

A guide to agricultural resources on the Net. Written by Wilfred Drew, this text directs the reader to all kinds of agricultural resources, including BBSs, mailing lists, and other important services.

Anonymous FTP:
Address: **ftp.sura.net**
Path: **/pub/nic/agricultural.list**

Nottingham Arabidopsis Stock Centre

The Nottingham Arabidopsis Stock Centre (NASC) distributes seed free of charge to Europe, Australasia, and Africa. To see a seed list, an order form, or just to ask questions, check out this web page.

World Wide Web:
URL: **http://nasc.nott.ac.uk/**

PENpages

International Food and Nutrition Database, National Family Database, The 4-H Youth Development Database, agricultural and weather statistics, market news, newsletters, and drought information. This resource is provided by the Penn State College of Agricultural Sciences.

Note: Login with the two-letter abbreviation for your state (for example: PA).

Telnet:
Address: **psupen.psu.edu**

A
B
C
D
E
F
G
H
I
J
K
L
M
N
O
P
Q
R
S
T
U
V
W
X
Y
Z

RiceGenes

RiceGenes is a genome database (a compilation of molecular and phenotypic information) about rice. This project is supported by the USDA Plant Genome Research Program.

Gopher:
 Name: Rice Genome Database
 Address: **nightshade.cit.cornell.edu**

Sustainable Agriculture

The politics and technology of ecologically sound agriculture.

Gopher:
 Name: North Carolina State University
 Address: **twosocks.ces.ncsu.edu**
 Choose: **National CES Information**

Mail:
 Address: **almanac@ces.ncsu.edu**
 Body: **send sust-ag-dir catalog**

Telnet:
 Address: **twosocks.ces.ncsu.edu**
 Login: **wais**
 Password: **swais**

Usenet:
 Newsgroup: **alt.sustainable.agriculture**

Sustainable Agriculture Information

This gopher provides access to discussion group archives, pesticide education resources, information on rural skills, the EnviroGopher, agronomy information, USDA statistics, and other gopher servers around the Net.

Gopher:
 Name: Sustainable Agriculture Information
 Address: **calypso.oit.unc.edu**
 Choose: **Worlds of SunSITE — by Subject | Sustainable Agriculture Information**

U.S.D.A. Economics and Statistics Gopher

A U.S.D.A. gopher offering data sets and other information about crops, farm economics, food, international agriculture, livestock, rural affairs, specialty agriculture, and other items of agricultural and economic interest.

Gopher:
 Name: USDA Economics and Stats Gopher
 Address: **usda.mannlib.cornell.edu**

U.S.D.A. Extension Service

An informal educational system that links the education and research resources and activities of the U.S.D.A., many universities, and thousands of county administrative offices. These web and gopher servers provide links to information from the Extension Service of the U.S.D.A. and other scientific agencies within the U.S.D.A.

Gopher:
 Name: U.S. Department of Agriculture
 Address: **esusda.gov**

World Wide Web:
 URL: **http://eos.esusda.gov/usda-es.html**

ANARCHY

Anarchist Resources

This document lists resources, both on the Internet and in the "real world", that are related to anarchy and anarchists. It includes lists of newsgroups, ftp sites, gophers, web pages, newsletters, mailing lists, publications, and more.

World Wide Web:
 URL: **http://www.cwi.nl/cwi/people/Jack.Jansen/spunk/Spunk_Resources.html**

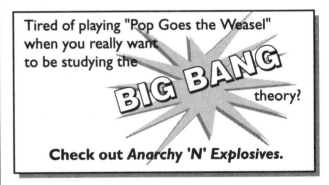

Tired of playing "Pop Goes the Weasel" when you really want to be studying the BIG BANG theory?

Check out *Anarchy 'N' Explosives*.

Anarchy Discussion List

The Anarchy list is a mailing list for discussing anarchism (society without government). There is also an archive of previous postings available and an introduction posting.

Internet Mailing List:
 List Address: **anarchy-list@cwi.nl**
 Subscription Address: **anarchy-list-request@cwi.nl**

World Wide Web:
 URL: **http://www.cwi.nl/cwi/people/Jack.Jansen/anarchy/anarchy.html**

Anarchy 'N' Explosives

Are you up to no good? Do you want to be? Delve into the archives of Anarchy 'N' Explosives and find new uses for all that liquid nitrogen you have sitting around the house.

Anonymous FTP:
Address: **ftp.eff.org**
Path: **/pub/Publications/CuD/ANE/***

Propaganda

Some people call it "disinformation." Some people call it "lies." The nicest word is "propaganda," and you will find a healthy dose of it at this site. Read this stuff and allow yourself to be mislead. Stop thinking for yourself and do as you are told. The Internet is Your Friend.

World Wide Web:
URL: **http://www.clark.net/pub/murple/propaganda.html**

The Seed

A collection of activist resources, including details of the Freedom Press, which publishes anarchist titles, European Counter Network (ECN), which exchanges news and information on the class war across Europe, Phoenix Press, giving practical support to anarchist voices, Class War, Spunk Press, news, events, and alerts. This site also offers many U.K. and Europe-specific anarchist issues and event details.

World Wide Web:
URL: **http://web.cs.city.ac.uk/homes/louise/seed2.html**

Spunk Press

Spunk Press collects and distributes electronic literature with an emphasis on anarchism and related issues. Their home page offers a manifesto, a large catalog of anarchy articles covering anarchist art, selected writings, anarchism around the world, anarchist prose, reviews, anarchist quotations, groups, bibliographies, publications, and images, flyers, calls for contribution, and a list of anarchist resources.

Anonymous FTP:
Address: **etext.archive.umich.edu**
Path: **/pub/Politics/Spunk/***

World Wide Web:
URL: **http://www.cwi.nl/cwi/people/Jack.Jansen/spunk/Spunk_Home.html**

ANIMALS AND PETS

Animal Resources

Archives and FAQs about many different animals, including exotic birds and pets, cats, dogs, chinchillas, goats, sheep, cows, horses, and gerbils.

See also: Agriculture, Zoology

Gopher:
Name: NETVET Veterinary Resources
Address: **netvet.wustl.edu**
Choose: **NETVET Veterinary Resources | Animal Resources**

Animals in the News

Don't take Mr. Ed's word for it. Read the latest news and information on animals.

Usenet:
Newsgroup: **clari.news.interest.animals**

Aquaculture Information Center

AquaNic offers news, images, newsletters, and other information about aquaculture.

Gopher:
Name: Aquaculture Information Center
Address: **thorplus.lib.purdue.edu**
Port: **Scholarly Databases | AquaNic**

Aquaria Mailing List

An open discussion about all things related to the hobby of keeping fish and other aquatic life in an aquarium.

Listserv Mailing List:
List Address: **aquarium@emuvm1.cc.emory.edu**
Subscription Address: **listserv@emuvm1.cc.emory.edu**

Aquariums

What does it mean when your gourami is leaning thirty degrees to the right? He could be trying to steer, but that's probably not the case. Splash around with other ichthiophiles as they explore the true nature of tropical fish. Learn a wide variety of new things, like the best way to earthquake-proof your tanks, how to name your fish after famous Internet book writers, or what to feed your black piranha when all he really wants is you.

Usenet:
Newsgroup: **alt.aquaria**
Newsgroup: **rec.aquaria**

Aquariums and Tropical Fish

Buyers' guides, filter information, magazine list, plant and water quality basics, and many more resources related to aquarium and fish keeping.

Anonymous FTP:
Address: **caldera.usc.edu**
Path: **/pub/aquaria/***

Bird Keeping

Bird magazines, books, terminology, buying guides, cage and toy reviews, diet and feeding information, training help, and other topics.

Anonymous FTP:
Address: **rtfm.mit.edu**
Path: **/pub/usenet/news.answers/pets-birds-faq/***

Birding

Do you like birds or birdwatching? If so, you might enjoy this web page. It includes links to FAQ lists about birds and birdwatching, information about mailing lists, images and photos, exhibits, book lists, announcements, event guides, and other items of interest to bird lovers.

World Wide Web:
URL: **http://compstat.wharton.upenn.edu:8001/ ~siler/birding.html**

Birds

They chirp and squawk and cheep. They execute graceful flight and dives. They also go to the bathroom on everything, but we'd rather ignore that part. Bird lovers can read notes on ecology, contact bird guides, and even download sound files on various birds. It's a nice thing to have if you are stuck in an office all day.

Gopher:
Name: University of Pennsylvania
Address: **simon.wharton.upenn.edu**
Choose: **BIRD THINGS**

Bird-Watching

This is a hobby that can be as simple or as elaborate as you wish. Basic pieces of equipment are a lawn chair, a bird book, and a pair of binoculars — and some birds, of course. On the high end, you can use complicated camouflage, blinds, and camera equipment. No matter what your aim is, bird-watching is an endlessly fascinating pastime.

Usenet:
Newsgroup: **rec.birds**

Bird-Watching Archives

A collection of over 50 gifs and jpgs of various types of birds, including parrots, hummingbirds, eagles, and siskins. There is also information accompanying each image as well as the sounds the birds make.

Anonymous FTP:
Address: **vitruvius.cecer.army.mil**
Path: **/pub/gifs/***

Address: **vitruvius.cecer.army.mil**
Path: **/pub/sounds/***

Bird-Watching Mailing Lists

BirdBand and **BirdChat** are for anyone interested in wild birds, including endangered and extinct birds, as well as common (but not pet) birds.

Listserv Mailing List:
List Address: **birdband@arizvm1.ccit.arizona.edu**
Subscription Address:
listserv@arizvm1.ccit.arizona.edu

List Address: **birdchat@arizvm1.ccit.arizona.edu**
Subscription Address:
listserv@arizvm1.ccit.arizona.edu

Cats

Basic cat care, guide to getting a cat, medical information, problem behaviors, entertainment, and much more related material all about cats.

Anonymous FTP:
Address: **rtfm.mit.edu**
Path: **/pub/usenet/news.answers/cats-faq/***

Dog Resources

This is a great compilation of doggy resources with frequently asked question lists, informative articles, poems about dogs, and technical information such as the Dog Genome Project. You can even learn the meaning of interesting terms like "flews" and "dewclaws."

World Wide Web:
URL: **http://www.sce.carleton.ca/comm/wilf/ doggy_info.html**

Dogs

Owner guides, puppy needs, health care issues, training tips, behavior understanding, kennel clubs, publications, resources, and much more material about man's best friend.

Anonymous FTP:
  Address: **rtfm.mit.edu**
  Paths: **/pub/usenet/news.answers/dogs-faq/***

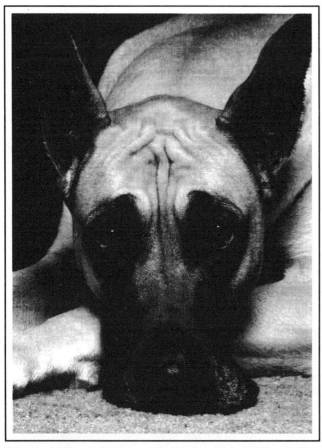

Pet lovers take heart. You're sure to find images of your favorite animals on the Net. From chinchillas to zebras, they're all here. If you think your pet is cuter than this, take a picture and post it for others to enjoy. This one is **saddog.jpg**.

Equestrian

Why do so many young women love to ride horses? Well, we know, but we can't tell. What we can tell you is that this newsgroup is the place to meet horse lovers of all types for a general discussion of horses, riding, and all-round good, clean equestrian fun.

Internet Mailing List:
  List Address: **horse@bbn.com**
  Subscription Address: **horse-request@bbn.com**

Usenet:
  Newsgroup: **rec.equestrian**

Exotic Pets

Do you have a fondness for exotic pets? Learn about special care for your special animals, including how to breed and feed animals, recognize illnesses, and develop an awareness of safety. Discussion is not limited to reptiles (herpetology).

Usenet:
  Newsgroup: **rec.pets.herp**

Ferrets

They are as playful as kittens, good-natured, energetic, and entertaining. Learn more about the suitability of ferrets as pets, get health information, and read ferret stories by owners and roommates of owners.

Internet Mailing List:
  List Address: **ferret@ferret.ocunix.on.ca**
  Subscription Address:
    ferret-request@ferret.ocunix.on.ca

Fish

If you think fish are for something besides eating, you have come to the right place, whether your interests lie in the freshwater, marine, tropical or temperate variety. Load up on FAQs for general fish care, or for reefkeeping, building and planning tanks and other large projects, and how-to's. Also available are interesting discussion archives and a catalog of fish, complete with pictures.

World Wide Web:
  URL: **http://www.actwin.com/fish/index.html**

Fish Cam

The Internet is great because it will allow you to look at pictures of fish whenever you want. And not just any fish. You can see live fish — fish that are still wiggling. (This is how they look before the chef gets to them.) You can also connect to other places on the Net where you can get information on sportfishing or raising fish as pets.

See also: Outdoor Activities

World Wide Web:
  URL: **http://mcom.com/fishcam/fishcam.html**

Writers, share your stories on the Net.

A
B
C
D
E
F
G
H
I
J
K
L
M
N
O
P
Q
R
S
T
U
V
W
X
Y
Z

Excerpt from the Net...

```
(from the standard message that explains the mailing list "petbunny")

...PetBunny is an open, unmoderated discussion list for owners of pet
rabbits.  Things such as how to care for a pet rabbit, rabbit diseases
and rabbit psychology are likely to be discussed.  The list is NOT
intended for rabbit bashing...
```

Fleas and Ticks

Learn how to rid your pet or home of fleas and what to do about ticks. (The ol' gasoline trick probably isn't a very good idea anymore.)

Anonymous FTP:
Address: **rtfm.mit.edu**
Path: **/pub/usenet/news.answers/fleas-ticks**

Golden Retrievers

These dogs are energetic mounds of golden fluff and enthusiasm. Retriever fans will tell you that golden retrievers are a joy to own, not only because they are happy and loving dogs, but because they fetch really well, too. Read up on news, articles, discussion of lines and breeds, shows, activities, and general I-love-my-dog posts.

Internet Mailing List:
List Address: **golden@hobbes.ucsd.edu**
Subscription Address:
   golden-request@hobbes.ucsd.edu

Horse Fanciers

There is no domestic animal that has a more powerful, yet graceful carriage than the horse. Join the discussion of all phases of horse ownership and management of all horse breeds and learn the truth in the phrase "poetry in motion."

Internet Mailing List:
List Address: **horse@world.std.com**
Subscription Address:
   horse-request@world.std.com

List Address: **equine-l@psuvm.psu.edu**
Subscription Address: **listserv@psuvm.psu.edu**

Kitten Page

Nobody can resist warming up to a cute little kitten. Someone thought their kittens were so cute that you should see them, too. Check out this page for a selection of pictures of cats and kittens.

World Wide Web:
   URL: **http://rhythm.com/keith/KeithHome.html**

Pets General Discussion

Learn about a wide variety of pets. Share information and experiences on a range of topics, including exotic animals, nutrition, grooming, behavior, and veterinary care.

Usenet:
   Newsgroup: **rec.pets**

Rabbits

Cuddly, soft, lovable little animals that you can dye pastel shades when Easter rolls around. Bunnies are not just for kids. They make great pets for everyone. Learn about how to care for a pet rabbit and get information about rabbit psychology and diseases that afflict bunnies. Non-bunny-lovers are not welcome unless you can mind your manners.

Listserv Mailing List:
   List Address: **petbunny@ukcc.uky.edu**
   Subscription Address: **listserv@ukcc.uky.edu**

Siamese Fighting Fish

A mailing list for people interested in keeping and breeding *Betta splendens* (Siamese fighting fish). This list is not for general aquaria information, but strictly for Siamese fighting fish.

Listserv Mailing List:
   List Address: **bettas@arizvm1.ccit.arizona.edu**
   Subscription Address:
      listserv@arizvm1.ccit.arizona.edu

This is the first book of the rest of your life.

Specific Domestic Pets

Kittens and puppies and birds, oh my! Learn the best methods of caring for your pet. Discover how to pick the best pet, analyze behavior, and find new ideas for making your pet the happiest pet ever. Read advice and anecdotes from experienced friends of animals.

Usenet:
>   Newsgroup: **rec.pets.birds**
>   Newsgroup: **rec.pets.cats**
>   Newsgroup: **rec.pets.dogs**

Treatment of Animals

What goes on in the lives of animals that are not just pets? Develop awareness on the use and abuse of animals.

Usenet:
>   Newsgroup: **talk.politics.animal**

ANTHROPOLOGY

Aboriginal Studies Archive

The Australian Institute of Aboriginal and Torres Strait Islander Studies maintains material in the Aboriginal Studies Electronic Data Archive. This archive is available to researchers subject to conditions. An online catalog gives brief details of material held at the Institute.

World Wide Web:
>   URL: **http://coombs.anu.edu.au/SpecialProj/ASEDA/ASEDA.html**

Evolution of Humans and Primates

Some days it's hard to believe that humans might have evolved from primates. Then on a very bad day you will encounter some Neanderthal whose vocabulary is limited to grunts varying only in pitch and perhaps resonance. On those days it's easy to believe in the theory of evolution. Get together with people who spend their days contemplating the anthropological aspects of the evolution of humans and primates.

Usenet:
>   Newsgroup: **sci.anthropology.paleo**

ARCHAEOLOGY

Archaeological Computing

A bibliography of archaeological computing resources in BibTeX format.

WAIS:
>   Database: **archaeological_computing**

ArchNet

The University of Connecticut's anthropology department runs the ArchNet server, which provides access to archaeological resources on the Internet. This web page has links to a huge number a really neat archaeological resources, and it won a PC Week Labs "Cool Web Page" award.

World Wide Web:
>   URL: **http://spirit.lib.uconn.edu/HTML/archnet.html**

Classics and Mediterranean Archaeology

Dedicated to information and other resources of interest to classicists and Mediterranean archaeologists. Offers access to journals, texts, spatially referenced data as well as information on museum and library exhibits.

Gopher:
>   Name: Classics and Mediterranean Archaeology
>   Address: **rome.classics.lsa.umich.edu**

Parents and children, take a look at: Families and Parenting, Kids, and Youth.

A
B
C
D
E
F
G
H
I
J
K
L
M
N
O
P
Q
R
S
T
U
V
W
X
Y
Z

Dead Sea Scrolls

"Scrolls from the Dead Sea: the Ancient Library of Qumran and Modern Scholarship" is a Library of Congress exhibit. It describes the historical context of the scrolls and the Qumran community where they may have originated.

Anonymous FTP:
>   Address: **calypso-2.oit.unc.edu**
>   Path: **/pub/academic/history/deadsea-scrolls/***

>   Address: **ftp.loc.gov**
>   Path: **/pub/exhibit.images/**
>   **deadsea.scrolls.exhibit/***

>   Address: **ftp.tex.ac.uk**
>   Path: **/tex-archive/language/hebrew**

Gopher:
>   Name: UK TeX Archive
>   Address: **gopher.tex.ac.uk**
>   Choose: **UK TeX Archive**
>   **| Archive directory**
>   **| language**
>   **| hebrew**
>   **| deadsea**

Egyptian Artifacts

You can be Indiana Jones without having to worry about sharp spikes being driven through your head or giant rolling rocks crushing you to death. Take a look at beautiful Egyptian artifacts at the Institute of Egyptian Art and Archaeology.

World Wide Web:
>   URL: **http://www.memphis.edu/egypt/**
>   **artifact.html**

National Archaeological Database

A database of over 100,000 reports of archaeological investigations. Search by keyword, location, author, and publication date.

Telnet:
>   Address: **cast.uark.edu**
>   Login: **nadb**

Treasure In Your Backyard?

How many people are unaware of important --and perhaps valuable--archaeological treasures right in their own backyard? This need never happen to you.

The
National Archaeological Database
contains information on more investigations than you can shake a 500-year-old stick at. Telnet to this bountiful resource and get the lowdown on what's low down.

Research into Artifacts Center for Engineering

Research into Artifacts Center for Engineering (RACE) hopes to reverse the trends of modern technology: the continuous subdivision and narrowing of science and the consequent loss of balance to society and the environment. Better buy a horse while you can still afford one.

World Wide Web:
>   URL: **http://brains.race.u-tokyo.ac.jp/**

University of Southampton Department of Archaeology

Descriptive material about the Department of Archaeology at the University of Southampton and the courses offered there, including online course notes for students, archives of articles and images, and an online journal of archaeological theory.

Gopher:
Name: University of Southampton
Address: **avebury.arch.soton.ac.uk**

World Wide Web:
URL: **http://avebury.arch.soton.ac.uk/**

ARCHITECTURE

Alternative Architecture

Discuss nontraditional building designs and techniques. Swap tips and techniques about solar energy, innovative designs, new materials, and much more.

Usenet:
Newsgroup: **alt.architecture.alternative**

Tired of the same old structures everywhere you look?
Try Alternative Architecture
for new thinking about old ideas.

ArchiGopher

A gopher at the University of Michigan that is dedicated to the dissemination of architectural knowledge. ArchiGopher resources include samples of five Kandinsky paintings, a sample of Andrea Palladio's architectural projects, computer images from the CAD group, and scenes and images from other projects and settings.

Gopher:
Name: University of Michigan
Address: **libra.arch.umich.edu**

Architectural Modeling

Projects at siteX were produced for an architectural modeling course at McGill University and the University of Waterloo. The course explores the differences between models produced in the traditional manner and models produced using computer technology.

World Wide Web:
URL: **http://architecture.mcgill.ca/siteX/homepage.html**

Architectural Visualization

Acording to ancient wisdom, architects make images from ideas. This site is a visualization of architects' ideas and models. It includes a gallery of images and ideas in and around architecture, reconstruction models of ancient buildings, an exploration of some computer applications, and computer graphics ideas and applications.

World Wide Web:
URL: **http://archpropplan.auckland.ac.nz/Archivis/archivis.html**

Architecture General Discussion

Talk about architecture-oriented topics: building design, construction, architecture schools, materials, and so on.

Usenet:
Newsgroup: **alt.architecture**

Architecture of the Tropics

Read about the architecture of the tropics and take a guided tour of Miami Beach sites. This web page is provided by the University of Miami School of Architecture.

World Wide Web:
URL: **http://rossi.arc.miami.edu/**

A
B
C
D
E
F
G
H
I
J
K
L
M
N
O
P
Q
R
S
T
U
V
W
X
Y
Z

Architronic

An electronic journal dedicated to the profession and issues of architecture.

Note: The FTP site is not anonymous; log in with the userid **architecture** and a password of **archives**.

Anonymous FTP:
>Address: **ksuvxa.kent.edu**

Gopher:
>Name: North Carolina State University
>Address: **dewey.lib.ncsu.edu**
>Choose: **NCSU's Library without Walls**
>   **| Electronic Journals and Books**
>   **| Architronic**

Listserv Mailing List:
>List Address: **arcitron@kentvm.bitnet**
>Subscription Address: **listserv@kentvm.bitnet**

Association of Collegiate Schools of Architecture

The ACSA is an association of professional schools of architecture in the U.S. and Canada. The stated purpose of ACSA is to improve the quality of architecture education. This web page also provides links to all the ACSA schools in the western region.

World Wide Web:
>URL: **http://uhunix.uhcc.hawaii.edu:3333/**

Classical Architecture of the Mediterranean

A huge database of more than 2,500 images of classical architecture of the Mediterranean basin. Allows you to search for images from a specific country, century, type of work, site, and title of work.

World Wide Web:
>URL: **http://rubens.anu.edu.au/**
>   **architecture_form.html**

Excerpt from the Net...

(from the Web: http://www.cis.upenn.edu/~mjd/otherwork/plumbing.html)

AN ARCHITECTURAL MANIFESTO

Buckminister Fuller said that the average person doesn't give a thought to the sophistication of the technology that allows him to flush the toilet on the 104th floor and have it work... I say, let's just cut holes in the floor and let the refuse fall into the basement.

However, architectural critics pick nits with this design:

>"This design is a crock. Although cheap and effective in low buildings, random air currents blowing this way and that will inevitably cause the material descending from higher floors to splatter on the edges of the holes in the floors below."

I say, no problem, just make the holes on the lower floors bigger.

Architectural critics still pick nits:

>"The hole in the first floor of a 104-story building would have to be at least 35 feet, 4 inches in diameter to be practical."

I say, so what, people will love 'em. What a conversation piece... Imagine this: you're sitting in your living room, eating toast points, drinking champagne before your maid serves dinner, and you see a piece of refuse fall through the 35-foot hole in the ceiling, silently descend the 12 feet to the 35 foot 4 inch hole in the floor, and vanish from sight. One of your guests remarks:

>"Looked to be about 6.5 feet in from the edge, there. I'd say it came from the 42nd floor..."

Contemporary Architecture in Hong Kong

An overview of the architecture of Hong Kong, images of buildings and prints, a national gallery, and other resources and papers on the architecture of Hong Kong.

World Wide Web:
> URL: **http://www.ncsa.uiuc.edu/SDG/ Experimental/anu-art-history/hongkong.html**

Images of Architecture and Sculpture in Turkey

This web page has pointers to images of the sculptured theater "frons scenae" at the Roman theater at Perge in Turkey, images of 2nd century A.D. Roman sarcophagi, and other great archaeological sites in Turkey.

World Wide Web:
> URL: **http://www.ncsa.uiuc.edu/SDG/ Experimental/anu-art-history/ architecture.images.html**

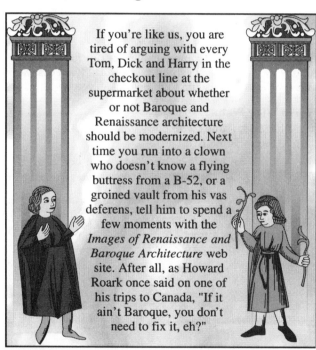

If you're like us, you are tired of arguing with every Tom, Dick and Harry in the checkout line at the supermarket about whether or not Baroque and Renaissance architecture should be modernized. Next time you run into a clown who doesn't know a flying buttress from a B-52, or a groined vault from his vas deferens, tell him to spend a few moments with the *Images of Renaissance and Baroque Architecture* web site. After all, as Howard Roark once said on one of his trips to Canada, "If it ain't Baroque, you don't need to fix it, eh?"

Images of Renaissance and Baroque Architecture

Images of Renaissance and Baroque architecture that show basic design and building principles of typical architecture of the time.

World Wide Web:
> URL: **http://www.lib.virginia.edu/dic/ class/arh102/**

Lighthouses in the Eastern U.S.

A guide to images and notes about lighthouses in New England, the Outer Banks of North Carolina, and California.

World Wide Web:
> URL: **http://gopher.lib.utk.edu:70/0/ Other-Internet-Resources/pictures/lights/ lights.html**

ART

911 Gallery

So you just don't see what's so appealing about ancient art. It's old, dusty, and it smells bad. You want something new, shiny and fast. Check out this gallery of electronic media, including computer graphics, video and music. As with all galleries, the exhibits on display will change, so keep checking in to see new things.

World Wide Web:
> URL: **http://www.iquest.net/911/iq_911.html**

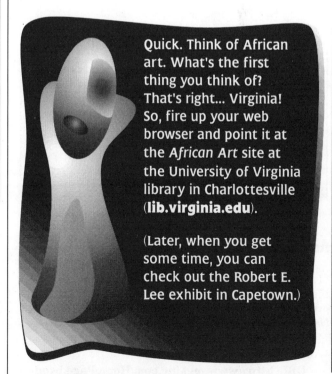

Quick. Think of African art. What's the first thing you think of? That's right... Virginia! So, fire up your web browser and point it at the *African Art* site at the University of Virginia library in Charlottesville (**lib.virginia.edu**).

(Later, when you get some time, you can check out the Robert E. Lee exhibit in Capetown.)

A B C D E F G H I J K L M N O P Q R S T U V W X Y Z

Aart Gallery

Be an armchair art lover. The Aart Gallery exhibits the work of various artists. The images at this site change, just like a museum or gallery show changes, so make this a place to frequent. More traditional media are carried here while digital media can be found at the Drux gallery.

World Wide Web:
    URL: **http://www.wimsey.com/Generality/
    aart_Gallery.html**

Ah, we love poetry readings and that is why we love to hang out at *The Anecdote*. In fact, just for the occasion, we have composed a special poem. So for the moment, pretend you are sitting at The Anecdote Club in Ann Arbor, Michigan, a long, cool espresso in front of you, eyes closed, listening closely to the clinking of cutlery, the dull buzz of quiet conversation, and the expectant aura of collective delight as Harley approaches the microphone to read one of his poems:

> *There once was a girl from Nantucket,*
> *Who told all her boyfriends to –*

Oh sorry, wrong poem, here we go...

TRASH CAN

I see the empty trash can of life
Thrown carelessly along the roadside of existence.
How empty and meaningless seem the old candy
*   bar wrappers*
How futile and existential are yesterday's newspapers.
Surely the dump truck of the universe is at once
Our salvation and our nemesis.
Are we fated to one day lie in the trash can ourselves
Or will we be recycled?
I see the empty trash can of life
But no one has discarded the answers.

Access Art

Medium for Global Access, Inc (MGA) offers Access Art, the largest virtual art gallery on the Internet. Access Art presents fine art for your browsing pleasure and for sale. New artists and works are added monthly.

World Wide Web:
    URL: **http://www.mgainc.com/HomePage.html**

African Art

See elements of the African aesthetic and their meaning in relation to culture and morality. Images are included at this site.

World Wide Web:
    URL: **http://www.lib.virginia.edu/
    dic/African.html**

The Anecdote

Experience the virtual equivalent of the Anecdote — a real club in Ann Arbor, Michigan. See the gallery of art and hear poetry readings and segments of performances by bands.

World Wide Web:
    URL: **http://anecdote.com/**

Ansel Adams

Experience the beauty and technical perfection of Ansel Adams by viewing this exhibit of his work. Read essays and shop at this museum's online bookstore.

World Wide Web:
    URL: **http://bookweb.cwis.uci.edu:8042/
    AdamsHome.html**

Ansel Adams is our main pic man, Man. Check out his web site and see how, even when you have to wait a long time for something to develop, photography doesn't have to be a negative experience.

Art Crimes

Graffiti is often referred to as "art crime" because even though it can sometimes be beautiful, it's still illegal. Take a photo-tour of art crimes around the world. Many of these places no longer exist, so this will be your only chance to see them.

World Wide Web:
    URL: **http://www.gatech.edu/desoto/graf/
    Index.Art_Crimes.html**

Art Criticism Forum

A mailing list open to anyone interested in the visual arts. Topics are often political.

Listserv Mailing List:
 List Address: **artcrit@vm1.yorku.ca**
 Subscription Address: **listserv@vm1.yorku.ca**

Art Educational Materials

Varieties of image project work, including an interactive student tutorial on the history of prints, architecture and architectural sculpture of the Mediterranean basin, and visual materials from the National Gallery of Australia.

See also: Education

World Wide Web:
 URL: **http://www.ncsa.uiuc.edu/SDG/ Experimental/anu-art-history/home.html**

Art Exploration

Explore the art of many cultures using the multimedia capabilities of the Web.

World Wide Web:
 URL: **http://solar.rtd.utk.edu/friends/art/art.html**

Art Gallery

This gopher features a large repository of artwork. Works are arranged on the gopher menu by the names of artists.

Gopher:
 Name: Art Gallery
 Address: **unix5.nysed.gov**
 Choose: **K-12 Resources
 | Arts & Humanities
 | Gallery**

Art History Server

This server offers a variety of image collections and small presentations, all of which deal in some way with art history. There are over 2,800 images of prints, largely from the 15th century to the end of the 19th century, and 2,500 images of mainly classical architecture and architectural sculpture from around the Mediterranean.

See also: History

World Wide Web:
 URL: **http://rubens.anu.edu.au/**

Art and Images

Links to thousands of animations and gifs, including weather, space, satellite images, clip art, and many other pictures and graphics.

Gopher:
 Name: Art & Images
 Address: **cs4sun.cs.ttu.edu**
 Choose: **Art & Images**

Art Museums and Exhibits

Access to commercial art galleries, electronic art galleries, Krannert Art Museum, the Louvre, the Museum of New Zealand, photography exhibits, the REIFF II Museum, and many other links.

See also: Museums

World Wide Web:
 URL: **http://www.yahoo.com/Art/Museums/**

Art Network for Integrated Media Applications

Links to many different resources relating to digital art, multimedia, the integration of art and technology, online arts and media publications, programs, tools and applications, and discussion groups.

World Wide Web:
 URL: **http://www.wimsey.com/anima/ ANIMAhome.html**

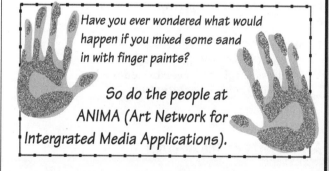

Have you ever wondered what would happen if you mixed some sand in with finger paints?

So do the people at ANIMA (Art Network for Intergrated Media Applications).

Art News

The real story on the art scene. Get news on drama, music, and other fine arts.

Usenet:
 Newsgroup: **clari.news.arts**

A B C D E F G H I J K L M N O P Q R S T U V W X Y Z

Art Nouveau

An overview of the Art Nouveau movement, a sensitive map of the major European centers of Art Nouveau, information on famous artists of the movement, what kind of art they created, and a section on architecture.

World Wide Web:
URL: **http://www.enst.fr/~derville/AN/AN.html**

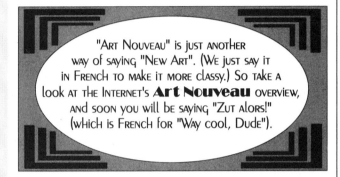

"Art Nouveau" is just another way of saying "New Art". (We just say it in French to make it more classy.) So take a look at the Internet's **Art Nouveau** overview, and soon you will be saying "Zut alors!" (which is French for "Way cool, Dude").

Art on the Net

Galleries, artists, current art happenings, links to other art sites, copyrights, and other information about art resources on the Net.

World Wide Web:
URL: **http://www.art.net/**

Art Papers

A collection of art-related papers and documents, including aesthetic perspectives, bibliography of arts, and catalog reviews.

Gopher:
Name: Carnegie Mellon University
Address: **english-server.hss.cmu.edu**
Choose: **Art and Architecture**
| **Text**

Art Projects on the Internet

The Syracuse University Computer Graphics for the Arts server offers details and images from many projects, encouraging collaboration between artists across the Internet. It includes such projects as Digital Journeys, ChainArt, Search for the Lost Souli, as well as links to many more.

World Wide Web:
URL: **http://ziris.syr.edu/home.html**

Art Reviews

booknews features reviews of new and forthcoming books, as well as CDs, and music videos.

Listserv Mailing List:
List Address: **booknews@columbia.ilc.com**
Subscription Address: **listserv@columbia.ilc.com**

Artistic Expression

A web page devoted to the free expression and distribution of artistic ideas. It is composed of independent artists and supports independent artists. It includes stories, images, poems, technical articles and photographs.

World Wide Web:
URL: **http://www.wimsey.com/~jmax/index.html**

Artistic Melange

Find out about music, opera, plays. Read reviews and interviews. If you've been looking for art in all the wrong places, you will definitely be able to find it here.

Usenet:
Newsgroup: **rec.arts.misc**

Arts Online

A bibliography of arts-related resources available on the Internet and other networks.

Anonymous FTP:
Address: **ftp.funet.fi**
Path: **/pub/doc/library/artbase.txt.Z**

ArtSource

A gathering point for networked resources on art and architecture. This web page is large and eclectic and includes links to resources around the Net as well as original materials submitted by librarians, artists, and historians.

See also: Architecture

World Wide Web:
URL: **http://www.uky.edu/Artsource/
artsourcehome.html**

ArtWorld

A large collection of pointers and information about all areas of online arts, including visual, performance, literature, video, mass media, and design.

World Wide Web:
>   URL: **http://wimsey.com/anima/**
>   **ARTWORLDhome.html**

ASCII Cartoons

A selection of ASCII art, including *The Simpsons*, cows, smileys, spaceships, dragons, and Slimer.

Gopher:
>   Name: Universitaet des Saarlandes
>   Address: **pfsparc02.phil15.uni-sb.de**
>   Choose: **Fun (Spass & Spiel, etc.)**
>   **| Cartoons**

Basic Design in Art and Architecture

There is more to art and architecture than just expressing yourself. You have to do it in a way in which nobody gets killed. At least in architecture. (In the art world, you just call it "performance art" and that makes it okay.) Participate in discussion relating to basic and applied design as it relates to both art and architecture.

Listserv Mailing List:
>   List Address: **design-l@psuvm.psu.edu**
>   Subscription Address: **listserv@psuvm.psu.edu**

Beauty for Ashes

A collection of art by Christian artists who believe that "art should be a reflection of the soul" and that they should bring "the eternal and ethereal into everyday existence." As well as images, there are poems and stories. You will need a graphical browser to enjoy this.

World Wide Web:
>   URL: **http://enuxsa.eas.asu.edu:8080/public/**
>   **fetters/ashes.html**

Book of Kells

Sample pages from the *Book of Kells*, an eighth-century illuminated gospel, housed in the Long Room of the Old Library at Trinity College, Dublin.

World Wide Web:
>   URL: **http://www.tcd.ie/kells.html**

Brian Eno

He's more than an artist — he's a musician, a producer, a man who can't just settle on one thing to do. Therefore, it is fitting that this group doesn't concentrate on just one topic. As well as discussing Brian Eno, this forum covers any related video artists, avant-garde music, and museum gallery installations.

See also: Music

Internet Mailing List:
>   List Address: **nerve_net@noc.pue.udlap.mx**
>   Subscription Address:
>   **nerve_net-request@noc.pue.udlap.mx**

Cadence Design Systems

A mailing list for users, and potential users, of the software tools from Cadence Design Systems.

Internet Mailing List:
>   List Address: **artist-users@uicc.com**
>   Subscription Address:
>   **artist-users-request@uicc.com**

Carlos Museum of Art

Get your daily dose of culture by looking at images of ancient Egypt, the ancient Americas, art from Asia, Greece, Rome, and sub-Saharan Africa. You will see ancient artifacts such as a cuneiform tablet, a mummy, and an engraved effigy, among others. Also available are later works on paper, such as manuscripts and scrolls.

See also: World Cultures, History, Archaeology

World Wide Web:
>   URL: **http://www.cc.emory.edu/CARLOS/**
>   **carlos.html**

Ceramic Arts Discussion List

A mailing list of interest to folks into ceramic arts and pottery. Discuss any related subject you like, including aesthetic issues and concerns, grant information, and exhibition opportunities.

Listserv Mailing List:
>   List Address: **clayart@ukcc.uky.edu**
>   Subscription Address: **listserv@ukcc.uky.edu**

A B C D E F G H I J K L M N O P Q R S T U V W X Y Z

Ceramic City

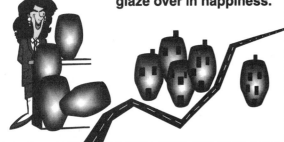

Yes, it's true: in Ceramic City there are two pots for every guy (and gal).

Join the **clayart** mailing list and have your mailbox filled with information and discussion that will bring fire to your life and make your eyes glaze over in happiness.

Ceramics Gopher

An experimental database of glazes, clay recipes, and other items of interest to pottery fans.

Gopher:
> Name: San Diego State University
> Address: **athena.sdsu.edu**
> Choose: **SDSU Campus Topics**
> | **Departmental Information**
> | **Art Department**
> | **The Ceramics Gopher**

Chesley Bonestell

We are all familiar with how space is portrayed in the movies of the '40s and '50s, in which costumes were made of tin foil and all aliens were small and green. (This was before they became cute and cuddly in the '80s.) But when people sat under the stars at night and imagined what it would be like to really be in space, how did they see it? Chesley Bonestell, an artist and architect popular in the '40s and '50s, had his own dreams of space and put those images onto canvas. They are available for viewing at this web site.

See also: Astronomy

World Wide Web:
> URL: **http://www.secapl.com/bonestell/top.html**

Contemporary Russian Fine Arts Gallery

A bilingual excursion through halls of Russian paintings, standing sculptures, and decorative art.

World Wide Web:
> URL: **http://www.kiae.su/www/wtr/artinfo/begin.html**

CyberNet's Art Gallery

Links to many cool art sites, including the Louvre and the Ansel Adams archive.

World Wide Web:
> URL: **http://venus.mcs.com/~flowers/html.art.html**

Digital Art Archives

An assortment of scanned images from Dali, Degas, da Vinci, and others.

See also: Computers: Pictures

Gopher:
> Name: Delft University of Technology
> Address: **olt.et.tudelft.nl**
> Choose: **Fun and Leisure Box**
> | **Digital Picture Archive of the 17th Floor**
> | **art**

Digital Journeys

An ongoing collaborative art project by various people on the Internet. You need to have a graphical browser to really appreciate this work. Read the writing, look at the pictures, and if you feel inspired you can add to them. It's free-form and fun.

World Wide Web:
> URL: **http://ziris.syr.edu/digjourney.html**

One of the best things about the Internet is how people share their creations. (It's also one of the worst things about the Internet.)

If you feel like collaborating —or seeing how others collaborate—

take a look at **Digital Journeys** and see how the Internet can bring out the best in people.

Drux Electronic Art Gallery

Discover the magic of digital art by taking a tour of the work of artists who are on the cutting edge of technology. The collection changes periodically, so what you see today may not be available for viewing tomorrow.

World Wide Web:
URL: **http://www.wimsey.com/ Generality/Drux.HTML**

Electric Gallery

Discover the wonders of the primitive and naive art of Haiti. Walk through an exhibit of artwork by Haitian artists. A selection of the artwork is also for sale.

World Wide Web:
URL: **http://www.egallery.com/egallery/**

Electronic Resources for Art Historians

Don't consign yourself to a life of blowing dust off old books. Immerse yourself in the sea of electronic resources that are available: CD-ROMs, tape drives, video disks, as well as things on the Net — gophers, webs, ftp sites, and discussion groups.

See also: History

World Wide Web:
URL: **http://www.uky.edu/Artsource/ sourcelists/electresources.txt**

Enfolding Perspectives

A collection of photo collages, landscapes, self-portraits and thoughtful writing.

World Wide Web:
URL: **file://netcom13.netcom.com/pub/simran/ shows/shows.html**

Expo Exhibit

Start your exhibit tour by virtual shuttle bus at the charming and friendly Expo ticket office. You will be offered tours of a variety of interesting exhibits: Vatican, Soviet Archive, 1492, Paleontology, Spalato, and the Dead Sea Scrolls. Round out your excursions with a French cooking demo by notable chefs. The Expo comes complete with a post office and bookstore.

World Wide Web:
URL: **http://sunsite.unc.edu/expo/ ticket_office.html**

Fine Art Forum

Delve into the mystery and meaning of art. Artists come together for lively exploration of the meaning, impact, responsibility, and history of art. This forum is scholarly, but not intimidating, and can provide answers to the most obscure technical or theoretical questions. Because artists are always in the studio, this is a great way to finally get them all in one place.

Listserv Mailing List:
List Address: **fine-art@rutvm1.rutgers.edu**
Subscription Address:
listserv@rutvm1.rutgers.edu

Usenet:
Newsgroup: **rec.arts.fine**

Fine Art Pictures

The modern age means art for everyone. Digitized fine art pictures are available here for downloading. The .d list is exclusively for discussion of the posting of pictures. Both groups are moderated.

Usenet:
Newsgroup: **alt.binaries.pictures.fine-art.d**
Newsgroup: **alt.binaries.pictures.fine-art.digitized**

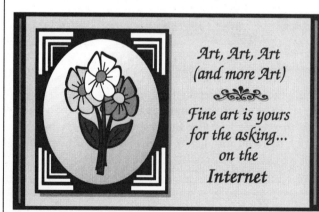

Art, Art, Art (and more Art)
Fine art is yours for the asking... on the Internet

FineArt Forum's Directory of Online Resources

An excellent directory of Internet resources relating to the arts.

Anonymous FTP:
Address: **ra.msstate.edu**
Path: **/pub/archives/fineart_online/ Online_directory**

Graphics

Graphics is on the rise as an art form. Capture some of your favorites. This group is moderated.

Usenet:
 Newsgroup: **alt.binaries.pictures.fine-art.graphics**

Grotesque in Art

This is an exhibit of visual images that explores violence, horror, and the grotesque in art. Send the kids out of the room, don't eat before viewing, and don't meditate on these just before bedtime because they can be very graphic.

World Wide Web:
 URL: **http://www.ugcs.caltech.edu/~werdna/ grotesque/grotesque.html**

 If you are an ordinary mortal, you may not be aware that *grotesque* – just like *sfumato*, *profil perdu* or *horror vacuii* – is an actual technical term among art historians. So when you cop a look at the ***Grotesque in Art*** resource, you are actually dropping in on a scholarly exhibit, designed to educate, enlighten, and generally raise men above the base level of beasts. To use another technical term favored by the people who like to drive students crazy by making them mindlessly memorize slides of famous paintings, it's way cool.

H.P. Lovecraft Image Gallery

The fiction of horror writer H.P. Lovecraft has inspired many artists to explore the darker regions of their creativity. The Lovecraft Image Gallery brings some of the more obscure and rare images inspired by Lovecraft's work to the Internet.

World Wide Web:
 URL: **http://daneel.acns.nwu.edu:8082/lovecraft/ lovecraftinfo.html**

Hot Wire

Hot Wire is a newsletter put out by Art Wire, a network for artists. This newsletter is made available at no charge, although other services offered by Art Wire are not free.

Gopher:
 Name: The Meta Network
 Address: **tmn.com**
 Choose: **Arts Wire**
  | **Hot Wire Archive**

International Internet ChainArt Project

This project began as a class effort and developed into a project that resulted in more than 100 images involving people in ten countries. The documentation and images are available for viewing.

World Wide Web:
 URL: **http://ziris.syr.edu/chainartdocs/ chainart.html**

Japanese Animation

Immerse yourself in the magical world of Japanese animation (anime). Devotees of animation provide information not only on this art form, but also movie reviews, schedules of showings, announcements of new releases, conventions, and club meetings.

Usenet:
 Newsgroup: **rec.arts.anime.info**

Kaleidospace

A gallery that displays artists' work that is available for purchase. Wander through the newsstand which features interviews of artists and songwriters and a reading room with excerpts from featured authors.

World Wide Web:
 URL: **http://kspace.com/**

Krannert Art Museum

Sculptures, paintings, antiquities, and other works of art from all over the world, housed at the Krannert Art Museum, located on the campus of the University of Illinois at Champaign-Urbana.

World Wide Web:
 URL: **http://www.ncsa.uiuc.edu/General/UIUC/ KrannertArtMuseum/KrannertArtHome.html**

Le Louvre

Here's your chance to visit Paris free of charge. Get a ticket to the virtual Louvre, which is conducting tours around the city. You will see the Eiffel Tower and the Champs Elysees, among other sights. At the Louvre itself, they offer tours of a collection of famous paintings and a demonstration of French Medieval art. You have to bring your own pastries.

World Wide Web:
    URL: **http://www.yahoo.com/Art/Museums/
    Le_louvre/**

Lexia

A forum for the arts, artists, and others concerned with the humanities. This web site presents art, information on ongoing projects, and other items of interest.

World Wide Web:
    URL: **http://crash.cts.com/lexia/**

Mona Lisa

DaVinci's famous painting in gif format. Download this file and replace your Windows startup screen with the Mona Lisa!

Anonymous FTP:
    Address: **ftp.wustl.edu**
    Path: **/multimedia/images/gif/monalisa.gif**

Museum of New Zealand

The Museum of New Zealand Te Papa Tongarewa represents the amalgamation of the National Museum and National Art Gallery. On this multimedia audio/visual tour you will see and learn about some of the museum's diverse collections of Maori, natural environment, history, and art objects.

See also: History, Museums

World Wide Web:
    URL: **http://www.uni-passau.de/forwiss/
    mitarbeiter/freie/ramsch/Museum/
    Museum_of_New_Zealand.html**

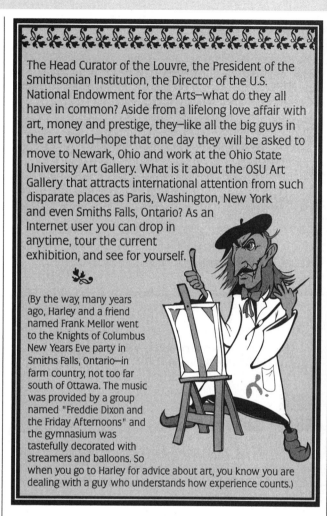

The Head Curator of the Louvre, the President of the Smithsonian Institution, the Director of the U.S. National Endowment for the Arts–what do they all have in common? Aside from a lifelong love affair with art, money and prestige, they–like all the big guys in the art world–hope that one day they will be asked to move to Newark, Ohio and work at the Ohio State University Art Gallery. What is it about the OSU Art Gallery that attracts international attention from such disparate places as Paris, Washington, New York and even Smiths Falls, Ontario? As an Internet user you can drop in anytime, tour the current exhibition, and see for yourself.

(By the way, many years ago, Harley and a friend named Frank Mellor went to the Knights of Columbus New Years Eve party in Smiths Falls, Ontario—in farm country, not too far south of Ottawa. The music was provided by a group named "Freddie Dixon and the Friday Afternoons" and the gymnasium was tastefully decorated with streamers and balloons. So when you go to Harley for advice about art, you know you are dealing with a guy who understands how experience counts.)

Nexus

A collection of network projects by artists investigating the interface between art and technology. They vary from the literary and critical to the expressive and visual, including a network imagined as "a spiral, a nerve, a mathematical phrase, molecular, monocular, rhythmic or knot tree form."

World Wide Web:
    URL: **http://wimsey.com/anima/
    NEXUShome.html**

Off the Wall Gallery

View works of original art in a variety of media, not exclusively digital. The gallery features new artists in each issue, so the images on this site change and you are consistently offered new things to see.

World Wide Web:
URL: **http://nearnet.gnn.com/arcade/gallery/art.html**

URL: **http://nearnet.gnn.com/mag/1_94/gallery/art.html**

Online Art References

A web page with links to art shows, galleries, resources, organizations, and museums.

World Wide Web:
URL: **http://www.art.net/Links/artref.html#organizations**

OSU Art Gallery

A view of the art on display at the Ohio State University at Newark: photography, ceramics, painting, cultural art, and notables such as Roy Lichtenstein. Biographical information on artists is available.

World Wide Web:
URL: **http://www.cgrg.ohio-state.edu/mkruse/osu.html**

OTIS Project

OTIS (Operative Term Is Stimulate) distributes original artwork and photographs over the network for public perusal, scrutiny, and distribution. OTIS also offers a forum for critique and exhibition of your works. A virtual art gallery that never closes and exists in an information dimension where your submissions will hang as wallpaper on thousands of glowing monitors.

Anonymous FTP:
Address: **sunsite.unc.edu**
Path: **/pub/multimedia/pictures/OTIS/***

World Wide Web:
URL: **http://sunsite.unc.edu/otis/otis.html**

Images of original art, such as the Mona Lisa, are widely available on the Net. This version of monalisa.gif was downloaded from Washington University at St. Louis (**ftp.wustl.edu**). Use archie to find the current directory or other sites. (Search for **monalisa**.)

Pixel Pushers

Pixel Pushers is an electronic gallery of artworks on paper.

World Wide Web:
URL: **http://www.wimsey.com/Pixel_Pushers/**

Playground Gallery

A continually expanding collection of artwork, and links to other galleries and arts. It offers graphic works, written works, multimedia publications, and art resource and organization lists.

World Wide Web:
URL: **http://oz.sas.upenn.edu/gallery/gallery.html**

Prints Database

Compiled into this database is a huge list of artists who have done printmaking. Search the database by toggling through artists, method of print, subject matter or type, or you may search by title or date.

World Wide Web:
URL: **http://rubens.anu.edu.au/prints_form.html**

RoboGopher

With a shower of sparks and a flash of colorful light, art meets technology. Perhaps it's not quite that dramatic, but it's at least as interesting. The Robot Group puts out a weekly newsletter about art and technology as well as listing current projects.

Gopher:
Name: University of Texas at Austin
Address: **cs.utexas.edu**
Choose: **Other Interesting Gophers and Information Servers | RoboGopher**

Need Unix help? See Harley's book "Unix Unbound."

Rome Reborn

An electronic exhibition of the Vatican library and Renaissance culture in the form of texts, image captions, and jpeg images.

Anonymous FTP:
Address: **ftp.lib.virginia.edu**
Path: **/pub/alpha/vat/***

Gopher:
Name: University of Virginia
Address: **gopher.virginia.edu**
Choose: **Library Services**
| University Library GWIS Collections (alpha and subj. organization)
| Alphabetic Organization
| Vatican Library Exhibition

Rosen Sculpture Exhibition

A collection of photos of sculptures, with the artists' statements, presented by ten artists in the Rosen Outdoor Sculpture Competition and Exhibition.

World Wide Web:
URL: **http://xx.acs.appstate.edu/art/rosen/main_menu.html**

Roy Lichtenstein Pre-Pop 1948-1960

Over thirty works from the famous American artist, the majority of which have never been seen by the public before. Includes some of his early works, medieval period, American period, abstract expressionism and pop periods.

World Wide Web:
URL: **http://www.cgrg.ohio-state.edu/mkruse/lichten1.html**

Sleeping Dog

The Sleeping Dog is a periodical review of visual and verbal art designed specifically for the printed page. These reviews are produced by the computer imaging lab of the Department of Fine Arts of the University of Colorado.

World Wide Web:
URL: **http://cuboulder.colorado.edu/FineArt/FineArts.html**

Spectrum

A collection of arts and media publications, including issues from *Front* magazine, *MediaWest*, and *Ctheory*.

World Wide Web:
URL: **http://wimsey.com/anima/SPECTRUMhome.html**

A B C D E F G H I J K L M N O P Q R S T U V W X Y Z

Strange Interactions

A moving and professional collection of oil and acrylic paintings, drawings, woodcuts, etchings, and lithographs by John Jacobsen. View his concrete aspect of the subconscious.

Gopher:
> Name: Rice University
> Address: **riceinfo.rice.edu**
> Choose: **Information by Subject Area**
> | **Arts**
> | **Strange Interactions**

World Wide Web:
> URL: **http://amanda.physics.wisc.edu/show.html**

Virtual Art Gallery

Collection of canvas, photos, and images from selected artists.

World Wide Web:
> URL: **http://www.nets.com/site/art/art.html**

ASTROLOGY

Astrology Collection

The next time you are in charge of a competitive business meeting or you have to set up a special date to win the heart of that special someone, plan the date to your advantage. Don't just check the weather — look at the stars and planets and compare their alignment to your birthchart. Avoid disastrous retrogrades and perilous planetary pitfalls that may be in store for you. Find out everything you need to know about astrology with introductory lessons by Maggie McPherson, lists of books, software and organizations, and Astrolog and STAR demos.

See also: Religion: Alternative

Anonymous FTP:
> Address: **hilbert.maths.utas.edu.au**
> Path: **/pub/astrology/***

Astrology Discussion Group

You've discovered that Uranus is in conjunction with your ascendant ruler, Jupiter. And as if that's not enough, Uranus also squares Mercury, your tenth house ruler, and you have four yods that are creating frustration and dissatisfaction in your life. What's a person to do? Besides calling the psychic hotline, you can post queries or hints

to stargazers across the globe or even — depending on whom they know — across the universe.

Usenet:
> Newsgroup: **alt.astrology**

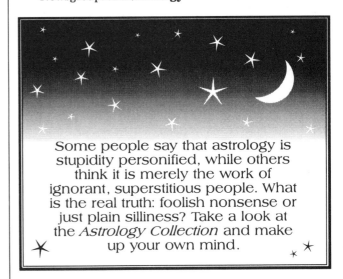

Some people say that astrology is stupidity personified, while others think it is merely the work of ignorant, superstitious people. What is the real truth: foolish nonsense or just plain silliness? Take a look at the *Astrology Collection* and make up your own mind.

Astrology Resources

Stars are more than just pretty lights you sit under at night. You can make wishes upon them, navigate ships by them, or record their positions to make up an astrological chart that you can consult for all your important decisions. Learn the basics of astrology, including its history and related topics like solar magnetism and etheric planets. If it's good enough for a First Lady, it's good enough for...someone.

See also: New Age

World Wide Web:
> URL: **http://err.ethz.ch/~kiwi/Spirit/Astro/Overview.html**

Horoscopes by Yul and Doc X

Check out these strange and short horoscopes from Yul Moonglow and Doctor Xavier Jenkins from the Vasco de Gama Institute of Planetology.

World Wide Web:
> URL: **http://alfred1.u.washington.edu:8080/~roland/horoscope/horoscope.html**

Do you like weirdness? Check out Usenet Curiosities.

Interactive Astrology Chart

Don't wander through life wondering if you are going in the right direction. Use this interactive web page to learn exactly what your next move should be. If your browser supports forms, you can fill in the required information and the computer will whip out your astrological chart faster than you can say, "What's your sign, baby?"

World Wide Web:
    URL: **http://err.ethz.ch/~kiwi/Spirit/Astro/
    astro-chart.html**

ASTRONOMY

Amateur Radio Transmissions

Technical details and considerations relating to radio transmissions and telemetry data to and from space (for amateurs).

Usenet:
    Newsgroup: **rec.radio.amateur.space**

out of This world

The best thing about astronomy is that it keeps all its stuff out in the sky where it won't get in your way. However the Internet's astronomical resources are down here on Mother Earth. If you have stars in your eyes check out

Astro FTP List

Never again will you be caught without an interesting FTP site when your date comes up to your place for a nightcap.

Astro FTP List

A list with descriptions of ftp sites that contain astronomy and space research material.

Anonymous FTP:
    Address: **plaza.aarnet.edu.au**
    Path: **/micros/pc/garbo/pc/astronomy**

Astrometry Science Team

If you had a telescope, would you study heavenly bodies? Well, that's exactly what the folks at the University of Texas are doing with the Hubble Telescope. Point your web browser here for images, data, and other items of interest from the folks who use the fine guidance sensors aboard the Hubble Space Telescope to study the stars and other celestial bodies.

World Wide Web:
    URL: **http://dorrit.as.utexas.edu/**

Astronomical Internet Resources

The AstroWeb page connects you to dozens of interesting astronomical resources available on the Internet.

World Wide Web:
    URL: **http://marvel.stsci.edu/net-resources.html**

Astronomical Museum

Instruments used by Bolognese astronomers from the early 18th to mid-19th century are on display here in the same rooms of the ancient tower originally devoted to observations. A history of the museum and astronomy in Bologna, Italy, and a guided tour of the Meridian, Globe, and Turret Rooms are available here. There are gif images of the early scientific equipment, along with lengthy descriptions.

World Wide Web:
    URL: **http://boas3.bo.astro.it/dip/Museum/
    MuseumHome.html**

Astronomy General Discussion

Stars, planets, telescopes, cosmology, and all aspects of astronomy and astrophysics. Talk with people who really do understand black holes.

Usenet:
    Newsgroup: **sci.astro**

A
B
C
D
E
F
G
H
I
J
K
L
M
N
O
P
Q
R
S
T
U
V
W
X
Y
Z

Astronomy HyperTextbook

Back in the old days, most of us had to lug around 150 pounds of dull, dry textbooks, and the only fun that could be had was to devise ways of writing graffiti in them without getting caught. With hypertext languages, textbooks become interactive and fun. Plus, you can sneak around and play games on the computer while the teacher isn't looking. Check out this fun and informative textbook that gives learning a whole new twist.

See also: Space

World Wide Web:
>   URL: **http://zebu.uoregon.edu/text.html**

Astronomy Programs

Programs for all popular systems, texts, documents, pictures, news, and equipment information about astronomy and stargazing.

Anonymous FTP:
>   Address: **ftp.funet.fi**
>   Path: **/pub/astro/***

Astronomy Servers

Large collection of links to astronomy-related servers around the globe. Each link has the institution's logo beside it, making it clear what is available.

World Wide Web:
>   URL: **http://info.er.usgs.gov/network/science/ astronomy/index.html**

Astrophysics Data System

The ADS Abstract Service allows access to more than 160,000 astronomy abstracts provided by the NASA/STI program.

World Wide Web:
>   URL: **http://adswww.harvard.edu/**

Astrotext

This project is an online hyper-textbook on astronomy which is being compiled from information gathered from people on the Net. In exchange for accessing files, send in some information of your own, or offer evaluations and critiques of available material. This isn't mandatory, but is encouraged.

World Wide Web:
>   URL: **http://uu-gna.mit.edu:8001/uu-gna/text/ astro/index.html**

Earth Views

It's all a matter of perspective. No matter where you go on the Earth, you can never see the entire thing. These days, you don't have to be an astronaut to enjoy a nice view of the Earth from space. Check out this collection of photos of the Earth. If you know the latitude and longitude of your house, you can find the corresponding pictures and make a map with a big X and label it "You are here."

See also: Computers: Pictures

World Wide Web:
>   URL: **http://images.jsc.nasa.gov/html/home.htm**

Flexible Image Transport System (FITS)

Technical discussion about FITS (Flexible Image Transport System), a computer data format used to exchange astronomical data. FITS is designed to facilitate convenient data transfer between different types of computer systems.

Usenet:
>   Newsgroup: **sci.astro.fits**

HEASARC Astronomical Browser

Search for entries from various NASA documents detailing what launched satellites see. Available are records for the Rontgen satellite, Compton Gamma-Ray Observatory, high energy astrophysics observatories, the European X-ray Astronomy satellite, the Astro 1 Broad Band X-ray telescope, and many other satellite missions.

See also: Physics

World Wide Web:
>   URL: **http://heasarc.gsfc.nasa.gov/StarTrax/ Browse.html**

Hubble Telescope

Mull over data and observations from the Hubble Telescope. This moderated newsgroup contains technical information released as part of the Hubble project.

Usenet:
>   Newsgroup: **sci.astro.hubble**

Institutes of Astronomy

This web page has a collection of many links to institutes and universities with centers for astronomy and astrophysics.

World Wide Web:
>   URL: **http://www.yahoo.com/Science/ Astronomy/Institutes/**

Mars Atlas

This atlas is just as good as being on Mars. Better, really, if you think about how much you save in gas money by not going there. This is not just any atlas. You can scroll around and zoom in on the surface of the planet to see exactly what you want. If you look hard enough, maybe you will see those little men that Ray Bradbury is always going on about.

Note: Your browser must support in-line images to use this.

World Wide Web:
URL: **http://fi-www.arc.nasa.gov/fia/ projects/bayes-group/Atlas/Mars/**

National Optical Astronomy Observatories

NOAO is operated by the Association of Universities for Research in Astronomy in agreement with the NSF. The NOAO server contains the NOAO newsletter, ftp archives, IRAF (Image Reduction and Analysis Facility), info on astronomical conferences, and links to other astronomical communities.

World Wide Web:
URL: **http://www.noao.edu/noao.html**

Observatories

Links to observatories all over the world, including Australia, Columbia, Canada, France, the U.K., Hawaii, Arizona, California, and many others.

World Wide Web:
URL: **http://www.yahoo.com/Science/ Astronomy/Observatories/**

Planetariums

Do you think that planetariums can be used for more than laser light shows to Pink Floyd music? If so, you can discuss issues with people who plan and implement planetarium programs.

Usenet:
Newsgroup: **sci.astro.planetarium**

Planetary Tour Guide

Make plans for where you want to go when Planet Earth gets too crowded. NASA offers several tour guides that will show you just what is hanging out in the sky above us. Even if you don't want to relocate, it's a nice way to plan your next vacation.

World Wide Web:
URL: **http://ranier.oact.hq.nasa.gov/ Sensors_page/Planets.html**

Planets

If you've never had occasion to visit another planet, you don't have to feel that you are missing out on anything. Check out this colorful display of planetary "snapshots." If you move your chair around really fast while you look at these, you can almost pretend you are flying through space.

World Wide Web:
URL: **http://stardust.jpl.nasa.gov/planets/**

Planets and the Solar System

The planets, asteroids, and other bodies that make up our solar system. Discuss astronomical details as well as space missions sent to explore these places.

Usenet:
Newsgroup: **alt.sci.planetary**

Shoemaker-Levy Comet

In July 1994, pieces of the Shoemaker-Levy comet struck Jupiter. This site contains pictures from various ground-based and space-based observatories. There are some movies of fragment impacts and plenty of detailed reports on the phenomenon.

World Wide Web:
URL: **http://newproducts.jpl.nasa.gov/ sl9/sl9.html**

A B C D E F G H I J K L M N O P Q R S T U V W X Y Z

Sloan Digital Sky Survey (SDSS)

The goal of the SDSS project is to build and operate a dedicated telescope suitable for wide-angle surveys of the sky that will address critical issues in extragalactic astronomy, especially in the field of large-scale structure. For more information on the research going on at SDSS, see their web server.

World Wide Web:
URL: **http://www-sdss.fnal.gov:8000/**

Space Telescope Science Institute

This organization is responsible for the scientific operations of the Hubble Space Telescope. The organization is operated by Associated Universities for Research in Astronomy, is under contract to NASA, and is located on the campus of Johns Hopkins University in Baltimore, Maryland.

World Wide Web:
URL: **http://marvel.stsci.edu/top.html**

Starlink

The Starlink Project at the Rutherford Appleton Laboratory is a computing facility designed to support U.K. astronomers. The Starlink software includes major packages covering a range of astronomical data reduction and analysis techniques. There is also a support group that manages Starlink sites.

World Wide Web:
URL: **http://star-www.rl.ac.uk/**

Star*s Family

A collection of directories, dictionaries, databases, star guides, and other products related to astronomy and other space sciences.

World Wide Web:
URL: **http://cdsweb.u-strasbg.fr/~heck/sf.htm**

Strasbourg Astronomical Data Center

A large collection of astronomical data, including tables and abstracts from *Astronomy and Astrophysics* and other major journals, two online databases, organizations, services, and links to other related resources.

World Wide Web:
URL: **http://cdsweb.u-strasbg.fr/CDS.html**

Sunspots

Satellite tracking, sunspots, daily corona maps, plus Jupiter info and images.

Anonymous FTP:
Address: **susnpot.noao.edu**
Path: **/pub/sunspots, /pub/corona.maps/*, /pub/jupiter**

Views of the Solar System

Take an educational tour of the solar system. See images and information about the sun, planets, moons, asteroids and comets that are found within our solar system. In addition, you can read up on a little space history and space terms to gain some background knowledge.

World Wide Web:
URL: **http://www.c3.lanl.gov:1331/c3/people/calvin/homepage.html**

THERE'S NO PLACE ON EARTH LIKE THE WORLD!

But when you get tired of the same old planet, it's time to broaden your outlook and point your mind outwards.

Spend a few hours with *Views of the Solar System* and see why our solar system is one of the most popular in the galaxy. Find the facts and hints that can make your next vacation a trip to remember.

WebStars: Astrophysics in Cyberspace

Virtual reality, software, cyberspace quotes, links to space science web groups, and pointers to many other astronomy and astrophysics resources on the Internet.

World Wide Web:
URL: **http://guinan.gsfc.nasa.gov/**

AUTOMOTIVE: CARS

Air-Cooled Volkswagens

You never see high-action adventure movies using Volkswagens in their chase scenes. Why is that? Admittedly, they are probably not on anyone's top ten high-performance cars list, but that's no call for discrimination. Owners and enthusiasts of air-cooled Volkswagens exchange information on the care and maintenance of their cars.

Listserv Mailing List:
>   List Address: **vintagvw@sjsuvm1.sjsu.edu**
>   Subscription Address: **listserv@sjsuvm1.sjsu.edu**

Alfa Romeo Home Page

Information about Alfa Romeo cars, pictures of cars, both static and racing, services, model information, mailing lists, and many other items of interest to Alfa enthusiasts.

World Wide Web:
>   URL: **http://amdahl1.cs.latrobe.edu.au:8080/**
>   **~baragry/AlfaRomeo/HomePage.html**

Antique Cars

Wash it, buff it, tuck your baby in at night. Antique automobiles hold a special place in everyone's heart. Care and feeding of all older automobiles is covered in **alt.autos.antique**. Automobiles over 25 years old are parked in **rec.autos.antique**.

Usenet:
>   Newsgroup: **alt.autos.antique**
>   Newsgroup: **rec.autos.antique**

Audi

Not just any car will do. There is a particular make of automobile that inspires your fantasies. You can just imagine running your hands across her, buffing her finish, sliding inside and pressing on the gas pedal, making the engine rev. Indulge in your Audi fantasies with other Audiphiles and discuss maintenance procedures, parts sources, personal experiences, and the latest Audi news.

Majordomo Mailing List:
>   List Address: **quattro@swiss.ans.net**
>   Subscription Address: **majordomo@swiss.ans.net**

Auto Racing

It's not enough to be able to get in the car and go. You have to go fast. You have to go so fast that rubber burns, that the friction of the wind heats the metal on your car and nearly blisters the paint, that the G-forces press you into the fine Italian upholstery and any planetary geophysical disturbance threatens to rocket you into outer space. Now, that's what we call fun. And when you are not driving, participate in discussion of wheel-to-wheel racing for drivers, workers and crew.

Internet Mailing List:
>   List Address:
>   **wheel-to-wheel@abingdon.eng.sun.com**
>   Subscription Address:
>   **wheel-to-wheel-request@abingdon.eng.sun.com**

Automobile General Discussion Groups

Everything to do with automobiles, including design, construction, service, tires, competitions, driving, manufacturers, and antique cars.

Usenet:
>   Newsgroup: **alt.autos.karting**
>   Newsgroup: **alt.autos.rod-n-custom**
>   Newsgroup: **alt.hotrod**
>   Newsgroup: **rec.autos**
>   Newsgroup: **rec.autos.sport**
>   Newsgroup: **rec.autos.tech**
>   Newsgroup: **rec.autos.vw**

Beemer List

A mailing list for owners, or anyone else interested in cars made by BMW.

Internet Mailing List:
>   List Address: **bmw@balltown.cma.com**
>   Subscription Address:
>   **bmw-request@balltown.cma.com**

No need to be bored. Try Parties and Entertainment.

A B C D E F G H I J K L M N O P Q R S T U V W X Y Z

BMW Information

Do you like beemers? Check out this web page where you can get information about BMW cars and upcoming events of interest to the beemer set.

World Wide Web:
> URL: **http://cbsgi1.bu.edu/bmw/bmw.html**

British Cars

Of owning, repairing, racing, cursing, and loving British cars, especially sports cars, and some Land Rover topics.

Internet Mailing List:
> List Address: **british-cars@autox.team.net**
> Subscription Address:
>> **british-cars-request@autox.team.net**

World Wide Web:
> URL: **http://www.law.indiana.edu/misc/**
>> **b-cars.html**

Camaros and Firebirds

What a thrill to be cruising down the highway in a Camaro or Firebird. You are drawing stares from hot babes and getting the attention of everyone in general, including the policeman you happen to speed past. Not to worry, we heard somewhere that for Camaro and Firebird drivers, the first ticket is always free. (Freely given, at least.) Commune with other Camaro and Firebird fans on this mailing list designed especially for you.

Internet Mailing List:
> List Address:
>> **f-bodyt@boogie.ebay.sun.com**
> Subscription Address:
>> **f-bodyt-request@boogie.ebay.sun.com**

Car Audio

"My woofer is bigger than your woofer!" Make the most of your automobile's audio system by learning about installation, trouble shooting, and consumer information.

Usenet:
> Newsgroup: **rec.audio.car**

Corvette

What a spiffy car! The Corvette is one of those cars that has been hot for years. Race around the block with other Corvette owners and enthusiasts, and discuss ideas and experiences related to this fine automobile.

Internet Mailing List:
> List Address: **vettes@compaq.com**
> Subscription Address:
>> **vettes-request@compaq.com**

Datsun Roadsters

Forget driving that namby-pamby family-sized car with the childproof locks in the back seat. Or that mile-long luxury car that is impossible to parallel park without demolishing the cars on either side of you. Try a Datsun roadster and impress your friends with your good taste in cars. Roadster fans get together to discuss all aspects of owning, showing, repairing, and driving Datsun roadsters.

Internet Mailing List:
> List Address: **datsun-roadsters@autox.team.net**
> Subscription Address:
>> **datsun-roadsters-request@autox.team.net**

Datsun Z Car

If you liked your Z, check out this web page. It offers a history of the Z, technical information, and pictures.

World Wide Web:
> URL: **http://www.cs.princeton.edu/grad/snd/**
>> **z-car/zpage.html**

This image was downloaded from Northern Arizona University (**ftp.nau.edu**). The file is **/graphics/gif/digi/ferrarigto.gif** and was originally located with an archie substring search for **ferrari**.

Dodge Stealth/Mitsubishi 3000GT

Stealth. The name alone is so... James Bond-like. There you are in your car, sliding silently through dark streets and hidden alleys. Almost makes you want to find a covert operation to jump in on. Fans of the Dodge Stealth and Mitsubishi 3000GT join together to discuss anything related to these cars, whether it is of a personal or technical bent.

See also: Hobbies

Internet Mailing List:
List Address:
stealth-request%jim.uucp@wupost.wustl.edu
Subscription Address:
stealth-request%jim.uucp-request@wupost.wustl.edu

Driving

Slide into your car, start her up, see the road race beneath you. Make your driving experience exquisite. Keep informed on driving laws and learn how to better handle your car.

Usenet:
Newsgroup: **rec.autos.driving**

Driving in California

Material concerning driving, parking tickets, traffic laws, insurance, Highway Patrol, and other aspects of driving in California.

Anonymous FTP:
Address: **rtfm.mit.edu**
Path: **/pub/usenet/news.answers/ca-driving-faq**

Driving Schools

The desire is there, but your skill leaves a great deal to be desired. Don't try high performance driving without a little training under your belt or you might end up with your high performance automobile sliding on its side around a hairpin turn. Not only will this damage you and your ego, make your health and car insurance premiums rise, but it's not good for your paint job, either. Join the discussion of high performance driving schools and maybe you can get a job driving in one of those cool commercials on television.

Internet Mailing List:
List Address: **school@balltown.cma.com**
Subscription Address:
school-request@balltown.cma.com

Electric Vehicles

How many automobile technicians does it take to screw in a lightbulb? It depends where on the car they are trying to screw it in. Catch up on the state of the electric vehicle technology and the future of electric vehicles. How close are we to affordable electric cars? Will we be able to plug them into the wall of our garage? This list is not to argue about whether we should have electric vehicles or to compare EVs to other modes of driving. (So don't even try it.)

See also: Technology

Listserv Mailing List:
List Address: **ev@sjsuvm1.sjsu.edu**
Subscription Address: **listserv@sjsuvm1.sjsu.edu**

Exotic Cars

Imagine the awe you would inspire in everyone around you if you were the lucky owner of an exotic or limited edition automobile. Neighbors would ask you to drive them to the grocery store, people's chatter would die down to a respectful whisper as they passed your car, and the insurance agent would beg you to please leave the car in the garage. But there is more to exotic cars than just good looks. Merge with other exotic car enthusiasts to talk about maintenance, driving experiences, and any other aspects of these rare and desirable cars.

Internet Mailing List:
List Address: **exotic-cars@sol.asl.hitachi.com**
Subscription Address:
exotic-cars-request@sol.asl.hitachi.com

Ford Mustangs

The Ford Mustang has had some good days. It's probably had its dog days as well. Get together with other late model (1980+) Ford Mustang owners to discuss technical issues, problems, solutions, and modifications relating to these cars.

Internet Mailing List:
List Address: **mustangs@cup.hp.com**
Subscription Address:
mustangs-request@cup.hp.com

High Performance Cars

Don't just drive your car, experience it. Which cars perform the best? How can you increase your auto's performance? Learn safety, technical aspects, and techniques.

Usenet:
Newsgroup: **alt.autos.rod-n-custom**
Newsgroup: **rec.autos.rod-n-custom**

A
B
C
D
E
F
G
H
I
J
K
L
M
N
O
P
Q
R
S
T
U
V
W
X
Y
Z

Life in the Fast Lane

We all know that fast, high-performance cars are just a substitute for you-know-what. (Well we do know, but we aren't allowed to talk about stuff like that in a family-oriented book.) Join the boys in the **rod-n-custom** Usenet groups and fin out how to soup-up your performance and enhance your experience with high speed and quick starts.

Hot Rods

Rev your engine and burn rubber. Find out the do's and don'ts of working with high-speed automobiles. Hot rod enthusiasts know the nuts and bolts. This group is moderated.

Internet Mailing List:
List Address: **hotrod@dixie.com**
Subscription Address: **hotrod-request@dixie.com**

Usenet:
Newsgroup: **alt.hotrod**

Kit Cars

For years you have been putting model cars together, and now you can do it without gluing your fingers together. It's time to graduate to the real thing. Find out about purchasing, building, driving, and maintaining kit cars — full-size and fully functioning cars you build from scratch. Then when people give you compliments on your smooth ride, you can say, "Thanks. I made it myself."

Internet Mailing List:
List Address: **kitcar@cs.usask.ca**
Subscription Address: **kitcar-request@cs.usask.ca**

Lancia

Links to Lancia-related information on the web. Check out the model list and a history of the Lancia in competition, as well as links to other car-related pages and resources.

World Wide Web:
URL: **http://www.c2.org/~mark/lancia /lancia.html**

Offroad Driving

There is something exciting and rebellious about not sticking to the road when you drive. Day in and day out you are forced to stay between the lines in the road and be orderly like every other motorist around you. Find your release in offroad driving. Rev up the 4x4 and take off over hill and dale. Other driving maniacs make a pitstop on this unmoderated list and talk about technical or mechanical problems, driving techniques, safety, and experiences. You can also receive this list in digest form.

Internet Mailing List:
List Address: **offroad@ai.gtri.gatech.edu**
Subscription Address:
offroad-request@ai.gtri.gatech.edu

Porsche

What is it about a Porsche that makes everyone's blood race? Is it the design or just that it's an expensive car? Porsche lovers gather to talk about questions, mechanics, aesthetics, and pricing of Porsches.

Internet Mailing List:
List Address: **porschephiles@tta.com**
Subscription Address:
porschephiles-request@tta.com

Porschephiles Home Page

The premier online resource about Porsche automobiles. This web page offers information about a Porsche mailing list, racing schedules and information, and links to a frequently asked question list, archives, and other automotive resources.

World Wide Web:
URL: **http://tta.com/Porschephiles/home.html**

Racing

Put the pedal to the metal and aim for the checkered flag. Discover the thrill of all aspects of organized racing competition.

Usenet:
Newsgroup: **rec.autos.sport**

RoverWeb

A web page for Land Rover enthusiasts with links to the Land Rover FAQ list, a picture library, stories, and information about a Land Rover mailing list.

World Wide Web:
URL: **http://whitman.gar.utexas.edu/roverweb/roverweb.html**

Saturn

The Saturn web server is an example of the enthusiasm Saturn cars generate in their owners. Get information about the newest models, features and specs, financial information, reviews, comparisons, and a link to the referenced Saturn ftp site. If you like the Saturn, you'll like these resources!

Anonymous FTP:
Address: **ftp.hmc.edu**
Path: **/pub/saturn**

Address: **ftp.oar.net**
Path: **/pub/saturn/***

World Wide Web:
URL: **http://www.physics.sunysb.edu/Saturn/**

Solar Cars

All about solar-powered car races and related events, including information on the Sunrayce races, race routes, participating teams, and official results.

World Wide Web:
URL: **http://www-lips.ece.utexas.edu/~delayman/solar.html**

Solar Vehicles at UC Berkeley

The University of California at Berkeley solar vehicle race team has its own web page. Find out how they plan to beat the competition this year!

World Wide Web:
URL: **http://www-lips.ece.utexas.edu/~delayman/calsol.html**

Spare time? Take a look at Games.

Solar Vehicles at the University of Michigan

Information about the University of Michigan Solar Car Team including a history of the team, the races they've participated in and won, and links to other solar racing teams, races, and even T-shirts!

World Wide Web:
URL: **http://www.engin.umich.edu/solarcar/homepage.html**

Team.Net Automotive Information Archives

A collection of automotive-related mailing lists, including Autocrossing, British Cars, BMW, Datsun Z-Cars, Fieros, Porsches, and many more, an automotive flea market, images, digests, FAQs, and ftp archives.

World Wide Web:
URL: **http://triumph.cs.utah.edu/team.net.html**

Technical Automotive Discussion

Points, carbs, blocks, calibration: what's it all mean? A wide variety of topics are discussed. If you absorb only half the information offered by these enthusiasts, you will be highly informed.

Usenet:
Newsgroup: **rec.autos.tech**

Toyota

You can putter, race, or rough-ride in a Toyota. It's nice to have choices. You even have choices of mailing lists if you are an owner or prospective owner of a vehicle made by Toyota. The **toyota** list is for general discussion, **corolla** is for talk about older models of Corolla and the newer offshoots, and **mr2-interest** covers MR2s.

Internet Mailing List:
List Address: **mr2-interest@validgh.com**
Subscription Address:
mr2-interest-request@validgh.com

List Address: **corolla@mcs.com**
Subscription Address: **corolla-request@mcs.com**

List Address: **toyota@quack.kfu.com**
Subscription Address:
toyota-request@quack.kfu.com

Volkswagen

Volkswagens have a unique following. Learn the ins and outs of your VW. Share your experiences or benefit from the experience of others.

Usenet:
Newsgroup: **rec.autos.vw**

Volkswagen Names

A list of names people have given their Volkswagen cars, and why.

Anonymous FTP:
Address: **ftp.spies.com**
Path: **/Library/Document/names.vw**

Gopher:
Name: Internet Wiretap
Address: **wiretap.spies.com**
Choose: **Wiretap Online Library**
  | **Assorted Documents**
  | **The Grand VW Car Name List**

AUTOMOTIVE: MOTORCYCLES

Motorcycle Archive

FAQs, photo images in gif format, and "Denizens of Doom" (DoD) information.

Anonymous FTP:
Address: **cerritos.edu**
Path: **/DOD/***

Motorcycle Design

People do it all the time — make things to suit themselves. Programmers customize programs, people sew their own clothes and build their own homes. Why not design your own motorcycle? This mailing list is devoted to the theory and practice of motorcycle chassis design and construction.

Internet Mailing List:
List Address: **moto.chassis@oce.orst.edu**
Subscription Address:
  moto.chassis-request@oce.orst.edu

Motorcycle Racing

What a rush it is to be racing at high speeds with nothing between you and the air except a flimsy little jumpsuit that will disintegrate upon impact with the asphalt. Motorcycle racing enthusiasts discuss roadracing from the racer's point of view as well as the pit crew's.

Majordomo Mailing List:
List Address: **race@thumper.lerc.nasa.gov**
Subscription Address:
  majordomo@thumper.lerc.nasa.gov

Motorcycle Reviews

A large collection of motorcycle and accessory reviews written by readers of the Usenet **rec.motorcycles** groups and based on their own experiences. New reviews are always welcome. Includes some motorcycle pictures.

Anonymous FTP:
Address: **ftp.cecm.sfu.ca**
Path: **/pub/RMR/***

Address: **ftp.cs.dal.ca**
Path: **/comp.archives/rec.motorcycles/***

Motorcycles

Anything named "Harley" is bound to be sexy. No doubt that is why so many people just love their motorcycles. If you just can't live without something hard and powerful, this is the place to be.

Internet Mailing List:
List Address: **harleys@thinkage.on.ca**
Subscription Address:
  harleys-request@thinkage.on.ca

Usenet:
Newsgroup: **alt.motorcycles.harley**
Newsgroup: **rec.motorcycles**
Newsgroup: **rec.motorcycles.dirt**
Newsgroup: **rec.motorcycles.harley**
Newsgroup: **rec.motorcycles.racing**

Excerpt from the Net...

Your bike can be as clean as you want, and it'll always look dirty.

AVIATION

Aerospace Engineering

A mailing list dedicated to the theoretical side of aerospace engineering. Includes discussion on aerospace technology, calls for papers, seminar anouncements, and other related topics.

Internet Mailing List:
List Address: **aviation-theory@mc.lcs.mit.edu**
Subscription Address:
aviation-theory-request@mc.lcs.mit.edu

> Little know fact: Charles and Diana met in alt.romance.

Aircraft Discussion Forum

A mailing list forum for people interested in aircraft and helicopters, both new and old. The list also includes information about air shows and similar events.

Listserv Mailing List:
List Address: **aircraft@grearn.csi.forth.gr**
Subscription Address: **listserv@grearn.csi.forth.gr**

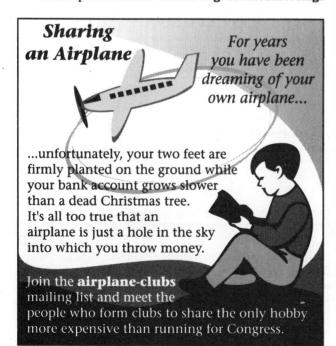

Sharing an Airplane

For years you have been dreaming of your own airplane...

...unfortunately, your two feet are firmly planted on the ground while your bank account grows slower than a dead Christmas tree. It's all too true that an airplane is just a hole in the sky into which you throw money.

Join the **airplane-clubs** mailing list and meet the people who form clubs to share the only hobby more expensive than running for Congress.

Aircraft Group Ownership

Ever wonder how you could afford to own an airplane? Group ownership may be one way you can. This mailing list will fill you in on all you need to know.

Internet Mailing List:
List Address: **airplane-clubs@dg-rtp.dg.com**
Subscription Address:
airplane-clubs-request@dg-rtp.dg.com

Aircraft Images

This ftp site features jpeg images of many different aircraft and flying formations, including the F-4 Phantom Tiger, F-16, Harrier, Mirage-4000, Tiger Moth, and others.

Anonymous FTP:
Address: **ftp.cs.ruu.nl**
Path: **/pub/AIRCRAFT-IMAGES/***

Airline and Airliner Discussion List

A mailing list featuring airlines, airliners, and other civil aircraft and related topics. Modelers are welcome, too.

Listserv Mailing List:
List Address: **airline@cunyvm.cuny.edu**
Subscription Address: **listserv@cunyvm.cuny.edu**

Airline Travel

Solve travel problems before they happen. If you are traveling, scope out trials that may occur between your departure and destination with ticket purchases, layovers, connecting flights, luggage dramas, and airline strikes. Information is available for the entire planet. Next stop: the rest of the universe.

Usenet:
Newsgroup: **rec.travel.air**

Airport Codes

The three-letter identification codes for nearly every airport in the world.

Anonymous FTP:
Address: **ftp.spies.com**
Path: **/Library/Article/Aero/airport.lis**

Gopher:
Name: Internet Wiretap
Address: **wiretap.spies.com**
Choose: **Wiretap Online Library**
  | Articles
  | Aeronautics and Space
  | Airport 3 Letter Abbreviations

A
B
C
D
E
F
G
H
I
J
K
L
M
N
O
P
Q
R
S
T
U
V
W
X
Y
Z

Aviation Archives

In-flight cockpit visits to aviation jokes, humor, trivia, and so on.

Anonymous FTP:
Address: **rascal.ics.utexas.edu**
Path: **/misc/av/***

Aviation Enthusiast Corner

A forum dedicated to furthering interest in aviation-related hobbies. It offers an aircraft reference, air events guide, a large list of aviation museums and displays, and links to other aviation- and aerospace-related sites.

World Wide Web:
URL: **http://www.brooklyn.cuny.edu/rec/
air/air.html**

Aviation General Discussion

You'll go into a flat spin when you see all the information you can find in this group. If you don't know how to choose one of the specific aviation groups, this is a great place to start. There are often cross-postings from other groups to **.misc**, so you'll see a wide variety of topics, including comparisons of different types of planes, what to do about engine fires, pros and cons of leasing, and what happens when an instrument malfunctions. There's something for everyone.

Usenet:
Newsgroup: **rec.aviation.misc**

This image was downloaded from Northern Arizona University (**ftp.nau.edu**). The file is **/graphics/gif/misc/x29.gif**. This file also exists on many other sites around the world.

Aviation Gopher

These gophers have bundles of information about aviation and contain most of the subjects covered in the Usenet newsgroup **rec.aviation**. They offer numerous articles, pictures, stories, and also weather and fly-in information.

Gopher:
Name: Embry-Riddle Aeronautical University
Address: **gopher.db.erau.edu**

Name: University of Nebraska at Omaha
Address: **gopher.unomaha.edu**
Choose: **UNO Student Organizations
| UNO Aviation**

Aviation Technology

Don't be content to just fly: dig deep into what makes aeronautics work. See the latest NASA press releases and learn about the physics of flight, pitch moment damping, aircraft stability, boarding design, and technical safety.

Usenet:
Newsgroup: **sci.aeronautics**
Newsgroup: **sci.aeronautics.airliners**

Canadian Airlines International

Canadian Airlines International (CAI) is the first airline in the world to offer a web server. Their web page provides information about their airline, routes, destinations, weather, and leisure information, and won PC Week Labs "Cool Web Site" award.

World Wide Web:
URL: **http://www.cdnair.ca/**

Dryden Photo Archive

Large collection of aircraft and spacecraft photos in jpeg format from Edwards Air Force Base in California. Includes pictures of the X Series and F Series research aircraft, the space shuttle, lifting bodies, and many other vehicles.

World Wide Web:
URL: **http://www.dfrf.nasa.gov/Dryden/Photos.html**

DUAT

If you're a pilot, this is the place to get your weather briefings, plan your flight, and even file your flight plan. DUAT also offers other valuable services. Check it out the next time you plan a cross-country flight. The **duat** address is for pilots only; **duats** is for pilots and non-pilots, but non-pilots are charged a fee.

Telnet:
Address: **duat.gtefsd.com**
Address: **duats.gtefsd.com**

Flight Planning

Public domain flight-planning software and data, written in C and complete with source.

Anonymous FTP:
Address: **eecs.nwu.edu**
Path: **/pub/aviation/***

Address: **lifshitz.ph.utexas.edu**
Path: **/pub/aviation/***

Flying

Material about learning how to fly, technical information, ownership costs, equipment guides, aviation policies, and many more related FAQs.

Anonymous FTP:
Address: **rtfm.mit.edu**
Path: **/pub/usenet/news.answers/aviation/***

Flying and Aviation

Topics of interest to pilots, including training systems, laws, airports, planes, procedures, characteristics of aircraft and avionic products, as well as comments on commercial aviation and much more.

Internet Mailing List:
List Address: **aviation@mc.lcs.mit.edu**
Subscription Address:
aviation-request@mc.lcs.mit.edu

Gliding

Follow the example of the eagle and experience the powerful magic of gliding. Using sailplanes and hang-gliders has its own unique set of considerations. Learn about glide ratios, wind, flying in the rain, good places to glide, safety, gliding championships, and more.

Internet Mailing List:
List Address: **hang-gliding@virginia.edu**
Subscription Address:
hang-gliding-request@virginia.edu

Usenet:
Newsgroup: **rec.aviation.soaring**

Hang Gliding Server

The site for the foot-launched flying community, offering a large gallery of hang gliding photographs, digests, movies, weather updates, software, manufacturer contact list, a FAQ, paraglider designs, and much more.

See also: Outdoor Activities, Sports and Athletics

World Wide Web:
URL: **http://cougar.stanford.edu:7878/HGMPSHomePage.html**

Instrument Flight Rules

Find out the concerns of flying under Instrument Flight Rules. Alternative mnemonics and IFR tasks just scratch the surface of the topics covered.

Usenet:
Newsgroup: **rec.aviation.ifr**

Learning to Fly

What a wonderful new experience: learning to fly. It's nice to know you have a place to ask questions or share your experiences with people who enjoy the same hobby or way of life. Find out all the questions new students are asking, and learn about instructors, lessons, equipment, PPL qualifications, and airspace.

Usenet:
Newsgroup: **rec.aviation.student**

Excerpt from the Net...

```
Newsgroup: rec.aviation.student
Subject: Nausea and Learning to Fly

> I'm at about 15 hours now, and the
> nausea has pretty much entirely sub-
> sided. Anyone else have stress-
> related nausea while flying?

You're most definitely not alone there.
As a student I don't think that I know
of anyone as stressed out as I was in
my learning days. All I can say to oth-
ers as unfortunate is stick it out, it
WILL go away if you want.
```

McDonnell Douglas Aerospace

The McDonnell Douglas web server has information about the company in general and special projects/research interests including info on automation and robotics, guidance, navigation and control, mission analysis and integration, and rendezvous and proximity operations.

World Wide Web:
URL: **http://pat.mdc.com/**

Military Aircraft

From the Sopwith Camel to the F-117A Stealth Fighter and beyond, experience the thrill of military aircraft. See the past, present, and even the future, as aviation devotees share their ideas on what are the best planes, who are the most notorious pilots in history, and how military aircraft of various countries compare to one another.

Usenet:
Newsgroup: **rec.aviation.military**

MIT Soaring Association

The MIT Soaring Association offers information on soaring contests, competitions, aviation and soaring photos, newsgroups, club and association details, events guide, fuel prices, rental surveys, list of aircraft owners and builders, publication guides, and links to other aviation servers.

World Wide Web:
URL: **http://adswww.harvard.edu/MITSA/ mitsa_homepg.html**

NASA Aviation Server

A large collection of aviation information, including NASA aeronautical research servers, flight planning software, newsgroups, FAQs, piloting tips, federal aviation regulations, weather information, radio alphabet, flying jokes and poetry, details of aviation BBSs, Civil Air Patrol archives, and links to aircraft simulator ftp and gopher sites.

World Wide Web:
URL: **http://aviation.jsc.nasa.gov/**

News About the Aviation and Aerospace Industries

What's going on in the aviation and aerospace industries? Read the real news and get the facts.

Usenet:
Newsgroup: **clari.news.aviation**
Newsgroup: **clari.tw.aerospace**

Owning Airplanes

Don't you wish owning an airplane were as simple as installing a bigger garage door on your house? Learn the joys and travails of being the owner of a powerful flying machine. If you are interested in building or restoring aircraft, check out **.homebuilt** to indulge in your aviation obsession. A word of warning: one of the questions in the homebuilt FAQ list is, "Will my marriage survive?"

Usenet:
Newsgroup: **rec.aviation.homebuilt**
Newsgroup: **rec.aviation.owning**

Piloting

The tower says you're clear for takeoff into the wide world of piloting. You'll discover handy tips on priming cold engines, how to deal with rough weather, safety hints, and announcements on flying seminars.

Usenet:
Newsgroup: **rec.aviation.piloting**

Products for Pilots

Flight computers, sectionals, avionics, Snoopy scarves, and leather bomber jackets — find out what's new and useful for pilots.

Usenet:
Newsgroup: **rec.aviation.products**

Q & A About Aviation

Looking for thorough, well-researched information on aviation? Or are you willing to pass on your knowledge through concise, streamlined postings? This is the place for you. This group is moderated, and it would be in your best interest to read the FAQ list before posting.

Usenet:
Newsgroup: **rec.aviation.answers**

Your own airplane

Oh, how these three simple words invoke deep feelings in all of us.

Wouldn't it be great to be able to fly

Join the discussion on Usenet (rec.aviation.homebuilt and rec.aviation.owning) **and share ideas about what might well be the personal transportation vehicle of the 21st century.**

Stories about Flying

How does it feel to be so high above the Earth? What was it like the first time you went solo? What excites you about flying? Read anecdotes of flight experiences and share yours. Even if you don't fly, you can experience the thrill of the moment in the stories of others.

Usenet:
Newsgroup: **rec.aviation.stories**

Planning a picnic? Check the weather using the Net.

Ultralight Flying

Don't let the testosterone take over and convince you that you have to fly a jumbo jet. Experience the joy of ultralight aircraft and discuss with list members the joy of flying and the cost of maintaining ultralight aricraft.

See also: Hobbies

Internet Mailing List:
List Address: **ultralight-flight@ms.uky.edu**
Subscription Address:
ultralight-flight-request@ms.uky.edu

Upcoming Aviation Events

What's going on? Do you have an open weekend you want to fill? Are you going to be traveling to a new city and want to catch some aviation action? Find out what's happening on the aviation scene.

Usenet:
Newsgroup: **rec.aviation.announce**

All revved up and nowhere to go?

Check out Aviation UPCOMING EVENTS

Xpilot Game

Xpilot, a game for X Window, is one you really have to try if you like games and flying. Enthusiasts provide tips on sensors and cloaking devices, suggestions for saving disk space, special options to add to your game, ideas for team playing, and even homemade programs to enhance Xpilot.

Usenet:
Newsgroup: **alt.games.xpilot**

World Wide Web:
URL: **http://www.cs.uit.no/XPilot/**

URL: **http://www.nada.kth.se/htbin/ d-sektionen/xpilot**

A
B
C
D
E
F
G
H
I
J
K
L
M
N
O
P
Q
R
S
T
U
V
W
X
Y
Z

BBSs (BULLETIN BOARD SYSTEMS)

Auggie BBS

A widely varied BBS, with a wide spread of discussion boards, public files, chat and talk facilities. Friendly people are always ready to chat, day or night, through the numerous online communication programs.

Telnet:
>Address: **bbs.augsburg.edu**
>Login: **bbs**

BBS Access via Gopher

Access more BBSs than you can imagine through gopher. Just choose the BBS you wish to use from the large list available and you will be connected. Get rid of those long cumbersome BBS lists.

Gopher:
>Name: Texas A&M University
>Address: **gopher.tamu.edu**
>Choose: **Hot Topics: What's New And What's Popular**
> **| Hot Topics: A&M's Most Popular Items**
> **| Bulletin Boards**

>Name: Texas Tech University
>Address: **gopher.cs.ttu.edu**
>Choose: **Other Information Sources And Services**
> **| Bulletin Board Systems**

>Name: University of Texas at Austin
>Address: **actlab.rtf.utexas.edu**
>Choose: **Networks**
> **| The Internet**
> **| Bulletin Board Systems**

BBS Acronyms

Do the acronyms of the BBS and computer worlds have you feeling dyslexic, dazed and confused? Well, NAM (not any more)! Check out this file and LYAO at some of these.

Anonymous FTP:
>Address: **ftp.spies.com**
>Path: **/Library/Cyber/acronyms.bbs**

Gopher:
>Name: Internet Wiretap
>Address: **wiretap.spies.com**
>Choose: **Wiretap Online Library**
> **| Cyberspace**
> **| Common BBS Acronyms**

BBS General Discussion

These Usenet groups are for general discussions on understanding, using, and even running a bulletin board system.

Usenet:
>Newsgroup: **alt.bbs**
>Newsgroup: **comp.bbs.misc**

Need help understanding BBSs? Read **comp.bbs.misc**

BBS Information

Frequently asked questions (FAQ) and answers about Internet bulletin boards.

Anonymous FTP:
>Address: **nigel.msen.com**
>Path: **/pub/gopher/stuff/stuff.old/inet-bbs-faq/***

Archie:
>Pattern: **inet-bbs-faq**

Usenet:
>Newsgroup: **alt.bbs.internet**

BBS Lists

CC's list, Zamfield's BBS list, and Yanoff's Internet List together form the most complete updated source of all the Internet BBS addresses and like-minded services that you will ever need. Endless hours of roaming the Net await within their pages.

Anonymous FTP:
>Address: **aug3.augsburg.edu**
>Path: **/files/bbs_lists**

>Address: **oak.oakland.edu**
>Path: **/pub/misc/bbslists**

Mail:
>Address: **bbslist@aug3.augsburg.edu**

BBS Programs

Here are a number of Usenet discussion groups devoted to particular BBS software packages. If you're interested in any of these packages, you'll want to be in constant contact with the experts.

Usenet:
> Newsgroup: **alt.bbs.first-class**
> Newsgroup: **alt.bbs.gigo-gateway**
> Newsgroup: **alt.bbs.majorbbs**
> Newsgroup: **alt.bbs.metal**
> Newsgroup: **alt.bbs.pcboard**
> Newsgroup: **alt.bbs.renegade**
> Newsgroup: **alt.bbs.searchlight**
> Newsgroup: **alt.bbs.waffle**
> Newsgroup: **alt.bbs.watergate**
> Newsgroup: **alt.bbs.wildcat**
> Newsgroup: **comp.bbs.tbbs**
> Newsgroup: **comp.bbs.waffle**

BBSs Around the World

Information and advertisements describing various BBSs to which you can connect.

Usenet:
> Newsgroup: **alt.bbs.ads**
> Newsgroup: **alt.bbs.internet**
> Newsgroup: **alt.bbs.lists**
> Newsgroup: **alt.bbs.lists.d**

Bulletin Boards Around the World

There was a time when computerized bulletin board systems (BBSs) were accessible only by their very own phone number. Not any more. As an Internet user, you can telnet to many different BBSs without making the slightest dent in your phone bill. Even government agencies have BBSs, putting the "bull" back in "bulletin" and the "bored" back in "board".

Cetys-BBS

A Mexican BBS, with many Spanish discussion groups. An interesting place to practice your Spanish, but English speakers are welcome also.

Telnet:
> Address: **infrs.mxl.cetys.mx**
> Login: **bbs**

Citadel

A Unix BBS software package with add-ons, complete with source code and editor.

Anonymous FTP:
> Address: **quartz.rutgers.edu**
> Path: **/pub/citadel/***

Gopher:
> Name: Rutgers University
> Address: **quartz.rutgers.edu**
> Choose: **Citadel/UX BBS Software and Add-ons**

Csb/Sju BBS

This easy-to-use menu-driven BBS, with its simple and unique message navigating commands and use of graphics, allows for quick scanning of all the different topics it has to offer.

Telnet:
> Address: **tiny.computing.csbsju.edu**
> Login: **bbs**

CueCosy

A conferencing system in Canada allowing posting and reading of messages on many topics. There is a special education section called TIX, the Teachers Information Exchange.

Telnet:
> Address: **cue.bc.ca**
> Login: **cosy**

Cybernet BBS

Offers many interesting and varied resources, including Internet mail, limited Usenet, hytelnet, finger, talk, multiuser chat, file downloading, games, and even a matchmaking program for lonely hearts.

Telnet:
> Address: **cybernet.cse.fau.edu**
> Login: **bbs**

A
B
C
D
E
F
G
H
I
J
K
L
M
N
O
P
Q
R
S
T
U
V
W
X
Y
Z

Doors

External programs (doors) that are integrated into a BBS in order to provide access to special services.

Usenet:
    Newsgroup: **alt.bbs.doors**

DUBBS

A quiet little BBS in the Netherlands, offering message and bulletin board systems, and lots of downloadable computer files. If you have a flair for Dutch, check it out.

Telnet:
    Address: **tudrwa.tudelft.nl**
    Login: **bbs**

Eagles' Nest BBS

Offers lots of variety in its discussion groups, including two public chat rooms.

Note: After you log in, you'll be asked for a userid and a password. Use **guest** for both.

Telnet:
    Address: **seabass.st.usm.edu**
    Login: **bbs**

Endless Forest BBS

Some say alternate space/time continuums exist for the known reality—the Endless Forest is one. Here the Forest dwellers roam, purely for the exchange of technical information, controversial debate, inane babble, and general fun.

Telnet:
    Address: **ef.creighton.edu**
    Login: **ef**

    Address: **forest.creighton.edu**
    Login: **ef**

European Southern Observatory Bulletin Board

A bulletin board system for people involved in, or interested in, the European Southern Observatory. Discussion and information regarding astronomy and telescopes.

Telnet:
    Address: **bbhost.hq.eso.org**
    Login: **esobb**

Foothills Multiuser Chat

A very popular chat system, and a great place to relax and talk. Foothills provides a nice secure environment in which you can converse, with a multitude of features that make life easier.

Telnet:
    Address: **marble.bu.edu**
    Port: **2010**

> # The Bizarre section has some cool stuff.

Government-Sponsored Bulletin Boards

A list of U.S. government bulletin boards. This list is compiled by the Department of Commerce, Economics and Statistics Administration and lists many BBSs by government agency.

Gopher:
    Name: Library of Congress
    Address: **marvel.loc.gov**
    Choose: **Government Information**
      | Federal Information Resources
      | Information By Agency
      | General Information
      | Federal Bulletin Boards (List)

Excerpt from the Net...

```
(from "Government Sponsored Bulletin Boards")

NATIONAL INSTITUTE FOR STANDARDS AND TECHNOLOGY

Microcomputer Electronic Information Exchange
     Voice Number:  301-975-3359
     Data Number:   301-948-5717 (2400 bps)
                    301-948-5718 (9600 bps)


Describes software, systems, and techniques that combat unauthorized access to your
computer, and contains files that describe computer viruses and how to prevent them.
```

ISCA BBS

The largest and most popular BBS on the Internet (and the largest nonprofit BBS in the world). There are discussion groups to fit all tastes, especially some of a more esoteric nature that seem to be lacking from Usenet. ISCA is often full, with users from all over the globe busily rambling away.

Telnet:
> Address: **bbs.isca.uiowa.edu**
> Login: **guest**
>
> Address: **whip.isca.uiowa.edu**
> Login: **guest**

Launchpad BBS

Much more than a BBS, this Internet service mediator welcomes all new users with open arms. Offering complete network news, local mail, wais, gopher, and access to many other information systems, it is well worth investigating.

Telnet:
> Address: **launchpad.unc.edu**
> Login: **launch**
>
> Address: **launchpad.unc.edu**
> Login: **launch**

The Launchpad Spoonfeeder

We know that you are a cool dude who has memorized all the commands that you need to use the Internet. But we are sure you have a friend (probably a Mac user) who always expects things to be "easy". Send him to Launchpad: a BBS that allows you to access Internet services by choosing items from a menu. If you know how to order food in a restaurant, you can use Launchpad.

Monochrome

Monochrome is a sophisticated multiuser messaging system. This includes its local messages, multitudes of files, a multiuser talker, and a unique presentation capability which takes full advantage of your terminal type, throwing delightful quotes and scrolling messages at you constantly.

Telnet:
> Address: **neutron.city.ac.uk**
> Login: **mono**

NCTU CIS BBS

A friendly BBS located in the heart of Taiwan. It offers an amazing selection of resources, including local discussion boards, games, Usenet news, gopher, and great chat facilities. Can display everything in Chinese if you download the necessary client, which is an interesting touch.

Telnet:
> Address: **bbs.cis.nctu.edu.tw**
> Login: **guest**

OuluBox

A small BBS located in Finland offering bulletins, a selection of discussion conferences, and downloadable files. A great place to practice your Finnish, but there is also an English language menu option.

Telnet:
> Address: **tolsun.oulu.fi**
> Login: **box**

Powertech BBS

Powertech Information Systems is a BBS in Oslo, Norway, with a web server that provides many types of Internet services, including IRC, editions of *Netsurfer Digest* and other electronic documents, keyword searches, and links to many other interesting services.

World Wide Web:
> URL: **http://www.powertech.no/**

Want some fun?
Read the Fun section

A B C D E F G H I J K L M N O P Q R S T U V W X Y Z

Prism Hotel BBS

The Prism Hotel is divided into multiple floors, each with its own subject area. On each floor there are numerous rooms that you can enter to view the discussion posts therein. Message bases include arts and entertainment, music, business, and science and technology. It all makes for an interesting BBS experience.

Telnet:
>Address: **bbs.fdu.edu**
>Login: **bbs**

Quartz BBS

One of the oldest BBSs on the Internet. Age has only enhanced it, as there are many interesting discussion topics here, including personals, jobs, computer topics, movies, education, sports, pets, history, comics, and also a useful Internet information system.

Telnet:
>Address: **quartz.rutgers.edu**
>Login: **bbs**

Radford University BBS

Offers an amazing number of services, including general discussion groups, IRC, public files, local mail, access to libraries, and games.

Telnet:
>Address: **bbs.runet.edu**
>Login: **bbs**

Skynet BBS

A friendly BBS based in Norway offering varied and interesting discussion groups. The policy of no censorship has led to many diverse and informative topics, covering a wide spectrum of life's mysteries.

Telnet:
>Address: **hpx6.aid.no**
>Login: **skynet**

Softwords COSY

A friendly conferencing system with a variety of discussion groups, including many technical and business issues such as animation and multimedia, philosophy, programming, and the Internet. Also offers Internet mail access to its users.

Telnet:
>Address: **softwords.bc.ca**
>Login: **cosy**

Sunset BBS

A programming project of the University of Arizona. Lots of varied discussion groups, including the Hardware and Computing Knowledge Society. Forums include *Star Trek*, religion, careers, networks, VAX systems, music, and comics. Sunset also offers local mail, and a scenic login screen.

Telnet:
>Address: **paladine.hacks.arizona.edu**
>Login: **bbs**

Sysop Information

A forum for BBS system operators — a bunch that likes to call themselves "sysops."

Usenet:
>Newsgroup: **alt.bbs.allsysop**

Unix and BBSs

Information about BBS software for Unix systems and the UUCP mail facility.

Usenet:
>Newsgroup: **alt.bbs.pcbuucp**
>Newsgroup: **alt.bbs.unixbbs**
>Newsgroup: **alt.bbs.unixbbs.uniboard**
>Newsgroup: **alt.bbs.uupcb**

UTBBS

Based in Holland, with both English and Dutch-speaking users, UTBBS offers public and personal messaging, online chat, and a very large file selection covering many areas such as astronomy, biology, chemistry, computing, and more.

Telnet:
>Address: **utbbs.civ.utwente.nl**
>Login: **bbs**

Web BBS List

Do you get tired of having all those little pieces of paper with the name of your favorite BBSs scribbled on them? Throw them out and join the electronic age. On the Web you can find a list of BBSs, and by selecting the link, you will automatically be connected to whatever BBS you choose.

World Wide Web:
>URL: **http://bbs.augsburg.edu/ ~schwartz/ebbs.html**

BIOLOGY

Ageing

There's more to ageing than getting old. Despite what skin cream commercials say, you age from the inside out and no amount of Oil of Olay will cure that. Learn about cellular and organismal ageing and go on your quest for the fountain of youth.

Usenet:
Newsgroup: **bionet.molbio.ageing**

THE WORST PART OF AGEING IS GETTING OLD (THE REST ISN'T SO BAD). Still, AT LEAST YOU CAN BE WELL-INFORMED ABOUT WHAT YOUR CELLS ARE DOING BY READING **bionet.molbio.ageing.**

American Type Culture Collection

A natural language database. Compose your queries in plain English and the system will provide documents relating to your queries.

Telnet:
Address: **atcc.nih.gov**
Login: **search**
Password: **common**

Animal Behavior

The Center for the Integrative Study of Animal Behavior works with a number of diverse organisms, including rabbits, bats, rodents, birds, amphibians, fish, mollusks, flies, and wasps to study animal behaviour. Check out their web page and see what they're up to.

World Wide Web:
URL: **http://www.cisab.indiana.edu/index.html**

Arabidopsis Project

Imagine how carefree you would feel running through a huge field of arabidopsis, your lab coat flapping behind you. Capture that experience, or at least the next best thing, by discussing the arabidopsis project with others who share your interest in these little herbs.

Usenet:
Newsgroup: **bionet.genome.arabidopsis**

BioBox Wonder World

BioBox Wonder World is a collection of the favorite web pages of anyone involved with biology. If you like biology, you simply must check this out, and if your favorite page isn't there, add it!

World Wide Web:
URL: **http://shamrock.csc.fi:81/cgi-bin/topbio**

Biochemistry

The world would not be the same without nucleic acids. After all, without them, what would biochemists do for a living? The Netbiochem page offers information on macromolecules, nucleic acids, heme and iron metabolism, and more.

World Wide Web:
URL: **http://ubu.hahnemann.edu/Heme-Iron/NetWelcome.html**

Where would we be without biochemistry? Well, for some of us, pre-med studies would have been a lot easier. On the other hand, with no biochemistry, all we would be is a bunch of organic chemicals lying in a pool on the floor, so there are definite trade-offs. For those of us stuck in the real world of exquisitely shaped enzymes and long, silly chains of carbon that don't seem to know when to stop, the *Biochemistry* web site can provide a biodegradable home away from home.

A
B
C
D
E
F
G
H
I
J
K
L
M
N
O
P
Q
R
S
T
U
V
W
X
Y
Z

Biochemistry Graphics Room at Aberdeen University

Some of the cool projects here include database visualization using 3-D graphics; Assassin, a constraints-based assignment system for protein 2-D nuclear magnetic resonance; object-oriented database development for antibody modeling; and an integrated knowledge base for protein structure and sequence. There are links to many servers on biotechnology, biochemistry and other related fields.

World Wide Web:
URL: **http://www.biochem.abdn.ac.uk/**

BioData Cyberspace Launching Pad

Yet another list of Internet hot spots for biology resources. This one is designed as a launch pad for users of the BioData Navigator. Begin your excellent adventure into the biosciences right here!

World Wide Web:
URL: **http://www.biodata.com/launch.html**

Biodiversity

Men and women — that's about as diverse as biology gets. Unfortunately, this forum doesn't offer any insight on that issue, but it does offer discussion on technical opportunities, administrative and economic issues, limitations and scientific goals relating to the biodiversity network.

Listserv Mailing List:
List Address: **biodiv-l@bdt.ftpt.ansp.br**
Subscription Address: **listserv@bdt.ftpt.ansp.br**

Bioethics

What happens when you cross a philosopher with a biologist? You get a very interesting gopher server with a huge amount of information on bioethics. Connect with online discussion groups, read news alerts, and flip through various papers on bioethics.

Gopher:
Name: Medical College of Wisconsin
Address: **post.its.mcw.edu**
Port: **72**

Bioinformatics Resource Gopher

The Bioinformatics gopher at the University of West Florida develops and operates DNA and protein sequence analysis software. Analysis software includes vertebrate genomic DNA analysis, vertebrate cDNA analysis, and protein analysis.

Gopher:
Name: University of Florida
Address: **dna.cedb.uwf.edu**

Biological Databases

For seemingly endless amounts of information, check out these biological databases. Find computer applications to suit your biological needs, so to speak.

Gopher:
Name: Cornell University
Address: **muse.bio.cornell.edu**

Usenet:
Newsgroup: **bionet.molbio.bio-matrix**

Biological Sciences Conferences

A large list of mailing lists related to the biological sciences, divided into subject areas.

Anonymous FTP:
Address: **ksuvxa.kent.edu**
Path: **/library/acadlist.file5**

Gopher:
Name: Sam Houston State University
Address: **niord.shsu.edu**
Choose: **anonymous ftp archives at niord.shsu.edu**
 I **acadlist**
 I **acadlist.file5**

Biological Scientist's Network Guide

Useful FAQs, papers, press releases, announcements, and project information for biological scientists who work on a variety of computer networks.

Gopher:
Name: World Data Center on Microorganisms
Address: **fragrans.riken.go.jp**
Choose: **About bioinfo resources on Internet**
 I **Useful articles from BIOSCI-BIONET newsgroups**

Biologist's Guide to Internet Resources

This document explains how to find everything of use to a biologist on the Internet.

Anonymous FTP:
Address: **rtfm.mit.edu**
Path: **/pub/usenet-by-group/biology/guide/***

Gopher:
Name: Center for Scientific Computing
Address: **gopher.csc.fi**
Choose: **Information in English**
| **Scientific Topics**
| **Finnish EMBnet BioBox**
| **FAQ Files**
| **A Biologist's Guide..**

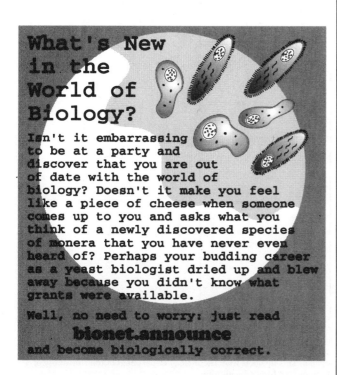

What's New in the World of Biology?

Isn't it embarrassing to be at a party and discover that you are out of date with the world of biology? Doesn't it make you feel like a piece of cheese when someone comes up to you and asks what you think of a newly discovered species of monera that you have never even heard of? Perhaps your budding career as a yeast biologist dried up and blew away because you didn't know what grants were available.

Well, no need to worry: just read **bionet.announce** and become biologically correct.

Biology and Information Theory

A text file containing discussions on the applications of information theory to biological research.

Anonymous FTP:
Address: **ftp.hmc.edu**
Path: **/pub/science/sci.answers/.mirror.OLD/**
biology/info-theory

Biology Announcements

This newsgroup is the loudspeaker of Bionet, Usenet's hierarchy of biology-oriented newsgroups. Find out what's going on in the wide world of biology: new electronic journals, conference announcements, calls for research papers, and new databases are a few of the things that people are shouting about. This group is moderated.

Usenet:
Newsgroup: **bionet.announce**

Biology General Discussion

This forum covers all the biological sciences. Catch glimpses of a little bit of everything that makes up the world around us. Discover what makes your body tick, what's in that yeast bread you've been eating, and how everything you touch teems with life. Your life will never be the same.

Usenet:
Newsgroup: **bionet.general**

Biology Information Theory

Speculation, brainstorming, and sharing of ideas is what happens when you get everyone together to talk about biological information theory.

Usenet:
Newsgroup: **bionet.info-theory**

Biology Job Opportunities

Why be a telemarketer when you can have a job in the exciting field of biology? See cells reproduce right before your eyes, cut up small unsuspecting micro-organisms with lightning speed, and create new life forms seemingly from scratch. Opportunities abound for pre- or post-docs, undergraduates looking for something to keep them out of trouble for the summer, assistant professors who don't mind grading papers, and for upwardly mobile tenure-track seekers.

Usenet:
Newsgroup: **bionet.jobs**

Biology Journals

If you like biological journals, or even if you don't and have to read them anyway, check the **.contents** for a brief outline of what's in the latest journals. Look at the **.note** group for advice on using biology journals.

Usenet:
Newsgroup: **bionet.journals.contents**
Newsgroup: **bionet.journals.note**

WAIS:
Database: **biology-journal-contents**

A
B
C
D
E
F
G
H
I
J
K
L
M
N
O
P
Q
R
S
T
U
V
W
X
Y
Z

Biology Newsletter

Selection of newsletters about agriculture, botany, ecosystems, genetics, and general biology, including publications such as *Starnet*, *Tiempo*, and *Flora* online.

Anonymous FTP:
Address: **nigel.msen.com**
Path: **/pub/newsletters/Bio/***

Biology Resources

Explore the many biology-related resources available on the Internet via the gopher. Contains FAQs, ftp sites, book lists, and access to many bio servers around the globe.

Gopher:
Name: Center for Scientific Computing
Address: **gopher.csc.fi**
Choose: **Information in English**
  | **Scientific Topics**
  | **Finnish EMBnet BioBox**

Biology Software and Archives

An extensive collection of more than 70 biology resources available via the Internet. Includes a gene server, molecular graphics, software, project information, and access to many more biological tools and programs.

Anonymous FTP:
Address: **ftp.bio.indiana.edu**
Path: **/biology/***

Gopher:
Name: Johns Hopkins University
Address: **gopher.gdb.org**
Choose: **FTP Sites, Software and Data Archives for Biology**

Biology Software Search

Search and retrieve biology-related software for all the popular computers.

Gopher:
Name: Johns Hopkins University
Address: **gopher.gdb.org**
Choose: **Search and Retrieve Software**
  | **Search and Retrieve Software for Biology**

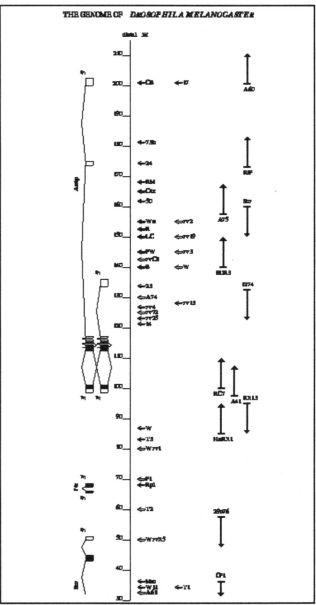

Computer pictures aren't only for fun. This image is the genome of a drosophila melanogaster (whatever that is). Many university science departments store image files on their systems that could be of interest to you. This image is from the Biology Department of the University of Indiana (**ftp.bio.indiana.edu**).

Biomechanics

A mailing list intended for members of the International, European, American, Canadian and other Societies of Biomechanics, and anyone else interested in this field.

Listserv Mailing List:
List Address: **biomch-l@nic.surfnet.nl**
Subscription Address: **listserv@nic.surfnet.nl**

The Net is mankind's greatest achievement.

BioMOO

BioMOO is the biologists' virtual meeting place, where people come to meet colleagues in biology studies and related fields, to hold discussions and conferences, and to explore the serious side of this new medium. You can also view recordings of previous meetings or browse the reference files.

World Wide Web:
URL: **http://bioinformatics.weizmann.ac.il:70/1s/ biomoo**

Biosphere and Ecology

Life does not exist in a vacuum. Ecology cannot exist strictly in a lab. For you rugged, active types, try studying the relations between living organisms and their environment.

Usenet:
Newsgroup: **bit.listserv.biosph-l**
Newsgroup: **sci.bio.ecology**

Biotechnology

Biotechnology is not simply the clicking of switches and the turning of dials. It's the graceful application of science and technology to all aspects of biology, but especially to molecular and cellular biology and genetics. Catch technology hot off the presses.

Usenet:
Newsgroup: **sci.bio.technology**

Bird Studies in the Australian National Botanic Gardens

A tour of the common birds of the Australian National Botanic Gardens, including sketches in gif format, information about the birds, and **.au** audio files of many bird calls.

World Wide Web:
URL: **http://osprey.erin.gov.au/projects/birds/ bird-studies.html**

Brazilian Tropical Databases

Brazilian biological information, including tropical plants and animals, census of animals in Brazilian zoos, antimicrobials, and discussions of biodiversity.

Gopher:
Name: Base de Dados Tropical
Address: **bdt.ftpt.br**
Choose: **BDTNet - Tropical Data Base Network**

Catalog of Marine Fish and Invertebrates

A catalog of more than 200 pictures of marine fish and invertebrates. The catalog can be searched by type, scientific name, or common name. There are also pictorial guides to angelfish, butterfly fish, clownfish, and tangs (surgeonfish).

World Wide Web:
URL: **http://www.actwin.com/fish/species.html**

Cell Biology

This is where life happens, in tiny units of protoplasm. Unless you are a robot, cell biology concerns you. Cell scholars from all over the world dissect studies, research, and experiments that relate to cell biology.

Usenet:
Newsgroup: **bionet.cellbiol**

Excerpt from the Net...

```
Newsgroup: sci.bio.ecology
Subject: Why are foxes the main carrier of rabies in the wild?

In Ontario [Canada], foxes are definitely one of the main vectors (skunks are good vec-
tors too). I think that the reason for this is as simple as the fact that there is a
specific rabies strain which attacks foxes but doesn't kill them very quickly. This
would allow the number of foxes with rabies to build up due to contact with others be-
fore its death. I think that the primary vector depends on which strain of rabies pre-
dominates in a particular area.
```

A B C D E F G H I J K L M N O P Q R S T U V W X Y Z

Chromosome 22

Play Chromatin Lotto, the game of human chance. If 22 is your lucky number, you've hit the jackpot. Get all sorts of information on Chromosome 22 and its function in the larger scheme of things.

Usenet:
Newsgroup: **bionet.genome.chrom22**

Collaborative Clickable Biology

Collaborative Clickable Biology is a collection of published biological data, including many articles and journals. The biological community world-wide is invited to organize and use this information.

World Wide Web:
URL: **http://s-crim1.dl.ac.uk:8000/HOME.html**

Computers and Mathematics

There's more to life than just cells and DNA. (Not much more, but more.) Feeding in data, spitting out numbers, running this, programming that — it's all part of computer and mathematical biology. This group is moderated.

Usenet:
Newsgroup: **bionet.biology.computational**

Counting on your genes to pull you through?

Read
bionet.biology.computational

Conservation Biology

The planet is relatively resilient, but there is only so much it can take. Science has taken up the cause of helping to protect, maintain, and restore life to the Earth, its species, and its ecological and evolutionary environment. That is the goal of conservation biology as well as of the members of this list.

Listserv Mailing List:
List Address: **consbio@uwavm.u.washington.edu**
Subscription Address:
listserv@uwavm.u.washington.edu

Drosophila

The media is always reporting recent exploits of the pesky fruit fly in its travels around the globe. More amazing is the fact that there are people who study these critters for long periods of time. If you are one of those special people, find kinship with your peers as they discuss the biology of drosophila.

Usenet:
Newsgroup: **bionet.drosophila**

EMBL Nucleic Acid Database

If you're searching for information on EMBL nucleic acids, this is the place for you. People from all over the world feed this database with information.

Usenet:
Newsgroup: **bionet.molbio.embldatabank**

Entomology at Colorado State University

The CSU Entomology web server provides links to various entomology resources, including insect drawings, an insect database, publications such as *The Aquatic Invertebrate Ecologist*, and entomology resources at other universities.

World Wide Web:
URL: **http://www.colostate.edu/Depts/Entomology/ent.html**

European Molecular Biology Net

The European Molecular Biology Net was established in 1988 and currently has 22 nodes with full connectivity to most European countries. This server is the entrypoint to a commonwealth of information on the network, including its services and projects, its history and its members.

World Wide Web:
URL: **http://beta.ebmnet.unibas.ch/ebmnet/info.html**

Evolution of Genes and Proteins

You won't see it happen right before your eyes (unless you are watching a bad science fiction movie) but evolution is nevertheless happening around us all the time. Study ideas and research on the evolution of genes and proteins.

Usenet:
Newsgroup: **bionet.molbio.evolution**

Frog Dissection Kit

Here's one of the hottest biology resources on the Net. The interactive web frog dissection kit is for use in high school biology classrooms. It uses photo images to allow you to perform a virtual dissection including preparation, skin incisions, muscle incisions and examination of internal organs.

Note: Requires that your browser be graphical and support a forms-based interface.

World Wide Web:
   URL: **http://curry.edschool.Virginia.EDU:80/ ~insttech/frog/**

   URL: **http://george.lbl.gov/ITG.hm.pg.docs/ dissect/info.html**

Funding and Grants

Don't wait for your million dollar sweepstakes check to come in. Where are some of the funding agencies in biology? Who's giving out research grants? Find out who has the money and how you can get some, too.

Usenet:
   Newsgroup: **bionet.sci-resources**

Funding and Grants in Biology

So you've got this great idea for developing wheat that grows in thin rows, just perfect for making sliced bread. But what can you do for seed money?

Participate in the **bionet.sci-resources** discussion group and perhaps, just perhaps, you will find the financial source that will send you on your way to becoming the next Internet Nobel prize winner.

Fungi

It's safe to say that fungi are just about everybody's favorite biological kingdom (although some people do prefer monera). Find out what makes these multicelled, eukaryotic heterotrophs so much fun. Whether saprobic or parasitic, these cool organisms will well repay a lifetime of study. Join the crowd.

Usenet:
   Newsgroup: **bionet.mycology**

G Protein-Coupled Receptor Database

A molecular biology protein research site that provides information about diseases caused by or linked to G protein-coupled receptors.

World Wide Web:
   URL: **http://receptor.mgh.harvard.edu/ GCRDBHOME.html**

GenBank Database

It's not just a database, it's a way of life. Not only is the GenBank nucleic acid database available, but the **.updates** group has the most recent news about GenBank.

Usenet:
   Newsgroup: **bionet.molbio.genbank**
   Newsgroup: **bionet.molbio.genbank.updates**

Genetic Linkage

How many genes does it take to organize a chromosome? It's not a joke, it's Genetic Linkage Trivia. Read linkage analyses on **gene-linkage**. On **gene-org**, experience how genes are organized on chromosomes. They would put any board of directors to shame.

Usenet:
   Newsgroup: **bionet.molbio.gene-linkage**
   Newsgroup: **bionet.molbio.gene-org**

Genetics Resources

This genetics gopher provides access to fly, mouse, and human genomic databases, culture collections, ftp repositories, protein sites and patterns, nucleic acid database, protein sequence database, vectors, promoters, and sequence tags.

Gopher:
   Name: Genetics Resources
   Address: **una.hh.lib.umich.edu**
   Choose: **science**
      | **Life Sciences**
      | **Genetics Resources**

A
B
C
D
E
F
G
H
I
J
K
L
M
N
O
P
Q
R
S
T
U
V
W
X
Y
Z

GenomeNet

A network for genome research and related research areas in molecular and cellular biology. The Human Genome Center (HGC) and the Supercomputer Laboratory (SCL) provide database services that are available through GenomeNet.

Gopher:
Name: GenomeNet
Address: **gopher.genome.ad.jp**

World Wide Web:
URL: **http://www.genome.ad.jp/**

Genome Research at Harvard Biological Laboratories

This web page provides access to BioInfomatics and biotechnology information, including model organism databases software and documentation.

World Wide Web:
URL: **http://golgi.harvard.edu/**

Globin Gene Server

The Globin Gene Server provides access to information about the regulation of gene expression within the beta-like globin gene cluster. The page also has related information and links to other web pages.

World Wide Web:
URL: **http://globin.cse.psu.edu/**

Human Genome Project

Join the discussion about the Human Genome Project, the massively ambitious scheme to ferret out and document all of the genes in human chromosomes. Maybe one day they will find the gene for TV watching and we will all be saved.

Gopher:
Name: UK Medical Research Council
Address: **gopher.hgmp.mrc.ac.uk**

Usenet:
Newsgroup: **bionet.molbio.gdb**
Newsgroup: **bionet.molbio.genome-program**

Immunology

Bigger, stronger people mean quicker and faster viral mutations. Why do you get sick, but your co-worker doesn't? Immunology reveals the magic of our ability to withstand the effects of disease and sickness.

Usenet:
Newsgroup: **bionet.immunology**

Jackson Laboratory

The Jackson Laboratory in Maine has a threefold mission: to conduct research in basic genetics and the role of genes in health and disease; to educate the scientific community; and to provide genetically defined mice and other genetic resources to the world. For more information about the lab and their projects, see the server.

World Wide Web:
URL: **http://www.jax.org/**

Japan Animal Genome Database

This genome database offers genome data for cattle, pigs, and mice and includes information on cytogenetic maps and linkage maps.

World Wide Web:
URL: **http://ws4.niai.affrc.go.jp/jgbase.html**

Kinetics and Thermodynamics

Kinetics and thermodynamics are fitness programs for cells, except that cells don't wear little spandex suits. Discuss the dynamics of chain reactions at the cellular level.

Usenet:
Newsgroup: **bionet.metabolic-reg**

Mapping Chromosomes

Much like the quest of Indiana Jones, only on a smaller scale (much smaller), mapping and sequencing eucaryote chromosomes can be mysterious and revealing. Join the discussion and find out the why and how.

Usenet:
Newsgroup: **bionet.genome.chromosomes**

Methods and Reagents

Develop some flair when experimenting. Show a little imagination when you stain your DNA or measure your plasma renin activity. See your peers use PCR to introduce silent mutations — the genetic ninjas of biology. Learn the methods and reagents that work and run quickly away from the ones that don't.

Usenet:
Newsgroup: **bionet.molbio.methds-reagnts**

Microbiology at the Technical University of Denmark

The home page of the Department of Microbiology at the Technical University of Denmark offers information about the department, the University, and the Cellstat program — a graphical, automated cell detection and quantification program for X Window.

World Wide Web:
URL: **http://ftp.lm.dtu.dk/**

Molecular Biology Laboratory

The European Molecular Biology Laboratory web server provides information about the scientific programs, the network, courses, and other information and activities at the lab.

World Wide Web:
URL: **http://www.embl-heidelberg.de/**

Molecular Biology Network

The European Molecular Biology Network (EMBnet) operates 22 nodes in most European countries and is working on the development of new techniques in biological database access and utilization.

World Wide Web:
URL: **http://beta.embnet.unibas.ch/embnet/info.html**

Molecular Biology of HIV

There is so much information going around about the family of HIV viruses. Every day it seems there are new studies, new research. See it broken down to a molecular level and learn how HIV operates.

Usenet:
Newsgroup: **bionet.molbio.hiv**

Molecular Modeling

A central source of information for the National Institute of Health research community and others interested in molecular modeling methods and possible applications. This page also provides a link to the "Molecules R Us" database at the NIH.

World Wide Web:
URL: **http://www.nih.gov/molecular_modeling/mmhome.html**

Motif BioInformatics Server

From the Department of Biochemistry at Stanford University, this page includes information on Stanford's programs in molecular and genetic medicine and features links to X Window software for biology.

World Wide Web:
URL: **http://motif.stanford.edu/**

Mouse Biology

A genomic database of the mouse, genetic maps of the mouse, mouse and locus data, and a mouse locus catalog.

Telnet:
Address: **morgan.jax.org**
Login: **guest**

Neuroscience

When you tell someone you are a bundle of nerves, you are telling more of the truth than you probably realize. Neuroscience involves the study of the nervous system, its structure and diseases. Join the discussion and meet the pros.

Usenet:
Newsgroup: **bionet.neuroscience**

Nitrogen Fixation

Most people don't think of bacteria as handy and useful things to have around. You clean them, spray them, call them bad names. Just hope they don't go on strike and stop carrying ammonia-bound nitrogen to their designated delivery areas, causing the collapse of the food chain right at the weakest link (you). See such nitrogen fixing in action and discover how this process keeps us in pizza and Chinese food.

Usenet:
Newsgroup: **bionet.n2-fixation**

Population Biology

The biology of populations used to be as simple as counting the legs and dividing by two. Modern methods are a lot more complex and require considerable biological, mathematical, and computational expertise. Visit this newsgroup when you need to swap stories with the experts.

Usenet:
Newsgroup: **bionet.population-bio**

Primates

A gopher dedicated to primate biology, including discussions, directory of primatology, newsletters, behavioral patterns, animal welfare legislation, and other items of interest.

Gopher:
Name: Primate Info Net
Address: **saimiri.primate.wisc.edu**

Protein

How many angels can dance on the head of a lutropin beta chain? We don't know, but we know whom to ask. If you are into protein, check out these protein databases. Several databases are linked together covering sequencing, structure, enzyme classification, and comparisons of DNA and protein sequences. Protein: it's not just for carnivores.

World Wide Web:
URL: **http://expasy.hcuge.ch/sprot/ sprot-top.html**
URL: **http://www.gdb.org/hopkins.html**

Protein Crystallography

Discover the latest thoughts on the form, structure, and properties of crystallized protein. It's not recommended for trail mix, but it certainly has its merits.

Usenet:
Newsgroup: **bionet.xtallography**

Protein Databases

Are you into protein? These resources are facilities for constructing and analyzing protein databases with the goal of encouraging the construction of numerous such protein databases for scientific investigations.

Gopher:
Name: Protein Data Bank
Address: **pdb.pdb.bnl.gov**

Usenet:
Newsgroup: **bionet.molbio.proteins**

World Wide Web:
URL: **http://siva.cshl.org/**

Randomly Amplified Polymorphic DNA

It's late in the day. You have optimized your PCR reaction conditions with a pair of specific primer sets. You then switch to random primers from UBC to do RAPD (not forgetting to lower the annealing temperature to 35 degrees C). However, you try 30 random primers and still do not get any good results. Isn't it good to know you have a place to turn for help?

Usenet:
Newsgroup: **bionet.molbio.rapd**

Related Sciences

Unbutton your top button and roll up your sleeves in preparation for some lively biological bantering. While informative and educational, subjects are never strictly hard-core science. Debate is sparked by such topics as evolution, the ethics of cloning, and the instinctual mating habits of animals and humans.

Usenet:
Newsgroup: **sci.bio**

Salk Institute for Biological Studies

The University of California at San Diego's NeuroWeb, an online resource focused on the neurosciences.

World Wide Web:
URL: **http://salk.edu/**

Society for Neuroscience

Information on joining the society, and available newsletters and journals relating to neuroscience.

Gopher:
Name: Society for Neuroscience
Address: **gopher.sfn.org**

Nattering Nabobs of Neuroscience

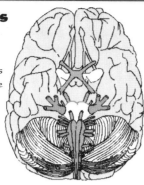

In his lifetime, Harley has dissected two and a half brains and, he can tell you, it is a rare privilege. There is something about holding a human brain in your hand that makes you humble. Imagine standing there, contemplating 1500 grams of recently organic matter, and thinking to yourself: this was once a living, thinking person. Everything that he knew about poetry, love, trees, Australia, television-all of it was contained in this small organ sitting in my hand.

The search for understanding of our nervous system is nothing less than the search for what makes us animate and human. If you want to find out what the professionals are up to, point your gopher to the *Society for Neuroscience* and take a look at their publications. Maybe you can find a clue to help you figure out a way to regenerate stem cells or a better method for using intracellular calcium buffers. If so, let us know and we will put your picture in the next edition of this book.

Software

Computers lighten your workload, if you have the right tools. The right tools are available, if you know where to look. There are many software sources for general biology or for more specific needs listed here.

Usenet:
Newsgroup: **bionet.software**
Newsgroup: **bionet.software.acedb**
Newsgroup: **bionet.software.gcg**
Newsgroup: **bionet.software.sources**
Newsgroup: **bit.listserv.info-gcg**

Taxacom FTP Server

Technical information, software, and information on standards, and workshops in the field of systematic biology.

Anonymous FTP:
Address: **huh.harvard.edu**
Path: **/pub/README.TAX**

Taxacom Listserv Lists

Taxacom Bitnet Listserv mailing lists focus on systematic biology and accept mail messages from any network source and then distribute those messages to list subscribers. The Listserv is capable of delivering mail to users on Bitnet, the Internet, or to any mail service on a gatewayed network. There are no restrictions on participation, and there is no cost.

Anonymous FTP:
Address: **huh.harvard.edu**
Path: **/pub/taxacom/taxacom.txt**

Tropical Biology

Imagine being on the beach, the wind whispering through your hair, sand between your toes — a scalpel in one hand, a mollusk in the other. What could be more beautiful? Experience the exotic essence of tropical biology with other people who think life is one long spring break. The only thing that could make it more interesting would be a drink with a little umbrella in it.

Usenet:
Newsgroup: **bionet.biology.tropical**

University of Minnesota Medical School

This web page provides access to various research projects, genome centers, the human brain project, and lots of other neat biological services.

World Wide Web:
URL: **http://lenti.med.umn.edu/**

Virology

Nobody likes to invite a virus to the party, but biologists have a knack for making virology appealing. Talk often turns speculative, as topics include such debatable issues as destroying the last remaining specimens of the smallpox virus or whether certain viruses are capable of cross-species infection.

Usenet:
Newsgroup: **bionet.virology**

Virtual Genome Center

Find out what's hot and what's not in the genome world. Software and applications are available as well as documentation and images of some very unusual yeast sequences.

World Wide Web:
URL: **http://alces.med.umn.edu/VGC.html**

A
B
C
D
E
F
G
H
I
J
K
L
M
N
O
P
Q
R
S
T
U
V
W
X
Y
Z

Who's Who in Biology

Who was that guy who wrote the article on yeast vector shuttles? If you are looking for someone particular in the field of biology, check here. While the Bionet is a small world, it covers a huge area. It has been said that you are only six people away from any person in the world. Try out this newsgroup and skip the five missing links.

Usenet:
Newsgroup: **bionet.users.addresses**

Whole Frog Project

The goal of the Whole Frog Project is to provide high school biology classes the ability to explore the anatomy of a frog by using data from high resolution MRI imagining and mechanical sectioning, together with 3-D surface and volume rendering software to visualize the anatomical structures of the original animal. Details about the project, including a technical report, mpeg and quicktime movies of a rotating transparent frog, examples, ftp archives, technique discussions, and more can be found here.

World Wide Web:
URL: **http://george.lbl.gov/ITG.hm.pg.docs/Whole.Frog/Whole.Frog.html**

Women in Biology

Women share why the field of biology is important to them. Discover gender-related issues and other concerns that are specifically tied to women in this career. This group is not just about science; it has that added touch of something special that only women can give.

Usenet:
Newsgroup: **bionet.women-in-bio**

**Parents and children,
take a look at:
Families and Parenting,
Kids, and Youth.**

Yale Peabody Museum of Natural History

A Museum of biodiversity and biological information with searches of Peabody collections for entomology, ichthyology, mammalogy, mineralogy, ornithology, paleobotany, zoology, and paleontology.

Gopher:
Name: Yale University, Peabody Museum of Natural History
Address: **gopher.peabody.yale.edu**

Yeast

Yeast is good for more than bread and beer. It's a fascinating, multiuseful mass of minute fungi. Find out what the molecular biology and genetics of yeast are all about. Maybe you'll even get some good recipes for bread and beer.

Usenet:
Newsgroup: **bionet.molbio.yeast**

Zebrafish Information Server

This Zebrafish web provides fish and aquarium tips from a collection of Internet databases.

World Wide Web:
URL: **http://zebra.scarolina.edu/**

BIZARRE

Aleister Crowley

Documents and texts by Aleister Crowley, including *Book 4*, *Magick Without Tears*, *Book of the Law*, *Magick in Theory and Practice*, and *Equinox*.

Anonymous FTP:
Address: **ftp.funet.fi**
Path: **/pub/doc/occult/occult/magick/magick/Crowley/***

Anonymity

Greta Garbo used to participate in this discussion group, but under a pseudonym. Want to be alone with other people? This is the place to be or not to be.

Usenet:
Newsgroup: **alt.anonymous**

Arcana Arcanorum

Arcana Arcanorum, the playing-card oracle, is a method of fortune telling using an ordinary deck of playing cards.

Anonymous FTP:
Address: **ftp.spies.com**
Path: **/Library/Document/arcana.doc**

Gopher:
Name: Internet Wiretap
Address: **wiretap.spies.com**
Choose: **Wiretap Online Library**
  Ι Assorted Documents
  Ι Arcana Arcanorum (Playing-Card Oracle)

Yes, the Internet is large, but there is only one biancaTroll and only one Smut Shack. From time to time we talk about risqué items in our books, but this is one web site that even we won't discuss in detail. Just check it out for yourself. (And don't tell anyone where you read about it.)

biancaTroll's Smut Shack

This will be a treat for all you voyeurs. Explore the rooms of biancaTroll's Smut Shack. Read and write graffiti on the walls of her bathroom, read her diary, flip through books on her shelves, explore her closet, talk to her troll, and otherwise put your nose where it doesn't belong.

World Wide Web:
URL: **http://bianca.com/shack/**

**Bored? Try Fun.
Still bored? Try Games.**

Bigfoot

I saw Bigfoot, the animal/man/monster, in K-Mart, reading *The Internet Complete Reference*. Immediately, I ran to share my experience with the people in this, my favorite Usenet newsgroup. Honest, it's true, I really saw him. (He was looking up archie servers.)

Usenet:
Newsgroup: **alt.bigfoot**

Bizarre General Discussion

The unusual, curious, and often stupid: here is Usenet's newsgroup for canonical strangeness. Just don't make the mistake of sending in an article that is not bizarre enough.

Usenet:
Newsgroup: **talk.bizarre**

Bizarre Literature

A mailing list devoted to bizarre, disturbing, and offensive short stories and ramblings, but not humor.

Listserv Mailing List:
List Address: **weird-l@brownvm.brown.edu**
Subscription Address:
  listserv@brownvm.brown.edu

Callahan's Bar

A home away from home: meet the regular patrons of Callahan's Bar, a virtual bar for real people. Friends, fellowship, good will, and bad puns.

Usenet:
Newsgroup: **alt.callahans**

Life can be tough.
Take a break at
Callahan's Bar

Cesium

How much can you say about the element cesium? You would be surprised — you *will* be surprised — when you join this discussion group: the group that proves that, truly, Usenet has something for everyone.

Usenet:
Newsgroup: **alt.cesium**

> ## Excerpt from the Net...
> ```
> Newsgroup: alt.cesium
> Subject: Cesium in water
>
> > What would happen if Cesium were to
> > be thrown into water?
> > Would it cause an explosion?
>
> No. In fact, it would not. It would
> just sit there like a lump of cesium
> thrown into water...which would then,
> of course, explode with the force of a
> billion suns. Don't try this at home,
> kids (unless your home happens to be in
> Jersey).
> ```

Church of the SubGenius

Find out about the Church of the SubGenius, Bob and his pipe, and slack. The Church of the SubGenius is a cult parody that sharply satirizes what's wrong with religion and society in general.

Anonymous FTP:
Address: **quartz.rutgers.edu**
Path: **/pub/subgenius/***

Gopher:
Name: Rutgers University
Address: **quartz.rutgers.edu**
Choose: **SubGenius-The Church of the SubGenius**

Usenet:
Newsgroup: **alt.slack**

Complaining

Welcome to the Usenet complaint department. Complain about anything you want and read other people's pet peeves. Just the thing to get you back in a good mood after reading **alt.good.morning**.

Usenet:
Newsgroup: **alt.peeves**

THE USENET COMPLAINT DEPARTMENT

We all need to complain. The trouble is, most of our complaints are heard only by people in our immediate vicinity. Much better to send your complaints to alt.peeves.

That way, anyone on the Internet will have a chance to find out what you think of parents who can't keep their kids quiet in public, or talk show hosts who swank around like they own the place.

Cryonics

We all have to go sometime, but maybe a lucky few will actually get to come back. Is it possible to have yourself frozen, in preparation for the time when unspecified future technology will be ready to bring you back to the future? If you are deadly serious about an encore, this is a newsgroup you will not want to miss. To start, read the frequently asked question list (available from the ftp site). Next, decide whether you should have your whole body frozen or just your head (neuropreservation). Why let yourself get carried away, when you can chill out?

Anonymous FTP:
Address: **rtfm.mit.edu**
Path: **/pub/usenet/news.answers/cryonics-faq/***

Usenet:
Newsgroup: **sci.cryonics**

> ## Got too much stuff?
> ## Need some more stuff?
> ## Try Buying and Selling.

Excerpt from the Net...

```
Newsgroup: sci.cryonics
Subject: Expiring minds want to know...

Neuropreservation is a form of cryonic
suspension in which only the patient's
head or brain is preserved. It clearly
is less expensive than whole-body
cryonic suspension. Being more compact,
the patient (normally) is more port-
able, too, enabling faster escape from
disaster. Furthermore, neuropatients ar-
guably can get better perfused brains
than whole-body patients, since the per-
fusion protocol can focus only on their
brains rather than all their other or-
gans, too. The most obvious disadvan-
tage of neuropreservation, however, is
the lack of a body.

At first glance, lacking a body sounds
like a fatal flaw in the plan...

Question sent to sci.cryonics:

> Do you have to be DEAD to have this
> done? Is there any way that I could
> have them do it to me when I'm 90 or
> so? And then specify to warm me back
> up in another 75 years?
```

Cult of the Dead Cow

Are you mad at the world? Do you have disdain for those who have any semblance of normal societal ties? Do you sit in your apartment with the blinds closed and think of new ways to cause discord? Join the Cult of the Dead Cow. Even if you don't care about any of that other stuff, they have a really cool ASCII logo.

See also: Cyberpunk

Anonymous FTP:
  Address: **ftp.eff.org**
  Path: **/pub/Publications/CuD/CDC/***

Gopher:
  Name: Electronic Frontier Foundation
  Address: **gopher.eff.org**
  Choose: **Publications**
    | **CuD**
    | **CDC**

Dark Side of the Net

A list of gothic, vampire, occult, and various other dark resources; including IRC channels, mailing lists, ftp sites, Usenet newsgroups, and e-zines. To subscribe, send mail to the address below. In addition, this list is posted regularly to the **alt.gothic** and **news.lists** newsgroups.

Mail:
  Address: **carriec@eskimo.com**
  Body: **subscribe dark side** *yourname@host*

Devilbunnies

What are these devilbunnies? Tiny little creatures that seem to pop up everywhere and make the best laid plans of mice and men gang aft agley. Are they real, or figments of warped imaginations that have spent too long glued to the computer? Tune in for the latest update on the spiritual descendants of the gremlins of World War II.

Usenet:
  Newsgroup: **alt.devilbunnies**

Discord and Destruction

Serious talk about serious talk. Destroy the earth or just our way of life: it's up to you. Remember, life is stern and earnest and nobody gets out of here alive.

Usenet:
  Newsgroup: **alt.destroy.the.earth**
  Newsgroup: **alt.discordia**

Explosions and Blowing Things Up

Okay, we know it sounds weird, but we all have a primal urge to blow things up. Well, guys do, anyway. Well, some guys. Okay, so we like things that go boom in the night. Check out Usenet's answer to the big bang. (Kibo, of course, is just along for the ride.)

Usenet:
  Newsgroup: **alt.exploding.kibo**

Fiction Therapy Group

Spin bizarre tales of adventure, romance, mystery. Get your hero into a terrible mess and leave the story sitting for someone else to figure out a way to get him out of it, preferably alive. Random people create surreal scenarios, taking turns bringing stories to life.

World Wide Web:
  URL: **http://www.galcit.caltech.edu/**
    ~ta/fiction/fiction.html

A
B
C
D
E
F
G
H
I
J
K
L
M
N
O
P
Q
R
S
T
U
V
W
X
Y
Z

Furry Animals

Whether live or stuffed, there's something about small furry animals that brings out the latent anthropomorphism in us all. They are just too cute for words, so we won't even try.

Usenet:
Newsgroup: **alt.fan.furry**

Future Culture Digest Archives

Collection of archives for the Future Culture mailing list, which brings tomorrow's reality today, including the Future Culture and **alt.cyberpunk** FAQs.

Anonymous FTP:
Address: **ftp.cic.net**
Path: **/pub/e-serials/alphabetic/f/future-culture/***

Gateway to Darkness

A collection of sounds, images, text, and other links to the gothic genre and other places of darkness on the Internet.

World Wide Web:
URL: **http://coe1.engr.umbc.edu/~vijay2/ home.html**

Geeks and Nerds

Remember, if it weren't for geeks and nerds, there wouldn't be an Internet (and you wouldn't be able to read this totally cool Internet book). Pay tribute to these unsung heroes of the *Star Trek* generation. Join Usenet's own mutual admiration society: take a nerd to lunch today.

Usenet:
Newsgroup: **alt.geek**

Excerpt from the Net...

```
Newsgroups: alt.geek
Subject: Excitement, nerd-style


Hey guys, am I the only one this
happens to?


I get excited when I see a female
logged on our system very very late on
a Friday night!  It's even cooler when
she and I are the only ones logged on
the system :)
```

Excerpt from the Net...

```
Newsgroup: alt.geek
Subject: What the well-dressed geek is wearing
```

While we are discussing various facets of geek paraphernalia, I just wanted to mention something which *seems* to be becoming extinct: horned-rim glasses.

As I mentioned before, I'm only 14; but I have a NIFTY pair of horned-rim glasses straight out of any high school picture from 1964. I don't know about you, but I think extra-thick horned-rims are a classic geek symbol. Maybe I'm wrong. However, they look pretty good with tape.

My grandpa bestowed me his leather slide-rule case. I don't wear it much anymore because I tend to use my graphics calculator and my palmtop a bit more. I don't have a holster for my calc, but I do have a clip (which I'm sure is not as good). My palmtop, on the other hand, is a different story. I can't find anything with which I can attach it to my belt.

Regarding pocket-protectors. I agree with what someone said earlier: you should only wear them to suit a cause. Any other reason would be stupid and (dare I say it) rather superficial. If you like to have your pens and screwdrivers at hand like I do, then a protector is a good idea. I have a day-glo neon yellow protector that says "Kiss me, I'm a Physicist". Of course, I'm not a physicist, but a friend of mine who works at a research lab gave it to me.

Gross and Disgusting

Tales to make you cringe, poems to offend you, and bets you wouldn't believe, all utterly tasteless!

Anonymous FTP:
    Address: **ftp.spies.com**
    Path: **/Library/Fringe/Gross/***

Gopher:
    Name: Internet Wiretap
    Address: **wiretap.spies.com**
    Choose: **Wiretap Online Library**
    | **Fringes of Reason**
    | **Gross and Disgusting**

Happy Birthday

Wish yourself a happy birthday and see if anyone cares. Gather round for birthday greetings from all over the world in this once-a-year newsgroup for everybody. In case you are wondering: Harley's birthday is December 21 and Rick's is October 9. (And money is always in good taste.)

Usenet:
    Newsgroup: **alt.happy.birthday.to.me**

High Weirdness

Incredible collection of information and lists, telling you where to locate the more esoteric and weird resources on the Internet.

Anonymous FTP:
    Address: **slopoke.mlb.semi.harris.com**
    Path: **/pub/weirdness/weird***

HyperDiscordia

This is the leading source for confusion, chaos, and discord. Intone the reverent "Hail Eris!" and you will be welcome here. If you are looking for a little peace and quiet, walk quickly away from this site.

World Wide Web:
    URL: **http://vaxa.stevens-tech.edu:8000/jofo/
    hyperdiscordia.html**

The Net is cool because YOU are cool.

Jihad to Destroy Barney on the Web

Not everyone feels that Barney is a lovable dinosaur. In fact, there is a group that insists he is responsible for subversive mind control techniques being used on today's youth. The Jihad has put together a collection of FAQs, their basic beliefs and terminology, lists of the Original Sponge Minions (read "bad guys") and lists of the members of the Jihad (read "good guys"), parodies, stories, insults, Barney trivia, and an occasional thoughtful and reasonable article.

World Wide Web:
    URL: **http://sdeeptht.armory.com/~deadslug/
    Jihad/jihad.html**

Lemurs

What is it that makes these monkey-like mammals from Madagascar so adorably desirable? Serious lemur-lovers hang out in the **.lemurs** group. Those who prefer their lemurs broiled with a touch of paprika will be more at home in **lemurs.cooked**.

Usenet:
    Newsgroup: **alt.fan.lemurs**
    Newsgroup: **alt.fan.lemurs.cooked**

Lips

Some people like legs, some people are fascinated by eyes. View this person's lip obsession: a collection of the lips of many famous statues of Europe.

World Wide Web:
    URL: **http://oz.sas.upenn.edu/lynn/lips/lips.html**

Ludvigsen Residence — A Family Server

This web server in Loshavn, Norway, is a bit different from any other you are likely to encounter. Here, in addition to a wide variety of Internet services, you can actually meet the members of the family who run the server! There is video tape of their house, pets, and Loshavn, and a guestbook of visitors who can leave postcards.

World Wide Web:
    URL: **http://www.ludvigsen.dhhalden.no/**

A
B
C
D
E
F
G
H
I
J
K
L
M
N
O
P
Q
R
S
T
U
V
W
X
Y
Z

Lunch Servers

This is perfect for those really busy times when you're stuck in the office and you don't have time to do much more than cram a sandwich into your mouth before you have to get back to work. That doesn't leave much time to cultivate a good social atmosphere in the staff lunchroom. Now you can experience lunch with another person on the Web. See what other people are having for lunch, including pictures, descriptions, and perhaps even some live video. It's almost as good as the real thing.

World Wide Web:
>URL: **http://grissom.larc.nasa.gov/misc/lunchserver.html**
>URL: **http://hp8.ini.cmu.edu:5550/lunch.html**
>URL: **http://oz.sas.upenn.edu/miscellany/lunch.html**
>URL: **http://physics.purdue.edu/~sho/lunch_main.html**
>URL: **http://speckle.ncsl.nist.gov/greg-bin/lunch**

Mkzdk

Techno-shamanic digital art, ambient world trance dance music, scientific visualization, cosmology, trance-mutation playlists, and interesting meta-news, such as an article on the discovery of the largest structure in the universe.

World Wide Web:
>URL: **http://www.nets.com/site/mkzdk/mkzdk.html**

Naked Guy

Andy Martinez is a man of conviction. In order to make a point, he started coming to class at U.C. Berkeley dressed only in a small loincloth and, eventually, completely naked. Well, Martinez — now affectionately known as The Naked Guy — got thrown out, but he did make his point (at least in the summer). Read this newsgroup and follow the career of one who, arguably, can be described as the best man.

Usenet:
>Newsgroup: **alt.fan.naked-guy**

The Net is for smart people (like you).

Necromicon

This is a multipurpose group, whether it started out that way or not. Necromicon literally translates to "The Book of Dead Mice" and is a spoof on *The Necronomicon*, which is a handbook for people who make a hobby of using dead people as a means of divination. If either of these topics appeals to you, pull up a keyboard and get in on the conversation. This is as lively as the dead get.

See also: Paranormal

Usenet:
>Newsgroup: **alt.necromicon**

Negative Emotions

Angst, bitterness, misanthropy, fear, disgust, anxiety, and just plain being in a bad mood. Join the folks down at the not-OK corral for some roll-up-your-sleeves-and-get-down-to-it homestyle bitchin'. As John Milton put it (when they took away his Internet account), "So little is our loss. So little is our gain."

Usenet:
>Newsgroup: **alt.angst**
>Newsgroup: **alt.bitterness**
>Newsgroup: **alt.misanthropy**

Pantyhose

We know a newsgroup devoted to pantyhose sounds a little strange, but, after all, you have to admit that there is something about long, sensuous legs wrapped in sheer black stockings that will turn even the most dignified gentleman into a wild jungle cat with the morals of a U.S. senator. Check out the ftp site too.

Anonymous FTP:
>Address: **alycia.andrew.cmu.edu**
>Path: **/pub/graphics/over_age_18_only/hosiery/***

Internet Relay Chat:
>Channel: **#pantyhose**

Usenet:
>Newsgroup: **alt.pantyhose**

Paving the Earth

Have you ever wondered what it would be like to pave the Earth? No more grass to stain your white pants, no more insects to eat your picnic food, no more dirt on your new sneakers. Just imagine everything nice and smooth and hard. Seriously. (Do you think we make this stuff up?)

Usenet:
>Newsgroup: **alt.pave.the.earth**

Too much spare time? Explore a MUD.

Porter List

High Weirdness by mail — some very interesting lists and mail addresses you can use to get bizarre and esoteric information. Find the home of the Church of Spam, subscribe to *Moot News for Modern Man*, or find out where you can get Paul Spinrad's *Bodily Functions Survey* covering nasal hygiene, vomiting, urination, defecation, and flatus expulsion. (Whew, what a relief it is that this entry is done.)

Anonymous FTP:
    Address: **nexus.yorku.ca**
    Path: **/pub/Internet-info/high-weirdness**

Positive Emotions

As if there isn't enough to deal with already, here are newsgroups devoted to good feelings and happiness. Bah, humbug. If God had wanted us to hear good news, he wouldn't have given us television and newscasters with bad toupees. And most sickening of all has to be the **.good.morning** group: people from all over the world, wishing each other a good morning. As Butthead says: "I don't like stuff that sucks."

Usenet:
    Newsgroup: **alt.good.morning**
    Newsgroup: **alt.good.news**
    Newsgroup: **alt.hi.are.you.cute**
    Newsgroup: **clari.news.goodnews**

Excerpt from the Net...

```
Newsgroup: alt.hi.are.you.cute
Subject: A Cute Thing at Disney!

Today I did a temp assignment working
at the reception desk at Disney Studios.
Today the man and woman who do the
voices for Mickey and Minnie Mouse
came in and entertained us with some
samples of their vocal talents.
But the cutest thing is that they
are married to each other.  They met
while doing the voices of Mickey
and Minnie, and fell in love...
I think that is so cute!
```

Profanity and Insult Server

For those of you who just like to be insulted, are looking for a new pack of insults, or just want to leave some insults of your own behind, the Profanity and Insult Server is for you! Be warned, however, that it is not for everyone. You may be offended!

World Wide Web:
    URL: **http://www.scrg.cs.tcd.ie/cgi-bin/profanity**

Roadkill R Us

Get the going prices for roadkill and find out what makes or breaks a good roadkill sale — bloat, availability, and completeness of parts. Roadkill news, history of the Roadkill R Us corporation and an occasional recipe.

World Wide Web:
    URL: **http://hostname.pencom.com/rru.html**

Roommates from Hell

Next time your roommate borrows your girlfriend without asking, count yourself lucky. Tune in to the roommate version of "Can You Top This?" and it won't be long before you realize that some people have *real* trouble.

Usenet:
    Newsgroup: **alt.flame.roommate**

Rumors

Check out all the new rumors, both serious (Elvis and aliens) and less serious (the FBI and CIA). Did you know that readers of this book are entitled to free admission to Disney World?

Usenet:
    Newsgroup: **talk.rumors**

Santa Claus

Ho! Ho! Ho! Santa is real. Search your hearts for the truth; celebrate the magic of the Christmas season by joining in with other devout Santa believers. Just don't forget to be good for goodness sake.

Usenet:
    Newsgroup: **alt.religion.santaism**

Schizophrenia Nervosa

Tour this "maze" called The Low Road, which takes you on a grim tour of one man's idea of a mental hospital. Links in the text take you to different parts of the hospital and by the time you get through, you will be inspired to act sane, even if you aren't.

World Wide Web:
    URL: **http://www.rpi.edu/~pier1/lowroad.html**

A B C D E F G H I J K L M N O P Q R S T U V W X Y Z

Social Deviants

It's a great deal of hard work to be normal, and not everyone is up to the strain. As long as you are not involved, it's fun to read about bizarre, disgusting, and socially unacceptable acts by people who simply do not have all of their eggs in one basket. Check out the rantings, ravings, news, and theories on cults, freaks, criminals, and other social deviants.

Internet Mailing List:
List Address: **deviants@csv.warwick.ac.uk**
Subscription Address:
deviants-request@csv.warwick.ac.uk

Somerville Stories

A collection of short stories by Thomas Colthurst written for the newsgroup **talk.bizarre**. Includes such titles as "Conversation with an Ex-Girlfriend," "Mirror Mirror," "The Social Psychology of Dragon Hoards," "Initiation," and many more ordered by character, chronological order, subject, and title.

World Wide Web:
URL: **http://www.mit.edu:8001/afs/ athena.mit.edu/user/t/h/thomasc/Public/ stories/stories.html**

Stories by RICHH

These quick, little stories will make you look at the world differently. Or at least Norway. The stories are randomly chosen, so it is unpredictable which story you will get to read. To get the gopher to randomize, you must go up one menu level then back down and re-select Random Stories. The web page has pointers to the complete collection of RICHH stories.

See also: Humor, Fun

Gopher:
Name: University of Trondheim, Norway
Address: **gopher.nvg.unit.no**
Choose: **Help, I don't know a single word in Norwegian**
 I Humor and other Exciting Stuff
 I Random Stories by RICHH

World Wide Web:
URL: **http://www.mit.edu:8001/afs/ athena.mit.edu/user/t/h/thomasc/Public/ richh/richh.html**

Strange Rantings

Rantings and ravings about a number of topics including the Dead Sea Scrolls, the Holocaust, the Waco siege, and other topics.

Anonymous FTP:
Address: **ftp.std.com**
Path: **/obi/Rants/***

Address: **ftp.uu.net**
Path: **/doc/literary/obi/Rants/***

Strange Tales

A collection of weird articles; subjects include hedgehog songs, recursive storytelling, the Kloo Gnomes, and other strange tales.

Anonymous FTP:
Address: **ftp.spies.com**
Path: **/Library/Fringe/Weird/***

Gopher:
Name: Internet Wiretap
Address: **wiretap.spies.com**
Choose: **Wiretap Online Library**
 I Fringes of Reason
 I Very Strange

Swedish Chef

Remember that lovable Swedish chef on the Muppets? The one who would chase little chickens with a meat cleaver, talk with a Swedish accent, and say "Bork, bork, bork"? Well, he is alive and well on the Internet. Read this newsgroup and find out how to get the encheferizer program: software to turn regular English text into a speech from the Swedish chef. Und noo, buys und gurls, ve-a veell leern hoo tu cuuk cheeckees. Bork bork bork!

Usenet:
Newsgroup: **alt.swedish.chef.bork.bork.bork**

Talk.Bizarre Web Page Thing

Meet the readers and writers from the newsgroup **talk.bizarre** through this page of links to their home pages. Mail **page@cs.odu.edu** with your web address to be added, but no lurkers need apply.

World Wide Web:
URL: **http://sunsite.unc.edu/boutell/tb/tb.html**

Tapestry

The Tapestry is a place for exploration, a place for you to learn about things you've never heard before, a place for you to renew that which you already know. It contains many articles and links about the occult, the spiritual, and the bizarre.

See also: Paranormal

World Wide Web:
URL: **http://io.com/user/blade/tapestry.html**

Tasteless Tales

Dozens of the best tales from the Usenet group **alt.tasteless** divided into anecdote, prank, tasteless fact, and art sections.

Anonymous FTP:
Address: **ftp.spies.com**
Path: **/Library/Fringe/Gross/tasteles.92**

Gopher:
Name: Internet Wiretap
Address: **wiretap.spies.com**
Choose: **Wiretap Online Library**
 l **Fringes of Reason**
 l **Gross and Disgusting**
 l **Alt.Tasteless 26 Best of 1992**

Tasteless Topics

All that is tasteless. Say whatever you want: just make sure it is disgusting. This is not the place to bring your grandmother for her birthday.

Usenet:
Newsgroup: **alt.tasteless**

Three-Letter Acronyms

Join the only worldwide discussion group devoted to three-letter acronyms and extended three-letter acronyms. FYI, IMHO, you will love TLAs and ETLAs. (Don't forget to RTFM in order to CYA.)

Usenet:
Newsgroup: **alt.tla**

Unplastic News

An electronic magazine devoted to the aberrant, bizarre, and preposterous, containing weird and humorous quotes from the computer undergound.

Anonymous FTP:
Address: **etext.archive.umich.edu**
Path: **/pub/Zines/Unplastic_News**

Vampire Chat Channel

Do you feel like you need to liven up your night life? Drop into the **#vampire** IRC channel and see what everyone else does between dusk and dawn.

Internet Relay Chat:
Channel: **#vampire**

BOATING AND SAILING

Boating Discussion Groups

Moving on water, how basic a feeling it invokes within us. Join the boating crowd and discuss all aspects of things that float. The **.paddle** newsgroup is specifically for canoes, rowboats, and so on.

Usenet:
Newsgroup: **rec.boats**
Newsgroup: **rec.boats.paddle**

Boating Web Server

This web server has links to information on boating mailing lists, Usenet groups, other web servers with boating resources, a charter boat directory, and classified ads for boats.

World Wide Web:
URL: **http://www.recreation.com/boating/**
URL: **http://www.recreation.com:80/boats/**

Decavitator

Decavitator is a human-powered hydrofoil which attained a world-record speed of 18.5 knots in 1991, and which won the DuPont prize for human-powered water speed. This web page offers background information, a history of the project, time line, specifications, descriptions of the methods and materials used in the project, gif images, mpeg video segments, a bibliography, and more.

World Wide Web:
URL: **http://lancet.mit.edu:80/decavitator/**

Marine Signal Flags

A collection of the international maritime signal flags. Ships at sea use signal flags to spell out short messages or to communicate speeds and course changes. This page shows alphabetic flags, answering pennants, numeric pennants, substitute pennants, and the semaphore flag waving system.

World Wide Web:
URL: **http://155.187.10.12/flags/signal-flags.html**

Paddling Web Server

This server has information about paddling sports, including canoeing, kayaking, and rafting. It offers plan and kit sources, paddling classifieds, paddling clubs and associations details, publications, magazines, newsletters, a manufacturer directory, mailing lists, newsgroup FAQs and a list of whitewater outfitters and dealers.

World Wide Web:
URL: **http://www.recreation.com/paddling/home.html**

River and Rowing Museum

This page gives details of the River and Rowing Museum at Henley, England, and offers rowing-related resources, including links to a rowing page, a fishing page, a map of the U.K. with rivers, and thoughts on a virtual reality rowing machine.

World Wide Web:
URL: **http://www.comlab.ox.ac.uk/archive/other/museums/rowing.html**

Sailing

Experience the freedom and grace of operating a traditional sailing vessel. Just you and your ship against the wind and water. When they are not on the sea, sailors hang out on this mailing list to discuss experiences and techniques relating to owning and managing sailing vessels.

Listserv Mailing List:
List Address: **tallship@vccscent.bitnet**
Subscription Address: **listserv@vccscent.bitnet**

Sailing Laser Boats

Information on sailing laser boats, including newsletters, race results, an ftp server, regatta guidelines, and mailing lists.

World Wide Web:
URL: **http://www.law.indiana.edu/misc/laser.html**

Sailing Mailing List

A typical sailing fantasy is being on a well-crafted yacht while healthy winds snap the sails, sending you cruising toward paradise as you relax and drink an umbrella-adorned beverage. But this is not a typical sailing list. These sailors want to go fast. Primary topics for discussion are racing, regattas, and high performance sailing vessels. If they could burn rubber, they would.

Listserv Mailing List:
List Address: **sailing-l@cornell.edu**
Subscription Address: **listserv@cornell.edu**

Sailing Page

The sailing page has answers to frequently asked questions about sailing, sailing movies, a link to the Usenet group **rec.boats**, tidbits, mailing lists, and information about sailing opportunities, sailing texts, maritime museums online, and other sailing resources.

World Wide Web:
URL: **http://community.bellcore.com/mbr/sailing-page.html**

BOOKS

Alternative History

What would happen if...? People love the concept of taking history and twisting and turning it, trying to imagine how things might be different today if one little thing were changed way-back-when. For example, if there had never been an Internet, you might be out discovering an important cure for writer's cramp right now. See this gigantic list of books that have alternative history as a common denominator.

Anonymous FTP:
Address: **rtfm.mit.edu**
Path: **/pub/usenet/news.answers/sf/alt_history/part***

**Need Unix help?
See Harley's book
"Unix Unbound."**

Book FAQs and Info

FAQs about books, list of bookstores, bibliography of quotation compilations, list of recommended Unix books, book reviews, and reading lists.

Anonymous FTP:
Address: **quartz.rutgers.edu**
Path: **/pub/books/***

Gopher:
Name: Rutgers University
Address: **quartz.rutgers.edu**
Choose: **Book FAQs and Info**

Book and Publishing News

Find out the real news on books and the publishing industry. What's hot off the press, and which Internet book by Hahn and Stout is on the bestseller list?

Usenet:
Newsgroup: **clari.news.books**

Book Reviews

Why waste your time and money on an unrewarding book? Read the reviews in this newsgroup and find out the real scoop before you make a serious commitment. Save your excess time and money for unrewarding people. The Usenet newsgroup is for ongoing discussion and current reviews. To take a look at previous reviews, use the gopher reference, or download reviews by anonymous ftp.

Anonymous FTP:
Address: **csn.org**
Path: **/pub/alt.books.reviews/***

Gopher:
Name: Whole Earth Lectronic Link
Address: **gopher.well.sf.ca.us**
Choose: **Whole Earth Review, the Magazine**
  | Book Reviews

Usenet:
Newsgroup: **alt.books.reviews**

Book Stacks Unlimited

An online bookstore and reader's conference system that allows you to search for books by author or title, or just browse by subject.

Telnet:
Address: **books.com**
Login: RETURN

Books General Discussion

A good place to find a variety of information about books. This newsgroup covers books of all genres, including reviews and discussion of reviews. This is a fairly free forum provided you know something about your topic. Moreover, talk is not limited to books: there is much discussion of the publishing industry as well as requests for information on interesting bookstores and hard-to-find bargains.

Usenet:
Newsgroup: **rec.arts.books**

Books Online

Page after page of books. This site has local books, as well as links to mirror sites. Each title indicates whether it is local or not and whether it is plain text or hypertext.

Note: These pages are searchable by title or author depending on the address you use.

World Wide Web:
URL: **http://www.cs.cmu.edu:8001/Web/ bookauthors.html**

URL: **http://www.cs.cmu.edu:8001/Web/ booktitles.html**

Bookstore Reviews

Reviews and interesting information about bookstores, from the motif of the store to ratings on salespeople. These reviews are done by book buffs, and their works are compiled and categorized by region and city on this gopher server.

Anonymous FTP:
Address: **rtfm.mit.edu**
Path: **/pub/usenet/news.answers/books/stores/***

Gopher:
Name: University of Minnesota
Address: **gopher.micro.umn.edu**
Choose: **Fun & Games**
  | Games
  | Bookstores

Buying and Selling Books

Get a piece of the buying and selling action. See what's hot and what's not. Book reviews and business news make up the bulk of the traffic in this newsgroup.

Usenet:
Newsgroup: **biz.books.technical**
Newsgroup: **rec.arts.books.marketplace**

A
B
C
D
E
F
G
H
I
J
K
L
M
N
O
P
Q
R
S
T
U
V
W
X
Y
Z

Computer Books

Offers news, book descriptions, lists, and ordering information for publications from O'Reilly & Associates.

Gopher:
Name: O'Reilly & Associates
Address: **ora.com**

Doomsday Brunette

This is a fun interactive book. It's a futuristic mystery complete with a detective. Read the book from a realistic point of view, from the detective's point of view, or switch back and forth. Select the hero's actions and be responsible for the outcome. A three-chapter demo is available, but the rest is shareware.

Gopher:
Name: The Doomsday Brunette
Address: **zeb.nysaes.cornell.edu**

World Wide Web:
URL: **http://zeb.nysaes.cornell.edu/CGI/ddb/demo.cgi**

If you are one of those people who likes to switch, take a look at *The Doomsday Brunette*. As you read this detective story, you can jump back and forth from one point of view to another. (Rumor has it that the author used to be a speechwriter for Bill Clinton.) The first few chapters are free, after that you need to pay. (Now we know that the author used to work for Clinton.)

Electronic Books at Wiretap

A huge index of full-length electronic books on the Internet Wiretap gopher and ftp site.

Anonymous FTP:
Address: **ftp.spies.com**
Path: **/Library/Classic/***

Gopher:
Name: Internet Wiretap
Address: **wiretap.spies.com**
Choose: **Electronic Books at Wiretap**

Etext Resources

Access to many gophers and archives around the world offering various electronic books and online texts.

Gopher:
Name: Internet Wiretap
Address: **wiretap.spies.com**
Choose: **Various ETEXT Resources on the Internet**

Internet Book Information Center

A huge selection of book information, including Internet book resources, newsgroups, authors, publishers, booksellers, libraries, online books, book reviews, and a reference shelf. Also available is "The Commonplace Book" which is an interesting collection of thought-provoking excerpts that people have transcribed.

See also: Literature, Publishing

Anonymous FTP:
Address: **sunsite.unc.edu**
Path: **/pub/electronic-publications/ibic/***

Gopher:
Name: University of North Carolina
Address: **sunsite.unc.edu**
Choose: **Worlds of SunSITE — by Subject | The Internet Book Information Center...**

World Wide Web:
URL: **http://sunsite.unc.edu/ibic/IBIC-homepage.html**

Book lovers: Have you seen the
Internet Book Information Center?

Internet Books

A list of recommended Internet books with a short comment, ISBN number, and price for each.

Anonymous FTP:
Address: **nysernet.org**
Path: **/pub/guides/surfing.***

Gopher:
Name: NYSERNet
Address: **nysernet.org**
Choose: **Special Collections: Internet Help
| Good Books about the Internet**

Internet Books List

An Internet RFC (1432), containing a list of books related to using the Internet, divided into category types.

Anonymous FTP:
Address: **athos.rutgers.edu**
Path: **/rfc/rfc1432.txt**

Address: **ftp.denet.dk**
Path: **/pub/rfc/rfc1432.txt**

Address: **sunsite.unc.edu**
Path: **/pub/docs/rfc/rfc1432.txt**

Archie:
Pattern: **rfc1432.txt**

Gopher:
Name: NYSERNet
Address: **nysernet.org**
Choose: **Special Collections: Internet Help
| Internet Books**

Microsoft Windows 3.1 Book List

A list of books about Microsoft Windows 3.1 covering topics ranging from those of interest to beginners, to programming for Windows.

Anonymous FTP:
Address: **sunsite.unc.edu**
Path: **/pub/UNC-info/IAT/guides/irg-09.txt**

O'Reilly & Associates

News, book descriptions and information, a complete listing of book titles, online indexes, instructions on obtaining book samples and archives.

Anonymous FTP:
Address: **ftp.ora.com**
Path: **/pub**

Gopher:
Name: O'Reilly & Associates
Address: **ora.com**
Choose: **Book & Tape Descriptions**

O'Reilly Book Samples

Sample text from many of the computer books published by O'Reilly & Associates.

Anonymous FTP:
Address: **ftp.uu.net**
Path: **/published/oreilly**

Need a good book?
"The Internet Complete Reference"
is the best.
Need another book?
Try the **NYSERNet gopher.**

Online Book Initiative

The Online Book Initiative offers freely redistributable collections of information such as books, journals, catalogs, magazines, manuals, and maps. The **obi** list is for general discussion and the **obi-announce** group is for announcements.

Gopher:
Name: Software Tool & Die
Address: **gopher.std.com**
Choose: **OBI The Online Book Initiative**

Internet Mailing List:
List Address: **obi@world.std.com**
Subscription Address: **obi-request@world.std.com**

List Address: **obi-announce@world.std.com**
Subscription Address:
obi-announce-requests@world.std.com

A
B
C
D
E
F
G
H
I
J
K
L
M
N
O
P
Q
R
S
T
U
V
W
X
Y
Z

Free Books

There is a lot to read on the Internet. Many well-known (and not so well-known) books are available to you to download from the Online Book Initiative.

Snarf a couple for yourself and spend tonight cuddled up with a warm display screen. Moreover, since the text is stored electronically, you can make changes. . .

Think what you can do with Albert Hoffman's story of how he discovered LSD, or Conan Doyle's Sherlock Holmes tales. This time, you can let Moriarty win.

Online Bookstore

An online bookstore that carries computer and other books. Mail for more information. Order extra copies of *this* book for all your friends.

Mail:
Address: **obs@tic.com**

Pulp Fiction

Pulp magazines existed in America from the turn of the century to the early 1950s. They offered an impressive array of stories about crime, mystery, detectives, war, love, romance, science fiction, horror, sports, westerns, and adventure. The spirit of pulp fiction is alive today in modern paperback adventure series and in this Usenet newsgroup. Did you know that the Shadow was really Kent Allard, a World War I ace and spy? Lamont Cranston was merely a disguise. If you listen to the radio show, you will be misinformed, but if you read this newsgroup, you will know the truth.

Usenet:
Newsgroup: **alt.pulp**

Spare time? Take a look at Games

Rare Books

People always want what they can't have. If it's rare, it's bound to be popular. Take rare books, for example. People collect them, and most of the time they just store the books and never look at them. Join the forum where the topic for discussion is rare book and manuscript librarianship along with special collections issues. Anyone can subscribe, but most of the membership consists of those librarians who wear the little white gloves when they work.

See also: Libraries

Listserv Mailing List:
List Address: **exlibris@rutvm1.rutgers.edu**
Subscription Address: **listserv@rutvm1.rutgers.edu**

Reviews of Children's Books

See what's hot and what's not in the world of children's books. Read this wide selection of reviews, not only on books for kids, but also books about kids.

World Wide Web:
URL: **file://ftp.armory.com/pub/user/web**

Roswell Internet Computer Bookstore

An online computer bookstore devoted exclusively to computer books, with a database listing over 7,000 titles. Browse the list by subject or search by author, title, or ISBN.

Gopher:
Name: Nova Scotia Technology Network
Address: **gopher.nstn.ca**
Choose: **CyberMall | Bookstores | Roswell Internet Computer Books**

World Wide Web:
URL: **http://www.nstn.ca/cybermall/roswell/roswell.html**

Science Fiction Reviews

This is the place to find reviews of your favorite (or not so favorite) books, magazines, movies, and videos. Although the name implies science fiction only, you will also find speculative fiction, fantasy, horror, and even (sometimes) comics. This group is moderated.

Usenet:
Newsgroup: **rec.arts.sf.reviews**

Technical Books

If you have a squeak in your clicker or you can't get slot A to line up with tab B, check into this newsgroup to see if there is a technical book that can help. Just the place to look when you need to decide which Unix book to give your grandmother for her birthday.

Usenet:
> Newsgroup: **alt.books.technical**
> Newsgroup: **misc.books.technical**

Travels with Samantha

Philip Greenspun writes of his travels across North America. Images are included. This is a 19-chapter travelogue complete with a slide show, maps and photo tips.

World Wide Web:
> URL: **http://www-swiss.ai.mit.edu/ samantha/travels-with-samantha.htm**

Unix Book Lists

A bibliography of some of the best books and documentation on Unix, the C programming languages, and other related areas.

Anonymous FTP:
> Address: **ftp.rahul.net**
> Path: **/pub/mitch/YABL/**
>
> Address: **rtfm.mit.edu**
> Path: **/pub/usenet/news.answers/books**
>
> Address: **ucselx.sdsu.edu**
> Path: **/pub/doc/general/Unix-C-Booklist**

Gopher:
> Name: O'Reilly & Associates
> Address: **ora.com**
> Choose: **Bibliographies**

> # Planning a picnic? Check the weather using the Net.

Unofficial Internet Book List

According to Kevin Savetz, this list is "the most extensive bibliography of books about the Internet" and we believe it. Actually, it's more than just a list — Savetz does concise and interesting (and accurate) reviews of each of the books in his list. How do we know his reviews are accurate? Because he says we've done *The Internet Golden Directory* right!

Anonymous FTP:
> Address: **rtfm.mit.edu**
> Path: **/pub/usenet/news.answers/ internet-services/book-list**

Mail:
> Address: **savetz@rahul.net**
> Subject: **subscribe booklist**

BOTANY

Agroforestry

As the population grows, the need for better crops and soil increases. Agroforestry studies plant growth and nutrition in an effort to find crops and soil that are compatible with each other and with the rest of the surrounding environment.

Usenet:
> Newsgroup: **bionet.agroforestry**

Australian National Botanic Gardens

It's not every day that most of us (or any of us) get to stroll through the botanic gardens in Australia. Via the Web, you can see what flowers are in bloom this week and learn about the plants, frogs and birds of the gardens. For those who are more technical and managerial, there are many things labeled in Latin, in addition to plans of management and fire emergency procedures.

World Wide Web:
> URL: **http://155.187.10.12/anbg.html**

Botanical Gardens at the University of Delaware

A hypermedia map which allows you to click on various botanical gardens that you would like to visit.

World Wide Web:
> URL: **http://indri.cns.udel.edu/udgarden.html**

A B C D E F G H I J K L M N O P Q R S T U V W X Y Z

Botany Database

A database of nearly 100,000 records in the Type Specimen Register for the U.S. National Herbarium.

Gopher:
> Name: Smithsonian Institution
> Address: **smithson.si.edu**
> Choose: **Department of Botany at the Smithsonian Institution**

Bromeliaceae

There's little that would be more alarming than jumping into bed on a cold night and finding a bromeliaceae under the covers. But it doesn't have to happen, not if you take the time to educate yourself. Taxonomy, phylogeny and evolution, culture and ethnobotany of the Bromeliaceae plant family are just a few of the things discussed on this mailing list.

Listserv Mailing List:
> List Address: **brom-l@ftpt.br**
> Subscription Address: **listserv@ftpt.br**

Carnivorous Plants

It has been said that people should stick to eating vegetables because it's not polite to eat animals. But here is a group of plants that put a new kink in that argument. Carnivorous plants are a whole new reason to eat more vegetables: eat or be eaten. Learn about cultivation, field observation, and make some connections to trade plants and offer or obtain advice. The information you get on this list could one day save your life.

Listserv Mailing List:
> List Address: **cp@opus.hpl.hp.com**
> Subscription Address: **listserv@opus.hpl.hp.com**

> List Address: **cp@hpl-opus.hpl.hp.com**
> Subscription Address:
> **listserv@hpl-opus.hpl.hp.com**

Chlamydomonas

Chlamydomonas reproduces faster than that blue fuzzy stuff in the refrigerator. Learn about this happy little algae as it works its way through life making a pest of itself with neighboring filtration plants.

Usenet:
> Newsgroup: **bionet.chlamydomonas**

Endangered Australian Flora and Fauna

A guide to endangered Australian plants and animals. The lists include other vulnerable and already extinct species.

Gopher:
> Name: Australian Environmental Resources Information Network
> Address: **kaos.erin.gov.au**
> Choose: **Biodiversity**

International Organization of Paleobotany

The Paleobiology Research Unit (PRU) is comprised of people interested in past environments and how their paleobiology can be investigated. Most of the work is paleobotanical, and centers around the Plant Fossil Record Database.

See also: Biology

World Wide Web:
> URL: **http://sunrae.uel.ac.uk/palaeo/index.html**

Mammal Database

A database of all the known mammals of the world, with a variety of information, including the scientific names for each species.

Gopher:
> Name: Smithsonian Institution
> Address: **smithson.si.edu**
> Choose: **Vertebrate Zoology at the Smithsonian Institution**

Missouri Botanical Garden

Take a tour of the Missouri Botanical Garden and see images and details about the latest plants in bloom. Also on offer are details of the Flora of North America project, access to a database of over 600,000 Wais-indexed records on gymnosperms and angiosperms and links to many other related sites.

Gopher:
> Name: Missouri Botanical Garden
> Address: **gopher.mobot.org**

World Wide Web:
> URL: **http://straylight.tamu.edu/MoBot/welcome.html**

There's no getting around it: plants are cool. And the Missouri Botanical Garden is farm out.

Photosynthesis

Plants kissed by the sun get their own version of a tan. See green plant cells become little organic factories as their chlorophyl explodes into action. Read about the ins and outs of photosynthesis: the original food processor.

Usenet:
Newsgroup: **bionet.photosynthesis**

Plant Biology

How does your garden grow? Discover the myth and mystery of plant growth and reproduction. Discussion of all aspects of plant biology are encouraged. You'll never have a guilt-free salad again.

Usenet:
Newsgroup: **bionet.plants**

Smithsonian Botany Gopher

This gopher contains information resources that are compiled and maintained by Smithsonian staff and includes newsletters and projects as well as pointers to other network resources of interest to researchers in botany.

Gopher:
Name: Smithsonian Institution
Address: **nmnhgoph.si.edu**
Choose: **Botany at the Smithsonian Institution**

**Spare time?
Take a look at Games.**

Smithsonian Vertebrate Zoology Gopher

A database of the thousands of currently recognized species of mammals, in a taxonomic hierarchy that includes order, family, subfamily, and genus.

Gopher:
Name: Smithsonian Institution
Address: **nmnhgoph.si.edu**
Choose: **Vertebrate Zoology**

BUSINESS AND FINANCE

Advertising and Marketing

Information about how advertising on the Internet would differ from current advertising methods, a marketing agencies directory, and a link to a FAQ list about advertising on the Internet.

World Wide Web:
URL: **http://www.yahoo.com/Business/Marketing/**

American Risk and Insurance Association

Information about the programs and services of the American Risk and Insurance Association. This page includes links to newsletters, journals, seminar and meeting information, and other items of interest.

World Wide Web:
URL: **http://riskweb.bus.utexas.edu/aria.html**

Asia Online

Asia Online provides information on commercial and investment opportunities in Asia. It offers a worldwide marketing service for Asian suppliers of products and services as well as a global distribution channel for publishers of Asian electronic directories and magazines.

World Wide Web:
URL: **http://www.ncb.gov.sg:1080/**

Asia Pacific Business and Marketing Resources

Articles about business and management in China, Asia, Japan, and Korea.

Gopher:
Name: Simon Fraser University
Address: **hoshi.cic.sfu.ca**
Choose: **David See-Chai Lam Centre for International Communications | Asia Pacific Business & Marketing Resources**

A
B
C
D
E
F
G
H
I
J
K
L
M
N
O
P
Q
R
S
T
U
V
W
X
Y
Z

Banks and Financial Industries News

Learn why lending rates fluctuate and how it affects you. News on banks and financial industries will keep you up to date.

Usenet:
> Newsgroup: **clari.biz.finance.services**
> Newsgroup: **clari.biz.industry.banking**

Business and Commerce

I'll give you one bag of flour and two chickens for three bags of grain. While business and commerce are not quite this simple, it still doesn't have to be over your head. Read about business and commerce of all kinds.

Usenet:
> Newsgroup: **alt.business.misc**

Business and Industry

Newsbytes offer insights on the real stories in business and industry news. Don't settle for less than the facts.

Usenet:
> Newsgroup: **clari.nb.business**

Business Archives

A listing of businesses on the Web, with a specific computer company hotlist covering many of the large computer companies.

World Wide Web:
> URL: **http://www.cen.uiuc.edu/~rs4184/businessa.html**

Little known fact: Charles and Diana met in alt.romance.

Business Conferences

A list of mailing list discussion groups related to the business world.

Anonymous FTP:
> Address: **ksuvxa.kent.edu**
> Path: **/library/acadlist.file7**

Gopher:
> Name: Sam Houston State University
> Address: **niord.shsu.edu**
> Choose: **Network Based Information and References**
> | **Directory of Scholarly Electronic Conferences (8th edition)**
> | **ACADLIST.FILE7 (Business, Economics, Publishing, News)**

Business Electronic Mail Addresses

A large list of business mail addresses, including names and descriptions.

Gopher:
> Name: NYSERNet
> Address: **nysernet.org**
> Choose: **Special Collections: Business and Economic Development**
> | **Business and Academic Related Email Addresses**

Business Information Resources

A large collection of pointers to business information resources on the Net, including the Internet Business Center, a FAQ about advertising on the Internet, newsletters, national directory listings, laws concerning unsolicited faxing, and much more.

World Wide Web:
> URL: **http://sashimi.wwa.com/~notime/eotw/business_info.html**

Business Information Server

The Dun & Bradstreet business server has articles on marketing your business globally, strategic business planning, tactical marketing, effective research, and a series of tutorials to help the small business owner.

World Wide Web:
> URL: **http://www.dbisna.com/**

Business News

Survey what's going on around you in the business world. There is a little of everything here to provide you with a healthy overview of business, even if it's just to decide that you want someone else to handle it for you.

Usenet:

Newsgroup: **clari.biz.misc**

Business Statistics

General business indicators, commodity prices, construction and real estate stats, and many more indicators and statistics. Also includes industry statistics for the food industry, leather, lumber, metals, manufacturers, and so on.

Gopher:

Name: University of Michigan
Address: **una.hh.lib.umich.edu**
Choose: **ebb**
   | **Current Business Statistics**

Businesses on the Internet

Links to information about thousands of businesses with a presence on the Internet. Companies are grouped according to the products they make or sell.

World Wide Web:

URL: **http://www.yahoo.com/Business/ Corporations/**

BusinessWeb

A comprehensive guide to business-related information on the Internet. Contains many clear and easy links to important information, including economics and trade, transportation schedules, securities and investment schedules, and government and law sections.

World Wide Web:

URL: **http://venus.mcs.com/~cascade/html/biz/ main.html**

Case Online Information System

The Case Online Information System is a collection of business case study material from Harvard Business School, the University of Western Ontario, and the European Case Clearinghouse. This database has over 10,000 case studies, videos, technical notes, and industry notes. First you pick a category (eg. accounting, finance, management, human resources, marketing, etc.), then you can search the database by a single word, or by groups of words. This is an invaluable research tool.

Telnet:

Address: **ecch.babson.edu**
Login: **colis**

China Import/Export News

Trade is fun. You get to take ordinary stuff that you see every day of your life and trade it for cool and exotic things like seaweed and little statues of gods you have never heard of. If you are hot to get into the import/export business with China or if you just want to get an edge in your present dealings, check out this moderated newsletter.

Listserv Mailing List:

List Address: **china-link@ifcss.org**
Subscription Address: **listserv@ifcss.org**

Cogeneration

Tired of paying the electric company? Join this list and learn how to generate your own power — even how to sell your excess power to the utility company at their rates! The ftp site is an archive for the mailing list.

Anonymous FTP:

Address: **ftp.iup.edu**
Path: **/cogeneration/***

Internet Mailing List:

List Address: **cogeneration@grove.iup.edu**
Subscription Address:
   cogeneration-request@grove.iup.edu

Commerce Business Daily

A publication that announces invitations to bid on proposals requested by the U.S. government. This information is updated every business day.

Gopher:

Name: CNS, Inc.
Address: **cscns.com**
Choose: **Internet Express Gopher by Subject**
   | **Business - Commerce Business**
     Daily - Softshare

Commercial Use of the Internet

Greed is good. Money is the root of all evil. So which is it? (Hint: It depends on whether you are cross-posting mass advertising across Usenet groups.) Find out strategies for using the Internet in your commercial ventures. Includes statistics, informational lists, and links to various commercial sites.

World Wide Web:

URL: **http://pass.wayne.edu/business.html**

A B C D E F G H I J K L M N O P Q R S T U V W X Y Z

Commodities

Trading commodities is a great way to grasp financial defeat from the jaws of victory. Why wait for the newspaper to check on how Arkansas pork bellies are doing? Check this newsgroup for up-to-date news and price reports.

Usenet:
Newsgroup: **clari.apbl.reports.commodity**
Newsgroup: **clari.biz.commodity**
Newsgroup: **clari.biz.market.commodities**

Corporate Finance News

Exchange rates, percentages, the value of the ruble. Get real news on finance and currency.

Usenet:
Newsgroup: **clari.biz.finance**

Currency Converter

The Koblas Currency Converter is simple to use. You select the desired country and all the other countries' currencies will be converted relative to the one you selected. The name of the currency will appear as part of your selection.

World Wide Web:
URL: **http://www.ora.com/cgi-bin/ ora/currency?United_States**

Earnings and Dividend Reports

Track your earnings and dividends by staying informed. See up-to-date news on earnings and dividend reports and make the most of your money.

Usenet:
Newsgroup: **clari.biz.finance.earnings**

Eastern Europe Trade Leads

A repository of requests from entrepreneurs in Eastern European countries seeking business partners and trade leads in the U.S.

Gopher:
Name: University of California San Diego
Address: **infopath.ucsd.edu**
Choose: **News & Services**
  | **Economic..**
  | **Eastern Europe trade..**

Eastern European Business Network

If you're interested in helping the countries of Eastern Europe (including the former Soviet Union) in their transition to market economies, this list will help you link up with business persons in Eastern Europe.

Listserv Mailing List:
List Address: **e-europe@pucc.princeton.edu**
Subscription Address:
  listserv@pucc.princeton.edu

EBB and Agency Information

The Economic Bulletin Board (EBB) is an electronic bulletin board run by the U.S. Department of Commerce, Office of Business Analysis, and provides a one-stop source of current economic information. The EBB contains press releases and statistical information from the Bureau of Economic Analysis, the Bureau of the Census, the Federal Reserve Board, the Bureau of Labor Statistics, the Department of Treasury, and several other Federal Government agencies. A menu-driven system.

Gopher:
Name: University of California San Diego
Address: **infopath.ucsd.edu**
Choose: **News & Services**
  | **Economic..**
  | **EBB and Agency Info..**

Economic Indicators

The raw data for the leading (and lesser) economic indicators in the U.S.

Gopher:
Name: University of California San Diego
Address: **infopath.ucsd.edu**
Choose: **News & Services**
  | **Economic..**
  | **Economic Indicators**

Economy

If you're like us, the economy is one of your favorite parts of the social infrastructure. Get the latest poop on what money and labor are doing in the U.S. and worldwide.

Usenet:
Newsgroup: **clari.apbl.reports.economy**
Newsgroup: **clari.biz.economy**
Newsgroup: **clari.biz.economy.world**

EDGAR Mutual Funds

Want to see what is happening in the world of mutual funds? Get fast information on a huge selection of various mutual funds — find out what's been going on in the past months or just the last few days.

World Wide Web:
> URL: **http://edgar.stern.nyu.edu/mutual.html**

Entrepreneurs

Tired of being manacled to that creaking metal desk with the file drawer that always sticks? Take charge of your life: own your own business. See the pitfalls and glories that await you, the entrepreneur.

Usenet:
> Newsgroup: **misc.entrepreneurs**

Your Own Business

What could be more fun than running your own business?

Why let someone else worry about health care, liability insurance, meeting the payroll, and making a profit, when you can do so yourself?

(Of course, there are drawbacks as well.)

If you are starting your own business, make sure to read **misc.entrepreneur**. There are a lot of people just like you.

$$$$$$$$$$$

Entrepreneurs on the Web

A place where entrepreneurs the world over can find useful business information and offer their goods and services to other entrepreneurs. There is a large collection of links to business information resources, details on how to advertise through NoTime Enterprises, the creators of this web page, and a list of commercial services available from businesses on the Net.

World Wide Web:
> URL: **http://sashimi.wwa.com/~notime/ eotw/EOTW.html**

European Commission Host Organization

ECHO offers scientific, language, business, and research databases in any of eight languages.

Telnet:
> Address: **echo.lu**
> Login: **echo**

Export Guide

For the ambitious entrepreneur — read an entire textbook devoted to information, tips, and strategies on exporting goods. This is thorough and informative writing, with 19 chapters and several appendices.

Gopher:
> Name: University of Missouri St. Louis
> Address: **umslvma.umsl.edu**
> Choose: **The Library**
>   **I Government Information**
>   **I Basic Guide to Export**

Have you got an extra amount of something that someone, somewhere, might need? Would you like to send that something to someone who in return would send you something else (or maybe even money)?

If so, point your gopher to the *Exporting Guide* and enter the exciting world of moving stuff from here to there.

Feature Stories

Read real news stories on the movers and shakers of the business world. Feature stories relate to all aspects of business.

Usenet:
> Newsgroup: **clari.biz.features**

Federal Information Exchange

Federal Information Exchange, Inc., is a company that provides database services, software development, and technical support to the government, private sector, and academic communities.

Gopher:
Name: Federal Information Exchange
Address: **gopher.fie.com**

Name: University of California San Diego
Address: **infopath.ucsd.edu**
Choose: **The World**
  | Miscellaneous Special Topics or Reference Sources
  | Federal Government
  | FEDIX

Telnet:
Address: **fedix.fie.com**
Login: **new**

FinanceNet

FinanceNet links government financial management professionals in an effort to optimize the way government manages taxpayer resources. FinanceNet is associated with Vice President Gore's office of the National Performance Review.

World Wide Web:
URL: **http://www.financenet.gov/**

Financial Executive Journal

A cooperative venture between the Legal Information Institute at the Cornell Law School and the NASDAQ Stock Exchange. This quarterly journal covers major issues relating to finance.

World Wide Web:
URL: **http://www.law.cornell.edu/nasdaq/ nasdtoc.html**

Financial Ratios for Manufacturing Corporations

Supporting data and computations of financial ratios for manufacturers.

Gopher:
Name: University of California San Diego
Address: **infopath.ucsd.edu**
Choose: **News & Services**
  | Economic..
  | Special Studies and Reports

Goethe Investment Heimatseite

If you happen to read and write German and you've got a few extra marks to invest, check out the Goethe Investment Heimatseite — a German Investment Club.

World Wide Web:
URL: **http://www.wiwi.uni-frankfurt.de/AG/ JWGI/JWGIhome.html**

Hot News

Get the latest news in business and get it fast. When the market has a wild swing, it might pay to know it right away.

Usenet:
Newsgroup: **clari.biz.urgent**

Income Taxation Information

This web site points to income tax information that is available on the Internet, CD-ROM, and on bulletin board systems.

World Wide Web:
URL: **ftp://ftp.netcom.com/pub/ftmexpat/ home.html**

Industry Statistics

Benchmark and periodic statistics for a number of industry segments. Includes quarterly financial reports and technical documents.

Gopher:
Name: University of California San Diego
Address: **infopath.ucsd.edu**
Choose: **News & Services**
  | Economic..
  | Industry Statistics

Information Technology Laboratory

The importance of information technology to financial institutions led the Union Bank of Switzerland to become active in research. UBILAB, the corporate information technology innovation center of the Union Bank of Switzerland, conducts research in areas of expert systems, human-computer interaction, data and network security, voice and image recognition, and data management.

See also: Computers: Technology, Technology

World Wide Web:
URL: **http://www.ubilab.ubs.ch/**

International Business Practices Guide

Just like you have to remember not to scratch your nose at an auction, there are things you have to realize about international business. Read this guide, designed to provide business firms with an overview of the legal practices of over one hundred countries as well as hints to solve practical problems as they arise.

Gopher:
Name: University of Missouri St. Louis
Address: **umslvma.umsl.edu**
Choose: **The Library**
| **Government Information**
| **International Business**

International Business

Are you interested in starting a ski resort in the Bahamas (where there is no income tax, inheritance tax, or sales tax)? Or maybe you want to set up an Eskimo Pie business in Iceland, and you need to decide which of the three different forms of business you should use. Or maybe all you want to do is form a shell corporation in Uruguay to surprise your wife on your next anniversary. All this and more is available from the **International Business Practices Guide** at the University of Missouri at St. Louis. (Of course, it is up to you to supply your own snow, Eskimo Pies, and wife.)

International Market Insight Reports

Market briefs on opportunities and news in international and foreign markets.

Gopher:
Name: University of California San Diego
Address: **infopath.ucsd.edu**
Choose: **News & Services**
| **Economic..**
| **International Market...**

Internet Better Business Bureau

The Internet Better Business Bureau is a central repository for complaints about people and businesses that abuse the Internet or Usenet. Complaints are processed, compiled, and then are presented to the local Better Business Bureau where the offending person or business resides. Point your browser here to file a complaint.

World Wide Web:
URL: **http://ibd.ar.com/IBBB/IBBB.html**

Internet Business Center

The Internet Business Center (IBC) is a web server for information specifically related to business use of the Internet. It offers important Internet statistics, maps, charts, links to Internet business sites and services, articles relating to business on the Internet, and Net Nuggets, which are links to information about Internet infrastructure elements.

World Wide Web:
URL: **http://tig.com/IBC/**
URL: **http://www.tig.com/IBC/index.html**

Investments

Mutual funds, IRAs, discount brokerages, margin terms — do you sometimes feel like your head is going to spin around? Learn everything you need to know about investments and handling money. Make your money work for you.

Usenet:
Newsgroup: **clari.biz.invest**
Newsgroup: **misc.invest**
Newsgroup: **misc.invest.funds**
Newsgroup: **misc.invest.stocks**

Japanese Business Studies

The times are more civilized and international business is a little safer than it used to be because nowadays people leave their swords at home when they come to the bargaining table. This is not to say that negotiations can't get brutal. As the saying goes, "The pen is mightier than the sword," and that especially holds true for signing contracts. Japan scholars, students, government and business researchers, and executives devote themselves to discussion regarding Japanese economy and business systems.

Listserv Mailing List:
List Address: **japan@pucc.princeton.edu**
Subscription Address:
listserv@pucc.princeton.edu

A B C D E F G H I J K L M N O P Q R S T U V W X Y Z

Labor

Even more fun than actually working is reading about other people who do (or don't, as the case may be). Read this group for the latest news on strikes, unions, and labor relations.

Usenet:
    Newsgroup: **clari.biz.labor**

Leasing a Web Server

If you can't run your own web server or don't want to, several sites allow you to use or lease space from them. Other services, such as preparing HTML documents or providing ftp access, are also available. This page, called "HyperNews," is a list of available sites.

World Wide Web:
    URL: **http://union.ncsa.uiuc.edu/www/
    leasing.shtml**

Legal News

Who's suing whom? Find out the latest news on America's favorite pastime: litigation. News items cover any business-related legal matter.

Usenet:
    Newsgroup: **clari.biz.courts**

Libraries

If you are interested in more than saving loose bills in a sock in a coffee can buried under Aunt Grace's gladioli, then pull up a chair and do some research. If you can't find the information you need in business libraries, you just don't need to know it. Or you can ask Aunt Grace.

Usenet:
    Newsgroup: **bit.listserv.buslib-l**

Mail Addresses of Ukraine Businesses

This file contains the mail addresses of nearly 200 businesses and entrepreneurs in the Ukraine.

Anonymous FTP:
    Address: **infomeister.osc.edu**
    Path: **/central_eastern_europe/ukrainian/
    business/commercial.directory**

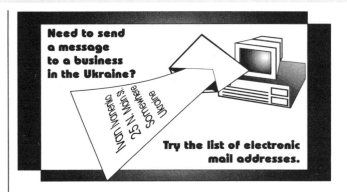

Need to send a message to a business in the Ukraine?

Try the list of electronic mail addresses.

Mergers and Acquisitions

Stay on top of the turbulent world of business mergers and acquisitions. This group has the lowdown on everything that is going on.

Usenet:
    Newsgroup: **clari.biz.mergers**

Mortgage Calculator

If you have your eye on that choice piece of property down the road and you want to see just how bad the mortgage will bite into your wallet, put this mortgage calculator to work. Simply enter the buying price and interest rate and a few other simple fields, and the computer will give you a fully amortized schedule or a brief summary of what you will be paying in principle and interest, your monthly payments, and what you should be earning to be able to afford the house.

See also: Real Estate

World Wide Web:
    URL: **http://ibc.wustl.edu/mort.html**

Do you want to ruin your day?

Use the **Mortgage Calculator** and find out how much you are *really* paying for your house.

Multilevel Marketing

The great pyramids are not just in Egypt. Learn all about the "trickle-up theory" and hear stories of why multilevel marketing is the greatest money-making scheme, er... plan, ever. Don't settle for a rattling car and a rental home. Sell Amway so you can drive a Rolls Royce and own a yacht. These folks can show you how.

Anonymous FTP:
Address: **rtfm.mit.edu**
Path: **/pub/usenet-by-group/alt.answers/mlm-faq**

Usenet:
Newsgroup: **alt.business.multi-level**

Question List

Need the scoop on serious multi-level marketing?

Download the frequently asked question list, then tell five friends, who will tell five friends, who will. . .

Mutual Fund Price Movement Chart

Discover what mutual funds are doing these days. This site is not updated automatically, so you might not get daily information, but they have a nice selection of funds with all the historical data.

World Wide Web:
URL: **http://www.ai.mit.edu/stocks/mf.html**

National Trade Data Bank

Information on exporting, background on various countries of the world, breaking into exporting, licensing, investment, tariffs, and more. More than one hundred items.

Anonymous FTP:
Address: **ftp.stat-usa.gov**
Path: **/pub/NTDB/***

Gopher:
Name: Department of Commerce, Economics and Statistics Administration
Address: **gopher.stat-usa.gov**
Choose: **National Trade Data Bank**

World Wide Web:
URL: **http://www.stat-usa.gov/BEN/Topics/TradePromo.html**

NETworth

Money markets, stocks, bonds, mutual funds — if your vault is getting overcrowded, maybe you need to invest. Arm yourself with a load of information before making investments with the help of this free investing service. While the service is free, you do have to register with the company that sponsors the service and inevitably you will find yourself on a mailing list, so read the fine print.

World Wide Web:
URL: **http://networth.galt.com/**

New Products and Services

Think what an advantage you would have over the rest of the world if you were the first to find out about all kinds of cool, new stuff. Here is a quick update on innovative products and services while they are still hot off the economic griddle.

Usenet:
Newsgroup: **clari.biz.products**

Non-Profit Organizations

These days the fastest way to see money come pouring in is to operate a non-profit business. The only problem is that you can't keep all the money. Learn about forming non-profit organizations, how to be a wise donor, tips on fund raising, annual reports of non-profit organizations, and philanthropy in general.

Gopher:
Name: EnviroLink Network
Address: **envirolink.org**
Choose: **EnviroOrgs — Environmental Organizations On-Line**
| Internet NonProfit C

Office Automation

A paper discussing the methods necessary for an office to thrive, by having a hierarchy of well-defined realms which are controlled by and support the needs of each group.

Gopher:
Name: Whole Earth Lectronic Link
Address: **gopher.well.sf.ca.us**
Choose: **Whole Systems**
| Good Office Patterns

A
B
C
D
E
F
G
H
I
J
K
L
M
N
O
P
Q
R
S
T
U
V
W
X
Y
Z

Penn World Trade Tables

An expanded set of international economic and business comparisons and statistics from 1950-1988, including population and GDP data.

Anonymous FTP:
Address: **nber.harvard.edu**
Path: **/pub/pwt55/***

Gopher:
Name: National Bureau of Economic Research
Address: **nber.harvard.edu**
Choose: **Penn-World Tables v. 5.5**

Personal Finance

It was so much easier when you were a kid. Your biggest money worry was trying to figure out how to break the piggy open without anybody noticing. Now there's all this tax stuff, deductions and annuities, investments and exemptions. At least people on the Net are making it a little easier to sort out all the information. Find great tips on managing your personal finances.

World Wide Web:
URL: **http://www.thegroup.net/green.htm**

Personal Investing and Finance News

It's hard to decide the best place to put your money. Take the mystery out of investing by keeping up on the latest investing and finance news.

Usenet:
Newsgroup: **clari.biz.finance.personal**

World Wide Web:
URL: **http://www.yahoo.com/Economy/ Markets_and_Investments/Personal_Finance/**

Price and Volume Charts

Information on the price and volume of more than 300 stocks. Prices show recent closing information.

World Wide Web:
URL: **http://www.ai.mit.edu/stocks/graphs.html**

QuoteCom

This service provides financial market data to Internet users. Services include stock quoting and portfolio updates. Not all services are free.

World Wide Web:
URL: **http://www.quote.com/**

RISKWeb

RISKWeb's primary purpose is to serve information to academics and professionals whose research and/or teaching interests are in the area of risk and insurance. Offered are risk and insurance database search engines, meeting details, a working paper archive, teaching notes, software, and much more.

World Wide Web:
URL: **http://riskweb.bus.utexas.edu/riskweb.htm**

Savage Archive

Information on mutual funds, stock market, Canadian market, futures, exchange rates, spreadsheets, graphs, and strategies.

World Wide Web:
URL: **file://dg-rtp.dg.com/pub/misc.invest**

Security APL Quote Server

Watch your stack of money rise and fall as the minutes pass. The APL Quote Server states the current S&P 500 Index, offers a graphical representation of the Dow Jones Industrial Average and the daily volume at the New York Stock Exchange. The news is updated from Wall Street approximately every fifteen minutes, so you will have that much of a head start if you have to leave town.

World Wide Web:
URL: **http://www.secapl.com/cgi-bin/qs**

Small Business Administration

Running your own business can be a delight or a hassle, depending on how you approach it. It helps to have as much information at your fingertips as possible. The Small Business Administration is now online, and you can read about business development, government contracting, minority business, and financial assistance.

Gopher:
Name: Small Business Administration
Address: **gopher.sbaonline.sba.gov**

Standard & Poors 500 Index

A constantly updated, real-time graph showing the most recent day's activity of the Standard & Poors 500 Index. Historical graphs of the last twelve months, the last five years, and the last ten years are also available.

World Wide Web:
URL: **http://www.secapl.com/secapl/quoteserver/ sp500.html**

Stock Market

Get the latest in stock market closing quotes and comments. These sites house current information as well as archives and reports from recent dates.

Gopher:
Name: Poudre-R1 School District
Address: **alpha.pr1.k12.co.us**
Choose: **Other Information Services
| Stock Market Closing Quotes**

Name: Washington University St. Louis Economics Department
Address: **wuecon.wustl.edu**
Port: **671**
Choose: **Holt's Stock Market Reports**

Stock Market Data

Stock market information is updated daily and shows stock charts of prices and movement, top stocks, stock quotes, and historical data.

World Wide Web:
URL: **http://www.ai.mit.edu/stocks.html**

Stock Market Discussion Groups

Whether you are the head investor of a multimillion dollar mutual fund, or simply the CEO of a large, international corporation, stock market news is important to you. Check these newsgroups for the latest numbers and reports.

Usenet:
Newsgroup: **clari.apbl.stocks**
Newsgroup: **clari.apbl.stocks.analysis**
Newsgroup: **clari.apbl.stocks.dow**
Newsgroup: **clari.apbl.stocks.tech**
Newsgroup: **clari.biz.market**
Newsgroup: **clari.biz.market.amex**
Newsgroup: **clari.biz.market.commodities**
Newsgroup: **clari.biz.market.dow**
Newsgroup: **clari.biz.market.misc**
Newsgroup: **clari.biz.market.news**
Newsgroup: **clari.biz.market.ny**
Newsgroup: **clari.biz.market.otc**
Newsgroup: **clari.biz.market.report**
Newsgroup: **clari.biz.market.report.asia**
Newsgroup: **clari.biz.market.report.europe**
Newsgroup: **clari.biz.market.report.top**
Newsgroup: **clari.biz.market.report.usa**
Newsgroup: **clari.biz.market.report.usa.nyse**

Stock Market Report

Telnet into the daily stock market summary report provided as a free service of a2i, or receive quotes daily by electronic mail.

Mail:
Address: **martin.wong@eng.sun.com**

Telnet:
Address: **a2i.rahul.net**
Login: **guest**
Choose: **MENU: Current system information
| Market report**

Stock Market Simulations

Welcome to Rotisserie Investing, "your greed-o-matic virtual portfolio". Where else can you start out with $100,000 for nothing at all? These market simulations will follow the actual performance of the real markets. See for yourself how easy it is to make a $100,000 on cattle futures.

Telnet:
Address: **castor.tat.physik.uni-tuebingen.de**
Login: **games**

Address: **mammon.media.mit.edu**
Port: **10900**

StrategyWeb

StrategyWeb uses the web environment to provide business consulting, advice, and information — a great resource for business people of any size organization. StrategyWeb offers advices from experts, answers to frequently asked questions, and even an interactive stock pricing system.

World Wide Web:
URL: **http://fender.onramp.net/~atw_dhw/precom.htm**

Taxing Times

Ah, the glorious month of April. The birds rejoice at the dawn of spring. Earthworms happily aerate the soil to stimulate new growth. A delicate breeze blows. And you are stuck inside doing your taxes. Isn't life cruel? Try to make it as painless as possible by planning ahead. Get handy instructions and forms available in TIFF, PostScript, and Adobe Portable Document Format. Then go catch some rays.

World Wide Web:
URL: **http://www.scubed.com:8001/tax/tax.html**

Tax Forms

Yes, you really can get tax forms—American and Canadian—and all kinds of tax information for free over the Internet (courtesy of the S-Cubed Division of Maxwell Labs). There is a *lot* of stuff here, including the entire tax code (all 22 megabytes), so what are you waiting for?

Technical Aspects

This is where money and math collide. Flying formulas, staggering statistics, and profitable predictions abound to provide the basis for economic decision-making. How do you know when to buy a mutual fund? What good is a regression analysis? Take part in the discussion and learn how to buy and sell by the numbers.

Usenet:
Newsgroup: **misc.invest.technical**

Top News

Find out the big financial events. If you don't have time to wade through all the news, at least get the top stories.

Usenet:
Newsgroup: **clari.biz.top**

Trademark Act of 1946

Are you interested in trademark law or in establishing your own trademark? Cornell University's law school has put the full text of the Lanham Act (the Trademark Act of 1946) on this web page.

World Wide Web:
URL: **http://www.law.cornell.edu/lanham/lanham.table.html**

Trademarks

A list of all of the International Trademark Classes in order of class, including a detailed description of each. The list starts with Class 1 (Chemicals) and goes through Class 42 (Miscellaneous services).

World Wide Web:
URL: **http://www.naming.com/naming/icclasses.html**

Vienna Stock Exchange

If you can read German, take a look at this telnet site, which will give you information about the Vienna Stock Exchange.

Telnet:
Address: **fiivs01.tu-graz.ac.at**
Login: **boerse**

World Bank

The World Bank is comprised of the International Bank for Reconstruction and Development (IBRD), the International Development Association (IDA), the International Finance Corporation (IFC), and the Multilateral Investment Guarantee Agency (MIGA). Through its gopher, the World Bank offers economic reports, environmental assessments and analysis, environmental data sheets, project information documents, national environmental action plans, and many other publications with a wealth of economic and social data.

World Wide Web:
URL: **http://www.worldbank.org/**

World of Coca-Cola

An article about the Coca-Cola Company of Atlanta, Georgia: a "tribute to a unique product and the consumers who have made it the world's favorite soft drink."

Gopher:
Name: Carnegie Mellon University
Address: **english-server.hss.cmu.edu**
Choose: **Cultural Theory**
    l **Friedman - World of Coca Cola**

BUYING AND SELLING

Anime

Buy and cell — sorry, sell — all types of items related to anime (Japanese animation).

Usenet:
Newsgroup: **rec.arts.anime.marketplace**

Bicycles

Drop in to the bicycle marketplace: buying, selling, and reviews. Soon you'll be bopping around town on your very own bicycle built for one.

Usenet:
Newsgroup: **rec.bicycles.marketplace**

Bootleg Music

Surely this isn't the illegal activity it looks like. Everyone knows that it's against the law to sell bootleg copies of recordings or amateur recordings of live performances. Don't they?

See also: Music

Internet Relay Chat:
Channel: **#bootlegs**

Computers

Buying a computer? Check out the **clari** newsgroup for the latest prices. For buying and selling particular machines, see the specialized groups. The **.d** group is for discussion of the computer buy-and-sell groups. Here is our hint for the day: it is difficult to buy too much speed, too much memory, or too much video resolution.

Usenet:
Newsgroup: **clari.streetprice**
Newsgroup: **comp.sys.amiga.marketplace**
Newsgroup: **comp.sys.apple2.marketplace**
Newsgroup: **comp.sys.next.marketplace**
Newsgroup: **misc.forsale.computers.d**
Newsgroup: **misc.forsale.computers.mac**
Newsgroup: **misc.forsale.computers.other**
Newsgroup: **misc.forsale.computers.pc-clone**
Newsgroup: **misc.forsale.computers.workstation**

MarketBase Online Catalog

The MarketBase Online Catalog of Goods and Services is a unique online service dedicated to providing a forum where buyers and sellers meet to exchange the attributes of products and services electronically.

Gopher:
Name: University of North Carolina
Address: **gopher.ncsu.edu**
Choose: **Entertainment**
  | Online Mall

Marketplace, Buy and Sell

Here is the main Usenet marketplace: buy, sell, or trade anything. If you need it and someone has it, this is the place to find it.

Usenet:
Newsgroup: **misc.forsale**

Pinball and Video Game Machine Auctions

Results and prices of video game software, equipment, and pinball machines sold at auction around the U.S.

Anonymous FTP:
Address: **ftp.spies.com**
Path: **/game_archive/auction/***

Satellite TV Equipment

All manner of home satellite equipment to buy, sell, and talk about. Just the place to pick up an extra Ku LNB. (By the way, for information about economical Usenet feeds using a personal satellite dish, send mail to **pagesat@pagesat.com**.)

Usenet:
Newsgroup: **alt.satellite.tv.forsale**

Science Fiction

Do you need a replacement for your old tricorder? Is your communicator or phaser malfunctioning? Check out the science fiction marketplace. If they don't have it, or know about it, it hasn't been replicated.

Usenet:
Newsgroup: **rec.arts.sf.marketplace**

Selling on IRC

If you've got to get rid of something fast, come to the **#forsale** channel to dump those unwanted items. People come here to buy, sell, and barter. They even hold live auctions from time to time.

Internet Relay Chat:
Channel: **#forsale**

Video Games

When you are not playing a video game, you are wasting your time (unless you are talking about video games). If God didn't want us to spend all our time staring at the screen and manipulating a surrogate being, why did he give us this newsgroup?

Usenet:
Newsgroup: **rec.games.video.marketplace**

A
B
C
D
E
F
G
H
I
J
K
L
M
N
O
P
Q
R
S
T
U
V
W
X
Y
Z

CANADA

British Columbia Regional Information

This web page has a detailed map of British Columbia that serves general and local tourist information. To use the map, just click on the area of the map in which you're interested.

World Wide Web:
URL: **http://www.cg94.freenet.victoria.bc.ca/ tourism/regions/regions.html**

British Columbia Tourism Information

The home page for information about beautiful British Columbia.

World Wide Web:
URL: **http://www.cg94.freenet.victoria.bc.ca/ tourism/tourismhome.html**

British Columbian Web Servers

A comprehensive list of web servers in British Columbia, Canada.

World Wide Web:
URL: **http://freenet.victoria.bc.ca/bcw3list.html**

Canadian Business Information

Links to a Canadian business directory, a business resource center, and a job center.

World Wide Web:
URL: **http://csclub.uwaterloo.ca/u/nckwan/ index.html**

Canadian Discussion

Channels where Canadians and their friends meet, talk and jest. French is spoken on the **#quebec** channel.

Internet Relay Chat:
Channel: **#canada**
Channel: **#quebec**

Canadian Geographical Web Server

A geography server for Canada via the Web. Start by choosing a province or territory, then choose from one of the submaps to focus in on the area of your interest.

World Wide Web:
URL: **http://www.sal.ists.ca/services/w3_can/ maps.html**

Canadian Government Documents

The Canada Meech Lake Accord, Charlottetown Constitutional Agreement, excerpts from the Canada Constitution Act, and proposals for shaping the future of Canada (in both French and English).

Anonymous FTP:
Address: **ftp.spies.com**
Path: **/Gov/Canada/***

Gopher:
Name: Internet Wiretap
Address: **wiretap.spies.com**
Choose: **Government Docs (US & World)**
 | **Canadian Documents**

MANY people think that government documents are dull. Well, like Marlon Brando in *A Streetcar Named Desire*, we say "Ha...ha ha!" One needs only to point to the wonderful treasure house of fascinating information available from various British Columbian provincial government departments. For example, when you are looking for a romantic evening to share with a date, there is really no substitute for firing up your gopher and displaying documents from the Provincial Advisory Committee on Education Technology; or holding hands, looking into one another's eyes with silent devotion, and browsing through General Information Items from the Ministry of Education. And, if things threaten to get a little too hot to handle, you can always jump to the Government of Ontario gopher and go wild (not recommended for beginners or anyone with a weak heart).

Canadian Government Gophers

Documents and information services from the ministries of various Canadian provinces and other governmental organizations.

Gopher:
Name: Community Learning Network
Address: **cln.etc.bc.ca**
Choose: **B.C. and Canadian Government Gophers**

Canadian History

A web page provided by the Mississippi State University that offers access to Mississippi State's Canadian history ftp site and the "Canada on Heidelberg History Gopher."

Anonymous FTP:
Address: **ftp.msstate.edu**
Path: **/docs/history/Canada/***

World Wide Web:
URL: **http://history.cc.ukans.edu/history/
reading_rooms/canada.html**

Canadian Investment

If you're looking to spread your money around a little, try investing in Canada. Learn about Canadian money markets, investment clubs, financial publications, and the government. (And, if you have a little extra money, we have a snow farm you might want to invest in.)

Usenet:
Newsgroup: **misc.invest.canada**

Canadian Issues Forum

A mailing list discussion forum for political, social, cultural, and economic issues in Canada.

Listserv Mailing List:
List Address: **canada-l@vm1.mcgill.ca**
Subscription Address: **listserv@vm1.mcgill.ca**

Canadian Music

After more than 25 years of federal "Canadian content" rules, Canadian music is alive and well and living in...ahem...Canada. Join the discussion of your favorite musicians from the land where a rich musical tradition resonates from sea to shining sea. (Bagpipes and accordians are optional.)

Usenet:
Newsgroup: **alt.music.canada**

Canadian News

An American magazine once referred to Canada as "the retarded giant on our doorstep." Read the Clarinet Canadian newsgroups and get the real scoop. You will find that Canadian news is about as exciting as... well... Canadian news.

Usenet:
Newsgroup: **clari.canada.biz**
Newsgroup: **clari.canada.briefs**
Newsgroup: **clari.canada.briefs.ont**
Newsgroup: **clari.canada.briefs.west**
Newsgroup: **clari.canada.features**
Newsgroup: **clari.canada.general**
Newsgroup: **clari.canada.gov**
Newsgroup: **clari.canada.law**
Newsgroup: **clari.canada.newscast**
Newsgroup: **clari.canada.politics**
Newsgroup: **clari.canada.trouble**
Newsgroup: **clari.news.canada**
Newsgroup: **clari.world.americas.canada.business**

Canadian Resource Page

The Canadian Resource Page has links to news, statistics and figures about Canada, travel and tourism information, government services, politics and history, education and culture.

World Wide Web:
URL: **http://www.cs.cmu.edu:8001/Web/
Unofficial/Canadiana/README.html**

Canadian Stock Archives

What's happening in the financial world of Canada? See daily and historical stock data for more than 300 Canadian stocks.

Anonymous FTP:
Address: **dg-rtp.dg.com**
Path: **/pub/misc.invest/Canadian/***

A B C D E F G H I J K L M N O P Q R S T U V W X Y Z

Investing in Canada

No financial portfolio is complete without a healthy collection of Canadian stock. But don't let your holdings in the country just north of the Land-of-the-Free-and-the-Home-of-the-Brave expire from benign neglect. Keep track of what is moving and grooving in the country that boasts the best baseball team in the world: Use the *Canadian Stock Archives*. Our personal favorite is a long-term investment in beaver futures.

Canadian Web Master Index

The central index of Canadian World Wide Web servers at the Space Astrophysics Laboratory in North York, Ontario.

World Wide Web:
> URL: **http://www.sal.ists.ca/services/w3_can/www_index.html**

Censorship and Intellectual Freedom in Canada

Censorship is a global issue and Canada is not immune to the effects. Assert your intellectual freedom and see what everyone else has to say on censorship challenges in Canada. This forum is open to faculty members, librarians, researchers, teachers and anyone else interested in being alert to events that pose a threat to intellectual freedom.

Internet Mailing List:
> List Address: **ifreedom@snoopy.ucis.dal.ca**
> Subscription Address:
> **ifreedom-request@snoopy.ucis.dal.ca**

Charlottetown Agreement

Consensus Report of the Canadian Charlottetown Constitutional Agreement of August 28th, 1992, including highlights, fact sheets, legal text, and the report itself.

Gopher:
> Name: Nova Scotia Technology Network
> Address: **nstn.ns.ca**
> Choose: **Other Information**
> **| Constitutional Kit**

Culture

There is an old riddle: What is Canadian culture? The answer is, "Mostly American." Some people feel that "Canadian culture" is an oxymoron. What do they know? Haven't they ever heard of the Blue Jays? William Shatner? Rick Moranis (with whom Harley went to summer camp)? After all, if Canadian culture is good enough for Wayne Gretzky, it should be good enough for Doug and Bob.

Usenet:
> Newsgroup: **soc.culture.canada**

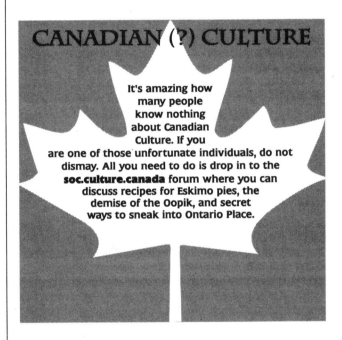

CANADIAN (?) CULTURE

It's amazing how many people know nothing about Canadian Culture. If you are one of those unfortunate individuals, do not dismay. All you need to do is drop in to the **soc.culture.canada** forum where you can discuss recipes for Eskimo pies, the demise of the Oopik, and secret ways to sneak into Ontario Place.

Halifax Nova Scotia

Pay a virtual visit to Halifax and Nova Scotia via the World Wide Web.

World Wide Web:
> URL: **http://aton.hypercomp.ns.ca/pix/halifax.html**

Maritimes Web Servers

Select a web site on the map of Canada by clicking on the name of the organization that sponsors the site.

World Wide Web:
> URL: **http://www.sal.ists.ca/services/w3_can/maritimes.html**

Official Touring Guide to New Brunswick

Check out the culture of Canada's only officially bilingual province. Read the official touring guide of New Brunswick in either French or English.

World Wide Web:
    URL: **http://www.cuslm.ca/tourist/welcome.htm**

Ottawa

See photos of beautiful Ottawa, check out the art galleries and museums in a virtual tour of Canada's capital city.

World Wide Web:
    URL: **http://www.scs.carleton.ca/ottawa/
    ottawa.html**

Jokes? Try Humor.

Prince Edward Island

Need a getaway? Check out this information about Prince Edward Island, Canada. They offer photographs, an event guide, entertainment hot spots, and the history of the area — and they'd love to see you there!

See also: Travel

Gopher:
    Name: PEI Crafts Council
    Address: **gopher.crafts-council.pe.ca**
    Choose: **Prince Edward Island: Electronic
      Visitors Guide**

World Wide Web:
    URL: **http://www.crafts-council.pe.ca/
    vg/index.html**

Statistics Canada Daily Reports

Reports on international transactions, agricultural, and other key Canadian economic statistics.

Gopher:
    Name: Carleton University
    Address: **gopher.carleton.ca**
    Choose: **Access to Remote Gophers and
      Information Services**
    | **Canadian Government Gophers**
    | **Statistics Canada**

Tour Canada Without Leaving Your Desk

A tour of Canada and collection of links to resources describing Canadian locales and events. It includes images and articles on Vancouver, Ontario, Ottawa, Quebec, New Brunswick, British Columbia, and many other places in Canada. Some of the information is also available in French.

World Wide Web:
    URL: **http://www.cs.cmu.edu:8001/afs/
    cs.cmu.edu/user/clamen/misc/Canadiana/
    Travelogue.html**

Web Servers in Quebec

A geographical web gateway to the web servers of Quebec. Just click on a web server on the map of Quebec for information and a direct link.

World Wide Web:
    URL: **http://www.sal.ists.ca/services/w3_can/
    qc.html**

CHEMISTRY

American Chemical Society

The American Chemical Society gopher contains items of interest to chemists, including supplementary material pages from the *Journal of the American Chemical Society*.

Gopher:
    Name: American Chemical Society
    Address: **acsinfo.acs.org**

Center for Atmospheric Science

The Center for Atmospheric Science is part of the chemistry department at Cambridge University. Their server contains atmospheric data, current weather information and links to the Atmospheric Chemistry Modeling Support Unit in addition to links to other Internet services.

See also: Weather

World Wide Web:
    URL: **http://www.atm.ch.cam.ac.uk/**

A B C D E F G H I J K L M N O P Q R S T U V W X Y Z

Chemical Engineering

Discuss the various aspects of chemical engineering in this Usenet group, or check out the Chemical Engineering web page and its pointers to chemical engineering-related resources all over the Internet.

Usenet:
Newsgroup: **sci.engr.chem**

World Wide Web:
URL: **http://www.yahoo.com/Science/ Engineering/Chemical_Engineering/**

Hey guys:

Want to make lots of money and meet beautiful women? Maybe it's time to check out

Chemical Engineering

Chemical Engineering List

A mailing list forum focused on the role of chemical engineering in a changing technology and world economy, and new research trends in industry and academia.

Listserv Mailing List:
List Address: **cheme-l@psuvm.psu.edu**
Subscription Address: **listserv@psuvm.psu.edu**

Chemical Information Sources

Don't get your chemicals off the street — you never know who could be hiding a little machine gun beneath their roomy labcoat. Instead, learn about chemistry and various chemical compounds from this listserv list. Catch news about existing reference sources, the appearance of printed or machine-readable new resources, and prices and availability of chemicals. Any topic is okay as long as it relates to chemistry in some way.

Listserv Mailing List:
List Address: **chminf-l@iubvm.ucs.indiana.edu**
Subscription Address:
listserv@iubvm.ucs.indiana.edu

Chemical Physics Preprint Database

The Chemical Physics Preprint Database is a fully automated electronic archive and distribution server for the international theoretical chemistry community.

World Wide Web:
URL: **http://www.chem.brown.edu/chem-ph.html**

Chemistry Art Gallery

Spectacular visualization and animations in chemistry. Among the offerings are animations of small molecule diffusion in polymers, protein cellobihydrolase I (CBHI), visualization of chromosomes and viruses based on electron microscopy tomography, visualization of micelles, and a visualization of the dynamics of spreading of small droplets of chainlike molecules on surfaces. There are also links to other chemistry visualizations and animations.

World Wide Web:
URL: **http://www.csc.fi/lul/chem/graphics.html**

Chemistry in Israel

A mailing list for discussion of the science of chemistry in Israel. Topics can include lectures, workshops, seminars, colloquia, and funding opportunities.

Listserv Mailing List:
List Address: **chemic-l@vm.tau.ac.il**
Subscription Address: **listserv@vm.tau.ac.il**

The Net is mankind's greatest achievement.

Chemistry Information

An electronic reference source providing answers to frequently asked chemistry questions through library resources. It covers nomenclature, compound identification, properties, structure determination, toxicity, synthesis, and registry numbers. For each component it lists the most appropriate reference resources (online catalog, indexes, journals, etc.).

Anonymous FTP:
> Address: **ucssun1.sdsu.edu**
> Path: **/pub/chemras/***

Chemistry Talk

Let's talk chemistry! (This isn't about how we get along, it's strictly business.) If you're interested in any aspect of chemistry or its related sciences and fields, join the discussion group **sci.chem** and explore your chemistry with others of similar interests.

Usenet:
> Newsgroup: **sci.chem**

Chemistry Telementoring

A mailing list to foster the exchange of ideas and information between chemistry students and teachers from high schools to universities.

Internet Mailing List:
> List Address: **chemistrytm@dhvx20.csudh.edu**
> Subscription Address:
> **chemistrytm-request@dhvx20.csudh.edu**

College of Chemistry at Berkeley

The College of Chemistry at Berkeley offers a hypertext periodic table with details available on all the elements, mpeg movies of vibrational modes of benzene and some interesting chemical reactions, chemistry-related software, and links to other chemistry resources on the Net.

World Wide Web:
> URL: **http://www.cchem.berkeley.edu/**

Excerpt from the Net...

```
Newsgroup: sci.chem
Subject: (fwd) Re: Strange properties of cornstarch slurr

>> The other night I was making a sauce and noticed that the cornstarch
>> and water had the bizzare property of solidifying when pressure was
>> applied and returning to a liquid when released. Is anyone familiar
>> with this phenomenon?


> This property is called thixotropy. I haven't tried this, but
> hitting the cornstarch/water slurry with a blunt object is supposed
> to cause it to crack, yet it can also be poured like a liquid.

I think the proper term is dilatancy.

Pseudoplastic fluids:
- thin with increasing shear rate and are not time dependent

Thixotropic fluids:
- thin with increasing shear rate and are time dependent

Newtonian fluids:
- are not effected by shear rate or time dependent

Dilatant fluids:
- thicken with increasing shear rate and are not time dependent

Rheopectic fluids:
- thicken with increasing shear rate and are time dependent
```

A B C D E F G H I J K L M N O P Q R S T U V W X Y Z

Computational Chemistry List

A mailing list for the discussion of quantum chemistry, molecular mechanics and dynamics, and other fields related to computational chemistry.

Internet Mailing List:
List Address: **chemistry@osc.edu**
Subscription Address: **chemistry-request@osc.edu**

Hydrogen Bond Calculation Program

This program, called HBPLUS, calculates hydrogen bonds. If that's something you do occasionally, check this out before you get out the old HP calculator.

World Wide Web:
URL: **http://bsmcha1.biochem.ucl.ac.uk/ ~mcdonald/hbplus/home.html**

Hyperactive Molecules

Molecular coordinates are stored in a large number of formats, and originate from some of the most interesting sources, like crystallography, quantum chemistry calculations, molecular mechanics or dynamics runs. Check out this page to see how one organization proposes to store molecular coordinates.

World Wide Web:
URL: **http://www.ch.ic.ac.uk/ chemical_mime.html**

Institute for Molecular Science

The IMS server contains information from the Department of Applied Molecular Science in Japan, information from the CMC (Chemical Materials Center), a search of the Quantum Chemistry Literature Database and various journals (including the ACS journals).

World Wide Web:
URL: **http://ccinfo.ims.ac.jp/**

Organometallic Chemistry

Chemistry and techniques used in working with organometallic compounds.

Usenet:
Newsgroup: **sci.chem.organomet**

Periodic Table of the Elements

A graphical DOS program that displays the periodic table. Select an element with the cursor for detailed information on any of the elements. (The only bad thing is that they have renamed Hahnium [element 105] to Unnilpentium.)

Anonymous FTP:
Address: **freebsd.cdrom.com**
Path: **/.1/games/msdos/educate/periodic.zip**

Archie:
Pattern: **periodic.zip**

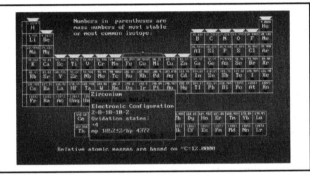

On the Internet, software programs are available by the tens of thousands for just about anything you can think of. This program shows the Periodic Table of the Elements. You move a cursor around to choose an element, then press ENTER, and the program will give you more detailed information about that element. This program is available on most University systems. This copy was obtained from **freebsd.cdrom.com** in the file **/.1/games/msdos/educate/periodic.zip**.

Periodic Table of the Elements (Online)

An online periodic table of the elements. A handy tool to have, since the periodic table changes so frequently.

Telnet:
Address: **camms2.caos.kun.nl**
Port: **2034**

Address: **kufacts.cc.ukans.edu**
Login: **kufacts**
Choose: **Reference Shelf**
  | Miscellaneous Resources
  | Periodic Table

Periodic Table in Hypertext Format

A hypertext version of the Periodic Table that allows you to click on any individual element to obtain details of that element. The details include standard state, color, discoverer, date discovered, name meaning, radii, valency, electronegativities, effective nuclear charge, bond enthalpies, temperatures, enthalpies, ionization enthalpies, isotopic abundances, and more.

World Wide Web:
URL: **http://www.cchem.berkeley.edu/Table/index.html**

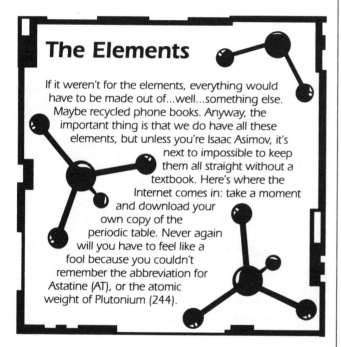

The Elements

If it weren't for the elements, everything would have to be made out of...well...something else. Maybe recycled phone books. Anyway, the important thing is that we do have all these elements, but unless you're Isaac Asimov, it's next to impossible to keep them all straight without a textbook. Here's where the Internet comes in: take a moment and download your own copy of the periodic table. Never again will you have to feel like a fool because you couldn't remember the abbreviation for Astatine (AT), or the atomic weight of Plutonium (244).

Polymer Science and Technology

The home page for the Interdisciplinary Research Centre in Polymer Science and Technology — a consortium of groups involved in polymer research in the Universities of Leeds, Bradford and Durham, England.

World Wide Web:
URL: **http://irc.leeds.ac.uk/**

Ponder Lab Web Server

A laboratory server focused on computational chemistry and molecular modeling.

World Wide Web:
URL: **http://dasher.wustl.edu/**

Short-Lived Reactive Pollutants

What's the average life-span of a pollutant? We're not sure, but anything over a minute is probably too long. If chemistry and the environment make your Bunsen burner hot, then get in on this discussion and exchange of information about air sampling and monitoring short-lived reactive pollutants.

See also: Environment

Listserv Mailing List:
List Address: **reactive@vm1.mcgill.ca**
Subscription Address: **listserv@vm1.mcgill.ca**

Virtual Library of Chemistry

A web page with links to all the most important chemistry-related resources on the Internet — a veritable virtual library!

World Wide Web:
URL: **http://www.chem.ucla.edu/chempointers.html**

WebElements

The Department of Chemistry at the University of Sheffield runs an experimental service called WebElements, a web periodic table database and utility package constructed with data abstracted from the HyperCard program MacElements and which has a periodic table of elements database, an interactive isotope pattern calculator and an element percentage calculator.

World Wide Web:
URL: **http://www2.shef.ac.uk/chemistry/web-elements/web-elements-home.html**

World Association of Theoretical Organic Chemists

This server is supported by the Department of Chemistry, Imperial College, London. It has information on upcoming conferences, registration info, *Chemical Physics* reprints, online presentations, and much more.

World Wide Web:
URL: **http://www.ch.ic.ac.uk/watoc.html**

A B C D E F G H I J K L M N O P Q R S T U V W X Y Z

COMIC BOOKS

Alternative Comics

Keep up with the latest news and gossip in the alternative comics scene. In this group you will find information on artists, stories, and comic book companies, and discussion on the philosophy and sociological aspects of comic books.

Usenet:
    Newsgroup: **alt.comics.alternative**

Comic Book Mailing List

If you're into comic books, this mailing list is the place for stimulating and exhilarating discourse about rare and exotic comic books. If you've got 'em, want 'em, or just want to banter about 'em, try **comix**.

Internet Mailing List:
    List Address: **comix@world.std.com**
    Subscription Address:
        comix-request@world.std.com

Comics Archives

Discussions about the comic book *Watchmen*, and a bibliography, episode guide, and glossary for the comic book *Cerebus*.

Anonymous FTP:
    Address: **ftp.white.toronto.edu**
    Path: **/pub/comics/***

Comics Marketplace

What do you do when it's 2 A.M. and you just have to lay your hands on the *Superman* comic in which Lois Lane pretends to marry Peewee Herman, but it turns out to be a hoax? Fire up the old computer and visit the Usenet comics marketplace.

Usenet:
    Newsgroup: **rec.arts.comics.marketplace**

Bored? Try Fun.
Still bored? Try Games.

Comics Newsgroups

Zap! Biff! Pow! Action dialogue brings comics to life. Whether you are a collector or just a person who likes to read comics now and then, you'll love the variety of discussion you can find in Usenet.

Usenet:
    Newsgroup: **alt.comics.batman**
    Newsgroup: **alt.comics.buffalo-roam**
    Newsgroup: **alt.comics.elfquest**
    Newsgroup: **alt.comics.lnh**
    Newsgroup: **alt.comics.superman**
    Newsgroup: **rec.arts.comics.info**
    Newsgroup: **rec.arts.comics.misc**
    Newsgroup: **rec.arts.comics.strips**
    Newsgroup: **rec.arts.comics.xbooks**

Need to know when the next meeting of the **Jimmy Olsen Fan Club** will be held? Send your request to one of the Usenet comic book discussion groups.

Comics Resource Center

Go on a comics binge and stuff yourself full of information on comic strips, books, and animation. You will find links to archives, Usenet groups, gophers and ftp sites.

See also: Fun, Role-Playing

World Wide Web:
    URL: **http://www.yahoo.com/Entertainment/ Comics/**

More Comics

Graphics and album lists from a selection of comics, including *Tintin*, and the French *Valerian*.

Anonymous FTP:
    Address: **ftp.funet.fi**
    Path: **/pub/culture/comics/***

The Net is for smart people (like you).

Superhero Comic Writing

Experience the dynamic fun of being in control of a superhero universe and all the people in it. At the flourish of a penstroke you can be faster than a speeding bullet and able to leap tall buildings in a single bound. Read the works in progress of budding comic writers and perhaps submit some work of your own.

Usenet:
Newsgroup: **rec.arts.comics.creative**

X-Men

Follow this group of mutants as they fight crime and try to help bridge the gap between mutants and non-mutants. Read up on the history and creators of the X-Men as well as reviews and trivia. You can also find out about various mailing lists available on the Net. The **stripe-l** list is a mailing list for fans of Rogue.

See also: Art

Listserv Mailing List:
List Address: **stripe-l@netcom.com**
Subscription Address: **listserv@netcom.com**

Usenet:
Newsgroup: **rec.arts.comics.xbooks**

World Wide Web:
URL: **http://www.santarosa.edu/~sthoemke/x.html**

Excerpt from the Net...

```
Newsgroup: rec.arts.comics.creative
Subject: The Impending Storm: An Introduction

    THE IMPENDING STORM: AN INTRODUCTION

The following are excerpts from past postings to The Impending Storm Saga...

What has gone before:

Our valiant heroes have been transported by the Holy Savant to a world
known as the Arena in order to find the 12 Cross-Time X-piators in
order to save their world from the unravelling of time. Before the
Holy Savant left our heroes to their own devices (for they had no more
mutant powers), he left images in their minds of the 12. They were
then captured and thrown into a cell. The heroes escaped from said
cell, chased by Bill the Axe-man, nearly flooded, and separated.

Vod and the Outrider came upon Captain Ultra and an unconscious White
Knave. Bill the Axe-man sent a raven named Ailli (who may be a dark
horse, later) to spy on the heroes. So far, only the Outrider, who can
speak to the raven, trusts her.

White Knave:
   [finally regaining consciousness]
  Uuuuhhhnnn. What the hell happened?
   [Seeing Vod, he quickly jumps to his feet and unsheathes his sword]
  And what the hell is she doing with us?

Captain Ultra:
  Whoa, easy there big fella. Calm down. She is one of us now. She
  is not under the control of her dark self...
```

A B C D E F G H I J K L M N O P Q R S T U V W X Y Z

COMPUTERS: COMMODORE

Amiga Archives

AmiNet: Demos, games, utilities, programming tools, mailing list information, and documentation for people with Commodore Amiga computers.

See also: Software

Anonymous FTP:
Address: **ftp.cdrom.com**
Path: **/pub/aminet/***

Address: **ftp.luth.se**
Path: **/pub/aminet/***

Address: **ftp.wustl.edu**
Path: **/pub/aminet/***

Gopher:
Name: EUnet in Slovakia
Address: **gopher.eunet.sk**
Choose: **Archive of EUnet Slovakia | Amiga Archive**

Amiga Information Resources

A nicely presented web page offering a large collection of Amiga resources, including magazines, newsletters, rumors, hardware details, software resources, mailing lists, newsgroups, user groups, lists of developers, manufacturers, retailers, and links to the home pages of other Amiga users divided by geographical region.

World Wide Web:
URL: **http://www.cs.cmu.edu:8001/Web/People/ mjw/Computer/Amiga/MainPage.html**

Amiga Mosaic

Amiga Mosaic for the Commodore Amiga computer is based on NCSA's Mosaic. This page details installation instructions, specific features, developers list, known bugs, program status, screen shots from the program, and a link to the ftp archive where it is available.

See also: Software: Internet

World Wide Web:
URL: **http://insti.physics.sunysb.edu/AMosaic/**

Writers, share your stories on the Net.

Amiga Pictures

Pictures and related material for those wonderfully equipped Amiga computers.

See also: Computers: Graphics

Usenet:
Newsgroup: **comp.sys.amiga.graphics**

Amiga Sounds

Have you ever wondered how the professionals create and mix sound for interesting effects? The people on this newsgroup know how and they're ready to share their knowledge with you. Of course, this group is about creating sounds specifically on Amiga computers.

See also: Computers: Multimedia, Computers: Sounds

Usenet:
Newsgroup: **comp.sys.amiga.audio**

Amiga Talk

A popular channel where you can discuss anything and everything to do with the Commodore Amiga. This is a good place to seek answers to your Amiga questions or problems.

Internet Relay Chat:
Channel: **#amiga**

Amiga Telecom

Discussions about telecommunications for Amiga computer systems.

See also: Telecommunications

Usenet:
Newsgroup: **comp.sys.amiga.datacomm**

Amiga Unix

And you thought Commodore's Amiga computers were just toys! Well, a computer that can run a full-fledged Unix is not a toy. Ah, but is it a full-fledged Unix?

See also: Operating Systems: Unix Systems

Usenet:
Newsgroup: **comp.binaries.amiga**
Newsgroup: **comp.sys.amiga.unix**
Newsgroup: **comp.unix.amiga**

Commodore 64/128 Archive

Large archive of information, graphics, games, utilities, and other material for the Commodore 64 and Commodore 128 computers.

See also: Games, Software

Anonymous FTP:
Address: **ccnga.uwaterloo.ca**
Path: **/pub/cbm/***

Commodore-64 Chat

Discuss the Commodore-64 computer, its software, emulators, Commodore users and their unique computer culture.

Internet Relay Chat:
Channel: **#C-64**
Channel: **#C=64**

COMPUTERS: COMPANIES

BTG

BTG specializes in open systems development, systems engineering, reusable software, document management, and value-added reselling. This web page points to a number of their press releases, product details, and information about the BTG AXP275 RISC computer.

See also: Computers: Software

World Wide Web:
URL: **http://www.btg.com/**

Celerity Systems

It has been said that size isn't everything and in this case it happens to be true. Participate in discussion pertaining to superminicomputer systems manufactured by Celerity.

Internet Mailing List:
List Address: **info-celerity@dolphin.bu.edu**
Subscription Address:
info-celerity-request@dolphin.bu.edu

The Net is for smart people (like you).

Digital Equipment Corporation

DEC's home page sports system and options catalogs, customer updates, performance reports, press releases, newsletters, the *Digital Technical Journal*, software product descriptions, and facilities to search for specific documents or products by name.

World Wide Web:
URL: **http://www.digital.com/info/ info.home.html**

Hewlett-Packard

See the latest news, services, contacts, and products offered by Hewlett-Packard.

World Wide Web:
URL: **http://www.hp.com**

Microsoft Archives

If your best pal's birthday is coming around, or perhaps Valentine's Day, and you have to get a special gift at the last minute, check out the supermarket of software via ftp. This is not a Microsoft support site, but they do have a variety of interesting items such as product updates, the famous Microsoft Knowledgebases for each of the main desktop applications, documentation, updated drivers, utilities, and other interesting items.

Anonymous FTP:
Address: **ftp.microsoft.com**

Microsoft Gopher Server

Access the official knowledge bases for each of Microsoft's products, and hundreds of files in the software library area. Files include utility programs, device drivers, application examples, and much more for MS-DOS, Microsoft Windows, and Windows NT.

Gopher:
Name: Microsoft Corporation
Address: **gopher.microsoft.com**

Microsoft Research

See the areas of computer science in which Microsoft is working: decision theory, program analysis, natural language, operating systems, speech recognition, and user interfaces. You can also read technical reports about these and other subject areas.

World Wide Web:
URL: **http://www.research.microsoft.com**

A
B
C
D
E
F
G
H
I
J
K
L
M
N
O
P
Q
R
S
T
U
V
W
X
Y
Z

WHAT IS MICROSOFT UP TO?

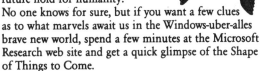

We all know that virtually everything that is important in Modern Life comes from Microsoft, and for that we are grateful. We doubt if there is anyone even remotely concerned with information and computing who doesn't rest easy at night knowing that Uncle Bill and his trained seals are on the job. However, what does the future hold for humanity? No one knows for sure, but if you want a few clues as to what marvels await us in the Windows-uber-alles brave new world, spend a few minutes at the Microsoft Research web site and get a quick glimpse of the Shape of Things to Come.

NEC

NEC's web server offers an overview of the company, news, details of products and services, research and development, a link to the NEC U.S.A. web server, and other information about this Japanese electronics company. There are both English and Japanese versions of this page.

World Wide Web:
    URL: **http://www.nec.co.jp/**

Santa Cruz Operation

The Web page from SCO Open Systems Software offers a company overview, product information including data sheets, questions and answers, sample SCO UNIX tutorial, sample man pages, service details, developer programs, third party products and services, and much more.

See also: Consumer Information

World Wide Web:
    URL: **http://www.sco.com/**

> **Parents and children,
> take a look at:
> Families and Parenting,
> Kids, and Youth.**

Sun Microsystems

Product overviews, service and support details, business articles, a technology and research section, news, and a company overview from Sun Microsystems. Sun supplies distributed computing technologies, products, and services, including networked workstations and servers, operating system software, Silicon Designs, and other value-added technologies.

See also: Consumer Information

World Wide Web:
    URL: **http://www.sun.com/**

COMPUTERS: CULTURE

Art of Technology Digest

Set of journals dedicated to sharing information among computerists and to the presentation and debate of diverse views.

Anonymous FTP:
    Address: **ftp.wustl.edu**
    Path: **/doc/misc/aot/***

Byte Bandit

The Baudy World of the Byte Bandit is a postmodernist interpretation of the computer underground.

Anonymous FTP:
    Address: **ftp.spies.com**
    Path: **/Library/Cyber/meyer.cu**

Gopher:
    Name: Internet Wiretap
    Address: **wiretap.spies.com**
    Choose: **Wiretap Online Library**
        | **Cyberspace**
        | **Computer Underground (Meyer & Thomas)**

Code of the Geeks

Are you a geek? Do you want to be? Check out the Code of the Geeks and see how you rate. Put this rating in your **.signature** file and let the world know that you are geeky and darn proud of it.

Finger:
    Address: **hayden@vax1.mankato.msus.edu**

Computer Professionals for Social Responsibility

Computer Professionals for Social Responsibility (CPSR) is a non-profit organization concerned with the effects of computers on society. CPSR is supported by its membership and has chapters throughout the country. This web page has links to discussion lists on similar topics and numerous publications.

World Wide Web:
  URL: **http://www.cpsr.org/dox/home.html**

Computer Underground Digest

The complete collection of the *Computer Underground Digest*, a weekly electronic publication covering matters concerning the computer underground.

Anonymous FTP:
  Address: **ftp.eff.org**
  Path: **/pub/Publications/CuD/CuD/***

Computer-Generated Writing

This is the early-'70s nightmare revisited, in which the world's computers develop a mind of their own and try to take over the planet. Except this time they aren't into politics. This time they want to write novels and poetry, subtly influencing the minds of young children. Read sample texts of computer-generated stories and poems and see links to other resources relating to computer-generated writing. Software for generating text is also included at this site.

See also: Software

World Wide Web:
  URL: **http://www.uio.no/~mwatz/c-g.writing/index.html**
  URL: **http://www.uio.no:80/~mwatz/c-g.writing/**

The Internet will set you free.

Excerpt from the Net...

Newsgroup: alt.comp.acad-freedom.talk
Subject: Usenet Censorship

The censors at the State Board for Comprehensive Technical Education have removed my access to the group alt.sexual.abuse.recovery. It has the word sex in it you see, and it MUST be obscene if it has the word sex in it.

They also removed all groups with the word "game" in it because the fools who make the Internet decisions for South Carolina Technical Colleges actually think people PLAY games in those groups. This was clearly stated in the rational for the block, that people will tie up the lines playing games. The people who are deciding what to censor don't even understand that these are discussion groups, not video parlors. The blind leading the sighted.

They excluded all binary/picture groups because they think people are going to be gumming up the system looking at pictures, and used alt.sex.aluminum.baseball.bat, a joke group, as an example of the kind of immoral obscene decadent pervertedness that is to be found on the Net.

They have blocked "flame" because there are insults and bad words in there.

These people haven't a clue as to the what or how or why of the Net, and yet somehow they are in a position to determine what I have access to. In this shotgun attempt to censor my reading material, they have not achieved their purpose, as I can still access the very types of materials which they are attempting to stop me from obtaining and which I have no interest in to begin with, yet have been deprived of access to other groups which I do read and which are legitimate.

A B C D E F G H I J K L M N O P Q R S T U V W X Y Z

Computers and Academic Freedom

Discussion about everything to do with computers and academic freedom, and how it should be applied to university computers and networks.

Anonymous FTP:
Address: **ftp.eff.org**
Path: **/pub/CAF/academic/***

Gopher:
Name: Electronic Frontier Foundation
Address: **gopher.eff.org**
Choose: **Computers & Academic Freedom mailing list archives & info**

Usenet:
Newsgroup: **alt.comp.acad-freedom.news**
Newsgroup: **alt.comp.acad-freedom.talk**

Concerning Hackers...

"Concerning Hackers Who Break into Computer Systems" is a paper that addresses hackers and the hacker community.

Anonymous FTP:
Address: **ftp.spies.com**
Path: **/Library/Cyber/denning.txt**

Gopher:
Name: Internet Wirenet
Address: **wiretap.spies.com**
Choose: **Wiretap Online Library**
  I **Cyberspace**
  I **Concerning Hackers who Break into Systems**

Cyberspace

Articles about cyberspace and the cyberspace culture, including papers on hackers, the computer underground, MUDs, and IRC.

Anonymous FTP:
Address: **ftp.spies.com**
Path: **/Library/Cyber/***

Gopher:
Name: Internet Wiretap
Address: **wiretap.spies.com**
Choose: **Wiretap Online Library**
  I **Cyberspace**

Ethics

Dissertations on the computer ethics policies of many universities and organizations.

Anonymous FTP:
Address: **ariel.unm.edu**
Path: **/ethics/**

Future Culture

These forward-thinking people want to contemplate the Internet, the concept of the global community, and technology and how these affect our culture and make us interact with each other in new and different ways. The Web site contains FAQs, documents relating to Future Culture, and links to related resources. Or you can just join the mailing list and get a daily dose of technocultural philosophy.

Listserv Mailing List:
List Address: **futurec@uafsysb.uark.edu**
Subscription Address: **listserv@uafsysb.uark.edu**

World Wide Web:
URL: **http://www.uio.no/~mwatz/futurec/index.html**

Excerpt from the Net...

(from the article "Concerning Hackers Who Break into Computer Systems")

A diffuse group of people, often called "hackers," has been characterized as unethical, irresponsible and a serious danger to society, for actions related to breaking into computer systems. This paper attempts to construct a picture of hackers, their concerns and the discourse in which hacking takes place. My initial findings suggest that hackers are learners and explorers who want to help rather than cause damage, and who often have very high standards of behavior... Based on my findings, I recommend that we work closely with hackers, and suggest several actions that might be taken...

A
B
C
D
E
F
G
H
I
J
K
L
M
N
O
P
Q
R
S
T
U
V
W
X
Y
Z

> ## Too much spare time?
> ## Explore a MUD.

Hackers

Peer in on clever hacking discussions and learn not only how to hack computer hardware and software, but anything in everyday life, including loose shower tiles, vibrating air conditioning vents and dust-spewing vacuum cleaners.

Usenet:
   Newsgroup: **alt.hackers**

Excerpt from the Net...

```
Newsgroup: alt.hackers
Subject: cheap grad-student food hack

With $5 to spend and 15 minutes to make
a dish for a potluck dinner:

1 can condensed cream of mushroom soup
1 package frozen chopped spinach

Place both in microwave-safe dish.
Microwave 4 min. Stir.
Microwave another 4 min.
Top with random cheeses.
```

IBM Songbook

Songs of life and inspiration at Big Blue. "Onward we'll ever go, in strong array; our thousands to the fore, nothing can stem, our march forevermore, with IBM."

Anonymous FTP:
   Address: **ftp.uu.net**
   Path: **/doc/literary/obi/IBM/songbook**

League for Programming Freedom/Free Software Foundation

A subdirectory containing articles and publications from the LPF and FSF, which are dedicated to the purchaser's right to use, copy, modify, and distribute software as he or she sees fit.

Anonymous FTP:
   Address: **ftp.uu.net**
   Path: **/doc/literary/obi/LPF/***

Nerd Page

If it's been a minimum of two days since you have seen the sun and if you can't see the top of your desk because it's covered with scraps of paper, pens and empty soda cans, then it's likely that you are a Nerd. Being a Nerd entitles you to check out this home page. It's cool, even though it's really nerdy. It's loaded with links to things around the Net that Nerds are guaranteed to love.

World Wide Web:
   URL: **http://www.engr.scarolina.edu/nerd/**

Social Organization of Computer Underground

A thesis paper examining the social organization of computer hackers, phone phreaks, and software pirates.

Anonymous FTP:
   Address: **ftp.spies.com**
   Path: **/Library/Cyber/hacker.ths**

Gopher:
   Name: Internet Wiretap
   Address: **wiretap.spies.com**
   Choose: **Wiretap Online Library**
      I **Cyberspace**
      I **Soc Organiz of Comp Underground (thesis)**

If you like studying ants or bees... take a look at *Social Organization of the Computer Underground*

WebWorld

Create your own little section of WebWorld by establishing links and paths within the community. Just like in real life, once you make something it's yours to take care of and maintain. The cool thing is there are no mortgages, evil landlords or housing inspectors.

World Wide Web:
   URL: **http://sailfish.peregrine.com/WebWorld/welcome.html**

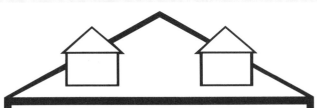

Build Your Own Web House

Are you one of those people who always dreamed of building a house of your own, only to be foiled by the high cost of real estate, construction, and not knowing what you were doing? Well, WebWorld is for you. Stake out a claim of your own and build that home page away from home that will give you the peace of mind you need to be a secure and fulfilled member of our information-savvy society.

Women and Computer Science

This is a great collection of online writings by women, in the form of essays and speeches. In addition, there are lists of women's organizations, resources, and gender bender anecdotes.

World Wide Web:
URL: **http://www.ai.mit.edu/people/ellens/ gender.html**

It is a well-known fact that men love a woman who understands Bachus-Naur form and optimizing compilers that use recursive descent and B+ trees. What is less well known is that there is a special place on the Net for Women of Computer Science to find out what other Women of Computer Science think about Women of Computer Science. (Boy, talk about recursive descent.) So don't let yourself burn out, you are not alone. Remember, "A woman who is tired of Tchebyshev polynomials is tired of Life."

COMPUTERS: GRAPHICS

Acid Warp

A much sought-after graphics program, with a wonderful psychedelic graphics display.

Anonymous FTP:
Address: **csd4.csd.uwm.edu**
Path: **/pub/aragorn/acidwarp.zoo**

Annotated Scientific Visualization Weblet Bibliography

This page is an annotated bibliography of many scientific visualization weblets and includes links to visualization software archives, and projects such as the REINAS Project at UC Santa Cruz — a realtime, data acquisition, data management, and visualization system.

World Wide Web:
URL: **http://www.nas.nasa.gov/RNR/ Visualization/annotatedURLs.html**

Computer Graphics Bibliography

A database of computer graphics bibliographic references, covering a wide span of the field. Organized by year and formatted in the BibTeX bibliography format.

Gopher:
Name: ACM SIGGRAPH
Address: **siggraph.org**
Choose: **Publications | Bibliography**

Telnet:
Address: **siggraph.org**
Login: **biblio**

Computer Graphics Information

Here are a couple of great starting points if you're looking for information on computer graphics. This web page has many links to university and government labs, newsgroups, ftp sites, software, and FAQs. The gopher offers information on computer graphics techniques, online bibliographies, conference news, utilities, and other items of interest.

Gopher:
Name: ACM SIGGRAPH
Address: **siggraph.org**

World Wide Web:
URL: **http://mambo.ucsc.edu/psl/cg.html**

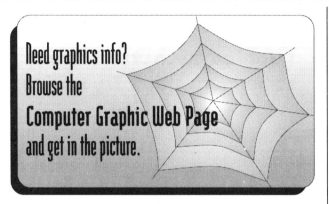

Need graphics info?
Browse the
Computer Graphic Web Page
and get in the picture.

Cool Demos

Cool demos is a web page at the Stanford Computer Graphics Laboratory. The page has links to neat demonstrations, including a morph from a human head to an orangutan head, movies of a zippered polygon mesh model of a plastic toy lyon, and information about annual competitions.

World Wide Web:
URL: **http://www-graphics.stanford.edu/demos/**

Figlet Fonts

Don't settle for the same old dull, boring strings of letters. Spice things up with some ASCII fonts. This server will allow you to select a font and modify the size and design to exactly what you want.

World Wide Web:
URL: **http://www.inf.utfsm.cl/cgi-bin/figlet**

Fract Int

A popular freeware fractal generator for DOS, Windows, OS/2, and Unix X Window. Fract Int is available in source code as well as in executable form.

Anonymous FTP:
Address: **ftp-os2.nmsu.edu**
Path: **/os2/2_x/graphics/pmfra2.zip**

Address: **ftp.uni-koeln.de**
Path: **/windows/xcontrib/xfract***

Address: **ftp.wustl.edu**
Path: **/systems/ibmpc/simtel/graphics/frasr***

Address: **ftp.wustl.edu**
Path: **/systems/ibmpc/simtel/graphics/frain***

Fractal Images

A collection of fractal images in gif format, fractal documents, formulas, and programs.

Anonymous FTP:
Address: **csus.edu**
Path: **/pub/alt.fractals.pictures/***

Address: **spanky.triumf.ca**
Path: **/fractals/***

World Wide Web:
URL: **http://www.cnam.fr/fractals.html**

Fractal Movie Archive

More than fifty fractal animations in different formats, including mpeg, Fli, Flc, and QuickTime. Fast-fly through fractal-generated landscapes and canyons or zoom into the Mandelbrot set.

World Wide Web:
URL: **http://www.cnam.fr/fractals/anim.html**

Fractals

All you ever wanted to know about fractals, including reading and resource lists, FAQs about chaos, the Mandelbrot set, Julia set, quaternion arithmetic, plasma clouds, and other related subjects.

Anonymous FTP:
Address: **rtfm.mit.edu**
Path: **/pub/usenet/news.answers/fractal-faq**

Archie:
Pattern: **fractal-faq**

Usenet:
Newsgroup: **sci.fractals**

Fractals and Chaos

This exhibition of sonic and visual art at the Australian National University is a celebration of fractals, feedback and chaos. An online catalog of submitted works is available, along with a brief history of fractals, feedback and chaos, and a tutorial.

World Wide Web:
URL: **http://acat.anu.edu.au/contours.html**

A B C D E F G H I J K L M N O P Q R S T U V W X Y Z

Gallery of Images from Silicon Graphics

Links to many graphics and 3D images from customers and partners of Silicon Graphics. The Gallery has general artistic images as well as technical and scientific images. A few examples of image titles are "Motorcycle Race," "Flat World," and "Crash Dummy." There are also links to movies, including an overview of SGI Products, and some fun ones like "Airbag Demo," "Ford Airflow," and "Extreme Sports." (These movies are in QuickTime format — the web page has information on getting a viewer for these.)

World Wide Web:
    URL: **http://www.sgi.com/free/gallery.html**

Genetic Movies

Browse an interesting selection of nine genetic mpeg movies, and then take part in this interactive art piece by voicing your own opinion. After ten votes have been collected, the votes are counted and the results are used by a genetic algorithm to create new art pieces. In this way, the collection is constantly evolving and creating new movies.

World Wide Web:
    URL: **http://robocop.modmath.cs.cmu.edu:8001/ htbin/moviegenform**

Geometry Sender

The Geometry Sender is a network file system dedicated to the distribution of geometric structures. This page offers manuals and tutorials, geometry data, interactive software for many platforms, interactive examples, links to related resources, details of external viewers for the Web and where to get them, and much more.

World Wide Web:
    URL: **http://synap.neuro.sfc.keio.ac.jp/~aly/ polygon/polygon.html**

Hyperbolic Movies

Collection of hyperbolic and fractal movies, including hyperbolic motion, a fractal octopus, and Noh men. There are also HyperCard interactive versions for some movies.

World Wide Web:
    URL: **http://andro.sfc.keio.ac.jp/~aly/ mpeg/mpeg.html**

Got too much stuff? Need some more stuff? Try Buying and Selling.

Hyperbolic Tiles

Hyperbolic tile images in jpeg format, and the Unix source code for the hyperbolic tiler that created them are available from this page. Immerse yourself in hyperbolic spheres and tiles of money, weird patterns, and even portraits.

World Wide Web:
    URL: **http://www.cs.cmu.edu:8001/Web/People/ jmount/moretilings.html**

Icon Browser

If you spend more time on your computer than you do wandering around the house, put a little effort into fixing it up nice by scattering some clever icons around. The icon browser has over three thousand icons from which to choose.

World Wide Web:
    URL: **http://www.di.unipi.it/iconbrowser/ icons.html**

PERSONALLY, we believe that icons belong in Russian churches. Still, in this post-Bill Gates world of pull-down menus and one-size-fits-all-if-you-know-what's-good-for-you, you never know when you will be called upon to lay your hands on a new icon. Not to worry. The **Icon Browser** is to icon creation what magazines with colorful pictures are to people who actually believe that making collages is an art form.

(Actually, the legend is that Bill Gates incurred the wrath of the gods by revealing the secrets of icons to mankind and, as a punishment, an eagle attacks him each day at lunchtime in the Microsoft cafeteria, forcing him to eat a plate full of liver.)

Image and Audio File Formats

Documents and descriptions of image and sound data file formats.

See also: Computers: Programming

Anonymous FTP:
    Address: **ftp.wustl.edu**
    Path: **/doc/graphic-formats/***

    Address: **rtfm.mit.edu**
    Path: **/pub/usenet-by-group/comp.answers/
      audio-fmts**

Archie:
    Pattern: **audio-fmts**

Internet Font Browser

The Internet Font Browser allows you to browse many hundreds of font samples stored as gif images. The fonts are available in PostScript Type 1 format, and you can search for a specific font, use the alphabetic listing, or select a font from the miniature images available in the thumbnail sheets.

World Wide Web:
    URL: **http://cui_www.unige.ch/
      InternetFontBrowser**

JPEG File Viewer for Macintosh

A program for viewing jpeg format graphics files. Do an archie search for **jpeg-view** for other locations and newer versions.

Anonymous FTP:
    Address: **ftp.std.com**
    Path: **/src/macintosh/graphics/jpeg-view-20.hqx**

    Address: **ftp.wustl.edu**
    Path: **/systems/mac/info-mac/grf/util/
      jpeg-view-30.hqx**

    Address: **plaza.aarnet.edu.au**
    Path: **/micros/mac/info-mac/grf/util/
      jpeg-view-31.hqx**

Archie:
    Pattern: **jpeg-view**

Professionally created images are yours for the taking. This image is one of many similar images based on the floating metallic ball concept. This one is called **balls2.gif**. Others have similar names.

JPEG File Viewer for Windows

A Windows 3.x-based jpeg file viewer. This type of file gets moved around a lot. Do an archie substring search for **winecj** for the most current locations.

Anonymous FTP:
    Address: **ftp.cica.indiana.edu**
    Path: **/pub/pc/win3/desktop/winecj.zip**

    Address: **plaza.aarnet.edu.au**
    Path: **/micros/pc/oak/windows3/winecj12.zip**

    Address: **wcarchive.cdrom.com**
    Path: **/.2/simtel/msdos/windows3/winecj12.zip**

Macintosh Graphics

Spice up your boring papers and word processing projects with graphics help from Macintosh. Learn about the various software available as well as fonts, hints about methods and style, and even the more technical aspects of hardware needed to achieve your artistic vision.

Usenet:
    Newsgroup: **comp.sys.mac.graphics**

Mandelbrot Explorer

Be a Mandelbrot artist without having to strain your brain. All you have to do is enter some coordinates, and the computer will do the work for you. Print out the results and stick them on the wall, and when everyone asks about your cool wallpaper you can act casual and say, "Oh, this? I made it myself."

World Wide Web:
    URL: **http://www.ntua.gr/mandel/mandel.html**

A
B
C
D
E
F
G
H
I
J
K
L
M
N
O
P
Q
R
S
T
U
V
W
X
Y
Z

Do you like those cool Mandelbrot patterns that everyone talks about but no one really understands? If so, try the **MANDELBROT EXPLORER.**

Mosaic Gizmos

A collection of small figures and images to give your HTML documents a more attractive look. It includes images of small balls, lines, buttons and pointers, pictures, and links to other icon resources and pages.

World Wide Web:
URL: **http://colargol.edb.tih.no/~geirme/ gizmos/gizmo.html**

Persistence of Vision

The Persistence of Vision Ray Tracer (POV-Ray) is a freeware program that allows a user to easily create fantastic, three dimensional, photo-realistic images on many computer platforms. This page offers POV news bulletins, FAQs, links to the official distribution sites, POV utilities, documentation, ready-made POV objects, and links to galleries of images created with POV.

World Wide Web:
URL: **http://www.uio.no/~mwatz/pov/index.html**

Pixel-Planes Graphics Machine

A web page for the graphics machine called Pixel Planes, which was developed at the computer science department of the University of North Carolina at Chapel Hill. This page has links to a project overview, history, information about the current version of the Pixel Planes, including hardware and software information, and the next version of the machine.

World Wide Web:
URL: **http://www.cs.unc.edu/~pxpl/home.html**

Radiance

Radiance is a package for the analysis and visualization of lighting in design. Radiance is used by architects and engineers to predict illumination, visual quality and appearance of innovative design space, and by researchers to evaluate new lighting and daylighting technologies. Radiance images, user documentation, technical papers, ftp distribution sites, and digests are available here.

World Wide Web:
URL: **ftp://hobbes.lbl.gov/www/radiance/ radiance.html**

Raytrace Graphics

Whether you want to make simple spheric shapes or plot three-dimensional movements of a human figure through space, this raytracing Usenet group will have something for you. Discussion covers software, tools and methods of raytracing for the novice or wizard. The web page has pointers to FAQs, bibliography, documentation, software packages, ftp archives, many raytraced images, links to other raytracing related sites, and much more to do with raytracing.

Usenet:
Newsgroup: **comp.graphics.raytracing**

World Wide Web:
URL: **http://www.cm.cf.ac.uk/Ray.Tracing/**

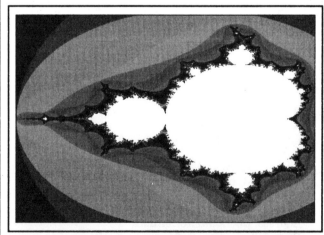

To view the graphics files you download from the Internet, you need software capable of displaying graphics. This software is just as free and just as available as all of the images themselves. Once you've got software that can display graphic images, you can download and display images of images being displayed! This picture is **mandelbr.gif** (for Mandelbrot [the fractal guy]).

Rayshade

Rayshade is an extensible system for creating ray-traced images. It's written in C and available for many different platforms. This site offers the Rayshade software, user's guide, quick-reference sheet, Rayshade images, a magnificent Rayshade Gallery, mailing list archives, tutorials, and much more.

World Wide Web:
URL: **http://www.cs.princeton.edu/grad/ cek/rayshade/rayshade.html**

Rob's Multimedia Lab

Rob's Multimedia Lab (RML) is a massive collection of images, sounds, and movies. It contains gif images, audio files, and mpeg movies. The images and sounds are categorized into sections, and there are links to many other sites containing picture, sound, or movie archives. If you are looking for a specific picture or sound, there is a good chance that you can find it here.

See also: Computers: Sounds

World Wide Web:
URL: **http://www.acm.uiuc.edu:80/rml/**

Silicon Graphics Gallery

Graphics and 3-D galleries that have come from Silicon Graphics customers and partners. The images are divided into general and scientific sections. The winning entries from the eleven categories in the Silicon Graphics International Visual Computing Awards are also on display. There is a section with Single Image Random Dot Stereograms (SIRDS), also called Rastergrams, which are images that can only be seen when viewers allow their eyes to relax and create multiple focal points. Finally, there are also QuickTime movie clips, including product movies and other fun stuff.

World Wide Web:
URL: **http://www.sgi.com/free/ gallery.html#movie**

**Need Unix help?
See Harley's book
"Unix Unbound."**

Silicon Graphics Silicon Surf

Silicon Surf is a service for the Silicon Graphics community of users offering press releases, product announcements, product catalog with descriptions of both Silicon Graphics and partners' products, a classroom section with course descriptions of both lecture-led courses and self-paced courses, software and images, and technical information.

See also: Consumer Information

World Wide Web:
URL: **http://www.sgi.com/ss.home.page.html**

Text-based Animation

Files that produce interesting animation sequences when routed to a vt100 terminal.

Anonymous FTP:
Address: **quartz.rutgers.edu**
Path: **/pub/computer/vt100/***

Gopher:
Name: Rutgers University
Address: **quartz.rutgers.edu**
Choose: **Computer-Sources, Documentation, Comp.Sci
| vt100 Animations**

Thant's Animations Index

More than one hundred short descriptions and links to servers on the Web which offer computer generated animations, visualizations, movies and interactive images. It includes an mpeg movie of the Big Bang, calculus visualizations, movies of NASA LaRC's F-16 project, 3-D visualization of a frog, cosmic movies, sports movies, scenery movies, *Star Trek* movies, and many more. The movies and animations are in varying formats.

World Wide Web:
URL: **http://mambo.ucsc.edu/psl/thant/ thant.html**

Tomservo Raytraced Images

A large collection of raytraced images, in jpeg format, from the POV-ray raytracing program, and other sources. The images are divided into directories depending on the time it took to actually raytrace the images.

World Wide Web:
URL: **http://www.hmc.edu/~awells/files/ raytrace.html**

A B C D E F G H I J K L M N O P Q R S T U V W X Y Z

Virtual Reality Markup Language

An open forum discussion for the design and implementation of a platform-independent language for virtual reality scene design. Includes links to many proposed Virtual Reality Markup Language (VRML) systems, visions, goals, hypermail archive, VRML concepts, papers, and much more.

World Wide Web:
URL: **http://www.wired.com:80/vrml/**

VuSystem

The VuSystem is a programming system for the dynamic manipulation of temporally sensitive data. It was designed at MIT and runs on any Unix workstation with the X Window system. Details of its video applications, demonstrations, and some source distribution can be found here.

World Wide Web:
URL: **http://tns-www.lcs.mit.edu/vs/ vusystem.html**

Web Page Graphics and Icons

A list of pointers and links to many different icons and graphic images you can use with HTML documents (web pages). These collections include arrows, bullets, buttons, dingbats, dots, 3-D icons, Greek symbols, NCSA icons, violent crime symbols, monochrome icons, gopher icons, flags, mail, movies, daemons, globes, houses, palettes, musical instruments, dividers, logos, and many more. Most of these graphics are in xbm and gif formats.

World Wide Web:
URL: **http://www.yahoo.com/Computers/ World_Wide_Web/Programming/Icons/**
URL: **http://www-pcd.stanford.edu/gifs/**
URL: **http://www.bsdi.com/icons/misc.html**

WebOOGL Home Page

WebOOGL is a format for distributing and linking multidimensional objects across the Web, in much the same way that HTML is used to distribute text-based hypermedia. A guide to WebOOGL, which contains details of what you need to view it, examples of linked WebOOGL worlds, a visualizing webspace example, instructions on how to make your own WebOOGL files, and a WebOOGL repository, can be found here.

World Wide Web:
URL: **http://www.geom.umn.edu/docs/weboogl/ weboogl.html**

COMPUTERS: HARDWARE

386BSD Unix Supplements for Compaq Computers

The original 386BSD 0.1 file systems with bootstrap programs modified to boot on Compaq hardware.

See also: Operating Systems: Unix Systems

Anonymous FTP:
Address: **ftp.compaq.com**
Path: **/pub/386bsd/***

Apple IIgs

Fans of the venerable Apple IIgs meet here to discuss everything you can imagine about this still popular computer.

Internet Relay Chat:
Channel: **#appleIIgs**

Compaq Fixes and Patches

All the available fixes and patches for Compaq hardware in SoftPaq form. Read the file **patches.1st** for more information.

See also: Operating Systems: Unix

Anonymous FTP:
Address: **ftp.compaq.com**
Path: **/pub/softpaq**

Computer Information

Information on many different types of computers and software, including IBMs, Macintosh computers, NeXT and Sun workstations, and others. The information includes valuable instructions for complex operations such as configuring network file systems, CD-ROM drives, development systems, Apple's A/UX, Claris software, and so on.

Gopher:
Name: University of Minnesota
Address: **gopher.micro.umn.edu**
Choose: **Computer Information**

Do you like weirdness? Check out Usenet Curiosities.

EPROM Models and Manufacturers List

A list of manufacturers, models, and statistics for many EPROM (Erasable/Programmable Read-Only Memory) chips.

Anonymous FTP:
Address: **oak.oakland.edu**
Path: **/pub/misc/eprom/eprom-types.list**

Hard Disk Guide

Comprehensive dictionary of hard drives, floppy drives, optical drives, drive controllers, and host adapters. Designed to help the novice and pro alike with integration problems and system setups.

Anonymous FTP:
Address: **ftp.uwasa.fi**
Path: **/pc/doc-hard/harddisk.zip**

Address: **ftp.wustl.edu**
Path: **/systems/ibmpc/garbo/doc-hard/ harddisk.zip**

Address: **nic.funet.fi**
Path: **/pub/doc/HW/harddisks/***

Hardware Architectures

Technical information and tutorials about some of the large IBM systems, including the ES/9000, RS600, and the Scalable Powerparallel systems.

Gopher:
Name: Cornell University
Address: **gopher.tc.cornell.edu**
Choose: **Hardware Platforms**

Hardware News

Read about news events and discussions relating to computers, printers, companies, software, and even calculators and palmtops. This directory is a veritable scrapbook of all the most interesting clippings from usenet newsgroups and other sources.

Anonymous FTP:
Address: **csd4.csd.uwm.edu**
Path: **/pub/Portables/News/***

Hardware Technical Material

Details on various hardware, including S100 bus pins, Multimedia PC specification, hard disk interleave factors, and Multibus II.

Anonymous FTP:
Address: **ftp.spies.com**
Path: **/Library/Techdoc/Hardware/***

Gopher:
Name: Internet Wiretap
Address: **wiretap.spies.com**
Choose: **Wiretap Online Library**
  | **Technical Information**
  | **Hardware**

How Computers Work

A list of articles on the basic workings of the computer. Includes sections on ASCII, bits and bytes, memory, operating systems, files and directories, and software programs.

Gopher:
Name: La Trobe University
Address: **gopher.latrobe.edu.au**
Choose: **Computing Services**
  | **1993 Handbook**
  | **Introduction to Computing Services**

What is the magic inside the box?

Take a look at **HOW COMPUTERS WORK**

Microprocessor Instruction Set Cards

A number of microprocessor and microcomputer instruction set cards in a common format, including microprocessors from Motorola, Intel, Rockwell, National Semiconductor, DEC, and others. There is also a Unix shell script to process the cards for output on a single page of an A4 PostScript printer.

Anonymous FTP:
Address: **ftp.comlab.ox.ac.uk**
Path: **/pub/Cards/***

World Wide Web:
URL: **http://www.comlab.ox.ac.uk/ archive/cards.html**

A
B
C
D
E
F
G
H
I
J
K
L
M
N
O
P
Q
R
S
T
U
V
W
X
Y
Z

Modems

Discussion, reviews, comparative statistics, program source code, and much more for and about modems.

Anonymous FTP:
    Address: **oak.oakland.edu**
    Path: **/pub/misc/modems**

MODEMS and FUN

Modems are now an indispensible accoutrement of modern life. However, anyone who has ever tried to get a recalcitrant modem to cooperate understands just how much fun these delightful little devices can be. When your modem gets its back up, turn to the modem information site for help and enlightenment.

Parallel Computing Archive

Offers papers, software, technical documentation, programming environment packages, event details, bibliographies, book lists, documents and standards, FAQs, journals, mailing list archives, and much more relating to the world of parallel computing.

Anonymous FTP:
    Address: **unix.hensa.ac.uk**
    Path: **/parallel/***

World Wide Web:
    URL: **http://www.hensa.ac.uk/parallel/**

PC and Macintosh Guides

Information sheets, articles, hints, and tricks for people with PCs or Macintosh computers.

Anonymous FTP:
    Address: **ftp.spies.com**
    Path: **/Library/Techdoc/Micro/***

Gopher:
    Name: Internet Wiretap
    Address: **wiretap.spies.com**
    Choose: **Wiretap Online Library**
      | Technical Information
      | PCs and Macintoshes

PC Hardware

Computing is no fun if you have to work on a slow dinosaur of a PC that creaks when it starts up or blows dust out of its cracks every time you change directories. Keep up with the latest in hardware changes and make your machine state-of-the-art.

Usenet:
    Newsgroup: **comp.sys.ibm.pc.hardware.cd-rom**
    Newsgroup: **comp.sys.ibm.pc.hardware.chips**
    Newsgroup: **comp.sys.ibm.pc.hardware.comm**
    Newsgroup: **comp.sys.ibm.pc.hardware.misc**
    Newsgroup: **comp.sys.ibm.pc.hardware.networking**
    Newsgroup: **comp.sys.ibm.pc.hardware.storage**
    Newsgroup: **comp.sys.ibm.pc.hardware.systems**
    Newsgroup: **comp.sys.ibm.pc.hardware.video**

Performance Database Server

A web page interface to the Performance Database Server — a database with information on benchmarking computer hardware. Links on the page allow you to search the database, or to browse articles directly. Article topics include the Dhrystone, Fhourstone, Flops, and many other benchmarking methods.

World Wide Web:
    URL: **http://netlib2.cs.utk.edu/performance/html/PDStop.html**

Portable Computer Information

Everything you could possibly wonder about portable computers, including laptops, subnotebooks, Personal Digital Assistants (PDAs), and high-end calculators. Subdirectories contain frequently asked questions, and reviews and information about specific models. From PCMCIA Ethernet adapters to cheap palmtops, here's the place to look for information.

Anonymous FTP:
    Address: **csd4.csd.uwm.edu**
    Path: **/pub/Portables/***

Powerful Computer List

A list of the world's most powerful computing sites.

Mail:
> Address: **gunter@yarrow.wt.uwa.edu.au**

Sinclair ZX-Spectrum Web server

Software and documents for fans of the Sinclair ZX-Spectrum. This page has links to emulators, frequently asked questions, hardware information, ROM routines, game maps, and a hacker's guide.

World Wide Web:
> URL: **http://www.nvg.unit.no/Sinclair/Spectrum/**

Supercomputer Documentation

Collection of information about applications packages, graphics software, languages and compilers, and scientific libraries available for supercomputers.

Gopher:
> Name: Texas A&M University
> Address: **gopher.tamu.edu**
> Choose: **TAMU Service & Agency Gophers**
>   **| Supercomputer Center gopher**

Transputer Archive

The Transputer Archive contains information relevant to the Transputer microprocessor designed by Inmos. It includes mailing list archives, addresses of Occam/Transputer companies, calls for papers, contacts for the Occam user group, jokes, surveys, technical notes, articles from the newsgroup **comp.sys.transputer**, and pointers to related sites.

Anonymous FTP:
> Address: **ftp.comlab.ox.ac.uk**
> Path: **/pub/Transputer/***

World Wide Web:
> URL: **http://www.comlab.ox.ac.uk/archive/ transputer.html**

Spare time? Take a look at Games.

Troubleshooting Your PC

Guide to the built-in diagnostic procedures that help identify computer component problems.

Anonymous FTP:
> Address: **ftp.spies.com**
> Path: **/Library/Techdoc/Micro/diagnose.txt**

Gopher:
> Name: Internet Wiretap
> Address: **wiretap.spies.com**
> Choose: **Wiretap Online Library**
>   **| Technical Information**
>   **| PCs and Macintoshes**
>   **| Troubleshooting your IBM PC**

Ultrasound

An area devoted to information and utilities supporting the Gravis Ultrasound card for ISA-based computers, including IBM/PCs. Includes demos, digests, games, bulletins, sounds, and utilities.

Anonymous FTP:
> Address: **ftp.wustl.edu**
> Path: **/systems/ibmpc/ultrasound/***

Vaxbook

A guide made by users for users of VAX/VMS, available in PostScript and TeX formats.

Anonymous FTP:
> Address: **decoy.uoregon.edu**
> Path: **/pub/vaxbook/***

> Address: **ftp.uga.edu**
> Path: **/pub/vms/***

COMPUTERS: LITERATURE

Alice in Unix Land

Jump through your monitor with Alice and go on a wild and woolly chase through the strange and mysterious Unix Land. This fun story is based on the Wonderland tales by Lewis Carroll.

See also: Humor

Gopher:
> Name: University of Minnesota
> Address: **gopher.micro.umn.edu**
> Choose: **Fun & Games**
>   **| Humor**
>   **| Alice in UNIX Land**

A B C D E F G H I J K L M N O P Q R S T U V W X Y Z

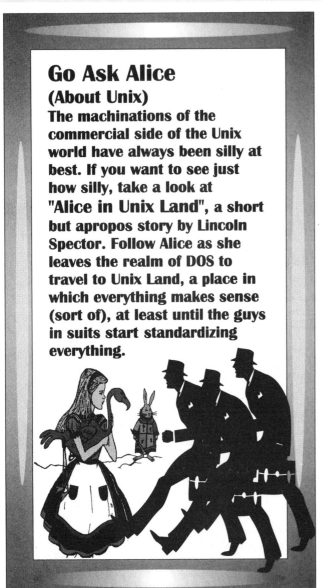

Go Ask Alice
(About Unix)

The machinations of the commercial side of the Unix world have always been silly at best. If you want to see just how silly, take a look at "Alice in Unix Land", a short but apropos story by Lincoln Spector. Follow Alice as she leaves the realm of DOS to travel to Unix Land, a place in which everything makes sense (sort of), at least until the guys in suits start standardizing everything.

Amateur Computerist

Complete run of the *Amateur Computerist* newsletter, and archives from the **alt.amateur-comp** Usenet group, dedicated to inform people of developments in an effort to advance computer education.

Anonymous FTP:
   Address: **ftp.wustl.edu**
   Path: **/doc/misc/acn/***

Be cool! Join a mailing list.

Artificial Intelligence Journal

Back issues of the *Artificial Intelligence Journal* in PC file formats.

Anonymous FTP:
   Address: **ftp.cic.net**
   Path: **/pub/nircomm/gopher/e-serials/alphabetic/a/aijournal**

Archie:
   Pattern: **aijournal**

Gopher:
   Name: CICNet
   Address: **gopher.cic.net**
   Choose: **Electronic Serials**
      | **Alphabetic List**
      | **A**
      | **Artificial Intelligence Journal**

   Name: Software Tool & Die
   Address: **gopher.std.com**
   Choose: **Periodicals, Magazines, and Journals**
      | **Artificial Intelligence Journal**

BBS Issues

Items of interest to BBS operators, including the text and analysis of lawsuits, FCC regulations, opinions, and more.

Anonymous FTP:
   Address: **oak.oakland.edu**
   Path: **/pub/misc/bbs**

Computer Emergency Response Team

Lots of technical and advisory documents about specific computer security problems and bugs from the Computer Emergency Response Team.

Anonymous FTP:
   Address: **cert.org**
   Path: **/pub/***

   Address: **ftp.uu.net**
   Path: **/doc/security/cert_advisories**

Planning a picnic? Check the weather using the Net.

> ## No one understands the Internet, so relax and enjoy.

Computer Science Technical Papers Archive

This web page has links to computer science technical reports in PostScript format. Pointers include papers from the Computer Science Division, Robotics Institute, and Center for Machine Translation, categorized by year.

World Wide Web:
    URL: **http://www.cs.cmu.edu:8001/afs/
    cs.cmu.edu/user/clamen/mosaic/
    reports/README.html**

Computer Science Technical Reports

Gopher and ftp access to a large archive of technical computer science reports from a number of sources and institutions.

Anonymous FTP:
    Address: **fas.sfu.ca**
    Path: **/pub/cs/techreports**

Gopher:
    Name: Simon Fraser University
    Address: **fas.sfu.ca**
    Choose: **Internet Resouce Projects**
    | **EPiCS**
    | **Technical Report Archives in Computer
    Science**

HACKING for FUN and PROFIT

The hacker community is a lot more convoluted and sophisticated than you might think. If you are a teenager looking for something exciting that your parents and teachers will never understand, take a look at the literature of the *Computer Underground.*

Computer Underground

Largest collection of hacker, phreaker, anarchist, cyberpunk, and underground material to be found anywhere on the Internet. Includes such fabled publications as *Phrack*, *Magik*, *Phantasy*, and *The Legion of Doom Technical Journals*.

Anonymous FTP:
    Address: **ftp.eff.org**
    Path: **/pub/Publications/CuD/***

Computer Virus Technical Information

Detailed technical information about many of the known viruses, including how to detect them, the damage they cause, and eradicating them. Includes entries for MS-DOS, Amiga, and Macintosh viruses.

Anonymous FTP:
    Address: **oak.oakland.edu**
    Path: **/pub/misc/virus**

Computing Across America

Tales of adventure from Nomad and his electronic cottage, as he traveled across America on a techno-gizmo encumbered recumbent bicycle.

Anonymous FTP:
    Address: **ucsd.edu**
    Path: **/nomad/Nomadness/***

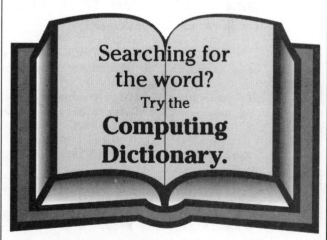

Searching for the word? Try the **Computing Dictionary.**

Computing Dictionary

Abbreviations, a list of over 2,100 computer languages, available compilers and interpreters, hacker jargon file, STING hypertext computing glossary, and links to other interesting computer resources.

World Wide Web:
    URL: **http://wombat.doc.ic.ac.uk/**

A B C D E F G H I J K L M N O P Q R S T U V W X Y Z

Computing Newsletters

Selection of newsletters and articles about operating systems, software, and other technical computer topics.

Anonymous FTP:
> Address: **nigel.msen.com**
> Path: **/pub/newsletters/Computing/***

Desktop Publishing

FAQs, current job opportunities, accounting database and cashbook programs, for Pagemaker users and desktop publishers in general.

Anonymous FTP:
> Address: **ftp.wustl.edu**
> Path: **/doc/misc/pagemakr/***

Gopher:
> Name: University of Texas at Austin
> Address: **gopher.cc.utexas.edu**
> Choose: **UT-Austin**
> > | **Computation Center**
> > | **Desktop Publishing..**

Usenet:
> Newsgroup: **alt.aldus.pagemaker**

Jump into the Net.

EFF's Guide to the Internet

Formerly the *Big Dummy's Guide to the Internet*, this text is an entertaining guide to surviving on the Net. The guide covers everything from using electronic mail to Usenet and MUDs.

Note: Also check out the FAQ file at EFF's ftp site.

Anonymous FTP:
> Address: **ftp.eff.org**
> Path: **/pub/Net_info/EFF_Net_Guide/netguide.eff**

> Address: **ftp.germany.eu.net**
> Path: **/pub/books/big-dummys-guide/***

> Address: **ftp.vifp.monash.edu.au**
> Path: **/pub/userdocs/bdgtti/***

Gopher:
> Name: Electronic Frontier Foundation
> Address: **gopher.eff.org**
> Choose: **Net Info (EFF's Guide to the Internet, FAQs, etc.)**

Excerpt from the Net...

```
(from "Alice in Unix Land")

..."Well," responded the Sun Bear, "we've got to do something to
make them want to switch to Unix."

"Do you think," said a Woodpecker who had been busy making a hole in
the table, "that there might be a problem with the name 'Unix?' I mean,
it does sort of suggest being less than a man."

"Maybe we should try another name, " suggested the Job Sparrow, "like
Brut, or Rambo."

"Penix," suggested a Penguin.

"Mount," said the Frog, "spawn."

Alice slapped him. "Nice?" he asked.

"But then again," suggested the Woodpecker, "what about the shrinkwrap
issue?"

Suddenly, everyone leaped up and started dashing about, waving their
hands in the air and screaming. Just as suddenly, they all sat down
again...
```

Hacker Crackdown

A subdirectory of text files containing the book *The Hacker Crackdown*, by Bruce Sterling.

Anonymous FTP:
 Address: **ftp.uu.net**
 Path: **/doc/literary/obi/Bruce.Sterling/**
 The.Hacker.Crackdown/*

Hacker's Dictionary

A comprehensive compendium of hacker slang illuminating many aspects of hackish tradition, folklore, and humor. Also known as the "jargon file."

Gopher:
 Name: Kent State University
 Address: **nimitz.mcs.kent.edu**
 Choose: **Documentation**
  | **General Computer**
  | **Hacker's Dictionary**

Hacker's Technical Journals

The infamous Legion of Doom has put together several journals full of technical information for those of you who like to know exactly how things work. What's nice about these archives is that they are multi-purpose: they can probably get you out of as much trouble as they get you into.

See also: Cyberpunk, Computers: Technology

Anonymous FTP:
 Address: **ftp.eff.org**
 Path: **/pub/Publications/CuD/LOD/***

Be informed. Check out Consumer Information.

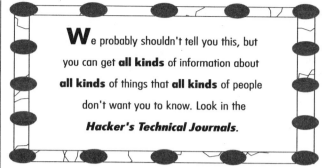

We probably shouldn't tell you this, but you can get **all kinds** of information about **all kinds** of things that **all kinds** of people don't want you to know. Look in the *Hacker's Technical Journals*.

How to Steal Code

Also known as "Inventing the Wheel Only Once." A guide by Henry Spencer on the merits of using the wealth of existing software and libraries instead of writing programs from scratch.

Anonymous FTP:
 Address: **rohan.sdsu.edu**
 Path: **/pub/doc/general/steal.doc**

 Address: **relay.cs.toronto.edu**
 Path: **/doc/programming/steal.doc**

HPCwire

HPCwire publishes a weekly news bulletin on high-performance computing, distributed to thousands of users on the Internet. Topic matter ranges from workstations through supercomputers, with news briefs, feature stories, and in-depth, exclusive interviews.

Telnet:
 Address: **hpcwire.ans.net**
 Login: **hpcwire**

Internet Bibliography

An extensive list of Internet-related books compiled by the Institute for Academic Technology at the University of North Carolina.

Anonymous FTP:
 Address: **sunsite.unc.edu**
 Path: **/pub/UNC-info/IAT/guides/ug-14.txt**

Gopher:
 Name: University of North Carolina
 Address: **sunsite.unc.edu**
 Choose: **UNC-Gopherspace**
  | **UNC-CH Information Center**
  | **Publications**
  | **Institute for Academic Technology**
  | **Resource Guides and Bibliographies**
  | **Internet Bibliography**

Internet Computer Index

The Internet Computer Index is a central repository for all resources relating to PCs, Macintosh, and Unix systems. Searching is made easy by categorizing resources into newsgroups, mailing lists, gopher servers, web pages, ftp sites, FAQs, online publications, and commonly downloaded files.

See also: Computers: PC, Computers: Macintosh

World Wide Web:
URL: **http://ici.proper.com/**

Internet Overview

An interesting history and overview of the Internet written by cyberpunk author Bruce Sterling.

Gopher:
Name: University of Texas at Austin
Address: **actlab.rtf.utexas.edu**
Choose: **Networks**
| The Internet
| An Article on the Internet...

Introduction to HTML

Get creative with Hypertext Markup Language (HTML) and make impressive web pages. Use this detailed documentation to get an overview of HTML, learn about attractive design, markup elements, see examples and pointers to other HTML resources as well as quite a few other helpful links.

World Wide Web:
URL: **http://www.utirc.utoronto.ca:3232/ HTMLdocs/NewHTML/intro.html**

DO YOU WANT TO CREATE YOUR OWN WEB PAGE?

Start with the **Introduction to HTML**

IRC Thesis

An honors thesis entitled "Electropolis: Communication and Community on IRC," by E.M. Reid, detailing the culture and ways of Internet Relay Chat.

Anonymous FTP:
Address: **ftp.spies.com**
Path: **/Library/Cyber/electrop.txt**

Kermit Manual

Sixth edition of the manual for the Kermit file transfer protocol, the protocol often used by communications programs to transfer files using a modem.

Anonymous FTP:
Address: **ftp.funet.fi**
Path: **/pub/kermit/docs/***

Address: **kermit.columbia.edu**
Path: **/kermit***

Gopher:
Name: Int. Centre for Genetic Engineering and Biotechnology
Address: **genes.icgeb.trieste.it**
Choose: **General Computing Services**
| File Transfer
| Kermit
| General Kermit Documentation

LAN Management

Text file containing the book *LAN Management*, by Charles Hedrick.

Anonymous FTP:
Address: **ftp.uu.net**
Path: **/doc/literary/obi/Charles.Hedrick/ lan.management**

Logintaka

An entertaining guide to becoming a Unix wizard.

Gopher:
Name: Oregon State University
Address: **gopher.fsl.orst.edu**
Choose: **Other Sources of Information**
| Hugo's Lore-House
| Where the Sun Doesn't Shine & Other Bottomless Pits
| The Logintaka

Network Bibliography

A list of many of the world's most important computer networks.

Mail:
Address: **comserve@rpiecs.bitnet**
Body: **send compunet biblio**

Network Newsletters

Selection of newsletters related to networks, including discussion of their social aspect and impact.

Anonymous FTP:
Address: **nigel.msen.com**
Path: **/pub/newsletters/Networker/***

Networking Computers

Lots of information on computer networking, school computing, hardware for networking, Unix networking, and programming languages.

Gopher:
Name: Pacific Systems Group
Address: **gopher.psg.com**
Choose: **Networking...**

PC Downloading

A guide to downloading Internet files to a PC, using the Procomm or Kermit communications programs and protocols.

Anonymous FTP:
Address: **ftp.funet.fi**
Path: **/pub/doc/library/download.txt**

PC/MS-DOS: The Essentials

A brief guide for beginners with MS-DOS/PC-DOS computers. Written by George Campbell, this guide starts at the very beginning and takes it one step at a time.

Anonymous FTP:
Address: **ucselx.sdsu.edu**
Path: **/pub/doc/general/msdos.txt**

If you weren't lucky enough to buy one of the older Peter Norton DOS books (when Harley was working on them), you may need some help with your PC.

Try
PC/MS-DOS:
The Essentials

Tao of Programming

A humorous guide to programming and otherwise living with computers in the modern age. "Something mysterious is formed, born in the silent void. Waiting alone and unmoving, it is at once still and yet in constant motion. It is the source of all programs. I do not know its name, so I will call it the Tao of Programming."

Anonymous FTP:
Address: **ucselx.sdsu.edu**
Path: **/pub/doc/etext/tao-of-programming.txt**

Technical Reports Online

Many pointers to resources for online computer science technical reports and papers from academic and research centers all over the world.

World Wide Web:
URL: **http://www.cs.cmu.edu:8001/Web/techreport.html**

Tipsheet

A computer help and tip exchange where people can discuss a project or ask questions and get answers.

Listserv Mailing List:
List Address: **tipsheet@wsuvm1.csc.wsu.edu**
Subscription Address:
listserv@wsuvm1.csc.wsu.edu

Zen and the Art of the Internet

The first edition of the booklet by Brendan Kehoe, which covers all the basics of the Internet, including mail, ftp, Usenet, telnet, and other tools.

Anonymous FTP:
Address: **ftp.cs.widener.edu**
Path: **/pub/zen/***

Address: **ftp.csn.org**
Path: **/pub/net/zen**

Address: **quartz.rutgers.edu**
Path: **/pub/internet/docs/zen/***

A B C D E F G H I J K L M N O P Q R S T U V W X Y Z

COMPUTERS: MACINTOSH

Buying and Selling Macs

Here is the Usenet swap meet for Macs. The **.wanted** newsgroup is the place to send a request for Macintosh-related hardware or software. The **.computers** group is more for buying and selling systems and components.

Usenet:
   Newsgroup: **comp.sys.mac.wanted**
   Newsgroup: **misc.forsale.computers.mac**

Internet Macintosh Resources

Access to Mac resources on the Net, including prices on used Macintosh equipment, the Info-Mac HyperArchive, and "The Weird, the Wild, and the Wonderful on the WWW."

World Wide Web:
   URL: **http://raptor.sccs.swarthmore.edu/jahall/ dox/Mac.html**

Mac Hardware

General discussion about Macintosh hardware of all types. The **.portable** newsgroup is for anything small and easy to move: laptops, notebooks, and so on.

Usenet:
   Newsgroup: **comp.sys.mac.hardware**
   Newsgroup: **comp.sys.mac.portables**

MacinTalk

Discuss any and all aspects of the Apple Macintosh computers with other Mac users and enthusiasts. There is also an online MacServ Deluxe bot offering many services and files, although user privileges are required to access some of these.

Internet Relay Chat:
   Channel: **#macintosh**

Excerpt from the Net...

(from "An Article on the Internet" by Bruce Sterling)

Some thirty years ago, the Rand Corporation, America's foremost Cold War think-tank, faced a strange strategic problem. How could the U.S. authorities successfully communicate after a nuclear war?...

Rand mulled over this grim puzzle in deep military secrecy, and arrived at a daring solution. The Rand proposal (the brainchild of Rand staffer Paul Baran) was made public in 1964. In the first place, the network would have no central authority. Furthermore, it would be designed from the beginning to operate while in tatters...

In fall 1969, the first such node was installed in UCLA. By December 1969, there were four nodes on the infant network, which was named ARPANET, after its Pentagon sponsor...

It wasn't long before the invention of the mailing-list, an ARPANET broadcasting technique in which an identical message could be sent automatically to large numbers of network subscribers. Interestingly, one of the first really big mailing-lists was "SF-LOVERS," for science fiction fans. Discussing science fiction on the network was not work-related and was frowned upon by many ARPANET computer administrators, but this didn't stop it from happening...

ARPA's network, designed to assure control of a ravaged society after a nuclear holocaust, has been superceded by its mutant child the Internet, which is thoroughly out of control, and spreading exponentially through the post-Cold War electronic global village...

Macintosh Announcements

This moderated newsgroup contains announcements related to the Macintosh and to Apple: hardware and software, problems and solutions.

Usenet:
Newsgroup: **comp.sys.mac.announce**

Macintosh General Discussion

Discussion and commentary on every topic under the Macintosh sun. The **.advocacy** newsgroup is for debate and opinion. The **.digest** is a moderated magazine that contains articles of interest to Mac people. The **.misc** group is a forum for general discussion.

Usenet:
Newsgroup: **comp.sys.mac**
Newsgroup: **comp.sys.mac.advocacy**
Newsgroup: **comp.sys.mac.digest**
Newsgroup: **comp.sys.mac.graphics**
Newsgroup: **comp.sys.mac.misc**

Macintosh Index

A wealth of information on Mac-related contests, ftp sites, gophers, Web servers, mailing lists, online publications, FAQs, and reviews of products.

World Wide Web:
URL: **http://ici.proper.com/1/mac**

Macintosh News

Breaking news stories and events involving Apple Computer, Inc. and Macintosh computers.

Usenet:
Newsgroup: **clari.nb.apple**

Macintosh Resources

Access to Mac network resources such as HyperSAM — a hypertext document on interface guidelines, Macintosh FAQs, mailing lists, and even a link that lets you listen in on the Space Shuttle!

World Wide Web:
URL: **http://www.astro.nwu.edu/lentz/ mac/home-mac.html**

Macintosh in Science and Technology

Discussions about using the Macintosh for science and technological work. Just the place, for example, to ask if anyone knows of a catalog for organic chemical substances to use with a Mac.

Usenet:
Newsgroup: **comp.sys.mac.scitech**

Macintosh User's Group

If you speak German and you're into Macintosh computers, this could be the place for you! A Mac group for Austrians and Germans.

Telnet:
Address: **amdalinz.edvz.uni-linz.ac.at**
Login: **guest**
Password: **guest**

Macintosh User's Group at Arkansas College

The Arkansas College and University Macintosh User's Group (ACUMUG) offers access to Apple and Macintosh resources, including links to the Apple Higher Education gopher, Apple's ftp site, and a direct link to the Arizona Macintosh User's Group.

World Wide Web:
URL: **http://acumug.ualr.edu/**

Macintosh User's Group at Johns Hopkins

The home page for the Johns Hopkins Macintosh Users Group. This page has some interesting links, including pricing for Macintosh equipment through JHU, links to the Welch Medical Library, the Genome database, and JHU's gopher.

World Wide Web:
URL: **http://mug.welch.jhu.edu/**

Resources for Apple Users

A web page that collects some of the more interesting Macintosh resources. This page offers access to Apple's Internet servers, ftp sites, Macintosh user groups, software archives, material on A/UX, and more.

World Wide Web:
URL: **http://www.apple.com/Documents/ ResourcePointers.html**

A
B
C
D
E
F
G
H
I
J
K
L
M
N
O
P
Q
R
S
T
U
V
W
X
Y
Z

Source Code for Macintosh

Share your Macintosh source code with the rest of the world by posting it to this Usenet group. **alt.sources.mac** is only for source code, so if you want to discuss code that is posted at the newsgroup, use **alt.sources.mac.d**. If you want to make a request for source code, you should post on **alt.sources.wanted**.

Usenet:
> Newsgroup: **alt.sources.mac**
> Newsgroup: **alt.sources.mac.d**
> Newsgroup: **alt.sources.wanted**

Need to keep up with the MacJoneses? Read **TidBITS**

TidBITS

A weekly electronic publication that reports on products and events in the world of the Macintosh.

Anonymous FTP:
> Address: **ftp.halcyon.com**
> Path: **/pub/tidbits/issues/***

> Address: **ftp.uu.net**
> Path: **/doc/literary/obi/Macintosh/**
> **TidBITS-digests/***

Listserv Mailing List:
> List Address: **tidbits@ricevm1.rice.edu**
> Subscription Address: **listserv@ricevm1.rice.edu**

World Wide Web:
> URL: **http://www.dartmouth.edu/Pages/**
> **TidBITS/TidBITS.html**

COMPUTERS: MULTIMEDIA

Audio Slideshow Guide

Illustrated instructions on how to add slideshow capabilities to your Sun or Linux system, using isplay and isunpack. This page has links to both the source code and binaries, as well as sample audio/visual files for testing.

See also: Computers: Pictures

World Wide Web:
> URL: **http://zaphod.cc.ttu.ee/vrainn/illaud.html**

Illustrated Audio Slide Show Technology

Illustrated Audio is new technology that synchronizes graphic image and text displays with a sound track. This technology is under development at the Communications Research Centre in Canada and the Canadian Broadcasting Corporation, and allows for computer-based slide shows and for distributing video programs over low-bandwidth networks where full-motion video is not possible. Illustrated Audio source code is available for Unix computers running X Window; binaries are also available for Sun SPARCstations and Linux systems.

World Wide Web:
> URL: **http://debra.dgbt.doc.ca/ia/ia.html**

Image Processing with Live Video Sources

Experiment with various image processing filters on different video sources. You can choose from a variety of filters and configuration variables. This page uses the vvdemo VuSystem application from MIT.

Note: Requires NCSA Mosaic for the X Window System, version 2.0 or higher.

World Wide Web:
> URL: **http://tns-www.lcs.mit.edu/cgi-bin/**
> **vs/vvdemo**

MPEG Animation Shows

Dozens of mpeg binary animation files containing a dizzying array of clips from waterskiing feats to space aliens.

Gopher:
> Name: National Chung Cheng University
> Address: **gopher.ccu.edu.tw**
> Choose: **miscellanies**
>   **| mpeg**

MPEG Movie Archive

Hundreds of megabytes of animations, supermodels, music, space, and R-rated and various other mpeg movies. There is also an mpeg FAQ and a hotlist showing the top 25 movies of the day.

World Wide Web:
URL: **http://w3.eeb.ele.tue.nl/mpeg/index.html**

MPEG Movies

Large collection of mpeg movies containing everything from Homer Simpson to juggling, waterskiing, and *Star Trek*.

World Wide Web:
URL: **http://www.cs.ucl.ac.uk/movies/**

MPEG Movies from JRC

A collection of mpeg movies, all under 650K in size, including a space flight, global weather, a helicopter flight, gas reactions, Taylor instability, 3-D salinity, and lake upwelling.

World Wide Web:
URL: **http://esba-www.jrc.it/dvgdocs/dvg1.html**

Multimedia in Education

Computing doesn't have to be complicated, dull or boring. Not with multimedia. Pictures, sounds, graphics, and animations all make computers come to life. Learn about using multimedia as a teaching tool and find out places where you can be taught to use multimedia effectively.

Usenet:
Newsgroup: **misc.education.multimedia**

QuickTime Movies

A small collection of QuickTime movies, used as examples of standard analog video converted to digital QuickTime, which allows for the display of digital video combined with sound. It includes a 1994 Distinguished Teaching Award Slide Show, and links to using QuickTime movies with NCSA Mosaic.

World Wide Web:
URL: **http://oms1.berkeley.edu/Video/QTlist.html**

Video Webalog

The Video Webalog is an information source for the exciting and fast-paced world of desktop video. It offers informative reviews of the technology underlying multimedia video and descriptions of video products in ten different product categories, allowing you to review and compare products and mail questions to the manufacturers.

World Wide Web:
URL: **http://figment.fastman.com/vweb/html/ vidmain.html**

COMPUTERS: NETWORKS

Bibliography of Internetworking Information

Technical information about connecting computer networks. This document is RFC-1175.

Anonymous FTP:
Address: **ds.internic.net**
Path: **/rfc/rfc1175.txt**

Bitnet Network

Information on the Bitnet network, including a node list and introductory guide.

Anonymous FTP:
Address: **quartz.rutgers.edu**
Path: **/pub/internet/misc/bitnet-intro.gz**

Gopher:
Name: Rutgers University
Address: **quartz.rutgers.edu**
Choose: **Internet Information and Documentation | Miscellaneous Internet Material**

Looking for special fun? Turn to the Vice section.

Campus Computing Newsletter Editors

If you are organized enough to have a campus computing network, you are probably going the next step and creating a newsletter to go along with it. Luckily, if you are the editor you are no longer alone. Gather with other editors to exchange ideas, problems, and experiences in editing, producing, and circulating printed and electronic newsletters.

Listserv Mailing List:
List Address: **ccnews@bitnic.educom.edu**
Subscription Address: **listserv@bitnic.educom.edu**

Cisco Information Archive

Information from Cisco Systems, Inc., a networking and router company, including Cisco's user magazine *The Packet*, news, contacts, product information, software image library, service and support details, conference programs, the Cisco educational archive and resources catalog, and a utility to find the Cisco office nearest you.

World Wide Web:
URL: **http://sunsite.unc.edu/cisco/cisco-home.html**

Computer and Networking Column

Converse with Fred about computers and networking in his electronic newspaper column.

Gopher:
Name: Software Tool & Die
Address: **gopher.std.com**
Choose: **Periodicals, Magazines, and Journals | Middlesex News | Columns | Fred**

Cyberspace Communications

A collection of articles covering communications in cyberspace and the Internet, and what we have to gain or lose with these new technologies.

Gopher:
Name: Whole Earth Lectronic Link
Address: **gopher.well.sf.ca.us**
Choose: **Communications and Media**

Data Communications and Networking Links

Information and links to resources about data communications and networking. This page includes tutorials, FAQ lists about networking, and information about networking companies and organizations, magazines, and mailing lists.

World Wide Web:
URL: **http://www.racal.com/networking.html**

Datagram

Forming and maintaining networks for schools is tricky business. This newsletter contains articles that discuss how to construct, maintain, and use networks for educational purposes.

See also: Education: Colleges and Universities

Mail:
Address: **jdltech@mr.net**
Subject: **subject: subscribe**

European Academic Research Network

The world gets smaller and smaller as the Internet gets bigger. The European Academic Research Network has established a discussion group to promote and help integrate new computer networks in eastern Europe into the rest of the networking world. Discussion is primarily in English and is conversational as well as technical.

Listserv Mailing List:
List Address: **euearn-l@ubvm.cc.buffalo.edu**
Subscription Address: **listserv@ubvm.cc.buffalo.edu**

The Internet has lots and lots (and lots) of free software.

FORTHnet

FORTHnet is the "first, largest, most advanced, and most central multiprotocol computer network" in Greece. It is headquartered in Crete and connects many networks all over Greece to the Internet, providing a full range of network services. FORTHnet also serves as the backbone for EUnet in Greece, providing UUCP mail and Usenet news services.

See also: Internet: Resources

World Wide Web:
    URL: **http://www.forthnet.gr/**

High Performance Computing Gopher

This gopher provides information on the Federal High Performance Computing and Communications Program and on the burgeoning National Information Infrastructure. There are also links to other government, public interest, and private sector gopher servers related to HPCC and the Internet.

Gopher:
    Name: National Coordination Office for HPCC
    Address: **gopher.hpcc.gov**

Inter-Network Mail Guide

A publication by John Chew and Scott Yanoff that documents methods for sending mail from one network to another. If you're not sure how to mail someone on CompuServe, America Online, to someone on Compuserve from Prodigy, or any of many different networks, this document has the information with detailed instructions.

Anonymous FTP:
    Address: **csd4.csd.uwm.edu**
    Path: **/pub/internetwork-mail-guide**

Finger:
    Address: **yanoff@csd4.csd.uwm.edu**

Usenet:
    Newsgroup: **alt.internet.services**

Does your postman never even ring once?

Try the
Inter-Network Mail Guide

Mail Gateway Guide

Jeremy Smith's *Getting Through the Matrix*, a guide to sending mail from one network to another through gateway computers.

Gopher:
    Name: Oregon State University
    Address: **gopher.fsl.orst.edu**
    Choose: **Other Sources of Info**
      | **Hugo's Lore-House**
      | **Dr.Fegg's Big House o'Fun..**
      | **Jeremy Smith's Guide to Gateways**

Managing Networked Information

A compendium of papers on network information management from the "Drinking from a Firehose" VALA Conference.

Gopher:
    Name: La Trobe University
    Address: **gopher.latrobe.edu.au**
    Choose: **Library Services**
      | **VALA Conference Papers**

Matrix News

Samples and information about *Matrix News*, a newsletter about cross-network issues.

Anonymous FTP:
    Address: **tic.com**
    Path: **/matrix/news/***

Gopher:
    Name: Texas Internet Consulting
    Address: **tic.com**
    Choose: **Matrix Information...**
      | **About Matrix News, the..**

Microsoft Windows Networking Environment

Getting a network running is often troublesome. Have some back-up help ready in the form of Usenet groups. These groups offer a good source of information on general networking, TCP/IP, and network programming with the Microsoft Windows operating system.

Usenet:
    Newsgroup:
        comp.os.ms-windows.networking.misc
    Newsgroup:
        comp.os.ms-windows.networking.tcp-ip
    Newsgroup:
        comp.os.ms-windows.networking.windows
    Newsgroup:
        comp.os.ms-windows.programmer.networks

A B C D E F G H I J K L M N O P Q R S T U V W X Y Z

National Information Infrastructure Agenda

The text of the executive order dated September 15, 1993, that creates an advisory council of 25 appointed members to advise the Secretary of Commerce on ways to integrate hardware, software, and skills to facilitate interaction between people. (No doubt, they will begin by reading this book as well as *The Internet Complete Reference*.)

Gopher:
> Name: U.S. Department of Agriculture
> Address: **ace.esusda.gov**
> Choose: **Americans Communicating Electronically**
>   **I National Policy Issues**
>   **I National Information Infrastructure (NII)**

Network Hardware Suppliers List

A list of dealers in new and used telecommunications and computer equipment. These companies have been recommended by a variety of people on the Net and the entries include helpful comments.

World Wide Web:
> URL: **http://www.ai.mit.edu/datawave/ hardware.html**

Network Maps

A color geographical map of the world, showing the main global networks in the matrix of computer networks that exchange electronic mail.

Anonymous FTP:
> Address: **tic.com**
> Path: **/matrix/maps/***

Gopher:
> Name: Texas Internet Consulting
> Address: **tic.com**
> Choose: **Matrix Information..**
>   **I Maps of Networks**

Network Politics

The more people who are on the Internet, the more complex the politics get. Read discussion on media and government action relating to networking including topics such as privacy, freedom of speech, democracy and virtual communities.

Usenet:
> Newsgroup: **alt.politics.datahighway**

Excerpt from the Net...

(from the "Information Infrastructure Executive Order 9/15/93")

THE WHITE HOUSE
Office of the Press Secretary

For Immediate Release   September 15, 1993

EXECUTIVE ORDER
- - - - - - -

UNITED STATES ADVISORY COUNCIL
ON THE NATIONAL INFORMATION INFRASTRUCTURE

By the authority vested in me as President by the Constitution and the laws of the United States of America, including the Federal Advisory Committee Act, as amended (5 U.S.C. App. 2) ("Act"), and section 301 of title 3, United States Code, it is hereby ordered as follows:

Section 1. Establishment. (a) There is established in the Commerce Department the "United States Advisory Council on the National Information Infrastructure"...

Networking Articles

Articles on all aspects of networking including TCP/IP LANs, ethernet, Internet protocols, and the Wiretap Algorithm.

Anonymous FTP:
Address: **ftp.spies.com**
Path: **/Library/Techdoc/Network/***

Gopher:
Name: Internet Wiretap
Address: **wiretap.spies.com**
Choose: **Wiretap Online Library**
| **Technical Information**
| **Networking**

NeuroNet

NeuroNet is the European neural network's "Network of Excellence." NeuroNet attempts to better coordinate the high level of neural network activity in Europe with the goal of both increasing awareness and doing work in theory, applications, and implementation of neural networks.

World Wide Web:
URL: **http://www.neuronet.ph.kcl.ac.uk/**

OS/2 Networking Environment

If you love the OS/2 operating system and want to get it networked, check out these discussion groups relating to the OS/2 environment. You will find general discussion and information on TCP/IP as well as trouble-shooting opportunities. Don't leave your home directory without it.

Usenet:
Newsgroup: **comp.os.os2.networking**
Newsgroup: **comp.os.os2.networking.misc**
Newsgroup: **comp.os.os2.networking.tcp-ip**

Rockwell Network Systems

Rockwell Network Systems is a leading supplier of high performance standards-based networking equipment. Their web page offers product information, new release news, upgrade details, a special Guru's Corner that provides new and engaging insights into networking technologies, Internet project information, and an Internet resource discover tool called Nomad.

World Wide Web:
URL: **http://www.rns.com/**

TCP/IP Introduction

An introduction to the TCP/IP set of networking protocols, and advice on what to read for more information.

Anonymous FTP:
Address: **ftp.spies.com**
Path: **/Library/Techdoc/Network/intro.tcp**

Gopher:
Name: Internet Wiretap
Address: **wiretap.spies.com**
Choose: **Wiretap Online Library**
| **Technical Information**
| **Networking**
| **TCP/IP Introduction**

Vnet Outdial Servers

Vnet is a commercial Internet provider which also offers a global access gateway. This gives access to networks and services far beyond the reach of the Internet by dialing in to or out from modems in more than 1,500 cities around the world.

See also: Consumer Information

Telnet:
Address: **char.vnet.net**
Login: **new**

WWPing

WWPing is a program for "pinging" web servers—that is, checking if a particular web server or Internet site is alive and well. It will also tell you what server type and protocol a particular web server is running.

World Wide Web:
URL: **http://www.stir.ac.uk/jsbin/wwping**

Z39.50 Resources

A reference point for resources related to the Information Retrieval Service and Protocol standard, ANSI/NISO Z39.50. There is a layman's guide, implementation details, software, and development news.

World Wide Web:
URL: **http://ds.internic.net/z3950/z3950.html**

A
B
C
D
E
F
G
H
I
J
K
L
M
N
O
P
Q
R
S
T
U
V
W
X
Y
Z

COMPUTERS: PCs

Building PC Hardware

This is a group for the do-it-yourselfer. There's nothing more satisfying than lying in a hammock having a cold drink after a hard back-breaking day trying to build your own PC. Get tips on upgrading or building your own PC and avoiding hardware problems. Ask and answer questions and learn where to buy cheap hardware. This list is for DOS, Windows, or OS/2-based machines.

Listserv Mailing List:
List Address: **pcbuild@tscvm.trenton.edu**
Subscription Address: **listserv@tscvm.trenton.edu**

IBM News

News stories about IBM and its products.

Usenet:
Newsgroup: **clari.nb.ibm**

Magazine

This moderated newsgroup is an electronic magazine devoted to PCs.

Usenet:
Newsgroup: **alt.znet.pc**

PC Catalog

An online catalog of over 2,000 PC products and nearly 200 computer companies. This gopher also sports new technology annoucements, price information, shopper's checklists, and other items of interest if you're in the market for equipment.

Gopher:
Name: PC Catalog
Address: **pccatalog.peed.com**

PC Clones

If you are in the market for PC clone or if you already have one and want some peer support, look to **pc-clone** groups for information. Here you will read smart shopping tips, technical questions and answers, horror stories and praise for various brands of clones.

Usenet:
Newsgroup: **alt.sys.pc-clone.dell**
Newsgroup: **alt.sys.pc-clone.gateway2000**
Newsgroup: **alt.sys.pc-clone.zeos**

Watcha gonna do when your cheap PC clone takes a dive in the second round and no one at the company wants to talk to you? Complain to your friends in the Usenet PC clone discussion groups.

PC General Discussion

General discussion about PCs and related hardware and software topics. The **.misc** group is an open forum.

Usenet:
Newsgroup: **comp.sys.ibm.pc.digest**
Newsgroup: **comp.sys.ibm.pc.misc**

PC Hardware

General discussion of all types of PC hardware. The **.pc** newsgroup is for any type of PC hardware from any vendor; the **.ps2** group is for PS/2 and Microchannel hardware. The **.gateway2000** group is devoted to products from the Gateway 2000 company. The **.pcmcia** group is for discussion of PCMCIA add-in cards for portable computers.

Usenet:
Newsgroup: **alt.periphs.pcmcia**
Newsgroup: **alt.sys.pc-clone.gateway2000**
Newsgroup: **comp.sys.ibm.pc.hardware**
Newsgroup: **comp.sys.ibm.ps2.hardware**

**Want some fun?
Read the Fun section.**

PC Hardware

Ah, those halcyon days of our youth when--screwdrivers and chip pullers in hand--we spent so many wonderful hours working on the innards of our PCs. What could be more fun on a summer's afternoon than discussing PC hardware when everybody else is wasting their time at the beach?

(Tip for the guys: women really go for men who know their hardware.)

PC Hardware Introduction

After you read this article you'll understand the ads in magazines, and you may even make a better choice the next time you buy a PC.

World Wide Web:
URL: **http://pclt.cis.yale.edu/pclt/pchw/
platypus.htm**

PC Index

This page features extensive information about PCs and the Internet, including links to PC-related gopher and web servers, info about PC mailing lists, Usenet groups, and many other online resources of interest.

World Wide Web:
URL: **http://ici.proper.com/1/pc**

PC Lube and Tune

A campy motif is used to bring you in-depth technical information as well as background documents on PC usage. PC Lube and Tune is billed as a service station located at an off-ramp of the Information Superhighway where you can do self-service maintenance or repairs. Beneath its lighthearted exterior, this site has thorough files on Windows, Ethernet, APPC, TCP/IP and PC hardware.

See also: Computers: Networks

World Wide Web:
URL: **http://pclt.cis.yale.edu/pclt/default.html**

PowerPC News

What's the latest news about the IBM/Motorola/Apple microprocessor systems? Read the full text of this electronic magazine at its web site or receive a list of the table of contents every two weeks and send for just the articles in which you are interested.

Mail:
Address: **add@power.globalnews.com**

World Wide Web:
URL: **http://power.globalnews.com/**

COMPUTERS: PICTURES

alt.binaries.pictures Image Server

This page helps you select and retrieve files distributed on the **alt.binaries.pictures** newsgroups in the last few days. The nice thing about it is that you can view miniature pictures of the images through your browser and read the picture description before you actually decide if you want to download the whole file.

World Wide Web:
URL: **http://web.cnam.fr/Images/Usenet/**

Cartoon Pictures

Pictures of your favorite cartoon characters — Rescue Rangers, Snow White, Ren and Stimpy, Chip 'n' Dale, Bill and Hillary — here they are, waiting for you to download.

Usenet:
Newsgroup: **alt.binaries.pictures.cartoons**
Newsgroup: **alt.toon-pics**

Chinese GIF Collection

A collection of more than 50 gif image files which you can view through gopher (if you have the appropriate software).

Gopher:
Name: National Chung Cheng University
Address: **gopher.ccu.edu.tw**
Choose: **miscellanies**
| Beautiful Pictures

Clip Art

In case your art skills are limited to stick figures who look like they have nervous disorders, there is another outlet for your creative side. Clip art is available for DOS, Macintosh and Unix so you can make your projects come alive with snappy pictures and graphics.

Usenet:
> Newsgroup: **alt.binaries.clip-art**

Digital Picture Archive on the 17th Floor

This archive contains hundreds of megabytes of gif and jpeg pictures. It offers art, paintings, and computer-generated images, including cars, airplanes, faces, nature, technology, space, pornography, and all pictures which were transmitted via Usenet in the past week.

See also: Art

Gopher:
> Name: Delft University of Technology
> Address: **olt.et.tudelft.nl**
> Choose: **Fun and Leisure Box**
> | **Digital Picture Archive of the 17th Floor**

World Wide Web:
> URL: **http://olt.et.tudelft.nl/fun/pictures/**
> **pictures.html**

Fantasy Images

Collection of gif and jpeg fantasy and mythical images, including dragons, waterfalls, Gandalf, moons, whales, orcas, castles, and more.

Anonymous FTP:
> Address: **orangutan.cv.nrao.edu**
> Path: **/pub/images/fantasy/***

World Wide Web:
> URL: **http://orangutan.cv.nrao.edu/images/**
> **fantasy**

Make sure you are prepared: Read Emergency and Disaster.

Fine Art

As Tennyson said when he first started using the Internet, "The fact that picture newsgroups exist for more than just erotica proves that man can rise on the stepping stones of his lower self to better things." Participate and download fine art, suitable for framing. The **.d** newsgroup is for discussion. The other groups are for pictures only. The rules (if you care to follow them) are that **.digitized** is for original, digitized artwork; **.graphics** is for original pictures created with a computer.

Usenet:
> Newsgroup: **alt.binaries.pictures.fine-art.d**
> Newsgroup: **alt.binaries.pictures.fine-art.digitized**
> Newsgroup: **alt.binaries.pictures.fine-art.graphics**

Fractals

Ah, fractals: those wonderful fractional dimensional thingies that nobody understands, but that lend themselves to such totally cool pictures that really blow you away for the first five minutes. Get some for yourself.

Usenet:
> Newsgroup: **alt.binaries.pictures.fractals**

GIF Image Files

A collection of interesting gif files including a Pepsi can, Reagan, and Bush images.

Anonymous FTP:
> Address: **aug3.augsburg.edu**
> Path: **/files/other_gifs/***

Girls, Girls, Girls

Pictures, mostly in jpeg format, of many top models, including Stephanie Seymour, Niki Taylor, Claudia Schiffer, Cindy Crawford, and many more.

World Wide Web:
> URL: **http://www.cnuce.cnr.it/**
> URL: **http://www.ifi.uio.no/~steinho/dame.htm**
> URL: **http://www.nis.garr.it/**
> URL: **http://www.pi.infn.it/**
> URL: **http://www.unipi.it/**

Icons

Interesting collection of icons in gif or xbm format. Includes icons of stickups, muggings, skiing accidents, coffins, auto-theft, and many more.

World Wide Web:
> URL: **http://www.cis.upenn.edu/~mjd/icons**

Image and Movie Archives

Large collection of images and movies, divided into categories such as animals, astronomy, X11 bitmaps, cartoons, computers, dinosaurs, fantasy, fine art, fractals, nature, scenic, space, *Star Trek*, and more.

Anonymous FTP:
Address: **orangutan.cv.nrao.edu**
Path: **/pub/images/***

World Wide Web:
URL: **http://orangutan.cv.nrao.edu/images/summary.html**

Japanese Animation Images

A large collection of Japanese anime images in jpeg format.

Anonymous FTP:
Address: **ftp.tcp.com**
Path: **/pub/anime/Images/***

Gopher:
Name: National Chung Cheng University
Address: **gopher.ccu.edu.tw**
Choose: **miscellanies**
   I Japanese Anim Picture

JPEG Files

Graphic image files in the jpeg format. Selections include aliens, punisher, wolverine, and saddog.

Anonymous FTP:
Address: **aug3.augsburg.edu**
Path: **/files/jpeg/***

Kandinsky Image Archive

This archive has gif images of paintings by Vasili Kandinsky, abstract artist.

Gopher:
Name: University of Michigan
Address: **libra.arch.umich.edu**
Choose: **The Kandinsky Image Archive**

Need a quick artistic fix?
Try the Kandinsky Image Archive

Lighthouses

See the magic and mystery of the lighthouses of New England. Pictures and stories almost make you feel the ocean spray, see the fog roll in, and hear the soulful wail of the foghorn.

World Wide Web:
URL: **http://gopher.lib.utk.edu:70/0/Other-Internet-Resources/pictures/**

URL: **http://www.lib.utk.edu:70/1/Other-Internet-Resources/pictures/**

What could be more romantic and satisfying than using the Internet to look at pictures of lighthouses?

Well...lots of things actually, but if your life is otherwise devoid of romance and satisfaction, you might try looking at lighthouses. At least you won't have to worry about getting your clothes all wet.

Mandelbrot Images

A collection of Mandelbrot images in gif format.

Anonymous FTP:
Address: **ftp.ira.uka.de**
Path: **/pub/graphic/fractals/***

Miscellaneous Pictures

General Usenet groups devoted to the sharing of pictures. The **.d** newsgroup is for discussion about pictures. The other groups are for pictures only.

Usenet:
Newsgroup: **alt.binaries.misc**
Newsgroup: **alt.binaries.pictures**
Newsgroup: **alt.binaries.pictures.d**
Newsgroup: **alt.binaries.pictures.misc**

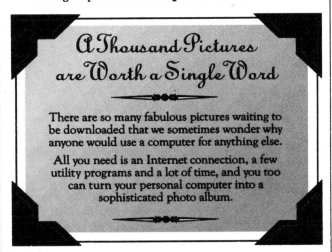

A Thousand Pictures are Worth a Single Word

There are so many fabulous pictures waiting to be downloaded that we sometimes wonder why anyone would use a computer for anything else.

All you need is an Internet connection, a few utility programs and a lot of time, and you too can turn your personal computer into a sophisticated photo album.

Picture-Related Files FTP Site List

Large list of anonymous ftp sites that contain files related to viewing, extracting, encoding, compressing, archiving, converting, and anything else you can do to pictures of all format types.

Anonymous FTP:
Address: **ftp.cc.utexas.edu**
Path: **/gifstuff/ftpsites**

Picture Viewing Software

Before you can view pictures on your own computer, you need the appropriate software. Read this newsgroup to get info on what programs are available and how to use them.

Usenet:
Newsgroup: **alt.binaries.pictures.utilities**

Satellite Images of Europe

Europe, as seen by the Meteosat weather satellite, in gif and jpeg formats.

Anonymous FTP:
Address: **cumulus.met.ed.ac.uk**
Path: **/images/***

Address: **liasun3.epfl.ch**
Path: **/pub/weather/***

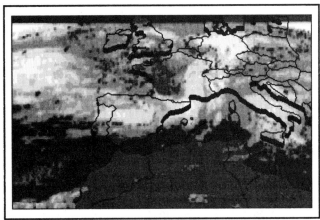

Weather satellite images available on the Internet are updated daily, if not more often. These images are almost always in standard gif or jpg formats.

Sex Pictures

Let's take a minute to stop and appreciate the vast resources of the Internet: all those computers, communications lines, satellites. Not to mention the tens of thousands of people working day and night to ensure that it all hangs together. All of this, just so you can download sexy...err...erotic pictures to display on your own computer. Usenet, mirroring the world at large, has a large selection of newsgroups devoted to various aspects of visual gratification. The **.d** newsgroups are for discussion. All the other groups are for pictures only. (Note: If you want to learn how to download pictures and what software you need, read *The Internet Complete Reference*.)

See also: Sex, X-Rated Resources

Usenet:
Newsgroup: **alt.binaries.pictures.erotica**
Newsgroup: **alt.binaries.pictures.erotica.blondes**
Newsgroup: **alt.binaries.pictures.erotica.d**
Newsgroup: **alt.binaries.pictures.erotica.female**
Newsgroup: **alt.binaries.pictures.erotica.male**
Newsgroup: **alt.binaries.pictures.erotica.orientals**
Newsgroup: **alt.sex.pictures**
Newsgroup: **alt.sex.pictures.d**
Newsgroup: **alt.sex.pictures.female**
Newsgroup: **alt.sex.pictures.male**

Shuttle and Satellite Images

Photographs in electronic formats of spacecraft and spectacular views from Earth and space.

Anonymous FTP:
Address: **sseop.jsc.nasa.gov**

Gopher:
Name: NASA Goddard Space Flight Center
Address: **gopher.gsfc.nasa.gov**
Choose: **Nasa information**
  I **Space images and information**

Smithsonian Photographs

Photographs of gems, jungles, stars, and artifacts, taken by the Smithsonian Institution. Available with viewing software in jpeg and jfif formats.

Gopher:
Name: The Pipeline Gopher
Address: **pipeline.com**
Choose: **Arts and Leisure**
  I **Smithsonian photographs and viewing software**

Supermodels

The next best thing to living next door to a supermodel is being able to download one whenever you want. Just the thing to look at when you get tired of fractals.

Usenet:
Newsgroup: **alt.binaries.pictures.supermodels**

Tasteless Pictures

Here is a newsgroup for the posting of tasteless, bizarre, and grotesque pictures only. For the truly demented: get your fill of car wrecks, mangled bodies, freaks, and so on. What is tasteless? Well, all we can say is that this newsgroup is not for the faint of heart. You will see pictures of things that we can't even mention in a family book. Suffice it to say that if you are the type of person who likes to look at things that make other people cringe, this group is for you.

Usenet:
Newsgroup: **alt.binaries.pictures.tasteless**

Washington, D.C.

Everyone loves cherry blossom time in Washington, D.C. This is a nice collection of photographs relating to the White House and includes beautiful scenery as well as pictures of the Clinton administration. You can download them and have them printed up in wallet size so when you travel to other countries you can whip out the photograph and say, "See this? This is my President."

Gopher:
Name: University of North Carolina
Address: **calypso.oit.unc.edu**
Choose: **Worlds of SunSITE — by Subject**
  I **US and World Politics**
  I **Multimedia (White House Pictures)**

COMPUTERS: PROGRAMMING

Ada

Public library containing compilers, tools, documentation, FAQs and other software for the Ada programming language, as used by the U.S. Department of Defense.

Anonymous FTP:
Address: **ftp.wustl.edu**
Path: **/languages/ada/***

Basic Programming Language

Questions and answers on topics relating to the Basic programming language.

Usenet:
Newsgroup: **alt.lang.basic**
Newsgroup: **comp.lang.basic.misc**
Newsgroup: **comp.lang.basic.visual**

C Programs

Some interesting little C programs for the Unix gurus amongst you; some require you to have root privileges to run them.

Anonymous FTP:
Address: **ftp.cs.widener.edu**
Path: **/pub/brendan/***

C++ Frequently Asked Questions

Answers to hundreds of the most frequently asked questions about the C++ programming language. Nearly one hundred pages of densely packed information for programmers interested in C++.

Anonymous FTP:
Address: **sun.soe.clarkson.edu**
Path: **/pub/C++/FAQ***

If you're thinking of making the most serious commitment that a computer programmer can make, jumping into C++, stop, take a deep breath, and read the frequently asked question list.

CCMD Source Code in C

The complete source code and makefiles to a user-interface program based on the COMND jsys from tops20. This program gives escape completion on many different types of data (filenames, users, groups, keywords, etc.). Columbia's MM (Mail Manager) program is written with it.

Anonymous FTP:
Address: **oak.oakland.edu**
Path: **/pub/misc/ccmd/***

CompuServe B File Transfer Protocol

The complete C source code and documentation for implementing the CompuServe B file transfer protocol. Other files in the same directory document many other communications protocols including xmodem, ymodem, zmodem, SLIP, UUCP, and others.

Anonymous FTP:
Address: **oak.oakland.edu**
Path: **/pub/misc/protocols/bproto.doc**

> ## Gopher problems? Read the "The Internet Complete Reference."

> ## The Bizarre section has some cool stuff.

CPUs and Assembly Language

Tutorials, opcode listings, compatibility issues, articles, and reports about programming on a variety of different CPUs.

Anonymous FTP:
Address: **ftp.spies.com**
Path: **/Library/Techdoc/Cpu/***

Gopher:
Name: Internet Wiretap
Address: **wiretap.spies.com**
Choose: **Wiretap Online Library**
 | Technical Information
 | CPU's and Assembly Language

Free Language Tools

Extensive list of free language tools with source code, including compilers and interpreters.

Gopher:
Name: Pacific Systems Group
Address: **gopher.psg.com**
Choose: **Programming Languages**
 | List of Free Compilers...

FSP

Information, utilities, and the latest Unix FSP software, an alternative file transfer protocol to ftp.

Anonymous FTP:
Address: **plaza.aarnet.edu.au**
Path: **/usenet/comp.sources.misc/volume34/fsp/***

Address: **usc.edu**
Path: **/archive/usenet/sources/**
 comp.sources.misc/volume34/fsp

Gnuplot Tutorial

A Postscript file containing a tutorial to teach you the nuances of gnuplot, a graph plotting program.

Anonymous FTP:
Address: **ccosun.caltech.edu**
Path: **/pub/documents/gnuplot-tutorial.ps**

Gopher and Utilities for VMS

Collection of files and programs for VMS, which can be browsed or downloaded. Includes latest gopher client, compression and archive utilities, and more.

Gopher:
> Name: Sam Houston State University
> Address: **niord.shsu.edu**
> Choose: **VMS Gopher-related file library**

Hello World!

The classic neophyte program in many different languages.

Anonymous FTP:
> Address: **ocf.berkeley.edu**
> Path: **/pub/Library/Hello_World**

Interactive Fiction Game Programming

Interactive fiction games, development tools, game solutions, and programming examples from the Usenet newsgroups **rec.arts.int-fiction** and **rec.games.int-fiction.**

Anonymous FTP:
> Address: **ftp.wustl.edu**
> Path: **/doc/misc/if-archive/***

Language FAQs

FAQs on many programming languages and tools, including C, C++, Forth, Lisp, Perl, Prolog, and Scheme.

Anonymous FTP:
> Address: **quartz.rutgers.edu**
> Path: **/pub/computer/languages/***

Gopher:
> Name: Rutgers University
> Address: **quartz.rutgers.edu**
> Choose: **Computer-Sources, Documentation, Comp.Sci**
> **| Computer Science, AI, Languages**

WE'VE GOT THE ANSWERS TO ALL OF YOUR QUESTIONS
If they are about computer languages, that is. The quartz archive at Rutgers University has a wealth of frequently asked question (FAQ) lists about all kinds of languages. Here's an idea: why not connect to the Gopher and check out a programming language you have never heard of? It's a great way to impress a date.

Language List

An extensive list of collected information on more than 2,000 computer languages, past and present.

Gopher:
> Name: Pacific Systems Group
> Address: **gopher.psg.com**
> Choose: **Programming Languages**
> **| List of 'All' Programming...**

Linear Programming Answers

Selected postings to the Usenet newsgroup **sci.op-research** about linear computer programming, including tips on where to find source code to solve linear programming problems.

Anonymous FTP:
> Address: **ftp.hmc.edu**
> Path: **/pub/science/sci.answers/.mirror.OLD/ linear-programming-faq**

Nonlinear Programming Facts

A text file listing reference books that answer frequently asked questions raised about nonlinear programming in the Usenet newsgroup **sci.op-research**.

Anonymous FTP:
> Address: **ftp.hmc.edu**
> Path: **/pub/science/sci.answers/.mirror.OLD/ nonlinear-programming-faq**

Obfuscated C Code

Entries and winners for the International Obfuscated C Code Contest, which asked people to write, in 512 bytes or less, the worst complete C program. The **ftp.uu.net** site shows the winners of past contests.

Note: This is an annual contest so different sites may maintain these files each year. Use archie and veronica to find other sites.

Anonymous FTP:
> Address: **ftp.cs.yale.edu**
> Path: **/pub/obfuscated-c/***

> Address: **ftp.uu.net**
> Path: **/doc/literary/obi/Nerd.Humor/ObfuscatedC**

Archie:
> Pattern: **obfuscated**

If you like trouble, take a look at Mischief.

Object-Oriented Programming Using C++

A class put together specifically for the Internet environment. Get a solid introduction to C++ programming with emphasis on object-orientation.

World Wide Web:
URL: **http://info.desy.de/gna/html/cc/index.html**

OS/2 Programming

Questions and answers relating to object-oriented programming and using programming tools in an OS/2 environment.

Usenet:
Newsgroup: **comp.os.os2.programmer.oop**
Newsgroup: **comp.os.os2.programmer.tools**

Parallel Programming Laboratory

The Parallel Programming Laboratory (PPL) researches tools and techniques for programming parallel processing systems as well as applications. Most of the research is centered around the Charm parallel programming system.

World Wide Web:
URL: **http://charm.cs.uiuc.edu/**

Pascal to C Translator

This Unix program translates Pascal programs to C programs, just like that!

Anonymous FTP:
Address: **ccosun.caltech.edu**
Path: **/pub/misc/p2c-1.18.tar.Z**

Programming Examples

Programming examples, code fragments, and helpful hints for many different computer languages.

Anonymous FTP:
Address: **ftp.uu.net**
Path: **/languages/***

Programming for Microsoft Windows

Questions and answers relating to general programming in the Microsoft Windows environment as well as more specific topics such as controls, dialogs and VBXs, graphics and printing, memory management, multimedia and network programming.

Usenet:
Newsgroup: **comp.os.ms-windows.programmer**
Newsgroup:
   comp.os.ms-windows.programmer.controls
Newsgroup:
   comp.os.ms-windows.programmer.drivers
Newsgroup:
   comp.os.ms-windows.programmer.graphics
Newsgroup:
   comp.os.ms-windows.programmer.memory
Newsgroup:
   comp.os.ms-windows.programmer.misc
Newsgroup:
   comp.os.ms-windows.programmer.multimedia
Newsgroup:
   comp.os.ms-windows.programmer.networks
Newsgroup:
   comp.os.ms-windows.programmer.ole
Newsgroup:
   comp.os.ms-windows.programmer.tools
Newsgroup:
   comp.os.ms-windows.programmer.win32
Newsgroup:
   comp.os.ms-windows.programmer.winhelp

Programming General Discussion

General discussion about DOS programming: tips, questions and answers.

Usenet:
Newsgroup: **alt.msdos.programmer**
Newsgroup: **comp.os.msdos.programmer**

Programming in Ada

Tips, tricks, utilities, source code, and complete programs for users of this programming language.

Anonymous FTP:
Address: **oak.oakland.edu**
Path: **/pub/msdos/ada/***

This is the first book of the rest of your life.

Programming Language Material

Articles and guides on computer languages, including C, Ada, and Protolo object code format.

Anonymous FTP:
  Address: **ftp.spies.com**
  Path: **/Library/Techdoc/Language/***

Gopher:
  Name: Internet Wiretap
  Address: **wiretap.spies.com**
  Choose: **Wiretap Online Library**
    | Technical Information
    | Languages

Programming Languages

Information on lots of computer programming languages, including C++, Modula 2, Oberon, and Pascal.

Gopher:
  Name: Pacific Systems Group
  Address: **gopher.psg.com**
  Choose: **Programming Languages**

World Wide Web:
  URL: **http://www.yahoo.com/Computers/Languages/**

Ravel

A C-like interpreted programming language for the IBM-PC, that directly supports MIDI music constructs. The package includes music files and source code.

Anonymous FTP:
  Address: **ftp.cs.pdx.edu**
  Path: **/pub/music/ravel/***

TCP/IP Development Tools

This directory contains instructions and C source code for a mail program, and for implementing the TCP/IP protocol on PCs and Macintosh computers.

Anonymous FTP:
  Address: **athene.uni-paderborn.de**
  Path: **/pcsoft2/msdos2/ka9q-tcpip**

  Address: **ftp.uni-kl.de**
  Path: **/pub3/pc/net/ka9q-tcpip**

  Address: **oak.oakland.edu**
  Path: **/pub/misc/protocols/SLIP**

Turbo Vision

Programming using Borland's Turbo Vision: text-based object-oriented application libraries and development tools.

Usenet:
  Newsgroup:
    comp.os.msdos.programmer.turbovision

Twisted Code

Humorous articles relating to computer code and languages, including an electronic C Christmas card, funny **man** pages, and a rude C program.

Anonymous FTP:
  Address: **ftp.spies.com**
  Path: **/Library/Humor/Code/***

Gopher:
  Name: Internet Wiretap
  Address: **wiretap.spies.com**
  Choose: **Wiretap Online Library**
    | Humor
    | Code

X Window Software Index

An index of public domain software to exploit or enhance the X Window system. It lets you peruse archives and tells you what software exists, with a brief description of each item and where to find it.

Gopher:
  Name: University of Edinburgh
  Address: **gopher.ed.ac.uk**
  Choose: **Index to public domain X sources**

A B C D E F G H I J K L M N O P Q R S T U V W X Y Z

COMPUTERS: SECURITY AND PRIVACY

Computer Security Gopher

The DFN-Cert gopher in Germany offers lots of information about computer security through their archives, including information on firewalls, worm attacks, and Unix security.

Anonymous FTP:
Address: **ftp.informatik.uni-hamburg.de**
Path: **/pub/security/***

Gopher:
Name: University of Hamburg
Address: **gopher.informatik.uni-hamburg.de**

Computer Security Sites

A web page with links to a number of web sites relating to computer and network security, including Yahoo's Security and Encryption Page, the NIST Computer Security page, Trusted Information Systems, Bennet Yee's Security Page, and Quadralay's Cryptography Archive.

World Wide Web:
URL: **http://mls.saic.com/mls.sec_sites.html**

Computers and the Law

Who would have thought that "breaking and entering" would apply to computers one day? Now that people spend more and more time on the Net not only socializing but doing business as well, the environment becomes ripe for intrigue and sneaky activity. This moderated list covers all aspects of computers and law.

Internet Mailing List:
List Address: **info-law@brl.mil**
Subscription Address: **info-law-request@brl.mil**

Show some enterprise and explore the **Hacker Sites on the Net:** Go boldly where no mortal man (and very few women) have gone before.

Hacker Sites on the Net

Want to explore all the nooks and crannies in which hackers hang out? Here are a few sites that are run or frequented by hackers. But be careful. These are the people your mother warned you about.

World Wide Web:
URL: **http://dfw.net/~aleph1/sites.html**

Incident Response Teams

In case of a security emergency, follow the directions in the manual. No manual? Don't panic. Look here for the names and phone numbers of various incident response teams. You can trust them. They are the good guys.

World Wide Web:
URL: **http://dfw.net/~aleph1/teams.html**

Incident Response Team

An old woman calls the **Incident Response Team** and says, "A young man tried to violate me."

The expert listens to her and then asks, "Ma'am, when did this happen?"

She answers, "Forty-five years ago."

So the expert says, "And why do you want to report it now?"

The old woman replies, "I don't want to report it, I just want to talk about it."

Internet Security Firewalls

A definitive collection of information about Internet firewalls, including a tutorial and private presentations. This web page is maintained by Great Circle Associates.

World Wide Web:
URL: **http://www.greatcircle.com/gca/tutorial/main.html**

Network and Computer Security Reference Index

This web page is a veritable "everything you ever wanted to know about computer security" resource. Links here point to FAQs, documents about firewalls, security, vendors, Pretty Good Privacy (PGP), Riordan's Internet Privacy Enhanced Mail, other web information sources, Usenet newsgroups, ftp sites, and mailing lists.

World Wide Web:
URL: **http://www.tansu.com.au/Info/ security.html**

PGP Keyservers

Public PGP keyservers which allow you to exchange public PGP encryption keys running through the Internet and UUCP mail systems.

Mail:
Address: **pgp-public-keys@demon.co.uk**
Subject: **help**

Address: **pgp-public-keys@dsi.unimi.it**
Subject: **help**

Address: **pgp-public-keys@pgp.iastate.edu**
Subject: **help**

Address: **pgp-public-keys@pgp.mit.edu**
Subject: **help**

Privacy and Anonymity Issues

Details on encryption, mail and account privacy, anonymous mailing and posting, and other Internet and global network privacy issues.

Anonymous FTP:
Address: **rtfm.mit.edu**
Path: **/pub/usenet/news.answers/net-privacy/***

Address: **rtfm.mit.edu**
Path: **/pub/usenet/news.answers/net-anonymity/***

Gopher:
Name: Oregon State University
Address: **gopher.fsl.orst.edu**
Choose: **Other Sources of Info**
| **Hugo's Lore-House**
| **Where the Sun Doesn't Shine..**
| **Identity, Privacy and Anonimity on the Internet**

Privacy Forum Digest

A moderated digest for the discussion and analysis of the legal aspects of privacy in the information age.

Anonymous FTP:
Address: **ftp.vortex.com**
Path: **/privacy/***

Gopher:
Name: Vortex Technology
Address: **cv.vortex.com**
Choose: **Privacy Forum**

RIPEM Resources

This web page contains links to many resources related to RIPEM, Riordan's Internet Privacy Enhanced Mail. It includes a FAQ, an article on RIPEM vulnerabilities and defenses, cryptography issues, user guides, and details on how to access the special security ftp site for the source. RIPEM is available to citizens and permanent residents of the U.S.

See also: Internet

World Wide Web:
URL: **http://cs.indiana.edu/ripem/dir.html**

RSA Data Security, Inc.

RSA Data Security, Inc., is a recognized world leader in cryptography, with millions of copies of its encryption and authentication software installed and in use worldwide. RSA's home page offers announcements, press releases, factsheets, cryptography FAQs, and a software archive of data security-related tools and documents.

World Wide Web:
URL: **http://www.rsa.com/**

Security Resources

Yet another web page with links to security resources. Some of these are the same as other security pages, but there is also unique information, as well as new pointers. The resources here include cryptography news bulletins, Clipper information, the Electronic Frontier Foundation's response to an FBI draft bill about digital telephony, information on the anonymous credit card protocol, and much more.

World Wide Web:
URL: **http://www.cs.cmu.edu:8001/afs/ cs.cmu.edu/user/bsy/www/sec.html**

A B C D E F G H I J K L M N O P Q R S T U V W X Y Z

Security Web

You can never tell when a hacker is going to come racing up through the wires straight into your computer and wreak some kind of unsuppressible havoc on your system. As they say, the best defense is a good offense. Learn about security, cryptography, and hacking at this web page full of links to additional related topics.

World Wide Web:
URL: **http://dfw.net/~aleph1/**

Stalking the Wily Hacker

Author and astronomer Cliff Stoll gave a presentation at Cisco NetWorkers '94 on "Stalking the Wily Hacker." Stoll is the author of *The Cuckoo's Egg*, a true story of intrigue and suspense about how Stoll discovered a 75-cent computer accounting error and tracked it all the way to a European ring of KGB spies. Stoll tells his story with a sequence of still photos and audio files. This multimedia presentation is captivating, but be aware that some of the audio sequences are large.

World Wide Web:
URL: **http://town.hall.org/university/security/stoll/cliff.html**

Unix Security

This web page lists programs you can use to improve the security of computers running Unix. Some of these programs also run on other operating systems. The list includes COPS, Crack, Npasswd, Passwd+, PGP, Socks, Tripwire, and others.

World Wide Web:
URL: **http://www.alw.nih.gov/~jbk/sec-prog.html**

Unix Security Tutorial

A detailed guide to improving the security of your Unix system.

Anonymous FTP:
Address: **quartz.rutgers.edu**
Path: **/pub/computer/security/unix-security-tutorial**

Gopher:
Name: Rutgers University
Address: **quartz.rutgers.edu**
Choose: **Computer-Sources, Documentation, Comp.Sci**
| **Computer Security Info**
| **unix-security-tutorial**

COMPUTERS: SOUNDS

AsTeR

AsTeR (Audio System for Technical Readings) is a computing system for rendering technical documents in audio. It uses the display-independent nature of electronic documents to verbally deliver technical documents produced in LaTeX. This hypertext document contains examples and audio renderings generated by AsTeR, covering many areas of mathematical notation and representation.

World Wide Web:
URL: **http://www.cs.cornell.edu/Info/People/raman/aster/aster-toplevel.html**

Index of Sounds

A giant collection of .au sound files, divided into songs, percussion, sound effects, animal sounds, hal9000, and other categories.

World Wide Web:
URL: **http://www.it.kth.se/sounds**

Macintosh Sounds

No Macintosh is a real computer unless you make it erupt into various sounds of James Brown, The Beatles, or just plain beeping and whistling. Find all these plus sound clips from movies at these Macintosh sound archives. Your friends will be impressed and your mom will be happy because you can stop showing off your armpit noises when her bridge club comes over.

Anonymous FTP:
Address: **ftp.std.com**
Path: **/src/macintosh/sound/***

Address: **joker.optics.rochester.edu**
Path: **/mac/sounds/***

MIDI Archives

Put away that CD player and download some MIDI sound files. If you don't have the software, don't worry. The MIDI Archives has gone on safari in the wilds of Michigan to find all the software you need to process MIDI sound files.

Gopher:
Name: Merit Network
Address: **gopher.archive.merit.edu**
Choose: **Merit Software Archives**
| **Macintosh Archive**
| **sound**
| **midi**

Miscellaneous Sounds

Aren't sounds great? Without them there would be nothing to listen to. Join the Usenet group devoted to sharing sounds of all types. Music, people, things, and lots of what-have-you. The **.misc** group is for sounds only. The **.d** group is for discussion about sounds and the requisite hardware and software, especially audio formats.

Usenet:
Newsgroup: **alt.binaries.sounds.d**
Newsgroup: **alt.binaries.sounds.misc**

Tired of the silence? Download some sounds!!

Movies and Television

Bring movies and television to life on your computer with sound files you can download from Usenet. You can get sounds from movies like *The Princess Bride*, *Star Wars*, *Forrest Gump*, and *Aliens*. Television is equally as popular with sounds from *Hawaii 5-0*, *The Simpsons*, *Beavis and Butthead*, *Mission Impossible*, and *Star Trek*.

Usenet:
Newsgroup: **alt.binaries.sounds.movies**
Newsgroup: **alt.binaries.sounds.tv**

Music

All types of music, especially classical music. Endow your computer with the charms it needs to tame the savage beast within you.

Usenet:
Newsgroup: **alt.binaries.sounds.music**

NeXT Sounds

Hundreds of megabytes of sounds for the NeXT machine, including lots of theme songs and samples from well-known artists.

Anonymous FTP:
Address: **csus.edu**
Path: **/pub/NeXT/sounds/***

Address: **ftp.wustl.edu**
Path: **/pub/NeXT-Music/***

Number Synthesizer

Type in a number and this program will read it out loud for you.

World Wide Web:
URL: **http://www.cs.yale.edu/cgi-bin/saynumber.au**

PC Sounds

Blow the dust out of your PC's speakers with some hair-raising, skin-tingling audio files guaranteed to liven up any dull, boring computer. Impress your friends by making your stuffy PC do imitations of movie actors and cool special effects.

Anonymous FTP:
Address: **oak.oakland.edu**
Path: **/pub/msdos/sound/***

Address: **sunsite.unc.edu**
Path: **/pub/micro/pc-stuff/sounds/***

Address: **winftp.cica.indiana.edu**
Path: **/pub/pc/win3/sounds/***

Rplay

A Sun software package that allows you to play multiple sounds at once on the same, and on different machines. Also supports sound broadcasting. Make your office sound like the bridge of the starship Enterprise!

Anonymous FTP:
Address: **ftp.sdsu.edu**
Path: **/pub/rplay/***

Sex Sounds

Simon and Garfunkel used to wax eloquent about the sounds of silence. Come on, who are we fooling? Check out this newsgroup and download some sounds of you-know-what. Of course, in order to really enjoy the experience you will need the proper hardware (as if you didn't know).

Usenet:
Newsgroup: **alt.sex.sounds**

If you're feeling risque, take a look at the X-Rated Resources.

A
B
C
D
E
F
G
H
I
J
K
L
M
N
O
P
Q
R
S
T
U
V
W
X
Y
Z

Sound Archives

Special occasions call for special sounds. Some days you will need a little Beavis and Butthead. Some days you will need some classic Monty Python or maybe a friendly cartoon sound file. Never again will you have to listen to the sounds of silence at your computer. Check out the many sound archives available on the Net.

Anonymous FTP:
Address: **ee.lbl.gov**
Path: **/sounds/***

Address: **f.ms.uky.edu**
Path: **/pub3/sounds/***

Address: **plan9.njit.edu**
Path: **/pub/sounds/***

Address: **sol.ctr.columbia.edu**
Path: **/pub/DA/sounds/***

Address: **valhalla.ee.rochester.edu**
Path: **/pub/sound/***

Address: **vela.acs.oakland.edu**
Path: **/pub/sound/***

Sound Cards

For a PC to play any sounds worth listening to, it needs a sound card. Join these discussion groups and swap hints and tips about PC sound cards. The **.soundcard** newsgroup is for all hardware and software aspects of such cards. The **.sb** group is for the Sound Blaster card. The **.gus** group is for the Gravis Ultrasound card.

Usenet:
Newsgroup: **alt.sb.programmer**
Newsgroup: **comp.sys.ibm.pc.soundcard**
Newsgroup: **comp.sys.ibm.pc.soundcard.advocacy**
Newsgroup: **comp.sys.ibm.pc.soundcard.games**
Newsgroup: **comp.sys.ibm.pc.soundcard.gus**
Newsgroup: **comp.sys.ibm.pc.soundcard.misc**
Newsgroup: **comp.sys.ibm.pc.soundcard.music**
Newsgroup: **comp.sys.ibm.pc.soundcard.tech**

Sound Tools

A collection of tools for dealing with .au sound files for MS-DOS, Windows Mosaic, Mac, and Amiga. Available in executable and compressed formats.

World Wide Web:
URL: **http://debra.dgbt.doc.ca/cbc/tools/tools.html**

Sound Utility Programs

There are sounds available all over the Internet, but that doesn't help you unless you know how to use them on your particular system. Find the information you need to play, convert or create sounds and soon you will have your computer making enough noise to cause the neighbors to start complaining.

Usenet:
Newsgroup: **alt.binaries.sounds.utilities**

Star Trek Sounds

Imagine having the voices and sounds of your favorite Star Trek episodes coming out of your very own computer. You can almost pretend you are right there in the sound stage or better yet, you are flying through space at high speeds seeking out new life and new civilizations — boldly going where no net.geek has gone before. Use these sounds to create some ambiance in your computing environment.

Anonymous FTP:
Address: **info2.rus.uni-stuttgart.de**
Path: **/pub/audio/sounds/startrek/***

Address: **plan9.njit.edu**
Path: **/pub/sounds/startrek/***

Address: **sunsite.unc.edu**
Path: **/pub/multimedia/sun-sounds/startrek/***

Sun Sound Files

Large collections of songs, rooster crows, cackles, gongs, dial tones, and other miscellaneous sounds to play on your Sun Sparcstation. Includes the Sparctracker software.

Anonymous FTP:
Address: **rutgers.edu**
Path: **/src/sun-sources/sounds/***

Address: **sunsite.unc.edu**
Path: **/pub/multimedia/sun-sounds/***

Gopher:
Name: National Chung Cheng University
Address: **gopher.ccu.edu.tw**
Choose: **miscellanies**
 | Funny Sounds

COMPUTERS: TECHNOLOGY

Artificial Life

Getting tired of real life? Try a little artificial life. It's low in calories, high in fiber, and while it might run up your electricity bill, it will certainly keep you from being lonely. MIT Press makes available this collection of resources relating to artificial life.

See also: Technology

World Wide Web:
URL: **http://alife.santafe.edu/**

Chinese Computing and Word Processing

A mailing list discussion group on technology relating to the use of Chinese text on computers. A forum for both experts and regular users that reaches from North America to the Far East.

Listserv Mailing List:
List Address: **ccnet-l@uga.cc.uga.edu**
Subscription Address: **listserv@uga.cc.uga.edu**

Complex Systems Resources

Links to many resources related to complex systems, including ftp and web sites, specific programs and papers, newsgroups, journals and mailing lists, bibliographies, and some pictures.

World Wide Web:
URL: **http://www.seas.upenn.edu/~ale/cplxsys.html**

Computer Aided Detector Design

The aim of the Computer Aided Detector Design (CADD) initiative is the integrated management of data concerning the LHC detectors throughout their lifetime. From this, three main tasks have been indentified: link event simulation with engineering design; link engineering tools among themselves; and provide a framework for management of engineering data. CADD provides several services for these tasks.

World Wide Web:
URL: **http://cadd.cern.ch/cadd_front.html**

Computer Lore

Famous computer bugs, unofficial Unix horror stories, *Old Iron at Home* stories, and much more computer folklore.

Anonymous FTP:
Address: **ftp.spies.com**
Path: **/Library/Techdoc/Lore/***

Gopher:
Name: Internet Wiretap
Address: **wiretap.spies.com**
Choose: **Wiretap Online Library**
| Technical Information
| Computer Lore

Computer Science Conferences

A large list of mailing lists related to computer science, the social, cultural, and political aspects of computers, and academic computing support.

Anonymous FTP:
Address: ksuvxa.kent.edu
Path: **/library/acadlist.file8**

Gopher:
Name: Coalition for Networked Information
Address: **gopher.cni.org**
Choose: **Coalition Ftp Archives**
| Publically Accessible Documents
| Guides to Network Use
| Kovacs, Diane; Directory of Scholarly Electronic Conferences
| File 8; Computer Science

Computer Speech

Archives and information about computer speech technology and speech science.

Anonymous FTP:
Address: svr-ftp.eng.cam.ac.uk
Path: **/comp.speech/***

Computer Standards

Technical documents on many standards, including gif, ymodem, zmodem, rich text format, and binhex.

Anonymous FTP:
Address: **ftp.spies.com**
Path: **/Library/Techdoc/Standard/***

Gopher:
Name: Internet Wiretap
Address: **wiretap.spies.com**
Choose: **Wiretap Online Library**
| Technical Information
| Computer Standards

Computer Viruses

FAQs and articles on viruses, including Bulgarian and Soviet virus factories, boot sector viruses, Bitnet and Internet viruses, and virus protection.

Anonymous FTP:
Address: **ftp.spies.com**
Path: **/Library/Techdoc/Virus/***

Gopher:
Name: Internet Wiretap
Address: **wiretap.spies.com**
Choose: **Wiretap Online Library**
  | **Technical Information**
  | **Viruses**

Computers and Technology in the Home

Wouldn't it be cool to be like the Jetsons? You could have everything automated so you never had to do dishes, mow the lawn or walk the dog. Discuss the development and use of telecommunication, information technology and automation in the private home environment.

Usenet:
Newsgroup: **comp.home.misc**

Cybernetics

Even though it's glorified in movies and science fiction, cybernetics is still a developing technology. Join this unmoderated list to see discussions on cybernetics and systems science. You might pick up a few good tips on how to make your own Terminator.

Listserv Mailing List:
List Address:
  cybsys-l@bingvmb.cc.binghamton.edu
Subscription Address:
  listserv@bingvmb.cc.binghamton.edu

Hebrew Users Group

Beyond its charming name (E-HUG), this mailing list is a useful resource covering all topics relating to the use of Hebrew, Judesmo, Yiddish and Aramaic when computing. This group is open to new users and old pros.

Anonymous FTP:
Address: **ftp.std.com**
Path: **/pub/obi/Zines/Hebrew.Users.Group/***

Listserv Mailing List:
List Address: **e-hug@dartcms1.dartmouth.edu**
Subscription Address:
  listserv@dartcms1.dartmouth.edu

Human and Computer Interaction

Documents, collections, directories, organizations, and resource lists relating to human and computer interaction. It includes links to bibliographies, research labs and projects, associations, guides, standards, software, tools, and much more.

World Wide Web:
URL: **http://galaxy.einet.net/galaxy/**
  Engineering-and-Technology/
  Computer-Technology/
  Human-computer-Interaction.html

Japanese Research

Text files giving accounts of what the Japanese are currently doing in all aspects of computer development.

Anonymous FTP:
Address: **ftp.uu.net**
Path: **/doc/literary/obi/HighTechReports/Japan/***

National Center for Supercomputing Applications

The birthplace of Mosaic, the NCSA is the mecca for fans of high-performance computing. Read news and announcements, information on software, publications, and computer resources, and see a nice selection of multimedia exhibits.

World Wide Web:
URL: **http://www.ncsa.uiuc.edu/**

New and Trendy Protocols

Articles, overviews, working groups, specifications, mailing lists, implementations, FAQs, and more to do with new protocols, such as SIPP (Simple Internet Protocol Plus) and TUBA (TCP and UDP with Bigger Addresses), which form the IP next generation (IPng).

World Wide Web:
URL: **http://town.hall.org/trendy/trendy.html**

SFI BBS

A research BBS devoted to complex systems.

Telnet:
Address: **bbs.santafe.edu**
Login: **bbs**

Speech Generator

Enter a sentence: it will be passed through a text-to-speech translator and thrown out your speaker. Both single line and multiline processing are available. Now the computer can swear back.

World Wide Web:
    URL: **http://utis179.cs.utwente.nl:8001/say/**

Techne

A forum for experimental research projects, tools, and issues in interface and information design, presented in the form of hypertext papers and discussions.

World Wide Web:
    URL: **http://wimsey.com/anima/**
        TECHNEhome.html

Technology Magazines

Sample articles and subscription information for computer technology and network-related magazines.

Gopher:
    Name: The Electronic Newsstand
    Address: **gopher.enews.com**
    Choose: **Magazines, Periodicals, and Journals**
        | Titles Arranged by Subject
        | Technology, Computers, Networks

Upcoming Events in the Computer Industry

A web page that points to numerous tidbits of information about upcoming events, seminars, expos, workshops, and meetings in the computer and software industries.

World Wide Web:
    URL: **http://www.yahoo.com/Events/**

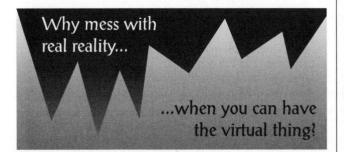

Why mess with real reality...

...when you can have the virtual thing!

Virtual Reality

This menu contains items relevant to the concept of a single-user virtual reality. It includes some interesting articles and access to the interactive fiction archive.

Anonymous FTP:
    Address: **ftp.u.washington.edu**
    Path: **/public/VirtualReality/***

VuSystem and VuNet Demonstrations

Live video and audio, and other demonstrations of the VuSystem and VuNet hardware developed by the Telemedia, Networks, and Systems Group at MIT. This won a technical award in the WWW Best Pages contest.

Note: Requires NCSA Mosaic for the X Window System, version 2.0 or later.

World Wide Web:
    URL: **http://tns-www.lcs.mit.edu/vs/demos.html**

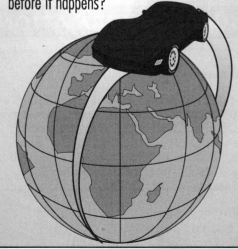

Your Internet Autopilot

Wouldn't it be great if you could use an automated program to travel around the World Wide Web and find things for you? Well, you can. Just take a look at **Wanderers, Robots, and Spiders,** and find out how to put these strange Internet creatures to work for you. It's just like living in the future, except that the food is better. Why not take a moment and imagine how good it all is, right now. After all, how often do you get to be nostalgic about something before it happens?

Wanderers, Robots, and Spiders

Make use of automation on the Web. Get information on how to use programs that travel on autopilot to conduct searches for you. See a list of known robots, how to use them, tips to help write one, and pitfalls to avoid.

World Wide Web:
URL: **http://web.nexor.co.uk/mak/doc/robots/ robots.html**

Wombat Dictionaries

A glossary of programming languages, architectures, networks, domain theory, mathematics, and, in fact, anything to do with computing.

Gopher:
Name: Imperial College
Address: **wombat.doc.ic.ac.uk**

Xtoys Gallery

This is a collection of images created by Xtoys programs, which are a set of cellular automata simulators. View pictures and details of classic life cellular automata, ants, Fredkin's modulo 2 rule, an avalanche in a sandpile model, Isling models, and more.

World Wide Web:
URL: **http://penguin.phy.bnl.gov/www/xtoys/ gallery/gallery.html**

CONSUMER INFORMATION

California Yellow Pages

A large list of retail businesses, realtors, restaurants, radio stations, sports and recreation, shopping centers, large and small companies, Internet service providers, magazines, and other organizations with World Wide Web offerings in California. Also offers an alphabetical listing of California web servers, and a "California: What's New" section.

World Wide Web:
URL: **http://www.research.digital.com/SRC/ virtual-tourist/CaliforniaYP.html**

For advice on using the Internet, read "The Internet Complete Reference."

Computer and Communication Companies

Hundreds of links to web pages of computer and communication companies around the globe, updated on a regular basis. Also includes links to other more generally related lists of commercial companies on the Internet.

World Wide Web:
URL: **http://www-atp.llnl.gov/atp/ companies.html**

Consumer Information

Here is Usenet's general consumer forum. And, since we are all consumers, there is something for everyone. Send in your questions, share your answers, read the reviews, opinions, and general bad-mouthing of the bad guys. Before you spend your next dime, check with the world at large.

Usenet:
Newsgroup: **misc.consumers**

Consumer Issues

Be a smart shopper and keep up with the latest news relating to consumer issues like product safety, value, new products, recalls. This is real news from Clarinet — hot off the wire.

Usenet:
Newsgroup: **clari.living.consumer**

Consumer News

Real news about real products bought by real consumers (you). Find out what is happening before the Joneses do.

Gopher:
Name: CICNet
Address: **gopher.cic.net**
Choose: **Electronic Serials**
 l **General Subject Headings**
 l **Business**
 l **Consumer News (UIUC)**

Usenet:
Newsgroup: **clari.news.consumer**

Credit Information

A FAQ list detailing everything you need to know about consumer credit.

Anonymous FTP:
Address: **rtfm.mit.edu**
Path: **/pub/usenet/news.answers/ consumer-credit-faq/***

Gopher:
Name: Oregon State University
Address: **gopher.fsl.orst.edu**
Choose: **Other Sources of Info**
  | Hugo's Lore-House
  | Where the Sun Doesn't Shine & Other Bottomless Pits
  | All you should ever need..

Dell Web Server

Dell Computer's web server is available for customers and interested parties. There are parts information, technical support, press releases, and online services available.

World Wide Web:
URL: **http://www.us.dell.com/**

Downtown Anywhere

Located in central cyberspace, Downtown Anywhere is a great place to browse, learn, share, and trade. This virtual city has many of the amenities of a real city, including libraries, newsstands, museums, bookstores, video and computer stores, art galleries, a post office, and a souvenir shop. Visit the financial district, or drop by the sports arena to see who's playing. This page won a "Cool Web Site" award from PC Week Labs.

See also: Internet: Resources

World Wide Web:
URL: **http://www.awa.com/**

Electronic Mail Directory of Companies

A directory of electronic mail addresses for companies that provide information about their products and services via email. To obtain a copy of the directory, or to request a free listing for your company in the directory, send mail to the address below.

Mail:
Address: **bbrca@aol.com**

Fair Credit Reporting Act

The full text of this Congressional act.

Gopher:
Name: Internet Wiretap
Address: **wiretap.spies.com**
Choose: **Government Docs (US & World)**
  | Fair Credit Reporting Act

Just the Fax, Ma'am

Now that we have the Internet, are faxes obsolete? Not really, because there are times when you will need to send material to someone not smart enough to have e-mail access. Not to worry, use the FAXNET service and send your fax from the comfort of your Internet account. It does cost money, but when you figure it out in dollars/dot, it's really quite reasonable.

FaxGate

This file will explain how to send a fax over the Internet. (You do have to register with them before you can use this service.)

Anonymous FTP:
Address: **ftp.pandora.sf.ca.us**
Path: **/pub/elvis/faxgate.help**

Look around. Is anyone watching? Good. Take a look at the X-Rated section. (But remember, you didn't read it here.)

Lonely? Try the Personals.

Faxnet

Send and receive faxes to and from anywhere in the world from your computer or terminal. All you need is to be able to send mail on the Internet. Send a mail message to the address below for a FAQ list about this service. (This is a service of AnyWare Associates, and they do charge fees.)

Mail:
Address: **info@awa.com**

Free Offers

There is free stuff out there in the world, just waiting for you to ask for it. You can get all kinds of cool things for free like phone calls, food, clothes, recipes, tickets and endless samples of miscellany — just for asking. All the information is here, so clean out the garage in order to make room for more stuff.

Usenet:
Newsgroup: **alt.consumers.free-stuff**

Houses

What did you ever do with your weekends before you bought a house? Don't you feel sorry for all those people who have nothing better to do than go out and have fun? Share your experiences with hardwood floors, mortgages, roofing repairs, plumbing, carpeting, contractors, real estate agents, painting, ventilation systems, and all the other great ways to spend your short, all-too-brief time on planet Earth.

Usenet:
Newsgroup: **misc.consumers.house**

Excerpt from the Net...

```
Newsgroup: misc.consumers.house
Subject: Too much house?

> Has anyone bought or rented a house
> and discovered that there was
> too much space for you?

I don't know if you're going to get
much sympathy for your problems.
It is far easier to make a house
smaller than to make it larger...
```

Excerpt from the Net...

```
Newsgroup: alt.consumers.free-stuff
Subject: Ways to Get Free Music

Join a record club and get your promised 10 free CDs, tapes, or
whatever they have promised. They make you pay shipping charges, but
it's only about $2 per CD or tape. Then, when they want you to buy
more CDs or tapes at the regular price you:

a) Say that you are a minor. Write a note from your parent saying they
   didn't know you were in this club.

b) Say you are devastated by society's pressures -- for example, you
   are 21 and pregnant, trying to resist everyday pressures etc
   -- and the last thing you can worry about is belonging to a stupid
   record club.

c) Say that you decided to give the money instead to charity.

This also works great with magazines to get a couple of issues free.

Trust me...
```

Infinite Illusions Home Page

Infinite Illusions Juggling Supplies is an online juggling store which not only offers its extensive catalog of juggling and related fun equipment, but also juggling graphics, tutorials, and links to other neat juggling resources on the Net.

See also: Hobbies

World Wide Web:
URL: **http://io.com/usr/infinite**

Internet Consultants Directory

A list of consultants with skill sets encompassing the Internet and World Wide Web. Use this list to find a consultant in your neighborhood!

World Wide Web:
URL: **http://www.commerce.net/directories/ consultants/consultants.html**

Internet Mall

A huge list of commercial products available online. This virtual department store is organized by floors: the first floor is media, the second personal items, the third is computer hardware and software, and the fourth floor is services. If you need to buy something, check here first. From CDs to sunglasses, those other online malls have nothing on the Internet Mall.

Anonymous FTP:
Address: **ftp.netcom.com**
Path: **/pub/Gu/Guides/***

Finger:
Address: **taylor@netcom.com**

Listserv Mailing List:
List Address: **imall-l@netcom.com**
Subscription Address: **listserv@netcom.com**

List Address: **imall-chat@netcom.com**
Subscription Address: **listserv@netcom.com**

World Wide Web:
URL: **ftp://ftp.netcom.com/pub/Guides/ Internet.Mall**
URL: **http://www.elf.com/gilly/mall/ mall.intro.html**
URL: **http://www.kei.com/ internet-mall.html**

Internet Services Directory

A directory of the huge number of companies, services and organizations available on the Internet, what they offer, and how to contact them. You can use several search methods through the web form-based interface, including searches by organization type, field of interest, and geographical location.

World Wide Web:
URL: **http://www.bbcnc.org.uk/babbage/ market.html**

Travel Marketplace

Offers many reviews, samples, images, ordering information and advisories from travel books and travel companies. Displaying and offering their products and views of many areas around the world are DeLorme Mapping, Lonely Planet Publications, Mountain Travel Sobek, Travelers' Tales Books, and Fodors WorldView Systems. The information is updated on a regular basis.

See also: Travel

World Wide Web:
URL: **http://nearnet.gnn.com/gnn/meta/travel/ mkt/index.html**

Xerox Corporation

Information about Xerox products, document solutions, contact methods, overview and news of Xerox Corporation, press releases, and links to Xerox Research servers.

World Wide Web:
URL: **http://www.xerox.com/**

Your Complete Guide to Credit

A consumer guide by Mark J. Allen.

Anonymous FTP:
Address: **oak.oakland.edu**
Path: **/pub/misc/consumers/credit.txt**

If you would like to send us a comment, mail to: catalog@rain.org

A B C D E F G H I J K L M N O P Q R S T U V W X Y Z

CRAFTS

Arts and Crafts Information Service

Search a database with references to over 5,000 craft product suppliers across North America. There is even a tutorial and a quick reference to help you get started using the database.

Gopher:
Name: PEI Crafts Council
Address: **gopher.crafts-council.pe.ca**
Choose: **Crafts Information Service: search for sources of crafts**

Craft Resources

A web page with links to many craft-related resources on the Internet. Some of the links are about making kites, metalworking, plastics, fibers, cross-stitching and bear-making.

World Wide Web:
URL: **http://www.crafts-council.pe.ca/crafts.html**

Craft Suppliers

A collection of U.S. toll-free telephone numbers for many crafts suppliers, categorized alphabetically by the type of craft products they supply. The list includes advertising, bearmaking, candlemaking, crocheting, fibre, lace, paper, quilting, sewing, stone, and many others.

Gopher:
Name: PEI Crafts Council
Address: **gopher.crafts-council.pe.ca**
Choose: **Other Crafts Information**
  | General Information
  | Toll-Free

Crafting on the Internet

A collection of FAQs, tutorials and links to craft resources on the Internet. Includes sections on craft events, fine art, photography, quilting, rug making, marketing, telephony, wood, and more.

Gopher:
Name: PEI Crafts Council
Address: **gopher.crafts-council.pe.ca**
Choose: **Other Crafts Information**

Crafts

Relax and be creative with a craft. Anyone can make a craft out of anything. (Remember pop-top art?) Dried flowers, matting, calligraphy, basket-weaving — the list goes on and on — but we have to get on to the next item.

Usenet:
Newsgroup: **rec.crafts.misc**

Jewelry

What a great feeling it is to be dressed up for a night on the town when someone compliments you on your stunning cufflinks and you can say, "Thanks. I made these myself while I was watching the ballgame." Learn the find craft of jewelry making or share your jewelry secrets with others. Topics of discussion include gems, settings, beadmaking and even selling jewelry.

Usenet:
Newsgroup: **rec.crafts.jewelry**

Needlework

This delicate and skillful craft takes time, patience and devotion. Read up on all manner of needlework including tips and techniques on tatting, pettipoint, cross stitch, and embroidery. Share patterns, design ideas and time-saving hints on this age-old craft.

Usenet:
Newsgroup: **rec.crafts.textiles.needlework**

Is the world of needlework confusing you? Start reading **rec.crafts.textiles.needlework** and get the point

Yarn

The world would be a dull place if it were not for yarn. There would be no cozy sweaters or lumpy slippers to wear. Whether you like knitting, crocheting, using a machine or just your hands, this group will have something you like as long as you are a lover of yarn.

Usenet:
Newsgroup: **rec.crafts.textiles.yarn**

CRYPTOGRAPHY

All About Cryptography

Articles about aspects of cryptography, including DES, Clipper, wiretaps, and other security issues.

Anonymous FTP:
Address: **ftp.spies.com**
Path: **/Library/Article/Crypto/***

Gopher:
Name: Internet Wiretap
Address: **wiretap.spies.com**
Choose: **Wiretap Online Library**
 | **Articles**
 | **Cryptography**

Crypto Glossary

Glossary of cryptography-related terms, from the Cypherpunks mailing list.

Anonymous FTP:
Address: **ftp.spies.com**
Path: **/Library/Document/crypto.dic**

Gopher:
Name: Internet Wiretap
Address: **wiretap.spies.com**
Choose: **Wiretap Online Library**
 | **Assorted Documents**
 | **Crypto Glossary (cyberpunks)**

Cryptography General Discussion

A general discussion on all aspects of data encryption and decryption.

Usenet:
Newsgroup: **sci.crypt**

Cryptography and the Government

How the government is involved with cryptography. Do they want to protect us all, or snoop on our private lives?

Usenet:
Newsgroup: **talk.politics.crypto**

Cryptography Sources on the Internet

This web page has links to a bunch of cryptography sources on the Internet, including Usenet groups, archives and a monstrous FAQ about cryptography.

World Wide Web:
URL: **http://www.beckman.uiuc.edu/groups/biss/people/gross/crypto.html**

Cryptography, PGP, and Your Privacy

Do you have a secret? If you do or if you just want the right to have a secret, check out this privacy page. It includes PGP documentation, links to PGP FAQs, newsgroups, and the actual program. In addition, there are links to other cryptography, PGP, and privacy pages as well as information on the notorious Clipper chip.

World Wide Web:
URL: **http://draco.centerline.com:8080/~franl/crypto.html**

Want to send and receive secret messages with your best friend? Get PGP (the **PRETTY GOOD PRIVACY** software package) and you can be as private as you want.

A
B
C
D
E
F
G
H
I
J
K
L
M
N
O
P
Q
R
S
T
U
V
W
X
Y

Cypherpunks

Clipper documents, cryptanalysis tools, crypt ftp site list, FAQs, PGP, and other cryptography-related material can be found at this Cypherpunk mailing list archive.

Anonymous FTP:
Address: **ftp.csua.berkeley.edu**
Path: **/pub/cypherpunks/***

Address: **ftp.funet.fi**
Path: **/pub/doc/cypherpunks/***

World Wide Web:
URL: **ftp://ftp.csua.berkeley.edu/pub/cypherpunks/Home.html**

Can't cope with PGP? Use PGPShell to make sending secret messages easy. But don't tell anyone, it's a secret.

PGP Encryption/Decryption Program

Where to get and how to use the ubiquitous PGP (Pretty Good Privacy) encryption package. Use it to send secret messages to your friends.

Anonymous FTP:
Address: **net-dist.mit.edu**
Path: **/pub/PGP/README**

Usenet:
Newsgroup: **alt.security.pgp**

Sending Secret Messages with PGP

The best things in life may be free, but if you don't want to share, you may have to hide them. The most widely used encryption program on the Net is **PGP**, written by Phil Zimmerman who, single handedly, deep-sixed all the government's plans to control encryption by offering a free, high-quality software package to everyone.

Using **PGP** requires two passwords called "keys". One of these is public; the other one is secret. You give your public key to anyone whom you want to be able to send secret notes to you. They use this key (and the **PGP** software) to encode a message which they then send to you. The beauty of the system is that a person can only decode the message if they have the private key (which you keep only for yourself).

The **PGP** program helps you create public and private keys that will work properly. Then you can give out your public key to your friends and start sending secrets around the Net. Similarly, if you have a friend who uses **PGP**, you can use his public key to encode a message to him that only he can read (because only he has the corresponding private key). Truly, Phil Zimmerman is one of the heroes of the 1990's.

PGPShell

If you've tried PGP and it's just too much for you to handle, get the friendlier PGPShell so you can frustrate the Feds with a smile on your face.

See also: Computers: Security and Privacy

Anonymous FTP:
Address: **oak.oakland.edu**
Path: **/pub/msdos/security/pgpshe31.zip**

Want to trade secrets? I'll show you my public key if you show me yours.

Need help reading the Usenet news? Try "The Internet Complete Reference."

Public Key Exchange

Share your public key with everyone else so you can send and receive secret encoded messages.

Usenet:
Newsgroup: **alt.security.keydist**

Quadralay Cryptography Archive

Quadralay Corporation maintains this vast repository of information about cryptography and security. This web page has links to resources at Quadralay and all over the Net.

World Wide Web:
URL: **http://www.quadralay.com/www/Crypt/Crypt.html**

HIDING SECRETS WITHIN PICTURES USING STEGO

Stego is the most amazing, cool thing you have ever seen. You can encode secret information inside a **PICTURE**—within the little tiny dots. To anyone else, it looks like a regular picture (say, of you shaking hands with the Pope at Princess Diana's birthday party). But to anyone in the know, it is a **SECRET MESSAGE**. You can send it all around the Net if you want, and no one can extract the information unless they have the password.

How totally radical. Only you know that the picture contains information hidden within the dots. All you need is a Macintosh and a modem and you can open your own spy agency. If you do, make sure you remember what Harley's sister told him years ago: It's nice to be important, but it's important to be nice.

Stego

Where are you going to hide Aunt Effie's secret recipe that you plan to use for the chili cook-off? The county championship is at stake, and you are determined not to let a spy slip in and ruin your chances. Don't settle for mere PGP encryption. Use Stego to hide your encrypted recipe inside a Macintosh PICT file. After you win, you can send us the recipe.

Anonymous FTP:
Address: **scss3.cl.msu.edu**
Path: **/pub/crypt/other/stego1.0a2.sit.hqx**

CYBERPUNK

Agrippa: A Book of the Dead

The complete text of this cyberpunk tale by William Gibson.

Gopher:
Name: Whole Earth Lectronic Link
Address: **gopher.well.sf.ca.us**
Choose: **Authors, Books, Periodicals, Zines | Poetry | Agrippa...**

Bruce Sterling Articles

A selection of essays and articles by Bruce Sterling, the renowned cyberpunk author, covering a variety of topics about cyberspace and its surrounding culture.

Anonymous FTP:
Address: **ftp.eff.org**
Path: **/pub/Publications/Bruce_Sterling**

Gopher:
Name: Whole Earth Lectronic Link
Address: **gopher.well.sf.ca.us**
Choose: **Cyberpunk and Postmodern Culture | Bruce Sterling**

Cyberspace City

Fans of Bruce Sterling (Mr. Cyberspace) can rejoice. Selected articles are available by Anonymous FTP or via a Gopher. Why go all the way to the library or bookstore just to read something on...ugh... paper. Read Sterling the way God meant you to read him: on your computer screen.

Cyberculture

A collection of articles, papers, and FAQs pertaining to cyberspace and electronic culture.

Anonymous FTP:
> Address: **quartz.rutgers.edu**
> Path: **/pub/cyberculture/***

Gopher:
> Name: Rutgers University
> Address: **quartz.rutgers.edu**
> Choose: **Cyberculture Papers and Info**

Cyberkind

Cyberkind, a web publication, offers prosaics and poetics for a wired world. It contains non-fiction, fiction, poetry, and art galleries, and is updated periodically. Writers' guidelines, details of how to write to the editor, a notification mailing list, and the publication itself.

World Wide Web:
> URL: **http://sunsite.unc.edu/ckind/title.html**

Lots and lots of music on the Internet: check out the Music category.

Cybermind

This web page offers archives from the Cybermind mailing list, Cybermind texts, many articles covering the themes of cybermind and cyberspace, and links to Cybermind-related online resources.

World Wide Web:
> URL: **http://www.uio.no:80/~mwatz/cybermind/**

Cyberpunk News

Collection of cyberpunk-related material, including *Locus* magazine, Bruce Sterling articles, and the latest information about cyberpunk conventions, those mind-blowing meetings of the computer underground.

Gopher:
> Name: Whole Earth Lectronic Link
> Address: **gopher.well.sf.ca.us**
> Choose: **Cyberpunk and Postmodern Culture**

Cyberpunk Reading List

A long list of cyberpunk-related books, novels, and material, arranged by author.

Anonymous FTP:
> Address: **ftp.spies.com**
> Path: **/Library/Media/Sci-Fi/cyber.lis**

Gopher:
> Name: Internet Wiretap
> Address: **wiretap.spies.com**
> Choose: **Wiretap Online Library**
>   **| Mass Media**
>   **| Science Fiction and Fantasy**
>   **| Cyberpunk Reading List**

Future Culture and Cyberpunks Mailing List

Discussion and news about tomorrow's reality today. Become a dreamer of the dreams.

Internet Mailing List:
> List Address: **uafsysb@uark.edu**
> Subscription Address: **uafsysb-request@uark.edu**

Usenet:
> Newsgroup: **alt.cyberpunk**
> Newsgroup: **alt.cyberpunk.movement**
> Newsgroup: **alt.cyberpunk.tech**

DANCE

Ballet and Modern Dance

The only thing that is not cool about ballet and modern dance is that you can't do it on the Internet. The closest thing you will find is a place where people talk about their experiences in the dance scene and share information on upcoming dance tours as well as dance opportunities. Strap yourself into some shoes and sashay on over to where the dance action is happening.

Usenet:
Newsgroup: **alt.arts.ballet**

Dance Archives and Discussion

Discussion and materials of interest to fans of dance, including swing, ballroom, rock and roll, and others. Materials include information on places to dance, events, new CDs, and steps.

Anonymous FTP:
Address: **ftp.cs.dal.ca**
Path: **/comp.archives/rec.arts.dance/***

Address: **ftp.cs.dal.ca**
Path: **/comp.archives/rec.folk-dancing/***

Address: **fuzzy.ucsc.edu**
Path: **/pub/bds93.Z**

Internet Mailing List:
List Address: **ballroom@athena.mit.edu**
Subscription Address:
ballroom-request@athena.mit.edu

Dance General Discussion

Are you wondering what is the theme of this year's Winter Biannual Formal Dance at the University of Wisconsin, Madison? Perhaps you have a less esoteric question about choreography, dance videos, stretching exercises, or how to do the tango. Step along with dance folk of all types in this general bop-till-you-drop discussion group.

Usenet:
Newsgroup: **rec.arts.dance**

The Net is mankind's greatest achievement.

Dance Resources on the Internet

Information about dance instruction on the Internet, and links to other dance-related resources, including the American Dance Fest, Galaxy Einet, the Tango Server, the Music & Dance page, and others.

World Wide Web:
URL: **http://www.cs.fsu.edu/projects/group4/dance.html**

Folk and Traditional Dance Mailing List

A global forum for information exchange for those interested in folk dance and traditional dance.

Listserv Mailing List:
List Address: **dance-l@nic.surfnet.nl**
Subscription Address: **listserv@nic.surfnet.nl**

Folk Dancing

There aren't too many ways to have fun, get exercise, listen to music, enjoy your friends, and act like a jerk, all at the same time. Whether you are into folk, dance, or folk dance, this is the place to meet the kind of people who like lining up and stepping out.

Usenet:
Newsgroup: **rec.folk-dancing**

It takes three to *tango:* you, your partner, and an Internet connection to the *Tango* site on the web.

Scottish Dancing

Forget the bar scene and the pick-up lines. Try some Scottish country dancing. Even though there is no actual dancing on this mailing list, you can talk about the history of dancing and share descriptions of dance as well as your experiences and helpful hints. You can join in the discussion of the dance even if you have two left feet. If you don't tell, no one will ever know.

See also: Hobbies, World Culture

Internet Mailing List:
List Address: **strathspey@math.uni-frankfurt.de**
Subscription Address:
strathspey-request@math.uni-frankfurt.de

Tango

Find out what is so appealing, so passionate, so captivating about tango. Choreography, lyrics, discussion groups, video clips, and photos. Warning: the Surgeon General has declared that doing the tango can be hazardous to your libido.

World Wide Web:
URL: **http://imtsun3.epfl.ch:8000/tango/welcome.html**

UK-Dance

UK-Dance is a web page and mailing list about the dance music culture in the UK, including clubs, parties, special events, record shops, radio, records, and anything else to do with the underground scene. The web page presents features from the mailing list and also archives the music reviews on the list.

World Wide Web:
URL: **http://www.tecc.co.uk/public/tqm/uk-dance/**

Western Square Dancing

"Chicken in the bread pan kickin' out dough; Skip to the lou my darling!" or "Parlez-vous square dance?" This web page is the place to be if you like square dancing. It has call lists, articles, humor, and much more.

World Wide Web:
URL: **http://suif.stanford.edu/~rfrench/wsd/wsd.html**

Square Dancing
The Pastime of Kings

Who has not fantasized about meeting their perfect man or woman in the middle of a square dance? There is something about this honestly American tradition that fans the flames of grace and mobility in all of us. The next time you are sitting home on a Saturday night, wondering if there are people out there who really know how to have more fun than you, take a look at the Western Square Dancing web site and eat your heart out. Then, stop feeling sorry for yourself and get out on the floor.

DISABILITIES

Americans with Disabilities Act

The full text of the 1990 act that was signed into law. The University of Maryland site has manuals and other documents regarding the Act.

Gopher:
Name: University of California Santa Cruz
Address: **scilibx.ucsc.edu**
Choose: **Electronic Books and Other Texts**

Name: University of Maryland
Address: **info.umd.edu**
Choose: **Academic Resources By Topic**
  | **Disability Resources**
  | **Cornucopia of Disability Information**
  | **Government Documents**
  | **Americans with Disabilities Act**

Blind News Digest

This newsletter is a digest format of posts to the Blind News list. It covers issues relating to being partially or totally blind and ways to deal with such an impairment. Topics include experiences and anecdotes as well as medical and technical information about blindness. This group is moderated.

Listserv Mailing List:
List Address: **blindnws@ndsuvm1.bitnet**
Subscription Address: **listserv@ndsuvm1.bitnet**

Usenet:
Newsgroup: **bit.listserv.blindnws**

Blind and Visually Impaired Computer Usage

Using the computer is tricky enough when you don't have a vision impairment. This list provides a forum for the discussion of computer use by the blind and visually impaired and offers a place to discuss problems and solutions relating to VM/CMS, PCs, and other systems.

Listserv Mailing List:
List Address: **blind-l@uafsysb.uark.edu**
Subscription Address: **listserv@uafsysb.uark.edu**

Deaf Magazine

One of the great things about the Net is that it offers people additional resources that are valuable. A great example is this weekly magazine with issues relating to hearing impairment.

Internet Mailing List:
List Address: **deaf@clark.net**
Subscription Address: **deaf-request@clark.net**

Deaf-Blind Discussion List

This is a multi-purpose list devoted to the topic of dual sensory impairment or deaf-blindness. Not only is it a place where professionals can discuss problems and solutions, but it's also a space in which individuals with DSI or families and friends can share information, inquiries, ideas and opinions.

Listserv Mailing List:
List Address: **deafblnd@ukcc.uky.edu**
Subscription Address: **listserv@ukcc.uky.edu**

Deafness

The deaf, hearing impaired, researchers, and family members of the deaf gather to discuss issues relating to deafness. Topics include medical and technical subjects as well as experiences and problems with having little or no ability to hear.

Listserv Mailing List:
List Address: **deaf-l@siucvmb.bitnet**
Subscription Address: **listserv@siucvmb.bitnet**

Usenet:
Newsgroup: **bit.listserv.deaf-l**

Developmentally Disabled and Autism

A mailing list for those who are developmentally disabled, their teachers, or anyone interested in the subject.

Listserv Mailing List:
List Address: **autism@sjuvm.stjohns.edu**
Subscription Address: **listserv@sjuvm.stjohns.edu**

Disability Aid

Information on federal aid programs, sources of income and information for the disabled, and business and employment opportunities.

Gopher:
Name: University of Michigan
Address: **vienna.hh.lib.umich.edu**
Choose: **Social Issues & Social Services | Disability and Rehabilitation**

If you or a loved one is disabled, remember that there are many people on the Net who are glad to help. There are many sites that offer information for the disabled and they are open 24 hours a day.

Excerpt from the Net...

```
Newsgroup: bit.listserv.deaf-l
Subject: Hard of Hearing in the Hearing World

...I figured out that this is all physics. I have an 80 dB loss.
You hear half with every loss of 20 dB. So it goes like this:

      -20 dB   you hear   1/2 the sound
      -40                 1/4
      -60                 1/8
      -80                 1/16
```

Assuming I'm still at -80, I hear 1/16 what you hear. That means the person
I am listening to [in a lecture hall] has to be 16 times closer...

Once I understood what was wrong, I could understand that if I am
sitting down and the person speaking to me is standing up, I can't hear
them. It's obvious why...

When people get high frequency deafness, the ability to pick out
consonants fails as well as the hearing itself. People do not realise
that when they raise their voice to communicate with people who are
hard of hearing, they automatically destroy the very consonants that
cannot be heard. The vowels distort and completely cover up the
consonants.

Please never ask us to "listen harder". We are already trying to
outguess the 70 percent or more of the consonants we cannot hear. We
hear all languages like a foreign language, English included...

When you talk us, DO talk in a normal soft voice, very close in the
ear. If this will not work, write it down. If we can't hear it close
and soft, we will not be able to hear it louder or "enunciated" either.

Please understand that lip reading is nothing but a guessing game, and
we are really tired of guessing. There is not even one lip pattern
that unambiguously means one thing only.

At the same time, we are sick of being alone, sick of eating by
ourselves (since almost no one takes the trouble to learn how to talk
to us), sick of being unable to communicate.

So there you have it: how it is to be hard of hearing in a hearing world.

Disability Information

Pointers and access to many disability-related resources,
including recordings for the blind and deaf education
information.

Gopher:
   Name: University of Wisconsin Madison,
      Trace Center
   Address: **trace.waisman.wisc.edu**

World Wide Web:
   URL: **http://www.eskimo.com/~dempt/**
   URL: **http://www.eskimo.com/~jlubin/**
   URL: **http://www.usfca.edu/usf/westford/**
      westford.html

Need a laugh? Check out Humor.

Disability Information Archive

Provides disability information, including digests, computing information, legal issues, college guides, government documents, employment, the Directory of Assisted Living Centers, and the National Rehabilitation Information Center (NARIC).

Gopher:
    Name: CODI
    Address: **val-dor.cc.buffalo.edu**

Disabled Computing

Articles and information about computing for those with physical disabilities.

Gopher:
    Name: CODI
    Address: **val-dor.cc.buffalo.edu**
    Choose: **Computing**

Disabled Student Services in Higher Education

It's frustrating for disabled students when colleges and universities don't have enough curb cuts, ramps, wide doorways, or elevators where they are needed. The purpose of this discussion group is to provide a forum to share information among providers of services for disabled students in higher education. Common issues for discussion are service delivery models and legal issues relating to the Americans with Disabilities Act.

See also: Education: Colleges and Universities

Listserv Mailing List:
    List Address: **dsshe-l@ubvm.cc.buffalo.edu**
    Subscription Address:
      listserv@ubvm.cc.buffalo.edu

Do-It Disability Program

The Do-It program offers a list of mailing lists, newsletters, newsgroups, and gopher sites which contain information of interest to people with disabilities. This list is not long, but it is thorough and provides a wealth of interesting information for the disabled.

Gopher:
    Name: University of Washington
    Address: **hawking.u.washington.edu**

Fathers of Children with Disabilities

Being a dad can be tough. If your child has a disability or special health needs, you may need some extra support. Fathers, professionals, and any other persons who care for children with disabilities are welcome to join this list, but the mission of this group is to share information, inquiries, ideas, and opinions on matters relating to the experiences of fathers of children who are disabled or have special health care needs.

Listserv Mailing List:
    List Address: **dadvocat@ukcc.uky.edu**
    Subscription Address: **listserv@ukcc.uky.edu**

Handicap BBS Lists

Lists of more than eight hundred dial-up BBSs that offer disability-related information.

Anonymous FTP:
    Address: **handicap.shel.isc-br.com**
    Path: **/pub/bbslists/***

Handicap Issues

If you have a handicap, you will find something helpful from these groups. Useful information and personal support covers topics such as problems facing amputees, medical issues for the disabled, handicap access concerns, politics, and personal interest stories such as biographies of famous people.

Usenet:
    Newsgroup: **bit.listserv.l-hcap**
    Newsgroup: **misc.handicap**

Mentally Retarded Deaf

There are many resources for the deaf or for the mentally retarded, but not for those who are both. This list has been created to fill a great need and is open to teachers, parents, students, administrators, therapists, researchers, and anyone who has an interest in the mentally retarded deaf.

Majordomo Mailing List:
    List Address: **mrdeaf-l@bga.com**
    Subscription Address: **majordomo@bga.com**

**Need that special something?
Try Romance.**

A B C D E F G H I J K L M N O P Q R S T U V W X Y Z

Reading Disabilities

A scientific paper discussing reading disabilities.

Anonymous FTP:
Address: **ftp.spies.com**
Path: **/Library/Article/Misc/disable.rd**

Gopher:
Name: Internet Wiretap
Address: **wiretap.spies.com**
Choose: **Wiretap Online Library**
 | **Articles**
 | **Misc**
 | **Reading Disabilities**

SAIDIE: The Intellectual Disability Network

Articles and information about intellectual disabilities, including policy, psychology, medicine, and education.

Gopher:
Name: MedCal
Address: **gopher.vifp.monash.edu.au**
Choose: **Medical**
 | **SAIDIE - The Intellectual Disability Network**

Software and Information for the Handicapped

This ftp site has many directories of informational files of interest to the handicapped.

Anonymous FTP:
Address: **handicap.shel.isc-br.com**

DRAMA

Dramatic Exchange

The Dramatic Exchange is an archive for storing and distributing play scripts. This web server is a vehicle for experienced or budding playwrights to publish and distribute their works, and a place for producers to look at new material. Anyone else interested in drama is also welcome here.

World Wide Web:
URL: **http://www.cco.caltech.edu/~rknop/ dramex.html**

Ahoy Scriptwriters!

The *Dramatic Exchange* is a place for you to share your work and read what other people are doing. Just the place to show off the great script that Warren Beatty refuses to read, about a surfing detective who writes Internet books.

Hollyweb Film Guide

What's on at the movies? Pop a little popcorn, grab a cold drink, and point your web browser toward Hollyweb. Read reviews, articles, top movie and video picks, history, and find out the top money-makers in the industry.

World Wide Web:
URL: **ftp://ftp.netcom.com/pub/spease/ hollyweb.html**

Musicals

It's too bad life isn't like a musical. When you are stressed or unhappy or madly in love, you could just burst into song and all the people around you would stop what they are doing and sing with you. In fact, you might want to try it, but we can't be held responsible for what happens. Get a good dose of musical theater by talking to other lovers of the musical genre. Any topic is acceptable as long as it relates to musical theater, though sometimes list members will get carried away and even talk about a little non-musical theater.

Internet Mailing List:
List Address: **musicals@world.std.com**
Subscription Address:
 musicals-request@world.std.com

Usenet:
Newsgroup: **rec.arts.theatre.musicals**

Opera Schedule Server

A web server dedicated to opera, with schedules and reviews of performances for opera houses around the world.

World Wide Web:
URL: **http://www.fsz.bme.hu/opera/main.html**

Remember,
it's not over until the fat woman
has checked out the Opera
Schedule Server.

Play Scripts

Numerous play scripts and other drama-related materials, including reviews, Shakespeare's plays, and Shakespearean information.

Gopher:
Name: Carnegie Mellon University
Address: **english-server.hss.cmu.edu**
Choose: **Drama**

Shakespeare Discussion

A global discussion open to all persons interested in Shakespeare, offering announcements, scholarly papers, and informal discussion.

Listserv Mailing List:
List Address: **shaksper@utoronto.bitnet**
Subscription Address: **listserv@utoronto.bitnet**

Look around. Is anyone
watching? Good. Take a
look at the X-Rated section.
(But remember, you didn't
read it here.)

Shakespeare Glossary

A glossary of Shakespearean terms.

Gopher:
Name: Carnegie Mellon University
Address: **english-server.hss.cmu.edu**
Choose: **Language**
  | Shakespeare Glossary

Stagecraft

The lure of the theater is hard to resist and even if you have no acting talent, this doesn't mean that you have to miss out on the magic. Arm yourself with tools, gadgets, plans, and a great imagination and you can be one of the all-important backstage magicians who create the stage, sets, and costumes of the theater. This newsgroup discusses the more technical aspects of theater.

See also: Fashion and Clothing

Usenet:
Newsgroup: **alt.stagecraft**
Newsgroup: **rec.arts.theatre.stagecraft**

Theater

There is magic in the stage with the lights and sound and hush of the finely-dressed audience as they breathlessly await the curtain's rise. Whether you are an actor, a techie or a fan, you can find great discussions between people immersed in the drama scene.

Usenet:
Newsgroup: **rec.arts.theatre.misc**
Newsgroup: **rec.arts.theatre.plays**

Theater Plays and Musicals

Theater FAQs, musical lyrics, reviews, guides, and other material relating to the theater.

Anonymous FTP:
Address: **quartz.rutgers.edu**
Path: **/pub/theater/***

Gopher:
Name: Rutgers University
Address: **quartz.rutgers.edu**
Choose: **Theater-Plays and Musicals**

Theatre Home Page

This web page offers information on some famous playwrights and links to more information on theater and performance art.

World Wide Web:
URL: **http://www.cs.fsu.edu/projects/group4/ theatre.html**

DRUGS

Anti War-on-Drugs Activist List

A list of organizations that are active in drug law reform.

Anonymous FTP:
Address: **ftp.uu.net**
Path: **/usenet/news.answers/drugs/ law-reformers.Z**

Address: **rtfm.mit.edu**
Path: **/pub/usenet-by-group/alt.answers/drugs/ law-reformers.Z**

Blotter Art Collection

Who says art is only for cultured people? Check out interesting ways in which people decorate their drugs. When you look at this web page they will encourage you to lick your screen, but don't do it. Just say no.

World Wide Web:
URL: **http://www.acpub.duke.edu/~eja/ blotter.html**

Caffeine

Start reading this newsgroup and find out everything you always wanted to know about the world's most overused stimulant. Do you know how to make really sludgy, sweet espresso? Are you wondering how much caffeine is in Jello Pudding Pops? Don't let it keep you up at night.

Usenet:
Newsgroup: **alt.drugs.caffeine**

World Wide Web:
URL: **http://www.quadralay.com/www/Caffeine/ Caffeine.html**

Have trouble staying awake at night? Try reading **alt.drugs.caffeine.**

Drug Abuse Education Information and Research

There is more to drug abuse education than just saying no to over-the-counter diet pills. This list was created for people interested in issues related to community drug abuse education and the epidemiology and study of drug abuse.

See also: Health

Listserv Mailing List:
List Address: **drugabus@umab.bitnet**
Subscription Address: **listserv@umab.bitnet**

> **THEY don't want you to know, but we'll tell you: take a look at Secret Stuff.**

The Internet will set you free.

Drug Chemistry and Synthesis

Where do you turn when it's late and you have a cold and all the pharmacies are closed? Check out this newsgroup and see if you can find a nice recipe for a decongestant or perhaps some LSD. That won't help your cold, but at least it will take your mind off your symptoms. Chemists and fans of chemistry chat about what how drugs are constructed and synthesized.

Usenet:
Newsgroup: **alt.drugs.chemistry**

Drug Culture

There is an entire group of people who choose not to hang out in reality some of the time. Instead of going to Disneyland, they like to spend lots of money on chemicals that are illegal and bad for their health. Commune with members of the drug culture as they talk about various drugs, music to trip to, and becoming one with nature and getting in touch with themselves and on special occasions with each other.

Usenet:
Newsgroup: **alt.drugs.culture**

Drug Information Resources on the Net

This web page offers links to many drug-related resources on the Internet, including ftp sites, gophers, mailing lists, newsgroups, IRC bots, and organizations.

World Wide Web:
URL: **http://stein1.u.washington.edu:2012/pharm/misc/resources.html**

Drug News

What would life be like without drugs? There would be less criminal activity and not as much money passing back and forth between South America and the rest of the world. There would also be less Clarinet news to read. Get the latest news on drug wars, politics, legislation, and top stories relating to drugs and drug testing and remember, without drugs, this group would not exist.

Usenet:
Newsgroup: **clari.news.drugs**

Drug Talk

Chat about all kinds and colors of drugs — what to do with them, and where they'll take you.

Internet Relay Chat:
Channel: **#drugs**

Drug Use History

A brief history of drug use and prohibition beginning around 5000 B.C.

Anonymous FTP:
Address: **ftp.spies.com**
Path: **/Library/Fringe/Pharm/drug.use**

Gopher:
Name: Internet Wiretap
Address: **wiretap.spies.com**
Choose: **Wiretap Online Library**
| Fringes of Reason
| Pharmacological Cornucopia
| A brief history of drug use

Drug Web Servers

These web pages offer all kinds of interesting items about drug tests, medical information, drug humor, politics, programs, and information on specific types of drugs.

World Wide Web:
URL: **http://www.yahoo.com/Health/Pharmacology/Drugs/**
URL: **http://cyborganic.com/drugz/**
URL: **http://www.pitt.edu/~mbtst3/druginfo.html**
URL: **http://www.ramp.com/misc/drugs/**

Do you have a favorite item that is not in the catalog? Let us know by sending mail to catalog@rain.org

A B C D E F G H I J K L M N O P Q R S T U V W X Y Z

Ecstasy

What a nice name for a drug. An intense, yet delicate labeling. Contrary to what most people believe, Ecstasy (or MDMA) is not a new drug. Read about the history, effects, dangers, and usage of Ecstasy, the drug that even the U.S. Army likes to use.

See also: Chemistry, Freedom

World Wide Web:
URL: **http://stein1.u.washington.edu:2012/ pharm/e4x-ht/**

General Drug Information

A directory containing subdirectories, each of which deals with a different drug and the issues surrounding its use, including LSD, peyote (mescaline), marijuana, opiates, stimulants, and others. Some nested subdirectories contain medical and legal information and one is devoted solely to drug-oriented humor.

Anonymous FTP:
Address: **ftp.hmc.edu**
Path: **/pub/drugs/***

Hints for Marijuana Growers

A guide for the aspiring farmer. A subdirectory containing compressed text files that tell you everything you ever wanted to know (but were afraid to ask) about how to grow marijuana.

Anonymous FTP:
Address: **ftp.hmc.edu**
Path: **/pub/drugs/marijuana/growers/***

Illegal Recreational Drug Information

Lots of information about drugs, including drug tests, FAQs, statistics, growing methods, chemical notes, marijuana-brownie recipes, and much more.

Anonymous FTP:
Address: **anubis.ac.hmc.edu**
Path: **/pub/drugs/***

**If you like trouble,
take a look at Mischief.**

Did you know there are many different books that you can download to your own computer? See Literature for the details.

LSD: My Problem Child

The father of LSD, Albert Hofmann, discusses his discovery and career as a research chemist, in this book translated by Jonathan Ott.

Anonymous FTP:
Address: **ftp.std.com**
Path: **/obi/A.Hofmann/probchild.Z**

Gopher:
Name: Software Tool & Die
Address: **gopher.std.com**
Choose: **OBI The Online Book Initiative
I The Online Books
I A. Hofmann**

Marijuana Discussion

It's a drag when you have a residue in your bong and you just don't know how to clean it out. Should you use acetone or windshield washer fluid? Or what do you do when your marijuana plants are not getting enough nitrogen? Or maybe you just need a good brownie recipe for when friends stop by for a visit. Find out the solutions to all these dilemmas by dropping in on the folks who really know their weed.

Usenet:
Newsgroup: **alt.drugs.pot**

Marijuana Fiction

A subdirectory containing marijuana-oriented stories in compressed text files.

Anonymous FTP:
Address: **ftp.hmc.edu**
Path: **/pub/drugs/marijuana/fiction/***

Marijuana Usage

Who gets to light the joint? A subdirectory containing compressed text files that deal with the practice and etiquette of smoking marijuana.

Anonymous FTP:
Address: **ftp.hmc.edu**
Path: **/pub/drugs/marijuana/usage/***

Medical Information About Marijuana

A subdirectory containing compressed text files dealing with medical issues involving marijuana, including data on possible therapeutic uses.

Anonymous FTP:
Address: **ftp.hmc.edu**
Path: **/pub/drugs/marijuana/medical/***

Neuropharmacological Anarchy

This web page is a database of information and links to many resources on the Internet about illegal and recreational drugs.

World Wide Web:
URL: **http://stein1.u.washington.edu:2012/pharm/pharm.html**

News About Drugs

All the news about drug-related crimes and newsworthy events. Tonight, read your kids something relevant instead of Barney the Dinosaur.

Usenet:
Newsgroup: **clari.news.law.drugs**

Nitrous Oxide FAQ

Learn what it is, what it is used for besides dentistry (whipped cream, dairy production, and auto racing), how to use it for recreational purposes.

See also: Health

World Wide Web:
URL: **http://www.resort.com/~banshee/Info/N2O/N2O.html**

Nitrous Oxide: Your Friend in the World of Nitrogen

A long, long time ago, Harley and his partner accidentally killed a mouse in the Neuroscience lab by using too much nitrous oxide. Make sure that this embarrassing experience does not happen to you. Stop whatever you are doing *right now* and read the **NITROUS OXIDE** frequently asked question list.

Nitrous Oxide Synthesis

Compressed text file containing instructions on how to synthesize nitrous oxide (laughing gas) at home.

Anonymous FTP:
Address: **ftp.hyperreal.com**
Path: **/drugs/inhalants/n2o.synth**

Nootropics (Intelligence-Enhancing Drugs)

A subdirectory containing compressed text files that deal with nootropics, the so-called intelligence-enhancing drugs.

Anonymous FTP:
Address: **ftp.hmc.edu**
Path: **/pub/drugs/nootropics/***

**Bored? Try Fun.
Still bored? Try Games.**

A
B
C
D
E
F
G
H
I
J
K
L
M
N
O
P
Q
R
S
T
U
V
W
X
Y
Z

Pharmacological Cornucopia

A collection of drug information, including a brief history of drug use, and articles and FAQs on absinthe, ecstasy, hemp, LSD, mushrooms, marijuana, opium, and psychedelic drugs.

Anonymous FTP:
Address: **ftp.spies.com**
Path: **/Library/Fringe/Pharm/***

Gopher:
Name: Internet Wiretap
Address: **wiretap.spies.com**
Choose: **Wiretap Online Library**
  | **Fringes of Reason**
  | **Pharmacological Cornucopia**

PiHKAL

An acronym for *Phenelthylamines I Have Known and Loved*, PiHKAL is a "love story" about a man and his favorite chemicals. Read excerpts from the book and see clever chemical breakdowns of everyone's favorite phenylethyl radical.

See also: Health, Medicine, Chemistry

World Wide Web:
URL: **http://stein1.u.washington.edu:2012/pharm/pihkal-ht/pihkal.index.html**

Politics and Drugs

Politicians, reporters, professors, doctors, and Ann Landers all have it wrong. Read what the people who really understand drugs and politics have to say.

Usenet:
Newsgroup: **talk.politics.drugs**

The Net is for smart people (like you).

Politics of Contraband

A directory of subdirectories which contain text files, each one of which deals with a different issue involving the politics and legality of drug use.

Anonymous FTP:
Address: **ftp.hmc.edu**
Path: **/pub/drugs/politics/***

JUST SAY "NO"

That's right, just say "no" to computer networks that do not offer you enough information to make intelligent decisions about drugs. Fortunately, that's not a problem on the Internet. All you have to do is read the information in *Pharmacological Cornucopia* and your brain cells will never be the same again.

Psychoactive Drugs

The Internet is just a crutch for people who can't cope with drugs. But if you happen to be one of those lucky few who can handle both at the same time, join the discussion about psychoactive drugs, legal and illegal. Just don't let it go to your head.

Usenet:
Newsgroup: **alt.psychoactives**

Recreational Drugs

Drugs for fun, not for profit. Where else can you go for advice on what to do with a pot of leftover phenyl acetic acid? How do you tell the difference between *Amanita Muscaria, Psilocybe Cubensis,* and Chinese take-out? Turn on, tune out, and drop into the only Usenet newsgroup where "Better Living Through Modern Chemistry" is more than just a slogan.

Usenet:
Newsgroup: **alt.drugs**

EARTH SCIENCE

Earth Observation System

You never know when the day will come that you will be called upon to know the salinity of coastal air or even how you find out stuff like that. To make an airborne salinity mapper, what wavelengths of microwave and IR-bands do you use and what's the conversion algorithm? No need to worry about bothersome details. NASA has it all worked out for you with their Earth Observation System. They're keeping an eye on the planet so you can rest easy at night.

Usenet:
 Newsgroup: **sci.geo.eos**

Earth Science Data Directory

The Earth Science Data Directory (ESDD) is being developed by the U.S. Geological Survey as a system for readily determining the availability of specific earth-science and natural-resource data. It offers access to a USGS computer repository of information about earth-science and natural-resource databases.

Gopher:
 Name: University of California Santa Cruz
 Address: **scilibx.ucsc.edu**
 Choose: **The Researcher**
  | **Science and Engineering**
  | **Earth and Marine Sciences**
  | **USGS Earth Science Data Directory**

Oceanplanet.gif is available from Northern Arizona University (**ftp.nau.edu**) in the directory **/graphics/gif/digi**.

Earth Sciences Resources

A list of earth-science-related Internet resources.

Anonymous FTP:
 Address: **ftp.csn.org**
 Path: **/COGS/internet.resources.earth.sci**

Gopher:
 Name: Oregon State University
 Address: **gopher.fsl.orst.edu**
 Choose: **Other Sources of Info**
  | **Hugo's Lore-House**
  | **Where the Sun Doesn't Shine..**
  | **Internet Resources for the Earth Sciences**

Planet Earth Images and Movies

Images of the Earth by region, movies of the Earth rotating, images of the Earth from space and the moon, Earth icons, details of the xearth globe picture creation program, and more.

World Wide Web:
 URL: **http://white.nosc.mil/earth_images.html**

Pictures of Your Planet

If you are like us, the Earth is one of your favorite planets in the entire universe. But what do you do when you meet an alien who pulls out a wallet and starts showing you photos of his home planet? Invite him over to your computer, fire up your web browser, and point it to "Planet Earth Images and Movies." Never again will you have to let a foreigner one–up you when it comes to civic pride.

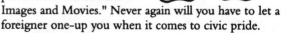

Polar Research

Information from the Polar Research Center, including Antarctic imagery, Earth pictures, animations of the rotating Earth, hardware and software details, and other interesting links.

See also: Geography

World Wide Web:
 URL: **http://www.mps.ohio-state.edu/**

Smithsonian Natural History Gopher

This gopher contains information resources that are compiled and maintained by Smithsonian staff, and includes newsletters and projects as well as pointers to other network resources of interest to researchers in natural history.

Gopher:
> Name: Smithsonian Institution
> Address: **nmnhgoph.si.edu**

> Name: U.S. Military Academy
> Address: **euler.math.usma.edu**
> Choose: **Reference_Section**
>   **I Other Neat Stuff**
>   **I Smithsonian Institution's Natural History Gopher**

xearth Graphics Software

xearth changes your X Window system's root window to an image of the Earth from your favorite vantage point in outer space. xearth updates the image every five minutes and produces gif or ppm files. Point your browser to the web page here for the man pages, examples, and the history of xearth, as well as the software.

Anonymous FTP:
> Address: **cag.lcs.mit.edu**
> Path: **/pub/tuna/xearth***

World Wide Web:
> URL: **http://cag-www.lcs.mit.edu/~tuna/xearth/**
> URL: **http://www.mps.ohio-state.edu/xearth/xearth.html**

Do you have **X Window**? Do you feel lost in space? Get the "xearth" program and never again worry about losing that home-sweet-home feeling.

ECONOMICS

British Economics Research

View and search hundreds of the latest economic research papers and statistics on the British economy.

Anonymous FTP:
> Address: **netec.mcc.ac.uk**
> Path: **/pub/NetEc/***

Gopher:
> Name: Manchester Computing Centre
> Address: **gopher.mcc.ac.uk**
> Choose: **Economics — NetEc**

Telnet:
> Address: **netec.mcc.ac.uk**
> Login: **netec**
> Password: **netec**

Need to know what those in England in the need to know need to know? If so, British Economics Research is waiting for you.

Community Economic Development

A discussion forum for anyone interested in trends, opportunities and changes in community economic development. The focus is on what communities can do for themselves in terms of achieving access to knowledge, programs, markets, and funds.

Majordomo Mailing List:
> List Address: **ced-net@sfu.ca**
> Subscription Address: **majordomo@sfu.ca**

Jokes? Try Humor.

Computational Economics

Working papers, handbooks, conferences, software, and more related to computational economics.

Gopher:
Name: SARA (Stichting Academisch Rekencentrum Amsterdam)
Address: **gopher.sara.nl**
Choose: **Computational Economics**

Directory of Economists

A large alphabetical list of economists on the Internet, including their mail addresses and other contact and research information.

Gopher:
Name: SARA (Stichting Academisch Rekencentrum Amsterdam)
Address: **gopher.sara.nl**
Choose: **Computational Economics**
  | **Directory of Economists (by name)**

Finding an Economist

How many times has this happened to you?
    You are planning a big party to impress your friends and neighbors and – while making out the guest list – you realize that you don't know any economists. And, as we all know, a party without at least one economist is like. . . well. . . a party without an economist.
    No need to panic. Just point your gopher to the Directory of Economists as you need. Remember, a man who knows his numbers is a man you can count on.

Excerpt from the Net...
(from the Computational Economics gopher)

```
Using Randomization to Break the Curse of Dimensionality
============================================================
```

Abstract:

This paper presents random versions of successive approximations and multigrid algorithms for solving a class of finite and infinite horizon Markovian decision problems known as discrete decision processes (DDP's). A DDP has a d-dimensional state space but a finite number |A| of possible actions in each state s in S. Monte Carlo integration is used to approximate the d-dimensional integrals required to solve the Bellman equation characterizing the optimal value function V.

The convergence of the random successive approximations and multigrid algorithms is shown to depend on the convergence of a "random Bellman operator". We appeal to the Central Limit Theorem in Banach Spaces and a version of Pollard's 1989 maximal inequality for empirical processes to prove that the maximum expected error in the random Bellman operator decreases at rate 1/\sqrt N independent of the dimension of the state space. These results imply that randomization succeeds in breaking the "curse of dimensionality" for this class of problems.

A B C D E F G H I J K L M N O P Q R S T U V W X Y Z

Economic Bulletin Board

The Economic Bulletin Board is operated by the U.S. Department of Commerce. It has 20 separate file areas that contain current economic and trade information, such as economic indicators, U.S. Treasury auction results, and employment statistics.

Gopher:
>   Name: University of Michigan
>   Address: **gopher.lib.umich.edu**
>   Choose: **Social Sciences Resources**
>   **| Economics**

Telnet:
>   Address: **ebb.stat-usa.gov**
>   Login: **guest**

Economic Experts Predict...

No more will you be at the mercy of economic experts when you need to decide where to take your vacation, or whether or not to finance your next purchase at the grocery store.

Just connect to the U.S. Department of Commerce's

Economic Bulletin Board

and you can get all the information you need to make your own predictions.

Astound your friends and family with your bold observations and wry comments.

Are you a know-it-all? Check in Trivia for tidbits of useless information.

Economic Development

It all started with a few beads, a handful of corn, and maybe a button or two. Who was to know that that functional system would turn into mutual funds, stocks, and IRAs? Economic development is where the little fish grow up to be the big fish who eat other little fish. Of course, it's not quite that simple, which is why you should read this list to find out how small, innovative companies can gain sophisticated tools that help them compete in a global economy.

See also: Business and Finance

Majordomo Mailing List:
>   List Address: **econ-dev@csn.org**
>   Subscription Address: **majordomo@csn.org**

Excerpt from the Net...

(from "Resources for Economists on the Internet")

While relatively few economists use the Internet, there is a surprising amount of very useful information on it. For instance, there are two very extensive sets of macro data, a bibliography of some 20,000 working papers in economics, household surveys from 21 countries, two interactive electronic markets, 24 mailing lists and two Usenet newsgroups.

Economic Problems in Less Developed Countries

Some countries have such cool sounding currencies: korunas, rupees, ringgits. Unfortunately, having interesting money doesn't solve the economic problems of less-developed countries. Professionals in the economic field study the economy and economic problems of these countries to not only enhance the field of study, but to examine the countries in relation to economic policy measures. Tune in with other economy buffs and analyze economic problems, theories, policies, social conditions, and political effects in less-developed countries and their relationship with the rest of the world.

See also: Business and Finance

Listserv Mailing List:
>   List Address: **economy@acadvm1.uottawa.ca**
>   Subscription Address:
>   **listserv@acadvm1.uottawa.ca**

Economics on the Net

It all started with Classical economics and moved through Marxism, the Neoclassical schools, Keynesian economics, Monetarism, right through to supply-side economics. Where does that leave us now? Good question. All we can tell you is try to get paid in advance and carry a big stick.

However, if you want to understand even more, there are substantial economics resources on the Net. Download the frequently asked question list and you will have more economic resources than you can shake a big stick at. Never again need you feel left out when the people in the checkout line at the supermarket start discussing the contributions of the neoclassicists to microeconomics.

Economic Resources

A document with a list of resources available on the Internet of interest to economists. Each resource has a brief description and the Internet address to access it. This information is updated every six weeks and currently contains a great deal of resources.

Anonymous FTP:
> Address: **rtfm.mit.edu**
> Path: **/pub/usenet/sci.econ.research/**
> **econ-resources-faq**

Economics Discussion

A mailing list forum for discussion of issues relevant to economics and distribution of new research papers.

Listserv Mailing List:
> List Address: **corryfee@hasara11.bitnet**
> Subscription Address: **listserv@hasara11.bitnet**

Economics Gopher

A wide array of economics-related information, including discussion list archives, census summaries, budget reports, directory of economists, and access to other economic resources.

Gopher:
> Name: Sam Houston State University
> Address: **niord.shsu.edu**
> Choose: **Economics (SHSU Network Access Initiative Project)**

Economics Resources on the Web

This web page has a great list of links to economics goodies such as price indexes, budgets, accounting information, and economic databases.

World Wide Web:
> URL: **http://fisher.ecn.bris.ac.uk/Subjects/econ.html**

Economies of the Caribbean Basin

Articles, information, and opinions concerning the economies of the Caribbean Basin as well as the overall economic health of the region.

Internet Mailing List:
> List Address:
> **caribbean-economy@vela.acs.oakland.edu**
> Subscription Address:
> **caribbean-economy-request@vela.acs.oakland.edu**

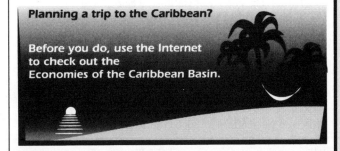

Economist Resources

A list of resources for economists on the Net, covering archives, gophers, library catalogs, Usenet newsgroups, and mailing lists.

Gopher:
> Name: NYSERNet
> Address: **nysernet.org**
> Choose: **Special Collections: Business and Economic Development**
> **I Resources for Economists on the Internet**

Employment Statistics

Civilian and government labor force statistics and unemployment information by state.

Gopher:
Name: University of California San Diego
Address: **infopath.ucsd.edu**
Choose: **News & Services**
  | **Economic..**
  | **Employment Statistics**

Wondering who's working at what? Take a look at the **Employment Statistics**

Foreign Trade

Statistics and data on U.S. foreign trade of merchandise and textiles. Includes import and export data, as well as foreign spending, capital expenditures, and summaries.

Gopher:
Name: University of California San Diego
Address: **infopath.ucsd.edu**
Choose: **News & Services**
  | **Economic..**
  | **Foreign Trade**

General Agreement on Tariffs and Trade (GATT)

This web page offers a link to the text of the GATT Act, as well as many commentary discussion areas including other similar agreements and the Uruguay Round Agreements.

World Wide Web:
URL: **http://ananse.irv.uit.no/trade_law/gatt/nav/toc.html**

The Net is mankind's greatest achievement.

Gross State Product Tables

The gross state product data tables estimate the value of goods and services produced for 61 industries in 50 states, eight regions, and the nation as a whole. The value is the sum of four components: compensation of employees; proprietors' income with inventory valuation adjustment and capital consumption allowances; indirect business tax and nontax liability; and other, mainly capital-related, charges.

Gopher:
Name: University of Michigan
Address: **gopher.lib.umich.edu**
Choose: **Social Sciences Resources**
  | **Economics**
  | **Gross State Product Tables from US Bureau of Econ. Analysis**

Marketing

Marketing people have such power. Imagine being able to take a film or a jingle, combine it with a promotional idea, and suddenly have a million people foaming at the mouth to buy your product. This is the basis of all good mind control. Marketing academics and practitioners join up to discuss marketing-related topics such as pricing tactics, distribution, promotion and advertising, segmentation, surveys, service quality, marketing planning for non-profits, exporting, product design, and more.

Internet Mailing List:
List Address: **elmar@columbia.edu**
Subscription Address: **elmar-request@columbia.edu**

List Address: **market-l@nervm.nerdc.ufl.edu**
Subscription Address:
  listserv@nervm.nerdc.ufl.edu

Monetary Statistics

Foreign exchange rates, aggregate reserves, daily bond rates, consumer credit, flow of funds, savings bond rates, treasury yields, and much more.

Gopher:
Name: University of California San Diego
Address: **infopath.ucsd.edu**
Choose: **News & Services**
  | **Economic..**
  | **Monetary Statistics**

Morningstar Spotlight

Morningstar, Inc. is the leading provider of mutual fund performance information. This web page sports their top five aggressive equity/growth funds, top five hybrid income investment funds, and the top five no-load small cap funds.

World Wide Web:
> URL: **http://networth.galt.com/www/home/ mutual/morning/mspot.htm**

Mutual Fund Market Manager

The Mutual Fund Market Manager claims to be the first to offer mutual fund information all the way down to the prospectus level on the Internet.

World Wide Web:
> URL: **http://networth.galt.com/www/home/ mutual/mutualmn.htm**

Mutual Fund Quotations

The NETnavs page offers a number of great resources including free mutual fund quotes, a portfolio management tool, a fund manager, S&P market indices, Market Fundamentals, and much more.

World Wide Web:
> URL: **http://networth.galt.com/www/home/nav/ netnav.htm**

Mutual Funds Phone Numbers

Need to call about a mutual fund? We do it all the time (sure we do). Well, if you need to call, the phone number will surely be here. This web page has a huge list of phone numbers for many mutual funds.

World Wide Web:
> URL: **http://www.cs.cmu.edu:8001/afs/cs.cmu.edu/ user/jdg/invest/info/funds-phones**

National Income and Products Accounts

Annual income statistics for past years, estimates, gross domestic product tables, quarterly and annual NIPA reports, and source statistics used to calculate GDP.

Gopher:
> Name: University of California San Diego
> Address: **infopath.ucsd.edu**
> Choose: **News & Services**
> I **Economic..**
> I **National Income..**

Press Releases from U.S. Trade Representative

A collection of the press releases from the U.S. Trade Representative. Releases are named by subject.

Gopher:
> Name: University of Michigan
> Address: **gopher.lib.umich.edu**
> Choose: **Social Sciences Resources**
> I **Economics**
> I **Economic Bulletin Board**
> I **Press Releases from U.S. Trade Representative**

Price and Productivity Statistics

Supporting data and statistics used in computation of the Consumer Price Index, import and export price indexes, the producer price index, and productivity and cost statistics.

Gopher:
> Name: University of Michigan
> Address: **gopher.lib.umich.edu**
> Choose: **Social Sciences Resources**
> I **Economics**
> I **Economic Bulletin Board**
> I **Price and Productivity Statistics**

Regional Economic Statistics

Supporting data and computations of disposable per capita income by state, total personal incomes, metropolitan, state, and regional incomes. Also includes wage and salary data by industry, by state, by region, and U.S. totals.

Gopher:
> Name: University of Michigan
> Address: **gopher.lib.umich.edu**
> Choose: **Social Sciences Resources**
> I **Economics**
> I **Economic Bulletin Board**
> I **Regional Economic Statistics**

A B C D E F G H I J K L M N O P Q R S T U V W X Y Z

Russian Economics

Information on the transition in Russia's economy and international business information.

World Wide Web:
URL: **http://solar.rtd.utk.edu/friends/economics/ economics.html**

Securities and Exchange Commission's Database

The SEC's Internet EDGAR Dissemination project allows you to get any current filings to the Securities and Exchange Commission that are available to the public.

Gopher:
Name: Internet Town Hall
Address: **town.hall.org**

World Wide Web:
URL: **http://town.hall.org/edgar/edgar.html**

Summaries of Current Economic Conditions

Government and industry statistical summaries on trade, the balance of payments, the consumer price index, retail sales, inventories, construction, durable goods, employment cost index, housing starts, production and capacity, plant and equipment spending, and much more.

Gopher:
Name: University of Michigan
Address: **gopher.lib.umich.edu**
Choose: **Social Sciences Resources**
| **Economics**
| **Economic Bulletin Board**
| **Summaries of Current Economic Conditions**

Thoughts on Economics

A collection of articles relating to economics, business, and finance, including a Christmas price index, investment guide, and the lawnmower strategy.

Anonymous FTP:
Address: **quartz.rutgers.edu**
Path: **/pub/economics/***

Gopher:
Name: Rutgers University
Address: **quartz.rutgers.edu**
Choose: **Economics, Business, Finance**

Bored? Try Fun.
Still bored? Try Games.

U.S. Economic Statistics

A subdirectory of files containing U.S. economic statistics for 1981-1991, including retail and home sales figures, and individual and corporate income taxes.

Note: These files are formatted for printing, not for viewing on your screen.

Anonymous FTP:
Address: **ftp.uu.net**
Path: **/doc/literary/obi/Economics/***

Working Paper Archive

An archive of working papers on economics, grouped in 21 subject areas with abstracts.

Anonymous FTP:
Address: **econwpa.wustl.edu**
Path: **/econ-wp/***

Gopher:
Name: Washington University St. Louis
Address: **gopher.wustl.edu**
Choose: **Departmental Gopher Servers**
| **Economics Department**
| **Economics Working Paper Archive**

EDUCATION

Academic Technology

Don't get behind in the race for information. Wield your computer like a sword and cut through all the useless or frivolous information that you don't have time for. Subscribe to **infobits** and read their hand-selected tidbits about information technology and instruction technology sources. It will leave you with more time for the important things in life, like teaching more students or perhaps having a cold drink while you work on your tan.

See also: Technology

Listserv Mailing List:
List Address: **infobits@gibbs.oit.unc.edu**
Subscription Address: **listserv@gibbs.oit.unc.edu**

Adult Education and Literacy

These forums offer interesting discussion on ways to educate adults. Topics cover textbooks, education using an interactive computer environment like MOOs and IRC, learning by audio tapes and more conventional environments such as a classroom setting.

Listserv Mailing List:
List Address: **aednet@suvm.syr.edu**
Subscription Address: **listserv@suvm.syr.edu**

Usenet:
Newsgroup: **misc.education.adult**

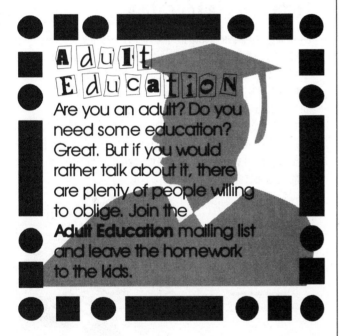

Are you an adult? Do you need some education? Great. But if you would rather talk about it, there are plenty of people willing to oblige. Join the **Adult Education** mailing list and leave the homework to the kids.

Adult Literacy

Learning to read when you are an adult can sometimes be tough — just like trying to learn a new language. Practice is the crucial ingredient for being able to read well and with **learner**, a moderated discussion group for adult learners, you can practice reading and writing skills by posting to the group. Since the group is for adults, it provides a safe and helpful environment for new learners to share ideas, meet other people, and establish pen-pal contacts.

Listserv Mailing List:
List Address: **learner@nysernet.org**
Subscription Address: **listserv@nysernet.org**

AERA SIG/ENET Discussion

Forget plastics and natural resources. *Information* is the key investment for the future. (Remember that you heard it here first.) This discussion group is for educators and educational researchers interested in information technology and resources.

See also: Education: Teachers, Technology

Listserv Mailing List:
List Address: **enet-l@uhccvm.uhcc.hawaii.edu**
Subscription Address:
listserv@uhccvm.uhcc.hawaii.edu

Alternative Approaches to Learning

Members of this mailing list discuss all aspects of alternative and new approaches to education and learning.

Listserv Mailing List:
List Address: **altlearn@sjuvm.stjohns.edu**
Subscription Address: **listserv@sjuvm.stjohns.edu**

Armadillo

The Texas Studies Gopher, Armadillo, has been designed with the middle-school teacher and student in mind, and presents information about Texas natural and cultural history.

Gopher:
Name: Rice University
Address: **chico.rice.edu**
Port: **1170**

Want to talk about new ways to learn? Join altlearn, the mailing list for discussions about Alternative Approaches to Learning.

A
B
C
D
E
F
G
H
I
J
K
L
M
N
O
P
Q
R
S
T
U
V
W
X
Y
Z

Association for Experiential Education

The AEE is a non-profit organization that encourages learning through experience. With international membership, the AEE offers diversity in their professional and special interest groups. Find out more information about the group and other resources for experiential education at AEE's home page.

World Wide Web:
URL: **http://www.princeton.edu/~rcurtis/aee.html**

Biology Education

It's 6:00AM and you need a quick answer for your biology homework due at 8:00. Never fear — fire off a question into the **biopi-l** mailing list. Within a few minutes you may get your answer!

See also: Biology

Listserv Mailing List:
List Address: **biopi-l@ksuvm.ksu.edu**
Subscription Address: **listserv@ksuvm.ksu.edu**

Commonwealth of Learning

The purpose of the Commonwealth of Learning is to create and widen access to education and improve its quality by using techniques and technologies designed to meet the requirements of its member countries. To learn about the different areas of focus of this organization, see their server.

World Wide Web:
URL: **http://www.col.org/**

Computer Networking

A mailing list for discussing the use of computer networking within today's education systems.

Listserv Mailing List:
List Address: **cneduc-l@tamvm1.tamu.edu**
Subscription Address: **listserv@tamvm1.tamu.edu**

The Net is for smart people (like you).

Computers in Education

Gone are the days of doing your homework on portable blackboard slates. Education has gone high-tech. Read about the use of computers in elementary, secondary, and higher education. Topics covered include authoring tools, programming languages, applications, and artificial intelligence. Because of all this, kids have had to change their tactics and learn to say, "I did my homework, but the dog ate my floppy disk."

Listserv Mailing List:
List Address: **infed-l@ccsun.unicamp.br**
Subscription Address: **listserv@ccsun.unicamp.br**

Computers in Education

We love computers in education. When Harley was in school, he had his own personal robot to help him with his homework, and look how good he turned out. What could be better than a mechanical teacher that tells you stories about aliens and doesn't mind when you throw spitballs?

If you think education is more than the three R's (reading the "Internet Yellow Pages," 'riting, and 'rithmetic) join the **infed-l** mailing list and see what is new and wonderful in the world of computers and education.

Curriculum Materials and Ideas

A collection of pointers to curriculum resources on the Net, including curriculum guides, lesson plans, ideas and resources.

Gopher:
Name: AskERIC
Address: **gopher.cua.edu**
Choose: **Special Resources**
  | ERIC Clearinghouse on Assessment and Evaluation
  | **Curriculum guides, lesson plans, ideas, & resources**

Daily Report Card

Up-to-date information on the state of educational concerns in the U.S.

Gopher:
> Name: NYSERNet
> Address: **nysernet.org**
> Choose: **Special Collections:Empire Internet Schoolhouse (K-12)**
> **I School Reform and Technology Planning Center**
> **I Daily Report Card News Service**

Education Mailing Lists

Here's an assortment of education-related mailing lists: **sigtel-l** is about telecommunications in education, **vocnet** is about vocational education, **susig** is about math education — especially with spreadsheet programs, **stlhe-l** is about higher education, and **school-l** is about primary and post-primary education.

Listserv Mailing List:
> List Address: **sigtel-l@unmva.unm.edu**
> Subscription Address: **listserv@unmva.unm.edu**

> List Address: **susig@miamiu.acs.muohio.edu**
> Subscription Address:
> **listserv@miamiu.acs.muohio.edu**

> List Address: **stlhe-l@unb.ca**
> Subscription Address: **listserv@unb.ca**

> List Address: **school-l@irlearn.ucd.ie**
> Subscription Address: **listserv@irlearn.ucd.ie**

> List Address: **vocnet@cmsa.berkeley.edu**
> Subscription Address: **listserv@cmsa.berkeley.edu**

> No matter who you are, no matter what your interests, if you are in the world of education, there is a mailing list for you.

Education Policy

A mailing list forum for discussing education policy analysis in the U.S. The **edpolyar** list is an archive for the **edpolyan** list.

Listserv Mailing List:
> List Address: **edpolyan@asuvm.inre.asu.edu**
> Subscription Address:
> **listserv@asuvm.inre.asu.edu**

> List Address: **edpolyar@asuvm.inre.asu.edu**
> Subscription Address:
> **listserv@asuvm.inre.asu.edu**

Educational Listserv Lists

A guide to mailing lists relating to all aspects of education, arranged by subject area.

Anonymous FTP:
> Address: **nic.umass.edu**
> Path: **/pub/ednet/educatrs.lst**

Gopher:
> Name: NYSERNet
> Address: **nysernet.org**
> Choose: **Special Collections: Internet Help**
> **I Guide to Educational Listservs**

Educational Newsgroups

A guide to education-related Usenet groups, cataloged by subject area.

Anonymous FTP:
> Address: **nic.umass.edu**
> Path: **/pub/ednet/edusenet.gde**

Gopher:
> Name: NYSERNet
> Address: **nysernet.org**
> Choose: **Special Collections: Internet Help**
> **I Guide to Educational Newsgroups**

> **Parents and children, take a look at: Families and Parenting, Kids, and Youth.**

A
B
C
D
E
F
G
H
I
J
K
L
M
N
O
P
Q
R
S
T
U
V
W
X
Y
Z

Educational Reform

A mailing list about innovations in educational reform, as well as other educational issues, including performance assessment, nongraded primary education, and multicultural education.

Listserv Mailing List:
  List Address: **ukera-l@ukcc.uky.edu**
  Subscription Address: **listserv@ukcc.uky.edu**

Education and Usenet

Usenet has many newsgroups related to teaching, schools and education in general. You could spend time in all of them - what a learning experience that would be! - but it would take the rest of your life.

Better to use the guide in **Educational Newsgroups** and narrow your focus. That way, you can spend more time reading jokes.

EDUPAGE

An education-related news service provided by EDUCOM, a consortium of leading colleges and universities seeking to transform education through the use of information technology. The vehicle for news delivery is periodical mail messages with summary news briefs.

Mail:
  Address: **edupage@educom.edu**

The Internet will set you free.

Eisenhower National Clearinghouse

The Eisenhower National Clearinghouse (ENC) provides K-12 teachers a central source of information on mathematics and science curriculum materials and encourages the adoption and use of these materials. ENC is funded by the U.S. Department of Education.

World Wide Web:
  URL: **http://kepler.enc.org/**

Engines for Education

Everybody's complaining about education reform, but nothing seems to get done. Now you can read a hyperbook called *Engines for Education* which tells you exactly what's wrong with education and what should be done about it.

World Wide Web:
  URL: **http://www.ils.nwu.edu/~e_for_e/**
  URL: **http://www.ils.nwu.edu:80/~e_for_e/**

Global Schoolhouse Project

The Global Schoolhouse is a project that connects schools and students nationally and internationally using the Internet and modeling classroom applications of Internet tools and resources. Collaborative research is conducted between the schools, and students interact using a variety of Internet tools including live video conferences with Macintosh computers and PCs.

World Wide Web:
  URL: **http://k12.cnidr.org/gshwelcome.html**

Want to talk to other kids in strange exotic places (like Nebraska or Vermont)? Join the Global Schoolhouse.

This is the first book of the rest of your life.

GNA Virtual Library

A collection of links to numerous reference sources, online bookstores, electronic texts, and GNA course-related articles.

World Wide Web:
URL: **http://www.mit.edu:8001/afs/ athena.mit.edu/user/d/j/djkahle/www/library2**

Grants, Scholarships, and Funding

A lengthy list of organizations that offer funding in one form or another. Newsletters and bulletins about grants and funding are also available.

Gopher:
Name: Rice University
Address: **riceinfo.rice.edu**
Choose: **Information by Subject Area | Grants, Scholarships and Funding**

MONEY FOR YOU!

If you are one of those rare people in the educational community who needs more money, the Internet can help you. Point yourself at the Rice University gopher and take a look at their **Grants, Scholarships and Funding** list. Perhaps with some good begging skills and a little bit of luck, you too can ride to school each day in a chauffeured limousine and, better yet, afford anything you want in the school cafeteria.

Writers, share your stories on the Net.

Excerpt from the Net...

```
Newsgroup: misc.education.home-school.misc
Subject: How do you cope with four at home?

Hey, congrats on your plunge into what I think is the most rewarding
part of my life.  I have four, like you.  Mine are 9, 7, 4 and 1, my
boys are the older and girls the younger...

It is pretty hard to attend to all their differing needs.  I'm sure it
will take awhile for you to get into a routine, and I don't think it's
REAL important to worry too much about lots of structure right away.
When my boys were 7 and 5 we did very little schooling at all (we have
always homeschooled) — I sort of waited for them to indicate a
willingness and readiness.  We did lots of reading to them, which my
daughter (3) enjoyed, even the books geared to older kids.  And we did
lots of our work just talking about things: phonics/math/history/science
and they all seem to retain most of what we would talk about if it was
on their level at all.

I think your 2 year old will probably stop her sabotage if you can
involve her by letting her participate...  If it's way beyond her
level, she will probably get bored and turn to a different activity.
My three older kids all do pretty much the same work, but I don't
expect my four year old's stuff to be "correct" and I make sure she
knows it's optional, especially if she gets frustrated...
```

A B C D E F G H I J K L M N O P Q R S T U V W X Y Z

Health Sciences Libraries Consortium

The Health Sciences Libraries Consortium (HSLC) Computer Based Learning Software Database contains listings of PC-compatible and Macintosh programs used in health sciences education.

Telnet:
>Address: **shrsys.hslc.org**
>Login: **cbl**

Home School Discussion

As home schooling becomes more popular, it is easier to find resources relating to the process of teaching children in the home environment. Take advantage of the Internet as one of these resources and discuss with other home schoolers the trials and rewards of teaching your kids at home. The **misc.education.home-school.christian** group is specifically for Christians who home school.

Usenet:
>Newsgroup: **misc.education.home-school.christian**
>Newsgroup: **misc.education.home-school.misc**

Home School Resources

People home-school their children for cultural, social and religious reasons. Whatever the reason, it's good to have as many resources as possible if you are going to take on the home-schooling task. On the Net there are many options. This web page will not only offer you articles on home-schooling, but it will also show you available mailing lists where you can talk with other Net folk who are interested in home-schooling.

World Wide Web:
>URL: **http://www.armory.com/~jon/hs/ HomeSchool.html**

IBM Kiosk for Education

A gopher-based server offering IBM information, application software, and a bulletin board for IBM users in the higher education community. The system is funded by IBM and developed and operated by the Center for Information Systems Optimization at the University of Washington.

Gopher:
>Name: University of Washington
>Address: **ike.engr.washington.edu**

Telnet:
>Address: **isaac.engr.washington.edu**
>Login: **register**

Incomplete Guide to the Internet

The Incomplete Guide to the Internet and Other Telecommunications Opportunities Especially for Teachers and Students, K-12 is a resource guide and how-to manual for beginning and intermediate Internet users as well as an excellent reference for advanced users.

Anonymous FTP:
>Address: **ftp.ncsa.uiuc.edu**
>Path: **/Education/Education_Resources/ Incomplete_Guide/***

Indigenous Peoples

All explorers feel compelled to run out and find natives and quickly bring them up to date on how life is in the modern world. It's a tough choice — would you give up being able to run naked in the woods for indoor plumbing? Exchange information and ideas with other people interested in the educational needs of the world's indigenous peoples.

Listserv Mailing List:
>List Address: **nat-edu@miamiu.muohio.edu**
>Subscription Address: **listserv@miamiu.muohio.edu**

Institutional Communications Network

The INet project, which is run by the U.S. Department of Education, is intended to facilitate communication and information sharing among the major education research, development, and dissemination institutions that OERI (Office of Educational Research and Improvement) supports. But beyond its institutional purpose, INet also provides Internet access through its web server to a broad range of databases and files containing both statistical data and research and development information aimed at improving teaching and learning.

Gopher:
>Name: U.S. Department of Education
>Address: **gopher.ed.gov**

World Wide Web:
>URL: **http://www.ed.gov/**

Want to know what makes the Internet run? Read Internet: RFCs.

JANET Network

Long- and short-term information on the JANET network, the U.K.'s academic network.

Gopher:
Name: Joint Academic Network
Address: **news.janet.ac.uk**

K12 Internet School Sites

Before you know it, nobody will have to go to school anymore. We can all just sit home and learn from the Internet. See elementary, junior high, and high schools on the Web. Kids and teachers work together to make interesting home pages for their schools. There are also links to school districts and the U.S. Department of Education.

World Wide Web:
URL: **http://toons.cc.ndsu.nodak.edu/~sackmann/k12.html**

K12 Resources

A great source of links to many education resources for all K12 levels.

World Wide Web:
URL: **http://edu-153.sfsu.edu/k12/k12.html**
URL: **http://galaxy.einet.net/galaxy/Social-Sciences/Education.html**

Latin Language Textbook

A subdirectory of text files that together comprise a Latin language textbook.

Anonymous FTP:
Address: **ftp.uu.net**
Path: **/doc/literary/obi/Classics/CHAP***

Math Information Server

This site was a nominee for the Best Overall Site in the 1994 Best of the Web awards. It offers some excellent teaching and lecture notes from the undergraduate and masters degrees available at Cardiff, including course documentation on C programming, X Window, hypertext, image processing, computer graphics, artificial intelligence, vision systems, and more. There is also a great page on raytracing, a video games database, hotlist database, and other fun resources.

See also: Internet: Resources

World Wide Web:
URL: **http://www.cm.cf.ac.uk/**

Media in Education

A mailing list for discussing the use of media in the classroom and the use of media in education in general.

See also: Journalism and Media

Listserv Mailing List:
List Address: **media-l@bingvmb.cc.binghamton.edu**
Subscription Address:
listserv@bingvmb.cc.binghamton.edu

MicroMUSE Learning Community

MicroMUSE is an educational environment for children from kindergarden through the 12th grade as well as adults. MicroMUSE is a learning environment and the public is invited.

Telnet:
Address: **michael.ai.mit.edu**
Login: **guest**

Ministry of Education in Singapore

Discover how children in Singapore are educated. The Ministry of Education has its own web site as well as links to other educational resources.

World Wide Web:
URL: **http://www.moe.ac.sg/**

Multilingual Classrooms

A mailing list for discussing teaching, language, and education in multilingual environments.

See also: Language

Listserv Mailing List:
List Address: **multi-l@vm.biu.ac.il**
Subscription Address: **listserv@vm.biu.ac.il**

Cool words? Look in Quotations.

A
B
C
D
E
F
G
H
I
J
K
L
M
N
O
P
Q
R
S
T
U
V
W
X
Y
Z

National Education BBS

A system sponsored by the National Education Supercomputing Program (NESP). Full access is only available to NESP members, but limited access is granted to guests. Includes files, news, talk, and chat.

Telnet:
Address: **nebbs.nersc.gov**
Login: **nebbs**

National Referral Center Master File

The National Referral Center Master file (NRCM) provides thousands of descriptions of organizations qualified and willing to answer questions and provide information on many topics in science, technology, and the social sciences. The file is updated weekly and each entry in the file lists the name of the organization, mailing address, and other information.

Telnet:
Address: **locis.loc.gov**

New Patterns in Education

Discussion about new patterns in education, including new teaching methods, new challenges, and new ways to get parents involved in education.

Listserv Mailing List:
List Address: **newedu-l@uhccvm.uhcc.hawaii.edu**
Subscription Address:
listserv@uhccvm.uhcc.hawaii.edu

Newbie Newz

Newbie Newz is for teachers and students who are new Internet users. It aims to teach the basics of ftp, telnet, and the Web, and give pointers to interesting resources.

Internet Mailing List:
List Address: **newbienewz@io.com**
Subscription Address: **newbienewz-request@io.com**

Newton

A BBS for anyone teaching or studying science, math, or computer science.

Telnet:
Address: **newton.dep.anl.gov**
Login: **bbs**

Online Journal of Education and Communication

Issues of the OJEC, which is dedicated to publishing articles about educating children all over the world through instruction by computer network.

Anonymous FTP:
Address: **ftp.uu.net**
Path: **/doc/literary/obi/Jnl.Distance.Ed/***

Perkins Vocational and Applied Technology Education

Vocational and applied technology colleges don't always get the first pick of monetary grants and financial aid packages. The Perkins Act is an act of Congress that established monetary grants for vocational and career education. Unfortunately, it was like handing the keys to the 18-wheeler to someone who's never driven anything but a station wagon. This list was established to make implementing the mandates of the Perkins act less confusing and time-consuming.

Listserv Mailing List:
List Address: **perkact@siucvmb.bitnet**
Subscription Address: **listserv@siucvmb.bitnet**

Project Kaleidoscope

Weekly seminars over the Internet to exchange ideas and information about reforming American undergraduate science and mathematics educational programs.

Anonymous FTP:
Address: **aug3.augsburg.edu**
Path: **/files/pkal**

Quality of Education

A forum for anyone concerned with the quality of education. If you're a parent, teacher, administrator, or student, join the **bgedu-l** list to share ideas and to discuss better alternatives for education.

Listserv Mailing List:
List Address: **bgedu-l@ukcc.uky.edu**
Subscription Address: **listserv@ukcc.uky.edu**

Scholarly Conferences

Descriptions of mailing lists, Internet interest groups, Usenet newsgroups, electronic journals, ftp sites, and more of interest to students and scholars.

Anonymous FTP:
Address: **ksuvxa.kent.edu**
Path: **/library/acad***

Gopher:
Name: Coalition for Networked Information
Address: **gopher.cni.org**
Choose: **Coalition FTP Archives**
 I **Publicly Accessible Documents (/pub)**
 I **Guides to Network Use**
 I **Kovacs, Diane; Directory of Scholarly Education Conferences, 8th edition**

Academic Excellence on the Internet

Do you like to tell other people what to think?
Do you love to pontificate using sentences that start with "It turns out that. . ."?

Do you want to work for an organization that never makes a profit?

If so, academia may be for you.

The only trouble is that you may have to do research, which can really eat into your spare time.

Not to worry. Use the

Scholarly Conferences
resource and find out what's already there for the taking.

School Nurse Network

Being a school nurse is more than handing out aspirin and Band-Aids. This list provides information and networking opportunities for anyone related to the field of school nursing. Discussion covers research and technological advancements, legislation, policy and regulations, educational opportunities, new grants, and information on professional organizations.

See also: Health, Medicine

Listserv Mailing List:
List Address: **schlrn-l@ubvm.cc.buffalo.edu**
Subscription Address: **listserv@ubvm.cc.buffalo.edu**

Schoolnet

An educational networking initiative of Industry and Science Canada. It provides educational information, discussion areas, and learning tools. Eventually, every school in Canada will be hooked up to Schoolnet.

Anonymous FTP:
Address: **schoolnet.carleton.ca**
Path: **/pub/schoolnet/***

Gopher:
Name: Schoolnet Gopher
Address: **gopher.schoolnet.carleton.ca**

Schoolnet Resource Manual

Details of more than one hundred science, engineering, and technology resources available on the Internet and of special interest to schools. Available in ASCII text and various word processor formats.

Anonymous FTP:
Address: **ftp.ccs.carleton.ca**
Path: **/pub/schoolnet/manuals/Resource.***

Schoolnet's News Flash

Contains information on current events in the real world, on the Internet, and in Canada's Schoolnet.

Gopher:
Name: Schoolnet Gopher
Address: **gopher.schoolnet.carleton.ca**
Choose: **SchoolNet Gopher**
 I **Electronic News Stand**

Schools on the Internet

This web page collects a list of links to all the known high schools and elementary schools on the Internet.

World Wide Web:
URL: **http://hillside.coled.umn.edu/others.html**

Science Education

This list is a forum for discussing the reform of science education. If you believe that science education should — or should not — undergo fundamental change, join **ncprse-l** and let your feelings be known.

Listserv Mailing List:
List Address: **ncprse-l@ecuvm.cis.ecu.edu**
Subscription Address: **listserv@ecuvm.cis.ecu.edu**

A B C D E F G H I J K L M N O P Q R S T U V W X Y Z

Shadowy Science Projects

A collection of articles, discussions, and projects about shadows, the sun, solar noon, Earth's rotation, and related topics.

Gopher:
Name: Ralph Bunche School
Address: **ralphbunche.rbs.edu**
Choose: **Shadows Science Project**

Simultaneous Projects

Information and details about school projects that make use of the Internet.

Gopher:
Name: Schoolnet Gopher
Address: **gopher.schoolnet.carleton.ca**
Choose: **SchoolNet Gopher**
| **Classroom & Academic Projects**
| **Offers To Join Simultaneous Projects**

Talented and Gifted

A forum has been established for the discussion of special programs for children who show exceptional skill, intelligence or creativity. Learn about resources, research, and experience relating to Talented and Gifted educational programs.

Listserv Mailing List:
List Address: **tag-l@vm1.nodak.edu**
Subscription Address: **listserv@vm1.nodak.edu**

Teaching and Learning with the Web

Reports of international conference workshops, details on future projects, participation, working groups, and reference material.

World Wide Web:
URL: **http://tecfa.unige.ch/edu-ws94/ws.html**

Technet

Technical Support for Education and Research is an open, unmoderated discussion list for technical support staff at universities and other nonprofit educational and research institutions worldwide. Discussions may cover such topics as electronic and software design, interfacing of laboratory equipment to computers, construction of unique laboratory equipment, data collection methods, and more.

Listserv Mailing List:
List Address: **technet@acadvm1.uottawa.ca**
Subscription Address:
listserv@acadvm1.uottawa.ca

> # Do you like weirdness?
> # Check out Usenet Curiosities.

Technology and Information Education Services

TIES provides leadership in the application of technology to education by means of support services and training. Their gopher provides access to many K12 educational resources.

Gopher:
Name: TIESnet Internet Gopher
Address: **tiesnet.ties.k12.mn.us**

Technology in the Classroom

Here are two forums for discussing educational technology — both the state of technology today and where we're headed in the future.

Listserv Mailing List:
List Address: **edtech@msu.edu**
Subscription Address: **listserv@msu.edu**

List Address: **jte-l@vtm1.cc.vt.edu**
Subscription Address: **listserv@vtm1.cc.vt.edu**

U.S. Department of Education

As part of the Institutional Communications Network project, the U.S. Department of Education has established this site to provide information to educators and researchers interested in education. You will find a wide variety of files on K12 education as well as vocational and adult education, goals of the Department of Education, programs, announcements and press releases, and educational software.

See also: Education: Teachers

Anonymous FTP:
Address: **ftp.ed.gov**
Path: **/gopher/***

Gopher:
Name: U.S. Department of Education
Address: **gopher.ed.gov**

World Wide Web:
URL: **http://www.ed.gov/**

44545545455

U.S. National K12 Gopher

The National School K12 Gopher is a national research and development resource in which schools, school districts, and community organizations can experiment with applications that bring significant new educational benefits to teachers and students.

Gopher:
Name: US National K12 Gopher
Address: **copernicus.bbn.com**

Vocational Education

Network with teachers and administrators of vocational education systems as they explore new ways to pass on needed skills to people heading into the work force. Discover interesting projects designed to make learning interesting and see how educators use the Internet to enhance the learning environment.

Listserv Mailing List:
List Address: **vocnet@ucbcmsa.bitnet**
Subscription Address: **listserv@ucbcmsa.bitnet**

Usenet:
Newsgroup: **bit.listserv.vocnet**

EDUCATION: COLLEGES AND UNIVERSITIES

Academic Electronic Mail Addresses

A long list of e-mail addresses of academic institutions, including names and descriptions of the organizations.

Gopher:
Name: NYSERNet
Address: **nysernet.org**
Choose: **Special Collections: Business and Economic Development**
| **Business and Academic Related Email Addresses**

Apple Computer Higher Education Gopher

This gopher at Apple Computer offers product information, news, publications, and support from Apple. You can post information to this gopher using mail.

Gopher:
Name: Apple Computer
Address: **info.hed.apple.com**

Brown University Alumni

A mailing list for friends and alumni of Brown University. Discussions involve issues affecting the university and its students, faculty, staff, and alumni.

Listserv Mailing List:
List Address: **brunonia@brownvm.brown.edu**
Subscription Address:
listserv@brownvm.brown.edu

Campus Climate

Campuses have their own special environment, made up of rule-makers, rule-followers, and rule-breakers. It's a breeding ground for diversity, and that has advantages and disadvantages of its own. This open forum invites discussion on the personal, educational, and physical environments of campuses, including topics like race relations, sexual harrassment, safety, and handicapped access.

Listserv Mailing List:
List Address: **campclim@uafsysb.uark.edu**
Subscription Address: **listserv@uafsysb.uark.edu**

Campus Parking

Rumor has it that when naughty college students die they go to the Perpetually Crowded Parking Lot down below and are doomed to spend eternity driving around in circles looking for a place to park while thinking they have only three minutes to make it to their Econ midterm. That's enough to make anyone develop better religious hygiene. Parking problems on campus are universal, so a forum was started in which you can discuss administrative and technical questions and concerns and work toward a resolution that will make everyone happy. (Paving the Earth is not an option.)

Listserv Mailing List:
List Address: **cpark-l@psuvm.psu.edu**
Subscription Address: **listserv@psuvm.psu.edu**

Campus-Wide Information Systems

A large list of many campus-wide information systems, providing local and regional information from academic institutions worldwide.

Anonymous FTP:
Address: **ftp.oit.unc.edu**
Path: **/pub/docs/about-the-net/cwis/cwis-l**

Gopher:
Name: National Chung Cheng University
Address: **gopher.ccu.edu.tw**
Choose: **Internet Resources**
| **Information Servers via Telnet**
| **cwis**

Community Colleges

A collection of links to community college gophers in Canada and the United States.

Gopher:
Name: Fayetteville Technical Community College
Address: **gopher1.faytech.cc.nc.us**
Choose: **Community College Gophers**

Diversity University

Diversity University is a virtually real university campus where teachers are welcome to bring their classes for interactive sessions. Diversity University is helping to bring educational services to the Internet.

World Wide Web:
URL: **http://pass.wayne.edu/DU.html**
Funding

It costs a great deal of money to keep educational institutions running, and poor college students can only pay so much. Learn where institutions and departments can apply for outside funding support from places like government agencies, corporations, and private foundations. This list will assist faculty in locating sources of support as well as pass on news from potential sponsors.

Listserv Mailing List:
List Address: **research@vm.temple.edu**
Subscription Address: **listserv@vm.temple.edu**

Globewide Network Academy

GNA is a non-profit corporation affiliated with the Usenet University project. In the long term, it hopes to create a fully accredited online university. Currently it offers hypertextbooks and online consultants. Real-time interaction is provided through a text-based virtual reality system.

World Wide Web:
URL: **http://uu-nna.mit.edu:8001/uu-gna/**

Graduate Students

Graduating from college is so much fun that some people like to do it multiple times. If you are heading for your second phase of being a college student or if you are already doing time in graduate school, join up with other grads to talk about requirements, entrance exams, curriculum, grants and other issues relating to graduate school.

Usenet:
Newsgroup: **soc.college.graduation**

Higher Education Resources and Opportunities

A 24-hour, online database service that provides access to valuable information from colleges and universities on scholarships, grants, fellowships, conferences, faculty and student development, research opportunities, partnership initiatives, and other opportunities for minorities and women.

Telnet:
Address: **fedix.fie.com**
Login: **new**

College students!!

Need a scholarship, grant, fellowship or just plain money to buy some books?

Telnet to the *HERO* database for info.

Maricopa Center for Learning and Instruction (MCLI)

The MCLI, located at the district office of the Maricopa Community Colleges, Arizona, is considered a national model for motivating, infusing, and promoting innovation and change in the community college environment.

World Wide Web:
URL: **http://hakatai.mcli.dist.maricopa.edu/**

Minority College and University Information

This resource provides comprehensive information on minority colleges and universities, such as institutional capabilities, student and faculty profiles, educational programs, research centers, scholarships, and other points of interest.

Telnet:
Address: **fedix.fie.com**

> **Spare time? Take a look at Games.**

Research and Advanced Study: Canada, Italy

The Canadian Academic Centre in Italy sponsors this forum for the research communities in Canada and Italy. Researchers in all fields and disciplines are invited to subscribe.

Listserv Mailing List:
  List Address: **caci-l@vm.ucs.ualberta.ca**
  Subscription Address: **listserv@vm.ucs.ualberta.ca**

Student Financial Aid Administration

"But I need my money and I need it now!" How many times have you heard that? (How many times have you *said* that?) No matter which side of the checkbook you are on, processing financial aid is a grueling and painful process designed by fans of the Spanish Inquisition. On this interactive informational network, you can discuss administrative concerns and discover resolutions to common problems in the student financial aid community. Share your expertise with fellow administrators and related personnel.

Listserv Mailing List:
  List Address: **finaid-l@psuvm.psu.edu**
  Subscription Address: **listserv@psuvm.psu.edu**

Theta Xi Fraternity

College is not just for learning. It's also good to attend so you can join a fraternity and have lots of parties and participate in wild pranks that you can tell your grandkids about later in life. Join up with your Theta Xi brothers electronically and the fun really will never stop. Any brother can subscribe, even if you are not currently affiliated with a chapter.

Listserv Mailing List:
  List Address: **thetaxi@gitvm1.bitnet**
  Subscription Address: **listserv@gitvm1.bitnet**

Two-Year Colleges

Join this global network of educators who teach in two-year colleges. They are interested in facilitating instant communication by means of this discussion group, bringing together faculty, administrators, and staff at two-year institutions around the world.

Listserv Mailing List:
  List Address: **commcoll@ukcc.uky.edu**
  Subscription Address: **listserv@ukcc.uky.edu**

U.S. Colleges

This is almost as good as a "try before you buy" plan. Check out the rumors and reputations of colleges and universities around the United States or discuss the merits of various departments as well as opportunities available at different schools. Discussion includes input from students, professors and alumni.

Usenet:
  Newsgroup: **alt.college.us**

Excerpt from the Net...

```
Newsgroup: alt.college.us
Subject: Studio Art Programs

> Can anyone recommend reputable colleges/universities for studio art?
> My brother is an aspiring comic book artist who is unsure of which
> schools he should consider...

One of the most important things that your brother needs to look into
when he checks on schools is their attitude toward "comic book art" or
other "alternative" forms of art.  By alternative, I mean
"non-traditional".  I can tell you from experience that no matter how
good the school or the instructors, if they don't feel that what he
does is "real art", he is going to end up either squelching his natural
inclinations or spend four or five years fighting the
administration.
```

A B C D E F G H I J K L M N O P Q R S T U V W X Y Z

Ultralab — Learning Technology Research Center

Ultralab is Anglia Polytechnic University's learning technology research center. This lab is for parents and teachers who want to explore new learning techniques and education.

World Wide Web:
>   URL: **http://deep.ultralab.anglia.ac.uk/Scripts/ Homes/Main.html**

University and College Education

This web page collects links to the home pages of American Universities and International Universities.

World Wide Web:
>   URL: **http://www.cs.fsu.edu/projects/group11/ combined.hotlist.html**

Usenet University

FAQs, history, ideas, papers, and newsgroup lists for the Usenet University, a society of people interested in learning, teaching, and tutoring.

Anonymous FTP:
>   Address: **ftp.funet.fi**
>   Path: **/pub/doc/uu/***

Virtual Online University

The Virtual Online University is a liberal arts university located online in the form of a virtual education environment. It offers online lectures and seminars using a variety of interactive techniques, including simulations and cooperative learning.

Telnet:
>   Address: **coyote.csusm.edu**
>   Port: **8888**

World Wide Web:
>   URL: **http://symnet.net/~VOU**

Need help with the morons around you? Try Psychology.

EDUCATION: ELEMENTARY

Arbor Heights School

Arbor Heights Elementary in Seattle, Washington, is the home of the Earth Day Groceries project. When the project was run in April 1994, more than 10,000 students decorated over 13,000 grocery bags, which were then distributed to shoppers on Earth Day. A full report of the project can be found here.

World Wide Web:
>   URL: **http://www.halcyon.com/arborhts/ arborhts.html**

Kidcafe

The Kidcafe list is part of the Kidlink project and is meant for direct dialog among youth between the ages of 10 and 15. It is a place where kids can meet and chat.

See also: Kids, Youth

Listserv Mailing List:
>   List Address: **kidcafe@vm1.nodak.edu**
>   Subscription Address: **listserv@vm1.nodak.edu**

Kidlink

A mailing list for planning Internet activities for younger network users. The **kidlink** list is for administrative information and announcements. The **kids-act** list is part of the Kidlink project and discusses activity projects for kids.

Listserv Mailing List:
>   List Address: **kidlink@vm1.nodak.edu**
>   Subscription Address: **listserv@vm1.nodak.edu**
>
>   List Address: **kidplan@vm1.nodak.edu**
>   Subscription Address: **listserv@vm1.nodak.edu**
>
>   List Address: **kids-act@vm1.nodak.edu**
>   Subscription Address: **listserv@vm1.nodak.edu**

Plugged In

Plugged In is a non-profit group dedicated to bringing the educational opportunities created by new technologies to children and families from low-income communities. This server has a newsletter, online projects and project ideas, and a directory of community-based computer learning groups.

World Wide Web:
>   URL: **http://netmedia.com/ims/pi/PluggedIn/ PluggedIn.html**

EDUCATION: STUDENTS

Academic Advice

Sound suggestions for attacking poor study habits, relieving stress, and making it happily through college — and life.

Gopher:
Name:
University of Montana Healthline Gopher Server
Address: **selway.umt.edu**
Port: **700**
Choose: **General Health Information
| Academic Help**

Telnet:
Address: **selway.umt.edu**
Login: **health**

Academic Magazines

Sample articles and subscription information for scholarly, academic, and university-related magazines.

Gopher:
Name: The Electronic Newsstand
Address: **gopher.enews.com**
Choose: **Magazines, Periodicals, and Journals
| Titles Arranged by Category
| Scholarship - Culture, Politics, History,
Ethics, Medicine**

The Exploratorium

The Exploratorium is absolutely our favorite place in the San Francisco Bay Area (except for the offices of our publisher Osborne McGraw-Hill, in Berkeley, where they write the royalty checks). The next time you are in San Francisco, be sure to visit The Exploratorium, the greatest hands-on science museum in the world. There are hundreds of things to do and zillions of buttons to push. Before you go, get the lowdown by connecting to the Exploratorium's Internet facilities.

If you have a graphical web browser (like Mosaic) or a graphical gopher client, you can display all kinds of interesting pictures to give you a preview of what you will find at the museum itself. You can even try experiments, right in the privacy of your own computer.

(Hint for afterwards: When you are finished at the Exploratorium, go across the bay to Berkeley and drop into Osborne McGraw-Hill. Ask for our editor, Scott Rogers, and tell him that because you are a reader of this book, he must take you out to dinner.)

Exploratorium

Science is fun. You can blow things up, stick things together, make things float and create loud noises that will guarantee you a trip to the principal's office. The Exploratorium in San Francisco creates an environment of hands-on, fun learning and now they have a home on the Internet.

See also: Science

Anonymous FTP:
Address: **ftp.exploratorium.edu**

Gopher:
Name: The Exploratorium
Address: **gopher.exploratorium.edu**

World Wide Web:
URL: **http://www.exploratorium.edu/**

Math Problem-Solving Skills

Sometimes math is not fun. At least not as fun as playing hookey to go swimming on a hot summer day. But now there is MathMagic — a mailing list on which you can team up with other students to solve challenging math problems. You'll get to solve problems, learn communication skills, and meet people at the same time. You can join the general group for open discussion or join the group specific to a grade level: K-3, 4-6, 7-9, 10-12.

See also: Education: Teachers, Mathematics

Majordomo Mailing List:
List Address:
mathmagic-k-3-open@forum.swarthmore.edu
Subscription Address:
majordomo@forum.swarthmore.edu

List Address:
mathmagic-4-6-open@forum.swarthmore.edu
Subscription Address:
majordomo@forum.swarthmore.edu

List Address:
mathmagic-7-9-open@forum.swarthmore.edu
Subscription Address:
majordomo@forum.swarthmore.edu

List Address:
mathmagic-10-12@forum.swarthmore.edu
Subscription Address:
majordomo@forum.swarthmore.edu

List Address:
mathmagic-general-open@forum.swarthmore.edu
Subscription Address:
majordomo@forum.swarthmore.edu

A B C D E F G H I J K L M N O P Q R S T U V W X Y Z

Scavenger Hunt

Learn to use the Internet in a fun and entertaining way by following these scavenger hunts for school kids. Elementary school and secondary school editions are available, as well as a special hunt focusing on space resources.

Gopher:
  Name: Schoolnet Gopher
  Address: **gopher.schoolnet.carleton.ca**
  Choose: **SchoolNet Gopher**
   | **Virtual School**
   | **Recess**
   | **Scavenger Hunts**

School Humor

Humor related to school, including fifty ways to confuse a roommate, fun things to do in a final, and math professor quotes.

Anonymous FTP:
  Address: **quartz.rutgers.edu**
  Path: **/pub/humor/School/***

Gopher:
  Name: Rutgers University
  Address: **quartz.rutgers.edu**
  Choose: **Humor**
   | **School**

Looking for Stuff

Students: Learn how to use the Internet by looking for stuff. Yes, there is a lot of stuff out there, and it is your job to find it. Check out

Scavenger Hunt

for some cool stuff to look for. Stuff, stuff . . . find more stuff . . .

Planning a picnic? Check the weather using the Net.

Excerpt from the Net...

```
(from "School Humor")

Fun things to do during a final exam:

-- When you get a copy of the exam, run out screaming "Andre, Andre, I've got the
   secret documents!!"

-- Walk in, get the exam, sit down.  About five minutes into it, loudly say to the
   instructor, "I don't understand ANY of this. I've been to every lecture all semester
   long!  What's the deal?  And who the hell are you?  Where's the regular guy?"

-- Find a new, interesting way to refuse to answer every question. For example: I
   refuse to answer this question on the grounds that it conflicts with my religious
   beliefs.

-- Run into the exam room looking about frantically.  Breathe a sigh of relief.  Go to
   the instructor, say "They've found me, I have to leave the country" and run off.
```

Student Governments

Today's student body will be tomorrow's civic and political leaders. If that scares you, at least you can take comfort in the fact that they can organize themselves on the Internet. This universal home page leads to many student government organizations at colleges and universities across the United States.

World Wide Web:
URL: **http://www.cs.cmu.edu:8001/afs/andrew/ usr/ss2p/www/sga.html**

EDUCATION: TEACHERS

AskERIC

ERIC (Educational Resources Information Center) is a taxpayer-funded information system that provides access to education-related literature for teachers, library media specialists, administrators, and others.

Gopher:
Name: Syracuse University
Address: **ericir.syr.edu**

Mail:
Address: **askeric@ericir.syr.edu**

Best of K12

A large selection of educational resources for grades K12 and teachers, including news, guides, books, exchange information, and information about access to other education-related gophers and BBSs.

Gopher:
Name: TIESnet Internet Gopher
Address: **tiesnet.ties.k12.mn.us**

Business School Faculty

A mailing list to allow business school faculty all over the world to share problems, discuss solutions, and research ideas.

Listserv Mailing List:
List Address: **busfac-l@cmuvm.csv.cmich.edu**
Subscription Address:
listserv@cmuvm.csv.cmich.edu

Catalyst for College Educators

College educators have concerns that often differ from other educators. This quarterly journal published by the National Council on Community Services and Continuing Education has been created to meet the needs of educators in community, junior, and technical colleges.

Listserv Mailing List:
List Address: **catalyst@vtvm1.cc.vt.edu**
Subscription Address: **listserv@vtvm1.cc.vt.edu**

CD-ROM Activities

Nearly 150 activities that make use of scientific data on CD-ROMs in K-12 classrooms. There is a full catalog of activities and descriptive titles for the files to aid in choosing your activities.

Anonymous FTP:
Address: **jei.umd.edu**
Path: **/pub/jei/Teacher Developed Activities**

Gopher:
Name: Joint Education Initiative
Address: **jei.umd.edu**
Choose: **Teacher Developed Activities**

Chronicle of Higher Education

Offers information about job openings, best-selling books on campuses, and news articles from the *Chronicle of Higher Education* in its free online service "Academe this Week."

Gopher:
Name: Merit Network
Address: **chronicle.merit.edu**

Name: University of Colorado Boulder
Address: **gopher.colorado.edu**
Choose: **Academe this Week**

World Wide Web:
URL: **http://chronicle.merit.edu/**

College and University Teaching Assistants

Remember how in school everyone wanted to do stuff for the teacher, like clean the chalkboard, bang erasers, or grade papers? Most of us got over that urge, but there are some who never did and now they are hanging out in the big league academic scene wearing tweed and discussing philosophy at the off-campus coffeehouse. But that's not all they do. Sometimes they are found on the Internet discussing the roles of teacher and student with other teaching assistants on this listserv list. It's a nice space in which to talk about teaching techniques and the responsibilities of being a teaching assistant.

Listserv Mailing List:
List Address: **t-assist@unmvma.unm.edu**
Subscription Address: **listserv@unmvma.unm.edu**

Dead Teacher's Society

A mailing list for broad discussions of teaching and learning.

Listserv Mailing List:
List Address: **dts-l@iubvm.ucs.indiana.edu**
Subscription Address:
listserv@iubvm.ucs.indiana.edu

Discovery Communications Online Listings

The Discovery Channel and the Learning Channel are great resources for teachers because programs on those channels make learning fun. It's better than sitting in a stuffy classroom with a musty teacher who drones on and on about The Life and Times of the West Indian Batfish. This listserv list makes available advanced listings and curriculum material for educational programming on the Discovery and Learning Channels.

See also: Television

Listserv Mailing List:
List Address: **disc-l@sendit.nodak.edu**
Subscription Address: **listserv@sendit.nodak.edu**

Education Net

Ednet is for those interested in exploring the educational potential of the Internet. Discussions range from K12 through postsecondary education.

Listserv Mailing List:
List Address: **ednet@nic.umass.edu**
Subscription Address: **listserv@nic.umass.edu**

Educational Administration

A mailing list for educators who teach in the K-12 levels and are interested in educational administration.

Listserv Mailing List:
List Address: **k12admin@suvm.syr.edu**
Subscription Address: **listserv@suvm.syr.edu**

Educational K12 Resources

An educational Web containing K12 programs and projects, a "what's new" section, a list of good education gophers, art resources, schools that have their own web pages, K12 virtual libraries, notices about contests, and much more. This is a great collection.

World Wide Web:
URL: **http://k12.cnidr.org/janice_k12/k12menu.html**

Effectiveness of Teachers

A mailing list for discussing teaching effectiveness, including ways to increase effectiveness in all aspects of education.

Listserv Mailing List:
List Address: **teacheft@lyra.wcupa.edu**
Subscription Address: **listserv@lyra.wcupa.edu**

Electronic Book Discussion

Before networking was common, students had to sit in class and read boring literature and listen to the teacher discuss what it all meant. With the BookRead and BR_Match programs, students and teachers can interactively discuss literature not only with other schools online, but with authors as well. Join the BR_Match mailing list to get information on schools looking for partner schools and to find out more about participating in the BookRead program.

Mail:
Address: **mailserv@wcu.edu**
Body: **subscribe BR_Match**

Explorer

A remarkable collection of ideas, lesson plans, and general information for educators and students that is easy to work with and simple to understand. Outlines for math and science lessons, newsletters, and resource keyword searching capabilities.

World Wide Web:
URL: **http://unite.tisl.ukans.edu/xmintro.html**

Globe and Mail

Classroom and teacher editions of the *Toronto Globe and Mail*'s monthly Infoglobe, a service aimed at bringing news and events into the classroom.

Gopher:
Name: Schoolnet Gopher
Address: **gopher.schoolnet.carleton.ca**
Choose: **SchoolNet Gopher**
  | **Electronic News Stand**
  | **Newspapers**
  | **The Globe & Mail**

KIDSPHERE

A mailing list for teachers (grades K12), school administrators, scientists, and others around the world. Send a mail message to join the list.

Internet Mailing List:
List Address: **kidsphere@vms.cis.pitt.edu**
Subscription Address:
  kidsphere-request@vms.cis.pitt.edu

Kindergarten to Grade 6 Corner

Learn interesting facts, neat tricks, things to try, and penpals to meet in this educational forum for kids.

Gopher:
Name: Schoolnet Gopher
Address: **gopher.schoolnet.carleton.ca**
Choose: **SchoolNet Gopher**
  | **Kindergarten to Grade 6 Corner**

Lesson Plans

This gopher is used to test ways of making a database of lesson plans available, and contains sample school lessons that can be searched and viewed.

Gopher:
Name: US National K12 Gopher
Address: **copernicus.bbn.com**
Choose: **National School Network Testbed**
  | **UCSD InternNet Lesson Plans**

Free Lesson Plans

IF YOU ARE A TEACHER YOU KNOW HOW EMBARRASSING IT CAN BE TO TEACH SOMETHING UNEXPECTED BY ACCIDENT. USE THE

Lesson Plan Gopher

AND YOU CAN COORDINATE YOUR PLANS WITH TEACHERS ALL OVER THE INTERNET. JUST THE THING WHEN YOUR LESSON BOOK IS EMPTY AND THE INSPECTOR IS DUE FOR A VISIT.

Neat Educational Tricks

A collection of teaching tricks — including how to see a hole in your hand, how to make your arms float, and how to move things with your mind — aimed at teaching basic human biology to younger students.

Gopher:
Name: Schoolnet Gopher
Address: **gopher.schoolnet.carleton.ca**
Choose: **SchoolNet Gopher**
  | **Kindergarten to Grade 6 Corner**
  | **Neat tricks you can do...**

Physics Teachers

Physics is comforting because you get to study gravity and learn all the reasons why we are not at risk of being flung off the planet at high speeds. It makes going to bed at night that much easier. So physics teachers are really doing everyone a favor by imparting information that is vital to the mental well-being of Earth's population. Meet physics teachers from colleges and universities around the world as they discuss teaching, laboratory experiments, and classroom experiences.

Listserv Mailing List:
List Address: **phys-l@uwf.cc.uwf.edu**
Subscription Address: **listserv@uwf.cc.uwf.edu**

A B C D E F G H I J K L M N O P Q R S T U V W X Y Z

Excerpt from the Net...

```
Newsgroup: bit.listserv.tesl-l
Subject: What's a good post?

Fellow netters: I am writing this both as an active teacher and as the
founder of TESL-L, and I am answering the claim that netters are using
this list just to get "quick fixes" to help them with their next class.

Well, I can't see anything wrong with that... TESL-L was founded and
is funded to help teachers help students.  In particular, my vision for
TESL-L was that teachers who are professionally or geographically
isolated would have a forum where they could get the information they
needed and couldn't get elsewhere.

I think it is *wonderful* if teachers can get help with their next
TESL/FL class...

To demand that teachers not use the net if the information requested is
available in libraries denies the value of electronic communications,
and it denies the facts of many teachers' lives: They do not have ready
access to libraries, journals, and professional development....
```

Reading Room

A large collection of journals, newsletters, and texts (as well as access to other subject-related gophers) at the University of Maryland.

Gopher:
>Name: University of Maryland
>Address: **info.umd.edu**
>Choose: **Educational Resources**
>   **| Academic Reading Room**

Satellite Communications for Learning Associated

The Satellite Communications for Learning Associated (SCOLA) is a non-profit consortium of thousands of schools, colleges, universities, governments and businesses that receive television programming from more than forty different countries in the original languages.

Gopher:
>Name: Creighton University
>Address: **bluejay.creighton.edu**
>Choose: **Auxiliary Services**
>   **| Satellite Communicatoins for Learning (SCOLA)**

Special Education

There are a great deal of unique concerns when dealing with the field of special education. It's great to be able to network with other teachers, clinicians and researchers to discuss current issues about practices, policies and new developments. This list is open to anyone who has an interest in special education.

Majordomo Mailing List:
>List Address: **spedtalk@virginia.edu**
>Subscription Address: **majordomo@virginia.edu**

Teaching English as a Second Language

Imagine the thrill of teaching people to speak English — that every word you say is going to be mimicked and all across the globe there will be people who talk just like you. Take advantage of networking opportunities by looking at what other teachers of English are doing with lesson plans, multi-cultural classroom environments, helpful hints for pronunciation and other important issues.

Usenet:
>Newsgroup: **bit.listserv.tesl-l**

No one understands the Internet, so relax and enjoy.

Teaching Health and Physical Education

Talk to people who teach health and physical education. Trade ideas, tips, and stories. Find out if it is really true that "Those who can, do. Those who can't, teach. And those who can't teach, teach P.E."

Usenet:
Newsgroup: **k12.ed.health-pe**

Worldwide Education Net

A group at CalPoly has committed to the ambitious task of forming a virtual subnetwork exclusively for educators. Within this network, they intend to connect people, not by simply maintaining a mailing list or a newsgroup, but by bringing education professionals together with e-mail interaction on a one-on-one basis according to their interests.

Mail:
Address: **worldwide@csupomona.edu**

ELECTRONICS

Circuit Analysis Discussion List

A mailing list for anyone interested in the discussion of circuit analysis and design.

Internet Mailing List:
List Address: **circuits-l@uwplatt.edu**
Subscription Address:
circuits-l-request@uwplatt.edu

Computer-Aided Design

Computer-aided electronics design beats writing on a napkin at the coffeehouse any day of the week. Check out information on hardware, software, programming, techniques and helpful hints from the folks who never get their wires crossed — or at least never accidentally.

Usenet:
Newsgroup: **sci.electronics.cad**

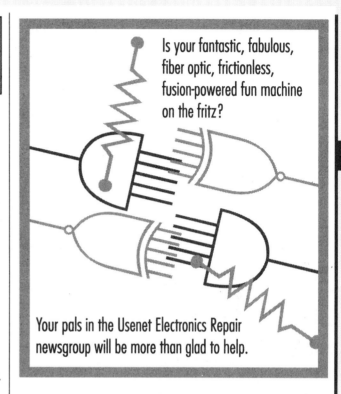

Is your fantastic, fabulous, fiber optic, frictionless, fusion-powered fun machine on the fritz?

Your pals in the Usenet Electronics Repair newsgroup will be more than glad to help.

Electronic Design and Development

We love gadgets — ones that have switches, blink on and off, or make noise. But to some people, it's not just love. It's a passion that keeps them up at night, that makes them stagger to the design table before that first cup of coffee, that compels them to tell their blind dates all about circuit boards. For the electronically active technicians, technologists and engineers who are involved in the design and development of analog and digital electronic circuitry, this is your release. Never again will you have to ruin your Friday night. Get it all out of your system by discussing circuit design, electronic components, PC-board layout, and getting information on workshops and seminars.

See also: Technology

Listserv Mailing List:
List Address: **edesign@acadvm1.uottawa.ca**
Subscription Address:
listserv@acadvm1.uottawa.ca

A
B
C
D
E
F
G
H
I
J
K
L
M
N
O
P
Q
R
S
T
U
V
W
X
Y
Z

Electronics Repair

What a feeling of power to wield your mighty soldering iron knowing that you can fix anything. Share the thrill of wiring up the world with other electronics pros and enthusiasts and hear adventure stories about sparking microwave ovens, glowing Halloween gadgets, and televisions that generate X-rays. The talk is technical in detail, but these electronics gurus have a sense of humor (and the joy buzzers to prove it).

Usenet:
Newsgroup: **sci.electronics.repair**

English-Chinese Electronics Terms

An English-Chinese, Chinese-English dictionary of electronic and electrical terms.

Note: Requires Chinese viewing software.

See also: Software: Utilities

Gopher:
Name: National Chung Cheng University
Address: **gopher.ccu.edu.tw**
Choose: **micscellanies**
 | **English <-> Chinese Electric Term**

HP Calculator BBS

A BBS just for users of HP calculators. Chat with or send messages to other users and enthusiasts of HP scientific and business calculators. The HP Calculator Bulletin Board is a free service to allow for the exchange of software and information between HP calculator users, software developers, and distributors.

Telnet:
Address: **hpcvbbs.cv.hp.com**
Login: **new**

IEEE Gopher

The IEEE Computer Society is a world-renowned source of information relating to all aspects of computer science, electronics, and engineering, including the publication of periodicals and newsletters, sponsoring conferences, workshops, and symposiums, and the development of standards. *Computer Society Online* now offers an electronic source of this information, in many cases before the information is published in hard copy.

Gopher:
Name: IEEE Computer Society
Address: **info.computer.org**

EMERGENCY AND DISASTER

California Emergency Services

Known for its earthquakes, fires and mudslides, California certainly deserves to have an Office of Emergency Services. You just never know when you might have a disaster — like a plague of locusts descending on the entire city of Los Angeles. Read documents and factsheets compiled to make sure that everyone is in a state of readiness.

Telnet:
Address: **oes1.oes.ca.gov**
Port: **5501**

World Wide Web:
URL: **http://www.oes.ca.gov:8001/**

CALIFORNIA EMERGENCY SERVICES

California has its own types of special emergencies. For example, what if your agent is coming over to dinner and you are all out of Chardonnay? Or what do you do when the heater on your hot tub goes on the fritz and it's too late to call a repairman? Or, even worse, what if you have a fabulous breakthrough in your emotional and intellectual growth program, and there is no one around to help you relate to the experience?

Not to worry: As long as you have a web browser, the California Emergency Services Internet site is there to help. And, if you get bored, you can always display a photo of a large fire or other natural disaster, or a picture of the Chief Deputy Director of the Governor's Office of Emergency Services.

Disaster Management

Selection of resources related to disasters and how to deal with them, including access to the Australian Disaster Management Information Network, earthquake information, Emergency Preparedness Information eXchange, and others.

Gopher:
Name: Monash University
Address: **gopher.vifp.monash.edu.au**
Choose: **Disaster Management**

Disaster Situation and Status Reports

Information and reports about natural disasters and events from agencies like the U.S. Weather Service and the U.S. Geological Survey. Information includes earthquake reports, weather reports, and hurricane forecasts.

See also: Environment, Weather

Gopher:
Name: Disaster Information Center
Address: **vita.org**

Natural Disasters and You!

One of the best parts of life is reading about natural disasters that happen to other people. What could be more fun than waking up each morning, logging in to your favorite Internet connection, and checking out all the disasters that happened overnight to people who aren't as smart and good looking as you? (And, if truth be told, may not even be smart enough to read *The Internet Golden Directory*.)

Earthquakes in Alaska

If you are planning that trip to Alaska to see the migration of the barren ground caribou, it would be nice to check the latest earthquake info just to assure yourself that while you are up there, the Big One is not going to hit. See the latest Alaskan earthquake shakings that register over a magnitude of 2.0 on the Richter scale.

See also: Geology, Geography

Finger:
Address: **quake@fm.gi.alaska.edu**

Earthquakes in California

It's not a big surprise to most people when there is an earthquake in California. In fact, it's almost becoming routine. Keep up on the hectic business of California seismic activity with just a few keystrokes. The **caltech** site will give you information on Southern California and the **usgs** site will tell you about Northern California.

Finger:
Address: **quake@andreas.wr.usgs.gov**
Address: **quake@scec2.gps.caltech.edu**

We will let you in on a secret: There are no earthquakes in California. It's all a myth that is carefully nurtured to keep out the riff-raff. Don't believe us? Check out the California earthquake finger services and see how elaborate the big lie has become.

Emergency Medical Services

911, along with the iron lung and the electric sewer rooter, is an awesome invention that we all hope we never have to use. It's nice to know that in the event of a personal disaster, an emergency medical team will come racing to help you. In an effort to continually update information and to improve services, EMS providers discuss protocols, rules, policies, and hospital regulations. **ems-c** discusses emergency medical services and general emergency medical care for children.

See also: Medicine

Listserv Mailing List:
List Address: **ems-c@lists.colorado.edu**
Subscription Address: **listserv@lists.colorado.edu**

List Address: **emsny-l@albnydh2.bitnet**
Subscription Address: **listserv@albnydh2.bitnet**

A B C D E F G H I J K L M N O P Q R S T U V W X Y Z

Emergency Preparedness Information eXchange (EPIX)

The Emergency Preparedness Information eXchange (EPIX) is dedicated to the promotion of networking in support of disaster mitigation research and practice. Offers information on emergency and disaster management organizations, topics, conferences, and access to other emergency management resources.

Gopher:
>Name: EPIX
>Address: **hoshi.cic.sfu.ca**
>Port: **5555**

Fire Safety Tips

Information and tips on how to prevent all types of house fires and wildland fires. There is also a tutorial with diagrams explaining how to create a firebreak to save your home.

World Wide Web:
>URL: **http://www.abag.ca.gov/abag/local_gov/city/ san_carlos/fire/firedept.html**

HungerWeb

This web page provides information about world hunger with a special section on current crises. There's also an interactive quiz about world hunger, an mpeg movie, research articles, statistics, and links to related resoures.

World Wide Web:
>URL: **http://www.het.brown.edu/hungerweb/**

Newcastle Earthquake

A well-written and horrific account of the deadly Newcastle, Australia, earthquake in December, 1989, the first known Australian quake to result in fatalities.

Gopher:
>Name: Monash University
>Address: **gopher.vifp.monash.edu.au**
>Choose: **Disaster Management**
> l **Aust. Disaster Management Information Network**
> l **Disaster Management - General Interest**
> l **What If - The Newcastle Earthquake**

ReliefNet

A non-profit service that enables major charitable organizations to accept pledges online and share information about disaster areas and relief projects around the world.

Gopher:
>Name: Earthweb
>Address: **earthweb.com**
>Port: **2801**

World Wide Web:
>URL: **http://www.earthweb.com:2800/**

ENERGY

Energy Statistics

Compilations of statistics on energy consumption, requirements, and reserves in the U.S., including specific information on coal, crude oil, natural gas, and other energy sources.

Gopher:
>Name: University of California San Diego
>Address: **infopath.ucsd.edu**
>Choose: **News & Services**
> l **Economic..**
> l **Energy Statistics**

National Renewable Energy Laboratory (NREL)

NREL is the nation's primary federal laboratory for renewable energy research and performs functions assigned by the Department of Energy in research, development, and testing. NREL conducts and coordinates research and development that private industry cannot reasonably be expected to undertake. The key mission is facilitating the transfer of its technologies to private industry for commercialization.

World Wide Web:
>URL: **http://www.nrel.gov/**

Oak Ridge National Laboratory

The Oak Ridge National Laboratory conducts basic and applied research and development to advance the nation's energy resources, environmental quality scientific knowledge, and educational foundations. The Oak Ridge server has information about programs, technologies, and publications of the lab.

World Wide Web:
URL: **http://www.orn.gov/**

Renewable Energy

Right now, as you read this there are clever people around the world thinking about ways to use renewable energy. They are coming up with new designs for batteries, generators, pumps and chargers to use wind, water and sun for fuel. Read about the neat gadgets they have modified or invented or just check out the ideas and philosophy behind using renewable energy.

Usenet:
Newsgroup: **alt.energy.renewable**

ENGINEERING

Advanced Nuclear Reactor Technology

A mailing list to facilitate substantive discussion on the worldwide advocacy, design, and deployment of advanced nuclear reactor technology.

Listserv Mailing List:
List Address: **anurt-l@vm1.hqadmin.doe.gov**
Subscription Address:
listserv@vm1.hqadmin.doe.gov

Build a Flying Saucer

An essay in speculative engineering on how to build a flying saucer.

Anonymous FTP:
Address: **ftp.spies.com**
Path: **/Library/Fringe/Ufo/build.ufo**

Gopher:
Name: Internet Wiretap
Address: **wiretap.spies.com**
Choose: **Wiretap Online Library**
  | **Fringes of Reason**
  | **UFO's and Mysterious Abductions**
  | **How to Build a Flying Saucer**

No need to put up with rush hour traffic. Build your own flying saucer.

The plans are free for the downloading on Build a Flying Saucer.

CAD Mailing Lists

Mailing lists devoted to CAD (Computer Aided Design), CAM (Computer Aided Manufactering), and other related interests and subjects.

Listserv Mailing List:
List Address: **cadam-l@suvm.syr.edu**
Subscription Address: **listserv@suvm.syr.edu**

List Address: **vtcad-l@vtvm1.cc.vt.edu**
Subscription Address: **listserv@vtvm1.cc.vt.edu**

List Address: **cadlist@suvm.syr.edu**
Subscription Address: **listserv@suvm.syr.edu**

List Address: **caeds-l@suvm.syr.edu**
Subscription Address: **listserv@suvm.syr.edu**

Civil Engineering

This web page has links to civil engineering resources including construction information, institutes and water resources.

World Wide Web:
URL: **http://www.yahoo.com/Science/
Engineering/Civil_Engineering/**

Congress of Canadian Engineering Students

A mailing list forum for Canadian Federation of Engineering Students to discuss current topics and exchange information.

Listserv Mailing List:
List Address: **cces-l@unbvm1.csd.unb.ca**
Subscription Address: **listserv@unbvm1.csd.unb.ca**

The Internet has lots and lots (and lots) of free software.

A
B
C
D
E
F
G
H
I
J
K
L
M
N
O
P
Q
R
S
T
U
V
W
X
Y
Z

Electrical Engineering

Links to electrical engineering resources including institutes, signal and image processing resources, neural networks, nanostructures, terms, and newsletters.

World Wide Web:
URL: **http://www.yahoo.com/Science/ Engineering/Electrical_Engineering/**

Facilities and Services

What a madhouse it would be if everyone had to take care of everything themselves and nobody was in charge of organizing anything. As much as we don't like to drive at the speed limit, it's still nice to know there are rules and regulations — even if some people don't follow them. Get in on the discussion of facilities and services such as physical plant operations, security and public safety, transportation and parking, telephone and mail service, environmental health and safety, capital planning, and facilities utilization.

Listserv Mailing List:
List Address: **facser-l@wvnvm.wvnet.edu**
Subscription Address: **listserv@wvnvm.wvnet.edu**

Fluid Mechanics

A mailing list for Ph.D. students for discussing all aspects of fluid mechanics and the J.M. Burgers Centre.

Listserv Mailing List:
List Address: **burg-cen@nic.surfnet.nl**
Subscription Address: **listserv@nic.surfnet.nl**

Mechanical Engineering

Links to mechanical engineering resources including institutes, manufacturing information, microelectromechanical systems, and robotics.

World Wide Web:
URL: **http://www.yahoo.com/Science/ Engineering/Mechanical_Engineering/**

Nuclear Engineering

Links for items such as the Defense Nuclear Facilities Safety Board, and other nuclear engineering resources and information.

World Wide Web:
URL: **http://www.yahoo.com/Science/ Engineering/Nuclear_Engineering/**

Optical Engineering

Links to photonics information, the Optical Society of America, and The International Society for Optical Engineering.

World Wide Web:
URL: **http://www.yahoo.com/Science/ Engineering/Optical_Engineering/**

What do you do if you happen to be married to a member of the British royal family and want to learn to relate to your mate? Not to worry. The Net has lots and lots of resources to help you understand robotics.

Robotics

Archives, software, and FAQs related to robotics and any preprogrammable, electromechanical devices that perform useful functions.

Anonymous FTP:
    Address: **ftp.cs.yale.edu**
    Path: **/pub/nisp/***

    Address: **kame.media.mit.edu**
    Path: **/pub/el-publications/EL-Memos**

    Address: **rtfm.mit.edu**
    Path: **/pub/usenet/news.answers/robotics-faq/***

    Address: **wilma.cs.brown.edu**
    Path: **/pub/comp.robotics/***

Archie:
    Pattern: **robotics**

World Wide Web:
    URL: **http://www.yahoo.com/Science/Engineering/Mechanical_Engineering/Robotics/**

Software Engineering

Links to software engineering resources including institutes, libraries, and various web pages relating to software engineering.

World Wide Web:
    URL: **http://www.yahoo.com/Computers/Software/Software_Engineering/**

Virtual Library of Engineering

This web page has links to many fields of engineering from aerospace to software.

World Wide Web:
    URL: **http://epims1.gsfc.nasa.gov/engineering/engineering.html**

ENVIRONMENT

2020 News & Views

A bimonthly newsletter which seeks to identify and discuss solutions for meeting future world food needs while reducing poverty and protecting the environment.

Gopher:
    Name: CGNET
    Address: **gopher.cgnet.com**
    Choose: **CGIAR news and information | 2020 News & Views Newsletter**

Listserv Mailing List:
    List Address: **2020-news@cgnet.com**
    Subscription Address: **listserv@cgnet.com**

40 Tips to Go Green

A flyer distributed by the Jalan Hijau Environmental Action Group during Earth Day 1992 in Singapore.

World Wide Web:
    URL: **http://www.ncb.gov.sg/jkj/env/greentips.html**

Air Pollution BBS

A BBS devoted to the collection and dissemination of pollution and pollution control information.

Telnet:
    Address: **ttnbbs.rtpnc.epa.gov**

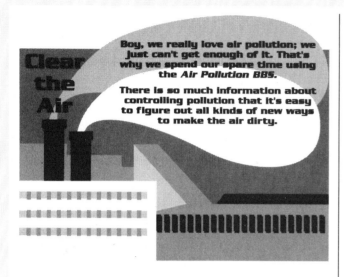

Boy, we really love air pollution; we just can't get enough of it. That's why we spend our spare time using the *Air Pollution BBS*.

There is so much information about controlling pollution that it's easy to figure out all kinds of new ways to make the air dirty.

Australian Environmental Resources Network

The Environmental Resources Information Network (ERIN) aims to provide geographically related data for planning and decision making. The ERIN Program is based on cooperative efforts between agencies interested in environmental information.

World Wide Web:
   URL: **http://kaos.erin.gov.au/erin.html**

Biosphere Mailing List and Discussion Group

Discussions related to the environment and the biosphere, including such topics as wind power, whaling, wildlife conservation, and fossil fuels.

Listserv Mailing List:
   List Address: **biosph-l@ubvm.cc.buffalo.edu**
   Subscription Address: **listserv@ubvm.cc.buffalo.edu**

Usenet:
   Newsgroup: **bit.listserv.biosph-l**

Biosphere Newsletter

Back issues of this newsletter discussing environmental topics with both scientific and reader-friendly articles.

Note: Hours are 6 PM-10 AM EST.

Anonymous FTP:
   Address: **ftp.cic.net**
   Path: **/pub/nircomm/gopher/e-serials/alphabetic/ b/biosphere**

California Rivers Assessment

The California Rivers Assessment (CARA) provides a comprehensive inventory and evaluation of California's river resources. The initial focus of CARA is on the riparian and aquatic components of rivers and the value of rivers and streams as natural resources.

World Wide Web:
   URL: **http://ice.ucdavis.edu/Rivers/ Rivers_main_page.html**

Canadian Forest Service

The Canadian Forest Service (CFS) promotes the sustainable development and competitiveness of the Canadian forest sector for the well-being of Canadians. CFS researchers use up-to-date science and technology to improve awareness and forest management techniques.

World Wide Web:
   URL: **http://www.nofc.forestry.ca/**

Centre for Landscape Research (CLR)

The research arm of the Programme in Landscape Architecture at the University of Toronto. This server provides a collaborative environment for the exploration of ideas related to the design, planning, and policies of the environment. Its primary focus is on using electronic media to foster more informed decision making.

World Wide Web:
   URL: **http://www.clr.toronto.edu:1080/clr.html**

Chemical Substance Factsheets

Information from the EPA on hundreds of chemicals, elements, and compounds. Factsheets include data on toxicity, identification, reason for citation, how to determine if you've been exposed, OSHA safety limits, ways to reduce exposure, and more relevant information.

Gopher:
   Name: University of Virginia
   Address: **ecosys.drdr.virginia.edu**
   Choose: **Education**
    | **Environmental Fact Sheets**
    | **EPA Chemical Substance Factsheets**

Chernobyl Nuclear Accident

A web page with information on the Chernobyl nuclear power plant accident, including the last official version of events, which was published in 1992. This page also has links to materials about the Chernobyl Kurchatov Institute Expedition and a number of publications from scientific and mass media.

World Wide Web:
URL: **http://polyn.net.kiae.su/polyn/manifest.html**

Coalition to Ban Dihydrogen Monoxide

The home page of this coalition informs us that dihydrogen monoxide is a colorless, odorless, and tasteless gas that kills many thousands of people each year.

World Wide Web:
URL: **http://www.circus.com/~no_dhmo/**

Coastal Management and Resources

People think that the coast is all fun and sun with the ocean crashing against the beach and the sun setting across the water. Well, it's that very water that makes the coast so tricky to manage. And then there's that theory that has been going around about California falling off into the ocean. It's enough to give anyone a headache. Fortunately, there is a list that deals with topics related to coastal management and resources, so there is a place to turn when it's time to do some brainstorming or to discuss revolutionary ideas that pop up in the coastal management field.

See also: Geography, Geology

Listserv Mailing List:
List Address: **coastnet@uriacc.uri.edu**
Subscription Address: **listserv@uriacc.uri.edu**

Conservation OnLine

Conservation OnLine (CoOL) is a full text database of conservation information. This database covers a wide spectrum of topics of interest to anyone involved with the conservation of libraries, archives and museum materials.

World Wide Web:
URL: **http://palimpsest.stanford.edu/**

The Net is cool because YOU are cool.

Earth and Environmental Science

The U.S. Geological Survey maintains this registry of Earth and Environmental Science Internet resources as a service to the research community. Web servers in the registry are identified by an icon.

World Wide Web:
URL: **http://info.er.usgs.gov/network/science/ earth/earthquake.html**

Earth Day Bibliography

A bibliography of environment-related books, including those about global warming, environmental ethics, nuclear waste, ecology, energy, and other topics.

Anonymous FTP:
Address: **mthvax.cs.miami.edu**
Path: **/pub/biosph/earthday.bib.Z**

Gopher:
Name: EnviroLink Network
Address: **envirolink.org**
Choose: **EnviroPublications
| EnviroBooks**

Earth Negotiations Bulletin

This web page offers the Earth Negotiations Bulletin in hypertext as well as links to UN documentation and background materials on the environment and developmental negotiations.

World Wide Web:
URL: **http://www.iisd.ca/linkages/**

Ecological Economics

What does economics have to do with the environment? According to this list, we should make a major change in the way we think about economics in order to respond to environmental threats to the planet. If you love the Earth more than you love your money, this might be the place for you. Join in on discussions about alternatives to prevailing economic systems.

See also: Economics, Business and Finance

Listserv Mailing List:
List Address: **ecol-econ@csf.colorado.edu**
Subscription Address: **listserv@csf.colorado.edu**

Need Unix help? See Harley's book "Unix Unbound."

EcoNet

EcoNet is a network for sharing information and enhancing cooperation among people and organizations interested in environmentally-oriented programs and activities.

World Wide Web:
URL: **http://www.igc.apc.org/igc/en.html**

EcoWeb

Do your part for Mother Earth by checking in at the EcoWeb, a network for the environmentally conscious. EcoWeb has audio clips, movies, links to an EcoGopher and EcoChat — a place where you can chat with other green people. Connect to more than 25 mailing lists sponsored by the Students Environmental Action Coalition. Explore other environment related resources on the Net through links that offer everything from simple text to the whole multimedia shebang.

World Wide Web:
URL: **http://ecosys.drdr.virginia.edu/ EcoWeb.html**

Edwards Aquifer Research and Data Center

Established in 1979 by Southwest Texas State University, the EARDC provides a public service in the study and use of the fragile Edwards Aquifer, which supplies water to the people of San Antonio. To learn more about the aquifer and the Center, check out this web page.

World Wide Web:
URL: **http://eardc.swt.edu/**

Electronic Membrane Information Library

The Electronic Membrane Information Library (EMILY) is the electronic library for membrane users and researchers. EMILY was established to publicize and transfer membrane information to interested users, researchers and scientists around the world.

Anonymous FTP:
Address: **aqua.ccwr.ac.za**
Path: **/pub/emily**

World Wide Web:
URL: **ftp://aqua.ccwr.ac.za/pub/emily//emily/html**

Endangered Species

The U.S. Fish and Wildlife Service has a division for endangered species, which offers to keep you informed of what animals are on the brink of extinction. Send for this help file which will tell you how to access the List of Threatened and Endangered Species, the Plant Notice of Review, the Endangered Species Act of 1973, and species maps.

See also: Animals and Pets

Mail:
Address: **r9irmlib@mail.fws.gov**
Subject: **send help**

Energy and the Environment

Exactly how did those holes get in the ozone? Could it be all the hairspray women had to use in the '50s for those tricky bouffant hairdos? Find out the facts about the ozone, UV radiation, and the status of the northern and southern ozone holes. Also available is historical information on gas prices and energy consumption.

See also: Science

World Wide Web:
URL: **http://zebu.uoregon.edu/energy.html**

EnviroLink Network

A large resource of environmental information from the EnviroLink Network. It covers all aspects of the environment, including environmental action, issues, media, networks, organization, and politics, and gives easy access to other environmental gopher servers.

Gopher:
Name: Carnegie Mellon University
Address: **english-server.hss.cmu.edu**

Name: EnviroLink Network
Address: **envirolink.org**

World Wide Web:
URL: **http://envirolink.org/**

Before you go on a trip, use the Net to help you plan. Read the Travel section.

Environmental Education Database

The Directory of Environmental Education Resources (DEER) is a joint project between many organizations and individuals that distribute environmental education resources.

World Wide Web:
URL: **http://www.einet.net/hytelnet/FUL008.html**

Environmental Engineering

It's like any picnic — when you have people hanging around they are bound to make trash that you have to deal with and dealing with trash is what environmental engineers do, except on a much larger scale. Read about all topics relating to environmental engineering, including water and waste water treatment, air pollution control, solid waste management, and radioactive waste treatment.

Listserv Mailing List:
List Address: **enveng-l@vm.temple.edu**
Subscription Address: **listserv@vm.temple.edu**

Environmental Factsheets

Articles and facts about automobiles, climate, energy, meat, ozone depletion, chemical substances, and other environmental issues.

Gopher:
Name: EcoGopher at the University of Virginia
Address: **ecosys.drdr.virginia.edu**
Choose: **Education: The EcoGopher Environmental Library | Environmental Factsheets**

Environmental Issues

A variety of stories, essays, and book reviews covering various environmental issues and ideas, including disaster management, solid waste landfill info, and several environmental publications.

Gopher:
Name: Whole Earth Lectronic Link
Address: **gopher.well.sf.ca.us**
Choose: **Environmental Issues and Ideas**

Why be normal? Read Bizarre.

Did you know that this book, and "The Internet Complete Reference," are used at the South Pole?

Environmental Protection Agency

The EPA has collected a massive amount of information on the environment with regard to legislation, regulations, job vacancies, grants, newsletters and journals, press releases, announcements and consumer information.

Gopher:
Name: Environmental Protection Agency
Address: **gopher.epa.gov**

Environmental Resource Center

The Environmental Resource Center (ERC) provides timely and cost effective access to environmental data and information.

World Wide Web:
URL: **http://ftp.clearlake.ibm.com/ERC/ HomePage.html**

Environmental Scorecard

See how EcoNet rates your representatives' voting records on environmental issues. Use your mouse to select the state for which you would like to view environmental voting records. This page also has links to bill descriptions, information about the state of the environmental movement, the League of Conservation Voters, and EcoNet.

World Wide Web:
URL: **http://www.econet.apc.org/lcv/ scorecard.html**

Environmental Services Data Directory

A large database that provides detailed and diverse information on Earth's environment.

Gopher:
Name: The National Oceanic and Atmospheric Administration
Address: **esdim1.nodc.noaa.gov**

Name: The National Oceanic and Atmospheric Administration
Address: **gopher.esdim.noaa.gov**

A B C D E F G H I J K L M N O P Q R S T U V W X Y Z

EnviroWeb

The EnviroWeb server has information on its many projects and services, including the Virtual Environment Library — a comprehensive clearinghouse of environmental info, an environmental resource directory — which provides users with a list of all environmental information services that provide important resources to the public, Online Environmental Project info, and information about environment-friendly products.

World Wide Web:
URL: **http://envirolink.org/start_web.html**

FireNet

An information service for everyone interested in any aspect of rural and landscape fires. The information concerns all aspects of fire science and management, including fire behavior, fire weather, fire prevention, mitigation and suppression, plant and animal responses to fire, and fire effects.

Anonymous FTP:
Address: **life.anu.edu.au**
Path: **/pub/landscape_ecology/firenet**

Gopher:
Name: Australian National University
Address: **life.anu.edu.au**
Choose: **Landscape Ecology, Fire,..**
 | firenet

Forest Science

This web page offers access to a forest science ftp server and academic information including undergraduate and graduate programs in the field of forestry and forest science.

World Wide Web:
URL: **http://www.forsci.ualberta.ca/**

Forests

Reference materials relating to forest environments, forest-related industries, and other documents of interest regarding forests.

Gopher:
Name: University of Minnesota
Address: **forestry.umn.edu**
Choose: **Forestry Library**

Global Change and Climate History

Data sets from the U.S.G.S. are available here, as well as abstracts on current research activities and results.

World Wide Web:
URL: **http://geochange.er.usgs.gov/gch.html**

Global Recycling Network

Global Recycling Network is an information service set up on the Internet to aid businesses around the world in recycling resources, surplus manufactured goods and outdated or used machinery.

World Wide Web:
URL: **http://clinet.fi/grn/**

Global Warming

This web page offers information summaries and data on trends and other anomalies regarding global warming.

World Wide Web:
URL: **http://www.ncdc.noaa.gov/gblwrmupd/ global.html**

Great Lakes Information Network

A network to store and disseminate bi-national data and information regarding environmental issues, resource management, transportation, demographic and development data, and other information and resources in the Great Lakes region of the U.S. and Canada.

Gopher:
Name: CICNet
Address: **gopher.cic.net**

Green Manufacturing

Nobody likes it when the Earth is unhappy, because we get all these earthquakes and storms and floods. So, in an effort to please Mother Nature, someone came up with the concept of green manufacturing — a means of manufacturing that is environmentally friendly. Scholars, manufacturers, and students interested in the environment should check out background information and studies on green manufacturing.

World Wide Web:
URL: **http://euler.berkeley.edu/green/cgdm.html**

GreenDisk Environmental Information

GreenDisk is a forum for the publication of research reports, press releases, action alerts, and news summaries from the world's environmental groups and governmental agencies.

Gopher:
Name: University of Maryland
Address: **info.umd.edu**
Choose: **Educational Resources**
 | Academic Reading Room
 | Academic Resources By Topic
 | Agriculture and Environment Resources
 | The GreenDisk Paperless Environmental Journal

Greenpeace

If the military is not your style, but you want a sense of adventure on the open seas, check out Greenpeace. Read up on ship movements, press releases, latest demonstrations, job opportunities; see pictures and publications of this environmental activist group. You will also find a link to other environmental gophers.

Gopher:
    Name: Greenpeace
    Address: **adam.greenpeace.org**

International Arctic Buoy Program

The home page of this organization that monitors data collecting buoys in the Arctic Basin. The buoys collect data on synoptic-scale fields of pressure, temperature fluctuation, and ice motion throughout the Arctic Basin.

World Wide Web:
    URL: **http://iabp.apl.washington.edu/**

Joshua Tree National Monument

Learn about this fascinating and unique area located 140 miles east of Los Angeles. The web page has introductory material, a slide show of images from the park, and a new series of high quality images.

World Wide Web:
    URL: **http://quests.com/jt/**

League of Conservation Voters

The League of Conservation Voters (LCV) is a political arm of the environmental movement. The LCV hopes to sway the balance of power in the U.S. Congress to reflect its pro-environmental concerns.

World Wide Web:
    URL: **http://www.econet.apc.org/lcv/lcv_info.html**

Man and the Biosphere

Man And the Biosphere (MAB) provides access to various databases of fauna, biological information servers, international organizations, images, and maps.

World Wide Web:
    URL: **http://ice.ucdavis.edu/MAB/ MAB_main_page.html**

Next time you are at the supermarket, show them this book and ask for a discount (you never know...).

National Environmental Data Referral Service

This National Oceanic and Atmospheric Administration (NOAA) database documents environmental data from the sun, the atmosphere, the Earth, and the oceans. Solar and upper atmosphere physics, satellite remote sensing, oceanography, climatology, meteorology, pollution, toxic substances, geophysics and geology, geochemistry, and freshwater and marine fisheries are some of the disciplines included.

Gopher:
    Name: University of California Santa Cruz
    Address: **scilibx.ucsc.edu**
    Choose: **The Researcher**
      | Science and Engineering
      | Environmental Science
      | NOAA Nat. Env. Referral Service

National Wetlands Inventory

You can check on America's wetlands without having to put on the waders and slosh about in the muck. Graphical maps will show you the status of the wetlands using color-coding. A master map will give you the availability of digital maps, but others are available only in print. If you don't have a graphical browser you will need to download the images, or the information at this site won't make much sense.

World Wide Web:
    URL: **http://www.nwi.fws.gov/**

Want some fun? Read the Fun section.

A B C D E F G H I J K L M N O P Q R S T U V W X Y Z

National Wildlife Refuges

This server provides information about the National Wildlife Refuge System and topics of interest related to wildlife management and natural resources management.

World Wide Web:
URL: **http://bluegoose.arw.r9.fws.gov/**

Natural Environment Research Council

This organization plans, encourages and carries out research in the physical and biological sciences to explain the natural processes of the environment.

World Wide Web:
URL: **http://www.nerc.ac.uk/**

Northridge Earthquake Simulation

This page offers simulations, patterns, and other data about the great California earthquake.

World Wide Web:
URL: **http://www.scubed.com:8001/products/ Tres3D.northridge.html**

Ozone Depletion

FAQs discussing the depletion of the ozone layer, including the Antarctic ozone hole and ultraviolet radiation.

Anonymous FTP:
Address: **rtfm.mit.edu**
Path: **/pub/usenet/news.answers/ozone-depletion/***

Usenet:
Newsgroup: **sci.environment**

World Wide Web:
URL: **http://icair.iac.org.nz/ozone/index.html**

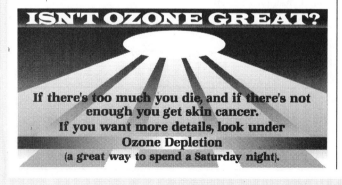

ISN'T OZONE GREAT?

If there's too much you die, and if there's not enough you get skin cancer. If you want more details, look under Ozone Depletion (a great way to spend a Saturday night).

Paleoenvironmental Records of Past Climate Change

Archives from geologic and biologic proxy climate indicators which are used to understand natural climate variability for times prior to the existence of instrumental climate records.

World Wide Web:
URL: **http://www.ngdc.noaa.gov/paleo/paleo.html**

Pollution and Groundwater Recharge

A mailing list discussing the vulnerability of aquifers to pollution, and what can be done about it.

Listserv Mailing List:
List Address: **aquifer@ibacsata.bitnet**
Subscription Address: **listserv@ibacsata.bitnet**

Pollution Research Group

The Pollution Research Group (PRG) is in the Department of Chemical Engineering at the University of Natal, Durban, South Africa. It is dedicated to the application of chemical engineering principles in the solution of environmental problems (dealing mostly with water and waste water management).

World Wide Web:
URL: **http://www.und.ac.za/prg/prg.html**

Sea Level Increase

A document discussing a possible increase in sea level and whether the previously suspected global warming could be the cause of such a phenomenon.

Anonymous FTP:
Address: **ftp.hmc.edu**
Path: **/pub/science/sci.answers/.mirror.OLD/ sea-level-faq**

South African Environmental Information Gateway

ECOSERV is an independent research and consulting company that provides technical environmental consulting services.

World Wide Web:
URL: **http://www.iaccess.za/ecoserv/index.html**

U.S. Environmental Protection Agency

A menu-driven system that provides information on the U.S. Environmental Protection Agency (EPA) and what they're up to, including a database of EPA documents searchable online by author, title, keywords, and year of publication.

Telnet:
Address: **epaibm.rtpnc.epa.gov**

ULS Report

A bimonthly newsletter that helps people "use less stuff" and become more friendly to the environment. The list also serves as a discussion group for anyone interested in activities and occasionally features guest experts who respond to reader questions and comments.

Majordomo Mailing List:
List Address: **uls@mail.msen.com**
Subscription Address: **majordomo@mail.msen.com**

UNESCO World Heritage List

A list of historic and cultural properties and parks throughout the world that have been nominated for inclusion on the World Heritage list of historic and cultural properties. The list of properties include both man-made and natural sites, and the list is arranged alphabetically by the nominating country.

World Wide Web:
URL: **http://www.ccsf.caltech.edu/~roy/world.heritage.html**

Waste Reduction

Information about the most efficient and effective way to reduce waste and conserve resources. The focus is on source reduction and reuse rather than just recycling. Also here are current and back issues of the *ULS Report* and articles pertaining to packaging and waste reduction.

Anonymous FTP:
Address: **ftp.cygnus-group.com**
Path: **/pub/vendor/cygnus/***

Gopher:
Name: Cygnus-Group
Address: **gopher.cygnus-group.com**
Port: **9011**

World Wide Web:
URL: **http://www.cygnus-group.com:9011**

TOO MUCH STUFF?

The Net has lots and lots of resources for Waste Reduction

Wilderness Society

An archive of factsheets from the Wilderness Society, the nation's only conservation organization devoted primarily to public lands protection and management issues. There are sheets for such topics as the Everglades, the Grand Canyon, wetlands, forest fires and forest health.

World Wide Web:
URL: **http://town.hall.org/environment/wild_soc/wilderness.html**

A
B
C
D
E
F
G
H
I
J
K
L
M
N
O
P
Q
R
S
T
U
V
W
X
Y
Z

FAMILIES AND PARENTING

Babies

Babies want most of all to be fed, loved and changed. But when there's something wrong, it can be hard to tell what the problem is — or even if there is one. Parenting can be frustrating sometimes. Read articles here about caring for babies — things to do and things not to do.

See also: Health, Medicine, Psychology, Youth

Gopher:
>   Name: University of Minnesota
>   Address: **tinman.mes.umn.edu**
>   Choose: **National Extension Children...**
> | **Other CYF Information Servers**
> | **Children, Youth and Family Consortium**
> | **Brochures, Newsletters & Short Articles**
> | **Bringing Up Baby**

Child Support

How do you stand on issues of custody and child support? Find out the thoughts of others affected by these issues and learn about current legislation.

Usenet:
>   Newsgroup: **alt.child-support**

If you need some quiet, non-controversial conversation to relax you, try the IRC **alt.child-support** newsgroup

there are only two things worth remembering (but I can't remember the other one)

Excerpt from the Net...

```
Newsgroups: misc.kids
Subject: Re: "My daddy dressed me"

>> Well, Carrie's Daddy dressed her yesterday, and what a combination
>> he came up with!  She was wearing a pair of overalls, bright red
>> with...
>>
>> Normally, if Daddy dresses the kids, I leave on what he puts on
>> them, not wanting to belittle his efforts.  But normally he does
>> better than yesterday.

> I've been away from misc.kids for a while and, on tuning in today, it
> is disappointing to see that this sexist crap is still going on.  The
> traditional "this colour goes with that" attitude has clearly long
> been dropped from fad wear, in which any and every colour is worn
> together.

Sorry, but I have to disagree.  While I personally do not care if my son matches when he
plays, my wife and I do try to make sure he "matches" if we go out.  (Of course, I tend
to have a little more liberal interpretation of what matches than my wife does, but that
seems to be common given the father/mother responses. :-)

Now, I'm not saying it is important for a young child to match.  I don't place that much
weight on it.  However, one of the things I see later on in life, especially with males,
is that wearing the appropriate clothes to work/interviews, etc, one feels much more
confident when one isn't concerned about whether their tie matches their suit or if it
clashes...
```

Childcare Newsletters

This ftp site features a collection of newsletters about kids and childcare in general.

Anonymous FTP:
   Address: **nigel.msen.com**
   Path: **/pub/newsletters/Kids/***

Children General Discussion

Kids say the darnedest things. Impart your information and experience regarding children from the cradle onward. Anecdotes, advice on doctors, behavior, activities, discipline, and schooling legislation are just a few of the topics covered.

Usenet:
   Newsgroup: **misc.kids**

Family Childcare Newsletter

It's no longer fashionable to park a child in front of a television set. They end up growing into people who have to be surgically removed from the couch after their skin has grafted to the upholstery. Creative and responsible childcare takes a great deal of work. Read articles and papers on many issues relating to children, including shyness, fear, discipline, safety, and fun activities.

See also: Psychology, Youth

Gopher:
   Name: University of Minnesota
   Address: **tinman.mes.umn.edu**
   Choose: **National Extension Children...**
      I **Other CYF Information Servers**
      I **Children, Youth and Family Consortium**
      I **Brochures, Newsletters...**
      I **Family Childcare Newsletters 1987 - Current**

Family Discussions

Discussion and sharing of family experiences and values, and chat about family life in general.

Internet Relay Chat:
   Channel: **#family**

Family Life Newsletter

Raising kids is tricky business. How did people do it before there were all these helpful books and newsletters? Check out the information compiled in the Family Life Newsletter. There are articles on almost any subject that relates to being a parent, including tantrums, patience, learning, communication, and napping, which happens to be our personal favorite.

See also: Youth

Gopher:
   Name: University of Minnesota
   Address: **tinman.mes.umn.edu**
   Choose: **National Extension Children...**
      I **Other CYF Information Servers**
      I **Children, Youth and Family Consortium**
      I **Brochures, Newsletters...**
      I **Family Life Newsletters 1987 - Current**

Family News

Read the latest news on the family, marriage and adoption in Clarinet — a source of real news on the Internet. This group offers the latest news stories about court cases, laws, and unusual occurrences relating to the family like custody cases, the legality of nannies, visitation rights, adoption, and non-traditional family environments.

Usenet:
   Newsgroup: **clari.news.family**

Family Web Page

The family that Webs together stays together. This web page covers family topics like adolescence, pre-school, infants, children and marriage. Links on these topics will result in a list of related articles that will lead you to even more links for hours of interesting reading.

World Wide Web:
   URL: **http://www.einet.net/galaxy/Community/The-Family.html**

A B C D E F G H I J K L M N O P Q R S T U V W X Y Z

FatherNet

It gets tiring hearing Mr. Mom jokes after a while. Dads, here is a little portion of the Internet just for you. Read through papers on men and children, information on interaction with kids, connect to an electronic bulletin board and chat system for dads, get a newsletter called *At-Home Dad*, and send in your opinions and experiences about fatherhood.

Gopher:
Name: University of Minnesota
Address: **tinman.mes.umn.edu**
Choose: **National Extension Children...**
 | **Other CYF Information Servers**
 | **Children, Youth and Family Consortium**
 | **FatherNet: The Role of Men in Children's Lives**

Great Beginnings Newsletter

A newsletter that provides tips to help make the job of parenting easier and more rewarding.

Gopher:
Name: University of Delaware
Address: **gopher.udel.edu**
Choose: **UD Department & College Information Services**
 | **AGINFO: College of Agricultural Sciences**
 | **Information by Type of Publication**
 | **Newsletters**
 | **Great Beginning**

Missing Children

Help locate a missing child. Read descriptions of missing children that have been posted by concerned individuals.

Usenet:
Newsgroup: **alt.missing-kids**

Missing Children Database

Information and pictures of children who are missing in the United States. This database is maintained by the national Center for Missing and Exploited Children. It includes points of contact for anyone who might have information about the whereabouts of these children.

World Wide Web:
URL: **http://www.scubed.com:8001/ public_service/missing.html**

News on Children

What is going on with children these days? Read news regarding children and parenting.

Usenet:
Newsgroup: **clari.news.children**

News on the Family

Keep current on issues that concern the family, child abuse, and other subjects concerning children and families.

Usenet:
Newsgroup: **clari.news.issues.family**

Parent Trap

A news column featuring stories of parents about life, love, and raising children.

Gopher:
Name: Software Tool & Die
Address: **gopher.std.com**
Choose: **Periodicals, Magazines, and Journals**
 | **Middlesex News**
 | **Columns**
 | **The Parent Trap**

Parents and Teens

What works? What doesn't? Share your experiences with other parents, give advice, ask questions.

Usenet:
Newsgroup: **alt.parents-teens**

Vacationing with Children

When you plan your next vacation, include reading Usenet to find out helpful hints on how to make travelling with your children easier. Find money-saving ideas, new ways to entertain kids while on the road, information on travel safety as well as funny travel anecdotes from parents.

Usenet:
Newsgroup: **misc.kids.vacation**

FASHION AND CLOTHING

Clothes Moths

It's that special night on the town and you are hustling to get ready. You drag out the sexy dress you have been saving just for tonight, only to discover some pesky moth with a big appetite has been munching on your favorite garment for quite some time. Protect your clothes as well as carpets and curtains by learning all about those annoying lepidoptera.

Gopher:
> Name: Virginia Cooperative Extension
> Address: **gopher.ext.vt.edu**
> Choose: **VCE Subject Matter**
> | **Entomology**
> | **Insect Factsheets**
> | **Household**
> | **Lepidoptera (Butterflies/Moths)**
> | **Clothes Moth**

General Fashion

It's a nice feeling when you're dressed in a spiffy new outfit with all the right accessories and people turn to look as you walk down the street. Impress your friends, family, and total strangers with your fashion sense and the clothing tips you've learned while hanging out on the Internet. Clothing pros, trendsetters, and the hopelessly unfashionable find their way to these newsgroups to share ideas or get answers to questions.

Usenet:
> Newsgroup: **alt.clothing**
> Newsgroup: **alt.fashion**

Stay cool and trendy: read the fashion newsgroups.

Historical Costuming

Pattern and supplier lists, a bibliography, and information relevant to the Society for Creative Anachronism (SCA). The SCA re-creates the history of the Middle Ages and Renaissance.

Anonymous FTP:
> Address: **cs.columbia.edu**
> Path: **/archives/mirror2/faq/alt.answers/crafts/historical-costuming**
>
> Address: **plaza.aarnet.edu.au**
> Path: **/usenet/FAQs/alt.answers/crafts/historical-costuming**
>
> Address: **rtfm.mit.edu**
> Path: **/pub/usenet/news.answers/crafts/***
>
> Address: **svin02.info.win.tue.nl**
> Path: **/pub/usenet/news.answers/crafts/historical-costuming**

Historical Costuming Discussion

Laces and ruffles and corsets and buttons — these are just a few of the things that make historical costuming so interesting and elaborate. Whether you love the detailed intricacies of Elizabethan garb or the comfortable simplicity of a toga, you will be able to find someone with whom you have something in common. Get together with the people who know that playing dress-up is not just for kids.

See also: History, Hobbies

Internet Mailing List:
> List Address: **h-costume@andrew.cmu.edu**
> Subscription Address:
> **h-costume-request@andrew.cmu.edu**

Lingerie

Lingerie is fun and sexy, but the bad thing about it is you can't parade around outdoors while wearing it. Or at least you're not supposed to. For discussion about garments that you wear for limited viewing, check out this Usenet group, where they talk about things with straps and things with no straps, garments that hold you in and ones that let you hang out, and outfits that make you look naked even when you're not.

See also: Sex

Usenet:
> Newsgroup: **alt.clothing.lingerie**

A B C D E F G H I J K L M N O P Q R S T U V W X Y Z

Sewing Discussions

Some people are truly amazing. They lose a button or tear their hem while waiting in line at the grocery store and out of nowhere they whip out a little sewing kit and make the repair before the checker can say "paper or plastic." Whether you are like that or just want to be, stop in at this newsgroup to read up on the latest information about sewing textiles.

See also: Hobbies

Usenet:
Newsgroup: **rec.crafts.textiles.sewing**

Textiles Discussion Groups

Rough and soft, shiny and crinkled, textiles come in a variety of colors, weights, and textures. Some are made from natural materials like plants and animals or even metal. Others are invented in a lab, fibers woven out of who-knows-what kind of synthetic material with a 12-syllable name. Fashion designers, students, people who sew, or just folks who love fashion — you will find them all on Usenet.

Usenet:
Newsgroup: **rec.crafts.textiles**
Newsgroup: **rec.crafts.textiles.misc**

Textiles Mailing List

You can make it a hobby, a science, or a way of life. This list covers the development, science, chemistry, engineering, technology, and management of textiles. Discussion is open to any researchers, students, academics, or industrialists who are interested in clothing and textiles.

Listserv Mailing List:
List Address: **textiles@vm3090.ege.edu.tr**
Subscription Address: **listserv@vm3090.ege.edu.tr**

Textiles Reference Material

There is a ton of printed information on textiles, sewing and fashion. And someone has compiled the information for you. See this list of books and periodicals covering topics such as sewing, tailoring, men's fashion, quick tips, fitting, and pattern drafting.

Anonymous FTP:
Address: **rtfm.mit.edu**
Path: **/pub/usenet-by-group/news.answers/crafts/textiles/books/***

Textiles and Sewing Archives

If you aren't a sewing adept, you should be. There's enough information on the Net to guarantee that you could sew a formal gown out of a paper bag and make any fashion designer envious. A list of frequently asked questions has been compiled and covers topics such as sewing, fitting, pattern drafting, costuming, supplies, and even how to work on that antique sewing machine that's been taking up space in your attic.

Anonymous FTP:
Address: **rtfm.mit.edu**
Path: **/pub/usenet-by-group/news.answers/crafts/textiles/faq**

Vintage Clothing and Costume Jewelry

If you save something long enough, it will come back into style. (Unless it's from the '70s. . . in that case, you will just have to take your chances.) Vintage clothing is fun. Some people collect it for preservation. Others acquire vintage clothing and costume jewelry to actually wear and create unique combinations that are interesting and attractive. Join the rest of the clothes scavengers and compare notes on all subjects relating to vintage clothing and costume jewelry.

Internet Mailing List:
List Address: **vintage@presto.ig.com**
Subscription Address:
vintage-request@presto.ig.com

FLIGHT SIMULATORS

Aeronautics Simulation

Imagine being able to zip through the air at high speeds while being in total control of a state-of-the-art aircraft that responds to your every command. And you don't even have to pay the gas bill or worry about scratching the paint. Flight simulation is not just for games, but can be a serious learning tool. Explore the developmental and technical side of flight simulation from people who fly while keeping their feet on the ground.

Usenet:
Newsgroup: **sci.aeronautics.simulation**

> ## Bored? Try Fun.
> ## Still bored? Try Games.

> ## The Net is for smart people
> ## (like you).

Air Warrior

Files and patches to improve the cockpit detail in some of the planes in the video game Air Warriors. Also, a program that can manipulate the pilot roster. Air Warrior is a PC flight simulator that makes full use of SVGA video and sound cards.

Anonymous FTP:
Address: **cactus.org**
Path: **/pub/genie/airwar/***

Falcon 3.0 Archives

This site has lots of upgrade files and utility programs for Falcon 3.0, a popular PC flight simulator from Spectrum HoloByte. Included here are demos, documentation, a FAQ list, hints, information on a mailing list, mission files, pilot files, recorded flights, scenarios, and other items of interest.

Anonymous FTP:
Address: **cactus.org**
Path: **/pub/falcon3/programs/***

Address: **ftp.informatik.uni-rostock.de**
Path: **/pub/msdos/falcon3**

Flight Simulator Utilities and Scenery

Flight simulation theory, products, reviews, scenery for specific software, and other material related to air and spacecraft simulators.

Anonymous FTP:
Address: **ftp.funet.fi**
Path: **/pub/X11/contrib/acm4.0.tar.Z**

Address: **ftp.ulowell.edu**
Path: **/msdos/Games/FltSim/***

Address: **onion.rain.com**
Path: **/pub/falcon3/***

Address: **rtfm.mit.edu**
Path: **/pub/usenet/news.answers/aviation/
flight-simulators**

WAIS:
Database: **flight_sim**

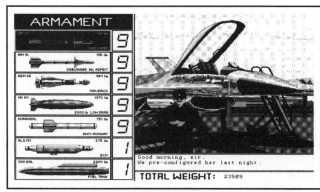

The Internet is a marvelous source for items of interest to the game player. Just teach yourself how to use Anonymous FTP and you can find not only free software and shareware games, but utilities, hints, cheats, additional scenery, missions and more. This image you see here is **cockpit.gif** from Northern Arizona University (**ftp.nau.edu**). If you use archie to search for **cockpit**, you will find much more specific images, such as **F111C-cockpit.jpg** and **falconcockpit.gif**.

Crash and Burn

The great thing about flight simulators is that you can do anything you want and not get into real trouble. (The only drawbacks are that you have to bring your own salted peanuts and you don't get any frequent flyer miles.) The Internet has a gaggle of FTP sites with information about flight and space simulators. Never again will you have to settle for the real thing.

Flight Simulators

Don't worry if you can't fly a plane; simulators are the next best thing. Be bold, be daring, get crazy, and never have to worry about unscheduled landings. The **.flight-sim** newsgroup concentrates on PC flight simulators, touching on such topics as bugs and bug fixes, simulator missions and objectives, and game reviews. If your interest in simulation goes beyond games, check out **.simulators** which deals with flight simulation on all levels.

See also: Games

Usenet:
>   Newsgroup: **comp.sys.ibm.pc.games.flight-sim**
>   Newsgroup: **rec.aviation.simulators**

IFR Flight Simulator

A demo of a PC program that simulates IFR flight training. This directory also contains numerous scenery and utility files for Microsoft Flight Simulator.

Note: This computer is a VMS system. After you log in, enter the command **cd xevious:** (note the colon). Then you can **get** files in the usual manner.

Anonymous FTP:
>   Address: **ftp.iup.edu**
>   Path: **xevious:/ift5demo.zip**

Microsoft Flight Simulator

Tons of files for Microsoft Flight Simulator, including scenery of dozens of cities and landscapes throughout the world (check out the Hawaiian Islands). Also static display files, aircraft (both civil and military), and utility programs.

Note: This computer is a VMS system. After you log in, enter the command to change to the appropriate directory **cd xevious:** (note the colon) or **cd flight-sim**. Then you can get and display files in the usual manner.

Anonymous FTP:
>   Address: **ftp.iup.edu**
>   Path: **xevious:/***

>   Address: **ftp.iup.edu**
>   Path: **flight-sim/***

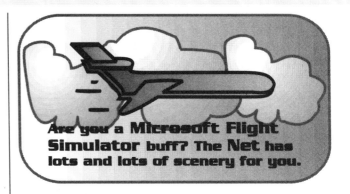

Are you a Microsoft Flight Simulator buff? The Net has lots and lots of scenery for you.

FOLKLORE AND MYTHOLOGY

Bulfinch's Mythology

Bulfinch weaves tales of mythological times and characters. Recorded in this electronic book are the antics of gods and goddesses as viewed in ancient times. Experience the era where swans were gods and women were darn proud of it.

Gopher:
>   Name: Virginia Tech
>   Address: **gopher.vt.edu**
>   Choose: **Information for Students**
>   l **Electronic Books**
>   l **Bulfinch's Mythology**

Greek Mythology

Brush up on your ancient Greek mythology by reading stories about gods, goddesses, heroes and creatures. This Web page will not only give you an overview, but will also diagram a family tree so you can keep all your characters straight.

World-Wide Web:
>   URL: **http://info.desy.de/gna/interpedia/**
>   **greek_myth/greek_myth.html**

Lore

A broad-based mailing list that examines and discusses all aspects of folklore.

Listserv Mailing List:
>   List Address: **lore@vm1.nodak.edu**
>   Subscription Address: **listserv@vm1.nodak.edu**

Mythical Animals

As cute as they are, little ground hogs and frolicking squirrels can get tiresome after a while. Imagine a world in which all sorts of bizarre creatures were alive and roaming your neighborhood. What fun it would be to have to worry about gorgons and harpies hastening your demise, mischievous satyrs, graceful unicorns, and beautiful mermaids who nip at your toes as you tread water. Read about all forms of mythical creatures and their origins.

Usenet:
   Newsgroup: **alt.mythology.mythic-animals**

We had some really important things to say about oral traditions but we can't find where we wrote down our notes. Oh well, it's probably more important to make sure that we remember to tell you where on the Net people talk about this kind of stuff. Now, where was it? It was on a yellow piece of paper somewhere. Hmm.. well, I guess it wasn't that important. Oh well, nevermind.

Net Legends

Learn the stories behind all your favorite or most-hated Net legends. Lists of FAQs and stories about people who are notorious on the Net or about strange occurrences that you have only heard about in rumors.

See also: Usenet Curiosities

Gopher:
   Name: University of Illinois
   Address: **dixie.aiss.uiuc.edu**
   Port: **6969**
   Choose: **urban.legends**
     | **Net.legends FAQ**

Excerpt from the Net...

```
Newsgroup: alt.folklore.science
Subject: See the Ultraviolet


> According to Hecht's "Optics", people who have cataract surgery can
> see into the ultraviolet. The removed lens no longer filters out the
> ultraviolet.

The late Walter Scott Houston, who wrote the Deep Sky Wonders in Sky &
Telescope, mentioned this once in a while. The central star in the
ring nebula (M57 in Lyra) is brightest in the ultraviolet. This star
is considered a challenge to see since there is so little "visible"
light emitted. After cataract surgery (in which the eye's lense is
replaced with a plastic one), he claimed that the star was easy to see
with that eye.
```

A
B
C
D
E
F
G
H
I
J
K
L
M
N
O
P
Q
R
S
T
U
V
W
X
Y
Z

Oral Tradition

Centuries ago, tradition was passed on orally. A woman would teach her daughter the "women's ways." Grandmothers would tell stories about the old days when gods and spirits came down to the Earth. Join in the discussion of the oral traditions of the African, Hispanic and Native American peoples, and discussions about texts with a history of oral tradition, such as the Mahabharata, the Iliad, and the Old and New Testaments.

Listserv Mailing List:
List Address: **ortrad-l@mizzou1.missouri.edu**
Subscription Address:
listserv@mizzou1.missouri.edu

Scientific Urban Legends

There are all sorts of nasty rumors flying around about science. And we know just where they are coming from. Check out the latest outlandish tales of science which often sound like they come straight from the set of a 1950's science fiction movie. Help discern the truths from the myths by reading up on what the folks in Usenet have to say.

Usenet:
Newsgroup: **alt.folklore.science**

Urban Folklore

The Rutgers gopher and ftp site houses frequently asked question lists about urban and college folklore, articles, and other craziness such as Snopes' Unusual Fact & Fiction (SNUFF) List and a story about pull-tab collectors for charity.

Anonymous FTP:
Address: **quartz.rutgers.edu**
Path: **/pub/folklore/***

Gopher:
Name: Rutgers University
Address: **quartz.rutgers.edu**
Choose: **Folklore - Urban and Other**

Urban Legends

Stories, trivia, old wives' tales, and a place for confirming or disproving beliefs and rumors of all kinds.

Anonymous FTP:
Address: **balder.nta.no**
Path: **/pub/alt.folklore.urban/***

Address: **cathouse.org**
Path: **/pub/cathouse/urban.legends/***

Usenet:
Newsgroup: **alt.folklore.gemstones**
Newsgroup: **alt.folklore.military**
Newsgroup: **alt.folklore.suburban**
Newsgroup: **alt.folklore.urban**

FOOD AND DRINK

Austrian Beer Guide

An unfinished guide to some great Austrian beers along with information about good places to drink beer in Austria.

World Wide Web:
URL: **http://www.lib.uchicago.edu/keith/ austrian-beer.html**

Don't you just love those unbelievable stories that always happen to a "friend of a friend"? These are urban legends and the Net has several newsgroups devoted to such tales. (We wonder, is there any truth to the story about the man whose life was saved by a copy of *The Internet Complete Reference*?)

Writers, share your stories on the Net.

Beer

Making, choosing, and imbibing: these discussion groups will help you find out everything you want to know about beer and related beverages. Read the regular posting on which beers are best, based on the votes of Usenet participants. (Anyone can vote, although you do have to supply your own beer.) For specialists, the **.zima** group discusses this odd, beer-like drink.

Usenet:
    Newsgroup: **alt.beer**
    Newsgroup: **alt.zima**
    Newsgroup: **rec.crafts.brewing**
    Newsgroup: **rec.food.drink.beer**

World Wide Web:
    URL: **http://www.eff.org/dan/beer.html**

Beer Archive

This web page offers a beer FAQ from the Usenet newsgroup **alt.beer**, lists of beer magazines, and information about CAMRA (the Campaign for Real Ale).

Anonymous FTP:
    Address: **ftp.cwru.edu**
    Path: **/pub/alt.beer/***

Beer Judging

Imagine milling through a room of people who are murmuring about the subtleties of the fine beer they are sipping. A tuxedo-clad man with a napkin draped over his arm comes by and shows you the selection of beer on his tray. As you choose a dark domestic beer he says, "Might I offer you some cheese to clear your palate?" What a life that would be, eh? Most people don't realize it, but beer is not just for guzzling. Connoisseurs of fine beer will tell you that there is a great deal more to judging beer than knowing what chip it goes with. Join in the discussion of beer judging and competition organization.

Internet Mailing List:
    List Address: **judgenet@synchro.com**
    Subscription Address:
        judgenet-request@synchro.com

Beer Page

If you like beer and you're curious about some of the more esoteric aspects of homebrewing, check out this web page. There's a beer FAQ, links to archive sites, recipe files, and a growing collection of beer-related documents.

World Wide Web:
    URL: **http://guraldi.hgp.med.umich.edu/Beer/**

Beer Ratings

Mike's Beer Ratings includes full descriptions of beers (in Mike's opinion, of course), as well as images of a few beer logos, and links to other beer resources.

World Wide Web:
    URL: **http://www.mit.edu:8001/afs/
    athena.mit.edu/user/m/j/mjbauer/WWW/
    beer-ratings.html**

Big Drink List

Mixing hints, tips, and recipes for hundreds of mixed drinks, including such favorites as the Alexander, Highball, Rickey, Alabama Slammer, and many more.

Anonymous FTP:
    Address: **ftp.ocf.berkeley.edu**
    Path: **/pub/Library/Recreation/big-drink-list**

Gopher:
    Name: University of California Berkeley
    Address: **gopher.ocf.berkeley.edu**
    Choose: **ftp.ocf.Berkeley.EDU Anonymous FTP
        Archive/**
        l **The OCF On-line Library**
        l **Recreation**
        l **big-drink-list**

Boat Drinks

The Parrotthead Madness Boat Drink Mixer page has recipes to dozens of aquatic drinks including such favorites as Cuba Libre, Jolly Mon, Oyster Shooter, Pina Colada, Tampico Trauma, Mai Tai, Banana Republic, the Expatriated American and many others.

World Wide Web:
    URL: **http://www.ils.nwu.edu/~april/buffett/
    tobyboat.html**

Booze Cookbook

More drink recipes, including Hemorrhaging Brain and the Vulcan Death Grip.

Anonymous FTP:
    Address: **ftp.ocf.berkeley.edu**
    Path: **/pub/Library/Recreation/Booze_Cook**

A B C D E F G H I J K L M N O P Q R S T U V W

Creative Drinking

Has this ever happened to you?

It's your turn to mix the drinks, but you can't remember the recipes. So you end up putting in some Drano and nobody will ever speak to you again.

Next time, take a moment and check with the

Booze Cookbook

Novelty images abound on the Internet. Think of it as your world-spanning repertoire of color photographic clipart. Finding images is usually easy. We found this image by doing an archie search for **pepsi**.

Coca-Cola World

An article about the Coca-Cola Company of Atlanta, Georgia: a "tribute to a unique product and the consumers who have made it the world's favorite soft drink."

Gopher:
Name: Carnegie Mellon University
Address: **english-server.hss.cmu.edu**
Choose: **Cultural Theory**
| **Friedman - World of Coca Cola**

Coffee

Some people like to sip it, some gulp it down in the morning before their eyes are open. Some people like to have it flavored and run through various elaborate preparations which result in a thick, syrupy brew or a decadent foamy concoction. And then there are the hard core people who don't bother brewing and simply munch on the beans themselves. If your drug of choice is coffee, you will feel right at home in these newsgroups where people talk about preparation, storage, growth and sale of this popular beverage.

Usenet:
Newsgroup: **alt.coffee**
Newsgroup: **alt.food.coffee**
Newsgroup: **rec.food.drink.coffee**

Coffee Lover's Resourcess

Dedicated to coffee lovers all over the world, this resource features links to a glossary of coffee terminology, a list of mail order coffee and tea vendors, the coffee file archives, newsgroups about coffee, coffee recipes, books, FAQs, and even a traveler's guide to coffee houses.

World Wide Web:
URL: **http://www.infonet.net:80/showcase/coffee/**

Cereal

Cereal is not just for the first meal of the day. In fact, it's more than just something to put in your mouth. It's not only nutrition and sustenance — it's fun and if you read the box, you could even call it a literary experience. More than that, it's a facilitator of a great social experience by bringing people together on Usenet to talk about how cereal makes an impact on all our lives. Don't be left out of the cereal movement. Grab a spoon and dig in.

Usenet:
Newsgroup: **alt.cereal**

Coca-Cola

Talk to fans of Coca-Cola, the most important beverage in the refrigerator of American hegemony.

Usenet:
Newsgroup: **alt.food.cocacola**

Cola: Make Your Own

Make your own cola with this recipe. It looks time-consuming, but could be worth the trouble for the true Coke connoisseur or the budding chemist.

Anonymous FTP:
Address: **ftp.spies.com**
Path: **/Library/Article/Food/newcoke.txt**

Gopher:
Name: Internet Wiretap
Address: **wiretap.spies.com**
Choose: **Wiretap Online Library**
 I **Articles**
 I **Food and Drink**
 I **Laszlo Nibble: The New Coke**

College Food

Ah, those good old college days. How nostalgic we will be when our hair turns silver and we wax eloquent about mystery meat burgers and the blue-green algae surprise. Come on in and discuss college dining halls, cafeterias, and pay-for-it-even-if-you-don't-want-it food plans.

Usenet:
Newsgroup: **alt.college.food**

Are you young? Are you a gourmet? Then discussing college food on the Net is for you.

Complete Guide to Guinness Beer

Everything you could ever want to know about this great Irish beer, including facts, FAQs, "Black and Tan," specifications of the various types of Guinness, and some of those great Guinness advertisements.

World Wide Web:
URL: **http://wombatix.physics.ucg.ie/misc/guinness.html**

Cookie Recipes

Have you ever wanted to know why Mrs. Fields' cookies are soooo good? Well, here is her recipe — yes, the real McCoy. There are also recipes here for several other kinds of cookies. (This entry is giving us the munchies.)

Anonymous FTP:
Address: **quartz.rutgers.edu**
Path: **/pub/food/cookie.recipes**

Gopher:
Name: Rutgers University
Address: **quartz.rutgers.edu**
Choose: **Food, Recipes, and Nutrition**
 I **cookie.recipes**

Cooking

International conversion helper, food terms, liquid measures, ingredient guides, and Usenet discussions related to cooking.

Anonymous FTP:
Address: **rtfm.mit.edu**
Path: **/pub/usenet/news.answers/cooking-faq**

Usenet:
Newsgroup: **alt.cooking-chat**
Newsgroup: **alt.creative-cook**
Newsgroup: **alt.creative-cooking**

Crackers

To some people, crackers are just a carrier for bits of cheese or some form of food spread. Broaden your horizons by experiencing the passion and exotic gourmet side of cracker-eating by rubbing virtual elbows with people who know their water crackers from their stoned wheat thins. Never again will you be satisfied with merely crumbling saltines in your soup.

Usenet:
Newsgroup: **alt.crackers**

Diabetic Recipes

A collection of recipes for diabetics, including some dishes you would think diabetics could never eat, like apple dumplings, double fudge balls, fruit cookies, and others. There is also information on powdered sugar replacements.

World Wide Web:
URL: **http://www.vuw.ac.nz/who/Amy.Gale/special/diabetic-coll.html#1**

A B C D E F G H I J K L M N O P Q R S T U V W X Y Z

Dining Out on the Web

A collection of pointers to restaurant reviews and resources around the world. The list of U.S. resources is organized by state, and there is also a list of restaurant reviews from across the country, and a list of vegetarian restaurants.

World Wide Web:
URL: **http://cornelius.ucsf.edu/~troyer/dish/ diningout.html**

Fat-Free Food

Remember, just because it has no taste doesn't mean it's good for you. Immerse yourself in the world of fat-free fanatics and lower your cholesterol, blood pressure, and enjoyment quotient.

Usenet:
Newsgroup: **alt.food.fat-free**

Food and Beverages

General discussion group for people who think that eating is more than putting stuff into your mouth.

Usenet:
Newsgroup: **rec.food.drink**

Food-related Topics

A collection of assorted recipes and food-related links for cheese, crockpotting, pies, souffles, vegetables and diet recipes.

World Wide Web:
URL: **http://zaphod.cc.ttu.ee/vrainn/nox/ recipes.html**

Good Food

Discussion of cooking techniques, equipment, recipes, vegetarianism, restaurants, and food and drink in general.

Usenet:
Newsgroup: **alt.food**
Newsgroup: **rec.food.cooking**
Newsgroup: **rec.food.drink**
Newsgroup: **rec.food.recipes**
Newsgroup: **rec.food.restaurants**
Newsgroup: **rec.food.veg**

Grapevine

Grapevine is a Web-accessible magazine for wine lovers. It has archives to **rec.food.drink** and does reviews of wines and vintages.

World Wide Web:
URL: **http://www.opal.com/grapevine**

Are you a wine lover? Try the **Grapevine**.

Herbs

Do you wonder how your favorite chili would do on the Scoville Organoleptic Test? Do you have a cold and want to know whether to eat the zinc before or after the garlic? Get together with the Herbs-R-Us people and discuss all manner of herbal lore and treatments.

Usenet:
Newsgroup: **alt.folklore.herbs**

Excerpt from the Net...

```
Newsgroup: alt.folklore.herbs
Subject: Food for thought

Gotu Kola and Ginkgo are both used in
Ayurvedic medicine as brain tonics.

One's supposed to help clear and focus
the mind, the other's supposed to give
your thoughts energy, but I forget
which is which.
```

History of Food

Where do you ask for information on what type of food the peasants ate during the French Revolution? What do you do when the in-laws are due any moment and you need the recipe for figgy pudding? Check out this newsgroup and move forward into the past.

Usenet:
Newsgroup: **rec.food.historic**

Homebrew Mailing List

All about making and tasting beer, ale, and mead. This mailing list also covers related issues such as breweries, books, judging, commercial beers, and beer festivals.

Anonymous FTP:
Address: **mthvax.cs.miami.edu**
Path: **/pub/homebrew/***

Internet Mailing List:
List Address: **homebrew@hpfcmi.fc.hp.com**
Subscription Address:
homebrew-request@hpfcmi.fc.hp.com

Homebrewing

All kinds of material related to beer and homebrewing, including recipes, *Homebrew Digest* archives, color images of various beer labels and coasters, and much more.

Anonymous FTP:
Address: **ftp.funet.fi**
Path: **/pub/culture/beer/***

How to Make Your Own Booze

A guide to making alcoholic beverages, including recipes for vodka, rum, moonshine, whiskey, beer, wine, and hard cider.

Anonymous FTP:
Address: **ftp.spies.com**
Path: **/Library/Untech/alcohol.mak**

Gopher:
Name: Internet Wiretap
Address: **wiretap.spies.com**
Choose: **Wiretap Online Library**
  | **Questionables**
  | **How To Make Alcohol**

Why pay for the real thing when you can make your own? Check out *How to Make Your Own Booze* Just be sure to watch out for revenooers.

Ice Cream

If you want to try every different flavor of ice cream in the world or every way that ice cream can be prepared, then it's best to start when you are very young. Explore those ice cream avenues left untouched by human lips by checking out the newsgroup where the connoiseurs of frozen dairy products talk about the object of their desire.

Usenet:
Newsgroup: **alt.food.ice-cream**

Japanese Food and Culture

Slip off your shoes, pull up a tatami mat and dig into Japanese food and culture with other fans of the Orient.

See also: World Cultures

Listserv Mailing List:
List Address: **j-food-l@jpnknu01.bitnet**
Subscription Address: **listserv@jpnknu01.bitnet**

Jewish Recipes

A collection of Jewish recipes, including bagels and bialys, latkes, hamantaschen, schnecken, turkey steaks with herbs, and others.

Gopher:
Name: Jerusalem One
Address: **jerusalem1.datasrv.co.il**
Choose: **THE Board**
  | **Recipe Board**

Ketchup

A whole newsgroup devoted to this most wondrous of tomato foodstuffs. Ketchup, ketchup, ketchup...wowie, zowie...just keep it away from us.

Usenet:
Newsgroup: **alt.ketchup**

A B C D E F G H I J K L M N O P Q R S T U V W X Y Z

McDonald's

If your junk food is missing that *je ne sais quoi* that makes all the difference, perhaps you should share the experience. Come on in and discuss McDonald's, everybody's favorite home away from home.

Usenet:
> Newsgroup: **alt.food.mcdonalds**
> Newsgroup: **alt.mcdonalds**

Mead Maker's Resources

These resources are just for brewers of mead, an alcoholic beverage made from honey. The web page has links to recipes and other information and items of interest to mead lovers.

Anonymous FTP:
> Address: **ftp.spies.com**
> Path: **/Library/Article/Food/mead.rcp**

Gopher:
> Name: Internet Wiretap
> Address: **wiretap.spies.com**
> Choose: **Wiretap Online Library**
>   **| Articles**
>   **| Food and Drink**
>   **| Mead Recipes**

World Wide Web:
> URL: **http://www.atd.ucar.edu/rdp/gfc/mead/ mead.html**

Milwaukee Frozen Custard

If it's definitely not pudding and it's not ice cream, but it's cool and creamy, it could be Milwaukee's famous frozen custard. This web page has links to vendors, and information on the flavors about the town.

World Wide Web:
> URL: **http://www.mixcom.com/milwaukee/ custard.html**

MotherCity Coffee — A Guide to Seattle Coffee

This server claims that unless you are sitting in Milano, Italia, you're not in a city that consumes as much coffee as Seattle. The MotherCity home page is a compendium of a select number of Seattle coffee roasters and coffeehouses.

World Wide Web:
> URL: **http://www.seas.upenn.edu/~cpage/ mothercity.html**

Pancakes

Pancakes are more than just a carrier for fancy syrup. They are the basis for a creative cooking and eating experience. Discover all the new and unusual things you can do with a pancake including, but not necessarily limited to, eating them.

Usenet:
> Newsgroup: **alt.food.pancakes**

Recipe Archives

Out of ideas for dinner tonight? With this archive at your fingertips, you need never run dry on ideas. Search this large database of recipes for that special dish.

Anonymous FTP:
> Address: **ftp.cs.ubc.ca**
> Path: **/pub/local/RECIPES**

> Address: **ftp.neosoft.com**
> Path: **/pub/rec.food.recipes**

> Address: **ftp.wustl.edu**
> Path: **/usenet/rec.food.recipes/recipes**

> Address: **gatekeeper.dec.com**
> Path: **/pub/recipes**

> Address: **mthvax.cs.miami.edu**
> Path: **/pub/recipes**

> Address: **quartz.rutgers.edu**
> Path: **/pub/food/***

Gopher:
> Name: Albert Einstein College of Medicine
> Address: **gopher.aecom.yu.edu**
> Choose: **Internet Resources**
>   **| Miscellaneous**
>   **| Search the Food Recipes Database**

WAIS:
> Database: **recipes**
> Database: **usenet-cookbook**

**Need Unix help?
See Harley's book
"Unix Unbound."**

A
B
C
D
E
F
G
H
I
J
K
L
M
N
O
P
Q
R
S
T
U
V
W
X
Y
Z

Recipe Assortments

Numerous food and drink recipes, including beef jerky, fajitas, vegan recipes, the ultimate mixed drink list, and instructions for a medieval pig feast.

Anonymous FTP:
Address: **ftp.spies.com**
Path: **/Library/Article/Food/***

Address: **ftp.uu.net**
Path: **/doc/literary/obi/HM.recipes/TheRecipes**

Address: **ftp.uu.net**
Path: **/doc/literary/obi/Recipes**

Address: **ftp.uu.net**
Path: **/doc/literary/obi/Usenet.Cookbook**

Gopher:
Name: Internet Wiretap
Address: **wiretap.spies.com**
Choose: **Wiretap Online Library**
    | Articles
    | Food and Drink

Recipes

What do you do when your boss and his family are coming over for dinner and all you have is a couple of frozen armadillos? Connect to Usenet and check out the recipe groups. The **.gourmand** and **.recipes** groups are moderated. The **.cooking** group is open to all.

Usenet:
Newsgroup: **alt.gourmand**
Newsgroup: **rec.food.cooking**
Newsgroup: **rec.food.recipes**

Recipes from Slovakia

Do you like Slovakian food? Try some new recipes from the Slovakian recipe archives. How about "Bryndzove pirohy" (dumplings filled with feta cheese) tonight?

Gopher:
Name: Academy of Sciences, Bratislava
Address: **savba.savba.sk**
Choose: **Slovakia**
    | Recipes of Grand Mother

Do you like weirdness?
Check out Usenet Curiosities.

Restaurant Le Cordon Bleu

The EXPO Restaurant Le Cordon Bleu is an exhibit of L'Art Culinaire. This web page contains numerous menus and recipes for fine French cuisine.

World Wide Web:
URL: **http://sunsite.unc.edu/expo/restaurant/restaurant.html**

Restaurants

Tips on where to go for good eats; complaints about the stinkers. This is the place to read about dining out.

Usenet:
Newsgroup: **rec.food.restaurants**

Eating Out is Good

These days, more and more people who go to restaurants are going to restaurants. (Strange, but true.)

But where's the best place to go?
No need to guess.

Before you spend your hard-earned cash for stuff to put in your mouth, check with your friends on

rec.food.restaurants

Restaurants on the Web

Check out the menus of these fine restaurants on the Web. See their menus, gift catalogs, and maybe even fax in your order! The restaurants include the Binary Cafe in Toronto, Burk's Creole & Cajun in Seattle, Red Sage in Washington, D.C., the London Underground Pub, Fuji-Ya in Hardwood Heights, Illinois, and many others.

World Wide Web:
URL: **http://www.yahoo.com/Economy/Business/Corporations/Restaurants/**

Snapple on the Net

This is the first automatic Snapple delivery system on the Web! The page has an image of Ralph, a Snapple lover, as well as images of the wrappers for orange, lemon, and raspberry flavored ice teas. These images are actually buttons that you can click for some great sound effects. Be ready by having a glass of at least an 8-ounce capacity nearby — you won't have much warning. There are also links to scratch and lick samplers.

World Wide Web:
URL: **http://pcd.stanford.edu/~mogens/ snapple.html**

Sourdough

The best thing in the world: sourdough bread as originally baked in San Francisco. Discuss the ins and outs of making this tricky but pleasingly addictive foodstuff.

Usenet:
Newsgroup: **rec.food.sourdough**

Spam

To quote *The Encyclopedia of Bad Taste* by Jane and Michael Stern, "Spam is ground pork shoulder and ground ham combined with salt, sugar, water and sodium nitrite, stuffed into a can, sealed, cooked, dried, dated, and shipped." It's hard to explain the world's love affair with this most versatile of foods. Join Spam enthusiasts as they debate the pros and cons of this 20th century culinary wonder. As the Sterns point out, "Next to spit-roasted dog meat, Spam is just about Korea's favorite delicacy."

Usenet:
Newsgroup: **alt.spam**
Newsgroup: **alt.spam.conspiracy**

Sporks

Simple, yet utilitarian. Graceful in its functional elegance. Along with lasers and automatic bread slicers, the Spork is one of the greatest inventions of the Modern Age. (The Modern Age officially began the day that Alice Cooper first appeared on Hollywood Squares, bringing the culture of the 1970's Disco Era to its timely conclusion.) Fans of the Spork post laudatory comments on the merits of this plastic eating utensil.

Usenet:
Newsgroup: **alt.utensils.spork**

Sugar Cereals

Sweetness is as sweetness does. Start your day with a sugar-charged bang. Check out the latest scoop on sugar cereals and related issues of importance.

Usenet:
Newsgroup: **alt.food.sugar-cereals**

Sushi

What is it about small, strange hunks of biological material wrapped in seaweed that makes you want to put them in your mouth? It has been said that sushi is to the 1990s what roasted chunks of meat were to the 1530s. Still, you don't need to take our word for it. Your friends on Usenet are ever-ready to talk sushi-talk regardless of how compelling your needs may be.

Usenet:
Newsgroup: **alt.food.sushi**

Unusual Foods of the World

Pictures and details of a small selection of unusual foods from around the world, including snail livers, and Gatorade Spritzer.

World Wide Web:
URL: **http://town.hall.org/food/unusual.html**

Vegans

If it came out of an animal, vegans want no part of it. That means all the rich yummy foods are off limits — butter, milk, cheese, and eggs are among the things that will not pass a vegan's lips. This active forum is for vegans or aspiring vegans to share thoughts and ideas. Available in digest format as well.

Listserv Mailing List:
List Address: **vegan-l@vm.temple.edu**
Subscription Address: **listserv@vm.temple.edu**

Vegetarian Archives

General information on all aspects of vegetarianism, answers to common questions, vegetarian recipes, and a world guide to vegetarianism.

Anonymous FTP:
Address: **flubber.cs.umd.edu**
Path: **/other/tms/veg/***

Address: **rtfm.mit.edu**
Path: **/pub/usenet/rec.answers/vegetarian/faq**

A
B
C
D
E
F
G
H
I
J
K
L
M
N
O
P
Q
R
S
T
U
V
W
X
Y
Z

Vegetarianism

Is it worth living forever if you can't have a hot dog? That seems to be the central issue of our times, and here is the place to talk about it. Share your thoughts, hopes, dreams, and vegetarian recipes.

Internet Mailing List:
>List Address: **veggie@maths.bath.ac.uk**
>Subscription Address:
>>**veggie-request@maths.bath.ac.uk**

>List Address: **veggie@gibbs.oit.unc.edu**
>Subscription Address: **listserv@gibbs.oit.unc.edu**

Usenet:
>Newsgroup: **rec.food.veg**
>Newsgroup: **rec.food.veg.cooking**

Virtual Pub & Beer Emporium

Forget beer brewing, how about a little (or a lot) of beer drinking? Settle into the "tasting room" at the Pub to see current reviews of beer and the review archives as well. Find beer guides, pictures of collector beer glasses, results of beer contests, FAQs on tasting and measuring beer, Usenet archives, information on brewing mead, and links to brewing pages. See the German version of the Reinheitsgebot (Pure Beer Law of 1516) as well as the English translation.

World Wide Web:
>URL: **http://www.planetary.brown.edu:8080/virtual-pub/**

Wine

Tired of the pedestrian charms of beer? Move up to the big time where drinking is an art form and 1983 was a good year. Join the Bacchus society, wine lovers extraordinaire, and maybe even make your own homegrown vino. Oenophiles of the world unite: you have nothing to lose but your grains.

Usenet:
>Newsgroup: **alt.bacchus**
>Newsgroup: **alt.food.wine**
>Newsgroup: **rec.crafts.winemaking**

Need a refresher on using archie to find files? You can find a picture of practically anything in less than a minute. *The Internet Complete Reference* shows you how. This picture is **jemerson.gif**.

Wine Page

The Wine Page includes many interesting resources for wine lovers, including pictures of Wine Valley, links to tasting archives, other wine pages, the Virtual Tasting Group, the Wine Net Newsletter, and other items of interest.

World Wide Web:
>URL: **http://augustus.csscr.washington.edu/personal/bigstar-mosaic/wine.html**

FREEDOM

ACLU Reading Room

Speeches, publications, reports, legislative alerts, Supreme Court filings, and other information from the American Civil Liberties Union.

Gopher:
>Name: American Civil Liberties Union
>Address: **aclu.org**
>Choose: **Society, Law, Politics**
>>**I American Civil Liberties Union**

Hungry? Try Food and Drink. Hungry for Love? Try Romance.

Banned Computer Material

A list of computer material that has been banned or challenged in academic institutions.

Anonymous FTP:
Address: **ftp.eff.org**
Path: **/pub/CAF/banned***

Address: **ftp.spies.com**
Path: **/Library/Article/Rights/banned.91**

Gopher:
Name: Internet Wiretap
Address: **wiretap.spies.com**
Choose: **Wiretap Online Library**
| **Articles**
| **Civil Rights and Liberties**
| **Banned Computer Material of 1991**

Censored Books and News Stories

A list of more than fifty books that were challenged, burned, or banned somewhere in the United States in the last fifteen years, and the top ten censored news stories from Project Censored in 1989.

Anonymous FTP:
Address: **ftp.spies.com**
Path: **/Library/Article/Rights/censored.***

Gopher:
Name: Internet Wiretap
Address: **wiretap.spies.com**
Choose: **Wiretap Online Library**
| **Articles**
| **Civil Rights and Liberties**
| **Censored Books (and Waldenbooks Promotion)**

Civil Rights and Liberties

Articles about instances of censorship, banned computer material, firearms, copyright laws, and legal information.

Anonymous FTP:
Address: **ftp.spies.com**
Path: **/Library/Article/Rights/***

Gopher:
Name: Internet Wiretap
Address: **wiretap.spies.com**
Choose: **Wiretap Online Library**
| **Articles**
| **Civil Rights and Liberties**

File Room

A large collection of occurrences of censorship, mostly in art or public display and performances. It's best if you have a graphical browser to look at this site, but it's not absolutely necessary. You can still read the case histories and descriptions of the artwork. You can also add your own information if you know of a significant case of censorship. The information is global, concerning censorship issues around the world.

See also: Art

World Wide Web:
URL: **http://fileroom.aaup.uic.edu/FileRoom/ documents/homepage.html**

Censorship, Boo!

All of us, of course, are against censorship (except when the censored item is something that offends *us*). If you've got a hankering to see what sorts of things people don't want you to see, visit *The File Room*. (Actually, the most important act of censorship of modern times occurred when "They" would not let us explain the real meaning of "rtfm" in *The Internet Complete Reference*.)

Free Speech

A forum for discussing free speech issues. Topics here include current and historical issues in freedom of expression, reviews of recent books and articles related to free speech, constitutional interpretation, research opportunities, privacy, censorship, and other areas relating to freedom of expression in the United States and elsewhere.

Listserv Mailing List:
List Address: **amend1-l@uafsysb.uark.edu**
Subscription Address: **listserv@uafsysb.uark.edu**

A B C D E F G H I J K L M N O P Q R S T U V W X Y Z

Freedom of Information Act

A publication from the federal government that explains to citizens how to use the Freedom of Information Act and the Privacy Act of 1974.

Anonymous FTP:
Address: **ftp.spies.com**
Path: **/Gov/foia.cit**

Gopher:
Name: Internet Wiretap
Address: **wiretap.spies.com**
Choose: **Government Docs (US & World)
| Citizens Guide to Using the FOIA**

Liberty Web

Links to various places on the Web that concern freedom, Libertarian Party Headquarters, selected articles from *Reason* magazine, information on firearms and the NRA, *Terrorist's Handbook*, cypherpunk and cryptography home pages.

World Wide Web:
URL: **ftp://ftp.netcom.com/pub/jamesd/world.html**

Piss List

A compilation of companies that do some form of Human Quality tests that violate your right to privacy. Who wants urine? Who wants blood? Who wants to crack open your skull and look inside? Helpful hint: Whatever happens, you can always say that you didn't inhale.

World Wide Web:
URL: **http://rafferty.com/~piss/**

FREQUENTLY ASKED QUESTIONS

IRC Questions

Once you immerse yourself in an IRC environment, so many questions are going to come up about all the commands you can use whether they are simple beginning commands or complicated issues like creating an IRC robot. FAQs are available, but it's also nice to know there is a more interactive option. Post your questions on this newsgroup and not only will you get the answer, but you will meet some interesting people in the process.

Usenet:
Newsgroup: **alt.irc.questions**

Newsgroups

The reason for frequently asked question lists is that newcomers to a Usenet discussion group often seem to ask the same questions. Veterans don't mind answering new questions, but nobody wants to explain, over and over and over, what "Unix" means.

Through the years, many newsgroups have developed a frequently asked question (FAQ) list that contains all the common questions that have been answered repeatedly in that group. Some FAQ lists are so large as to be divided into several parts. Whenever you start reading a new group, look for a FAQ list to orient yourself. More important, before you post a question to the group, check the FAQ list to see if your question has already been answered.

The people who maintain FAQ lists post them regularly, not only to their own newsgroup, but to special newsgroups that have been created just to hold FAQ lists and related material. The **news.answers** group contains FAQ lists from every possible source. The other **.answers** groups contain FAQ lists for their respective hierarchies. For example, **comp.answers** contains computer FAQ lists. When you have a spare moment, check out these groups, especially **alt.answers**. You will see a lot of interesting and strange stuff that you might never encounter otherwise. These groups contain not only FAQ lists, but important summaries of information not tied to specific newsgroups.

Usenet:
Newsgroup: **alt.answers**
Newsgroup: **comp.answers**
Newsgroup: **misc.answers**
Newsgroup: **news.answers**
Newsgroup: **rec.answers**
Newsgroup: **sci.answers**
Newsgroup: **soc.answers**
Newsgroup: **talk.answers**

Usenet FAQ List Archive

It's the middle of the night. An emergency arises that requires you to read one of the Usenet frequently asked question lists. So you fire up your favorite newsreader program only to find that the article you want has expired. Never you mind. Many of the Usenet FAQ lists are available from the Usenet archive maintained by Jonathan Kamens.

Anonymous FTP:
Address: **rtfm.mit.edu**
Path: **/pub/usenet/news.answers/***

FUN

Adventures of Cyber Cat

Every time you connect to this web page, you get a new picture showing the adventures of Cyber Cat.

World Wide Web:
URL: **http://www.cityscape.co.uk/cgi-bin/cyber-cat**

Anagrams

Anagrams are something you can do no matter where you are or what is going on. For instance, if you're in traffic and there is nothing on the radio but ads for hair replenishing cream, you can make up all sorts of anagrams by rearranging the letters of all of Henry the VIII's wives' names. This will be good practice so when you are at a party and word gets around that you are the county anagram champion you will be able to demonstrate your talents with grace and elegance.

Usenet:
Newsgroup: **alt.anagrams**

ASCII Art Bazaar

It's much more fun to read a book or story that has pictures in it. (That's why men's magazines seem to be so popular.) See what creative people have done using ASCII art to illustrate stories they've written.

Gopher:
Name: The ASCII Art Bazaar
Address: **twinbrook.cis.uab.edu**
Choose: **The Continuum**
 | The ASCII Art Bazaar

DO YOU LIKE **free pictures?** Take a moment to visit the ASCII ART BAZAAR. Find out why ASCII art is now an accepted topic among the New York intelligentsia, and why ASCII animation may be added to the next Cannes Film Festival.

Ask Joe

Forget Abby, Ann, and Miss Manners. Ask Joe for advice on any kind of question. Even if he isn't helpful, he will at least take your mind off the problem.

World Wide Web:
URL: **http://fishwrap.mit.edu/News/AskJoe/AskJoe.html**

Check out the **Big Fun Lists** and you can have fun, fun, fun until Daddy takes your Internet account away.

Barney's Page

A humorous page dedicated to this big purple TV star. It includes Barney's Chant, a forms-based question and answer room, photos, cartoons, ASCII images, many short **.au** audio sound clips, a case history, and links to other sites with Barney material.

World Wide Web:
URL: **http://www.galcit.caltech.edu/~ta/barney/**

Big Fun Lists

Big fun in the Internet. Lists of fun resources on the net from Uncle Bert and Conan.

Anonymous FTP:
Address: **owl.nstn.ns.ca**
Path: **/pub/netinfo/bigfun.***

Address: **quartz.rutgers.edu**
Path: **/pub/internet/sites/internet-bigfunlist.gz**

**No need to be bored.
Try Parties and
Entertainment.**

A
B
C
D
E
F
G
H
I
J
K
L
M
N
O
P
Q
R
S
T
U
V
W
X
Y
Z

Bluedog Can Count

Let Bluedog solve all your research problems. Fill in the simple mathematical formula in the form provided, and Blue Dog will bark the result for you.

World Wide Web:
URL: **http://hp8.ini.cmu.edu:5550/bdf.html**

Boredom

Bored? Share your boredom with others who have nothing better to do than listen.

Internet Relay Chat:
Channel: **#bored**

Cartoon Collection

This web page features a small, but exquisite collection of cartoons displayed as in-line images.

World Wide Web:
URL: **http://acorn.educ.nottingham.ac.uk/ ShellCent/distract/cartoons/**

Chat

Looking for some conversation? Here are a couple of great places to come and chew the fat with other Internet folks.

Internet Relay Chat:
Channel: **#chat**
Channel: **#hello**

Confession Booth

With this web page, almost anyone can feel like a Catholic. Confess your sins by checking the appropriate boxes and receiving your penance.

World Wide Web:
URL: **http://anther.learning.cs.cmu.edu/ priest.html**

Spare time? Take a look at Games

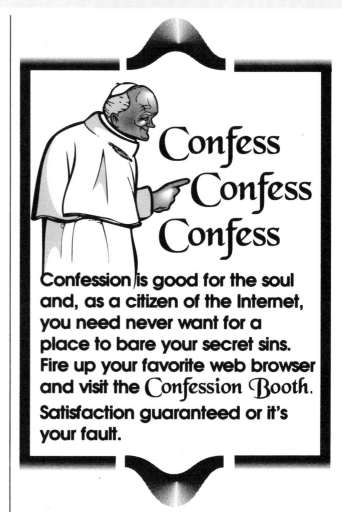

Confession is good for the soul and, as a citizen of the Internet, you need never want for a place to bare your secret sins. Fire up your favorite web browser and visit the Confession Booth. Satisfaction guaranteed or it's your fault.

Conversational Hypertext Access Technology

CHAT (Conversational Hypertext Access Technology) is a natural language database query engine. Take part in a simulated conversation with a dragon or a woman named Alice. They correctly understand just about anything you say to them. Be careful, though: it takes skill and cunning to talk the dragon out of flaming you on the spot.

Telnet:
Address: **debra.dgbt.doc.ca**
Port: **3000**

Cool Site of the Day

Every day, this page offers a link to a cool site on the Web. You never know where you are going until you get there. Every midnight, the link is changed so that you can have a constant new web fix, every day! Check out today's cool site! There are also links to previous cool sites.

World Wide Web:
URL: **http://www.infi.net/cool.html**

Crosswords

Dictionary, word-list books, technical paper guides, software pointers, solution tips, and other material about crosswords.

Anonymous FTP:
Address: **rtfm.mit.edu**
Path: **/pub/usenet/news.answers/crossword-faq/***

CyberNet

This home page declares that newsgroups have become inundated with stuffy people who are boring, and that *their* site offers lots of fun stuff to combat boredom. They have selections categorized as hazardous, funky, kitsch, noise, and popular culture, so there is something interesting and strange enough for everyone.

World Wide Web:
URL: **http://venus.mcs.com/~flowers/html/cybernet.html**

Cybersight

An information arcade that makes the Net an even cooler place to be than it already is. This page offers a "What You Want List" with sections on cybversive stuff, art, electric dinosaurs, noise, kitsch, sports and leisure.

Note: After connecting to this web site, select **Cybersight**.

World Wide Web:
URL: **http://cybersight.com/**

Digital Movies

If you are planning your hot date for Saturday night, consider catching a movie. Or more than one, even. Impress your date with your technical prowess by checking out these places on the Internet where you can see digital movies. It's fun, it's safe and best of all, it's free.

See also: Computers: Technology

World Wide Web:
URL: **http://www.digital.com/gnn/special/drivein/screening.room.html**

Disney

Interesting facts, animated feature film guides, character notes, event news, and more about Disney movies, Disneyland, Walt Disney and the magic kingdom he created.

Anonymous FTP:
Address: **rtfm.mit.edu**
Path: **/pub/usenet/news.answers/disney-faq/***

Usenet:
Newsgroup: **rec.arts.disney**

Disneyland: The Real Poop

Going to Disneyland is such a Big Deal that it's silly not to be prepared. Don't even think about stepping into the Magic Kingdom without first reading the **Disney** frequently asked question list. (When you go there, see if you can find the secret Club 33, the only place in Disneyland where where liquor is served.)

Distractions

A web page containing various entertaining items of varying degrees of educational value. It includes cartoons, humourous tutorial computer projects and more.

World Wide Web:
URL: **http://acorn.educ.nottingham.ac.uk/ShellCent/distract/**

Druid Science Reading Room

The Druid Science Reading Room has nothing to do with Druids and very little to do with science. It does, however, have lots to do with fun and reading. It includes such articles as "The Shadow of the Shark and Surfin' Sin Jonz," the argument against artificial belligerence, Grandma Death column, Cyberia, and Dr. Bean.

World Wide Web:
URL: **http://www.wimsey.com/Generality/Druid.html**

Dysfunctional Family Circus

A parody on *The Family Circus*. They offer do-it-yourself manipulation of *Family Circus* cartoons. This is a family for the '90s.

World Wide Web:
URL: **http://www.cis.upenn.edu/~mjd/dfc/dfc.html**

A
B
C
D
E
F
G
H
I
J
K
L
M
N
O
P
Q
R
S
T
U
V
W
X
Y
Z

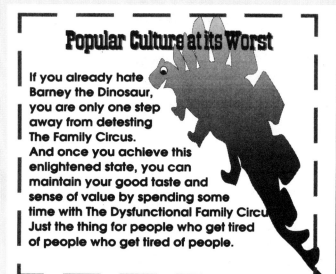

Popular Culture at its Worst

If you already hate Barney the Dinosaur, you are only one step away from detesting The Family Circus. And once you achieve this enlightened state, you can maintain your good taste and sense of value by spending some time with The Dysfunctional Family Circu Just the thing for people who get tired of people who get tired of people.

Froggy Page

Froggy pictures, froggy sounds in **.au** format, froggy tales, songs of the frog, articles from *Scientific Amphibian*, details of famous frogs such as Kermit from the Muppets, froggy ftp archives, and much more to do with these little green guys.

World Wide Web:
URL: **http://www.cs.yale.edu/HTML/YALE/CS/ HyPlans/loosemore-sandra/froggy.html**

Get Hooked on the Internet

A list with links to many handy facts and fun stuff that you will find yourself using on a daily basis. Includes "Things you do almost daily" and "Things you do occasionally" sections, offering links to the latest news, stock quotes, movie details, television listings, pictures, sports, and much more.

World Wide Web:
URL: **http://stingray.ess.harris.com/ gethooked.html**

Happy People

Tired of talking to crotchety people? Want to talk with happy people, or just to be silly and not have to feel guilty about it? These IRC channels are places where you can hang out and be yourself. Check out the **#penpals** channel if you'd like to find others with whom you can correspond.

Internet Relay Chat:
Channel: **#happy**
Channel: **#penpals**
Channel: **#silly**

Hypermedia Star

"So you want to be an Internet Hypermedia Star?" A humorous sing-along guide to how to become an Internet Hypermedia Star, including links to web browsers, HTML guides, NSF charts, NCSA's "What's New" and more.

World Wide Web:
URL: **http://155.187.10.12/fun/ hypermedia-star.html**

Internet Candy Dish

When you connect to this URL, five random sweetheart images are presented, complete with those cute little quotes on the front. "Be Good to Me," "As You Like It," "Jet Set," "Dearest," and "You're So Cool."

World Wide Web:
URL: **http://orange-room.cc.nd.edu/ToyBox/ ICD/ICD.exe**

Internet Hunt

A monthly scavenger hunt for facts and trivia on and about the net. Be the first to submit the correct answers to the questions and win fame and notoriety. Participate in the individual category, or work with friends in the team category. Look for the hunt questions on Usenet.

Anonymous FTP:
Address: **ftp.cic.net**
Path: **/pub/hunt/***

Gopher:
Name: CICNet
Address: **gopher.cic.net**
Choose: **The Internet Hunt**

Usenet:
Newsgroup: **alt.internet.services**

IRC Bar

Come drink and chat in the IRC bar. Descriptions of over sixty cocktails are available from the barman who is more than happy to serve or even sober you up. The web site offers gossip, news, help, and gif pictures, and plans of the real-life meetings that the bar's frequenters hold every so often. Come drink and be merry in the bar that never sleeps. Cheers!

Internet Relay Chat:
Channel: **#ircbar**

World Wide Web:
URL: **http://http2.brunel.ac.uk:8080/ ~cs93jtl/IRCBar.html**

Joe's Adventure

Wouldn't it be fun to be omnipotent just for a little while? Get a taste of that power by having total control over Joe's life. You can operate him by multiple choice or, if your browser supports forms, you can simply write out what Joe has to do for the day.

World Wide Web:
    URL: **http://cybersight.com/cgi-bin/cs/idic/joe/**

Juggling

Several large collections of information, news, FAQs, animations, publications, help, programs, and archives to do with juggling. Learn how to juggle the cascade, fountain, or shower patterns in no time.

Anonymous FTP:
    Address: **moocow.cogsci.indiana.edu**
    Path: **/pub/juggling/***

World Wide Web:
    URL: **http://www.hal.com/~nathan/Juggling/**
    URL: **http://www.hal.com/services/juggle/**

Madlibs

If your Web browser has forms, you will have loads of fun filling in nouns, adjectives, and other words out of which the computer will weave a story. This is just like the paper Madlibs, only you don't need a group of friends to play it.

World Wide Web:
    URL: **http://www.mit.edu:8001/madlib**

Marshmallow Peanut Circus Home Page

The Marshmallow Peanut Circus is a geekhouse located at 211 Pearl St., Santa Cruz, California. The house is painted screaming orange — you can't miss it. This site contains details about the folks who live there, their nutty buddies, Santa Cruz information, their "cool pages," and links to other geekhouses.

World Wide Web:
    URL: **http://samsara.circus.com/**

Movie of the Week

You no longer have to wait in line for tickets and then wait in line for popcorn and crawl over people who won't move their legs to let you by. And more importantly, you won't have to worry about your feet sticking to the floor because of gooey cola residue. Catch the Movie of the Week on your computer. Short digital movies are highlighted at this web page and made available for viewing.

World Wide Web:
    URL: **http://www.digital.com/gnn/special/**
    drivein/mov.of.week.html

Multiple Choice Quiz

This weekly quiz is a blast for trivia buffs. Answer questions on a variety of topics—music, movies, culture, history, women—and let the computer keep score. Make up questions of your own for other people to answer.

World Wide Web:
    URL: **http://altair.herts.ac.uk:8000/html/**
    WebQuiz.html

NetBoy

A weird but cool comic strip about the adventures of NetBoy. There is a new strip each week, and as one happy reader said, "NetBoy is 200k this week... but worth every penny."

World Wide Web:
    URL: **http://www.interaccess.com/netboy.html**

Nicecafe

A nice little cafe in the realms of IRC, where people sit and watch the world go by.

Internet Relay Chat:
    Channel: **#nicecafe**

Nude Beaches

Lists of some magnificent beaches, hot springs, and parks around the world where clothing is optional.

Anonymous FTP:
    Address: **rtfm.mit.edu**
    Path: **/pub/usenet/rec-answers/nude-faq/***

Orange Room Toy Box

A collection of unique toys and resources. Includes sounds, cartoons, candy hearts, images, and more.

World Wide Web:
    URL: **http://orange-room.cc.nd.edu/ToyBox/**
    ToyBox.html

Pawn Shop

Come and browse the fine wares in this pawn shop. You don't need any money here, since it operates on the honor system. If you see something you like, select it from the list, and it will be removed from the shop. If you have something to sell, you enter it in the form provided, with an optional URL that points to a description of your object.

World Wide Web:
    URL: **http://hp8.ini.cmu.edu:5550/cgi-bin/**
    pawnshop

A B C D E F G H I J K L M N O P Q R S T U V W X Y Z

Penn and Teller

Even if you can't do it, magic is fun to watch, and Penn and Teller are masters of the trade. Read interviews, see pictures, and get information on upcoming gigs of this mismatched but perfect-for-each-other duo.

See also: Hobbies

World Wide Web:
> URL: **http://www.portal.com/~gambler/ PennandTeller/penn-n-teller.html**

Pizza Server

Ever spent a late night coding or MUDing and get the hankering for a steaming hot pizza? (Or even a stale, cold pizza?) Well, now you can order that customized pizza you have been wanting and get it within a delivery time that puts Domino's to shame. Send for the help file to see how it all works.

Mail:
> Address: **pizza@ecst.csuchico.edu**
> Subject: **help**

Poeticus

Collection of poetry and other literature articles, including "The Chime of Ages," the epic musings of a Discordian bard, an Internet writing game, and a discourse on literature and the new technology of hypertext.

World Wide Web:
> URL: **http://daneel.acns.nwu.edu:8082/ poeticus/poeticus.html**

Puzzles

Hundreds of puzzles to open your mind, complete with solutions. If six cats can kill six rats in six minutes, how many cats does it take to kill one rat in one minute?

Anonymous FTP:
> Address: **rtfm.mit.edu**
> Path: **/pub/usenet/news.answers/puzzles/***

Pyramix

A solution to the Pyramix, the tetrahedral pyramid puzzle where each face is divided into nine segments, written by the Oxford University Programming Research Group.

Anonymous FTP:
> Address: **ftp.comlab.ox.ac.uk**
> Path: **/pub/Cards/Pyramix.Z**

QuarkWeb

A secret facility located hundreds of feet below the Nevada desert in an abandoned UFO research facility. The supercomputers here that once calculated top-secret UFO data have been retrofitted with the latest TCP/IP networking hardware to provide the world with access to the legendary QuarkWeb node sites — a collection of unique, fun web pages.

World Wide Web:
> URL: **http://alfred1.u.washington.edu:8080/ ~roland/quarkweb/quarkweb.html**

Recreational Arts

A collection of fun and interesting recreational documents, articles, and factsheets.

Gopher:
> Name: NYSERNet
> Address: **nysernet.org**
> Choose: **Reference Desk**
> | **Arts and Recreation**
> | **Recreational Arts**

Roller Coasters

All sorts of goodies about roller coasters, including images, animations, a FAQ, and descriptions and reviews of parks and coasters.

Anonymous FTP:
> Address: **gboro.rowan.edu**
> Path: **/pub/Coasters/***

Rubik's Cube

A solution to this mind-bending 3x3x3 puzzle cube, written by Jonathan Bowen of the Oxford University Programming Research Group.

Anonymous FTP:
> Address: **ftp.comlab.ox.ac.uk**
> Path: **/pub/Cards/Rubik.Z**

Rubik's Revenge

A solution to Rubik's Revenge, the 4x4x4 puzzle cube, written by the Oxford University Programming Research Group. Astound your friends with your ability to solve this master puzzle.

Anonymous FTP:
> Address: **ftp.comlab.ox.ac.uk**
> Path: **/pub/Cards/Revenge.Z**

Silicon Sister's Java Hut

Here's an interesting page laid out as a hut with rooms paneled in light pine that smells softly of the forest. You can wander around the hut and look at the sights and sounds, including the bulletin board, table, salon, gallery, and the rest of the hut.

World Wide Web:
URL: **http://www.indra.net/julie/ssjh/ main/main.html**

Time Wasting

It's a moral imperative that everyone spend at least part of every day wasting some time or else we would have all this extra time that we would have to fill or worse — recycle. If you have too much time on your hands, waste a little of it here learning new ways to creatively fritter a good portion of your day away.

Usenet:
Newsgroup: **alt.timewasters**

Toys

Admit it. You love toys. Not only are they fun, but they are a great thing to keep you busy so you don't have to work. The only thing that could possibly be better than playing with toys is actually getting paid to play with toys. Enter the world's largest playroom and meet other people who love toys. These groups cover toys from the simplest plastic legos to the most complicated technical gadgetry.

Usenet:
Newsgroup: **alt.toys.high-tech**
Newsgroup: **alt.toys.lego**
Newsgroup: **alt.toys.transformers**
Newsgroup: **rec.toys.lego**
Newsgroup: **rec.toys.misc**

Universe of Discourse

A great page of words, pictures, and toys, including "Guess the Animal" game, Hexapawn, the Dysfunctional Family Circus, and The Temptation of Saint Anthony, where the focus is on the seven deadly sins (envy, gluttony, greed, lust, pride, sloth and wrath).

World Wide Web:
URL: **http://www.cis.upenn.edu/~mjd/**

URouLette

URouLette is a random URL generator. By clicking on the picture of the floating roulette wheel, you are connected to a random location on the Web. You won't know where you're going until you get there.

World Wide Web:
URL: **http://kuhttp.cc.ukans.edu/cwis/ organizations/kucia/uroulette/uroulette.html**

Void

"If we're not in your hotlist, then you suck." The void is an interesting place to hang out, with amusements such as the barking Blue Dog, a Pawn Shop, a Transporter Room controlled by Kirk and Picard zapping you to the far outreach of Web space, a lunch server, and some radio stuff.

World Wide Web:
URL: **http://hp8.ini.cmu.edu:5550/**

Walking Man

A web writing game that forms a collaborative visualization, a hyperfiction dreamscape, of a guy who is walking, perceiving everything along the way until he meets his end. Read the story and add your own tales to the legend.

World Wide Web:
URL: **http://daneel.acns.nwu.edu:8082/poeticus/ walk/walkhome.html**

Web Addict's Pop-Culture Scavenger Hunt

Play detective on the Internet. Get a list of easy, medium, hard, or impossible questions and start hunting for the answers that will give you the password to the winner's page where you can record your name and a message for posterity. Hint: the impossible questions really are impossible.

World Wide Web:
URL: **http://www.galcit.caltech.edu/ ~ta/wwwhunt.html**

Whole Internet Scavenger Hunt

Join the Whole Internet Scavenger Hunt (WISH) and try to be the first to acquire all the requisite Internet gems on this trek through the Internet.

World Wide Web:
URL: **http://zaphod.cc.ttu.ee/vrainn/whome.html**

GAMES

AD&D Discussion

Everything to do with *Advanced Dungeons and Dragons,* especially for Dungeon Masters.

Internet Relay Chat:
Channel: **#ad&d**

Addventure!

Play this "choose your own adventure" game with rooms that have been created by previous players of the game. While there is a definite starting point, the game diverges into a wide variety of unknown plot twists. You select which rooms and paths you wish to investigate by clicking on the hypertext links. Unix source code and full instructions are also available here.

World Wide Web:
URL: **http://acm.rpi.edu/~prisoner/addv-docs/**

Advanced Dungeons and Dragons

Lots of Advanced Dungeons and Dragons role-playing material, including spell and priest books, campaigns, modules, new monsters, new spells, rules, interactive games, comments, and anything else to do with AD&D.

Anonymous FTP:
Address: **ftp.cs.pdx.edu**
Path: **/pub/frp/***

Listserv Mailing List:
List Address: **adnd-l@utarlvm1.uta.edu**
Subscription Address: **listserv@utarlvm1.uta.edu**

Advanced Dungeons and Dragons Character Creator

A Windows 3.1 program you can use to create new characters for *Advanced Dungeons and Dragons.*

Anonymous FTP:
Address: **ftp.iastate.edu**
Path: **/pub/frp/incoming/Programs/Dos/**
  creator.zip

Aerial Combat Simulation

A multiplayer network-based aerial combat simulation game. With ACM, players engage in air-to-air combat against one another using heat seeking missiles and cannons.

Note: ACM is a client/server program for Unix systems that comes complete with source code, and is as much for demonstrating client/server technology as it is for fun.

Anonymous FTP:
Address: **ftp.x.org**
Path: **/contrib/games/acm-*.tar.Z**

Anime Video Games

A list of anime-related video games available for many game systems. Includes a list of U.S. stores that sell Japanese video game cartridges.

Anonymous FTP:
Address: **romulus.rutgers.edu**
Path: **/pub/anime/misc/anime-games.Z**

Apogee Games

A multitude of fantastic games from Apogee, including such favorites as Commander Keen and Cosmo.

Anonymous FTP:
Address: **ftp.std.com**
Path: **/src/msdos/games/apogee/***

Arcade Video Game Tricks

A large list of tricks and cheats for many of the classic video arcade games. Lists are arranged by skill level (i.e., beginner, intermediate, and advanced).

Anonymous FTP:
Address: **ftp.spies.com**
Path: **/game_archive/cheatList/***

Gopher:
Name: Internet Wiretap
Address: **wiretap.spies.com**
Choose: **Wiretap Online Library**
  | Mass Media
  | Games and Video Games
  | Definitive Arcade Video Game Cheats

Atari Archive

Huge archive for all Atari computers, including the 8-bit machines, ST range, Falcon, and Lynx.

Anonymous FTP:
Address: **atari.archive.umich.edu**
Path: **/atari/***

Atari Jaguar Game Archive

This web page has links to lots of game FAQs, cheats for games, product information, contests, tips, and links to game pages.

World Wide Web:
URL: **http://www2.ecst.csuchico.edu/ ~jschlich/Jaguar**

Atomic Cafe

The way cool home page of Avalon Hill Games, the producers of *Operation Crusader* and other great games.

World Wide Web:
URL: **http://atomic.neosoft.com/Atomic.html**

Autospamosaurus

Autospamosaurus is a netrek hockey playing robot. Download the source code for Autospamosaurus and improve it yourself.

World Wide Web:
URL: **http://www.arl.wustl.edu/~flan/ Autospamosaurus/Welcome.html**

Backgammon Server

Play backgammon with others around the world via the Internet.

Telnet:
Address: **fraggel65.mdstud.chalmers.se**
Port: **4321**
Login: **guest**

Backgammon with Strangers

These days you have to be careful who you mix with. Playing backgammon in person presents all kinds of potential problems. For example, someone might sneeze on you and give you pneumonia, or your opponent could get mad and stab you with an ice pick.

Much better to play it safe: telnet to the *Backgammon Server,* where you can depend on the kindness of strangers. Moreover, you can play in your underwear and no one will care.

Battleships

Play Battleships through the Web, and if you've got what it takes, all shall remember your name in the Hall of Fame.

World Wide Web:
URL: **http://aurora.york.ac.uk/~steer/ cgi-bin/bships_win.sh**

Bizarre Board Game

Rules, instructions, and board diagrams for playing *T.B., the Board Game*, a game that duplicates all the action of a typical month on the Usenet newsgroup **talk.bizarre**.

Anonymous FTP:
Address: **ftp.spies.com**
Path: **/Library/Fringe/Weird/bizarre.gam**

Gopher:
Name: Internet Wiretap
Address: **wiretap.spies.com**
Choose: **Wiretap Online Library**
| **Fringes of Reason**
| **Very Strange**
| **The Talk.Bizarre Board Game**

A B C D E F G H I J K L M N O P Q R S T U V W X Y Z

Blackjack

If you can't make it to a casino this weekend, this is the next best thing. Play Blackjack with other Internet folks and become a Net billionaire or downright penniless. There are help files available and records are kept of rankings, cash won and lost, top players, and other table statistics. Join the table today.

Internet Relay Chat:
Channel: **#blackjack**

Board Game Rules and Information

Rules, rule variations, reviews, clubs, distributors, charts, and more about board games from around the world. This web page caters mainly to family and strategy games.

World Wide Web:
URL: **http://web.kaleida.com/u/tidwell/ GameCabinet.html**

Boggle

The robot on this channel hosts a game patterned after the popular Boggle word game. You are presented with a grid of letters, and you must form words that are at least three letters long, created out of adjoining letters. Full instructions are available from the bot online.

Internet Relay Chat:
Channel: **#boggle**

Bolo

Bolo is a multiplayer graphical networked realtime tank battle game for the Macintosh that you play against opponents over the Internet. Read the FAQ or check out the web pages for more information.

Anonymous FTP:
Address: **rtfm.mit.edu**
Path: **/pub/usenet/news.answers/games/bolo-faq**

Telnet:
Address: **gwis.circ.gwu.edu**
Port: **50000**

World Wide Web:
URL: **http://compstat.wharton.upenn.edu:8001/ ~frazier/Bolo/BoloHome.html**
URL: **http://www.uio.no/~mwatz/bolo/**

Bolo Tracker

A program that keeps track of and reports all the Bolo games currently under way, including the number of players and sides, as well as the number of neutral bases and pills available. It also gives addresses and IP numeric addresses to join these games.

Telnet:
Address: **gwis.circ.gwu.edu**
Port: **1234**

The World of Bolo

Bolo is a magnificent computer game–developed by a programmer named Stuart Cheshire–in which you play against other people over a network. Bolo is like chess in that it is simple to learn, but difficult to master. There are Bolo players (and fanatics) all over the Internet who have developed sophisticated systems of strategies and ethos, and whose devotion to this pastime transcends the ordinary.

The idea of Bolo is to control a tank that travels around a landscape (called a "map") containing trees, water, swamps, roads and so on. The map also contains "pillboxes" and "bases", structures which have certain characteristics and important strategic value. Your tank has bullets and shields, which you can use for offense and defense, respectively.

It takes a while to learn how to play Bolo well, but if you like strategy and arcade games, any time you put in will be well repaid. Remember, you play in real time against other people, and much of the strategy involves making (and breaking) alliances, and anticipating the actions of the other players. It is not unknown to hear of serious players working in teams during 12-hour long games.

To play Bolo, you need (1) a Macintosh (and only a Macintosh), and (2) a network connection to other Bolo players. This connection can be on your local network or on the Internet. However, the Internet connection should be direct; a phone hookup, even with SLIP or PPP, will be too slow. Before you start, be sure to read the frequently asked question (FAQ) list and the documentation.

Bridge

Bridge is such a fun game for couples. Most men take up bridge when they get married and discover their wives won't let them watch football. The only thing left to do is to sit with another couple and play cards all night. Perfect your bridge skills so you can learn to play a killer game. If you're clever, you can even make it a contact sport so you won't even miss football.

World Wide Web:
 URL: **http://www.cs.vu.nl/users/staff/sater/ bridge/bridge-on-the-web.html**

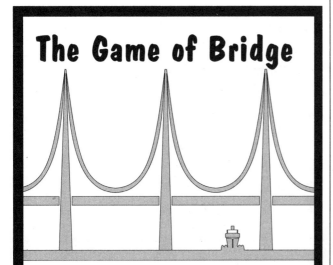

The Game of Bridge

Well, it's time to write another advertisement and I was asked to do one about the game of bridge. Actually, I don't normally even think of it as a game, per se. More like a thing that you build or perhaps even a structure. Okay, it's important to have bridges–after all, if we didn't have any bridges, all the cars on the highway would just fall off into nothingness, and you wouldn't be able to get across rivers and things–but still, I hardly see where that qualifies as a game. And I'm dashed if I can figure out why they wanted me to write an ad for the "game" of bridge. I mean, I know that there are people out there who build bridges and roads and things, civil engineers and what not, but why anyone would think that that belongs in an Internet book, or why it requires an advertisement... What's that? You don't mean building bridges? You mean the card game? Do you mean all that stuff with spades and hearts and two no-trump and so on? Oh... *that* bridge game.

Oh... Nevermind.

Car Wars

A mailing list about the Steve Jackson game Car Wars. Topics of discussion include rules, debates, tournament organization, and computer versions.

Listserv Mailing List:
 List Address: **carwar-l@ubvm.buffalo.edu**
 Subscription Address: **listserv@ubvm.buffalo.edu**

Chess Archives

Many freeware chess programs for different machines and operating systems, game scores, and other chess-related material.

Anonymous FTP:
 Address: **chess.uoknor.edu**
 Path: **/pub/chess/***

CHESS LOVERS, the Net has a lot for you. The Chess Archives are just full of things and stuff and so on.

Chess Discussion List

A mailing list for discussing chess, tournament announcements, specific interesting chess games, strategies, lore, and even programming chess logic.

Internet Mailing List:
 List Address: **chessnews@tssi.com**
 Subscription Address: **chessnews-request@tssi.com**

Chess Discussion and Play

Play chess with other Internet chess players using chess notation, or simply chat about tactics and the grandmasters.

Internet Relay Chat:
 Channel: **#chess**

A B C D E F G H I J K L M N O P Q R S T U V W X Y Z

Chess News

News, events, and up-to-date moves from the world of international chess.

Gopher:
>Name: Software Tool & Die
>Address: **gopher.std.com**
>Choose: **Periodicals, Magazines, and Journals**
> | **Middlesex News**
> | **Columns**
> | **Your Move (chess)**

Chess Servers

Meet and play chess with other chess enthusiasts throughout the world. Watch others play or join in and play a game of your own. You can save a game and return to it later.

Note: Mail addresses are for questions; telnet addresses are for playing.

Finger:
>Address: **chess@ics.onenet.net**

Mail:
>Address: **danke@daimi.aau.dk**
>Address: **tange@daimi.aau.dk**

Telnet:
>Address: **anemone.daimi.aau.dk**
>Port: **5000**
>Login: *your name*

>Address: **ics.onenet.net**
>Port: **5000**
>Login: *your name*

>Address: **iris4.metiu.ucsb.edu**
>Port: **5000**
>Login: *your name*

>Address: **lux.latrobe.edu.au**
>Port: **5000**
>Login: *your name*

>Address: **telnet dds.hacktic.nl**
>Port: **5000**
>Login: *your name*

Usenet:
>Newsgroup: **alt.chess.ics**

Jokes? Try Humor.

Cool words? Look in Quotations.

Chinese Chess

Here are two telnet ports for fans of the ancient game of chess—Chinese chess.

Telnet:
>Address: **coolidge.harvard.edu**
>Port: **5555**

>Address: **hippolytos.ud.chalmers.se**
>Port: **5555**

Civilization Editor

An editor for the popular DOS game called Civilization.

Anonymous FTP:
>Address: **cs.uwp.edu**
>Path: **/pub/msdos/romulus/misc/civedit3.zip**

Connect-4

Play this web game against the Cambridge computer, where the object is to be the first player to connect four of his or her colors in a row on the 7x6 square board.

World Wide Web:
>URL: **http://pelican.cl.cam.ac.uk/people/dlg10/c4.html**

Conquest

"Kill a man, you are an assassin. Kill millions of men, you are a conqueror." Play IRC Conquest, a strategy war game set in the Middle Ages — a time of battles, alliances, and spies.

Internet Relay Chat:
>Channel: **#conquest**

Core War

Offers documents, tutorials, source code, and system information for a variety of formats for Core War, a system where programs battle other programs and try to destroy each other in cyberspace.

Anonymous FTP:
>Address: **ftp.csua.berkeley.edu**
>Path: **/pub/corewar/***

Cribbage

Why work when you can play games? Play this fun card game on any Unix system. It's easy to extract and compile, and comes complete with directions and rules. The hard part is beating the computer.

Anonymous FTP:
Address: **ftp.std.com**
Path: **/src/games/cribbage/***

Crossfire

Crossfire is a multiplayer graphical arcade and adventure game for the X Window environment. Shooting and blowing things up is an excellent source of entertainment as well as a great stress-reliever. Fans of Crossfire discuss the development of the game as well.

Internet Mailing List:
List Address: **crossfire@ifi.uio.no**
Subscription Address: **crossfire-request@ifi.uio.no**

World Wide Web:
URL: **http://web.cs.city.ac.uk/games/crossfire/crossfire.html**

**Do you need a word?
Don't be cross.
Use a Crossword server.**

Crossword Servers

Internet servers devoted to crossword games such as Scrabble.

Telnet:
Address: **next7.cas.muohio.edu**
Port: **8888**

Address: **seabass.st.usm.edu**
Port: **7777**

CyberMUD Web Game

A text adventure with links that lead you through the story. Even though this is a mini-adventure, you don't save your character or keep score.

World Wide Web:
URL: **http://web.mit.edu/afs/athena.mit.edu/user/r/e/rei/WWW/GAME/in**

Diplomacy

A game you play by mail. The setting is pre-WWI Europe. Players send in their moves once a week and results are distributed each week. Conspire with your neighbors to conquer the Old World.

Mail:
Address: **judge@dipvax.dsto.gov.au**
Address: **judge@morrolan.eff.org**
Address: **judge@shrike.und.ac.za**

Diplomacy Discussion List

Some people were born to be diplomats. Then there are the rest of us who fumble our way around hoping we can get what we want without messing things up too badly. If you feel you were destined to be a great diplomat but can't seem to give up your job at the 7-11, then you can live vicariously through the game Diplomacy. This list coordinates with the play-by-mail game.

Listserv Mailing List:
List Address: **dipl-l@mitvma.mit.edu**
Subscription Address: **listserv@mitvma.mit.edu**

Doom Discussion and Realtime Chat

Have you been dreaming about Cacodemons, Imps, and Barons of Hell? If not, you're not playing enough Doom. Join with others hooked on this incredible, virtually real, shoot 'em all game from id Software. Ask about tips and tricks, find out where to get the game, or ask how to play the game against others over the Internet. The DoomServ bot on the IRC channel offers many files, including patches, FAQs, modem init strings, cheats, help files, editors, tutorials, and much more.

Internet Relay Chat:
Channel: **#doom**

Usenet:
Newsgroup: **alt.games.doom**
Newsgroup: **alt.games.doom.announce**
Newsgroup: **alt.games.doom.newplayers**

A B C D E F G H I J K L M N O P Q R S T U V W X Y Z

*If you are a **Doom** fan, the Net has lots of stuff for you. Then you can hunt and kill things to your heart's content in the privacy of your very own computer.*

Are you a know-it-all? Check in Trivia for tidbits of useless information.

Doom Information and Files

These unofficial Doom web pages offer the official Doom FAQ, tutorial guides, update news, Doom specifications, graphics from the game, great utilities available in zip format (such as map editors and level creators) to use with Doom, and links to other Doom related pages. The file specified at the ftp site is a text version of the FAQ file.

Anonymous FTP:
  Address: **archive.orst.edu**
  Path: **/pub/gaming/doom/text/dmfaq58.txt**

World Wide Web:
  URL: **ftp://ftp.netcom.com/pub/vhold/
    doom/doom.html**

  URL: **http://www.cedar.buffalo.edu/
    ~kapis-p/doom/DOOM.html**

DoomWeb Node

A web page dedicated to Doom, the 3-D, action-packed game from id Software. It offers version information, editing and hacking details, the Doom story, several FAQs, discussion forums, ftp sites, and links to other DoomWeb nodes.

World Wide Web:
  URL: **http://www.cs.hmc.edu/people/tj/docs/
    doom/**

Excerpt from the Net...

```
Newsgroup: alt.games.doom
Subject: Real Men Use the Keyboard

>>> I've played keyboarders before.  Pretty decent keyboarders.
>>> And you know what? I won.
>>> You also know what? I use the mouse.
>>> You also know what?
>>> I've never had less than a 3-to-1 frag ratio against a keyboarder...

>> I've also played decent keyboarders.
>> And you know what? I beat them too.
>> Your point?

> None of you are "real men".  Real men have better things to do than
> sit behind a computer (keyboard or mouse) wasting their lives away
> playing video games...

Right.  Real men are those who have nothing better to do than sit
behind a computer (keyboard or mouse) wasting their life away, telling
people that they waste their lives away playing video games...
```

Drool

In this text adventure, you are a dog. It's up to you what kind of dog — size, shape and gender. Once you have your doghood established, you can cavort off into the story where you will proceed through the harrowing experience of interacting with stick-throwing masters and children who look very tasty.

See also: Fun

World Wide Web:
URL: **http://www.mit.edu:8001/afs/athena.mit.edu/ user/j/b/jbreiden/game/entry.html**

Empire

Home of the famous game of Empire, the real-time strategy wargame played by up to eighty people across the Internet. This page offers Empire news, FAQs, and archive services to obtain the necessary software.

World Wide Web:
URL: **http://www.engg.ksu.edu/empire/ home.html**

Fascist

Fascist is a variation on the game called Nomic, which was invented by Peter Suber and described by Douglas Hofstadter in *Scientific American*. Fascist is designed to be completely undemocratic, at least to start with. There are a few initial rules, players propose new rules or rule changes, and the Imperious Emperor says whether they are accepted or not.

World Wide Web:
URL: **http://wombat.doc.ic.ac.uk/fascist/ fascist.html**

Flat Top

Combat is fun as long as it's simulated. There is little joy in being shot at in real life. With Flat Top, a World War II naval combat simulation game by Avalon Hill Game Company, you can have all the fun of combat without the worry or post-traumatic stress disorder. Join this list to talk about the game, scenarios, the bimonthly newsletter, and find out how you can even play Flat Top by electronic mail.

Internet Mailing List:
List Address: **flattop@aclcb.purdue.edu**
Subscription Address:
flattop-request@aclcb.purdue.edu

Game Bytes

Game reviews, interviews, reports, and actual screen shots from games can be found in this free electronic gaming magazine.

Anonymous FTP:
Address: **ftp.uml.edu**
Path: **/msdos/Games/Game_Bytes/***

Address: **ftp.wustl.edu**
Path: **/pub/msdos_uploads/games/Game_Bytes**

World Wide Web:
URL: **http://wcl-rs.bham.ac.uk/GameBytes**

Game Information Archive

Articles, rules, tips, spoilers, reviews, and FAQs for popular games and video games.

Anonymous FTP:
Address: **ftp.spies.com**
Path: **/Library/Media/Games/***

Gopher:
Name: Internet Wiretap
Address: **wiretap.spies.com**
Choose: **Wiretap Online Library**
  | **Mass Media**
  | **Games and Video Games**

Game of Life

Is it about life or is it just a game? Are we just cosmic chickens in the barnyard of the universe? Pit yourself against the skills of the computer in this game of logic and strategy and discover why nobody makes playing God a full-time job.

World Wide Web:
URL: **http://www.research.digital.com/nsl/ projects/life/life.html**

Game Server

Choose from a multitude of exciting online games including Bucks, Moria, Tetris, Sokoban, Reversi, Nethack, and many adventure games, including MUDs.

Gopher:
Name: University of Stuttgart
Address: **gopher.uni-stuttgart.de**
Choose: **Fun & Games**

A B C D E F G H I J K L M N O P Q R S T U V W X Y Z

Game Solutions

Hints and solutions to more games than you will ever have time to play. Covers hundreds of popular adventure games.

Anonymous FTP:
>Address: **ftp.funet.fi**
>Path: **/pub/doc/games/solutions/***

Games Domain

The Games Domain has pointers to frequently asked question lists, articles, game solutions and walk-throughs, ftp sites, company lists, and many other games-related links, and details are here for those who just like to play.

World Wide Web:
>URL: **http://wcl-rs.bham.ac.uk/GamesDomain**

Games and Recreation

This page sports an interactive list of computer games and recreational activities — mostly those that involve the Internet or the Web. The list has all the favorite titles like Paradise Netrek, Netrek, XPilot, Bolo, Nethack, Crossfire, Empire, and others. The page also has links to a vast list of MUDs and web pages with card games.

World Wide Web:
>URL: **http://www.cis.ufl.edu/~thoth/library/recreation.html**

GNU Chess

A chess complete with source code for X Window, Suntools, curses, ASCII, and IBMPC character set displays.

See also: Software: Unix

Anonymous FTP:
>Address: **aeneas.mit.edu**
>Path: **/pub/gnu/gnuchess***

>Address: **prep.ai.mit.edu**
>Path: **/pub/gnu/gnuchess***

>Address: **sunsite.unc.edu**
>Path: **/pub/gnu/games/gnuchess***

Archie:
>Pattern: **gnuchess**

GNU Go

The ancient Japanese board game Go, complete with source for Unix systems.

Anonymous FTP:
>Address: **aeneas.mit.edu**
>Path: **/pub/gnu/gnugo***

>Address: **sunsite.unc.edu**
>Path: **/pub/gnu/games/gnugo***

Archie:
>Pattern: **gnugo**

Go

Play Go with other admirers of this popular Japanese game. Watch others play, join in, or discuss strategy with the masters. The ftp site contains information of interest to Go players.

Anonymous FTP:
>Address: **bsdserver.ucsf.edu**
>Path: **/Go/prog**

Telnet:
>Address: **hellspark.wharton.upenn.edu**
>Port: **6969**

Guess the Animal

A very old and traditional computer game. You think of an animal, and the game will ask you questions and try to deduce what animal you are thinking of. The game currently knows almost 400 animals, and it learns about new ones from the players.

World Wide Web:
>URL: **http://www.cis.upenn.edu/cgi-bin/mjd/animal?intro**

Guess the Disease

Do you have fever or spots or scales between your fingers? These are just a few of the questions you will be asked when you and the computer play *Guess the Disease*. Pick a disease, then try to stump the computer as it asks you questions. If the computer can't figure out what disease you have in mind, you can teach it something about your disease. For entertainment, not medicinal purposes.

World Wide Web:
URL: **http://www.reed.edu/cgi-bin/karl-animal**

Hangman

Play hangman through the Web and win yourself a gold star or the hangman's rope!

World Wide Web:
URL: **http://www.cm.cf.ac.uk/htbin/RobH/ hangman?go**

Head to Head Daemon Resources

An archive and mailing list for anyone interested in producing software that allows you to play multiuser realtime PC games over the Internet. For example, you can play certain flight simulators and other games such as Doom "head to head" — that is, against another real person when you connect your PCs via modem. Members of this mailing list are interested in producing dialers and other driver programs that convince your game software to play in a multiuser mode over the Internet. Some of these dialers are already finished and are in use. Join the list to find out which games you can play head to head over the Internet and where to find the necessary utilities.

Anonymous FTP:
Address: **cactus.org**
Path: **/pub/IHHD/***

Listserv Mailing List:
List Address: **ihhd@cactus.org**
Subscription Address: **listserv@cactus.org**

Hexapawn

Hexapawn is a game played against the computer on a 3x3 square board. Each player has three chess pawns, which move as they do in traditional chess. Initially the computer will be untrained, but as it plays games against you, it will never make the same mistake twice, eventually making it unbeatable, at least by you.

World Wide Web:
URL: **http://www.cis.upenn.edu/cgi-bin/mjd/ hexapawn**

Home Video Games History

The history of video games, including all the interesting turns of events that make today's games what they are.

Anonymous FTP:
Address: **ftp.spies.com**
Path: **/Library/Media/Games/videogam.his**

Gopher:
Name: Internet Wiretap
Address: **wiretap.spies.com**
Choose: **Wiretap Online Library**
I **Mass Media**
I **Games and Video Games**
I **Home Video Games History**

Howitzer95

A Super-VGA game for PCs where tanks do battle on a 2-D field in realtime.

Anonymous FTP:
Address: **ftp.wustl.edu**
Path: **/pub/games/hwitz095.exe**

Hunt the Wumpus

It's big, it's ugly, and it smells bad. Your job is to find the Wumpus and kill it before it gets you. In the meantime, watch the bats which will carry you away, be careful of the pit into which you can plummet, and oh, yes, there are other people wandering around in the cave who could prove to be lethal. You need graphics to play this successfully.

See also: Fun

World Wide Web:
URL: **http://www.bu.edu/htbin/wcl**

Illuminati Online Games

Illuminati Online makes available a web page with links to a great selection of games. On the first page, you choose the category of game that you're interested in such as war games, multiplayer games, brain teasers, card games, adventure games, and so on. When you choose a link, you go to another page that features nice descriptions of each of the games and links to the games themselves.

World Wide Web:
URL: **http://io.com/help/online.games.html**

Initgame

Playing Initgame is just like playing the guessing game 20 Questions, except that you have to try and guess the famous person that the gamemaster is thinking of. There is an iSRV bot with help files and tips for playing the game.

Internet Relay Chat:
Channel: **#initgame**

Interactive Fiction

Archives for interactive fiction games, development tools, game solutions, programming examples, and the interactive fiction Usenet newsgroups.

Anonymous FTP:
Address: **ftp.gmd.de**
Path: **/if-archive/***

Address: **ftp.wustl.edu**
Path: **/systems/ibmpc/msdos-games/TextAd/***

Interactive Web Games

Here's a fun web page with several interactive games. Just the ticket when work gets slow. The games are Tic Tac Toe, Pegs, Hunt the Wumpus, and 9 Puzzle.

World Wide Web:
URL: **http://www.bu.edu/Games/games.html**

Internet Modem Players Listing

The Internet Modem Players Listing (IMPL) is a contact service to all modem gamers. It offers lists of all signed-up players by area codes, sign-up and request forms, and details of the Internet Head-to-Head Daemon, which enables people with Internet access to play games on the Net.

World Wide Web:
URL: **http://chemotaxis.biology.utah.edu/IMPL/home.html**

Jeopardy

An online Jeopardy host asks a multitude of questions in many different categories, awarding points to the first person to answer correctly. Win enough points and you can play Final Jeopardy on this popular channel.

Internet Relay Chat:
Channel: **#jeopardy**

Lynx Cheats

Cheat sheets and passwords for Atari Lynx video games.

Anonymous FTP:
Address: **atari.archive.umich.edu**
Path: **/atari/Lynx/cheats.zoo**

Magic Square Puzzle

Play the 4 by 4 Magic Square Puzzle and figure out just what is going on in the picture it forms. There is a new picture for every game.

World Wide Web:
URL: **http://www.cm.cf.ac.uk/htbin/AndrewW/Puzzle/puzzle4x4image**

Magic: The Gathering

This is a dungeons-and-dragons-type game that is played with collectible cards. The site has tips on strategies, rules, different ways to play. It has links to other pages and sources for gaming materials.

World Wide Web:
URL: **http://www.parasoft.com/whicken/magic/magic.html**

Modem Doomer's Hangout

Compete against Doom addicts in the killing game of Modem Doom. Leave your mail or phone number, using this Mosaic form, for others to play against you, or search the list of players already signed up. You can specify your preferred mode of play, and your approximate rank and skill. To play over a modem link, all you need is a 9600bps or faster full duplex (V.32) modem.

World Wide Web:
URL: **http://lilly.ping.de/~sven/doom/ modem.html**

Multi-Trek

Multi-Trek is a multiuser trek-based game that you can play from either a character-based terminal or an X terminal. From the comfort of your own starship, blast your friends and collect gold.

Telnet:
Address: **mtrek.internex.net**
Port: **1701**

World Wide Web:
URL: **http://www.cygnus.com/jeffrey/ mtrekguide.html**

Multiuser Games

Forget competing against the computer. Match your wits against the unpredictability of the human mind and play games against your friends. These Usenet groups will give you a huge amount of information about various multiuser games. Work your way up through the ranks and before long you will be known as the neighborhood champion of network computer games, and when you are at the grocery store, the people will be yelling throughout the produce section, saying, "Hey, you're the champ, aren't you? How are those brussel sprouts?"

Usenet:
Newsgroup: **alt.games.mtrek**
Newsgroup: **alt.games.netrek.paradise**
Newsgroup: **rec.games.bolo**

No need to be bored. Try Parties and Entertainment.

Nethack

The famous game of Nethack for Unix systems, where avid adventurers travel deep into dungeons unknown.

Anonymous FTP:
Address: **aeneas.mit.edu**
Path: **/pub/gnu/nethack***

Address: **sunsite.unc.edu**
Path: **/pub/gnu/games/nethack***

Archie:
Pattern: **nethack**

Usenet:
Newsgroup: **rec.games.roguelike.nethack**

Netrek

Netrek is a multiuser graphical real-time battle simulation with a *Star Trek* theme. Two teams dogfight each other and attempt to conquer their opponent's planets. Choose from several different types of ships, including fast but fragile scouts, or big, slow, and well-armored battleships. Netrek runs on Unix systems with X Window and an Internet connection.

World Wide Web:
URL: **http://obsidian.math.arizona.edu:8080/ netrek.html**
URL: **http://web.city.ac.uk/~cb165/netrekFAQ.html**

Othello Home Page

Official rules, articles, statistics, links to software sites, Internet Othello servers, and tournament information, available in French as well as English.

World Wide Web:
URL: **http://web.cs.ualberta.ca/~brock/ othello.html**

Outburst

The robot on this channel hosts a game patterned after the popular party game Outburst. It gives a category and you must provide answers that fit that category. You play as teams and full instructions are available online.

Internet Relay Chat:
Channel: **#outburst**

A B C D E F G H I J K L M N O P Q R S T U V W X Y Z

Paintball Server

This web page and Usenet group are dedicated to the sport of paintball. There are links to a FAQ and other information for newbies, Team Internet, and other web pages relating to paintball. The web page also has a direct link to the Usenet group.

Usenet:
Newsgroup: **rec.sport.paintball**

World Wide Web:
URL: **http://warpig.cati.csufresno.edu/**

PC Games Frequently Asked Question List

An invaluable document for PC gamers providing related Usenet newsgroups, ftp guide, acronym list, computer issues, software issues, and much essential information.

Anonymous FTP:
Address: **rtfm.mit.edu**
Path: **/pub/usenet/comp.answers/PC-games-faq/***

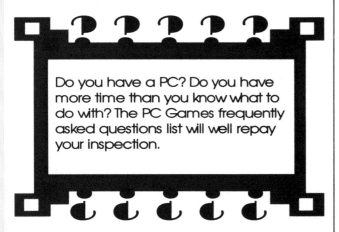

Do you have a PC? Do you have more time than you know what to do with? The PC Games frequently asked questions list will well repay your inspection.

Pinball Pasture

A source for pinball-related information, including an extensive bibliography, help section, FAQs, rules, reviews, articles, glossary, a pinball showroom with gif images of pinball machines, and details and cheats for computer pinball games.

Usenet:
Newsgroup: **rec.games.pinball**

World Wide Web:
URL: **http://www.lysator.liu.se:7500/pinball/**

Play-by-Mail Archives

Not everyone has time to spend hours gaming or interacting on the computer in real time. Play-by-mail games can give you the opportunity to participate in games at your leisure. Plus, you can have fun gaming without having to invite people over and giving them the opportunity to trash your living room. A variety of games are offered.

Gopher:
Name: Delft University
Address: **orion.cp.tn.tudelft.nl**
Choose: **Play-By-Mail Archives**

World Wide Web:
URL: **http://fermi.clas.virginia.edu/ ~gl8f/pbm.html**

Poker

Play or watch multiuser poker, administered by the IRC Poker Bot. The bot can provide complete instructions and a command summary.

Internet Relay Chat:
Channel: **#poker**

Prairie Dog Hunt for Windows

A refreshingly politically incorrect shoot 'em up game for Windows. Choose between a pellet gun, .44 magnum, or shotgun to blow away cute little prairie critters that pop out of their mounds. Be quick, though, or they'll give you rabies before you get them all.

Anonymous FTP:
Address: **ftp.cica.indiana.edu**
Path: **/pub/pc/win3/games/windog10.zip**

Address: **ftp.luth.se**
Path: **/pub/msdos/win3/games/windog10.zip**

Address: **nic.switch.ch**
Path: **/mirror/win3/games/windog10.zip**

Archie:
Pattern: **windog**

Praser Maze

A great adventure game where you wander around the Web by solving puzzles that are posed. Eventually you win or give up. Initially only some parts of the Maze are open to you, but as you solve more puzzles you will find URLs (web links) which give you access to more of the game.

Note: Requires a web client which supports forms.

World Wide Web:
URL: **http://orac.andrew.cmu.edu:5823/pra5**

Risk

A Windows version of the classic game of world conquest. You start with a number of countries chosen at random by the computer, and a number of armies determined by the number of players. You can then use your base to fulfill your Napoleonic fantasies of conquering the world.

Anonymous FTP:
Address: **ftp.monash.edu.au**
Path: **/pub/win3/games/winrisk.zip**

Address: **nic.switch.ch**
Path: **/mirror/win3/games/winrisk.zip**

Address: **winftp.cica.indiana.edu**
Path: **/pub/pc/win3/games/winrisk.zip**

Rubik's Cube

It's not the craze it used to be, but there are still people who love Rubik's Cube. If you like the Cube from a mathematical point of view or just from a puzzle-loving point of view, this list is for you. Discussions range from simple ideas to complex mathematical notation. And you don't even have to know how to solve the thing.

See also: Fun

Internet Mailing List:
List Address: **cube-lovers@ai.ai.mit.edu**
Subscription Address:
cube-lovers-request@ai.ai.mit.edu

Sega Game Secrets

A lists of secrets and cheats for Sega Genesis and Sega CD video games.

Anonymous FTP:
Address: **rtfm.mit.edu**
Path: **/pub/usenet/news.answers/games/video-games/sega/***

Sega Hardware

Details and information about Sega video game systems hardware, including Genesis joystick pinouts and Genesis hardware internals.

Anonymous FTP:
Address: **ftp.spd.louisville.edu**
Path: **/pub/sega/***

Super Secret Stuff for Sega Supporters

Attention Sega game players: Wouldn't you like to know all the secret stuff that the men in suits want desperately to keep hidden? Of course you do, and now you can have it all. Just use Anonymous FTP to connect to the Usenet archive (**rtfm.mit.edu**), and the secret list of special stuff is yours for the downloading.

Shogi

Once and for all, Shogi is not another name for chess. We heard it from the experts who are trying to set everyone straight. Yes, Shogi is a two-player game, the object of the game is to capture your opponent's king, and it is played on a board with squares. Don't let any of those facts confuse you. It's fun, challenging, and knowing how to play will make you look cultured. Other Shogi buffs gather to discuss the details and strategy of this Japanese board game.

Anonymous FTP:
Address: **ftp.funet.fi**
Path: **/pub/gnu/gnushogi***

Address: **ftp.funet.fi**
Path: **/pub/gnu/xshogi***

Address: **sunsite.unc.edu**
Path: **/pub/gnu/xshogi***

Address: **sunsite.unc.edu**
Path: **/pub/gnu/gnushogi***

Archie:
Pattern: **gnushogi**
Pattern: **xshogi**

Listserv Mailing List:
List Address: **shogi-l@technion.technion.ac.il**
Subscription Address:
listserv@technion.technion.ac.il

A B C D E F G H I J K L M N O P Q R S T U V W X Y Z

Snackman

Here's a fun little PacMan knockoff that supports advanced graphics and sound.

Anonymous FTP:
Address: **ftp.wustl.edu**
Path: **/pub/msdos_uploads/games/snackman.zip**

Sokoban

A fun and challenging game with very simple rules. It's not for mental wimps, though. It's great exercise for your brain if you need to think in an orderly, logical manner.

World Wide Web:
URL: **http://www.contrib.andrew.cmu.edu:8001/ sokoban**

Source Code to Omega

Complete C source code to Omega, a popular role-playing game. This source also exists in a number of other locations.

Anonymous FTP:
Address: **sun.soe.clarkson.edu**
Path: **/pub/src/games/omega/***

Archie:
Pattern: **omega**

Tic Tac Toe

Play the original game of Tic Tac Toe against the computer through the Web. Available as either a graphic image or a text-based game, depending on the capabilities of your web browser.

World Wide Web:
URL: **http://www.willamette.edu/htbin/tic-tac-toe**

Tiddlywinks

Learn the rules, history, and terminology of this complex game of strategy and tactics.

Anonymous FTP:
Address: **rtfm.mit.edu**
Path: **/pub/usenet/alt.games.tiddlywinks/***

Top 100 PC Games

A weekly list of the top one hundred PC games, as voted by game players on the Internet.

Usenet:
Newsgroup: **comp.sys.ibm.pc.games.announce**

TradeWars Discussion

Chat and discussion about the multiuser TradeWars game, popular on BBSs, and also available through the Internet.

Internet Relay Chat:
Channel: **#tradewars**
Channel: **#tw2002**

TrekMUSE Gateway

TrekMUSE is a text-based virtual reality game with a Star Trek flavor. This web page has links to instructions on how to play the game, ftp sites with binaries and source code, and other Star Trek resources on the Net.

World Wide Web:
URL: **http://grimmy.cnidr.org/trek.html**

Truth or Dare

Play Truth or Dare with other Internet folks on this popular channel. You'll be surprised by what you hear and what you're asked!

Internet Relay Chat:
Channel: **#truthdare**

Vectrex Arcade System

Service manual, games, music, instructions, internals guide, programming notes, and more relating to the Vectrex Arcade System.

Anonymous FTP:
Address: **csus.edu**
Path: **/pub/vectrex/***

Video Game Archive

An archive of material related to video games, including images of ROMs from arcade video games, repair hints, game lists, switch settings, cheats, FAQs, and other items of interest.

Anonymous FTP:
Address: **ftp.spies.com**
Path: **/game_archive/***

Gopher:
Name: Internet Wiretap
Address: **wiretap.spies.com**
Choose: **Wiretap Online Library**
 l **Mass Media**
 l **Games and Video Games**

Video Game Collecting

Why bother collecting stamps or bottles when you can collect something really cool like video and arcade games? What better way to pass the time than trying to find, repair and maintain games that most people consider dead and gone forever. Make Usenet your first stop on the quest for new games to add to your collection. Post

Jump into the Net

requests, information or just let everyone know if you have a surplus of your own.

Usenet:
  Newsgroup: **rec.games.video.arcade.collecting**

Excerpt from the Net...
(from the Video Game Archive)

```
[The following is from a frequently asked question (FAQ) list, explaining the best
strategies for buying a used video game.]

Q: What happened to my favourite game while it was at the arcade, and where did it go
   when it left?
A: Here's a rough sketch, based on the authors' experiences, of what the first few years
   of a game's life is like.

An OPERATOR (the owner of video arcade games) makes money by buying video games for
$2500-$3000 and running them for several months... After the first week of operation, the
operator will probably have $200-$400 inside.  If a game costs $3200 and the operator
gets $200/week, it takes the operator 16 weeks to make back his original investment.
Anything that comes in after that is pure profit.

Unless you can offer the operator more than he will make from a machine over the next
three months or so, you can forget it.  This is why you never hear of anybody buying new
machines from an operator.

Q: What makes operators tick?
A: Very simply.  In fact, one word will suffice: MONEY.

Q: So this is the MONEY principle, right?
A: Right.  The MONEY principle is simple:  OPERATORS LOVE MONEY.

It's a simple rule, but its importance cannot be overstated.  MONEY gets you in the door,
MONEY talks to the operator, MONEY pays your way when you're inside, and MONEY can even
help you get your favourite game away from the operator at the lowest price possible.
The strategy section of this FAQ will describe all of this (and more) in detail.

Operators own games for one reason: to make MONEY.  If operators were allowed to run
porno shows on their games in order to collect quarters, they'd do it.  Operators are not
interested in the art of game design. They are not interested in the impact that these
games have had upon society.  And they are certainly not interested in packaging up the
boards for your favourite game and sending it halfway across the country -- not for you
or anyone else -- not when he can make several times as much money by sitting back and
letting players pump quarters into his games.

        AGAIN, ONLY ONE THING MATTERS TO OPERATORS:
        GETTING THE MOST MONEY OUT OF THE GAMES THEY OWN

             Read that sentence again.

You and I, however, only want to wrestle our favourite games away from these "operators".
So how do we do it?  Suffice to say that whatever the answer is, it lies in MONEY. This
should be kept in mind as you read the remainder of this FAQ, and should be foremost in
your mind whenever you deal with an operator...
```

A
B
C
D
E
F
G
H
I
J
K
L
M
N
O
P
Q
R
S
T
U
V
W
X
Y
Z

Video Game Database Browser

Search a massive database of video game titles with information on the number of players, the genre, platforms available, release company, the year it came out, and a list of cheats for each title. There is a voting system which shows how popular each title is, along with FAQs, images, archives, magazines, links to other gaming Web sites, and video gaming newsgroup lists and archives. New games are added to the database on a regular basis.

World Wide Web:
URL: **http://www.cm.cf.ac.uk/Games**

Video Game Debates

Video games are not all fluff and fun. There is serious business involved when thinking about the philosophical and social aspects of the games. Get in on the discussion of game design, manufacture and sale of video games, and hear debates between people who take their game-playing seriously.

Usenet:
Newsgroup: **rec.games.video.advocacy**

Video Game Discussions

Discussion groups relating to many popular video and arcade games.

Usenet:
Newsgroup: **rec.games.video.arcade**

Video Game List

A huge list of coin-operated video and arcade games, including descriptions and comments on each.

Anonymous FTP:
Address: **ftp.spies.com**
Path: **/Library/Media/Games/videogam.lis**

Gopher:
Name: Internet Wiretap
Address: **wiretap.spies.com**
Choose: **Wiretap Online Library**
  | **Mass Media**
  | **Games and Video Games**
  | **The Killer List of Video Games**

Video Game Systems

The suspension of reality is fun as long as you are not driving a car or operating heavy machinery. Video games are a great method of escape. Find out all about various video game systems by reading Usenet. Fans of video games talk about their favorite company, new games, hints and strategies for playing video games.

Usenet:
Newsgroup: **alt.atari-jaguar.discussion**
Newsgroup: **alt.sega.genesis**
Newsgroup: **alt.super.nes**
Newsgroup: **rec.games.video.3do**
Newsgroup: **rec.games.video.atari**
Newsgroup: **rec.games.video.atari**
Newsgroup: **rec.games.video.cd32**
Newsgroup: **rec.games.video.nintendo**
Newsgroup: **rec.games.video.sega**

Video Games Frequently Asked Questions

Questions and answers about video game systems, equipment, magazines, cartridges, cheats, terms, developments, problems, and more.

Anonymous FTP:
Address: **rtfm.mit.edu**
Path: **/pub/usenet/news.answers/games/video-games/faq/***

Video Puzzle with Live Video Sources

Play the magic square puzzle with a live video source. Uses the vspuzzle VuSystem application with a live video source.

Note: Requires NCSA Mosaic for the X Window System, version 2.0 or higher

World Wide Web:
URL: **http://tns-www.lcs.mit.edu/cgi-bin/vs/vspuzzle**

Walkthroughs

If you are having problems with your text adventure and you need just a teeny-tiny hint, help is on the way. By checking here, nobody will know you had to cheat. Hints available for Myst, Beyond Zork, Ultima Underworld 2, and Ultima 8.

World Wide Web:
URL: **http://wcl-rs.bham.ac.uk/~djh/walkthru.html**

x4war

An X Window, four-player, chess-like fighting game that is played over the Internet. Unix source and instructions are available.

Anonymous FTP:
> Address: **bigbang.phy.duke.edu**
> Path: **/pub/feng/x4war.gz**

> Address: **ftp.funet.fi**
> Path: **/pub/archive/comp.sources.games/ volume13/x4war/***

> Address: **ftp.inria.fr**
> Path: **/X/contrib-R5/games/x4war1.1.tar.Z**

Archie:
> Pattern: **x4war**

x4war Players

Find out where current x4war games — the multiuser chess-like fighting game — are in play on the Net. You can also ask for advice about the game from other players or watch a current battle.

Internet Relay Chat:
> Channel: **#x4war**

Bored?

Zarf's List of Interactive Games will provide you with as many interesting games as you want, so there is no excuse for actually doing any work.

xsokoban

An X Window version of the popular game Sokoban. This page has links to the man page for xsokoban, the source code for the latest version, installation notes, and instructions.

World Wide Web:
> URL: **http://clef.lcs.mit.edu/~andru/ xsokoban.html**

Zarf's List of Interactive Games on the Web

A fantastic list of many, many games available on the Web. This list is divided into two sections: the first section covers interactive games, like multiplayer games, user-versus-computer games, and adventure games, and the second section covers interactive toys, which are things you can fool around with that don't necessarily have a real goal.

World Wide Web:
> URL: **http://www.cs.cmu.edu:8001/afs/ cs.cmu.edu/user/zarf/www/games.html**

GARDENING

Annuals, Perennials and Bulbs

Are you supposed to put the bulbs into the ground before or after a frost? And why do annuals come and go when perennials keep returning? Get all the answers to your questions about annuals, perennials and bulbs at this informative cooperative extension service.

See also: Agriculture

Gopher:
> Name: Virginia Cooperative Extension
> Address: **gopher.ext.vt.edu**
> Choose: **VCE Subject Matter**
>   **I Horticulture**
>   **I Consumer Horticulture**
>   **I Question Box & Press Releases**
>   **I Annuals, Perennials and Bulbs**

Bonsai

Develop patience and an appreciation for long-term planning by practicing the fine art of bonsai. You will be rewarded with plants that are exquisite in form and grace. If you feel your skill or attention span is not up to the task, you can always try Zen rock gardening.

Anonymous FTP:
> Address: **bonsai.pass.wayne.edu**
> Path: **/pub/GIFS/***

> Address: **bonsai.pass.wayne.edu**
> Path: **/pub/Information/***

> Address: **rtfm.mit.edu**
> Path: **/pub/usenet/news.answers/bonsai-faq/***

Listserv Mailing List:
> List Address: **bonsai@waynest1.bitnet**
> Subscription Address: **listserv@waynest1.bitnet**

Usenet:
> Newsgroup: **alt.bonsai**
> Newsgroup: **rec.arts.bonsai**

A B C D E F G H I J K L M N O P Q R S T U V W X Y Z

Bonsai Mailing List

The art and craft of Bonsai and related art forms. Bonsai is the oriental art of dwarfing trees and plants into forms that mimic nature. Anyone interested, whether novice or professional, may join this mailing list.

See also: Hobbies

Listserv Mailing List:
    List Address: **bonsai@cms.cc.wayne.edu**
    Subscription Address: **listserv@cms.cc.wayne.edu**

Chia Pets

They're quiet, easy to care for and you don't have to potty train them. Chia pets are the perfect pet for the busy executive or absent-minded bachelor. They come in all shapes and sizes and even have their own newsgroup, which makes them all the more special. Chia owners and fanciers talk about what it is to love and be loved by these friendly little plants.

Usenet:
    Newsgroup: **alt.pets.chia**

Children's Gardening

Encouraging your children to work in the garden is not only healthy, good exercise, and a great learning experience, but it will also wear them out fast so they will go to bed earlier. Discover a myriad of fun activities that you can organize in the garden that will incorporate the interests and talents of children.

See also: Families and Parenting, Youth

Gopher:
    Name: Virginia Cooperative Extension
    Address: **gopher.ext.vt.edu**
    Choose: **VCE Subject Matter**
      | Horticulture
      | Consumer Horticulture
      | General Horticulture Information
      | Children's Gardening

Flower Gardens

Wouldn't it be great to have flowers all over the house and yard so that when you wake up in the morning, the air is all fragrant with natural perfume? With time, patience, a bit of a green thumb and some Usenet newsgroups, you can turn your home into a floral paradise. Gardeners offer tips and general information on the care and feeding of specific flowers.

Usenet:
    Newsgroup: **rec.gardens.orchids**
    Newsgroup: **rec.gardens.roses**

Fruit Growing

Experience the thrill of harvesting your own fruit to sell, eat, or to just give to friends. Use these helpful articles to learn tips for successfully growing a variety of fruits, such as berries, grapes, pomegranates, pears, apples, and kiwis.

See also: Agriculture

Gopher:
    Name: Virginia Cooperative Extension
    Address: **gopher.ext.vt.edu**
    Choose: **VCE Subject Matter**
      | Horticulture
      | Consumer Horticulture
      | Question Box & Press Releases
      | Fruit Growing

Fruit Growing

Ah . . . who has not relaxed in the quiet peace of an evenfall, listening to the dozy buzzing of the bees and wallowing in the still, relaxed atmosphere of the earth as it slowly closes its petals for the night? And what could be more intoxicating than lying quietly in your hammock as night falls, enjoying the smooth, subtle fragrances of your very own fruit trees as their gentle scents calmly and tenderly caress your face?

    Yes, there is something about fruit–your own fruit–that speaks to the depths of all of us. In a world of noise and international conflict and general brouhaha, where you can't pick up a newspaper without reading about some fiend with a hatchet slaying six or a gas explosion on the Indian subcontinent wiping out a village, and you can't turn on the TV without hearing about children who get arrested for anti-social behavior or husbands sneaking 'round the corner to do things that right-minded people don't even discuss, isn't it nice to know that in your very own garden, with your very own fruit trees, you can find a spot of peace and a tiny portion of tranquility?

Garden Encyclopedia

Flip through this easy-to-use encyclopedia of gardening and get information on soils, plants, tools, trimming, digging, mulching, and more. Never again will you have to wonder how much osmunda fiber to use for your epiphitic orchids or what the difference is between a bush hook and a sickle.

World Wide Web:
URL: **http://www.btw.com/garden_archive/ toc.html**

Gardener's Assistant

A PC program to help aspiring gardeners choose plants according to growing conditions.

Anonymous FTP:
Address: **ftp.wustl.edu**
Path: **/systems/ibmpc/msdos/database/ gardener.zip**

Address: **plaza.aarnet.edu.au**
Path: **/micros/pc/oak/database/gardener.zip**

Address: **rigel.acs.oakland.edu**
Path: **/pub/msdos/database/gardener.zip**

Archie:
Pattern: **gardener.zip**

Gardening Information

A large collection of material about fertilizers, herbs, peppers, ivy, poisonous plants, pruning, roses, seeds, fruit trees, turf grasses, and much more. If your thumb doesn't turn green with all this help, give it up.

Anonymous FTP:
Address: **sunsite.unc.edu**
Path: **/pub/academic/agriculture/ sustainable_agriculture/gardening/***

Gopher:
Name: Texas A&M Agricultural Extension Service
Address: **taex-gopher1.tamu.edu**
Choose: **Master Gardener Information**

Gardens and Plants

If things aren't going right in the garden, don't just raze everything with the roto-tiller — turn to your fellow Internet buddies for ideas. For the organically challenged, you have the opportunity to cry, scream, and beg for help. Bragging is also welcome; you can pass on the news that it was your 25-pound tomato that made the cover of the *National Enquirer*.

Usenet:
Newsgroup: **rec.gardens**

Excerpt from the Net...

Newsgroup: rec.gardens
Subject: Plants that attract birds?

> Has anyone had any particular success
> attracting birds to their yard
> with particular plants? I've bought
> a book called "How to Attract
> House and Feed Birds" which contains
> a list of trees and shrubs that
> birds are attracted to, but it lists
> several dozen and I'm having a
> hard time choosing among them.

If I had room for just one bird-feeding plant, it would be a serviceberrry (Amelenchier species): either a shrub or tree. Robins and other birds love the berries. In addition, the plants have beautiful spring blooms and great fall color.

Growing Herbs

Herbs are great for so many things. You can eat them, make decorations out of them, and use them as medicine (or even as a recreational activity provided you don't inhale). Learn how to grow your very own herbs. This guideline will tell you about the care and feeding of common garden herbs.

See also: Medicine: Alternative, Agriculture, Health

Gopher:
Name: Utah State University
Address: **extsparc.agsci.usu.edu**
Choose: **Selected Documents (Utah State Extension)**
| **Fact Sheets**
| **Agriculture**
| **Gardens**
| **Herbs**

Growing Vegetables

A guide to planting and growing vegetables.

Gopher:
Name: University of Delaware
Address: **gopher.udel.edu**
Choose: **UD Department..**
| **AGINFO: College of Agricultural Sciences**
| **Info by Type of Publication**
| **Fact Sheets | Vegetables**

Many people do not appreciate their friends in the vegetable kingdom. Why not grow your own? Take a look at **Growing Vegetables.**

Herb Information

Growing herbs can be rewarding, fun and profitable if you know what you are doing. Read these herb journals, resource and book lists, and a lengthy herb FAQ that will turn your thumb green in no time.

See also: Agriculture

Gopher:
Name: SunSITE
Address: **calypso-2.oit.unc.edu**
Choose: **Worlds of SunSITE — by Subject**
  l **Sustainable Agriculture Information**
  l **Gardening**
  l **Miscellaneous Information on Herbs**

Herb Mailing List

When they're not actually digging around in the garden or making nifty things from plants, herb lovers participate in this mailing list about growing herbs and using them for cooking, decorations, and medicine. Join in and meet the people who really know their hemp from their hemlock.

See also: Medicine: Alternative, Hobbies, Health

Listserv Mailing List:
List Address: **herb@trearn.bitnet**
Subscription Address: **listserv@trearn.bitnet**

Herbal Variations

Learn to play games with herbs or to make gifts out of them. Explore new ways to grow and mark the little wonders that grow in your garden, on the windowsill, or near the porch steps. There are lots of interesting things you can do with a few herbs and some imagination.

See also: Hobbies, Medicine: Alternative, Agriculture

Gopher:
Name: Virginia Cooperative Extension
Address: **gopher.ext.vt.edu**
Choose: **VCE Subject Matter**
  l **Horticulture**
  l **Consumer Horticulture**
  l **General Horticulture Information**
  l **Children's Gardening**
  l **4-H Horticulture Publications at Va Tech**
  l **Herb Garden**

Home Gardening Mailing List

Gardens and gardening mailing list promotes and exchanges information about home gardening. Topics include vegetable gardens, herbs, flowers, ornamental gardening, and other topics. Both novice and experienced gardeners are welcome.

Listserv Mailing List:
List Address: **gardens@ukcc.uky.edu**
Subscription Address: **listserv@ukcc.uky.edu**

Hydroponic Gardening

Why get your hands dirty when you can grow your crops hydroponically? Hydroponic gardening is on the rise everywhere. Hydroponics fans get together to discuss technical aspects and personal experiences relating to growing plants without the mechanical support of soil.

See also: Agriculture

Majordomo Mailing List:
List Address: **hydro@hawg.stanford.edu**
Subscription Address:
  majordomo@hawg.stanford.edu

Indoor Plants

The cat has eaten half of your dieffenbachia and the leaves on your African violet are turning yellow. What should you do? Check out the helpful hints at the Virginia Cooperative Extension. Articles cover topics such as container drainage, decorating with houseplants, feeding and watering, and making terrariums.

Gopher:
Name: Virginia Cooperative Extension
Address: **gopher.ext.vt.edu**
Choose: **VCE Subject Matter**
  I **Horticulture**
  I **Consumer Horticulture**
  I **Question Box & Press Releases**
  I **Indoor Plants**

Landscaping and Lawns

It's a fear that strikes deep in your gut. You really want to go out in the backyard, but you just can't stand the thought of what might be lurking around in the uncut grass and wild, thorny shrubbery. Make a bold move and turn "Night of the Living Greenery" into "The Garden of Earthly Delights." These helpful articles will give you information on landscaping and lawn care and you don't even have to spend a fortune to do it. They include tips to save time and money.

See also: Home Maintenance

Gopher:
Name: Virginia Cooperative Extension
Address: **gopher.ext.vt.edu**
Choose: **VCE Subject Matter**
  I **Horticulture**
  I **Consumer Horticulture**
  I **Question Box & Press Releases**
  I **Landscaping and Lawns**

Master Gardener

The Master Gardener offers advice on the care and production of fruits and nuts, flowering plants — both annual and perennial, ornamental trees and shrubs, turf grasses and vegetable crops.

Gopher:
Name: Master Gardener
Address: **leviathan.tamu.edu**
Choose: **Master Gardener Information**

World Wide Web:
URL: **http://leviathan.tamu.edu:70**

> ## Do you like the "Final Frontier?" Take a look at Star Trek (or Space).

Pest Management

"Pest management" is the politically correct term for figuring out effective ways to destroy, obliterate, or otherwise get rid of those nasty creatures that feed on your plants. Form your strategic battle plan with the help of this extension service. It offers insect factsheets, information on exotic pests, and even images of insects so you can accurately identify the enemy.

See also: Agriculture

Gopher:
Name: Virginia Cooperative Extension
Address: **gopher.ext.vt.edu**
Choose: **VCE Subject Matter**
  I **Horticulture**
  I **Consumer Horticulture**
  I **Pest Management**

Pests, Diseases and Weeds

What is it that causes swarms of creeping, crawling, out-of-control nasties to infest your garden? If you're doing battle with aphids, cutworms, lace beetles, spider mites, or a particularily persistent white pine weevil, read articles here that cover the bug and weed basics and soon you will have a pest-free environment.

Gopher:
Name: Virginia Cooperative Extension
Address: **gopher.ext.vt.edu**
Choose: **VCE Subject Matter**
  I **Horticulture**
  I **Consumer Horticulture**
  I **Question Box & Press Releases**
  I **Pests, Diseases, and Weeds**

Questions about plants? The Plant Factsheets are for you.

Plant Factsheets

The key to being a successful gardener is to make sure you are well-informed. One way you can do that is by having a look at these factsheets, which cover topics like ground covers, poisonous plants, shrubs, vines, trees, flowering potted plants, and even cut flowers. The factsheets give a brief overview of each item and basic information on how to care for them. This directory offers a keyword search if you are looking for something specific.

See also: Agriculture

Gopher:
Name: Virginia Cooperative Extension
Address: **gopher.ext.vt.edu**
Choose: **VCE Subject Matter**
 | **Horticulture**
 | **Consumer Horticulture**
 | **Plant Fact Sheets**

Trees

All you need to know about tree selection, planting, and care.

Gopher:
Name: University of Delaware
Address: **gopher.udel.edu**
Choose: **UD Department Program**
 | **AGINFO: College of Agricultural Sciences**
 | **Information by Type of Publication**
 | **Fact Sheets**
 | **Ornamental Horticulture**

N0 NEED to stay ignorant about trees. Point your gopher to the Ornamental Horticulture resource at the University of Delaware and spend some time with these wonderful perennial plants that boast single woody self-supporting stems.

Vegetable and Herb Growing

If you ignore the back-breaking intensity and the fact that it's really hard on your nails, gardening can be fun. Read this large collection of articles on growing herbs and vegetables and get hints on things like making container gardens, storing and drying herbs, choosing vegetable varieties, and planting early crops.

Gopher:
Name: Virginia Cooperative Extension
Address: **gopher.ext.vt.edu**
Choose: **VCE Subject Matter**
 | **Horticulture**
 | **Consumer Horticulture**
 | **Question Box & Press Releases**
 | **Vegetable and Herb Growing**

Woody Plants

There is more to landscaping than willowy flowers and delicate groundcover. Shrubs and trees offer sturdy variety for your yard and garden. Learn about planting, growing, feeding, and trimming shrubs and trees as well as how to avoid diseases and pests that afflict them.

See also: Agriculture

Gopher:
Name: Virginia Cooperative Extension
Address: **gopher.ext.vt.edu**
Choose: **VCE Subject Matter**
 | **Horticulture**
 | **Consumer Horticulture**
 | **Question Box & Press Releases**
 | **Woody Plants**

GAY, LESBIAN, BISEXUAL

Assorted Resources

Years ago, gay, lesbian and bisexual resources were harder to find. Now, on the Net, information is freely disseminated and can be found in a variety of places. This archive houses a variety of national and international resources including GLB organizations, AIDS and HIV organizations, and links to other archives such as the Queer Resource Directory.

Gopher:
Name: University of California Berkeley
Address: **uclink.berkeley.edu**
Choose: **Other U.C. Berkeley Information Servers**
 | **Community Topics**
 | **Multicultural/Bisexual Lesbian Gay Alliance**

Bear Code

You are a bear and you want everyone to know it. But bears come in all shapes and sizes (within limits). Have a look at the bear code and categorize yourself so you can let the world know just how big, furry and squeezable you are.

Internet Relay Chat:
Channel: **#bearcave**

World Wide Web:
URL: **http://www.cs.cmu.edu:8001/afs/cs.cmu.edu/ user/scotts/bulgarians/bear-code.html**

Bears

This web page offers information on bears, bear clubs, and links to other related resources for big, furry, lovable men.

World Wide Web:
URL: **http://www.skepsis.com/.gblo/bears/ index.html**

Bears in Movies

The next time you decide to go bear watching, check out this list of bears in movies. What better way to spend a Sunday afternoon than watching films of large, hairy men who are really built.

World Wide Web:
URL: **http://www.skepsis.com/.gblo/bears/ bears_in_movies.html**

Bible's View of Homosexuality

Are homosexuality and Christianity at odds? Read this lengthy paper that discusses how Jesus and the Bible view homosexuality.

See also: Religion: Traditional

World Wide Web:
URL: **http://www.acs.appstate.edu/~hb6399/stale/ rainbow/bible.homos**

Bisexual Resource List

These web pages are compilations of resources useful to bisexual and bifriendly people. They include a calendar of events, mailing lists, newsgroups, newsletters, literature, radio shows, and HIV and AIDS education.

World Wide Web:
URL: **http://vector.casti.com/QRD/.html/BRC/ brl-toc.html**
URL: **http://www.cis.ohio-state.edu/hypertext/faq/ usenet/bisexual/resources/faq.html**

Bisexuality

The Internet offers some important forums for bisexuals (people who are attracted to both men and women). The **biact-l** mailing list is for bisexual activists; **bifem-l** is for female bisexuals; **bisexu-l** is for general discussion.

Usenet:
Newsgroup: **soc.bi**

Listserv mailing list:
List Address: **biact-l@brownvm.brown.edu**
Subscription Address:
listserv@brownvm.brown.edu

List Address: **bifem-l@brownvm.brown.edu**
Subscription Address:
listserv@brownvm.brown.edu

List Address: **bisexu-l@brownvm.brown.edu**
Subscription Address:
listserv@brownvm.brown.edu

Bisexuality and Gender Issues

For some hard-hitting theoretical discussion of bisexuality and gender issues, look in on the dialogue from this newsgroup. It's strongly recommended that you realize that this is not a social group, support group or forum for news and announcements. This is purely intellectual stuff and cross-postings are discouraged. The **alt.moss.bisexua-l** newsgroup is a more relaxed atmosphere.

Listserv Mailing List:
List Address: **bithry-l@brownvm.brown.edu**
Subscription Address:
listserv@brownvm.brown.edu

Usenet:
Newsgroup: **alt.motss.bisexua-l**

Brochure on Sexual Orientation

A brochure called *Someone You Know Is Gay* offers information on sexual orientation and tries to answer questions about why people are gay. It also addresses the process of coming out and stereotypes such as "what gay people look like."

See also: Sex, Sexuality

World Wide Web:
URL: **http://www.acs.appstate.edu/~hb6399/ stale/rainbow/someone**

A B C D E F G H I J K L M N O P Q R S T U V W X Y Z

Collected Queer Information

A large collection of gay, lesbian, and bisexual resources including articles, a list of gay, lesbian, bisexual, and supportive businesses, film lists, news, a bisexual resource list, advice, a link to the Queer National Homeland in Webworld, and links to other related resources.

World Wide Web:
> URL: **http://www.cs.cmu.edu:8001/Web/People/ mjw/Queer/MainPage.html**

Coming Out

Discussion of the process through which individuals come to terms with their lesbian or gay sexual orientations.

Gopher:
> Name: University of Montana Healthline Gopher Server
> Address: **selway.umt.edu**
> Port: **700**
> Choose: **Sexuality | Coming Out**

Telnet:
> Address: **selway.umt.edu**
> Login: **health**

Domestic Partners

It's amazing that problems can be caused by not having a little piece of paper. Even if you have signed on to your relationship for life, it doesn't legally count without the certificate. Domestic partners gather to discuss issues concerning domestic partnerships, such as how to obtain benefits from places of employment, what tactics work and don't work, the cost of benefits, and any other issue related to domestic partners.

See also: Law, Politics, Government, Sex

Internet Mailing List:
> List Address: **domestic@tattoo.mti.sgi.com**
> Subscription Address:
> **domestic-request@tattoo.mti.sgi.com**

Planning a picnic? Check the weather using the Net.

Don't Ask; Don't Tell

Next to advertising agencies, the government is the best at coming up with nifty expressions like "information superhighway" and "don't ask; don't tell." Underneath that glib exterior, there are important issues that arise with the "don't ask; don't tell" policy. Concerned people gather to discuss the effects of this policy on military institutions.

See also: Government, Military, Politics

Internet Mailing List:
> List Address: **dont-tell@choice.princeton.edu**
> Subscription Address:
> **dont-tell-request@choice.princeton.edu**

Electronic Mailing Lists

Mailing lists are fun because the information comes straight to you — you don't have to go out to get it (sort of like pizza). There is a huge amount of mailing lists dedicated to gays, lesbians and bisexuals, including regional lists. With this file, you don't have to wade through all the other mailing lists offered by listserv — it's already sorted for you.

Mail:
> Address: **listserv@umdd.umd.edu**
> Body: **get lesbigay lists wmst-l**

Faces Quiz

Who are those people you have been hanging out with in Usenet? See pictures and try to match up the names. Hints are provided to help you figure it out if you have trouble.

World Wide Web:
> URL: **http://www.skepsis.com/.gblo/motss/quiz/**

Gay FTP Site

Gay and lesbian stories, campaign information, queer resources directory, mailing lists, laws, AIDS information, event guide, newspaper articles, and much more.

Anonymous FTP:
> Address: **nifty.andrew.cmu.edu**
> Path: **/pub/***

Gay, Lesbian, and Bisexual Resources

This web page collects links to many local and national gay, lesbian, and bisexual resources on the Internet.

World Wide Web:
> URL: **http://www.yahoo.com/ Society_and_Culture/Sex/ Gay_Lesbian_and_Bisexual_Resources/**

No one understands the Internet, so relax and enjoy.

Gay, Lesbian, and Bisexual Trivia Game

Help build the **soc.motss** trivia game by adding in your trivial tidbits. Select the category, type in the question and answer and you'll be in on helping compile this fun trivia database.

World Wide Web:
URL: **http://www.skepsis.com/.gblo/motss/ triv_form.html**

Gay, Lesbian, and Bisexual White Pages

Keep in touch with the **soc.motss** crew. Add your name and vital statistics to the database.

World Wide Web:
URL: **http://www.skepsis.com/.gblo/motss/ motss_dir.html**

Gay Public Officials

Discover more about public officials than just their political leanings. Read this list of government people who are publicly out.

See also: Government, Politics

World Wide Web:
URL: **http://www.acs.appstate.edu/~hb6399/ stale/rainbow/officials**

Gay TV Listings of the Week

This weekly column outlines movies and television programs that are showing on network or cable television. The guide tells you whether it's pay-per-view, on premium channels, or whether to check your local television listing for viewing times.

See also: Television

World Wide Web:
URL: **http://www.acs.appstate.edu/~hb6399/stale/ rainbow/tv**

Need help with the morons around you? Try Psychology.

Excerpt from the Net...

Newsgroup: alt.homosexual
Subject: Are You Gay or is it a Phase?

> After all these years, my mother still thinks I'm going through a
> phase. It's the longest phase I'm going through :-) and I'm
> wondering if anyone here has parents, friends or other loved one's
> who think the same thing.

For almost seven years, my mother began all our phone conversations
with: "Are you normal yet? When will you get over that silly phase?
Your father and I are getting older and we want grandchildren from you."

I put a stop to this, but every now and then my mother still surprises
me with: "Do you have any female friends that you find attractive?"
I always disappoint her by saying: "I do mom, but I'm lucky in that we
cruise different types of men..."

A B C D E F G H I J K L M N O P Q R S T U V W X Y Z

Gays in Russia

Homosexuals are regarded differently by each culture. Read articles and informative texts on being gay in Russia and find out about clubs for homosexuals in that country.

See also: World Culture, Politics

Anonymous FTP:
Address: **nic.funet.fi**
Path: **/pub/culture/russian/sex/sodomy/***

Hanky Codes

Advertising can be subtle, but effective. Get out your hankies and bedeck yourself in colors that tell the world what you will and won't do. Stick this code up on your refrigerator so you can use it as a handy quick-reference in case unexpected guests drop by.

See also: Sex

World Wide Web:
URL: **http://www.cs.cmu.edu:8001/afs/cs.cmu.edu/ user/scotts/bulgarians/hanky-codes.html**

Historical and Celebrity Figures

When you're famous, you can't expect to have your privacy. Just look at headlines of the tabloids and other gossip sheets. Here is a list of people who are out by choice or by force, so take it for what you think it's worth.

See also: Sex, Sexuality

Anonymous FTP:
Address: **ftp.spies.com**
Path: **/Library/Article/Sex/glbo.lis**

Homosexuality

Members of the same sex (MOTSS) discuss their thoughts, feelings, and experiences about being gay. The general group on homosexuality covers a wide range of topics on how gays relate to the rest of the world, while the **.motss** newsgroups discuss how gays relate to one another.

Usenet:
Newsgroup: **alt.homosexual**
Newsgroup: **alt.sex.homosexual**
Newsgroup: **alt.sex.motss**
Newsgroup: **soc.motss**

Homosexuality and the Church

It's tricky being homosexual and Christian at the same time. Unless you can alternate days, you have to deal with the views of the church regarding being gay. Read this lengthy article, which outlines how various denominations deal with homosexuals who embrace Christianity.

See also: Religion: Traditional

World Wide Web:
URL: **http://www.cs.cmu.edu:8001/afs/cs.cmu.edu/ user/scotts/bulgarians/church.html**

Homosexuality and Gay Rights

Don't be taken in by rumors and gossip. Read the real news on homosexuality and gay rights. Significant upcoming events and current events are highlighted.

Usenet:
Newsgroup: **clari.news.gays**
Newsgroup: **clari.news.group.gays**

Homosexuality in the Middle Ages

It's obvious from studying Greek history that homosexuality was not invented in this century. And you can ask anybody who studies the Middle Ages, too. In fact, there is even an official list of the Society for the Study of Homosexuality in the Middle Ages. They discuss all aspects of homosexuality in the medieval era. It's almost better than watching reruns of *Flipper*.

See also: History, Philosophy

Listserv Mailing List:
List Address: **medgay-l@ksuvm.ksu.edu**
Subscription Address: **listserv@ksuvm.ksu.edu**

International Association of Gay Square Dance Clubs

This web page has information about conventions and related events, info on clubs, and other square dance resources.

World Wide Web:
URL: **http://molscat.giss.nasa.gov/IAGSDC/.html**

Don't be left out among the left out.
THE
Lesbian Lexicon
will ensure that you will at least know
what the words mean.

Lesbian Lexicon

Everyone needs a good lexicon now and then. Read up on terms relevant to lesbians and lesbianism since the birth of feminism, and learn the meaning of phrases like "lesbian bed death" and "serial monogamy."

See also: Sexuality, Women

World Wide Web:
URL: **http://bianca.com/shack/bedroom/lesbian.html**

Lesbian Love

Meet and talk with other lesbians and bisexual women from around the world.

Internet Relay Chat:
Channel: **#lesbian**
Channel: **#lesbos**

Lesbian Mothers

This list is for women only and relates to special issues that are faced by lesbian mothers or lesbian mom-wannabes, either single or partnered. The list is private so only members of the list will have access to information on or about the list.

Majordomo Mailing List:
List Address: **moms@qiclab.scn.rain.com**
Subscription Address:
majordomo@qiclab.scn.rain.com

Lesbian, Gay, and Bisexual Mailing Lists

List of more than 50 lesbian, gay, bisexual, and transgender mailing lists, and information about them.

Anonymous FTP:
Address: **nifty.andrew.cmu.edu**
Path: **/pub/QRD/qrdinfo**

The Out List

Stop speculating on whether your favorite famous person is out or not. Read this lengthy list of notable people who have publicly acknowledged that they are gay, lesbian or bisexual.

World Wide Web:
URL: **http://orange-room.cc.nd.edu/toybox/WrittenWord/OutList.html**

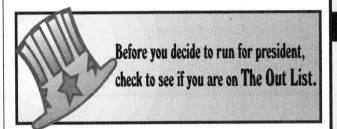

Before you decide to run for president, check to see if you are on **The Out List.**

Politics and Homosexuality

Gays in the military and child custody battles put the politics of homosexuality on the front page. Discuss the latest civil rights cases, pending legislation, and whom to boycott (or not). Keep informed so you can make a difference in your community.

Usenet:
Newsgroup: **alt.politics.homosexuality**

Politics and Sex

For some reason, politics and sex are inseparable (and it's not just the Kennedys). What do Gennifer Flowers, Donna Rice, and Jessica Hahn know that Dr. Ruth has never figured out? Join the discussion and see what strange bedfellows politics and sex really make.

Usenet:
Newsgroup: **alt.politics.sex**

Looking for special fun?
Turn to the Vices section.

A B C D E F **G** H I J K L M N O P Q R S T U V W X Y Z

Queer Resources Directory

Resources for gay interests and issues, including civil rights and AIDS information. The wais database has pointers to more information. The web page is an electronic research library dedicated to sexual minorities, and features links to information and resources of interest to the gay community.

Anonymous FTP:
Address: **nifty.andrew.cmu.edu**
Path: **/pub/QRD**

WAIS:
Database: **Queer-Resources**

World Wide Web:
URL: **http://vector.casti.com/QRD/.html/ QRD-home-page.html**

Queer Zines

Looking for something good to read? Have a look at this list of zines that relate to gays, lesbians and bisexuals. This informative list covers print zines that are not accessible on the Net, but it gives all the details on how to subscribe or find the publications in question.

See also: Zines

World Wide Web:
URL: **http://boothp1.ecs.ox.ac.uk:5705/zines/ qz/LIST.html**

Queers 'R' Us

A web page with links to several gay resources including "People, Places & Things" from Washington State Queers, and CyberQueers, a gay advocacy group.

World Wide Web:
URL: **http://sparky.cyberzine.org/html/Queer/ queerpage.html**

Stonewall Images

See images of the Stonewall march on the United Nations, including the logo, the Rainbow Flag, and pictures of the host city. This site also has links to papers on AIDS, the Gay Games, and inspirational writings by notable gays.

See also: Government, Politics

World Wide Web:
URL: **http://www.rpi.edu/~gey2/ Stonewall-images.html**

Stonewall Riot

New York City, 1969. The raid and closing of the Stonewall Inn is one of the landmarks in the history of the gay movement. Read articles which offer varied points of view on the Stonewall riot.

See also: Government, Politics

World Wide Web:
URL: **http://www.cs.cmu.edu:8001/afs/cs.cmu.edu/ user/scotts/bulgarians/NY-DN_Stonewall.txt**
URL: **http://www.cs.cmu.edu:8001/afs/cs.cmu.edu/ user/scotts/bulgarians/stonewall.txt**

Twink Code

A twink is characterized by his stylish clothing and the perfection of his hair. Whether you are a BeachTwink, a StreetTwink or a EuroTwink, there will be something here for you. Scan the list and see how you rate on the twink scale.

World Wide Web:
URL: **http://www.cs.cmu.edu:8001/afs/cs.cmu.edu/ user/scotts/bulgarians/twink-code.txt**

GENEALOGY

Canadian Genealogy Resources

Searching through the records of another country is often difficult and time consuming. Get an advantage by doing preliminary research on the Net. Search through bibliographies and catalogs, census directories, name indexes, and find a long list of addresses for Canadian genealogy researchers.

See also: Libraries

Gopher:
Name: Queens University, Canada
Address: **gopher.queensu.ca**
Choose: **Library Services & Information
| Library Subject Guides
| Genealogy**

The Internet has lots and lots (and lots) of free software.

CyberRoots

Here is a demonstration of a great way to organize your family tree. Take advantage of today's computer technology to construct intricate record-keeping structures that are interesting to look at, as well as functional. Store your information in a multimedia environment that, with the addition of pictures and sounds, makes for hours of fun browsing.

World Wide Web:
URL: **http://irpsbbs.ucsd.edu/gene/ genedemo.html**

Database

Don't bother trying to invent a genealogy database to suit your needs. Someone has already done it. This might be the only resource you need, or you might choose to use it along with other freeware or perhaps some commercial software.

See also: Software: DOS, Software: Macintosh

Anonymous FTP:
Address: **mintaka.lcs.mit.edu**
Path: **/pub/map/genealogy/***

When Harley was growing up in Canada, he would have given anything for access to the Canadian Genealogy Resources that you can get for free whenever you want. (Well, not really, but he did want to say something nice about Canada...)

Family History Research

This web page features family history research resources offered by Brigham Young University's Interactive Software Systems Laboratory.

World Wide Web:
URL: **ftp://issl.cs.byu.edu/FamHist/home.html**

Genealogical Smorgasbord

Pick and choose what you like from this large selection of resources — software, how-tos, and documents are just a few things you will find here.

See also: Libraries

Gopher:
Name: University of Alabama
Address: **twinbrook.cis.uab.edu**
Choose: **Internet Resource Discovery**
| The Interdex
| genealogy

Genealogy Newsgroups and Mailing Lists

The Internet is a global community — a great place from which to track down family members from way-back-when. Newsgroups and mailing lists not only provide convenient forums for the discussion of research techniques, genealogy software, and genealogical resources, but are also great places to ask for information on family names and swap anecdotes about your family history quests. Plenty of sharing goes on here. Find that long-lost second-half-cousin-twice-removed who broke all your crayons when you were seven and remind him you want all 64 colors, plus the built-in sharpener.

Listserv Mailing List:
List Address: **roots-l@vm1.nodak.edu**
Subscription Address: **listserv@vm1.nodak.edu**

Usenet:
Newsgroup: **alt.genealogy**
Newsgroup: **soc.roots**

Genealogy Software for the PC

Find all the software you will need to store and process all your family records.

See also: Software: PC

Anonymous FTP:
Address: **archive.umich.edu**
Path: **/pub/msdos/genealogy/***

Address: **oak.oakland.edu**
Path: **/pub/msdos/genealgy/***

Gopher:
Name: Merit Network
Address: **gopher.archive.merit.edu**
Choose: **Merit Software Archives**
| MSDOS Archive
| genealogy

Genealogy Web

Check in here to see what is new in the Net's genealogy scene. This site offers access to a variety of other resources — ftp sites and gophers — for software, documents and general information.

World Wide Web:
>   URL: **http://www.yahoo.com/Science/Genealogy/**
>   URL: **http://ftp.cac.psu.edu/~saw/genealogy.html**
>   URL: **http://wood.cebaf.gov/~saw/genealogy.html**

Handy Tips and How-To's

Looking at the big genealogical picture is overwhelming. Get helpful hints and some how-to documents that will make tracing your family tree much easier. When you start searching back, it's amazing who you will find. Perhaps you will be the one to find The Missing Link.

See also: Libraries

Gopher:
>   Name: University of Toledo
>   Address: **gopher.utoledo.edu**
>   Choose: **Research Resources**
>   **| Genealogy**

Jewish Mailing List

This mailing list specifically addresses special issues involved when tracing Jewish lineage and is a great companion to **soc.roots** and **roots-l**.

Listserv Mailing List:
>   List Address: **jewishgen@shamash.nysernet.org**
>   Subscription Address:
>   **listserv@shamash.nysernet.org**

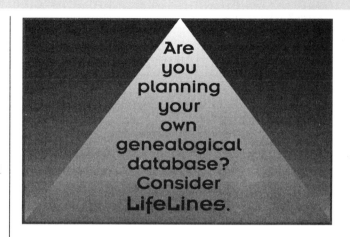

Are you planning your own genealogical database? Consider LifeLines.

LifeLines Database

LifeLines is a software program that runs on Unix systems. It is remarkably flexible in that it allows a maximum amount of manipulation to the database. Entries can easily be added, removed, swapped, or merged with each other. There is no limit to the size of the entries. LifeLines is written to accommodate itself to fit your needs. This software will also support GEDCOM, another genealogical database. **lines-l** is a mailing list that covers discussion of all topics concerning LifeLines.

See also: Software: Unix

Listserv Mailing List:
>   List Address: **lines-l@vm1.nodak.edu**
>   Subscription Address: **listserv@vm1.nodak.edu**

Need a laugh?
Check out Humor.

Excerpt from the Net...

```
Newsgroup: alt.genealogy
Subject: The Oldest U.S. Surname

This was in a local newspaper...
"Surname of the oldest surviving family in the United States reportedly
is Sonan.  Descended from settlers at Florida's St. Augustine."

The next clip said: "When your father's father, or his, was a lad, men
usually lived longer than women.  And that had always been true.
Worldwide.  But by 1920, women lived a little longer.  And for the last
generation or so, they've stabilized, evidently, outliving men by about
seven years."
```

> **Parents and children, take a look at: Families and Parenting, Kids, and Youth.**

National Archives and Records Administration

See what NARA has to offer in the way of instructional leaflets and helpful searching tips for genealogical research. They also give you a glance at microfiche records for census and federal court information such as bankruptcy records, naturalization records, land grant claims and more.

Gopher:
Name: National Archives and Records Administration
Address: **gopher.nara.gov**
Choose: **Genealogy**

Non-DOS Software

Non-DOS genealogical software is very hard to find as freeware or shareware on the Net, but we found one secret hideaway for it. Not only is software available here, but a nice selection of census transcripts, research group information, how-tos, and files on Jewish lineage.

Anonymous FTP:
Address: **ftp.cac.psu.edu**
Path: **/pub/genealogy/***

Gopher:
Name: Pennsylvania State University
Address: **ftp.cac.psu.edu**
Choose: **genealogy**

State by State

The Mormons have put together an impressive amount of information on family research, little of which is made available on the Internet. Fortunately, there are a few archives of how-to documents written for each state. These provide library and document information and hints on efficient methods of research.

See also: Libraries

Anonymous FTP:
Address: **hipp.etsu.edu**
Path: **/pub/genealogy/***

United Kingdom

If you are doing extensive research in the U.K., it will be helpful to have census data and the necessary documents to get the information you need. This site has a lot of items pertinent to research involving the United Kingdom.

Anonymous FTP:
Address: **ftp.essex.ac.uk**
Path: **/pub/genealogy/***

Vital Records in New York State

Digging up old documents is hard enough to do without the added hubbub of the New York environment. Arm yourself with all the information necessary to get through the bureaucracy quickly and efficiently. Available are addresses to send for records and the necessary forms to use. You will also find writings on the Adoption Information Registry.

See also: Libraries

Gopher:
Name: New York State Department of Health
Address: **gopher.health.state.ny.us**
Choose:
NYSDOH — Consumer Health Information | Vital Records in NYS

WHAT'S IN A NAME?

WE ALL KNOW THAT IT IS IMPORTANT TO KNOW EVERYTHING POSSIBLE ABOUT YOUR ANCESTORS BECAUSE...UH...WELL...I GUESS I FORGET BUT IT IS A PRETTY IMPORTANT REASON. AFTER ALL, IF YOU DON'T KNOW WHERE YOU CAME FROM THEN YOU CERTAINLY WON'T KNOW WHERE YOU ARE AND...HMMM... SOMETHING OR OTHER ANYWAY.

LET'S JUST SAY THAT GENEALOGY IS COOL AND LEAVE IT AT THAT. AFTER ALL, IF IT WASN'T FOR OUR ANCESTORS, WE WOULDN'T BE HERE. (WELL, WE MIGHT BE HERE BUT WE WOULD HAVE DIFFERENT PARENTS AND GRANDPARENTS, AND WE WOULDN'T KNOW ANYONE'S BIRTHDAY, AND EVERYTHING WOULD BE ALL MIXED UP AND, WELL... YOU GET THE IDEA.)

A B C D E F G H I J K L M N O P Q R S T U V W X Y Z

What's in a Name?

Access some of the Mormon genealogical archives as well as all of the files stored by Roots-L. This site has an incredible collection of family names that have been donated by people around the world via the Net. Search by browsing or by keyword.

Gopher:
>Name: Brigham Young University
>Address: **ucs2.byu.edu**
>Choose: **General Information & Services**
> **| LDS Information**
> **| Genealogy**

GEOGRAPHY

Antarctica Resource Guide

Details and links to Internet resources related to the Antarctica, including first hand reports, research reports, news articles, images, general information, and book lists.

World Wide Web:
>URL: **http://http2.sils.umich.edu/Antarctica/ Bibliography/Bib.html**

Antarctica, Noble America

Has this ever happened to you? You have planned a picnic on Antarctica for all your friends and, after taking several months to get there by ship, you find that it is the cold season and all your food freezes as soon as you lay it out on the tablecloth. What's worse, you didn't bother to check out the facilities and you find that it is 4700 kilometers to the nearest restroom. So, when you go to wash your hands, by the time you get back they are dirty again.

What a pickle.

But, since you are Net person, this need never happen to you. Just remember: Before you plan your next trip to everyone's favorite continent, take a few moments with the Antarctica Resource Guide. No need for *you* to be caught short of penguin food or find yourself at the South Pole without a reservation.

Whatever you do, do *not* forget that a list of Australian Postal Codes is available whenever you want. They might even save your life some day. Don't laugh: if it wasn't for Australian Postal Codes we wouldn't be rich and famous. (Sorry, we don't have the space to tell the story here.)

Australian Postal Codes

Search a database for Australian postal codes by keywords, including state, city, and more.

Gopher:
>Name: Austin Hospital
>Address: **gopher.austin.unimelb.edu.au**
>Choose: **General Information and Resources**
> **| Look Up Australian Post Codes**

CIA World Factbook

The complete text. Detailed information about every country and territory in the world. Includes geographic, climate, economic, and political information.

Anonymous FTP:
>Address: **ucselx.sdsu.edu**
>Path: **/pub/doc/etext/world.text.Z**

Gopher:
>Name: Internet Wiretap
>Address: **wiretap.spies.com**
>Choose: **Electronic Books at Wiretap**
> **| CIA World Factbook**

>Name: University of Minnesota
>Address: **gopher.micro.umn.edu**
>Choose: **Libraries**
> **| Reference Works**
> **| CIA World Fact Book**

WAIS:
>Database: **world-factbook**

CIA INFO FOR YOU

The U.S. Central Intelligence Agency is so secret that its budget is not even made public. (We don't even know if they have enough money to buy copies of our Internet books.)

What we do know is that they spend a lot of time and effort keeping track of all the countries of the world. And you can get it all (the non-secret stuff anyway) for free. The CIA World Factbook resource is invaluable for anyone who is planning to create their own military alliance.

Earth

A world factbook, world map, and topological relief database about the Earth. There's also a directory of Meteostat images.

Anonymous FTP:
Address: **ftp.funet.fi**
Path: **/pub/doc/world/***

European Postal Codes

A list of postal country codes used by most European and Mediterranean countries.

Anonymous FTP:
Address: **ftp.funet.fi**
Path: **/pub/doc/mail/stamps/finnish/**
postimerkit.tar.gz

Federal Geographic Data Products

This web page is the Manual of Federal Geographic Data Products, a government program that attempts to create a cohesive geographic resource system available to all areas of government on the Internet.

World Wide Web:
URL: **http://info.er.usgs.gov/fgdc-catalog/**
title.html

Geodetic Survey of Canada

This web page offers geographic and geodetic information about Canada. The page has both English and French interfaces and features links to other Canadian geographic and geodetic servers including the Canada Centre for Surveying Information and Canadian archives.

World Wide Web:
URL: **http://www.geod.emr.ca/**

Geographic Information and Analysis Laboratory

The Geographic Information and Analysis Laboratory (GIAL) server at the University of Buffalo is a multi-purpose resource center for the study of geography. This page has links to many kinds of geographical resources and information. There is also a link to the National Center for Geographic Information and Analysis.

World Wide Web:
URL: **http://www.geog.buffalo.edu/**

Geographic Information System

A collection of geographic data. Search the database first, then request specific items via mail.

Gopher:
Name: Oregon State University
Address: **gopher.fsl.orst.edu**
Choose: **Corvallis FSL GIS Data Catalog**

Need an idea for a great way to spend a Saturday night? Take a look at the Geodetic Survey of Canada and see if you can find the place where Harley was born. (If that is too easy, look for the plaque that commemorates Harley's leaving the country for California.)

A B C D E F G H I J K L M N O P Q R S T U V W X Y Z

Geographic Resources Analysis Support System

Read about how the U.S. Army Construction Engineering Research Laboratory attempts to maximize the Army's use of land for training while protecting valuable natural and cultural resources and ecosystems.

World Wide Web:
URL: **http://www.cecer.army.mil/grass/ GRASS.main.html**

Geographische Informationssyteme

An Austrian list for discussion and other postings regarding geography, cartography, and geographic information processing.

Listserv Mailing List:
List Address: **acdgis-l@vm.akh-wien.ac.at**
Subscription Address: **listserv@vm.akh-wien.ac.at**

Geography Discussion

Imagine what life would be like if there was no geography. There would be no road maps to have to re-fold. There would be no grueling hours of having to memorize the capitals of third world countries. And worse, there would be no map showing what hills and dales you have to go over to get to Grandma's house. In fact, geography is so important that you can find a lively discussion about it in Usenet. Go hang out with the people who know the planet like the backs of their hands.

Usenet:
Newsgroup: **bit.listserv.geograph**

Geography Education Software

Project GeoSim is a joint research project between the computer science and geography departments at Virginia Tech to produce educational software modules for introductory geography courses. The software runs on DOS, Macs, and X Window systems.

World Wide Web:
URL: **http://geosim.cs.vt.edu/index.html**

Geography Server

Get information about cities, regions, countries, etc., including population, latitude and longitude, elevation, and so on.

Telnet:
Address: **martini.eecs.umich.edu**
Port: **3000**

Global Land Information System

Download land use and geological survey maps of the United States.

Telnet:
Address: **glis.cr.usgs.gov**
Login: **guest**

International Background Information

Take a peek at other countries through the U.S. State Department's keyhole. Read background information on 170 countries and organizations around the world.

See also: Government

Gopher:
Name: University of Missouri St. Louis
Address: **umslvma.umsl.edu**
Choose: **The Library
  I Government Information
  I Background Notes**

Super-Secret Information About Any Country in the World

Do you need to know something about a country? The U.S. State Department has all kinds of information just for you. **INTERNATIONAL BACKGROUND INFORMATION** is a terrific resource for students doing research or just the average Joe who needs to know the names of the principal cities of Mauritania (Nouakchott, Nouadhibou, Kaedi, Zouerate, Kiffa, and Rosso).

Local Times Around the World

Local times in many cities around the world. This gopher menu connects to a computer in your city of interest, which reports the local time.

Gopher:
   Name: Austin Hospital
   Address: **gopher.austin.unimelb.edu.au**
   Choose: **General Information and Resources
      | Local Times**

Map Related Web Sites

Pointers to many web sites that contain maps of all types including relief maps, historic maps, and railroad maps.

World Wide Web:
   URL: **http://www.lib.utexas.edu/LibrariesList/
      PCL/Map_collection/map_sites.html**

Maps

Get a bird's-eye view of the world via the Web. See relief maps, weather maps, census maps, and the clever "You are here" map.

World Wide Web:
   URL: **http://www.yahoo.com/Science/
      Geography/Maps/**
   URL: **http://www.delorme.com/maps/
      mapurls.htm**

The New South Polar Times

This bi-weekly newsletter gives an ongoing, first hand account of life at the South Pole. Back issues, data about the South Pole, a history of South Pole exploration, and classroom ideas can also be found here.

See also: Education

World Wide Web:
   URL: **http://www.deakin.edu.au/edu/
      MSEE/GENII/NSPT/NSPThomePage.html**

New York State Statistics

Figures and data on New York state, including population, crime, education, industry, and vital information.

Gopher:
   Name: State University of New York
   Address: **gopher.acsu.buffalo.edu**
   Choose: **Miscellany
      | New_York_State_Facts**

Pathfinder Land Data Sets

This web page sponsored by NOAA and NASA offers satellite data sets of geographic information. The page also has links to archives, geography software to process the data sets, and video sequences from satellites.

World Wide Web:
   URL: **http://xtreme.gsfc.nasa.gov/**

Excerpt from the Net...

(from U.S.A. Statistics)

Area	3,618,770 sq mi
Population 1975	213,559,000
Population 1990	250,442,000
Population 2000	273,646,000
Population Doubling Time	78 years
Urbanization	22.5 %
Life Expectancy (Male)	72.0 years
Life Expectancy (Female)	79.0 years

-- Principal Language: English. Spanish is spoken by 9%.
-- Americans comprise many diverse ethnic groups.
-- Independence and entrepreneurship are highly regarded.

A B C D E F G H I J K L M N O P Q R S T U V W X Y Z

U.S. Geographic Name Server

Obtain geographic position, population, elevation, state, and other statistics for a U.S. city or zip code.

Gopher:
Name: NASA Goddard Space Flight Center
Address: **gopher.gsfc.nasa.gov**
Choose: **Virtual Reference Shelf**
  | **US geographic name server**

U.S. Snow Cover Maps

Images and snow cover maps for the U.S., updated regularly and available in gif and other formats, from the National Weather Service.

Anonymous FTP:
Address: **snow.nohrsc.nws.gov**
Path: **/pub/bbs/***

U.S.A. Statistics

Facts, figures, statistics, and other information about the United States of America.

Gopher:
Name: State University of New York
Address: **gopher.acsu.buffalo.edu**
Choose: **Miscellany**
  | **American_Facts**

World City Maps

This web page offers maps of many cities, countries, and regions of the world. Most of these maps (and there are many, many of them) were produced by the CIA. To select a map, you first choose a continent, then a country, and so on.

World Wide Web:
URL: **http://www.lib.utexas.edu/Libs
    PCL/Map_collection/Map_collection.html**

> **Next time you are at the supermarket, show them this book and ask for a discount (you never know...)**

World Map Collection

Maps covering every area of the world, from the Perry-Castaneda Library Map Collection at the University of Texas at Austin.

World Wide Web:
URL: **http://www.lib.utexas.edu/LibrariesList/
    PCL/Map_collection/Map_collection.html**

Xerox Map Viewer

The PARC Web Map Viewer is an experiment in providing dynamic information retrieval via the Web. It allows you to zoom in and out of a map of the world and takes many options that you can supply to instantly make custom Web maps of any location in the world. This page won the Most Technical Merit and the Best Use of Interaction sections in the 1994 Best of the Web Awards.

World Wide Web:
URL: **http://pubweb.parc.xerox.com/map**

Zip Codes of the U.S.

The ftp site has a file with all the zip codes in the U.S. and the city and state of their location. The gopher is a geographic name server. To use it, you type in the zip code, and it displays information about the location for the zip code.

Anonymous FTP:
Address: **freebsd.cdrom.com**
Path: **/.8/cdrom/zipcodes.zip**

Archie:
Pattern: **zipcode**

Gopher:
Name: University of Oregon
Address: **gopher.uoregon.edu**
Choose: **Desktop Reference**
  | **Geographic & Travel Information**
  | **U.S. Zip Code Directory**

World Wide Web:
URL: **http://www.ucsd.edu/library/reference_shelf/**

GEOLOGY

For **vasquez.jpg** and other interesting photographs, you can go to the University of North Carolina (**sunsite.unc.edu**). This one is **Gallery/Photo/Kliendenst F.** in the directory **/pub/multimedia/pictures/OTIS/photos**.

Earthquake Information

Get up-to-date news about earthquakes that have occurred around the world.

Finger:
Address: **quake@geophys.washington.edu**

Gopher:
Name: St. Olaf College
Address: **gopher.stolaf.edu**
Choose: **Internet Resources**
I Weather and Geography

Telnet:
Address: **geophys.washington.edu**
Login: **quake**
Password: **quake**

Geological Time Scale

A time scale charting the eras and events of the last 4 to 5 million years.

Anonymous FTP:
Address: **ftp.spies.com**
Path: **/Library/Document/geologic.tbl**

Gopher:
Name: Internet Wiretap
Address: **wiretap.spies.com**
Choose: **Wiretap Online Library**
I Assorted Documents
I Geologic time table

National Geophysical Data Center

The National Geophysical Data Center (NGDC) manages environmental data in the fields of solar-terrestrial physics, solid earth geophysics, marine geology and geophysics, paleoclimatology and glaciology.

See also: Physics, Environment

Anonymous FTP:
Address: **ftp.ngdc.noaa.gov**

Gopher:
Name: National Oceanic and Atmospheric Administration
Address: **gopher.ngdc.noaa.gov**

World Wide Web:
URL: **http://www.ngdc.noaa.gov**

Oklahoma Geological Survey Observatory

Near real-time seismic and magnetic data, Oklahoma earthquake catalog, a catalog of known nuclear explosions, and the text of nuclear testing treaties.

Gopher:
Name: Oklahoma Seismic Gopher
Address: **wealaka.okgeosurvey1.gov**

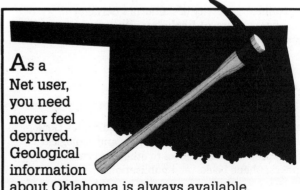

As a Net user, you need never feel deprived. Geological information about Oklahoma is always available, day and night. (Now, how did we ever get by without the Internet?)

Seismic Information

A large list of seismic information resources available on the Internet via finger, ftp, mail, telnet, and on the Web. These resources are categorized into sections by the Interent tools you use to access them.

World Wide Web:
URL: **http://www.geophys.washington.edu/ seismosurfing.html**

Smithsonian Gem & Mineral Collection

A collection of almost 50 images and descriptions of different types of gems and minerals. This page presents you with a thumbnail picture of the images available, then you can select these to view the gem or mineral in more detail in a full-size image.

World Wide Web:
URL: **http://galaxy.einet.net/images/gems/ gems-icons.html**

U.C. Berkeley Museum of Paleontology

Information on museum collections and paleontological database information. Also includes nature and science images; images of animals and birds; biology image archive; animal sounds; and an online *On the Origin of Species* complete text.

Gopher:
Name: University of California Berkeley
Address: **ucmp1.berkeley.edu**

U.S. Geological Survey Gopher

This gopher is sponsored by the United States Geological Survey. This system has geographic and geological information as well as links to other government gophers, phone books, and publications.

Gopher:
Name: U.S. Geological Survey
Address: **info.er.usgs.gov**

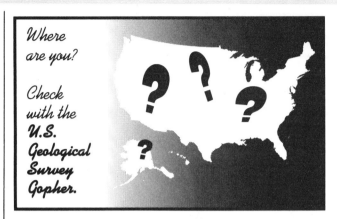

Where are you? Check with the U.S. Geological Survey Gopher.

U.S.G.S. Seismology Reports

Weekly and historical seismic reports and data as well as programs and source code for crunching seismic data.

Gopher:
Name: Northwestern University
Address: **somalia.earth.nwu.edu**
Choose: **Seismology Resources
| USGS Seismology and Tectonophysics Information**

Volcanoes

It used to be that the only thing you could do with a volcano was to throw a virgin into it and hope that the gods were appeased. Now you can hook up all sorts of wires and gadgets to it and use X-ray fluorescence to examine trace elements and use aerial photographs to analyze pumiceous pyroclastic flow. This site presents detailed descriptions of several volcanoes and includes pictures.

World Wide Web:
URL: **http://vulcan.wr.usgs.gov/home.html**
URL: **http://www.geo.mtu.edu/volcanoes/**

Volcanology

The NASA Volcanology page features some spectacular images of volcanos and their results. The page also has information about the NASA's volcanology team and educational information about volcanoes.

World Wide Web:
URL: **http://www.geo.mtu.edu/eos/**

Volcanoes

What can you say about volcanoes and their almost magnetic attraction to us all? We could remind you that they are holes or cracks in the Earth's surface that release molten lava, ash or other products from underground magma chambers. (Now *that's* a word: "magma". Bet you can't say it ten times real fast.)

Anyway, we could wax eloquent about the runny volcanic outpourings and how they build basalt beds, or how the more viscous types of lava form steep-sided volcanoes, or how ash residue tends to build cone-like peaks. Or, we could go on and on about how volcanoes erupt where one lithospheric plate is forced beneath another, or where two such plates diverge.

Yes, there is a lot to say about volcanoes and, if truth be told, they are among our favorite large-scale geological formations. Still, there is something unsatisfying about mere talk and, if you are like us, you will want some pictures, and that is where the Net comes in. Take a cruise to volcano web sites and we guarantee that you will find more than a few shots suitable for framing.

World Paleomagnetic Database

This program allows remote users to search the Abase ASCII version of the World Paleomagnetic Database. The search program is simple to use and will search the Soviet, non-Soviet, rock unit, and reference databases and create output files that can be downloaded to a researcher's local system via anonymous ftp.

Telnet:
>   Address: **earth.eps.pitt.edu**
>   Login: **Search**

GOVERNMENT

Bureau of Justice Statistics Documents

Statistics on a plethora of justice-related topics, including drug enforcement and treatment in prisons, jail inmates, drunk driving, police departments, felony sentences, prisoner statistics by year, women in prison, capital punishment, and other subjects.

See also: Law

Gopher:
>   Name: University of Albany
>   Address: **uacsc2.albany.edu**
>   Choose: **United Nations Justice Network
> | Bureau of Justice Statistics Documents**

Make Yourself Feel Bad

No need to walk around always feeling good. Use your Gopher and take a look at the crime statistics from the *Bureau of Justice Statistics Documents.*

Just the thing to take the edge off a beautiful spring day.

Canadian Government

Explore segments of the Canadian federal government, including the House of Commons, the Senate, the Supreme Court, and federal departments and agencies. These pages are in both French and English.

World Wide Web:
>   URL: **http://debra.dgbt.doc.ca:80/opengov/**

Catalog of Federal Domestic Assistance

A search program interface to a catalog of the many federal assistance programs.

Gopher:
   Name: Library of Congress
   Address: **marvel.loc.gov**
   Choose: **Government Information**
     I **Federal Information Resources**
     I **Information by Agency**
     I **General Information Resources**
     I **Catalog of Federal Domestic Assistance**

Census Data for Massachusetts

A document with the data from the 1990 census for the state of Masschusetts.

Anonymous FTP:
   Address: **ftp.uu.net**
   Path: **/doc/literary/obi/Census/mass.census.1**

Code of the Federal Register

The Federal Register is responsible for central filing of original acts enacted by Congress, original documents containing executive orders and proclamations of the President, and other official documents and regulations. This resource contains the full text of the law granting this authority and responsibility to the Federal Register.

Gopher:
   Name: Counterpoint Publishing
   Address: **gopher.counterpoint.com**
   Choose: **Code of Federal Regulations**

   Name: The Internet Company
   Address: **gopher.internet.com**
   Choose: **Counterpoint Publishing**
     I **Code of Federal Regulations**

Cooperative Extension System

A gopher system sponsored by the U.S. Department of Agriculture Children Youth Family Education Research Network (CYFER-net). CYFER-net provides access to information from the USDA Extension Service and the National Agriculture Library. Also accessible here are Americans Communicating Electronically, and the USDA's Food and Nutrition Center.

Gopher:
   Name: U.S. Department of Agriculture
   Address: **cyfer.esusda.gov**

Copyright Information

Works registered for copyright since 1978. These include books, films, music, maps, sound recordings, software, multimedia kits, drawings, posters, sculpture, etc.

Gopher:
   Name: Library of Congress
   Address: **gopher.loc.gov**
   Choose: **Copyright**

Department of Commerce

Information about the U.S. Department of Commerce and the people in charge. This site also offers links to other government resources.

World Wide Web:
   URL: **http://www.doc.gov/**

Economic Conversion Information Exchange

Compiled data on state and local laws, adjustment programs, technology, and non-governmental programs relating to economic conversion.

See also: Economics

Gopher:
   Name: Economic Conversion Information Exchange
   Address: **ecix.doc.gov**

Federal Highway

The Federal Highway Administration Electronic Bulletin Board System offers public messages, discussions of FHWA activities, and discussions about computers and related topics.

Note: Hit RETURN once you are connected.

Telnet:
   Address: **152.120.108.19**

Federal Information Processing Standards

A publication of the U.S. Department of Commerce describing standards for information processing.

Anonymous FTP:
   Address: **oak.oakland.edu**
   Path: **/pub/misc/standards**

Federal Register

Documents from the Federal Register and information on how to gain full access to the daily U.S. Federal Register via the Internet. Documents include proclamations, executive orders, and so on.

Gopher:
Name: Counterpoint Publishing
Address: **gopher.counterpoint.com**
Choose: **United States Federal Register**

Name: Texas A&M University
Address: **gopher.tamu.edu**
Choose: **Browse Information By Subject**
 | **Government Information**
 | **Federal Register**

Name: The Internet Company
Address: **gopher.internet.com**
Choose: **Counterpoint Publishing**
 | **United States Federal Register**

FedWorld

An enormous resource for scientific, technical, and other information provided by the federal government. FedWorld is taxpayer-supported through the National Technical Information Service (NTIS). It is an easy-to-use system that offers information on a wide variety of subjects.

Telnet:
Address: **fedworld.gov**

World Wide Web:
URL: **http://www.fedworld.gov/**

GAO (General Accounting Office) Reports

Reports from the GAO on budget issues, investment, government management, public services, health care, energy issues, and virtually every other area of government on which the GAO may have reported.

Anonymous FTP:
Address: **ftp.cu.nih.gov**
Path: **/gao-reports**

Gopher:
Name: Internet Wiretap
Address: **wiretap.spies.com**
Choose: **Government Docs (US & World)**
 | **GAO Transition Reports**

**Lonely?
Mail to Famous People.**

General Accounting Office Transitional Reports

A series of reports on the effectiveness of government social programs.

Gopher:
Name: University of Colorado Boulder
Address: **gopher.colorado.edu**
Choose: **Online Library Catalogs...**
 | **Information from the U.S. Federal Government**
 | **US General Accounting Office Transitional Reports**

Government and Civics Archives

A large collection of laws, treaties, and historical and legal documents.

Anonymous FTP:
Address: **ftp.spies.com**
Path: **/Gov/***

Gopher:
Name: Internet Wiretap
Address: **wiretap.spies.com**
Choose: **Government Docs (US & World)**

Government Corruption

We don't want to talk behind anyone's back, but rumor has it that there is corruption in government. We thought that if you were going to hear it, you should get the news from us. It's up to you to dig out the truth and, as you know, the press always gives you the facts. Read the latest stories about the government's dirty laundry in this Clarinet newsgroup.

Usenet:
Newsgroup: **clari.news.corruption**

Jump into the Net.

Too much spare time? Explore a MUD.

Government Information Sources on the Internet

Sources of U.S. federal government information compiled by Blake Gumprecht.

Anonymous FTP:
Address: **ftp.nwnet.net**
Path: **/user-docs/government/
gumprecht-guide.txt**

Gopher:
Name: NYSERNet
Address: **nysernet.org**
Choose: **Special Collections: New York State and
Federal Info**

Name: OARnet
Address: **gopher.oar.net**
Choose: **Services and Information Resources
on the Internet**

Name: University of Michigan
Address: **gopher.lib.umich.edu**
Choose: **Social Sciences Resources**
 I **Government And Politics**
 I **Guide to Government Internet Resources**

Name: University of Virginia
Address: **gopher.virginia.edu**
Choose: **Library Services**
 I **Worldwide Internet Services**
 I **Internet Resources**
 I **Internet Resources By Subject**
 I **Clearinghouse of Subject Oriented
 Resource Guides**
 I **Guides on the Social Sciences**

Government Policy

If there's one thing the government is good at, it's passing around paper and making policies. That is their job. Keep up with the latest product of the U.S. government's brainstorming by reading stories from the press regarding domestic and foreign policy.

Usenet:
Newsgroup: **clari.news.usa.gov.foreign_policy**
Newsgroup: **clari.news.usa.gov.misc**

For Lovers of Exotic Government Documents

Here's the scene. You are a young man who has just met a beautiful woman whom, you suspect, might be the woman of your dreams. You invite her up to your place where you have prepared a gourmet meal of spaghetti and inexpensive wine, and you are reclining in front of the stereo listening to a Bach concerto and watching the dancing shadows on your walls where they reflect the ever-changing luminescence of those candles that your sister got you for your last birthday and that you finally found a use for.

And, as the music lulls you into a romantic idyll, you turn to your date with a lingering look and slightly parted moist lips. And as you bend over to whisper gently in her ear, you hear her say, "Do you have any information from the official residence of the Japanese Prime Minister?" "No," you stammer, "what with one thing or another I never actually got a chance to take a look at that web site and, well... you know...".

But by that time it is too late. Your date has left, leaving you alone with a half bottle of Australian table wine and a roomful of regrets. "If only..." you say to yourself, but the words freeze in your mouth. Truly, of all the words of tongue and pen, the saddest are these: you should have checked it out on the Net when you had the chance.

Government Publications Network

The government has published a wide variety of books and newsletters electronically so that they could use the paper they saved for printing money. See official publications of the U.S. government and the European Community, and rest assured that thousands of squirrels still have homes to go to after a hard day of nut-gathering.

See also: Publishing

Telnet:
Address: **kraus.com**
Login: **gpn**

Japanese Prime Minister's Official Residence

This web server is located in the Prime Minister's official residence, Tokyo, Japan. If offers information, speeches, and press releases from the Japanese Prime Minister, in both Japanese and English.

World Wide Web:
    URL: **http://www.kantei.go.jp/**

National Archives and Records Administration

National archives for still pictures, motion pictures, sound and video recordings, World War II pictures, and electronic records.

Gopher:
    Name: Library of Congress
    Address: **gopher.loc.gov**
    Choose: **Government Information**
      | Federal Information Resources
      | National Libraries and National Archives

National Performance Review Web Site

The government is trying hard to get you in on the action — at least they'd like you to think so. The National Performance Review has a more interactive site which includes not only information, but an actual "toolkit to help reinvent government" so you can do your own political version of *Home Improvement*.

World Wide Web:
    URL: **http://www.npr.gov/**

NetResults

A network of people working to reinvent government. (No, really.) They have pulled together in an attempt to implement changes recommended by the National Performance Review. Information on the NPR and NetResults are available at the USDA's Extension Service gopher.

Gopher:
    Name: U.S. Department of Agriculture
    Address: **ace.esusda.gov**
    Choose: **Americans Communicating Electronically**
      | National Performance

Excerpt from the Net...

(from the North American Free Trade Agreement)

PREAMBLE

The Government of Canada, the Government of the United Mexican States
    and the Government of the United States of America, resolved to:

STRENGTHEN the special bonds of friendship and cooperation...
CONTRIBUTE to the harmonious development and expansion of...
CREATE an expanded and secure market for the goods and services...
REDUCE distortions to trade
ESTABLISH clear and mutually advantageous rules...
ENSURE a predictable commercial framework for business...
BUILD on their respective rights and obligations...
ENHANCE the competitiveness of their firms in global markets
FOSTER creativity and innovation, and promote trade...
CREATE new employment opportunities and improve working conditions...
UNDERTAKE each of the preceding in a manner consistent with...
PRESERVE their flexibility to safeguard the public welfare
PROMOTE sustainable development
STRENGTHEN the development and enforcement of environmental laws...
PROTECT, enhance and enforce basic workers' rights

HAVE AGREED as follows...

A
B
C
D
E
F
G
H
I
J
K
L
M
N
O
P
Q
R
S
T
U
V
W
X
Y
Z

If you like trouble, take a look at Mischief.

North American Free Trade Agreement

The full text of the controversial law that purports to open the economic borders between the U.S., Canada and Mexico.

Gopher:
Name: Internet Wiretap
Address: **wiretap.spies.com**
Choose: **Government Docs (US & World)**
  | North American Free Trade Agreement

Name: University of Nevada Reno
Address: **gopher.scs.unr.edu**
Choose: **Selected Information Resources by Topic**
  | Government and Politics
  **| NAFTA ... North American Free Trade
  Agreement**

Patent Office Reform Panel Report

The final report of a committee sponsored by the U.S. Patent Office considering a switch from a first-to-invent to a first-to-file patent policy.

Gopher:
Name: Internet Wiretap
Address: **wiretap.spies.com**
Choose: **Government Docs (US & World)**
  | Patent Office Reform Panel Final Report

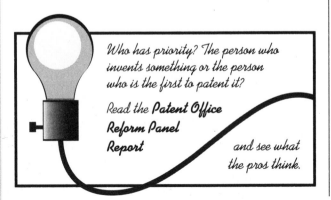

Who has priority? The person who invents something or the person who is the first to patent it?

*Read the **Patent Office Reform Panel Report*** *and see what the pros think.*

Pennsylvania Census, Housing Information

Income and poverty statistics as well as housing information, population, race and sex mixes, and other statistical data.

Gopher:
Name: University of Pennsylvania
Address: **gopher.upenn.edu**
Choose: **Penninfo via Gopher**
  | Penninfo
  | Libraries
  | Electronic Reference Desk
  | US Census and Statistical Data
  | Pennsylvania & Philadelphia

Personalities

The media is great because it helps you keep up with all the things you need to know, like rumors about the First Lady being pregnant, which government officials have died, and other interesting tidbits about the personal lives of the folks in Washington.

Usenet:
Newsgroup: **clari.news.usa.gov.personalities**

Social Security Administration

The Social Security Administration Office Support System Information Server (OSS-IS) offers data on monthly benefits, current operating statistics, history of benefits paid, and income data on the aged.

Anonymous FTP:
Address: **ftp.ssa.gov**
Path: **/pub/***

Social Security Administration Information

Information about the Social Security Administration, Social Security numbers, and obtaining information on others for genealogical purposes.

Anonymous FTP:
Address: **oak.oakland.edu**
Path: **/pub/misc/ss-info**

The Internet is PEOPLE, not computers.

> **Reality is dull. Try Science Fiction.**

Social Security Administration Online

Learn more about where a large portion of your paycheck is going. The Social Security Administration makes available news, legislation, press releases, and speeches by the Commissioner of Social Security. See policy handbooks and a handy feedback form on which you can write your praise or gripes. This page has links to other places on the Web that have Social Security resources. Information is available in English, Spanish, Armenian, Japanese and Vietnamese.

World Wide Web:
    URL: **http://www.ssa.gov/SSA_Home.html**

U.S. Census Information for 1990

The information at the first site is organized by state. The second site is organized by county, metro areas, state, and location, and includes tables in text and Lotus 1-2-3 format.

Gopher:
    Name: University of Minnesota
    Address: **gopher.micro.umn.edu**
    Choose: **Libraries**
     | Electronic Books
     | By Title
     | 1990 USA Census Information

    Name: University of Missouri
    Address: **bigcat.missouri.edu**
    Choose: **Reference and Information Center**
     | United States and Missouri Census
       Information
     | United States Census Data

U.S. Census Information Server

How many cool male Internet authors live on the north side of any given street in any given city? The Census Bureau can't tell you if the authors are cool, but they do know the rest. They also store financial data on state and local governments and schools, poverty in the United States, and housing changes.

World Wide Web:
    URL: **http://www.census.gov/**

Need some numbers?

Check out the
U.S. Census Information Server.

U.S. Department of Housing and Urban Development

Descriptions of the mission and functions of HUD, reports, news, information about the Partnerships Against Violence programs, research findings on violence issues, and links to other federal, commercial, and educational servers. Enjoy the window dressing, but keep your hands on your First Amendment rights.

Gopher:
    Name: U.S. Department of Housing and
      Urban Development
    Address: **gopher.hud.gov**

U.S. Federal Government Information

Don't take the politicians' word. Look up government data yourself and make your own decisions. Information is categorized by source (for example, Government Accounting Office). Choose a source, then a document.

Gopher:
    Name: University of Minnesota
    Address: **gopher.micro.umn.edu**
    Choose: **Libraries**
     | Information from the US Federal Government

A B C D E F G H I J K L M N O P Q R S T U V W X Y Z

U.S. Government BBS List

List of dial-up U.S. government department bulletin boards, including BBSs for the Commerce, Customs, Defense, Energy, and Justice departments.

Gopher:
Name: Panix Public Access Unix
Address: **gopher.panix.com**
Choose: **Society for Electronic Access**
 | List of U.S. Government BBSs

U.S. Government Gophers

An informal list of gopher servers that are either operated or funded by the federal government. Gophers in this list are arranged by government agency.

Gopher:
Name: National Science Foundation
Address: **stis.nsf.gov**
Choose: **Other U.S. Government Gopher Servers**

U.S. Government Today

Current information about the U.S. government, including the House of Representatives and Senate memberships, Congressional phone and fax numbers, and the U.S. budget.

Anonymous FTP:
Address: **ftp.spies.com**
Path: /Gov/US-Gov/*

Gopher:
Name: Internet Wiretap
Address: **wiretap.spies.com**
Choose: **Government Docs (US & World)**
 | US Government Today

GOVERNMENT: U.S. CONGRESS

Bibliography of Senate Hearings

North Carolina State University produces monthly bibliographies of Senate hearings, prints, and publications from title page proofs received weekly from the Senate library.

Anonymous FTP:
Address: **ftp.ncsu.edu**
Path: **/pub/ncsu/senate/***

Gopher:
Name: North Carolina State University
Address: **dewey.lib.ncsu.edu**
Choose: **NCSU's Library without Walls**
 | Study Carrels
 | Government and Law
 | Bibliography of Senate Hearings

Budget of the United States Government

Past budgets and proposed budgets for the upcoming fiscal year in total and broken down by sections.

Gopher:
Name: University of North Carolina
Address: **sunsite.unc.edu**
Choose: **Worlds of SunSITE — by Subject**
 | US and World Politics
 | Sunsite Political Science Archives
 | US-Budget...

Congress Members

Search a database containing the names, addresses, and phone numbers of members of Congress for all fifty states.

Gopher:
Name: Library of Congress
Address: **marvel.loc.gov**
Choose: **U.S Congress**
 | Congressional Directories

Congressional Committee Assignments

Committee assignments for Congressional, Senate, and joint committees and subcommittees.

Gopher:
> Name: University of Michigan
> Address: **gopher.lib.umich.edu**
> Choose: **Social Science Resources**
> | **Govt and Politics**
> | **US Govt Resources: Legislative**
> | **US Congress : Committee Assignments**

Congressional Firsts

A list of racial firsts in the 103rd Congress.

Gopher:
> Name: University of Maryland
> Address: **info.umd.edu**
> Choose: **Educational Resources**
> | **Government**
> | **United States**
> | **Legislative (Congress)**
> | **103rd Congress firsts**

Congressional Legislation

These files track and describe legislation (bills and resolutions) introduced in the Congress, from 1973 (93rd Congress) to the current Congress (103rd). Each file covers a separate Congress.

Telnet:
> Address: **locis.loc.gov**

Congressional Quarterly

A newsletter that offers the latest dirt — or rather, news from Capitol Hill. The information is nonpartisan and in-depth, so it offers good coverage and analysis. The gopher also has reports, book reviews, and other items relating to Congress.

Gopher:
> Name: Congressional Quarterly
> Address: **gopher.cqalert.com**

Edward Kennedy

You don't have to be in Washington to march right into Ted Kennedy's office and see what's going on with the senator. Kennedy's electronic home away from home is now on the Web. Get the latest news that relates to Kennedy's office and the Senate.

See also: Politics, Government

World Wide Web:
> URL: **http://www.ai.mit.edu/projects/iiip/
> Kennedy/homepage.html**

Do you plan on visiting Massachusetts in the near future? Check with Ted Kennedy's office to see if you can get a seat on one of his world-famous motor tours of the countryside. (Just be sure not to forget your swimsuit.)

Legislative Branch Resources

Keep up with what's going on in the U.S. legislative branch of the government. The Library of Congress has put together a nice selection of resources pertaining to Congress, including links to web pages of various members of Congress and notations on the members' voting records.

World Wide Web:
> URL: **http://lcweb.loc.gov/global/congress.html**

GOVERNMENT: U.S. EXECUTIVE BRANCH

Clinton's Cabinet

The résumés of President Clinton's cabinet, including contact information for them — updated hourly.

Anonymous FTP:
> Address: **nifty.andrew.cmu.edu**
> Path: **/pub/QRD/usa/federal/cabinet-resumes**

> Address: **vector.casti.com**
> Path: **/pub/QRD/usa/federal/cabinet-resumes**

Stay cool: read Fashion and Clothing.

A
B
C
D
E
F
G
H
I
J
K
L
M
N
O
P
Q
R
S
T
U
V
W
X
Y
Z

Clinton's Inaugural Address

The full text from Project Gutenberg.

Gopher:
>   Name: University of Minnesota
>   Address: **gopher.micro.umn.edu**
>   Choose: **Libraries**
> | **Electronic Books**
> | **By Title**
> | **Clinton's Inaugural Address**

Executive Branch Information via Gopher

Cabinet members' addresses and phone numbers, how to access White House mail, NAFTA, budget information, the Federal Register, and other items provided by the executive branch of the federal government.

Gopher:
>   Name: University of Michigan
>   Address: **gopher.lib.umich.edu**
>   Choose: **Social Sciences Resources**
> | **Government and Politics**
> | **U.S. Government Resources: Executive Branch**

Executive Branch Resources via the Web

Never again will you have to hotfoot it around the Net looking for government information. The Library of Congress has compiled a web page that covers resources pertaining to the executive branch of the federal government and its various departments, as well as independent executive agencies.

World Wide Web:
>   URL: **http://lcweb.loc.gov/global/executive.html**

Impeaching Clinton

Nobody said being President was fun. Sure, you get to have as many Big Macs as you like, but that doesn't mean it's fun. Consider, for example, this discussion group. Imagine how hurt Clinton's feelings are going to be when he cranks up his newsreader only to find that there are even people on the Internet who don't like him.

Usenet:
>   Newsgroup: **alt.impeach.clinton**

**Like mysteries?
Look at Intrigue.**

National Performance Review

Clinton's "reinventing government" program — the full 180-page text.

Gopher:
>   Name: University of North Carolina
>   Address: **sunsite.unc.edu**
>   Choose: **Worlds of SunSITE — by Subject**
> | **Browse All Sunsite Archives**
> | **Politics**
> | **National Performance Review...**

President's Daily Schedule

Ever wonder what the President of the United States is doing today? Examine the public schedule for the current month or previous months.

Gopher:
>   Name: Texas A&M University
>   Address: **gopher.tamu.edu**
>   Choose: **Hot Topics: What's New & What's Popular**
> | **Hot Topics: A&M's Most Popular Items**
> | **White House Information**
> | **1994 White House Information**
> | **President's Daily Schedule**

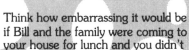

There is absolutely no excuse for not knowing what the President of the United States is doing when all you have to do is check the *President's Daily Schedule Gopher.* Maybe you should take a moment now and do so.

Think how embarrassing it would be if Bill and the family were coming to your house for lunch and you didn't even know.

President's Economic Plan

The details of the President's economic plan.

Gopher:
>   Name: Internet Wiretap
>   Address: **wiretap.spies.com**
>   Choose: **Government Docs (US & World)**
> | **Clinton's Economic Plan**
>
>   Name: University of California San Diego
>   Address: **infopath.ucsd.edu**
>   Choose: **News & Weather**
> | **National News**
> | **Economic Bulletin Board**
> | **Summaries of current economic conditions**
> | **President Clinton's Economic Plan**

Presidential Documents

Lots of information from the White House, including domestic, international, business and economic affairs, and the President's daily schedule.

Gopher:
Name: Texas A&M University
Address: **gopher.tamu.edu**
Choose:
    Hot Topics: What's New & What's Popular
    | **Hot Topics: A&M's Most Popular Items**
    | **White House Information**

U.S. Government Reports

Here's a number of U.S. government publications including the budget for the fiscal year 1994, and even an old GAO report on the feasibility of the strategic defense initiative (Star Wars).

Anonymous FTP:
Address: **ftp.uu.net**
Path: **/doc/literary/obi/USG/***

White House

Information and details about the White House, including the electronic mail system, press conferences, information policy, and the federal budget.

Gopher:
Name: Texas A&M University
Address: **gopher.tamu.edu**
Choose: **Hot Topics: What's New & What's Popular**
    | **A&M's Most Popular Items**
    | **White House Information**

Name: University of North Carolina
Address: **sunsite.unc.edu**
Choose: **Worlds of SunSITE — by Subject**
    | **US and World Politics**
    | **Sunsite Political Science Archives**
    | **whitehouse-papers...**

Name: Whole Earth Lectronic Link
Address: **gopher.well.sf.ca.us**
Choose: **Politics**
    | **The White House Information Archive**

World Wide Web:
URL: **http://sunsite.unc.edu/white-house/white-house.html**

Why be normal? Read Bizarre.

White House Archives

Texas A&M's White House Archives offers information about the executive branch of the government in the areas of domestic affairs, international affairs, the economy and budget, press briefings, speeches, and the President's daily schedule.

World Wide Web:
URL: **http://www.tamu.edu/~/cdl7435/wh.html**

White House News

This news isn't just the small stuff, like what the interior decorators are doing with the Yellow Room these days. This is hard-core news about what the President is doing with appointments, foreign relations, domestic policy and even his spare time.

Usenet:
Newsgroup: **clari.news.usa.gov.white_house**

White House Papers

White House press briefings and other papers dealing with the President, Vice President, First Lady, the Cabinet, Socks (the First Cat), and other important White House personalities.

WAIS:
Database: **White-House-Papers**

White House Press Releases

Press releases and other information about White House characters.

Anonymous FTP:
Address: **ftp.spies.com**
Path: **/Clinton/***

Gopher:
Name: Internet Wiretap
Address: **wiretap.spies.com**
Choose: **Government Docs (US & World)**
    | **White House Press Releases**

World Wide Web:
URL: **http://www.ee.pdx.edu/cat/enchanter/html/wh.html**

White House Press Releases: Daily

Receive by mail daily summaries of the activities and goings-on at the White House and U.S. government. Send a mail message to start the service with the line "subscribe wh-summary" in the body of your message.

Mail:
Address: **almanac@esusda.gov**

A
B
C
D
E
F
G
H
I
J
K
L
M
N
O
P
Q
R
S
T
U
V
W
X
Y
Z

HEALTH

Addictions

A mailing list for mature discussion of addictions, including food disorders, sex, codependency, nicotine, and other addictions.

Listserv Mailing List:
List Address: **addict-l@kentvm.kent.edu**
Subscription Address: **listserv@kentvm.kent.edu**

AIDS Information

AIDS statistics, including daily summaries from newspaper articles, details of those at risk, and the full text of *AIDS Treatment News*.

See also: Medicine

Anonymous FTP:
Address: **nifty.andrew.cmu.edu**
Path: **/pub/QRD/aids/***

Address: **vector.casti.com**
Path: **/pub/QRD/aids/***

Gopher:
Name: National Institute of Health
Address: **odie.niaid.nih.gov**
Choose: **AIDS Related Information**

Name: University of Montana Healthline Gopher Server
Address: **selway.umt.edu**
Port: **700**
Choose: **Sexuality**
 I Acquired Immune Deficiency Syndrome (AIDS)

AIDS News

News about AIDS: stories, research, new treatments and political issues.

Usenet:
Newsgroup: **clari.tw.health.aids**

Attention Deficit Disorder Archive

Information about Attention Deficit Disorder (ADD) including its diagnosis, questions to ask, articles, and other resources relating to ADD.

World Wide Web:
URL: **http://www.seas.upenn.edu/ ~mengwong/add/**

Cancer Mailing List

Discussion of any aspect of cancer, including diagnosis, treatments, self-examination, living with cancer, and more.

Listserv Mailing List:
List Address: **cancer-l@wvnvm.wvnet.edu**
Subscription Address: **listserv@wvnvm.wvnet.edu**

Children with Special Needs

A mailing list dedicated to children with special health care needs and their families, as well as pediatric health care in general.

Listserv Mailing List:
List Address: **cshcn-l@nervm.nerdc.ufl.edu**
Subscription Address:
 listserv@nervm.nerdc.ufl.edu

Communicable Diseases

Information on 60 different diseases — how you catch them, how you get rid of them, and what happens while you have them.

Gopher:
Name: New York State Department of Health
Address: **gopher.health.state.ny.us**
Choose: **NYSDOH — Consumer Health Information**
 I Communicable Diseases

Computers and Health

Is your computer emitting gamma rays that are slowly eating out the gray matter in your brain? Read about computers and health, and get up-to-date facts, opinions, and fallacies about this and other timely topics.

Usenet:
Newsgroup: **bit.listserv.c+health**
Newsgroup: **clari.nb.health**

World Wide Web:
URL: **http://www-penninfo.upenn.edu:1962/ tiserve.mit.edu/9000/25204.html**

Dental Poisoning

A mailing list for the discussion and dissemination of information about dental amalgam and mercury poisoning.

Listserv Mailing List:
List Address: **amalgam@vm.gmd.de**
Subscription Address: **listserv@vm.gmd.de**

Diabetes

Need the latest info about diabetes? Will new immune-desensitizing therapies provide a much-needed preventative measure or even a cure? Read all about the management, treatment, and research of diabetes. Talk with other diabetics who share their experiences, tips, and opinions.

Usenet:
  Newsgroup: **misc.health.diabetes**

Dietary Information

Diet goals, cholesterol statistics, fat and calorie information, and other guides to healthy eating.

Gopher:
  Name: University of Montana Healthline Gopher
    Server
  Address: **selway.umt.edu**
  Port: **700**
  Choose: **General Health Information
  | Dietary Information**

Telnet:
  Address: **selway.umt.edu**
  Login: **health**

Dieting

Does your diet work? Or like the other 99.9 percent of humanity, do you have to suffer to lose excess weight? Join ultra-nutrition-conscious people around the world who will thank you for sharing. Trade stories, scientific trivia, and leftover Weight Watchers' menus. Are you just about ready for your own zip code? Lonely no more.

Usenet:
  Newsgroup: **alt.support.diet**

> ## Learn Unix and
> ## walk with the gods.

Drug and Alcohol Information

Detailed documents and guides about the risks involved with drug and alcohol use, blood alcohol concentration statistics, state laws, and other related facts.

Gopher:
  Name: University of Montana Healthline Gopher
    Server
  Address: **selway.umt.edu**
  Port: **700**
  Choose: **Drug & Alcohol Information**

Listserv Mailing List:
  List Address: **alcohol@lmuacad.bitnet**
  Subscription Address: **listserv@lmuacad.bitnet**

Telnet:
  Address: **selway.umt.edu**
  Login: **health**

Exercise

If you are not exercising right now, you should be feeling guilty. Still, the next best thing is reading about it. Check out the discussion and trade info with some of the best-looking fanatics on the Internet. Are you embarrassed that you still mix up endomysium, perimysium and epimysium? All you have to do is read the regularly posted "Stretching and Flexibility" frequently asked question list.

Usenet:
  Newsgroup: **misc.fitness**

Excerpt from the Net...

```
Newsgroup: alt.support.diet
Subject: Bodyfat Measurement

Hi all.  Since a lot of people have been asking me about various methods of bodyfat measure-
ment, I figured I ought to post something.

There are a variety of methods used to measure bodyfat, each with their own pros and cons.

The most accurate method is to have the body dissected, and then to separate and weigh the
fat cells.  This will give the most accurate value but is rather inconvenient as you have
to be dead for it to work...
```

A B C D E F G H I J K L M N O P Q R S T U V W X Y Z

Eye Care

An informational guide that explains how your eyes work and how to prevent eye problems.

Gopher:
Name: University of Montana Healthline Gopher Server
Address: **selway.umt.edu**
Port: **700**
Choose: **General Health Information**
I How Do Your Eyes Work?

Telnet:
Address: **selway.umt.edu**
Login: **health**

Food and Drug Administration BBS

Sponsored and operated by the FDA, this BBS offers drug and device product approval lists, reports from the Center for Devices and Radiological Health, AIDS information, *FDA Consumer* magazine index and selected articles, veterinary medicine news, import alerts, and other topics.

Telnet:
Address: **fdabbs.fda.gov**
Login: **bbs**

Food Labeling Information

Rulings on labeling requirements for ingredients, serving sizes, terms, fat and cancer, fruits and vegetables, nutritional claims, and other related topics.

Gopher:
Name: U.S. Department of Agriculture
Address: **esusda.gov**
Choose: **USDA and Other Federal Agency Information**
I Food Labeling Information

Headaches

It could be one of those dull, throbbing ones. Or it could be a sharp, aching one. Or maybe it starts slow when the back of your neck is tense and works its way up until it feels like your eyeballs will pop out. If you have personal or professional interest in headaches of any sort, this is a mailing list and ftp archive that will interest you. Discussion covers the physical, emotional, social, and economic impact of recurring headaches.

Anonymous FTP:
Address: **niord.shsu.edu**
Path: **/headache.dir/***

Listserv Mailing List:
List Address: **headache@shsu.edu**
Subscription Address: **listserv@shsu.edu**

Does your head feel okay? Well, we can fix that.

Take a look at the *Headaches* resource and see what you've been missing.

Health Care Reform Act

Documents, reports, and the text of briefings and press releases regarding the Health Security Act of 1993. The documents here only support the proposal.

Anonymous FTP:
Address: **sunsite.unc.edu**
Path: **/pub/academic/political-science/ Health-Security-Act**

Gopher:
Name: U.S. Department of Agriculture
Address: **ace.esusda.gov**
Choose: **Americans Communicating Electronically**
I National Policy Issues
I Health Care Reform Agenda
I Health Security Act

Name: University of North Carolina
Address: **gopher.unc.edu**
Choose: **Worlds of SunSITE — by subject**
I Browse All Sunsite Archives
I Politics
I Health-Security-Act

Telnet:
Address: **fedworld.gov**

World Wide Web:
URL: **http://sunsite.unc.edu/nhs/NHS-T-o-C**

Clinton's Health Care Package

Personally, we wouldn't get sick if you paid us. The trouble is, no one will pay us, and sometimes we get sick anyway. So, if you're going to be sick, you might as well read all about the Clintons' plans for reforming the American health care system.

Health General Information

Documents and guides on many health dysfunctions, including asthma, back pain, headaches, and sleeping disorders.

Gopher:
Name: University of Montana Healthline Gopher Server
Address: **selway.umt.edu**
Port: **700**
Choose: **General Health Information**

Telnet:
Address: **selway.umt.edu**
Login: **health**

Health Info-Com Network Newsletter

A biweekly publication by medical professionals that addresses issues and concerns about medicine and health.

Gopher:
Name: University of Maryland
Address: **info.umd.edu**
Choose: **Computer Resources**
 I Network Information
 I Newsletters
 I Health Info Com

Don't worry about technology, just enjoy yourself.

Health Issue Discussion

Usenet and electronic mail discussion groups on health issues, including health-related archives.

Gopher:
Name: University of Montana Healthline Gopher Server
Address: **selway.umt.edu**
Port: **700**
Choose: **Internet Health-related Resources**
 I Usenet News & Electronic Mail Discussion Groups on Health Issue

Telnet:
Address: **selway.umt.edu**
Login: **health**

Health News

Read the news about health care and medicine. Find out if there is a cure for what ails ya.

Usenet:
Newsgroup: **clari.tw.health**

Health Newsletters

Selection of newsletters covering medicine, medical research, disease, and therapy.

Anonymous FTP:
Address: **nigel.msen.com**
Path: **/pub/newsletters/Health/***

KEEP A HEALTHY INTEREST IN HEALTH. SEE **HEALTH NEWSLETTERS**

Health Resources

A collection of links to health-related resources and sites, including the World Health Organization, Rights and Health Care, and the National Institutes of Health.

World Wide Web:
URL: **http://access.cs.fsu.edu:1992/healthdir/TOC.health.html**
URL: **http://zaphod.cc.ttu.ee/vrainn/nox/health.html**

Jokes? Try Humor.

Health Science Resources

A large list of Internet and Bitnet resources related to the health sciences.

Gopher:
Name: NYSERNet
Address: **nysernet.org**
Choose: **Reference Desk**
  | **600 - Applied Science and Technology**
  | **610 - Medical Sciences**
  | **Internet Health Sciences Resources 3-94**

Health Sciences Libraries Consortium

The Health Sciences Libraries Consortium (HSLC) Computer Based Learning Software Database, begun in 1987, contains listings of PC-compatible and Macintosh programs used in health sciences education. This project has been endorsed and funded by the American Medical Informatics Association's Education Working Group. Records have also been contributed by the University of Michigan's Software for Health Sciences Education.

Telnet:
Address: **hslc.org**
Login: **cbl**

Healthline

Documents and information on a wide range of topics from migraine headaches to health products.

Gopher:
Name: University of Montana Healthline Gopher Server
Address: **selway.umt.edu**
Port: **700**

Telnet:
Address: **selway.umt.edu**
Login: **health**

HEALTH INFO GOPHER

No need to wonder about what ails you.
Connect to the *Healthline* Gopher and get the facts.

(Then you can really worry.)

Excerpt from the Net...

```
Newsgroup: alt.backrubs
Subject: Michelle Loves Back Rubs

> My name is Michelle. I'm 19 years old, and I live in Michigan.

> I am 5'6", 125 lbs, long, blonde hair. I love getting back rubs from
> cute guys (mainly ones who like country music).

> Is there anyone who would like to give me a back rub?
> I'll be wearing nothing but a pair of black silky pantyhose.

Michelle,

Too bad you are in Michigan because I love back rubs too.
The funny thing is that I like to wear black silky panty hose too.

Aching in Salt Lake,
     Dave
```

HealthNet

A project to help highlight the potential of existing communications technologies being applied toward a health care information infrastructure in Canada. This project provides demonstrations of possible health care applications and links to other related resources.

World Wide Web:
    URL: **http://hpb.hwc.ca/healthnet/**

Massage

Just by using your fingers, you can turn someone into a noodle. Massage is a delicious and therapeutic way to alleviate the effects of tension and ill health. Discover new techniques and new methods of massage along with recommendations for oils and additional accoutrements that can take massage to a new level.

Anonymous FTP:
    Address: **ftp.csd.uwo.ca**
    Path: **/pub/news/alt.backrubs**

Usenet:
    Newsgroup: **alt.backrubs**

Material Safety Data Sheets

A database of information on hundreds of chemicals and compounds. Includes scientific data such as molecular formulas and atomic weights as well as health hazards and fire-fighting procedures.

Gopher:
    Name: Iowa State University
    Address: **isumvs.iastate.edu**
    Choose: **ISU Research**
      **I EPA Chemical Substances Database
      (Univ. of Virginia)**

Migraine Headaches

Information about the symptoms of, and how to cope with, migraine headaches, which affect one out of every 20 people.

Gopher:
    Name: University of Montana Healthline Gopher
      Server
    Address: **selway.umt.edu**
    Port: **700**
    Choose: **General Health Information
      I Migraine Headaches**

Telnet:
    Address: **selway.umt.edu**
    Login: **health**

Morbidity and Mortality Weekly Report

Current and back issues of the *Morbidity and Mortality Weekly Report.*

Gopher:
    Name: National Institute of Health
    Address: **odie.niaid.nih.gov**
    Choose: **AIDS Related Information
      I Morbidity and Mortality Weekly Report**

National Institute of Allergy and Infectious Disease

The NIAID gopher offers up-to-date information on a wide variety of health topics.

Gopher:
    Name: National Institute of Health
    Address: **gopher.niaid.nih.gov**

National Institute of Health

Announcements, information for researchers, a molecular biology database, library and literature resources, the NIH phone book, and more.

Gopher:
    Name: National Institute of Health
    Address: **gopher.nih.gov**

    Name: University of California San Diego
    Address: **infopath.ucsd.edu**
    Choose: **The World
      I Misc Special Topics or Reference Sources
      I Federal Government
      I National Institute of Health (NIH) Gopher**

New York State Department of Health

Archives and information on communicable diseases, consumer health information, health publications and other resources.

Gopher:
    Name: New York State Department of Health
    Address: **gopher.health.state.ny.us**

> **To dream is human,
> to telnet is divine.**

A
B
C
D
E
F
G
H
I
J
K
L
M
N
O
P
Q
R
S
T
U
V
W
X
Y
Z

Nutrition

Should you eat the Twinkie or opt for another seaweed sandwich? Join the conversation and talk about all aspects of diet and eating. Vitamins, carbohydrates, proteins, fats, minerals, fiber — the usual gang of suspects is waiting for you here.

Usenet:
   Newsgroup: **sci.med.nutrition**

Physical Sciences Conferences

A long list of mailing lists related to the physical sciences, arranged by subject area.

Anonymous FTP:
   Address: **ksuvxa.kent.edu**
   Path: **/library/acadlist.file6**

Gopher:
   Name: Oregon State University
   Address: **gopher.kerr.orst.edu**
   Choose: **Internet Resources Grouped by Subject
   l Directory of Scholarly Electronic Conferences
   l Physical Sciences**

   Name: University of Notre Dame
   Address: **gopher.nd.edu**
   Choose: **Non-Notre Dame Information Sources
   l Electronic Journals, Periodicals, Etc.
   l Directory of Scholarly Electronic Conferences**

Public Health Information Guide

A guide to help you locate public health-related resources on the Internet. Resources include links to documents, ftp sites, web pages and gopher servers.

World Wide Web:
   URL: **http://128.196.106.42/ph-hp.html**

Sexual Health Topics

Guides to many sex-related health topics, including contraception, STDs, AIDS, cervical cancer, and other health issues.

Gopher:
   Name: University of Montana Healthline Gopher
      Server
   Address: **selway.umt.edu**
   Port: **700**
   Choose: **Sexuality**

Telnet:
   Address: **selway.umt.edu**
   Login: **health**

Do you like weirdness? Check out Usenet Curiosities.

Sleeping Problems

Antidepressant and sleep disorder guides and advice on how to get a good night's sleep.

Gopher:
   Name: University of Montana Healthline Gopher
      Server
   Address: **selway.umt.edu**
   Port: **700**
   Choose: **General Health Information
   l Antidepressants and Sleep Disorders**

   Name: University of Montana Healthline Gopher
      Server
   Address: **selway.umt.edu**
   Port: **700**
   Choose: **General Health Information
   l Do's and Dont's for Poor Sleepers**

Telnet:
   Address: **selway.umt.edu**
   Login: **health**

Snakebites

Learn how to prevent and treat bites from poisonous North American snakes. Also includes information on the effects of snakebites.

Anonymous FTP:
   Address: **ftp.spies.com**
   Path: **/Library/Article/Outdoors/snake.bc**

Gopher:
   Name: Internet Wiretap
   Address: **wiretap.spies.com**
   Choose: **Wiretap Online Library
   l Articles
   l Backcountry and Outdoors
   l BC: Snakebite Distilled Wisdom**

Surgeon General's Warning on AIDS

A message from the Surgeon General of the United States about AIDS.

Anonymous FTP:
   Address: **ftp.spies.com**
   Path: **/Library/Article/Sex/aids.sg**

Typing Injuries

All the information about typing injuries and their solutions. Includes a long list of keyboard alternatives and some related gif pictures.

Anonymous FTP:
Address: **ftp.csua.berkeley.edu**
Path: **/pub/typing-injury/***

World Wide Web:
URL: **http://www.cis.ohio-state.edu/hypertext/ faq/usenet/typing-injury-faq/top.html**

U.S. Department of Health and Human Services

The DHHS web server provides information on the mission, programs, organization, initiatives, activities, and impact of the DHHS on the health and well-being of the American public. In addition, this server provides access to information and resources made available by the various organizations that comprise DHHS.

World Wide Web:
URL: **http://www.os.dhhs.gov/**

Wellness Mailing List

This mailing list is for discussing issues of health, nutrition, wellness, life expectancy and fitness. You can also come here for advice on books and the personal experiences of other participants. If you're interested in your health, check out the healthy recipes and other good advice you can get here — free!

Majordomo Mailing List:
List Address: **wellnesslist@wellnessmart.com**
Subscription Address:
majordomo@wellnessmart.com

World Health Organization

This gopher and web page are home to the World Health Organization (WHO) located in Switzerland. Information on the projects supported by WHO and upcoming events are available on this server.

Gopher:
Name: World Health Organization
Address: **gopher.who.ch**

World Wide Web:
URL: **http://www.who.ch/**

Yoga

Everyone is looking for a way to save time these days. Yoga is the way to do it. Not only can you prepare your mind for enlightenment, but you can get some great exercise at the same time. Get information on a variety of yoga paths including Karma, Kriya, Bhakti, Surat Shabd, and Astanga, among others.

See also: Health, New Age

World Wide Web:
URL: **http://err.ethz.ch/~kiwi/Spirit/Yoga/ Overview.html**

HISTORICAL DOCUMENTS

American Historical Documents

The Constitution, Amendments to the Constitution, Annapolis Convention, Articles of Confederation, Bill of Rights, Charlottetown Resolves, Continental Congress Resolves, Japanese and German surrenders, "I Have a Dream" speech, inaugural addresses, the Monroe Doctrine, *Rights of Man*, treaties, and more.

Anonymous FTP:
Address: **ftp.spies.com**
Path: **/Gov/US-History/***

Gopher:
Name: Internet Wiretap
Address: **wiretap.spies.com**
Choose: **Government Docs (US & World)
  I US Historical Documents**

Name: University of Minnesota
Address: **gopher.micro.umn.edu**
Choose: **Libraries
  I Electronic Books
  I By Title
  I Historical Documents**

A
B
C
D
E
F
G
H
I
J
K
L
M
N
O
P
Q
R
S
T
U
V
W
X
Y
Z

Constitution of the United States of America

The complete text of the Constitution of the United States.

Anonymous FTP:
Address: **ocf.berkeley.edu**
Path: **/pub/Library/Politics/U.S._Constitution.gz**

Address: **ucselx.sdsu.edu**
Path: **/pub/doc/etext/USConstitution.txt**

Gopher:
Name: University of Maryland
Address: **info.umd.edu**
Choose: **Educational Resources**
  | **Academic Resources By Topic**
  | **United States and World Politics, Culture and History**
  | **United States**
  | **Historical Documents**
  | **The Constitution of the United States**

Declaration of Arms, 1775

The complete text of the Declaration of the Causes and Necessity of Taking Up Arms—July 6, 1775.

Anonymous FTP:
Address: **ftp.spies.com**
Path: **/Gov/US-History/arms1775.txt**

Gopher:
Name: Internet Wiretap
Address: **wiretap.spies.com**
Choose: **Government Docs (US & World)**
  | **US Historical Documents**
  | **Declaration of Arms, 1775**

Declaration of Independence

The complete text of the Declaration of Independence.

Anonymous FTP:
Address: **ocf.berkeley.edu**
Path: **/pub/Library/Politics/Declaration_of_Independence.gz**

Address: **ucselx.sdsu.edu**
Path: **/pub/doc/etext/Declaration.txt**

Document Archive

An archive of historical documents, including the Magna Carta, the U.S. Bill of Rights, Lincoln's Second Inaugural Address, the Monroe Doctrine, the Mayflower Compact, the Emancipation Proclamation, and many others.

Anonymous FTP:
Address: **ftp.uu.net**
Path: **/doc/literary/freedom-shrine/***

Emancipation Proclamation

Lincoln's Emancipation Proclamation of 1862, with comments and explanations.

Anonymous FTP:
Address: **ftp.spies.com**
Path: /Gov/US-History/emancip.txt

Gopher:
Name: Internet Wiretap
Address: **wiretap.spies.com**
Choose: **Government Docs (US & World)**
  | **US Historical Documents**
  | **Emancipation Proclamation**

The *Declaration of Independence*

Few written documents are as important and well-written as the Declaration of Independence. (In fact, the only one we can think of is **The Internet Complete Reference.**) *Download a copy and take a few minutes to examine this crucial piece of history. After all, if it wasn't for the Declaration of Independence, America would still be British and the whole country would have to eat boiled food and worry about Charles and Diana.*

The next time your teacher or your boss tries to tell you what to do, download the Emancipation Proclamation and mail them their own personal copy.

Everything in this book is free.

Federalist Papers

The full text from Project Gutenberg.

Gopher:
Name: University of Minnesota
Address: **gopher.micro.umn.edu**
Choose: **Libraries**
  | **Electronic Books**
  | **By Title**
  | **Federalist Papers, The**

Who Killed JFK?

We know. Our research on the Internet has uncovered hitherto secret documentation explaining beyond the tiniest shadow of a doubt who killed President Kennedy.

Of course, you can do your own research (there are several good sites on the Net), but we were particularly lucky in finding several pieces of the puzzle that, frankly, we couldn't expect to figure out except by pure serendipity.

So, as a public service, we will now explain exactly what happened with Kennedy, Mrs. Kennedy, John Connally, Lee Harvey Oswald and Jack Ruby. Once and for all, we are going to

explain this tantalizing and seemingly insolvable mystery. So here it is:

What *really* happened is as follows: It seems that... hold on...

What's this? We're out of space? Are you sure? Well...okay.

Sorry folks, there just isn't space to explain it all right now. Maybe in the next edition.

Gulf War Announcement Speech

The text of the speech President Bush gave to the nation on January 16, 1991 announcing Operation Desert Shield.

Anonymous FTP:
Address: **ftp.uu.net**
Path: **/doc/literary/obi/George.Bush/ Desert.Shield**

JFK Conspiracy Documents

Various works and documents describing conspiracy theories about the assassination of John Kennedy and the evidence supporting them.

Anonymous FTP:
Address: **ftp.uu.net**
Path: **/doc/literary/obi/JFK/***

Usenet:
Newsgroup: **alt.conspiracy.jfk**

World Wide Web:
URL: **http://heiwww.unige.ch/jfk/**

Source Documents on the Holocaust

An archive of historical Nazi documents about the Jewish Holocaust.

Anonymous FTP:
Address: **ftp.uu.net**
Path: **/doc/literary/obi/Holocaust/***

U.N. Resolutions on Desert Storm

An archive of the United Nations resolutions relating to the Gulf War of 1991.

Anonymous FTP:
Address: **ftp.uu.net**
Path: **/doc/literary/Desert.Storm/UN.Res.***

Be informed. Check out Consumer Information.

A B C D E F G H I J K L M N O P Q R S T U V W X Y Z

HISTORY

Aegean Palaces

How and why did the first Aegean palaces end up where they did? This is one of the burning mysteries that keep historians up at night when even warm milk will not induce slumber. Documents of Aegean prehistory are now available on the Net, so when the urge to explore the origins of such palatial civilizations strikes, you will know just where to go.

World Wide Web:
    URL: **http://rome.classics.lsa.umich.edu/ 11.FirstPalaces.0393.html**

American Memory Collection

The Library of Congress has put together these "scrapbooks" of American history and culture. Flip through and look at Civil War photographs, portraits of literary figures, artists and celebrities, photos of rural America, and hear sound recordings of speeches that were delivered around the World War I era.

World Wide Web:
    URL: **http://rs6.loc.gov/amtitle.html**

American Studies

This is a great place to argue about who discovered America, because you can be sure these people know what they are talking about. And with American Studies there aren't as many dates to remember because the history is much shorter. Come dwell on the past with other scholars of American Studies and discuss issues relating to your field.

Listserv Mailing List:
    List Address: **h-amstdy@uicvm.uic.edu**
    Subscription Address: **listserv@uicvm.uic.edu**

Anglo-Saxon Mailing List

A mailing list for scholars and others interested in the culture and history of England in the later Middle Ages and early medieval periods.

Listserv Mailing Address:
    List Address: **ansax-1@wvnvm.wvnet.edu**
    Subscription Address: **listsev@wvnvm.wvnet.edu**

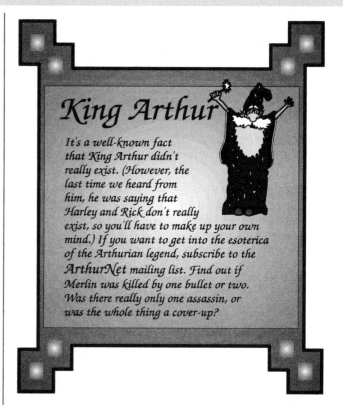

King Arthur

It's a well-known fact that King Arthur didn't really exist. (However, the last time we heard from him, he was saying that Harley and Rick don't really exist, so you'll have to make up your own mind.) If you want to get into the esoterica of the Arthurian legend, subscribe to the ArthurNet mailing list. Find out if Merlin was killed by one bullet or two. Was there really only one assassin, or was the whole thing a cover-up?

ArthurNet

Immerse yourself in the romance, mystery, and magic of the legendary age of King Arthur. Scholars and students of literature, history, mythology and philosophy discuss Arthurian subjects from the early Middle Ages to modern day.

See also: Literature

Listserv Mailing List:
    List Address: **arthurnet@morgan.ucs.mun.ca**
    Subscription Address:
        listserv@morgan.ucs.mun.ca

Aztec Studies

What is the Nahuatl for "Please hand me that spear — the explorers are coming?" We don't know and apparently the Aztecs didn't either. Nevertheless, the Aztec culture and language are fascinating and mysterious. Brush the dust off your linguistic skills and join in on this unmoderated discussion which focuses on Aztec studies in general and the Nahuatl language in particular.

See also: World Cultures

Internet Mailing List:
    List Address: **nahuat-l@fauvax.bitnet**
    Subscription Address:
        nahuat-l-request@fauvax.bitnet

Camelot

Mythology and history concerning King Arthur, the Knights of the Round Table, and the Holy Grail, including reenactments, literature, linguistics, archaeology, and mysticism. This ftp site contains archives, gifs of an Arthurian nature, FAQs, and other documents of interest.

Anonymous FTP:
   Address: **sapphire.epcc.ed.ac.uk**
   Path: **/pub/camelot/***

Charlotte, The Vermont Whale

Images, articles, and discussions about the discovery of the bones of a whale in the fields of rural Vermont.

World Wide Web:
   URL: **http://www.uvm.edu/whale/
      whalehome.html**

Civil War

Answers to dozens of interesting questions about the American Civil War. A good resource for historical information and trivia.

Anonymous FTP:
   Address: **etext.archive.umich.edu**
   Path: **/pub/Quartz/history/civil-war-faq.gz**

   Address: **ftp.cic.net**
   Path: **/pub/ETEXT/pub/Quartz/history/
      civil-war-faq.gz**

Gopher:
   Name: University of Toronto
   Address: **gopher.physics.utoronto.ca**
   Choose: **USENET News Frequently Asked
      Questions (FAQ)**
   | **FAQ - All FAQ listed by archive name**
   | **civil-war-faq**

Classical Studies

A FAQ list for the Usenet newsgroup **sci.classics**, which is devoted to the study of Greco-Roman civilization.

Anonymous FTP:
   Address: **rtfm.mit.edu**
   Path: **/pub/usenet/news.answers/classics-faq**

D-Day

In remembrance of D-Day, Patch American High School has put together a web page with documents from that notable day as well as World War II in general. This site has government documents, excerpts from *Stars and Stripes*, quotes, Quicktime and mpeg Army newsreels, photos, maps, declassified top-secret invasion documents, and interviews.

See also: Military, International Politics

World Wide Web:
   URL: **http://192.253.114.31/D-Day/
      Table_of_contents.html**

DINOSAURS

The fact is, just about everybody likes dinosaurs (unless they are named "Barney"). If you've got kids, show them how to use your web browser and point it at the DINOSAUR EXHIBIT at the Honolulu Community College. We owe it to ourselves to spend some time learning about these great beasts from the past and how they influence our modern culture. (After all, dinosaurs are people too.)

For example, few people realize it but, before David Letterman, the top-rated American nighttime TV talkshow host was a dinosaur. And fully 75% of modern American publishing companies are run by dinosaurs. Let's teach our kids to understand and appreciate our friends in the dinosaur kingdom, and soon we will all be living in peace and harmony.

A
B
C
D
E
F
G
H
I
J
K
L
M
N
O
P
Q
R
S
T
U
V
W
X
Y
Z

Dinosaur Discussion List

An open discussion about dinosaurs of the Mesozoic era. Discussion topics range from detailed theories to popular news items.

Listproc Mailing List:
List Address: **dinosaur@lepomis.psych.upenn.edu**
Subscription Address:
listproc@lepomis.psych.upenn.edu

Dinosaur Exhibit

Honolulu Community College is sponsoring an impressive dinosaur exhibit. For those of you who can't hop a plane to see the display, a guided tour has been made available on the Net. The tour will show you fossils and sculptures during a narrated tour complete with sound and images. This site also has links to other interesting dinosaur resources.

See also: Archaeology

World Wide Web:
URL: **http://www.hcc.hawaii.edu/dinos/ dinos.1.html**

Feudal Terms

A dictionary of terms from feudal times, including such words as "abbey," "Black Monks," "fief," and "yoke."

Anonymous FTP:
Address: **ftp.spies.com**
Path: **/Library/Article/Socio/feudal.dic**

Gopher:
Name: Internet Wiretap
Address: **wiretap.spies.com**
Choose: **Wiretap Online Library**
| Articles
| Sociological Issues
| Feudal Terms Dictionary

Hall of Dinosaurs

A magnificent multimedia tour of the Dinosaur Antechamber at the University of California's Museum of Paleontology. These pages are packed with facts, images, diagrams, skeletons, and history. Click on a specific area of the phylogeny diagram of Dinosauria and Ancestors to begin your tour.

World Wide Web:
URL: **http://ucmp1.berkeley.edu/exhibittext/ cladecham.html**

Hiroshima Accounts

Accounts and first hand experiences of survivors of the atomic bombing of Hiroshima.

Anonymous FTP:
Address: **ftp.uu.net**
Path: **/doc/literary/obi/Hiroshima/***

Historian's Database and Information Server

HNSource is the central information server for historians, located at the University of Kansas. This system allows users to browse through a wide variety of information resources related to the historical discipline.

Gopher:
Name: U.S. Military Academy
Address: **euler.math.usma.edu**
Choose: **USMA_Academic_Departments**
| Department of History
| History Source at the University of Kansas

Telnet:
Address: **hnsource.cc.ukans.edu**
Login: **history**

Address: **ukanaix.cc.ukans.edu**
Login: **history**

Historian's Newsletter

A newsletter for historians and anyone else interested in history.

Listserv Mailing List:
List Address: **histnews@ukanvm.cc.ukans.edu**
Subscription Address:
listserv@ukanvm.cc.ukans.edu

Historic American Speeches

The text of many historic American speeches and addresses, including some of those given by Washington, Jefferson, Martin Luther King, Lincoln, Kennedy, and others.

Anonymous FTP:
Address: **ftp.spies.com**
Path: **/Gov/US-Speech/***

Gopher:
Name: Internet Wiretap
Address: **wiretap.spies.com**
Choose: **Government Docs (US & World)**
| US Speeches and Address

Historical Sounds and Speeches

The Vincent Voice Collection of historical sounds and speeches contains many sound files of famous speeches including some from John F. Kennedy, Richard Nixon, Teddy Roosevelt, Babe Ruth, Betty Ford, and many more.

Gopher:
> Name: Michigan State University
> Address: **burrow.cl.msu.edu**
> Choose: **Libraries**
> | **Collections**
> | **Main Libraries/Collections**
> | **Vincent Voice Library**

History Archives

Archives of history material, including articles, bibliographies, databases, software, gif images, papers, newsletters, and diaries. Historical subjects include diplomacy, ethnicity, military, maritime, political, scientific, women, and many more.

Anonymous FTP:
> Address: **byrd.mu.wvnet.edu**
> Path: **/pub/history/***

> Address: **ra.msstate.edu**
> Path: **/pub/docs/history/***

History Discussion

The great thing about history is that you never run out of it. Every minute there is more history made and that just means there is more to memorize when you are in school. Stop in at Usenet and hang out with the people who love to dwell on the past.

Usenet:
> Newsgroup: **soc.history.moderated**

**Parents and children,
take a look at:
Families and Parenting,
Kids, and Youth.**

History Mailing Lists

Devoted to people interested in any aspect of history. Discussions range from trivial to very serious. Newcomers are welcome.

Listserv Mailing List:
> List Address: **hist-l@ukanvm.cc.ukans.edu**
> Subscription Address:
>   **listserv@ukanvm.cc.ukans.edu**

> List Address: **history@irlearn.ucd.ie**
> Subscription Address: **listserv@irlearn.ucd.ie**

> List Address: **history@vm1.mcgill.ca**
> Subscription Address: **listserv@vm1.mcgill.ca**

> List Address: **history@psuvm.psu.edu**
> Subscription Address: **listserv@psuvm.psu.edu**

> List Address: **history@ubvm.cc.buffalo.edu**
> Subscription Address:
>   **listserv@ubvm.cc.buffalo.edu**

> List Address: **history@earn.cvut.cz**
> Subscription Address: **listserv@earn.cvut.cz**

> List Address: **history@rutvm1.rutgers.edu**
> Subscription Address:
>   **listserv@rutvm1.rutgers.edu**

History of the Ancient Mediterranean

Debate, discussion, and the exchange of information by students and scholars of the history of the ancient Mediterranean.

Listserv Mailing List:
> List Address: **ancien-l@ulkyvm.louisville.edu**
> Subscription Address:
>   **listserv@ulkyvm.louisville.edu**

Holocaust Discussion

This list covers not only the Holocaust itself, but also related topics such as anti-semitism, Jewish history in the 1930s and 1940s, and any topics with related themes in the history of World War II and Germany. This list is sponsored by the history department of the University of Illinois and its Jewish Studies program.

Listserv Mailing List:
> List Address: **holocaus@uicvm.uic.edu**
> Subscription Address: **listserv@uicvm.uic.edu**

> List Address: **hlist@oneb.almanac.bc.ca**
> Subscription Address:
>   **listserv@oneb.almanac.bc.ca**

A B C D E F G H I J K L M N O P Q R S T U V W X Y Z

I Have a Dream

The text of Martin Luther King, Jr.'s "I Have a Dream" speech.

Anonymous FTP:
Address: **ocf.berkeley.edu**
Path: **/pub/Library/Politics/I_Have_a_Dream.gz**

Interactive Natural History Museum

Adventure through the exhibits and catalogs of the enormous collections of paleontological materials at the U.C. Berkeley Museum of Paleontology. Learn what fossils tell us about the ecologies of the past, about evolution, and about our place as humans.

World Wide Web:
URL: **http://ucmp1.berkeley.edu/**

Internet Timeline

A document showing the history of the development of the Internet from the 1956 Russian launch of Sputnik, which might have triggered it all, through ARPANET, UUCP in 1976, Usenet in 1979, the Internet Worm in 1988, and right up to the exponential growth that we see today.

See also: Internet

World Wide Web:
URL: **http://tig.com/IBC/Timeline.html**

Jesuits and the Sciences

A magnificent stone arch greets you on this web page, which offers rare scientific works from the Cudahy Collection of Jesuitica at the Science Library of Loyola University of Chicago. The exhibition is divided into four main time periods and offers a collection of images and text from rare works in astronomy, cosmology, engineering, mathematics and natural history. The text was written during the 17th and 18th centuries, and some of the original Latin is included beside the images.

See also: Science

World Wide Web:
URL: **http://www.luc.edu/~scilib/jessci.html**

If you lived here, you'd be home by now.

Marx and Engels' Writings

A library of major works by, and articles about, Karl Marx and Friedrich Engels, dating from 1837 to 1895.

Gopher:
Name: Carnegie-Mellon University
Address: **english-server.hss.cmu.edu**
Choose: **Marx and Engels**

World Wide Web:
URL: **http://english-server.hss.cmu.edu/Marx.html**

Medieval History

Never mind that people were dirty, smelly, poor, and ate rotten food. Medieval history is cool because people got to fight with swords. Anyone who studies the culture and history of the medieval era can tell you that people were very different back then, as is evidenced by their politics, art, philosophy and religion. Scholars and students of the Middle Ages (A.D. 476 to A.D. 1453) discuss this period in history.

See also: Philosophy

Listserv Mailing List:
List Address: **mediev-l@ukanvm.cc.ukans.edu**
Subscription Address:
listserv@ukanvm.cc.ukans.edu

North America

This web page is a starting point for learning about the history of various American states, including their constitutions, and the Library of Congress.

World Wide Web:
URL: **http://history.cc.ukans.edu/history/reading_rooms/north_america.html**

Palace of Diocletian

A story-book tour with inline images and detailed facts of a Roman Palace in the former Yugoslavia.

See also: Architecture

World Wide Web:
URL: **http://www.ncsa.uiuc.edu/SDG/Experimental/split/split1.html**

Prehistoric Flying Creatures

An article discussing large flying creatures of the distant past and how they overcame gravity.

Anonymous FTP:
    Address: **ftp.spies.com**
    Path: **/Library/Article/Misc/dinosaur.fly**

Gopher:
    Name: Internet Wiretap
    Address: **wiretap.spies.com**
    Choose: **Wiretap Online Library**
      | Articles
      | Misc
      | Prehistoric Flying Creatures and Gravity

Renaissance

What a creative time in history the Renaissance was. Beautiful art, architecture and clothing are just a few of the things that originate from that time period. If you can ignore the Plague, you can almost imagine it would be a great time in which to live. Scholars, students, and historians exchange information on the history of the Renaissance in the form of letters, papers, announcements of meetings and debates.

See also: Fashion and Clothing

Listserv Mailing List:
    List Address: **renais-l@ulkyvm.louisville.edu**
    Subscription Address:
      listserv@ulkyvm.louisville.edu

History buffs: join the Renaissance mailing list and see what other people have to say about art, beauty, architecture, and all the other things that people used to do before there was television.

Sardinia

An extensive history of Sardinia by Francesco Cesare Casula complete with gif pictures.

World Wide Web:
    URL: **http://www.crs4.it/~luigi/SARDEGNA/sardegna.html**

Spanish and Portuguese History

Spice up your mailbox with some discussion on Spanish and Portuguese historical studies. Most of this list is in English, but postings in Portuguese, Spanish or Catalan are welcome. This list is for both students and scholars.

Listserv Mailing List:
    List Address: **espora-l@ukanvm.cc.ukans.edu**
    Subscription Address:
      listserv@ukanvm.cc.ukans.edu

U.S. History

An archive on general American historical subjects.

Anonymous FTP:
    Address: **ftp.uu.net**
    Path: **/doc/literary/obi/History/***

Vatican Exhibit

Witness the rebirth of Rome with the multimedia version of the Vatican exhibit called "Rome Reborn." Links take you through a detailed, yet easy-to-read explanation of the history and culture of Rome. Also, jpeg images accompany the text.

World Wide Web:
    URL: **http://www.ncsa.uiuc.edu/SDG/Experimental/vatican.exhibit/Vati**

Vietnam War Information

Documents and reports about the Vietnam era, including the Senate Select POW-MIA Affairs Report.

Anonymous FTP:
    Address: **ftp.spies.com**
    Path: **/Gov/US-History/Vietnam/***

Gopher:
    Name: Internet Wiretap
    Address: **wiretap.spies.com**
    Choose: **Government Docs (US & World)**
      | US Historical Documents
      | Vietnam Era Documents

A B C D E F G H I J K L M N O P Q R S T U V W X Y Z

Vietnam War Mailing List

Sometimes even when things are over, they are never really over, and that's how it is with war. This list is a place for scholars, students, teachers, veterans, and family and friends of veterans to communicate their thoughts, feelings and ideas about the Vietnam War.

Listserv Mailing List:
List Address: **vwar-l@ubvm.cc.buffalo.edu**
Subscription Address:
listserv@ubvm.cc.buffalo.edu

Vikings

A web page dedicated to the Vikings. This page includes details of the Viking era (793-1050), the AEsir cult, a short Swedish-Viking-English Dictionary, and details and excerpts from the exhibition of Vikings in Russia at the Sigtuna Museum.

World Wide Web:
URL: **http://control.chalmers.se/vikings/ viking.html**

War

Whenever you have more than one person on the planet at the same time, there is always the chance that you are going to have a war. This sort of behavior has been going on for centuries and no amount of naps or "time-outs" is going to solve the problem. Historians and history lovers gather around the Usenet campfire to talk about anything relating to war.

Usenet:
Newsgroup: **soc.history.war.misc**

World War II

Military and history buffs discuss the history, strategy, technology, politics and sociology of World War II as well as toss around a few bits of interesting trivia.

See also: Military, Government, Politics: National (U.S.)

Listserv Mailing List:
List Address: **wwii-l@ubvm.cc.buffalo.edu**
Subscription Address:
listserv@ubvm.cc.buffalo.edu

Usenet:
Newsgroup: **soc.history.war.world-war-ii**

World War II Documents

Historical documents relating to incidents leading up to and during the Second World War.

Anonymous FTP:
Address: **ftp.spies.com**
Path: **/Gov/US-History/WWII/***

Gopher:
Name: Internet Wiretap
Address: **wiretap.spies.com**
Choose: **Government Docs (US & World)**
  I **US Historical Documents**
  I **World War II Documents**

HOBBIES

Amateur Radio

We all have a need to communicate — some of us just like to do it over long distances. Usenet provides a large number of newsgroups devoted to the enjoyment of amateur radio. Tune in, turn on, and drop whatever you are doing: whether you are a novice or a pro, there is a discussion group for you.

Usenet:
> Newsgroup: **rec.radio.amateur.antenna**
> Newsgroup: **rec.radio.amateur.digital.misc**
> Newsgroup: **rec.radio.amateur.equipment**
> Newsgroup: **rec.radio.amateur.homebrew**
> Newsgroup: **rec.radio.amateur.misc**
> Newsgroup: **rec.radio.amateur.packet**
> Newsgroup: **rec.radio.amateur.policy**
> Newsgroup: **rec.radio.cb**
> Newsgroup: **rec.radio.shortwave**
> Newsgroup: **rec.radio.swap**

Amateur Radio Information by Mail

Interested in amateur radio? This site has all the information, including how to get started in this exciting hobby. ARRL offers information and files by mail.

Mail:
> Address: **info@arrl.org**
> Body: **help**

Antique Newspaper Column

An electronic newspaper column offering advice and information on a variety of antique gadgets and furniture.

Gopher:
> Name: Software Tool & Die
> Address: **gopher.std.com**
> Choose: **Periodicals, Magazines, and Journals**
>   **I Middlesex News**
>   **I Columns**
>   **I Antiques**

Antiques

Capture the past by collecting antiques and vintage items. Learn to restore your old Victrola, music box, or clock. Find out where you can get issues of the *Charlie Chaplin* comics. Buy, sell, and trade.

Usenet:
> Newsgroup: **rec.antiques**

Archery

You don't have to wear a green outfit and tights to fit in here. You do have to have a passion for nocking an arrow onto a taut bowstring, pulling the string to its absolute limit, then letting go and seeing the arrow silently sink into your target. Archery is great for so many things — hunting, competition, relaxation — and they are all covered in this group.

Usenet:
> Newsgroup: **alt.archery**

ArtMetal

Do you have the mettle to work with metal? Find out by checking out the ArtMetal project. ArtMetal is a group of metalsmiths and artists interested in working with metal. If you've ever thought about getting into blacksmithing, metal shaping, jewelry making, casting, or spinning, check this out. There is also a gallery of art metalwork, and links to ftp archives, FAQs, and much information about metalworking.

See also: Art

World Wide Web:
> URL: **http://wuarchive.wustl.edu/edu/arts/**
>   **metal/ArtMetal.html**

Audio Experts

A real audio system will make your living room windows bulge. Take the squeak out of your tweeter and the growl out of your woofer with a few helpful hints from the folks who know audio. High-fidelity, high-end, and professional audio are some of the topics covered.

Usenet:
> Newsgroup: **rec.audio**
> Newsgroup: **rec.audio.high-end**
> Newsgroup: **rec.audio.pro**

Beads

Beads are not just for jewelry. You can make clothes, home decorations, toys, and much more. If you like making beads from scratch, your material is nearly limitless. Paper, clay, glass and synthetics are a few of the things that you can learn how to use. Share your ideas and tips with like-minded bead people.

Usenet:
> Newsgroup: **alt.beadworld**

A B C D E F G H I J K L M N O P Q R S T U V W X Y Z

Don't get strung out: join the
Usenet discussion about beads

Clocks and Watches

A mailing list for people interested in collecting clocks
and watches, timepiece repair, the history of
timekeeping, antique timepieces, and trading.

Listserv Mailing List:
List Address: **clocks@suvm.syr.edu**
Subscription Address: **listserv@suvm.syr.edu**

Don't be late.
Check out **clocks**,
the Internet's
most timely
mailing list.

Coins and Money

All about coins, tokens, and paper money the world over.
Historic U.S. pieces as well as ancient European and
Middle Eastern money are discussed.

Internet Mailing List:
List Address: **coins@iscsvax.uni.edu**
Subscription Address:
coins-request@iscsvax.uni.edu

List Address: **coins@rocky.er.usgs.gov**
Subscription Address:
coins-request@rocky.er.usgs.gov

Collecting

Is there anyone who doesn't collect anything? (We, for
example, collect Internet books.) Collecting seems to be
part of our nature as human beings. Thus, if you are
human, there is a place in this discussion for you. Use
your imagination: anything that can be quantified or
categorized is fair game. The **.cards** newsgroup is for
those who collect trading cards, both sport and nonsport.

Usenet:
Newsgroup: **rec.collecting**
Newsgroup: **rec.collecting.cards**

Collector's Network

Do you like stuff? Get all you can, where you can and as
fast as you can. Not only do collectors like to collect stuff,
but they apparently like to collect each other. Join this
network of collectors and find great resources about the
art of hunting and gathering.

World Wide Web:
URL: **ftp://ftp.netcom.com/pub/collector/
collect.html**

Comics

A channel for comic writers, artists, readers, publishers,
and lurkers.

Internet Relay Chat:
Channel: **#comics**

Doll Houses

Remember the fun of having a doll house with all the nice
rooms in which you could arrange furniture and enact
various domestic scenes, like the daddy being unable to
find his car keys when he is late for work or the kids
having a party and destroying the furniture? That was
just part of the fun as a kid. As an adult enthusiast of
doll houses, you can be more creative and elaborate with
furniture, architecture, paint and wallpaper and create
beautiful and intricate homes on a small scale. It's almost
like never growing up except now you can spend money
on whatever you want. Learn what designers, builders
and players of doll houses are doing in their spare time.

Listserv Mailing List:
List Address: **dollh-l@vm1.ferris.edu**
Subscription Address: **listserv@vm1.ferris.edu**

Drums and Marching

You've seen those rowdy children who sit in the middle of
the kitchen floor and beat pots and pans together. What
you may not know is that these very same children grow
up to be in the drum corps, where they can make lots of
noise and people praise them instead of sending them to
their rooms. Join high-spirited marching bands as they
talk tech and tell the world why their group is better
than your group.

Usenet:
Newsgroup: **alt.drumcorps**
Newsgroup: **rec.arts.marching.drumcorps**
Newsgroup: **rec.arts.marching.misc**

Drums and Marching

You may not know it, but there are a whole lot of people who march to someone else's drummer. Drum-corps groups and competitions are two of America's fastest growing leisure time activities. What better way could anyone find to spend a sunny weekend afternoon?

Fiber Arts

Textiles are so, well, earthy. Sewing, weaving, and knitting can be a lot of fun and certainly make for an enjoyable way to relax while creating something useful. Drop in to the ongoing discussion and meet the sort of people who can cross-stitch and latch-hook in their sleep.

Usenet:
Newsgroup: **rec.crafts.textiles**

Guns

Discussions and material about shooting sports, reloading, training, personal defense, gun laws, weaponry, and other topics related to firearms in general.

Anonymous FTP:
Address: **ftp.vmars.tuwien.ac.at**
Path: **/pub/misc/guns/***

Usenet:
Newsgroup: **rec.guns**

Juggling

Harley can juggle three oranges. Rick can juggle numbers. So when we tell you that juggling is a great way to make friends and influence people, you know we are telling the truth. Join the group and learn how to keep none of your eggs in one basket.

Usenet:
Newsgroup: **rec.juggling**

Juggling Archives

The archives for the newsgroup **rec.juggling**, including images, animations, the FAQ, other information and publications.

Anonymous FTP:
Address: **ftp.cogsci.indiana.edu**
Path: **/pub/juggling/***

Kites and Kiting Resources

Everything for the kite enthusiast, or all you need to know to get started with kites. Read kite reviews, stories, tips on flying, general information, event guides, and even graphic images of single, dual, and quadline kites. If you like kites, try all of these resources. Good winds to you.

Anonymous FTP:
Address: **ftp.hawaii.edu**
Path: **/pub/rec/kites**

Gopher:
Name: University of Surrey
Address: **gopher.cpe.surrey.ac.uk**
Choose: **Kites**

Internet Mailing List:
List Address: **kites@harvard.harvard.edu**
Subscription Address:
kites-request@harvard.harvard.edu

Usenet:
Newsgroup: **rec.kites**

World Wide Web:
URL: **http://www.latrobe.edu.au/Glenn/KiteSite/Kites.html**

Lacemaking

It's midnight and you want to put the finishing touches on that dress you've been working on, but you suddenly realize that you are out of lace and all the stores are closed. Do what anyone would do in this type of emergency and make the lace yourself. See this handy information on how to make bobbin lace, as well as postings about lacemaking and crocheting for historical costuming.

World Wide Web:
URL: **http://arachne.nyc.ny.us/**

The Internet is more fun than a barrel of cliches.

A B C D E F G H I J K L M N O P Q R S T U V W X Y Z

LEGO

Legos are not just for kids. At least, not anymore. Lego enthusiasts are making great architectural strides and have documented their building projects. See the pictures and read instructions and articles on building with Legos. Years from now, imagine what is going to be written in archaeological journals about this.

World Wide Web:
URL: **http://legowww.itek.norut.no/**

Living History

History seems so exciting in retrospect, much more exciting than it probably was when it was happening. (How interesting is *your* life?) Relive history by joining others who find delight in reenacting historical periods or events. Remember, those who remember history are fated to repeat it.

Usenet:
Newsgroup: **alt.history.living**

Magic

Even after seeing the cut-up tie trick or the lady and the tiger a hundred times, you still can't figure them out. Brush up on your magic and learn some trade secrets. Learn how to make your little brother disappear or how to change that pesky IRS auditor into a pen and pencil set. You don't have to sell your soul to the devil, you just have to be more clever than the rest of us.

Anonymous FTP:
Address: **quartz.rutgers.edu**
Path: **/pub/misc/magic-faq**

Address: **rtfm.mit.edu**
Path: **/pub/usenet/news.answers/magic-faq/***

Gopher:
Name: Rutgers University
Address: **quartz.rutgers.edu**
Choose: **Miscellaneous**
   | magic-faq

Internet Mailing List:
List Address: **magic@maillist.crd.ge.com**
Subscription Address:
   magic-request@maillist.crd.ge.com

Usenet:
Newsgroup: **alt.magic**

Metalworking

Get the hammer, the acetylene torch, a pair of tongs, the right side of your brain, and create wonderful new things made of metal. If you can't handle a scheme that elaborate, then get the box of paperclips from your desk and create a magnificent desk sculpture. Metalworkers find great variety in their metal and use it to their advantage.

Usenet:
Newsgroup: **rec.crafts.metalworking**

Metalworking. . . doesn't the very idea just make you so. . . malleable?

Models

Discussion groups for modeling enthusiasts. The **.rc** newsgroup is for discussion about radio-controlled models. **.rockets** is for model rockets; **.scale** for the building of scale models; and **.railroad** for all types of model railroads.

Usenet:
Newsgroup: **rec.models.railroad**
Newsgroup: **rec.models.rc**
Newsgroup: **rec.models.rockets**
Newsgroup: **rec.models.scale**

Nudity

Naturists are cool because they never have to iron their clothes. Sense the freedom and vitality of the human body unfettered by fabric. Nudists and naturists discuss the meaning, the legality, and the public's opinion of being naked. If you are looking for a hot game of strip poker, you are bound to be disappointed.

Usenet:
Newsgroup: **rec.nude**

Origami

Discussion of all facets of origami, the Japanese art of paper folding, including bibliographies, folding techniques, display ideas, materials, organizations, tips, tricks, and pointers.

Anonymous FTP:
Address: **nstn.ns.ca**
Path: **/listserv/origami-l/***

Internet Mailing List:
List Address: **origami@cs.utexas.edu**
Subscription Address:
origami-request@cs.utexas.edu

List Address: **origami-l@nstn.ns.ca**
Subscription Address: **listserv@nstn.ns.ca**

Origami is so beautiful. What compelling beauty there is in constructing something so delicate and exotic from a simple piece of paper.

Japanese Folding Tricks

Our favorite is the cute, little "PC with modem that doesn't work".

Postcards

One thing about electronic mail that's no fun is that you can't get postcards. (Undoubtedly someone is probably working to solve that problem right now.) Postcards were designed so that people who go on vacation could quickly and easily torture all those friends or family members who didn't get to go. Connect with other postcard collectors and discuss the history of picture postcards, information on research activities or find people with whom you can exchange postcards by mail.

Listserv Mailing List:
List Address: **postcard@idbsu.bitnet**
Subscription Address: **listserv@idbsu.bitnet**

Do you really exist? Check Philosophy and be sure.

Puzzles

What's a six-letter word for the best place to read the news? Drive your friends wild with an endless supply of puzzles, quizzes, and problems. Open yourself up for a little brain teasing or be merciless and create a puzzle that hardly anyone can solve. (!tenesU :rewsnA)

Anonymous FTP:
Address: **rtfm.mit.edu**
Path: **/pub/usenet/news.answers/puzzles/archive**

Usenet:
Newsgroup: **rec.puzzles**
Newsgroup: **rec.puzzles.crosswords**

Quilting

Do you like to take small, soft things and join them into large, soft things? Quilting is an old tradition kept alive in this age of information by Usenet-savvy enthusiasts. Join the folks who know how to get just the right tension in their hoops.

Listserv Mailing List:
List Address: **quilt@cornell.edu**
Subscription Address: **listserv@cornell.edu**

Usenet:
Newsgroup: **rec.crafts.quilting**
Newsgroup: **rec.crafts.textiles.quilting**

World Wide Web:
URL: **http://ttsw.com/MainQuiltingPage.html**

Radio-Controlled Models

Lots of information about all types of radio-controlled models for hobbyists.

Anonymous FTP:
Address: **rtfm.mit.edu**
Path: **/pub/usenet/rec.models.rc/***

Railroad

Who's been working on the railroad, all the live-long day? And what has Dinah been doing in the kitchen? Join the railroad fanatics and discuss real and model trains.

Listserv Mailing List:
List Address: **railroad@cunyvm.cuny.edu**
Subscription Address: **listserv@cunyvm.cuny.edu**

Usenet:
Newsgroup: **rec.railroad**

A B C D E F G H I J K L M N O P Q R S T U V W X Y Z

Railroad Databases

This web page offers lists of Internet-based archives and information relating to railroads and trains. There is also a list of resources that are not on the Internet. (But why would you bother?)

World Wide Web:
URL: **http://www-cse.ucsd.edu/users/bowdidge/ railroad/rail-databases.html**

Railroad Maps

Maps of subways and railroads located around the world including the London Underground, the BART system in the San Francisco Bay Area, the French Metro, Boston line maps, and many more.

World Wide Web:
URL: **http://www-cse.ucsd.edu/users/bowdidge/ railroad/rail-maps.html**

Railroad Modeling

Modeling techniques, railroading information sources, operation guides, and notes on real railroads.

Anonymous FTP:
Address: **rtfm.mit.edu**
Path: **/pub/usenet/rec.models.railroad/***

Railroad-Related Internet Resources

This web server provides pointers to interesting and important railroad-related information sources on the Internet including images, model-railroading, train schedules, newsletters, databases, specific area railfan information, ftp sites, and much more.

World Wide Web:
URL: **http://www-cse.ucsd.edu/users/bowdidge/ railroad/rail-home.html**

Hungry? Try Food and Drink.
Hungry for Love?
Try Romance.

Rock Collection

They're not friendly or cuddly, but you don't have to feed and water them and they don't make any noise. If you are into long-term commitment without the emotional sloppiness, rocks make perfect friends. Get together with other collectors to exchange ideas and share tips on gem, mineral, and fossil hunting and collecting.

See also: Geology, Archaeology

Internet Mailing List:
List Address: **rockhounds@infodyn.com**
Subscription Address:
rockhounds-request@infodyn.com

List Address: **rocks-and-fossils@world.std.com**
Subscription Address: **majordomo@world.std.com**

Roller Coasters

You are utterly terrified, screaming. Your heart is pounding and you think you might vomit. You love every minute of it and want more, more, more. You are addicted to roller coasters. It's okay, because you are not alone. Frenzied coaster fans review the best amusement parks and the top roller coasters in the country as well as discuss accidents and safety.

Usenet:
Newsgroup: **rec.roller-coaster**

Scouting Meets

The channel for scouting including Cubs, Scouts, Guides, and others. There is a bot online which contains a list of addresses of groups all over the world, so that groups can communicate with each other.

Internet Relay Chat:
Channel: **#scouting**

Scuba Diving

Information of interest to scuba divers, both recreational and professional. Destination reports, clubs, classified ads, diving agencies, diving gear info, images, and a wreck database.

Gopher:
Name: Aquanaut (Scuba, Techdiver, WreckDB)
Address: **gopher.opal.com**

World Wide Web:
URL: **http://www.recreation.com/scuba/**

Sewing

Your bobbin is tangled and your darts are crooked. Needle little advice? Ask questions, get answers, give answers, learn new sewing shortcuts. Whether you're a pro or someone who can't stitch your way out of a paper bag, you'll be able to gain insight on the theory and practice of sewing. (And remember, sewing is not just for women; it just seems that way because men don't do it.)

Usenet:
Newsgroup: **alt.sewing**

Sewing Archives

Get supply information, peruse the antique sewing machine guide, and trade tips, techniques and patterns with sewing buffs and professionals. Also includes pointers to historical costuming and textile-related books, and much more material about sewing, fitting, and pattern drafting.

Anonymous FTP:
Address: **rtfm.mit.edu**
Path: **/pub/usenet-by-group/alt.sewing**

Address: **rtfm.mit.edu**
Path: **/pub/usenet/news.answers/crafts/ textiles/books**

Address: **rtfm.mit.edu**
Path: **/pub/usenet/news.answers/crafts/textiles/***

Skateboarding

If you can't skateboard there, why bother going? Maybe because your law firm doesn't like it when you jump the ramp into the office, sliding your briefcase into the receptionist's hands before doing the slalom between all the associates' desks. Beyond that, there's no sense in ever getting off your board. Discover all the clever things you can do with wheels under your feet.

Usenet:
Newsgroup: **alt.skate-board**

Skating

Some people look like they were born with wheels or blades on their feet. The rest of us are like pigs on ice. Hockey, figure skating, and rollerblading are the mainstay of this group. Discuss trivia, learn new competition rules on routines and dance music, and discuss the physical rigors of being a skater.

Usenet:
Newsgroup: **alt.skate**

Society for Creative Anachronism

Step back in time to the Middle Ages, where chivalry lives and everyone's lives are ordered by the rising and setting of the sun. Watch people dress up in metal and hit each other with sticks. Experience the grace and beauty of period costuming. Discover the festivity of a real medieval feast. Members and friends of the SCA discuss how it feels to live life in the modern Middle Ages.

Internet Mailing List:
List Address: **sca@mc.lcs.mit.edu**
Subscription Address: **sca-request@mc.lcs.mit.edu**

List Address: **sca-west@ecst.csuchico.edu**
Subscription Address:
sca-west-request@ecst.csuchico.edu

Usenet:
Newsgroup: **alt.heraldry.sca**
Newsgroup: **rec.heraldry**
Newsgroup: **rec.org.sca**

The *Society for Creative Anachronism* is all about living simply using the tools and customs from a bygone era. See how much fun it can be living in the Middle Ages with an Internet account.

— Everything we tell you is true.
— The above sentence is only partially correct.
— Don't believe everything you read.

Stamp Collecting

If you like to collect stamps, these stamp collecting resources could be just the ticket for you! The ftp site has the Elvis stamp and a collage of other American postal stamps starting with a 1/2 cent stamp. Check out the mailing lists to horse trade for stamps or just chat with other collectors and hobbyists.

Note: Login as **pictures** instead of **anonymous**. Enter your address for the password.

Anonymous FTP:
   Address: **ftp.funet.fi**
   Path: **/pub/pics/misc/stamps**

Listserv Mailing List:
   List Address: **stamps@pccvm.bitnet**
   Subscription Address: **listserv@pccvm.bitnet**

   List Address: **stamps@cunyvm.cuny.edu**
   Subscription Address: **listserv@cunyvm.cuny.edu**

Usenet:
   Newsgroup: **rec.collecting.stamps**

Steam Engines

A list of more than 1,400 surviving steam engines in the United States, including location, line, and technical information on each.

Anonymous FTP:
   Address: **ftp.spies.com**
   Path: **/Library/Document/steam.lis**

Gopher:
   Name: Internet Wiretap
   Address: **wiretap.spies.com**
   Choose: **Wiretap Online Library**
     l **Assorted Documents**
     l **Steam Engines in the United States**

SurfNet

Don't allow yourself to be stranded in an office with an old fan that barely pushes the air around and your only hope of contact with the ocean being a scratched-up Beach Boys LP. Catch a wave on SurfNet, the refreshing multimedia web page with the sights and sounds of oceans around the world. Get surfing tips, news about the tide and wave conditions, and hear stories of the wave that got away. About the only thing you won't get here is sand in your shoes.

See also: Sports and Athletics

World Wide Web:
   URL: **http://sailfish.peregrine.com/surf/surf.html**

Catch a wave and you're sitting on top of the world. Yes, it's true that surfing is totally cool beyond words. And it is just as true that most people will never even get near a real surfboard. Still, if you are on the Net, you can always live vicariously on SurfNet.

Trading Cards

A forum for people interested in collecting, speculating, and investing in baseball, football, basketball, hockey, and other trading cards or memorabilia. Discussion is open to anyone and "wanted" and "for sale" lists are welcome.

Note: This cards list is not open to people from "pay to play systems" such as Compuserve and Prodigy.

Internet Mailing List:
   List Address: **cards@tanstaafl.uchicago.edu**
   Subscription Address:
     cards-request@tanstaafl.uchicago.edu

   List Address: **sports-cards@tanstaafl.uchicago.edu**
   Subscription Address:
     sports-cards-request@tanstaafl.uchicago.edu

Trains and Railways

Material relating to railways and trains, including the history of trains, a list of Amtrak and other trains, and an article on underground stations and wooden railways.

Anonymous FTP:
Address: **quartz.rutgers.edu**
Path: **/pub/railfan/***

Gopher:
Name: Rutgers University
Address: **quartz.rutgers.edu**
Choose: **Railfan Info**

Unicycling

Forget the romance of a bicycle built for two. In fact, forget two wheels, period. Unicycling may not catch on as an energy-saving way to commute to work, but it sure is fun. Unicycling enthusiasts have put together a FAQ list, mailing list, pictures and animation. Now, if they could only come up with a unicycle built for two.

Internet Mailing List:
List Address: **unicycling@mcs.kent.edu**
Subscription Address:
    unicycling-request@mcs.kent.edu

World Wide Web:
URL: **http://www.mcs.kent.edu/~bkonarsk/**

Usenet Hobby Groups

Discussion of pastimes, hobbies, crafts, and many other recreational activities.

Usenet:
Newsgroup: **rec.***

Woodworking

While it isn't the most forgiving medium, wood is rich in texture and color. Rev up your chainsaw or sharpen your chisel. Whatever your approach, the wood will yield to your skilled handling of the blade. Your neighbors will probably prefer the chisel approach, but if you use a chainsaw, they probably won't complain. At least not to your face.

Listserv Mailing List:
List Address: **woodwork@ipfwvm.bitnet**
Subscription Address: **listserv@ipfwvm.bitnet**

Usenet:
Newsgroup: **rec.woodworking**

Woodn't it Be Great?
Wood is so cool—and organic too. There is something about a nicely-shaped piece of wood that can turn on just about anybody. (We call it the Pinocchio factor.) Join the folks on **rec.woodworking** *and see what's happening wood-wise.*

Woodworking Archives

Discussions of tools, safety notes, FAQ, woodsmith plans, electric woodworking motor information, and supplier addresses.

Anonymous FTP:
Address: **ftp.cs.purdue.edu**
Path: **/pub/sjc/woodworking/***

Address: **ftp.cs.rochester.edu**
Path: **/pub/rec.woodworking/***

Address: **rtfm.mit.edu**
Path: **/pub/usenet/news.answers/woodworking/***

HOME MAINTENANCE

Controlling Pests

Information and control guides to common pests found in the home, yard, and garden, including fabric pests, house flies, Japanese beetles, and millipedes.

Gopher:
Name: University of Delaware
Address: **gopher.udel.edu**
Choose: **UD Department & College Information Services**
    | AGINFO: College of Agricultural Sciences
    | Information By Topic
    | Gardening
    | Home, Yard and Garden Factsheets
    | Pests

A B C D E F G H I J K L M N O P Q R S T U V W X Y Z

Home Repairs

It's midnight and the shower is creating a tsunami in the upstairs bathroom. The emergency plumber is out on a hot date and can't stop by. What do you do? Find out on this home fix-it list where handy people talk about home improvement, repairs, electricity, plumbing, and carpentry. These people really know their widgets, gadgets and whatchacallits.

Listserv Mailing List:
    List Address: **homefix@vm3090.ege.edu.tr**
    Subscription Address: **listserv@vm3090.ege.edu.tr**

Joist Span Calculator

Joists here and joists there, joists are everywhere. Make sure you have your joists the right distance apart or when your contractor friends come over and see what you've done they will be snickering behind your back and making jokes about you down at the neighborhood lumberyard. Enter all the joist information and let the computer calculate where your joists should be.

World Wide Web:
    URL: **http://www.btw.com/applets/ span_calc.html**

Paint Estimator

It's bound to happen. You've taken on the weekend painting project and here it is Sunday night at midnight and you are still at it. The really annoying thing is that you have about two feet of wall space left to cover and you've run out of paint. If you had used the paint estimator, you would be tucked cozy into bed dreaming of freshly painted homes. All you had to do was enter in the dimensions of your room and the calculator would tell you exactly how much paint you needed to buy.

World Wide Web:
    URL: **http://www.btw.com/applets/ paint_calc.html**

Don't get backed into a corner. Use the Paint Estimator *before* you start

Learn how to use anonymous ftp and the world is at your fingertips.

Repairs

It's an ideal setting — you have your own place, no landlord to deal with, you can paint that "Ode to Dead Rock Stars" mural that you have been wanting to do. But then the toilet backs up and the shower is leaking and when you went out to get the morning paper you noticed that the gutter is coming loose. Don't worry about a thing. Strap on that tool belt, fire up your favorite newsreader and find out all there is to know about home repair from people who are good with their hands.

Usenet:
    Newsgroup: **alt.home.repair**

Repairing Your Own Home

Oh, what could be more fun than spending all your spare time and most of your disposable income repairing your own home? And, if you are one of the lucky ones, there is no reason for you to feel all alone when it comes to those wonderful, enjoyable details that only homeowners can appreciate. Your friends on the Net are always there for you, ready to discuss the best way to do something-or-other, or to replace a whatchamacallit with a whosis.

Spills and Stains

If you have ever spilled coffee on your best business suit or have skunk odor in your favorite Permawicker chair, you know how nice it is to be able to have so much handy information at your fingertips. Spills and stains are easy to combat when you can use this wais searching tool to learn just the right cleanup strategy. Type in key words and learn all you need to know.

Gopher:
Name: North Carolina Cooperative Extension
Address: **twosocks.ces.ncsu.edu**
Choose: **NC Extension Information
| Search Home Care Database**

Vacuum Cleaners

We have this fantasy that one day someone will invent a riding vacuum cleaner and all our troubles will be over. You'd send the kids out to play, shut the cat in the bathroom, strap on your crash helmet and rev through the house. Moments later you would be finished with nothing worse than a little wind burn. Until that day, we'll have to be satisfied with reading about vacuum cleaners in Usenet.

Usenet:
Newsgroup: **alt.hoovers**

HUMANITIES

Aging

No matter how much Oil of Olay you smear on your body, you are still getting older. There's not much that can be done except talk about it, which is what people like to do. In this newsgroup, you probably won't get any tips on moisturizers or plastic surgeon referrals, but you can explore the more humanistic aspects of aging.

Usenet:
Newsgroup: **bit.listserv.humage-l**

Worried about getting older? You can either join the discussion of Aging, or you can buy every edition of **The Internet Yellow Pages** which will keep you young forever (at least in spirit).

Cognition

Selection of publications from the Indiana-based Center for Research on Concepts and Cognition, about cognition, the mind, and related subjects.

Anonymous FTP:
Address: **moocow.cogsci.indiana.edu**
Path: **/pub/***

You are what you think.

Excerpt from the Net...

```
Newsgroup: alt.hoovers
Subject: Just Wondering

> I was wondering: Is this a group for people named Hoover?
> Or is this a vaccuum discussion?

Must be a vacuum discussion of some sort.
All the posts seem to have been sucked out of here.
```

A B C D E F G H I J K L M N O P Q R S T U V W X Y Z

Coombspapers Social Sciences Data Bank

Electronic repository of social science and humanities papers, offprints, departmental publications, bibliographies, directories, abstracts of theses, and other material.

Anonymous FTP:
Address: **ftp.wustl.edu**
Path: **/doc/coombspapers/***

Gopher:
Name: Australian National University
Address: **coombs.anu.edu.au**
Choose: **Coombspapers Soc.Sci.Research.
Data Bank - Ftp Archives**

World Wide Web:
URL: **http://coombs.anu.edu.au/
CoombsHome.html**

Humanist Mailing List

A large international discussion group for humanists and for those who support and are interested in the application of computers in the humanities.

Listserv Mailing List:
List Address: **humanist@brownvm.brown.edu**
Subscription Address:
listserv@brownvm.brown.edu

Nobel Prize

This is it, your one and only chance to win an all-expenses-paid trip to a tropical island nobody has ever heard of. All you have to do is know who won the 1903 Nobel Prize for Chemistry and be the 189th caller to your radio station. You dash to the computer and fire up your favorite web browser, navigating straight to the Nobel Prize web page. And you see it, right there among the lists of all the winners in chemistry, physics, literature, and more, is his name: Svante Arrhenius. Just as you suspected.

World Wide Web:
URL: **http://www.chemie.fu-berlin.de/diverse/
bib/nobelpreise.html**

Proposed Idea Exchange

Were you one of those kids who had all the neighborhood clubhouses communicating through a network of tin cans and fishing line? If you are the type who has big ideas and wants to share, get feedback, or comment on someone else's ideas, then welcome to The Proposed Idea Exchange. The topics covered are community network development, linking LANs to the Net via cable television, educational reform, and technology transfer to low income areas via the Net.

Gopher:
Name: Consortium for School Networking
Address: **digital.cosn.org**
Choose: **Networking Information
I The Proposed Idea Exchange**

REACH

Research and Educational Applications of Computers in the Humanities (REACH) is a newsletter that is continually loaded with new resources for anyone who is interested in the humanities. They have software reviews, announcements of new ftp sites, and articles on new mailing lists.

Anonymous FTP:
Address: **ucsbuxa.ucsb.edu**
Path: **/hcf/***

Listserv Mailing List:
List Address: **reach@ucsbvm.ucsb.edu**
Subscription Address: **listserv@ucsbvm.ucsb.edu**

Resource Guides to the Humanities

Internet resource guides for diversity, linguistics, mysticism, philosophy, psychology, religious studies, and history.

Gopher:
Name: University of Michigan
Address: **una.hh.lib.umich.edu**
Choose: **inetdirs
I Guides on the Humanities**

HUMOR

Amusing Tests and Quizzies

A collection of humorous tests, including a life quiz, a nerd test, creativity test, and the feminist quiz.

Anonymous FTP:
Address: **quartz.rutgers.edu**
Path: **/pub/humor/Tests/***

Gopher:
Name: Rutgers University
Address: **quartz.rutgers.edu**
Choose: **Humor**
  | Tests

Ask Dr. Bean

Ask advice on all topics from Dr. Ignacious Bean, former Assistant Professor of Gyropsychopathetics at the St. Louis de Ha Ha Institute of Advanced Cartography.

World Wide Web:
URL: **http://www.wimsey.com/Generality/Bean.html**

Barney the Dinosaur

More enduring than the Energizer Bunny, more purple than a fine Reisling, able to leap small children in a single bound. He holds thousands of youngsters spellbound with his happy antics. Read the good, the bad, and the ugly about Barney the Dinosaur.

See also: Fun, Television

World Wide Web:
URL: **www.yahoo.com/Entertainment/Television/Shows/Cartoons**

Bastard Operator from Hell

A hilarious sequence of stories about a system operator you *don't* want running your system.

Anonymous FTP:
Address: **rs3.hrz.th-darmstadt.de**
Path: **/pub/docs/fun/bastard-operator.tar.Z**

Address: **sunsite.unc.edu**
Path: **/pub/docs/humor/bastard-operator**

Archie:
Pattern: **bastard-op**

Bastard Operator from Hell

There are those who say that humor and early training in computer science are mutually exclusive phenomena. As proof, they point to the level of humor in books such as this one.

Not that it is for us to argue. No, we simply point them to the classic computer-oriented stories called "The Bastard Operator from Hell." Not that hardly anyone even knows what a computer operator is any longer. Still, take our word for it: these stories are funny (and they make great birthday gifts for people who are not smart enough to buy *The Internet Golden Directory* for themselves).

Best of Usenet

Don't spend hours searching through thousands of newsgroups looking for the funny stuff. Someone has already done the dirty work for you. If you are in the market for humor, you can find lots of laughs with one-stop shopping by checking out the group that claims to have the best of what Usenet has to offer. The **alt.humor.best-of-usenet** group has the funny stuff and **alt.humor.best-of-usenet.d** is where you can talk about the funny stuff.

Usenet:
Newsgroup: **alt.humor.best-of-usenet**
Newsgroup: **alt.humor.best-of-usenet.d**

Better and Better

The Battle of the Sexes has been raging longer than any war in the history of man, er. . . humankind. This humor archive holds the secret of the mystery of the ages: who is better? Peruse list after list of reasons why cucumbers are better than men, why beer is better than women and for those of you who care about neither, see why a slide rule is better than an X workstation.

Gopher:
Name: University of Illinois
Address: **dixie.aiss.uiuc.edu**
Port: **6969**
Choose: **humor**
  | better

Bootsie Report

Experience life from an outlandish Bootsie point of view. Teetering on the edge of credibility, Juan Bootsie writes reports of his adventures and encounters with famous people in a fun and lively manner that will make you want to quit your job, stick a press badge in your hat band and take off in search of the newsmakers. Read the Bootsie reports to get a piece of the action without having to leave your seat.

Anonymous FTP:
>   Address: **ftp.webcom.com**
>   Path: **/pub/hamlet/ftp/juan/***

>   Address: **ftp.webcom.com**
>   Path: **/pub/hamlet/ftp/index.jb**

British Comedy

There is something so captivating about British comedy. Besides the accents, of course. It's dry, it's straight, it's unexpected. Whether you are a hardcore fan or just someone who wants to learn more about British humor, sign up on this mailing list for the discussion of British comedy shows like *Black Adder* and *Monty Python*.

Mail:
>   Address: **casino@pobox.upenn.edu**
>   Subject: **Britcomedy Digest**
>   Body: **your e-mail address**

World Wide Web:
>   URL: **http://cathouse.org:8000/BritishComedy/**

British Humor

England has a long tradition of world-famous comedians: Prince Charles, Margaret Thatcher, Neville Chamberlain, among others. If you are a fan of British "humour," tune in to this newsgroup and discuss your favorite TV shows, performers, movies and personalities.

Usenet:
>   Newsgroup: **alt.comedy.british**

Nothing is funnier than *British Humor*

(except maybe their food, or the weather, or the Royal Family, or. . .)

Canonical Lists

Need that joke for a special occasion? Check out the **rec.humor** archives where you can find not only canonical lists of jokes, but the canonical list of canonical lists. Blonde jokes, answering machine messages, lawyer jokes, things that are politically incorrect, and a list of people in need of a good, hard caning. The archives go on and on.

Anonymous FTP:
>   Address: **cco.caltech.edu**
>   Path: **/pub/humor/canonical.lists/***

World Wide Web:
>   URL: **http://www.cs.odu.edu/~cashman/humor.html**

Cathouse Archives

Hundreds of humorous and amusing files. Animal jokes, ASCII art, why a * is better than a *, British humour, holiday jokes, Dave Barry, geography, sex, jobs, life, politics, Murphy's laws, political correctness, quotes, religion, sports, and much more.

Anonymous FTP:
>   Address: **cathouse.org**
>   Path: **/pub/cathouse/humor**

Classic Practical Jokes

Read about some of the best practical jokes ever perpetrated and contribute your own experiences.

Anonymous FTP:
>   Address: **elf.tn.cornell.edu**
>   Path: **/shenanigans/***

Usenet:
>   Newsgroup: **alt.shenanigans**

College Humor

College humor has certainly come a long way since Max Shulman and Dobie Gillis. (Who?) Join the discussion and hear some real, honest-to-god stories, rumors, and anecdotes, some of which might even be true.

Usenet:
>   Newsgroup: **alt.folklore.college**

Excerpt from the Net...

```
Newsgroup: alt.folklore.college
Subject: Early birds

> Someone here just did a poll on vir-
> ginity at The University of
> Pennsylvania.
>
> The Results:
>    Over 50% of incoming freshman are
> virgins.
>    Less than 20% of outgoing seniors
> are virgins.
>
> What does this mean?

It means that if you're into virgins,
come and get it fast during freshman
orientation.
```

Comedy

We love jokes, so we are encouraging everyone to choose comedy as a career. Sure, the world will have to make do with less new inventions, scientific discoveries and medical miracles, but we will all be laughing too hard to notice. Comedy is an addiction and when people are not listening to it or watching it, they are talking about it on Usenet.

Usenet:
Newsgroup: **alt.comedy.british**
Newsgroup: **alt.comedy.british.blackadder**
Newsgroup: **alt.comedy.firesgn-thtre**
Newsgroup: **alt.comedy.slapstick.3-stooges**
Newsgroup: **alt.comedy.standup**
Newsgroup: **alt.comedy.vaudeville**
Newsgroup: **alt.tv.comedy-central**

Comix

Collection of graphical comic strips including *Doonesbury, Dilbert,* and *Dr. Fun.*

World Wide Web:
URL: **http://nearnet.gnn.com/arcade/comix/index.html**

Computer Cartoons

Computer related cartoons by John Zakour, with new cartoons added every weekend.

World Wide Web:
URL: **http://zeb.nysaes.cornell.edu/CGI/ctoons.cgi**

Computer Nerd Humor

Are you a *real* computer nerd? Take the hacker test and find out. Also discover the 20 things you'll never see on *Star Trek*.

Anonymous FTP:
Address: **ftp.uu.net**
Path: **/doc/literary/obi/Nerd.Humor/***

Computer-Oriented Humor

Humorous articles about computers and computer users. Included are a computer nerd's version of "The Night Before Christmas" and a file of hilarious misstatements by students.

Anonymous FTP:
Address: **ftp.uu.net**
Path: **/doc/literary/obi/DEC/humor/***

Contemporary Humor

Humor isn't just for fun. Some people study it or actually make a living out of it. This list has a dual purpose — to entertain, but to also provide a body of contemporary humor for people who take their jokes seriously. And who knows, you may find out why the chicken really did cross the road.

Listserv Mailing List:
List Address: **humor@uga.cc.uga.edu**
Subscription Address: **listserv@uga.cc.uga.edu**

Deep Thoughts

Do you ever look into people's eyes and wonder what bizarre thoughts are lurking around in their heads? Most normal people are occupied by thoughts of the upcoming meal or catching up on work or paying bills. And then there is Jack Handey. Is he funny or just plain strange? Read Handey's skewed thoughts and decide for yourself.

World Wide Web:
URL: **http://orange-room.cc.nd.edu/toybox/WrittenWord/JackHandey1.html**

Don't be a Web Potato: participate.

Dr. Fun

The popular single-panel cartoon by David Farley. A new cartoon is distributed everyday, and archives of all the ones you've missed are available, ensuring that this will become a permanent fixture on your hotlist.

Anonymous FTP:
Address: **sunsite.unc.edu**
Path: **/pub/electronic-publications/Dr-Fun/***

Usenet:
Newsgroup: **alt.binaries.pictures.misc**

World Wide Web:
URL: **http://sunsite.unc.edu/Dave/drfun.html**

Encheferizer

A program that converts written English text into English with a very thick Swedish accent as spoken by the Swedish Chef from the Muppets. There are versions of the Encheferizer program for PCs, for the Mac, Amiga, Vax, and any other Unix system.

Anonymous FTP:
Address: **ftp.hmc.edu**
Path: **/pub/chef/***

English is Tough Stuff

A humorous poem that was used to teach non-English speaking NATO officers correct English pronunciation. It uses contrasts like "corpse" and "corps" both for humor and as practice. A French general was quoted in the file as saying that he would rather do six months at hard labor than have to recite six lines of this poem.

Anonymous FTP:
Address: **ftp.uu.net**
Path: **/doc/literary/obi/Anonymous/
English.is.tough.stuff**

Fabio's Top Ten Pick-Up Lines

You probably think Fabio gets all those women because he has bulging muscles, a washboard stomach, strong jaw, and long, lustrous hair. It's not true. He gets the women because he has clever pick-up lines. Now you can experience Fabio's rich success with women. Practice these lines in front of a mirror, then go out on the town and try them out. Your clever approach combined with a little good hygiene will change your life.

World Wide Web:
URL: **http://orange-room.cc.nd.edu/toybox/
WrittenWord/FabiosPickUpLines.html**

Firesign Theater

Firesign Theater, an American comedy and satire group from the 1970s, has a cult following all their own. Join this group to discuss whatever-happened-to-so-and-so, as well as upcoming appearances by ex-FST members and a host of trivia questions. Read the regularly posted FAQ list and find out if we really are all bozos on this bus.

Usenet:
Newsgroup: **alt.comedy.firesgn-thtre**
Newsgroup: **alt.fan.firesign-theatre**

Don't Crush That Gopher, Hand Me the Telnet

Firesign Theater is one of the highest achievements of modern American theater. However, you need to have just the right type of warped mind to appreciate it. Fortunately, we do, and so can you.

Tune in to the **Firesign Theater** Usenet groups and join George Tirebiter, Ralph Spoilsport and Nick Danger back on the Internet (which is already in progress...)

Funny News

Every now and then, something funny happens in the real world (the one that you don't need a computer to access). Read about such happenings here.

Usenet:
Newsgroup: **clari.news.interest.quirks**

Funny People

Usenet has a whole set of newsgroups devoted to the worship and discussion of various famous people and their work. Humor, of course, is well represented. Join the disciples and discuss your favorite humorists: Bill Gates, Dave Barry, Andrew Dice Clay, the Goons (from the old *Goon Show*), David Letterman, *Monty Python*, Terry Pratchett, P.G. Wodehouse (pronounced "Woodhouse," please) and Woody Allen.

Usenet:
Newsgroup: **alt.fan.bill-gates**
Newsgroup: **alt.fan.dave_barry**
Newsgroup: **alt.fan.dice-man**
Newsgroup: **alt.fan.goons**
Newsgroup: **alt.fan.greg-kinnear**
Newsgroup: **alt.fan.letterman**
Newsgroup: **alt.fan.mel-brooks**
Newsgroup: **alt.fan.monty-python**
Newsgroup: **alt.fan.penn-n-teller**
Newsgroup: **alt.fan.pratchett**
Newsgroup: **alt.fan.wodehouse**
Newsgroup: **alt.fan.woody-allen**

Funny Texts

A selection of humorous articles and stories.

Gopher:
>Name: Universidade Nova de Lisboa
>Address: **gopher.fct.unl.pt**
>Choose: **Public info**
> | **Humor**
> | **Funny Texts**

Giggles

It's fun to let yourself go and collapse into a fit of giggles. We won't tell. In fact, you can do it now. Nobody is watching. Go ahead. Or if you want, you can save it for when you join this list and see all the funny jokes, stories and anecdotes people have to share. You can even post some yourself as long as what you send is not copyrighted and is related to humor.

See also: Fun

Listserv Mailing List:
>List Address: **giggles@vtvm1.cc.vt.edu**
>Subscription Address: **listserv@vtvm1.cc.vt.edu**

Guide to System Administrators

Get to know the breed of human called "System Administrator." Behavior has been scientifically studied and recorded in this helpful guide.

World Wide Web:
>URL: **http://www.seas.upenn.edu/~turnert/ sysadmins.html**

Hacker Test

Find out if you are a computer illiterate, nerd, hacker, guru, or wizard with this set of questions.

Gopher:
>Name: Universitaet des Saarlandes
>Address: **pfsparc02.phil15.uni-sb.de**
>Choose: **Fun (Spass & Spiel, etc.)**
> | **Hacker**

How to Confuse Your Roommate

There's nothing wrong with a little chaos on the homefront. If you feel the need to boggle your roommate's mind, try a few of these tricks. They range from the mildly annoying to the cruel and unusual. Don't try any of these experiments unless you are ready to advertise for a new roomie.

World Wide Web:
>URL: **http://orange-room.cc.nd.edu/toybox/ WrittenWord/ConfuseRoommate.html**

Humor Archives

Massive collections of jokes, anecdotes, humorous stories, one-liners, and riddles.

Anonymous FTP:
>Address: **donau.et.tudelft.nl**
>Path: **/pub/humor**

>Address: **ftp.cco.caltech.edu**
>Path: **/pub/bjmccall/non-political/Funny**

>Address: **ftp.cs.dal.ca**
>Path: **/comp.archives/rec.humor.d**

>Address: **ftp.cs.dal.ca**
>Path: **/comp.archives/alt.humor.oracle**

>Address: **ftp.cs.dal.ca**
>Path: **/comp.archives/rec.humor**

>Address: **ftp.funet.fi**
>Path: **/pub/doc/humour**

>Address: **ftp.spies.com**
>Path: **/Library/Humor/***

>Address: **ftp.uu.net**
>Path: **/doc/literary/obi/DEC/humor**

>Address: **gatekeeper.dec.com**
>Path: **/pub/misc/humour**

>Address: **ocf.berkeley.edu**
>Path: **/pub/Library/Humor**

>Address: **quartz.rutgers.edu**
>Path: **/pub/humor**

>Address: **rascal.ics.utexas.edu**
>Path: **/misc/funny**

>Address: **shape.mps.ohio-state.edu**
>Path: **/pub/jokes**

>Address: **sifon.cc.mcgill.ca**
>Path: **/pub/docs/misc/dave_barry**

>Address: **slopoke.mlb.semi.harris.com**
>Path: **/pub/doc/humor**

>Address: **theta.iis.u-tokyo.ac.jp**
>Path: **/JUNET-DB/jokes**

>Address: **tolsun.oulu.fi**
>Path: **/pub/humor**

Gopher:
>Name: Internet Wiretap
>Address: **wiretap.spies.com**
>Choose: **Wiretap Online Library**
> | **Humor**

> ## Using the Internet won't make you go blind.

Humor Mailing List

Why go out and hunt the humor down when you can have it come directly to you? Distract your co-workers by giggling as the mail pours in. **humor-l**: coming to a monitor near you — and you don't even have to tip the paper boy.

See also: Fun

Listserv Mailing List:
   List Address: **humor-l@cornell.edu**
   Subscription Address: **listserv@cornell.edu**

> ## Next time you are at the supermarket, show them this book and ask for a discount (you never know...).

Joke Collections

Irish jokes, condom jokes, elephant jokes, lightbulb jokes, sorority girl jokes, Clinton jokes, offensive jokes, math jokes, nun jokes, religion jokes, lawyer jokes, and blonde jokes — not necessarily in that order.

Anonymous FTP:
   Address: **ftp.spies.com**
   Path: **/Library/Humor/Jokes/***

Gopher:
   Name: Internet Wiretap
   Address: **wiretap.spies.com**
   Choose: **Wiretap Online Library**
   | Humor
   | Jokes

Jokes

This is the most important place on the entire Internet: the joke-telling newsgroup. Anyone may post a joke about anything (although truly tasteless jokes are best sent to **alt.tasteless.jokes**). Beginners note: The **.d** newsgroup is for the discussion of jokes or for requests (such as "Does anyone have the canonical list of Hillary and Beavis jokes?"). The **rec.humor** group is for jokes only.

Usenet:
   Newsgroup: **rec.humor**
   Newsgroup: **rec.humor.d**

Excerpt from the Net...

```
Newsgroup: rec.humor
Subject: Weirdness

For some reason I've always known that I'd never be psychic...

I used to be an astrologer, but I gave it up because I couldn't see any
    future in it...

I thought I was wrong once, but I was mistaken...

I used to be indecisive, but now I'm not so sure...

I've had amnesia for as long as I can remember...

That last thing I'd ever do is commit suicide...

People say I'm apathetic but I just don't care...
```

Wanna change the system? Try Anarchy.

Jokes and Fun Archive

It's that awkward silence that always makes you want to find a hole to crawl into. Never again will you have to suffer the embarrassment of being speechless. Just whip out the clever remark you got from this archive of jokes, anecdotes and funny stories.

World Wide Web:
URL: **http://www.yahoo.com/Entertainment/ Humor_Jokes_and_Fun/**

Jokes, Moderated

This moderated group is to **rec.humor** what Compuserve is to the Internet: there is Someone in Charge. All jokes are submitted to a moderator who posts the ones she thinks are funny. What this means is that, unlike **rec.humor**, you don't have to wade through a whole lot of junk, silliness, and bad jokes. It also means that you have to put up with irritating messages that are tacked on to the end of each joke, as well as regularly posted draconian ukases, setting out rules and regulations. Still, this newsgroup is one of the most popular on the entire Usenet (in our estimation, coming between **rec.arts.erotica** and **alt.sex.bondage**).

Usenet:
Newsgroup: **rec.humor.funny**

Excerpt from the Net...

```
Newsgroups: rec.humor.funny
Subject: Transcripts from the General Motors Help Line

General Motors doesn't have a help line for people who don't know how
to drive. Imagine if they did ...

HelpLine: "General Motors Help Line, how can I help you?"
Customer: "Hi, I just bought my first car, and I chose your car because it
     has automatic transmission, cruise control, power steering,
     power brakes, and power door locks."
HelpLine: "Thanks for buying our car. How can I help you?"
Customer: "How do I work it?"
HelpLine: "Do you know how to drive?"
Customer: "Do I know how to what?"
HelpLine: "Do you know how to drive?"
Customer: "I'm not a technical person. I just want to go places in my car."

---

HelpLine: "General Motors Help Line, how can I help you?"
Customer: "My car ran fine for a week and now it won't go anywhere!"
HelpLine: "Is the gas tank empty?"
Customer: "Huh? How do I know?"
HelpLine: "There's a little gauge on the front panel with a needle and
      markings from 'E' to 'F'. Where is the needle pointing?"
Customer: "It's pointing to 'E'. What does that mean?"
HelpLine: "It means you have to visit a gasoline vendor and purchase
      some more gasoline. You can install it yourself or pay the
      vendor to install it for you."
Customer: "What? I paid $12,000 for this car! Now you tell me that I
      have to keep buying more components? I want a car that comes
      with everything built in!"
```

A B C D E F G H I J K L M N O P Q R S T U V W X Y Z

Jokes and Stories

A collection of popular jokes and humorous stories, such as, "A Role-player's Famous Last Words" and "The Vaxorcist."

Gopher:
> Name: Technische Universitaet Muenchen
> Address: **gopher.informatik.tu-muenchen.de**
> Choose: **ISAR Gopher - Muenchen**
>   **(worldwide informationservices)**
>   I **Vershiedenes**
>   I **Satirische Texte und Witze (Englisch)**

Late Night Talk Show Monologues

Catch all the jokes you missed on the late night comedy shows with the VuSystem from MIT.

Note: Requires NCSA Mosaic for the X Window System, version 2.0 or higher

World Wide Web:
> URL: **http://tns-www.lcs.mit.edu/cgi-bin/ vs/vsjoke**

Library Humor

An archive of jokes and humorous or absurd stories from librarians.

Gopher:
> Name: State University of New York, Agriculture and Technical College
> Address: **snymorva.cs.snymor.edu**
> Choose: **Library Services**
>   I **Library Humor**

Limerick Server

Always funny, often raunchy — limericks can be useful for many occasions. You can recite them when you're nervous about giving the big presentation for your boss. You can confuse the mugger by telling him a limerick when he asks for your wallet. Or you can use one as a pick-up technique at the local singles bar. Get a daily limerick from the limerick server so you can always keep your material fresh.

Finger:
> Address: **limerick@bronze.coil.com**

Who says that librarians aren't funny? (Not us.) Take a look at Library Humor and see why more and more people in the know are choosing to become people in the know.

Manly Men's Ten Commandments

It is hoped that all men obey these sacred laws, for any breach of these written rules will be considered a sin against womanhood, and may result in the loss of manly privileges such as *Monday Night Football*.

Gopher:
> Name: Royal Postgraduate Medical School
> Address: **mpcc3.rpms.ac.uk**
> Choose: **Fun And Games**
>   I **Manly Men**

Michael Tucker

The Internet's foremost proponent of self-deprecating humor, Michael Tucker is, in reality, a mild-mannered computer trade journalist who, once a week, turns into a mild-mannered Internet columnist. Join the tens of thousands of Tucker's fans who have subscribed to his weekly column. It's free (and well worth every cent).

Majordomo Mailing List:
> List Address: **explosive-cargo@world.std.com**
> Subscription Address: **majordomo@world.std.com**

Miss Netters' Advice Column

She is the Miss Manners of the Internet. Have a question about how to deal with shameless users who propagate chain letters or whether to answer unsolicited talk requests from potential studly hunks of nerdflesh? Ask Miss Netters for her advice on netiquette.

World Wide Web:
    URL: **http://www.ugcs.caltech.edu/~mnetters/**

Monty Python's Flying Circus

Collection of all the popular *Monty Python* sketches and screenplays, including *The Holy Grail* and *Life of Brian*.

Anonymous FTP:
    Address: **ftp.funet.fi**
    Path: **/pub/culture/tv+film/series/MontyPython**

    Address: **ocf.berkeley.edu**
    Path: **/pub/Library/Monty_Python**

World Wide Web:
    URL: **http://alfred.u.washington.edu:8080/
    ~uffda/python.html**

Nothing to do?

Download some Monty Python skits and put on a show for your friends.

Nerd Humor

Computer humor of all sorts, including computer songs, smileys, Story of Creation, Turing Shroud, and Unix Wars.

Anonymous FTP:
    Address: **ftp.spies.com**
    Path: **/Library/Humor/Nerd/***

Gopher:
    Name: Internet Wiretap
    Address: **wiretap.spies.com**
    Choose: **Wiretap Online Library**
       I **Humor**
       I **Nerd Humor**

Netwit Mailing List

Netwit is a compilation of jokes and "net humor."

Mail:
    Address: **help@netwit.cmhnet.org**
    Body: **add** *your@own.address*

    Address: **netwit@netwit.cmhnet.org**
    Body: **add** *your@own.address*

Ollie the Ostrich

Learn about the myth of Ollie, and how in the beginning there was no Ollie, there were only the Waters, and how from these Waters came the One Egg. Read the vast catalog of Ollieisms, browse the Ollie Chronology or simply ponder the wise sayings of this Ostrich.

World Wide Web:
    URL: **http://pubweb.ucdavis.edu/Documents/
    Quotations/olliehome.html**

Oracle: Wisdom in Its Ultimate Form

No problem is too small, no quandry too big. Whatever you need, whenever you need it, the Usenet Oracle is there for you. Get in on the ground floor of what is sure to be the new computer-based religion of the Age of the Internet. Remember, even God started as a cult figure.

A
B
C
D
E
F
G
H
I
J
K
L
M
N
O
P
Q
R
S
T
U
V
W
X
Y
Z

Oracle

You send in any question you want to the Usenet Oracle. After a short wait, you receive your response. Great, you say, the wondrous powers of omnipotent wisdom are at my disposal whenever I want. Then you notice a catch: in return for answering your question, the Oracle sends *you* a question to answer."Why not?" you say, "Maybe the Oracle is overworked this week, and it is really quite a compliment to be asked for my opinion." Then you notice that whenever you ask a question, you are sent one in return. Eventually you catch on, "Why, we are all just answering..." Well, we're sure you don't need our help to figure it out (especially if you have ever sold Amway products). The Usenet Oracle is a time-honored tradition. Read the best of the Oracle's answers in the moderated group **rec.humor.oracle**. The **.d** group is unmoderated and is for an open discussion of the Oracle's wisdom.

Usenet:
Newsgroup: **rec.humor.oracle**
Newsgroup: **rec.humor.oracle.d**

Political Humor

Political humor, including *Ten Ways to Avoid the Draft* and *The Top 59 Mistakes Made by Adolf Hitler*.

Anonymous FTP:
Address: **quartz.rutgers.edu**
Path: **/pub/humor/Political/***

Gopher:
Name: Rutgers University
Address: **quartz.rutgers.edu**
Choose: **Humor**
 | Political

Politically Correct Primer

Ever wonder what it really means to be politically correct? Get the straight story from this primer.

World Wide Web:
URL: **http://www.umd.umich.edu/~nhughes/ htmldocs/pc.html**

Principia Discordia

The "Principia Discordia" or "How I Found the Goddess and What I Did to Her When I Found Her".

See also: Literature

World Wide Web:
URL: **http://www.willamette.edu/webdev/ principia/**

Project Galactic Guide

A large and humourous guide to everything real and unreal in the galaxy, written in the style of Douglas Adams' *Hitchhiker's Guide to the Galaxy*.

Anonymous FTP:
Address: **vela.acs.oakland.edu**
Path: **/pub/galactic-guide/***

World Wide Web:
URL: **http://web.cs.city.ac.uk/pgg/guide.html**

Puns

It has been said that puns are the lowest form of humor. The people who read this newsgroup either haven't heard or they just don't care. We have to warn you, if you want to read these puns you need to make sure you have a strong constitution. This is not for the weak or hesitant. These punsters take their word play seriously.

Usenet:
Newsgroup: **alt.humor.puns**

Selected Cartoons

A collection of cartoon pictures in gif format, ranging from Legally Blonde, to Pillar of Salt and Parenting Wonks.

World Wide Web:
URL: **http://orange-room.cc.nd.edu/Toybox/ Cartoons/Cartoons.html**

Seminars for Men

Men have been trying to understand women for years. See this list of seminars designed especially for men who are seeking to get more in touch with their feminine side.

World Wide Web:
URL: **http://orange-room.cc.nd.edu/toybox/ WrittenWord/SeminarsForMen.html**

Shakespearean Insults

Everytime you connect to this resource a different insult is thrown at you in perfect Shakespearean style. Examples: "Thou clouted knotty-pated maggot-pie," "Thou jarring plume-plucked measle," "Thou errant toad-spotted pignut," or "Thou dankish bat-fowling pumpion."

World Wide Web:
URL: **http://alpha.acast.nova.edu/cgi-bin/bard.pl**

Song and TV Show Parodies

This directory holds parodies of popular songs, including new lyrics to the tunes of "My Favorite Things," "I've Been Working on the Railroad," and "The Girl from Ipanema." There is also a spoof of *Star Trek* called "Star Coke," and two years of "Usenet Olympics."

Anonymous FTP:
Address: **ocf.berkeley.edu**
Path: **/pub/Library/Parodies**

Standard Disclaimer

Fear inspires people to put disclaimers on anything they produce. Most of us are smart enough to know not to eat the contents of the silica packages that come with our new shoes. Just to be safe, manufacturers slap a warning on them anyway. Here is a standard disclaimer that will cover just about any problem that may arise. Unless it doesn't.

World Wide Web:
URL: **http://orange-room.cc.nd.edu/toybox/ WrittenWord/StandardDisclaimer.html**

Witty? Read On

Do you want to be witty beyond the dreams of imagination? Well, you have two choices. You can stay up nights thinking about wry commentary and studying the human condition to the point of exhaustion. Or... you can use the Steven Wright Quote Server. As long as you confine yourself to people who have never heard of Steven Wright and have never used this particular Web site, you can pass off all his jokes as your own and be the life of several parties at the same time. No more will you have to depend upon your reputation as a structural engineer or an accountant. Now you can *really* be witty. The world may not be at your feet, but it will at least be at your kneecaps.

> **Ignoring this hint may be hazardous to your health.**

Steven Wright Quote Server

If you like Steven Wright, check out the Steven Wright Quote and Fortune Server. Each time you connect, out pops another witty saying!

World Wide Web:
URL: **http://ugcs.caltech.edu/htbin/werdna/ fortune?wright**

Swifties

The brainchild of Edward Stratemeyer, Tom Swift began as a fictional character who later became immortalized for his dramatic mannerisms. Today a "Tom Swifty" is a particularly stylized pun.

World Wide Web:
URL: **http://cad.ucla.edu/repository/library/ Cadlab/swifties**

Tag Lines Galore

You can wow all your friends by having thousands of tag lines at your fingertips. At this site you will find a line covering almost any topic. The listings are sorted in alphabetical order and by topic.

World Wide Web:
URL: **http://www.brandonu.ca/~ennsnr/Tags/**

Tasteless (and Dirty) Jokes

Don't read this newsgroup unless you want sickening, tasteless, repulsive, humiliating, insulting jokes and stories (many of which are silly, but — like Congressmen — you get what you pay for). Don't you dare post anything that is not tasteless. And don't you dare complain that anything in this newsgroup offends you. You have been warned... now check it out.

Usenet:
Newsgroup: **alt.tasteless.jokes**

A
B
C
D
E
F
G
H
I
J
K
L
M
N
O
P
Q
R
S
T
U
V
W
X
Y
Z

> ## There are only two things worth remembering in life (both of which I forget).

Ten Commandments for C Programmers

Example: "Thou shalt check the array bounds of all strings (indeed, all arrays), for surely where thou typest *foo* someone someday shall type *supercalifragilisticexpialidocious*."

Anonymous FTP:
Address: **ucselx.sdsu.edu**
Path: **/pub/doc/general/ten-commandments**

Ten Commandments for C Programmers (Annotated)

The annotated edition of this humorous document for C programmers.

Anonymous FTP:
Address: **ftp.spies.com**
Path: **/Library/Techdoc/Language/c-command.10**

Gopher:
Name: Internet Wiretap
Address: **wiretap.spies.com**
Choose: **Wiretap Online Library**
I **Technical Information**
I **Languages**
I **Ten Commandments for C Programmers**

Tintin

Extensive list of *Tintin* comic albums, and scanned images of album covers.

Anonymous FTP:
Address: **ftp.funet.fi**
Path: **/pub/culture/comics/Tintin/***

Top 10 Signs Your Web Homepage is Not Cool

Wanna know how you rate? Look at the checklist and see if you have any of these top ten signs — your early warning system for true uncoolness.

World Wide Web:
URL: **http://www.galcit.caltech.edu/~joe/ coolpage.html**

Toxic Custard Workshop Network

A dry, but hilariously funny newsletter about everything and nothing. It's occasionally available through Usenet, but send mail to the address below for more information.

Mail:
Address: **tcwf@gnu.ai.mit.edu**

Anonymous FTP:
Address: **ftp.cs.widener.edu**
Path: **/pub/tcwf/***

Wall O'Shame

These are news stories, old posters and documents, letters, advertisements, and anything else we should be ashamed of or embarrassed by. Contributions welcome.

World Wide Web:
URL: **http://web.kaleida.com/u/danfuzz/info/ words/wall_o_shame/**

Why?

A funny collection of questions like "If a cow were to laugh, would milk come out her nose?" and "If nothing ever sticks to Teflon, how do they get Teflon to stick to the pan?"

World Wide Web:
URL: **http://www.mit.edu:8001/afs/athena/ user/t/o/tomcat/Public/why_**

YourMom

A hilarious magazine — and good medicine for the blues.

World Wide Web:
URL: **http://www.cc.columbia.edu/~emj5/ yourmom/ymhome.html**

INTERNATIONAL POLITICS

African National Congress

Historical documents, policy statements, press releases, daily news briefings, graphics, and other documents relating to the African National Congress of South Africa.

Anonymous FTP:
    Address: **wn.apc.org**
    Path: **/anc/***

Gopher:
    Name: Southern Africa NGO Network
    Address: **wn.apc.org**
    Choose: **African National Congress Information**

American/Japanese Economic Relations

A collection of articles describing the cultural differences between the United States and Japan, and how these cultural differences can affect trade relations between the two countries.

Anonymous FTP:
    Address: **ftp.std.com**
    Path: **/obi/Japan/***

    Address: **ftp.uu.net**
    Path: **/doc/literary/obi/Japan/***

Arms and Disarmament

A mailing list for discussing politics, peace, war, the cold war, disarmament, and other related subjects.

Listserv Mailing List:
    List Address: **arms-l@buacca.bu.edu**
    Subscription Address: **listserv@buacca.bu.edu**

Crisis in Rwanda

Daily updates of information and press releases relating to the bloodshed and strife of the civil war in Rwanda. This web page also has maps of Africa, Rwanda, Burundi, and Kigali.

World Wide Web:
    URL: **http://www.intac.com/PubService/rwanda/**

Fighting Hate

Information about modern neo-fascist and neo-nazi groups, articles about the Holocaust, and the Holocaust denial archives.

Gopher:
    Name: Jerusalem One
    Address: **jerusalem1.datasrv.co.il**
    Choose: **Fighting Hate: Neo-Nazis, Facists and Holocaust Related Archives**

Global Topics

A collection of pointers that looks at information resources with a global scope. It includes such topics as environment, government, military, peace, health, education, general reference and more.

Gopher:
    Name: University of Southern California
    Address: **cwis.usc.edu**
    Choose: **Other Gopher and Information Resources**
    | Gopher Jewels
    | Community, Global and Environmental
    | Global or World-Wide Topics

Irish Politics

This list is for the discussion of the kinder, gentler side of Irish politics as defined by the 26 counties of the Republic of Ireland since 1922. Discussions of Northern Ireland are welcome only if they directly relate to the politics of the Republic.

See also: Government, World Cultures

Listserv Mailing List:
    List Address: **irl-pol@irlearn.ucd.ie**
    Subscription Address: **listserv@irlearn.ucd.ie**

Israeli Politics

A collection of news articles and reports about Israeli politics, including NATO reports, charters, covenants, the peace process, activist groups, and information about Arab terror organizations.

Gopher:
    Name: Jerusalem One
    Address: **jerusalem1.datasrv.co.il**
    Choose: **Politics**

Josip Broz Tito

Even dictators need love. And what better way to show your admiration than to set up an entire web page devoted to the object of your affection? Read speeches, articles, history and see pictures of Josip Broz Tito, former leader of Yugoslavia.

World Wide Web:
URL: **http://www.fer.uni-lj.si/tito/tito-eng.html**

NATO

Communiqués, studies, factsheets, fellowships, handbook, military, scientific, and other papers and positions of NATO.

Gopher:
Name: North Atlantic Treaty Organization
Address: **gopher.nato.int**

Name: University of North Carolina
Address: **sunsite.unc.edu**
Choose: **Worlds of SunSITE — by Subject**
 I **US and World Politics**
 I **Sunsite Political Science Archives**
 I **nato...**

NATO Handbook

Documents explaining NATO (North Atlantic Treaty Organization): how it works, the future role of the alliance, its organization and structure, and other related information.

Anonymous FTP:
Address: **ftp.spies.com**
Path: **/Gov/NATO-HB/***

Gopher:
Name: Internet Wiretap
Address: **wiretap.spies.com**
Choose: **Government Docs (US & World)**
 I **NATO Handbook**

NATO Press Releases

Press releases and news from NATO, the North Atlantic Treaty Organization.

Anonymous FTP:
Address: **ftp.spies.com**
Path: **/Gov/NATO/***

Gopher:
Name: Internet Wiretap
Address: **wiretap.spies.com**
Choose: **Government Docs (US & World)**
 I **NATO Press Releases**

NATODATA

A mailing list that distributes public information about the North Atlantic Treaty Organization, including press releases, communiqués, articles, factsheets, programs, speeches, and the NATO handbook.

Listserv Mailing List:
List Address: **natodata@cc1.kuleuven.ac.be**
Subscription Address: **listserv@cc1.kuleuven.ac.be**

Radio Free Europe/Liberty Research Institute

A daily report of the latest developments in Russia, Central Asia, and Central and Eastern Europe.

Anonymous FTP:
Address: **poniecki.berkeley.edu**
Path: **/pub/polish/publications/RFE-RL/***

Gopher:
Name: University of Michigan
Address: **gopher.lib.umich.edu**
Choose: **News Services**
 I **Radio Free Europe**

Listserv Mailing List:
List Address: **rferl-l@ubvm.cc.buffalo.edu**
Subscription Address:
 listserv@ubvm.cc.buffalo.edu

Speech by Philip Agee

The text of a speech delivered by Philip Agee, a former CIA agent, just prior to the outbreak of the Gulf War. In his speech, Agee describes what he feels to be America's true interest in the Iraqi invasion of Kuwait.

Anonymous FTP:
Address: **ftp.std.com**
Path: **/obi/Philip.Agee/Z**

Address: **ftp.uu.net**
Path: **/doc/literary/obi/Philip.Agee/Z**

> **There are only two things worth remembering in life (both of which I forget).**

Treaties

A number of treaties, including the Maastricht Treaty, Geneva Convention, North Atlantic Treaty of 1949, the Treaty on the Nonproliferation of Nuclear Weapons 1968, and other important agreements.

Anonymous FTP:
Address: **ftp.spies.com**
Path: **/Gov/Treaties/***

Gopher:
Name: Internet Wiretap
Address: **wiretap.spies.com**
Choose: **Government Docs (US & World)**
 I Treaties and International Covenants

Name: Swedish University Network
Address: **gopher.sunet.se**
Choose: **Subject Tree**
 I Politics

Treaties are made to be broken, of course, but unless you know exactly what was in a treaty, you can't tell who is breaking what rule. Take a moment and snarf your own personal copy of the Geneva Convention. Just the thing for really understanding reruns of Hogan's Heroes.

United Nations Gopher

This gopher has lots of information about the United Nations, including what it is and what it does, its organizations and resources, press releases, conference news, and much more.

Gopher:
Name: United Nations
Address: **nywork1.undp.org**

United Nations Resolutions

The text of some of the UN's resolutions on Iraq as well as covenants on civil and political rights, economic, social, and cultural rights, the Universal Declaration of Human Rights, and resolutions involving Israel, the Palestinians and Bosnia.

Anonymous FTP:
Address: **ftp.std.com**
Path: **/obi/United.Nations/***

Address: **ftp.uu.net**
Path: **/doc/literary/obi/United.Nations/***

Gopher:
Name: Internet Wiretap
Address: **wiretap.spies.com**
Choose: **Government Docs (US & World)**
 I United Nations Resolutions (selected)

INTERNET

Babbage's Best of the Internet

This is a hypertext guide to the services, resources, and people of the Internet. Because it contains new and exciting links, as well as a form-based interface to many Web search engines, this is not just another Internet guide.

World Wide Web:
URL: **http://www.bbcnc.org.uk/babbage/**

CU-SeeMe

CU-SeeMe is a real-time, multiparty video-conferencing system for the Internet. This site (Cornell University — the "CU" in "CU-SeeMe") offers source code for Mac, X Window, and Microsoft Windows versions, a FAQ, lists of reflector machines, those public Unix sites which allow multiparty conferencing with CU-SeeMe, and the source code to allow you to put up your own reflector site.

Anonymous FTP:
Address: **gated.cornell.edu**
Path: **/pub/video/***

If you like trouble, take a look at Mischief.

CU-SeeMe Reflector Sites

So much for fantasy. Until CU-SeeMe came along, you could be anyone you wanted and you didn't have to dress up or even brush your hair to sit in front of the computer. Now, with video added to your networking capabilities, you can't just stagger straight from bed to the computer for fear of scaring the wits out of some unsuspecting person at one of these reflector sites. Still, if you want to try out your CU-SeeMe setup, just connect to one of these sites and hope that whoever is sitting at the other end is as responsibly groomed as you are.

World Wide Web:
URL: **http://magneto.csc.ncsu.edu/ Multimedia/CU-SeeMe/reflect_list.html**

CU-SeeMe

One of the best things about the Internet is that you can hide behind your keyboard. Although you can communicate with people, they can't see you. Or can they?

The CU-SeeMe system developed at Cornell University (get it? See You, See Me? C.U.= Cornell University... it's a joke, son) allows you to view other people in almost real time. And, if you have a simple video card and miniature camera (less expensive than you might think), you can broadcast yourself all over the Net. Try it out. You will be surprised at how cool it is to watch someone on the other side of the Net, live and moving on your very own screen.

(You will also be surprised at how fast the whole thing gets old. Still, it's free and not fattening.)

Exploring the Internet

The Internet can seem like a pretty overwhelming place at times. This is a nice place to start for the beginner, because it has informative documents. If you are a pro, it's a great place from which to explore, because it has links to other cool web pages and tips on how to create your own page.

World Wide Web:
URL: **http://riskweb.bus.utexas.edu/explore.html**

Freenets

One of the great things about the Internet is that things are free. Sometimes even access itself is free. Find links to various freenets as well as articles on network communities and how to get a network up and running. There is a great deal of information here.

World Wide Web:
URL: **http://herald.usask.ca/~scottp/free.html**

GopherMail

A guide to accessing gopher resources via electronic mail. This is useful for people with no direct Internet access, but who have electronic mail.

Gopher:
Name: National Institute for Physiological Sciences
Address: **gopher.nips.ac.jp**
Choose: **About GopherMail**

Graphical Information Map Tutorial

A guide detailing how to create your own graphical maps of Internet resources. Let the world see your design talents!

World Wide Web:
URL: **http://wintermute.ncsa.uiuc.edu:8080/ map-tutorial/image-maps.html**

History and Uses of the Internet

This multimedia course presents the history and current uses of the Internet and serves as an introduction to the technical aspects of the Internet as well as its limitations and possible future uses.

World Wide Web:
URL: **http://www.nlm.nih.gov/LECTURES.dir/ internet_course.dir/starting_page.html**

Internet Conference Calendar

A list of upcoming conferences, symposia, courses, and workshops related to the Internet or to internetworking technologies. There is also a listing of related calls for papers. To add an announcement, send mail to **iconc@automatrix.com**.

World Wide Web:
URL: **http://www.automatrix.com/conferences/**

Internet Drafts

Working documents of the Internet Engineering Task Force, often relating to technical aspects of the Net, but sometimes including more readable files such as glossaries or "how to" texts. These draft documents are working proposals that might be later submitted to the IESG or RFC editors to become official RFC documents.

See also: Internet RFCs

Mail:
> Address: **Internet-drafts@nri.reston.va.us**
> Body: **help**

Internet Engineering

Charters, technical documents, service, and up-to-date activity information about the Internet Engineering Task Force (IETF).

Anonymous FTP:
> Address: **ftp.wustl.edu**
> Path: **/doc/ietf/***

Internet General Discussion

The next best thing to being on the Internet is talking about being on the Internet. Get your fix of Internet topics by checking out the newsgroup where anyone who thinks they are anyone chats about issues relating to the Internet.

Usenet:
> Newsgroup: **alt.internet.talk.haven**
> Newsgroup: **alt.internet.talk.of.the.town**

Internet Growth Statistics

Figures and statistics showing the growth of the Internet, as well as discussion of other global networks, including the Bitnet, uucp, and Fidonet.

Anonymous FTP:
> Address: **tic.com**
> Path: **/matrix/growth/internet/***

Gopher:
> Name: NYSERNet
> Address: **nysernet.org**
> Choose: **Special Collections: Internet Help | Growth information about the Internet**

Internet Society Gopher

Contains detailed information about the Internet Society, including conference news, charts and graphics, newsletters, and other general information related to the technical side of the Internet.

Gopher:
> Name: Corporation for National Research Initiatives
> Address: **ietf.cnri.reston.va.us**
> Choose: **Internet Society (includes IETF)**

Internet Talk Radio Traveling Circus

Details, reports, articles, pictures, highlights, and more from Internet-related conferences and meetings, including Cisco Systems NetWorkers, INET, Networld, and Interop Cyberstation.

World Wide Web:
> URL: **http://town.hall.org/circus/circus.html**

Internet Timeline

Web pages that show the history of the development of the Internet from the 1956 Russian launch of Sputnik, which might have triggered it all, through ARPANET, UUCP in 1976, Usenet in 1979, the Internet Worm in 1988, and right up to the exponential growth that we see today.

World Wide Web:
> URL: **http://tig.com/IBC/Timeline.html**
> URL: **http://www.ludvigsen.dhhalden.no/webdoc/timeline.html**

People talk a lot about the Internet and exaggerate a great deal. However, one thing that is not well understood is that the Net is older than most people think. In our minds, we tend to think of the Net as dating back only a short time to the publication of Ed Krol's seminal book (The Whole Internet User's Guide and Catalog). However, the Net actually started back in the mid-70s with the first experimental packet switching network done under the auspices of ARPA (the U.S. Advanced Research Projects Agency). When you get a few moments, take a look at the Internet Timeline. It will give you a perspective on the Net and allow your feelings of where you are in the course of human events to be all the more meaningful.

Excerpt from the Net...

(from Internet Growth Statistics)

Here is a graph (in logarithmic scale), showing the growth of the Internet. The "@" characters show an estimate of the number of hosts (that is, computers connected to the Internet) at various times.

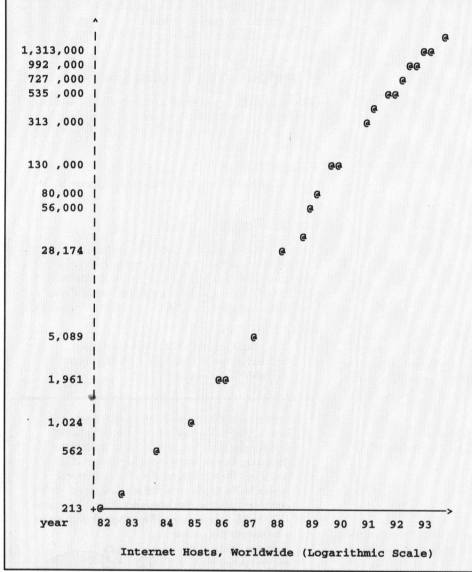

Internet Hosts, Worldwide (Logarithmic Scale)

**Want some fun?
Read the Fun section.**

**The Bizarre section has some
cool stuff.**

Internet University

This page contains excerpts of talks and tutorials from throughout the Internet on a variety of Internet-related topics. The talks are presented with **.au** audio files and graphics and include "Stalking the Wiley Hacker" by Clifford Stoll and "RSVP" by Deborah Estrin.

World Wide Web:
>   URL: **http://town.hall.org/university/index.html**

Internet Worm

Technical papers and reports about the Internet Worm, the program that crippled the Internet.

Anonymous FTP:
>   Address: **ftp.funet.fi**
>   Path: **/pub/doc/security/worm/***

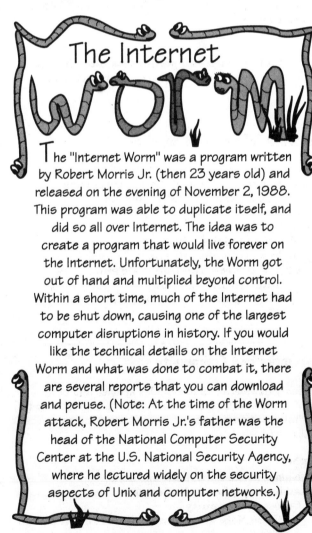

The Internet

The "Internet Worm" was a program written by Robert Morris Jr. (then 23 years old) and released on the evening of November 2, 1988. This program was able to duplicate itself, and did so all over Internet. The idea was to create a program that would live forever on the Internet. Unfortunately, the Worm got out of hand and multiplied beyond control. Within a short time, much of the Internet had to be shut down, causing one of the largest computer disruptions in history. If you would like the technical details on the Internet Worm and what was done to combat it, there are several reports that you can download and peruse. (Note: At the time of the Worm attack, Robert Morris Jr.'s father was the head of the National Computer Security Center at the U.S. National Security Agency, where he lectured widely on the security aspects of Unix and computer networks.)

InterNIC Information Services

Find information about people, organizations, and resources on the Internet. Also find and retrieve documents from all over the world with lookups by name or keyword.

Telnet:
>   Address: **ds.internic.net**
>   Login: **guest**

>   Address: **rs.internic.net**

InterText Magazine

A network-distributed, bi-monthly magazine with topics ranging from science fiction to humor, fantasy, and horror.

Gopher:
>   Name: CICNet
>   Address: **locust.cic.net**
>   Choose: **Zines**
> | **InterText**
> | **InterText Gopher Server**

IP Address Resolver

This resource will determine the IP address of an Internet site and send you a mail message with the address. Useful for people who don't have access to the **host** or **nslookup** command.

Mail:
>   Address: **dns@grasp.insa-lyon.fr**
>   Body: **site** *site name*

>   Address: **resolve@cs.widener.edu**
>   Body: **site** *site name*

IRC (Internet Relay Chat)

Using IRC is like going into a crowded bar only there is not as much smoke and no cover charge. Mingle with the crowds of people, make new friends, have philosophical discussions — use your imagination. Just about anything can happen when you're on IRC. Check out these Usenet newsgroups which cover topics like announcements, specific IRC channels, questions and servers relating to IRC.

Usenet:
Newsgroup: **alt.irc.announce**
Newsgroup: **alt.irc.hottub**
Newsgroup: **alt.irc.jeopardy**
Newsgroup: **alt.irc.questions**
Newsgroup: **alt.irc.undernet**

IRC channel #WWW

This web page and IRC channel #WWW are the places to talk and ask questions about the World Wide Web. The web page provides links to the home pages of regular users of #WWW, IRC help files, and links to other web pages which are dedicated to specific IRC channels.

Internet Relay Chat:
Channel: **#WWW**

World Wide Web:
URL: **http://www.ugcs.caltech.edu/ ~kluster/ircwww.html**

Loopback Service

Use this Internet address and you'll bounce back to your own system.

Telnet:
Address: **127.0.0.1**

Mail Robot

Details and instructions for the Unix mail robot, which maintains mailing lists and allows web documents to be retrieved by electronic mail.

World Wide Web:
URL: **http://info.cern.ch/hypertext/WWW/ MailRobot/Status.html**

Media Coverage

Listen to the latest hubbub by seeing what the media are saying about the Internet. You will find stories about new software releases, access providers, legal aspects of the Net and more.

Usenet:
Newsgroup: **alt.internet.media-coverage**

Mosaic Mail Gateway

Send mail conveniently and easily through your Mosaic interface using forms. Useful to have as a link on your web home page, allowing people to send comments to you quickly and easily.

Note: Requires Mosaic v2.4 or greater.

World Wide Web:
URL: **http://www.acm.uiuc.edu/acm-cgi-bin/ mailgateway**

Net Happenings

A mailing list of everything interesting going on with the Net. Includes interesting events such as the Geek of the Week contest, new mailing lists, electronic newsletters, and much more.

Listserv Mailing List:
List Address: **net-happenings@is.internic.net**
Subscription Address: **listserv@is.internic.net**

Network Information Services

Easy access to information about important networks and information services around the globe, including ASK, DDN, Hytelnet, Janet, MichNet, and others.

Gopher:
Name: Yale University
Address: **yaleinfo.yale.edu**
Choose: **Browse YaleInfo (Yale and Internet Information)**
  | Finding Information and Resources

Networks and Community

A weekly newsletter that compiles articles and news about the networking community. This is a great way to stay informed on new things as well as on Internet culture as a whole.

Gopher:
Name: Whole Earth Lectronic Link
Address: **gopher.well.sf.ca.us**
Choose: **Community**
  | Civic Nets, Community Nets, Free-Nets, and Toaster

Nixpub List

The Nixpub list is a comprehensive list of Internet providers. The list contains all the important information you need to find an Internet provider.

Anonymous FTP:
Address: **ftp.wustl.edu**
Path: **/systems/ibmpc/msdos/bbslist/nixpub.zip**

Address: **uceng.uc.edu**
Path: **/pub/wuarchive/systems/ibmpc/msdos/ bbslist/nixpub.zip**

NSFNET Traffic Analysis

This document illustrates the growth of the National Science Foundation Network (NSFNET) over the past five years, in terms of traffic traversing the backbone, as well as the number of networks connected to it. There are mpeg animations portraying this growth by use of a map of the United States, showing the states where traffic has increased the most, growing upward into 3-D space. There are animations available for T1 network packets, T3 network packets, and the number of networks in total, including a short discussion about the project.

World Wide Web:
URL: **http://www.internic.net/internic/ nsfnet-traffic.html**

Overview of the Internet and World Wide Web

A narrated multimedia introduction to the Internet and the Web, using the script and images from the original video produced by Xerox Corporation.

World Wide Web:
URL: **http://pubweb.parc.xerox.com/ hypertext/wwwvideo/wwwvideo.html**

People on the Internet

Collection of services to help you find that lost comrade on the Internet. It includes access to Knowbot, Netfind, PSI White Pages, U.K. searches, Whois, and X.500 searches.

Gopher:
Name: Yale University
Address: **yaleinfo.yale.edu**
Choose: **Browse YaleInfo (Yale and Internet Information)**
| People on the Internet

Political Implications of the Internet

An article discussing the political and social implications of the Internet.

Anonymous FTP:
Address: **ftp.spies.com**
Path: **/Library/Cyber/cyber.net**

Gopher:
Name: Internet Wiretap
Address: **wiretap.spies.com**
Choose: **Wiretap Online Library**
| Cyberspace
| Political & Social Implications of the Net

Search Engines

The Internet is huge, and it's growing by leaps and bounds. This access point makes the task of finding the resource you want less daunting. It offers more than twenty search tools, with the option of immediately using the search tool through the form-based interface, or obtaining the tool's web page if you are new to the program. A useful collection of invaluable Internet searching tools, including veronica, CUI World Wide Web Catalog, Nomad Search Engine, JumpStation, Global Network Academy Meta-Library, the Whole Internet Catalog, Archieplex, the Language list, Netfind, RFC index search, and many more.

World Wide Web:
URL: **http://www.bbcnc.org.uk/babbage/iap.html**

Excerpt from the Net...

(from "Political Implications of the Internet")

I have called the Net the last (accidentally) uncensored mass medium.
It does not take a rocket scientist to realize that they decide what appears in
newspapers, magazines, books, and on radio and TV, whereas we decide what will appear on
the Net...

A B C D E F G H I J K L M N O P Q R S T U V W X Y Z

Uniform Resource Identifiers

Documents related to the Working Group on Uniform Resource Identifiers. This group is attempting to develop a system whereby a Uniform Resource Identifier (URI) can uniquely identify resources on the Internet and provide persistent naming for networked objects — even if the resource is moved or renamed.

Anonymous FTP:
Address: **ftp.hmc.edu**
Path: **/pub/internet/uri-wg/***

Web Collaboration Projects

It's much more fun to work on a project with someone than to be stuck in a room brainstorming all by yourself. See works in progress that people want feedback on or get help with a project of your own.

World Wide Web:
URL: **http://union.ncsa.uiuc.edu/hypernews/related.shtml**

Web Mailing Lists

Join in discussions concerning the Web. A wide variety of topics are covered in the **www-announce** group. For more technical information, consider joining **www-talk**.

See also: Libraries

Listserv Mailing List:
List Address: **www-announce@info.cern.ch**
Subscription Address: **listserv@info.cern.ch**

List Address: **www-talk@info.cern.ch**
Subscription Address: **listserv@info.cern.ch**

Web Tutorial Slides

A set of web tutorial slides written in HTML. Although some parts of the tutorial are site-specific, they are still a valuable resource to anyone giving or in need of a web tutorial. The tutorial includes sections on background, exploring the Web, creating new documents, technical details, and discussions.

World Wide Web:
URL: **http://www.cs.cmu.edu:8001/afs/cs/usr/mwm/www/tutorial/**

You are what you think.

The WebCrawler

The WebCrawler is a web robot that builds indexes for documents it finds on the Web, making the resources it finds available as a broad, content-based index. It can also search for documents of particular interest to the user. Details of how it works, implementation status, and a search form are available here.

World Wide Web:
URL: **http://www.biotech.washington.edu/WebCrawler/WebCrawler.html**

WebWorld

A web-based cyberworld constructed entirely by the Internet community. It is a virtual world in which you can move around, build, and visually link to other parts of the Web. Allows you to construct your own containers and paths (which are yours to change or tear down), and you can even run into other pedestrians on your travels through the world. You traverse the world by moving around a massive, graphical 3-D map. So get your copy of the map and parachute in today.

World Wide Web:
URL: **http://sailfish.peregrine.com/ww/welcome.html**

Who's Who Online

People on the Internet have decided to share things about themselves and have offered up personal information for you to browse. Read autobiographical information of a professional and sometimes intimate nature. Each person has set up links to other pages that relate to items in their profiles. If you want to be included, there is also instruction on how to record your life story.

World Wide Web:
URL: **http://www.ictp.trieste.it/Canessa/whoiswho.html**

Yarn Server

Yarn is a text-based meeting system, allowing users to communicate with others across the Internet. One can connect to a Yarn server via the telnet interface, but there are also GUI client modules for X Window and Microsoft Windows NT. Details of how to use Yarn, acquiring Yarn binaries and clients, commands, server information, and a Yarn demo server can be found here.

World Wide Web:
URL: **http://dstc.bond.edu.au:91776/YarnMan.html**

INTERNET: HELP

Accessing the Internet by Mail

Learn how to use ftp, gopher, archie, veronica, wais, the Web, and Usenet, using mail as your only tool.

Anonymous FTP:
Address: **mailbase.ac.uk**
Path: **/pub/lists/lis-iis/files/e-access-inet.txt**

Address: **ubvm.cc.buffalo.edu**
Path: **/NETTRAIN/INTERNET.BY-EMAIL**

Mail:
Address: **mailbase@mailbase.ac.uk**
Body: **send lis-iis e-access-inet.txt**

Beginner's Guide to HTML

A primer for producing documents and presentations in HTML, the markup language used by the World Wide Web. Produce your own home page today!

World Wide Web:
URL: **http://www.ncsa.uiuc.edu/demoweb/ html-primer.html**

Composing Good HTML

Thousands of people are going to be looking at your web page. Don't embarrass yourself with shoddy workmanship. HTML can be a work of art if it's done right. Get handy tips on how to use HTML to produce beautiful and impressive web pages. Your mama will be proud.

World Wide Web:
URL: **http://union.ncsa.uiuc.edu/www/html/ guides.shtml**

URL: **http://www.willamette.edu/ html-composition/strict-html.html**

Entering the World Wide Web: Guide to Cyberspace

Don't allow yourself to get hopelessly lost and confused. Access this detailed guide to using the World Wide Web.

Anonymous FTP:
Address: **ftp.eit.com**
Path: **/pub/web.guide/guide.61/***

World Wide Web:
URL: **http://www.eit.com/web/www.guide/**

Guide to Network Resource Tools

An online guide to Internet tools such as gopher, the World Wide Web, wais, archie, Hytelnet, whois, netfind, trickle, bitftp, listserv, Usenet, and others.

World Wide Web:
URL: **http://www.earn.net/gnrt/notice.html**

Guide to SLIP and PPP

A guide to personal Internet access using SLIP or PPP, with details of how to use them and how each works. It gives a high-level overview of SLIP and PPP with pointers to where to find installation and configuration for particular SLIP or PPP software.

Anonymous FTP:
Address: **ftp.digex.net**
Path: **/pub/access/hecker/internet/slip-ppp.txt**

World Wide Web:
URL: **http://www.charm.net/ppp.html**

How to Find a Mail Address

To find someone's mail address when you only know their userid or real name, try this service.

Mail:
Address: **mail-server@rtfm.mit.edu**
Body: **send usenet-addresses/***name*

How to Make Movies

This is where budding filmmakers go to get their start in the Internet movie-making industry. Learn what hardware and software you need to make movies, and explore MBONE, mpeg, QuickTime, and other options for producing movies. And when you go up on stage to accept your Academy Award, don't forget to mention that we gave you your start.

World Wide Web:
URL: **http://www.digital.com/gnn/special/ drivein/projector.html**

A
B
C
D
E
F
G
H
I
J
K
L
M
N
O
P
Q
R
S
T
U
V
W
X
Y
Z

DO YOU WANT TO DIRECT? *You can, on the Internet. Check out the* HOW TO MAKE MOVIES *web site.*

How-to Collection

A large collection of "how-to" help files and guides to many different areas, including the Internet, physics, software packages, programming languages, research, advertising, and more.

World Wide Web:
URL:
http://zaphod.cc.ttu.ee/vrainn/nox/howto.html

Mr. Know-It-All

Remember Bullwinkle the Moose in his guise as Mr. Know-it-all, the Isaac Asimov of cartoon-land? Well, you too can be a pedant. All you need do is investigate the Internet's very own How-to Collection. Once you memorize everything in this collection, you will have more facts and ideas at your fingertips than there are tea leaves in China in a month of Sundays. (Well, something like that anyway...)

Hypertext Markup Language

You're at a party and you have your eye on a hot prospect that you've been dying to talk to. You stake your claim at the onion dip, knowing at any minute she will come over, because who can resist onion dip? Finally she does and you strike up a conversation, hoping to talk about something meaningful. And she asks, "Don't you find it terribly inconvenient that the PRE element is the only way in which structured tables can be properly formatted in HTML?" Be prepared for situations like this by reading up on all aspects of Hypertext Markup Language.

World Wide Web:
URL: **http://union.ncsa.uiuc.edu/www/html/lang.shtml**

Internet Access Providers List

This web page is a list of public Internet access providers sorted by the area codes they serve. Information for each provider includes the name of the organization, the telephone number, and an Internet mail address.

World Wide Web:
URL: **http://www.umd.umich.edu/~clp/i-access.html**

Internet Classroom

Experience hands-on learning about the Internet. Available are tutorials on the Web, Usenet, MOOs, ftp and mail. When you feel ready for it, try the problem sets — they are just like homework, except if you don't do them, you don't have to suffer through detention.

World Wide Web:
URL: **http://uu-gna.mit.edu:8001/uu-gna/text/internet/notes/index.h**

Internet Help

Collection of documents, guides, and publications to help you find your way around the vastness of the Internet. Includes a FAQ, *Hitchhiker's Guide to the Internet*, *Zen and the Art of the Internet*, and much more.

Gopher:
Name: Yale University
Address: **yaleinfo.yale.edu**
Choose: **Browse YaleInfo (Yale and Internet Information)**
  | **About the Internet**

Internet Information

Over fifty documents and resources detailing the Internet, its resources, its culture, and its technical features.

Gopher:
Name: Swedish University Network
Address: **gopher.sunet.se**
Choose: **Internet Information**

Internet Newbies

The Internet operates on a "learn as you go along" system which is a little like jumping into the lake and *then* trying to figure out how to swim. Fortunately, there is a place for new people to go if they have questions or problems or even if they just want some general information.

Usenet:
Newsgroup: **alt.newbie**
Newsgroup: **alt.newbies**

IRC Help

Has IRC got you scratching your head? Help on any aspect of IRC is available here. You can use the Helper bot to ask a question such as "What is a bot?" or "What is a client?" and there are many help topics available that you can list or search.

Internet Relay Chat:
Channel: **#irchelp**

Jargon File

Pronunciation, definitions, and examples of computer and Internet terms, acronyms, and abbreviations. (Humorous, but informative.) This file is available via anonymous ftp from many sites. One is listed below. Search for **jargon** with archie for other sites.

Anonymous FTP:
Address: **ftp.std.com**
Path: **/obi/Nerd.Humor/webster/jargon**

WAIS:
Database: **jargon**

JARGON
We are what we think, and we think with the words that we manage to scrape up off the sidewalk of life and somehow implant in non-volatile memory. The Jargon File is a wonderful resource that has, to coin a phrase, stood the test of time. In other words, someone smart and witty wrote it and it's a lot of fun to read. Take a few moments and check it out. If nothing else, you will see the human side of the techno-nerd part of our culture that is all too often hidden behind the glamour and the heartache of life in the technical/computer/rational fast lane.

John December's Internet Web Text

A hypertext guide to Internet resources offering orientation guides, tools, hints, and references. Flexible presentation gives you several ways to browse — icons or no icons, text only, images only, or a compact version.

World Wide Web:
URL: **http://www.rpi.edu/Internet/Guides/ decemj/text.html**

Let's Go Gopherin' Now

Everybody's learnin' how. Workshop tutorials to help the novice learn to surf the Net with a gopher board.

Anonymous FTP:
Address: **ubvmsb.cc.buffalo.edu**
Path: **internet/gophern/***

Gopher:
Name: University at Buffalo
Address: **ubvmsb.cc.buffalo.edu**
Choose: **Internet information**
  | **Let's Go Gophern' Workshop**

Usenet:
Newsgroup: **bit.listserv.gophern**

A B C D E F G H I J K L M N O P Q R S T U V W X Y Z

Listserv Information Home Page

A web page containing information on listserv lists. It consists of reference pages with lists grouped into specific topics and details on how to join, the number of members, archives, and more.

See also: Internet: Resources

World Wide Web:
URL: **http://www.clark.net/pub/listserv/listserv.html**

For some quick Internet information, try the **Merit Network Information Center Gopher.**

Merit Network Information Center

A gopher operated by the Merit network that provides information on a variety of topics, including how to connect to the Internet, how to anonymous ftp, the National Research Education Network, and links to the National Science Foundation Network.

Gopher:
Name: Merit Network
Address: **nic.merit.edu**

Mining the Internet

A tutorial on using the Internet from the University of California. Send a mail message to the address below to request this document.

Mail:
Address: **bljohnston@ucdavis.edu**

Newbie's Guide to the Net

This web page offers links to many tutorials and guides on computer and Internet related subjects, including Linux, PERL, C, C++, IRC, GNU, WWW, Unix, Macintosh computers, where to find online books, and Internet documents.

World Wide Web:
URL: **http://ug.cs.dal.ca:3400/franklin.html**

Real-Life on the Internet

Examples of real uses of the Internet. Real people working through real projects.

Anonymous FTP:
Address: **ftp.wustl.edu**
Path: **/doc/internet-info/user.profiles/***

Surfing the Internet

A short introduction to the Internet, by Jean Armour Polly. Jean wrote *Surfing the Internet* for librarians, but it has proven popular with Internet users everywhere.

Anonymous FTP:
Address: **nysernet.org**
Path: **/pub/resources/guides/surfing***

Gopher:
Name: NYSERNet
Address: **nysernet.org**
Choose: **Special Collections: Internet Help | Surfing the Internet**

If you are one of those many people who love and worship Jean Polly, you will enjoy her seminal work "Surfing the Internet" available for free. Hint: It is a great Mother's Day present.

Tutorial for PC Users

A computer-based tutorial, written by Pat Suarez, in the form of a DOS program that you can download and run on your own PC. The tutorial describes all the basic Internet services and is a good way for beginners to start learning about the Internet.

Note: The question marks represent the current version number.

Anonymous FTP:
Address: **oak.oakland.edu**
Path: **/pub/msdos/info/bgi??.zip**

**Tutorial for PC Users-
An Easy Way to Learn
About the Internet**

Are you new to the Internet?

**If you have a PC, download the tutorial by
Pat Suarez and start teaching yourself.
Then, rush out and buy a copy of**

The Internet Complete Reference

Web Introduction

Slides and transcription of the commentary for each slide
for an introductory presentation on the Web, suitable for
a variety of new users.

World Wide Web:
    URL: **http://melmac.corp.harris.com/www_intro/**

Why Are Internet Resources Free?

An article discussing why most of the resources on the
Internet are provided at no cost.

Anonymous FTP:
    Address: **ftp.spies.com**
    Path: **/Library/Cyber/freeserv.net**

Gopher:
    Name: Internet Wiretap
    Address: **wiretap.spies.com**
    Choose: **Wiretap Online Library**
        l **Cyberspace**
        l **Why are Internet Resources Free?**

INTERNET: RESOURCES

Announcements of Internet Services

Keep informed with what is happening with information
on the Internet. In this moderated newsgroup you will
find announcements for interesting resources as they are
made available, such as new web pages offered by NASA,
new gopher sites and cool places to ftp to get software.
You will never have to be bored again.

Usenet:
    Newsgroup: **comp.infosystems.announce**

Anonymous FTP Site List

This file contains a huge list of anonymous ftp sites on
the Internet where you can download software and data.

Anonymous FTP:
    Address: **ftp.shsu.edu**
    Path: **/pub/ftp-list/sitelist**

Awesome List

A list gathering together the glory and grandeur of the
Internet, divided into many interesting hypertext linked
categories.

World Wide Web:
    URL: **http://www.clark.net/pub/journalism/
    awesome.html**

Best of the Web '94 Recipients

The winner's circle for the 1994 Best of the Web Awards
presents awards in 13 categories, and underscores the
tremendous quality and rapidly growing popularity of the
World Wide Web. This page has direct links to the
winning pages to allow you to see for yourself the very
best of the Web.

World Wide Web:
    URL: **http://wings.buffalo.edu/contest/awards/**

A
B
C
D
E
F
G
H
I
J
K
L
M
N
O
P
Q
R
S
T
U
V
W
X
Y
Z

Carnegie Mellon School of Computer Science

This site got an honorable mention in the 1994 Best of the Web awards. It contains many computer science, library, and web resources, computing information, and great non-academic resources, including some interesting personal home pages and an "Eat, Drink, and Be Merry" page with many fun things to do.

World Wide Web:
URL: **http://www.cs.cmu.edu:8001/Web/ FrontDoor.html**

Clearinghouse for Networked Information Discovery

An organization that promotes the development of networked information discovery and retrieval software applications such as wide area information servers, the World Wide Web, gopher, and archie. This page has links to many of these and other similar applications.

World Wide Web:
URL: **http://kudzu.cnidr.org/welcome.html**

Clearinghouse for Subject-Oriented Internet Resources

A massive collection of subject-oriented guides to Internet resources organized by format or by information delivery tool. Offers hundreds of guides covering humanities, social sciences, sciences, and much more. Many of the guides are now available in HTML format, allowing instant access to resources through hypertext links.

World Wide Web:
URL: **http://www.lib.umich.edu/chhome.html**

Computer-Mediated Communication

This page describes information relating to a project to list information sources related to the Internet and computer-mediated communication. You can view a summary of the purpose, audience, assumptions, and notes about this information and get instructions on using the hypertext version. The list is also available in many formats, including ASCII, LaTeX, PostScript, HTML, and others. The list of resources itself contains many hundreds of links divided into subject areas.

Anonymous FTP:
Address: **ftp.rpi.edu**
Path: **/pub/communications/internet-cmc.readme**

World Wide Web:
URL: **http://www.rpi.edu/Internet/Guides/ decemj/internet-cmc.html**

Content Router

A query refinement and query routing system with access to hundreds of Wais servers, the Content Router is based on content labels which are constructed from Wais source and catalog files. The Router suggests terms that are related to the query, and when it chooses the relevant Wais servers, it searches them in parallel.

World Wide Web:
URL: **http://www-psrg.lcs.mit.edu/ content-router.html**

Cybersmith

Cybersmith Inc. runs a web server which provides many different types of services and amusements for its users. There is an Internet display service where you can buy books, get documents translated into other languages, shop for a house, play an adventure game in which you can explore and help design interactively, a sound byte archive, a movie archive, and many other neat tidbits!

World Wide Web:
URL: **http://www.csi.nb.ca/**

Data Explorer

Tutorials, news, examples, extensions, and other information for the IBM Visualization Data Explorer software.

Anonymous FTP:
Address: **ftp.tc.cornell.edu**
Path: **/pub/Data.Explorer**

Gopher:
Name: Cornell University
Address: **gopher.tc.cornell.edu**
Choose: **Anonymous FTP**
 | **Data Explorer Repository**

Database via finger

Several databases provided for public use by the University of Sydney in Australia. Finger for more information and instructions.

Finger:
Address: **help@dir.su.oz.au**

Databases via Telnet

Access major commercial and free databases around the world, including Nicolas, Penpages, Dow Jones, Epic/Firstsearch, and Orbit.

Gopher:
Name: Swedish University Network
Address: **gopher.sunet.se**
Choose: **Library Services**
 I **Databases via Telnet**

Name: Swedish University of Agricultural Sciences
Address: **pinus.slu.se**
Choose: **Databases via telnet**

Denver Freenet

Denver Freenet is a Community Computing System supported by the School of Nursing at the University of Colorado Health Sciences Center.

Gopher:
Name: University of Colorado Boulder
Address: **gopher.colorado.edu**
Choose: **Freenets and World Wide Web**
 I **Denver Freenet**

Telnet:
Address: **freenet.hsc.colorado.edu**

Directory Servers

Have you lost track of old friends? Not to worry. If they're associated with a university anywhere in the world, there is a directory server that can help you find them. This gopher at the University of Colorado ties all the world's university directories together. You can begin your quest by specifying the continent you're interested in, or you can go directly to the worldwide list of universities.

Gopher:
Name: University of Colorado Boulder
Address: **gopher.colorado.edu**
Choose: **Directory Servers**
 I **All the directory servers in the world**

If you're feeling risque, take a look at the X-Rated Resources.

Discovering Internet Resources

A document describing various methods to retrieve information from the Internet. The document covers archie, gopher, wais, and the Web.

Gopher:
Name: National Chung Cheng University
Address: **gopher.ccu.edu.tw**
Choose: **Information Resources**
 I **About Resource Discovery**
 I **About Networked Information Retrieval (NIR) Tools**
 I **intdiscovery.doc**

Distance Learning Resources

Dr. E's Eclectic Compendium of electronic resources for adult distance learning consists of information on related mailing lists, electronic journals, and other Internet resources.

Gopher:
Name: NYSERNet
Address: **nysernet.org**
Choose: **Special Collections: Higher Education**
 I **Distance Learning Resources**

EINet Galaxy

A guide to World Wide Web information and services, EINet Galaxy includes public information as well as commercial information and services provided by customers and affiliates. Information here is organized by topic, and you can search for what you need based on subjects or keywords. Categories include Arts and Humanities, Business and Commerce, Community, Engineering and Technology, Government, Law, Leisure and Recreation, Medicine, Science, Social Sciences, and many more.

World Wide Web:
URL: **http://www.einet.net/galaxy.html**

Electronic Cafe

A virtual community which provides numerous methods of accessing the Internet: mail, gopher, the Web, ftp, MUDs, and a list of other informative resources.

Mail:
Address: **ecafe@cyberspace.org**

World Wide Web:
URL: **http://www.cyberspace.org/u/ecafe/www/index.html**

A B C D E F G H I J K L M N O P Q R S T U V W X Y Z

FingerInfo

Using the **finger** command is a great way to learn more about people who have interesting things in their **.plan** or **.project** files. Scott Yanoff wrote a shell script that will present you with a menu of fingerable sites. The script is publicly available by ftp or the Web.

Anonymous FTP:
> Address: **csd4.csd.uwm.edu**
> Path: **/pub/fingerinfo**

World Wide Web:
> URL: **file://csd4.csd.uwm.edu/pub/fingerinfo**

Freenets via Gopher

Access freenets through a gopher menu. Simply choose the freenet you wish to reach from the menu and the gopher will make the connection for you automatically.

Gopher:
> Name: Texas A&M University
> Address: **gopher.tamu.edu**
> Choose: **Hot Topics: What's New & What's Popular | Hot Topics: A&M's Most Popular Items | FreeNets**

> Name: University of Colorado Boulder
> Address: **gopher.colorado.edu**
> Choose: **Freenets and WWW | Other Freenets and...**

FTP by Mail

The Dutch Unix Users Groups (NLUUG) Mail Server provides access to the combined NLUUG and EU.NET archives.

Mail:
> Address: **mail-server@nluug.nl**
> Subject: **help**
> Body: **help**

FTP Services for Non-FTP Users

A guide to ftp-by-mail and other ftp services for those without ftp.

Note: European addresses are for requests from Europe only.

Mail:
> Address: **bitftp@pucc.princeton.edu**
> Address: **bitftp@vm.gmd.de**

> Address: **ftpmail@decwrl.dec.com**
> Body: **help**

> Address: **ftpmail@grasp.insa-lyon.fr**
> Body: **help**

Global City

The Global City offers a collection of merchants (bookstores, Internet services, marketing, and consulting) and a newspaper that gladly accepts articles from authors around the globe. There is a variety of information and news concerning telecommunications, the Web/Internet and other advancing technologies, and products and services offered by clients and sponsors.

World Wide Web:
> URL: **http://kaleidoscope.bga.com/km/KM_top.html**

Global Electronic Marketing Service

A web page with links to guides on business, travel, real estate, and community affairs. Also there is a special section for companies to promote their products and services, a baseball information center for up-to-date baseball information, and information on fantasy leagues.

World Wide Web:
> URL: **http://www.gems.com/index.html**

Global Network Navigator

Global Network Navigator (GNN) provides current information about the World Wide Web. The focus of GNN is on what's new on the Web, and the service includes a newsletter, reviews, feature articles, advice, and commentary on the Web and the Internet in general. The GNN home page also provides direct links to an online version of *The Whole Internet Catalog*, the GNN Business Pages, and GNN NetNews.

World Wide Web:
> URL: **http://bond.edu.au/gnn/gnn.html**
> URL: **http://gnn.com/gnn.html**
> URL: **http://gnn.interpath.net/gnn/gnn.html**
> URL: **http://nearnet.gnn.com/gnn/gnn.html**
> URL: **http://quasar.sba.dal.ca:2000/gnn/gnn.html**
> URL: **http://src.doc.ic.ac.uk/gnn/gnn.html**
> URL: **http://www.digital.com/gnn/gnn.html**
> URL: **http://www.elvis.msk.su/gnn/gnn.html**
> URL: **http://www.germany.eu.net/gnn/gnn.html**
> URL: **http://www.iol.ie/gnn/gnn.html**
> URL: **http://www.ntt.jp/gnn/gnn.html**
> URL: **http://www.tu-chmnitz.de/gnn/gnn.html**
> URL: **http://www.wimsey.com/gnn/gnn.html**

Gopher Resources

A large list of gopher sites, divided by category for easy access to specific topics and subject areas.

Gopher:
>   Name: University of Southern California
>   Address: **cwis.usc.edu**
>   Choose:
>>   **Other Gophers and Information Resources**
> | **Gopher-Jewels**

Graphic Web Analysis Program

This program (gwstat) processes the html output from the wwwstat program and generates a set of gif graphs to illustrate the httpd server traffic by hour, day, week or calling country/domain. You can also plot traffic statistics for a particular URL from your server.

World Wide Web:
>   URL: **http://dis.cs.umass.edu/stats/gwstat.html**

Home Page Publisher

We like home pages. Every home should have at least one or two. They're like little electronic welcome mats. Friendly is good. If you can't get anyone at your site to put up your home page, then try the folks at Ohio State, who understand exactly how important it is to have a home page. If you have a forms-capable browser, you can create and edit your page with its own URL using the Home Page Publisher.

World Wide Web:
>   URL: **http://www.mps.ohio-state.edu/HomePage/**

Home Pages

Once you get caught up in the Web, it's hard to get away. Everywhere you look there are paths leading all over, and it's nearly impossible to get where you are going without getting sidetracked. If you love to explore new places, try the home page of home pages for some clever and interesting environments.

World Wide Web:
>   URL: **http://web.city.ac.uk/~cb157/pages.html**

> # This is the first book of the rest of your life.

IBM Whois Server

Use the IBM Whois server to find out if your favorite IBMer has an Internet mail address. All you have to do is send mail to the address below. You do not need a subject. In the body of the message, put the word **whois**, followed by the person's last name, a comma, a space, and their first name or initial. For example, **whois gates, bill**. For help, send a message that contains only the single word **help**.

Mail:
>   Address: **nic@vnet.ibm.com**
>   Body: **whois** *last name, first name*

InfoMatch

InfoMatch is a cutting-edge Internet software and services provider (including SLIP accounts) located in Vancouver, Canada. They offer software available online, daily news, games, and other products and services.

World Wide Web:
>   URL: **http://infomatch.com:70/**

Internet by E-Mail

Are you stuck with a commercial access provider who doesn't offer gopher, ftp, telnet and other nifty Internet services? Don't let that spoil your fun. There is a way to get access to cool stuff on the Internet just by using electronic mail. Find out how by sending for this informative file.

Note: Users in Europe should use the **.uk** site.

Mail:
>   Address: **listserv@ubvm.cc.buffalo.edu**
>   Body: **get internet by-email nettrain f=mail**

>   Address: **mailbase@mailbase.ac.uk**
>   Body: **send lis-iis e-access-inet.txt**

Internet Computer Index

Gain access to PC, Mac and Unix information available on the Internet and corraled into one location. Resources include Usenet, mailing lists, gopher servers, web servers, ftp sites, FAQs, online publications, and commonly downloaded files and indexes of reviews from popular magazines.

Gopher:
>   Name: Proper Publishing
>   Address: **proper.com**

World Wide Web:
>   URL: **http://ici.proper.com**

A B C D E F G H I J K L M N O P Q R S T U V W X Y Z

Internet Fax Server

The Internet Fax Server is an attempt to make it possible to send free faxes to many different parts of the world through Internet mail. The recipient's name and fax number are converted to an electronic mail address within the remote printing domain and the mail message is routed via the Internet to a computer near the destination. The receiving computer converts the mail message into a fax and transmits it through the local telephone network to the recipient's fax machine.

World Wide Web:
URL: **http://linux1.balliol.ox.ac.uk/fax/ faxsend.html**

Internet Mailing Lists

A comprehensive list of mailing lists you can join on the Internet. An electronic version of the Prentice Hall book *Internet: Mailing Lists*. Nearly 500 pages of detailed descriptions and instructions. Topics range from children's rights and other political issues to beekeeping and yachting.

Anonymous FTP:
Address: **dartcms1.dartmouth.edu**
Path: **/siglists/internet.lists**

Address: **ftp.concert.net**
Path: **/netinfo/interest-groups.txt**

Mail:
Address: **mail-server@sri.com**
Body: **send netinfo/interest-groups**

Usenet:
Newsgroup: **news.answers**

World Wide Web:
URL: **http://www.neosoft.com/internet/paml**

Internet Market Place

Products, services and resources on the Internet have been brought together in one spot. A few of the categories are business, computers, recreation, science, engineering, music and government.

World Wide Web:
URL: **http://www.cityscape.co.uk/inter-market/ index.html**

Internet Resource Guide

A comprehensive document listing Internet resources and how you can access them.

Mail:
Address: **info-server@nnsc.nsf.net**

Internet Resource Guides

A large collection of subject-oriented guides to Internet resources, provided by the Clearinghouse Project.

Anonymous FTP:
Address: **una.hh.lib.umich.edu**
Path: **/inetdirs/***

Gopher:
Name: University of Michigan
Address: **una.hh.lib.umich.edu**
Choose: **inetdirs**

Internet Resources Metamap

A graphical metamap of Internet information resource indexes and listings that can be accessed transparently. Just click on the information resource on the map that you wish to see.

World Wide Web:
URL: **http://www.ncsa.uiuc.edu/SDG/Software/ Mosaic/Demo/metamap.html**

Internet Services

Mail to the address below for a list of documents on how to find indexes to Internet services.

Mail:
Address: **fileserv@shsu.edu**
Body: **sendme MaasInfo.TopIndex***

Internet Services List

Also known as the Yanoff List, a comprehensive list of Internet resources.

Anonymous FTP:
Address: **csd4.csd.uwm.edu**
Path: **/pub/inet.services.txt**

Mail:
Address: **inetlist@aug3.augsburg.edu**

HOORAY FOR SCOTT YANOFF

If there is any single person who is most responsible for helping Internet users become aware of just what is available, it would have to be Scott Yanoff, the creator of the Yanoff Internet Services List.

In fact, you could consider this book to be the spiritual descendent of the Yanoff list. So, let us all take a moment and thank Scott for all his hard work...

(Okay, that's enough. You can get back to your reading now.)

Internet Services and Resources

This is a comprehensive collection of Internet resources presented in an easy-to-use, menu-driven interface. The system operates like a bulletin board, but offers direct access to remote resources.

Telnet:
> Address: **garam.kreonet.re.kr**
> Login: **nic**
>
> Address: **info.anu.edu.au**
> Login: **library**
>
> Address: **nessie.cc.wwu.edu**
> Login: **libs**

No need to be confused by the Internet. Take a look at Internet Services and Resources and try using the LIBS system, then choose whatever you want from the menus.

Internet Tools List

A brief and to-the-point summary of the tools available on the Internet for searching out files and information.

Anonymous FTP:
> Address: **ftp.rpi.edu**
> Path: **/pub/communcations/internet-tools**

InterNIC Directory of Directories

Over 30 categories of directories from which to choose. Topics cover arts, sciences, technical items, and even fun stuff.

Gopher:
> Name: InterNIC
> Address: **ds.internic.net**
> Choose: **InterNIC Directory and Database Services | InterNIC Directory**

World Wide Web:
> URL: **http://ds.internic.net/ds/dsdirofdirs.html**

InterNIC InfoGuide

The InterNIC InfoGuide web page offers access to lots of useful information on the Internet such as how to get connected, where to find resources, InterNIC Web Picks, and the weekly InterNIC Scout Report which keeps track of new sites on the Internet.

World Wide Web:
> URL: **http://www.internic.net/infoguide.html**

InterNIC Web Picks

Pack a picnic lunch and leave a note on the door that says you are going off to have an adventure. Fire up your favorite web browser and go straight to these general starting points for exploration. There is enough to keep you wandering the Net for hours or at least until the Search and Rescue team comes banging on the door to save you from yourself.

World Wide Web:
> URL: **http://www.internic.net/links/**

InterScape

InterScape is another Internet web server in Canada which offers all kinds of interesting diversions. There is an entertainment section which has movie and music reviews, comics, a multimedia gallery, and games; a sports section relating to Canadian sports; and corporate and technology sections for scientific/industry information.

World Wide Web:
> URL: **http://www.cimteg.ists.ca/**

A B C D E F G H I J K L M N O P Q R S T U V W X Y Z

Island Internet

Island Internet is an Internet connection provided for central and northern Vancouver Island. There are ranges of service, including shell, menu, or SLIP access. They provide custom information services as well, including access to the Cyber Mall and tourism information on British Columbia.

World Wide Web:
URL: **http://www.island.net/**

JumpStation

The JumpStation is a way of referencing web information by querying a large database of document information. To query the database you fill out a Mosaic form with the necessary details. You are then presented with a set of links relating to the query.

World Wide Web:
URL: **http://www.stir.ac.uk/jsbin/js**

Knowbot Information Service

Knowbot, or netaddress, is an information service that provides a uniform user interface to the various Internet information services. By learning the knowbot interface, you can query a variety of remote information services and see the results of your search in a uniform format.

Telnet:
Address: **info.cnri.reston.va.us**
Port: **185**

Listserv User Guide

Do you only put "subscribe" or do you add your name, too? And when you want to unsubscribe do you say "signoff" or "unsubscribe?" Getting on mailing lists is sometimes tricky. Getting off mailing lists is usually trickier. This guide is a nice thing to have at your fingertips. It gives all the commands for subscribing and unsubscribing, for getting archives, and setting list options. And you don't even have to subscribe to anything to get it.

World Wide Web:
URL: **http://www.earn.net/lug/notice.html**

Excerpt from the Net...

```
Sender:  Listserv list owners' forum <LSTOWN-L@SEARN.BITNET>
Subject:  Listserv stats

                    LISTSERV Statistics

            Overall: 1,086,800 subscribers
        An average of 215 subscribers per list


        ==================================
        The Top 20 Listserv Mailing Lists
        ==================================


        Subscribers   Name      Description
        -----------   ----      -----------
        18,062        MINI-AIR  The Mini-Annals of Improbable Research
        17,945        TOP-TEN   Late Show Top Ten List
        17,777        GOPHERN   Let's Go Gopherin'
         9,860        CNDPSU-L  China News Digest (Global Service)
         9,492        CCMAN-L   CND Chinese Magazine Network
         9,429        TIDBITS   A newsletter for Mac users
         8,840        NEW-LIST  New List Announcements
         8,755        CHINA-ND  China News Digest (US News)
         8,283        PACS-L    Public-Access Computer Systems Forum
         7,975        RFERL-L   RFE/RL Research Institute Daily Report
```

LYCOS Web Searcher

It's midnight and you've forgotten your best friend's birthday. Panic sets in. You have to find something fast and all the stores are closed. Maybe a poem would be nice, or a funny story or a web site with information about her favorite hobbies. But where can you find it? Use the LYCOS searching tool to search more than 390,000 web documents so you can find just what you need before anyone notices the slip-up.

World Wide Web:
    URL: **http://lycos.cmu.edu/**

MaasInfo Files

A particularly comprehensive collection of information about resources that you can use on the Internet.

Anonymous FTP:
    Address: **nic.wisc.edu**
    Path: **/userinfo/hints/maasinfo**

    Address: **ra.msstate.edu**
    Path: **/pub/docs/words-l/Net-Stuff/maas***

Gopher:
    Name: University of Minnesota Soil Science
    Address: **saturn.soils.umn.edu**
    Choose: **FAQS - Resource Listings - Netiquette
     | maas***

Mailbase Gopher

Mailbase aims to provide groups of people with the ability to have focused discussions by using several lists, each with a specific topic. Mailbase provides access to hundreds of mailing lists, including descriptions, contact addresses, and archive sites for each list.

Gopher:
    Name: U.K. Mailbase Gopher
    Address: **mailbase.ac.uk**

Telnet:
    Address: **mailbase.ac.uk**
    Login: **guest**
    Password: **mailbase**

Send your mother an email note. Right now.

Mailing List Search

Search and view the enormous selection of Listserv and Internet mailing lists through this easy-to-use gopher interface. Includes lists of recent additions, deletions, and updates.

Gopher:
    Name: Nova Scotia Technology Network
    Address: **nstn.ns.ca**
    Choose: **Internet Resources
     | Mail Lists**

MapMaker

This page allows you to create an image map of inline images on the World Wide Web. You specify the URL of the page with the inline image in which you're interested, and the program will do the rest. With a finished image map, you can transparently navigate the entire Internet with a click of your mouse.

See also: Computers: Graphics

World Wide Web:
    URL: **http://tns-www.lcs.mit.edu/cgi-bin/
    mapmaker**

Mother-of-All BBSs

A massive collection of web home pages for companies, universities, research centers, government agencies, and research projects, divided into a comprehensive list of subject categories.

World Wide Web:
    URL: **http://www.cs.colorado.edu/homes/
    mcbryan/public_html/bb/summary.html**

NandO.net (North Carolina Web Server)

The NandO.net server attempts to bring all the excitement of North Carolina over the phone lines and onto your computer screen. There are daily selections for the *News & Observer* (a N.C. newspaper), a sport server with coverage of baseball and football, an entertainment server, the Music Kitchen, and a popular attractions section.

World Wide Web:
    URL: **http://www.nando.net/**

A B C D E F G H I J K L M N O P Q R S T U V W X Y Z

Net-Happenings

Be on the super-sharp cutting edge of the latest in Net resources. Join the Net-Happenings mailing list or take advantage of their wais index of archives.

Majordomo Mailing List:
List Address: **net-happenings@is.internic.net**
Subscription Address: **majordomo@is.internic.net**

World Wide Web:
URL: **http://www.internic.net/internic/
net-happenings.html**

Net-Happenings

Okay, we all know that the world is just chock full to the Plimsoll line with fanatics. What is really great is when you can get some of that extreme energy working for you without having to do anything for yourself.

Enter Net-Happenings. Simply subscribe to the mailing list and your box will fill up with the latest info on more new and interesting Internet resources than you can shake several sticks at.

Even if you only subscribe for a little while, we guarantee that you will be impressed with all the new stuff on the Net. In fact, *we* are impressed (and we are hard to impress).

NetPages

It isn't true that all Internet users are red-eyed, information-grabbing night owls who are crazed with the feeling of all this power they have at their fingertips. (Just some.) When you have a lust for information, does it make you just want to yell, "More more more"? How about an electronic book with blue pages for general Net information, white pages for individual and business mail addresses, and yellow pages for classified advertising? The *NetPages*, which was once available only in print, is now available in these electronic formats: Acrobat, Replica and Postscript. Sections are also available by electronic mail.

Anonymous FTP:
Address: **ftp.sco.com**
Path: **/NetPages/***

Address: **ftp.spin.ad.jp**
Path: **/pub/doc/NetPages/***

Mail:
Address: **info@aldea.com**

World Wide Web:
URL: **ftp://ftp.spin.ad.jp/pub/doc/NetPages**
URL: **http://www.sco.com**

New Gophers

Access many of the latest new gopher sites on the Internet from this gopher.

Gopher:
Name: Washington & Lee University
Address: **liberty.uc.wlu.edu**
Choose: **Explore Internet Resources**
    | **New Internet Sites**
    | **New Gopher Sites**

New Sites

A list of new gopher, telnet, and wais sites on the Internet. This list is updated on a regular basis.

Gopher:
Name: Washington & Lee University Gopher
Address: **liberty.uc.wlu.edu**
Choose: **Explore Internet Resources**
    | **New Internet Sites**

You are what you think.

New telnet Sites

Explore the latest public access telnet sites on the Internet from this menu.

Gopher:
Name: Washington & Lee University
Address: **liberty.uc.wlu.edu**
Choose: **Explore Internet Resources**
 | **New Internet Sites**
 | **New Telnet Sites (Hytelnet)**

New Wais Sources

A gopher menu with pointers to all of the newest wais databases. Check here periodically to keep up with the latest wais resources.

Gopher:
Name: Washington & Lee University
Address: **liberty.uc.wlu.edu**
Choose: **Explore Internet Resources**
 | **New Internet Sites**
 | **New WAIS Server Databases**

NICOL

A gopher that brings together some of the best sources of Internet network information via wais, the Web, anonymous ftp, and gopher in a seamless and orderly manner.

Telnet:
Address: **nicol.jvnc.net**
Login: **nicol**

Nikos

Nikos is a project to create a large pool of replicated web resource locators. Documentation and a database search engine are available from this page.

World Wide Web:
URL: **http://www.rns.com/cgi-bin/nikos**

"THEY" don't want you to know, but we'll tell you: take a look at Secret Stuff.

Online Services

Life without the Internet is like being on a desert island with nothing but a year's supply of peanut butter sandwiches. Don't settle for less than you could have. Explore the variety of online services that are offered, some of which are absolutely free, and you will have the world at your fingertips.

Usenet:
Newsgroup: **alt.america.online**
Newsgroup: **alt.freenet**
Newsgroup: **alt.online-service**
Newsgroup: **alt.online-service.america-online**
Newsgroup: **alt.online-service.compuserve**
Newsgroup: **alt.online-service.delphi**
Newsgroup: **alt.online-service.freenet**
Newsgroup: **alt.online-service.genie**
Newsgroup: **alt.online-service.portal**
Newsgroup: **alt.online-service.prodigy**
Newsgroup: **clari.nb.online**
Newsgroup: **clari.tw.new_media**

Planet Earth Home Page

A magnificent collection of resources available on the Internet, with four format choices: text, graphical map interface, graphic panel for workstations, and graphic panel for personal computers. The panels are huge, clickable icon maps with links to many different Internet tools, clients, catalogs, search engines, information sources, world regions, universities, sciences, community, multimedia, government, and much, much more. There is a **.au** audio welcome file that will blow you out of your seat.

World Wide Web:
URL: **http://white.nosc.mil/info.html**

Popular FTP Archives

Browse some of the most popular ftp sites on the Internet from this menu. Just select the subject or system you wish to look at, and you will be connected.

Gopher:
Name: NASA Goddard Space Flight Center
Address: **gopher.gsfc.nasa.gov**
Choose: **FTP Archives**

Public Internet Encyclopedia

Discussions about an Internet encyclopedia, or Interpedia, and using the Internet as an encyclopedia.

Listserv Mailing List:
List Address: **interpedia@telerama.lm.com**
Subscription Address: **listserv@telerama.lm.com**

A B C D E F G H I J K L M N O P Q R S T U V W X Y Z

RTD Web Server

Located in Tucson, Arizona, RTD provides many Internet services, including access to various compilers, editors, shells, usenet, gopher, the Web, multiuser dungeon clients, conferencing, and other resources.

See also: Technology

World Wide Web:
   URL: **http://www.rtd.com/**

Scout Report

Stay on top of what is happening in the Net world, by getting weekly lists of the latest gophers, ftp and web sites. Experience the luxury of having someone else do the hard part while you get to have all the fun.

Gopher:
   Name: InterNic Information Services
   Address: **is.internic.net**
   Choose: **InterNIC Information Services
      | Scout Report**

Majordomo Mailing List:
   List Address: **scout-report@is.internic.net**
   Subscription Address: **majordomo@is.internic.net**

World Wide Web:
   URL: **http://www.internic.net/scout-report/**

Searching the Internet

A collection of the most useful tools to use in searching the Internet for that needed resource. It includes a FAQ about searches and archives, and describes all the important searching tools, including archie, Hytelnet, veronica, wais, and the Web.

Gopher:
   Name: Yale University
   Address: **yaleinfo.yale.edu**
   Choose: **The Internet
      | Searching the Internet with...**

Subject Trees

A collection of different subject trees maintained all over the Internet. Each tree acts like a gopher road map allowing you to find the subjects you want to investigate in the vastness of gopherspace.

Gopher:
   Name: Yale University
   Address: **yaleinfo.yale.edu**
   Choose: **The Internet
      | Subject Trees**

Subway

A graphical map, in the form of a colorful subway layout, which will take you to many virtual destinations throughout the Internet. Hop on that train and travel afar.

World Wide Web:
   URL: **http://ucmp1.berkeley.edu/subway.html**

SunSITE

SunSITE (Sun Information and Technology Exchange) is a Sun Microsystems sponsored program at key universities around the world. Its goals are to provide easy access to public domain software on the Internet, act as a repository for Sun and government information, promote development and research of new Internet tools, and archive material of general interest, including the Internet Underground Music Archive and various multimedia expositions. This page offers links to all SunSITEs around the world.

World Wide Web:
   URL: **http://www.sun.com/sunsite/sunsite.html**

SunSITE Classic

This site received a nomination for the Best Overall Site in the 1994 Best of the Web awards. It has a great graphical display from which you can choose such areas as the Heliocentric Information Map, Launchpad, U.S. government hypertexts, and exhibits, archives and expositions of multimedia projects at SunSITE.

World Wide Web:
   URL: **http://sunsite.unc.edu/**

> # Using the Internet won't make you go blind.

Surfers Web

The Surfers Web server contains related material to the Surfers interactive chat program. Surfers allows you to communicate with other people all over the world via your computer. The fact that it is utterly frivolous and a huge waste of your valuable time doesn't stop it from being great fun!

World Wide Web:
    URL: **http://flipper.csc.stu.mmu.ac.uk/**

Swiss Academic and Research Network

The Swiss Academic and Research Network (SWITCH) foundation was established in 1987 to promote modern methods of data transmission and to run an academic and research network in Switzerland. SWITCH offers many Internet services, including mail, archie, the Web, and a Swiss electronic phonebook.

See also: Computers: Networks

World Wide Web:
    URL: **http://www.switch.ch/**

Technical Report Index

The Web is a fun place to do research. For instance, if you are looking for technical papers on force dynamics, artificial intelligence, or objects that cannot be taken apart with two hands, type in your keywords and shazam! This index will search over eight thousand technical reports and find those that relate to your topic.

World Wide Web:
    URL: **http://cs.indiana.edu/cstr/search**

Thousand Points of Sites

They aren't kidding. There really are a thousand points and it's up to you to pick an image and go racing off across the Internet in a thousand random directions. If you don't have graphics, this page will not make any sense to you, because the links you select are images with no descriptions.

World Wide Web:
    URL: **http://legendre.ucsd.edu/y/
    randomjump1.html**

Today's Internet Highlights

News about the Internet as well as announcements of new resources and services. Updated regularly.

Gopher:
    Name: The Pipeline Gopher
    Address: **pipeline.com**
    Choose: **Today's Internet Highlights**

Traveler Memories

A set of specialized programs that travel regularly through gopherspace and ftp servers finding resources, omitting uninteresting items, and compiling the information.

Gopher:
    Name: Universidade Nova de Lisboa
    Address: **gopher.fct.unl.pt**
    Port: **4320**
    Choose: **Traveler Memories**

Trickle Server Documentation

All about trickle servers. What they are, how to use them, technical information and user tips.

Anonymous FTP:
    Address: **oak.oakland.edu**
    Path: **/pub/misc/trickle**

Wais Gateways

An easy-to-use interface to wais, the wide area information servers. This gopher offers information for the new user about wais, including concepts and an overview as well as references to wais sources and search tools.

Gopher:
    Name: University of Colorado Boulder
    Address: **gopher.colorado.edu**
    Choose: **WAIS Gateway**

Web fingerinfo

A large collection of sites and resources you can finger through the Web interface simply by selecting the resource to query. Based on Fingerinfo by Scott Yanoff, it offers sports reports, drink machine statistics, weather information, earthquake news, television ratings, weekly trivia, rock lyrics, and much more.

World Wide Web:
    URL: **http://sundae.triumf.ca/fingerinfo.html**

A B C D E F G H I J K L M N O P Q R S T U V W X Y Z

Web Power Index

Get ready for some premium web action. This site has links to a wide variety of fun and fascinating things to do and is updated on a daily basis. Don't bother to connect if you don't have hours to spend browsing. And whatever you do, don't use this to keep your date busy while you finish getting ready, unless you have a crowbar and four strong men on standby to pry him away from the computer.

World Wide Web:
URL: **file://netcom5.netcom.com/pub/css/www/index.html**

Web Search Engines

Archie and veronica are the two favorite searching tools on the Internet. Now there is something just as handy for the Web. Pick your favorite search engine and send it out looking for cool stuff. It's nice to have at least one thing at your beck and call at all times.

World Wide Web:
URL: **http://cuiwww.unige.ch/meta-index.html**
URL: **http://schiller.wustl.edu/DACLOD/daclod**

Web of Wonder

A web page with more than 1,500 links (and growing) to other web resources. The links are categorized by subject, including Art, Business, Computers, Education, Entertainment, Geography, Government, Health, Law, News, Reference, Science, and Weather.

World Wide Web:
URL: **ftp://ftp.netcom.com/pub/lweitzel/wow/home.html**

WebCrawler Top 25

The WebCrawler Top 25 is a list of the most frequently referenced (linked) URLs on the Web. You can immediately access these links from this page to sample some of the most popular web resources available.

World Wide Web:
URL: **http://www.biotech.washington.edu/WebCrawler/Top25.html**

webNews

This is a great resource for checking out news of the Web as it appears on Usenet. You don't have to spend hours looking through newsgroups to find what you want. This site will enable you to scan the list of articles or search by keyword to find exactly the item you want.

World Wide Web:
URL: **gopher://twinbrook.cis.uab.edu/hwebNews.80**

What's New with NCSA Mosaic and the Web

This document covers recent changes and additions to the universe of information available to Mosaic and the World Wide Web. The document is updated on a daily basis, but links to previous months and years are also available. You can register your own findings or sites by sending mail to **whats-new@ncsa.uiuc.edu**

World Wide Web:
URL: **http://www.ncsa.uiuc.edu/SDG/Software/Mosaic/Docs/whats-new.html**

Whole Internet Catalog

An Internet catalog based on the bestselling book *The Whole Internet Catalog*. New resources are added on a weekly basis, and the resources are divided into subject areas. There is also a list of the fifty most popular resources.

World Wide Web:
URL: **http://nearnet.gnn.com/wic/newrescat.toc.html**

WIT Interactive Talk Forum

WIT is a forms-based discussion system which is an attempt to improve upon newsgroups and mailing lists. Discussion groups are broken up into subject areas in which you may choose to participate.

World Wide Web:
URL:
http://info.cern.ch/hypertext/WWW/Discussion

World Wide Web Access Point

A text-based web server you can use if you don't have a browser program. (The preferable way to access the World Wide Web is to download a web browser, but this server will work in a pinch.)

See also: Internet: Software

Gopher:
Name: University of Colorado Boulder
Address: **gopher.colorado.edu**
Choose: **Freenets and World Wide Web
| World Wide Web**

Telnet:
Address: **info.cern.ch**

World Wide Web by Electronic Mail

This service allows you to request web pages through electronic mail. There are several commands available to help you retrieve URLs, including **deep**, which allows you to get all documents linked in the URL you mentioned.

Mail:
>   Address: **listproc@www0.cern.ch**
>   Body: **help**

World Wide Web Home

This is the home of the Web and it has everything you ever wanted to know about the Web, or a link to it. The definitive web project page, a list of client and server software, technical details, a searchable catalog, a list of all registered servers, and a virtual library of resources sorted by subject area are all available here. This site got an honorable mention in the 1994 Best of the Web Awards.

World Wide Web:
>   URL: **http://info.cern.ch/**

World Wide Web Worm

The Web Worm is a friendly critter that is sent out on the Net periodically to seek out new web pages and record them and all the connecting links. The last time anyone counted, the Worm had amassed over 100,000 multimedia objects, and they can all be accessed here. Search by title, keyword, or by a portion of the URL path. It's a clever project and worth checking out.

World Wide Web:
>   URL: **http://www.cs.colorado.edu/home/**
>   **mcbryan/WWWW.html**

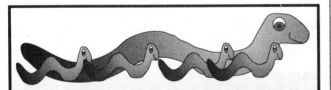

The Web Worm

Quick. What's so small that it takes up no space at all yet is so large that it is well beyond the comprehension of any single man (and even most women)? The answer is the Web Worm. Using a simple interface, you can search a vast number of web items for whatever you want. It's easy to say, but the Web Worm has to be seen to be believed. Warning: Don't start playing with it when you are in a hurry. It will take hours and hours of your time. (Time when you could be, say, out at a bookstore buying *The Internet Complete Reference* or *Unix Unbound*.)

INTERNET: RFCs

RFC Archive

The complete set of the Internet "Request for Comments" technical documents.

Anonymous FTP:
>   Address: **ftp.uu.net**
>   Path: **/inet/rfc/***

>   Address: **ftp.wustl.edu**
>   Path: **/doc/rfc/***

Connecting to the Internet

RFC 1359 outlines the major issues an institution should consider in the decision and implementation of a campus connection to the Internet.

Anonymous FTP:
>   Address: **ds.internic.net**
>   Path: **/rfc/rfc1359.txt**

Experienced Internet User Questions

RFC 1207 codifies the Internet lore so that network operations staff, especially for those networks just connecting to the Internet, will have an accurate and up-to-date reference.

Anonymous FTP:
>   Address: **ds.internic.net**
>   Path: **/rfc/rfc1207.txt**

Glossary of Networking Terms

RFC 1208 is a glossary adapted from *The INTEROP Pocket Glossary of Networking Terms*, which was originally distributed at the Interop Conference '90.

Anonymous FTP:
>   Address: **ds.internic.net**
>   Path: **/rfc/rfc1208.txt**

Instead of watching TV, read about it: take a look at the Television section.

A B C D E F G H I J K L M N O P Q R S T U V W X Y Z

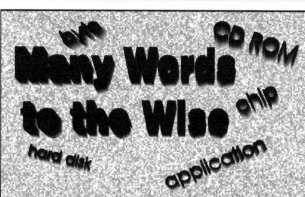

It's true. People do judge you by the words you use. So, if you want computer people to take you seriously, you need to learn their words. Still, it won't be long before you *are* a computer person and then they will be *your* words! So, download *RFC 1208* and check out more networking terms than you ever knew existed.

Hitchhiker's Guide to the Internet

RFC 1118 provides detailed hints to allow new network participants to understand how the direction of the Internet is set, how to acquire online information, and how to be a good Internet neighbor.

Anonymous FTP:
> Address: **ftp.wustl.edu**
> Path: **/doc/internet-info/hitchhikers.guide**

> Address: **nic.ddn.mil**
> Path: **/rfc/rfc1118.txt**

> Address: **nis.nsf.net**
> Path: **/documents/rfc/rfc1118.txt**

Internet Users' Glossary

RFC 1392 (*The Internet Users' Glossary*) is a networking glossary that concentrates on terms which are specific to the Internet.

Anonymous FTP:
> Address: **ds.internic.net**
> Path: **/rfc/rfc1392.txt**

Gopher:
> Name: Swedish University Network
> Address: **gopher.sunet.se**
> Choose: **Request for Comments (RFC)**
> | **rfc.1300-1399**
> | **rfc1392.txt**

What's the word, Snerd?
See the Internet User's Glossary
and never go wordless again.

New Internet User Questions

RFC 1325 can provide new users up-to-date basic Internet knowledge and experience, and at the same time move the repetitive questions away from electronic mailing lists.

Anonymous FTP:
> Address: **ds.internic.net**
> Path: **/rfc/rfc1325.txt**

Responsibilities of Host and Network Managers

RFC 1173 describes the conventions to be followed by those in charge of networks and hosts on the Internet and serves as the written documentation of the "oral tradition" of the Internet on this subject.

Anonymous FTP:
> Address: **ds.internic.net**
> Path: **/rfc/rfc1173.txt**

RFC Lists

An index of all the RFCs. Lists each RFC, starting with the most recent, and for each RFC provides the number, title, author, issue date, and number of hardcopy pages. In addition, it lists the online formats for each RFC and the number of bytes of each version online.

Anonymous FTP:
> Address: **isi.edu**
> Path: **/in-notes/rfc-retrieval.txt**

WAIS:
> Database: **internet-rfcs**

There's Gold in them thar Networks!

RFC 1402 (*There's Gold in them thar Networks!* or *Searching for Treasure in All the Wrong Places*) is an easy-to-read document that tries to make the Internet wanderer's life easier. Of course, you've already taken the best step — buying *The Internet Golden Directory*.

Anonymous FTP:
> Address: **ds.internic.net**
> Path: **/rfc/rfc1402.txt**

INTRIGUE

Conspiracies

Amazing conspiracies of all kinds, from AIDS being a government plot to Russia's operational Star Wars system, secret wars, what really happened at Waco, the final analysis of the JFK assassination, and much more.

Anonymous FTP:
Address: **ftp.spies.com**
Path: **/Library/Fringe/Conspiry/***

Gopher:
Name: Internet Wiretap
Address: **wiretap.spies.com**
Choose: **Wiretap Online Library**
  | **Fringes of Reason**
  | **Conspiracies**

Usenet:
Newsgroup: **alt.conspiracy**
Newsgroup: **alt.illuminati**

Don't look now but **they** are out to get you. Really. Better read all about **Conspiracies** before it's too late.

Wanna Change the system? Try Anarchy.

J.F.K. Conspiracy

John F. Kennedy assassination conspiracy material, and archives from the **alt.conspiracy.jfk** Usenet newsgroup.

Note: For the telnet site, use the Change_dir command to change to **/info/jfk**

Anonymous FTP:
Address: **grind.isca.uiowa.edu**
Path: **/info/jfk/***

Telnet:
Address: **grind.isca.uiowa.edu**
Login: **iscabbs**

Excerpt from the Net...

```
Newsgroups: alt.paranet.ufo,sci.skeptic,alt.conspiracy
Subject: The Case Against a Government UFO Conspiracy

One of the best UFO events occured on Guam... It seems that on some
summer evenings several fuzzy radar targets would appear on the U.S.
air base radar. When challenged with IFF they responded with the
correct code for the day before. Fighter aircraft could find no radar
or visual contact.

The problem was resolved by plotting the position of all equipment
within radar range (about 200 miles). Then 2 times radar range and so
forth.  At 5 times radar range there was an aircraft flying from Japan
to Hickam Air Force Base, Hawaii. When asked to turn their IFF off the
radar targets quit answering. The code for the day before was correct
because the aircraft was west of the international date line and was
the proper code for his position...
```

Lincoln Conspiracies

The Statute of Limitations has probably run out on the assassination of President Abraham Lincoln. But that certainly doesn't mean that people don't want to continue with the conspiracy theories involving the event. That puts Abe in good company with Elvis and JFK. Don't wait to hear the news from the National Enquirer — learn the latest conspiracy theories relating to Abraham Lincoln from Usenet.

Usenet:
  Newsgroup: **alt.conspiracy.abe-lincoln**

Taylorology

In 1922, one of Hollywood's top movie directors, William Desmond Taylor, was shot to death in his home. The killing was never solved and remains Hollywood's most fascinating murder mystery. *Taylorology* is a lengthy newsletter devoted to analyzing and reprinting source material pertaining to the crime and its coverage in the press.

Anonymous FTP:
  Address: **etext.archive.umich.edu**
  Path: **/Zines/Taylorology**

  Address: **ftp.uu.net**
  Path: **/doc/literary/obi/Zines/Taylorology**

Usenet:
  Newsgroup: **alt.true-crime**

> # Gophers are your friends.

Vigilantes

Just like the way of the Old West, vigilantism has its popularity in some circles of people who are fed up with going through "routine channels." Whether you agree or disagree with taking the law into your own hands, you can at least discuss the philosophy and see heated debates on the subject.

Usenet:
  Newsgroup: **alt.vigilantes**

WHO KILLED LINCOLN?

Hmmm...we are not sure. We think it had something to do with aliens and mass fluoridation of the water supply. Still, there is more to this than meets the eye of history and, if you have a spare moment, your friends on Usenet will be glad to show you the details. ("Aside from that, Mrs. Lincoln, how did you enjoy the show?")

Excerpt from the Net...

(From "Conspiracies", on the Wiretap gopher)

The following memorandum, written by J. Edgar Hoover [head of the FBI] immediately after his meeting with President Johnson, just seven days after the assassination of President Kennedy, is a remarkable document to say the least. There is much information imparted in the memo regarding just how fluid and unstable the cover story about who killed JFK still was shaping up to be at that time.

By analyzing the discrepancies between the story Hoover briefed Johnson about on November 29th, and what the final cover story handed down by the Warren Commission would claim almost a year later, we can better appreciate the degree to which the final "official report" was sculpted to fit the constraints the Commission was forced to adhere to, regardless of the actual facts of the assassination...

JOBS

Academic Jobs

The Academic Position Network is an online system for placing and reviewing currently open academic position announcements. Allows one to browse currently available positions, or place an advertisement for academic position openings.

Gopher:
> Name: Academic Position Network
> Address: **wcni.cis.umn.edu**
> Port: **11111**

American Astronomical Society Job Register

This web page is a registry of university jobs in the fields of astronomy and astrophysics.

World Wide Web:
> URL: **http://blackhole.aas.org/JobRegister/ aasjobs.html**

American Indian Work Issues

Sometimes there are special issues an American Indian has to address with respect to work and employment. Explore employment problems faced by American Indians, including cultural conflict, the culturally appropriate workplace, and other barriers that affect individuals as well as the American Indian population as a whole.

Listserv Mailing List:
> List Address: **nat-work@vm1.cc.uakron.edu**
> Subscription Address: **listserv@vm1.cc.uakron.edu**

Biological Sciences

If you have a shiny new biological sciences degree in your hand and can't decide what to do with it, consider turning to Usenet to supplement your job search. Post your qualifications and requirements to this newsgroup and see if anyone takes the bait.

Usenet:
> Newsgroup: **bionet.jobs.wanted**

> ## The Net is for smart people (like you).

> ## Need Unix help? See Harley's book "Unix Unbound."

Career Books

Details, reviews, and ordering information on a wide selection of career-oriented books and publications.

Gopher:
> Name: Msen
> Address: **garnet.msen.com**
> Port: **9062**
> Choose: **Career Assistance**

Career Events

Details of upcoming career fairs and other employment-related events.

Gopher:
> Name: Msen
> Address: **garnet.msen.com**
> Port: **9062**
> Choose: **Employment Events**

CareerMosaic

CareerMosaic is an online guide to in-depth information about employers, companies and job opportunities. Through a colorful interface, it presents information about where employers are, what they specialize in, and what's important to them.

World Wide Web:
> URL: **http://www.careermosaic.com/cm/**

Chronicle of Higher Education - Academe This Week

Job openings in academe from the current issue of the Chronicle. Search for your job either by the field in which you are interested, or the location where you would like to work.

World Wide Web:
> URL: **http://chronicle.merit.edu:8083/.ads/ .links.html**

Cinema Workers

Seeing all the free movies you want would almost be worth the agony of cleaning gum and sticky cola residue off the theater floor. Apparently there are a lot of in-jokes if you work in a cinema or film society, because the members of this list say that anyone is welcome to join, but if you aren't one of them, you are unlikely to understand most of the conversations. Maybe it's a cover to hide some trade secret involving the chemical formula for butter flavoring. Join up with the elite group of cinema workers and see what life is like on the business end of a projector.

Internet Mailing List:
   List Address: **exhibitionists@jvnc.net**
   Subscription Address:
      exhibitionists-request@jvnc.net

Contract Labor

More and more people are working from contract to contract. Aside from the cachet of getting to call yourself a "consultant," you will find that life is a lot more fun and challenging without fringe benefits. Here is the place to offer your services, look for a contract job, or swap experiences. (For hourly contracts, see **alt.sex.wanted**.)

Usenet:
   Newsgroup: **misc.jobs.contract**

Education-Related Jobs

Detailed descriptions of education-related jobs. Information includes required education and experience, and compensation levels.

Gopher:
   Name: Schoolnet Gopher
   Address: **gopher.schoolnet.carleton.ca**
   Choose: **SchoolNet Gopher**
    I **Career Centre**
    I **Job Descriptions**

Employee Search

Search through thousands of résumés in the Online Career Center database, from every corner of the U.S. and Canada, for just the right person. This resource is updated on a daily basis.

Gopher:
   Name: Msen
   Address: **garnet.msen.com**
   Port: **9062**
   Choose: **Search Resumes**

Employer Profiles

Details and other information about many of the companies that participate in the Online Career Center.

Gopher:
   Name: Msen
   Address: **garnet.msen.com**
   Port: **9062**
   Choose: **Company Sponsors and Profiles**

Need Work?

Are you. . . how shall we say it?. . . between jobs? The Internet can help you out. The Msen Gopher contains all kinds of information for the job seeker. Get the lowdown on many different companies, read helpful hints about the job market, take a peek at other people's resumes, and – best of all – upload your own resume to the data bank, where anyone on the Internet can look at it.

(Aww. . . on second thought forget it. What do you want to get a job for anyway? You'd only have to wake up early every day.)

Employment Opportunities at Microsoft

This page lists some of the employment opportunities currently available at Microsoft Corporation.

World Wide Web:
   URL: **http://www.microsoft.com/jobops/default.htm**

Before you go on a trip, use the Net to help you plan. Read the Travel section.

Entry Level Jobs Offered

What does an arts graduate say to a computer science graduate? "Would you like fries with your order?" If you are ready for an entry-level job, this is the newsgroup for you. Check out the jobs that offer you no place to go but up.

Usenet:
> Newsgroup: **misc.jobs.offered.entry**

Federal Jobs

Lists of federal job openings, including computer-related jobs and information for DOD employees in downsized agencies. Also includes information useful to applicants for federal jobs.

Gopher:
> Name: Dartmouth College
> Address: **dartcms1.dartmouth.edu**
> Choose: **Job Openings in the Federal Government**

Listserv Mailing List:
> List Address: **fedjobs@dartcms1.dartmouth.edu**
> Subscription Address:
>> **listserv@dartcms1.dartmouth.edu**

Interactive Employment Network

E-Span's Interactive Employment Network provides current, authoritative resources for the job seeker and the employer. It offers reference tools to select the best résumé format, practice exercises, a job library with job listings searchable by keyword, date posted, or job title, career fairs searchable by state and keyword, job search management tips, a searchable résumé database, and more. You can also submit your own résumé for inclusion in the database.

World Wide Web:
> URL: **http://www.espan.com/**

Job Search

Browse and search through a database of thousands of job advertisements in all disciplines and all over the U.S. and Canada. This resource is updated daily.

Gopher:
> Name: Msen
> Address: **garnet.msen.com**
> Port: **9062**
> Choose: **Search Jobs**

Aren't jobs great?
You sell your soul for a few pennies a week and then you grow old and die.
Still, if you really feel the need, the **JOB SEARCH** facilities on the Net are at your service.

Job Seeking

Having a job is really nice because when people ask you what you do for a living you don't have to say "Absolutely nothing." It will give them the impression that you are respectable. This forum has been established to assist people in sharing not only job opportunities, but ideas on how to gain employment.

Internet Mailing List:
> List Address: **employ@oti.disa.mil**
> Subscription Address:
>> **employ-request@oti.disa.mil**

Jobnet

This web page collects links to job-related resources all over the Internet. Links may take you to gopher servers, Usenet newsgroups, other web pages, and even mailing list servers. Check out Jobnet for information about employment trends, statistics, and information about career opportunities all over the world.

World Wide Web:
> URL: **http://sun.cc.westga.edu/~coop/localhome.html**

The Internet will set you free.

A
B
C
D
E
F
G
H
I
J
K
L
M
N
O
P
Q
R
S
T
U
V
W
X
Y
Z

Jobs General Discussion

Before you send away for instructions on how to make money at home stuffing envelopes, maybe you should check it out with your friends on the Net. Just as important, don't start your job hunt without finding out which companies allow their employees to wear long hair and earrings. If you need a job, have a job, or are offering a job, this newsgroup is the place to talk and trade tips about employment, the workplace, and careers.

Usenet:
> Newsgroup: **misc.jobs.misc**

Jobs Offered

Nothing to do all day? Perhaps you might like a job. Here are two general announcement forums for all types of employment.

Usenet:
> Newsgroup: **biz.jobs.offered**
> Newsgroup: **misc.jobs.offered**

Major Resource Kit

Entry-level job titles, job descriptions, and lists of the major employers for many of the common undergraduate degree programs.

Gopher:
> Name: University of Delaware
> Address: **gopher.udel.edu**
> Choose: **Student Information**
> | **Career Services**
> | **Career Services Major Resource Kit**

MedSearch America

Whether you are a healthcare professional or an employer wanting to fill a position quickly, MedSearch America is the place to look.

Gopher:
> Name: Msen
> Address: **gopher.medsearch.com**
> Port: **9001**

Need a laugh? Check out Humor.

Online Career Center

Career and employment-related information and advertisements, including huge job and résumé databases, an event guide, and company profiles.

Gopher:
> Name: Msen
> Address: **garnet.msen.com**
> Port: **9062**

Mail:
> Address: **occ-info@mail.msen.com**

Online Job Services

Some days the classifieds just don't have what you are looking for. With the Internet you have even more available resources. Link up to web sites, ftp sites, and gophers that have job listings.

World Wide Web:
> URL: **http://rescomp.stanford.edu/jobs.html**

Professional Career Organizations

Details and contact addresses of professional career organizations and networks.

Gopher:
> Name: Millsaps College
> Address: **gopher.millsaps.edu**
> Choose: **World Wide Information - Access The Internet**
> | **Internet Resources**
> | **Selected Internet Resources**
> | **Professional Societies and Organizations**

Résumé Database

Make your résumé available to thousands of employers across the United States by entering it in the Online Career Center database.

Gopher:
> Name: Msen
> Address: **garnet.msen.com**
> Port: **9062**
> Choose: **About Online Career Center**
> | **How to Enter Your Resume**

Mail:
> Address: **occ-resumes@msen.com**
> Subject: **Resume Title**
> Body: *text of your résumé*

Résumé Server

This web page has links to many people's résumés in HTML format. You can read people's résumés or post your own.

World Wide Web:
URL: **http://ibd.ar.com/Resume/**

Résumés

Here is the place to post your résumé (or look for ideas from other people's résumés to put on your own). Also the place to advertise that you would like a specific job.

Usenet:
Newsgroup: **misc.jobs.resumes**

Scientific Research

Scientists are like Sherlock Holmes. They spend their days looking for clues, gathering information and putting it together to solve the mysteries of the universe. If you have a career in scientific research or if you want one, examine all the issues relating to the topic by checking out this Usenet group. Researchers discuss the current projects, funding, job opportunities and post requests for information.

Usenet:
Newsgroup: **sci.research.careers**

SPIE Employment Service

SPIE is an online employment resource to help people in the scientific and engineering communities find jobs and to help employers in industry find qualified candidates. This service is free and available to anyone in a field related to optics.

World Wide Web:
URL: **http://www.spie.org/web/employment/
employ_home.html**

U.S. Department of Justice Job Listings

If you would like to be an attorney with the Department of Justice and you just happen to need a job, check out this gopher. Current job openings at the Department of Justice are listed here.

Gopher:
Name: U.S. Department of Justice
Address: **justice2.usdoj.gov**
Choose: **Justice Department Attorney Job listings**

> ## Spare time? Take a look at Games.

Virtual Library of Employment Opportunities

This web page lists many, many jobs available at colleges and universities across the United States. First choose an institution that you're interested in, then pick your job!

World Wide Web:
URL: **http://galaxy.einet.net/GJ/employment.html**

VMS Jobs

Jobs offered and wanted for people knowledgeable in DEC computers and the VMS operating system and network.

Usenet:
Newsgroup: **vmsnet.employment**

Women in Science and Engineering

Woman to woman, share your experiences, tips, and feelings about science and engineering, especially when it comes to jobs. For biologists, there is the **women-in-bio** group. For science and engineering in general, there is **wisenet** (the Women In Science and Engineering Network. Get it? W.I.S.E.NET... Oh, never mind. Silly acronyms are for men, anyway.).

Usenet:
Newsgroup: **bionet.women-in-bio**
Newsgroup: **info.wisenet**

Women in science: join the discussion in bionet.women-in-bio and info.wisenet

A B C D E F G H I J K L M N O P Q R S T U V W X Y Z

Women's Studies

If your field is women's studies or you want to work in a job related to women's issues and concerns, check out this list of employment opportunities. Scholarly, business and research positions are just a few of the careers that are open to you.

World Wide Web:
URL: **http://inform.umd.edu:86/ Educational_Resources/ AcademicResourcesByTopic/ WomensStudies/Employment**

JOURNALISM AND MEDIA

Broadcasting

Radio and television is a large and competitive business. Check out the latest news stories about current events in the broadcasting industry. Clarinet has the latest articles from the press.

Usenet:
Newsgroup: **clari.biz.industry.broadcasting**

Gonzo Journalism

In the tradition of Hunter Thompson, Gonzo journalism is the method of reporting in which the journalist is a participant in the series of events or story being reported on. Read discussion about Hunter S. Thompson and the concepts of gonzo journalism.

Usenet:
Newsgroup: **alt.journalism.gonzo**

Journalism

A mailing list and usenet newsgroup to facilitate communication between working journalists in any media, journalism educators, and news librarians and researchers. The main focus is on the use of computers in journalism, rather than general journalism.

Listserv Mailing List:
List Address: **carr-l@ulkyvm.louisville.edu**
Subscription Address:
listserv@ulkyvm.louisville.edu

Usenet:
Newsgroup: **alt.journalism**

Bedtime for Gonzo

Is there anyone who has read "Fear and Loathing in Las Vegas" and not felt Hunter Thompson to possess that spark of outrageous genius which is all too rare. Too bad, then, that the spark fanned into a dull flame that attenuated and died years ago, regretted by all. In its place, we have the legacy of Gonzo journalism, a largely mythical school of creation in which the writer is immersed in the events about which he is reporting. Still, as you might guess from reading this book, we firmly believe that irreverence is as irreverence does and that the spirit of Gonzo lives. So, if you are one of the atavistic intellectual hold-outs from the 70s, take some time and visit your friends in **alt.journalism.gonzo**. And if you happen to be reading this in a bookstore, buy this book or we will be forced to rip your lungs out.

Journalism Criticism

The media is taking a lot of heat for it's sensational tendencies. Take a close look at the criticism offered by the Usenet community about various journalists and the general media.

Usenet:
Newsgroup: **alt.journalism.criticism**

Journalism Discussions

Topics of interest to journalists and journalism educators, including issues related to magazine publishing.

Listserv Mailing List:
List Address: **magazine@vm.ecs.rpi.edu**
Subscription Address: **listserv@vm.ecs.rpi.edu**

List Address: **journet@qucdn.queensu.ca**
Subscription Address: **listserv@qucdn.queensu.ca**

Why be normal? Read Bizarre.

Mass Media

Articles about mass media, including sections on television, science fiction, video games, movies, comics, and books.

Anonymous FTP:
Address: **ftp.spies.com**
Path: **/Library/Media/***

Gopher:
Name: Internet Wiretap
Address: **wiretap.spies.com**
Choose: **Wiretap Online Library**
I Mass Media

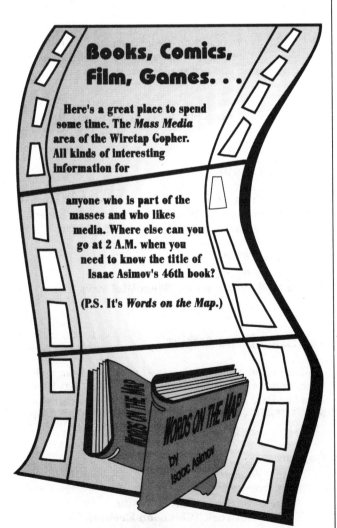

Books, Comics, Film, Games. . .

Here's a great place to spend some time. The *Mass Media* area of the Wiretap Gopher. All kinds of interesting information for

anyone who is part of the masses and who likes media. Where else can you go at 2 A.M. when you need to know the title of Isaac Asimov's 46th book?

(P.S. It's *Words on the Map*.)

Media List

You now have access to the untouchable media. Download a list of journalists and reporters who send and receive electronic mail. Radio stations, television stations, magazines and newspapers are included.

See also: News

Anonymous FTP:
Address: **ftp.std.com**
Path: **/customers/periodicals/ Middlesex-News/ medialist**

Majordomo Mailing List:
List Address: **medialist@world.std.com**
Subscription Address: **majordomo@world.std.com**

Media Magazines

Sample articles and subscription information for television and other media-related magazines.

Gopher:
Name: The Electronic Newsstand
Address: **gopher.enews.com**
Choose: **Magazines, Periodicals, and Journals (all titles)**
I Titles Arranged By Subject
I Media-Television

Music Journalism

Forget the blood and gore. Don't bother with the evening news and prime time telling of current events. Go for the glitz and the glory by following the music scene. Not only will you be able to wear rad clothes, but you can talk to cool rock stars and actually get paid for it. When you are a rich and famous music journalist and hosting your own show on M-TV you can say you got your start on the Internet.

Usenet:
Newsgroup: **alt.journalism.music**

Zines are cool.

News Media

News is constantly in the making. Keep up with news, news makers and reporters in this Usenet group that covers current events and concepts about the news media.

Usenet:
Newsgroup: **alt.news-media**

Lonely? Try the Personals.

Online Newspapers

Don't bother getting the newspaper anymore. Not only are you responsible for deforestation, but you also have stacks and stacks of paper to recycle. Having something to read over your Cheerios is just not worth the trouble. Now you have a choice of several newspapers that you can catch online, such as *USA Today*, the *San Francisco Chronicle and Examiner*, and everyone's favorite — the *Minnesota Daily*.

World Wide Web:
    URL: **http://www.nando.net/epage/htdocs/links/ newspapers.html**

Play-by-Play Sportscasters

Admit it. You've had the fantasy. In fact, we're betting when nobody is around you turn the sound down on the game and do the play-by-play yourself, doing your own impression of Howard Cosell. This discussion group offers a place for both students of sportscasting and hardened veterans to talk about broadcasting for radio or television.

See also: Sports and Athletics, Radio, Television

Listserv Mailing List:
    List Address: **pbp-l@etsuadmn.etsu.edu**
    Subscription Address: **listserv@etsuadmn.etsu.edu**

Hey, you know what? We could put on our own sports event: all we need is a play-by-play broadcaster. Not to worry. The PDP-1 mailing list is just the place to look.

Press Photographers

A press pass is a license to barge in where you are not wanted. If you're lucky you can snap pictures of famous movie stars and world leaders. If not, you end up doomed to take pictures of the winners of the Blizzard County's 94th Annual Chili Cook-Off. This list is sponsored by the National Press Photographers Association and offers a place for designers, educators and students to discuss this noble profession.

See also: Photography

Listserv Mailing List:
    List Address: **nppa-l@cmuvm.csv.cmich.edu**
    Subscription Address:
      listserv@cmuvm.csv.cmich.edu

Print Media

The media has to report on itself occasionally. Find real news stories through Clarinet and learn the latest news of the magazine and newspaper industry.

Usenet:
    Newsgroup: **clari.biz.industry.print_media**

Report on Waco

A file containing a report on the assault on the Branch Davidian compound in Waco, Texas, written by Robert McCurry, who takes an anti-government position.

Anonymous FTP:
    Address: **ftp.uu.net**
    Path: **/doc/literary/obi/Waco/McCurry**

Television News Archive

Abstracts from the big four news broadcasts from nightly evening news programs. Contains info from 1990-1994. Also has Persian Gulf War news coverage abstracts, in **Specialized News Collections | Persian Gulf War (1991)**.

Gopher:
    Name: Vanderbilt University, Television News
      Archive
    Address: **tvnews.vanderbilt.edu**
    Choose: **Network Television Evening News Abstracts**

KEYS AND LOCKS

Guide to Lock Picking

This page is Ted the Tool's Guide to Lock Picking. Start out by learning how a key opens a lock, and then build on your knowledge to learn about pin columns, scrubbing, and analytic thinking about lock-picking.

World Wide Web:
URL: **http://www.lysator.liu.se:7500/mit-guide/mit-guide.html**

THE KEY ᴛᴏ SUCCESS

One thing we have learned in life is that some of the most interesting things happen in places where people don't want us to be. All the more reason why the well-dressed man or woman should never be without a few lock picks and master keys. However, tools by themselves are useless, so before you even think about becoming a lock-and-key person, check out the Internet's *Lock Picking* archives.

(And remember, you should only use your lock picking skills to help friends who lose their keys. The last thing we want is for you to be sneaking into places just to see if anything interesting is happening.)

Lock Picking

Frequently asked questions about lock pick sets, skeleton keys, Kryptonite locks, automatic pickers, related books, legal issues, and more.

Anonymous FTP:
Address: **rtfm.mit.edu**
Path: **/pub/usenet/alt.locksmithing/***

Jump into the Net.

Lock Talk

Do you need the name of a book that will show you how to get into a locked, keyless automobile? How about a reference on safe-cracking? Or an electronic copy of *The MIT Guide to Lockpicking*, by Ted the Tool? Or are you an amateur locksmith with a picky problem? Check with the lock and key set for all your needs. Just don't tell anyone where you found out about it.

Usenet:
Newsgroup: **alt.locksmithing**

Excerpt from the Net...
(from the Locksmithing frequently asked question list)

How can I make my own picks and tension wrenches?

You can file or grind picks out of spring steel. It is best to use spring steel -- sources include hacksaw blades, piano wire, clock springs... In a pinch, safety pin steel, or even a bobby pin can be used...

Where can I get the "MIT Guide to Picking Locks"?

The author of the "MIT Guide to Picking Locks", Ted the Tool, has posted a Post-script version of the guide which can be retrieved via Anonymous FTP...

What are "pick guns" or "automatic pickers" and do they work?

A "pick gun" is a manual or powered device that uses a vibrating pin to try to bounce the pin tumblers so there are spaces at the shear line so the the plug can rotate. They are not a panacea, aren't always effective, and the Net seems to feel that these are no substitute for a little skill with a pick and learning how locks work...

(continued on next page)

(continued from previous page)

Can the Club be picked? Is the Club any good?

[Note: The "Club" is a widely-advertised automobile anti-theft device that you use to lock the steering wheel when you leave your car.]

"I used to have a Club, purchased on the recommendation of a coworker. The first time I tried picking it, it took me approximately 30 seconds, using the cap of a Papermate Flexgrip pen for tension, and a bent jumbo paperclip to rake the pins. With practice, I was able to reliably pick every "Club" I encountered in 5-30 seconds using these tools."

However, it doesn't really matter, no car thief is going to pick it, they are going to cut the soft plastic steering wheel with a hacksaw or bolt cutters and slip the Club off.

Here are some of the things collected about locations and availabilities (most are from alt.locksmithing). We do not endorse any of these, but feel that you can get information by reading.

PADLOCK SHIM PICKS. Open padlocks in seconds! Our new Padlock Shim pick's unique design makes them so successful that it is frightening! Simply slide the shim down between the shackle and the lock housing, twist and the lock is open. Works best on laminated type padlocks (the most popular type) but will open almost any type of padlock -- including the popular 3 number combination type...

PICK GUN. Picks locks FAST. Open locks in less than 5 seconds. Specifically designed for tumbler locks. Insert pick into key slot, then just pull trigger. Throws all pins into position at one time. Lock is then turned with tension bar. Used extensively by police and other government agencies...

PRO-LOK "CAR KILLER" KIT. Over the years we have had thousands of requests for a multi-vehicle opening kit. We are now able to offer the most complete kit that we have ever seen. This kit of tools will open over 135 automobiles, both domestic and foreign, on the road today. The opening procedure for each vehicle is diagrammed and explained in the instruction manual...

TUBULAR LOCK PICK. This tool is an easy and reliable method for picking tubular locks, as found on commercial vending machines, washers, dryers, etc...

HOW TO GET IN ANYWHERE, ANYTIME (video tape). Nearly two full hours of on-site techniques to get in any building, beat any lock, open any safe, enter any car...

TECHNIQUES OF BURGLAR ALARM BYPASSING.
Alarms covered include: Magnetic Switches, Window Foil, Sound and Heat Detectors, Photoelectric Devices, Guard Dogs, Central Station Systems, Closed-Circuit Television and more...

TECHNIQUES OF SAFECRACKING...

HIGH SPEED ENTRY: INSTANT OPENING TECHNIQUES (video tape)...

THE COMPLETE GUIDE TO LOCK PICKING by Eddie the Wire. The very best book ever written on how to pick locks...

CIA FIELD-EXPEDIENT KEY CASTING MANUAL. How to make a duplicate key when you can keep the original only a short time...

HOW I STEAL CARS: A REPO MAN'S GUIDE TO CAR THIEVES' SECRETS (video tape). How to open and enter practically any modern automobile and how to start them without the key...

Locksmithing Archives

Technical information and pictures related to locksmithing.

Anonymous FTP:
Address: **ftp.std.com**
Path: **/archive/alt.locksmithing/***

KIDS

Children's Discussion

Clubhouses and playhouses are always fun because it's a great place for kids to hang out and be themselves and no parents are allowed. There is a place like that on Usenet. Kids go to talk about anything they want and it's just for them, so parents — no peeking.

Usenet:
Newsgroup: **alt.kids-talk**

Interesting Projects for Young Children

The Schoolnet Gopher at Carleton University (Ottawa, Canada) has a wealth of resources for kids, parents and teachers. The *Cool Things to Try* section has ideas for interesting projects that you can do with your youngsters. for example, using common household articles, you can make your own thyxotropic substance. Not only will your kids have fun, but somebody (whose name we won't mention) might even learn something by accident.

Children's Stories, Poems and Pictures

Good collection of children's stories, poems, pictures, magazines, movie clips, cartoons, and links to other fun sites.

World Wide Web:
URL: **http://www.comlab.ox.ac.uk/oucl/users/ jonathan.bowen/children/**

Cool Things to Try

Have fun with a potato-powered clock, a liquid that changes to a solid under pressure, and other cool experiments.

Gopher:
Name: Schoolnet Gopher
Address: **gopher.schoolnet.carleton.ca**
Choose: **SchoolNet Gopher**
| SchoolNet Gopher
| Kindergarten to Grade 6 Corner
| Cool things to try...

Disney

FAQs about Disneyland, lyrics to Disney songs, EuroDisney reports, and other material from the Magic Kingdom.

Anonymous FTP:
Address: **quartz.rutgers.edu**
Path: **/pub/disney/***

Gopher:
Name: Rutgers University
Address: **quartz.rutgers.edu**
Choose: **Disney - The Wonderful World of Disney**

Disney Talk

Talk about Disney films, cartoons, Disneyland, Disney World, and anything else related to the Magic Kingdom.

Internet Relay Chat:
Channel: **#disney**

Field of Clovers

Search a field of clovers for that magical four leaf one.

World Wide Web:
URL: **http://orange-room.cc.nd.edu/ToyBox/ Clovers/Clovers.html**

A B C D E F G H I J K L M N O P Q R S T U V W X Y Z

How to Recycle Paper

A fun guide that teaches kids how to make paper from trash and old paper.

Gopher:
> Name: Schoolnet Gopher
> Address: **gopher.schoolnet.carleton.ca**
> Choose: **SchoolNet Gopher**
> | **Kindergarten to Grade 6 Corner**
> | **Cool things to try...**
> | **Learn How to Make Your Own Recycled Paper!**

Kid's Internet Delight

The KID Server is a gathering of pointers to sites that children might enjoy. There are dinosaurs, sports info, NASA and space info, the KidLink gopher, and various links to elementary schools across the country.

World Wide Web:
> URL: **http://www.clark.net/pub/journalism/kid.html**

KidArt

A gallery of computer art presenting works by kids. Pictures are stored in gif format, but the gallery supports MS-DOS, Mac, Amiga, Apple II, and Atari systems.

Gopher:
> Name: KIDLINK Gopher!
> Address: **kids.ccit.duq.edu**
> Choose: **KIDART Computer Art Gallery**

Kidlink

An educational project to encourage children between the ages of 10 and 15 to get involved in global dialog through mail, IRC, and other telecommunications technologies.

Gopher:
> Name: KIDLINK Gopher!
> Address: **kids.ccit.duq.edu**

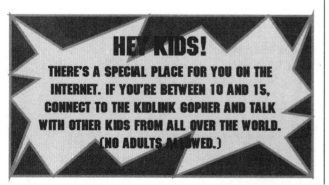

HEY KIDS!
THERE'S A SPECIAL PLACE FOR YOU ON THE INTERNET. IF YOU'RE BETWEEN 10 AND 15, CONNECT TO THE KIDLINK GOPHER AND TALK WITH OTHER KIDS FROM ALL OVER THE WORLD. (NO ADULTS ALLOWED.)

Kids and Computers

Put kids on the cutting edge by finding out the best kid-friendly computers and software.

Usenet:
> Newsgroup: **misc.kids.computer**

Kids Mailing List

A spin-off of the Kidsphere mailing list, KIDS exists for children to post messages to other children around the world. Send a mail message to the below address to join.

Mail:
> Address: **joinkids@vms.cis.pitt.edu**

MayaQuest

Pictures and information about a wholly kid-directed cycling expedition into the Mayan world of Central America to illuminate the great mystery of the collapse of the ancient Mayan civilization.

Gopher:
> Name: Minnesota K-12
> Address: **informns.k12.mn.us**
> Choose: **Minnesota K-12 Resources**
> | **MAYAQUEST**

World Wide Web:
> URL: **http://informns.k12.mn.us/mayaquest**

Neat Tricks

Learn how to make your friends' arms rise against their will, how to move things with your mind, and other neat tricks to impress your friends.

Gopher:
> Name: Schoolnet Gopher
> Address: **gopher.schoolnet.carleton.ca**
> Choose: **SchoolNet Gopher**
> | **Kindergarten to Grade 6 Corner**
> | **Neat tricks you can do**

Stories About Children

Parents share anecdotes about children and the funny things they do and say. This group is not only a relaxed atmosphere in which to talk about kids, but it's also a great way to pass along important, timely and useful information relating to children.

Usenet:
> Newsgroup: **misc.kids**

LANGUAGE

Acronym Servers and Archives

These servers contains thousands of acronyms and their meanings.

Anonymous FTP:
Address: **ucselx.sdsu.edu**
Path: **/pub/doc/general/acronyms.txt**

Gopher:
Name: Manchester Computing Centre
Address: **info.mcc.ac.uk**
Choose: **Miscellaneous items**
| **Acronym dictionary**

WAIS:
Database: **acronyms**

World Wide Web:
URL: **http://curia.ucc.ie/info/net/acronyms/acro.html**

American/British Lexicon

A dictionary of American and British language usage. A fun and useful reference for American travelers to Great Britain or British travelers to the U.S.

Gopher:
Name: Oregon State University
Address: **gopher.fsl.orst.edu**
Choose: **Other Sources of Info**
| **Hugo's Lore-House**
| **Dr.Fegg's Big House o'Fun..**
| **Jeremy Smith's American/British Lexicon**

Arabic

If Arabic is on your list of things to learn before retirement, you are in luck. Download audio lessons, films, music and pictures. This is only for hardcore Arabic lovers, because these files are very large and transferring them may take a great deal of time and disk space.

See also: World Cultures

World Wide Web:
URL: **http://philae.sas.upenn.edu/Arabic/arabic.html**

Catalan

When life is hectic, it's hard to keep up with your Catalan on a day-to-day basis. With Usenet, it's much easier. Discuss the language of Catalonia, Andorra and the Belearic Islands and get a little culture at the same time.

Usenet:
Newsgroup: **bit.listserv.catala**

Chinese Text Viewers

Programs, documents, and fonts for viewing Chinese text on IBM-PC and Unix systems.

Anonymous FTP:
Address: **ftp.funet.fi**
Path: **/pub/culture/chinese/***

Colibri

Colibri is an electronic newsletter and web service for people interested in the fields of language, speech, logic or information. The Colibri newsletter is sent out every week from the OTS, Utrecht University.

World Wide Web:
URL: **http://colibri.let.ruu.nl**

College Slang Dictionary

The official Usenet dictionary of college slang, as compiled by the readers of the Usenet **soc.college** newsgroup.

Anonymous FTP:
Address: **ftp.spies.com**
Path: **/Library/Article/Language/slang.col**

Gopher:
Name: Internet Wiretap
Address: **wiretap.spies.com**
Choose: **Wiretap Online Library**
| **Articles** | **Language**
| **College Slang Dictionary**

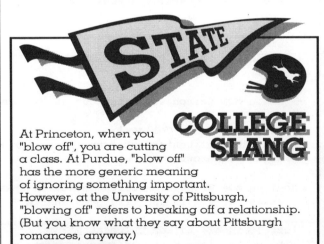

At Princeton, when you "blow off", you are cutting a class. At Purdue, "blow off" has the more generic meaning of ignoring something important. However, at the University of Pittsburgh, "blowing off" refers to breaking off a relationship. (But you know what they say about Pittsburgh romances, anyway.)

Clearly, you can get yourself into a lot of trouble just by using the wrong word. For some definitive info on college slang, check out the Usenet **College Slang Dictionary** as compiled by Jennifer Doyle.

Computation and Language E-Print Archive

This is a fully automated electronic archive and distribution server for papers on computational linguistics, natural language processing, speech processing, and related fields.

See also: World Cultures

World Wide Web:
   URL: **http://xxx.lanl.gov/cmp-lg/**

Cyrillic Text

Information about Russian Cyrillic text, including a basic tutorial and introduction to the Russian language.

World Wide Web:
   URL: **http://solar.rtd.utk.edu/friends/cyrillic/ cyrillic.html**

Zines are cool.

Czech Slovak

Come to this IRC channel to talk with others in the Eastern European tongues of Czech and Slovak.

Internet Relay Chat:
   Channel: **#cs**

Devil's Dictionary

A cynical, sarcastic lexicon of terms and phrases. This dictionary was completed in 1911 by Ambrose Bierce.

Anonymous FTP:
   Address: **ftp.std.com**
   Path: **/obi/Ambrose.Bierce/ The.Devils.Dictionary.Z**

Gopher:
   Name: Software Tool & Die
   Address: **gopher.std.com**
   Choose: **OBI The Online Book Initiative**
      | The Online Books
      | Ambrose.Bierce
      | The.Devils.Dictionary

Excerpt from the Net...

```
(from the "College Slang Dictionary")

Geek Box/Nerd Box [Purdue University]:
-- a container, usually a tackle box, carried by electrical engineering students and
containing the millions of electronic components needed in the lab

Plasma [MIT]:
-- caffeine, in any of its forms

Random [MIT]:
-- a non-MIT person who hangs out at MIT anyway

Sexile [Swarthmore College]:
-- the state of banishment from one's room while one's roommate is with his/her
   significant other

Shooting the Shabookie [Carnegie-Mellon University]:
-- taking it all in the card game Hearts

Slort [Carnegie-Mellon University]:
-- to go to class with the express purpose of sleeping through it

Tool [Princeton University]:
-- someone with political or business ambitions

Wendy [Wellesley College]:
-- to be like the stereotypically WASP'y Wellesley woman
```

Dictionary of Computing Terms

Detailed glossary of programming languages, architectures, domain theory, mathematics, networking, and many other computing areas.

Anonymous FTP:
   Address: **wombat.doc.ic.ac.uk**
   Path: **/pub/Dictionary.gz**

Gopher:
   Name: Imperial College
   Address: **wombat.doc.ic.ac.uk**
   Choose: **The Free On-Line Dictionary of Computing 800k <PC Bin>**

Dictionary Word Lists

Word lists for many languages and topics, including Dutch, German, Italian, Norwegian, Swedish, Finnish, Japanese, and Polish names. Also includes zip codes and *Star Trek* terms.

Anonymous FTP:
   Address: **black.ox.ac.uk**
   Path: **/wordlists/***

Dutch

Slip off your wooden shoes and cozy up to the keyboard for some discussion of Dutch language and literature. The newsgroup is moderated; the IRC channel isn't.

Internet Relay Chat:
   Channel: **#dutch**

Usenet:
   Newsgroup: **bit.lang.neder-l**

Echo Eurodictautom

This web page can translate words in French, German, Italian, Spanish, Danish, Dutch, or Portuguese to any other of those languages.

World Wide Web:
   URL: **http://www.uni-frankfurt.de/ ~felix/eurodictautom.html**

English Language

Lively discussion of the English language and the meaning of words. Besides learning quirky new meanings of words, you will have loads of fun on this newsgroup and mailing list, which have very friendly and relaxed atmospheres.

Listserv Mailing List:
   List Address: **words-l@uga.cc.uga.edu**
   Subscription Address: **listserv@uga.cc.uga.edu**

Usenet:
   Newsgroup: **bit.listserv.words-l**

English and Modern Language Graduate Students

Next to the language of love, English and the modern languages are the most handy languages to know. Graduate students get together for the exchange of academic and professional information about English and the modern languages.

Listserv Mailing List:
   List Address: **e-grad@rutvm1.rutgers.edu**
   Subscription Address:
      listserv@rutvm1.rutgers.edu

Excerpt from the Net...

```
Newsgroup: bit.listserv.words-l
Subject: Linguistic Terminology


> "Rhetorical device", "linguistic phenomenon", what's the deal with
> sullying the name of linguistics this way? I guess it's called
> metonymy. Of course for you guys everything is metaphor, right?

A man's reach should exceed his grasp, or what's a meta phor?
```

A B C D E F G H I J K **L** M N O P Q R S T U V W X Y Z

English-German Dictionary

Langenscheidt's English-German dictionary allows you to type in an English word and get an immediate translation for it. It will produce several possibilities for the translation if appropriate.

World Wide Web:
URL: **http://www.fmi.uni-passau.de/htbin/lt/lte**

English-Slovene Dictionary

This is something you should always keep handy in case some important Slovene dignitaries drop in for dinner. This dictionary has tens of thousands of entries and can be searched by keyword, wildcard, or regular expression match.

World Wide Web:
URL: **http://olymp.fer.uni-lj.si/dictionary/a2s.html**

Esperanto

Here are some forums for people interested in any aspect of the international language Esperanto. Participants are encouraged, but not required, to participate in the language.

Internet Mailing List:
List Address: **esperanto@lll-crg-llnl.gov**
Subscription Address:
esperanto-request@lll-crg-llnl.gov

List Address: **esperanto@rand.org**
Subscription Address:
esperanto-request@rand.org

List Address: **esper-l@vm3090.ege.edu.tr**
Subscription Address: **listserv@vm3090.ege.edu.tr**

Usenet:
Newsgroup: **alt.uu.lang.esperanto.misc**
Newsgroup: **soc.culture.esperanto**

Esperanto HyperCourse

A magnificent demonstration of the use of the Web as an interactive tutorial. You are presented with a picture of a normal office, and by clicking on any of the objects within the office you can hear its Esperanto name.

World Wide Web:
URL: **http://utis179.cs.utwente.nl:8001/esperanto/hypercourse/index.html**

URL: **http://utis179.cs.utwente.nl:8001/esperanto/hyperkursus/oficej_au.html**

Esperanto Introduction

This web page offers an introduction to Esperanto, a FAQ, Esperanto information-server details, introductory courses, event guides, pictures, **.au** audio files, texts, tools, links to other Esperanto resources, and much more.

World Wide Web:
URL: **http://utis179.cs.utwente.nl:8001/esperanto/index_en.html**

Esperanto-English Dictionary

Are you tired of not being able to understand everyone speaking Esperanto? Well, here's a dictionary you can use to translate Esperanto words into their English equivalents. Keep this with you — you never know when it might come in handy.

Anonymous FTP:
Address: **ftp.spies.com**
Path: **/Library/Article/Language/esperant.eng**

Gopher:
Name: Internet Wiretap
Address: **wiretap.spies.com**
Choose: **Wiretap Online Library**
l **Articles**
l **Language**
l **Esperanto English Dictionary**

European Network in Language and Speech

ELSNET seeks to encourage the development of language technology in Europe by helping coordinate progress on both scientific and technological fronts. There are research coordination, training and mobility, language and speech resources, and industrial links task groups. The server has info on these task groups and other projects, publications and newsletters of ELSNET.

World Wide Web:
URL: **http://www.cogsci.ed.ac.uk/elsnet/home.html**

Foreign Language Dictionaries

Dictionaries for a number of European languages, including Dutch, English, German, Italian, Norwegian, and Swedish.

Anonymous FTP:
Address: **ftp.uu.net**
Path: **/doc/dictionaries/DEC-collection/***

French

Pop the popcorn and sit down at your computer for this French slide show on the history and civilization of France. In addition, there are links to readers and games that can help you learn the language.

World Wide Web:
URL: **http://philae.sas.upenn.edu/French/french.html**

Gaelic and Gaelic Culture

Gaelic is the English word used to describe Irish Gaelic, Manx Gaelic, and Scottish Gaelic, the three languages that form one half of the Celtic language family group. This site offers examples of spoken Gaelic, a short history of the Celts, mailing list archives, lists of Gaelic books and tapes, Irish National Radio news, and links to many other Celtic-related topics and resources.

World Wide Web:
URL: **http://sunsite.unc.edu/gaelic/gaelic.html**

Gaelic Mailing List

A multidisciplinary discussion list for the exchange of news, views, and information between speakers of Scottish Gaelic, Irish, and Manx. Provides tuition for people learning to speak Gaelic.

Listserv Mailing List:
List Address: **gaelic-l@irlearn.ucd.ie**
Subscription Address: **listserv@irlearn.ucd.ie**

German

Sprechen sie Deutsch? Brush up on your German by asking questions, reading posts and practicing in this Usenet group. Discussion is held in both English and German. If you're up to a realtime test, try your skill on the IRC channels. English and beginners' German is spoken on the **#german** channel.

Internet Relay Chat:
Channel: **#german**
Channel: **#germany**

Usenet:
Newsgroup: **alt.usage.german**

German-English Dictionary

Langenscheidt's German-English dictionary allows you to type in a German word and get an immediate translation for it. It will produce several possibilities for the translation if appropriate.

World Wide Web:
URL: **http://www.fmi.uni-passau.de/htbin/lt/ltd**

Hawaiian Glossary

The Hawaiian language only has five vowels and twelve consonants, out of which twelve letters (a, h, i, k, l, m, n, o, p, t, u, and w) are represented here. By choosing a specific letter, you can see a selection of Hawaiian words beginning with that letter and their English translation.

World Wide Web:
URL: **http://bookweb.cwis.uci.edu:8042/Books/Moon/glossary.html**

Going to Maui soon? Perhaps a copy of the Hawaiian dictionary would help you. It really helps to be able to talk to the natives in their own language when you need to say, "Can I please have a condo that does not overlook the parking lot."

Hindi

This web page has video and written text that can help you learn to speak Hindi.

World Wide Web:
URL: **http://philae.sas.upenn.edu/Hindi/hindi.html**

History of Languages

A document containing condensations of postings to the Usenet newsgroup **sci.lang**, which is devoted to the scientific and historical study of language. Issues that are addressed in these postings include the physical nature of speech, the use of sounds in language, the meanings and history of words, and sentence structures.

Anonymous FTP:
Address: **ftp.hmc.edu**
Path: **/pub/science/sci.answers/.mirror.OLD/sci-lang-faq**

A
B
C
D
E
F
G
H
I
J
K
L
M
N
O
P
Q
R
S
T
U
V
W
X
Y
Z

Iceland

An IRC channel where people from Iceland and those who speak Icelandic congregate.

Internet Relay Chat:
Channel: **#iceland**

Italian Lessons

A set of Italian lessons for beginners, written by Lucio Chiappetti (sounds Italian to us). Pick your lesson right off the web page and learn to speak Italian!

World Wide Web:
URL: **http://www.willamette.edu/~tjones/
languages/Italian/Italian-lesson.html**

Japanese

No matter if your kanji is weak or if you just need some help on pronunciation, you can find assistance here. This group covers all aspects of the Japanese language — written and spoken. The next time you go out for sushi you won't have to just point at the menu and say "I'll have that thing."

Usenet:
Newsgroup: **sci.lang.japan**

Language Articles

Many language-related resources, including unusual language dictionaries, lists of mnemonics, spoonerisms, palindromes, and language guides.

Anonymous FTP:
Address: **ftp.spies.com**
Path: **/Library/Article/Language/***

Gopher:
Name: Internet Wiretap
Address: **wiretap.spies.com**
Choose: **Wiretap Online Library**
  I Articles
  I Language

**Planning a picnic? Check the
weather using the Net.**

Language IRC Channels

Here are a few IRC channels where you can try out new lines in a foreign language. Seriously, if you're learning a new language, you'll find experts here.

Internet Relay Chat:
Channel: **#espanol**
Channel: **#francais**
Channel: **#italia**
Channel: **#turks**

Languages of the World

A small collection of information about human languages, including sexist and non-sexist language, the Maori language, and a link to the large collection of texts at the Oxford Text Archive.

World Wide Web:
URL: **http://www.cs.cmu.edu:8001/Web/People/
mjw/Language/MainPage.html**

URL: **http://www.willamette.edu/~tjones/
Language-Page.html**

Latin Study Guides

Study guides to *Wheelock's Latin*, the most widely used introductory Latin textbook in American colleges and universities.

Anonymous FTP:
Address: **ftp.spies.com**
Path: **/Library/Article/Language/latin.stu**

Gopher:
Name: Internet Wiretap
Address: **wiretap.spies.com**
Choose: **Wiretap Online Library**
  I Articles
  I Language
  I Study Guide to Wheelock Latin

Learn Spanish in South America!

This web page is a program to help you learn to speak Spanish by going on a fully immersive trip to Ecuador.

World Wide Web:
URL: **http://www.comnet.com/ecuador/
learnSpanish.html**

Lessons in Spanish

Learn basic words, numbers, and pronuciation in Spanish. Each week, there's a new list of words to learn and a mini-curriculum put together by Tyler Jones.

World Wide Web:
URL: **http://www.willamette.edu/~tjones/ Spanish/lesson1.html**

Linguist List

This web page features a hypertext version of the Linguist list, the mailing list of the linguistics community.

World Wide Web:
URL: **http://www.ling.rochester.edu/linguist/ contents.html**

Linguistics

You won't find any puns, anagrams or palindromes here so if you are looking for fun or help with a crossword puzzle don't post to this newsgroup. This is where scholars of linguistics hang out to discuss the scientific and historical study of human language. Get in on some hot and heavy discussion of Latin declensions or a quick and dirty comparison of Frisian to Old English. It will certainly liven up any dull afternoon.

Usenet:
Newsgroup: **sci.lang**

No one understands the Internet, so relax and enjoy.

Lojban

Lojban is a made-up language that is based on logic and is designed to be good for interacting with computers. Lojban is said to be unambiguous, genderless, and easy to learn. See an electronic brochure complete with contact people and detailed information about the language, its history and how to learn it.

World Wide Web:
URL: **http://xiron.pc.helsinki.fi/lojban/ lojbroch.html**

Middle English

Search texts for words in Middle English. There are also texts for browsing and connections to other Middle English collections.

World Wide Web:
URL: **http://etext.virginia.edu/ Mideng.query.html**

Excerpt from the Net...

```
(from "Mnemonics", easy ways to remember sequences of words)

     To remember the hardness scale for minerals:

               1) Talc
               2) Gypsum
               3) Calcite
               4) Flurite
               5) Appetite
               6) Orthoclase
               7) Quartz
               8) Topaz
               9) Corumdum
              10) Diamond

          All you have to do is memorize:

     "Toronto girls can flirt and only quit to chase dwarves."

   [By the way, Harley was born in Toronto and he can assure you that the observation
   about Toronto girls is perfectly true.]
```

A B C D E F G H I J K L M N O P Q R S T U V W X Y Z

Mnemonics

A selection of mnemonics for remembering everything from trigonometric equations to resistor color codes, pi, and music scales.

Anonymous FTP:
Address: **ftp.spies.com**
Path: **/Library/Article/Language/mnemonic.txt**

Gopher:
Name: Internet Wiretap
Address: **wiretap.spies.com**
Choose: **Wiretap Online Library**
  | Articles
  | Language
  | Mnemonics

Name Guide

An interesting guide to naming conventions in many cultures around the world. This paper outlines differences between Mac and Mc, and many other cultural variations of names and naming conventions.

Gopher:
Name: World Data Center on Microorganisms
Address: **fragrans.riken.go.jp**
Choose: **Important note about Asian names**

Palindromes

A long list of palindromes — words and phrases that read the same way backward as they do forward. For example, "A man, a plan, a canal, Panama!"

Anonymous FTP:
Address: **ftp.spies.com**
Path: **/Library/Article/Language/palindro.txt**

Gopher:
Name: Internet Wiretap
Address: **wiretap.spies.com**
Choose: **Wiretap Online Library**
  | Articles
  | Language
  | Palindromes

Parler au Quotidien

Learn French in your spare time with this popular program from Radio France International. There are seven lessons, each one being a **.au** audio file typically between 2 and 2.5 megabytes.

World Wide Web:
URL: **http://town.hall.org/travel/france/rfi.html**

Looking for special fun? Turn to the Vices section.

Pronunciation

An interesting poem about pronunciation in the English language, written to help students learning English.

Anonymous FTP:
Address: **quartz.rutgers.edu**
Path: **/pub/misc/pronunciation.gz**

Gopher:
Name: Rutgers University
Address: **quartz.rutgers.edu**
Choose: **Miscellaneous**
  | pronunciation

Quick and Dirty Guide to Japanese

This useful information will help you learn to use Japanese in the shortest possible time. It places emphasis on communicating rather than complete correctness.

Anonymous FTP:
Address: **ftp.spies.com**
Path: **/Library/Article/Language/grammar.jap**

Gopher:
Name: Internet Wiretap
Address: **wiretap.spies.com**
Choose: **Wiretap Online Library**
  | Articles
  | Language
  | Quick & Dirty Guide to Japanese Grammar

Got a hot date at the sushi bar? Better take a moment to review the Quick and Dirty Guide to Japanese.

Rasta Dictionary

You be jammin' to that funky reggae music and suddenly the singer utters some words that you just don't understand. Don't let it ruin your great musical experience. Increase your rasta vocabulary by learning all the words in this online dictionary. That way, when you go to Jamaica and someone says they are in "agony," you won't rescue them, or if they call you "massive," you won't worry about your weight.

World Wide Web:
URL: **ftp://jammin.nosc.mil/pub/reggae/patois.txt**

Roget's Thesaurus

The complete reference, provided by Project Gutenberg. Search and consult the original 1911 *Roget's Thesaurus*.

Gopher:
Name: University of California San Diego
Address: **infopath.ucsd.edu**
Choose: **Reference Shelf**
 | **Dictionaries & Thesauri**
 | **Roget's 1911 Thesaurus**

Name: University of Minnesota
Address: **gopher.micro.umn.edu**
Choose: **Libraries**
 | **Reference Works**
 | **Roget's Thesaurus (Published 1911)**

Name: University of Oregon
Address: **gopher.uoregon.edu**
Choose: **Desktop Reference/Roget's Thesaurus**

Russian and East European Studies

This web page features a Russian word list with over 31,000 Russian words in alphabetical order.

World Wide Web:
URL: **http://www.pitt.edu/~cjp/rslang.html**

Russian Swear Words

More Russian swear words than you could learn even if you were Russian!

Anonymous FTP:
Address: **infomeister.osc.edu**
Path: **/pub/central_eastern_europe/russian/ obscenities/***

Russian Talk

Come and speak Russian with Russian speakers all around the world.

Internet Relay Chat:
Channel: **#russian**

Serbian

It has been said that Serbian is one of the easiest languages to learn to write because it is so phonetic. See if this is true, by brushing up on your Serbian as well as the Cyrillic and Latin alphabets.

See also: World Cultures

World Wide Web:
URL: **http://www.umiacs.umd.edu/research/lpv/ YU/HTML/jezik.html**

Shorter Oxford Dictionary

The complete shorter *Oxford Dictionary* word list, including part-of-speech information.

Anonymous FTP:
Address: **ftp.white.toronto.edu**
Path: **/pub/words/sodict.gz**

Slang Dictionary

The definitive, and complete, reference to street and trash talk.

Anonymous FTP:
Address: **ftp.spies.com**
Path: **/Library/Misc/slang.txt**

Gopher:
Name: Internet Wiretap
Address: **wiretap.spies.com**
Choose: **Wiretap Online Library**
 | **Miscellaneous**
 | **Slang Dictionary (Western PA, USA)**

A B C D E F G H I J K L M N O P Q R S T U V W X Y Z

Slang Dictionary

What do you do when your grandmother is coming over for dinner and you are sure that, once again, she is going to gross out the entire family with her expert knowledge of slang and odd expressions? Well, since you are a denizen of the Net, all you need to do is connect your gopher to the Slang Dictionary and you will have no problem finding all kinds of expressions that will put even the most earthy grandmother in her place.

Spoonerisms

A collection of malapropisms, mixed metaphors, and spoonerisms, bringing new communication possibilities to the English language.

Anonymous FTP:
>   Address: **ftp.spies.com**
>   Path: **/Library/Article/Language/spooner.lis**

Gopher:
>   Name: Internet Wiretap
>   Address: **wiretap.spies.com**
>   Choose: **Wiretap Online Library**
> | **Articles**
> | **Language**
> | **Spoonerisms and Malapropisms**

Technical Japanese Program

Provides education in Japanese language, culture, and technical management to American scientists and engineers. Conferences, workshops, research projects, newsletters, and links to other Japanese resources are also available.

World Wide Web:
>   URL: **http://www.uwtc.washington.edu/
>   Default.html**

Traveler's Japanese

They sprang the business trip to Japan on you at the last minute and you have to get prepared. It would be awful to go all the way to Japan and not be able to get any decent sushi. Do what any sensible Internet user would do in a case like this — take the laptop and cellular phone and learn Japanese during the long flight overseas.

See also: World Cultures

World Wide Web:
>   URL: **http://www.ntt.jp/japan/japanese/**

Urdu Dictionary

Here's an Urdu-English dictionary just in case you might find yourself among ancient Hindustanis. Have yaaraa and go with yazdaan.

Anonymous FTP:
>   Address: **ftp.spies.com**
>   Path: **/Library/Article/Language/urdu.dic**

Gopher:
>   Name: Internet Wiretap
>   Address: **wiretap.spies.com**
>   Choose: **Wiretap Online Library**
> | **Articles**
> | **Language**
> | **Small Urdu Dictionary**

Word Lists

Word lists for several languages, including Dutch, English, German, Italian, Norwegian, and Swedish. Useful for linguistic research and text-processing applications such as spelling checkers.

Anonymous FTP:
>   Address: **ftp.funet.fi**
>   Path: **/pub/doc/dictionaries/***

Word-a-Day

If someone calls you a "wowser" and you don't know whether to feel congratulated or insulted, then you might need to improve your vocabulary by joining this word-a-day list. Each day, a new word will come to your mailbox. Impress your friends and co-workers. Don't be caught verbally unaware.

Mail:
>   Address: **wsmith@wordsmith.org**
>   **Subject: subscribe** *your full name*

WORD-A-DAY

We all know that having a big vocabulary is essential if you want to know a lot of words. Still, there is no royal road to knowledge, and if you want to know a lot of words you are just going to have to know a lot of words. The easy way is to subscribe to the Word-a-Day mailing list and soon, you too, will be able to tergiversate with the best of them.

es·ta·mi·net   con·duc·to·met·ric
con·es·to·ga
apo·neu·ro·sis

LAW

Ananse - International Trade Law Project

An experimental web server that offers information about international trade law. Links point to areas about sales of goods and services, protection of intellectual property, carriage of goods, insurance, payment mechanisms, agency, limitation periods, and other areas of international law.

World Wide Web:
   URL: **http://ananse.irv.uit.no/trade_law/ nav/trade.html**

Artificial Intelligence and the Law

How do two such diverse topics as artificial intelligence and law come together to form the focus of a discussion list? That's what we'd like to know. If either of these is an interest of yours, let us know where they intersect.

Internet Mailing List:
   List Address: **ail-l@austin.onu.edu**
   Subscription Address:
      ail-l-request@austin.onu.edu

Australian Law

Learn the laws of the land down under. What can and can't you do with a kangaroo? What does the Declaration of Rights of the Indigenous People say? If you get thrown in jail, do you get a free phone call? E Law, the electronic journal of law at the Murdoch University in Australia, is archived here.

Anonymous FTP:
   Address: **ftp.spies.com**
   Path: **/Gov/Aussie/***

Gopher:
   Name: Internet Wiretap
   Address: **wiretap.spies.com**
   Choose: **Government Docs (US & World)
      | Australian Law Documents**

   Name: Murdoch University Library
   Address: **infolib.murdoch.edu.au**
   Choose: **Electronic Library
      | Electronic Journals
      | E Law: Murdoch Elec**

Did you know that in Australia it is illegal to download files by ftp after 9 PM on Sundays? Well, it isn't but it might be. So, if you are in any doubt whatsoever, you had better check with the Australian Law resources and keep yourself out of trouble.

Bruce Lavois Shooting

A document containing the story of the controversial shooting of Bruce Lavois by Nashua, New Hampshire police during a drug raid and the aftermath.

Anonymous FTP:
> Address: **ftp.uu.net**
> Path: **/doc/literary/obi/Police.Notes/Nashua.NH**

California Legal Codes

This web page offers links to the California Legal Code. To use the server, drill down into the code by first choosing the code area. Top level code categories include the Business and Professions Code, Civil Code, Commercial Code, Corporations Code, Education Code, Elections Code, and all the rest of the code sections of the official laws of the State of California.

World Wide Web:
> URL: **http://www.law.indiana.edu/codes/ca/codes.html**

Canadian Law

If you get arrested in Canada, do they give you one free phone call? If you plan on breaking the law in Canada or if you want to be the Canadian Perry Mason, then tune in to this discussion group. It's not limited to law; the list also welcomes discussion on Canadian society, so you will see a wide spectrum of subscribers from fields such as law, economics, sociology, political science, and criminology.

Internet Mailing List:
> List Address: **lawsoc-l@cc.umanitoba.ca**
> Subscription Address:
>   **lawsoc-l-request@cc.umanitoba.ca**

Computer Fraud and Abuse Act

The United States Computer Fraud and Abuse Statute (18 USC 1030).

Anonymous FTP:
> Address: **ftp.spies.com**
> Path: **/Gov/US-Docs/compfraud.act**

Gopher:
> Name: Internet Wiretap
> Address: **wiretap.spies.com**
> Choose: **Government Docs (US & World)**
>   l **US Miscellaneous Documents**
>   l **Computer Fraud and Abuse Act (18 USC 1030)**

> # The Internet has lots and lots (and lots) of free software.

Computer Laws

Collection of information about laws involving computers, including computer crime laws for many states and countries.

Anonymous FTP:
> Address: **ftp.eff.org**
> Path: **/pub/Publications/CuD/Law**

> Address: **ftp.eff.org**
> Path: **/pub/CAF/law**

Constitution in Cyberspace

A collection of articles from the Electronic Frontier Foundation regarding Constitutional liberties which are under attack. Numerous examples are included of regular U.S. government violations of citizens' Fourth Amendment rights against unreasonable search and seizure and First Amendment rights of free speech and press. Big Brother isn't coming, he's already here.

Anonymous FTP:
> Address: **ftp.uu.net**
> Path: **/doc/literary/obi/EFF/***

Copyright and Intellectual Property Forum

Archives of a mailing list covering discussions of copyright and intellectual property issues.

Gopher:
> Name: Coalition for Networked Information
> Address: **gopher.cni.org**
> Choose: **Coalition Working Groups**
>   l **WG E-mail forums**
>   l **(CNI-COPYRIGHT)**

Criminal Justice Country Profiles

Informational files on organizational structure and methods of criminal justice systems in many countries.

Gopher:
> Name: University at Albany
> Address: **uacsc2.albany.edu**
> Choose: **United Nations Justice Network (UNCJIN)**
>   l **UN Criminal Justice Country Profiles**

Criminal Justice Discussion Group

The Journal of Criminal Justice and Popular Culture is designed to serve the criminal justice community by providing film reviews and original essays on the intersection of popular culture with criminal justice.

Listserv Mailing List:
List Address: **cjmovies@albany.edu**
Subscription Address: **listserv@albany.edu**

CU-LawNet

Legal reference resource and information about Columbia University and the Columbia University Law School by the Columbia Law School Public Information Service. Also offers Columbia University and Law School catalogs.

Telnet:
Address: **lawnet.law.columbia.edu**
Login: **lawnet**

ElNet Galaxy Law List

A large list of law resources on the Internet, divided into the following sections: administrative, commercial, constitutional, criminal, environmental, intellectual property, legal profession, military, personal finance, research, societal, and tax. There are also lists of law collections, directories, and organizations on the Internet.

World Wide Web:
URL: **http://www.einet.net/galaxy/Law.html**

Electronic and Communications Privacy Act of 1986

Text file containing text of the Electronic and Communications Privacy Act of 1986 (Senate bill S.2575).

Anonymous FTP:
Address: **ftp.uu.net**
Path: **/doc/literary/obi/ECPA/S.2575**

European Law Students Association

A mailing list to improve the communication between ELSA members and other interested parties.

Internet Mailing List:
List Address: **all-of-elsa@jus.uio.no**
Subscription Address:
all-of-elsa-request@jus.uio.no

Federal Communications Law Journal

Back issues of the *Federal Communications Law Journal*. Use the wais indexing to cut down on your search time using keywords and phrases.

World Wide Web:
URL: **http://www.law.indiana.edu/fclj/fclj.html**

Hawaii Legislative Information Service

The Hawaii state legislature's information system offers access to legal documents, including the text of laws, pending bills, and a database of bills, as well as a keyword search.

Telnet:
Address: **access.uhcc.hawaii.edu**

Indiana University School of Law Web Server

An amazing, text-based, hypertext information retrieval service with topics such as information about the Indiana University School of Law, career services, libraries, Internet radio shorts, and other law-related resources on the Internet.

World Wide Web:
URL: **http://www.law.indiana.edu/**

Information Law Papers

Among other things, lawyers are notorious for being hard to get in touch with. If you just have to have law information at your fingertips fast and in an easy-to-read fashion, connect to the Center for Information Law and Policy at the Villanova Law School. A few of the resources available are electronic living wills, documents on network and computer law, and search warrants.

Gopher:
Name: Villanova Law School
Address: **ming.law.vill.edu**
Choose: **Information Law Papers**

World Wide Web:
URL: **gopher://ming.law.vill.edu:70/11/.efl/**

Parents and children, take a look at: Families and Parenting, Kids, and Youth.

A
B
C
D
E
F
G
H
I
J
K
L
M
N
O
P
Q
R
S
T
U
V
W
X
Y
Z

Jerry's Guide to Law

A collection of law resources divided into sections on commercial law, defense funds, human rights, institutes, intellectual property, international trade, law firms, legal agencies, libraries, newsletters, Supreme Court, and more.

World Wide Web:
URL: **http://www.yahoo.com/Law/**

Law Discussion

It's a Saturday night and you are anxious to discuss freedom of religion, libel and the concept of invasion of privacy with someone. When you have no place to go and you are just itching to talk law, check out Usenet where you will find lawyers, law students and lawyer wannabes chatting about legalities.

Usenet:
Newsgroup: **misc.legal**
Newsgroup: **misc.legal.moderated**

Law Resources

Long list of Internet resources related to the law, including mailing lists, law library catalogs, ftp sites, and Usenet newsgroups.

Gopher:
Name: NYSERNet
Address: **nysernet.org**
Choose: **Reference Desk**
| 300 - Social Science
| 340 - Law
| Law resources on the Internet

Law Schools

The great thing about going to law school is that it means when you graduate you will be in a profession that is so popular that people like to tell lots of jokes about it. Find out how law schools rank, discuss programs of study and methods of learning at various institutions.

Usenet:
Newsgroup: **bit.listserv.lawsch-l**

> ## Do you like the "final frontier"? Take a look at Star Trek (or Space).

STAY OUT OF TROUBLE: USE THE INTERNET'S LAW RESOURCES.

Law Schools and Law Firms on the Web

This web page offers direct links to many (many) law schools in North America and Europe.

World Wide Web:
URL: **http://www.law.indiana.edu/law/ lawother.html**

Law Server

Legal discussions and reference material for United States, foreign, and international law. Library resources, government agencies, periodicals, and lists of other legal resources on the Internet.

Gopher:
Name: Cleveland State University
Address: **gopher.law.csuohio.edu**

Name: Cornell University Law School
Address: **gopher.law.cornell.edu**

> ## Need Help? Try Internet: Help.

LawTalk

A service provided by the law school at Indiana University, LawTalk offers links to information about the amendments to the US Constitution, business and personal finance law, criminal law, and civil law.

World Wide Web:
URL: **http://www.law.indiana.edu/law/ lawtalk.html**

> # There are only two things worth remembering in life (both of which I forget).

League for Programming Freedom

The League for Programming Freedom (LPF) is a grassroots organization of professors, students, businessmen, programmers, and users dedicated to reversing the current trend toward copyright and patent laws covering software. This anonymous ftp site stores position papers, descriptions of events, and membership information for the LPF.

Anonymous FTP:
>Address: **ftp.cs.widener.edu**
>Path: **/pub/lpf/***

The League for Programming Freedom

Don't you just hate it when you develop your own operating system and then find out that you can't market it because it infringes on a copyright held by Microsoft? So do we (and, evidently, so does IBM). That's why we think that anyone who cares about software and the freedom that it brings to the emerging human species should find out about the League for Programming Freedom.

Legal and Criminal Articles

Documents about the law and lawbreakers, including adoption laws by state, definition and jurisdiction, law heritage, and more.

Anonymous FTP:
>Address: **ftp.spies.com**
>Path: **/Library/Article/Legal/***

Gopher:
>Name: Internet Wiretap
>Address: **wiretap.spies.com**
>Choose: **Wiretap Online Library**
>　| **Articles**
>　| **Legal and Criminal**

Legal Domain Network

This web server provides read-only access to law-related Usenet newsgroups.

World Wide Web:
>URL: **http://www.kentlaw.edu/lawnet/lawnet.html**

Legal News

Clarinet is a great source of news relating to legal matters. Get the latest stories on lawsuits, trials, legislation and more. You will find hundreds of news articles covering the subject of law in the Clarinet hierarchy.

Usenet:
>Newsgroup: **clari.biz.courts**
>Newsgroup: **clari.nb.law**
>Newsgroup: **clari.news.gov.taxes**
>Newsgroup: **clari.news.law**
>Newsgroup: **clari.news.law.civil**
>Newsgroup: **clari.news.law.crime**
>Newsgroup: **clari.news.law.crime.sex**
>Newsgroup: **clari.news.law.crime.trial**
>Newsgroup: **clari.news.law.crime.violent**
>Newsgroup: **clari.news.law.drugs**
>Newsgroup: **clari.news.law.investigation**
>Newsgroup: **clari.news.law.police**
>Newsgroup: **clari.news.law.prison**
>Newsgroup: **clari.news.law.profession**
>Newsgroup: **clari.news.law.supreme**
>Newsgroup: **clari.news.usa.law**
>Newsgroup: **clari.news.usa.law.supreme**

A B C D E F G H I J K **L** M N O P Q R S T U V W X Y Z

Gophers are your friends.

Net Law

Discussion of the various legal issues affecting the Internet community.

Gopher:
Name: Electronic Frontier Foundation
Address: **gopher.eff.org**
Choose: **Electronic Frontier Foundation files & information**
  I **Legal issues affecting computing & telecommunications**

Supreme Court Documents

Have you ever been in the situation of being introduced to the man or woman of your dreams, getting into a wonderful conversation, and then all of a sudden having that person turn you down like a bedspread because you have no knowledge of recent Supreme Court rulings? Fortunately, this all-too-common occurrence need not happen to you. All you need to do is take the simple precaution of checking on the Net for new Supreme Court opinions every day when you get up. Never again will you lose out on the relationship of a lifetime because of poor preparation.

Socio-Legal Preprint Archive

An archive of papers about the legal system and jurisprudence delivered at various major social science conferences.

See also: Sociology, Humanities

Gopher:
Name: Northwestern University
Address: **gopher.nwu.edu**
Port: **4200**

Steve Jackson Games

Collection of all the information surrounding the Secret Service raid on the Steve Jackson Games company, and the following court case.

Anonymous FTP:
Address: **ftp.eff.org**
Path: **/pub/EFF/Policy/SJG**

Gopher:
Name: Illuminati Online
Address: **io.com**
Choose: **SJ Games vs. the Secret Service**

Supreme Court Rulings

With Project Hermes, the United States Supreme Court makes its opinions and rulings available in electronic format within minutes of their release. Case Western Reserve University is one of the sites the Supreme Court supplies with this information. Get and read the files **info** and **readme.first**.

Anonymous FTP:
Address: **ftp.cwru.edu**
Path: **/hermes/***

Gopher:
Name: University of Maryland
Address: **info.umd.edu**
Choose: **Academic Resources by Topic**
  I **United States and World Politics, Culture and History**
  I **United States**
  I **Supreme Court Documents**

WAIS:
Database: **supreme-court**

World Wide Web:
URL: **http://www.law.cornell.edu/supct/**

Trade Law Library

A collection of links and pointers to Internet sites for law, economics, and commerce. It includes general lists of various law services, selected law sites, commerce-related material, law databases, law publishers, selected libraries, bookstores, and more.

World Wide Web:
URL: **http://ananse.irv.uit.no/law/nav/ law_ref.html**

U.S. Patent Database

Use this web page to perform searches of a U.S. patent database. Although this page is not supported by the U.S. Patent and Trademark office, it should be. The page also has links to interesting articles and bits of information such as "Can you really get a patent without a lawyer?"

World Wide Web:
URL: **http://town.hall.org/patent/patent.html**

Venable Attorneys at Law

This law firm in Washington D.C. offers this web server to provide information on the firm's legal services and legal materials, particularly issues of concern to electronic information providers.

World Wide Web:
URL: **http://venable.com/vbh.htm**

Virtual Law Library

A long list of hundreds of pointers to online legal information. This resource offers topical and alphabetical listings of organizations, and a list of United States government law servers.

World Wide Web:
URL: **http://www.law.indiana.edu/law/ lawindex.html**

Washburn School of Law

The web server at the Washburn School of Law offers links to subject areas including foreign and international law, United States law, government documents, law library catalogs, the Virtual Law Reference Desk, directories, and links to other law-related resources on the Net.

World Wide Web:
URL: **http://law.wuacc.edu/washlaw/ washlaw.html**

Washington and Lee University Law Library

Gateways to an amazing volume of Internet law resources, including many universities in the United States and around the world. Use an easy menu interface to navigate through law libaries all over the nation. Search for keywords, read the case law, or search for books, articles, and publications.

Gopher:
Name: Washington & Lee University
Address: **liberty.uc.wlu.edu**
Choose: **Libraries and Information Access | Law**

Telnet:
Address: **liberty.uc.wlu.edu**
Login: **lawlib**

LIBRARIES

Archives and Archivists List

Learn the finer points of being an archivist.

Listserv Mailing List:
List Address: **archives@miamiu.muohio.edu**
Subscription Address:
listserv@miamiu.muohio.edu

Automated Library Information Xchange

Check out the Automated Library Information Xchange (ALIX) for advice, opinions, and software by and for librarians. ALIX also includes newsletters and library job postings.

Telnet:
Address: **alix.loc.gov**
Port: **3001**

The Internet has lots of free software. Check out Computers, Software and Operating Systems.

A
B
C
D
E
F
G
H
I
J
K
L
M
N
O
P
Q
R
S
T
U
V
W
X
Y
Z

Billy Barron's Library List

Details of how to access hundreds of online bibliographic databases and libraries around the world.

Anonymous FTP:
　　Address: **ftp.utdallas.edu**
　　Path: **/pub/staff/billy/libguide/***

Gopher:
　　Name: NYSERNet
　　Address: **nysernet.org**
　　Choose: **Special Collections: Libraries**
　　　| **Billy Barron List**

　　Name: Yale University
　　Address: **yaleinfo.yale.edu**
　　Port: **7000**
　　Choose: **Libraries**
　　　| **Paper List (BBarrons' Accessing Online Bib Dbases)**

Carl System

A computerized network of library systems. Search for keywords from any of five databases (library catalogs, current articles, information databases, other library systems, library and system news).

Telnet:
　　Address: **pac.carl.org**

Cataloging

It's not a job that most people envy — all those books that have to be cataloged and kept track of in some manner. It takes someone with patience, perseverence and a good sense of organization. That's the kind of people who hang out in this newsgroup. Check out the raging debates over the modality and paradigms of cataloging.

Usenet:
　　Newsgroup: **bit.listserv.autocat**

Circulation Control

Anyone who has worked in a library knows how much can go wrong when it comes to circulation. Considering how many books are shuffled back and forth every day, it's an exemplary library system where few problems arise, and it's understandable why librarians often look stern. They are the scholarly version of the military's drill sergeant. This mailing list deals with issues related to circulation control in libraries, including shelving, reserve room operations, and stack maintenance.

Listserv Mailing List:
　　List Address: **circplus@idbsu.bitnet**
　　Subscription Address: **listserv@idbsu.bitnet**

College Libraries

So many backpacks to search, so little time. College librarians have to keep up with the ebb and flow of students who race in and out, who move and change addresses, forget to turn the books in, forget to pay fines, and get an occasional mean streak and decide to make off with the only copy of the 1952 version of a textbook on human sexuality. This list serves as a forum for discussing issues relevant primarily to college librarians and staff who hold down the fort at four-year undergraduate institutions.

Listserv Mailing List:
　　List Address: **collib-l@willamette.edu**
　　Subscription Address: **listserv@willamette.edu**

Current Cites

A monthly publication of the Library Technology Watch Program, which provides articles on modern technology and librarianship.

Anonymous FTP:
　　Address: **ftp.cni.org**
　　Path: **/pub/Current.Cites/***

Gopher:
　　Name: University of Virginia
　　Address: **gopher.virginia.edu**
　　Choose: **Library Services**
　　　| **University Library GWIS Collections**
　　　| **Alphabetic Organization**
　　　| **Current Cites**

Dental Librarians

It's amazing that such a small portion of the body, like your mouth, can have a whole library devoted to it. This discussion group is intended for librarians, educators, and persons who have an interest in dental and oral health information issues and wish to exchange information and ideas. Next time you are lying helpless in the dental chair with someone's hands stuck in your mouth, you can think how lucky you are that such a great resource exists.

Listserv Mailing List:
　　List Address: **dentalib@vm.usc.edu**
　　Subscription Address: **listserv@vm.usc.edu**

Lonely? Mail to Famous People.

Need to find the best places to read about gingivitis and the more obscure branches of the tregeminal nerve? No need to feel down in the mouth. The Dental Librarian mailing list awaits you.

Electronic Jewish Library

A large online library of Jewish-related material, including Holocaust archives, Hebrew and Jewish studies, historical documents, book reviews, journals, press clippings, and other items of interest.

See also: Historical Documents

Gopher:
Name: Jerusalem One
Address: **jerusalem1.datasrv.co.il**
Choose: **Electronic Jewish Library**

Eureka

An easy-to-use search service. With Eureka, any individual or institution can search the online resources of the Research Libraries Group (RLG), including the RLIN bibliographic files and the CitaDel article-citation and document-delivery service. Eureka contains information about more than 20 million books, serials, sound recordings, musical scores, archival collections, and other materials.

Telnet:
Address: **eureka-info.stanford.edu**

Government Document Issues

Besides whitewashing, the government is well-known for its paperwork and production of triplicates and quadruplicates resulting in the deforestation of small third world countries. All these documents have to go somewhere, so they end up at Federal Depository Libraries. What happens to them after that is up to the librarians. Topics discussed on this list are the electronic dissemination policies of the Government Printing Office, census documents and Freedom of Information Act issues.

Listserv Mailing List:
List Address: **govdoc-l@psuvm.psu.edu**
Subscription Address: **listserv@psuvm.psu.edu**

Hytelnet

This program assists people using library resources by automating the process. Hytelnet is a program that presents library resources on an easy-to-use menu interface. When you choose a resource, Hytelnet will show you how to access the resource, or even connect you to it automatically. Executables for various machines, as well as source, are available.

Anonymous FTP:
Address: **ftp.usask.ca**
Path: **/pub/hytelnet/pc/latest/hyteln***

Address: **liberty.uc.wlu.edu**
Path: **/pub/lawlib/hytelnet**

Archie:
Pattern: **hytelnet**

Telnet:
Address: **access.usask.ca**
Login: **hytelnet**

Address: **info.ccit.arizona.edu**
Login: **hytelnet**

Hytelnet

(1) Hytelnet is a library-inspired service that points to lots of stuff.
(2) Librarians love information.
(3) Hytelnet gives you access to lots of information.
(4) Therefore, if you use Hytelnet, librarians will love you.

Image Databases

Computers are a great help in the library system, not only for keeping track of things, but for storage of material as well. Photographs, artwork and more can be scanned and stored in a digital format. Get in on discussion of hardware, software, copyright legality and other aspects of image databases in library systems.

Usenet:
Newsgroup: **bit.listserv.imagelib**

A
B
C
D
E
F
G
H
I
J
K
L
M
N
O
P
Q
R
S
T
U
V
W
X
Y
Z

Launchpad

This system provides access to many library systems across the country. You can perform searches, download files, find other users, and even connect to the local gopher client. Try the CIA World Fact Book in the experimental gopherspace section.

Telnet:
Address: **launchpad.unc.edu**
Login: **launch**

Library Catalogs and Databases

A large document with detailed instructions on how to access the computerized library systems of many universities around the world.

Anonymous FTP:
Address: **ftp.funet.fi**
Path: **/pub/doc/library/internet.libraries.Z**

Address: **ftp.unt.edu**
Path: **/pub/library/libraries.txt**

Library Catalogs via telnet

Check out the library catalogs and online databases of the universities of Minnesota, Indiana, Michigan State, Northwestern, Ohio State, and the rest of the Big 10 schools.

Gopher:
Name: University of Colorado Boulder
Address: **gopher.colorado.edu**
Choose: **Online Library Catalogs...**

> ## MUDs are real (sort of).

Library of Congress

The Library of Congress maintains millions of records of publications in the United States, as well as legislative and copyright information. The web site has pointers to the LC Marvel (the Library of Congress' gopher system) and LOCIS (the Library's database retrieval system). The page also has links to thousands of images from the American Memory project.

Gopher:
Name: Library of Congress
Address: **marvel.loc.gov**

Telnet:
Address: **locis.loc.gov**

World Wide Web:
URL: **http://lcweb.loc.gov/homepage/lchp.html**

Need info on a book? Any book?

Try the Library of Congress Gopher.

Excerpt from the Net...

Library and Information Science

If there is anything in the world that you want to know, ask a librarian. Library and information science turns ordinary mortals into oracles of facts. Even if they don't know it off the tops of their heads, librarians will know where to find what you are looking for. See discussion on librarianship from a technical and a philosophical point of view.

Usenet:
Newsgroup: **bit.listserv.lis-l**

Library Newsletters

Selection of newsletters about the cataloging, indexing, collecting, and preserving of books.

Anonymous FTP:
Address: **nigel.msen.com**
Path: **/pub/newsletters/Libraries/***

Library Policy Archive

A collection of library policy statements, including the American Library Association's Freedom to Read statement and the ALA Library Bill of Rights.

Anonymous FTP:
Address: **ftp.eff.org**
Path: **/pub/CAF/library/***

Gopher:
Name: Electronic Frontier Foundation
Address: **gopher.eff.org**
Choose: **Computers and Academic Freedom archives & info | Library Policy Statements**

Library Resources

Access to many Internet library-related resources, including lists, articles, newsletters, archives, electronic journals, and library catalogs.

Gopher:
Name: NYSERNet
Address: **nysernet.org**
Choose: **Special Collections: Libraries**

Like mysteries? Look at Intrigue.

Stay cool: read Fashion and Clothing.

Library Resources on the Internet

This file contains strategies for the selection and use of library resources on the Internet. A 40+ page document for download via ftp that includes information on how to get started, road maps, travel guides, search strategies and information about other library resources.

Anonymous FTP:
Address: **dla.ucop.edu**
Path: **/pub/internet/libcat-guide**

Library Topic Lists

List of mailing lists and serials related to all aspects of libraries.

Gopher:
Name: NYSERNet
Address: **nysernet.org**
Choose: **Special Collections: Libraries | Library conferences**

Medianet OnLine Public Catalog Access

Search by title or subject for articles and videos on a vast number of topics. Then read a short description or check the availability of your finds for rental.

Gopher:
Name: University of Colorado Boulder
Address: **gopher.colorado.edu**
Choose: **Online Library Catalogs... | Medianet On-Line Public Catalogue Access**

Public Access Catalogs

A list of online Internet public access library catalogs and databases, and other related information.

Anonymous FTP:
Address: **ftp.std.com**
Path: **/obi/Access/***

Gopher:
Name: Software Tool & Die
Address: **gopher.std.com**
Choose: **OBI The Online Book Initiative | The Online Books | Access**

A
B
C
D
E
F
G
H
I
J
K
L
M
N
O
P
Q
R
S
T
U
V
W
X
Y
Z

University of Maryland Information Database

Information and documents on many subjects of interest.

Gopher:
Name: University of Maryland
Address: **info.umd.edu**
Choose: **Library Information and Resources**

Telnet:
Address: **info.umd.edu**

Using Internet Libraries

A multitude of software, documents, and resource guides, including those for archie, wais, ftp, mail and listserv, and resource lists for librarians and library users on the Internet.

Anonymous FTP:
Address: **ftp.funet.fi**
Path: **/pub/doc/library/***

The Internet, Librarian Style

Some of the most passionate users of the Internet are librarians. (Of course, this has nothing to do with the Internet: by their very nature, librarians are passionate people.) Indeed, there are so many resources on the Internet that only a librarian could really catalog and describe them all. Take a look at *Using Internet Libraries,* and see what the book people have to offer us civilians.

Washington University Services

Washington University in St. Louis provides an easy-to-use menu interface to university library systems and Internet resources all over the world.

Telnet:
Address: **library.wustl.edu**

Web Mailing List for Librarians

The Web is a remarkable source of information for librarians. **Web4lib** is a mailing list formed to discuss issues relating to creating and managing web servers and clients that are based in libraries. Topics cover not only staff usage of the resources, but also access to patrons.

Listserv Mailing List:
List Address: **web4lib@library.berkeley.edu**
Subscription Address:
listserv@library.berkeley.edu

Wiretap Online Library

A huge collection of useful and entertaining information, including articles, journals, technical information, and much more.

Anonymous FTP:
Address: **ftp.spies.com**
Path: **/Library/***

Gopher:
Name: Internet Wiretap
Address: **wiretap.spies.com**
Choose: **Wiretap Online Library**

Excerpt from the Net...

(from the "Questionables" area of the "Wiretap Online Services" gopher)

Outlaw Labs Atomic Bomb:

...Plastic explosives work best in this situation since they can be manipulated to enable both a Uranium bomb and a Plutonium bomb to detonate. One very good explosive is Urea Nitrate. The directions on how to make Urea Nitrate are as follows...

LITERATURE

American Literature Discussion List

Discussion of topics and issues in American literature among a worldwide community.

Listserv Mailing List:
List Address: **amlit-l@umcvmb.missouri.edu**
Subscription Address:
listserv@umcvmb.missouri.edu

Bibliographies of Literature

Reading lists and bibliographies on many literary subjects, including Arthurian legends, computer ethics, hypertext, medieval European, narrative theory, and modern drama.

Gopher:
Name: Carnegie Mellon University
Address: **english-server.hss.cmu.edu**
Choose: **Books**
| **Bibliographies**

Bryn Mawr Classical Review

Several hundred articles on classical literature topics.

Gopher:
Name: University of Florida
Address: **gaia.sci-ed.fit.edu**
Choose: **Subject Area Resources**
| **Language Arts**
| **Bryn Mawr Classical Review**

Name: University of Virginia
Address: **gopher.lib.virginia.edu**
Choose: **Electronic Journals**
| **Bryn Mawr Classical Review**

> **Need help with repairs? Try Home Maintenance.**

Classics

Provocative articles, reviews, conference news, and other information regarding the classics. The mailing lists are for discussions about classics, classical literature, and Latin in general.

Gopher:
Name: University of Tasmania
Address: **info.utas.edu.au**
Choose: **Publications**
| **Electronic Antiquity : Communicating The Classics**

Listserv Mailing List:
List Address: **latin-l@psuvm.psu.edu**
Subscription Address: **listserv@psuvm.psu.edu**

List Address: **classics@uwavm.u.washington.edu**
Subscription Address:
listserv@uwavm.u.washington.edu

Council of Remiremont

This is a story in Latin about naughty nuns who talk about what kind of men they like. It's in Latin, so if you don't know how to read it, you can't really tell how naughty they are. Who says scholars don't have any fun?

See also: Language

World Wide Web:
URL: **http://ccat.sas.upenn.edu/jod/remiremont.html**

Cthulhu

He's almost like a big friendly dog except for the fact that he's not really friendly and has the annoying habit of devouring unsuspecting virgins to fuel himself for the takeover of this section of the universe. Originating from the mind of H.P. Lovecraft, this evil creature has developed a following of horror fans around the world. Check out what mischief they are getting into as they try to think of new ways to bring Cthulhu out of his dormancy to wreak havoc on the world. Also available is an informative hypercard stack with pictures and sounds of various Cthulhu monsters.

See also: Bizarre, Games, Paranormal, Role-Playing

Anonymous FTP:
Address: **ftp.luth.se**
Path: **/pub/mac/card/fun/cthulhumonsters1.0.cpt.hqx**

Usenet:
Newsgroup: **alt.horror.cthulhu**

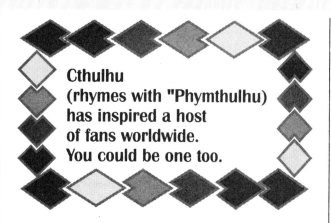

Cthulhu
(rhymes with "Phymthulhu)
has inspired a host
of fans worldwide.
You could be one too.

Dutch Literature

This moderated group offers a change of scenery with its concentration on the Dutch language and literature. You'll find yourself swept up in the culture and atmosphere of the Netherlands.

Usenet:
>   Newsgroup: **bit.lang.neder-l**

Electronic Text Resources

Pointers on where to obtain electronic text (etext) on the Internet and elsewhere. This information is from the Usenet **alt.etext** archives and is updated daily.

Anonymous FTP:
>   Address: **ftp.spies.com**
>   Path: **/alt.etext/***

Gopher:
>   Name: Internet Wiretap
>   Address: **wiretap.spies.com**
>   Choose: **Usenet alt.etext Archives**

English Server

A gopher dedicated to the sharing of texts in English and other languages. Titles include autobiographies, plays, essays, hypertexts, jokes, novels, poems, speeches, short stories, and other items of interest.

Anonymous FTP:
>   Address: **english-server.hss.cmu.edu**
>   Path: **/English Server/***

Gopher:
>   Name: Carnegie Mellon University
>   Address: **english-server.hss.cmu.edu**

Fun Reading

A collection of informative and entertaining stories, interviews, articles, and FAQ lists.

Gopher:
>   Name: University of Illinois
>   Address: **wx.atmos.uiuc.edu**
>   Choose: **Documents**
> | **fun**

Fun Reading

What a pickle. It's Saturday night and you have nothing to do, so you look for something to read. Unfortunately, you've already read every page of *The Internet Complete Reference*, and nothing else looks good. What to do? Connect to the Internet and immerse yourself in something light and diverting.

(Maybe, just maybe, it will let you forget how your ex-significant other took the television set when she left you for that jerk on the rugby team who doesn't even know how to use a computer.)

Gothic Literature Discussion List

An information network for researchers that includes book reviews, notices, conferences, publications, notes and queries. Discussion is welcome about any aspect of Gothic literature or the grotesque category including theories, practices, and strategies. Discussions are generally about Mary Shelley, Bram Stoker, the book *Mary Barton*, and so on.

Mail:
>   Address: **mailbase@mailbase.ac.uk**
>   Body: **JOIN gothic-literature** *your name*

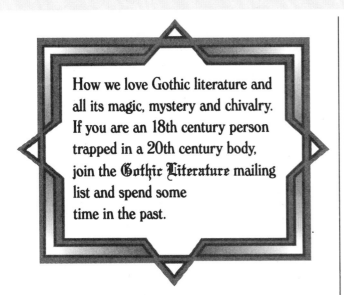

How we love Gothic literature and all its magic, mystery and chivalry. If you are an 18th century person trapped in a 20th century body, join the 𝔊𝔬𝔱𝔥𝔦𝔠 𝔏𝔦𝔱𝔢𝔯𝔞𝔱𝔲𝔯𝔢 mailing list and spend some time in the past.

Index to Literature Servers

This web page is the Rosetta Stone that bridges literature and computers. It has direct links to the Gutenberg Project, the Eris Project, the Internet Wiretap Collection, and the Online Book Initiative, as well as literature-related Usenet groups that are devoted to great authors.

World Wide Web:
    URL: **http://www.cs.fsu.edu/projects/group4/ litpage.html**

Information on Authors

Author information, including lists of works available on this ftp site.

Anonymous FTP:
    Address: **ftp.uu.net**
    Path: **/doc/literary/obi/Misc/Books**

Jewish Literature

A collection of Jewish fiction and poetry, including works entitled *The Isolated Jew*, *Birthright*, and *Hidden Face*.

Gopher:
    Name: Jerusalem One
    Address: **jerusalem1.datasrv.co.il**
    Choose: **Art of and About The Jewish People | Jewish Literature**

The Internet is PEOPLE, not computers.

Why are you reading this when you could be looking at the Sex section?

Literature Discussions

Discussions of favorite authors, favorite works, literary styles, and criticism.

Listserv Mailing List:
    List Address: **literary@ucf1vm.cc.ucf.edu**
    Subscription Address: **listserv@ucf1vm.cc.ucf.edu**

Literature General Discussion

Explore the subtle wonders of mainstream literature. Literary tradition will appeal to you because of the wide variety of its genre. Get frightened, get romantic, get nostalgic: all with a little help from some literary stimuli.

Usenet:
    Newsgroup: **bit.listserv.literary**

Modern British and Irish Literature

Wrap yourself up in a thick cable-knit sweater, grab a cup of tea, some biscuits, and settle down to discuss literature of Britain and Ireland. Any literature from 1895 to 1955 is considered an acceptable topic in this forum.

Listserv Mailing List:
    List Address: **modbrits@kentvm.kent.edu**
    Subscription Address: **listserv@kentvm.kent.edu**

Mysteries

Curling up with a mystery and cup of hot cocoa is a great way to spend the night — especially a dark and stormy night. And some people just can't get enough. This discussion group was formed to give mystery lovers a place to talk about their passion for the genre. The list was named after Dorothy L. Sayers, one of the great mystery writers of the century.

See also: Literature: Authors, Books

Listserv Mailing List:
    List Address: **dorothyl@kentvm.kent.edu**
    Subscription Address: **listserv@kentvm.kent.edu**

A B C D E F G H I J K L M N O P Q R S T U V W X Y Z

> **Reality is dull. Try Science Fiction.**

Mystery Genre

Most of us are not immersed in daily intrigue. Unless you consider trying to figure out what the cafeteria's mystery meat is. Beyond that, if you need a good brain-twister and suspense builder, curl up with a good mystery or detective novel. On this list you will meet fans of the mystery genre and discuss reviews of mystery books, movies and television series.

See also: Books

Internet Mailing List:
   List Address: **mystery@csd4.csd.uwm.edu**
   Subscription Address:
      mystery-request@csd4.csd.uwm.edu

Nancy Drew

You were a rare girl if, while growing up, you did not idolize Nancy Drew, girl detective. Inevitably, someone has taken Nancy Drew and turned her into a scholarly project by analyzing the history and symbology of these delightful teen mysteries.

World Wide Web:
   URL: **http://ils.unc.edu/keene/ktitle.html**

Native American Literature

Explore the writings of Native Americans through their literature. Scholars and other people interested in Native American literature share thoughts on book reviews, articles about poetry and fiction, offer criticism and information on new publications or conferences. Inclusive in the term "Native American" are indigenous peoples of the United States (including native Alaskans and native Hawaiians), Canada and Mexico.

See also: World Cultures

Listserv Mailing List:
   List Address: **nativelit-l@cornell.edu**
   Subscription Address: **listserv@cornell.edu**

Patchwork Electronic Literature

The great thing about having friends when you are a writer is that you can make them all read what you wrote and tell you how good it is. But after a while you run out of friends. With the Internet that just doesn't matter anymore. There are so many people out there sitting in front of their mailboxes just waiting for you to send in your poetry, essays, quotations, or even ASCII art. But as with all moments of shared creativity, you must be tender and polite. Don't send pornography or vulgar and obscene references or language. You never know when your mother might subscribe to the list.

See also: Writing

Internet Mailing List:
   List Address: **patchwork@nox.cs.du.edu**
   Subscription Address:
      patchwork-request@nox.cs.du.edu

Women's Book List

A list of books directly related to the role of women in society, including such topics as sexism, politics, jobs, and feminism.

Gopher:
   Name: Carnegie Mellon University
   Address: **english-server.hss.cmu.ecu**
   Choose: **Books**
      | **Bibliographies**
      | **Women's Center Book List**

Workshop on Electronic Texts

The Workshop on Electronic Texts drew together experts to compare ideas, beliefs, experiences, and, in particular, methods of placing and presenting historical textual materials in computerized form. The proceedings from this and other events are available here, as well as information on upcoming events.

Gopher:
   Name: University of Maryland
   Address: **info.umd.edu**
   Choose: **Computing Resources**
      | **Network Information**
      | **Reading Room**
      | **ElecWorkShop**

Writer Resource Guide

A list of magazines and newsletters accepting submissions by electronic mail, and other electronic resources for writers.

Anonymous FTP:
Address: **rtfm.mit.edu**
Path: **/pub/usenet/news.answers/writing/ resources**

Wanna Be a Writer?
Of course you do.
Who wouldn't want to be a respected, encultured member of the literary intelligenstia? More important, being an official writer means that you can stand in the special line at the library and that you get to read the newspaper first when there is only one copy. If this sounds like the life for you, just ftp the **Writer Resource Guide** and you are on your way to more happiness than a regular non-writing civilian will ever understand.

LITERATURE: AUTHORS

Jane Austen

A mailing list for fans of Jane Austen. Includes the discussion of her novels, as well as those of some of her contemporaries, including Fanny Burney, Maria Edgeworth, and Mary Wollstonecraft.

Listserv Mailing List:
List Address: **austen-l@vm1.mcgill.ca**
Subscription Address: **listserv@vm1.mcgill.ca**

L. Frank Baum

Two complete texts by L. Frank Baum, creator of *The Wonderful Wizard of Oz*.

Anonymous FTP:
Address: **ftp.funet.fi**
Path: **/pub/doc/literary/etext/wizoz.txt.gz**

Address: **ftp.funet.fi**
Path: **/pub/doc/literary/etext/ozland.txt.gz**

Ambrose Bierce

Complete texts by Ambrose Bierce, including *Can Such Things Be* and *The Devil's Dictionary*.

Anonymous FTP:
Address: **ftp.std.com**
Path: **/obi/Ambrose.Bierce/***

Gopher:
Name: Software Tool & Die
Address: **gopher.std.com**
Choose: **OBI The Online Book Initiative**
    | The Online Books
    | Ambrose.Bierce

Brontë Sisters

It doesn't seem quite fair that there is so much creativity coming out of one family. Because of this, according to the law of averages, someone else is having a great deal of trouble writing complete sentences. Fans of Emily, Charlotte and Anne Brontë gather to discuss all aspects of the Brontë lives and works, biographies and critical literature, social, cultural and historical perspectives, and any issues relating to the study and teaching of the Brontë works.

See also: Literature: Collections

Majordomo Mailing List:
List Address: **bronte@world.std.com**
Subscription Address: **majordomo@world.std.com**

Lewis Carroll

Several complete texts by Lewis Carroll.

Anonymous FTP:
Address: **ftp.funet.fi**
Path: **/pub/doc/literary/etext/snark.txt.gz**

Address: **ftp.funet.fi**
Path: **/pub/doc/literary/etext/carroll/***

Address: **ftp.funet.fi**
Path: **/pub/doc/literary/etext/jabber.txt.gz**

Address: **ftp.funet.fi**
Path: **/pub/doc/literary/etext/looking.txt.gz**

A B C D E F G H I J K L M N O P Q R S T U V W X Y Z

Geoffrey Chaucer Mailing List

A mailing list discussion group devoted to the works of Geoffrey Chaucer and medieval English literature and culture during the period 1100-1500.

Listserv Mailing List:
    List Address: **chaucer@unlinfo.unl.edu**
    Subscription Address: **listserv@unlinfo.unl.edu**

Joseph Conrad

Files containing text of novels *Heart of Darkness*, *Secret Sharer*, and *Lord Jim*. The file name is the book title in each case.

Anonymous FTP:
    Address: **ftp.uu.net**
    Path: **/doc/literary/obi/Joseph.Conrad/***

Ceanne DeRohan

The author of *The Right Use of Will, Healing and Evolving the Emotional Body* is the topic of discussion for this list. While most self-help books are warm and fuzzy, the writings of DeRohan are something else entirely. It is said that the insights from the book were received from God and that they are startling and unlike anything you would expect to hear, so the discussions on this list should be fairly startling, too.

Internet Mailing List:
    List Address:
      right_use_of_will@kether.webo.dg.com
    Subscription Address:
      right_use_of_will-request@kether.webo.dg.com

Philip K. Dick

Loyal followers of science fiction writer Philip K. Dick keep this list going with their talk about his books and stories, and writing about his life. Discussion sometimes touches on the subjects of reality, consciousness and religion as it relates to the author's work.

Internet Mailing List:
    List Address: **pkd-list@wang.com**
    Subscription Address: **pkd-list-request@wang.com**

> **The Net is mankind's greatest achievement.**

The Case of the Missing Password

"It was on a bitterly cold night and frosty morning, towards the end of the winter of '97, that I was awakened by a tugging at my shoulder. It was Holmes. The candle in his hand shone upon his eager, stooping face, and told me at a glance that something was amiss.

"'Come, Watson, come!' he cried. 'The game is afoot. Not a word! Into your clothes and come! We must track down the missing superuser password. . .'"

But who would steal a password? And what does this have to do with the giant rat of Sumatra? No need to die of suspense: download the stories of Arthur Conan Doyle and see for yourself.

Charles Dickens

Several complete novels by Charles Dickens.

Anonymous FTP:
    Address: **ftp.funet.fi**
    Path: **/pub/doc/literary/by-author/**
      Dickens,Charles/AChristmasCarol.gz

    Address: **ftp.funet.fi**
    Path: **/pub/doc/literary/etext/chimes.txt.gz**

    Address: **ftp.funet.fi**
    Path: **/pub/doc/literary/etext/cricket.txt.gz**

Gopher:
    Name: Software Tool & Die
    Address: **gopher.std.com**
    Choose: **OBI The Online Book Initiative**
      | The Online Books
      | Charles Dickens
      | AChristmasCaro.tar.Z

Frederick Douglass

The full text of this narrative of the life of an American writer, orator, abolitionist and former slave.

Gopher:
>Name: University of Minnesota
>Address: **gopher.micro.umn.edu**
>Choose: **Libraries**
>| **Electronic Books**
>| **By Title**
>| **Narrative of the life of Frederick Douglass**

Sir Arthur Conan Doyle

Several complete texts and stories by Sir Arthur Conan Doyle, author of the Sherlock Holmes series.

Anonymous FTP:
>Address: **ftp.funet.fi**
>Path: **/pub/doc/literary/etext/return.dyl.gz**

>Address: **ftp.funet.fi**
>Path: **/pub/doc/literary/etext/hound.dyl.gz**

>Address: **ftp.funet.fi**
>Path: **/pub/doc/literary/etext/lastbow.dyl.gz**

>Address: **ftp.funet.fi**
>Path: **/pub/doc/literary/etext/magicdoor.dyl.gz**

>Address: **ftp.funet.fi**
>Path: **/pub/doc/literary/etext/valley.dyl.gz**

>Address: **ftp.funet.fi**
>Path: **/pub/doc/literary/etext/memoirs.dyl.gz**

>Address: **ftp.funet.fi**
>Path: **/pub/doc/literary/etext/doyle/***

>Address: **ftp.funet.fi**
>Path: **/pub/doc/literary/etext/signfour.dyl.gz**

>Address: **ftp.funet.fi**
>Path: **/pub/doc/literary/etext/study.dyl.gz**

>Address: **ftp.funet.fi**
>Path: **/pub/doc/literary/by-author/Doyle,ArthurConan/TheAdventures***

>Address: **ftp.funet.fi**
>Path: **/pub/doc/literary/etext/casebook.dyl.gz**

Ernest Hemingway

It's tough to be a well-known writer. Adoring fans chase you down the street, send you bag after bag of fan mail, and ponder everything from your eating habits to your shoe size. And believe us, Hemingway has some really wild rumors going around about him. We just can't repeat them here. If you really want to know, stop in where Hemingway fans and experts hang out to discuss his life and literary achievements.

Majordomo Mailing List:
>List Address: **heming_l@mtu.edu**
>Subscription Address: **majordomo@mtu.edu**

Hermann Hesse

This mailing list is for scholars, researchers, and students interested in the life and works of Hermann Hesse. Subscribe to **hesse-l** to join in discussions about the life and accomplishments of this Swiss-German winner of the 1946 Nobel Prize.

Listserv Mailing List:
>List Address: **hesse-l@ucsbvm.ucsb.edu**
>Subscription Address: **listserv@ucsbvm.ucsb.edu**

Ingar Holst

A subdirectory of text files, each of which consists of one literary work by Holst.

Anonymous FTP:
>Address: **ftp.uu.net**
>Path: **/doc/literary/obi/Ingar.Holst/***

Katherine Kurtz

Reality is okay, but it occasionally gets tiresome. Don't let yourself get burned out. Hop in bed, prop yourself with lots of cozy pillows, and crack open a book of Katherine Kurtz fantasy. Explore Kurtz's Deryni universe, either through her books or through this discussion group, which consists of her fans all around the world. Discussion is not limited to Kurtz's Deryni writing.

Internet Mailing List:
>List Address: **deryni@mintir.fidonet.org**
>Subscription Address:
> **deryni-request@mintir.fidonet.org**

A B C D E F G H I J K **L** M N O P Q R S T U V W X Y Z

H.P. Lovecraft

Imagine being H.P. Lovecraft's roommate. You'd come home at midnight with the house all dark and you would have no idea what horrible creatures he might have concocted while you were away that he wants to tell you all about before you snuggle down under the bed covers. On the other hand, he'd be great on the planning committee of the annual Halloween party. Horror-lovers should check out the Lovecraft home page. It offers gopher searches for Lovecraft- and Cthulhu-related material, links to images, related resources and newsgroups.

World Wide Web:
URL: **http://elmer-fudd.cs.berkeley.edu/people/ davesimp/lovecraft/lovecraft.html**

Katherine Mansfield

A collection of works by Katherine Mansfield.

Anonymous FTP:
Address: **ftp.funet.fi**
Path: **/pub/doc/literary/etext/mansfield/***

John Milton

Several works by John Milton, including the classics *Paradise Lost* and *Paradise Regained*.

Anonymous FTP:
Address: **ftp.funet.fi**
Path: **/pub/doc/literary/etext/parlost.txt.gz**

Address: **ftp.funet.fi**
Path: **/pub/doc/literary/etext/pargain.txt.gz**

Edgar Allan Poe

Collection of works by Edgar Allan Poe. We've listed just a few of the filenames here, but there are many others.

Anonymous FTP:
Address: **ftp.funet.fi**
Path: **/pub/doc/literary/etext/Poe/***

Address: **ftp.funet.fi**
Path: **/pub/doc/literary/etext/cask.poe.gz**

Address: **ftp.funet.fi**
Path: **/pub/doc/literary/etext/telltale.poe.gz**

Address: **ftp.funet.fi**
Path: **/pub/doc/literary/etext/pit.poe.gz**

Address: **ftp.uu.net**
Path: **/doc/literary/obi/Edgar.Allan.Poe/***

Terry Pratchett

Archive of information about Terry Pratchett, a well-known author of humorous, fantasy-based science fiction novels, and his *Discworld* creations.

Anonymous FTP:
Address: **ftp.cs.pdx.edu**
Path: **/pub/pratchett/***

Saki

Two complete texts by the British writer known as Saki, including *Reginald*.

Anonymous FTP:
Address: **ftp.funet.fi**
Path: **/pub/doc/literary/etext/reginald.hh.gz**

Address: **ftp.funet.fi**
Path: **/pub/doc/literary/etext/russia.hh.gz**

William Shakespeare

The full text of Shakespeare's plays, poems, and sonnets. The gopher menu at the University of Minnesota is arranged by comedies, histories, poetry, tragedies, and so on.

Anonymous FTP:
Address: **ftp.funet.fi**
Path: **/pub/doc/literary/shakespeare/***

Address: **ftp.uu.net**
Path: **/doc/literary/shakespeare/***

Address: **ocf.berkeley.edu**
Path: **/pub/Library/Shakespeare/***

Gopher:
Name: University of Minnesota
Address: **spinaltap.micro.umn.edu**
Choose: **Gutenberg**
| **Complete Works of Shakespeare**

World Wide Web:
URL: **http://the-tech.mit.edu/Shakespeare.html**

Bored? Try Fun. Still bored? Try Games.

A Hint About Shakespeare

What can you say about Shakespeare? Truly, he was a happening dude for his day. Of course, there are ugly rumors that he didn't really write his own plays, that they were all done by someone else who happened to have the same name. In fact, if you take the soliloquy from Macbeth and run it through the Unix tr command you will find a secret message that says "This was really written by Shakespeare".

But don't believe us. Shakespeare's work is available for free on the Net. Download your favorite play or poem and perform your own analysis.

J.R.R. Tolkien

This site has an amazing amount of information on Tolkien. It has lists of books, societies, games, mailing lists, graphics, fonts and parodies. There are FAQs on Tolkien, TolkLang, a FAQ on more obscure questions, and a list of MUDs and MUSHs in the Tolkien genre. There are also databases and from this web site you can do veronica and jughead queries. Anyone who is interested in Tolkien's constructed language will like this site — many resources for linguists.

World Wide Web:
    URL: **http://csclub.uwaterloo.ca/u/relipper/ tolkien/rootpage.html**

This book is high in fiber.

J.R.R. Tolkien Discussions

Mailing lists for anyone interested in disussing the life and works of J.R.R. Tolkien.

Internet Mailing List:
    List Address: **tolklang@lfcs.ed.ac.uk**
    Subscription Address:
      tolklang-request@lfcs.ed.ac.uk

    List Address: **tolkien@jhuvm.hcf.jhu.edu**
    Subscription Address: **listserv@jhuvm.hcf.jhu.edu**

Mark Twain

Several complete texts by Mark Twain, including *Tom Sawyer*, *Extracts from Adam's Diary*, *A Ghost Story*, *Niagara*, as well as his more famous titles.

Anonymous FTP:
    Address: **ftp.funet.fi**
    Path: **/pub/doc/literary/etext/abroad.mt.gz**

    Address: **ftp.funet.fi**
    Path: **/pub/doc/literary/etext/adam.mt.gz**

    Address: **ftp.funet.fi**
    Path: **/pub/doc/literary/etext/detective.mt.gz**

    Address: **ftp.funet.fi**
    Path: **/pub/doc/literary/etext/ghost.mt.gz**

    Address: **ftp.funet.fi**
    Path: **/pub/doc/literary/etext/niagara.mt.gz**

    Address: **ftp.funet.fi**
    Path: **/pub/doc/literary/etext/sawyer.mt.gz**

    Address: **ftp.funet.fi**
    Path: **/pub/doc/literary/etext/pitcairn.mt.gz**

    Address: **ftp.funet.fi**
    Path: **/pub/doc/literary/etext/yankee.mt.gz**

Mark Twain Discussions

With a sharp sense of detail and a caustic wit, Twain wraps his fans up with his talent for observation and storytelling. Lovers and scholars of Mark Twain discuss his life and writing. Read queries, general discussion, conference announcements, calls for papers, and information on new publications relating to this author.

See also: Books

Listserv Mailing List:
    List Address: **twain-l@vm1.yorku.ca**
    Subscription Address: **listserv@vm1.yorku.ca**

A B C D E F G H I J K L M N O P Q R S T U V W X Y Z

Virgil

A collection of works in Latin by Virgil.

Anonymous FTP:
Address: **ftp.funet.fi**
Path: **/pub/doc/literary/etext/Virgil**

H.G. Wells

Complete texts by H.G. Wells, including *The Time Machine*, *The Invisible Man*, and *The War of the Worlds*.

Anonymous FTP:
Address: **ftp.funet.fi**
Path: **/pub/doc/literary/etext/warworld.txt.gz**

Address: **ftp.funet.fi**
Path: **/pub/doc/literary/etext/invisman.txt.gz**

Address: **ftp.funet.fi**
Path: **/pub/doc/literary/by-author/**
 Wells,HerbertGeorge/*

P.G. Wodehouse

A discussion group for fans of P.G. Wodehouse (pronounced "Woodhouse"). Wodehouse is the creator of many enduring characters, including Bertie Wooster and his valet Jeeves, Mr. Mulliner, Lord Emsworth and the Empress of Blandings, and Stanley Featherstonehaugh ("Fanshaw") Ukridge. The ftp site contains important Wodehouse information, including a full list of all his novels. He who has not met Wodehouse has not lived a full life.

Anonymous FTP:
Address: **cathouse.org**
Path: **/pub/cathouse/humor/authors/**
 p.g.wodehouse/*

Usenet:
Newsgroup: **alt.fan.wodehouse**

> P.G. Wodehouse was called "the best living writer of English prose". (That was when he was alive, of course.)
> Take a look at the Wodehouse archives and see what you're missing.

William Butler Yeats

The complete works of the Irish poet William Butler Yeats.

Anonymous FTP:
Address: **ftp.funet.fi**
Path: **/pub/doc/literary/etext/yeats/***

LITERATURE: COLLECTIONS

Anglo-Saxon Tales

Tales from the Anglo-Saxons, translated and annotated. Includes such classics as *Beowulf*.

Anonymous FTP:
Address: **ftp.std.com**
Path: **/obi/Anglo-Saxon/***

Gopher:
Name: Software Tool & Die
Address: **gopher.std.com**
Choose: **OBI The Online Book Initiative**
 | The Online Books
 | Anglo-Saxon

Anglo-Saxon Literature

In the fifth and sixth centuries, the Angles and the Saxons joined with the Jutes and headed over to England to see what they could dig up in the way of territory to conquer. Armed only with a few weapons, their wits, a tradition of bravery, and a boxful of copies of "The Internet Complete Reference", they managed to take over much of what we now call England, including the house in which Princess Diana used to entertain her male friends. One of the more important results of this invasion was the establishment of a culture that eventually led to a large number of works of literature including Beowulf, The Seafarer, Widsith, Deor's Lament and Walt Disney's Comics and Stories. If you want to download some Anglo-Saxon material for your next party, the Net will oblige with a nice selection of free literature.

Books in Zip Format

Many of the works mentioned elsewhere in this catalog in zip format. Other titles include *The Book of Mormon* and *Zen and the Art of the Internet*.

Anonymous FTP:
Address: **oak.oakland.edu**
Path: **/pub/misc/books**

Chinese Literature

A web page interface to ftp sites that store Chinese novels, poetry, and classics.

World Wide Web:
URL: **http://www.yahoo.com/Art/Literature/Ethnic/Chinese/**

Electronic Books

Access the Library of Congress records and a number of books in electronic form available to be read or downloaded. Titles include *Aesop's Fables*, *Agrippa*, *Aladdin and the Wonderful Lamp*, *Alice's Adventures in Wonderland*, and the *CIA World Factbook*. Search by author, call letter, title, or by specific strings of text. Entries are arranged alphabetically.

Gopher:
Name: University of Colorado Boulder
Address: **gopher.colorado.edu**
Choose: **Online Library Catalogs, Electronic Books and Reference Databases**

Name: University of Minnesota
Address: **gopher.micro.umn.edu**
Choose: **Libraries**
  | Electronic Books

Electronic Books in ASCII Text

ASCII text versions of more of your favorite novels than you could ever have imagined, all in one place.

Anonymous FTP:
Address: **ftp.funet.fi**
Path: **/pub/doc/literary/etext/***

> ## You are what you think.

Freethought Web

The Freethought Web is an archive of freely distributable freethought literature. The works are arranged alphabetically by author and have been made available either by the author or by the fact that the copyright has expired. Included here are works by Clarence Darrow, Theodore Dreiser, Thomas Paine, Upton Sinclair, and Charles Watts.

World Wide Web:
URL: **http://freethought.tamu.edu/freethought/**

French Literature

This web page has links to a textual database of French literature and philosophy from the 15th century, the Association des Bibliophiles Universels, a French encyclopedia, and le serveur litterature de l'université de Montréal.

World Wide Web:
URL: **http://www.yahoo.com/Art/Literature/Ethnic/French/**

> ## Before you go on a trip, use the Net to help you plan. Read the Travel section.

Gothic Tales

A bi-weekly mailing list of dark, bloody stories. This list includes material from classic authors such as Virginia Woolf, Edith Wharton, H.P. Lovecraft, and Poe, and includes old folk and fairy tales, ghost stories, and material written by Net denizens. This list has some really creepy stories that are not for the faint of heart.

Mail:
Address: **carriec@eskimo.com**
Body: **subscribe gothic** *yourname@host*

Hypertext Fiction

A collection of pointers to interactive hypertext fiction on the Internet. It includes "Stories from Downtown Anywhere," "Hypertext Hotel MOO," "Drool," "Postmodern Culture," "Bordeaux and Prague," and more.

World Wide Web:
URL: **http://is.rice.edu/~riddle/hyperfiction.html**

A
B
C
D
E
F
G
H
I
J
K
L
M
N
O
P
Q
R
S
T
U
V
W
X
Y
Z

Why be normal? Read Bizarre.

InterText Magazine

An electronic magazine of fiction published every two months. This page offers the current issue, an archive of back issues, an index of stories published by author, writers' guidelines, and links to other electronic publications.

See also: Zines

World Wide Web:
URL: **http://ftp.etext.org/Zines/InterText/
intertext.html**

Italian Literature

This web page has links to many works of Italian poetry, literature, and theatre, including titles such as *La Divina Commedia*, *I Sonetti*, *Dei Sepolcri*, and others; narratives including *I Promessi Sposi*, *Pinocchio*, *Una Giornata*, and many others.

World Wide Web:
URL: **http://www.yahoo.com/Art/Literature/
Ethnic/Italian/**

Philippine Literature

A collection of information on Filipino authors and their works, including details of Filipino writers published in the U.S., Philippine literature in English and Tagalog, and more.

World Wide Web:
URL: **http://www.teleport.com/~ria/index.html**

Excerpt from the Net...

(from the poetry collection at the Chung Cheng University gopher, Taiwan)

```
Oath of Friendship

Shang Ya!
I want to be your friend
For ever and ever without break or decay.
When the hills are all flat
And the rivers are all dry.
When it lightens and thunders in winter,
When it rains and snows in summer,
When Heaven and Earth mingle -
Not till then will I part from you.

-- Anonymous
   China, 1st centry B.C.
```

Poetry About Life

A collection of Chinese poetry, including *A Chinese Oath of Friendship* and other ponderings about life.

Note: Requires a Chinese text viewer.

Gopher:
Name: National Chung Cheng University
Address: **gopher.ccu.edu.tw**
Choose: **Life and Recreation
| Arts, Culture and Literature
| Chinese Poem**

Poetry Assortments

A large collection of poetry arranged by author. Includes works of Housman, Jeffers, Millay, O'Shaughnessy, Russell, Whitman, and Yeats.

Anonymous FTP:
Address: **ocf.berkeley.edu**
Path: **/pub/Library/Poetry**

Gopher:
Name: Carnegie Mellon University
Address: **english-server.hss.cmu.edu**
Choose: **Poetry**

Name: University of California Berkeley
Address: **ocf.berkeley.edu**
Choose: **Ocf On-line Library
| Poetry**

Project Gutenberg

Project Gutenberg is a storage- and clearinghouse for making books available very cheaply. Much of the work, so far, has focused on classic literature (for which the copyrights have expired). They have books by many authors, including Mark Twain and H.G. Wells. They also have the Bible and the *Book of Mormon* in ASCII format. Also available from **info.umnd.edu** is a collection of economic time series data from the federal government, as well as daily and long-term weather forecasts.

Anonymous FTP:
Address: **info.umd.edu**
Path: **/inforM/Educational_Resources/
ReadingRoom/Fiction/***

Address: **mrcnext.cso.uiuc.edu**
Path: **/pub/etext/etext/***

Gopher:
Name: University of Maryland
Address: **gopher.umd.edu**

Telnet:
Address: **info.umd.edu**

> # Wanna change the system?
> # Try Anarchy.

Science Fiction, Fantasy, and Horror

This page has links to Blake's 7, Douglas Adams, the SciFi Resource Guide, science fiction and fantasy reviews.

World Wide Web:
URL: **http://www.yahoo.com/Art/Literature/ Science_Fiction__Fantasy__Horror/**

Short Stories

An interesting collection of essays and short stories.

Gopher:
Name: Whole Earth Lectronic Link
Address: **gopher.well.sf.ca.us**
Choose: **Authors, Books, Periodicals, Zines | Miscellaneous Cyberprose**

Women and Literature

Experience the remarkable writing of women in literature. This site archives numerous women authors, including notables such as Louisa May Alcott, Jane Austen, Emily Brontë and Sylvia Plath.

World Wide Web:
URL: **http://sunsite.unc.edu/cheryb/women/ wlit.html**

LITERATURE: TITLES

Aeneid

The complete text of the *Aeneid* in Latin, by Virgil, the greatest of the Roman poets.

Anonymous FTP:
Address: **ftp.funet.fi**
Path: **/pub/doc/literary/etext/Vergil/aeneid*.tex**

Address: **ftp.std.com**
Path: **/obi/Classics/texts/vergil/aeneid***

Address: **ftp.uu.net**
Path:
/doc/literary/obi/Classics/texts/vergil/aeneid*

Aesop's Fables

Over three hundred of Aesop's fables from Project Gutenberg.

Anonymous FTP:
Address: **ftp.std.com**
Path: **/obi/Aesop/Fables.Z**

Gopher:
Name: University of Minnesota
Address: **gopher.micro.umn.edu**
Choose: **Libraries
| Electronic Books
| By Title
| Aesop's Fables**

Agrippa

The complete text by William Gibson.

Gopher:
Name: University of Minnesota
Address: **gopher.micro.umn.edu**
Choose: **Libraries
| Electronic Books
| By Title
| Agrippa**

Aladdin and the Wonderful Lamp

The complete text from Project Gutenberg.

Gopher:
Name: University of Minnesota
Address: **gopher.micro.umn.edu**
Choose: **Libraries
| Electronic Books
| By Title
| Aladdin and the Wonderful Lamp**

Alice's Adventures in Wonderland

The complete text of the novel by Lewis Carroll.

Anonymous FTP:
Address: **ftp.std.com**
Path: **/obi/Lewis.Carroll/AliceInWonderl.tar.Z**

Address: **ucselx.sdsu.edu**
Path: **/pub/doc/etext/alice*.txt**

Gopher:
Name: University of Minnesota
Address: **gopher.micro.umn.edu**
Choose: **Libraries
| Electronic Books
| By Title
| Alice's Adventures in Wonderland**

A B C D E F G H I J K L M N O P Q R S T U V W X Y Z

*Go ask Alice,
I think she'll know*

Anne of Green Gables

The complete text of the novel by Lucy Montgomery.

Anonymous FTP:
Address: **ftp.funet.fi**
Path: **/pub/doc/literary/etext/anne.txt.gz**

As a Man Thinketh

The full text by James Allen. "This little volume (the result of meditation and experience) is not intended as an exhaustive treatise on the much written upon subject of the power of thought. It is suggestive rather than explanatory, its object being to stimulate men and women to the discovery and perception of the truth that — they themselves are makers of themselves..." —James Allen

Anonymous FTP:
Address: **ftp.funet.fi**
Path: **/pub/doc/literary/etext/thinketh.txt.gz**

Address: **ftp.std.com**
Path: **/obi/James.Allen/As.a.Man.Thinketh**

Address: **ftp.uu.net**
Path: **/doc/literary/obi/James.Allen/
As.a.Man.Thinketh.Z**

The Call of the Wild

The complete text of the novel by Jack London.

Anonymous FTP:
Address: **ftp.funet.fi**
Path: **/pub/doc/literary/etext/callwild.txt.gz**

The Canterbury Tales

A text file containing *The Canterbury Tales* by Geoffrey Chaucer.

Anonymous FTP:
Address: **ftp.std.com**
Path: **/obi/Geoffrey.Chaucer/canterbury.txt.Z**

Address: **ftp.uu.net**
Path: **/doc/literary/obi/Geoffrey.Chaucer/
canterbury.txt.Z**

Cast Upon the Breakers

A document with the full text of the novel *Cast Upon the Breakers* by Horatio Alger, Jr.

Anonymous FTP:
Address: **ftp.std.com**
Path: **/obi/Horatio.Alger.Jr/
Cast.Upon.the.Breakers.Z**

Address: **ftp.uu.net**
Path: **/doc/literary/obi/Horatio.Alger.Jr/
Cast.Upon.the.Breakers.Z**

A Christmas Carol

The complete heartwarming tale by Charles Dickens.

Anonymous FTP:
Address: **ftp.funet.fi**
Path: **/pub/doc/literary/etext/carol.txt**

Address: **ftp.std.com**
Path: **/obi/Charles.Dickens/AChristmasCaro.tar.Z**

City of the Sun

A file containing the full text of the novel *City of the Sun* by Tommaso Campanello.

Anonymous FTP:
Address: **ftp.std.com**
Path: **/obi/Tommaso.Campanella/City.of.the.Sun.Z**

Address: **ftp.uu.net**
Path: **/doc/literary/obi/Tommaso.Campanella/
City.of.the.Sun.Z**

Have a Dickens of a Time

What could be more heartwarming than snuggling around the fire and reading aloud from

A Christmas Carol?

Download this wonderful tale and make your next holiday season one that your friends and loved · ones will treasure forever. (Our favorite part is where the guests are eating dinner and, all of a sudden, they realize that Dr. Franknfurter has actually cooked Eddie the delivery boy.)

Civil Disobedience

The full text of *Civil Disobedience* by Henry David Thoreau.

Anonymous FTP:
Address: **ftp.std.com**
Path: **/obi/Henry.David.Thoreau/
Civil.Disobedience.Z**

Address: **ftp.uu.net**
Path: **/doc/literary/obi/Henry.David.Thoreau/
Civil.Disobedience.Z**

Communist Manifesto

The complete text of the document by Marx and Engels.

Anonymous FTP:
Address: **ftp.funet.fi**
Path: **/pub/doc/literary/etext/manifesto.txt.gz**

A Connecticut Yankee in King Arthur's Court

The complete text of the novel by Mark Twain.

Anonymous FTP:
Address: **ftp.funet.fi**
Path: **/pub/doc/literary/etext/yankee.mt.gz**

Address: **ftp.std.com**
Path: **/obi/Mark.Twain/A.Connecticut.Yankee.Z**

Discourse on Reason

The complete essay by Descartes.

Anonymous FTP:
Address: **ftp.funet.fi**
Path: **/pub/doc/literary/etext/reason.txt.gz**

The Divine Comedy (La Divina Commedia)

Read or search for passages in Dante Alighieri's classic.

World Wide Web:
URL: **http://www.crs4.it/~riccardo/
DivinaCommedia/DivinaCommedia.html**

Dracula

The complete collection of texts written by Bram Stoker.

Anonymous FTP:
Address: **ftp.funet.fi**
Path: **/pub/doc/literary/etext/dracgst.txt.gz**

Essays in Radical Empiricism

The complete text by William James.

Anonymous FTP:
Address: **ftp.funet.fi**
Path: **/pub/doc/literary/etext/empiricism.txt.gz**

A B C D E F G H I J K L M N O P Q R S T U V W X Y Z

Fairy Tales

Wonderful collection of childhood magic. Tales of puffing wolves, little pigs, ugly ducklings, dwarves, princesses, and thieves. Text of numerous fairy tales, including *The Little Mermaid*, *Snow White*, *The Adventures of Aladdin*, *Beauty and the Beast*, *Hansel and Gretel*, *Jack and the Beanstalk*, *The Three Little Pigs*, *The Tin Soldier*, and many more.

Anonymous FTP:
Address: **ftp.funet.fi**
Path: **/pub/doc/literary/etext/fariy-tale/***

Address: **ftp.std.com**
Path: **/obi/Fairy.Tales/***

Address: **ftp.uu.net**
Path: **/doc/literary/obi/Fairy.Tales/***

Fanny Hill

The full text of the novel by John Cleland.

Anonymous FTP:
Address: **ftp.std.com**
Path: **/obi/John.Cleland/Fanny-Hill.Z**

Address: **ftp.uu.net**
Path: **/doc/literary/obi/John.Cleland/Fanny-Hill.Z**

Far from the Madding Crowd

The complete text of the novel by Thomas Hardy, provided by Project Gutenberg.

Gopher:
Name: University of Minnesota
Address: **gopher.micro.umn.edu**
Choose: **Libraries**
| Electronic Books
| By Title
| Far From the Madding Crowd

Flatland

The complete text of the novel *Flatland*, the story of the life of a two-dimensional being, by Edwin Abbott.

Anonymous FTP:
Address: **ftp.std.com**
Path: **/obi/Edwin.Abbott/flatland.***

Address: **ftp.uu.net**
Path: **/doc/literary/obi/Edwin.Abbott/flatland.***

Want to expand your mind? Read Flatland.

Frankenstein

The full text of the classic novel *Frankenstein* by Mary Shelley.

Anonymous FTP:
Address: **ftp.std.com**
Path: **/obi/Mary.W.Shelley/**
Frankenstein.cpt.hqx.Z

Address: **ftp.uu.net**
Path: **/doc/literary/obi/Mary.W.Shelley/**
Frankenstein.cpt.hqx.Z

The Gift of the Magi

The complete text of the O. Henry story, provided by Project Gutenberg.

Gopher:
Name: University of Minnesota
Address: **gopher.micro.umn.edu**
Choose: **Libraries**
| Electronic Books
| By Title
| Gift of the Magi, The

Harold and Maude

The full text of the novel *Harold and Maude* by Colin Higgins. This book was the basis for the cult movie by the same name.

Anonymous FTP:
Address: **ftp.std.com**
Path: **/obi/Colin.Higgins/harold.Z**

Address: **ftp.uu.net**
Path: **/doc/literary/obi/Colin.Higgins/harold.Z**

Herland

The complete text from Project Gutenberg.

Gopher:
> Name: University of Minnesota
> Address: **gopher.micro.umn.edu**
> Choose: **Libraries**
> | **Electronic Books**
> | **By Title**
> | **Herland**

Hippocratic Oath and Law

The text of the historical oath of physicians by Hippocrates. This is a must read — today's physicians should be held to the same standard as their counterparts of two millennia ago. If you think they *are* held to the same standard, you should read this.

Anonymous FTP:
> Address: **ftp.funet.fi**
> Path: **/pub/doc/literary/etext/hippoc.txt.gz**

The House of the Seven Gables

A file containing the full text of the novel by Nathaniel Hawthorne.

Anonymous FTP:
> Address: **ftp.std.com**
> Path: **/obi/Nathaniel.Hawthorne/**
>   **The.House.of.the.Seven.Gables.Z**

> Address: **ftp.uu.net**
> Path: **/doc/literary/obi/Nathaniel.Hawthorne/**
>   **The.House.of.the.Seven.Gables.Z**

The Hunting of the Snark

The complete text of a great poem by Lewis Carroll.

> "Just the place for a Snark!" the Bellman cried,
>   As he landed his crew with care;
> Supporting each man on the top of the tide
>   By a finger entwined in his hair.

Anonymous FTP:
> Address: **ucselx.sdsu.edu**
> Path: **/pub/doc/etext/snark11.txt**

Gopher:
> Name: University of Minnesota
> Address: **gopher.micro.umn.edu**
> Choose: **Libraries**
> | **Electronic Books**
> | **By Title**
> | **Hunting of the Snark, The**

The Invisible Man

The full text by H.G. Wells. "The stranger came early in February one wintry day, through a biting wind and a driving snow, the last snowfall of the year, over the down, walking as it seemed from Bramblehurst railway station and carrying a little black portmanteau in his thickly gloved hand."

Anonymous FTP:
> Address: **ftp.funet.fi**
> Path: **/pub/doc/literary/etext/invisman.txt.gz**

Jabberwocky

The complete text of the poem by Lewis Carroll.

Anonymous FTP:
> Address: **ftp.funet.fi**
> Path: **/pub/doc/literary/etext/jabber.txt**

Japan That Can Say No

Several enjoyable hours-worth of ranting and raving by a Japanese corporate leader with political designs. Find out what the Japanese really think of America and Americans. The Japanese wish this book had never left their shores, but this translation is provided by an anonymous group.

Anonymous FTP:
> Address: **rohan.sdsu.edu**
> Path: **/pub/doc/etext/japan-that-can-say-no.txt**

The Jungle Book

A document containing the classic collection of stories by Rudyard Kipling that became the basis for the Disney animated film of the same name. This subdirectory also has files that contain some of Kipling's poetry.

Anonymous FTP:
> Address: **ftp.std.com**
> Path: **/obi/Rudyard.Kipling/Jungle.Book.Z**

> Address: **ftp.uu.net**
> Path: **/doc/literary/obi/Rudyard.Kipling/**
>   **Jungle.Book.Z**

Spare time? Take a look at Games.

A B C D E F G H I J K L M N O P Q R S T U V W X Y Z

Just David

The full text of the novel *Just David* by the author of *Pollyanna*, Eleanor H. Porter.

Anonymous FTP:
Address: **ftp.std.com**
Path: **/obi/Eleanor.H.Porter/Just.David.Z**

Address: **ftp.uu.net**
Path: **/doc/literary/obi/Eleanor.H.Porter/
  Just.David.Z**

The Keepsake Stories

A subdirectory of files containing *The Keepsake Stories* by Sir Walter Scott.

Anonymous FTP:
Address: **ftp.std.com**
Path: **/obi/Walter.Scott/The.Keepsake.Stories**

Address: **ftp.uu.net**
Path: **/doc/literary/obi/Walter.Scott/
  The.Keepsake.Stories**

Anonymous FTP:
Address: **ftp.funet.fi**
Path: **/pub/doc/literary/etext/keepsake.txt.gz**

The Legend of Sleepy Hollow

The complete text of the story by Washington Irving.

Anonymous FTP:
Address: **ftp.funet.fi**
Path: **/pub/doc/literary/etext/sleepy.txt.gz**

Gopher:
Name: University of Minnesota
Address: **gopher.micro.umn.edu**
Choose: **Libraries**
  | Electronic Books
  | By Title
  | Sleepy Hollow

Mac Shrodinger's Cat

The complete text of the recent novel *Mac Shrodinger's Cat* by Reed de Buch. At the beginning of this document, the author requests feedback from readers and gives instructions on how to contact him.

Anonymous FTP:
Address: **ftp.std.com**
Path: **/obi/Reed.de.Buch/mac.cat.Z**

Address: **ftp.uu.net**
Path: **/doc/literary/obi/Reed.de.Buch/mac.car.Z**

Moby Dick

The complete text of the novel by Herman Melville, provided by Project Gutenberg.
Name: University of Minnesota
Address: **gopher.micro.umn.edu**
Choose: **Libraries**
  | Electronic Books
  | By Title
  | Moby Dick

Make Your Own Literature

Herman Melville labored for years writing *Moby Dick* and now you can read the whole thing for free anytime you want, just by using a Gopher. Better yet, download your favorite chapters and make changes. For example, use **vi** and enter the command **:%s/Dick/Rick/g**. You are now reading *Moby Rick*!

The New Atlantis

The text of the book by Francis Bacon.

Anonymous FTP:
Address: **ftp.std.com**
Path: **/obi/Francis.Bacon/The.New.Alantis.Z**

Address: **ftp.uu.net**
Path: **/doc/literary/obi/Francis.Bacon/
  The.New.Alantis.Z**

O Pioneers!

The complete text of the novel by Willa Cather, provided by Project Gutenberg.

Gopher:
Name: University of Minnesota
Address: **gopher.micro.umn.edu**
Choose: **Libraries**
  | Electronic Books
  | By Title
  | O Pioneers!

**Too much spare time?
Explore a MUD.**

The Oedipus Trilogy

The complete texts of the plays by Sophocles, provided by Project Gutenberg.

Gopher:
> Name: University of Minnesota
> Address: **gopher.micro.umn.edu**
> Choose: **Libraries**
> | **Electronic Books**
> | **By Title**
> | **Oedipus Trilogy, The**

> **Whatever else you say about Oedipus, you have to admit he *was* nice to his mother.**

On Liberty

A document with the full text of *On Liberty* by John Stuart Mill.

Anonymous FTP:
> Address: **ftp.std.com**
> Path: **/obi/John.Stuart.Mill/On.Liberty.Z**

> Address: **ftp.uu.net**
> Path: **/doc/literary/obi/John.Stuart.Mill/On.Liberty.Z**

Our Mr. Wrenn

A file with the full text of the novel *Our Mr. Wrenn* by Sinclair Lewis.

Anonymous FTP:
> Address: **ftp.std.com**
> Path: **/obi/Sinclair.Lewis/Our.Mr.Wrenn.Z**

> Address: **ftp.uu.net**
> Path: **/doc/literary/obi/Sinclair.Lewis/Our.Mr.Wrenn.Z**

Paradise Lost

The complete text of the epic poem by John Milton, provided by Project Gutenberg.

Gopher:
> Name: University of Minnesota
> Address: **gopher.micro.umn.edu**
> Choose: **Libraries**
> | **Electronic Books**
> | **By Title**
> | **Paradise Lost**

Parnassus on Wheels

A document file containing the novel *Parnassus on Wheels* by Christopher Morley.

Anonymous FTP:
> Address: **ftp.std.com**
> Path: **/obi/Christopher.Morley/Parnassus.on.Wheels.Z**

> Address: **ftp.uu.net**
> Path: **/doc/literary/obi/Christopher.Morley/Parnassus.on.Wheels.Z**

Peter Pan

The complete text of the story by J.M. Barrie, provided by Project Gutenberg.

Gopher:
> Name: University of Minnesota
> Address: **gopher.micro.umn.edu**
> Choose: **Libraries**
> | **Electronic Books**
> | **By Title**
> | **Peter Pan**

The Pit and the Pendulum

The complete text of the story by Edgar Allan Poe.

Anonymous FTP:
> Address: **ftp.funet.fi**
> Path: **/pub/doc/literary/etext/pit.poe.gz**

The Scarlet Letter

The complete text of the novel by Nathaniel Hawthorne, provided by Project Gutenberg.

Gopher:
> Name: University of Minnesota
> Address: **gopher.micro.umn.edu**
> Choose: **Libraries**
> | **Electronic Books**
> | **By Title**
> | **Scarlet Letter, The**

> **A sure-fire way to make all your dreams come true is to sleep with this book under your pillow.**

A B C D E F G H I J K L M N O P Q R S T U V W X Y Z

The Scarlet Pimpernel

The complete text by Baroness Orczy.

Anonymous FTP:
Address: **ftp.funet.fi**
Path: **/pub/doc/literary/etext/pimpernel.txt.gz**

Scientific Secrets, 1861

The complete text by Daniel Young.

Anonymous FTP:
Address: **ftp.funet.fi**
Path: **/pub/doc/literary/etext/science.txt.gz**

Sherlock Holmes Novels

A collection of novels by Sir Arthur Conan Doyle.

Anonymous FTP:
Address: **ftp.funet.fi**
Path: **/pub/doc/literary/etext/return.dyl.gz**

Address: **ftp.funet.fi**
Path: **/pub/doc/literary/etext/casebook.dyl.gz**

Address: **ftp.funet.fi**
Path: **/pub/doc/literary/etext/hound.dyl.gz**

Address: **ftp.funet.fi**
Path: **/pub/doc/literary/etext/lastbow.dyl.gz**

Address: **ftp.funet.fi**
Path: **/pub/doc/literary/etext/memoirs.dyl.gz**

Address: **ftp.funet.fi**
Path: **/pub/doc/literary/etext/signfour.dyl.gz**

Address: **ftp.funet.fi**
Path: **/pub/doc/literary/etext/study.dyl.gz**

Address: **ftp.funet.fi**
Path: **/pub/doc/literary/etext/valley.dyl.gz**

Address: **ftp.funet.fi**
Path: **/pub/doc/literary/etext/magicdoor.dyl.gz**

Address: **ftp.std.com**
Path: **/obi/Arthur.Conan.Doyle/***

Address: **ftp.uu.net**
Path: **/pub/literary/obi/Arthur.Conan.Doyle/***

Understanding Your Editor

One day, you may be faced with having to write a book. If so, you will find that one of the great privileges of writing is being able to work with editors. However, you may also find that your editors have only a rudimentary idea of how to deal with writers. If so, show them how to download a copy of "The Strange Case of Dr. Jekyll and Mr. Hyde". You may not know it , but that story is actually a metaphor for author/editor relations. We are sure that you will find the story to be useful in many ways, especially if you are trying to understand your husband or wife. (We use it to look for hints on how to negotiate for higher royalties.)

The Song of Hiawatha

The complete text of the poem by Henry Wadsworth Longfellow, provided by Project Gutenberg.

Gopher:
Name: University of Minnesota
Address: **gopher.micro.umn.edu**
Choose: **Libraries**
 I **Electronic Books**
 I **By Title**
 I **Song of Hiawatha**

The Strange Case of Dr. Jekyll and Mr. Hyde

The complete text of the novel by Robert Louis Stevenson, provided by Project Gutenberg.

Gopher:
Name: University of Minnesota
Address: **gopher.micro.umn.edu**
Choose: **Libraries**
 I **Electronic Books**
 I **By Title**
 I **Strange Case of Dr. Jekyll and Mr. Hyde**

Susan Lenox: Her Rise and Fall

A document file with the full text of David Graham Phillips' novel *Susan Lenox: Her Rise and Fall*.

Anonymous FTP:
Address: **ftp.std.com**
Path: **/obi/David.Graham.Phillips/Susan.Lenox.Z**

Address: **ftp.uu.net**
Path: **/doc/literary/obi/**
　　David.Graham.Phillips/Susan.Lenox.Z

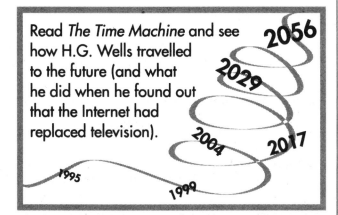

Read *The Time Machine* and see how H.G. Wells travelled to the future (and what he did when he found out that the Internet had replaced television).

The Time Machine

The complete text of the novel by H.G. Wells, provided by Project Gutenberg.

Gopher:
Name: University of Minnesota
Address: **gopher.micro.umn.edu**
Choose: **Libraries**
　| Electronic Books
　| By Title
　| Time Machine, The

Through the Looking-Glass

The complete text of the novel by Lewis Carroll.

Anonymous FTP:
Address: **ucselx.sdsu.edu**
Path: **/pub/doc/etext/lglass15.txt**

Gopher:
Name: University of Minnesota
Address: **gopher.micro.umn.edu**
Choose: **Libraries**
　| Electronic Books
　| By Title
　| Through the Looking Glass

Tom Sawyer

A collection of complete *Tom Sawyer* texts by Mark Twain.

Anonymous FTP:
Address: **ftp.funet.fi**
Path: **/pub/doc/literary/etext/detective.mt.gz**

Address: **ftp.funet.fi**
Path: **/pub/doc/literary/etext/sawyer.mt.gz**

Address: **ftp.funet.fi**
Path: **/pub/doc/literary/etext/abroad.mt.gz**

Why not take a few minutes and download TOM SAWYER. *Then, spend the rest of the afternoon reading it. (You can tell your boss that we said it was okay.)*

Umney's Last Case

English and German versions of this novel by the popular horror writer Stephen King.

See also: Literature: Authors

World Wide Web:
URL: **http://www.eunet.sk/king/king-intro.html**

A
B
C
D
E
F
G
H
I
J
K
L
M
N
O
P
Q
R
S
T
U
V
W
X
Y
Z

United Nations Declaration of Human Rights

Read what the U.N. considers to be basic human rights that should be conferred upon all the people in the world — by them.

Anonymous FTP:
　　Address: **ucselx.sdsu.edu**
　　Path: **/pub/doc/etext/un_declaration.txt**

United We Stand

The complete text, provided by Project Gutenberg.

Gopher:
　　Name: University of Minnesota
　　Address: **gopher.micro.umn.edu**
　　Choose: **Libraries**
　　　I **Electronic Books**
　　　I **By Title**
　　　I **United We Stand**

Up from Slavery

A document containing the book *Up from Slavery* by Booker T. Washington, in its entirety.

Anonymous FTP:
　　Address: **ftp.uu.net**
　　Path: **/doc/literary/obi/Booker.T.Washington/**
　　　Up.From.Slavery.Z

Voyage of the Beagle

Charles Darwin's story of his voyage on the *Beagle*, during which he gathered evidence for his theory of evolution that was later published in *The Origin of Species*.

Anonymous FTP:
　　Address: **ftp.uu.net**
　　Path: **/doc/literary/obi/Charles.Darwin/**
　　　Voyage.of.the.Beagle.Z

The War of the Worlds

The full novel by H.G. Wells that scared Americans out of their wits when Orson Welles performed a version of it on the radio air waves. *The War of the Worlds* may have been the genesis of today's space craze.

Anonymous FTP:
　　Address: **ftp.funet.fi**
　　Path: **/pub/doc/literary/etext/warworld.txt**

The Wonderful Wizard of Oz

The complete text of the novel by L. Frank Baum.

Anonymous FTP:
　　Address: **ftp.funet.fi**
　　Path: **/pub/doc/literary/etext/wizoz.txt.gz**

Wuthering Heights

The complete text of the novel by Emily Brontë.

Anonymous FTP:
　　Address: **ftp.funet.fi**
　　Path: **/pub/doc/literary/etext/wuther.txt.gz**

MAGAZINES

Blink Magazine

Blink magazine features articles, departments including an "Internet Hot List," "Telnet like it is," and "Cyberspace dispatch," as well as works of fiction, and other items of interest.

World Wide Web:
URL: **http://www.acns.nwu.edu/blink/**

bOING bOING

bOING bOING is a web-based news zine that bills itself as the flipside of serious culture. Check out the Happy Mutant Handbook, the bOING bOING Bazaar, the Merry Zine Review, and other tidbits and brain candy.

World Wide Web:
URL: **http://www.zeitgeist.net/public/Boing-boing/bbw3/boing.boing.html**

Byte Magazine

Back issues of *Byte* magazine in arc and zip format.

Anonymous FTP:
Address: **oak.oakland.edu**
Path: **/pub/misc/byte**

Chips Online

Back issues of *Chips* and *Chips Online* magazines.

Anonymous FTP:
Address: **oak.oakland.edu**
Path: **/pub/misc/nardac**

Computer-Mediated Communication

A magazine loaded with meaty articles, essays, and discussion of computer-mediated communication. This is not a haphazard publication, so if you are interested in ethics, philosophy, and actual thinking, you will enjoy this.

See also: Telecommunications, Zines

World Wide Web:
URL: **http://www.rpi.edu/~decemj/cmc/mag/current/toc.html**

CTHEORY

An international, electronic review of books on theory, technology and culture. CTHEORY has links to many articles, events, and reviews.

World Wide Web:
URL: **http://english-server.hss.cmu.edu/ctheory/ctheory.html**

Cultronix

A mixed format, multimedia journal that explores the cultural effects of technology on society. Cultronix features text, graphics, audio, video and interactive hypermedia technology.

World Wide Web:
URL: **http://english-server.hss.cmu.edu/cultronix.html**

Culture Magazines

Sample articles and subscription information for music, consumer, sports, and travel magazines.

Gopher:
Name: The Electronic Newsstand
Address: **gopher.internet.com**
Port: **2100**
Choose: **Titles Arranged by Subject**
  | **Culture - Music, Popular, Sport, Travel, Literature, etc**

Electronic Journals Project

A comprehensive collection of all public domain electronic journals currently available on the Internet. A complete list of the collection (with a description and topic information for each journal) is available for easy selection.

Anonymous FTP:
Address: **ftp.cic.net**
Path: **/pub/e-serials/***

Gopher:
Name: CICNet
Address: **gopher.cic.net**
Choose: **Electronic Serials**

Web users: if you are in a hurry, use Lynx.

Electronic Newspapers and Magazines

In the daily hubbub you seem to have misplaced your *Field and Stream* renewal notice. Now your subscription has lapsed. Don't let it get you down. There are lots of magazines and news publications on the Net. In fact, not only can you get electronic literature, you can discuss the evolution of newspaper and magazine experiments in electronic publishing. That sure beats learning the proper way to dig grubs or to gut a fish.

Majordomo Mailing List:
> List Address: **online-news@marketplace.com**
> Subscription Address:
> > **majordomo@marketplace.com**

Entertainment Magazines Online

The "Literary" web page has links to online magazines and e-zines including *Garrett Count Journal, Kyosaku, Postmodern Culture, The Morpo Review, The Unit Circle, TwentyNothing,* and *Verbiage Magazine*. The "Society" page has religious and sexual material including *Chariot Magazine, Out Magazine, Slippery When Wet*, and *Snake Oil*.

World Wide Web:
> URL: **http://www.yahoo.com/Entertainment/ Magazines/Literary/**

> URL: **http://www.yahoo.com/Entertainment/ Magazines/Society/**

Family Times

A family-oriented web magazine with links to many family resources, news, articles, a parents' forum, parenting tips, letters, back issues, and much more for you and your family.

World Wide Web:
> URL: **http://ssnet.com:8011/index.html**

Hacking

Based on the tone of 2600 magazine, this newsgroup is full of discussion about the technical, philosophical, ethical and sociologial aspects of hacking.

Usenet:
> Newsgroup: **alt.2600**

Do you like secrets? Try 2600. But don't tell anyone...it's a secret.

High Times News

This is one place you will not find many "Just Say No" slogans. Read select news articles from the magazine *High Times* and find out the latest news concerning drugs and freedom.

Gopher:
> Name: Echo
> Address: **echonyc.com**
> Choose: **Zines, Publications & Writings | High Times News**

Internaut

An online magazine for users of the Internet with links to online books, magazines, indexes, and resources available on the Internet.

World Wide Web:
> URL: **http://www.zilker.net/users/internaut/**

Internet with Attitude

An in-depth look in cyberculture on the Web. This web page features articles, information about the Internet, and a "Top Ten High-tech and Electronic Zines" list.

World Wide Web:
> URL: **http://www.3w.com/3W/index.html**

Internet Business Journal

Details about and samples from this publication exploring commercial opportunities in the networking age.

Anonymous FTP:
> Address: **ftp.fonorola.net**
> Path: **/Internet Business Journal**

Gopher:
> Name: Fonorola Network
> Address: **gopher.fonorola.net**
> Choose: **Internet Business Journal**

Internet Talk Radio

Internet Talk Radio is a new type of publication: a news and information service about the Internet, distributed on the Internet. Internet Talk Radio is modeled on National Public Radio and seeks to provide in-depth technical information about the Internet.

Mail:
Address: **info@radio.com**
Address: **questions@radio.com**
Address: **radio@ora.com**

Internet Mailing List:
List Address: **announce@radio.com**
Subscription Address:
announce-request@radio.com

Usenet:
Newsgroup: **alt.internet.services**

Magazine Summaries

This is better than going to the newsstand, because you don't have to take off your fuzzy slippers and leave the house. Check out zines, newsletters and magazines from your computer. Read contents and summaries of electronic and printed publications and find out how to get them.

Usenet:
Newsgroup: **rec.mag**

Meta

Meta is an electronic networking magazine focusing on the Internet, its growth and development, access, privacy, intellectual property, and related topics.

See also: Internet, Zines

Mail:
Address: **mlinksva@netcom.com**

World Wide Web:
URL: **ftp://ftp.netcom.com/pub/mlinksva/meta.html**
URL: **http://www.best.com/~au/meta/**

Make new friends on Internet Relay Chat (IRC).

Mother Jones

Mother Jones is a magazine of investigation and ideas for independent thinkers. It challenges conventional wisdom, exposes abuses of power, helps redefine stubborn problems, and offers fresh solutions. It's free and online.

Anonymous FTP:
Address: **mojones.com**
Path: **/pub/***

Gopher:
Name: Mother Jones Magazine
Address: **mojones.com**

Listserv Mailing List:
List Address: **motherjones-list@mojones.com**
Subscription Address: **listserv@mojones.com**

List Address: **motherjones-text@mojones.com**
Subscription Address: **listserv@mojones.com**

Netweaver

Back issues of *Netweaver*, the Journal of the Electronic Networking Association to promote electronic networking to enrich and enhance individuals and organizations and build global communities.

Anonymous FTP:
Address: **ftp.uu.net**
Path: **/doc/literary/obi/NetWeaver/***

Open Systems Today

The former *Unix Today!* magazine makes binary programs, source code, and other files of interest available via anonymous ftp and gopher.

Anonymous FTP:
Address: **ftp.uu.net**
Path: **/published/open-systems-today/***

A
B
C
D
E
F
G
H
I
J
K
L
M
N
O
P
Q
R
S
T
U
V
W
X
Y
Z

PC Magazine

PC Magazine, one of the most popular computer magazines, is also available online. This web page is maintained by Ziff-Davis and is actually an electronic version of the magazine. The page includes the current cover story, features, editorials, and even previous editions and previews of upcoming issues. The CalTech ftp site has back issues in arc and zip formats.

Anonymous FTP:
    Address: **ftp.cco.caltech.edu**
    Path: **/pub/ibmpc/pcmag/**

World Wide Web:
    URL: **http://www.ziff.com/~pcmag/**

PC Week Labs

PC Week Labs is a department of *PC Week*, a weekly newspaper for people in the computer and software industries. PC Week Labs' web page has great resources, including the "PC Week Labs Product of the Week," "Best of the Web," "What's New with NCSA Mosaic," and "Pages O' Pointers."

World Wide Web:
    URL: **http://www.ziff.com/~pcweek/**

Phrack

An electronic magazine devoted to hackers. Complete collection of the popular publication from the computer underground, containing technical and legal information relevant to hacking, phreaking, and other underground activities.

Anonymous FTP:
    Address: **aql.gatech.edu**
    Path: **/pub/eff/Publications/CuD/Phrack/***

    Address: **etext.archive.umich.edu**
    Path: **/pub/CuD/Phrack/***

    Address: **ftp.halcyon.com**
    Path: **/mirror1/cud/phrack**

    Address: **ftp.uu.net**
    Path: **/doc/literary/obi/Phracks**

Quanta

Back issues of *Quanta*, the "journal of fact, fiction, and opinion." *Quanta* is a literary magazine containing articles and short stories, many with a science/science fiction/fantasy theme.

Anonymous FTP:
    Address: **ftp.uu.net**
    Path: **/doc/literary/obi/Quanta/***

SCO World Magazine

There are times when you've read an article in *SCO World Magazine* and you are just aching to discuss it with someone. The problem is that you are the only person in your neighborhood who happens to read it. With Usenet, you never have to worry about not being able to find someone. The SCO world is suddenly a much bigger place. Tune in on the discussion of the magazine and its contents.

Usenet:
    Newsgroup: **biz.sco.magazine**

Skeptic

A list of all the tables of contents of back issues, selected articles from each issue, and subscription information. While the full issues of *Skeptic* magazine are not available online, there are several good articles to read.

Anonymous FTP:
    Address: **rtd.com**
    Path: **/pub/zines/skeptic/***

Soapbox

Soapbox magazine is a forum for varying and controversial opinions on all subjects.

Anonymous FTP:
    Address: **ftp.spies.com**
    Path: **/Library/Techdoc/Zines/soapbox/***

Gopher:
    Name: Internet Wiretap
    Address: **wiretap.spies.com**
    Choose: **Wiretap Online Library**
    | **Zines**
    | **soapbox**

> ## Learn Unix and walk with the gods.

Sound Site Newsletter

A monthly newsletter for PC sound enthusiasts. Tips on configuration, sound files, programming with sound, and much more.

Anonymous FTP:
    Address: **oak.oakland.edu**
    Path: **/pub/misc/sound/***

The Lynx

A real magazine with real reporters going to real places. Published via the Web, *The Lynx* offers coverage of alternative sides of the Web and the Internet, and promises to be entertaining, informative, and maybe a little anarchic.

World Wide Web:
    URL: **http://www.cityscape.co.uk/lynx/**

The Tech

The Tech is MIT's oldest and largest newspaper and is published at periodic intervals throughout the year. Back issues of the newspaper are available on this web server.

World Wide Web:
    URL: **http://the-tech.mit.edu/The-Tech**

Unix World

Program listings, articles, and other files of interest from *Unix World* magazine.

Anonymous FTP:
    Address: **ftp.uu.net**
    Path: **/published/unix-world/***

Gopher:
    Name: Software Tool & Die
    Address: **gopher.std.com**
    Choose: **Periodicals, Magazines, and Journals
    | UNIX World**

Virtual Library of Electronic Journals

A great page to access electronic journals available on the Internet. There are direct links to most magazines and descriptions to many more.

World Wide Web:
    URL: **http://info.cern.ch/hypertext/DataSources/
    bySubject/Electronic_Journals.html**

Voices from the Net

An electronic magazine filled with interviews and essays presenting the voices of folks from a wide variety of online environments. An entertaining and useful forum for net-literature and net-ethnography. An exploration of the odd corners of cyberspace. To subscribe, send mail to the address below. To download a back issue, use one of the ftp sites listed below.

Anonymous FTP:
    Address: **aql.gatech.edu**
    Path: **/pub/Zines/Voices_from_the_Net**

    Address: **etext.archive.umich.edu**
    Path: **/pub/Zines/Voices**

    Address: **ftp.spies.com**
    Path: **/Library/Zines/voices***

Internet Mailing List:
    List Address: **voices@andy.bgsu.edu**
    Subscription Address:
        voices-request@andy.bgsu.edu

Wired

Brought to you by the highly energized, highly caffeinated staff of *Wired* — interesting and fast-paced articles relating to the electronic and networking age, news and reviews, interviews and handfuls of fun tidbits. You'll miss *Wired*'s cool and creative graphics, but it's still very readable.

Gopher:
    Name: Wired Magazine
    Address: **gopher.wired.com**

Usenet:
    Newsgroup: **alt.wired**

World Wide Web:
    URL: **http://www.wired.com/**

A
B
C
D
E
F
G
H
I
J
K
L
M
N
O
P
Q
R
S
T
U
V
W
X
Y
Z

MAIL TO FAMOUS PEOPLE

Douglas Adams

The author of *The Hitchhiker's Guide to the Galaxy* and many other imaginative works has his own Usenet fan club. Drop in, chat with the fans, and maybe even send a line to the grand young man himself.

Mail:
> Address: **adamsd@cerf.net**

Usenet:
> Newsgroup: **alt.fan.douglas-adams**

World Wide Web:
> URL: **http://www.umd.umich.edu/~nhughes/dna/**

Scott Adams

Do you enjoy the *Dilbert* comic strip? Do you like the cute little dog that looks like a balloon with glasses? If so, tell the artist himself: Scott Adams.

Mail:
> Address: **scott.adams@aol.com**

John Perry Barlow

A man of many talents, Barlow left the Wyoming cattle ranching business to immerse himself in the world of music and computers. Lyricist for the Grateful Dead and co-founder of the Electronic Frontier Foundation, he can be found on the Net writing about computer freedom and culture.

Mail:
> Address: **barlow@eff.org**

World Wide Web:
> URL: **http://www.eff.org/homes/barlow.html**

Stewart Brand

Meet Stewart Brand, the original hippie-who-knows-how-to-make-money-without-selling-out-like- Jerry-Rubin. Brand, the creative force behind the *Whole Earth Catalog* and the *Whole Earth Review* is also the man behind the WELL, the electronic meeting place that reflects the best of the I-live-north-of-San-Francisco popular culture. Send him a message or check out the WELL itself by using their gopher.

Gopher:
> Name: Whole Earth Lectronic Link
> Address: **gopher.well.sf.ca.us**

Mail:
> Address: **sbb@well.sf.ca.us**

Excerpt from the Net...

```
Newsgroup: alt.internet.services
Subject: The Whitehouse Address

> Just clearing up a few points, the Whitehouse Internet address is:
>
>      whitehouse.gov
>
> The President's email address is:
>
>      president@whitehouse.gov
>
> and it works.  (You get a canned reply message, saying that they read
> all of the mail etc.)  If you ftp to this site, you can actually get
> a copy of the president's speeches.
>
> My girlfriend was wondering:
> Is there an e-mail address for Hillary Rodham Clinton?

I've heard that Hillary is root@whitehouse.gov
```

Bill Clinton

The President of the United States is a lot more than a good old boy from Arkansas: he's the Leader of the Free World, the Commander-in-Chief of the U.S. armed forces, and the Grand Poobah of the Illuminati. Drop him a note and tell him what is wrong with America and how to fix it. (You might also ask him if he knows where Hillary gets her hair done.)

Mail:
Address: **president@whitehouse.gov**

Want to talk to America's most Net-literate radio talk-show host? Drop a line to Alan Colmes. Better yet, listen to his daily program.

Alan Colmes

Here is the most computer-knowledgeable radio talk show host in America. Drop a note to Alan and let him know how much you like his show, his liberal point of view, and his wry sense of humor. Colmes is the inventor of "Radio Graffiti," where anyone can call in and say one sentence about anything they want.

Mail:
Address: **alan@pipeline.com**
Address: **alancolmes@aol.com**

Adam Curry

Adam Curry, the former MTV VJ (video jock) and gossip personality is forging the link between big-time, TV-oriented music entertainment and the Internet. Aside from having an Internet mailbox, Curry — something of a computer nerd himself — has established a gopher and an electronic magazine. For more information, finger him at the address below.

See also: Television

Gopher:
Name: Metaverse
Address: **metaverse.com**

Mail:
Address: **adam@metaverse.com**

Bill Gates

Isn't it great that we all get to live on this Earth at the same time as Bill Gates? Send Mr. Microsoft a note and tell him how much you appreciate his efforts to save mankind.

Mail:
Address: **billg@microsoft.com**

Al Gore

No, there is no truth that the Vice President of the United States is really a Turing Machine. (Actually, he couldn't pass the test.) Write him and tell him how nice he looks on TV.

Mail:
Address: **vice-president@whitehouse.gov**

Mike Jittlov

Filmmaker and animator, creator of such cult films as *Wizard of Speed and Time*, Mike Jittlov is one of those lucky few who have an adoring set of fans, a Usenet fan club group, and an Internet address.

Mail:
Address: **jittlov@gumby.gg.caltech.edu**

Usenet:
Newsgroup: **alt.fan.mike-jittlov**

A B C D E F G H I J K L **M** N O P Q R S T U V W X Y Z

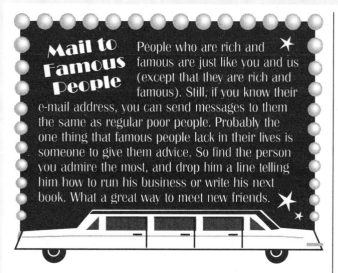

Mail to Famous People

People who are rich and famous are just like you and us (except that they are rich and famous). Still, if you know their e-mail address, you can send messages to them the same as regular poor people. Probably the one thing that famous people lack in their lives is someone to give them advice. So find the person you admire the most, and drop him a line telling him how to run his business or write his next book. What a great way to meet new friends.

Mitch Kapor

Introduce yourself to one of the pioneers of the personal computer era: Mitch Kapor, founder of Lotus (they make software, don't they?) and cofounder of the Electronic Frontier Foundation, staunch defender of your electronic rights.

Mail:
    Address: **mkapor@kei.com**

Edward Kennedy

Undoubtedly there is a thing or two you would like to say to Edward Kennedy — especially if you live in his political stomping ground. Now that the government has a passion for the Internet, you can find many politicians are becoming available electronically. Tell Ted what's on your mind, but be sure to include your snail mail address. He'll receive mail, but some regulation or other prevents him from replying electronically.

See also: Government, Politics

Mail:
    Address: **senator@kennedy.senate.gov**

Rush Limbaugh

Rush Limbaugh — the conservative radio and TV commentator with a huge audience of ditto-heads — is more an act of God than anything else. Send mail to the man who routinely performs with "half his brain tied behind his back." (If he were using his whole brain, he would be on the Internet, wouldn't he, not Compuserve.)

Mail:
    Address: **70277.2502@compuserve.com**

Roger McGuinn

Roger McGuinn, singer-songwriter, musician, and founder of the Byrds.

Mail:
    Address: **71571.672@compuserve.com**

Marvin Minsky

Talk to one of the fathers of artificial intelligence. Ask him if he knows if the Vice President of the U.S. is really a Turing Machine.

Mail:
    Address: **minsky@media.mit.edu**

Terry Pratchett

Humorous fantasy-based science fiction novelist Terry Pratchett has been compared to Douglas Adams and P.G. Wodehouse. Author of *Discworld*, Pratchett resides in England.

Mail:
    Address: **terryp@unseen.demon.co.uk**

Radio and TV Networks Electronic Mail Addresses

A list of mail addresses of many radio and television networks and stations around the world. For the United States section there are many specific programs or shows which can be contacted.

World Wide Web:
    URL: **http://www.helsinki.fi/~lsaarine/part2.html#RADIOs**

You Oughta Be On the TV

WHEN HARLEY WAS YOUNG, HE WAS ON THE RADIO, UNTIL ONE DAY HIS FATHER TOOK HIM OFF AND PUT THE LAMP ON INSTEAD.

IF YOU WANT YOUR SHOT AT THE BIG TIME, ALL YOU NEED TO DO IS CONTACT ONE OF THE MANY RADIO OR TV SHOWS WHOSE ELECTRONIC ADDRESS IS READILY AVAILABLE. TELL THEM WHO YOU ARE, HOW MUCH MONEY YOU EXPECT, AND THAT YOU ARE ONE OF OUR READERS. THE CONTRACT WILL, NO DOUBT, BE SENT TO YOU WITHIN A SHORT TIME.

Howard Rheingold

The author of *Higher Creativity, Tools for Thought,* and *Virtual Reality,* and former editor of the *Whole Earth Review.* His web page contains a few "Tomorrow" columns, speeches, bibliography, interviews, book reviews, and articles.

Mail:
Address: **hlr@well.sf.ca.us**

World Wide Web:
URL: **http://www.well.com/www/hlr**

Michael Tucker

Michael Tucker is a mild-mannered computer trade press writer who, at night, shucks off his stuffy journalist facade like a corn cob headed for the cooking pot and turns into a fast-stepping, high-spirited, Internet columnist who makes people laugh until they hurt. People all over the world are subscribing to Tucker's free weekly humor column. Be there or be square.

Mail:
Address: **mtucker@world.std.com**

James Woods

When not on the silver screen, this dynamic actor can be found catching up on his e-mail. Woods has starred in such movies as *Chaplin, The Specialist, Diggstown,* and *Citizen Cohn.*

Mail:
Address: **jameswoods@aol.com**

MATHEMATICS

Algebra Assistance

It's a total bummer when you are working on an equation at 3 o'clock in the morning and you have nobody to ask for help. Never again will you be left mathematically stranded. With this Usenet group, you will always have a place to turn. Too bad you can't take the computer in with you when you have a test.

Usenet:
Newsgroup: **alt.algebra.help**

American Mathematical Society

A variety of mathematical topics, including a moderation of Fermat's Last Theorem, mathematical publications, conference information, and access to other mathematical sites.

Gopher:
Name: American Mathematical Society
Address: **e-math.ams.com**

World Wide Web:
URL: **http://e-math.ams.org/**

Calculator

This probably won't help you with your 20-page mathematical theorem, but it will certainly do basic arithmetic. This is best used with a point-and-click browser.

World Wide Web:
URL: **http://www.charm.net/~web/Calc.html**

Need help with your Algebra?

Try **alt.algebra.help**. If anything goes wrong, tell your teacher that you can't hand in your homework because your dog ate the modem.

Calculus Graphics

A collection of graphical demonstrations in gif and mpeg formats for first year calculus. It includes sections on derivatives and differentials, computing the volume of water in a tipped glass, Archimedes' calculation of pi, and a bouncing ball.

World Wide Web:
URL: **http://www.math.psu.edu/dna/graphics.html**

Center for Geometry Analysis Numerics and Graphics

This web server focuses on the Center's research in differential geometry with particular emphasis on minimal surfaces, surfaces of constant mean curvature, surface and knot energies, along with applications of this research to material science and quantum physics.

World Wide Web:
URL: **http://www.gang.umass.edu/**

Center for Nonlinear Studies

The Center for Nonlinear Studies (CNLS) is a research institute devoted to nonlinear science. The CNLS coordinates a broad range of theoretical, experimental, and computational research programs. Check this page for more information on these programs and upcoming conferences and seminars.

World Wide Web:
URL: **http://cnls-www.lanl.gov/**

Centre for Experimental and Constructive Mathematics

The Centre for Experimental and Constructive Mathematics (CECM) explores and promotes the interaction of mathematics and modern computation and provides a computational environment for mathematical research.

World Wide Web:
URL: **http://www.cecm.sfu.ca/**

Chance Server

What exactly is a snowball's chance in hell? Check in at the Chance Server and you might find out. Get the Chance News, a bi-weekly report with popular news items that can be used in classroom settings to make teaching statistics and probability fun. (Not that it isn't normally fun, of course.) Teaching aids are also available.

World Wide Web:
URL: **http://www.geom.umn.edu/docs/snell/chance/welcome.html**

Commutative Algebra

A collection of abstracts and papers on the subject of commutative algebra in gzipped TeX format (.tex.gz).

Gopher:
Name: Commutative Algebra Gopher Server
Address: **hazlett.math.ndsu.nodak.edu**
Choose: **Commutative Algebra**

Consortium for Ordinary Differential Equations Experiments

Back issues of *The Journal of the Consortium for Ordinary Differential Equations Experiments*. Issues available are from 1992 and later.

Anonymous FTP:
Address: **ftp.hmc.edu**
Path: **/pub/CODEE/***

Differential Equations

The *Electronic Journal of Differential Equations* is a collection of academic papers that discuss all aspects of differential equations and is available in TeX and postscript formats.

Anonymous FTP:
Address: **ftp.unt.edu**
Path: **/EJDE/***

Guess how many items there are in the Trivia section.

E-Math BBS

The BBS of the American Mathematics Society. Offers conversation, software, and software reviews.

Telnet:
Address: **e-math.ams.com**
Login: **e-math**
Password: **e-math**

Electronic Journal of Combinatorics

Sponsored by the American Mathematical Society, this web page offers articles and research papers, and feature articles.

World Wide Web:
URL: **http://ejc.math.gatech.edu:8080/Journal/journalhome.html**

Electronic Journal of Differential Equations

The Electronic Journal of Differential Equations web server dedicated to all aspects of differential equations, integral equations, and functional differential equations and their applications.

World Wide Web:
URL: **http://ejde.math.swt.edu/**

Electronic Sources for Mathematics

This page links many mathematical resources on the Internet. It has links to electronic journals and zines, archives sites, and the home pages of other organizations such as the American Mathematical Society.

World Wide Web:
URL: **http://www.math.upenn.edu/MathSources.html**

Electronic Transactions on Numerical Analysis

This page, from Kent State University, is a yearly magazine with articles and abstracts about numerical analysis. There is a keyword index and prior issues are also online.

World Wide Web:
URL: **http://etna.mcs.kent.edu/**

Gallery of Interactive Online Geometry

If you're into geometry, this web page will get you off to a good start. Check out the QuasiTiler for visualizing plane cross-sections. Or check out Orbifold Pinball, the Teichmuller Navigator, or Cyberview-X.

World Wide Web:
URL: **http://www.geom.umn.edu/apps/gallery.html**

Geometry Center

The Geometry Center at the University of Minnesota is dedicated to computing and visualizing geometric structures and facilitates communication among mathematicians, and between mathematicians and the public.

World Wide Web:
URL: **http://www/geom.umn.edu/**

Geometry Literature Database

A BiBTeX database of papers on computational geometry at the University of Saskatchewan. This database is maintained by members of the computational geometry community.

World Wide Web:
URL: **http://www.cs.ruu.nl/people/otfried/html/geombib.html**

GNU Plot

Interactive Unix program for plotting mathematical expressions and data, complete with source.

Anonymous FTP:
Address: **aeneas.mit.edu**
Path: **/pub/gnu/gnuplot***

Archie:
Pattern: **gnuplot**

Hub Mathematics and Science Center

Take a few mathematicians and scientists, network them together, and suddenly you have The Hub, a service designed to help math and science researchers efficiently utilize telecommunications opportunities. The Hub offers a quarterly newsletter full of Internet usage tips and Internet and telecommunications resources. The Hub can also help you publish reports or requests for proposals.

World Wide Web:
URL: **http://hub.terc.edu/**

A B C D E F G H I J K L M N O P Q R S T U V W X Y Z

Illinois Mathematics and Science Academy

The Illinois Mathematics and Science Academy is a
public high school for students talented in science and
mathematics. The Academy's web server is administered
entirely by students and has information on clubs,
organizations, activities and events at the Academy.

World Wide Web:
URL: **http://www.imsa.edu/**

K-theory Preprint Archives

An archive of research papers in the mathematics field
of K-theory. Articles include *Adams operations on higher
K-theory*, *Finite domination and Novikov rings*, *An
Algorithmic Proof of Suslin's Stability Theorem for
Polynomial Rings*, and our favorite *Polylogarithmic
Extensions on Mixed Shimura varieties*.

World Wide Web:
URL: **http://www.math.uiuc.edu/K-theory/**

Logic

(1) The Internet is important to the human race. (2)
Before you can use the Internet, you must learn how it
works. (3) *The Internet Complete Reference* is the best
Internet book ever written. Therefore, it follows that (4)
anyone who has not bought *The Internet Complete
Reference* has not fulfilled his or her obligation as a
human being. For more complex questions of logic, read
this newsgroup, in which you will find discussions of
mathematics, philosophy and computation.

Usenet:
Newsgroup: **sci.logic**

Math Archives Gopher

Access to shareware and public domain software for both
PCs and Macs, as well as many other materials that can
be used to teach mathematics at the community college,
college, and university levels.

Gopher:
Name: University of Tennessee Knoxville
Address: **archives.math.utk.edu**
Choose: **Software (Packages, Abstracts and
Reviews)**

Math Articles

Documents on mathematics, including a fuzzy-logic tutorial,
FAQs, fractals, Putnam problems, the mathematics of
perspective, and other interesting topics.

Anonymous FTP:
Address: **ftp.spies.com**
Path: **/Library/Article/Math/***

Gopher:
Name: Internet Wiretap
Address: **wiretap.spies.com**
Choose: **Wiretap Online Library**
| **Articles**
| **Mathematics**

Math and Calculus Programs

Interesting and useful mathematics and calculus programs.

Anonymous FTP:
Address: **ftp.wustl.edu**
Path: **/edu/math/msdos/calculus/***

Math Gophers

A collection of over 100 gophers relating to mathematics.

Gopher:
Name: Lake Forest College
Address: **math.lfc.edu**
Choose: **Mathematics Related Items**
| **Other Mathematics Related Gophers**

Need Help? Try Internet: Help.

Math and Philosophy

Do you agree that even Frege can be faulted for insufficient tenacity in giving up his program after Russell's discovery of the eponymous paradox? Or do you think that ramified type theory, contextual definition of class abstracts, the doctrine of acquaintance, and the theory of proposition identity are just so much hot air? Sit in with people who really understand who shaves the barber (if the barber shaves everyone who does not shave himself). Just be careful to behave yourself: someone may prove that you do not really exist.

Usenet:
    Newsgroup: **sci.philosophy.tech**

Math Programs for the Mac

An ftp site that contains science and math software for Apple Macintosh computers.

See also: Software

Anonymous FTP:
    Address: **info.umd.edu**
    Path: **/software/Macintosh/Math-Science/***

Mathematical Association of America

The Mathematical Association of America is an organization of college and university mathematics teachers with the goal of advancing the mathematical sciences. This web page has links to math preprints, publications, career opportunities and other math resources on the Internet.

World Wide Web:
    URL: **http://www.maa.org/**

Mathematical Publications List

A copy of the *Literature Survey of Mathematica*, which lists publications dealing with math as applied in various areas such as physics and computers. The publications are broken down by field of application.

Anonymous FTP:
    Address: **ftp.uu.net**
    Path: **/doc/literary/obi/Mathematica/Lit.Survey**

Mathematical Research

Keep abreast of what is happening in the world of mathematics. Just the place to send your new proof of Fermat's Last Theorem that *does* fit in the margin of a book.

Usenet:
    Newsgroup: **sci.math.research**

Mathematical Sciences Server

The math server at the University of Durham has links to many mathematical-related services, including links to other math servers in the U.K. and elsewhere, the AMS gopher, the mathematics archive gopher, and Mathematics City.

World Wide Web:
    URL: **http://fourier.dur.ac.uk:8000/**

A B C D E F G H I J K L **M** N O P Q R S T U V W X Y Z

Excerpt from the Net...

```
Newsgroups: sci.math, sci.philosophy.tech, sci.lang, sci.logic
Subject: Is this finite or infinite?


> Well, then, if you're an ambitious logician, try your hand at
> describing the anaphoric construction (and finding the indirect
> quotation) in this example:
>      John didn't catch a fish, and he didn't eat it.

This is easy:  Quantify over concepts, and define the relation of things falling under
(singular or natural kind) concepts.  Then proceed to say that there is no object X
falling under the concept of fish, such that John caught X, or John ate X.  (Note that
this analysis works for unicorns just as well.)  As for the scope of indirect quotation,
it is implicit in the intentional aspect of John's sporting and alimentary failure --
since to catch X is to succeed in seeking that X comes in one's possession.  Again, all
of this is exceedingly well known from intensional logic.
```

Mathematics

The Queen of Sciences

What do you do when it's two in the morning and you need to remember all the characteristics of a vector space? You could go down to the all-night convenience store and ask the guy behind the counter. Or, you could call directory assistance and hope that the operator would know. But, if all else fails, why not send a request to the **sci.math** and let the Net help you.

(By the way, while we were researching this book, we came across a new proof for Fermat's Last Theorem that is more complete and easier to understand than Andrew Wiles' proof. His proof is long and cumbersome and runs into trouble in attempting to bound the order of a cohomology group which looks like a Selmer group for Sym^ 2 of the representation attached to a modular form. Our proof moves directly to elliptic curve theory and is much simpler. All in all, it is a marvellous proof but, unfortunately, there is not enough space here to write it down. What we can do, instead, is remind you that the largest known prime -- which is also the largest known Mersenne prime -- is 2^ 859433-1.)

Mathematical Topics at the Center for Scientific Computing

The Center for Scientific Computing in Finland collects together many gophers and web servers on the Internet that feature mathematic topics. This page also has a searchable database and information about how to get free mathematics software.

World Wide Web:
> URL: **http://www.csc.fi/math_topics/ General.html**

Mathematics City

Mathematics City is located in central WebWorld, and is a virtual city where you click on houses, doors, and streets to access mathematics resources on the Internet.

World Wide Web:
> URL: **http://sailfish.peregrine.com/wb/ww/ m(2,2,0,0)[Mathematics City]**

Mathematics General Discussion

A general discussion of things mathematical. Remember, a person who knows his numbers is a person you can count on.

Usenet:
> Newsgroup: **sci.math**

Mathematics Resource Pointers

This web page holds a collection of links to dozens of mathematical resources on the Internet including societies and organizations, universities and math software archives.

World Wide Web:
> URL: **http://www.ama.caltech.edu/ resources.html**

Mathematics Servers

A collection of links to university math departments, math organizations and math servers on the Internet.

World Wide Web:
> URL: **http://www.cs.fsu.edu/projects/group2/ math.html**

MathWorks

Discussions regarding Matlab, the calculation and visualization package from MathWorks.

Usenet:
> Newsgroup: **comp.soft-sys.matlab**

World Wide Web:
> URL: **http://www.mathworks.com/**

> **No need to get lost in gopher space. Try Veronica.**

NetLib Software Server

Math software programs via mail. Include the line **send index** in the body of a mail message.

Mail:
Address: **netlib@ornl.gov**
Address: **netlib@uunet.uu.net**

World Wide Web:
URL: **ftp://netlib.att.com/netlib/master/ readme.html**

New York Journal of Mathematics

Math is for mental studs. Get a good workout by reading various abstracts by smart people who know their numerical concepts.

World Wide Web:
URL: **http://nyjm.albany.edu:8000/nyjm.html**

Nonlinear Dynamics

Preprints and programs on nonlinear dynamics, signal processing, and related subjects, including fractal papers.

See also: Computers: Pictures, Computers: Sound

Anonymous FTP:
Address: **lyapunov.ucsd.edu**
Path: **/pub/***

Numerical Analysis

It's amazing how many people still don't know a Tchebyshev polynomial from a fourth-order Runge-Kutte algorithm. Join the discussion with people who want more out of life than the simple L2 norm that seems to satisfy a whole world of mathematically disadvantaged social scientists.

Usenet:
Newsgroup: **sci.math.num-analysis**

pi Page

The pi page has a link to the first 50,000 digits of pi, a program to compute pi to many more digits, information on arctangent formulae and other quaint numerical facts.

World Wide Web:
URL: **http://www.ccsf.caltech.edu/~roy/pi.html**

pi to 1 Million Digits

One million digits of the constant pi. Provided by Project Gutenberg.

Gopher:
Name: University of Minnesota
Address: **gopher.micro.umn.edu**
Choose: **Libraries**
| **Electronic Books**
| **By Title**
| **PI to One Million Digits**

pi to 1.25 Million Digits

The first 1.25 million digits of pi, that mathematical wonder!

Anonymous FTP:
Address: **ftp.wustl.edu**
Path: **/doc/misc/pi/***

A
B
C
D
E
F
G
H
I
J
K
L
M
N
O
P
Q
R
S
T
U
V
W
X
Y
Z

Society for Industrial and Applied Math

The Society for Industrial and Applied Mathematics gopher provides information about activities and issues of interest to applied and computational mathematicians, engineers, and scientists who use mathematics and computers.

Gopher:
Name: Society for Industrial and Applied Mathematics
Address: **gopher.siam.org**

Spanky Fractal Database

The Spanky Fractal Database (Spanky is the name of the computer) is a collection of fractal and fractal-related material for free distribution on the Net. There are links to fractal generating software, online images, documents, and other sites that offer fractal resources.

World Wide Web:
URL: **http://spanky.triumf.ca/**

Square Root of 2

The square root of 2 to many decimal places.

Gopher:
Name: University of Minnesota
Address: **gopher.micro.umn.edu**
Choose: **Libraries**
   | **Electronic Books**
   | **By Title**
   | **Square Root of 2**

Statistics

When you need a fuzzy clustering algorithm, do you go to a statistical mathematician or a mathematical statistician? Try both. Two complementary newsgroups for people who are approximately right, some or all of the time.

Usenet:
Newsgroup: **sci.math.stat**
Newsgroup: **sci.stat.math**

Statistics and Operations Research

In addition to links to math organizations and resources, this web page features statistics, constraints programming, and decision/risk analysis.

World Wide Web:
URL: **http://www.yahoo.com/**
   Science/Mathematics/
   Statistics_and_Operations_Research/

StatLib Archives

Programs, datasets, instructions, and help for statisticians. Include the line **send index** in the body of your mail message.

Gopher:
Name: StatLib Server
Address: **lib.stat.cmu.edu**

Mail:
Address: **statlib@lib.stat.cmu.edu**

StatLib Gopher Server

Presents a gopher view of the StatLib archives, a repository of statistical software and database archival material.

Gopher:
Name: Carnegie Mellon University
Address: **lib.stat.cmu.edu**
Choose: **StatLib Gopher Server**

Symbolic Algebra

The invention of symbolic computational programs has added a whole new set of tools to the arsenal of the practicing mathematician. This group discusses such tools, as well as the related mathematical issues. Talk about Mathematica, Maple, Macsyma, and Reduce. (My goodness, is Reduce still around? We remember using it back in the mid-1970s. Oh, how symbolic algebra makes one feel old.)

Usenet:
Newsgroup: **sci.math.symbolic**

Symbolic Mathematical Computation Information Center

SymbolicNet focuses on the areas of symbolic and algebraic computation known as computer algebra. SymbolicNet hopes to automate mathematical computations of all sorts. This web page is the home page of this organization and has links to many resources and documents relating to this area of mathematics.

World Wide Web:
URL: **http://symbolicnet.mcs.kent.edu/**

Teaching: Elementary and High Schools

If you hated math in school, how do you think your teachers felt? Find out by taking a look at these discussion groups: **k12** for teachers in all grades, **.stat** for teachers of statistics.

Usenet:
Newsgroup: **k12.ed.math**
Newsgroup: **sci.stat.edu**

Virtual Library of Math

A page of links to jokes, analysis, math gophers, newsgroups, and lots of other neat math stuff.

World Wide Web:
URL: **http://euclid.math.fsu.edu/Science/ math.html**

Weights and Measures

A detailed conversion table, including mathematical notation, metric interrelationships, and metric equivalents.

Gopher:
Name: University of Chicago
Address: **gopher.uchicago.edu**
Choose: **Browse resources . . .**
I **Texts, Data and Software**
I **Reference Works**
I **Weights and Measures**

MEDICINE

AIDS

Acquired Immune Deficiency Syndrome and the HIV virus. Read this moderated newsgroup to keep up to date on the medical treatments of AIDS, including the AIDS daily summary from the Centers for Disease Control and Prevention (CDC) National AIDS Clearinghouse.

Usenet:
Newsgroup: **sci.med.aids**

AIDS Frequently Asked Questions

Excerpts and highlights from the Usenet newsgroup **sci.med.aids** covering many aspects of the AIDS/HIV epidemic, including causes (with discussions of some controversial theories), treatment, prevention and political issues.

Anonymous FTP:
Address: **ftp.hmc.edu**
Path: **/pub/science/sci.answers/.mirror.OLD/ aids-faq/***

> ## You are what you think.

AIDS Information Newsletter

The *AIDS Information Newsletter* from the U.S. Department of Veterans Affairs AIDS Information Center is a biweekly electronic publication that serves VA medical facilities. The target audiences of this newsletter are health care professionals, librarians, and educators. Sections include safe sex information, women and HIV infection and tuberculosis and HIV.

World Wide Web:
URL: **http://cornelius.ucsf.edu/~troyer/safesex/ vanews/**

AIDS Information via CHAT Database

CHAT (Conversational Hypertext Access Technology) database system. You can ask questions of this database in plain English. It correctly interprets an amazing number of questions and instantly provides answers about AIDS — especially in Canada.

Telnet:
Address: **debra.dgbt.doc.ca**
Port: **3000**

AIDS Mailing List

A mailing list for medical issues related to AIDS, as well as some discussion of political and social issues.

Listserv Mailing List:
List Address: **aids@rutvm1.rutgers.edu**
Subscription Address:
listserv@rutvm1.rutgers.edu

AIDS Statistics

A mailing list for the distribution of the latest AIDS statistics, primarily from the Centers for Disease Control's monthly AIDS Surveillance Report. Other agencies' data is also disseminated when it's available.

Internet Mailing List:
List Address: **aids-stat@wubios.wustl.edu**
Subscription Address:
aids-stat-request@wubios.wustl.edu

AIDS Treatment News and Facts

AIDS treatment news, access to an AIDS BBS, newsletters, statistics, and much more AIDS-related information.

Gopher:
Name: National Institute of Health
Address: **odie.niaid.nih.gov**
Choose: **AIDS Related Information**

Allergies

Sneezing, coughing, runny nose, itchy eyes, funny red bumps and a general miserable feeling are a few of the symptoms of allergies which plague millions of people around the world. Find out more about this aggravating condition. Doctors, scientists, researchers and those who suffer from allergies gather to discuss causes and treatments for allergy conditions.

Usenet:
Newsgroup: **alt.med.allergy**

Anatomy Teaching Modules

Some days there are just not enough cadavers to go around. Not to worry. Learn anatomy online with these teaching modules. They come complete with information text as well as images.

See also: Health

World Wide Web:
URL: **http://www.rad.washington.edu/ AnatomyModuleList.html**

Anesthesiology

Discussion of topics and dissemination of information related to anesthesiology.

Gopher:
Name: State University of New York
Address: **eja.anes.hscsyr.edu**

Listserv Mailing List:
List Address: **anest-l@ubvm.cc.buffalo.edu**
Subscription Address:
listserv@ubvm.cc.buffalo.edu

World Wide Web:
URL: **http://www.med.nyu.edu/ruskin/ ruskin-intro.html**

Subscribe to the *Anesthesiology* mailing list and find out what happens when the lights go out.

Guess how many items there are in the Trivia section.

Biomedical Engineering

If you ever find medical imaging too boring, this is the place to be: signal processing, biomedical engineering — your cup will runneth over.

Usenet:
Newsgroup: **sci.engr.biomed**

Brain Tumors

Whether you are a patient, family member, or a professional who has had experience dealing with brain tumors, you are welcome here. This forum discusses topics related to brain tumors.

Listserv Mailing List:
List Address: **braintmr@mitvma.mit.edu**
Subscription Address: **listserv@mitvma.mit.edu**

Breast Cancer Information

This web page is a clearinghouse for information about breast cancer. Funded by the State of New York, this server has links to new information, detecting breast cancer, information for health professionals, and links to other cancer servers and resources.

World Wide Web:
URL: **http://nysernet.org/bcic/**

CancerNet

Health and clinical information about cancer and cancer research.

Gopher:
Name: National Institute of Health
Address: **gopher.nih.gov**
Choose: **Health and Clinical Information I CancerNet Information**

Mail:
Address: **cancernet@icicb.nci.nih.gov**

Chronic Fatigue Syndrome

It's no fun being tired all the time. You miss the end of movies, you can't get enough speed up to slide into home plate, and it's hard to make it across the intersection before the DON'T WALK sign lights up. Currently **cfs-med** membership is limited to physicians to discuss the diagnosis and treatment of chronic fatigue syndrome and related topics. Membership might become open to non-physician participation, so it doesn't hurt to inquire if you are interested in joining the group. The other lists, and of course, the newsgroup, are open to anyone interested in chronic fatigue syndrome.

Listserv Mailing List:
   List Address: **cfs-news@list.nih.gov**
   Subscription Address: **listserv@list.nih.gov**

   List Address: **cfs-med@list.nih.gov**
   Subscription Address: **listserv@list.nih.gov**

   List Address: **cfs-l@list.nih.gov**
   Subscription Address: **listserv@list.nih.gov**

Usenet:
   Newsgroup: **alt.med.cfs**

Croatian Medicine

Keep informed on the latest events in Croatian medicine. This is a good tool for organizing medical and humanitarian help for this country in distress.

Listserv Mailing List:
   List Address: **cromed-l@aearn.edvz.univie.ac.at**
   Subscription Address:
      listserv@aearn.edvz.univie.ac.at

Crohn's Disease and Colitis

Intestinal disorders are painful and debilitating. Sufferers of Crohn's disease and colitis can find support and information on this newsgroup. Friends and family members — as well as those who have intestinal disorders — participate in technical discussions about health and personal discussions about how these diseases affect their lives.

Usenet:
   Newsgroup: **alt.support.crohns-colitis**

Cryonics Frequently Asked Questions

Cryonics is the practice of freezing a recently deceased person in the hope that one day science will be able to cure the dead person's malady and restore him or her to life. This collection of documents deals with many of the issues involved in cryonics, including such gems as the question of whether it's better to freeze the whole body, or just the head.

Anonymous FTP:
   Address: **ftp.hmc.edu**
   Path: **/pub/science/sci.answers/.mirror.OLD/**
      cyonics-faq/*

Cystic Fibrosis

Cystic fibrosis is not just a medical issue. It's also a holistic and personal issue. Welcome to the discussion group that covers all these categories. You can get information on the latest medical advances as well as therapeutic and nutritional treatments. This is also a place for CF patients to share their frustrating encounters with the medical-industrial complex or with bias in school or at work.

Listserv Mailing List:
   List Address: **cystic-l@yalevm.cis.yale.edu**
   Subscription Address:
      listserv@yalevm.cis.yale.edu

Excerpt from the Net...

```
Newsgroups: sci.bio,sci.med,alt.sex,sci.engr.biomed
Subject: The Physiology of Being "Turned On".

When women are "turned on" they can go anything from being mildly dizzy
to nauseous (and almost vomiting) in extreme cases.

What released chemical in the body is causing this? Are there any
references for the physiology of being turned on?

Why doesn't this seem to happen to men?
```

A B C D E F G H I J K L M N O P Q R S T U V W X Y Z

Excerpt from the Net...

```
Newsgroup: sci.med.dentistry
Subject: Need stories about jaw wiring

I am looking for humorous anecdotes
about patients who have had their jaws
wired shut,especially for the purpose
of weight control.

Please E-mail me direct at:
xxxxx.ucla.edu

Thank you,
Xxxxxxx Xxxxxxxxx, D.M.D.
```

Dentistry

Long in the tooth or down in the mouth, everyone is welcome to this discussion on dentists, materials and dental techniques. Whether you need help on deciding if implants are better than a bridge, or you just want to read humorous stories about people who have had their jaws wired shut, nothing is more exciting and breathtaking than modern dentistry.

Usenet:
    Newsgroup: **sci.med.dentistry**

Dermatology List

If it's itchy or scratchy or blotching or peeling, it's probably a matter for the dermatologist. This list is moderated and is open to physicians who practice dermatology (the people who really know that beauty is only skin deep).

Listserv Mailing List:
    List Address: **derm-l@yalevm.cis.yale.edu**
    Subscription Address:
        listserv@yalevm.cis.yale.edu

Digital Imaging and Communications

Join discussions of the technical details of digital imaging and communications as practiced in bio-engineering and medicine.

Usenet:
    Newsgroup: **alt.image.medical**
    Newsgroup: **comp.protocols.dicom**

Immune System Talk

You can take our word for it. The immune system is where it's at -- medically speaking -- in the 21st Century. We prepict that all kinds of conditions will be treated by modifying the immune system and that desensitization by oral ingestion of particular substances will become the modality of choice for many illnesses that are being treated today by drugs. For example, certain types of arthritis will be treated by eating chicken soup (or at least the collagen by-products). We further predict that one day some smart fellow is going to take a close look at those homeopathic remedies that actually work, put them together with current immune system theory and treatment, and snarf a Nobel prize for him- or herself. In the meantime, there is no need for you to be out in the ether. You can follow what the specialists are saying by subscribing to the immune system mailing list.

Diseases Involving the Immune System

Having no immune system is like going away on a vacation and leaving all the doors and windows open. Diseases such as chronic fatigue syndrome, lupus, candida, hypoglycemia, and others manifest themselves in the immune system and wreak havoc on all the other systems in your body. This unmoderated forum is designed as a support group for people with immune-system breakdowns.

See also: Health

Internet Mailing List:
    List Address: **immune@weber.ucsd.edu**
    Subscription Address:
        immune-request@weber.ucsd.edu

Do Power Lines Cause Cancer?

A document that discusses scientific and medical aspects of the claims that electromagnetic fields generated by high-tension power lines cause cancer.

Anonymous FTP:
  Address: **ftp.hmc.edu**
  Path: **/pub/science/sci.answers/.mirror.OLD/
    powerlines-cancer-FAQ/***

Drugs Information

Read the latest reports and journals from the Food and Drug Administration's database. Called Medline, the database has the latest information.

Telnet:
  Address: **library.umdnj.edu**
  Login: **library**

  Address: **utmem1.utmem.edu**
  Login: **harvey**

E.T. Net

An information system run by the National Library of Medicine featuring conferences on computer-aided education in health sciences, hypermedia, expert systems, patient simulations, nursing care, computer hardware and software — including medical shareware.

Telnet:
  Address: **etnet.nlm.nih.gov**
  Login: **etnet**

Endometriosis

Read discussion on all aspects of endometriosis, with emphasis on coping with the disease and its treatment. Anyone is welcome to participate in the discussion whether or not they actually have the disease. This list offers a convenient way to exchange information and promote discussion of current treatments, research, and educational literature.

See also: Health, Women

Listserv Mailing List:
  List Address: **witsendo@dartcms1.dartmouth.edu**
  Subscription Address:
    listserv@dartcms1.dartmouth.edu

Epilepsy Information via CHAT Database

CHAT (Conversational Hypertext Access Technology) database system. You can ask questions of this database in plain English. It correctly interprets an amazing number of questions and instantly provides answers about epilepsy.

Telnet:
  Address: **debra.dgbt.doc.ca**
  Port: **3000**

Forensic Medicine

Articles on forensic medicine, the application of the principles and practice of medicine to the needs of the law, including diagnostic criteria in surgical pathology.

Gopher:
  Name: MedCal
  Address: **gopher.vifp.monash.edu.au**
  Choose: **Medical
    | Forensic Medicine**

MUDs are real (sort of).

Genetic Sequence Data Bank

Genetic sequence data, a database search utility, and other databases of interest to molecular biologists.

Gopher:
Name: National Institute of Health
Address: **gopher.nih.gov**
Choose: **Molecular Biology Databases**

DNA Cookbook

Boy, there's nothing we like more than sitting home on Friday night and cooking up a great big batch of DNA. Then we leave it in the bathtub for two or three million years and see if it evolves into anything. Unfortunately, the hardest part is getting new ideas about what base pair sequences to use. That's why we love the *Genetic Sequence Data Bank*: there are so many great patterns for making enzymes that you'll never get bored. Best of all, there are no service charges or snooty tellers to deal with.

Genetics Bank

A genetics database, including nucleic acid and protein sequence provided by the National Center of Biotechnology Information (part of the National Library of Medicine). You query this database by mail.

Mail:
Address: **blast@ncbi.nlm.nih.gov**
Body: **help**

Address: **gene-server@bchs.uh.edu**
Body: **help**

Address: **retrieve@ncbi.nlm.nih.gov**
Body: **help**

German Cancer Research Center

Medical and biological informatics, image processing research including images, and links to demonstrations and other servers.

World Wide Web:
URL: **http://mbi.dkfz-heidelberg.de/**

Hippocratic Oath

The full text of the oath written by Hippocrates in the fourth century B.C. Doctors should read this once every year.

Anonymous FTP:
Address: **ftp.std.com**
Path: **/obi/Hippocrates/Hippocratic.Oath**

Address: **ftp.uu.net**
Path: **/doc/literary/obi/Hippocrates/ Hippocratic.Oath**

History of Medicine Division

The web page of the National Institute of Health's History of Medicine Division. This page has links to articles and online exhibits, including a searchable database of over 60,000 images.

World Wide Web:
URL: **http://www.nlm.nih.gov/hmd.dir/hmd.html**

Home Test Kits

Information on home test kits for colorectal cancer, home pregnancy, and glucose. There is also a direct link to the UK Pharmacy home page.

World Wide Web:
URL: **http://kerouac.pharm.uky.edu/ testindex.html**

HyperDoc

The National Library of Medicine gives you electronic access to their online database services, multimedia exhibits on the history of medicine, and almost 60,000 medical-related images.

World Wide Web:
URL: **http://www.nlm.nih.gov/**

Infertility

If at first you don't succeed, try try again. If you still don't succeed, check out this newsgroup to see if you are doing something wrong. Discussion covers the causes, solutions and treatments for infertility in both men and women.

Usenet:
Newsgroup: **alt.infertility**

Life-Threatening Medical Emergencies

This server offers instructions on what to do when there is a medical emergency. There are separate threaded links to follow depending on the problem and whether the patient is a child or adult. Maladies include when breathing stops, the heart stops, choking and other airway obstructions.

World Wide Web:
URL: **http://www.seas.upenn.edu/ ~lzeltser/first.aid.html**

MEDCAL

The Medical Computer Assisted Learning Resource Archive contains information on research in progress, software packages, developmental tools, and other general information related to this field.

Gopher:
Name: MedCal
Address: **gopher.vifp.monash.edu.au**
Choose: **Medical**
 l **MEDCAL - Medical Computer Assisted Learning Resource Archive**

Medical Education Information Center

The Medical Education Information Center web page offers access to education programs, a library of publications, information for health care professionals and medical informatics.

World Wide Web:
URL: **http://hyrax.med.uth.tmc.edu/**

Looking for an anonymous ftp file? Try Archie.

Medical and Health Information

Offers access to a large number of medical resources from a single menu, including Camis, CancerNet, Medinfo, and many more.

Gopher:
Name: Albert Einstein College of Medicine
Address: **gopher.aecom.yu.edu**
Choose: **Internet Resources**
 l **Medical/Health Information**

Medical Libraries

Discussions on the care and feeding of medical libraries (and medical librarians).

Usenet:
Newsgroup: **bit.listserv.medlib-l**

Medical Physics

Here is the forum for medical physicists (those nice people who give you radiation therapy). Do they really glow in the dark or is that just an old wives' tale?

Usenet:
Newsgroup: **sci.med.physics**

Medical Resources

A guide to and large list of medical resources on the Internet.

Anonymous FTP:
Address: **ftp.funet.fi**
Path: **/pub/doc/library/medical_resources.txt.Z**

Medical Software

Macintosh software useful to the health science professional.

Anonymous FTP:
Address: **archie.au**
Path: **/micros/mac/umich/misc/medical/***

Address: **mac.archive.umich.edu**
Path: **/mac/misc/medical/***

Gopher:
Name: MedCal
Address: **gopher.vifp.monash.edu.au**
Choose: **Medical**
 l **MEDCAL - Medical Computer Assisted Learning Resource Archive**
 l **Software and Demos for downloading**

Medical Software and Data

An archive of software and documentation aimed at fostering educational and practical uses of computers in medicine and health sciences.

Anonymous FTP:
Address: **ftp.unicamp.br**
Path: **/pub/medicine/***

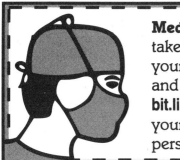

Med students: take time from your studies and check out **bit.listserv.medforum**, your own personal forum.

Medical Students

One would think that med students wouldn't have time to hang out on the Internet because they are always in a classroom somewhere with their hands thrust deep into some formaldehyde-soaked cadaver examining its medulla oblongata and vermiform appendix. But as addictive and distracting as the Internet can be, it's not surprising to find a place where medical students from around the world can gather to discuss anything relating to being a med student — labs, study habits, diseases, residencies, exhaustion, and overwork.

See also: Education: Students, Health

Listserv Mailing List:
List Address: **medstu-l@unmvma.unm.edu**
Subscription Address: **listserv@unmvma.unm.edu**

Medical Students Forum

Medical students voice their doubts and opinions in this moderated forum. Not a medical student yourself? Not to worry. Tune in and eavesdrop on what the future healers of America are up to.

Usenet:
Newsgroup: **bit.listserv.medforum**

Medicine General Discussion

Here is the agora of the Usenet medical community. Need to find out the etiology of kidney stones? Need to find out what "etiology" means? This is the place for you. General, free-flowing talk on everything medical. (Does anyone have a cure for a chrono-synclastic infidibulum?)

Usenet:
Newsgroup: **sci.med**

Mednews

An electronic journal dedicated to what is new and exciting in the field of medicine.

Usenet:
Newsgroup: **bit.listserv.mednews**

Mood Disorders Server

The Mood Disorders Server offers access to FAQ files on the drugs Prozac and Effexor, a hypertext FAQ on depression, other resources relating to depression, the writings of Ivan Goldberg, and links to other related resources including a server devoted to adult Attention Deficit Disorder.

World Wide Web:
URL: **http://avocado.pc.helsinki.fi/~janne/mood/ mood.html**

Multimedia Textbooks

Informative medical texts on such topics as pediatric airway disease, lung anatomy, pulmonary embolus, diffuse lung disease and gastrointestinal nuclear medicine.

See also: Health

World Wide Web:
URL: **http://indy.radiology.uiowa.edu/ MultimediaTextbooks.html**

National Cancer Center

CancerNet documents are available online which contain physician and patient diagnosis information on a wide variety of cancers.

Gopher:
Name: National Cancer Center (Tokyo, Japan)
Address: **gan.ncc.go.jp**

World Wide Web:
URL: **http://www.ncc.go.jp/**

National Cancer Center Database (Japan)

Database interfaces for physicians, patients, researchers, and other interested people. Other information includes design of clinical trials information, supportive care, cancer screening guidelines, news, and general information. A mailing list is also available.

Gopher:
Name: National Cancer Center (Tokyo, Japan)
Address: **gan.ncc.go.jp**
Choose: **CancerNet service**

National Library of Medicine

The National Library of Medicine is the world's largest library dealing with a single scientific/professional topic. It offers information about the library, factsheets about the commericial online services it provides, history of medicine exhibits and images, research and development activities, and links to other biomedical resources.

World Wide Web:
URL: **http://www.nlm.nih.gov/welcome.html**

National Library of Medicine Locator

The locator searches the book holdings database (CATLINE), the audiovisual holdings database (AVLINE), and the journal holdings database (SERLINE) of the U.S. National Library of Medicine. Information is also available on Library hours, policies, interlibrary loans and the National Network of Libraries of Medicine (NN/LM).

Gopher:
Name: Spencer S. Eccles Health Sciences Library Gopher
Address: **el-gopher.med.utah.edu**
Choose: **Health Sciences Resources on the Internet**

Telnet:
Address: **locator.nlm.nih.gov**
Login: **locator**

World Wide Web:
URL: **http://www.nlm.nih.gov/**

> ## Don't worry about technology, just enjoy yourself.

Nurses

Being an angel of mercy is not an easy chore. Not only is it hard work, but it can make your feet ache and give you varicose veins. This is not to say that it is without its rewards. Nurses have their own special places to talk on Usenet. Here they can share thoughts, ideas, anecdotes and technical information on all aspects of nursing.

Usenet:
Newsgroup: **alt.npractitioners**
Newsgroup: **bit.listserv.snurse-l**
Newsgroup: **sci.med.nursing**

Nursing

The Nightingale gopher and mailing list are all about nursing, including research, practice, education, nursing publications, professional nursing communications, and other nursing resources.

Gopher:
Name: Nightingale
Address: **nightingale.con.utk.edu**

Name: Warwick University
Address: **gopher.csv.warwick.ac.uk**
Port: **10001**

Listserv Mailing List:
List Address: **gradnrse@kentvm.kent.edu**
Subscription Address: **listserv@kentvm.kent.edu**

Nursing Web

The Nursing Web Information Service contains information on nursing, including archives for nursing issues, a nursing informatics and research list, links to Usenet newsgroups of interest to nurses, links to other nursing servers and gophers, and papers and conference information.

World Wide Web:
URL: **http//www.csv.warwick.ac.uk:8000/default.html**

Occupational Medicine

Need to pick out a back-friendly chair or an ergonomic keyboard? This discussion on occupational medicine will be just what the doctor would have ordered if he had thought of it.

Usenet:
Newsgroup: **sci.med.occupational**

A B C D E F G H I J K L **M** N O P Q R S T U V W X Y Z

Oncology

Not just for medical people, this multimedia oncology resource has a variety of information for patients, friends and family of patients as well as any medical field relating to cancer, including gynecology, pediatrics, and veterinary medicine. There is an art gallery which shows the creative endeavors of pediatric cancer patients. News, information, conferences, and more.

World Wide Web:
URL: **http://cancer.med.upenn.edu/**

Organ Transplant

One of the miracles of modern medicine is the ability to replace various body parts as needed. Of course, it's not that simple, but as the years go by the process becomes more advanced. This forum offers a means for organ transplant recipients, family members, and anyone interested in transplant issues to discuss their thoughts and experiences on the subject.

See also: Health

Listserv Mailing List:
List Address: **trnsplnt@wuvmd.wustl.edu**
Subscription Address: **listserv@wuvmd.wustl.edu**

Paramedics

If you have been eating an apple a day but you still need help, you may not be able to get the doctor to come over; however, the paramedics are always available. Join the discussion with paramedics and other emergency-oriented workers.

Usenet:
Newsgroup: **misc.emerg-services**

Pathology and Histology Server

Lessons in pathology, histology, and ENT, along with links to other medical resources.

World Wide Web:
URL: **http://virgil.mc.vanderbilt.edu/**

Pediatric Oncology Group

This web page is the Pediatric Oncology Group Statistical Office and it offers information on pediatric oncology protocols, and links to other pediatric oncology resources.

World Wide Web:
URL: **http://pog.ufl.edu/serv/htdocs/pog.html**

PET Scan Image Database

A database of Positron Emission Tomography (PET) scan images for a variety of human medical conditions. These images are accompanied by informative text files and are in jpeg format.

Gopher:
Name: Austin Hospital
Address: **gopher.austin.unimelb.edu.au**
Choose: **Digital Image Library**
| Austin Hospital PET Centre Image Database

Pharmacy

What a pickle. You are in charge of fundraising for the local PTA and you forgot the recipe for methylenedioxyamphetamine. Ask a pharmacist. Maybe you just need a pharmacist joke. (Did you hear about the pill counter who married the bean counter? They had a son who became a CPA, but would only work one hour before or three hours after meals.) Find out why pharmacy is the new glamour profession of the nineties.

Usenet:
Newsgroup: **sci.med.pharmacy**

World Wide Web:
URL: **http://157.142.72.77/pharmacy/pharmint.html**

Politics and Medicine

Talk is cheap, but medical care is not. What happens when an irresistible force (health care reform) meets an immovable object (the health care industry)? Join the ongoing debate and share your story of Uncle Willie and his gallbladder operation.

Usenet:
Newsgroup: **talk.politics.medicine**

TIRED OF EXPENSIVE MEDICAL BILLS? TALK IS CHEAP. DROP IN TO THE **talk.politics.medicine** DISCUSSION GROUP.

Post-Polio Syndrome

There are lingering disabilities associated with polio. A great deal of useful information has been compiled to educate people and assist sufferers in coping with this syndrome.

World Wide Web:
URL: **http://www.eskimo.com/~de**

Radiology

Just think, if people were like Superman, they could get jobs in hospitals and save everyone lots of money on X-rays. Realistically, this is pretty rare, so that's why radiologists are able to stay in the job market. This newsgroup discusses all aspects of radiology.

Usenet:
Newsgroup: **sci.med.radiology**

Repetitive Motion Injuries

A document containing a discussion of issues surrounding many types of stress-related repetitive motion injuries.

Anonymous FTP:
Address: **ftp.hmc.edu**
Path: **/pub/science/sci.answers/.mirror.OLD/ typing-injury-faq**

Repetitive Stress Injuries

A list for those in the Boston area interested in the Boston RSI (Repetitive Stress Injury) Support Group. Repetitive stress injuries — such as carpal tunnel syndrome, cumulative trauma disorders, tendonitis, and nerve compression — are caused by repetitive motion.

Internet Mailing List:
List Address: **boston-rsi@world.std.com**
Subscription Address:
boston-rsi-request@world.std.com

Telemedicine

Clinical consulting through computer networks. New technology for the world's second oldest profession.

Usenet:
Newsgroup: **sci.med.telemedicine**

Texas Cancer Data Center

This system provides computerized information on cancer demographics, resources, services and programs to anyone involved with cancer research or treatment in Texas.

Telnet:
Address: **txcancer.mda.uth.tmc.edu**
Login: **tcdc**

Topics In Primary Care

A web page with information and resources on many topics, including health promotion, cardiovascular, pulmonary, gatrointestinal, renal and urological, hematology and oncology, endocrinology, infectious diseases, geriatrics, and many other topics.

World Wide Web:
URL: **http://uhs.bsd.uchicago.edu/uhs/topics/ uhs-teaching.html**

Veterinary Medicine

If you were always the one to bring home the bird with the broken wing or if you liked to wrap the dog up in gauze bandages, then maybe your calling is veterinary medicine. There is a wealth of information on the Net about animals and the veterinary field.

See also: Zoology

Listserv Mailing List:
List Address: **vetinfo@ucdcvdls.bitnet**
Subscription Address: **listserv@ucdcvdls.bitnet**

List Address: **vetmed-l@uga.cc.uga.edu**
Subscription Address: **listserv@uga.cc.uga.edu**

World Wide Web:
URL: **gopher://netvet.wustl.edu:70/11n/vet**

Victorian Institute for Forensic Pathology

This organization specializes in histology, toxicology, microbiology and molecular biology. This server houses information and statistics on all of these subjects and others of interest, such as Sudden Infant Death Syndrome.

World Wide Web:
URL: **http://www.vifp.monash.edu.au/**

VIDIMED Project Image Gallery

A gallery of graphic images from the VIDIMED project. Images are medical in nature and mostly involve the human body and X-ray images.

World Wide Web:
URL: **http://www.artcom.de/projects/vidimed/**

Virtual Hospital

See this remarkable multimedia medical database that is available 24 hours a day. Multimedia textbooks and teaching files, lectures, clinical references, and medical history are just a few things offered here.

See also: Health

World Wide Web:
URL: **http://vh.radiology.uiowa.edu/**

Do you know someone who needs a doctor, but not right away?

Tell them to wait while you connect to the Virtual Hospital and teach yourself everything you need to know.

Virtual Library of Medicine

An index of links to many medical and bioscience resources and servers on the Internet.

World Wide Web:
URL: **http://golgi.harvard.edu/biopages/medicine.html**

MEDICINE: ALTERNATIVE

Alternative Medicine

Tired of legal drugs and poor bedside manner? Drop in to the alternative medicine forum where alternative-oriented people share alternative medical tips, alternative home remedies, and alternative approaches to healing. (If you can't make it, send an alternate.)

Usenet:
Newsgroup: **misc.health.alternative**

Alternative Medicine Home Page

Wander through this area and you will find link after link to interesting articles and files that pertain to alternative medicine whether it is for prevention or cure. Not only will you discover interesting methods of healing, but you will also be able to read medical conspiracy theories about surpressed cures, personal experiences of people who have been on the giving or receiving end of holistic treatments and some gentle philosophy about natural medicine.

World Wide Web:
URL: **http://www.yahoo.com/Health/Alternative_Medicine/**

Articles on Alternative Methods of Healing

Lots of people think they have discovered the secrets of health, vitality and the full-proof treatment of disease. Read articles on herbal cures for cancer, using light or oxygen for healing, vitamin usage and other files on alternative methods of healing.

World Wide Web:
URL: **http://werple.apana.org.au/sumeria/health.html**

If you lived here, you'd be home by now.

Ayurvedic Medicine

In Sanskrit, *Ayurveda* means "laws of health," and is the name of one of the four sacred Hindu texts. Ayurvedic medicine is based on Indian traditions over 3,000 years old. Read this newsgroup and learn about this ancient healing art and how it is practiced today.

Usenet:
> Newsgroup: **alt.health.ayurveda**

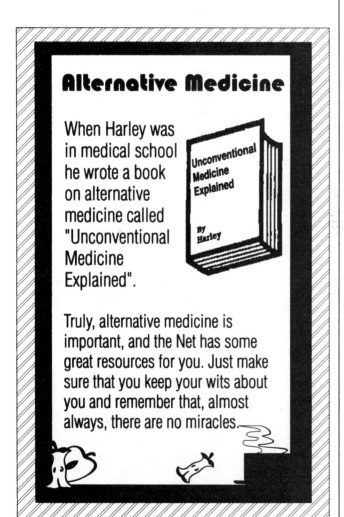

Alternative Medicine

When Harley was in medical school he wrote a book on alternative medicine called "Unconventional Medicine Explained".

Unconventional Medicine Explained
By Harley

Truly, alternative medicine is important, and the Net has some great resources for you. Just make sure that you keep your wits about you and remember that, almost always, there are no miracles.

Need a pick-me-up? Try a new Usenet group.

Essiac

It would be astounding to hear that someone had found a cure for cancer. According to some sources, this has already happened but it's not widespread knowledge. Read about the cure and the efforts made to suppress this information.

Anonymous FTP:
> Address: **werple.apana.org.au**
> Path: **/sumeria/health/essiac.txt**

> Address: **werple.apana.org.au**
> Path: **/sumeria/health/essiac2.txt**

World Wide Web:
> URL: **ftp://werple.apana.org.au/sumeria/ health/essiac.txt**

> URL: **ftp://werple.apana.org.au/sumeria/health/ essiac2.txt**

Good Medicine Magazine

While it's much more fun to smoke, drink and carouse, there is something to be said for the concept of prevention and caring for oneself. *Good Medicine Magazine* explores the ideas of prevention and the philosophy that traditional medicine and more holistic approaches to medicine should be combined to create a powerful method of healing. Read this bi-monthly online magazine and learn more about using prevention to combat sickness and disease.

World Wide Web:
> URL: **http://none.coolware.com/health/ good_med/**

Herb Archive

Text files give you all the details of medicinal herbs, such as the botanical name, where you can find them, the effects and side effects, and dosages. In addition, read related files on topics like herbs for animals, herbs to attract bees, and texts related to methods and philosophies of alternative medicine.

See also: Health

Gopher:
> Name: SunSITE Japan
> Address: **sunsite.sut.ac.jp**
> Choose: **SunSITE FTP Directory**
> | **academic-info**
> | **academic**
> | **medicine**
> | **alternative-healthcare**
> | **general**
> | **herbs**

A
B
C
D
E
F
G
H
I
J
K
L
M
N
O
P
Q
R
S
T
U
V
W
X
Y
Z

Herb Books and Sources

Herbal wisdom has been passed on from generation to generation by word of mouth. The occasional book on herbal medicine was written with delicate ink renderings of plant life and sage folk advice laid out beside the drawings. Now the information is much easier to find, and this list will tell you about books to read and sources from which you can get herb information.

See also: Books, Gardening, Hobbies

Gopher:
 Name: SunSITE Japan
 Address: **sunsite.sut.ac.jp**
 Choose: **SunSITE FTP Directory**
  | **academic-info**
  | **academic** | **medicine**
  | **alternative-healthcare**
  | **herbs**

Herb Hypercard Stack

Download this hypercard stack and you will have a nice batch of herb information at your fingertips. Flip through page after page of text on herbs, how to use them, and side effects, and see pictures that accompany the writing.

See also: Gardening, Health

Gopher:
 Name: Lund Institute of Technology
 Address: **nic.lth.se**
 Choose: **Arkiv**
  | **Lokal ftp** | **mac**
  | **info-mac** | **info**
  | **NonMacStuff**
  | **herbs-for-health-hc.hqx**

Herbal Caution

Just because an herb is good for you doesn't mean you should randomly stuff it into your mouth. Some herbs are toxic in high doses and some have side effects. (For instance, eating a huge amount of garlic before a blind date could result in a sudden loss of companionship.) Read up on cautionary use of medicinal herbs and learn how to be a prudent consumer.

See also: Gardening, Health, Medicine

Gopher:
 Name: Virginia Cooperative Extension
 Address: **gopher.ext.vt.edu**
 Choose: **VCE Subject Matter**
  | **Horticulture** | **Consumer Horticulture**
  | **Question Box & Press Releases**
  | **Vegetable and Herb Growing**
  | **Use Caution with Medicinal Herbs**

Herbal Medicine

Herbs have been used in healing for thousands of years, with their popularity occasionally rising and falling. Read these papers on how herbs are coming back into use in the medical world.

See also: Health

Gopher:
 Name: SunSITE Japan
 Address: **sunsite.sut.ac.jp**
 Choose: **SunSITE FTP Directory**
  | **academic-info**
  | **academic**
  | **medicine**
  | **alternative-healthcare**
  | **herbal-medicine**

Holistic Healing

Going to the doctor is no fun. Everyone is wearing a uniform, it's all sterile and rigid, and various people take turns poking you with sharp instruments. Experience a gentler alternative to medicine in the form of holistic concepts and methods of living, which are reported to be a more natural way of dealing with the hairpin turns on the road of life. A variety of holistic topics are discussed, such as states of consciousness, meditation, healthy diet, herbs, vitamins, rolfing, and massage.

See also: Medicine, New Age

Listserv Mailing List:
 List Address: **holistic@siucvmb.bitnet**
 Subscription Address: **listserv@siucvmb.bitnet**

Laetrile and Vitamin B17

Who would think that a little thing like a B-vitamin could cure cancer? Some researchers feel that it works, but usage of this treatment is not an accepted medical practice. Read up on the history and biology of how Laetrile and Vitamin B17 work.

World Wide Web:
 URL: **ftp://werple.apana.org.au/sumeria/health/laetrile.txt**

Anonymous ftp users: try logging in as "ftp".

Natural Childbirth Anecdotes

Long before drugs were invented and breathing exercises were developed, women were having babies. These anecdotes were compiled to show how there is something deep and instinctual inside a woman that makes her know how to do the right thing and when to do it during the birth process.

Anonymous FTP:
  Address: **werple.apana.org.au**
  Path: **/sumeria/health/birth.txt**

World Wide Web:
  URL: **ftp://werple.apana.org.au/sumeria/health/birth.txt**

Need to relax with some light reading? Try the Natural Childbirth Anecdotes.

Nutritional Healing

If we are what we eat, there is a lot of fast food running around on the planet. Discover ways to use food and nutrition for healing and prevention of sickness. This is probably the only medical advice you will see that actually says to eat cookies if you have a tummyache.

World Wide Web:
  URL: **ftp://werple.apana.org.au/sumeria/health/50tips.txt**

Oxygen and Ozone Therapy

Oxygen is one of our favorite things to breathe. It's handy because it keeps our brains and blood going and it's great when you want to keep experiencing the life process. See what else oxygen is good for by reading this article on oxygen and ozone therapy — a method of healing that is reported to be effective in combating lipid envelope virii such as AIDS and hepatitis.

Anonymous FTP:
  Address: **werple.apana.org.au**
  Path: /sumeria/health/h2o2.txt

World Wide Web:
  URL: **ftp://werple.apana.org.au/sumeria/health/h2o2.txt**

Excerpt from the Net...
(from the Nutritional Healing Web Site)

IMPOTENCE

...While surgery has been used to restore the blood flow, a low-fat diet may prove a more desirable cure. Dr. Padma-Nathan points out that an extremely low-fat, vegetarian, low-stress prescription has helped reverse coronary-artery blockage, so there's some reason to believe that whatever helps unblock one set of arteries could also help another. Even better: It's possible that men currently without problems may be able to prevent future impotence by carefully avoiding an artery-clogging diet to begin with...

A B C D E F G H I J K L M N O P Q R S T U V W X Y Z

MILITARY

Defense Conversion Subcommittee

Forums for associations, institutes, think tanks, and consultants for defense conversion. Includes weekly updates, government contacts, Russian conversion issues, and success stories.

Gopher:
Name: University of California San Diego
Address: **infopath.ucsd.edu**
Choose: **News & Weather | National News
| Economic Bulletin Board
| Defense Conversion Subcommittee**

Disarmament Discussion List

Discussion and monthly digests of military and political strategy, technology, sociology, and peace activism involved in accelerating disarmament of nuclear, conventional, and chemical weapons. **disarm-d** provides monthly digests of selected mail discussions that are posted to **disarm-l**. It also includes essays, papers, reviews, and excerpts from important publications.

Listserv Mailing List:
List Address: **disarm-d@uacsc2.albany.edu**
Subscription Address: **listserv@uacsc2.albany.edu**

List Address: **disarm-l@uacsc2.albany.edu**
Subscription Address: **listserv@uacsc2.albany.edu**

First World War

This international mailing list is a forum for discussing military history in general, World War I specifically, and the period from 1900 to 1920.

See also: History

Listserv Mailing List:
List Address: **wwi-l@ukanaix.cc.ukans.edu**
Subscription Address:
listserv@ukanaix.cc.ukans.edu

Military Collections

Collection of papers and viewpoints about the military, its people, policies, and practices, including book reviews and intelligence information.

Gopher:
Name: Whole Earth Lectronic Link
Address: **gopher.well.sf.ca.us**
Choose: **The Military, its People, Policies, and Practices**

Naval Fighting Ships

Information on American warships of World War II, including a directory battleships and cruisers. The data provided includes specifications and statistics. Also here is a career biography of Arleigh Burke, the Navy Cross winner for his leadership of the "Little Beavers" destroyer squadron.

Anonymous FTP:
Address: **ftp.spies.com**
Path: **/Gov/US-History/Naval/***

Gopher:
Name: Internet Wiretap
Address: **wiretap.spies.com**
Choose: **Government Docs (US & World)
| US Historical Documents
| Naval Fighting Ships**

Do you like ships that do not pass in the night?

Try the Naval Fighting Ships site. Maybe you can find something about the U.S.S. Stout (named after one of Rick's relatives).

Navy News Service

An electronic magazine with articles of interest to those in or interested in the Navy. Includes good articles on the Internet by famous authors and such items as the air show schedule for the Blue Angels. Mail for information on how to get on the mailing list, and where to ftp files.

Anonymous FTP:
>   Address: **ftp.ncts.navy.mil**
>   Path: **/pub/navpalib/news/navnews/Nnsinfo.txt**

Mail:
>   Address: **navnews@opnav-emh.navy.mil**

World Wide Web:
>   URL: **http://www.ncts.navy.mil/navpalib/news/**
>   **navnews/Nnsinfo.txt**

Generous movie fans take the time to create images of famous scenes and settings in their favorite movies. This means a wealth of art at your fingertips. You can easily import images you find on the Net into your favorite word-processing program.

> # The best way to make money is to give something away for free.

Navy Policy Book

The full text of the *United States Navy Policy Book*.

Gopher:
>   Name: Library of Congress
>   Address: **gopher.loc.gov**
>   Choose: **Government Information**
>   **| Federal Information Resources**
>   **| Information by Agency**
>   **| Military Agencies**
>   **| The Navy Policy Book**

NavyOnLine

A gateway to the Department of Navy's online resources. The NavyOnLine web page has links to many US Navy commands including the Naval Command Control and Ocean Surveillance Centers, Naval Postgraduate School, the Navy Public Affairs Library, the Naval Surface Warfare Centers, and many more. This page also has links to other Department of Defense resources.

World Wide Web:
>   URL: **http://www.navy.mil/**

Excerpt from the Net...

(from the electronic newspaper of the Australian Defence Force Academy)

```
ACC'S TATTOO FOR 11 DEC 93

Drill timings
Saturday 11 DEC 1993: Band, Pipes and Drums F/up 0845 Assembly Hall

0800: All Graduating Class to parade at the head of the parade ground for "reform"
      rehearsal.

0900: Corps in position to march onto practice parade ground (oval No.4).  Drum Corps
      required -- Band to rehearsals in the Assembly Hall.

1200: Corps dismissed.

NOTE: Everyone is to carry a water bottle on their belt.
```

A
B
C
D
E
F
G
H
I
J
K
L
M
N
O
P
Q
R
S
T
U
V
W
X
Y
Z

Siege Warfare

The neighboring castle has really been bothering you and now you feel that you should spend the weekend laying siege to it. The problem is, you just don't know where to start. Talk to the people who really know their siege warfare and can give you useful information on siege towers, sappers, ballistas, battering rams, catapults, and more. Get technical with the physics and mechanics of siege weapons or discuss the military strategies of attack and defense.

See also: History

Internet Mailing List:
List Address: **siege@bransle.ucs.mun.ca**
Subscription Address:
siege-request@bransle.ucs.mun.ca

Tattoo

The electronic newspaper of the Australian Defense Force Academy. Read about the daily regimen of cadets and other items of current interest.

Gopher:
Name: Australian Defense Force Academy
Address: **ccadfa.cc.adfa.oz.au**
Choose: **ACC Tattoos**

Technology Insertion

The Department of Defense likes to keep its war-fighters informed. We think that's a great idea, too. It keeps them from drag racing through quiet suburban neighborhoods. The DoD has put together a great deal of information on wireless communication, asynchronous transfer modes, and communication technology in general.

World Wide Web:
URL: **http://disa11.disa.atd.net/index.html**

U.S. Code of Military Justice

The first 12 chapters of this legal guide for the armed forces of the United States.

Anonymous FTP:
Address: **ftp.spies.com**
Path: **/Gov/UCMJ/***

Gopher:
Name: Internet Wiretap
Address: **wiretap.spies.com**
Choose: **Government Docs (US & World)
| Uniform Code of Military Justice**

The U.S. Code of Military Justice

Do you need an idea for a party game? Try this:

Download a copy of the U.S. Code of Military justice. Then, blindfold a "volunteer" and put him on trial. Arrange some chairs in a circle and interrogate the defendent until he "confesses". Now, you can choose your favorite part of the code and use it to select a suitable punishment.

Never again will people leave your parties complaining about being bored.

U.S. Military News

It's embarrassing when your country sends troops overseas to see some military action and you are the last one in the neighborhood to know about it. Especially if you are the General in charge. Don't be caught unawares. Keep up with U.S. Military news with the help of Clarinet.

Usenet:
Newsgroup: **clari.news.usa.military**

To dream is human, to telnet is divine.

Lots and lots of music on the Internet: check out the Music category.

War History

Speeches and editorial documents about wars and battles, mostly the Gulf War, but also World War II, Vietnam, secret wars of the CIA, and other conflicts.

Note: Notice the space in the path of the ftp site. If you're not using a graphical ftp interface, you can get into the "Gulf War" directory by typing: **cd Power/Gulf***

Anonymous FTP:
Address: **english-server.hss.cmu.edu**
Path: **Power/Gulf War/***

Gopher:
Name: Carnegie Mellon University
Address: **english-server.hss.cmu.edu**
Choose: **Government, Law and Society | Gulf War**

MISCHIEF

April Fools

The Ides of March is the least of the Internet's worries. The first day of April is the time when tricksters all over the world unleash their clever plots of lighthearted deceit. April Fools' pranks have been developed into an art form and are brought together in the form of archives which you can view from the safety of your own home. Archives date back to 1984.

Anonymous FTP:
Address: **sunsite.unc.edu**
Path: **/pub/academic/communications/ april-fools/***

World Wide Web:
URL: **http://sunsite.unc.edu/dbarberi/ april-fools.html**

There's no fool like an April Fool. Take a look at what other people have been doing and maybe you can get some good ideas for next year.

Big Book of Mischief

Information on how to make explosives, tennis ball cannons, carbide bombs, how to open locks, and other vital information for the budding soldier of fortune.

Anonymous FTP:
Address: **ftp.spies.com**
Path: **/Library/Untech/tbbom13.txt**

Gopher:
Name: Internet Wiretap
Address: **wiretap.spies.com**
Choose: **Wiretap Online Library | Questionables | The Big Book of Mischief**

Hack Gallery

Hack Gallery is a compendium of Interesting Hacks To Fascinate People (IHTFP) at MIT. The word "hack" refers to a clever, benign, and ethical prank which is challenging and amusing for the perpetrators. The gallery offers a large list of hacks sorted by topic, location, and the dates when they were perpetrated. There is also a FAQ, book list, and a "best of" hack list.

World Wide Web:
URL: **http://fishwrap.mit.edu/Hacks/ Gallery.html**

The Hack Gallery

Looking for a nice trick to play on someone? Try the MIT Hack Gallery for inspiration.

No need to put off putting off that special someone. The master hackers of the world have perpetrated all kinds of pranks and hoaxes and there is no reason why you can't join the ranks.

Practical Jokes

For serious enjoyment, what could be more good clean fun than embarrassing your friends and neighbors by making them look foolish? The dribble glass and plastic vomit are child's play. For real results, check out this newsgroup for ideas, techniques, and experiences with practical jokes. Make your loved ones say "uncle," and make your uncle say, "bork, bork, bork."

Usenet:
    Newsgroup: **alt.shenanigans**

Revenge

Landlord got you pissed? Teacher rapped you with a ruler? Your ex-SO (significant other) won't return your only copy of *The Little Prince*? Don't get mad, get even. Join the pros and find out just how smelly a fish in the ventilation duct can be. (Federal regulations require us to remind you of the ancient Chinese saying: "Before you set out for revenge, be sure to dig two graves.")

Usenet:
    Newsgroup: **alt.revenge**

Terrorist's Handbook

A few of the techniques and methods employed by people who use terror as a means to achieve their social and political goals. The web page is the entry point for a hypertext version of *The Terrorist's Handbook* that allows you to easily follow links between the sections of your interest. It includes sections on buying explosives and propellants, acquiring chemicals, explosive recipes, impact explosives, low order and high order explosives, ignition devices, projectile weapons, rockets and cannons, pyrotechnics, a list of suppliers, and even more.

Anonymous FTP:
    Address: **ftp.spies.com**
    Path: **/Library/Untech/terror.hb**

Gopher:
    Name: Internet Wiretap
    Address: **wiretap.spies.com**
    Choose: **Wiretap Online Library**
      | **Questionables**
      | **The Terrorist's Handbook**

World Wide Web:
    URL: **http://www.lysator.liu.se:7500/terror/
    thb_title.html**

Stuff You Are Not Supposed to Know About

Whether you are planning to blow up the World Trade Center, or merely explode a few small devices on the White House lawn, the *Terrorist's Handbook* is an invaluable guide to having a good time. Where else can you get such wonderful ideas about how to use up all that extra ammonium triiodide left over from last year's revolution?

MOVIES

Asian Movies

Experience the unique flavor of Asian movies. Fans and critics discuss action, adventure, horror and other genres of the Asian silver screen.

Usenet:
Newsgroup: **alt.asian-movies**

Blade Runner

A growing archive of all kinds of resources related to the movie *Blade Runner*. It includes FAQs, discussions, references, images from the movie, sound files, and links to other Blade Runner web pages.

World Wide Web:
URL: **http://kzsu.stanford.edu/uwi/br/off-world.html**

Blues Brothers

A hypertext FAQ with links to everything you could ever want to know about *The Blues Brothers* movie. Includes movie photos, lyrics, a transcript of the entire movie, sounds, fan club information, and other trivia and facts.

World Wide Web:
URL: **http://dec36.cs.monash.edu.au:1786/bluesbros/faq.html**

Cardiff's Movie Database Browser

This movie database allows you to search through a large movie database for your favorite movies, actors, quotes, and genres. Each movie selection has information about the movie, including a summary, awards, trivia, goofs, and movie rating information from users.

World Wide Web:
URL: **http://www.cm.cf.ac.uk/Movies/**

Cinema Discussion List

A mailing list dedicated to the discussion of cinema in all its aspects. Participants in this list hope to attract a variety of viewpoints and opinions.

Listserv Mailing List:
List Address: **cinema-l@american.edu**
Subscription Address: **listserv@american.edu**

Cinema Talk

Talk and idle chatter about the latest movies.

Internet Relay Chat:
Channel: **#cinema**
Channel: **#movies**

CinemaSpace

Film study is more than good popcorn and a comfortable seat. Learn more about cinema and the "new media" by reading scholarly articles and papers of a critical and philosophical nature. *CinemaSpace* is the name of a journal put out by the film studies program at U.C. Berkeley. Film clips are also available.

World Wide Web:
URL: **http://remarque.berkeley.edu:8001/~xcohen/**

Cult Movies

No matter how bad they get, no matter how outlandish they are or how far away from their origins they evolve, you will go see the hundredth version of a specific film. There are a few movies that have a cult following and fans feel so strongly about these films that they will see them at all costs. These newsgroups cover cult movies in general and some in particular like the *Evil Dead* movies and *Rocky Horror Picture Show*.

Usenet:
Newsgroup: **alt.cult-movies**
Newsgroup: **alt.cult-movies.evil-deads**
Newsgroup: **alt.cult-movies.rhps**
Newsgroup: **alt.cult-movies.rocky-horror**

Disney Comics and Cartoons

Wouldn't it be great if you could be a comic character for a day? You could fall off tall buildings and bounce, or have anvils drop out of the sky on your head without worrying about the repercussions. But life isn't the cartoons, so we have to make do with watching them on television or the movies, or even reading and discussing them on this mailing list.

See also: Fun, Television, Youth

Internet Mailing List:
List Address: **disney-comics@student.docs.uu.se**
Subscription Address:
disney-comics-request@student.docs.uu.se

Film Database

Search a database of synopses, cast lists, and other information on thousands of films released before 1987.

Gopher:
>   Name: Manchester Computing Centre
>   Address: **info.mcc.ac.uk**
>   Choose: **Miscellaneous items
> | Film database**

Mail:
>   Address: **movie@ibmpcug.co.uk**
>   Body: **help**

Film Mailing List

This mailing list is for the scholarly study of film, television, and radio, and the use of audiovisual materials as teaching tools. A forum where students of film can exchange ideas and research projects.

Listserv Mailing List:
>   List Address: **h-film@uicvm.uic.edu**
>   Subscription Address: **listserv@uicvm.uic.edu**

Film, Television, and Popular Culture

Scholars don't just study old stuff like dead languages and crumbling tombs. Some of them just watch movies and television. Now that is a fun way to be a scholar. Sit around with other people who study film, television and popular culture and the use of media in teaching. Read reviews of books, films and documentaries, announcements of grants, conferences and jobs, see course outlines, class handouts and syllabi, and participate in discussions on film history.

Listserv Mailing List:
>   List Address: **h-film@uicvm.bitnet**
>   Subscription Address: **listserv@uicvm.bitnet**

Film and TV Studies

Who knew there was so much to film and television? It's not just a matter of whether you enjoy it or not. There are all sorts of academic things involved like post-post-structuralist theory and pedagogical, historical and production issues to think about. This is a list for students, teachers and theorists who are interested in more than a good shoot-em-up flick or sitcom.

See also: Television

Listserv Mailing List:
>   List Address: **screen-l@ua1vm.ua.edu**
>   Subscription Address: **listserv@ua1vm.ua.edu**

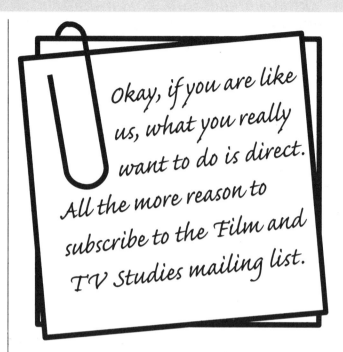

Okay, if you are like us, what you really want to do is direct. All the more reason to subscribe to the Film and TV Studies mailing list.

Film and Video Resources

A large guide to film and video resources on the Internet, including reviews, academic, popular, and technical discussions, filmographies, bibliographies, searchable databases, and much more.

World Wide Web:
>   URL: **http://http2.sils.umich.edu/Public/fvl/
>   film.html**

Filmmakers

Did you ever have fantasies about yelling "Roll 'em" and setting the movie-making process into motion with famous actors dashing about doing your directorial bidding? And if they don't do it your way, you can just yell "Cut!" and they stop? What power, what a heady feeling of creative control. Most of us will never have that thrill, but the next best thing is to have access to this list where people get together to discuss all aspects of motion picture production, with an emphasis on technical issues. The main topics of the list are construction and design issues for crews working on tight budgets. The subject of the list is film, not video.

Internet Mailing List:
>   List Address: **filmmakers@dhm.com**
>   Subscription Address:
>   **filmmakers-request@dhm.com**

Filmmaking and Reviews

Don't you hate it when you're sitting in a dark theater enjoying popcorn soaked in an obscene amount of butter and the hero of the flick has just been blown 30 feet into the sky by a car bomb when suddenly the guy behind you says, "Plastique does not have that sort of structured explosive radius. How unrealistic." Unfortunately, not everyone views movies in the same way. For some, film is art. For others, it is pure entertainment. It can also be a business or communications media. For amateur filmmakers, this list offers a source of help and a way to connect with other filmmakers and learn about new equipment and techniques.

Listserv Mailing List:
List Address: **film-l@itesmvf1.rzs.itesm.mx**
Subscription Address:
listserv@itesmvf1.rzs.itesm.mx

Horror Talk

Love a movie that scares you out of your wits? You're not alone. Join with other fans of horror films in this mailing list forum and talk about all your favorites.

Listserv Mailing List:
List Address: **horror@pacevm.dac.pace.edu**
Subscription Address:
listserv@pacevm.dac.pace.edu

Monster Movies

We love monsters. Even the bad ones. Monsters inevitably cause massive amounts of chaos, destruction, explosions and a variety of property damage, but that doesn't make them all bad. They are bound to be good for the economy in that they keep people employed — like construction workers, for instance. Check out the newsgroup devoted to the discussion of monster movies and get the real lowdown on Godzilla's family history.

Usenet:
Newsgroup: **alt.movies.monster**

> **Guys: The best way to impress a date is to invite her over and show her that you have a complete set of Harley's books.**

Movie Database Request Server

Perform detailed searches for movies by title, actor, or director. This database is large and contains a great deal of information.

Anonymous FTP:
Address: **cathouse.org**
Path: **/pub/cathouse/movies/database**

Address: **ftp.funet.fi**
Path: **/pub/culture/tv+film/lists**

Mail:
Address: **movie@ibmpcug.co.uk**
Body: **help**

Telnet:
Address: **ukanaix.cc.ukans.edu**
Login: **www**

World Wide Web:
URL: **http://www.cm.cf.ac.uk/Movies/moviequery.html**
URL: **http://www.msstate.edu/Movies/**

Movie and Film Festivals

This URL points to the "Movies and Films: Festivals" page on Stanford's web server. This page has direct links to information about the 11th World Festival of Animated Films, the Margaret Mead Film Festival, and the Philadelphia Festival of World Cinema. There is also a link to the International MPEG Bizarre.

World Wide Web:
URL: **http://www.yahoo.com/Entertainment/Movies_and_Films/Festivals/**

Movie Folklore

Interesting folklore about movies, including *The Wizard of Oz*, *The Little Mermaid*, *Beauty and the Beast*, and *Faces of Death*.

Anonymous FTP:
Address: **cathouse.org**
Path: **/pub/cathouse/urban.legends/movies/***

Address: **cathouse.org**
Path: **/pub/cathouse/urban.legends/movies/***

A
B
C
D
E
F
G
H
I
J
K
L
M
N
O
P
Q
R
S
T
U
V
W
X
Y
Z

> # Wanna change the system?
> # Try Anarchy.

Movie Information

A great listing of recent movie releases in the U.S., as well as movie reviews, filmographies, film facts, and access to many web pages devoted to specific movies.

World Wide Web:
URL: **http://www.cs.cmu.edu:8001/afs/cs.cmu.edu/ user/clamen/misc/movies/README.html**

Movie List

The canonical movie list, and more specific lists, including the James Bond movie list, railway movies, film noir list, Hitchcock information, vampire movie list, and others.

Anonymous FTP:
Address: **ftp.spies.com**
Path: **/Library/Media/Film/***

Gopher:
Name: Internet Wiretap
Address: **wiretap.spies.com**
Choose: **Wiretap Online Library**
| **Mass Media**
| **Film and Movies**

Movie Reviews

Thousands of reviews of all the popular movies, from a variety of different critics.

Anonymous FTP:
Address: **ftp.funet.fi**
Path: **/pub/culture/tv+film/reviews/***

Gopher:
Name: University of Minnesota
Address: **gopher.micro.umn.edu**
Choose: **Fun & Games**
| **Movies**

Usenet:
Newsgroup: **rec.arts.movies.reviews**

World Wide Web:
URL: **http://sfgate.com/~sfchron/movies/ videoguide.html**
URL: **http://www.service.com/PAW/thisweek/ movie_reviews.html**

Movies Archives

Volumes of movie information from the archives of Carnegie Mellon University including current and past Oscar information, film studios, Disney, and quotes from movies.

World Wide Web:
URL: **http://www.cs.cmu.edu:8001/afs/cs.cmu.edu/ user/mleone/web/movies.html**

Movies and Filmmaking

Movies are fun to watch from the audience, but don't you wonder what it would be like to be in on the action? Get in on the talk about movies and the making of movies from a creative or technical point of view. Fans and filmmakers frequent these newsgroups.

Usenet:
Newsgroup: **rec.arts.movies**
Newsgroup: **rec.arts.movies.production**

Movies News

Keep current on the latest news about movies and the movie industry. Clarinet offers you real news articles that will keep you up-to-date on the facts.

Usenet:
Newsgroup: **clari.apbl.movies**
Newsgroup: **clari.feature.movies**
Newsgroup: **clari.living.movies**
Newsgroup: **clari.news.movies**

If God really wanted us to live in the real world, why did he give us science fiction movies? (For that matter, why did he give us "The Internet Golden Directory?")

Science Fiction Movies

Movies of the science fiction genre are getting better all the time. Special effects are more creative and technically seamless, and the movie ideas are more outlandish. Discuss current science fiction movies as well as the more classical versions of the last few decades.

Usenet:
Newsgroup: **rec.arts.sf.movies**

weird movies

The only thing better than weird movies is reading about weird movies. If you think that the best things on film are the ones that make you scratch your head (or other parts of your anatomy), then this resource is for you. No need to feel left out when people at parties discuss films. Take a look at the Internet's weird movie list, and you will be more popular than a dog at a flea convention.

Society for the Preservation of Film Music

The home page of the Society for the Preservation of Film Music (SPFM) features information about the SPFM, and information about events, publications, and links to other film music resources.

World Wide Web:
URL: **http://www.electriciti.com/spfm/index.html**

Weird Movie List

A long, alphabetical list of weird movies, including descriptions.

Anonymous FTP:
Address: **ftp.spies.com**
Path: **/Library/Media/Film/weird.movi**

Gopher:
Name: Internet Wiretap
Address: **wiretap.spies.com**
Choose: **Wiretap Online Library**
   | Mass Media
   | Film and Movies
   | Weird Movie List

MUDS: GENERAL INFORMATION

Administrating MUDs

As a player, if you think it's an inconvenience when your MUD crashes, think how it would be if you were in charge of the machine that crashed it. Learn the ins and outs of being an administrator of a multiple user dimension. How do you start a MUD, and when you get it started, how in the world do you keep it going?

Usenet:
Newsgroup: **rec.games.mud.admin**

DikuMUDs

A DikuMUD is a text-based role-playing virtual reality. Slay a dragon, save a princess, drink a magic potion that will kill you (these are all optional, of course). If you love excitement, adventure, and fantasy, find out what DikuMUDs are all about.

Usenet:
Newsgroup: **rec.games.mud.diku**

A
B
C
D
E
F
G
H
I
J
K
L
M
N
O
P
Q
R
S
T
U
V
W
X
Y
Z

German Speakers

Sprechen Sie Deutsch? German-speaking MUDders not only experience the thrill of MUDding, but they can do it in German, making it extra special.

Usenet:
 Newsgroup: **alt.mud.german**

LPMUDs

Hack it, slash it, just make sure you clean up afterward. LPMUDs are text-based virtual realities where you can puzzle out a quest for advancement in the game or you can just find monsters to kill. Discover the adventurer within you. If you are already a hard-core MUDder and want to set up your own, check out **alt.mud.lp** to get tips on how to start.

Usenet:
 Newsgroup: **alt.mud.lp**
 Newsgroup: **rec.games.mud.lp**

MUD Announcements

What's new? What's passed away? Every Friday get the latest word on what MUD sites are up and running and which ones have been put to pasture. Did you lose your favorite MUD? Ask around here — someone will know the answer.

Usenet:
 Newsgroup: **rec.games.mud.announce**

MUD Documents

An interesting selection of information about MUDs, including a history of MUDs, inter-MUD communication, a MUD survey, and a paper on social virtual reality in the real world.

Gopher:
 Name: University of Stuttgart
 Address: **gopher.uni-stuttgart.de**
 Choose: **Fun & Game**
  | **MUD Gopher Tuebingen**
  | **Documents and papers about MUDs**

MUDs in the News

The best thing about MUDs is that they keep so many people away from real life, where they would otherwise get bored and cause trouble. (Just see how much trouble is caused by all the people who *don't* use MUDs.)

So, for all you MUDders, be sure to tune in to **rec.games.mud.announce** and find out what's new and exciting. Wouldn't it be awful to telnet to your favorite MUD and find out that everyone else has moved to Mars?

New to MUDding?

Try MUD Information. No point being more disoriented than is good for you.

Learn how to use anonymous ftp and the world is at your fingertips.

MUD Information

A large selection of information all about MUDs and the culture surrounding them, including research articles, clients, ftp sites, MUD lists, and descriptions of the various MUDs. It also catergorizes MUDs into their different types and allows you to connect directly to them from the gopher.

Gopher:
Name: University of Texas at Austin
Address: **actlab.rtf.utexas.edu**
Choose: **Virtual Spaces: MUD**

MUD List

List of all the Internet MUDs you will ever want to play. Classifies each MUD into its specific type, and provides both numeric and name addresses, status, and any further information. An updated list is released every Friday.

Anonymous FTP:
Address: **caisr2.caisr.cwru.edu**
Path: **/pub/mud**

MUD List

Defining a MUD is easy: it's a (usually) text-based virtual world in which people interact with one another as well as with the built-in inhabitants and objects of the MUD itself. Understanding a MUD is not so easy. There is something about these virtual worlds that appeals to certain types of people in ways that most of us can never understand. If you think that you might be one of these special people, try MUDding for a while and see how your life changes. Aside from making new friends and learning all kinds of esoteric information, you will connect yourself to a type of human/machine experience that just may change your life. (If it doesn't, an alternate method is to read the entire contents of "The Internet Complete Reference" backwards.

MUD as a Psychological Model

A theory discussing MUD as a psychological model, and issues concerning the separation of reality from virtual reality.

Anonymous FTP:
Address: **ftp.spies.com**
Path: **/Library/Cyber/realife.mud**

Gopher:
Name: Internet Wiretap
Address: **wiretap.spies.com**
Choose: **Wiretap Online Library**
| **Cyberspace**
| **MUD as a Psychological Model**

MUD Usenet Discussion Groups

Immerse yourself in the wonders of multiple user dimension games (MUDs). Text-based virtual realities provide you with an exciting realm in which to socialize or play adventure games. Find out what MUDding is all about, but be warned: the Surgeon General has declared MUDding to be addictive.

Usenet:
Newsgroup: **alt.mud**
Newsgroup: **rec.games.mud.***

MUDWHO Server

Shows the current players on various MUDs. Each MUDWHO server will know who is using various MUDs, so check the different servers to see which one keeps track of players on your favorite MUD.

Telnet:
Address: **nova.tat.physik.uni-tuebingen.de**
Port: **6889**

Address: **riemann.math.okstate.edu**
Port: **6889**

MUSH Documents

Enter the interactive social environment of MUSHs and create your own little corner of the world. Part of the charm of MUSHs is that anyone can do basic environmental programming. Read the tutorials that show you how to do this. There is also information on MUSH ethics, clients, and general startup help.

Anonymous FTP:
Address: **caisr2.caisr.cwru.edu**
Path: **/pub/mush/***

A B C D E F G H I J K L M N O P Q R S T U V W X Y Z

Tiny MUDs

Some MUDders consider adventuring and killing monsters barbaric. Imagine that. These social animals hang out on Tiny MUDs where social skill is a high art. If you are interested in chatting, making friends, or other socializing, you'll love Tiny MUDs (including MUSH, MUSE, and MOO).

Usenet:
> Newsgroup: **rec.games.mud.tiny**

MUDS: SPECIFIC TYPES

Actuator MUD

Actuator is about building cyberspace. It is for researching and designing drivers, clients, graphics, MUDlibs, worlds, networked objects, and social interaction.

Telnet:
> Address: **actlab.rtf.utexas.edu**
> Port: **4000**

Do you like to create?

Try the Actuator MUD.

Actuator MUD Gopher

Browse Actuator MUD, list its users, connect to other MUD gopher servers, or simply connect to Actuator MUD itself.

Gopher:
> Name: University of Texas at Austin
> Address: **actlab.rtf.utexas.edu**
> Port: **3452**

AlexMUD

The oldest DikuMUD on the Internet, started on March 9, 1991. Based in Sweden, it has its own distinctive style and depth, which accounts for its popularity.

Telnet:
> Address: **marcel.stacken.kth.se**
> Port: **4000**

> Address: **mud.stacken.kth.se**
> Port: **4000**

Apocalypse

A very popular DikuMUD with lots of extras. Seven different races, nine different character classes, chit-chat channels, and even color! Check it out.

Telnet:
> Address: **sapphire.geo.wvu.edu**
> Port: **4000**

Chupchups

MUDs come in all shapes and sizes. Chupchups is one of those MUDs with a very distinctive shape. It's so distinctive it gets its own newsgroup.

Usenet:
> Newsgroup: **alt.mud.chupchups**

Copper Diku

A highly customized DikuMUD with selection of hometown, special city for killers, battle arena, new areas, and even jail for law-breaking players.

Telnet:
> Address: **copper.denver.colorado.edu**
> Port: **4000**

Deeper Trouble

A classic fantasy-based LPmud with a Tolkienesque theme.

Telnet:
> Address: **alk.iesd.auc.dk**
> Port: **4242**

DikuMud II

Roam fantastic lands playing human, elf, dwarf, halfling, or gnome characters in the official Version Two of the original DikuMud-style MUD.

Telnet:
    Address: **mud.stacken.kth.se**
    Port: **4242**

Dirt

A classic adventure-style AberMUD.

Telnet:
    Address: **alkymene.uio.no**
    Port: **6715**

Discworld MUD

An LPMud based on the colorful *Discworld* books by the legendary Terry Pratchett. Discworld is, as the Wombles and Blues will tell you, where all your dreams can't come true.

Telnet:
    Address: **cix.compulink.co.uk**
    Port: **4242**

Discworld MUD Gopher

Allows one to view and find information about players of DiscWorld MUD, and offers easy access to other MUD and entertainment-related gophers.

Gopher:
    Name: Compulink
    Address: **cix.compulink.co.uk**
    Port: **3450**

htMUD

Web fever has struck the MUDders, so you can now expect rampant development of graphical MUD environments. It's already started: htMUD is a graphical tinyMUD consisting of one forms-capable web client window to allow for input and one telnet window for conversation output. If you want to see more about how this works, check out the web page, which will also tell you where you can catch the action.

World Wide Web:
    URL: **http://www.elf.com/~phi/htmud.html**

Island

A MUD with more than a passing resemblance to Oxford University.

Telnet:
    Address: **teaching4.physics.ox.ac.uk**
    Port: **2093**

Gopher to a MUD

Normally, you would telnet to your favorite MUD. However, there are times when telnet is just not available or when you want to browse a list of MUDs and try something new. At such times, you can use one of the Gophers devoted to MUD connections. Now you have no excuse whatsoever for actually doing any useful work with your computer.

LambdaMOO

A large and popular virtual reality with more varied sections and interesting objects than you'll ever be able to explore. Players are allowed to program and create their own sections.

Telnet:
    Address: **lambda.parc.xerox.com**
    Port: **8888**

A B C D E F G H I J K L M N O P Q R S T U V W X Y Z

MUD Access via Gopher

Access all your favorite MUDs through gopher. Simply select the MUD you wish to play from the massive selection available and you will be instantly connected. No more messing with lengthy MUD lists.

Gopher:
Name: Technische Universitaet Clausthal
Address: **solaris.rz.tu-clausthal.de**
Choose: **Student-Gopher**
  | Mud-Servers (for the REAL players!)

Name: University of Minnesota
Address: **gopher.micro.umn.edu**
Choose: **Fun & Games**
  | Games
  | MUDs

Nails

A popular and friendly MUD set in a modern day environment and using ANSI color.

Telnet:
Address: **flounder.rutgers.edu**
Port: **5150**

Nightfall MUD

Nightfall is an interactive, text-based, social Virtual Reality. It is an LPmud allowing you to adventure through strange lands solving puzzles, killing monsters, and selling treasures on your way.

Gopher:
Name: University of Stuttgart
Address: **rusinfo.rus.uni-stuttgart.de**
Choose: **Fun & Game**
  | GamerServer in Tuebingen Login: GAMES

Telnet:
Address: **nova.tat.physik.uni-tuebingen.de**
Port: **4242**

Nightfall MUD Information

This gopher offers information about Nightfall MUD and the MUD culture in general. It has access to the Nightfall MUD statistics and status, and it also allows you to connect to the MUD itself, or check who is currently playing.

Gopher:
Name: University of Stuttgart
Address: **gopher.uni-stuttgart.de**
Choose: **Fun & Game**
  | MUD Gopher Tuebingen

> ## Using the Internet won't make you go blind.

Nightmare MUD

Nightmare is a high-energy MUD with a variety of classes and races. Work your way up to be a High Mortal so you can beat up on the really studly monsters. Nightmare has high coding standards, so it's visually colorful and the settings are unique and imaginative.

Telnet:
Address: **nightmare.winternet.com**
Port: **1701**

PernMush

A popular MUD based on the *Pern* novels by Anne McCaffrey.

Telnet:
Address: **cesium.clock.org**
Port: **4201**

Regenesis

A virtual reality project with special clients available for X Window, Amiga, and PCs, which allow you to play with graphics.

Telnet:
Address: **regenesis.lysator.liu.se**
Port: **7475**

Star Wars

A MUSH-style MUD based on *Star Wars*, where the Force is always with you. Drop a note for more information.

Mail:
Address: **jharvey@netcom.com**

Three Kingdoms MUD

Three Kingdoms has a hierarchy based on a human monarchy, so it achieves variety through guild selection instead of races. This MUD is well-loved and full of life as evidenced by not only the traffic, but the high-spirited shouting that seems to be routine. Newbie documents are available at this site via anonymous FTP.

Telnet:
Address: **marble.bu.edu**
Port: **5000**

TrekMuse

A TinyMuse MUD based on the original *Star Trek* TV series.

Telnet:
Address: **siher.stanford.edu**
Port: **1701**

Zen

Meditate amidst the smell of incense and the sound of gongs and chanting in the great Zen MOO.

Telnet:
Address: **cheshire.oxy.edu**
Port: **7777**

MUSEUMS

Exploratorium

Science is fun. You can blow things up, stick things together, make things float and create loud noises that will guarantee you a trip to the principal's office. The Exploratorium in San Francisco creates an environment of hands-on, fun learning and now they have a home on the Internet.

See also: Science

Anonymous FTP:
Address: **ftp.exploratorium.edu**

Gopher:
Name: The Exploratorium
Address: **gopher.exploratorium.edu**

World Wide Web:
URL: **http://www.exploratorium.edu/**

Interactive Natural History Museum

Adventure through the exhibits and catalogs of the enormous collections of paleontological materials at the U.C. Berkeley Museum of Paleontology. Learn what fossils tell us about the ecologies of the past, about evolution, and about our place as humans.

World Wide Web:
URL: **http://ucmp1.berkeley.edu/**

Missing and Stolen Clearinghouse

Every year hundreds of thousands of books, manuscripts, photographs, color plates, maps, and other rare and valuable items are stolen from museums, libraries, book shops, and private collections. Most of these are stolen only to be sold to unsuspecting collectors, dealers, and institutions. The Interloc Missing and Stolen Books database is a central clearinghouse which lists such items in an easily searchable database, and provide an easy means to contribute news items.

Mail:
Address: **interloc@shaysnet.com**

Museums, Exhibits and Special Collections

Links to tours, exhibitions, and galleries, from museums and collections around the world. Most of these are available on gopher and ftp sites.

See also: Art

World Wide Web:
URL: **http://galaxy.einet.net/GJ/museums.html**

Museums on the Web

A collection of web links connecting museums and archives. This page offers pointers to such sights as the Hall of Dinosaurs, The Moscow Kremlin Online Excursion, the London Transport Museum, Native Vikings, and many other interesting destinations.

World Wide Web:
URL: **http://www.comlab.ox.ac.uk/archive/other/museums.html**

Natural History Museum, London

Reviews of the museums galleries, maps, visiting details, library catalog, newsletters, science information and images giving you a glimpse behind the scenes.

World Wide Web:
URL: **http://www.nhm.ac.uk/**

U.C. Berkeley Museum of Paleontology

Information on museum collections and paleontological database information. Also includes nature and science images, images of animals and birds; biology image archive; animal sounds; and an online *On the Origin of Species* complete text.

Gopher:
Name: University of California Berkeley
Address: **ucmp1.berkeley.edu**

MUSIC

4AD Eyesore

A searchable database of all releases from the music label 4AD. Search for groups, titles, tracks, or releases from specific people and years. There are also many interviews, hundreds of sleeve scans, and a FAQ file.

World Wide Web:
URL: **http://isvpc146.isv.uit.no/eyesore.html**

A Cappella

Discussion groups for people interested in music without instrumental accompaniment.

Usenet:
Newsgroup: **alt.music.a-cappella**
Newsgroup: **rec.music.a-cappella**

World Wide Web:
URL: **http://www.yahoo.com/Entertainment/ Music/Vocal/A_Cappella/**

Acid Jazz

Acid Jazz is music style that is part jazz, 70s funk, hip-hop, and soul. This is the home page for acid jazz and it has links to a mailing list, a mail archive, magazines, club information, and a regularly updated recording list.

World Wide Web:
URL: **http://www.cmd.uu.se/AcidJazz/**

Acoustic and Electric Bass

Techniques and equipment for both the double bass and electric bass.

Usenet:
Newsgroup: **rec.music.makers.bass**

> # A sure-fire way to make all your dreams come true is to sleep with this book under your pillow.

Acoustic Guitar Archive

Complete transcriptions with full lyrics of guitar music of all kinds, digests, and other related guitar information.

Anonymous FTP:
Address: **ftp.acns.nwu.edu**
Path: **/pub/acoustic-guitar/***

Gopher:
Name: NYSERNet
Address: **nysernet.org**
Choose: **Reference Desk**
| 700 - **Arts and Recreation**
| 780 - **Music**
| **Acoustic Guitar data**

Acoustic Guitar Digest

Check out this electronic magazine for acoustic guitar buffs.

Anonymous FTP:
Address: **casbah.acns.nwu.edu**
Path: **/pub/acoustic-guitar**

Acoustic Music Server

It's not just for hippies anymore. Enjoy the experience of hearing nimble fingers walk their way across the strings of a guitar. Catch your favorite artist on tour. Read articles on the latest acoustic music news, and let the FAQs answer all your questions.

World Wide Web:
URL: **http://kirk.cgrg.ohio-state.edu/Music.html**

Afro-Caribbean Music

An Afro-Caribbean music guide sorted by style, country, artist, and instrument, including album details and some song samples in **.au** format.

World Wide Web:
URL: **http://www.ina.fr/Music/**

Afro-Latin

Discussion of music with an African and Latin American flavor.

Usenet:
Newsgroup: **rec.music.afro-latin**

Articles of Music Composition

A number of articles about composing music. Hints, tips, tricks, and ideas of all sorts.

Anonymous FTP:
Address: **ftp.uwp.edu**
Path: **/pub/music/composition**

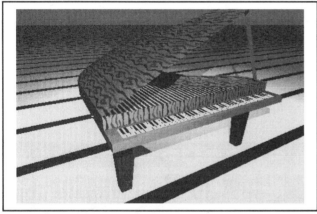

After a half hour with *The Internet Complete Reference*, you'll be an expert with ftp and archie, and you will be amazed at how much artwork is available on the Net. Millions of hours of artwork are in the public domain.

Bagpipes

Archive files and discussion of any topic related to bagpipes, with all manner of Scottish, Irish, English, and other instruments discussed. The ftp site contains FAQs, archives, and a bagpipe survey.

Anonymous FTP:
Address: **cs.dartmouth.edu**
Path: **/pub/bagpipes/***

Gopher:
Name: Dartmouth College
Address: **cs.dartmouth.edu**
Choose: **Bagpipe Archives**

Internet Mailing List:
List Address: **bagpipes@cs.dartmouth.edu**
Subscription Address:
bagpipes-request@cs.dartmouth.edu

Who hasn't heard a real Scotsman playing the bagpipes and not fallen in love with that sensuous, romantic, sophisticated sound that other, more euphonic musicians can only dream of?

Banjo Tablature Archive

Forget the guitar. Get down with some down-home banjo bluegrass. Tabs include classical works from Bach and Mozart (doesn't sound like bluegrass), as well as "traditional" selections such as "Whiskey before Breakfast" and "Wreck of the Old 97."

World Wide Web:
URL: **http://www.vuw.ac.nz/~gnat/banjo/tab/index.html**

Barbershop Quartets

Throw down your accordian, your bagpipes, your tin whistles, and join a barbershop quartet. More fun than a barrel of monkeys, able to leap octaves in a single bound, these singers are lively, energetic, and know how to have a good time. Check out their online organizations, calendar of events, FAQs, and other resource information.

Gopher:
Name: University of Pennsylvania
Address: **timc.pop.upenn.edu**

Bassoon and Oboe

Why is it that you never see street musicians playing the bassoon? It's because they get tired of people asking them "Is that a bassoon you're carrying or are you just glad to see me?" (Some people have no class.) Join this unmoderated list for bassoon and oboe performers, teachers and students to participate in the discussion of music, reed-making, performances, instruments, clinics and workshops, festivals, and other issues relating to double reed instruments.

Listserv Mailing List:
List Address: **doublereed-l@acc.wuacc.edu**
Subscription Address: **listserv@acc.wuacc.edu**

A B C D E F G H I J K L M N O P Q R S T U V W X Y Z

Big Band

While you can't hear the snappy, lively big band sound through this newsgroup, you can at least talk about all your favorite bands and musicians, and the history of the music and era.

Usenet:
Newsgroup: **alt.music.big-band**

Big band music is a gift of the gods.

Follow **alt.music.big-band** and see what the people with good taste have to say.

Bluegrass Music Discussion List

A mailing list for issues related to the International Bluegrass Music Association, and bluegrass music in general, including but not limited to recordings, bands, individual performers, and live performances.

Listserv Mailing List:
List Address: **bgrass-l@ukcc.uky.edu**
Subscription Address: **listserv@ukcc.uky.edu**

Blues

It's best played in tiny lounges with poor lighting. Maybe fill the room with some smoke. There is a true art to the mournful quality of the music. This is not just "crying in your beer" music. Explore the artist and picture archives that bring the blues to life on the Net.

Listserv Mailing List:
List Address: **blues-l@brownvm.brown.edu**
Subscription Address:
  listserv@brownvm.brown.edu

Usenet:
Newsgroup: **bit.listserv.blues-l**

World Wide Web:
URL: **http://dragon.acadiau.ca:1667/~rob/blues/blues.html**

Bottom Line Zine

It's what you usually hear when you are stuck in a nightclub and the speakers are turned up way too loud. Or worse, you can feel it somewhere between your stomach and your heart. But any bassist with class will keep his or her bottom line where it's supposed to be. We're not sure where that is exactly, but it's bound to be someplace respectable. This electronic zine has articles and information for bassists.

World Wide Web:
URL: **http://www.oulu.fi/tbl.html**

Brass Musicians

A discussion group for people interested in brass musical performance and related topics, especially small musical ensembles of all kinds. Woodwind, percussion, and other orchestral types are also welcome.

Internet Mailing List:
List Address: **brass@geomag.gly.fsu.edu**
Subscription Address:
  brass-request@geomag.gly.fsu.edu

How to Be Popular

Do you want to boost your popularity? Do you want to be invited to parties and be in demand in your social circle? All you need to do is download some Bulgarian sounds and keep them handy. Once people know that you are the guy or gal with the Bulgarian connection, you will have more offers than you can handle.

Bulgarian Sounds

Unleash the gypsy in you. Grab these sound files, close your eyes and crank up the volume. Allow the music to sweep over you — the sounds of the kaval, gadulka, gaida and tupan.

World Wide Web:
URL: **http://pisa.rockefeller.edu:8080/Bulgaria/sounds/**

Buying and Selling Music

People buying and selling musical instruments and equipment, records, tapes, and CDs.

Usenet:
Newsgroup: **rec.music.makers.marketplace**
Newsgroup: **rec.music.marketplace**

CDs

General discussion of music and CDs, including what's available, new releases, CDs wanted and for sale, and requests for information.

Usenet:
Newsgroup: **rec.music.cd**

Celtic Music

Music is something that the Celts do well. The soulful wail of the whistles and the primal beating of the drums would make just about anyone yearn to buy a plane ticket to Ireland. The proof is in the numbers. Fans of Celtic music are abundant on the Net and sponsor mailing lists and web pages with information about Celtic music magazines, live jam sessions, radio programs, and more.

Usenet:
Newsgroup: **rec.music.celtic**

World Wide Web:
URL: **http://celtic.stanford.edu/ceolas.html**

Christian Music

Discussion of contemporary and traditional Christian music.

Usenet:
Newsgroup: **rec.music.christian**

Clarinet Players Mailing List

News, information, research and teaching, and other items of interest to clarinet players, teachers, students, and enthusiasts.

Listserv Mailing List:
List Address: **klarinet@vccscent.bitnet**
Subscription Address: **listserv@vccscent.bitnet**

Classical Music

Talk to music aficionados about classical music in general, early preclassical European music, and the music of Shostakovitch.

Usenet:
Newsgroup: **alt.fan.shostakovich**
Newsgroup: **rec.music.classical**
Newsgroup: **rec.music.early**

World Wide Web:
URL: **http://www.yahoo.com/Entertainment/Music/Classical_Music/**

A B C D E F G H I J K L **M** N O P Q R S T U V W X Y Z

Classical Music Mailing List

The Classical Music List was created to discuss classical music of all kinds. All topics and periods are welcome, from Gregorian chants to George Crumb.

Listserv Mailing List:
List Address: **classm-l@brownvm.brown.edu**
Subscription Address:
listserv@brownvm.brown.edu

Complex Arrangements

Complex times call for complex musical arrangements. Composers and music lovers discuss the construction, styles and history of music in relation to complex arrangement.

Usenet:
Newsgroup: **alt.music.complex-arrang**

Computerized Music

A discussion group for exchanging music stored electronically on computers in MOD/669 format.

Usenet:
Newsgroup: **alt.binaries.sounds.music**

World Wide Web:
URL: **http://nmt.edu/~jefu/notes/notes.html**

Computers in Music Research

Forget sifting through dusty old archives of stained and smelly sheet music. Faster and more effective ways of conducting music research are being developed, and you can get in on the action along with musicologists, music analysts, computer scientists, and other people working on applications of computers in music research.

Internet Mailing List:
List Address:
music-research%prg.oxford.ac.uk@nss.cs.ucl.ac.uk
Subscription Address:
music-research%prg.oxford.ac.uk-request@nss.cs.ucl.ac.uk

Usenet:
Newsgroup: **comp.music**

Concert Information

This web page offers access to lists of concert schedules and information about where you can get tickets.

World Wide Web:
URL: **http://www.yahoo.com/**
Entertainment/Music/Events/Concerts/

Country and Western

Country and western music — love, marriage, divorce, truck driving, dogs, beer, intrigue — good old-fashioned American fun.

Usenet:
Newsgroup: **rec.music.country.western**

Country and Western Music

I love you b-a-a-by!

There is something about the steady thump, thump, twang, twang of country music that is so reassuring. *Country and Western* music serves up a heapin' platter of good ol' American culture at its finest: money, booze and bad love. Just the thing for tired Internet music lovers who have overdosed on bagpipes.

Creative Internet Home Page

Creative Internet provides interactive worlds for music and television. You can check out the ultimate list of links that can be updated by visitors, vote in the polls, see the hottest links, and advertise your links on the free-for-all.

See also: Television

World Wide Web:
URL: **http://www.galcit.caltech.edu/~ta/**
creative.html

Croatia

Civil unrest aside, Croatia has some good things going for it — like folk music. Experience the sounds of the Croatian culture from the safety of your own home.

World Wide Web:
URL: **http://tjev.tel.etf.hr/music/music.html**

Discographies

A large collection of discographies covering many bands and groups, including the Beatles, Genesis, Grateful Dead, New Order, Nirvana, Pink Floyd, Rolling Stones, and many others.

Anonymous FTP:
Address: **ftp.spies.com**
Path: **/Library/Music/Disc/***

Address: **ftp.spies.com**
Path: **/Library/Music/Label/***

Gopher:
Name: Internet Wiretap
Address: **wiretap.spies.com**
Choose: **Wiretap Online Library**
  | **Music**
  | **Discographies**

Name: Internet Wiretap
Address: **wiretap.spies.com**
Choose: **Wiretap Online Library**
  | **Music**
  | **Label Discographies**

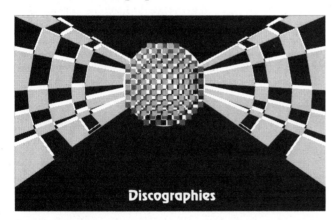

Discographies

Drums and Percussion

This is the part of the band that will never be able to sneak up on anybody. Read jokes, mailing lists, an encyclopedia of terms, and FAQs on how to make the kind of loud noises that people like.

World Wide Web:
URL: **http://www.cse.ogi.edu/Drum/**

Don't be a Web Potato: participate.

Early Music

Believe it or not, there really was music before rock and roll. And it was good music, too, but you can't do The Twist to it. If that doesn't bother you, you will probably love music from the Middle Ages and Renaissance. Early music lovers chat about records, books, performances, song texts, and translations as well as transcribing early music scores in electronic form.

Listserv Mailing List:
List Address: **earlym-l@aearn.edvz.univie.ac.at**
Subscription Address:
  listserv@aearn.edvz.univie.ac.at

Electric Music

The bad thing about electric music is that you can't play it during a power outage. So take advantage of the opportunity to download these audio files while the lights are still on. Do you think Ben Franklin had any idea that his little experiment would lead to this?

World Wide Web:
URL: **http://www.hike.te.chiba-u.ac.jp/eem/**

Electronic Music

Discussions and digests about electronic music, including composition, criticism, technology, and technique.

Listserv Mailing List:
List Address: **emusic-l@american.edu**
Subscription Address: **listserv@american.edu**

List Address: **emusic-d@american.edu**
Subscription Address: **listserv@american.edu**

Electronic Music and Synthesizers

Composing and playing electronic music, particularly music that uses synthesizers and MIDI.

Usenet:
Newsgroup: **alt.emusic**
Newsgroup: **alt.music.misc**
Newsgroup: **bit.listserv.emusic-l**
Newsgroup: **comp.sys.amiga.audio**
Newsgroup: **rec.music.makers.synth**
Newsgroup: **rec.music.synth**

A B C D E F G H I J K L M N O P Q R S T U V W X Y Z

Electronic/Industrial Music Zine List

A list of electronic/industrial/techno music-related zines with reviews and contact information for each.

Anonymous FTP:
    Address: **ftp.spies.com**
    Path: **/Library/Misc/electron.zin**

Gopher:
    Name: Internet Wiretap
    Address: **wiretap.spies.com**
    Choose: **Wiretap Online Library**
        | **Miscellaneous**
        | **Electronic/Industrial Zine List**

Ethnomusicology Research Digest

A periodical for professionals, librarians, and graduate students interested the field of ethnomusicology. (This is, of course, a subject of great global significance.)

Gopher:
    Name: University of Maryland
    Address: **info.umd.edu**
    Choose: **Educational Resources**
        | **The Reading Room**
        | **Newletters**
        | **Ethnomusicology**
        | **Digest**

Filk Music

Filking is the clever, but nearly irreverant art of taking an existing song, gutting it, and making it into something new using the same music, but different words. Join the rowdy crowd around the campfire as they belt out the ballads.

Usenet:
    Newsgroup: **alt.music.filk**

Film Music

Discussions of the music used in movies and television, including music reviews, film composers, film music history and theory, and requests for information about film music.

Listserv Mailing List:
    List Address: **filmus-l@iubvm.ucs.indiana.edu**
    Subscription Address:
        listserv@iubvm.ucs.indiana.edu

Usenet:
    Newsgroup: **alt.motherjones**

Folk Music Archives

Selection of folk music, country blues, and fingerstyle guitarists, discographies, and lyrics. Also offers lists of folk music societies, radio programs, publications, and other ftp sites.

Anonymous FTP:
    Address: **ftp.uwp.edu**
    Path: **/pub/music/folk/***

Folk Music Calendar

Search a list of upcoming folk music events and concerts in the United States by artist or by state. Gives booking details and is updated on a regular basis.

World Wide Web:
    URL: **http://pubweb.parc.xerox.com/hypertext/music/AboutDirtyLinen.html**

Folk Music Concerts

You will never have to worry about how to track down your favorite folk singer again. Find out concert dates and locations by searching under the artist's name or by state. Slip on those sandals, throw on some loose all-cotton clothing, load the community into a refurbished school bus, and roadtrip to a folk concert near you.

World Wide Web:
    URL: **http://pubweb.parc.xerox.com/hypertext/music/AboutDirtyLinen.h**

Folk Music Digital Tradition

The Digital Tradition is a huge database containing the words to over 4000 folk songs. It also contains nearly 2000 actual tunes that you can play using the speaker in your PC or Macintosh.

Anonymous FTP:
    Address: **parcftp.xerox.com**
    Path: **/pub/music/digital_tradition/***

World Wide Web:
    URL: **http://pubweb.parc.xerox.com/digitrad**

Folk Music Discussion

A discussion group about folk music of all types.

Usenet:
    Newsgroup: **rec.music.folk**

Folk Music Information

Access to albums, artists, concert schedules, the Digital Tradition Folk Song Database, the All-Music guide, and booking contacts.

World Wide Web:
URL: **http://www.eit.com/web/folk/folkhome.html**

Folk Music Lyrics

Lyrics to many ancient and new folk songs. Especially intriguing are the old English and Scottish songs. The lyrics are arranged in a hierarchy of directories, alphabetically by name. This site also has many contemporary lyrics, but the old folk songs make it quite interesting.

Anonymous FTP:
Address: **ftp.luth.se**
Path: **/pub/misc/lyrics/folk/***

Funk

Opera makes you homicidal, classical puts you to sleep, and country music makes you want to get in a monster truck and plow over any small cars in your path. For a change, try some funk. Funk is based on the rhythmic innovations of James Brown. Discussion includes not only funk, but some rap, hip-hop, soul, R&B, and related varieties. Artists of the genre include Funkadelic, Parliament, and Earth, Wind, and Fire. Not only does funk sound good, you can dance to it, too.

Internet Mailing List:
List Address: **funky-music@athena.mit.edu**
Subscription Address:
funky-music-request@athena.mit.edu

Usenet:
Newsgroup: **rec.music.funky**

Gothic Web Pages and Chat

Complete with images of Hell Fire, the Gothic home page offers a Goth image database of more than 120 pictures, text files from the **alt.gothic** newsgroup, Goth Club listings, and a list of other gothic resources on the Net.

Internet Relay Chat:
Channel: **#gothic**

World Wide Web:
URL: **http://www.yahoo.com/
Entertainment/Music/Gothic/**
URL: **http://www.acs.csulb.edu/~vamp/Gothic/**

Gregorian Chants

A feast day is coming up and you absolutely must find the perfect Gregorian chant. And it happens that your local chant expert is away for the weekend kayaking through the wild, white waters of Colorado without his cellular phone. Not to worry. Hook up to the database of Gregorian chants for the Divine Office and browse through antiphons assigned to the Magnificat of Vespers or the Benedictus of Lauds. You are sure to find a chant to suit your needs.

Gopher:
Name: Catholic University of America
Address: **vmsgopher.cua.edu**
Choose: **The Catholic University of America Gopher service**
| Special Resources
| Cantus-Database for Gregorian Chants . . .

Grunge

This is definitely not your parents' music. Let your hair down, rip the sleeves off your shirt, and hang loose. Hang out with other angst-consumed rebels and discuss the grunge scene. If it's neat, clean, or prepackaged, it doesn't belong here.

Listserv Mailing List:
List Address: **grunge-l@ubvm.cc.buffalo.edu**
Subscription Address:
listserv@ubvm.cc.buffalo.edu

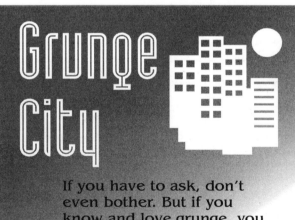

Grunge City

If you have to ask, don't even bother. But if you know and love grunge, you may want to subscribe to the **grunge-l** mailing list. Never again will you have to spend time in the real world without some grunge talk to bring you back to unreality.

A B C D E F G H I J K L M N O P Q R S T U V W X Y Z

Guitar

Guitar players, check out the discussion groups just for you. Tablature groups for sharing music and lyrics, as well as groups for general guitar, acoustic guitar, and classical guitar.

Usenet:
Newsgroup: **alt.guitar.tab**
Newsgroup: **rec.music.classical.guitar**
Newsgroup: **rec.music.makers.guitar**
Newsgroup: **rec.music.makers.guitar.acoustic**
Newsgroup: **rec.music.makers.guitar.tablature**

Guitar Archive

Large collection of guitar tab files, covering thousands of artists and groups, all organized in alphabetical order.

Anonymous FTP:
Address: **ftp.nevada.edu**
Path: **/pub/guitar/***

Address: **ftp.uwp.edu**
Path: **/pub/music/guitar/***

Guitar Chords for Popular Songs

Song lyrics and guitar chords for many popular songs. Songs are categorized by group or artist.

Anonymous FTP:
Address: **ftp.nevada.edu**
Path: **/pub/guitar**

Address: **ftp.uwp.edu**
Path: **/pub/music/guitar**

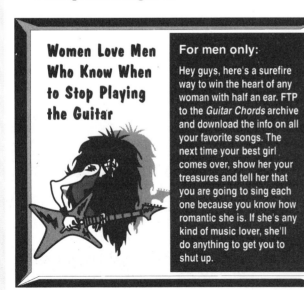

Hard Bop Cafe

Music knows no national borders because it can travel at the speed of sound. The Canadians have their own jazz scene and are documenting it on the Web. Schedules for jazz festivals, information on Canadian musicians as well as musicians of other nationalities, concert and album reviews, and pointers to mailing lists that you can join for more discussion.

See also: Canada

World Wide Web:
URL: **http://www.ee.umanitoba.ca/~mcgonig/ hardbop.html**

Harpsichord Exercises

This web page is an interactive tutor for some of Domenico Scarlatti's harpsichord exercises. You can select the number of exercises to be displayed on the page, and even the language in which you would like to work.

World Wide Web:
URL: **http://www.win.tue.nl/scarlatti**

Heavy Metal

Discuss metal and heavy metal music. Achieve total heavy-osity.

Internet Relay Chat:
Channel: **#metal**

Usenet:
Newsgroup: **alt.rock-n-roll.hard**
Newsgroup: **alt.rock-n-roll.metal**
Newsgroup: **alt.rock-n-roll.metal.death**
Newsgroup: **alt.rock-n-roll.metal.heavy**
Newsgroup: **alt.rock-n-roll.metal.progressive**

Heavy Thrash Music

A digest covering many aspects of grindcore, death metal, and other forms of heavy thrash music.

Internet Mailing List:
List Address: **grind@unh.edu**
Subscription Address: **grind-request@unh.edu**

Impulse

The Impulse mailing list is a comprehensive journal of music news, reviews, information and opinion.

Internet Mailing List:
List Address: **impulse@dsigroup.com**
Subscription Address:
impulse-request@dsigroup.com

Indian Classical Music

It's hard to dance to, but that doesn't mean it's not good. This music is best served with curry and perhaps some burning herbs. FAQs, bibliographies, and papers relating to all the genres of Carnatic and Hindustani music.

Usenet:
Newsgroup: **rec.music.indian.classical**
Newsgroup: **rec.music.indian.misc**

World Wide Web:
URL: **http://enuxsa.eas.asu.edu/~sridhar/music/**

Institutions of Music

Links to the music departments of a variety of universities.

World Wide Web:
URL: **http://www.yahoo.com/
Entertainment/Music/Organizations/**

Japanese Popular Music

This is just the thing to listen to over a bit of sushi, wasabi, and perhaps a little roasted wheat tea. Fans of Japanese popular music talk about the latest music, bands and issues.

Internet Mailing List:
List Address: **jpop@ferkel.ucsb.edu**
Subscription Address:
jpop-request@ferkel.ucsb.edu

Jazz/Blues/Rock and Roll Images

A large collection of gif photos and images of famous jazz, blues, and rock and roll performers and stars.

World Wide Web:
URL: **http://plan9.njit.edu/**

Jazz Clubs Around the World

A list of jazz clubs based on the information provided by the dedicated jazz fans who participate in the Usenet newsgroup **rec.music.bluenote**.

World Wide Web:
URL: **http://www.acns.nwu.edu/jazz/lists/
clubs.html**

Jazz Photography

Ray Avery is a well-known jazz photographer. (At least he is well-known in the jazz scene.) Believe it or not, Ray gave up fur farming to take up jazz photography and he began to document the birth of West Coast jazz. See this electronic exhibition of Avery's photographs.

World Wide Web:
URL: **http://bookweb.cwis.uci.edu:8042/
Jazz/jazz.html**

Jazz Server

Energetic is a good word to describe jazz music. Even the name sounds snappy. Read up on the history, news, and discussion about jazz. It's not just music, it's a whole culture.

Usenet:
Newsgroup: **rec.music.bluenote**

World Wide Web:
URL: **http://www.acns.nwu.edu/jazz/**
URL: **http://www.acns.nwu.edu/jazz/artists/
artist-index.html**

Jazz is cool, the Internet is cool, you are cool.

What are you waiting for? Take a look at rec.music.bluenote.

A B C D E F G H I J K L **M** N O P Q R S T U V W X Y Z

Jewish Music

This gopher has a large collection of Jewish tabs, chords, and lyrics, details of Jewish music groups, Jewish music FAQs, and event guides. Check out the newsgroup to take part in discussions about Jewish music.

Gopher:
Name: Jerusalem One
Address: **jerusalem1.datasrv.co.il**
Choose: **Art of and About The Jewish People | Jewish Music**

Usenet:
Newsgroup: **alt.music.jewish**

Lute

Discussion of lute playing and performance. The ftp site contains archives and the source for a Unix and Vax-VMS program to typeset tablature for the lute.

Anonymous FTP:
Address: **cs.dartmouth.edu**
Path: **/pub/lute/***

Gopher:
Name: Dartmouth College
Address: **cs.dartmouth.edu**
Choose: **Lute Files**

Internet Mailing List:
List Address: **lute@cs.dartmouth.edu**
Subscription Address:
lute-request@cs.dartmouth.edu

Lyrics Archive

Massive collection of song lyrics from thousands of artists and groups, with a variety of index methods for searching them.

Anonymous FTP:
Address: **ftp.uwp.edu**
Path: **/pub/music/lyrics/***

Address: **ocf.berkeley.edu**
Path: **/pub/Library/Lyrics**

Gopher:
Name: University of Wisconsin Parkside
Address: **gopher.uwp.edu**
Choose: **Music Archives | lyrics**

World Wide Web:
URL: **http://anxiety-closet.mit.edu:8001/ activities/russian-club/catalog.html**
URL: **http://www.ccs.neu.edu/USER/skilmon/ music/lyrics.html/**
URL: **http://www.mcc.ac.uk/Lyrics/**

> **There are only two things worth remembering in life (both of which I forget)**

Lyrics from Musicals

Lyrics to several musicals, including *Cats*, *Chess*, *Grease*, *Les Miserables*, *Phantom of the Opera*, and *The Rocky Horror Picture Show*.

Anonymous FTP:
Address: **quartz.rutgers.edu**
Path: **/pub/theater/musicals/***

Gopher:
Name: Rutgers University
Address: **quartz.rutgers.edu**
Choose: **Theater-Plays and Musicals | Musicals lyrics**

Mammoth Records Internet Center

A showcase for the best bands and albums that Mammoth has to offer. It offers band profiles, tour dates around the world, excerpts from the newest and hottest releases, video clips, singles samples, album covers and promo photos, reviews, and news.

World Wide Web:
URL: **http://www.nando.net/mammoth/ mammoth.html**

Marching Bands

This page collects direct links to the home pages of a variety of marching bands and drumcorps around the US, including Cal Berkeley, the California Aggies, Notre Dame, Columbia, Princeton, Virginia Tech, and other Ivy League and college bands.

World Wide Web:
URL: **http://www.yahoo.com/ Entertainment/Music/Marching_Bands/**

> **Do you really exist? Check Philosophy and be sure.**

Metaverse

A slick ftp site and gopher run by Adam Curry, the former MTV VJ, with tons of news and information about the music industry. The gopher features interviews with famous musicians, reviews of songs and albums, and even back issues of the Cybersleaze mailing list — the mailing list that gives you the lowdown on entertainers and the entertainment industry. To join the mailing list, send mail to the mail address below.

Finger:
  Address: **adam@metaverse.com**
  Address: **hotlist@metaverse.com**

Gopher:
  Name: Metaverse
  Address: **metaverse.com**

Mail:
  Address: **sleaze@metaverse.com**
  Body:
    subscribe cybersleaze *your email address*

World Wide Web:
  URL: **http://metaverse.com**

MIDI Home Page

Both beginners and advanced users of MIDI will find something useful on the MIDI home page. It offers an introduction to MIDI, simple and elaborate specifications of all the MIDI commands, SDS specifications, GS MIDI sequences, user groups, archives, and links to other MIDI related resources and web sites.

World Wide Web:
  URL: **http://www.eeb.ele.tue.nl/midi/index.html**

Music Archives

A gigantic collection of information about music, including artists, buying guides, picture files, lyrics, ftp site lists, and much more.

Anonymous FTP:
  Address: **ftp.uwp.edu**
  Path: **/pub/music/***

Gopher:
  Name: University of Wisconsin Parkside
  Address: **gopher.uwp.edu**
  Choose: **Research Information and Services**
    | Allmusic Music Archives

Music and Behavior

The Music and Science Information Computer Archive makes available a database of information relating to the study of the effects of music on behavior. You can search the database, or just read related news, notices, and other items of interest.

Telnet:
  Address: **mila.ps.uci.edu**
  Login: **mbi**
  Password: **nammbi**

Music Chat

Talk about music of all kinds. There is a MusicServ list with details of music, bootlegs, and live recordings for sale or trade.

Internet Relay Chat:
  Channel: **#altmusic**
  Channel: **#music**
  Channel: **#trax**

Music Composition

A Usenet discussion group dedicated to people interested in writing original music or lyrics.

Usenet:
  Newsgroup: **rec.music.compose**

Music Database

It's been on the tip of your tongue all morning, the name of that song running through your mind. It's driving you crazy. It has the word "grapefruit" in the title. Suddenly it hits you like wet fish — search the online music database. They have over two thousand albums that you can search by artist, title, track, language, country, style, or submitter. If you have album information, you may enter it in the database, too.

World Wide Web:
  URL: **http://www.cecer.army.mil/~burnett/MDB/**

A
B
C
D
E
F
G
H
I
J
K
L
M
N
O
P
Q
R
S
T
U
V
W
X
Y
Z

Music Discussion

A mailing list and Usenet groups devoted to discussion of all forms of music in all their aspects.

Listserv Mailing List:
List Address: **allmusic@american.edu**
Subscription Address: **listserv@american.edu**

Usenet:
Newsgroup: **alt.music.alternative**
Newsgroup: **alt.music.misc**
Newsgroup: **bit.listserv.allmusic**
Newsgroup: **rec.music.misc**

Music Facts

Facts and lists about all kinds of music, including a list of all-female bands, science fiction music list, and various band FAQs.

Anonymous FTP:
Address: **quartz.rutgers.edu**
Path: **/pub/music/***

Gopher:
Name: Rutgers University
Address: **quartz.rutgers.edu**
Choose: **Music**

Music FAQs

Without music the world would be a quieter and duller place. There would be no reason to call the police because of overcranked speakers. There would be no earplugs needed when people sing off-key. And there would be no reason for all the cool FAQs on Industrial, Reggae, Classical, Christian, Metal, and Ska music, to name a few. This site contains most of the frequently asked questions lists for the Usenet groups relating to music.

World Wide Web:
URL: **http://www.cis.ohio-state.edu/hypertext/faq/usenet/music/top.html**

Music Festival Information

This page brings together information on all kinds of music festivals, including the Colorado Music Festival, the New Orleans Jazz and Heritage Festival, WOMAD, and many more.

World Wide Web:
URL: **http://www.yahoo.com/Entertainment/Music/Events/Festivals/**

Music Kitchen

Discographies, press releases, movies, lyrics, pictures, audio files, and more for several bands and performers, including the Beastie Boys, Redd Kross, Breeders, Tracy Chapman, Meat Puppets, Bonnie Raitt, and Stephen Stills. Also includes some record company pages with catalogs, tour dates, and more.

World Wide Web:
URL: **http://www.nando.net/music/gm/**

Music Library Association

The issues and esoterica of music libraries around the world.

Usenet:
Newsgroup: **bit.listserv.mla-l**

Music List of Lists

The master list of music subjects.

Internet Mailing List:
List Address: **mlol@wariat.org**
Subscription Address: **mlol-request@wariat.org**

Music News

Gossip is fun, especially if it is true. Get the latest news of the music industry by reading these newsgroups. The latest articles hot-off-the-press are posted to the Clarinet groups so you can keep current on new releases, concerts, lawsuits and general industry buzz.

Usenet:
Newsgroup: **clari.apbl.music**
Newsgroup: **clari.living.music**
Newsgroup: **clari.news.music**
Newsgroup: **rec.music.info**

Music Performance

All aspects of musicmaking and performance. Be another Bob Dylan, Pete Townshend, or Billy Joel.

Usenet:
Newsgroup: **rec.music.makers**

Music Making Made Modern

Who can forget those fabulous musical film performances of the Lost Generation: Tom Cruise as the ultimate cool dude in "Risky Business"; or Garth, Wayne and the boys treating us to their special rendition of "Bohemian Rhapsody"? We know your secret: you too are a cool dude with unbelievable talent, and all you need is a break. Drop in to the **rec.music.makers** newsgroup and see what all the other talented Internet musicians are up to.

Music Resources

Discover this alternative to hanging out at the neighborhood jam session on a lazy Sunday afternoon. For those of you who just can't get enough music, check out the available academic sites, user-maintained information, and artist-specific sites at this web page.

World Wide Web:
URL: **http://www.music.indiana.edu/misc/music_resources.html**

Music Reviews

Reviews of all types of music. Read the opinions of people who have more knowledge of music in their whole body than you have in your little finger. A moderated group.

Usenet:
Newsgroup: **rec.music.reviews**

World Wide Web:
URL: **http://www.dcs.ed.ac.uk/students/pg/awrc/review/**

Music Samples

Sample the music of various performers in this web "try before you buy" setup.

See also: Music: Performers

World Wide Web:
URL: **http://actor.cs.vt.edu/~wentz/index.html**

Music Server

This site has just about anything a music fan might be interested in. Archives by artist name, music databases, classical, folk music, guitar TAB files, lyrics, MIDI files, picture files, release listings, mailing lists, and on and on.

Anonymous FTP:
Address: **ftp.uwp.edu**
Path: **/pub/music**

Music and Sound Files

The Internet is alive with the sound of music. No longer do you have to split your funds between your computer system and your stereo. Sink it all into the computer and with these files you can jam and might not even notice the difference. Music, sounds, Sun sounds, and radio programs are available from this site.

Anonymous FTP:
Address: **nic.funet.fi**
Path: **/pub/sounds/***

Music Underground Archive

"Free music from the media" is the motto of the Internet Music Underground. Archived at this site are mpeg sound files of bands, as well as their artwork. If you want to be heard, upload your music here — a place where it will be revered with absolutely no regard for your level of talent.

Gopher:
Name: SunSITE
Address: **calypso-2.oit.unc.edu**
Choose: **Worlds of SunSITE | Internet Music Underground Archive**

World Wide Web:
URL: **http://sunsite.unc.edu/ianc/index.html**

Music Videos

This Usenet group is the place to come to discuss music videos and music video software.

Usenet:
Newsgroup: **rec.music.video**

Isn't this more fun than watching television?

Musical Instrument Construction

What a satisfying feeling to be able to drag out a toolbox and some supplies and craft yourself a musical instrument. And what would be even better is if you can play it when you are finished building it. People who are good with their hands, gather to discuss the design, building and repair of musical instruments.

Usenet:
Newsgroup: **rec.music.makers.builders**

New Age Music

New Age music — Kitaro, Windham Hill, Steven Halpern, Enya, and so on—performers, recordings and general discussion.

Usenet:
Newsgroup: **alt.fan.enya**
Newsgroup: **alt.music.enya**
Newsgroup: **rec.music.gaffa**
Newsgroup: **rec.music.newage**

New Music

Discover music with a difference as you browse the online catalogs and playlists offering music and sound works that stretch the mind.

Gopher:
Name: Whole Earth Lectronic Link
Address: **gopher.well.sf.ca.us**
Choose: **Art and Culture**
  | New Music

Percussion

Techniques and equipment for drums and other percussion instruments.

Usenet:
Newsgroup: **rec.music.makers.percussion**

Performing Classical Music

Discussion for those who perform classical music. Pick up useful hints on style, logistics, and deciding how many encores to take. Check out the directions on how to get to Carnegie Hall (practice, practice, practice).

Usenet:
Newsgroup: **rec.music.classical.performing**

Pipe Organ

A programmable color organ program for the PC. Allows you to interchange music and graphics.

Anonymous FTP:
Address: **ftp.cs.pdx.edu**
Path: **/pub/music/ravel/pip.tar.Z**

Progressive

Progressive music: Yes, Marillion, Asia, King Crimson, and so on.

Usenet:
Newsgroup: **alt.music.progressive**

World Wide Web:
URL: **ftp://ortega.cs.ucdavis.edu/pub/
MSB/WWW/Prog.html**

Punk Rock

Punk rockers, head banging, thrashing, nose studs, dyed hair, and shaved heads — and what ever became of Jello Biafra? Share the punk experience.

Internet Relay Chat:
Channel: **#punk**
Channel: **#realpunk**
Channel: **#skinheads**

Usenet:
Newsgroup: **alt.punk**
Newsgroup: **alt.punk.straight-edge**

Rap

Rap music: no melody, heavy beat, full of words and rhythm, signifying nothing.

Usenet:
Newsgroup: **alt.rap**

Rare Groove

An electronic magazine on the groove music scene. This is not your typical "leaf through it" kind of document. Sample songs are included along with reviews that use such phrases as "vomit-inducing" or "this is a really ripping track." Immerse yourself in the techno intensity, man.

See also: Zines

World Wide Web:
URL: **http://rg.media.mit.edu/RG/RG.html**

Rave

Get into the ultimate techno-culture of music, dancing, drugs, and more illegal and excessive fun than most people can imagine. Learn to be the type of person that your parents warned you about.

Usenet:
Newsgroup: **alt.rave**

World Wide Web:
URL: **http://www.yahoo.com/ Entertainment/Music/Rave_and_techno/**

Do you still have some extra brain cells that you don't know what to do with?

Try Rave

Mr. Braincell
Mr. Braincell

Rave Discussion

Realtime discussion of techno, house, dance, ecstasy, all-weekend raves, and any other forms of rave.

Internet Relay Chat:
Channel: **#rave**

Record Production

To you, it's just a little sheet of vinyl or a small tape or CD that will fit in your backpack, but producing a record is a really big deal for everyone involved. Check out the details of deadlines, costs of production, contracts, technical miracles and equipment and develop a great appreciation for all the work that goes into creating your listening pleasure.

Usenet:
Newsgroup: **alt.music.producer**

Everything in this book is free.

Reggae

Reggae, including roots, rockers, and dancehall reggae. The web page has FAQ files, a list of radio shows and mailorder sources, pictures and lyrics, and links to **rec.music.reggae** and **soc.culture.caribbean**.

Usenet:
Newsgroup: **rec.music.reggae**

World Wide Web:
URL: **http://nyx10.cs.du.edu:8001/~damjohns/ reggae.html**

Renaissance Instruments

If you can't tell a zink from a flauto travelso, it's time to brush up on your music history. In very little time you will be able to impress your friends with knowledge gained while watching demonstrations of musical instruments of the Renaissance such as the shawm, Glastonbury pipe, tabor and crumhorn. Includes pictures and sounds.

World Wide Web:
URL: **http://www.hike.te.chiba-u.ac.jp/cons1/**

Rock and Classical Music

The melding of rock and classical music. Combining the great art of the past with the nostalgia of the future.

Usenet:
Newsgroup: **alt.rock-n-roll.symphonic**

Rock and Roll

Rock and roll is here to stay, I dig it till the end. It'll go down in history, just you wait, my friend.

Usenet:
Newsgroup: **alt.rock-n-roll**
Newsgroup: **alt.rock-n-roll.classic**
Newsgroup: **alt.rock-n-roll.oldies**

San Francisco Bay Area Concerts

Check out the upcoming concerts in the Bay Area with this web page.

World Wide Web:
URL: **http://www.usfca.edu/usf/neufeld/ concerts.html**

A B C D E F G H I J K L M N O P Q R S T U V W X Y Z

Scottish Style Drumming

It's almost like having an extra heartbeat. As the drums beat, the sound gets inside your head, chest, and gut, and calls to that primal part of you. This is the infectious charm of Scottish-style drumming, and if you've heard it you can understand why it's so popular. Drumming enthusiasts join this moderated list to ask questions and give answers about any issue relating to Scottish drumming, including the side, rhythm tenor, flourish tenor and bass drums.

See also: World Cultures

Listserv Mailing List:
    List Address: **sidedrum@sol1.solinet.net**
    Subscription Address: **listserv@sol1.solinet.net**

Sheet Music Collection

This collection of sheet music at Johns Hopkins University contains over 30,000 works of American music divided into dozens of topics.

World Wide Web:
    URL: **http://musicbox.mse.jhu.edu/**

Song Lyrics

Lyrics to popular (and not so popular) songs. This ftp server has an amazing volume of artists and songs. Directories are arranged alphabetically. Pick a directory for the band or artist (i.e., choose **J** for Elton John, then choose an album, then the song).

Anonymous FTP:
    Address: **cs.uwp.edu**
    Path: **/music/lyrics/***

Sonic

The *Sonic Verse Music* magazine highlights "underground" music and contains record reviews, interviews, and much more.

Listserv Mailing List:
    List Address: **sonic-l@vm.marist.edu**
    Subscription Address: **listserv@vm.marist.edu**

The Bizarre section has some cool stuff.

Southern Rock Music

This music is not just any old rock 'n' roll. Southern rock groupies talk about their favorite music and any news and information about the southern rock scene.

Listserv Mailing List:
    List Address: **soco-l@ubvm.cc.buffalo.edu**
    Subscription Address:
        listserv@ubvm.cc.buffalo.edu

Strange Sounds

Bizarre, esoteric, unusual music and sounds that are an acquired taste. Exotic music, skank, thrash, hardcore, industrial, electronic body music: not for those without an industrial-strength auditory cortex.

Usenet:
    Newsgroup: **alt.exotic-music**
    Newsgroup: **alt.music.ebm**
    Newsgroup: **alt.music.hardcore**
    Newsgroup: **alt.music.ska**
    Newsgroup: **alt.thrash**
    Newsgroup: **rec.music.industrial**

Techno/Rave Gopher

Archives, gif images, media reports, music reviews, ambient music survey, and more about raves and techno music.

Gopher:
    Name: Hyperreal Gopher
    Address: **gopher.hyperreal.com**

Top (and Bottom) 100 Lists

Various top 100 lists, including MTV top 100 videos, top 100 albums, and worst 100 singles of the last 25 years.

Anonymous FTP:
    Address: **ftp.spies.com**
    Path: **/Library/Music/Lists/***

Gopher:
    Name: Internet Wiretap
    Address: **wiretap.spies.com**
    Choose: **Wiretap Online Library**
        | Music
        | Various Top 100 Lists

Underground Music Archive

The Internet Underground Music Archive is the Internet's first free hi-fi music archive. This page has links to late-breaking news, legal issues, new features, information on alternative bands with audio excerpts, and links to the home pages of bands such as TeenBeat, Quagmire, Silent and Relentless Pursuit.

World Wide Web:
 URL: **http://www.iuma.com/**

Update Electronic Music Newsletter

An electronic newsletter for those interested in underground music.

Listserv Mailing List:
 List Address: **upnews@vm.marist.edu**
 Subscription Address: **listserv@vm.marist.edu**

Vibe Magazine

Vibe Magazine celebrates American urban youth music and the culture that inspires it. This web site includes excerpts from the latest issues, photographic images, sound clips from new albums, and video clips.

World Wide Web:
 URL: **http://www.vibe.com/**

Vibe Recording Studio

This page is a virtual recording studio where you will find all sorts of hot tracks from around the globe. There is a section with tracks distributed by Red Bullet Records, which has some good **.au** audio files. Be warned, though — the files average about two megabytes in size.

World Wide Web:
 URL: **http://metaverse.com/vibe/
 recording_studio/index.html**

Violin and Bow Makers

This page offers information about several violin and bow makers, as well as a few instrument makers that have mail addresses. One link is direct to the the American Federation of Violin and Bow Makers.

World Wide Web:
 URL: **http://www.eskimo.com/~dvz/
 violin-makers.html**

Virtual Radio

Samples and complete music tunes from all over America in **.wav** and aiff formats.

World Wide Web:
 URL: **http://www.microserve.net/vradio/**

Web Wide World of Music

The Web Wide World of Music offers the ultimate band list, with links for more than 150 bands, major music links, a place to post your own favorite music links on the Net, a trivia quiz, a forum for any thoughts on music, and a music poll where debates rage.

World Wide Web:
 URL: **http://www.galcit.caltech.edu/~ta/music/
 index.html**

WOMAD — World of Music, Arts, and Dance

WOMAD brings together artists from all over the world, and presents festivals and annual events in many countries. The WOMAD web page offers festival details, artists' biographies, interviews and samples.

World Wide Web:
 URL: **http://www.eunet.fi/womad/**

Woodstock '94 Multimedia Center

This site was created during Woodstock '94 by onsite participants, WELL users, and the Internet community. More than 300 web pages containing pictures, sound and text were created for people at the concert, providing a unique perspective of the concert from the people who were there. There are lots of images, stories, and gossip. This resource will remain on the Internet as an archive for generations of rock and roll lovers to savor.

World Wide Web:
 URL: **http://www.well.com/woodstock/**

World Music

Music from around the world: all types, all cultures, anything and everything.

Usenet:
 Newsgroup: **alt.music.world**

A
B
C
D
E
F
G
H
I
J
K
L
M
N
O
P
Q
R
S
T
U
V
W
X
Y
Z

MUSIC: PERFORMERS

Allman Brothers

A mailing list on the Allman Brothers Band and its derivatives. Tape trading, tour information, and other topics of interest to fans.

Internet Mailing List:
List Address: **allman@world.std.com**
Subscription Address:
allman-request@world.std.com

Tori Amos

Pictures, QuickTime movies, articles, mailing list archives, schedules, and a discography of Tori Amos.

Internet Mailing List:
List Address:
really-deep-thoughts@gradient.cis.upenn.edu
Subscription Address:
really-deep-thoughts-request@gradient.cis.upenn.edu

World Wide Web:
URL: **http://www.mit.edu:8001/people/nocturne/tori.html**

Art of Noise

A mailing list and an archive site about the music group Art of Noise. Solo works by the band members are also discussed here. The archive site has reviews, reprints, and a discography.

Anonymous FTP:
Address: **ftp.uwp.edu**
Path: **/pub/music/lists/aon/***

Internet Mailing List:
List Address: **aon@calpoly.edu**
Subscription Address: **aon-request@calpoly.edu**

Beastie Boys

Discography, newspaper and magazine articles, press releases, tour updates, pictures, movies, lyrics, and sound samples from this band.

World Wide Web:
URL: **http://www.nando.net/music/gm/BeastieBoys/**

Jimmy Buffett

Fans of this lively, energetic and upbeat performer talk about his music and concerts, articles and books about him and any other topic that might interest a "Parrothead."

Listserv Mailing List:
List Address: **buffett@miamiu.muohio.edu**
Subscription Address:
listserv@miamiu.muohio.edu

Kate Bush

A free-form, relaxed forum for the discussion of the music of Kate Bush. Don't be surprised if conversation wanders around a bit because Bush's fans have a wide variety of interests and don't always stick to the topic.

Internet Mailing List:
List Address: **love-hounds@eddie.mit.edu**
Subscription Address:
love-hounds-request@eddie.mit.edu

Christian Death Home Page

A complete Christian Death discography, details of other projects in which past or present members of Christian Death have been involved, a hypertext Cleopatra Catalogue, news on the UK Goth scene covering bands, clubs, gigs, and societies, and links to other Goth-related places of interest.

World Wide Web:
URL: **http://christian-death.acc.brad.ac.uk/**

Cocteau Twins Home Page

An introduction, latest news, members list, history, discography, pictures, lyrics, interview, sound and video clips, and more to do with this band.

World Wide Web:
URL: **http://garnet.berkeley.edu:8080/cocteau.html**

Concrete Blonde

Discuss the rock group Concrete Blonde and related artists.

Internet Mailing List:
List Address: **concrete-blonde@piggy.ucsb.edu**
Subscription Address:
concrete-blonde-request@piggy.ucsb.edu

Alice Cooper

This is not the guy you want picking up your sister for the prom. But other than that, he has some pretty great music and quite a few fans — people who stuck with him even through the *Hollywood Squares* days. Join in the unmoderated discussion of anything related to Alice Cooper including news, music, and tour dates. The list name is called Sickthings, but we can't imagine why.

Listserv Mailing List:
> List Address: **sickthings@wkuvx1.wku.edu**
> Subscription Address: **listserv@wkuvx1.wku.edu**

Elvis Costello

We can see why he changed his name from Declan Patrick Aloysius MacManus, but why did he pick Elvis? Find out this tidbit and more when you talk to Elvis Costello fans from around the world.

Internet Mailing List:
> List Address: **costello@gnu.ai.mit.edu**
> Subscription Address:
> **costello-request@gnu.ai.mit.edu**

Miles Davis

Mailing list for fans of the late jazz trumpeter Miles Davis.

Listserv Mailing List:
> List Address: **miles@hearn.bitnet**
> Subscription Address: **listserv@hearn.bitnet**

The Death of Rock 'n' Roll

The saying "It's better to burn out than to fade away" seems to be *the* motto for rock stars. Very few of them have gotten the chance to grow old gracefully except for Mick Jagger, and we're not sure if he can actually be called graceful. Read excerpts from the book *The Death of Rock 'n' Roll* and learn about the untimely demises of such stars as Elvis Presley, Sid Vicious, John Lennon and Marvin Gaye.

World Wide Web:
> URL: **http://alfred1.u.washington.edu:8080/~jlks/pike/DeathRR.html**

Depeche Mode

FAQ, discographies, lyrics, pictures, opinion polls, and links to other Depeche Mode sites.

World Wide Web:
> URL: **http://www.cis.ufl.edu/~sag/dm/**

Dire Straits

Get ready for some rock and roll overload. Put on headphones with your favorite Dire Straits album blaring and then read all the posts discussing the music of Dire Straits and associated side projects. This has got to be heaven.

Internet Mailing List:
> List Address: **dire-straits@merrimack.edu**
> Subscription Address:
> **dire-straits-request@merrimack.edu**

Bob Dylan

Large archive of information about Bob Dylan, including interviews, details of his life and events for over 30 years, and CD and book lists.

Anonymous FTP:
> Address: **ftp.cs.pdx.edu**
> Path: **/pub/dylan/***

Electric Light Orchestra

Without admitting that the Seventies might actually have had some good things about it, we would like to say that ELO cranked out some fun and energetic music. Discuss the works of the band as well as the later solo efforts of band members and former band members.

Internet Mailing List:
> List Address: **elo-list@andrew.cmu.edu**
> Subscription Address:
> **elo-list-request@andrew.cmu.edu**

Enya

A mailing list for fans of this new age Irish vocalist.

Majordomo Mailing List:
> List Address: **enya@cs.colorado.edu**
> Subscription Address:
> **majordomo@cs.colorado.edu**

Melissa Etheridge

She has a sound all her own, that dusky, powerful voice that generates a following that covers the globe. Meet other fans of Melissa Etheridge and discuss her life and music.

Internet Mailing List:
> List Address: **etheridge@krylov.cnd.mcgill.ca**
> Subscription Address:
> **etheridge-request@krylov.cnd.mcgill.ca**

A B C D E F G H I J K L M N O P Q R S T U V W X Y Z

Want to be relatively happy? Try Genealogy.

Favorite Musicians and Music Groups

There are many discussion groups devoted to popular musicians and music groups. Tune in for the latest in concert appearances, reviews, opinions, and esoterica. Look for your favorites!

Usenet:

Newsgroup: **alt.fan.barry-manilow**
Newsgroup: **alt.fan.blues-brothers**
Newsgroup: **alt.fan.david-bowie**
Newsgroup: **alt.fan.debbie.gibson**
Newsgroup: **alt.fan.devo**
Newsgroup: **alt.fan.frank-zappa**
Newsgroup: **alt.fan.jello-biafra**
Newsgroup: **alt.fan.jimmy-buffet**
Newsgroup: **alt.fan.michael-bolton**
Newsgroup: **alt.fan.oingo-boingo**
Newsgroup: **alt.fan.run-dmc**
Newsgroup: **alt.fan.spinal-tap**
Newsgroup: **alt.fan.sting**
Newsgroup: **alt.fan.u2**
Newsgroup: **alt.music.amy-grant**
Newsgroup: **alt.music.beastie-boys**
Newsgroup: **alt.music.bela-fleck**
Newsgroup: **alt.music.billy-joel**
Newsgroup: **alt.music.brian-eno**
Newsgroup: **alt.music.chapel-hill**
Newsgroup: **alt.music.danzig**
Newsgroup: **alt.music.deep-purple**
Newsgroup: **alt.music.dream-theater**
Newsgroup: **alt.music.elo**
Newsgroup: **alt.music.fates-warning**
Newsgroup: **alt.music.fleetwood-mac**
Newsgroup: **alt.music.james-taylor**
Newsgroup: **alt.music.jethro-tull**
Newsgroup: **alt.music.jimi.hendrix**
Newsgroup: **alt.music.kylie-minogue**
Newsgroup: **alt.music.led-zeppelin**
Newsgroup: **alt.music.marillion**
Newsgroup: **alt.music.monkees**
Newsgroup: **alt.music.moody-blues**
Newsgroup: **alt.music.nin**
Newsgroup: **alt.music.nirvana**
Newsgroup: **alt.music.pat-mccurdy**
Newsgroup: **alt.music.paul-simon**
Newsgroup: **alt.music.pearl-jam**
Newsgroup: **alt.music.peter-gabriel**
Newsgroup: **alt.music.pink-floyd**

Newsgroup: **alt.music.prince**
Newsgroup: **alt.music.queen**
Newsgroup: **alt.music.roger-waters**
Newsgroup: **alt.music.rush**
Newsgroup: **alt.music.smash-pumpkins**
Newsgroup: **alt.music.sonic-youth**
Newsgroup: **alt.music.sophie-hawkins**
Newsgroup: **alt.music.the-doors**
Newsgroup: **alt.music.the.police**
Newsgroup: **alt.music.tlc**
Newsgroup: **alt.music.tmbg**
Newsgroup: **alt.music.todd-rundgren**
Newsgroup: **alt.music.u2**
Newsgroup: **alt.music.ween**
Newsgroup: **alt.music.weird-al**
Newsgroup: **alt.music.yes**
Newsgroup: **alt.rock-n-roll.acdc**
Newsgroup: **alt.rock-n-roll.aerosmith**
Newsgroup: **alt.rock-n-roll.metal.gnr**
Newsgroup: **alt.rock-n-roll.metal.ironmaiden**
Newsgroup: **alt.rock-n-roll.metal.metallica**
Newsgroup: **alt.rock-n-roll.stones**
Newsgroup: **info.jethro-tull**
Newsgroup: **rec.music.beatles**
Newsgroup: **rec.music.dylan**
Newsgroup: **rec.music.gdead**
Newsgroup: **rec.music.phish**
Newsgroup: **rec.music.rem**

Front 242

Discography, lyrics, reviews, interviews, pictures, and items to buy and sell relating to Front 242.

See also: Music

World Wide Web:
URL: **http://www.ifi.uio.no/~terjesa/front242/ main.html**

Peter Gabriel

Lyrics, chords, articles, pictures, a discography, and a FAQ about the musical artist and his works.

World Wide Web:
URL: **http://www.cosy.sbg.ac.at/~bjelli/ Gabriel/Text/pg.faq**

There are only two things worth remembering in life (both of which I forget).

Be cool! Join a mailing list.

Marvin Gaye

What is it about performers who sing thought-provoking songs that make people want to shoot them? It's obvious in this particular case. Find out more about the life of Marvin Gaye, his career and the events that lead up to violent death.

World Wide Web:
> URL: **http://alfred1.u.washington.edu:8080/
> ~jlks/pike/mgaye.html**

The Internet has lots of free software. Check out Computers, Software and Operating Systems.

Debbie Gibson

A mailing list devoted to fans of Debbie Gibson.

Internet Mailing List:
> List Address: **btl@egbt.org**
> Subscription Address: **btl-request@egbt.org**

Grateful Dead

Files, information, and discussion lists for you Deadheads out there. At the gopher and ftp sites are numerous gems of interest: graphics, sound files, interviews, a conversation with Jerry Garcia, *the Hemporium*, and much more.

See also: Mail to Famous People

Anonymous FTP:
> Address: **gdead.berkeley.edu**
> Path: **/pub/gdead**

Gopher:
> Name: University of California Berkeley
> Address: **gdead.berkeley.edu**

Internet Mailing List:
> List Address: **dead-flames@virginia.edu**
> Subscription Address:
>   **dead-flames-request@virginia.edu**

> List Address: **dead-heads@virginia.edu**
> Subscription Address:
>   **dead-heads-request@virginia.edu**

A
B
C
D
E
F
G
H
I
J
K
L
M
N
O
P
Q
R
S
T
U
V
W
X
Y
Z

Excerpt from the Net...
(from the Grateful Dead Archives)

The Church of Unlimited Devotion is nothing if not eclectic...

The church's name can be found in a song by the Grateful Dead:

        "The Golden Road (to Unlimited Devotion)"

Members of the church -- which is based in Philo, California -- follow this rock band on most of its tours. Because of the spinning dance they perform both at concerts and as part of their religious devotions, they are know as "the Spinners." They are vegetarian, and take vows of poverty, chastity and obedience...

How did Jerry Garcia lose his finger ?

While they were chopping wood as children, his brother Tiff accidentally chopped it off with an axe.

**If Herman Melville
had written this book,
you would be reading a
metaphor right now.**

Jimi Hendrix

Even though he is long dead and hasn't had any new releases in the past twenty years, Jimi Hendrix is still popular and has a strong following. Hang out with other Hendrix worshippers and discuss his life and music.

Internet Mailing List:
    List Address: **hey-joe@ms.uky.edu**
    Subscription Address:
      hey-joe-request@ms.uky.edu

Allan Holdsworth

Stimulating discussions on the works of guitarist Allan Holdsworth.

Internet Mailing List:
    List Address:
      atavachron@msuacad.morehead-st.edu
    Subscription Address:
      atavachron-request@msuacad.morehead-st.edu

Indigo Girls

With voices that blend magically and fingers that dance across the guitar strings, the Indigo Girls have won the hearts of people all around the world. Fans talk about the artists' music, tour dates, concert reviews, and more. The list is also available in digest format if you want to get all the posts compiled in a single message.

Internet Mailing List:
    List Address: **indigo-girls@cgrg.ohio-state.edu**
    Subscription Address:
      indigo-girls-request@cgrg.ohio-state.edu

**The Internet is more fun than
a barrel of cliches**

Jean Michel Jarre

A mailing list for fans of this ambient/electronic performer.

Internet Mailing List:
    List Address: **jarre@cs.uwp.edu**
    Subscription Address: **jarre-request@cs.uwp.edu**

Jazz Performers

Imagine being in on the movement that created jazz. Who were the musicians who started jazz and kept the music alive? Check out this compilation of information on the hippest, baddest cats of jazz history.

World Wide Web:
    URL: **http://sccs.swarthmore.edu/~jbf/jazz.html**

**Learn HTML and create
your own web page
(see Internet: Resources).**

Billy Joel

Did Billy Joel ever put out a song that could be considered a real dog? Many performers have their selected following, but it's hard to imagine that there might be people who actually don't like Billy Joel's music. Fans of the Piano Man carry on lively discussion of his music, career, and life.

Listserv Mailing List:
    List Address: **pianoman@psuvm.psu.edu**
    Subscription Address: **listserv@psuvm.psu.edu**

Kiss

At the height of their popularity, Kiss was something pretty bizarre. But not anymore. They've revealed their true identities once and for all and are settling into the role of a "classic" rock band. Fans discuss any topic relating to Kiss, including news and opinions on albums. You might even pick up some good make-up tips.

Listserv Mailing List:
    List Address: **kissarmy@wkuvx1.wku.edu**
    Subscription Address: **listserv@wkuvx1.wku.edu**

John Lennon

John Lennon was taken early and has been mourned in the years since his death. Read a little about his history and music as well as his relationship with the other Beatles.

World Wide Web:
URL: **http://alfred1.u.washington.edu:8080/ ~jlks/pike/jolenno.html**

Paul McCartney

His career is reaching epic proportions. Paul started early and he's still going strong. Read about his rumored death and the ruckus it stirred up, as well as other topics of interest about Paul.

World Wide Web:
URL: **http://alfred1.u.washington.edu:8080/ ~jlks/pike/pmccar.html**

Paul McCartney Death Rumor

Rumors are fun, but they are only supposed to last a little while. Some rumors take on a life of their own and will not die, no matter how hard people try to make them go away. Beatles fans have been obsessed with Paul's "death" for years. Read all the theories and symbolism that have kept this joke going for so many years.

World Wide Web:
URL: **http://turtle.ncsa.uiuc.edu/alan/beatles/ pid.html**

Reba McEntire

Get the latest news on Reba McEntire: schedule of appearances, special events, reviews, fan club information, a bibliography of articles, and pictures of the country music goddess herself.

World Wide Web:
URL: **http://ruby.ph.utexas.edu/RebaWWW/ Reba.html**

> ## Do you have a favorite item that is not in the catalog? Let us know by sending mail to catalog@rain.org

> ## The Internet is low in cholesterol.

Nine Inch Nails

Lyrics, discography, reviews, tour information, FAQ, guitar tabs and chords, and mailing lists about Nine Inch Nails.

World Wide Web:
URL: **http://www.scri.fsu.edu/~patters/nin.html**

> ## Little known fact: Charles and Diana met in alt.romance.

Sinead O'Connor

There are not many women in the world who can shave their head and still be popular. Sinead O'Connor happens to be one of the few who can. Discuss O'Connor's music, lyrics, political antics and tour information with other fans of this songster.

Internet Mailing List:
List Address: **jump-in-the-river@presto.ig.com**
Subscription Address:
jump-in-the-river-request@presto.ig.com

Pink Floyd

We know what their name means, but we're not telling. You'll have to join the list to find out. Fans of Pink Floyd discuss the music and members of this unique band.

Mail:
Address: **echoserv@fawnya.tcs.com**
Body: **add echoes**

Internet Mailing List:
List Address: **echoes@fawnya.tcs.com**
Subscription Address:
echoes-request@fawnya.tcs.com

A B C D E F G H I J K L M N O P Q R S T U V W X Y Z

> **No matter who you are or what you believe, somewhere on the Internet, there are people like you.**

The Pogues

Images, discography, lyrics, and links to other sites for this Irish band with a name derived from the Gaelic "Pogue mahone," meaning "Kiss my ass."

World Wide Web:
   URL: **http://daneel.acns.nwu.edu:8082/kultur/ pogues/pogueroot.html**

> **The only place where Politics comes before Star Trek is in "The Internet Golden Directory."**

The Police

Nearly everyone loves The Police — the band, that is. Fans of this group talk about the music and lives of Sting, Stewart Copeland, and Andy Summers. All screaming groupies are welcome, but remember that on the Internet nobody can hear you scream.

Internet Mailing List:
   List Address: **police@cindy.ecst.csuchico.edu**
   Subscription Address:
   police-request@cindy.ecst.csuchico.edu

> **Parents and children, take a look at: Families and Parenting, Kids, and Youth.**

Elvis Presley

We have discovered where Elvis has been all along. He's really not dead. He has been living on the Internet. Take a tour of Graceland, hear sound clips, and learn all about the King.

Usenet:
   Newsgroup: **alt.elvis.king**
   Newsgroup: **alt.elvis.sighting**

World Wide Web:
   URL: **http://tamsun.tamu.edu/~ahb2188/ elvishom.html**

Elvis Forever

There is no doubt about it. Elvis died for your sins. Well . . . he died for someone's sins. Anyway, while you are thinking it over, point your web browser at the Elvis web site and see how the simple belief in America's favorite musical deity change your life.

Prince

He's not calling himself Prince anymore, but you know who we are talking about. We just can't pronounce his name. Follow his life, career, music and unusual philosophies with devotees of the performing-artist-formerly-known-as-Prince.

Internet Mailing List:
List Address: **prince@icpsr.umich.edu**
Subscription Address:
prince-request@icpsr.umich.edu

Rocker Group Web Pages

This page has links to the pages of hundreds of popular artists and bands as well as direct links to their respective Usenet newsgroups and FAQ files. If you thought you were the only fan of Alien Sex Fiend or Avocado Jungle Fuzz, well, apparently you were wrong.

World Wide Web:
URL: **http://www.yahoo.com/ Entertainment/Music/**

Want to know what makes the Internet run? Read Internet: RFCs.

Rolling Stones

This band has endless energy and will probably outlive most of us and be recording their last albums from the wing of a hospital for the Geriatric Rich and Famous. In the meantime, fans of the Stones get together to talk about music, guitar playing, books about the Stones, and review solo albums by members of the band. The web site is the home page for the Stones' Voodoo Lounge tour and won one of PC Week's "Cool Web Site" awards.

Internet Mailing List:
List Address:
undercover@snowhite.cis.uoguelph.ca
Subscription Address:
undercover-request@snowhite.cis.uoguelph.ca

World Wide Web:
URL: **http://www.stones.com/**

— Everything we tell you is true.
— The above sentence is only partially correct.
— Don't believe everything you read.

Rush

A few years ago when someone said the name "Rush" everyone thought about the rock group from Canada. Even though that has changed, the group's popularity certainly hasn't. Lovers of this band discuss the group and its music.

Internet Mailing List:
List Address: **rush@syrinx.umd.edu**
Subscription Address:
rush-request@syrinx.umd.edu

Severed Heads

A mailing list for fans of the Severed Heads, an Australian band that has been cranking it out since 1980. Members of this list also tend to like other bands on the Ralph label.

Internet Mailing List:
List Address: **adolph-a-carrot@andrew.cmu.edu**
Subscription Address:
adolph-a-carrot-request@andrew.cmu.edu

Frank Sinatra

A web page dedicated to undoubtedly one of the greatest musical artists of this century. It contains filmography, discography, interviews, music releases, International Sinatra Societies, and other tributes to this legendary singer.

World Wide Web:
URL: **http://www.io.org/~buff/sinatra.html**

The Internet is more fun than a barrel of cliches.

A
B
C
D
E
F
G
H
I
J
K
L
M
N
O
P
Q
R
S
T
U
V
W
X
Y
Z

Sisters of Mercy

Discography, interviews, pictures, sound files, lyrics, news, FAQ, concert reviews, artwork, and personal information on the various incarnations of the Sisters.

See also: Music

World Wide Web:
    URL: **http://www.cm.cf.ac.uk/Sisters.Of.Mercy/**

Bruce Springsteen

A mailing list for fans of the Boss.

Internet Mailing List:
    List Address: **backstreets@virginia.edu**
    Subscription Address:
      backstreets-request@virginia.edu

10,000 Maniacs

Audio files, pictures, and lyrics for the group 10,000 Maniacs.

See also: Music

World Wide Web:
    URL: **http://www.nd.edu/StudentLinks/
      mecheves/misc/10000.html**

Vangelis

Vangelis is a famous synthesizer guru who's made soundtracks for many movies. This web page has pictures, digitized music, and animations related to Vangelis.

World Wide Web:
    URL: **http://bau2.uibk.ac.at/perki/Vangelis.html**

Sid Vicious

Experience the tender tale of Sid Vicious, the perpetually violent punk-rocker and bassist of the Sex Pistols, who allegedly stabbed his girlfriend to death and who consumed heroin like a yuppie consumes Perrier.

World Wide Web:
    URL: **http://alfred1.u.washington.edu:8080/
      ~jlks/pike/svicio.html**

Doc Watson

A multimedia exhibit featuring North Carolina's Doc Watson, the American bluegrass and folk music legend. The exhibit includes a history of his career, samples of his music, details of other guitar players he met and worked with, and more. Let Doc sing the "Blue Railroad Train" for you.

World Wide Web:
    URL: **http://sunsite.unc.edu/doug/DocWat/
      DWCover.html**

XTC

Chalkhills is a mailing list for discussing the music and records of the band XTC.

Internet Mailing List:
    List Address: **chalkhills@presto.ig.com**
    Subscription Address:
      chalkhills-request@presto.ig.com

NEW AGE

Afterlife

Life is so much fun that it would be nice to believe we can experience it more than once. Listen to people share not only their thoughts and ideas on the concept of life after death, but also stories about experiences they have had with deceased loved ones coming back to visit and anecdotes of a paranormal type.

Usenet:
Newsgroup: **alt.life.afterlife**

THE AFTERLIFE

The question is not so much, is there life after death, but is there life before death? We have always thought it to be the ultimate cosmic joke. Here we are, trapped in mortal bodies that, through natural selection and evolution, have been programmed to not want to die. But we have brains that can not only understand the idea of death, but understand that, one day, we also will die and that will be the end of our existence. There are lots of ways to deal with this problem: religion, philosophy, ignorance, denial... But perhaps the most interesting is fostering the belief that there really is an afterlife. What a comforting feeling it must be to "know" that you do not cease to exist after you bite the big one. If you would like to see what such people believe (or if you perchance believe in an afterlife yourself), drop in on the discussion in **alt.life.afterlife**. Actually, we are beginning to suspect that the best thing might be to not even be conceived in the first place. Unfortunately, probably only one person in ten thousand is so lucky.

**Be cool!
Join a mailing list.**

AwareNet

Clear your seventh chakra, open your third eye, expand your consciousness, control your breathing — it's a fitness program for your psyche. If you like to be aware of what is going on in the universe besides stuffy physics and science, go where the enlightened people keep their archives of discussion on cosmic happenings, paranormal occurrences and astrological data. Get a free astrological chart personalized just for you or someone you love. It makes a great gift.

Gopher:
Name: AwareNET
Address: **awarenet.com**
Port: **8104**

Name: AwareNET
Address: **awarenet.com**
Choose: **AwareNET**

Biorhythms

This page will compute your biorhythm for you when you enter your birthdate. Results are presented in a statistical format.

World Wide Web:
URL: **http://cad.ucla.edu:8001/biorhythm**

Lucid Dreams

Having a lucid dream is sort of like directing your own movie except that it's a whole lot cheaper and you don't have to deal with unions. Lucid dreams are those in which you are totally aware of what is going on and you can control the outcome. Read about other people's dreams and share some of your own. It's fun and best of all it's free.

Usenet:
Newsgroup: **alt.dreams.lucid**

With lucid dreaming you can make sure that all your dreams can come true without having to pay taxes, change your clothes, or even leave your house.

Excerpt from the Net...

```
Newsgroup: alt.magick
Subject: End Of The World Party

Once again it's time to start planning
for the annual End Of The World Party.
This is an annual event invented by a
bunch of drunks in the backwoods of
Oregon with nothing better to do...
```

Magick

The good news for witches in the 90's is that nobody gets burned at the stake anymore. Whatever brand of magick you like to practice, Usenet has something to offer you. Get information on solitary witches, rituals, equipment and supplies, ethics and the hardships faced by today's practitioners of magick.

Usenet:

Newsgroup: **alt.magick**
Newsgroup: **alt.magick.chaos**
Newsgroup: **alt.magick.ethics**
Newsgroup: **alt.magick.order**
Newsgroup: **alt.magick.sex**
Newsgroup: **alt.magick.tyagi**

Magick Galore

You never know when you will need to immediately lay your hands on the Hymn to Osiris in the Egyptian Book of the Dead or perhaps look up the definition for the word "utok" in the Dictionary of Ouranos Barbaric. Have access to more magick than you can shake a bag of runes at.

See also: Paranormal, Religion: Alternative

World Wide Web:
URL: **http://www.nada.kth.se/~nv91-asa/ magick.html**

Masters, Extraterrestrials and Archangels

Quench that burning desire you have to know all about ascended masters, extraterrestrial beings, and other spiritual higher-ups. Read about and see pictures of such notables as Maitreya, Serapis-Bei, Melchizedek, Khutumi, Michael, and Ballerian.

See also: Paranormal, Religion: Alternative

World Wide Web:
URL: **http://err.ethz.ch/~kiwi/Spirit/ masters-ets-angels.html**

Zines are cool.

Excerpt from the Net...

```
Newsgroup: alt.meditation
Subject: Where Does the Deception Lie?

> I recall an article in Yoga Journal where they quote Yogananda's
> description of "levitation" as involving hopping in the early stages.

I am not aware of this reference to hopping or whether it has anything
to do with what Transcendental Meditation teaches.  Yogananda did refer
to saints who were able to levitate.  In fact he tells a story af a
Christian monk who could not perform his chores at the monastery
because he could not stay on the ground.

I should add that Yogananda repeatedly cautions the devotee to avoid
all psychic manifestations that are part of spiritual unfoldment.
They are maya and easily divert the devotee from the goal.  When
Brother Bhaktananda, one of Yogananda's most advanced disciples, was
asked about levitation, he gave the above warning and then commented
that it was better to devote all of your spiritual energy to meditation
and take the elevator.
```

Meditation

Close your eyes, breathe deep, relax. Clear your mind of all thoughts, free your body of all tension and float off to a world of pure spiritual essence. Explore the many methods of meditation, whether through yoga, visualization, traditional and philosophical processes, or by using more modern means. This newsgroup will give you information on the history and technique of all types of meditation.

Usenet:
Newsgroup: **alt.meditation**
Newsgroup: **alt.meditation.quanyin**

Mysticism

It's a dark and stormy night and during the dinner party someone brings up the subject of mysticism and begins telling about the seven layers of consciousness, time and the concept of becoming God. Then someone asks you what you think about the difference between the subconscient and the superconscient. Much to your embarrassment, the only response you can stammer is: "Anyone for dessert?" Raise your consciousness to a more mystical level by reading this newsgroup and never be caught with your aura down again.

Usenet:
Newsgroup: **alt.consciousness.mysticism**

New Age Talk

New Age believers encourage awareness, positive thinking, and healing with the mind, as well as offering information on many other topics.

Usenet:
Newsgroup: **talk.religion.newage**

Occult and Magick Talk

Chat, discussion, and talk of many areas of magick and occultism.

Internet Relay Chat:
Channel: **#babel**
Channel: **#magick**
Channel: **#omnet**
Channel: **#oto**
Channel: **#psimagick**
Channel: **#tarot**
Channel: **#thelema**

Occult Mailing List

No more will you wonder if the supernatural and existence-beyond-existence are real or just figments of your reality. Join the discussion about things hidden and esoteric, and learn about the history and theory of the occult.

Listserv Mailing List:
List Address: **arcana@unccvm.uncc.edu**
Subscription Address: **listserv@unccvm.uncc.edu**

Paganism

What are pagans about? Read the history, rituals, ethics, and methods of paganism.

Internet Mailing List:
List Address: **pagan@drycas.club.cc.cmu.edu**
Subscription Address:
pagan-request@drycas.club.cc.cmu.edu

Usenet:
Newsgroup: **alt.pagan**

Postmodern Culture

Back issues of *Postmodern Culture*, described as "an electronic journal of interdisciplinary criticism." *Postmodern Culture* examines all aspects of current society and how they relate to postmodernism.

Anonymous FTP:
Address: **ftp.uu.net**
Path: **/doc/literary/obi/Postmodern/***

Revelations of Awareness

The *New Age Cosmic Newsletter* is aimed at introducing people to cosmic awareness.

Anonymous FTP:
Address: **etext.archive.umich.edu**
Path: **/pub/Politics/Conspiracy/**
Cosmic.Awareness/*

**Ignoring this hint
may be hazardous
to your health.**

A B C D E F G H I J K L M N O P Q R S T U V W X Y Z

Make new friends on Internet Relay Chat (IRC).

Sex and Magick

An essay on sex and sex magick entitled "Liber Conjunctus," by Fr. Nigris.

Anonymous FTP:
> Address: **ftp.spies.com**
> Path: **/Library/Fringe/Occult/magick.sex**

Gopher:
> Name: Internet Wiretap
> Address: **wiretap.spies.com**
> Choose: **Wiretap Online Library**
> | **Fringes of Reason**
> | **Occult and Paranormal**
> | **Liber Conjunctus - Essay on Sex & Magick**

Usenet:
> Newsgroup: **alt.magick.sex**

Spirit Web

Do you ever get the feeling that there is more going on around you than you realize? What is it with all these alien sightings and interactions with ghosts and people who say they channel voices from the great beyond? Do they know something you don't? You don't have to feel left out any longer. Get information on channeling, alternative healing, UFOs, light technology, earth changes, out-of-body experiences, astrology and other subjects that really are out of this world.

See also: Paranormal

World Wide Web:
> URL: **http://err.ethz.ch/~kiwi/Spirit.html**

Spiritual Grab Bag

A buffet is nice because you can stroll along and sample a little of this and that as it strikes your fancy. That's what is great about this web site. You'll find articles, FAQs, and interesting tidbits on paganism, magick, the paranormal, UFOs, parapsychology, skepticism, and some really weird religions.

See also: Paranormal, Religion: Alternative

World Wide Web:
> URL: **http://x.pyramid.com/~mitch/kooks.html**

Spiritual Healing

A home page devoted to spiritual healing, such as the study of auras, chakras, energy work, Reiki, Shiatsu, and homeopathy. These methods are much easier to practice on your friends than a splenectomy, plus you can do these tricks at dinner parties and it won't make people lose their appetites.

See also: Health, Paranormal

World Wide Web:
> URL: **http://err.ethz.ch/~kiwi/Spirit/healing.html**

Sumeria Web Page

Articles on alternative science, suppressed and neglected medical ideas, areas for politics, fiction, animal issues, the immune system, alternative health and biology, short stories, an art gallery, and much more.

World Wide Web:
> URL: **http://werple.apana.org.au/sumeria/sumeria.html**

Tarot

You're minding your own business, laying your tarot cards out in a simple little Celtic Cross spread when all of a sudden the Nine of Swords pops up in a place where you least suspected. Now what does that mean? Don't let it stump you. Tarot fans and experts talk about this classical form of divination in Usenet. Get help, advice and hear interesting ideas about spreads, card meanings and different versions of tarot decks.

Usenet:
> Newsgroup: **alt.tarot**

Tarot Reading

Do you fear your future? Do you think that Tarot prophecy can actually affect your future? This server may provide (at least someone's) answers to these questions. You can get your own tarot card reading from this server. Of course, if you think this is what they make poi out of — never mind.

World Wide Web:
> URL: **http://cad.ucla.edu/repository/useful/tarot.html**

Urantia Book

What if someone were to tell you they could help you consolidate knowledge and all world views to improve life for everyone on Earth? Would you want to do it? If you would jump at the chance, then check out this list that discusses the Urantia material and is a forum for both scientific and theological perspectives for enhancing understanding of oneself using the Urantia material as a guide.

See also: Religion: Alternative

Listserv Mailing List:
    List Address: **urantial@uafsysb.uark.edu**
    Subscription Address: **listserv@uafsysb.uark.edu**

Visions of Jesus and Mary

Why waste your time on Elvis and Bigfoot sightings when you could be seeing someone really important, like Jesus and his mother, Mary? If you have seen apparitions of any members of the Holy Family or if you are interested in the significance of these experiences, gather with others to discuss what it all means.

Listserv Mailing List:
    List Address: **conyers@ubvm.cc.buffalo.edu**
    Subscription Address:
      listserv@ubvm.cc.buffalo.edu

Wicca

Documents detailing the Wiccan branch of the occult, including spells, beliefs, exercises, and much more.

Anonymous FTP:
    Address: **ftp.funet.fi**
    Path: **/pub/doc/occult/wicca/***

NEWS: U.S.

CBC Radio Trial

Daily news broadcasts, transcripts, program listings, sample radio programs, Radio Canada International information and schedules, a list of products, illustrated audio shows, and more from Canadian Broadcasting Corporation (CBC) Radio.

World Wide Web:
    URL: **http://debra.dgbt.doc.ca/cbc/cbc.html**

If you are one of those people lucky enough to get CBC (Canadian) Radio, you will appreciate their web site.

Clarinet

Many Usenet-like newsgroups devoted to real news. In order to access Clarinet, your news site must subscribe to it.

Usenet:
    Newsgroup: **clari.***

Commercial Online News Ventures

An article describing the various ways that publishers have tried to produce commercial electronic news services, including online services, independent bulletin board systems, and services available on the Internet. The article includes a list of commercial Internet-based news efforts as well as local BBS dialup services, America Online-based services, and others.

Mail:
    Address: **majordomo@marketplace.com**
    Body: **get online-news online-newspapers.list**

Current Affairs Magazines

Sample articles and subscription information for business, politics, and news magazines.

Gopher:
    Name: The Electronic Newsstand
    Address: **gopher.internet.com**
    Port: **2100**
    Choose: **Titles Arranged by Subject**
     | Current Affairs - Business, Politics, News

A
B
C
D
E
F
G
H
I
J
K
L
M
N
O
P
Q
R
S
T
U
V
W
X
Y
Z

Daily Sources of Business and Economic News

A large collection of links to free sources of daily news on the Internet. This page is divided into global news, regional news, national news, and links to specific general resources. It also offers newspaper, radio and television station electronic mail addresses.

World Wide Web:
URL: **http://www.helsinki.fi/~lsaarine/news.html**

News, News, and More News

Okay, so you are glued to your computer and fastened to the Net. Still there is no need to miss the news. All you need is a web browser and you can make sure that no event whatsoever escapes your attention.

EFFector Online and EFF News

The complete set of the *EFFector Online* magazine and EFF News publications, which tackle issues relating to computers, the law, and privacy.

Anonymous FTP:
Address: **ftp.eff.org**
Path: **/pub/EFF/Newsletters/***

Gopher:
Name: Electronic Frontier Foundation
Address: **gopher.eff.org**
Choose: **Electronic Frontier..**
| Back issues of EFF newsletters

Electric Examiner

The San Francisco Examiner offers web users this Virtual Newsroom, with links to current articles on sports, entertainment, science, columns and features, and national events.

World Wide Web:
URL: **http://sfgate.com/examiner**

Electronic Newsstand

Easy access to a wide range of interesting information and articles provided by U.S. and worldwide magazine publishers. Electronic Newsstand provides a window into the worlds of politics, science, business, foreign affairs, arts, travel, food, and sports.

Gopher:
Name: The Electronic Newsstand
Address: **gopher.internet.com**
Port: **2100**

Marla leaves Donald for a handsome Internet author!!   *Special Inside*

The Electronic Newsstand

How many times

have you held up the line in the supermarket reading the *National Enquirer* while everyone else encourages you to either buy it or move on? On the Net, you can take your time. Just connect to the *Electronic Newsstand* Gopher and browse until you're full. No, you won't find the *Enquirer*, but you will find a lot of other interesting items; certainly enough to keep you occupied when you should be working.

President consumes 32 million MacBurgers in effort to boost economy, and gains 576 lbs. as a result.

The Gate

This web page of the *San Francisco Chronicle* and the *San Francisco Examiner* offers news articles on business, sports, world news, Bay Area and California events, regular columns, movie reviews, book guides, and much more.

World Wide Web:
   URL: **http://cyber.sfgate.com/**

Headline and Business News

View video segments from recent news events on American television using the vsbrowser VuSystem from MIT.

Note: Requires NCSA Mosaic for the X Window System, version 2.0 or higher.

World Wide Web:
   URL: **http://tns-www.lcs.mit.edu/cgi-bin/vs/ vsbrowser**

Middlesex News

General interest newspaper from Metrowest, the high-tech region west of Boston. This electronic newspaper includes movie and restaurant reviews, event guides, tourist information, regular columns, and other items of interest.

Gopher:
   Name: Software Tool & Die
   Address: **gopher.std.com**
   Choose: **Periodicals, Magazines, and Journals I Middlesex News**

NASA Hot Topics

A hypertext collection of NASA news articles, subjects, and information sources of particular interest to the public, NASA *Hot Topics* is updated on a regular basis to keep you abreast of current events.

See also: Space

World Wide Web:
   URL: **http://hypatia.gsfc.nasa.gov/ nasa_hottopics.html**

National News Stories

Clarinet offers a great way to keep up with news about the United States. The **clari.news.usa** groups offer press articles on topics like government, law and the military.

Usenet:
   Newsgroup: **clari.news.usa.***

The News & Observer

Samples and articles from the latest edition of *The News & Observer* daily newspaper from North Carolina.

World Wide Web:
   URL: **http://www.nando.net/nando.html**

Newsletters and Journals Available via Gopher

A large collection of online newsletters and journals covering art, computing, education, humanities, languages, law, medicine, politics, religion, and more. They are all neatly categorized and available through gopher.

Gopher:
   Name: Swedish University Network
   Address: **gopher.sunet.se**
   Choose: **Library Services I Newsletters & Journals**

   Name: University of North Texas
   Address: **gopher.unt.edu**
   Choose: **Remote Information... I Electronic Documents**

Newspapers and Journalism Schools

The University of Florida's College of Journalism and Communications offers this list of links to commercial newspapers developing web editions, a list of Campus Newspapers on the Internet, and a collection of journalism and communications schools on the Web.

World Wide Web:
   URL: **http://www.jou.ufl.edu/commres/ webjou.htm**

San Francisco Examiner News Wires Page

Daily news reports wired to the World Wide Web from the *San Francisco Examiner*. Presented as a list of article headlines from which you can select the article of your choice.

World Wide Web:
   URL: **http://sfgate.com/examiner/ newswires.html**

MUDs are real (sort of).

A
B
C
D
E
F
G
H
I
J
K
L
M
N
O
P
Q
R
S
T
U
V
W
X
Y
Z

State News

Keep up to date with the news in your state by reading the **clari.local** groups offered by Clarinet news. These newsgroups are divided by state so you can keep up with news by specific locality.

Usenet:
Newsgroup: **clari.local.***

Submitting News via the Internet

Instructions on using the Internet to submit press releases, news tips, letters to the editor, op-ed pieces, and questions, through the Internet, to the *Middlesex News* newspaper, based near Boston.

Gopher:
Name: Software Tool & Die
Address: **gopher.std.com**
Choose: **Periodicals, Magazines, and Journals**
  | **Middlesex News**
  | **About the Middlesex News**

USA Today

Sample articles from the *USA Today* newspaper.

Gopher:
Name: Michigan State University
Address: **gopher.msu.edu**
Choose: **News & Weather**
  | **Electronic Newspapers**
  | **Sample Newspapers**
  | **USA Today**

Telnet:
Address: **freenet-in-a.cwru.edu**

Address: **freenet-in-b.cwru.edu**

Address: **freenet-in-c.cwru.edu**

Address: **yfn2.ysu.edu**
Login: **visitor**

Washington Post

Sample articles from the *Washington Post* newspaper.

Gopher:
Name: Michigan State University
Address: **gopher.msu.edu**
Choose: **News & Weather**
  | **Electronic Newspapers**
  | **Sample Newspapers**
  | **Washington Post**

NEWS: WORLD

ABC's World News Now

Not only can you catch the news on ABC, but you can talk about catching the news on ABC. *World News Now* is the popular overnight news show that covers a variety of interesting news topics. List discussion is open to anything related to *World News Now*, including the private lives of the anchors (for really hard-core fans who have nothing better to do with their lives).

Internet Mailing List:
List Address: **wnn@world.std.com**
Subscription Address: **wnn-request@world.std.com**

Australian News

News stories past and present from Australian newspapers.

Gopher:
Name: Universite de Montreal
Address: **megasun.bch.umontreal.ca**
Choose: **Australiana - News, sport, FAQ's...**
  | **News from Austrailian Newspapers**

Usenet:
Newsgroup: **soc.culture.australian**

Bosnia

Stay abreast of the action as it happens in Bosnia. Read news about the country as well as discussion of the news and what it means to the rest of the world. This newsgroup is moderated.

Usenet:
Newsgroup: **bit.listserv.bosnet**

A sure-fire way to make all your dreams come true is to sleep with this book under your pillow.

Chinese News Digest Server

China News Digest (CND) is a voluntary non-profit organization aimed at providing news and other information services to readers who are concerned primarily with China-related affairs. It offers both current news and an archive of previous global news, U.S., Canada, Europe, and Pacific regional news dating back many months, history, many scenic pictures from China, classic Chinese texts, and links to other news sites.

Gopher:
>Name: Chinese News Digest Server
>Address: **cnd.org**

World Wide Web:
>URL: **http://www.cnd.org/**

Croatian Ministry of Foreign Affairs

Daily news, bulletins and flashes, letters, and press releases.

Gopher:
>Name: Croatia
>Address: **rujan.srce.hr**
>Choose: **English Language**
> | **Actual News, Notices and Events**
> | **Croatian Homeland Association...**

Croatian News

This list carries articles and news about Croatia from sources like *Croatia Monitor*, Radio Free Europe, and UPI. This is a high volume list and reports come in English, Croatian, and sometimes Slovene.

Internet Mailing List:
>List Address: **cro-news@well.ox.ac.uk**
>Subscription Address:
>   **cro-news-request@well.ox.ac.uk**

Daily Newspaper Electronic Mail Addresses

A large list of mail addresses of contacts and reporters for daily newspapers around the world. This list includes mail addresses in Canada, Czech Republic, Europe, Germany, Namibia, Poland, U.K., and a large United States section. Send in your news tip today!

See also: News: U.S.

World Wide Web:
>URL: **http://www.helsinki.fi/~lsaarine/ part2.html#DAILY**

> ## Don't be a Web Potato: participate.

Ecuadoran Daily News Summaries

La Prensa newspaper (in Spanish).

Gopher:
>Name: Ministerio de Relaciones Exteriores del Ecuador
>Address: **gopher.mmrree.gov.ec**
>Choose: **Base de datos Documentales**
> | **PRENSA**

French Daily News Transcripts

Daily news reports in French from "Le service de presse de l'Ambassade de France á Washington." This page allows you to search the transcripts for a particular phrase or word, or click on the calendar for that particular date.

World Wide Web:
>URL: **http://phoebus.Colorado.EDU:8080/Revues/**

French Language Press Review

French summaries of news reported in the French language press, updated on an almost daily basis.

Gopher:
>Name: Michigan State University
>Address: **gopher.msu.edu**
>Choose: **News & Weather**
> | **Electronic Newspapers**
> | **General Newspapers**
> | **French Language Press Review**

French News

Daily newsbriefs in French about events in France, including a general discussion of the main articles published in the French press on that day, often quoting the articles extensively.

Gopher:
>Name: Yale University
>Address: **yaleinfo.yale.edu**
>Choose: **The Internet**
> | **News and weather**
> | **France**

A B C D E F G H I J K L M N O P Q R S T U V W X Y Z

Gazeta Wyborcza

The complete daily newspaper from Poland online, available in Polish only.

World Wide Web:
    URL: **http://info.fuw.edu.pl/gw/0/gazeta.htm**

German Language News Service

A German news digest with almost daily summaries of principal German news stories, provided in German.

Internet Mailing List:
    List Address: **germnews@vm.gmd.de**
    Subscription Address:
        germnews-request@vm.gmd.de

Islamic News

News, thoughtful articles and discussion about Islam. This group is moderated and comes in a digest format.

Usenet:
    Newsgroup: **bit.listserv.muslims**

Israeli News

Articles about the state of Israel, including Israel's Declaration of Independence, conference news, and newspaper reports.

Anonymous FTP:
    Address: **israel.nysernet.org**
    Path: **/israel/Israel_Info/***

Gopher:
    Name: NYSERNet
    Address: **israel.nysernet.org**
    Port: **71**
    Choose: **Israeli Business, Science and Projects
      | Israeli Information**

Moscow News

Sample of English articles from the *Moscow News* newspaper.

Gopher:
    Name: Michigan State University
    Address: **gopher.msu.edu**
    Choose: **News & Weather
      | Electronic Newspapers
      | Sample Newspapers
      | Moscow News**

Pakistan

These discussion, in digest format, offer a huge amount of information on the latest news about Pakistan. The newsletters offer timely and thoughtful articles, poems, news of politics and the social environment in Pakistan.

Usenet:
    Newsgroup: **bit.listserv.pakistan**
    Newsgroup: **bit.listserv.pns-l**

RTE Radio News

Listen to the Irish National Radio's (RTE) 8 A.M. morning and 8 P.M. evening world news broadcasts in English and Gaelic.

World Wide Web:
    URL: **http://sunsite.unc.edu:80/pub/academic/
        languages/gaelic/Rte/**

World News

Don't be the last person in the world to hear important news. Keep up with the day-to-day occurrences on the planet by checking out Clarinet news. This newsgroup will keep you current by showing you the top news stories from around the world and leaving out the fluff.

Usenet:
    Newsgroup: **clari.world.top**

OCEANOGRAPHY

Distributed Ocean Data System

The Oceanography Society maintains this online workshop as a national repository of reports, summaries, databases, and software tools of interest to oceanographers and other scientists interested in oceanographic data.

World Wide Web:
URL: **http://lake.mit.edu/dods.html**

Global Ocean Flux Study

The Joint Global Ocean Flux Study is a group of researchers studying the ocean's role in the global carbon cycle. They strive to better understand this cycle and ultimately offer a database and computer models. This page offers information about this study and the goals of the organization.

World Wide Web:
URL: **http://lake.mit.edu/jgofs.html**

Icelandic Fisheries Laboratories

The IFL server contains much information on Iceland and the waters surrounding it. Included are a tourist guide of Iceland, seafood recipes from various sources, and a fish database. There is also project information from the laboratories and other publications.

World Wide Web:
URL: **http://www.rfisk.is/**

Icelandic Fisheries Laboratories

Going to Iceland?
Make sure you
first check the IFL web site.

Index to Web Servers

This web page collects hypertext links to dozens of web servers in the U.S. and U.K. that feature oceanographic resources, including educational institutions, observatories and laboratories. If you're an oceanographer, you'll want this page in your hotlist.

World Wide Web:
URL: **http://www.whoi.edu/html/**
www-servers/oceanography.html

Institute for Remote Sensing Applications

The Marine Environment Unit of the Joint Research Center in Ispra, Italy, has information on European waters, including sea surface temperatures, pigment patterns, trends in the surface color field, and other data.

World Wide Web:
URL: **http://me-www.jrc.it/home.html**

Oceanic (The Ocean Network Information Center)

Oceanic data sets, research ship schedules and information, science and program information.

Gopher:
Name: University of Delaware
Address: **gopher.cms.udel.edu**

Telnet:
Address: **delocn.udel.edu**
Login: **info**

World Wide Web:
URL: **http://diu.cms.udel.edu/**
URL: **http://www.cms.udel.edu**

Oceanography Information

Exchange information with oceanographers and oceanography buffs. From fishery science to the effects of natural and man-made disasters on the ocean's ecology, this is the place to find the information.

Anonymous FTP:
Address: **biome.bio.dfo.ca**
Path: **/pub**

A
B
C
D
E
F
G
H
I
J
K
L
M
N
O
P
Q
R
S
T
U
V
W
X
Y
Z

Scripps Institute of Oceanography

There's a great deal of ocean waiting for someone to study it. If you love the ocean for more than surfing, check out all the information available on the Internet. Not only can you get information from Scripps, but you can also connect to other gophers that have oceanographic appeal.

Gopher:
Name: Scripps Institute of Oceanography
Address: **sio.ucsd.edu**

SeaWiFS Project

NASA's Goddard Space Flight Center is working on a global ocean color monitoring project called SeaWiFS. This page offers information about this project in addition to other similar projects and links to other NASA resources.

World Wide Web:
URL: **http://seawifs.gsfc.nasa.gov/scripts/ SEAWIFS.html**

OPERATING SYSTEMS: DOS

4DOS Command Processor

Discussion of the 4DOS command processor, a replacement for the standard COMMAND.COM.

Usenet:
Newsgroup: **comp.os.msdos.4dos**

Desqview

Discussion group devoted to Desqview — the multitasking task manager from Quarterdeck — and related products.

Usenet:
Newsgroup: **comp.os.msdos.desqview**

DOS News

Read the latest news about the DOS operating systems. Articles cover new releases and industry news relating to DOS.

Usenet:
Newsgroup: **clari.nb.dos**

Excerpt from the Net...

```
Newsgroup: comp.os.msdos.misc
Subject: What is this hidden file?

>> I have just discovered, on a quest to solve another mystery, the
>> following hidden system file in the root directory:
>>
>>      386spart.par
>>
>> with the incredible size of 12558336.  It carries today's date.
>>
>> What on earth is this file?

> This is a FAQ (frequently asked question).  The file is your 12 Mb
> permanent Windows swapfile.
>
> I wonder, is there an advantage for having a permanent swap file over a
> temporary one?

Yes.

A temporary swap file uses space that was available on your hard drive at the time you
started Windows: you have no control on how large this file will be.  Moreover, the file
may very well be fragmented.

The permanent swap file is constructed only of contiguous blocks on your hard drive.
This provides faster access.  In addition, you can specify how large the file should be.
With contiguous blocks, you will have faster access.  Working with a temporary swap file
may result in a slower speed, just as with a fragmented hard disk.
```

Mail and Usenet News

DOS-based mail and Usenet news systems.

Usenet:
Newsgroup: **comp.os.msdos.mail-news**

Miscellaneous DOS Topics

Discussion of topics relating to DOS and DOS machines.

Usenet:
Newsgroup: **comp.os.msdos.misc**

uucp for DOS

Why bother? Why not just get a system that comes with uucp? Well, if you're a diehard DOS user and you want to mimic yet another feature built into Unix, come check out this discussion group and find out how.

Usenet:
Newsgroup: **alt.bbs.pcbuucp**

OPERATING SYSTEMS: GENERAL TOPICS

Operating Systems General Discussion

General discussion about operating systems, not carried elsewhere.

Usenet:
Newsgroup: **comp.os.misc**

Research on Operating Systems

Join the **comp.os.research** newsgroup to get the latest on research and developments in operating systems technology.

Usenet:
Newsgroup: **comp.os.research**

Root Chatline

Discussion about computer systems, languages, operating systems, programming, and architectures.

Internet Relay Chat:
Channel: **#root**

OPERATING SYSTEMS: MICROSOFT WINDOWS

Announcements About Microsoft Windows

This moderated newsgroup contains announcements related to Microsoft Windows.

Usenet:
Newsgroup: **comp.os.ms-windows.announce**

Microsoft Windows

Isn't Windows great? Don't you just love those GPF (General Protection Faults)? And don't you look back with nostalgia on so many of those fabulous UAE's (Unidentified Application Errors)?

Come on guys, no complaining: GPFs and UAEs are just Microsoft's way of telling you to slow down. In fact, we bet that you love Windows so much that you would do anything to keep from missing out on all that's new and keen. Not to worry.

All you have to do is read
comp.os.ms-windows.announce
and you'll never be left behind.

Applications for Microsoft Windows

Discussion about Microsoft Windows programs and Windows itself. Read the lively debate about Windows 4 and jump into the fray if you dare.

Usenet:
Newsgroup: **comp.os.ms-windows.apps**
Newsgroup: **comp.os.ms-windows.apps.comm**
Newsgroup: **comp.os.ms-windows.apps.financial**
Newsgroup: **comp.os.ms-windows.apps.misc**
Newsgroup: **comp.os.ms-windows.apps.utilities**
Newsgroup: **comp.os.ms-windows.apps.word-proc**

A B C D E F G H I J K L M N O P Q R S T U V W X Y Z

Binaries for Windows

Binary (executable) programs for Microsoft Windows, ready to download and run.

Usenet:
>Newsgroup: **comp.binaries.ms-windows**

Microsoft Web Server

Microsoft's web server offers access to virtually all of Microsoft's resources on the Internet. This web page has links to information about Windows and Windows NT, standards and other programming information, and Microsoft's Knowledge Base and software archives. There are also direct links to Microsoft's gopher server and ftp site.

World Wide Web:
>URL: **http://www.microsoft.com/**

Microsoft Windows Developer Information

Items of interest to software and hardware developers for Microsoft Windows and Windows NT operating systems. Available information is from independent developers as well as from Microsoft.

See also: Operating Systems: Windows NT

World Wide Web:
>URL: **http://www-drg.microsoft.com/devinfo.htm**

Networking

Discussion relating to networking in the Microsoft Windows environment. Topics cover general networking, TCP/IP and built-in networking.

Usenet:
>Newsgroup:
>**comp.os.ms-windows.networking.misc**
>Newsgroup:
>**comp.os.ms-windows.networking.tcp-ip**
>Newsgroup:
>**comp.os.ms-windows.networking.windows**

This book is high in fiber.

Programming

A large selection of newsgroups devoted to the topic of programming in the Windows environment. Topics cover general programming as well as more specific subjects like controls, drivers, graphics, memory management, multimedia and networking.

Usenet:
>Newsgroup:
>**comp.os.ms-windows.programmer**
>Newsgroup:
>**comp.os.ms-windows.programmer.controls**
>Newsgroup:
>**comp.os.ms-windows.programmer.drivers**
>Newsgroup:
>**comp.os.ms-windows.programmer.graphics**
>Newsgroup:
>**comp.os.ms-windows.programmer.memory**
>Newsgroup:
>**comp.os.ms-windows.programmer.multimedia**
>Newsgroup:
>**comp.os.ms-windows.programmer.networks**
>Newsgroup:
>**comp.os.ms-windows.programmer.ole**
>Newsgroup:
>**comp.os.ms-windows.programmer.winhelp**

Sockets for Microsoft Windows

Discussions and programming considerations for sockets implementations under Microsoft Windows.

Usenet:
>Newsgroup: **alt.winsock**

Video

Discussion covering video adapters and drivers for the Microsoft Windows operating systems.

Usenet:
>Newsgroup: **comp.os.ms-windows.video**

Windows General Discussion

General discusssion about Microsoft Windows. The **.advocacy** newsgroup contains more controversial talk and debate.

Usenet:
>Newsgroup: **bit.listserv.win3-l**
>Newsgroup: **comp.os.ms-windows.advocacy**
>Newsgroup: **comp.os.ms-windows.misc**

Windows News

The latest news on the Windows family of operating systems, including the newest releases and upgrades.

World Wide Web:
    URL: **http://www.microsoft.com/chicago/ ms-www/ms-intro.htm**

Windows Setup

Installation and configuration of Microsoft Windows.

Usenet:
    Newsgroup: **comp.os.ms-windows.setup**

WordPerfect

Discussion about WordPerfect for Windows.

Usenet:
    Newsgroup: **bit.listserv.wpwin-l**

OPERATING SYSTEMS: MISCELLANEOUS SYSTEMS

AOS

Data General's AOS/VS operating system.

Usenet:
    Newsgroup: **comp.os.aos**

CP/M

One of the early microcomputer operating systems, CP/M is the spiritual ancestor of DOS and, in certain parts of the computing world, is still alive today.

Usenet:
    Newsgroup: **comp.os.cpm**
    Newsgroup: **comp.os.cpm.amethyst**

Geos

The Geos operating system from Geoworks.

Usenet:
    Newsgroup: **comp.os.geos**
    Newsgroup: **comp.os.msdos.pcgeos**

Geos Binaries

Binary postings for the GEOS operating system.

Usenet:
    Newsgroup: **comp.binaries.geos**

Internet Connectivity for PCs

Once upon a time, operating systems didn't directly support Internet access. If you still use DOS or Microsoft Windows, this web page can be your guide to getting your system on the Internet. Find out about terms like *TCP/IP* and *Sockets*, and find out exactly what software you need, and where you can get it (free, of course).

World Wide Web:
    URL: **http://pclt.cis.yale.edu/pclt/winworld/ winworld.htm**

Lynx

This Usenet group is the place to come to discuss the Lynx realtime operating system.

Usenet:
    Newsgroup: **comp.os.lynx**

WANT TO BUILD YOUR OWN OPERATING SYSTEM? NO PROBLEM. START WITH THE MACH KERNEL. IT'S AVAILABLE FOR DOWNLOADING ON THE INTERNET.

Mach

The famous Mach operating system and its ubiquitous kernel, as developed at Carnegie-Mellon University. The newsgroups are for ongoing discussion; the ftp sites contain source code, utilities, and documentation.

Anonymous FTP:
    Address: **ftp.uu.net**
    Path: **/systems/mach/***

    Address: **gatekeeper.dec.com**
    Path: **/pub/Mach/***

    Address: **mach.cs.cmu.edu**
    Path: **/usr/mach/public**

Usenet:
    Newsgroup: **comp.os.mach**
    Newsgroup: **info.mach**

Minix

The Minix operating system, designed by Andy Tannenbaum and described in his operating system book. The newsgroup is for ongoing discussion; the ftp site is for archives.

Anonymous FTP:
Address: **oak.oakland.edu**
Path: **/pub/misc/minix**

Usenet:
Newsgroup: **comp.os.minix**

Multics

The infamous Multics operating system, a dinosaur from days gone by at MIT.

Usenet:
Newsgroup: **alt.os.multics**

Nachos

Discussion of the Nachos operating systems used in teaching.

Usenet:
Newsgroup: **alt.os.nachos**

OS9

OS9 is a realtime, multiuser, multitasking operating system that runs on a wide variety of processors and has small memory requirements. The family of OS9 operating systems is based on the original OS9, developed by Microware Systems in the 1970s for the 6809 processor. Today, OS9 is supported by various other vendors and a disparate group of programmers around the world.

Usenet:
Newsgroup: **comp.os.os9**

Parix

Discussion of the Parix parallel operating system.

Usenet:
Newsgroup: **comp.os.parix**

QNX

Topics covering the QNX operating system.

Usenet:
Newsgroup: **comp.os.qnx**

RSTS

The old, venerable RSTS operating system for DEC's PDP-11 computers.

Usenet:
Newsgroup: **comp.os.rsts**

V

The V distributed operating system from Stanford. (Historical note: A windowing system named W was originally developed for V, and W is the ancestor of X Window.)

Usenet:
Newsgroup: **comp.os.v**

VMS

There are a large number of newsgroups devoted to discussions of various aspects of DEC's VMS operating system as well as related hardware, software, and networking.

Usenet:
Newsgroup: **bit.listserv.jnet-l**
Newsgroup: **bit.listserv.vmslsv-l**
Newsgroup: **comp.os.vms**
Newsgroup: **gnu.emacs.vms**
Newsgroup: **news.software.anu-news**
Newsgroup: **vmsnet.alpha**
Newsgroup: **vmsnet.announce.***
Newsgroup: **vmsnet.databases.rdb**
Newsgroup: **vmsnet.decus.***
Newsgroup: **vmsnet.infosystems.***
Newsgroup: **vmsnet.internals**
Newsgroup: **vmsnet.mail.***
Newsgroup: **vmsnet.misc**
Newsgroup: **vmsnet.networks.***
Newsgroup: **vmsnet.pdp-11**
Newsgroup: **vmsnet.sources.***
Newsgroup: **vmsnet.sysmgt**
Newsgroup: **vmsnet.tpu**
Newsgroup: **vmsnet.uucp**
Newsgroup: **vmsnet.vms-posix**

VSE/ESA Mainframe

Discussion of IBM's VSE/ESA mainframe.

Usenet:
    Newsgroup: **bit.listserv.vse-l**

VxWorks

Discussion of the VxWorks realtime operating system.

Usenet:
    Newsgroup: **comp.os.vxworks**

Xinu

The Xinu ("Xinu Is Not Unix") operating system from Purdue; from a project organized by Doug Comer.

Usenet:
    Newsgroup: **comp.os.xinu**

OPERATING SYSTEMS: OS/2

Announcements About OS/2

Announcements related to IBM's OS/2 operating system for PCs.

Usenet:
    Newsgroup: **comp.os.os2.announce**

OS/2 Announcements

Okay, we admit it, we like OS/2. But (we hear you say), don't you miss all those GFPs and UAEs? Isn't it boring to use an operating system that doesn't keep crashing?
Don't despair, OS/2 runs Windows, so you never need feel deprived. But don't run the risk of being left behind: find out what's new and exciting by reading **comp.os.os2.announce**.

(By the way, don't tell anyone, but we use OS/2 mostly to run our DOS programs...shh...it's a secret.)

Applications for OS/2

Are you an OS/2 fan? Well, Harley sure is. Join Harley and others here for lively discussion about OS/2 applications.

Usenet:
    Newsgroup: **comp.os.os2.apps**

Binaries for OS/2

Binary (executable) programs for OS/2 ready to download and run.

Usenet:
    Newsgroup: **comp.binaries.os2**

Games

OS/2 is not just a studly operating system. It's great for playing games, too. Check out the latest fun things you can do with OS/2 while nobody is looking.

Usenet:
    Newsgroup: **comp.os.os2.games**

Multimedia OS/2

Support and suggestions for implementing multimedia systems under OS/2.

Usenet:
    Newsgroup: **comp.os.os2.multimedia**

OS/2 Beta Releases

Problems, comments, and bugs in OS/2 beta releases.

Usenet:
    Newsgroup: **comp.os.os2.beta**

OS/2 Bugs and Fixes

Bug reports and fixes for the current version of OS/2. (What? OS/2 has a bug?)

Usenet:
    Newsgroup: **comp.os.os2.bugs**

A
B
C
D
E
F
G
H
I
J
K
L
M
N
O
P
Q
R
S
T
U
V
W
X
Y
Z

OS/2 Chat

A popular channel for discussing and exchanging information about OS/2. The OS2bot offers many commands, including a calendar, calculator, phone yellow pages, fortune, CD-ROM archive search, and help files. The OS2bot can search all the main OS/2 repositories in the world.

Internet Relay Chat:
Channel: **#os/2**

OS/2 General Discussion

General discussion about all aspects of OS/2. The **.advocacy** newsgroup contains more debate and controversial topics.

Usenet:
Newsgroup: **comp.os.os2**
Newsgroup: **comp.os.os2.advocacy**
Newsgroup: **comp.os.os2.misc**

OS/2 Home Page

Users and lovers of OS/2 will have lots to check out at these sites, which offer links to newsgroups, ftp sites, other web pages, and support groups relating to OS/2.

World Wide Web:
URL: **http://www.ccsf.caltech.edu/~kasturi/ os2.html**
URL: **http://www.cen.uiuc.edu/~rs9678/raj.html**
URL: **http://www.mit.edu:8001/activities/ os2/os2world.html**

OS/2 Information

Are you curious about OS/2? Well, here's the place to get the scoop. IBM's Almaden gopher has a wealth of information, tips, and tricks about OS/2. There are installation tips, problems, and workarounds, information about OS/2 development tools, networking, and software. This gopher also offers information about OS/2 user groups and new product announcements.

Gopher:
Name: IBM Corporation
Address: **index.almaden.ibm.com**
Choose: **OS/2 Information**

OS/2 Networking

OS/2 users come to these newsgroups to learn from the experts about networking OS/2.

Usenet:
Newsgroup: **comp.os.os2.networking**
Newsgroup: **comp.os.os2.networking.misc**
Newsgroup: **comp.os.os2.networking.tcp-ip**

OS/2 Setup

This Usenet group is just for installation and configuration problems you might have with OS/2.

Usenet:
Newsgroup: **comp.os.os2.setup**

OS/2 Versions 1.x

Discussion about OS/2 versions 1.0 through 1.3.

Usenet:
Newsgroup: **comp.os.os2.ver1x**

Programming in OS/2

Programming in the OS/2 environment. The **.porting** newsgroup is devoted to porting software from another system to OS/2.

Usenet:
Newsgroup: **comp.os.os2.programmer**
Newsgroup: **comp.os.os2.programmer.misc**
Newsgroup: **comp.os.os2.programmer.oop**
Newsgroup: **comp.os.os2.programmer.porting**
Newsgroup: **comp.os.os2.programmer.tools**

OPERATING SYSTEMS: SCO

Announcements About SCO Unix

This moderated newsgroup contains announcements regarding the Unix products and packages from the Santa Cruz Operation.

Usenet:
Newsgroup: **biz.sco.announce**

Binaries for SCO Unix

Binary (executable) programs for SCO Xenix, Unix or Open Desktop, ready to download and run.

Usenet:
> Newsgroup: **biz.sco.binaries**

Enhanced Feature Supplements

This directory on SCO's FTP server houses feature supplements and bug fixes for SCO's Unix operating systems. The supplements are contained within compressed Unix files and are keyed by floppy disk type (96 or 135 tpi installation drives).

Anonymous FTP:
> Address: **ftp.sco.com**
> Path: **/EFS**

Games for SCO Unix

This directory on SCO's FTP server contains games for SCO Unix systems.

Anonymous FTP:
> Address: **ftp.sco.com**
> Path: **/Games**

Hardware Compatibility Handbook

An electronic version of the *Hardware Compatibility Handbook* distributed with SCO products.

Anonymous FTP:
> Address: **ftp.sco.com**
> Path: **/HCH**

Open Desktop

Discussion about SCO's Open Desktop operating system and programming environment.

Usenet:
> Newsgroup: **biz.sco.opendesktop**

SCO General Discussion

General discussion about all of SCO's products.

Usenet:
> Newsgroup: **biz.sco.general**

SCO Magazine

An electronic magazine for users of SCO Unix operating systems.

Usenet:
> Newsgroup: **biz.sco.magazine**

SCO Unix Files for Compaq Computers

Patches for SCO Unix on Compaq computers. Download these files, make them executable by **root**, then just execute them as **root**.

See also: Unix: SCO

Anonymous FTP:
> Address: **ftp.compaq.com**
> Path: **/pub/SCO/patches**

SCO Unix Supplements: Compaq Computers

Enhanced function supplements for running SCO Unix specifically on Compaq computers.

Anonymous FTP:
> Address: **ftp.compaq.com**
> Path: **/pub/SCO/releases/***

A
B
C
D
E
F
G
H
I
J
K
L
M
N
O
P
Q
R
S
T
U
V
W
X
Y
Z

Source Code for Programs for SCO

If you need a program for SCO, check out **biz.sco.sources**. If they don't have it, they'll know where to get it.

Usenet:
> Newsgroup: **biz.sco.sources**

Support Level Supplements

Bug fixes and enhancements to SCO products. Includes an improved CD-ROM driver, console keyboard driver, TCP/IP daemon and driver, security supplements, an NFS supplement, and so on.

Anonymous FTP:
> Address: **ftp.sco.com**
> Path: **/SLS**

Technical Library Supplements

Experimental and educational files that are, in some cases, components and updates to existing SCO software. Not yet another archive for SCO products, but rather software that only SCO can provide or that is not available elsewhere.

Anonymous FTP:
> Address: **ftp.sco.com**
> Path: **/TLS**

Termcap and Terminfo Updates

Updated termcap and terminfo entries for many terminals.

Anonymous FTP:
> Address: **ftp.sco.com**
> Path: **/Term**

Widget Server

Discussion about the SCO widget server.

Usenet:
> Newsgroup: **biz.sco.wserver**

Xenix

SCO's version of the Xenix operating system.

Usenet:
> Newsgroup: **comp.unix.xenix.sco**

OPERATING SYSTEMS: UNIX IN GENERAL

Dial-Up Site List

A long listing of open access dial-up Unix sites, including both fee and no fee hosts. Contains detailed information on what each site has to offer.

Mail:
> Address: **archive-server@cs.widener.edu**
> Body: **send nixpub long**
>
> Address: **mail-server@bts.com**
> Body: **get pub nixpub**
>
> Address: **nixpub@access.digex.net**

DOS Under Unix

Talk and technical questions about all the different ways to run DOS and DOS programs under Unix.

Usenet:
> Newsgroup: **comp.unix.dos-under-unix**

Mainframes and Large Networks

Technical discussion about Unix systems that run on mainframes or on large networks.

Usenet:
> Newsgroup: **comp.unix.large**

News About Unix

News stories that involve the Unix industry.

Usenet:
> Newsgroup: **clari.nb.unix**

Open Software Foundation

Gossip, rumors, and technical debate regarding the Open Software Foundation and its machinations.

Usenet:
> Newsgroup: **comp.unix.osf.misc**

*What is the **Open Software Foundation** up to and how long until they are disbanded?*

Read all about it in comp.unix.osf.misc

PC and Macintosh Guides

Articles and FAQs on Berkeley Unix, USL Unix, Sun administration, the C-Shell, Zsh, Unix security, and other Unix subjects and variants of Unix.

Anonymous FTP:
  Address: **ftp.spies.com**
  Path: **/Library/Techdoc/Unix/***

Gopher:
  Name: Internet Wiretap
  Address: **wiretap.spies.com**
  Choose: **Wiretap Online Library**
    I **Technical Information**
    I **Unix Operating System**

Programming

So you want to be a Unix programmer, but you're spoiled by all the fancy DOS and Windows development systems. Well, you can still come here to talk with the experts at programming on Unix.

Usenet:
  Newsgroup: **comp.unix.programmer**

Questions and Answers About Unix

General Unix question and answer forums. Almost all questions should go to the **.questions** newsgroup. The **.wizards** group is only for real experts (stay away). You do not need to post a question to **.wizards** to make sure it is read by an expert — they read both groups.

Usenet:
  Newsgroup: **alt.unix.wizards.free**
  Newsgroup: **comp.unix.questions**
  Newsgroup: **comp.unix.wizards**

Security

Tired of hackers getting into your system and setting up Trojan horses? Join **comp.security.unix** and find out how to prevent this and other minor irritations.

Usenet:
  Newsgroup: **comp.security.unix**

Shells

Do you still use the C-Shell, or even the Bourne shell? It's time to join the '90s and find out about the modern command-line interpreters including bash (the Bourne Again SHell), the Tcsh, and the Zsh.

Usenet:
  Newsgroup: **comp.unix.shell**

Source Code to Unix Programs

Source programs to run under Unix. The **.sources** newsgroup contains programs ready to download and compile. The **.unix-sw** group has pointers to Unix software that is available by anonymous ftp.

Usenet:
  Newsgroup: **comp.sources.unix**
  Newsgroup: **info.unix-sw**

Free Unix source code — yours for the downloading.

Standards

Have you ever tried to make sense of the dizzying alphabet soup of Unix standards? If so, or if you're just interested, come here to find out about POSIX, ACE, and dozens of other standards both current and dead.

Usenet:
  Newsgroup: **comp.std.unix**

A B C D E F G H I J K L M N O P Q R S T U V W X Y Z

Text Formatter

A scaled down version of the nroff and troff text formatting software for Unix systems.

Anonymous FTP:
Address: **ftp.std.com**
Path: **/src/print/awf/***

Usenet:
Newsgroup: **comp.sources.unix**

Unix Administration

Discussion of all aspects of Unix administration.

Usenet:
Newsgroup: **comp.unix.admin**

Unix Chat and Help

Unix gurus chat, discuss, help, and argue everything and anything about the Unix operating system. This is a useful place to seek help when nobody else seems to have the answer or when you just can't wait for a Usenet reply.

Internet Relay Chat:
Channel: **#unix**

Unix General Discussion

Discussion of miscellaneous Unix topics that don't fit into any other newsgroup.

Usenet:
Newsgroup: **comp.unix.advocacy**
Newsgroup: **comp.unix.misc**

Unix Information Server

This page has a wealth of information about Unix online with links to pages on specific versions of Unix including AIX, A/UX, BSD, FreeBSD, Linux, and OSF/1 and others. This page also sports information about some Unix applications including Elm, the Z-shell, other Unix utilities, a complete set of Unix man pages online, and links to information about support groups, users groups, and other hot topics.

World Wide Web:
URL: **http://www.yahoo.com/
Computers/Operating_Systems/Unix/**

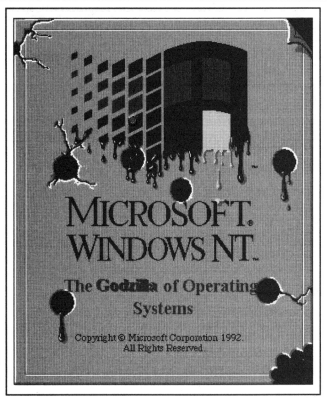

Humorous art and spoofs on common symbols are everywhere. This is **windoze.jpg** from **ftp.wustl.edu** (under **w**).

Unix Internals

Discussion about hacking deep inside Unix. Not for the faint of heart.

Usenet:
Newsgroup: **comp.unix.internals**

Unix Manual

Access the Unix manual by searching for keywords.

WAIS:
Database: **unix-manual**

Unix on PC Architectures

Talk and technical questions about running Unix on PCs. The **.16bit** newsgroup is for the older 16-bit machines. The **.32bit** group is for the more modern 32-bit machines.

Usenet:
Newsgroup: **comp.unix.pc-clone.16bit**
Newsgroup: **comp.unix.pc-clone.32bit**

RTFM

Yes, RTFM is the longest word in the English language with no vowels. It's also the single most important word in the Internet/Unix community. Originally, R.T.F.M. was an acronym that meant "Read the F. . . . . Manual". (Sorry, we are not allowed to print swear words where your parents might see them.)

Today, RTFM has a more refined meaning: it represents the idea that before you ask a question, you should try to answer it yourself. On the Internet, you are expected to (1) read the frequently asked question (FAQ) list for a Usenet newsgroup before sending in a question for the first time, and (2) check with the Unix manual before asking a question about a Unix command.

The FAQ lists are posted regularly to their respective newsgroups and to **news.answers**. They are also available by Anonymous FTP from **rtfm.mit.edu**. (Look in the directory **/pub/usenet/news.answers**.)

The Unix manual is a different story. All Unix systems should have a built-in command named **man** that will display the documentation for any Unix command. If for some reason this is not available on your system, you can search the Unix manual by using Wais. The name of the Wais database is **unix-manual**.

Unix Software and Source Code

A large general-purpose archive of systems software, utilities, and programs that have been published by several popular Unix magazines. Programs include source code and documentation for Unix.

Anonymous FTP:
Address: **ftp.uu.net**
Path: **/published/open-systems-today/***

Address: **ftp.uu.net**
Path: **/published/unix-world/***

Address: **ftp.uu.net**
Path: **/published/unix-review/***

User-Friendliness

A discussion of Unix and how it is (or is not) user-friendly. Lots of debate about whether Unix should (or should not) be user-friendly. The newsgroup is for ongoing discussion; the ftp site contains a frequently asked question list.

Anonymous FTP:
Address: **ftp.wfu.edu**
Path: **/usenet/cuuf.FAQ**

Usenet:
Newsgroup: **comp.unix.user-friendly**

vi Reference Card

A complete list of all the commands for the popular Unix vi text editor. The commands are suitably grouped into topics, so it's easy to locate the one you need.

Gopher:
Name: Scarborough College Computer Centre
Address: **wave.scar.utoronto.ca**
Choose: **Computing and Instructional Technology**
  l **Documentation, Reference and Training Material**
  l **vi.reference**

vi Tutorial

An interactive tutor teaching you all the basics of the popular Unix vi text editor. The file needs to be captured or downloaded and then used with vi.

Anonymous FTP:
Address: **ftp.mines.colorado.edu**
Path: **/pub/tutorials/vitutor***

Gopher:
Name: Scarborough College Computer Centre
Address: **wave.scar.utoronto.ca**
Choose: **Computing and Instructional Technology**
  l **Documentation, Reference and Training Material**
  l **vi tutorial**

Need help with the morons around you? Try Psychology.

A B C D E F G H I J K L M N O P Q R S T U V W X Y Z

OPERATING SYSTEMS: UNIX SYSTEMS

A/UX

Come to the answer guys for Apple's version of Unix. (Official technical support is too expensive anyway.) If you need to know the exit codes for the **fsck** program, the right kind of terminal server to get, or even where to find software for A/UX, this is the place.

Usenet:
>Newsgroup: **comp.unix.aux**

World Wide Web:
>URL: **http://jagubox.gsfc.nasa.gov/aux/**

AIX

IBM's version of Unix, running on the RS/6000 and other platforms. The newsgroups are for ongoing discussion; the FTP site contains archives, including articles from *AIXpert Magazine*.

Anonymous FTP:
>Address: **asterix.fi.upm.es**
>Path: **/pub/docs/ibm/***

Usenet:
>Newsgroup: **bit.listserv.aix-l**
>Newsgroup: **comp.unix.aix**

BSD Unix

The Berkeley Software Distribution (or BSD) Unix: one of the two ancestors of modern Unix. The newsgroups are for ongoing discussion; the ftp sites contain source code and documentation.

Anonymous FTP:
>Address: **ftp.uu.net**
>Path: **/systems/unix/bsd-sources/***

>Address: **gatekeeper.dec.com**
>Path: **/pub/BSD/***

Usenet:
>Newsgroup: **comp.bugs.2bsd**
>Newsgroup: **comp.bugs.4bsd**
>Newsgroup: **comp.bugs.4bsd.ucb-fixes**
>Newsgroup: **comp.unix.bsd**

BSD Unix for PCs

The version of BSD (Berkeley Unix) ported to the Intel PC architecture. The newsgroups are for ongoing discussion; the ftp site contains source code and documentation.

Anonymous FTP:
>Address: **gatekeeper.dec.com**
>Path: **/pub/BSD/***

Usenet:
>Newsgroup: **comp.os.386bsd.announce**
>Newsgroup: **comp.os.386bsd.apps**
>Newsgroup: **comp.os.386bsd.bugs**
>Newsgroup: **comp.os.386bsd.development**
>Newsgroup: **comp.os.386bsd.misc**
>Newsgroup: **comp.os.386bsd.questions**

BSD is one of the two ancestors of modern Unix (the other being System V). If you are interested in the version of BSD that runs on PCs, check out the **comp.os.386bsd.*** newsgroups. If you want, you can even download a free copy of the operating system and run it on your own PC.

BSDI

A commercial version of Berkeley Unix (BSD) as implemented by the BSDI company. The **.suit** newsgroup discusses the infamous and mean-spirited lawsuit between AT&T and BSDI.

Usenet:
>Newsgroup: **alt.suit.att-bsdi**
>Newsgroup: **info.bsdi.users**

Coherent

Coherent: an economical, Unix-like operating system that runs on PCs.

Usenet:
>Newsgroup: **comp.os.coherent**

Cray

Unix systems that run on Cray supercomputers.

Usenet:
>Newsgroup: **comp.unix.cray**

FreeBSD

FreeBSD: A 32-bit multitasking Unix-like operating system for PC or Intel-based systems. FreeBSD is developed and maintained as a labor of love by hackers around the Net and is available for free and unlimited distribution. You will find the FAQs and current version of FreeBSD at the FTP site. Sending a help message to **info@freebsd.org** will result in the latest information on where to get FreeBSD and related resources. Sending the **lists** command to the majordomo server will allow you to receive a listing of all the mailing lists which relate to FreeBSD such as new announcements, bugs, security, and more. Hint: If you are looking for a free Unix-like operating system, you should also take a look at Linux.

Anonymous FTP:
Address: **ftp.freebsd.org**
Path: **/pub/FreeBSD/FreeBSD.FAQ**

Address: **ftp.freebsd.org**
Path: **/pub/FreeBSD/FreeBSD-current/***

Mail:
Address: **info@freebsd.org**
Body: **help**

Address: **majordomo@freebsd.org**
Body: **lists**

World Wide Web:
URL: **http://hermes.cybernetics.net/**
URL: **http://minnie.cs.adfa.oz.au/BSD-info/BSD.html**

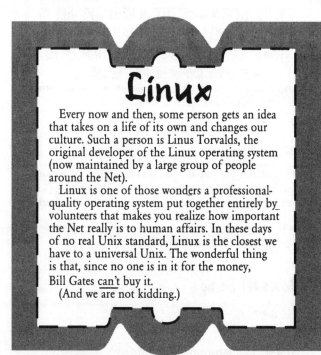

Linux

Every now and then, some person gets an idea that takes on a life of its own and changes our culture. Such a person is Linus Torvalds, the original developer of the Linux operating system (now maintained by a large group of people around the Net).

Linux is one of those wonders a professional-quality operating system put together entirely by volunteers that makes you realize how important the Net really is to human affairs. In these days of no real Unix standard, Linux is the closest we have to a universal Unix. The wonderful thing is that, since no one is in it for the money, Bill Gates can't buy it.

(And we are not kidding.)

Linux

Linux: the free Unix clone, developed and maintained by Linus Torvalds and a gaggle of hackers around the Internet. Linux was written completely from scratch (using no "official" Unix code) for 386- and 486-based PCs. The world of Linux is huge and is one of the most important (and unsung) achievements in the history of operating system development. The newsgroups are for ongoing discussion; the FTP sites contain source code, documentation, and archives.

Anonymous FTP:
Address: **ftp.funet.fi**
Path: **/pub/OS/Linux/***

Address: **ftp.informatik.tu-muenchen.de**
Path: **/pub/comp/os/linux**

Address: **sunsite.unc.edu**
Path: **/pub/Linux/***

Address: **tsx-11.mit.edu**
Path: **/pub/linux/***

Usenet:
Newsgroup: **alt.uu.comp.os.linux.questions**
Newsgroup: **comp.os.linux**
Newsgroup: **comp.os.linux.admin**
Newsgroup: **comp.os.linux.announce**
Newsgroup: **comp.os.linux.development**
Newsgroup: **comp.os.linux.help**
Newsgroup: **comp.os.linux.misc**

World Wide Web:
URL: **http://www.yahoo.com/Computers/Operating_Systems/Unix/Linux/**

Linux Chat and Support

Popular and friendly channels for discussing and asking questions about the Linux PC Unix operating system. The Linbot online bot offers help files, information on the latest kernel status, a short description of Linux, support availability information, and hardware and software requirements.

Internet Relay Chat:
Channel: **#linux**
Channel: **#linpeople**

Be cool! Join a mailing list.

A B C D E F G H I J K L M N **O** P Q R S T U V W X Y Z

OSF/1

The flagship operating system from the Open Software Foundation.

Usenet:
> Newsgroup: **comp.unix.osf.misc**
> Newsgroup: **comp.unix.osf.osf1**

World Wide Web:
> URL: **http://wsspinfo.cern.ch/file/osfsp**

Solaris

Get help from the real experts from all over the world on Sun's newest version of Unix — Solaris. Solaris runs on Sun's Sparc computers as well as on PCs. There are fans, critics, experts, and newbies, and they all seem to meet in this newsgroup.

Usenet:
> Newsgroup: **comp.unix.solaris**

System V

System V: one of the two ancestors of modern Unix.

Usenet:
> Newsgroup: **comp.bugs.misc**
> Newsgroup: **comp.unix.sys3**
> Newsgroup: **comp.unix.sys5.misc**
> Newsgroup: **comp.unix.sys5.r3**
> Newsgroup: **comp.unix.sys5.r4**

Ultrix

This group is devoted to Ultrix, one of DEC's versions of Unix.

Usenet:
> Newsgroup: **comp.unix.ultrix**

Xenix

The very old version of Unix designed to run on PCs.

Usenet:
> Newsgroup: **comp.unix.xenix.misc**
> Newsgroup: **comp.unix.xenix.sco**

OPERATING SYSTEMS: WINDOWS NT

Windows NT General Discussion

Discussion about any and all topics involving Microsoft's Windows NT operating system.

Usenet:
> Newsgroup: **comp.os.ms-windows.nt.misc**

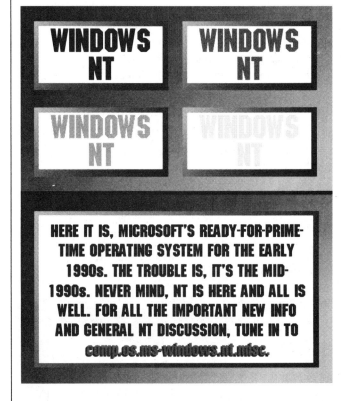

HERE IT IS, MICROSOFT'S READY-FOR-PRIME-TIME OPERATING SYSTEM FOR THE EARLY 1990s. THE TROUBLE IS, IT'S THE MID-1990s. NEVER MIND, NT IS HERE AND ALL IS WELL. FOR ALL THE IMPORTANT NEW INFO AND GENERAL NT DISCUSSION, TUNE IN TO comp.os.ms-windows.nt.misc.

Windows NT News

There's no need for you to stay on the edge of your seat about what is going on in the world of Windows NT. Get the latest news stories from Clarinet so you can stay informed.

Usenet:
> Newsgroup: **clari.nb.windows**

Windows NT Setup

Installing and configuring Windows NT.

Usenet:
> Newsgroup: **comp.os.ms-windows.nt.setup**

ORGANIZATIONS

Amnesty International

The Amnesty International web site offers the full text of the *Universal Declaration of Human Rights* as well as information about the organization and a membership application.

World Wide Web:
URL: **http://cyberzine.org/html/Amnesty/aihomepage.html**

Association for Computing Machinery

The Association for Computing Machinery (ACM) is the largest and oldest educational and scientific computing organization in the world today, and access to current information about the association's activities is readily available here, including many technical computing areas.

Gopher:
Name: Association for Computing Machinery
Address: **gopher.acm.org**

World Wide Web:
URL: **http://info.acm.org/**

Center for Civil Society International

This web page is a collection of points of interest to organizations and associations in the United States and the former Soviet Union.

See also: Business and Finance

World Wide Web:
URL: **http://solar.rtd.utk.edu/~ccsi/ccsihome.html**

Civil Society: USA

This web page provides an overview of the role that associations and private voluntary organizations play in American society. There is detailed information on more than 140 American organizations classified into categories from agriculture to social welfare.

World Wide Web:
URL: **http://solar.rtd.utk.edu/~ccsi/csusa/cshome.html**

Earth First

This environmentally friendly group discusses ways to put the earth first. Read news about environmental causes, organizations, movements and alerts that are essential in saving the planet.

Usenet:
Newsgroup: **alt.org.earth-first**

Electronic Frontier Foundation

The Electronic Frontier Foundation ensures that the new communications technology era is available to all, and that individuals' constitutional rights are preserved therein. Plenty of legal information, EFF publications, and many related articles and zines are available here.

Anonymous FTP:
Address: **ftp.eff.org**
Path: **/pub/EFF/***

Gopher:
Name: Electronic Frontier Foundation
Address: **gopher.eff.org**

World Wide Web:
URL: **http://www.eff.org/**

THE ELECTRONIC FRONTIER FOUNDATION

The Electronic Frontier Foundation (EFF) is a non-profit organization dedicated to maintaining your rights within the American electronic infrastructure. They publish an electronic newsletter (*EFFector Online*) that is freely available for reading or downloading, and they furnish expert testimony and financial support in various court cases. Isn't it nice to know that concerned **net.anti-police** are ready to jump in and fight for your right to privacy and access to public information? Why not take a look at some of their publications and see if you want to support them.

A
B
C
D
E
F
G
H
I
J
K
L
M
N
O
P
Q
R
S
T
U
V
W
X
Y
Z

Gophers are your friends.

History of Philosophy of Science

An informal, international working group of scholars who share an interest in promoting serious, scholarly research on the history of the philosophy of science and related topics.

Gopher:
    Name: Occidental College
    Address: **apa.oxy.edu**
    Choose: **Other Societies and Associations**
      I History of Philosophy of Science Working
      Group (HOPOS)

If you like science, and you like philosophy, and you like history, you'll just *love* the history of the philosophy of science.
Join the rest of the hoposophiles on the Occidental College Gopher.

Do you like weirdness? Check out Usenet Curiosities.

Excerpt from the Net...

```
Newsgroup: rec.org.mensa
Subject: sample test questions for Mensa

(Here are the first five questions from a fifteen question sample Mensa test)

1. Which of the lettered designs best completes the following sequence?

      [o]     [.]     (o)

      A: (.)
      B: (o)
      C: [.]
      D: [o]

2. Sally likes 225 but not 224; she likes 900 but not 800; she likes 144
   but not 145.  Does she like 1600 or 1700?

3. Only one other word can be made from the letters of INSATIABLE.   Can
   you find it?

4. Put the appropriate plus or minus signs between the numbers,  in  the
   correct places, so that the sum total will equal 1.

      0   1   2   3   4   5   6   7   8   9  = 1

5. What is the word coiled inside this circle?

                     T  P
                  I        U
                  A        N
                     L  S
```

Hume Society

The Hume Society invites anyone interested in the philosophy and writings of David Hume to become a member. Founded in 1974, the Hume Society is an international organization with approximately 300 members around the world.

Gopher:
> Name: Occidental College
> Address: **apa.oxy.edu**
> Choose: **Other Societies and Associations
> | The Hume Society**

Institute for Global Communications

This is an activist's dream. See a variety of resources covering peace, human rights, justice, and environmental protection. This organization has created four subnetworks — PeaceNet, EcoNet, ConflictNet and LaborNet — and provides a way to network with thousands of activists worldwide.

Gopher:
> Name: Institute for Global Communications
> Address: **gopher.igc.apc.org**

Jewish Organizations

Information and details about Jewish commercial and non-profit organizations, including some newsletters.

Gopher:
> Name: Jerusalem One
> Address: **jerusalem1.datasrv.co.il**
> Choose: **Jewish Organizations**

Mensa

Do you fancy yourself in the ranks of Adrian Cronauer, Marilyn Vos Savant, Geena Davis, and other smart people? If so, you should join Mensa so you can hang out on this elite list and talk about subjects that are calisthenics for your brain. The **mensatalk** list is exclusively for Mensa members, but **rec.org.mensa** is open to everyone.

Internet Mailing List:
> List Address: **mensatalk@psg.com**
> Subscription Address:
> **mensatalk-request@psg.com**

Usenet:
> Newsgroup: **rec.org.mensa**

National Child Rights Alliance

This organization, formed by survivors of child abuse and neglect, offers the youth bill of rights, many articles on children's rights, and a history of the NCRA.

World Wide Web:
> URL: **http:/www.ai.mit.edu/people/ellens/NCRA/ncra.html**

National Institute of Standards and Technology

The National Institute of Standards and Technology (NIST) gopher offers news, details of measurement services and laboratory programs, newsletters, budget information, factsheets, and industrial impact reports.

Gopher:
> Name: The National Institute of Standards and Technology
> Address: **gopher-server.nist.gov**

Nonprofit Organizations

Learn the ins and outs of running a nonprofit organization. Get ideas about raising money, hints on record keeping and how to start a nonprofit organization from scratch.

Usenet:
> Newsgroup: **soc.org.nonprofit**

Partnerships Against Violence

Partnerships Against Violence offers information and statistics about violence and youth at risk, including gang problems, drugs, rehabilitation of criminals, programs for violence prevention, including community violence, family violence, substance abuse, and youth violence.

Gopher:
> Name: Department of Housing and Urban Development
> Address: **gopher.hud.gov**
> Choose:
> **PAV*NET: Partnerships Against Violence**

Peace Corps

Interested in making a difference in the world, but don't know where to start? Try the Peace Corps. Find out more information on joining, travel in foreign countries, and the perils and rewards of being a Peace Corps volunteer.

Listserv Mailing List:
> List Address: **pcorps-l@cmuvm.csv.cmich.edu**
> Subscription Address:
> **listserv@cmuvm.csv.cmich.edu**

Usenet:
> Newsgroup: **alt.peace-corps**

A B C D E F G H I J K L M N O P Q R S T U V W X Y Z

Peace Watch

An independent watchdog group established to monitor Israeli and PLO compliance with the Declaration of Principles and other agreements. You can find Peace Watch information, news, and reports here.

Gopher:
Name: Jerusalem One
Address: **jerusalem1.datasrv.co.il**
Choose: **Politics**
| **The Peace Process**
| **Peace Watch Group - Monitoring**

SEA Gopher

The Society for Electronic Access (SEA) works to educate people about computer networks and how to use them to communicate and find information. Their gopher includes a list of U.S. government BBSs, articles, archives, and telecom law information.

Gopher:
Name: Panix Public Access Unix
Address: **gopher.panix.com**
Choose: **Society for Electronic Access (SEA)**

Service Organizations

Spending most of the day in front of the television is not the fastest way to feel fulfilled as a human being. Pull yourself out of the sofa and join a service organization. Check out this newsgroup to see which one would be right for you.

Usenet:
Newsgroup: **soc.org.service-clubs.misc**

Toastmasters

Join the club for people who love to make toasts. Hone your public speaking skills so you will be sought after when it comes time to do eulogies or partake in a celebrity roast.

Usenet:
Newsgroup: **alt.org.toastmasters**

World Organizations

The United Nations and other world organizations are busy making headlines. Read the latest stories from the press as they are posted to Clarinet.

Usenet:
Newsgroup: **clari.world.organizations**

OUTDOOR ACTIVITIES

Backcountry Home Page

An archive of backcountry-related resources, covering hiking, camping, and climbing. Contains trip reports, technical advice and tutorials, gear reviews and recommendations, places of interest, a gallery of some wonderfully scenic pictures, hiking club details, and links to other related pages.

World Wide Web:
URL: **http://io.datasys.swri.edu/**

Ballooning

A mailing list for discussing anything about the sport and preoccupation of ballooning.

Internet Mailing List:
List Address: **balloon@lut.ac.uk**
Subscription Address: **balloon-request@lut.ac.uk**

This image, **balloons.gif**, was retrieved from Washington University in Saint Louis (**ftp.wustl.edu**). This site is arranged in a hierarchical directory structure. Within the directory **/multimedia/images/gif** are directories for each letter of the alphabet. Just **cd** into the **b** directory for "balloon", and have a look.

Climbing

Open discussion about climbing techniques, specific climbs, and competition announcements.

Usenet:
Newsgroup: **rec.climbing**

Climbing Archive

Rock-climbing FAQs, upcoming event guides, route descriptions, trip reports, body tuning programs, images, songs, network advertisements, ropes, shops, and hardware-related reviews and information about this breathtaking sport.

World Wide Web:
URL: **http://www.dtek.chalmers.se/ Climbing/orig-index.html**
URL: **http://www.dtek/chalmers.se/Climbing/ index.html**

Diving Server

The UK Diving Server allows divers in the UK to share information about dive sites, air fill stations, slipways, and equipment. This web page also features diving pictures, and links to information about upcoming events and diving gear for sale.

World Wide Web:
URL: **http://www.cru.uea.ac.uk/ukdiving/ index.htm**

Fishing

Put an end to the stories about "the one that got away." Get tips on fishing and fly fishing. Images are available as well as archives to **rec.fishing** and **alt.outdoors.fishing**.

See also: Sports and Athletics

Usenet:
Newsgroup: **rec.outdoors.fishing.fly**
Newsgroup: **rec.outdoors.fishing.saltwater**

World Wide Web:
URL: **http://www.geo.mtu.edu/~jsuchosk/ fish/fishpage**

Hiking

Articles and guides about hiking and the great outdoors. Includes hiking songs, a snakebite guide, campfire lore, water filtering information, and other topics of interest to campers.

Anonymous FTP:
Address: **ftp.spies.com**
Path: **/Library/Article/Outdoors/***

Gopher:
Name: Internet Wiretap
Address: **wiretap.spies.com**
Choose: **Wiretap Online Library**
| **Articles**
| **Backcountry and Outdoors**

Kayaking

These kayaking pages offer information about this popular activity including several FAQ files, information about specific trips that paddlers have taken, pictures, kayak plans and kits, and links to other kayaking resources on the Net.

World Wide Web:
URL: **http://salk.edu/~preston/kayak/**
URL: **http://www.recreation.com/paddling/**

Mountain Biking

A set of web pages dedicated to mountain bikes, with links to newsgroups, mailing lists, magazines, race results, and even a BBS.

World Wide Web:
URL: **http://catless.ncl.ac.uk/mtb/**

Mountain Biking Areas

Descriptions of mountain biking in specific areas, including trails in the San Francisco Bay Area, Northern California, Colorado, Pittsburgh, Utah's legendary Slickrock Trail, and New Zealand.

World Wide Web:
URL: **http://xenon.stanford.edu/~rsf/ mtn-bike.html**

Orienteering and Rogaining

Grab a map and a sack lunch and head to the woods for some exciting, competitive, cross-country navigation. If you think trying to read a map while driving through Los Angeles is bad, try doing it in the middle of a forest where all the trees look the same and there are no road signs or even flushable toilets. Learn about orienteering and rogaining — the rules, how to compete, and what mailing lists are available.

Internet Mailing List:
List Address: **orienteering@graphics.cornell.edu**
Subscription Address:
orienteering-request@graphics.cornell.edu

World Wide Web:
URL: **http://www2.aos.princeton.edu/rdslater/ orienteering/**

A
B
C
D
E
F
G
H
I
J
K
L
M
N
O
P
Q
R
S
T
U
V
W
X
Y
Z

Outdoors Discussion Group

While the wilderness is not quite as scary as the city, it still has its potential for adventure. If you aren't already captivated with the outdoors, shame on you. It's natural, magical, and pure. It also has snakes and poison ivy and, oh yeah, a bear or two. Any activity you can think of doing outdoors is discussed. (Well, almost any activity.) Learn about good camping and hiking equipment, survival training, sledding, safety, and much more.

Usenet:
   Newsgroup: **rec.backcountry**

Paddling

Terminology, river ratings, equipment information, safety guides, books, and addresses for canoeing, kayaking, and rafting.

Anonymous FTP:
   Address: **rtfm.mit.edu**
   Path: **/pub/usenet/news.answers/paddling-faq**

Internet Mailing List:
   List Address: **whitewater@gynko.circ.upenn.edu**
   Subscription Address:
      whitewater-request@gynko.circ.upenn.edu

Rowing

This is not the rowing of a boat down a gentle stream. This rowing is muscle-rippling, back-bending, sweat-manufacturing athletic labor that would make a Viking proud. Newsgroup archives and other information are available.

World Wide Web:
   URL: **http://www.comlab.ox.ac.uk/archive/other/rowing.html**

Scouting

Scouting material for both scouts and leaders, including campfire songs, games, history, world news, unit administration information, and official policies.

Anonymous FTP:
   Address: **ftp.ethz.ch**
   Path: **/rec.scouting/***

   Address: **rtfm.mit.edu**
   Path: **/pub/usenet/news.answers/scouting/***

Snowmobiles

A snowmobile is one thing at which you won't have to yell, "Mush!" Feed it some gas, tell it you love it, then ride like a maniac across the frozen tundra (or whatever happens to be in front of you). Avid snowmobile fans tell how they keep their machines happy, safe, and healthy.

Usenet:
   Newsgroup: **alt.snowmobiles**

Spelunking

If you like crawling around in something that is cool, dark, and wet, you are digging in the right place. Here you will find connections to the National Speleological Society and other speleological societies around the world. There are archives of *Cavers Digest* here as well as a calendar of events. They have clip art, cartoons, images, newsletters and periodicals, cave studies, and writings about equipment used when caving. If you just want to talk about caving, check out **alt.caving** and the mailing list.

Internet Mailing List:
   List Address: **cavers@vlsi.vu.edu**
   Subscription Address: **cavers-request@vlsi.vu.edu**

Usenet:
   Newsgroup: **alt.caving**

World Wide Web:
   URL: **http://speleology.cs.yale.edu/**

Surfing Tutorial

Learn how to catch those waves with this short tutorial on a long and radical subject.

World Wide Web:
   URL: **http://sailfish.peregrine.com/surf/learning.html**

Windsurfing

Information on windsurfing at various areas in the United States. Get the scoop on windsurf shops, launch sites, and conditions. You can also participate in lively discussion topics and download cool windsurfing bitmaps.

Anonymous FTP:
   Address: **lemming.uvm.edu**
   Path: **/rec.windsurfing**

Internet Mailing List:
   List Address: **windsurfing@gcm.com**
   Subscription Address:
      windsurfing-request@gcm.com

World Wide Web:
   URL: **http://www.dsg.cs.tcd.ie/dsg_people/afcondon/windsurf/windsurf_home.html**

PARANORMAL

Alien Cultures

It's important to understand how to entertain when you have unexpected guests drop in from other planets and galaxies. Do you put the salad fork on the right or left? Learn about alien cultures such as the Pleiades, Zeta-Reticula, Lyra, Vega, and a few that are closer to home.

See also: New Age

World Wide Web:
URL: **http://err.ethz.ch/~kiwi/Spirit/ alien-cultures.html**

ALIEN CULTURES

As a member of our modern day, information-oriented culture-in-the-fast-lane, it behooves you to understand a few of the more important alien cultures. No problem. All you have to do is connect to the *Alien Cultures* web site and you will be in-the-know faster than you can say, "I see Elvis." Never again will you have to worry about what the dining customs are in the Pleiades or how much to tip a New York City cab driver.

Astral Projection

It gets boring being in the same old body all the time. Try something new. Dust off the ol' astral body and try cruising around the neighborhood or perhaps just fly off to another country and see the sights. It's liberating, enlightening, and best of all, it's free. This astral projection journal will give you some handy tips on how to get out of your body.

World Wide Web:
URL: **http://err.ethz.ch/~kiwi/Spirit/ tvos-astral.html**

Tired of moving **SLOWLY** in the *FAST LANE*? Try Astral Projection.

Channeling

The problem with people on the astral plane is that they have a hard time communicating with all the rest of us who are still hanging out on earth. That's where channeling comes in. Channelers have the great job of talking for these bodiless folks who still have a lot of things to say. Read stories, articles, and experiences relating to the process of channeling.

See also: New Age

Usenet:
Newsgroup: **alt.paranormal.channeling**

World Wide Web:
URL: **http://err.ethz.ch/~kiwi/Spirit/ channelings.html**

Zines are cool.

A B C D E F G H I J K L M N O **P** Q R S T U V W X Y Z

Freud's Occult Studies

A paper on Sigmund Freud's research into the paranormal.

Anonymous FTP:
Address: **ftp.spies.com**
Path: **/Library/Fringe/Occult/freud.occ**

Gopher:
Name: Internet Wiretap
Address: **wiretap.spies.com**
Choose: **Wiretap Online Library**
| **Fringes of Reason**
| **Occult and Paranormal**
| **Freud's Studies of the Occult**

Lightful Images

If seeing is believing, then this will put you one step closer to believing that some really strange stuff is going on in the universe. Stuff that maybe you would rather not know. So maybe it would be best if you didn't look at these pictures of aliens and other paranormal occurrences.

World Wide Web:
URL: **http://err.ethz.ch/~kiwi/Spirit/Images/List.html**

Near-Death Experiences

It doesn't count if someone scares you so bad that you think you nearly have a heart attack. This newsgroup talks about real near-death experiences like actually going out of your body and wisping around the room in an ethereal form before being yanked back to consciousness. Read studies on the near-death concept as well as anecdotes from people who have had these experiences.

Usenet:
Newsgroup: **alt.consciousness.near-death-exp**

Necronomicon

Material about this near-legendary text written in Damascus in 730 A.D. Includes documents about the Voymich Manuscript. Also contains the FAQ from **alt.necromicon** (a put-on).

Anonymous FTP:
Address: **ftp.funet.fi**
Path: **/pub/doc/occult/necronomicon/***

Usenet:
Newsgroup: **alt.necromicon**

Occult Archives

A collection of occult material and pictures, covering such subjects as astrology, druidism, herbs, magick, rituals, tarot, and wicca.

Anonymous FTP:
Address: **etext.archive.umich.edu**
Path: **/pub/Quartz/occult/***

Address: **ftp.cic.net**
Path: **/pub/ETEXT/pub/Quartz/occult/***

Address: **ftp.funet.fi**
Path: **/pub/doc/occult/***

Occult and Mysticism Network

The Occult and Mysticism Network (OMNet) is dedicated to facilitating public access to occult and mystical documents and social groups, and to promoting interdisciplinary information exchange. Its home page offers a foundation document, the Mage's Guide to the Internet, and links to useful resources on the occult and mysticism.

World Wide Web:
URL: **http://www.contrib.andrew.cmu.edu:8001/usr/sk4p/om**

Occult and Paranormal

A collection of articles on the occult and paranormal, including the "Eight Sabbats of Witchcraft," "The Runes," and "The Chalice of Ecstasy."

Anonymous FTP:
Address: **ftp.spies.com**
Path: **/Library/Fringe/Occult/***

Gopher:
Name: Internet Wiretap
Address: **wiretap.spies.com**
Choose: **Wiretap Online Library**
| **Fringes of Reason**
| **Occult and Paranormal**

Occultist Temple of Set

Material, guides, and rituals relating to the Occultist Temple of Set.

Anonymous FTP:
Address: **etext.archive.umich.edu**
Path: **/pub/Quartz/occult/set/***

Orvotron Newsletter

Sisters and Brothers of the Light can read up on the latest from Star People hanging out in North Carolina trying to awaken humankind's cellular memory so they will realize their origins and become one with each other so we can exist in a reality of wholeness and cosmic citizenship. And that's just the pre-lunch agenda. You should see their schedule for the entire week.

World Wide Web:
URL: **http://err.ethz.ch/~kiwi/Spirit/orvotron.html**

Out-of-Body Experiences

The best cure for indigestion is to just leave your body behind and let it work out the details for itself. Read up on astral projection, out-of-body healing, meditation, lucid dreaming, theories about higher realms, and tips on how to have an out-of-body experience.

See also: New Age

Usenet:
Newsgroup: **alt.oobe**
Newsgroup: **alt.out-of-body**

World Wide Web:
URL: **http://err.ethz.ch/~kiwi/Spirit/obe.html**

Paranormal Phenomena General Discussion

Freewheeling discussion of things that have to be believed to be seen. The weird, the unexplained, the things that go bump in the night. We love stories, especially ones that give us goose bumps and make the hair stand up on the back of our neck. Read stories and theories about paranormal phenomena.

Usenet:
Newsgroup: **alt.paranet.paranormal**
Newsgroup: **alt.paranormal**

Parapsychology

Remember all those nights you'd stay up late with friends, turn out the lights, and by the eerie glow of a flashlight you would tell ghost stories and creepy folk legends? None of that has changed, it's just that the scary stories get more complicated and sophisticated. Believers of the weird get together to talk about experiences, thoughts and questions such as ESP, out-of-body experiences, dreams and altered states of consciousness. The forum is not to debate whether psi exists, but to discuss the nature of it.

Listserv Mailing List:
List Address: **psi-l@vm.ecs.rpi.edu**
Subscription Address: **listserv@vm.ecs.rpi.edu**

Psi Phenomena

You're sitting at the bus stop when a beautiful woman sits down next to you. The bus arrives and she stands up to get on board. She turns to look at you and without speaking you hear her say "Going my way?" You are astounded. Could it be that you read her mind? Or maybe she used psychic ability to put the thought in your head. Or maybe it's a lot of wishful thinking. Find out the scoop on psi phenomena so if this happens again, you will know just what to do.

Usenet:
Newsgroup: **alt.paranet.psi**

Scientific Theories behind Paranormal Events

Ghosts, UFOs, poltergeists and other paranormal events are the stuff that makes urban folklore so rich. Skeptics and believers discuss scientific theories behind these paranormal phenomena.

Usenet:
Newsgroup: **alt.paranet.science**

Skepticism

It's not easy being the bad guy, but someone has to do it. Take a look into this debunker's paradise and read skeptics' opinions on topics like UFOs, the Shroud of Turin, firewalking, faith healing, and, yes, even home schooling.

Listserv Mailing List:
List Address: **skeptic@jhuvm.hcf.jhu.edu**
Subscription Address: **listserv@jhuvm.hcf.jhu.edu**

Usenet:
Newsgroup: **bit.listserv.skeptic**
Newsgroup: **sci.skeptic**

World Wide Web:
URL: **http://dragon.acadiau.ca:1667/~860099w/skeptic/skeptic.html**

Spaceships

If you are planning on taking a trip off the planet, be sure you're prepared. Besides supplies, you will need the ever-important spaceship. Then comes the dilemma of trying to decide if you should use an internally or externally created beam-ship. You also need to make sure your male and female aspects are balanced so the male will be able to bend the space/time continuum while the female will be able to balance the bend and control the destiny of your voyage. On second thought, maybe you should just stay home and watch more re-runs of the *Twilight Zone*.

World Wide Web:
URL: **http://err.ethz.ch/~kiwi/Spirit/RKMCorner/ spaceships.html**

Starbuilders

The Starbuilders are extraterrestrial "walk-ins" who are hanging out here on earth, probably because we have the best french fries this side of Zeta-Reticula. If you are interested in their mission on earth, check out this web page, because these ETs have Net access.

See also: New Age

World Wide Web:
URL: **http://err.ethz.ch/~kiwi/Spirit/ starbuilders.html**

> **Reality is dull.**
> **Try Science Fiction.**

Excerpt from the Net...

```
Newsgroup: alt.alien.visitors
Subject: Alien Visits and UFOs

There is no doubt in my mind that we will be "invaded". But they are
not hostile. In fact, these "aliens" are merely Satan's angels. Satan
will soon be thrown out of the heavenly realm, and in order to appear
legitimate he will arrive as "space aliens" and in peace. The whole
world will marvel at the aliens, at the miracles that these "aliens" can
perform, but do not be decieved. They are coming with the aid and
support of the government to bring us hell and destruction...


----------


I have seen them. I never was a believer until last weekend.

They came to my house looking for pretzels and beer. They had large
glossy red eyes and long scraggly beards and wore flannel shirts and
mud boots. Their ship sort of resembled a Chevy pick up...

It wasn't until later I realized what they really wanted: they had
really come for my body. They wanted to impregnate me with an alien
fetus and later take over the world. Disguised at Lumberjacks they
raided the fridge...

I am writing this from their ship.... They do not know I am here.
This is my only chance for help. Help me please...
Oh no! Here they come........ Ahhhhhh


----------


My husband and I were out of town for a day trip and when we returned
there was a foot print on top of our glass dining room table. What was
strange was that the foot print only has 3 toes. If you have heard
anything similar to that, please let me know.
```

UFOs - Discussion Groups

A cool, rational, scientific, intellectual, well-reasoned, plausible discussion about aliens visiting the Earth and swanking around like they own the place. Investigate, in person, the theory that man is really nature's last word. Just the place to spend your time when the TV is on the fritz.

Usenet:
> Newsgroup: **alt.alien.visitors**
> Newsgroup: **alt.paranet.abduct**
> Newsgroup: **alt.paranet.ufo**
> Newsgroup: **alt.paranormal**

UFOs - Incident in Roswell

A collection of UFO articles, including abduction stories and reports about the incident in Roswell, New Mexico, in 1947, when, some claim, a UFO crashed and was captured by the U.S. government.

Anonymous FTP:
> Address: **ftp.uu.net**
> Path: **/doc/literary/obi/UFO/***

UFOs - Mysterious Abductions

A collection of articles and FAQs about visitors from outer space, crop circles, Project Blue Book, UFO conspiracies, and other interesting and unexplainable incidents. The **uiowa.edu** sites are offered by the Paranet Association.

Anonymous FTP:
> Address: **ftp.spies.com**
> Path: **/Library/Fringe/Ufo/***
>
> Address: **grind.isca.uiowa.edu**
> Path: **/info/paranet/***

Gopher:
> Name: Internet Wiretap
> Address: **wiretap.spies.com**
> Choose: **Wiretap Online Library**
>   **| Fringes of Reason**
>   **| UFO's and Mysterious Abductions**

Telnet:
> Address: **bbs.isca.uiowa.edu**
> Login: **guest**

A Secret

We are going to tell you a secret. We are not real. None of the people around you are real. Everybody except you is a robot. The robots were designed by aliens to populate the Earth, just to give YOU the illusion of real life. Every night, after you fall asleep, the aliens take you aboard a space ship where they download your thought patterns and examine you. Of course, you know nothing about this because, each time they let you go, they wipe out your memory of the encounter. The aliens have allowed a few resources dealing with UFOs and alien abductions to appear on the Internet just to see what you do. It's an intelligence test.

PARTIES AND ENTERTAINMENT

Drinking Games

Magnificent collection of nearly one hundred beer drinking games, including such gems as Beat the Barman, Kings and Blood, and Viking.

Anonymous FTP:
> Address: **ocf.berkeley.edu**
> Path: **/pub/Library/Recreation/drinking.games**
>
> Address: **sauna.cs.hut.fi**
> Path: **/pub/drinking_games/***

Mardi Gras

Hedonism is fun and gratifying. At least, until the next morning. For the hard-core self-indulgent, try Mardi Gras, which translates as Fat Tuesday. Lovers of Mardi Gras discuss the New Orleans carnival celebration, parades, customs and traditions. Discussion about carnivals in other cities or countries is also welcome.

See also: Fun, Food and Drink

Internet Mailing List:
> List Address: **mardi_gras@mintir.fidonet.org**
> Subscription Address:
>   **mardi_gras-request@mintir.fidonet.org**

Party Ideas

Whose bright idea was it to give this party in the first place? You are a nervous wreck. What if nobody comes? What if everybody comes, but nobody has fun? How do you break the ice? The host and hostess are supposed to be cool and graceful under pressure, so before the party check out this gopher for great ideas on games, get-to-know-you exercises, songs, and other ways to have fun at parties. People will be talking about your party for weeks.

Gopher:
Name: Brigham Young University
Address: **acs1.byu.edu**
Choose: **Computing Information**
    | **Shaffer's test gopher**
    | **Social Recreation Resourc**

Need some party games? Check the gopher at Brigham Young University for ideas.

Party Time

On the Internet, it's party time all the time. At least in Usenet. Thousands of people around the world crash **alt.party** to see the latest business in the party scene. Talk about upcoming parties, ideas and plans for parties, or wild party experiences. And you don't have to worry about regretting anything in the morning.

See also: Fun, Games, Food and Drink

Usenet:
Newsgroup: **alt.party**

Lots and lots of music on the Internet: check out the Music category.

PARTY TILL YOUR MODEM CONNECTION DROPS

Hey, all you Internet party animals. Your friends on Usenet are ready to talk about partying until the sun comes up. **alt.party**:

be there or be square.

Toasts

Do you need some words for a special occasion and you just can't think of a creative thing to say? Check out this collection of sometimes funny, sometimes sentimental toasts for all occasions.

World Wide Web:
URL: **http://cad.ucla.edu/repository/library/ Cadlab/toasts**

PEOPLE

Albert Einstein

Discussions of the life and works of Albert Einstein, including topics indirectly related to his life.

Listserv Mailing List:
List Address: **epp-l@buacca.bu.edu**
Subscription Address: **listserv@buacca.bu.edu**

Buckminster Fuller

What do you do in your spare time? Most people read, play sports, or watch TV. Not many could say, "Well, I had a lot of time on my hands last weekend, so I invented the geodesic dome." Get to know Bucky Fuller, his works and philosophy.

Listserv Mailing List:
List Address: **geodesic@ubvm.cc.buffalo.edu**
Subscription Address:
    listserv@ubvm.cc.buffalo.edu

Buckminster Fuller

Richard Buckminster Fuller was a genius in that he could shed light on just about any area to which he turned his attention. During his lifetime, he received 39 honorary degrees and became the inspiration for a cult-like following based not so much on a belief system, but on a way of looking at the world and solving its problems. He described himself as an "engineer, inventor, mathematician, architect, cartographer, philosopher, poet, cosmologist, comprehensive designer and choreographer."

What we like best about Bucky is how he dedicated his life as an experiment, and his recognition that if one contributes to one's culture, the economy will lend support in an appropriate manner. Although this may seem far-fetched, it is this Fuller-inspired philosophy that has helped Harley to choose his lot in life and is indirectly responsible for the book you are now reading.

If you would like to learn more about Bucky, his teachings and his followers, subscribe to the geodesic mailing list. It is wonderful to contemplate the work of someone who has the capacity to rise above the petty concerns of day to day life and to see the universe with the eyes of enlightened curiosity.

Celebrities

You've devoured every newspaper, magazine and tabloid in sight and you still want more news and information about celebrities. Here is a source that is available 24 hours a day, so you can always get a fix. Read stories, news and rumors of old and new famous people.

Usenet:
Newsgroup: **alt.celebrities**
Newsgroup: **clari.living.celebrities**

Elders

It's nice to have an older person to talk with or look up to. As an elder, it's fun to get together with other people and work on projects or discuss political and social issues and find new friends. If you are an elder and want to network with other people or if you want the opportunity to act as an electronic grandparent or mentor, this is the perfect place for you, carved out by St. John's University.

Listserv Mailing List:
List Address: **elders@sjuvm.stjohns.edu**
Subscription Address: **listserv@sjuvm.stjohns.edu**

John Muir Exhibit

A collection of materials on the life and legacy of John Muir, the Scottish-born American pioneer of nature conservation. It includes factsheets, a chronology of important events in the life of John Muir, tributes, guides, memorial association details, historic sites, bibliographic materials, gif pictures, and a link to the John Muir Internet Center.

World Wide Web:
URL: **http://aldo.des.ucdavis.edu/John_Muir/ John_Muir_Exhibit.html**

National Press Club Luncheon Addresses

A large collection of recent speeches given at the National Press Club Luncheon. For each large audio file, which typically lasts about an hour, there is an overview of the speaker. New addresses are added on a regular basis.

World Wide Web:
URL: **http://www.cmf.nrl.navy.mil/radio/ club_HALL.html**

Nerd Club

Never again will you have to hang your head in shame. Being a nerd is something to be proud of, especially when you have your own mailing list. What started as a local group has gained international popularity. This is a place for nerds to gather for chit-chat and to share information. If you stick around long enough, you might even get to learn the secret handshake.

Internet Mailing List:
List Address: **nerdnosh@clovis.felton.ca.us**
Subscription Address:
nerdnosh-request@clovis.felton.ca.us

Hang out with the nerds. join the **nerdnosh** mailing list.

A B C D E F G H I J K L M N O **P** Q R S T U V W X Y Z

Obituary Page

Don't settle for reading the obituaries in your local paper, go global. Get a list of people, well-known or obscure, who have died, as well as information on various death hoaxes. Lists are arranged alphabetically or by category. Also available: movie stars who were born or died today.

Usenet:
Newsgroup: **alt.obituaries**

World Wide Web:
URL:
http://catless.ncl.ac.uk/Obituary/README.html

Wondering who's dead?
Read the **Obituary Page**.

(As a matter of fact, why not look for your own name? No need to wait until the last moment.)

Random Portrait Gallery

The Random Portrait Gallery contains self-portraits from the home pages of web users around the world. The gallery is divided into rooms, including the Variable Room, which displays different portraits each time you visit it.

World Wide Web:
URL: **http://oz.sas.upenn.edu/portraits/portraits.html**

Who's Who in Russia

A large list of important people in Russia.

Anonymous FTP:
Address: **ftp.spies.com**
Path: **/Library/Document/russia.who**

Gopher:
Name: Internet Wiretap
Address: **wiretap.spies.com**
Choose: **Wiretap Online Library**
| **Assorted Documents**
| **Who's Who in Russia**

PERSONALS

41 Plus

A friendly channel for those reaching the summit of the hill — oh sorry — just reaching the prime of life.

Internet Relay Chat:
Channel: **#41plus**

Bisexuals

Response will come easy for people posting to this personals group since they are not limited by gender classification. Bisexuals from around the world post ads for friendship, love, and encounters of an intimate nature.

Usenet:
Newsgroup: **alt.personals.bi**

Feel lucky?
Try **alt. personals.bi.** the bisexual discussion group. Right away you will double your chances of getting a date for Friday night.

Chit-Chat

If you want someone to talk to, why not check out **hottub** and **talk2me**? You never know who you might meet!

Internet Relay Chat:
Channel: **#hottub**
Channel: **#talk2me**

Electronic Matchmaker

A free, global matching service for anyone over 18 years of age. Fill out the detailed questionnaire and the perfect date could be yours.

Finger:

    Address: **perfect@match.com**

Mail:

    Address: **info.finger@match.com**

Fat People

Don't bother with skinny, insubstantial waifs when you can go for the gusto. Place your ad expressing your desire to interact with fat people.

Usenet:

    Newsgroup: **alt.personals.fat**

Friendly Folk

A place to stop and chat with friendly people.

Internet Relay Chat:
    Channel: **#friendly**

Large People

Big and tall people or those who are seeking big and tall people will love this newsgroup. Post your requests and see what happens. You will probably find just the response you are looking for. Or at least some response.

Usenet:

    Newsgroup: **alt.personals.big-folks**

Meeting People

Welcome to the smorgasbord of personal ads. There is something for everyone, and you can take as much as you like. Non-fattening, hypo-allergenic, 100 percent of your recommended daily allowance of fun and good times. Participate in one of these Usenet groups and maybe you'll meet the man, woman, or none-of-the-above of your dreams.

Mail:

    Address: **info@nook.com**

Usenet:

    Newsgroup: **alt.personals**
    Newsgroup: **alt.personals.ads**
    Newsgroup: **alt.personals.misc**

Polyamory

The Law of Romantic Physics states that when there is too much love to go around the excess has to go somewhere. We've found where it goes, and if you want to get some of it to take home with you, feel welcome. Polyamorous people share themselves with you (and you and you and you).

Usenet:

    Newsgroup: **alt.personals.poly**

World Wide Web:
    URL: **http://www.hal.com/~landman/Poly/**

Spanking

Everyone needs a good spanking now and then. If you like getting your bottom blistered or warming up someone else's backside, try placing an ad here to find a spanking partner.

Usenet:

    Newsgroup: **alt.personals.spanking**
    Newsgroup: **alt.personals.spanking.punishment**

Virtual MeetMarket

Need a hot date, a friend, or just someone to talk to? Place a personal ad using the latest hypertext environment — the Web. You can retain anonymity with your personal ad, as your identity is kept hidden and responses are forwarded to you from a server.

See also: Romance, Sex

World Wide Web:
   URL: **http://wwa.com:1111/**

PHILOSOPHY

American Philosophical Association

A BBS offering information about philosophical societies, grants, fellowships, seminars, and institutes. Also a mail directory of the APA membership and bibliographical and journal information.

Gopher:
   Name: Occidental College
   Address: **apa.oxy.edu**

An Enquiry Concerning Human Understanding

The text of David Hume's philosophical book *An Enquiry Concerning Human Understanding*.

Anonymous FTP:
   Address: **ftp.uu.net**
   Path: **/doc/literary/obi/David.Hume/
      Human.Understanding**

Ancient Philosophy

Do you ever get tired of the same old chit-chat at parties? Brush up on your ancient philosophy and you'll be able to discuss Hesiod over the clam dip and ponder Iamblichus while munching on meatballs.

Listserv Mailing List:
   List Address: **sophia@liverpool.ac.uk**
   Subscription Address: **listserv@liverpool.ac.uk**

David Hume

This well-known 18th Century Scottish philosopher managed to bring Western culture that certain something that was missing in the work of Locke and Berkeley. He suggested that the mind contained only a series of "impressions" (sensations) and thus discounted the possibility of certainty in knowledge. Although his underlying assumptions might be considered somewhat naive and primitive by modern standards, he was able to engender a posture of skepticism that was important not only to his fundamental work, but to his commentaries on religion.
If you are interested in Hume and his thinking, you can download one of his most important works, "An Enquiry Concerning Human Understanding," from the Net.

Buddhist Studies

There is more to Buddhism than just sitting around thinking about what some short, fat guy said many centuries ago. It's a whole way of living. The Coombs Computing Center offers an entire library relating to Buddhist studies.

World Wide Web:
   URL: **http://coombs.anu.edu.au/
      WWWVL-Buddhism.html**

Common Sense

The text of Thomas Paine's philosophical work.

Anonymous FTP:
   Address: **ftp.uu.net**
   Path: **/doc/literary/obi/Thomas.Paine/
      Common.Sense**

Electronic Journal of Analytic Philosophy

This journal is peer-reviewed and has an interesting selection of articles and topics relating to analytic philosophy. Skim through the current hypertext issue or look at back issues. Also available are subscription and referee registration forms and submission guidelines.

World Wide Web:
URL: **http://www.phil.indiana.edu/ejap/ejap.html**

Extropians

It's not an alien life form, nor is it a variety of insectoid species. Extropians are people who are interested in anarchocapitalist politics, cryonics and other life extension techniques, the technological extension of human intelligence and perception, and nanotechnology. It's not just another little hobby. It's a way of life.

Internet Mailing List:
List Address: **extropians@extropy.org**
Subscription Address:
extropians-request@extropy.org

Why die when you can become an EXTROPIAN?

Hakim Bey

This web page offers texts by Hakim Bey in HTML and ASCII format including *Temporary Autonomous Zone*, *The Radio Sermonettes*, and *The Evil Eye*, information about Bey (including a contact address), and a collection of works related to Bey's writing, such as *Incunabula* and *Aspects of Chaosophy*.

World Wide Web:
URL: **http://www.uio.no:80/~mwatz/bey/**

I Ching

Let the yin and yang lines of the I Ching predict your future with this reading of the forces that may affect your life.

World Wide Web:
URL: **http://cad.ucla.edu/repository/useful/
iching.html**

Immanuel Kant

Get your blood racing with a little cerebral stimulation in the form of Kant's philosophy. Scholars and philosophers sit and think about thinking. Check in to see if they're getting anywhere, or to add your own thoughts to the intellectual whirlwind.

Listserv Mailing List:
List Address: **kant-l@coral.bucknell.edu**
Subscription Address: **listserv@coral.bucknell.edu**

Soren Kierkegaard

"Truth is subjectivity," according to Soren Kierkegaard. What exactly does that mean? Some people make their living pondering that question. You can meet them on this list and discuss not only the works of this 19th century Danish philosopher, but also the works of related thinkers.

Internet Mailing List:
List Address: **kierkegaard@stolaf.edu**
Subscription Address:
kierkegaard-request@stolaf.edu

J. Krishnamurti

Krishnamurti (1895-1986) was a world-renowned teacher who conducted deep investigation on the nature of humanity and the Self, and gave talks and wrote books on love, religion, belief, relationships, death, thought, time, fear, envy, meditation and beauty. Gather around to talk about the teachings of J. Krishnamurti and join with others in some deep self-questioning.

Internet Mailing List:
List Address: **listening-l@cs.tu-berlin.de**
Subscription Address:
listening-l-request@cs.tu-berlin.de

Maximizing Life's Choices

Some days it's just too much. Life goes too fast, there are too many choices, things are too loud, too bright, too busy. There are people who have chosen to work toward having a positive, healthy lifestyle without giving in to heavy consumerism. They are simplifying their lives, getting rid of "stuff," and managing their money in creative ways. Join them in the quest for simplicity and see how nice it is to take pleasure in the little things.

Listserv Mailing List:
List Address: **maxlife@gibbs.oit.unc.edu**
Subscription Address: **listserv@gibbs.oit.unc.edu**

Memetics

There is a theory that ideas can propagate biologically. So, if you start getting funny thoughts in your head and you don't know where they came from, you can blame it on your parents and the theory of Memetics. Never again will you have to take responsibility for those strange ideas that keep coming to mind. Learn about memes and their effects on humanity.

Usenet:
Newsgroup: **alt.memetics**

World Wide Web:
URL:
http://www.uio.no/~mwatz/memetics/index.html

Metaphysics

Do you ever get the impression that there is more going on in the universe than you realize? Sit around with the folks on Usenet who love to contemplate the philosophical aspects of our "beingness" as well as the workings of the cosmos.

Usenet:
Newsgroup: **alt.paranet.metaphysics**

New Ways of Thinking

Break away from the herd and think for yourself, like those who find inspiration in Timothy Leary, Robert Anton Wilson and John Lilly. Push Darwin aside and help speed up the evolution of humankind by developing new ways of thinking and expanding consciousness. This is the fast food of philosophy.

Listserv Mailing List:
List Address: **fnord-l@ubvm.cc.buffalo.edu**
Subscription Address:
listserv@ubvm.cc.buffalo.edu

Objectivism

Ayn Rand created the philosophy of Objectivism. She summarizes: "My philosophy, in essence, is the concept of man as a heroic being, with his own happiness as the moral purpose of his life, with productive achievements as his noblest activity, and reason as his only absolute." Here is a web page and an ftp site dedicated to things of interest to Ayn Rand fans.

Anonymous FTP:
Address: **ftp.hmc.edu**
Path: **/pub/science/sci.answers/objectivism/faq**

World Wide Web:
URL:
http://www.rpi.edu/~pier1/phil/objectivism.html

Objectivism Mailing List

Students of objectivism and Ayn Rand discuss their ideas, issues, and exchange news. Any issue of relevance to objectivists is welcomed.

Internet Mailing List:
List Address: **objectivism@vix.com**
Subscription Address: **objectivism-request@vix.com**

Objectivism in the 1990s

There are some who find Ayn Rand's philosophy of Objectivism as relevant today as it was many years ago when she first started explaining what was wrong with the world. There are others who say that her ideas were fine for the time but are atavistic and irrelevant to modern life. Then, there are still others who say "Ayn who?".

Whichever camp you find yourself in–slavish follower, skeptical cynic, or just plain ignorant everyman–the Objectivism mailing list will furnish you with enough food for thought to have your own pseudo-intellectual picnic. Just remember: Ayn Rand refused to compromise her ideals in her work and in her life, and look where she is today.

We are not sure what she would make of the Internet. What we are sure of is that she would buy at least several copies of *The Internet Golden Directory* to impress her friends. As Howard Roark would say, "I don't care what you or anyone else may think, *I* am going to buy as many copies of *The Internet Golden Directory* as I want. To do less would be to compromise my inner self and would make all that I stand for a sham and a farce."

Want some fun?
Read the Fun section.

Oceania

Dreams of paradise are wonderful. Imagine a Utopian society where everything is perfect. What if you could start from scratch and form a new country, designing it exactly as you want it? This ambitious project is actually in effect. Read the development plans, constitution, and laws of this new country called Oceania, and ponder how they plan to pull the whole thing off.

See also: Politics, Government

World Wide Web:
URL: **http://saturn.uaamath.alaska.edu/~kane/ oceania_start.html**

Personal Idealogies

Everyone has an opinion, and some people even have opinions by which they consistently stand. If you feel strongly about your beliefs and want to share them, or want to hear others, join in the discussion of **belief-l**. This group will not tolerate religious proselytizing or flame wars, so consider sending listserv's **review** command to get a feel of the group before posting.

Listserv Mailing List:
List Address: **belief-l@brownvm.brown.edu**
Subscription Address: **listserv@brownvm.brown.edu**

Philosophical Discussions

Mailing lists for philosophers worldwide. Discuss jobs, conferences, works in progress, newsletters, journals, and other topics.

Listserv Mailing List:
List Address: **philosed@suvm.syr.edu**
Subscription Address: **listserv@suvm.syr.edu**

List Address: **philosop@vm1.yorku.ca**
Subscription Address: **listserv@vm1.yorku.ca**

List Address: **phil-l@vm.ucs.ualberta.ca**
Subscription Address: **listserv@vm.ucs.ualberta.ca**

Do you like to talk about Life and other Important Stuff?
Join one of the *Philosophical Discussions* mailing lists and talk with the pros.

Philosophy at the University of Bologna

If your Italian is up to snuff and you would like to investigate philosophy Mediterranean-style, check out this web page, which has links to other philosophy resources and departments at the University of Bologna.

World Wide Web:
URL: **http://www.philo.unibo.it/**

Philosophy of the Middle Ages

Every period has its great thinkers and the Middle Ages is no exception. Scholars examine the philosophy and socio-political thought of the medieval era, ask questions and share insights, as well as post announcements of conferences and calls for papers.

See also: History

Listserv Mailing List:
List Address: **mdvlphil@lsuvm.sncc.lsu.edu**
Subscription Address: **listserv@lsuvm.sncc.lsu.edu**

Plato

The full text of Plato's works *The Republic* and *Crito*.

Anonymous FTP:
Address: **ftp.std.com**
Path: **/obi/Plato/***

Address: **ftp.uu.net**
Path: **/doc/literary/obi/Plato/***

Principia Cybernetica Web

The Principia Cybernetica Project (PCP) is a collaborative, computer-supported attempt to develop a complete cybernetic and evolutionary philosophy. This page offers many articles and links to discussions of tools, structure, topics, philosophy, and the practical organization of the PCP.

World Wide Web:
URL: **http://pespmc1.vub.ac.be/nutshell.html**

University of Chicago Philosophy Project

Access to various discussions of theories and thought, and links to other philosophy resources and servers.

World Wide Web:
URL: **http://csmaclab-www.uchicago.edu/ philosophyProject/philos.html**

Utopia

The text of the classic of political philosophy by Thomas More.

Anonymous FTP:
  Address: **ftp.uu.net**
  Path: **/doc/literary/obi/Thomas.More/Utopia.Txt**

Zen

Experience the serenity and logic of Zen philosophy. Learn the ways of action through non-action and how to get there from here without even trying.

Usenet:
  Newsgroup: **alt.philosophy.zen**
  Newsgroup: **alt.zen**

Excerpt from the Net...

```
Newsgroup: alt.zen
Subject: Why learn Zen?

> What can I do to learn Zen?

Look both ways, inside and out.

> And why?

There is heavy traffic out there,
Lighter traffic in here,
Please take care of yourself and others
in crossing.

> Would I get something out of it?

No, sorry. Nothing for sale.
```

PHOTOGRAPHY

California Museum of Photography

A sample of some of the photographs on display at the California Museum of Photography.

Gopher:
  Name: University of California at Riverside
  Address: **galaxy.ucr.edu**
  Choose: **Campus Events**
   | **California Museum of Photography**
   | **Network Exhibitions**

Darkroom Photography

Photographic creativity certainly doesn't stop with a click of the shutter. When you head to the darkroom you have to ask youself all sorts of questions like "Should I print on warm or cold tone paper?" and "What kind of developer should I use?" Topics cover being creative in the darkroom as well as technical issues such as chemical usage, paper, tools, and equipment.

Usenet:
  Newsgroup: **rec.photo.darkroom**

Room in the Darkroom

Some of the most mysterious things in the world go on in a darkroom. If you are not a photographer, sorry, this part of human culture is closed to you and there's not much you can do about it except feel wistful in a polite sort of way. If however, you are among the cognoscenti who can distinguish between lith processing and posterization, the discussion group **rec.photo.darkroom** is waiting for you. Join the club and see what develops.

Photo Database

Material relating to photography, including technique guides, paper and film data sheets, and chemistry formulae and information.

Gopher:
  Name: Panix Public Access Unix
  Address: **gopher.panix.com**
  Choose: **The Panix Photography Database**

Photography Archives

Lexicon of terms, FAQs, equipment reviews, lens information, useful addresses and phone numbers, and archives having to do with photos and cameras.

Anonymous FTP:
> Address: **moink.nmsu.edu**
> Path: **/rec.photo/***

> Address: **rtfm.mit.edu**
> Path: **/pub/usenet/news.answers/rec-photo-faq**

Photography General Discussion

Whether you are just a snapshot shooter or a pro with hundreds of pounds of equipment, there is a newsgroup that is perfect for you. Fans of photography hang out and talk about taking pictures from a creative as well as a technical point of view.

Usenet:
> Newsgroup: **rec.photo**
> Newsgroup: **rec.photo.advanced**
> Newsgroup: **rec.photo.misc**

Photography Mailing List

Discussion of all aspects of photography, including aesthetics, equipment, and shooting technique.

Listserv Mailing List:
> List Address: **photo-l@buacca.bitnet**
> Subscription Address: **listserv@buacca.bitnet**

Photography Questions and Answers

No matter what the problem is, there is someone on Usenet who is bound to have an answer for you. Post questions or help someone solve a photography dilemma and pick up some helpful hints about shooting and developing photos as well as tips on using equipment.

Usenet:
> Newsgroup: **rec.photo.help**

The only place where Politics comes before Star Trek is in "The Internet Golden Directory."

Pinhole Camera

We know a secret. We know what you can do with an oatmeal box, some tape, aluminum foil and a pin. Unfortunately, it's not as big a secret since this list was formed. Users of pinhole cameras talk about camera construction, techniques and style when using pinhole cameras. You can get as simple or elaborate as you like, and you'd be surprised by the great results you can get with such a simple little gadget.

See also: Art

Internet Mailing List:
> List Address: **pinhole@mintir.fidonet.org**
> Subscription Address:
> **pinhole-request@mintir.fidonet.org**

Power Tips and Tricks for Photoshop

This web page features a hypertext version of Kai Krause's *Kai's Power Tips and Tricks for Adobe Photoshop*. Jump right in at Tip 1 (Secrets of Chops) and work your way down to Tip 23 (Complexity-city! The Snowy Mask Technique).

World Wide Web:
> URL: **http://the-tech.mit.edu/KPT/KPT.html**

Stereograms and 3-D Images

This web page collects an assortment of links to fun 3-D images and stereograms. There are also links to other web pages and ftp sites that store archives and galleries of stereograms.

World Wide Web:
> URL: **http://www.yahoo.com/Art/
> Computer_Generated/Stereograms/**

PHYSICS

American Institute of Physics

The American Institute of Physics home page offers information about the AIP, links to AIP publications, newsletters and mailing lists, and links to other physics resources and the gopher and ftp servers of the AIP.

World Wide Web:
> URL: **http://www.aip.org/**

A B C D E F G H I J K L M N O **P** Q R S T U V W X Y Z

Austin Fusion Studies

This web server offers information about the fusion research program conducted by the Fusion Research Center and the Institute for Fusion Studies at the University of Texas. It is the repository of physics and fusion newsletters and software, and provides pointers to physics information and white pages information for fusion labs, technical reports, and papers.

World Wide Web:
URL: **http://w3fusion.ph.utexas.edu/**

Center for Particle Astrophysics

The home page of the Center for Particle Astrophysics offers many physics resources and information, including information about the Center, and links to astrophysics resources and other servers.

World Wide Web:
URL: **http://physics7.berkeley.edu/home.html**

Early Instruments

A historical overview of instruments used in the field of physics: optics, heat, and electromagnetism. The information is very detailed and will show you images if you have a graphical browser.

World Wide Web:
URL: **http://hpl33.na.infn.it/Museum/Museum.html**

Einstein in 3-D

Experience Einstein's theory of relativity in a graphical, three-dimensional environment. Mathematical equations are turned into pictures for a much more visual physics experience.

See also: Science

World Wide Web:
URL: **http://www.ncsa.uiuc.edu/Apps/GenRel/SC93/HOME_sc93.html#workb**

Electromagnetic Fields and Microwave Electronics

This web page is provided by the Swiss Federal Institute of Technology and offers information on the institute's research into electromagnetic field theory and high-frequency electronics. The page also has links to other related resources.

See also: Technology

World Wide Web:
URL: **http://www.ifh.ee.ethz.ch/**

Electromagnetics

Old Ben Franklin would have had fun with this. It's amazing what you can do with a little metal, some wire, and a charge of electricity. When you're not in the lab flipping switches, subscribe to this mailing list to read about issues relating to electromagnetics, including book reviews, techniques, and code problems.

See also: Science, Technology

Internet Mailing List:
List Address: **em@decwd.ece.uiuc.edu**
Subscription Address:
em-request@decwd.ece.uiuc.edu

European Group for Atomic Spectroscopy

The EGAS organization is open to all European physicists working in the field of atomic physics. It aims to promote international cooperation between its members through the dissemination of information.

Gopher:
Name: EGAS
Address: **ipne.pne.ulg.ac.be**
Choose: **IPNE**
| **EGAS**

Can you name this molecule? Well, at least you can find its picture at Northern Arizona University (**ftp.nau.edu**) in **/graphics/gif/ray**. The filename is **molecule.gif**.

Fermilab

The Fermi National Accelerator Laboratory is a high-energy physics lab and home of the world's most powerful particle accelerator, the Tevatron. Scientists from the U.S. and elsewhere use the lab's resources in experiments to explore the most fundamental particles and forces of nature. This page has news updates, documents, and information about ongoing research projects at Fermilab.

World Wide Web:
URL: **http://fnnews.fnal.gov/**

Fusion

This web page offers links to fusion resources and pages at a number of institutions—including the University of Texas, MIT, UC Berkeley, and the Office of Fusion Energy—an index of fusion research and related sites, and a link to the Usenet newsgroup **sci.physics.fusion**.

World Wide Web:
URL: **http://www.yahoo.com/Science/Physics/Fusion/**

HEP Data Archive

The Durham-Rutherford HEP Data Archive provides you with interactive access to databases containing reaction data from particle physics experiments, information on past, current, and proposed experiments, data on particle properties, and the electronic mail addresses of HEP physicists.

Telnet:
Address: **durpdg.dur.ac.uk**
Login: **PDG**
Password: **hepdata**

High Energy Physics Information Center

The High Energy Physics Information Center (HEPIC) web page and gopher provide access to information about this organization, documentation and publications of HEPIC, information about HEPIC experiments, high energy physics software, and links to other high energy physics resources including web pages, ftp sites and gophers.

Gopher:
Name: HEP Network Resource Center
Address: **gopher.hep.net**

World Wide Web:
URL: **http://www.hep.net/**

Index of Abstracts

This is the perfect place to find papers relating to high energy physics, astrophysics, condensed matter theory, general relativity, quantum cosmology, and nuclear theory. A keyword search will help you track down the information you need.

See also: Astronomy, Space

World Wide Web:
URL: **http://xxx.lanl.gov/**

Institute of High Energy Physics

This page is the home page of the Institute of High Energy Physics, located in Beijing, China. Through this server, you can find out about current projects at IHEP and partnerships with other institutions.

World Wide Web:
URL: **http://www.ihep.ac.cn/ihep.html**

A B C D E F G H I J K L M N O P Q R S T U V W X Y Z

KVI Research Network

Read about research projects and get technical information about the fields of atomic, nuclear, and applied nuclear physics.

Gopher:
    Name: KVI Network
    Address: **kviexp.kvi.nl**

World Wide Web:
    URL: **gopher://kviexp.kvi.nl/**

National Nuclear Data Center Online Service

All the data you could possibly want regarding nuclear physics and statistical measurements, including radiation levels and other information for the U.S.

Telnet:
    Address: **bnlnd2.dne.bnl.gov**
    Login: **nndc**

OpticsNet

OpticsNet is the home page of the Optical Society of America (OSA). It covers all aspects of optical physics and engineering. The server provides information about quantum electronics, photonics, and vision.

See also: Technology

World Wide Web:
    URL: **http://www.osa.org/homepage.html**

Particles

A list of elementary and fundamental particles, giving the mass, lifetime, and properties of each.

Anonymous FTP:
    Address: **ftp.spies.com**
    Path: **/Library/Document/particle.tbl**

Gopher:
    Name: Internet Wiretap
    Address: **wiretap.spies.com**
    Choose: **Wiretap Online Library**
    | **Assorted Documents**
    | **Elementary & fundamental particles**

Physics Discussion Groups

Without physics, the world would be much more dull and life would be much too easy to understand. Exercise your brain by getting in on some physics discussion.

Usenet:
    Newsgroup: **alt.sci.physics.acoustics**
    Newsgroup: **alt.sci.physics.new-theories**
    Newsgroup: **alt.sci.physics.plutonium**
    Newsgroup: **alt.sci.physics.spam**
    Newsgroup: **bionet.biophysics**
    Newsgroup: **bit.listserv.physhare**
    Newsgroup: **sci.astro.research**
    Newsgroup: **sci.med.physics**
    Newsgroup: **sci.physics**
    Newsgroup: **sci.physics.accelerators**
    Newsgroup: **sci.physics.computational.fluid-dynamics**
    Newsgroup: **sci.physics.electromagnetics**
    Newsgroup: **sci.physics.fusion**
    Newsgroup: **sci.physics.particle**
    Newsgroup: **sci.physics.plasma**
    Newsgroup: **sci.physics.research**

Physics Gopher

Access to lots of physics resources and information, including the areas of astrophysics, general relativity and quantum cosmology, high energy physics, and nuclear theory.

Gopher:
    Name: University of Chicago
    Address: **granta.uchicago.edu**
    Choose: **Miscellaneous Physics Resources**

The Physics Gopher

Physics is great.

If we didn't have physics, there wouldn't be any gravity or light or sound (and we would all be floating around silently in the dark).

So, when you need to indulge yourself, try the physics Gopher at the University of Chicago: a great source for all types of things physical.

Physics Information Service

An information service for nuclear and particle physics that provides access to nuclear and high-energy physics-related preprint listings. Both the abstracts and the papers themselves are available through this gopher, as well as text searches of the abstracts, authors, and titles.

Gopher:
Name: LANL Physics Information Service
Address: **mentor.lanl.gov**

Physics Mailing Lists

These mailing lists cover current developments in theoretical and experimental physics, including plasmaphysics, particle physics, and astrophysics.

Internet Mailing List:
List Address: **physics@unix.sri.com**
Subscription Address:
physics-request@unix.sri.com

List Address: **physics@qedqcd.rye.ny.us**
Subscription Address:
physics-request@qedqcd.rye.ny.us

List Address: **physics@vm.marist.edu**
Subscription Address: **listserv@vm.marist.edu**

Physics on the Net

A condensation of postings to Usenet newsgroups about some cutting edge issues in physics, including black holes and what happens inside of them, gravitational radiation, the paradox of Einstein's relativity, tachyons, and the theoretical possibilities of time travel.

Anonymous FTP:
Address: **ftp.hmc.edu**
Path: **/pub/science/sci.answers/.mirror.OLD/ physics-faq/***

Physics Student Discussion List

A mailing list for physics students covering physics experiments, computer simulations, and other topics of interest.

Listserv Mailing List:
List Address: **phys-stu@uwf.cc.uwf.edu**
Subscription Address: **listserv@uwf.cc.uwf.edu**

Relativity

This page offers links to pages on mathematical relativity, gravitational physics and geometry, hyperspace, and the home pages of several organizations with interests in relativity.

World Wide Web:
URL: **http://www.yahoo.com/ Science/Physics/Relativity/**

Sounds from Chaos

Papers, sounds, and references about Chua's Circuit, one of the most interesting chaotic systems. Chua's Oscillator Circuit generates many strange and varied sounds and is one of the few physical systems for which the presence of chaos has been observed experimentally, verified by computer simulations, and proven mathematically.

See also: Computers: Sounds

World Wide Web:
URL: **http://www.ccsr.uiuc.edu/People/gmk/ Papers/ChuaSndRef.html**

Stanford Linear Accelerator Center

This is a national laboratory operated by Stanford University for the U.S. Department of Energy that does experimental and theoretical research in elementary particle physics and other diciplines. This server details projects and upcoming events at Stanford Linear Accelerator Center.

World Wide Web:
URL: **http://heplibw3.slac.stanford.edu/ FIND/slac.html**

Theoretical Physics Pre-print List

Papers on general relativity and quantum cosmology, and high energy physics.

Anonymous FTP:
Address: **xxx.lanl.gov**
Path: **/gr-qc/***

Address: **xxx.lanl.gov**
Path: **/hep-th/***

Mail:
Address: **gr-qc@xxx.lanl.gov**
Subject: **help**

Address: **hep-th@xxx.lanl.gov**
Subject: **help**

A B C D E F G H I J K L M N O P Q R S T U V W X Y Z

WebStars: Astrophysics on the Web

WebStars is about astronomy and astrophysics, cyberspace, data formats, virtual reality, and much more. It offers some thought-provoking articles on subjects such as how astrophysics information systems might be built and quotes from eminent authors, as well as a list of other web sites related to astronomy .

World Wide Web:
URL: **http://guinan.gsfc.nasa.gov/WebStars/About.html**

POETRY

William Blake

A collection of the poetry of William Blake, including "The New Jerusalem" which was made into the song "Jerusalem" by Emerson, Lake and Palmer.

Anonymous FTP:
Address: **ftp.uu.net**
Path: **/doc/literary/obi/William.Blake/***

Chinese Poetry

A mailing list dedicated to sharing and discussing Chinese poetry.

Listserv Mailing List:
List Address: **chpoem-l@ubvm.cc.buffalo.edu**
Subscription Address: **listserv@ubvm.cc.buffalo.edu**

Chinese Poetry
We love Chinese poetry and you will too once you give it half a chance. Our favorite Chinese poem is that traditional work from the Chi'ing dynasty that starts, "There was a young girl from Beijing...". If you would like to be involved in one of the most beautiful artforms and its oriental incarnations, subscribe to the **chpem-1** mailing list.

Dogwood Blossoms

Lovers of haiku join together to discuss their favorite haiku or to show something they have written in haiku form. This digest is compiled approximately once a month and is receptive to new haiku and to suggestions and input from readers. It's a friendly poetic community.

World Wide Web:
URL: **http://199.20.16.10/dbindex.html**

Exquisite Sonnet Project

A set of collaborative sonnets. Each sonnet was written by 14 people who wrote one line each and saw only the line they were to follow. See the interesting results of this project, which was organized through mail and Usenet groups.

World Wide Web:
URL: **http://oz.sas.upenn.edu/surreal/sonnets.html**

Robert Herrick

Poems by Robert Herrick including "To The Virgins" and "Upon Scobble."

Anonymous FTP:
Address: **ftp.uu.net**
Path: **/doc/literary/obi/Robert.Herrick/***

Internet Poetry Archive

This is a wonderful project from the University of North Carolina — famous poets can be experienced through pictures, sound files and text. Even if you don't have a graphical browser, you can still read the poetry from writers around the world, including Nobel Prize winners.

World Wide Web:
URL: **http://sunsite.unc.edu/dykki/poetry/home.html**

John Keats

A collection of poems by John Keats.

Anonymous FTP:
Address: **ftp.uu.net**
Path: **/doc/literary/obi/John.Keats/***

Poems

Spirits soar free on the wings of poetry. Show your verses to like-minded, creative people. If you ask, you can get advice, but there are more poems posted than critiques.

Usenet:
Newsgroup: **rec.arts.poems**

Poems and Prose

A collection of original poems and prose composed by people on the Internet.

Anonymous FTP:
Address: **quartz.rutgers.edu**
Path: **/pub/origworks/***

Gopher:
Name: Rutgers University
Address: **quartz.rutgers.edu**
Choose: **QuartzBBS Original Works Archive**

Poet's Cafe

Imagine sitting at a table wearing all black. You have a cup of coffee that is as thick as sludge. The room is dark and heavy, and even though you are with others, you feel isolated. Suddenly a voice speaks out of the darkness reciting a lovely, angst-ridden poem, and you know you are not alone. This is the atmosphere created at the Poet's Cafe, a gallery of poetry written by people on the Net. Bring your poems; the Cafe is always open for submissions.

Gopher:
Name: University of Alabama
Address: **twinbrook.cis.uab.edu**
Choose: **The Continuum**
  | The Poet's Cafe

Poetry Archives

The English Server sports a huge list of links to many fantastic poems and other poetry sites and servers.

World Wide Web:
URL: **http://english-server.hss.cmu.edu/
Poetry.html**

This is the first book of the rest of your life.

Poetry Index

A collection of poems and song lyrics mostly written by Howard Landman. This page also has a link to other haiku resources.

World Wide Web:
URL: **http://www.hal.com/~landman/Poetry/**

Poetry Workshop

It's hard to get an objective opinion from your friends because either they can't be objective or they're afraid to be. But you can get all the critiques you want from this group of aspiring poets. As long as you give as much as you get, this will be a nice source of suggestions and ideas about your work in progress.

See also: Writing

Internet Mailing List:
List Address: **poet@scruz.ucsc.edu**
Subscription Address: **poet-request@scruz.ucsc.edu**

Percy Bysshe Shelley

The text of several poems by Shelley, including the classic "Ozymandias."

Anonymous FTP:
Address: **ftp.uu.net**
Path: **/doc/literary/obi/Percy.Bysshe.Shelley/***

Shiki Internet Haiku Salon

An introduction to Haiku, including its history, information about Shiki Masaoka, the founder of modern Haiku, and links to many Haiku poems and resources including mailing lists and poetry servers.

World Wide Web:
URL: **http://mikan.cc.matsuyama-u.ac.jp/~shiki/**

Song

The complete text of the poem "Song", by John Donne.

Anonymous FTP:
Address: **ftp.std.com**
Path: **/obi/John.Donne/Song**

Address: **ftp.uu.net**
Path: **/doc/literary/obi/John.Donne/Song**

Algernon Charles Swinburne

A collection of poetry by Algernon Charles Swinburne.

Anonymous FTP:
Address: **ftp.uu.net**
Path: **/doc/literary/obi/**
Algernon.Charles.Swinburne/*

Terance, This Is Stupid Stuff

The text of the poem "Terance, This Is Stupid Stuff" by A. E. Housmann.

Anonymous FTP:
Address: **ftp.uu.net**
Path: **/doc/literary/obi/A.E.Housmann/Terance**

Alfred Lord Tennyson

Poetry by Tennyson, including the classic "The Charge of the Light Brigade."

Anonymous FTP:
Address: **ftp.uu.net**
Path: **/doc/literary/obi/Tennyson/***

To His Coy Mistress

A file containing "To His Coy Mistress" by Andrew Marvell.

Anonymous FTP:
Address: **ftp.uu.net**
Path: **/doc/literary/obi/Andrew.Marvell/**
To.His.Coy.Mistress

What the Welsh and Chinese Have in Common

"What the Welsh and Chinese Have In Common," a collection of poems by Paul Jones, is the winner of the 1990 Poetry Chapbook Competition sponsored by the North Carolina Writers' Network.

World Wide Web:
URL: **http://sunsite.unc.edu/pjones/poetry/**

When Lilacs Last in the Dooryard Bloomed

The full text of the poem "When Lilacs Last in the Dooryard Bloomed," by Walt Whitman.

Anonymous FTP:
Address: **ftp.std.com**
Path: **/obi/Walt.Whitman/**
When.Lilacs.Last.in.the.Dooryard.

Address: **ftp.uu.net**
Path: **/doc/literary/obi/Walt.Whitman/**
When.Lilacs.Last.in.the.Dooryard.

John Greenleaf Whittier

A collection of poems by John Greenleaf Whittier.

Anonymous FTP:
Address: **ftp.uu.net**
Path: **/doc/literary/obi/John.Greenleaf.Whittier/***

William Wordsworth

A collection of the poetry of Wordsworth.

Anonymous FTP:
Address: **ftp.uu.net**
Path: **/doc/literary/obi/William.Wordsworth/***

World War I Poetry

The poetry of Wilfred Owen, who wrote about World War I from the soldier's perspective.

Anonymous FTP:
Address: **ftp.uu.net**
Path: **/doc/literary/obi/Wilfred.Owen/***

POLITICS: NATIONAL (U.S.)

'60s Left Today

Up the revolution! Off the pigs! For those of you who miss '60s style leftist political rhetoric, here is a collection of articles, poems, and song lyrics from *The Activist Times, Inc.*, an organization devoted to promoting the political ideas of the '60s left in today's "Amerika."

Anonymous FTP:
Address: **ftp.uu.net**
Path: **/doc/literary/obi/ATI/***

21st Century Constitution

Barry Krusch's idea of an updated constitution to reflect the advancement of technology and society. This document is billed as a resource for people interested in political science or the Constitution.

Anonymous FTP:
Address: **ftp.netcom.com**
Path: **/pub/kr/krusch/21st.***

Address: **ftp.std.com**
Path: **/obi/Barry.Krusch/21st.txt**

Animal Defense Network

The Animal Defense Network brings together the many different faces and ideas of the animal rights/defense movement into one comprehensive listing.

World Wide Web:
URL: **http://orca.envirolink.org/elink/
adnmain.html**

Clinton Jokes

A Clinton joke for every occasion. Hillary, Bill, Chelsea, even Socks. No one is spared.

Anonymous FTP:
Address: **cco.caltech.edu**
Path: **/pub/humor/political/clinton.jokes***

Clinton Watch

Clinton Watch is the first political column on the Internet devoted to the critical analysis of the policies and actions of the Clinton administration. The main focus is to fill in the gaps on issues that are overlooked by the mainstream media.

Gopher:
Name: Clinton Watch
Address: **dolphin.gulf.net**
Port: **3000**

Coalition for Networked Information

Search databases for interesting publications, transcripts of congressional sessions, and other political events.

See also: Education, Internet

Telnet:
Address: **a.cni.org**
Login: **brsuser**

Conservation Action

What do you think would happen if instead of going to the polls to vote, democratic countries held Olympics to see who was able to get into office? This list explores the idea that in democratic elections, conservative and leftist voters balance each other out, but that the balance is limited to the electoral contest.

Majordomo Mailing List:
List Address: **conservative-action@world.std.com**
Subscription Address: **majordomo@world.std.com**

Conservative Discussion Lists

It's not easy being a conservative these days. But now you have your own support group in which to discuss the GOP and conservative movement, national conventions, conservative talk show hosts, and elections.

See also: Government, Mail to Famous People

Listserv Mailing List:
List Address: **gop-l@occvm.bitnet**
Subscription Address: **listserv@occvm.bitnet**

List Address: **repub-l@vm.marist.edu**
Subscription Address: **listserv@vm.marist.edu**

Conservative Political News

What is the latest news in the world of conservative politics? Find out about the most recent buzz in Washington and read about political agendas that relate to conservatives. This is not a discussion group, but rather a news list to stir discussion in other groups and to keep you informed on the latest political happenings.

Majordomo Mailing List:
List Address: **c-news@world.std.com**
Subscription Address: **majordomo@world.std.com**

Feminism and Liberty

Libertarian feminists discuss news and information relevant to their political philosophy. For discussion about the concepts of feminism and liberty, check out **libfem-talk**, which includes postings from **libfem-news**.

Internet Mailing List:
List Address: **libfem-news@math.uio.no**
Subscription Address:
libfem-news-request@math.uio.no

List Address: **libfem-talk@məth.uio.no**
Subscription Address:
libfem-talk-request@math.uio.no

A B C D E F G H I J K L M N O P Q R S T U V W X Y Z

Human Rights

Animal rights, equal rights, unborn rights — everyone wants rights. It's part of the human spirit to fight for a cause. Human rights is a great cause. Get the latest alerts, news, information on prisoners, read discussions about activism, and learn what you can do to help.

Internet Mailing List:
    List Address: **hr-l@vms.cis.pitt.edu**
    Subscription Address:
        hr-l-request@vms.cis.pitt.edu

World Wide Web:
    URL: **ftp://ftp.netcom.com/pub/ariel/www/
        human.rights/human.rights.html**

Libertarian Manifestos

A collection of political statements by the Boston Anarchist Drinking Brigade, a group with a generally libertarian attitude although they're not associated with the Libertarian Party. The articles from the BAD Brigade tend to skewer both the traditional left and right.

Anonymous FTP:
    Address: **ftp.uu.net**
    Path: **/doc/literary/obi/Anarchist/BadBrigade/***

Libertarian Student Network

Gone are the days of picking between just the Republicans and Democrats. Make your parents proud by showing your independent way of thinking: hook up with the Libertarians. Share ideas with other student Libertarian clubs, spread news, help form new groups, and make contacts. This mailing list is geared toward the formation of Libertarian clubs, and subscription is best limited to one member per group. As long as list objectives are kept in mind, though, the subscription limitation will not be strictly enforced.

Mail:
    Address: **mcpherso**
    Subject: **lumina.ucsd.edu**

Libertarians

These pages explain the Libertarian philosophy and party politics. They include a FAQ, ftp archives, a political quiz, Libertarian programs and platforms, and links to university/college Libertarian groups and other liberty-minded web pages.

World Wide Web:
    URL: **http://www.yahoo.com/Politics/
        Parties_and_Groups/Libertarian_Party/**

    URL: **http://w3eax.umd.edu/libertarian.html**

Liberty Network

Liberty is not something to be taken lightly. Pull up a soapbox and participate in quality discussion for anyone interested in the politics and philosophy of liberty.

Internet Mailing List:
    List Address: **libernet@dartmouth.edu**
    Subscription Address:
        libernet-request@dartmouth.edu

National Research and Education Network Bill

The full text of the bill to provide for a national networking backbone, including editorial comments.

Gopher:
    Name: University of Minnesota
    Address: **gopher.micro.umn.edu**
    Choose: **Libraries**
        | Electronic Books
        | By Title
        | NREN

The New Republic Magazine

A weekly political opinion magazine. The current issue and back issues are online.

Gopher:
    Name: The Internet Company
    Address: **gopher.internet.com**
    Choose: **The Electronic Newsstand**
        | Magazines, Periodicals, and Journals
        | Titles Arranged By Subject
        | Opinion - General, Politics
        | Politics
        | New Republic, The

No Treason — The Constitution of No Authority

A series of documents by Lysander Spooner that are based on the premise that since the U.S. Constitution was a contract between the people who signed it, and since all of those people are now dead, the U.S. Constitution has no legal force and is null and void.

Anonymous FTP:
    Address: **ftp.std.com**
    Path: **/obi/Lysander.Spooner/***

    Address: **ftp.uu.net**
    Path: **/doc/literary/obi/Lysander.Spooner/***

Political Discussions

Mailing lists for serious discussions of politics in the United States.

Listserv Mailing List:
   List Address: **politics@ucf1vm.cc.ucf.edu**
   Subscription Address: **listserv@ucf1vm.cc.ucf.edu**

   List Address: **statepol@umab.umd.edu**
   Subscription Address: **listserv@umab.umd.edu**

Political Forum

A one-stop political web server, the Political Forum offers information and articles about current political debates and discussions, a "who's who" in political science, and links to government web servers and other government information.

World Wide Web:
   URL: **http://garnet.acns.fsu.edu/~gmitchel/**

Political Party Platform Statements

The political platform statements of the Democratic, Green, and Libertarian political parties.

Gopher:
   Name: Internet Wiretap
   Address: **wiretap.spies.com**
   Choose: **Government Docs (US & World)**
    | Political Platforms of the US

Politics and the Network Community

Information concerning several areas of politics, but especially those issues concerning politics, computers, and the network communities.

Gopher:
   Name: Whole Earth Lectronic Link
   Address: **gopher.well.sf.ca.us**
   Choose: **Politics**

Position Papers of Senator Harkin

A collection of Tom Harkin's position papers from his 1992 campaign, including his positions on civil rights, disabilities, economics, education, the environment, health, and women's issues.

Anonymous FTP:
   Address: **ftp.std.com**
   Path: **/obi/Harkin/***

   Address: **ftp.uu.net**
   Path: **/doc/literary/obi/Harkin/***

Right Side of the Web

This web server provides a forum for the conservative point of view. It includes current political information, some online magazines (including *Wired*) and services (such as the D.C. Metro Prolife News/Events Line), and links to other conservative resources, such as the *National Review* archive.

World Wide Web:
   URL: **http://www.clark.net/pub/jeffd/index.html**

Rush Limbaugh Archives

Frequently asked question list and summaries of this popular radio and TV personality's shows. Show summaries are arranged chronologically by year and month. These archives are part of the Catstyle archives.

Anonymous FTP:
   Address: **cathouse.org**
   Path: **/pub/cathouse/rush.limbaugh/***

The Mouth that Roared

There's a lot you can say about Rush Limbaugh--the conservative political commentator and talk show host--and just about anyone you meet is ready to say it. Still, you have to admire anyone who can sell 1.4 million books in a month. (Well, maybe you don't have to admire that, but we find it hard not to.) *The Rush Limbaugh Archives* provide a wealth of information for dittoheads around the world. Rush, of course, can't read it because he isn't on the Internet, but you are, so go wild.

If you would like to send us a comment, mail to: catalog@rain.org

A B C D E F G H I J K L M N O P Q R S T U V W X Y Z

Did you know there are many different books that you can download to your own computer? See Literature for the details.

Rush Limbaugh Political Discussion

There's politics and then there's Rush Limbaugh politics. For those of you who enjoy caustic wit and exploration of politics from a Limbaugh point of view, this list will make your day. Discussion is dedicated to "shining the light of truth on politics, providing edification, inspiration and amusement needed to fill your days with optimism and good cheer." It sounds like a tall order, but check it out. Liberals are welcome. (Otherwise there would be nobody to pick on.)

Internet Mailing List:
   List Address: **rushtalk@ohionet.org**
   Subscription Address:
      rushtalk-request@ohionet.org

Scandals of the Clinton Administration

This web page is a collection of links to information about the scandals afflicting the Clinton administration including Whitewater, dodging the draft, the White House travel office, Clinton's drug usage, questionable commodities and stock investments, charges of sexual harassment, the use of Arkansas state troopers for questionable purposes, and many more. There are also links to other related resources including Clinton humor and Usenet discussions.

World Wide Web:
   URL: **http://www.cs.dartmouth.edu/~crow/
      whitewater/scandal.html**

Vince Foster

The Vince Foster web page puts forth a theory of what really happened to Vince Foster.

World Wide Web:
   URL: **http://www.cs.dartmouth.edu/~crow/
      foster/foster.html**

Vote Smart

Going into the voting both unprepared is worse than going to the grocery store when you are hungry. At least in the grocery store everything looks good and you have lots of choices. Be a smart voter and thoroughly check out the available candidates. With Project Vote Smart, you can access the voter hotline and find out how your candidate voted on key issues, the biographical details of their service in Congress, read evaluations by more than 70 political organizations, find out who paid for their campaign, and get the Congressional candidates' addresses and telephone numbers. Also available are the *Voter's Self-Defense Manual* and the *Government's Owners Manual* which will give you key information about voting and elected officials. This is just a little bit of what is available. There is a huge amount of information just waiting for you: read it and vote smart.

See also: Government

Gopher:
   Name: Northeastern University
   Address: **gopher.neu.edu**
   Choose: **Project Vote Smart**

Weird Politics and Conspiracy

Lots of documents and archives from some of the more unusual political movements. Includes *Arm the Spirit*, *The Disability Rag*, NativeNet archives, *Workers World*, and more.

Anonymous FTP:
   Address: **red.css.itd.umich.edu**
   Path: **/pub/Politics/***

   Address: **red.css.itd.umich.edu**
   Path: **/pub/Zines/***

Whitewater Scandal

A web page with information about the people and corporations involved with Clinton's Whitewater scandal, and the investigations and hearings.

World Wide Web:
   URL: **http://www.cs.dartmouth.edu/~crow/
      whitewater/whitewater.html**

The Internet is low in cholesterol.

POLITICS: STATE AND LOCAL (U.S.)

Bay Area Libertarians

Discussion and announcements of meetings, activities, and outings of Libertarians in the San Francisco Bay area.

Majordomo Mailing List:
List Address: **ba-liberty@shell.portal.com**
Subscription Address:
majordomo@shell.portal.com

California Libertarians

Meetings, events, activities, and schedules for the Libertarian party in California.

Majordomo Mailing List:
List Address: **ca-liberty@shell.portal.com**
Subscription Address:
majordomo@shell.portal.com

Colorado Legislative Information

Colorado state government reports, a library of legislative bills, newslines, issue papers, and updates on house and senate bills.

Gopher:
Name: University of Colorado Boulder
Address: **gopher.colorado.edu**
Choose: **Online Library Catalogs, Electronic Books and Reference Databases**
| Colorado Legislative Information

Iowa Political Stock Market

Buy and sell shares in political candidates. This is a nonprofit research project.

Telnet:
Address: **ipsm.biz.uiowa.edu**

MUDs are real (sort of).

Jim Warren Gopher

A collection of electronic newsletters and other information distributed by Jim Warren, a noted figure in computer magazine publishing, on political action and access to the government through the use of computer communications and the Internet. Included is text regarding a number of legislative bills especially relevant to Californians.

Gopher:
Name: Jim Warren Gopher
Address: **path.net**
Port: **8102**

PSYCHOLOGY

American Psychological Society

The gopher and web server of the American Psychological Society (APS) offer articles from publications of the APS, as well as information about membership, teaching psychology, doing research, job support services, publishers, and links to psychology software archives.

Gopher:
Name: Hanover College
Address: **gopher.hanover.edu**
Choose: **Public**
| American Psychology Society (APS) Gopher Directory

World Wide Web:
URL: **http://psych.hanover.edu/APS/**

Brainwashing

A discussion of the history, problems, and techniques of brainwashing, and ways that it is used in modern society.

Anonymous FTP:
Address: **ftp.spies.com**
Path: **/Library/Article/Misc/brainwa.txt**

Gopher:
Name: Internet Wiretap
Address: **wiretap.spies.com**
Choose: **Wiretap Online Library**
| Articles
| Misc
| The Battle for your Mind: Brainwashing

Cognitive and Psychological Sciences Index

This web page is a huge index to academic programs, organizations and conferences, journals and magazines, Usenet newsgroups, mailing lists, announcements, publishers, and many more resources relating to cognitive and psychological sciences.

World Wide Web:
>   URL: **http://matia.stanford.edu/cogsci/**

Cognitive Science

Cognition is neat because it keeps people from mistaking you for an amoeba. Well, that and the ability to walk upright. Faculty and students from a variety of disciplines, including psychology, philosophy, linguistics, computer science and music, have an electronic meeting of the minds to discuss cognition in all its forms. Come hang out with the people who think and therefore are.

Listserv Mailing List:
>   List Address: **cogsci-l@vm1.mcgill.ca**
>   Subscription Address: **listserv@vm1.mcgill.ca**

Consciousness

Consciousness is a good thing, especially when you are driving a car or operating heavy machinery. A Bitnet digest has been created to offer people the chance to share ideas and discuss research in the area of consciousness and to talk about articles that appear in the journal *Psyche*.

Listserv Mailing List:
>   List Address: **psyche-d@nki.bitnet**
>   Subscription Address: **listserv@nki.bitnet**

Creativity and Creative Problem Solving

That problem has really been nagging at you. It sits in the back of your mind taunting you, demanding attention, begging to be dealt with. No ordinary problem solving is going to take care of it. What's the difference between plain old problem solving and creative problem solving? Discover the answer to that question by examining stimulating factors for creativity in product development, strategic issues, and organizational settings.

Listserv Mailing List:
>   List Address: **crea-cps@nic.surfnet.nl**
>   Subscription Address: **listserv@nic.surfnet.nl**

Depression Disorders

Contrary to what many people believe, depression is not always about being sad. Sometimes it's biochemical as opposed to psychological. Whatever the cause, it's nice to have a place to discuss depression disorders of all kinds, including bipolar disorder. This list is for sufferers of depression as well as friends and family.

Internet Mailing List:
>   List Address:
>   **walkers-in-darkness@world.std.com**
>   Subscription Address:
>   **walkers-in-darkness-request@world.std.com**

Family Science

Life should be just like *Family Circus* — the round-faced little children and happy mom and dad bringing cheer to each other's lives. But for those of you not into fantasy, explore the field of family science, which focuses on marriage and family therapy, family sociology, and the behavioral science aspects of family medicine. This is a great opportunity to communicate with other family scientists and to learn about research programs in family science.

Listserv Mailing List:
>   List Address: **famlysci@ukcc.uky.edu**
>   Subscription Address: **listserv@ukcc.uky.edu**

Family Violence

Home is supposed to be a haven, a place for nurturing and safety. But life doesn't always quite go the way you expect it to and sometimes home is the place you feel the least safe. A networking system has been established to study all aspects of family violence. It is not limited to topics of child abuse or violence within the family, but serves a wide range of areas covered by the term "intimate violence."

Listserv Mailing List:
>   List Address: **intvio-l@uriacc.uri.edu**
>   Subscription Address: **listserv@uriacc.uri.edu**

Intimate Violence

"Intimate violence" refers to destructive contact in any relationship, whether it is with family members or lovers. The *Electronic Journal of Intimate Violence* reports on the latest research and treatment of intimate violence. Some of the topics discussed are physical or sexual child abuse, child neglect, physical or sexual spouse abuse, psychological abuse, elder abuse, and dating violence.

See also: Health

Listserv Mailing List:
>   List Address: **ejintvio@uriacc.uri.edu**
>   Subscription Address: **listserv@uriacc.uri.edu**

Excerpt from the Net...

(from "The Battle for Your Mind: Brainwashing")

To begin, I want to state the most basic of all facts about
brainwashing:

> In the entire history of man, no one has ever
> been brainwashed and realized, or believed, that
> he had been brainwashed.

Those who have been brainwashed will usually passionately defend their manipulators,
claiming they have simply been "shown the light", or have been transformed in miraculous
ways...

Cults and human-potential organizations are always looking for new converts. To attain
them, they must also create a brain-phase. And they often need to do it within a short
space of time -- a weekend, or maybe even a day. The following are the six primary
techniques used to generate the conversion.

The meeting or training takes place in an area where participants are cut off from the
outside world... In human-potential trainings, the controllers will give a lengthy talk
about the importance of "keeping agreements" in life. The participants are told that if
they don't keep agreements, their life will never work. It's a good idea to keep
agreements, but the controllers are subverting a positive human value for selfish
purposes. The participants vow to themselves and their trainer that they will keep their
agreements. Anyone who does not will be intimidated into agreement or forced to leave.
The next step is to agree to complete training, thus assuring a high percentage of
conversions for the organizations. They will USUALLY have to agree not to take drugs,
smoke, and sometimes not to eat, or they are given such short meal breaks that it creates
tension. The real reason for the agreements is to alter internal chemistry, which
generates anxiety and hopefully causes at least a slight malfunction of the nervous
system, which in turn increases the conversion potential.

Before the gathering is complete, the agreements will be used to ensure that the new
converts go out and find new participants. They are intimidated into agreeing to do so
before they leave. Since the importance of keeping agreements is so high on their
priority list, the converts will twist the arms of everyone they know, attempting to
talk them into attending a free introductory session offered at a future date by the
organization. The new converts are zealots. In fact, the inside term for merchandising
the largest and most successful human-potential training is, "sell it by zealot!"...

Panic Disorders

It grips your heart and throat. Panic is a debilitating
disorder that strikes people when they try to do some of
the things the rest of us take for granted, like go to the
grocery store, ride in an elevator, or go in the water. This
support group has been formed for people with panic
disorders or those who have recovered from panic
disorders.

See also: Health

Internet Mailing List:
   List Address: **panic@gnu.ai.mit.edu**
   Subscription Address:
      panic-request@gnu.ai.mit.edu

Practical Psychology Magazine

A hypertext magazine "dedicated to the art of living well -
off the net." Practical Psychology features articles by
renowned psychologists and respected experts. There are
also links to departmental areas where you can find more
articles and information on subjects such as
relationships, sexuality, addictions, family, sports
psychology and health.

World Wide Web:
   URL: **http://www.thegroup.net/
   ppm/ppmhome.htm**

Jokes? Try Humor.

Psychological Help

There are days when things seem overwhelming and unpleasant or you encounter a problem and you don't know exactly what to do with it. Check out the newsgroup that offers discussion about the problems people face. Maybe you will find an answer or just someone to talk to.

Usenet:
>   Newsgroup: **alt.psychology.help**

Psychology Graduate Student Journal

Professional-level articles in the field of psychology, compiled by and tailored to graduate students.

Listserv Mailing List:
>   List Address: **psygrd-j@acadvm1.uottawa.ca**
>   Subscription Address:
>   **listserv@acadvm1.uottawa.ca**

Is life too much (right now)?
Try **alt.psychology.help.**

Psycoloquy

A regularly published collection of articles from all areas of psychology. This resource is sponsored by the American Psychological Association.

Anonymous FTP:
>   Address: **princeton.edu**
>   Path: **/pub/harnad/Psycoloquy/***

Gopher:
>   Name: CICNet
>   Address: **gopher.cic.net**
>   Choose: **Electronic Serials**
> | **General Subject Headings**
> | **Psychology**
> | **Psycoloquy**

>   Name: University of Michigan Libraries
>   Address: **gopher.lib.umich.edu**
>   Choose: **Social Sciences Resources**
> | **Psychology, Sociology, and Anthropology**
> | **Psychology Journals**
> | **Psycoloquy**

>   Name: University of Virginia
>   Address: **gopher.virginia.edu**
>   Choose: **Library Services**
> | **University Library GWIS Collections**
> | **Alphabetic Organization**
> | **Psycoloquy**

World Wide Web:
>   URL: **http://info.cern.ch/hypertext/DataSources/
>   bySubject/Psychology/Psycoloquy.html**

PSYCOLOQUY

What do you do when you have a house guest you are just too busy to entertain? Sit him down at the computer, connect him to a Gopher, and have him read back issues of *Psycoloquy*, a refereed psychology journal.

Just listen to this:
"According to Wallis (1992), philosophers of mind agree that a successful theory of representation must 'describe conditions for representation in nonintentional and nonsemantic terms.' If we restrict representation talk to what goes on in frogs, the visual systems of humans, etc., then perhaps Wallis is right. But once we count beliefs as representations, there is no such agreement. Indeed..."

Your friends will be coming back to visit you, again and again.

Schizophrenia

Look into this unmoderated discussion list devoted to schizophrenia research. This is a place for researchers and medical professionals to explore this mental illness, facilitate collaborations between investigators, and foster discussion on published and unpublished findings and ideas.

See also: Medicine, Health

Listserv Mailing List:
List Address: **schiz-l@umab.bitnet**
Subscription Address: **listserv@umab.bitnet**

Stuttering

It's not painful or fatal, but it's certainly frustrating. Researchers and clinicians are continually working toward a solution to the problem of stuttering, and one helpful tool is networking on the Internet. Discussion of projects, procedures and theories are a few of the things relating to stuttering on this list. The **stutt-l** list is for professionals and the **stut-hlp** is a support list for people who stutter, as well as for their families. Both lists have their own distinctive environment and do not mingle.

Listserv Mailing List:
List Address: **stut-hlp@bgu.edu**
Subscription Address: **listserv@bgu.edu**

List Address: **stutt-l@vm.temple.edu**
Subscription Address: **listserv@vm.temple.edu**

Suicide Prevention

Sometimes life is frightening and miserable, and even though the pain won't last forever, it's still hard to deal with. If you feel like you've had all you can take and you're not sure what to do next, try getting in touch with the Samaritans. This is not a religious organization, but a group of people who want to give you a place to reach out to, confidentially. Their charity has been offering emotional support by phone, personal visits, and snail mail for 40 years, and now they are offering help electronically. Members of their staff are trained volunteers.

Mail:
Address: **jo@samaritans.org**
Address: **samaritans@anon.petit.fi**

PUBLICATIONS

Dartmouth College Library Online System

Search and browse a wealth of database files. Get information about titles, authors, and their publications. You can even search books and periodicals for keywords and view the text.

Telnet:
Address: **library.dartmouth.edu**

Journalism

Try these wais keywords for more than 10,000 published journals and periodicals.

WAIS:
Database: **journalism.periodicals**

Journals with a Difference

Selection of journals covering some of the more unusual topics in life. Includes such publications as *The Unplastic News*, *Athene*, *Scream Baby*, and *Quanta*.

Anonymous FTP:
Address: **etext.archive.umich.edu**
Path: **/pub/***

A B C D E F G H I J K L M N O P Q R S T U V W X Y Z

Newsletters, Electronic Journals, Zines

A wide selection of online publications covering biology, computing, health, kids, libraries, networks, politics, and space.

Anonymous FTP:
   Address: **nigel.msen.com**
   Path: **/pub/newsletters/***

Online Publications

Multitudes of online zines, essays, and articles covering lots of varied and unusual subjects. Includes articles from such publications as *Mondo 2000*, *Whole Earth Review*, *Locus*, and *The Unplastic News*.

Gopher:
   Name: Whole Earth Lectronic Link
   Address: **gopher.well.sf.ca.us**
   Choose: **Authors, Books, Periodicals, Zines**

Publisher's Catalogs

Browse catalogs from publishing companies, including Addison-Wesley, MIT Press, O'Reilly, Prentice Hall, and others.

Gopher:
   Name: University of Virginia
   Address: **gopher.virginia.edu**
   Choose: **Library Services**
   I **University Library GWIS Collections**
   I **Alphabetic Organization**
   I **Publisher's Catalogs**

If Herman Melville had written this book, you would be reading a metaphor right now.

Whole Earth Review Articles

A selection of articles from the *Whole Earth Review* magazine, which is dedicated to demystification, to self-teaching, and to encouraging people to think for themselves.

Gopher:
   Name: Whole Earth Lectronic Link
   Address: **gopher.well.sf.ca.us**
   Choose: **Whole Earth Review, the Magazine**

PUBLISHING

Association of American University Presses

Electronic publishing and other issues of interest to university presses.

Listserv Mailing List:
   List Address: **aaup-l@psuvm.psu.edu**
   Subscription Address: **listserv@psuvm.psu.edu**

Copy Editors Mailing List

A mailing list for copy editors and other defenders of the King's English who wish to discuss editorial problems, client relations, Internet resources, dictionaries, or whatever.

Listserv Mailing List:
   List Address: **copyediting-L@cornell.edu**
   Subscription Address: **listserv@cornell.edu**

Want to converse with the people whoze job it iss to find3e mistakess? Jpin the copy editor's maleing list.

Electronic Publishing

Important articles about publishing an electronic journal or paper, including ISSN and copyright information, resource guide, and the functions of the Library of Congress.

Anonymous FTP:
    Address: **ftp.loc.gov**
    Path: **/pub/lc.online**

    Address: **ftp.spies.com**
    Path: **/Library/Article/Publish/***

Gopher:
    Name: Internet Wiretap
    Address: **wiretap.spies.com**
    Choose: **Wiretap Online Library**
     | **Articles**
     | **Electronic Publishing**

McGraw-Hill Internet Resource Area

Samples and introductions for Internet-related books published by McGraw-Hill.

Gopher:
    Name: The Electronic Newsstand
    Address: **gopher.internet.com**
    Port: **2100**
    Choose: **Electronic Bookstore**
     | **McGraw-Hill Internet Resource Area**

Publisher's Catalogs

A large collection of catalogs showing what publishers have to offer. Catalogs from mainstream, computer and university presses.

World Wide Web:
    URL: **http://herald.usask.ca/~scottp/publish.html**

Look around. Is anyone watching? Good. Take a look at the X-Rated section. (But remember, you didn't read it here.)

Sci-Fi Publishers Newsletters

Find out about the latest science fiction and fantasy releases directly from the publishers. These newsletters contain information not only on new books, but works in progress and where to find excerpts online.

See also: Literature: Collections, Books

World Wide Web:
    URL: **http://www.lysator.liu.se/sf_archive/sf-texts/publisher_newsletters/**

Tor Books

Keep informed on what is happening with Tor Books, a major publisher of science fiction and fantasy. See a list of recent releases and forthcoming books, read their newsletter *Near Futures*, and have a taste of some book excerpts. If you are a writer, you will be interested in learning more about Tor's submission guidelines, which are outlined here.

See also: Science Fiction, Books

Gopher:
    Name: Panix
    Address: **gopher.panix.com**
    Choose: **Tor Books (SF and fantasy)**

Mail:
    Address: **pnh@tor.com**
    Subject: **near futures**

World Wide Web:
    URL: **http://sunsite.unc.edu/ibic/Tor-homepage.html**

Ventana Press Internet Resource Area

Samples and introductions for Internet-related books and software published by Ventana Press.

Gopher:
    Name: The Electronic Newsstand
    Address: **gopher.internet.com**
    Port: **2100**
    Choose: **Electronic Bookstore**
     | **Ventana Press Internet Resource Area**

Little known fact: Charles and Diana met in alt.romance.

QUOTATIONS

Woody Allen

You probably think that we have a good sense of humor but, actually, we've just memorized all of Woody Allen's famous quotes. No reason why you can't do the same.

Anonymous FTP:
> Address: **cathouse.org**
> Path: **/pub/cathouse/humor/quotes/woody.allen**

Beavis and Butthead Quotables

Is your significant other bringing the in-laws over for dinner tonight? Don't worry about getting caught short with nothing to say. Take a look at some quotes from Beavis and Butthead, two of America's foremost cultural philosophers.

Anonymous FTP:
> Address: **quartz.rutgers.edu**
> Path: **/pub/tv+movies/beavis/bnb-quotes**

Gopher:
> Name: Rutgers University
> Address: **quartz.rutgers.edu**
> Choose: **Television and Movies**
>   **| beavis**
>   **| bnb-quotes**

Bible Quotes

Quotations from the Bible, courtesy of *Christian Computing* magazine.

See also: Religion

Gopher:
> Name: University of Alabama
> Address: **twinbrook.cis.uab.edu**
> Choose: **The Continuum**
>   **| The Heavens**
>   **| The Gabriel's Horn**

If you like trouble, take a look at Mischief.

Lenny Bruce

Here's a man who knew how to talk dirty and influence people. Lenny Bruce was truly one of the illegitimate fathers of modern popular culture. You can draw a straight line from Lenny Bruce through George Carlin right to Beavis and Butthead. But what would be the point?

Anonymous FTP:
> Address: **cathouse.org**
> Path: **/pub/cathouse/humor/standup/lenny.bruce**

Andrew Dice Clay

If you're tired of plain old traditional nursery rhymes, read what Andrew Dice Clay has to say about Mother Hubbard and what else was bare besides her cupboard.

Anonymous FTP:
> Address: **cathouse.org**
> Path: **/pub/cathouse/humor/standup/andrew.dice.clay**

Cyberspace Quotations

Collection of quotations about cyberspace and virtual realities from eminent authors, including Lewis Carroll, Isaac Asimov, John D. Barrow, Michael Heim, and more.

World Wide Web:
> URL: **http://guinan.gsfc.nasa.gov/WebStars/Quotes.html**

Rodney Dangerfield

We get no respect. We went to use our Internet account the other day, and found that somebody had changed our username to **shicklegruber**. But we've got nothing to complain about; take a look at what Rodney has to say.

Anonymous FTP:
> Address: **cathouse.org**
> Path: **/pub/cathouse/humor/standup/rodney.dangerfield**

FOR MEN ONLY

Hey guys, need a quick way to impress a woman?

If she is under 20 years old, quote Beavis and Butt-head.

If she is between 20 and 30, quote Jerry Seinfeld.

If she is between 30 and 40, quote Steven Wright.

If she is between 40 and 50, quote Woody Allen.

If she is over 50, quote Rodney Dangerfield.

W.C. Fields

Even today, W.C. Fields' wit is still legendary. After all, anyone who hates kids, dogs, and books for dummies can't be all bad.

Anonymous FTP:
Address: **cathouse.org**
Path: **/pub/cathouse/humor/quotes/w.c.fields**

Gophers are your friends.

Excerpt from the Net...

```
            (from the "Fortune Quotes" archive)

Tie?  You want me to wear a TIE?  Listen: there's only one time in a man's life when he
should have a rope knotted around his neck, and that time ain't yet come for me.
   -- Canada Bill Jones

The secret of my success is that at a very early age I discovered that I'm not God.
   -- Oliver Wendell Holmes

...Fortunately, AT&T couldn't sell drugs at a Grateful Dead show.
   -- Bob Stratton

Time, because it is so fleeting, time, because it is beyond recall, is the most precious
of human goods, and to squander it is the most delicate form of dissipation in which man
can indulge.
   -- W. Somerset Maugham, "The Bum"

A fool with a spreadsheet is still a fool.
   -- Paul Abrahams

I love deadlines.  I like the whooshing sound they make as they fly by.
   -- Douglas Adams

Emacs is not an editor.  Emacs is a way of thinking about the world and, as such, is a
way of thinking about editors.  The process of editing is Emacs, but Emacs is more than
the process of editing.

When you ask what Emacs does, you are asking a question with no answer, because Emacs
doesn't do, it is done to.  Emacs just is.
...I hope this makes things clearer.
   -- Scott Dorsey

Not only did they all laugh at Christopher Columbus, they also laughed at Bozo the Clown.
   -- Peter Reiher

Shouldn't "anal rententive" have a hyphen?
   -- unidentified passing t-shirt
```

A B C D E F G H I J K L M N O P Q R S T U V W X Y Z

Hungry? Try Food and Drink. Hungry for Love? Try Romance.	**Make sure you are prepared: Read Emergency and Disaster.**

Excerpt from the Net...

(from the Samuel Goldwyn quotation archive)

Note: Samuel Goldwyn was an American immigrant who became one of the most powerful film producers in Hollywood. He controlled MGM (Metro-Goldwyn-Mayer) and was well-known for his emminently quotable remarks, many of which are, no doubt, apocryphal.

"It rolled off my back like a duck."

[When told his son was getting married]
"Thank heaven. A bachelor's life is no life for a single man."

"I can give you a definite maybe."

"Gentleman, include me out."

"A verbal contract isn't worth the paper its printed on."

Bookkeeper: Mr. Goldwyn, our files are bulging with paperwork we no longer need. May I
             have your permission to destroy all records before 1945?
Goldwyn: Certainly. Just be sure to keep a copy of everything.

"I can tell you in two words: im possible."

[On being told that a friend had named his son Sam, after him]
"Why did you do that? Every Tom, Dick and Harry is named Sam!"

"I paid too much for it, but its worth it."

"Don't worry about the war. It's all over but the shooting."

"Gentlemen, for your information, I have a question to ask you."

"I read part of it all the way through."

"If I could drop dead right now, I'd be the happiest man alive."

"I never put on a pair of shoes until I've worn them at least five years."

"I don't think anyone should write their autobiography until after they're dead."

"Anyone who goes to a psychiatrist ought to have his head examined.

"Gentlemen, listen to me slowly."

[in discussing Lillian Hellman's play, "The Children's Hour"]
  Goldwyn: Maybe we ought to buy it?
Associate: Forget it, Mr. Goldwyn, it's about Lesbians.
  Goldwyn: That's okay, we'll make them Americans.

Fortune Cookie Database

A large collection of quotes for fortune programs. Includes weasel quotes, strong quotes, Moriarty quotes, and fortune cookies.

Anonymous FTP:
Address: **quartz.rutgers.edu**
Path: **/pub/computer/fortune/***

Gopher:
Name: Rutgers University
Address: **quartz.rutgers.edu**
Choose: **Computer-Sources, Documentation...**
| **fortune**

Samuel Goldwyn

Are all the Samuel Goldwyn quotes real? We can tell you in two words: a pocryphal.

Anonymous FTP:
Address: **cathouse.org**
Path: **/pub/cathouse/humor/quotes/sam.goldwyn**

High Culture

Every time you connect to this resource, you are presented with a different poem excerpt or quote from famous poets and people.

World Wide Web:
URL: **http://cybersight.com/cgi-bin/cs/s?poem.gmml**

Humorous Quotations

A long list of topics from which to choose. Random quotation generators or files of one-liners, jokes and other humorous tidbits. Wide variety of subjects.

See also: Humor

World Wide Web:
URL: **http://meta.stanford.edu/quotes.html**

> **The best way to make money is to give something away for free.**

David Letterman

Everybody who loves David Letterman loves his top ten lists. But what do you do in the middle of the night when you wake up in a sweat because you can't remember what was number 5 on the list of top ten Dear Abby letter signatures from July 23, 1987? No problem. Connect to the Internet and the information is only a few keystrokes away.

Anonymous FTP:
Address: **cathouse.org**
Path: **/pub/cathouse/television/david.letterman**

Address: **quartz.rutgers.edu**
Path: **/pub/tv+movies/letterman/top-ten**

Gopher:
Name: Rutgers University
Address: **quartz.rutgers.edu**
Choose: **Television and Movies**
| **letterman**
| **top-ten**

loQtus

You're sitting at your desk and they come racing in — the women from the office down the hall. It's someone's birthday and they need a clever quote for the handmade birthday card they have whipped up at the photocopier. They have come to you because they know you have an entire quote database at your fingertips. It's someone's big day. Don't let them down.

World Wide Web:
URL: **http://pubweb.ucdavis.edu/Documents/Quotations/homepage.html**

Groucho Marx

Groucho Marx was one of America's funniest funny men. Check out some of his quotes and maybe you can pass them off as your own.

Anonymous FTP:
Address: **cathouse.org**
Path: **/pub/cathouse/humor/standup/groucho.marx**

> **Like mysteries?
> Look at Intrigue.**

A B C D E F G H I J K L M N O P Q R S T U V W X Y Z

Norm Peterson from Cheers

One of the troubles with witty sayings is that they are often difficult to understand if you've been drinking too much beer. Just the time to download a few Normisms ("How's life in the fast lane, Norm? Beats me, I can't find the on-ramp.").

Anonymous FTP:
   Address: **quartz.rutgers.edu**
   Path: **/pub/tv+movies/cheers/norm-sayings**

Gopher:
   Name: Rutgers University
   Address: **quartz.rutgers.edu**
   Choose: **Television and Movies**
      | **cheers**
      | **norm-sayings**

Quotation Reference Books

A comprehensive bibliography of books of quotations. Why waste your time being creative when borrowing is so easy?

Anonymous FTP:
   Address: **quartz.rutgers.edu**
   Path: **/pub/books/quote-books**

Gopher:
   Name: Rutgers University
   Address: **quartz.rutgers.edu**
   Choose: **Book FAQs and Info**
      | **quote-books**

Quotations Archive

A large selection of quotes from all walks of life. "Truth is more of a stranger than fiction." — Mark Twain.

Anonymous FTP:
   Address: **wilma.cs.brown.edu**
   Path: **/pub/alt.quotations/Archive/***

Usenet:
   Newsgroup: **alt.quotations**

Quotation Archives

The Internet has a number of anonymous FTP sites at which you can find all kinds of quotations. Just the thing for spicing up your conversation and enhancing your reputation. Here is a typical example showing how it works.

[You are talking to your teacher or boss.]

Teacher/Boss:

So what do you have to say for yourself?

[At this point you repeat a quote that you downloaded the night before from one of the Internet quotation archives.]

You:

Well, I think blah, blah blah, blah, blah...

Teacher/Boss:

Wow, you really are terrific. I'm going to give you an A (or a raise).

Very good looking woman/man who happens to be listening:

You are an unbelievably attractive person. Would you like to have dinner with me tonight?

Quotes About Religion

A document containing a variety of quotations about religion, and how it should relate to a secular society. Many of the quotations are from American founding fathers.

Anonymous FTP:
   Address: **ftp.uu.net**
   Path: **/doc/literary/obi/Quotes/religion**

Random Quotes

Random quotes from Dave Barry, Jack Handey, Steven Wright, *Star Trek*, *The Simpsons* and others. Also available is the Fortune Cookie and the Shakespearean Insult Server.

World Wide Web:
   URL: **http://alpha.acast.nova.edu/quotes.html**

Ren and Stimpy

Do you know the Ren and Stimpy fan club oath? Well, you should. Check out the Ren and Stimpy quotes and find all kinds of good stuff.

Anonymous FTP:
> Address: **quartz.rutgers.edu**
> Path: **/pub/tv+movies/renstimpy/quotes**

Gopher:
> Name: Rutgers University
> Address: **quartz.rutgers.edu**
> Choose: **Television and Movies**
> | **renstimpy**
> | **quotes**

Seinfeld Quotes

Too many people spend too much time watching Jerry Seinfeld and his friends on TV when they should be reading *The Internet Complete Reference*. But what can we do about it? Probably nothing, so you might as well use the Internet to download all those swell quotes that sounded so good the night before the morning after.

Anonymous FTP:
> Address: **quartz.rutgers.edu**
> Path: **/pub/tv+movies/seinfeld/Quotes**

Gopher:
> Name: Rutgers University
> Address: **quartz.rutgers.edu**
> Choose: **Televison and Movies**
> | **seinfeld**
> | **Quotes**

World Wide Web:
> URL: **http://www.yahoo.com/Entertainment/**
> **Television/Shows/Comedies/Seinfeld/**

Star Trek

Dammit, Jim, we're Internet writers, not trivia buffs. If you want quotes from the original *Star Trek, the Next Generation*, the *Star Trek* movies, or *Deep Space Nine*, you'll have to get them yourself.

Anonymous FTP:
> Address: **quartz.rutgers.edu**
> Path: **/pub/tv+movies/startrek/trek-quotes**

Gopher:
> Name: Rutgers University
> Address: **quartz.rutgers.edu**
> Choose: **Television and Movies**
> | **startrek**
> | **trek-quotes**

Mark Twain

Everybody talks about putting up an archive site for Mark Twain quotations, but nobody does anything about it. Except Jason Heimbaugh, that is. Take a look at Jason's Cathouse archives, and see what the father of modern American literature has to say for himself (Mark Twain, not Jason).

Anonymous FTP:
> Address: **cathouse.org**
> Path: **/pub/cathouse/humor/quotes/mark.twain**

WebWisdom

A graffiti wall of wisdom. Read the quips and quotes from other Net people or write your own and live in infamy.

World Wide Web:
> URL:
> **http://keck.tamu.edu/cgi/staff/webwisdom.html**

Oscar Wilde

According to Oscar Wilde, the only way to get rid of a temptation is to yield to it. So don't wait, rush out and buy ten copies of *The Internet Complete Reference*.

Anonymous FTP:
> Address: **cathouse.org**
> Path: **/pub/cathouse/humor/quotes/oscar.wilde**

> Address: **ftp.uu.net**
> Path: **/doc/literary/obi/Oscar.Wilde/quotes**

Steven Wright

Probably one of the things that makes you so popular is your ability to tell Steven Wright jokes at parties. But what do you do when you run out of material? Here's a large archive of Steven Wright quotations that will last you for years.

Anonymous FTP:
> Address: **cathouse.org**
> Path: **/pub/cathouse/humor/standup/**
> **steven.wright**

**Writers,
share your stories on the Net.**

A B C D E F G H I J K L M N O P **Q** R S T U V W X Y Z

RADIO

Amateur Radio

Radio is a great hobby and one day when you are an expert, you can have your own nationally syndicated talk show and screaming fans will throw themselves at your feet when you go out in public. Until then, you can spend time reading Usenet groups especially for amateur radio enthusiasts. Topics cover construction, packet and digital radio modes, transmission, regulations, repair and other general topics.

Usenet:
> Newsgroup: **rec.radio.amateur.antenna**
> Newsgroup: **rec.radio.amateur.digital.misc**
> Newsgroup: **rec.radio.amateur.equipment**
> Newsgroup: **rec.radio.amateur.homebrew**
> Newsgroup: **rec.radio.amateur.misc**
> Newsgroup: **rec.radio.amateur.packet**
> Newsgroup: **rec.radio.amateur.policy**
> Newsgroup: **rec.radio.amateur.space**

Need to spread the word? Try Amateur Radio

Campus Radio Disk Jockeys

What a cool job it is to sit in a climate-controlled booth jamming out to the latest tunes for hours on end. And in between the songs you get to offer some profound remarks that will reach the ears of every student on campus. What power! Hone your communication skills by hearing what other DJs and station managers discuss on this mailing list about college radio, federal and campus regulations, station policies, and equipment reviews.

See also: Journalism and Media

Listserv Mailing List:
> List Address: **dj-l@vm1.nodak.edu**
> Subscription Address: **listserv@vm1.nodak.edu**

Campus Radio Disc Jockeys

When Harley was an undergraduate at the University of Waterloo, Canada, he was a CRDJ. Actually, he was a CCCRDJ (Cool Canadian Campus Radio Disc Jockey). If you too are a member of this elite corps, join the dj-l mailing list and see what your fellow CRDJs are up to.

Canadian Broadcasting Corporation

The Canadian Broadcasting Corporation (CBC) has taken the first steps towards making CBC radio programming available over the Internet. This experimental database contains sound and text files from such CBC programs as *Quirks and Quarks*, *Basic Black*, and *Sunday Morning*.

World Wide Web:
> URL: **http://debra.dgbt.doc.ca/cbc/cbc.html**

Citizens Band Radio

Breaker breaker, anybody got your ears on? While the CB craze is not what it used to be, there are still a load of CB radio fans looking for people to talk to. Check out the citizens band action on Usenet.

Usenet:
> Newsgroup: **rec.radio.cb**

Digital Audio Broadcasting

Imagine: your voice — static-free, flying silky smooth through the air at the speed of sound, straight into someone's ear. They turn and could swear that you were right there behind them. This is the wonder of digital audio broadcasting with its improved sound quality and technical superiority. Join with other DAB enthusiasts to talk not only about the technological merits of digital audio broadcasting, but also the social and economic issues.

See also: Journalism and Media

Listserv Mailing List:
List Address: **radio-l@vm1.spcs.umn.edu**
Subscription Address: **listserv@vm1.spcs.umn.edu**

Usenet:
Newsgroup: **alt.radio.digital**

FM Broadcasting

Imagine having the kind of broadcasting power that would enable you to send your voice all across the globe — or better yet, way out into outer space to share news and rock 'n' roll with aliens across the galaxy. What a nice way to be heard. Radio techies get together to talk about modifications, enhancements and uses of the Ramsey FM-10 and other BA-1404-based FM stereo broadcasters, along with some discussion of FM pirate radio.

Internet Mailing List:
List Address: **fm-10@dg-rtp.dg.com**
Subscription Address:
fm-10-request@dg-rtp.dg.com

Ham Radio Archives

Archives of interest to ham radio buffs.

Anonymous FTP:
Address: **ftp.cs.buffalo.edu**
Path: **/pub/ham-radio/***

Address: **ftp.cs.tamu.edu**
Path: **/pub/hamradio/***

Address: **oak.oakland.edu**
Path: **/pub/misc/hamradio**

Gopher:
Name: Texas A&M University
Address: **gopher.cs.tamu.edu**
Choose: **Access to TAMU CS Anonymous FTP Files**
| hamradio

Ham Radio Callbooks

The national ham radio call-sign book. Search for ham radio users by call-sign, name, city, or by combining criteria.

Telnet:
Address: **callsign.cs.buffalo.edu**
Port: **2000**

Address: **pc.usl.edu**
Port: **2000**

Monitor Radio

Monitor Radio, a broadcast service of the *Christian Science Monitor*, is heard on countless Public Radio International stations and by shortwave listeners worldwide. It is now available daily on RT-FM, an Internet audio multicast channel from the Internet Multicasting Service. This page offers details about that channel, audio highlights from Monitor Radio, program schedules, and feed times.

World Wide Web:
URL: **http://town.hall.org/radio/Monitor/**
index.html

Radio Broadcasting

Boy, radio has just got to be the best invention since television. Join the folks who love to listen. The **.broadcasting** newsgroup is for discussing local broadcast radio. The **.info** group is for informative postings about radio in general. Both of these groups are moderated. For those who hate advertising, **.noncomm** is for talking about noncommercial radio. Finally, the **.scanner** group is for utility broadcasting, above 30 MHz. (Just the place to learn how to eavesdrop on your neighbor's cordless phone.)

Usenet:
Newsgroup: **alt.radio.scanner**
Newsgroup: **rec.radio.broadcasting**
Newsgroup: **rec.radio.info**
Newsgroup: **rec.radio.noncomm**
Newsgroup: **rec.radio.scanner**

Shortwave Radio

Shortwave radio enthusiasts talk tech-talk about what makes shortwave radio work. Learn tips about building, repairing and operating shortwave radios.

Usenet:
Newsgroup: **rec.radio.shortwave**

A B C D E F G H I J K L M N O P Q R S T U V W X Y Z

Voice of America

People all over the world tune in to the *Voice of America* to hear news and special programs not only on the radio, but on the Internet as well. Scan through the list of broadcasts to select just the news item that you want to hear.

Gopher:
> Name: Voice of America
> Address: **gopher.voa.gov**

REAL ESTATE

Commercial Real Estate

You are really getting into the big leagues when you start dealing with commercial real estate. This is a great all-purpose list where real estate professionals involved in sales, acquisitions, management, and development of commercial property can post press releases and information about available property and can ask and answer questions.

Listserv Mailing List:
> List Address: **commercial-realestate@syncomm.com**
> Subscription Address: **listserv@syncomm.com**

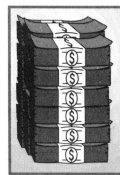

Are you into land, money, and buying and selling? Once you outgrow Monopoly, try the **commercial-realestate** mailing list.

Global Real Estate Guide

Whether you want a ranch that sprawls across 700 acres, a quaint Victorian home, or a loud Art Deco building made entirely of synthetic material, the Global Real Estate Guide is a good place to start. You can search by state or country, accessing thousands of listings of residential and commercial properties.

World Wide Web:
> URL: **http://www.gems.com/realestate/index.html**

Homebuyer's Fair

Buying a house is a little different than running to the corner market to pick up an extra package of hot dog buns. Get answers to questions about buying a home, learn information about mortgages and how to avoid "junk fees". You can even view images of homes for sale.

World Wide Web:
> URL: **http://www.homefair.com/homepage.html**

Real Estate Brokers

The great thing about being a real estate broker is that you get money whether you make a sale or not. So you can spend more time checking your mail to see if anything new has been posted to this list for brokers, investors, management companies and developers. The list is not for home buyers who are looking to have their questions answered, but is a list for professionals in real estate brokering.

See also: Business and Finance

Listserv Mailing List:
> List Address: **residential-realestate@property.com**
> Subscription Address: **listserv@property.com**

Real Estate Discussion Group

It's just like a Monopoly game, except you use real money and the bail is higher if you end up in jail. Learn tips on acquiring real estate: how to choose a good agent, perks for first-time homebuyers, and how to avoid the rental property blues. Invest in something tangible.

Usenet:
> Newsgroup: **misc.invest.real-estate**

REAL ESTATE REALITY

Isn't it great? All you have to do is spend some money and you can own your very own piece of an actual planet (Earth).

We love real estate because it brings out the best in people; and some of the best real estate people hang out in **misc.invest.real-estate**.

Remember, though, talking on the Net is no substitute for experience: the smart way is to "walk the dirt, smell the dirt and feel the dirt". (Fortunately, there's no shortage of dirt.)

Real Estate News

Get the latest news on the real estate industry such as housing costs, interest rates and other new developments.

Usenet:
 Newsgroup: **clari.biz.industry.real_estate**

Research and Data

When you are into real estate, you don't just tromp around in the woods or traipse through people's homes. You have to do paperwork, research, and learn laws and banking regulations. Real estate researchers and students gather to discuss research problems, data gathering, and other matters that relate to the roll-up-your-sleeves-and-get-down-to-it parts of real estate.

Listserv Mailing List:
 List Address: **re-forum@utarlvm1.uta.edu**
 Subscription Address: **listserv@utarlvm1.uta.edu**

RELIGION

Anglican Christianity

Join the **anglican** mailing list to discuss any topic relating to the Episcopal Church and the worldwide Anglican Communion.

Listserv Mailing List:
 List Address: **anglican@auvm.american.edu**
 Subscription Address: **listserv@auvm.american.edu**

Articles on Religion

Numerous documents and discussions, including an atheist manifesto, religion in American schools, Gideons, Mormonism, Baha'i faith, shamanism, Vedic civilization, and Taoism.

Anonymous FTP:
 Address: **ftp.spies.com**
 Path: **/Library/Article/Religion/***

Gopher:
 Name: Internet Wiretap
 Address: **wiretap.spies.com**
 Choose: **Wiretap Online Library**
  I Articles
  I Religion and Philosophy

Atheism

If you are one of those people who thinks "god" is just "dog" spelled backwards, this may be the group for you. Discuss how, why and where there is no God, and what this means for ordinary people who must pay their bills and remember their computer password. Atheists take their beliefs seriously and so should you.

Anonymous FTP:
 Address: **rtfm.mit.edu**
 Path: **/pub/usenet/alt.atheism/***

Usenet:
 Newsgroup: **alt.atheism**
 Newsgroup: **alt.atheism.moderated**
 Newsgroup: **alt.christnet.atheism**

World Wide Web:
 URL: **http://mantis.co.uk/atheism/**

Atheist Manifesto

The Atheist Manifesto is an article in support of the atheist theology.

Anonymous FTP:
 Address: **ftp.spies.com**
 Path: **/Library/Article/Religion/atheist.mf**

Gopher:
 Name: Internet Wiretap
 Address: **wiretap.spies.com**
 Choose: **Wiretap Online Library**
  I Articles
  I Religion and Philosophy
  I Atheist Manifesto

Baptist Discussion List

A list for the discussion of any and all topics relating to the Baptist experience. It includes all nationalities and denominations of Baptists, and is a forum for sharing information, ideas, and opinions.

Listserv Mailing List:
 List Address: **baptist@ukcc.uky.edu**
 Subscription Address: **listserv@ukcc.uky.edu**

Bible Browser for Unix

A program for browsing the Bible.

Anonymous FTP:
 Address: **cs.arizona.edu**
 Path: **/icon/contrib/bibl_tar.Z**

A B C D E F G H I J K L M N O P Q R S T U V W X Y Z

Excerpt from the Net...

```
Newsgroup: alt.atheism
Subject: Question for fellow atheists

> Although I am an atheist, I have always been fascinated by the
> beliefs of religions around the world.  Is this unusual for an
> atheist?
>
> I do not believe in God, but I see in the world's religions some
> vital information and insight into the nature of man.  When I explore
> various religions -- taking them as metaphors -- I learn a great deal
> about myself and my fellow human beings.  I have assumed that most
> atheists are more interested and educated in the world's religions,
> even after their acceptance of atheism, than most followers of
> individual faiths.  Is this true?

I don't know.  It's hard to speak authoritatively for "most atheists".
Certainly among those who participate in discussions of religion and atheism on the Net,
this seems to be the case.

In my own case, early exposure to other religions was instrumental in the development of
my atheism.  I was always interested by religious mythology, both as story and as it
related to the development of our culture.

Interestingly, I tended to give a fairly wide berth to Christianity and the major modern
religions until around the time I started participating in alt.atheism.  Since then, it's
been a fairly major topic with me.


--
"A little rudeness and disrespect can elevate a meaningless interaction to a battle of
 wills and add drama to an otherwise dull day." -- Calvin
```

Bible Gateway

You can use the Bible Gateway interactively to search and read specific passages, or you can turn scripture references into hyperlinks. There are also examples, instructions, and additional information about the gateway.

World Wide Web:
URL: **http://unicks.calvin.edu/cgi-bin/bible**

Bible Online

The complete Bible online with a gopher interface. There actually are many places where you can read the Bible online. Use veronica to find other sites.

Anonymous FTP:
Address: **ftp.uu.net**
Path: **/doc/literary/obi/Religion/KingJamesBible**

Gopher:
Name: University of Minnesota
Address: **gopher.micro.umn.edu**
Choose: **Libraries**
  | **Electronic Books**
  | **By Title**
  | **King James Bible**

THE BIBLE

By far, the most popular book In the history of mankind is the Bible (even more popular than *The Internet Complete Reference*). If you are a Bible scholar, or even a casual reader, you will be glad to know that the entire bible is available on the Net for downloading and perusing.

Bible Program

The complete online Bible program, with instructions for installation on a PC or Mac.

Anonymous FTP:
Address: **ftp.wustl.edu**
Path: **/doc/bible/***

Bible Promises Macintosh Hypercard Stack

A Hypercard program for the Macintosh.

Anonymous FTP:
>   Address: **f.ms.uky.edu**
>   Path: **/pub/mac/hypercard/**
>   **bible-promise-stack.cpt.bin**

Bible Quiz Game

A character-mode DOS program with more than a thousand questions about the books, characters, events, and other interesting aspects of the Bible.

Anonymous FTP:
>   Address: **oak.oakland.edu**
>   Path: **/pub/msdos/bible/bibleq.zip**

Bible Retrieval System for Unix

A Bible query system for Unix systems.

Anonymous FTP:
>   Address: **ftp.uu.net**
>   Path: **/doc/literary/obi/Religion/**
>   **Bible.Retrieval.System/***

Bible Search Program

A shareware version of a Bible search program called "The Word" Search. The shareware version contains only the book of Colossians, but you can get the information you need to obtain the full version.

Anonymous FTP:
>   Address: **oak.oakland.edu**
>   Path: **/pub/msdos/bible/bible14.zip**

Bible Search Tools

Assorted Bible search utilities.

Anonymous FTP:
>   Address: **oak.oakland.edu**
>   Path: **/pub/msdos/bible/kjv-tool.zip**

Make new friends on Internet Relay Chat (IRC).

Bible Study

When Paul said not to "forsake the gathering of ourselves together," the odds are this is not how he anticipated things would evolve. But if he were here today he would be telling you to stop MUDding and join this forum of people interested in studying the Bible together electronically. The assumption is made that participants consider the Bible authoritative, so it's not a sparring ground for belief systems, nor is it for purely academic purposes. The Usenet groups have similar objectives.

Majordomo Mailing List:
>   List Address: **bible@virginia.ed**
>   Subscription Address: **majordomo@virginia.ed**

Usenet:
>   Newsgroup: **alt.christnet.bible**
>   Newsgroup: **soc.religion.christian.bible-study**

Bible Text

The complete text of the Bible.

Anonymous FTP:
>   Address: **oak.oakland.edu**
>   Path: **/pub/msdos/bible/journey.zip**
>
>   Address: **ocf.berkeley.edu**
>   Path: **/pub/Library/Religion/Bible**

WAIS:
>   Database: **Bible**

Bible Translations

The Bible online in German, English, Swahili, and Swedish.

Anonymous FTP:
>   Address: **ftp.spies.com**
>   Path: **/Library/Religion/Bible/***

Gopher:
>   Name: Internet Wiretap
>   Address: **wiretap.spies.com**
>   Choose: **Wiretap Online Library**
>   **| Religion**
>   **| Bible**

Bible Verses

A memory resident pop-up TSR for DOS computers.

Anonymous FTP:
>   Address: **oak.oakland.edu**
>   Path: **/pub/msdos/bible/biblepop.zip**

A
B
C
D
E
F
G
H
I
J
K
L
M
N
O
P
Q
R
S
T
U
V
W
X
Y
Z

Bible Word, Phrase Counts: King James Version

Word counts, phrase counts, and other statistics for the King James Bible.

Anonymous FTP:
Address: **oak.oakland.edu**
Path: **/pub/msdos/bible/kjvcount.txt**

Bible Stats

Ahoy Bible scholars: if you are interested in analyzing the Bible from a statistical point of view, raw material is easy to come by on the Net. In just a few minutes, you can download all the word and phrase counts for the King James Bible. Great for programmers who want to devise their own computer analysis.

Give it a try and, who knows, maybe you'll be able to prove that the Bible was really written by Sir Francis Bacon.

Biblical Search and Extraction Tool

Another shareware Bible search program. This one is also a character-based DOS program, but it comes with the whole Bible.

Anonymous FTP:
Address: **oak.oakland.edu**
Path: **/pub/msdos/bible/refrkjv***

Biblical Timeline

A Jewish biblical timeline, based on the ages shown in the Torah.

Anonymous FTP:
Address: **ftp.spies.com**
Path: **/Library/Article/Religion/biblical.tl**

Gopher:
Name: Internet Wiretap
Address: **wiretap.spies.com**
Choose: **Wiretap Online Library**
  | **Articles**
  | **Religion and Philosophy**
  | **Biblical Timeline**

Who did what, when, and to whom? Take a look at the *Biblical Timeline* and bring some order to **the chaos.**

Book of Mormon

The complete text of the Book of Mormon in zip format. Also in this directory are some additional sets of scripture in ASCII format.

Anonymous FTP:
Address: **ftp.uu.net**
Path: **/systems/msdos/simtel/mormon/bom.zip**

Address: **ocf.berkeley.edu**
Path: **/pub/Library/Religion/Book_of_Mormon**

WAIS:
Database: **Book_of_Mormon**

Buddhism

Lots of documents about different types of Buddhism and Taoism, including mail addresses of individuals and organizations interested in Buddhism and Zen around the world.

Anonymous FTP:
Address: **coombs.anu.edu.au**
Path: **/coombspapers/otherarchives/
electronic-buddhist-archives/***

Buddhism Discussion

A mailing list and Usenet newsgroup for exchanging information and views about Buddhism.

Listserv Mailing List:
List Address: **buddha-l@ulkyvm.louisville.edu**
Subscription Address:
listserv@ulkyvm.louisville.edu

Usenet:
Newsgroup: **alt.religion.buddhism.tibetan**

Catholic Christianity

This mailing list is open for discussing anything of interest to all Catholics, including Roman Catholics. As the range of topics of this list is very broad and interest widespread, this tends to be a busy forum.

Listserv Mailing List:
List Address: **catholic@auvm.american.edu**
Subscription Address:
listserv@auvm.american.edu

Catholic Doctrine

There is more to being an orthodox Catholic than saying a rosary and partaking in the occasional consumption of the body of Christ. Immerse yourself in the discussion of all aspects of Catholic theology and get information on some great archives of Catholic art and magisterial documents. This group is moderated and offers no room for attacks on the Church, so don't try it lest you find yourself whacked on the knuckles with a ruler.

Internet Mailing List:
List Address: **catholic@sarto.gaithersburg.md.us**
Subscription Address:
catholic-request@sarto.gaithersburg.md.us

Catholic Evangelism

A mailing list about Catholic evangelism, church revitalization, and preservation of Catholic teachings, traditions, and values.

Internet Mailing List:
List Address: **catholic-action@cvpnet.chi.il.us**
Subscription Address:
catholic-action-request@cvpnet.chi.il.us

List Address: **catholic-action@vpnet.chi.il.us**
Subscription Address:
catholic-action-request@vpnet.chi.il.us

Catholicism

Information and articles on the Catholic church, including its rituals, Vatican II material, and statements of the popes.

Anonymous FTP:
Address: **ftp.spies.com**
Path: **/Library/Religion/Catholic/***

Gopher:
Name: Internet Wiretap
Address: **wiretap.spies.com**
Choose: **Wiretap Online Library**
| **Religion**
| **Catholic**

Chabad Lubavitch Judaism

This gopher server is the official home of the world Chabad-Lubavitch movement. There are many Jewish resources here including articles, inspirational passages, a glossary of Jewish words and terms, and links to many other Jewish and Judaism resources. Check the gopher for a current web address.

Gopher:
Name: Chabad-Lubavitch
Address: **lubavitch.chabad.org**

Christia

Free-spirited discussions about practical Christian life among strongly motivated Christians who agree to disagree. Immerse yourself in the everyday culture of people who practice their religion with the volume turned up.

Usenet:
Newsgroup: **bit.listserv.christia**

Christian Discussion

Christianity is a blanket that manages to cover a great deal of area. If you happen to be covered by that blanket, so to speak, take advantage of this forum provided to allow Christians of all denominations to discuss Christianity. Non-Christians are welcome to listen in, but debates over the issue of Christianity itself are not welcome and are best confined to the more appropriate Usenet newsgroups.

Internet Mailing List:
List Address: **christian@grian.cps.altadena.ca.us**
Subscription Address:
christian-request@grian.cps.altadena.ca.us

List Address: **mailjc@grian.cps.altadena.ca.us**
Subscription Address:
mailjc-request@grian.cps.altadena.ca.us

Christian Leadership Forum

Nobody said it was easy being a Christian leader, but at least you know you are not the only one who's struggling. Meet other Christian leaders and share with them your concerns, problems, ideas and insights. Christians from around the world participate, and you can hear their various struggles and pray for one another.

Majordomo Mailing List:
List Address: **leadership@iclnet93.iclnet.org**
Subscription Address:
majordomo@iclnet93.iclnet.org

A B C D E F G H I J K L M N O P Q R S T U V W X Y Z

Christian Resources

This page is a collection of links to many Christian resources including mailing lists, home pages of churches on the Web, music, ministries, hypertext bibles, executible outlines, a guide to Christian literature on the Net, and much more.

Anonymous FTP:
Address: **iclnet93.iclnet.org**
Path: **/pub/resources/christian-resources.txt**

World Wide Web:
URL: **http://www.yahoo.com/
Society_and_Culture/Religion/Christianity/**

Christian Thought and Literature in Late Antiquity

Enjoy fascinating discussion about thought and literature of Christianity during the period of 100 A.D. to 500 A.D. Patristics, gnosticism, asceticism, monasticism, archaeology, the Nag Hammadi and Manichaean corpora, and translation of scriptures are a few of the topics discussed.

Listserv Mailing List:
List Address: **elenchus@acadvm1.uottawa.ca**
Subscription Address:
listserv@acadvm1.uottawa.ca

Christian Visions

A mailing list primarily for Christian discussion about visions, prophecies, private revelations, miracles, spiritual experiences, and other gifts of God. Share your experiences or join in discussion and interpretation.

Listserv Mailing List:
List Address: **vision@ubvm.cc.buffalo.edu**
Subscription Address:
listserv@ubvm.cc.buffalo.edu

Christianity

Discover important topics on Christianity. Fundamentalism, evangelism, interfaith marriages, the Trinity, biblical history, tithing, holidays, and the effects of the New Age movement are just a taste of what you will find.

Usenet:
Newsgroup: **alt.christnet**
Newsgroup: **alt.christnet.evangelical**
Newsgroup: **alt.christnet.hypocrisy**
Newsgroup: **alt.christnet.philosophy**
Newsgroup: **alt.christnet.theology**
Newsgroup: **alt.religion.christian**
Newsgroup: **soc.religion.christian**
Newsgroup: **soc.religion.christian.youth-work**

Christianity and How It Relates to Society

A collection of the thoughts of John Henry Newman on Christianity and society.

Anonymous FTP:
Address: **ftp.uu.net**
Path: **/doc/literary/obi/John.Henry.Newman/***

Christianity and Literature

There is a close relationship between Christianity and literature — just look at the Bible. Holy books are about as heavy as literature gets. This forum is not intended for theological dispute, but if you want to discuss and explore the interrelations between Christianity and literature, this would be a good list to join.

Listserv Mailing List:
List Address: **christlit@bethel.edu**
Subscription Address: **listserv@bethel.edu**

Coptic

Material on the Coptic Lectionary.

Anonymous FTP:
Address: **ftp.spies.com**
Path: **/Library/Religion/Coptic/***

Address: **pharos.bu.edu**
Path: **/CN/***

Gopher:
Name: Internet Wiretap
Address: **wiretap.spies.com**
Choose: **Wiretap Online Library**
 | Religion
 | Coptic

Croatian Christian Information Service

An organization established to collect and distribute information about Christian church life. News distributions from various religious communities with regard to social, cultural, and scientific issues that are of interest to Christians in Croatia and elsewhere.

Gopher:
Name: Croatia
Address: **rujan.srce.hr**
Choose: **English Language**
 | Information - Various Institutions..
 | Christian Information Service

Different Christianities Dialogue

There are many different varieties of Christianity and this discussion explores those varieties, opening up tolerant and respectful dialogues between them.

Listserv Mailing List:
List Address: **diftx-l@yalevm.cis.yale.edu**
Subscription Address:
listserv@yalevm.cis.yale.edu

Eastern Orthodox Christianity

A mailing list for discussing the Eastern Orthodox family of Christianity.

Listserv Mailing List:
List Address: **eochr-l@qucdn.queensu.ca**
Subscription Address: **listserv@qucdn.queensu.ca**

Eastern Religions

If you are interested in Eastern enlightenment, read about Buddhism, Hinduism, and other Eastern religions. Often points are related through the tradition of parable, illustrating the beauty of the spiritual path. This group is moderated. (What is the sound of one hand holding open an Internet book?)

Usenet:
Newsgroup: **soc.religion.eastern**

Electric Mystic's Guide to the Internet

A complete bibliography of electronic documents, online conferences, serials, software, and archives relevant to religious studies.

Anonymous FTP:
Address: **panda1.uottawa.ca**
Path: **/pub/religion/electric-mystics-guide**

Episcopal Beliefs and Practices

Commune in this non-hostile environment to discuss Episcopal beliefs and practices. Non-Anglicans and non-Christians are welcome to join the list provided that it doesn't erupt in flaming debates between Anglicans and Protestants, Roman Catholics or non-Christians. Holy wars are best left to the appropriate Usenet newsgroups.

Listserv Mailing List:
List Address: **episcopal@american.edu**
Subscription Address: **listserv@american.edu**

First Century Judaism

Join in on this electronic seminar devoted to the exploration of first century Judaism. It's just the thing for those of you who can't get enough of the writings of Flavius Josephus or Philo of Alexandria.

See also: History, World Cultures

Listserv Mailing List:
List Address: **ioudaios@vm1.yorku.ca**
Subscription Address: **listserv@vm1.yorku.ca**

Gabriel's Horn

Returns a Bible verse from the Old or the New Testament.

Telnet:
Address: **twinbrook.cis.uab.edu**
Port: **7777**

Need some quick inspiration? Try Gabriel's Horn

Genesis

A study aid and reference for the King James Bible.

Anonymous FTP:
Address: **oak.oakland.edu**
Path: **/pub/msdos/bible/genaidc.zip**

Global Christianity Discussion

A mailing list dedicated to the discussion and study of global Christianity.

Listserv Mailing List:
List Address: **globlx-l@qucdn.queensu.ca**
Subscription Address: **listserv@qucdn.queensu.ca**

Hebrew Quiz

A biblical Hebrew language tutor.

Anonymous FTP:
Address: **oak.oakland.edu**
Path: **/pub/msdos/hebrew/hebquiz.zip**

A B C D E F G H I J K L M N O P Q R S T U V W X Y Z

Hindu Dharma

The Hindu religious philosophy is accepted by millions of people around the world. Followers of this way of life discuss the idea of many religious paths, the universal family and how Hinduism applies to everyday life. Topics also include other issues that might affect Hindu living, such as war and politics.

See also: Philosophy

Listserv Mailing List:
    List Address: **hindu-d@arizvm1.ccit.arizona.edu**
    Subscription Address:
      listserv@arizvm1.ccit.arizona.edu

Hinduism

A moderated discussion group, devoted to practice and scriptures of Hinduism.

Usenet:
    Newsgroup: **bit.listserv.hindu-d**

History of American Catholicism

A mailing list for those interested in the history of American Catholicism.

Listserv Mailing List:
    List Address: **amercath@ukcc.uky.edu**
    Subscription Address: **listserv@ukcc.uky.edu**

Islam

Discuss a variety of issues that are important in the Islamic faith. While topics cover the Qur'an, judgement day, Jesus, prophets and religious traditions, there is also spirited discussion regarding current events in the Middle East. This group is moderated.

Usenet:
    Newsgroup: **alt.religion.islam**
    Newsgroup: **soc.religion.islam**

Islam Discussion

Islam and the Qur'an. There is a bot that provides information about where and how to get a translation of the Qur'an.

Internet Relay Chat:
    Channel: **#islam**

Issues in Religion

Sit in on discussions that are religious, ethical, and moral in nature. Talk includes reference to scriptures and parables, but much of it concerns heavily debatable topics — for example, does the Pope use the Internet? — all of which makes for lively banter.

Usenet:
    Newsgroup: **talk.religion.misc**

Jainism

A course on the fundamentals of Jainism, human virtues, and articles on Jainism with other related material.

Anonymous FTP:
    Address: **ftp.spies.com**
    Path: **/Library/Religion/Jainism/***

Gopher:
    Name: Internet Wiretap
    Address: **wiretap.spies.com**
    Choose: **Wiretap Online Library**
     | Religion
     | Jainism

Jewish Culture and Religion

Enjoy a mix of culture and religion. This lively group covers a wide range of topics including the Torah, keeping kosher, traditions, history, and Middle Eastern current events. Learn how to offer too much food to people who visit you.

Usenet:
    Newsgroup: **soc.culture.jewish**

World Wide Web:
    URL: **http://sleepless.cs.uiuc.edu/signet/**
     JHSI/judaism.html

Jewish Law

As if government law is not enough, Jewish people get to add a bunch of their own law on top of it. Discuss Jewish topics with an emphasis on Jewish law relating to the Halakhic system. Debates between Jews and non-Jews or between factions of Judaism are best kept to the Usenet group **talk.religion.misc.**

See also: World Cultures

Listserv Mailing List:
    List Address: **jewish@israel.nysernet.org**
    Subscription Address: **listserv@israel.nysernet.org**

Jewish Mailing List

A list focusing on issues and questions of concern to observant Jews.

Listserv Mailing List:
  List Address: **baltuva@shamash.nysernet.org**
  Subscription Address:
    listserv@shamash.nysernet.org

Jewish Religious Institutions

Information about Jewish religious institutions, including the basics of Judaism, Aish HaTorah, Ohr Somayach, Root and Branch, and many others.

Gopher:
  Name: Jerusalem One
  Address: **jerusalem1.datasrv.co.il**
  Choose: **Religious Institutions and Information**

Judaica Collection

This page collects many links to Judaica resources, including sites for Israel such as the current Kol Israel shortwave schedule, the newsgroup **soc.culture.jewish**, FAQs, and other links including one to the U.S. Holocaust Memorial Museum.

World Wide Web:
  URL: **http://www.cs.cmu.edu:8001/afs/cs.cmu.edu/
    user/clamen/misc/Judaica/README.html**

Koran (or Qur'an)

The verses of the Koran, each in a separate file compressed with gzip.

Anonymous FTP:
  Address: **etext.archive.umich.edu**
  Path: **/pub/Religious.Texts/Quran/***

  Address: **ocf.berkeley.edu**
  Path: **/pub/Library/Religion/Koran**

  Address: **oes.orst.edu**
  Path: **/pub/data/etext/koran/koran**

WAIS:
  Database: **Quran**

The Quran

Strictly speaking, the Quran (Islamic Holy text) should be read in the original Arabic and is not considered to be correct when translated into another language. Still, if your Arabic skills are a bit rusty, you might get more out of reading the Quran in English. Download it and give it a try. Hint: If you want to search for a particular verse, use Wais. (Allaah yusallimukum.)

Mennonites

They are characterized by their clothes, simple living, and pacifistic lifestyles. This list has been formed for people to discuss the Anabaptist/Mennonite faith and Mennonite traditions. Topics can also include Amish, Hutterites, or simple living and pacifism. Most of the members of this group are Mennonite, but you don't have to be Mennonite to join.

Listserv Mailing List:
  List Address: **menno@uci.com**
  Subscription Address: **listserv@uci.com**

Moorish Orthodox Church

A history and catechism of the Moorish Orthodox Church of America.

Anonymous FTP:
  Address: **ftp.spies.com**
  Path: **/Library/Article/Religion/moorish.usa**

Gopher:
  Name: Internet Wiretap
  Address: **wiretap.spies.com**
  Choose: **Wiretap Online Library**
    | **Articles**
    | **Religion and Philosophy**
    | **Moorish Orthodox Church in the USA**

A
B
C
D
E
F
G
H
I
J
K
L
M
N
O
P
Q
R
S
T
U
V
W
X
Y
Z

Mormon

Material on the Mormon scriptures including The Book of Mormon, The Doctrine and Covenants, and The Pearl of Great Price.

Anonymous FTP:
  Address: **ftp.spies.com**
  Path: **/Library/Religion/Mormon/***

Gopher:
  Name: Internet Wiretap
  Address: **wiretap.spies.com**
  Choose: **Wiretap Online Library**
    | **Religion**
    | **Mormon**

Internet Mailing List:
  List Address: **lds@decwrl.dec.com**
  Subscription Address:
    lds-request@decwrl.dec.com

Usenet:
  Newsgroup: **alt.religion.mormon**

Mysticism Discussion

Discussion, chat, and arguments on many areas of mysticism from Christianity to Satanism, and everything in between.

Internet Relay Chat:
  Channel: **#asatru**
  Channel: **#atheism**
  Channel: **#buddhist**
  Channel: **#christ**
  Channel: **#christian**
  Channel: **#islam**

Orthodox Christianity

Orthodox Christianity is not just any old Christianity. It's vitamin-fortified, steel-belted Christianity. This list is dedicated to the discussion of this religion on a worldwide basis, in particular its recent rise in popularity within Russia and its neighboring countries. These lists are moderated.

Listserv Mailing List:
  List Address: **orthodox@iubvm.ucs.indiana.edu**
  Subscription Address:
    listserv@iubvm.ucs.indiana.edu

  List Address: **orthodox@miamiu.muohio.edu**
  Subscription Address:
    listserv@miamiu.muohio.edu

Period Calendar

A guide to taking modern month-and-day dates and converting them to old church-style dating by feasts and seasons.

Anonymous FTP:
  Address: **ftp.spies.com**
  Path: **/Library/Document/calendar.sca**

Gopher:
  Name: Internet Wiretap
  Address: **wiretap.spies.com**
  Choose: **Wiretap Online Library**
    | **Assorted Documents**
    | **Creative Anachronism Period Calendar**

Practical Christian Life

A mailing list for discussions on practical Christian life.

Listserv Mailing List:
  List Address: **christia@finhutc.bitnet**
  Subscription Address:
    listserv@finhutc.bitnet

Religious Denominations

Material on many Christian denominations, including Anglican, Catholic, Coptic, Mormon, Presbyterian, and others.

Anonymous FTP:
  Address: **ftp.spies.com**
  Path: **/Library/Religion/***

Gopher:
  Name: Internet Wiretap
  Address: **wiretap.spies.com**
  Choose: **Wiretap Online Library**
    | **Religion**

Religious News

Read what's going on with religion and religious leaders of the world. This is where you will find the facts on current religious events.

Usenet:
  Newsgroup: **clari.news.religion**

Religious Studies Publications

An electronic journal that disseminates tables of contents, abstracts, reviews, and ordering information on new, recently released, and electronic publications relevant to religious studies.

Listserv Mailing List:
List Address: **contents@acadvm1.uottawa.ca**
Subscription Address:
listserv@acadvm1.uottawa.ca

Religious Studies experts: keep up on what's new and exciting by subscribing to the **contents** *mailing list.*

Sexuality and Religion

Everyone knows you are not supposed to talk about sex and religion at the same time, so you should only read this paragraph if nobody is looking. These newsgroups actually do talk about sex in relation to Christianity. Understand the Christian's viewpoint of sex and get in on the "to do or not to do" debate.

Usenet:
Newsgroup: **alt.christnet.sex**
Newsgroup: **alt.religion.sexuality**

Shakers

Everyone would like a little utopia in their life. There are actually people who have figured out a way to get it — or at least get closer to it than the rest of us. The United Society of Believers (Shakers) hold to the fact that a pure life is one that is lived simply. On this mailing list, discussion covers anything related to the Shakers including their history, religious beliefs, culture, and furniture.

See also: Philosophy

Listserv Mailing List:
List Address: **shaker@ukcc.uky.edu**
Subscription Address: **listserv@ukcc.uky.edu**

Society of Friends

Commonly referred to as Quakers, Friends discuss on this list their natural way of living and their distaste for violence.

Listserv Mailing List:
List Address: **quaker-l@vmd.cso.uiuc.edu**
Subscription Address: **listserv@vmd.cso.uiuc.edu**

Usenet:
Newsgroup: **soc.religion.quaker**

Soka Gakkai International

This web page is for Buddhists who follow the practice of Nichiren Daishonin. The page has a link to daily guidance and Soka Gakkai web pages in Japan and elsewhere.

World Wide Web:
URL: **http://www.halcyon.com/lchinet/menu.html**

Vedic Civilization

Examples of Vedic ideas concerning time and human longevity, as detailed by the Vedic literature of India.

Anonymous FTP:
Address: **ftp.spies.com**
Path: **/Library/Article/Religion/marriage.ved**

Address: **ftp.spies.com**
Path: **/Library/Article/Religion/vedic.txt**

Address: **ftp.spies.com**
Path: **/Library/Article/Religion/vedic.wst**

Gopher:
Name: Internet Wiretap
Address: **wiretap.spies.com**
Choose: **Wiretap Online Library**
  | Articles
  | Religion and Philosophy
  | Vedic Civilization

World Wide Web:
URL: **http://err.ethz.ch/~kiwi/Spirit/Veda/**

Zen Buddhist Texts

Primary Zen texts, texts from the Southwest Zen Academy, and links to other Buddhist sources.

World Wide Web:
URL: **http://oac11.hsc.uth.tmc.edu/zen/index.html**

A B C D E F G H I J K L M N O P Q **R** S T U V W X Y Z

Zoroastrianism

Originating in ancient Iran, today Zoroastrianism has a small following in isolated areas of Iran and India. Join discussion on this religion founded in 6th century B.C. and hear the stories of Ahura Mazda as he battles his evil twin, Ahriman. This is the stuff good movies are made of.

Usenet:
Newsgroup: **alt.religion.zoroastrianism**

RELIGION: ALTERNATIVE

Ahmadiyya

Learn about Ahmadiyya, a messianic movement based on the principles of the Qur'an and founded in the late nineteenth century by Mirza Ghulam Ahmad. (Can you say that name fast ten times?) Unlike traditional Muslims, adherents of Ahmadiyya believe Qadiyani to be a prophet after Muhammad.

Usenet:
Newsgroup: **alt.sect.ahmadiyya**

World Wide Web:
URL:
http://www.umn.edu/nlhome/g626/ahma0011/
URL: **http://look1.apmaths.uwo.ca/sultan/amni**
URL: **http://www.utexas.edu/students/amso/**

Need spiritual guidance? You're on your own. Need a good laugh? Follow Brother Jed.

Baha'i Faith

Who was Baha'u'llah (a.k.a. Mirza Husayn Ali)? What did he do in Iran in the mid-19th century that was so important? Was he really the Bab (with a direct line to the twelfth Imam)? Learn about the message of the Baha'u'llah and the Baha'i view of life. Read quotes from Baha'i scriptures and discuss such topics as gender equality and spiritual revelations.

Anonymous FTP:
Address: **ftp.spies.com**
Path: **/Library/Article/Religion/bahai.int**

Gopher:
Name: Internet Wiretap
Address: **wiretap.spies.com**
Choose: **Wiretap Online Library**
| **Articles**
| **Religion and Philosophy**
| **Introduction to Baha'i Faith**

Internet Mailing List:
List Address: **bahai-faith@oneworld.wa.com**
Subscription Address:
bahai-faith-request@oneworld.wa.com

Usenet:
Newsgroup: **soc.religion.bahai**

World Wide Web:
URL: **http://herald.usask.ca/~maton/bahai.html**

Brother Jed

Follow the comings and goings of Brother Jed (George E. Smock) as his itinerent travels take him from campus to campus throughout America, spreading the word that Christianity is incompatible with homosexuality, long hair, drugs, and rock music. (Yes, it's true. Would we make up something like this?)

Usenet:
Newsgroup: **alt.brother-jed**

Eckankar

Join Eckists as they explore visualization, reality, and waking dreams. Book lists, exercises, and historical origins are a few of the topics covered.

Usenet:
Newsgroup: **alt.religion.eckankar**

Generic Religions and Secret Societies

The Generic Religions and Secret Societies (GRASS) mailing list is a forum for the development of religions and secret societies for use in role-playing games.

See also: Role-Playing

Mail:
Address: **grass-server@wharton.upenn.edu**
Body: **subscribe name**

Gnosticism

Take a few Christian terms, add in a liberal dose of Greek philosophy, a dash of mythology and a handful of magickal rituals. Let sit for several centuries and voila! You end up with a religion that can serve millions and is very low in calories. Learn more about Gnosticism, it's origins and tenets. The **soc.religion.gnosis** group is moderated.

Usenet:
Newsgroup: **alt.religion.gnostic**
Newsgroup: **soc.religion.gnosis**

World Wide Web:
URL: **http://www.webcom.com/~gnosis/**

Goddess Spirituality and Feminism

Hera really did give goddesses a bad name, but they are finally starting to become popular, and not just with women, either. Men and women alike are interested in goddess spirituality, feminism, and the incorporation of the feminine/feminist idea in the study and worship of the divine. Listen in on their discussions of spirituality in relation to the goddess.

See also: Women

Listserv Mailing List:
List Address: **wmsprt-l@ubvm.cc.buffalo.edu**
Subscription Address: **listserv@ubvm.cc.buffalo.edu**

Kriya Yoga

An introduction to the original Kriya practice and the keys of the Kriya path.

Anonymous FTP:
Address: **ftp.spies.com**
Path: **/Library/Article/Religion/kriya.yog**

Gopher:
Name: Internet Wiretap
Address: **wiretap.spies.com**
Choose: **Wiretap Online Library**
| **Articles**
| **Religion and Philosophy**
| **Original Kriya Yoga at a Glance**

Mage's Guide to the Internet

Details of how to find and use the many occult, magick, and mysticism-related resources on the Internet, including mailing lists, BBSs, IRC, ftp sites, gopher sites, web pages, and much more.

Anonymous FTP:
Address: **etext.archive.umich.edu**
Path: **/pub/Quartz/occult/mages-guide.gz**

Address: **ftp.lysator.liu.se**
Path: **/pub/magick/Net/Guides/***

World Wide Web:
URL: **http://err.ethz.ch/~kiwi/Spirit/mages-guide.html**
URL: **http://www.contrib.andrew.cmu.edu:8001/usr/sk4p/omnet/misc/MAGI**

New Religious Movements

From what we have seen, there is big money and fame in the business of religion. In addition to that, you can get all the women you want. This academic group discusses new religious movements. If you are interested in becoming a deity in this lifetime, you might check in and see if you can get any helpful hints.

Listserv Mailing List:
List Address: **nurel-l@listserv.ucalgary.ca**
Subscription Address: **listserv@listserv.ucalgary.ca**

Pagan Religion and Philosophy

It's hard to get bored with paganism because there are so many different gods you can worship and you get to do fun things like celebrate the solstice wearing little more than your birthday suit. Learn more about pagan religion and philosophy and see what you might have been missing all these years.

See also: New Age

Internet Mailing List:
List Address: **pagant@drycas.club.cc.cmu.edu**
Subscription Address:
pagant-request@drycas.club.cc.cmu.edu

List Address:
uther+pagan@drycas.club.cc.cmu.edu
Subscription Address:
uther+pagan-request@drycas.club.cc.cmu.edu

Pagan Yule Customs

An Asatru viewpoint of Yule customs and traditions.

Anonymous FTP:
Address: **ftp.spies.com**
Path: **/Library/Fringe/Occult/pagan.yul**

Gopher:
Name: Internet Wiretap
Address: **wiretap.spies.com**
Choose: **Wiretap Online Library**
 | **Fringes of Reason**
 | **Occult and Paranormal**
 | **Pagan Yule Customs**

Sabaean Religious Order

The origins, history, and philosophy of the Sabaeans and Sheba.

Usenet:
Newsgroup: **alt.religion.sabaean**

Satanism

Discover what Satanists feel are the misconceptions about their beliefs. See what Satanism means and discuss how Satanists feel their beliefs relate to Christianity. Other topics include music, books, and news items.

Usenet:
Newsgroup: **alt.satanism**

Scientology

Invite yourself into the house that Ron built: Scientology and Dianetics. Learn about becoming a *clear*: eliminate all your engrams, your first step towards becoming an operating thetan. Find out what is new and exciting in this oft-misunderstood marriage of science, religion, applied psychology, and science fiction. (Be sure to take along plenty of money.)

Usenet:
Newsgroup: **alt.clearing.technology**
Newsgroup: **alt.religion.scientology**

Secular Web

A server of secular concerns with sections for atheists and agnosticists, magazines such as *Free Inquiry* and *Skeptical Inquirer*, religious parodies, satire, and links to many other organizations and resources of secular interest.

World Wide Web:
URL: **http://freethought.tamu.edu/**

The Secular Web

Sometimes, "alternative religion" means a type of thought or belief that is so far into the ether as to be seriously wacko. However, another way to think about it is that "alternative" also means a thoughtful, skeptical, and perhaps lighthearted (or even satirical) approach to answering those deep questions that keep you up late at night. If this is your bent, take a look at the *Secular Web* wherein you will encounter the work of other similarly-minded atheists and agnostics.

Shamanism

Delve into the natural spiritual practices of the shaman. Discover the full range of the shamanic experience, which includes such things as drumming, vision quests, and visiting sacred sites.

Usenet:
Newsgroup: **alt.religion.shamanism**
Newsgroup: **soc.religion.shamanism**

Theosophy

Take a little religion, some Hindu philosophy, add a dash of mysticism, pantheism, or magic and you get Theosophy. If you like going on your own and not having to confess, tithe, or be organized in general, you might want to try this. Get an overview of what Theosophy is all about by reading selected papers and posts from related newsgroups.

See also: New Age, Paranormal

World Wide Web:
URL: **http://err.ethz.ch/~kiwi/Spirit/Theosophy/Overview.html**

Unitarianism

Share thoughts and opinions with the people who address their prayers "to whom it may concern." Discuss issues of interest to members of the Unitarian-Universalist church: the most free-thinking, tolerant, diverse, and intellectual group of people since the Nixon White House.

Listserv Mailing List:
List Address: **uus-l@info.terraluna.org**
Subscription Address: **listserv@info.terraluna.org**

List Address: **uus-l@ubvm.cc.buffalo.edu**
Subscription Address: **listserv@ubvm.cc.buffalo.edu**

Usenet:
Newsgroup: **bit.listserv.uus-l**

RELIGION: HUMOR

Atheism Satire

The Surgeon General's priest warns that reading this newsgroup could be hazardous to your spiritual health. But it's so much fun that it doesn't really matter. Put off your eternal damnation until tomorrow for hours of chuckles today.

Usenet:
> Newsgroup: **alt.atheism.satire**

Bible in Pig Latin

If you are not afraid of being struck by lightning or plagued by locusts, check out this version of the bible translated into Pig Latin.

Anonymous FTP:
> Address: **ftp.netcom.com**
> Path: **/pub/ea/earl/Ible-bay/***

World Wide Web:
> URL: **ftp://netcom.com/pub/earl/Ible-bay/**
>   **Ible-bay.html**

Religious Humor

If you are sensitive about your religion, don't come here. You *will* be offended — guaranteed. But if your spiritual skin is not too thin, check out *The Pagan Song* and *Shit-Religions*.

Anonymous FTP:
> Address: **quartz.rutgers.edu**
> Path: **/pub/humor/Religion/***

Gopher:
> Name: Rutgers University
> Address: **quartz.rutgers.edu**
> Choose: **Humor**
> | **Religion**

Do you really exist?
Check Philosophy and be sure.

Need Help?
Try Internet: Help.

ROLE-PLAYING

Chill Horror Role-Playing Game

It's not enough that you torture yourself at the movie theater by watching the latest in heart-stopping horror films. You have to get into the ultra-scary business of actually role-playing the horror. Chill is a game that will be of interest to anyone who loves the horror genre and thinks elves and faeries are for wimps. Discussion covers Chill, rules, and nifty role-playing ideas. If you like to get a group of people together and try to scare each other to death, it's okay, but leave us out of it. We don't like to have to sleep with the lights on.

Note: This list is manually maintained so there might be a slight delay in confirming that you have been added.

Internet Mailing List:
> List Address: **chill@callamer.com**
> Subscription Address: **chill-request@callamer.com**

Dark-Sun

Fantasy is fun. Immerse yourself in the *Advanced Dungeons and Dragons* world of *Dark-Sun* and meet with other people who revel there. Enjoy yourself, but don't forget to come up for air once in a while.

Listserv Mailing List:
> List Address: **dark-sun@le.ac.uk**
> Subscription Address: **listserv@le.ac.uk**

Fantasy Role-Playing

Magic, mystery, and adventure await you once you step across the line that separates fantasy from reality. Tag along with role-players in Dragon's Inn, Haven's Rest, and Cloven Shield as they weave a web of tales in front of this virtual fireplace. The **rec.games.frp** newsgroup offers discussion about fantasy role-playing.

Usenet:
> Newsgroup: **alt.dragons-inn**
> Newsgroup: **alt.pub.cloven-shield**
> Newsgroup: **alt.pub.havens-rest**
> Newsgroup: **rec.games.frp**
> Newsgroup: **rec.games.frp.archives**

A B C D E F G H I J K L M N O P Q R S T U V W X Y Z

Excerpt from the Net...

Newsgroup: alt.pub.dragons-inn
Subject: Guess What's Coming to Dinner

Synopsis:
    The party members have been ambushed at a dinner given by their host, the vampire
    Pericles. A great battle has just begun...

Unable to enjoy her food and not really interested in dessert, Matte had just begun to
try to excuse herself from the table when the servants attacked. Halfway out of her seat
already, she quickly leapt upon her chair and picked up a piece of cutlery from the
table. She attempted to hit one of the creatures attacking Moria on the opposite side of
the room, but was picked up from behind as she drew her arm back, the knife falling
harmlessly to the floor.

Matte felt the grip of the armoured servant tighten as she was lifted from her feet. The
creature's grasp was very firm, and she was unable to free herself to conjure assistance
or use her weapon. She grunted and kicked at her captor but to no avail.

Suddenly, she felt the iron grip give way as she landed on her feet and heard the clatter
of armour fall to the floor above the din of battle in the room.

She turned to see Tomonobu behind her, his sword flashing at more armoured servants
further away. "Rescuing you is getting to be a habit, Little One," he said as he moved
away to deal with problems of his own...

Fantasy Role-Playing Games

This site has a number of role-playing games to choose from, such as Empire of the Petal Throne.

Gopher:
    Name: University of Minnesota
    Address: **gopher.micro.umn.edu**
    Choose: **Fun & Games**
        | **Games**
        | **Fantasy Role-Playing Games**

Flashlife

There's no better way to spend your spare time than by thinking up cool ways to kill imaginary people, or at least to put them in severe peril. Role-playing is fun that way. You can take all the risks you want and never have to worry about hurting yourself. Join the mailing list for GMs of Shadowrun and other cyberpunk role-playing games to discuss rules, scenarios, ask questions, and give answers.

See also: Hobbies

Internet Mailing List:
    List Address: **flashlife@netcom.com**
    Subscription Address:
        flashlife-request@netcom.com

Illuminati Online

This contains information about Steve Jackson Games, the popular role-playing game company. Information about new and upcoming products, writing, art and playtesting for SJ Games, a link to Metaverse Moo, and some information on RPGing.

Gopher:
    Name: Illuminati Online
    Address: **io.com**

Live-Action Role-Playing

What a great way to spend the evening — dress up as someone else and take on a whole new life. Say goodbye to reality by doing some live-action role-playing where you talk to other characters and solve a mystery or a problem the way your character would. You'll never be able to go back to ordinary board games again.

Usenet:
    Newsgroup: **rec.games.frp.live-action**

**Spare time?
Take a look at Games.**

Miniatures

It's best if you have good eyesight and a steady hand, but anybody can have fun painting, sculpting, or decorating miniatures. Mostly miniatures are used in wargames or for fantasy role-playing games, but any hobbyist would find these tiny works of art fascinating. Get together with other fans of miniatures and talk about how bigger is not always better.

See also: Hobbies

Internet Mailing List:
List Address: **minilist@cs.unc.edu**
Subscription Address: **minilist-request@cs.unc.edu**

Pern Role-Playing

Calling all Dragon-Riders! Join forces with McCaffrey fans around the globe as they discuss all aspects of role-playing based on the Pern novels.

See also: MUDs: Specific Types

Listserv Mailing List:
List Address: **pern-rp@cornell.edu**
Subscription Address: **listserv@cornell.edu**

Role-Playing

A large collection of information connected to role-playing, including convention reports, ftp site lists, list of games and companies, and game-system specifics.

Gopher:
Name: University of San Diego
Address: **teetot.acusd.edu**
Choose: **Everything..**
    | **Entertainment and Food**
    | **Role-Playing**

Looking for special fun? Turn to the Vices section.

Role-Playing Games

Sometimes we wonder why people even bother with real life. Not only is it always in your face, but so much of the time it is noisy and ugly.
Take our advice: find out about role-playing games and leave reality to the grown-ups.

Role-Playing Archives

Large archives of role-playing materials — pictures, programs, game sheets, stories, specific systems, and texts on all aspects of role-playing. Includes AD&D, Traveller, Champions, Navero, Runequest, and others.

Anonymous FTP:
Address: **ftp.csua.berkeley.edu**
Path: **/pub/***

Address: **ftp.funet.fi**
Path: **/pub/doc/games/roleplay/***

Address: **ftp.white.toronto.edu**
Path: **/pub/frp/***

Address: **ics.uci.edu**
Path: **/usenet/rec.games.frp/***

Address: **ocf.berkeley.edu**
Path: **/pub/Traveller/***

Gopher:
Name: Youngstown Freenet
Address: **yfn.ysu.edu**
Choose: **The Public Forum**
    | **Sigs**
    | **Role-Playing Sig**

A
B
C
D
E
F
G
H
I
J
K
L
M
N
O
P
Q
R
S
T
U
V
W
X
Y
Z

Role-Playing Famous Last Words

When your role-playing character commits the most amazing blunder of all time, you become a legend. It's a tradition to be ridiculed for the rest of your days about it. At least you are not alone. See page after page of other players' famous last words and take comfort that nobody is laughing at you — they are laughing near you.

World Wide Web:
    URL: **http://cad.ucla.edu/repository/library/ Cadlab/lastwords**

Role-Playing Games

Materials to buy and sell role-playing and fantasy games.

Usenet:
    Newsgroup: **rec.games.frp.marketplace**

Reality is for people who aren't smart enough for role playing games

RuneQuest

The house is a mess, you have a deadline at work, and your mother-in-law is coming to visit. There's nothing left to do but simply skip out on reality with a little fantasy role-playing. RuneQuest is the perfect choice. Find out more about the game by reading articles and discussion between fans. There's plenty of time for reality later.

Internet Mailing List:
    List Address:
        rune-quest@glorantha.holland.sun.com
    Subscription Address:
        rune-quest-request@glorantha.holland.sun.com

ShadowRun

There are more fantasy role-playing games on the market than you can shake your Ares Predator II pistol at. Take the opportunity to learn about ShadowRun, an exciting fantasy game that's more than just fantasy. Take some trolls, elves, and dwarves, add some wires and computer chips, a few Native American totem spirits, and suddenly you have a cyberfantasy game that will provide you with hours of enjoyment. If you are a veteran of the game, you can answer questions, share comments, ideas and stories about ShadowRun. No matter what your mother says, there's no such thing as too much fun.

Listserv Mailing List:
    List Address: **shadowtk@nic.surfnet.nl**
    Subscription Address: **listserv@nic.surfnet.nl**

    List Address: **shadowrn@nic.surfnet.nl**
    Subscription Address: **listserv@nic.surfnet.nl**

ShadowRun on the Web

This web page is dedicated to the role-playing game ShadowRun. It offers archives of mailing lists, web forms to help issue listserv commands for the ShadowRun mailing lists, links to ftp sites containing ShadowRun and general cyberpunk information, FAQs, and links to other ShadowRun and cyberpunk resources.

World Wide Web:
    URL: **http://www.ip.net/shadowrun/**

Star Trek Role-Playing

Don't settle for just watching or reading *Star Trek*. You can actually be a *Star Trek* character. Trekkies discuss the game and its enhancements as well as putting together a group to play the game. It's not just fun, it's a way of life.

See also: Star Trek

Listserv Mailing List:
    List Address: **stargame@pccvm.bitnet**
    Subscription Address: **listserv@pccvm.bitnet**

Usenet:
    Newsgroup: **alt.starfleet.rpg**

Cool words?
Look in Quotations.

Tekumel

We wanted you to hear it from us: Tekumel is not a real world. As cool as the place sounds, someone just made it up. Of course, that doesn't mean you can't go there. Unleash your imagination and experience the Empire of the Petal Throne or the Man of Gold. Tekumel experts and novices talk about game modifications, old and new campaigns, and tips for enhancing play.

Internet Mailing List:
  List Address: **tekumel@ssdc.honeywell.com**
  Subscription Address:
    tekumel-request@ssdc.honeywell.com

Torg

There is a twisted appeal to certain death and destruction. And it's fun to be able to feel, for one night, like you are in charge of the salvation of Planet Earth. Gather with other adventurers to fight the Possibility Wars and discuss rules, ideas, and experiences of this lively and imaginative game.

Internet Mailing List:
  List Address: **torg@cool.vortech.com**
  Subscription Address:
    torg-request@cool.vortech.com

Traveller

Take a trip to a new world without having to bother with a passport or all those painful inoculations. The Traveller science fiction role-playing game lets you be the person you always fantasized about being. You are master of your fate. Hook up with other Traveller fans and explore all aspects of this science fiction game.

Internet Mailing List:
  List Address: **traveller@dadla.wr.tek.com**
  Subscription Address:
    traveller-request@dadla.wr.tek.com

  List Address: **traveller@engrg.uwo.ca**
  Subscription Address:
    traveller-request@engrg.uwo.ca

The Net is mankind's greatest achievement.

Vampire

Most normal people run in fear at the thought of being a vampire's midnight snack. Then there are those who actually go out looking for it. We're not saying there is anything wrong with that, of course, as long as they keep their teeth to themselves. Enthusiasts of the game Vampire discuss settings, rules, and ideas about this dark genre.

Internet Mailing List:
  List Address: **vampire@math.ufl.edu**
  Subscription Address:
    vampire-request@math.ufl.edu

ROMANCE

Couples

It's the best of times, it's the worst of times. Relationships have their ups and downs, but like a roller coaster, it's fun and thrilling, makes you afraid, and makes you laugh. See what is going on in the lives of other couples. Get ideas for romantic outings, anniversaries, how to patch up a fuss, or what to do with in-laws.

Listserv Mailing List:
  List Address: **couples-l@cornell.edu**
  Subscription Address: **listserv@cornell.edu**

Usenet:
  Newsgroup: **soc.couples**
  Newsgroup: **soc.couples.intercultural**

Love

For Cupid's own, those who seek love, or those who just want to talk about it.

Internet Relay Chat:
  Channel: **#love**
  Channel: **#love_nest**

Men and Women

We all got along fine when we were algae. But somewhere between floating gently on the lake and the invention of the bikini, men and women started to have their differences. Get up close and personal. See what the factions are saying about each other. It's not too much of a secret since there is a lot of crossposting.

Usenet:
  Newsgroup: **soc.men**
  Newsgroup: **soc.women**

A B C D E F G H I J K L M N O P Q R S T U V W X Y Z

Excerpt from the Net...

Newsgroup: soc.men
Subject: Marriage Makes Men Fearless

Al Bundy's T-shirt said it best: "Kill Me, I'm Married." There seems to be nothing more courage hardening than being trapped in a marriage. Men will willingly work a hundred hours a week to avoid going home, even if the work has an early death warranty. Men go to war, to sea, to space, and anywhere they can avoid facing their wives with no fear of the risks they are taking; because they have nothing to lose. Marriage must be one of the most powerful tools a culture has for its own protection. Without the terror of "going home" how would any country get hundreds of thousands of men to head off to war? Couldn't happen. We aren't protecting our country, we are protecting ourselves...

Love and Romance

Where would we be without love and romance? Probably at home in front of the TV. At least with romance we can be in front of the TV with someone to keep us company. As a Net person, you never need to worry about getting your share. There are lots of resources for the romantically inclined (and even for the romantically challenged). Just remember, the only place where "love" comes before "romance" is in The Internet Yellow Pages.

Penpals

It's so much fun to make new friends. Get a penpal (or two or three) and find out what is going on outside your world. Stick close to home or experience the other side of the planet through someone else's eyes. Take a little time and reach out to someone.

Usenet:
Newsgroup: **soc.penpals**

Excerpt from the Net...

Newsgroup: soc.women
Subject: Women Aren't Automobiles

>>> What I disagree with, however, is the notion that the man is in any
>>> way responsible for the woman's EXTRAVAGANT ways of dealing with
>>> such reproductive "accidents". That's like saying if I put a dent
>>> in the bumper of someone's Yugo in a parking lot, and they decide
>>> to replace the entire car with a Rolls Royce, that I'm liable for
>>> the entire cost of the "replacement".

>> Uhhh... women aren't automobiles. Perhaps your seeming to consider
>> them such is partially the cause of your being a "voluntary chaste
>> virgin".

> Alright. Then how do you explain the TV classic "My mother the car"?

Well, of course *some* women are automobiles. I don't think that anyone was denying this. But I still don't think that you can make the sweeping generalization that *all* women are automobiles. I did date a Ford Pinto once, but the relationship ended tragically...

Polyamory

Whether it's a big heart or a big ego, if you have the desire to love more than one person at a time, you can be in for quite a wild emotional ride. Don't get caught with your pants down. Learn the pros and cons of polyamory from some of the pros.

Usenet:
Newsgroup: **alt.polyamory**

Romance

Have you noticed life isn't quite like the covers of paperback romance novels (or the inside of the romance novels, for that matter)? Do something about that by generating a romantic fire with others who mourn the death of romance. Remember Cyrano de Bergerac and his words that could melt the hair off a moose? Where do you think he got his start?

Usenet:
Newsgroup: **alt.romance**
Newsgroup: **alt.romance.chat**

Romance Readers Anonymous

You've been sucked in. It's impossible to walk past a rack of romance novels without picking up at least one. The bronzed man holding the lithe woman with the heaving bosom makes your heart beat quickly, loud enough for everyone else in the store to hear. The television has cobwebs and you haven't been out of the house in months since you got a subscription to Romance of the Week. Get help now. You are not alone.

Listserv Mailing List:
List Address: **rra-l@kentvm.kent.edu**
Subscription Address: **listserv@kentvm.kent.edu**

Usenet:
Newsgroup: **bit.listserv.rra-l**

Romantic Whisperings

A place to whisper sweet nothings and tell tales of candlelight dinners, moonlight strolls, and hearts shared with other romantics from around the globe.

Internet Relay Chat:
Channel: **#romance**

The Internet will set you free.

Singles

Your mother probably said that anyone you can pick up in a bar is not someone with whom you want to develop a serious relationship. (What you probably didn't want to tell her was that you weren't looking for a serious relationship.) In the event that you change your mind, stop in at the nicest singles hangout in Usenet and the IRC and find that special someone just right for you.

Internet Relay Chat:
Channel: **#singles**

Usenet:
Newsgroup: **soc.singles**

Soulmates

There is a moment when you look into someone's eyes and you feel, in an instant, that you have known this person your entire life and that you can never bear to be seperated from him or her again. This is the feeling of finding a soulmate, someone who feels like the other half of you. Read anecdotes about people who have found their soulmates, people who are looking for soulmates and discuss the writings of Richard Bach, who writes extensively on the concept of soulmates.

Usenet:
Newsgroup: **alt.soulmates**

Unhappy Romances

The only thing worse than no romance is unhappy romance. Unrequited love, romance gone bad or people who are inept in the romance department — these are all topics that are fair game in this newsgroup.

Usenet:
Newsgroup: **alt.romance.unhappy**

Weddings

Don't let your wedding be a remake of *Father of the Bride* (or the Bay of Pigs). Learn what is proper and what is not. Find out shortcuts from folks who have done this before (or again and again). Topics cover a wide range, such as invitations, RSVPs, dresses, parties, garters, underclothes, and much more.

Usenet:
Newsgroup: **alt.wedding**

A B C D E F G H I J K L M N O P Q R S T U V W X Y Z

SCIENCE

Annealing (Simulated)

Discussion of simulated annealing techniques and analysis, as well as other related issues, including stochastic optimization, Boltzmann machines, metricity, etc.

Internet Mailing List:
List Address: **anneal@sc.ucla.edu**
Subscription Address: **anneal-request@sc.ucla.edu**

List Address: **anneal@sti.com**
Subscription Address: **majordomo@sti.com**

Simulated Annealing

Have you ever had the experience of being really heated up by something and then, after slowly cooling down, found yourself to be tougher and stronger? Well, that's annealing, and it happens to metal and glass as well. Physicists and engineers use simulated annealing (mathematical techniques based on this idea) to solve all kinds of interesting problems. If you want to see what the simulated annealing pros are up to, join the **anneal** mailing list.

Anthropology Mailing List

Discussions of various techniques and fields of research in anthropology, including computation in anthropology, graphics in archaeology, programs anthropologists use, and so on.

Listserv Mailing List:
List Address: **anthro-l@ubvm.cc.buffalo.edu**
Subscription Address:
listserv@ubvm.cc.buffalo.edu

Aquaculture Discussion List

A mailing list on farming aquatic species, including what is involved, technology, problems and solutions, who is doing it now, and where they're doing it.

Listserv Mailing List:
List Address: **aqua-l@uoguelph.bitnet**
Subscription Address: **listserv@uoguelph.bitnet**

Black Holes

A document by Stephen Hawking discussing his theories about black holes.

Anonymous FTP:
Address: **xcf.berkeley.edu**
Path: **/pub/misc/hawking.2**

Gopher:
Name: University of Illinois
Address: **wx.atmos.uiuc.edu**
Choose: **Documents**
   | **FUN**
   | **hawking.black.holes**

California Academy of Sciences

Pull the computer up by the fireplace and settle in with some cozy scientific reading. The Academy has a little bit of everything on anthropology, botany, entomology, herpetology, ichthyology, invertebrate zoology, geology, ornithology and aquatic biology. And there's probably even stuff here that we can't pronounce.

Gopher:
Name: California Academy of Sciences
Address: **cas.calacademy.org**

Color Perception

This group explores color concepts by drawing from color studies in anthropology, linguistics, philosophy, psychology and cognitive science.

Listserv Mailing List:
List Address: **colorcat@brownvm.brown.edu**
Subscription Address:
listserv@brownvm.brown.edu

Color and Vision

It's embarrassing to leave the house in the morning, go to work, and discover that your clothes don't match. And you could have sworn they matched while you were dressing. Color and lighting are cruel that way. Researchers conduct discussions about color science and vision research. Joining this list might not help with your fashion sense, but it will enlighten you about color and vision.

Listserv Mailing List:
List Address: **live-eye@vm1.yorku.ca**
Subscription Address: **listserv@vm1.yorku.ca**

Earth and Sky

Read the dialogs from this radio program heard across the United States, which deals with various popular science subjects, ranging from astronomy and Earth science to the environment. Today's program as well as archives of the older programs are available, brought to you by Quadralay Corporation.

World Wide Web:
URL: **http://www.quadralay.com/EarthSky/ es_home.htm**

Electromagnetics in Medicine, Science and Communication

What good is electromagnetics? Is it likely that it will improve how pizza tastes or help the Dodgers win their next game? According to the Electromagnetic Society, there is more to life than good pizza. Read literature concerning the interaction between electromagnetic fields and biological systems. Yes, there is even data on 60 Hz and microwave radiation.

See also: Medicine, Physics

Listserv Mailing List:
List Address: **emflds-l@ubvm.cc.buffalo.edu**
Subscription Address:
listserv@ubvm.cc.buffalo.edu

Energy Research in Israel

Get this Bitnet newsletter on energy research in Israel so you can keep up-to-date on energy in the Middle East.

Listserv Mailing List:
List Address: **energy-l@vm.tau.ac.il**
Subscription Address: **listserv@vm.tau.ac.il**

Ethology

It would be nice to know the meaning of all those gestures that the cat is making. What does it mean when he twitches his tail or moves his ears back and forth? People who study animal behavior and behavioral ecology have it all figured out. Discover new or controversial theories, new research methods, and discuss equipment, books, papers, conferences, and new software pretaining to behavioral analysis. You might even learn why a dog's leg twitches when you scratch him just right.

Listserv Mailing List:
List Address: **ethology@finhutc.hut.fi**
Subscription Address: **listserv@finhutc.hut.fi**

Global Positioning System

Information on the Australian global positioning navigation system, including the locations of base stations and other topics of interest.

Gopher:
Name: Australian Environmental Resources
Information Network
Address: **kaos.erin.gov.au**
Choose: **ERIN Information
| Global Positioning System**

Hiroshima

This server is operated by RERF (Radiation Effects Research Foundation), which is a bi-national organization dedicated to the discovery, application, and dissemination of knowledge about health effects in survivors of the atomic bombings of Hiroshima and Nagasaki.

See also: Health

World Wide Web:
URL: **http://www/rerf.or.jp/**

History of Science and Technology

A biannual journal that features articles, research notes, communications, book reviews, and electronic resource information.

Anonymous FTP:
Address: **epas.utoronto.ca**
Path: **/pub/ihpst/***

A
B
C
D
E
F
G
H
I
J
K
L
M
N
O
P
Q
R
S
T
U
V
W
X
Y
Z

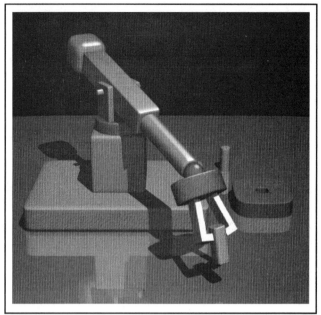

Simulating the operation of machines that aren't even built is a major application of computers in the world of engineering and science. Combine this technology with graphics and you get pictures of things that have never existed! You can find this image on the NASA system **aftnic.gsfc.nasa.gov** in **images/gifs/computer-art/robotarm.gif**

International System of Units

A list of SI units, conversion of non-SI units to SI units, fundamental constants, and elemental unit definitions.

Anonymous FTP:
Address: **ftp.spies.com**
Path: **/Library/Document/si.tbl**

Gopher:
Name: Internet Wiretap
Address: **wiretap.spies.com**
Choose: **Wiretap Online Library**
| **Assorted Documents**
| **International System of Units**

> — Everything we tell you is true.
> — The above sentence is only partially correct.
> — Don't believe everything you read.

The Mind

Explore the mysteries of the mind by taking part in serious discussion of the mind and how it learns, processes information and creates the body's reactions. Experiment with a little transcutaneous electrical neural stimulation or perhaps those of you who need a little break from everything can spend the day in a sensory deprivation tank. Just remember — wherever you go, there you are.

Note: Papers and archives are available by anonymous ftp.

Anonymous FTP:
Address: **asylum.sf.ca.us**
Path: **/pub/mind-l/***

Internet Mailing List:
List Address: **mind-l@asylum.sf.ca.us**
Subscription Address:
mind-l-request@asylum.sf.ca.us

Mini-Journal of Irreproducible Results

The Official Electronic Mini-Organ of the Society for Basic Irreproducible Research. The *Mini-Journal of Irreproducible Results* publishes news about overly stimulating research and ideas.

Listserv Mailing List:
List Address: **mini-air@mitvma.mit.edu**
Subscription Address: **listserv@mitvma.mit.edu**

National Institute of Health Projects

A subdirectory containing descriptions of projects currently being funded by NIH grants, plus instructions on how to apply for such a grant.

Anonymous FTP:
Address: **ftp.uu.net**
Path: **/doc/literary/obi/NIH/***

National Science Foundation Publications

Access the publications of the National Science Foundation, including awards information, letters, program guidelines, and reports for each directorate.

Gopher:
Name: National Science Foundation
Address: **stis.nsf.gov**

NCSA Digital Gallery CD-ROM Science Theater

A collection of mpeg movies and gif files submitted from researchers around the world for inclusion on the Digital Gallery CD-ROM. Available are sections on Earth sciences, fluid dynamics, medical sciences, planetary sciences, and volume visualization.

World Wide Web:
>URL: **http://www.ncsa.uiuc.edu/SDG/**
>**DigitalGallery/DG_science_theater.html**

Origin of the Universe

A document by Stephen Hawking discussing his theory on the origin of the universe.

Anonymous FTP:
>Address: **xcf.berkeley.edu**
>Path: **/pub/misc/hawking.1**

Gopher:
>Name: University of Illinois
>Address: **wx.atmos.uiuc.edu**
>Choose: **Documents**
>| **fun**
>| **hawking.origin**

Do you like the universe? (It's always been one of *our* favorite places.)

If so, read what Steven Hawking has to say about it.

Radiocarbon Gopher

Radiocarbon is the main international journal of record for research articles and datelists related to C-14 and other radioisotopes and techniques used in archaeological, geophysical, oceanographic, and related dating. This site offers related news and announcements, abstracts, datasets, and information about radiocarbon publications and links to other relevant resources.

Gopher:
>Name: Radiocarbon Gopher
>Address: **packrat.aml.arizona.edu**

World Wide Web:
>URL: **http://packrat.aml.arizona/**

Radiocarbon and Radioisotopes Mailing List

A mailing list for researchers and others involved in radiocarbon dating, the use of other radioisotopes in dating, and other scientific dating issues in general.

Listserv Mailing List:
>List Address: **c14-l@listserv.arizona.edu**
>Subscription Address:
>**listserv@listserv.arizona.edu**

Research Methods

You need a certain kind of mind to be an organized and efficient researcher. Here is a list that helps researchers in classification, clustering, phylogeny estimation, and related methods of data analysis to contact other researchers in the same fields. All professions are welcome to the list.

Listserv Mailing List:
>List Address: **class-l@ccvm.sunysb.edu**
>Subscription Address: **listserv@ccvm.sunysb.edu**

Resource Guides to Science

Internet resource guides for agriculture, biological sciences, computing, earth sciences, health sciences, mathematics, and physical sciences.

Anonymous FTP:
>Address: **una.hh.lib.umich.edu**
>Path: **/inetdirsstacks/***

Gopher:
>Name: University of Michigan
>Address: **una.hh.lib.umich.edu**
>Choose: **inetdirstacks**
>| **Guides on the Sciences (UMich)**

Science Beat

Science Beat is a synopsis of story ideas from the National Institute of Standards and Technology. It's published six times a year and contains brief articles on NIST research, programs and services. The publication also includes media contact phone numbers and electronic mail addresses.

Gopher:
>Name: The National Institute of Standards and Technology
>Address: **gopher-server.nist.gov**
>Choose: **NIST News & General Information**
>| **NIST Science Beat (story ideas for journalists)**

A
B
C
D
E
F
G
H
I
J
K
L
M
N
O
P
Q
R
S
T
U
V
W
X
Y
Z

Science Fraud

A mailing list dedicated to the discussion of fraud in science, including current and recent events, and historic accounts of fraudulent science. Also available is a database on fraud in science with over 4,000 references.

Listserv Mailing List:
List Address: **scifraud@uacsc2.albany.edu**
Subscription Address: **listserv@uacsc2.albany.edu**

Science Magazines

Sample articles and subscription information for science-related magazines.

Gopher:
Name: The Electronic Newsstand
Address: **gopher.internet.com**
Port: **2100**
Choose: **Titles Arranged by Subject**
| **Science - Ecology, Gardening, General**

Science and Technology Information System

STIS offers discussion, help, and a number of interesting topics for people interested in science and technology.

Telnet:
Address: **stis.nsf.gov**
Login: **public**

Scientific Articles

Contains some interesting online science articles and book reviews, such as a scientific article about forecasting eclipses.

Gopher:
Name: Whole Earth Lectronic Link
Address: **gopher.well.sf.ca.us**
Choose: **Science**

Scientific Ponderings

A collection of science articles covering topics such as perpetual motion, cold nuclear fusion in condensed matter, and quantum information processing in animals.

Anonymous FTP:
Address: **ftp.spies.com**
Path: **/Library/Article/Sci/***

Gopher:
Name: Internet Wiretap
Address: **wiretap.spies.com**
Choose: **Wiretap Online Library**
| **Articles**
| **Science**

Excerpt from the Net...

(from the collection of scientific ponderings on the "Wiretap" gopher)

OBSERVATION OF COLD NUCLEAR FUSION IN CONDENSED MATTER
by S. E. Jones et al

Department of Physics and Chemistry
Brigham Young University -- Utah, USA

March 23, 1989

Fusion of isotopic hydrogen nuclei is the principal means of producing energy in the high-temperature interior of stars. In relatively cold terrestrial conditions, the nuclei are clothed with electrons and approach one another no closer than allowed by the molecular Coulomb barrier...

We have discovered a means of inducing nuclear fusion without the use of either high temperatures or radioactive muons. We will present direct experimental results as well as indirect geological evidence for the occurrence of cold nuclear fusion.

DETECTION OF COLD FUSION NEUTRONS

We have observed deuteron-deuteron fusion at room temperature during low-voltage electrolytic infusion of deuterons into metallic titanium or palladium electrodes...

Scientific Skepticism

A text file containing almost 150K of postings from the Usenet newsgroup **sci.skeptic**, which is devoted to turning the cold light of scientific study onto all kinds of paranormal subjects, such as ESP and UFOs, among others.

Anonymous FTP:
Address: **ftp.hmc.edu**
Path: **/pub/science/sci.answers/.mirror.OLD/skeptic-faq**

The Scientist

Online version of current issues of *The Scientist*, a biweekly tabloid newspaper for science professionals.

Anonymous FTP:
Address: **ds.internic.net**
Path: **/pub/the-scientist/***

Gopher:
Name: The Jackson Laboratory
Address: **hobbes.jax.org**
Choose: **Journals**
 | **The Scientist - Newsletter**

Name: University of Florida
Address: **gaia.sci-ed.fit.edu**
Choose: **Subject Area Resources**
 | **Science**
 | **The Scientist - Newsletter**

WAIS:
Database: **the-scientist**

Scientist's Workbench

An X Window-based application designed to bring together a set of tools for enhancing the development, testing, and execution of scientific codes.

Anonymous FTP:
Address: **info.tc.cornell.edu**
Path: **/pub/swb/***

Gopher:
Name: Cornell University
Address: **gopher.tc.cornell.edu**
Choose: **Anonymous FTP**
 | **Scientist's Workbench**

The Internet is more fun than a barrel of cliches.

Virtual School of Natural Sciences

A Globewide Network Academy school focusing on collaboration with real colleges and educational institutions for natural sciences, with an emphasis on the development of web and moo based online courses. Plans to offer courses on biocomputing, structural biology, quantum mechanics in simple matrix form, and more.

World Wide Web:
URL: **http://uu-gna.mit.edu:8001/uu-gna/schools/vsns/index.html**

If Herman Melville had written this book, you would be reading a metaphor right now.

Women in Science Hypercard Project

A color hypercard project commemorating more than 35 women in the field of science. This project was compiled and designed by seventh and eighth grade students.

See also: History, People, Technology

Anonymous FTP:
Address: **vela.acs.oakland.edu**
Path: **/pub/eabyrnes/wis***

SCIENCE FICTION

Alien III Script

A script for a new Alien movie written by sci-fi novelist William Gibson. Apparently, the script won't be produced, but it's a good read.

World Wide Web:
URL: **http://www.umd.umich.edu/~nhughes/cyber/gibson/alien3.html**

A B C D E F G H I J K L M N O P Q R S T U V W X Y Z

Ansible Newsletter

Get the latest buzz on the Sci-Fi scene. *Ansible*, a Hugo award-winning newsletter, will give you news and gossip about your favorite authors, dates for conferences and conventions, book reviews and releases, as well as the occasional obituary. *Ansible* is archived at the web site, but is also available by electronic subscription.

See also: Zines

Internet Mailing List:
    List Address: **ansible@dcs.gla.ac.uk**
    Subscription Address:
        ansible-request@dcs.gla.ac.uk

World Wide Web:
    URL: **http://www.lysator.liu.se/sf_archive/**
        sf-texts/Ansible/

Who Wrote What?

It's late at night. You get a mysterious phone call. A stranger with an Armenian accent makes you an astounding offer: If you can tell him, within five minutes, who wrote *The Package in Hyperspace*, he will send you a million dollars plus an autographed copy of *The Internet Complete Reference*. No problem. Simply point your browser at the **Bibliographies of Science Fiction** web site and within a few minutes you will have your answer, a million dollars, and a copy of the best Internet book ever written. (By the way, the answer is "Janet Asimov.")

Bibliographies of Science Fiction

You no longer have to wonder if you have read everything written by your favorite science fiction or fantasy author. This list of bibliographies arranged alphabetically by author will give you a brief biography of the writer, a list of pseudonyms, listings of books and stories, and other related information, such as movie adaptations or collaborations.

See also: Literature: Authors, Publishing

World Wide Web:
    URL: **ftp://gandalf.rutgers.edu/pub/sfl/**
        sf-resource.guide.html#Bibliographies

    URL: **http://www.lysator.liu.se/sf_archive/**
        sub/jwenn.html

> ## There are only two things worth remembering in life (both of which I forget).

Bruce Sterling

The author of several science fiction novels, Sterling delves into the world of cyberpunk, computers, and virtual communities. Online resources include *The Hacker Crackdown* — his nonfiction work on computer corruption, magazine articles, bibliography, and speeches.

See also: Cyberpunk

World Wide Web:
    URL: **http://riceinfo.rice.edu/projects/RDA/**
        VirtualCity/Sterling/index.ntml

Classic Science Fiction and Fantasy Reviews

Old news is good news. At least in this case. Dani Zweig has amassed a large collection of reviews of science fiction and fantasy books that have been in circulation for quite a while. Read his analysis of such authors as Lovecraft, Burroughs, Wyndham, Zelazny, and LeGuin.

See also: Literature: Collections

World Wide Web:
    URL: **http://www.lysator.liu.se/sf_archive/sub/**
        belated.html

Complete Bibliographies of Major Authors

A subdirectory of text files, each of which contains the complete bibliography of a major science fiction writer. Each file name is the name of the author in question.

Anonymous FTP:
    Address: **ftp.uu.net**
    Path: **/doc/literary/obi/Misc/Books/***

Conan the Barbarian

What would life be like if everyone was like Conan the Barbarian? Sure, men would be fun to look at but nobody would ever get any work done. This doesn't stop the Conan fandom, though, which is alive and well in this newsgroup. Discuss the movies, books and other genres in which Conan appears.

Usenet:
    Newsgroup: **alt.fantasy.conan**

```
Make new friends on
Internet Relay Chat (IRC).
```

Dragons and Dragonlance Fantasy

Do you ever wish that fantasy were actually true to life? Like dragons. Wouldn't it be neat to go fight a dragon and risk being made into a human shishkabob for all the gold and jewels that can be found in the dragon's lair? That would be a much more exciting way to make a living than being a parking attendant. Experience the fantasy of dragons and Dragonlance fantasy through Usenet.

Usenet:
    Newsgroup: **alt.fan.dragonlance**
    Newsgroup: **alt.fan.dragons**

Dune Home Page

Sounds from the movie *Dune*, pictures, cover art from the *Dune* novels, articles, documents, FAQs, a newsgroup, and more about the series of science fiction books by Frank Herbert.

World Wide Web:
    URL: **http://www.princeton.edu/~cgilmore/
    dune/dune.html**

Fandom

Fans from all over the world live, eat, and breathe science fiction. They travel in packs, eager to suck the nectar out of the sci-fi flower. If you have a taste for something out of the ordinary, join the crowd, go to cons, and be a groupie.

Usenet:
    Newsgroup: **alt.fandom.cons**
    Newsgroup: **rec.arts.sf.fandom**

Fans of Science Fiction Writers

Lose yourself in the fantasy worlds that come pouring out of the minds of great science fiction writers. Anne McCaffrey, Piers Anthony, and Terry Pratchett are creators who have a strong following.

Usenet:
    Newsgroup: **alt.fan.pern**
    Newsgroup: **alt.fan.piers-anthony**
    Newsgroup: **alt.fan.pratchett**

Fantastic Fantasies

An interesting collection of fantasy pictures, some in gif and some in jpeg formats, including art based on *Dungeons and Dragons*, Lovecraft, Tolkien, *Elfquest*, and others.

See also: Computers: Graphics

Anonymous FTP:
    Address: **ftp.sunet.se**
    Path: **/pub/pictures/fantasy/***

Fantasy, Science Fiction, Horror Calendar

A calendar of upcoming events in the U.S. in the worlds of science fiction, fantasy, and horror. Updated regularly.

Gopher:
    Name: Panix Public Access Unix
    Address: **gopher.panix.com**
    Choose: **Fantasy, SF, and Horror Calendar**

Furry Stuff

Being a human is really overrated. You don't have much license to romp and play, and most people frown upon licking yourself at the table after a satisfying meal. At least there is a way to redirect your energy. Furry fans will rejoice to see this list of artists, publishers, and publications that cover anthropomorphic or "furry" art.

Anonymous FTP:
    Address: **ftp.halcyon.com**
    Path: **/local/phaedrus/furrylist/***

Highly Imaginative Technologies

There's nothing wrong with suspending reality. It's certainly a great way of brainstorming. Science fiction writers and movie makers get paid to sit around all day and invent cool things, and they don't even have to worry about laws of physics or people being blown up. Get together with other techies and talk about technology that can or can't be implemented in the future. Any advanced technology, such as interactive video, artificial reality, and speech-commanded devices, is a fair topic for discussion.

See also: Technology

Listserv Mailing List:
    List Address: **hit@ufrj.bitnet**
    Subscription Address: **listserv@ufrj.bitnet**

A B C D E F G H I J K L M N O P Q R S T U V W X Y Z

**Learn HTML and
create your own web page
(see Internet: Resources).**

Hugo Awards of 1990

A subdirectory containing text files that list the nominees
and winners of the 1990 Hugo Awards.

Anonymous FTP:
    Address: **ftp.uu.net**
    Path: **/doc/literary/obi/Hugo.Awards/***

Infinity City

A series of science fiction books about Infinity City, an
incredible world within a black hole. These books were
written by Douglas K. Bell, who will mail you an electronic
copy free of charge. The first books in the series are *Van
Gogh in Space*, *Jason the Rescuer*, and *Search for Katz*,
but there is a lot more. For information, send mail to
Doug at the address below.

Mail:
    Address: **dougbell@netcom.com**

Mystery Science Theater 3000

There are worse things in life than being consigned
to review bad sci-fi for your entire life. Experience the
hilarity of *Mystery Science Theater 3000* with other fans.

Internet Mailing List:
    List Address: **soln@gynko.circ.upenn.edu**
    Subscription Address:
      soln-request@gynko.circ.upenn.edu

    List Address: **mst3k@gynko.circ.upenn.edu**
    Subscription Address:
      mst3k-request@gynko.circ.upenn.edu

Usenet:
    Newsgroup: **alt.tv.mst3k**

Red Dwarf

Red Dwarf is a British science fiction comedy series. The
premise of the show is described by an opening used on
the first series: "This is an S.O.S. distress call from the
mining ship Red Dwarf. The crew are dead, killed by a
radiation leak. The only survivors are Dave Lister, who
was in suspended animation during the disaster, and his
pregnant cat, who was safely sealed in the hold. Revived
three million years later, Lister's only companions are a
life form who evolved from his cat, and Arnold Rimmer,
a hologram simulation of one of the dead crew."

Listserv Mailing List:
    List Address: **reddwarf@uel.ac.uk**
    Subscription Address: **listserv@uel.ac.uk**

Usenet:
    Newsgroup: **alt.tv.red-dwarf**

World Wide Web:
    URL: **http://http2.brunel.ac.uk:8080/**

Sci-Fi Books

Popularity rating for science fiction books, followed by a
large bibliography arranged by author.

Anonymous FTP:
    Address: **ftp.spies.com**
    Path: **/Library/Media/Sci-Fi/books.sf**

Gopher:
    Name: Internet Wiretap
    Address: **wiretap.spies.com**
    Choose: **Wiretap Online Library**
     I Mass Media
     I Science Fiction and Fantasy
     I Science Fiction Books (poll & biblio)

Sci-Fi Lovers

Discussions of any science fiction or fantasy-related
subjects, ranging from stories, reviews and conventions,
to movies and television.

Anonymous FTP:
    Address: **gandalf.rutgers.edu**
    Path: **/pub/sfl/***

Internet Mailing List:
    List Address: **sf-lovers@rutgers.edu**
    Subscription Address:
      sf-lovers-request@rutgers.edu

Science and Science Fiction

Stretch your mind by pushing your imagination to the limit. How real is the science in science fiction? A wide variety of topics are covered, such as the possibility of forcefields, transcendental engineering, and Hawking radiation. Invent your own theories or pick apart someone else's.

Usenet:
Newsgroup: **rec.arts.sf.science**

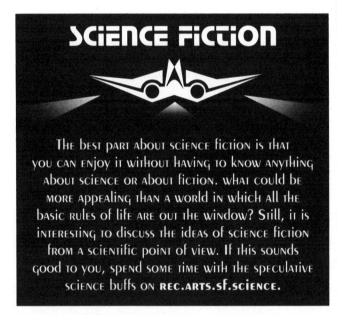

The best part about science fiction is that you can enjoy it without having to know anything about science or about fiction. What could be more appealing than a world in which all the basic rules of life are out the window? Still, it is interesting to discuss the ideas of science fiction from a scientific point of view. If this sounds good to you, spend some time with the speculative science buffs on **REC.ARTS.SF.SCIENCE.**

Science Fiction and Fantasy

Articles, guides, FAQs, reading lists, and other documents regarding science fiction, fantasy, and cyberpunk. Examples include "The Bad Guide to *Star Wars*," the *Blade Runner* FAQ, and "The Isaac Asimov Fiction Timeline."

Anonymous FTP:
Address: **ftp.spies.com**
Path: **/Library/Media/Sci-Fi/***

Gopher:
Name: EUnet in Slovakia
Address: **gopher.eunet.sk**
Choose: **Archive of EUnet Slovakia | Science Fiction Archive**

Name: Internet Wiretap
Address: **wiretap.spies.com**
Choose: **Wiretap Online Library | Mass Media | Science Fiction and Fantasy**

Science fiction fanatics: keep up on what's happening by reading **rec.arts.sf.announce.**

Science Fiction and Fantasy Archive

Science fiction and fantasy are the perfect things to read when you don't want to study for a test or work on something around the house. Cozy up to the computer and read these science fiction and fantasy archives, which will not only give you some great stories, but will also show you reviews of books, movies, and point you toward newsletters and zines that relate to the genre.

See also: Books, Literature

World Wide Web:
URL: **http://www.lysator.liu.se:7500/sf_archive/ sf_main.html**

Science Fiction Announcements

Attention science fiction buffs! Find out what's up and coming in sci-fi land. This moderated group will provide you with all the information you need on new movies, books, television shows, anything that is new in science fiction.

Usenet:
Newsgroup: **rec.arts.sf.announce**

Science Fiction Forum

Science fiction isn't a hobby: it's a lifestyle. Are you one of those people whose walls and cabinets (and floors) are covered with sci-fi books, magazines, tapes and memorabilia? Scoot all of it out of the way so you can get to the computer and find your sci-fi soulmates. Anything science fiction goes.

Usenet:
Newsgroup: **rec.arts.sf.misc**

Science Fiction Marketplace

Are you looking to trade your extra copy of the *Pegasus* episode of *Battlestar Galactica* for a signed copy of a *Friday* print by Whelan? Shop at the science fiction flea market — rare commodities for rare people. Buy, sell, or trade. Display your merchandise in this shoplifter-free environment.

Usenet:
Newsgroup: **rec.arts.sf.marketplace**

A B C D E F G H I J K L M N O P Q R S T U V W X Y Z

Ignoring this hint may be hazardous to your health.

Science Fiction Movies

You just saw the best movie ever and you have to tell someone or you'll explode. You can either run screaming through the parking lot of the movie theater and risk being arrested for disturbing the peace, or you can tell the sci-fi movie fans on the Internet.

Usenet:
    Newsgroup: **rec.arts.sf.movies**

Science Fiction Resource Guide

"More information on science fiction than any one person can comfortably keep track of." It has everything under the sun about science fiction, including details on authors, awards, bibliographies, bookstores, fan clubs, movies, publishers, role-playing games, television, newsgroups, and zines, as well as archives, reviews and criticism, fiction writing, and more, all arranged as hypertext links. This page received a Best of the Net Award.

World Wide Web:
    URL: **ftp://gandalf.rutgers.edu/pub/sfl/ sf-resource.guide.html**

Science Fiction Reviews

Zip up your spacesuit, fire all thrusters and launch into a review of the best and worst of science fiction. Don't hesitate to tell how you feel, because no one else does. Sometimes sublime, but more often not, reviews are always revealing and informative.

Usenet:
    Newsgroup: **rec.arts.sf.reviews**

Science Fiction Television

It's natural to feel like you can never get enough science fiction. Your mouth goes dry, your hands press continually on the remote control even though you know it will not make science fiction magically appear before you. You need a source or you are going to lose your mind. When you can't find it on the tube, seek your sci-fi television support group and get a quick fix.

Usenet:
    Newsgroup: **rec.arts.sf.tv**

Need a pick-me-up? Try a new Usenet group.

Excerpt from the Net...

Newsgroup: rec.arts.sf.written
Subject: Secret Messages in DNA

> There is quite a bit of "junk" DNA lying around a genome.
> Theoretically, there shouldn't be any reason for this DNA not to hide
> a message (mind you, you'd have to be pretty clever in finding the
> key to decode those base pair sequences). And a lot of this is
> supercoiled and packaged by histone and non-histone proteins that
> prevent DNA degradation, so if the message lay in introns in that
> "protected" section, it could remain largely unevolved/altered.

Well, the issue is not really how the DNA is packaged. The problem is
that there would be a steady accumulation of errors occurring during
the replication or repair of DNA. Not to mention more dramatic errors
caused by chromosomal rearrangements, unequal crossing over, etc. etc.
So if the message was going to last a long time, you would need to
incorporate some pretty complex error correction.

Science Fiction TV Series Guides

This server contains a number of guides to sci-fi shows such as *Star Trek*, *Dr. Who*, and *Blakes' 7*. There are extensive guides which include up-to-date episode summaries, cast lists, and trivia, and there are short form guides which give information on little known science fiction shows no longer in production.

World Wide Web:
URL: **http://www.ee.survey.ac.uk/Personal/sf.html**

Science Fiction Writing

Allow yourself to linger on the words, your eyes playing gently back and forth across the pages of your latest sci-fi novel. There is something tangible about a book which you just can't get from television or movies. Discuss your favorite book, hear about someone else's. Find out what's new and what is hopelessly out of print.

Usenet:
Newsgroup: **rec.arts.sf.written**

Speculative Fiction Clearing House

When you get tired of reality, or just want to explore a new one, check out this huge archive of science fiction and fantasy. Find links to other sci-fi archives, databases of information about authors and bibliographies, a list of science fiction awards as well as the winners of the awards. There are also links to contests, conferences, publishers, writing resources and zines.

World Wide Web:
URL: **http://thule.mt.cs.cmu.edu:8001/
sf-clearing-house/**

Star Wars

What would happen if... ? Speculation abounds regarding the Star Wars universe. Star Wars fans reinvent the movies daily, wondering what would happen if certain characters had done things differently. Discover inconsistencies you may have missed in the movies and learn what has happened to everyone involved, from the big screen to the cutting room floor.

Usenet:
Newsgroup: **rec.arts.sf.starwars**

Star Wars Archive

Everything you could want to know about the *Star Wars* movies including stories, pictures, magazines, interviews, scripts for *Star Wars*, *The Empire Strikes Back* and *Return of the Jedi*, music lists, book guides, character assessments, slide shows, FAQs, information about the actors, and much more.

See also: Movies

Anonymous FTP:
Address: **wpi.wpi.edu**
Path: **/starwars/***

World Wide Web:
URL: **http://stwing.resnet.upenn.edu:8001/
~jruspini/starwars.html**

Remember Star Wars?

It was a series of science fiction movies a long time ago, when you were young. Well, if you want to be obsessively nostalgic, there is an Internet archive waiting for you.

Transformations

It's really embarrassing and inconvenient when you have just dashed to the corner store to get a pack of gum only to be hit by the unmistakable feeling that you are turning into a werewolf. And it really happens. Don't be caught unawares. Learn what people do in books when this occurs so you will know the best way to handle it when it happens to you. This booklist is lengthy and covers just about any type of unnatural transformation, so you can always be prepared for the worst.

Anonymous FTP:
Address: **ftp.halcyon.com**
Path: **/local/phaedrus/translist/***

A B C D E F G H I J K L M N O P Q R **S** T U V W X Y Z

Xanth Series

Piers Anthony can certainly turn out the books. Fans of his *Xanth* series have loyally compiled a huge amount of information on the series' titles, characters and trivia about the *Xanth* world. There is also fan club information, as well as pictures of Anthony's book covers, the author and his dog.

See also: Books, Literature: Authors, Literature: Collections

World Wide Web:
 URL: **http://www.cs.indiana.edu/hyplan/ awooldri/Xanth.html**

SECRET STUFF

2600

A channel dedicated to the 2600 magazine, *Hacker Quarterly*. There are monthly meetings, usually on the 26th of the month, and subjects include phreaking, hacking, cellular phones, scanners, hardware, credit cards, and much more secret stuff.

Internet Relay Chat:
 Channel: **#2600**
 Channel: **#2600talk**

Easter Eggs

Instructions on how to view secret screens (easter eggs) in many PC and Macintosh software products.

Anonymous FTP:
 Address: **ftp.spies.com**
 Path: **/Library/Techdoc/Micro/secret.scr**

Gopher:
 Name: Internet Wiretap
 Address: **wiretap.spies.com**
 Choose: **Wiretap Online Library**
  | **Technical Information**
  | **PCs and Macintoshes**
  | **Secret Screen Cheat Sheet**

Easter Eggs

𝕺ne of the most important legends of Western culture is the story of how Jesus was put to death by the Romans and how, a short time later, was resurrected, symbolizing God's devotion to mankind and showing us that the devout and the faithful will themselves be resurrected at the appropriate time.

Today, these occurrences are remembered during the various Easter observances around the world, one of the most notable being the insertion of secret actions within important computer programs. These so-called "Easter Eggs" are found in a number of PC and Macintosh programs and are documented in the **Wiretap Online Library**. So, if you are feeling especially devotional one day, take a moment to find out about these Easter Eggs and demonstrate them for yourself. After all, it is all too easy to concentrate exclusively on work and other secular matters, and a few moments spent in a spiritual activity would be good for just about anybody.

Macintosh Secret Tricks List

Details of amusing and interesting hidden screens in Macintosh programs.

Anonymous FTP:
 Address: **ftp.spies.com**
 Path: **/Library/Techdoc/Micro/macintos.sec**

Gopher:
 Name: Internet Wiretap
 Address: **wiretap.spies.com**
 Choose: **Wiretap Online Library**
  | **Technical Information**
  | **PCs and Macintoshes**
  | **Macintosh Secret Tricks List**

Are you a Mac person? Take a look at the Macintosh Secret Tricks List and amaze your friends.

Phreaking

Discussion about telephones, exchanges, toll fraud, kodez, signaling, and much more to do with phones and phreaking. Some of the world's top phreakers, a few of whom have spent time behind bars and are known by the FBI for their phreaking and hacking activities, make an appearance every so often.

See also: Telephones

Internet Relay Chat:
Channel: **#phreak**

Questionables

Information and material of a questionable nature, including articles on ATM secret codes, garage door opener plans, pyrotechnics, police scanner codes, and pay-TV decoder plans.

Anonymous FTP:
Address: **ftp.spies.com**
Path: **/Library/Untech/***

Gopher:
Name: Internet Wiretap
Address: **wiretap.spies.com**
Choose: **Wiretap Online Library**
 | Questionables

Do not look in the *Questionables* archive. And once you get there, do not read anything. And once you read something, do not do what it says. And, most important, do not tell people that you learned about it here.

Warez

Discussion of where and how to obtain the latest cracked and pirated software, much of it available through hidden sites on the Internet. Some of the channels are often by invitation only, so you will require contacts to get inside.

See also: Software

Internet Relay Chat:
Channel: **#warez**
Channel: **#warez1**
Channel: **#warez2**
Channel: **#warez3**
Channel: **#warez4**
Channel: **#warez5**
Channel: **#warez6**
Channel: **#warez7**

SEX

Adult Movies

Step aside, Siskel and Ebert. Meet the pros: people who really know their films intimately. Learn what movies are hot and what movies are not worth warming the television up for. Who are the superstars of sexy films and what movies actually have plots? Bone up on your erotic movie trivia.

Usenet:
Newsgroup: **alt.sex.movies**

Adult Movies

Lights, camera, and lots and lots of action. If you are at all visually inclined, you may want to look in on the **alt.sex.movies** discussion group and find out what the cognoscenti think about the latest adult films. Our favorite is *Beyond the Internet Golden Directory, Part III.*

> A sure-fire way to make all your dreams come true is to sleep with this book under your pillow.

Bondage

All tied up with no place to go? You're in the right place. If having the most toys means having the most fun, then this is the zenith of extracurricular sexual activity. Read stories, share experiences, and discuss techniques and safety tips. If you love something, set it free; if it comes back to you, tie it up again.

Usenet:
    Newsgroup: **alt.personals.bondage**
    Newsgroup: **alt.sex.bondage**

Bondage Talk

Come here for idle chatter about whips, chains, handcuffs, bondage, and sado-masochism.

Internet Relay Chat:
    Channel: **#bdsm**
    Channel: **#bondage**

Clothespins as Toys

Just because you are an adult doesn't mean you shouldn't get to play with toys. In fact, you can even make your own toys out of common household items like clothespins. Read up on all the fun you can have with these simple little inventions.

Gopher:
    Name: Wiretap
    Address: **wiretap.spies.com**
    Choose: **Wiretap Online Library**
        | **Articles**
        | **Sex**
        | **On Clothespins as Toys**

Cross-Dressing Chat

Why is it normal for a woman to dress like a man, but bizarre for a man to don lace and satin? Maybe someone on the **#crossdres** IRC channel will have the answer (or at least a reaction).

Internet Relay Chat:
    Channel: **#crossdres**

Diaper Fetish

Diaper fetish discussions.

Usenet:
    Newsgroup: **alt.sex.fetish.diapers**

Discussion of Sex Stories

Discussion of stories of sexual encounters in **alt.sex.stories**.

Usenet:
    Newsgroup: **alt.sex.stories.d**

Exhibitionism

If you've got it, flaunt it. Or even if you don't have it, flaunt it. Exhibitionism is not for the faint of heart. Be gutsy, be bold. Hear stories of the exploits of the daring. Bring your own raincoat.

Usenet:
    Newsgroup: **alt.sex.exhibitionism**

Fat Fetish

Do you find the '90s body image preposterous? Don't continue to mourn the lost days when Rubenesque women were the norm. Revel in the rich, full quality of people who are fat and proud of it.

Usenet:
    Newsgroup: **alt.sex.fat**
    Newsgroup: **alt.sex.fetish.fa**

> You are what you think.

Foot Fetish

Discussions all about foot fetishes. You don't have to be a shoe salesman to enjoy yourself here.

Usenet:
Newsgroup: **alt.sex.fetish.feet**

Hair Fetish

Montel Williams and Jean-Luc Picard hold no appeal for you. If it's not hairy, it's not interesting. Don't think you're alone in your fantasies about Cousin It.

Usenet:
Newsgroup: **alt.sex.fetish.hair**

How to Use a Condom

Take advantage of the expertise offered in this lengthy how-to paper.

See also: Health, Sexuality, X-Rated Resources

World Wide Web:
URL: **gopher://gopher.uiuc.edu/00/UI/CSF/ health/heainfo/sex/birthcon/condom**

Intergenerational Relationships

Relationships are tricky enough when you have more than one person involved. There are special considerations when there is a significant age difference between partners and this group was created as a space to talk about problems, stories and theories relating to intergenerational relationships.

Usenet:
Newsgroup: **alt.sex.intergen**

Masturbation

Discussion of all topics concerning masturbation.

Usenet:
Newsgroup: **alt.sex.masturbation**

Masturbation Index

Read up on masturbation facts, hints, and techniques at this World Wide Web site.

See also: Sexuality, X-Rated Resources

World Wide Web:
URL: **http://www.psych.nwu.edu/biancaTroll/ vibrations/index.html**

Guys: The best way to impress a date is to invite her over and show her that you have a complete st of Harley,s books.

Oriental Fetish

Worship the exotic. Experience the mystery of the Far East and learn the secrets of Oriental sexuality.

Usenet:
Newsgroup: **alt.sex.fetish.orientals**

Pantyhose and Stockings

Soft, sleek, sensual... and more. Talk to the people who really appreciate what the well-dressed leg is wearing this season. Share your opinions and read provocative stories.

Anonymous FTP:
Address: **alycia.andrew.cmu.edu**
Path: **/pub/graphics/over_age_18_only/hosiery/***

Usenet:
Newsgroup: **alt.pantyhose**

There are only two things worth remembering in life (both of which I forget).

A B C D E F G H I J K L M N O P Q R S T U V W X Y Z

Pick-Up Lines

Are you running out of lines and still haven't found Ms. Right? Here's a batch that may help (but we doubt it). Even if you don't win her heart, at least she will know you have a sense of humor.

See also: Humor, X-Rated Resources

World Wide Web:
URL: **http://cad.ucla.edu/repository/library/ Cadlab/pickups**

Playboy

A mailing list and information on *Playboy* magazine, products, and yes, the Playmates. (The bad news is that there are no pictures here.)

Anonymous FTP:
Address: **ftp.css.itd.umich.edu**
Path: **/users/lovesexy/pei/***

Internet Mailing List:
List Address: **playboy@umich.edu**
Subscription Address:
playboy-request@umich.edu

Usenet:
Newsgroup: **alt.mag.playboy**

NEED TO CONVINCE YOUR COMPANY THAT THE INTERNET IS CRUCIAL TO YOUR ECONOMIC FUTURE? JUST SHOW THEM HOW EASY IT IS TO ACCESS THE VITAL STATISTICS FOR PLAYBOY CENTERFOLDS.

Playboy Centerfolds

Names and vital statistics for U.S.-edition *Playboy* centerfolds and playmates.

Anonymous FTP:
Address: **ftp.spies.com**
Path: **/Library/Article/Sex/playboy.l***

Gopher:
Name: Internet Wiretap
Address: **wiretap.spies.com**
Choose: **Wiretap Online Library**
| **Articles**
| **Sex**
| **Playboy Centerfolds**

Polyamory

An article describing this lifestyle, in which multiple intimate relationships are pursued simultaneously.

Anonymous FTP:
Address: **ftp.spies.com**
Path: **/Library/Article/Sex/polyamor.txt**

Gopher:
Name: Internet Wiretap
Address: **wiretap.spies.com**
Choose: **Wiretap Online Library**
| **Articles**
| **Sex**
| **Polyamory**

Pornographic Pictures

A large collection of X-rated photos and pictures, divided by subject area. This is one of the few public sites on the Internet that offers such a collection of X-rated pictures. Be warned, though: there is a daily downloading limit that prevents you from downloading huge numbers of pictures.

World Wide Web:
URL: **http://olt.et.tudelft.nl/fun/pictures/ porno.html**

Prostitute Prices

Detailed prostitute prices for many cities around the world.

Anonymous FTP:
Address: **ftp.spies.com**
Path: **/Library/Article/Sex/whore.pr**

Gopher:
Name: Internet Wiretap
Address: **wiretap.spies.com**
Choose: **Wiretap Online Library**
| **Articles**
| **Sex**
| **Whore Prices**

Purity Tests

Purity tests have long been a staple of Usenet humor groups. These tests consist of many sexually oriented questions designed to help you find out just how "pure" you are. Hint: The best such test is the one with 400 questions.

Anonymous FTP:
Address: **ftp.funet.fi**
Path: **/pub/doc/fun/tests/purity***

Address: **ftp.spies.com**
Path: **/Library/Article/Sex/purity***

Address: **quartz.rutgers.edu**
Path: **/pub/purity/***

Archie:
Pattern: **purity**

Gopher:
Name: Internet Wiretap
Address: **wiretap.spies.com**
Choose: **Wiretap Online Library**
  | Articles | Sex
  | The 400 Question Purity Test

World Wide Web:
URL: **http://www.circus.com/~omni/purity.html**

Excerpt from the Net...

(from the Pick-Up Lines web site)

I heard this one at a yuppie night club:

  "So... are you the one who is going to carve my heart out at midnight?"

It was appropriate because the female to whom this comment was directed considers herself a ritualistic priestess.

  "What do you like for breakfast?"

  "Say, didn't we go to different schools together?"

The best pickup line I've heard recently was something a friend of mine heard at the bar where he works. He told a girl that he would like to get her phone number. Came her casual reply:

  "Oh, you can just read it off of my phone in the morning."

The best pickup line I witnessed was a friend of mine who walked up to a young lady in a club and asked "Are you ready to go home now?".
They left together.

  "Hi, the voices in my head told me to come over and talk to you."

  "Can I buy you a drink, or do you just want the money?"

Safe Sex

We've all heard the stories, the advice, the lectures, the arguments, excuses and rumors. Safe sex is the buzz phrase for the next decade, so acquire good habits — like brushing your teeth before bed or combing your hair before you go to work. Learn the do's and don't's, the in's and out's and all the in-betweens of sexual safety. And if you still want to take risks, you can always jump out of an airplane.

See also: Sexuality, X-Rated Resources

World Wide Web:
> URL: **http://cornelius.ucsf.edu/~troyer/ safesex.html**
> URL: **http://www.cs.cmu.edu:8001/afs/ cs.cmu.edu/user/scotts/bulgaria**

Sex, Censorship, and the Internet

Normal is boring. Don't follow the rules, make your own. Take advantage of the Internet as a marvelous place to be free in your speech. Read about censorship and the Internet and how some people want to put a stranglehold on your electronic freedom.

World Wide Web:
> URL: **http://www.eff.org/CAF/cafuiuc.html**

Sex Experts

You're in the heat of the moment and a problem arises. What do you do? There's no time to write a letter to Dear Abby. Admittedly, this is not going to happen often, but if you want answers or information from sex experts, they are available with a few keystrokes. Don't you wish everything was this easy?

Usenet:
> Newsgroup: **alt.sex.wizards**

Sex Questions and Answers

All your wildest questions answered, including a special list of FAQs for sex wizards. Includes sex terms and acronyms, purity test guides, and truly much more.

Anonymous FTP:
> Address: **rtfm.mit.edu**
> Path: **/pub/usenet/news.answers/alt-sex/***

> ## The Internet is low in cholesterol.

Sex-Related Articles

Lots of interesting articles, purity tests, FAQs, *Playboy* centerfold lists, strip joint reviews, smurfs' code, prostitute pricing, and other valuable information. Whether you need to check the price of a prostitute in Halifax, Canada, or just read a review of your favorite strip joint, this is the place to be.

Anonymous FTP:
> Address: **ftp.spies.com**
> Path: **/Library/Article/Sex/***

Gopher:
> Name: Internet Wiretap
> Address: **wiretap.spies.com**
> Choose: **Wiretap Online Library**
> | Articles
> | Sex

Sex and Humor

Yes, it's true, sex is funny (if you do it right). For a nice collection of instantly-available sex-related humor, try the *Quartz* Gopher and archive. Just the place to look for interesting stories before you go to a family reunion.

Sex-Related Humor

Humor about sex, including bedroom golf, pick-up lines, sex colors, literary works and a chemical analysis of women.

Anonymous FTP:
> Address: **quartz.rutgers.edu**
> Path: **/pub/humor/Sex/***

Gopher:
> Name: Rutgers University
> Address: **quartz.rutgers.edu**
> Choose: **Humor**
> | Sex

Sex Sounds

Check out this newsgroup for some interesting sound-bytes. Post your own, too! Sounds come through here in **.wav** and other formats for most popular machines and software.

Usenet:
> Newsgroup: **alt.sex.sounds**

Sex Talk

What's the weirdest place you have ever had sex? Care to share? Even if you don't, there are hordes of people who do. Not only will they tell you about the weirdest place, but also about the weirdest accident they've ever had during sex, how many times they had sex, and what was going on around them before, during, and after. Be informed as you are entertained. Read about birth control, STDs, virginity (or lack of), and other topics of a sexual nature.

Usenet:
> Newsgroup: **alt.sex**

Sex Wanted

Forget love, forget romance. If you're looking to cut to the chase, then cut in here. Don't bother being coy or shy, state what you want and let the good times roll.

Usenet:
> Newsgroup: **alt.sex.wanted**

Sexual Identity and Gender Glossary

As times change, the language changes, and what was an acceptable label a few years ago is a serious faux pas today. Learn the difference between transgendered, transsexual, and transvestite, and why you shouldn't call a bisexual "confused."

See also: Gay, Lesbian, Bisexual

Anonymous FTP:
> Address: **ftp.spies.com**
> Path: **/Library/Article/Sex/gender.dic**

Excerpt from the Net...

```
Newsgroup: alt.sex
Subject: Is this sexy or what?

> ...it is a decoy.  I also found something in my smoke detector even
> more sinister, a cylindrical metallic case which cannot be opened and
> is covered with warnings and threats with vague references to radio
> activity...

Yes, if you open the secret metallic cylinder, you will find a fascinating substance.  It
may take some work to open the box up, but you should be able to pry it with a
screwdriver.  The substance in the smoke detector -- Hydropolyruthenium -- has some
amazing properties.

This substance was shown to the U.S. government by those almond-eyed aliens without any
hair, but superdeveloped brains and telepathic ability.  By eating enough of this
substance, a transformation takes place in humans.  They begin to lose their hair and
exhibit telepathic abilities.

It is this radio frequency wave which may be used to listen in on folks.  By eating the
substance and gaining those abilities, one can not only listen in to other's thoughts at
will, but shield oneself from others listening in (like the government).

Our government has a secret division of people who have developed this ability and patrol
the streets listening in on people where there aren't "smoke detectors".  These folks are
almost always completely bald and usually wear baseball caps.  Their eyes are larger than
normal.

I'm posting this anonymously for obvious reasons.
```

A
B
C
D
E
F
G
H
I
J
K
L
M
N
O
P
Q
R
S
T
U
V
W
X
Y
Z

Spanking

Have you ever just been sitting around the house and suddenly you think, "Hmm, I think I need a good spanking"? Don't feel alone, we've all had that experience (not really, but you can think that). Gather with others who like to take physical intimacy to another dimension. You'll recognize them: they're the ones who can't sit down.

Usenet:
Newsgroup: **alt.sex.spanking**

Stories

There's nothing like curling up with a provocative story and a hot cup of tea or a little classical music. You won't find tea or music here, but you will never want for a good, sexy story (or a bad one, for that matter). Stories range from mildly erotic mainstream to bold, raunchy kink. There's something for everyone. And if you'd like to hang around afterwards over coffee or a smoke and discuss the literary merit of the writing, check out **alt.sex.stories.d** for discussion.

Usenet:
Newsgroup: **alt.sex.stories**
Newsgroup: **alt.sex.stories.d**

Strip Joint Reviews

Detailed reviews of many American and Canadian strip joints.

Anonymous FTP:
Address: **ftp.spies.com**
Path: **/Library/Article/Sex/strip.rv**

Gopher:
Name: Internet Wiretap
Address: **wiretap.spies.com**
Choose: **Wiretap Online Library**
  | **Articles**
  | **Sex**
  | **Review of Strip Joints**

U.K. BDSM Scene

The home page of the U.K.'s bondage and discipline, dominance and submission, and sadism and masochism scene. Lists club happenings, special events like the Planet Sex Ball, and various marches and workshops. Read reviews and news on political issues. Open to anything on the BDSM topic.

World Wide Web:
URL: **http://www.ccs.neu.edu/USER/pallando/ BDSM/**

Urban Sex Legends

Amusing stories and urban legends with a sexual twist.

Anonymous FTP:
Address: **cathouse.org**
Path: **/pub/cathouse/urban.legends/sex/***

Voyeurism

There's something exciting about forbidden observation, peeking through the slats of the venetian blinds, pressing your ear against the cool, smooth wall, opening the door just a crack and watching. If you are more of a watcher than a doer, or you like doing while watching, post your thoughts, ideas, and stories here.

Usenet:
Newsgroup: **alt.sex.voyeurism**

Watersports

If you are looking for a good place to discuss your skill as a water-skier, go someplace else. For watersports of a more personal nature, like enemas and related fetishes, this is your place.

Usenet:
Newsgroup: **alt.sex.enemas**
Newsgroup: **alt.sex.fetish.watersports**
Newsgroup: **alt.sex.watersports**

SEXUALITY

Abuse and Recovery

Here is a safe place where you will be welcome. Spend some time reading stories of hurt as well as stories of healing. Sexual abuse brings people with sadness and anger together, but sharing and caring can inspire you to comfort and recovery.

Usenet:
Newsgroup: **alt.sexual.abuse.recovery**
Newsgroup: **alt.sexual.abuse.recovery.d**

Amazons International

Amazons of the world unite! *Amazons International* is an electronic digest newsletter for, about, and by Amazon women.

Internet Mailing List:
List Address: **amazons@math.uio.no**
Subscription Address:
  amazons-request@math.uio.no

Cross-Dressing

It's fun to play dress-up, but for some it's not just play: it's a way of life. This digest provides support and discussions, and allows people to share experiences about gender-related issues. Cross-dressing, transvestism, and transsexualism are all appropriate topics for discussion.

Internet Mailing List:
List Address: **cd-forum@valis.biocad.com**
Subscription Address:
  cd-forum-request@valis.biocad.com

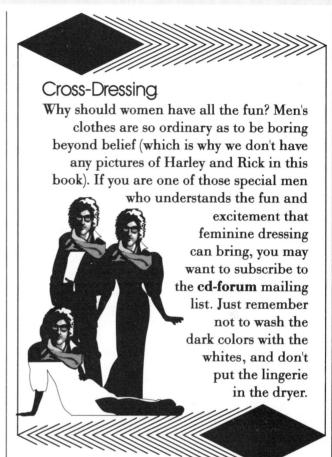

Cross-Dressing

Why should women have all the fun? Men's clothes are so ordinary as to be boring beyond belief (which is why we don't have any pictures of Harley and Rick in this book). If you are one of those special men who understands the fun and excitement that feminine dressing can bring, you may want to subscribe to the **cd-forum** mailing list. Just remember not to wash the dark colors with the whites, and don't put the lingerie in the dryer.

Gender Collection

A gigantic collection containing a wide variety of documents about women, men, gays, straights. There is history, politics and even some plain old fun. This is an excellent source of gender information.

See also: Gay, Lesbian, Bisexual

Gopher:
Name: American Civil Liberties Union
Address: **aclu.org**
Choose: **Society, Law, Politics**
  | A gender miscellany

Kinsey Questions and Answers

Read features from the Kinsey Institute and get real answers from the real pros. Why pick up your information from the gutter when Usenet is only a few keystrokes away?

Usenet:
Newsgroup: **clari.feature.kinsey**

A B C D E F G H I J K L M N O P Q R S T U V W X Y Z

Polyfidelity

The general idea behind marriage is that you say "I do" and then you are supposed to stay with that one special person for the rest of your lifetime. It's simple in theory and tricky in practice. That's why someone, probably a man, came up with the idea of polyfidelity. This unmoderated group is a forum in which all people can discuss the concept of non-monogamous relationships and the various issues that arise in relation to them, such as jealousy, sex, and marriage laws. Learn the real meaning of the phrase "the more, the merrier."

See also: Sex, X-Rated Resources

Internet Mailing List:
    List Address: **triples@hal.com**
    Subscription Address: **triples-request@hal.com**

Sex Addiction Recovery

There are worse things than sex that a person could be addicted to and maybe that makes it even harder to recover from the addiction. This support group offers a way for recovering sex addicts to share feelings and get ideas on the recovery process.

Usenet:
    Newsgroup: **alt.recovery.addiction.sexual**

Sex in the News

Sex isn't just fun and games (mostly, but not completely). When it's time to find out the hard news on the facts of life, turn to these two Clarinet newsgroups for your fix.

Usenet:
    Newsgroup: **clari.news.crime.sex**
    Newsgroup: **clari.news.law.crime.sex**
    Newsgroup: **clari.news.sex**

Sexual Assault and Sex Abuse Recovery

Documents and discussions to help deal with traumatic experiences, recover from sexual assault, and prevent acquaintance and date rape.

Gopher:
    Name: University of Montana Healthline Gopher
    Address: **selway.umt.edu**
    Port: **700**
    Choose: **Sexual Assault Recovery Service (SARS)**

Telnet:
    Address: **selway.umt.edu**
    Login: **health**

Usenet:
    Newsgroup: **alt.sexual.abuse.recovery**

We have heard a rumor that people judge you by the words you use. If you need to remove any lingering ambiguity in your life, a few moments spent with the *Sexual and Gender Identity Glossary* may make all the difference.

Sexual and Gender Identity Glossary

Basic information and a glossary of words and terms used in the gay and bisexual communities.

Anonymous FTP:
    Address: **ftp.spies.com**
    Path: **/Library/Article/Sex/lesbian.dic**

Gopher:
    Name: Internet Wiretap
    Address: **wiretap.spies.com**
    Choose: **Wiretap Online Library**
    | **Articles**
    | **Sex**
    | **Les/Bi/Gay & Transgender Glossary**

Do you really exist? Check Philosophy and be sure.

Excerpt from the Net...

Newsgroup: alt.transgendered
Subject: Mirrors

Who was he? The strange man in the mirror. I never knew. I laughed with him sometimes, cried with him more, yet I never knew who he was. We often stared at each other but he never spoke to me or betrayed his secrets to me.

I've heard that some people believe the mirror holds their soul and provides them a short visitation of it. Yet each time I came to the mirror, I was met by this cold stranger. I was forced by him to search within me to find my soul.

After long searching I finally came to her, sealed behind many walls and buried beneath tears and lies. I looked to her and cried, embracing her after so long. I began tending her wounds and helped her from that place, giving her freedom. She smiled and rose, filling me and embracing me. Now when I meet the mirror, I see her and she smiles tenderly to me. We share our thoughts and secrets. I speak fondly to her and feel her reply.

But I wonder what happened to the man in the mirror and who he was. I wish I could have known him and spoken to him. He is gone forever now. Perhaps he never existed, except as the guardian protecting my soul until she was strong enough to stand alone.

Transgender

Changing your gender is not an easy thing to do. (Now that's an understatement.) Talk with people who think it's okay for you to be who you really are. Here is an informative forum with technical and emotional support for anyone in the transgender process.

Listserv Mailing List:
    List Address: **transgen@brownvm.brown.edu**
    Subscription Address:
        listserv@brownvm.brown.edu

Usenet:
    Newsgroup: **alt.sex.trans**
    Newsgroup: **alt.transgendered**
    Newsgroup: **soc.support.transgendered**

SOCIOLOGY

Alternative Institutions

A mailing list on alternative ways to run conversations, countries, households, markets, and so on.

Internet Mailing List:
    List Address: **altinst@cs.cmu.edu**
    Subscription Address: **altinst-request@cs.cmu.edu**

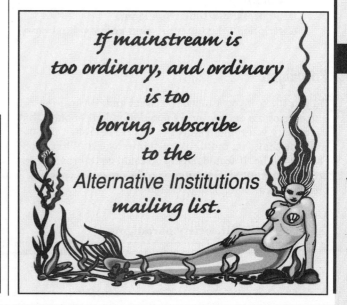
A B C D E F G H I J K L M N O P Q R S T U V W X Y Z

Demography and Population Studies

This page keeps track of leading information facilities of value and significance to researchers in the field of demography. It includes links to census information, social science data services, population studies, Wais databases, and many gopher and web servers of interest to demographers.

World Wide Web:
> URL: **http://coombs.anu.edu.au/ResFacilities/ emographyPage.html**
> URL: **http://www.psc.lsa.umich.edu/**

Family Times Online

Make the Internet a place for the entire family. This electronic magazine has information and links to family-oriented resources around the Net. The Internet isn't just for researchers or computer geeks. It has things for everyone in the family to enjoy.

World Wide Web:
> URL: **http://ssnet.com:8011/times.html**

Men's Issues

Believe it or not, men have their own issues, too. People always say that men are only interested in sex and that's just not true. (Or at least, not entirely accurate.) This mailing list is open to everyone, but is intended to provide an open and understanding atmosphere in which to discuss being male in today's world.

Internet Mailing List:
> List Address: **mail-men@usl.com**
> Subscription Address: **mail-men-request@usl.com**

Paradigms

Do you think if you studied the social and cultural patterns of the entire world's population long enough that eventually you could predict the future? And then if you could do that, you could rule the entire world. What a job that would be. It would mean you could get all the free ice cream you wanted. Get a jump on the crowd by checking out the discussion about paradigms.

Usenet:
> Newsgroup: **alt.society.paradigms**

> ## Zines are cool.

Social Science Gateway

The Social Science Information Gateway at the University of Bristol provides social scientists (hey, an oxymoron) with a centralized means of accessing relevant information sources over the networks. Resources include links to anthropology, economics, law, politics, sociology, and much more.

World Wide Web:
> URL: **http://sosig/esrc.bris.ac.uk/**

Social Science Information Gateway

Research in the social sciences has never been so easy. No matter what topic you are looking for, you can scan down this long list of links and make your selection. You can also look for resources by keyword in order to narrow down your search. This is an invaluable web page for anyone interested in social sciences.

World Wide Web:
> URL: **http://sosig.esrc.bris.ac.uk/**

Social Sciences Resource Guides

Internet resource guides for education, anthropology, bisexuality, business, economics, geography, government, journalism, law, library, social science, and women's studies.

Anonymous FTP:
> Address: **una.hh.lib.umich.edu**
> Path: **/inetdirs/socsciences/***

Gopher:
> Name: University of Michigan
> Address: **una.hh.lib.umich.edu**
> Choose: **inetdirs**
> | **Guides on the Social Sciences**

Society and Underwear

What is wrong with a society that is so repressed about underwear that we all have to wear it under our clothes? There is some really neat underwear in existence and it's a shame that we can't show it off in public. Read about the effects of underwear on society and if you want to read these newsgroups wearing only your underclothes, your secret will be safe with us.

Usenet:
> Newsgroup: **alt.society.underwear**

It's What's Underneath That Counts

The mark of real men (and most real women) can be found in what they wear under their clothes. Your friends on the Net recognize how important such things are and are ready to discuss the intimate details in **alt.society.underwear**

To get you started, we will tell you what we are wearing under our clothes at this very moment. We are wearing... oh, sorry ... we are out of room. Maybe in the next edition.

Sociological Issues

Articles about subjects such as neolithic warfare, anarchy, Celtic mythology, history of the Red Army Faction, and more.

Anonymous FTP:
    Address: **ftp.spies.com**
    Path: **/Library/Article/Socio/***

Gopher:
    Name: Internet Wiretap
    Address: **wiretap.spies.com**
    Choose: **Wiretap Online Library**
        | **Articles**
        | **Sociological Issues**

Sociology and Science

We've all heard the rumors — that sociology is one of those fluffy topics that people are required to take in college. Well, we are here to tell you that it's not so. Get into the hardcore science of sociology and talk down and dirty with people who know their people.

Usenet:
    Newsgroup: **sci.sociology**

SOFTWARE

Academic Software Development

If you're into academic software, you should check out the **acsoft-l** mailing list. On this list, you can join in discussion of all aspects of academic and educational software. Topics can include courseware development tools, research tool development, development practices, design techniques, and others.

Listserv Mailing List:
    List Address: **acsoft-l@wuvmd.wustl.edu**
    Subscription Address: **listserv@wuvmd.wustl.edu**

ASK Software Information System

A bilingual BBS that offers a searchable database for software, news, and information. Choose option 3 on the main menu to change from German to English.

Telnet:
    Address: **askhp.ask.uni-karlsruhe.de**
    Login: **ask**
    Password: **ask**

BrainWave Systems Users Group

Some people use brainwaves to make their computer run. If you are a BrainWave user, communicate with other users and gain information on software, data, and utility programs relating to BrainWave Systems.

Listserv Mailing List:
    List Address: **bixanet@jhuvm.hcf.jhu.edu**
    Subscription Address: **listserv@jhuvm.hcf.jhu.edu**

Bristol Technology

Bristol Technology is a leading developer of GUI-development tools and provides software which allows Microsoft Windows software developers quick and cost-effective access to the Unix system-based market. To learn more about this company, see their server.

See also: Technology

World Wide Web:
    URL: **http://bristol.com/**

Looking for an anonymous ftp file? Try Archie.

A
B
C
D
E
F
G
H
I
J
K
L
M
N
O
P
Q
R
S
T
U
V
W
X
Y
Z

Encryption Archives

This ftp site stores some interesting encryption routines and software, information, algorithms, hardware, and other related material.

Anonymous FTP:
Address: **ftp.funet.fi**
Path: **/pub/crypt/***

Do you like to be mysterious? Check the *Encryption* archive for everything you need to send and receive secret messages, even if you don't have a Masked Avenger Secret Decoder Ring.

GNU

A large, multi-faceted software project to create and distribute free software.

Usenet:
Newsgroup: **gnu.***

GNU for PCs

GNU-style programs and utilities for the PC, including **emacs**, **make**, **grep**, **sed**, and **sort**.

Anonymous FTP:
Address: **ftp.wustl.edu**
Path: **/systems/ibmpc/gnuish/***

Graphics Software Search

Search and retrieve graphics software and data with this gopher tool, including ftp sites, bibliography, FAQs, and other resources.

Gopher:
Name: Johns Hopkins University
Address: **gopher.gdb.org**
Choose: **Search and Retrieve Software**
    | **Search and Retrieve Graphics Software and Data**

GNU for You

GNU (pronounced "guh-new" to rhyme with "canoe") is a large software project managed by the Free Software Foundation (FSF). The original goal of the FSF was to create an entire Unix-like operating system that would be available free of commercial charges to anyone who wanted it. That goal is still unfulfilled (although the Linux and FreeBSD systems are readily available). However, the GNU project has created a lot of important software: compilers (gcc, g++), debuggers (gdb), games (GNU chess, GNU go), and—most important—all kinds of utilities: (emacs, bash, gzip, GNU plot, ghostscript, groff and on and on). If you would like to pick up any of this software for free, all you need to do is ftp to any of the GNU archives around the Net. For serious GNU users, there is an entire hierarchy of Usenet discussion groups (**gnu.***).

Info und Softserver

Journals, Unix programs and utilities, recipes, online cookbook. A bilingual (but mostly German) BBS.

Telnet:
Address: **rusinfo.rus.uni-stuttgart.de**
Login: **info**

Everything in this book is free.

Jewish Software

Jewish and Hebrew software and materials for the Macintosh, MS-DOS computers, and Unix systems.

Anonymous FTP:
Address: **israel.nysernet.org**
Path: **/israel/***

Gopher:
Name: NYSERNet
Address: **israel.nysernet.org**
Port: **71**
Choose: **Jews and Computers**

K-Sculpt Music Software

It's what you have been wishing someone would write and now it's finally been done. Get Ben Hall's freeware for Kawai K1, K1m and K1r synthesizers.

See also: Music

World Wide Web:
URL: **http://web.city.ac.uk/~cb170/ksclpt.html**

NASA's Computer Software Management and Information Center

COSMIC has been located at the University of Georgia since 1966. They presently have more than 1,200 computer programs that were originally developed by NASA and its contractors for the U.S. space program. Software is available for a number of areas of interest, including artificial intelligence, fluid dynamics, structural analysis, fluid flow, and much more. Programs are priced on a cost-recovery basis and usually include source code.

World Wide Web:
URL: **http://www.cosmic.uga.edu/**

NCSA Telnet

A TCP/IP telnet program for PCs and Macintosh computers from the same people who developed the excellent NCSA Mosaic graphical web browser. Both the source code and binaries (ready-to-run programs) are available here.

Anonymous FTP:
Address: **ftp.ncsa.uiuc.edu**
Path: **/Telnet/DOS/***

Address: **ftp.ncsa.uiuc.edu**
Path: **/Telnet/Mac/***

Non-English Software

Not everyone in the world speaks English, so it's great to have a resource where you can get information on non-English software. Post your queries or your finds on this Usenet group.

Usenet:
Newsgroup: **comp.software.international**

Nutshell Code

These directories contain many of the software tools and programs presented as examples in a number of the books published by O'Reilly & Associates.

Anonymous FTP:
Address: **ftp.ora.com**
Path: **/pub/examples**

Address: **ftp.uu.net**
Path: **/published/oreilly**

OS/2 Archive

Archiving programs, communications programs, demos, drivers, editors, games, graphics, patches, utilities, and other software for all versions of OS/2.

Anonymous FTP:
Address: **ftp-os2.nmsu.edu**
Path: **/os2/***

Software for the Masses

The Internet has fantastic collections of PC software, all of it free, and all of it just waiting for you to download. When you have an idea of what you want but you're not sure where to look, try the *PC Software Search* facility. Just the place to look for a Father's Day present.

PC Software Search

Search and retrieve MS-DOS software from popular ftp sites by either browsing or using program description keyword search.

Gopher:
> Name: Johns Hopkins University
> Address: **gopher.gdb.org**
> Choose: **Search and Retrieve Software**
> | **Search and Retrieve DOS Software**

Perl Archives

These sites offer Perl (Practical Extraction and Report Language) scripts, FAQs, hints, help guides, source code and other utilities and useful items for Perl.

Anonymous FTP:
> Address: **ftp.demon.co.uk**
> Path: **/pub/perl/***

> Address: **ftp.ee.umanitoba.ca**
> Path: **/pub/msdos/perl/***

> Address: **ftp.metronet.com**
> Path: **/pub/perl/***

Gopher:
> Name: Texas Metronet
> Address: **gopher.metronet.com**
> Choose: **The PERL programming language**

Perl Scripts

Perl scripts for many purposes, including system administration, database tools, menu applications, processes, and networks.

Anonymous FTP:
> Address: **ftp.metronet.com**
> Path: **/pub/perl/scripts/***

Gopher:
> Name: Texas Metronet
> Address: **gopher.metronet.com**
> Choose: **The PERL programming language**
> | **PERL Scripts for Many Purposes**

Searching for Software

The links and directories here will allow you to easily search for and retrieve software from ftp archives all over the world.

Gopher:
> Name: Johns Hopkins University
> Address: **gopher.gdb.org**
> Choose: **Search and Retrieve Software**

SIMTEL Software Archives

A huge repository of all types of software for all types of computers. These archives are mirrored at many sites around the world.

Anonymous FTP:
> Address: **ftp.uu.net**
> Path: **/systems/***

> Address: **oak.oakland.edu**
> Path: **/pub/msdos**

Software Archives

Information about archive sites around the Internet from which you can download programs via anonymous ftp. The **.announce** newsgroup is moderated and contains announcements regarding DOS archives. The **.d** group is for the discussion of related topics. This is a good place to ask where a particular program is available.

Usenet:
> Newsgroup: **comp.sources.***

Software Sites

Some of the most well-known software archive sites. They contain far more than we could ever print in this book. These are good for weeks of exploration.

Anonymous FTP:
> Address: **export.lcs.mit.edu**
> Path: **/pub/***

> Address: **ftp.cc.utexas.edu**
> Path: **/pub/***

> Address: **ftp.funet.fi**
> Path: **/pub/***

> Address: **ftp.rahul.net**
> Path: **/pub/***

> Address: **ftp.uu.net**
> Path: **/systems/***

> Address: **ftp.uu.net**
> Path: **/systems/ibmpc/msdos/simtel/***

> Address: **ftp.wustl.edu**
> Path: **/pub/***

> Address: **garbo.uwasa.fi**

> Address: **oak.oakland.edu**
> Path: **/pub/***

Web users: if you are in a hurry, use Lynx.

System Software

Here is a large software and documentation archive for a bunch of different systems, including Xenix, Unix, Sinclair, Novell, DOS, HPUX, Apple II, and VAX-VMS.

Anonymous FTP:
Address: **ftp.wustl.edu**
Path: **/systems/***

TeX Text Typesetter

Bundles of information about TeX, the software system written by Donald Knuth to typeset text, including access to archives, font information, FAQ lists, and LaTeX information.

Gopher:
Name: Sam Houston State University
Address: **niord.shsu.edu**
Choose: **TeX-related Materials**

Thesaurus Construction Program

Tim Craven's thesaurus construction program for the PC. Assists in creating, modifying, viewing, and printing out a small thesaurus. Includes source code and is in self-extracting archive form.

Anonymous FTP:
Address: **ftp.funet.fi**
Path: **/pub/doc/library/thesauri.exe**

There's something undeniably attractive about someone who has created their own thesaurus. And now, you can be that person. Just download the *Thesaurus Construction Program* and even Roget will eat your dust.

VAX/VMS Software List

An extensive list with hundreds of software applications for VAX/VMS systems and where to find them.

Note: Restrict ftp usage to times other than weekdays 10AM-10PM PST (GMT-0800).

Anonymous FTP:
Address: **pomona.claremont.edu**
Path: **/vax_list.dir/vax_list.txt**

Gopher:
Name: ISW, National Chung Cheng Univ.
Address: **isw2.sw.ccu.edu.tw**
Choose: **VAX/VMS Public Domain Files | The VAX Software List**

Mail:
Address: **vmsserv@pomona.claremont.edu**
Body: **send vax_list.package**

X-10 Protocol

Technical information about the X-10 remote control standard.

Anonymous FTP:
Address: **oak.oakland.edu**
Path: **/pub/misc/x-10/***

ZIB Electronic Library

The telnet site offers software, hot links to NetLib, archives, and catalogs.

Telnet:
Address: **elib.zib-berlin.de**
Login: **elib**

Zmodem

Complete C source, including makefiles, for the **sz** and **rz** Unix programs for sending and receiving with the Xmodem, Ymodem, and Zmodem protocols. You can download these programs and type **make** to produce the executables.

Anonymous FTP:
Address: **oak.oakland.edu**
Path: **/pub/misc/zmodem**

SOFTWARE: ARCHIVES

Apple II Archive

Large archive of games, demos, utilities, source code, and other material for the Apple II range of computers.

Anonymous FTP:
   Address: **ccosun.caltech.edu**
   Path: **/pub/apple2/***

Atari

Bundles of programs, source code, graphics, sounds, magazines, and documentation for the Atari ST range of computers.

Anonymous FTP:
   Address: **ftp.wustl.edu**
   Path: **/systems/atari/***

CPM Archives

Tips, tricks, utilities, source code, and complete programs for users of CPM computers.

Anonymous FTP:
   Address: **oak.oakland.edu**
   Path: **/pub/cpm/***

DECUS Library

A library catalog of software for various operating systems. Includes utilities, programs, and games for CPM, DEC, Ultrix, and VAX.

Gopher:
   Name: La Trobe University
   Address: **gopher.latrobe.edu.au**
   Choose: **Computing Services
      | DECUS Library**

> ## Learn how to use anonymous ftp and the world is at your fingertips.

> ## Don't be a Web Potato: participate.

Garbo (University of Vaasa, Finland)

Software, software, software! This anonymous ftp site has gobs of software for DOS, Windows, Macs, and Unix machines. Demos, utilities, screen savers, fonts, bitmaps, icons, games, patches, programs from astronomy and business to virus interceptors, and more games.

Anonymous FTP:
   Address: **garbo.uwasa.fi**
   Path: **/mac/***

   Address: **garbo.uwasa.fi**
   Path: **/windows/***

   Address: **garbo.uwasa.fi**
   Path: **/unix/***

   Address: **garbo.uwasa.fi**
   Path: **/pc/***

   Address: **garbo.uwasa.fi**
   Path: **/next/***

Hebrew Software Archive

The largest collection on the Internet of Hebrew and Jewish software for Unix, DOS, and the Macintosh. This archive has special areas for Hebrew tutorials and Jewish educational software, Hebrew screen drivers, databases, Hebrew font collections, clip art, a programmers' library, and more.

Anonymous FTP:
   Address: **jerusalem1.datasrv.co.il**
   Path: **/jer1/***

Gopher:
   Name: Jerusalem One
   Address: **jerusalem1.datasrv.co.il**
   Choose: **Hebrew Software Archives**

Macintosh Archives

Tips, tricks, utilities, source code, and complete programs for users of Macintosh computers.

Anonymous FTP:
   Address: **oak.oakland.edu**
   Path: **/pub2/macintosh/***

Free PC Software

If you have a PC, there is no reason why you should pay money for software. There is enough free software available on the Net to choke a virtual horse. Take some time and check out the **PC software archives** and save your money for important things (like buying copies of **The Internet Golden Directory** for all your friends).

PC Archives

Probably one of the largest collections of PC-related material to ever exist in one place. There are mirrors from several other large sites also. You name it, it's here.

Anonymous FTP:
Address: **ftp.wustl.edu**
Path: **/systems/ibmpc/***

PC Game Archives

Central repository for the PC gaming community, containing all manner of freely distributable games and accessories that run under MS-DOS or MS-Windows.

Anonymous FTP:
Address: **ftp.ulowell.edu**
Path: **/msdos/Games/***

Address: **ftp.wustl.edu**
Path: **/systems/ibmpc/msdos-games/***

PC Games for You

It's a sad day when you run out of new games for your PC and you are left with no alternative but to actually do some work.

But, as an Internet user, this unfortunate situation will never happen to you. All you have to do is look in the **PC Game Archives** and you will find enough diversions to keep you busy until it is time to retire.

Sinclair Archive

Dedicated to those wonderful creations of Clive Sinclair. If you're looking for information or specs for a ZX-81, QL, or Cambridge Z88, this is the place to find it.

Anonymous FTP:
Address: **ftp.wustl.edu**
Path: **/systems/sinclair/***

TeX Archive

Large repository of TeX-related material, accumulated by the Comprehensive TeX Archive Network (CTAN). It offers TeX digests, documentation, fonts, graphics, listings, macros, and much more.

Anonymous FTP:
Address: **ftp.shsu.edu**
Path: **/tex-archive/***

A B C D E F G H I J K L M N O P Q R S T U V W X Y Z

Unix C Archive

More serious software for Unix than you could ever imagine, much of it written in C or related tools and complete with source. Included are database utilities, editors, graphics, languages, and much more.

Anonymous FTP:
Address: **ftp.wustl.edu**
Path: **/systems/***

SOFTWARE: INTERNET

AirMosaic

A time-limited demo of a commercial version of Mosaic, the graphical Internet browser. AirMosaic includes some nice enhancements and features, but this demo version runs for only six minutes at a time.

See also: Internet

Anonymous FTP:
Address: **ftp.spry.com**
Path: **/vendor/spry/demo/**

Archie

The source code and binaries for the great little Internet search program written by Brendan Kehoe. There are versions in C for Unix or VMS, as well as versions for emacs, perl, X11, and Macintosh computers. The **widener** site has ready-to-run Archie clients.

Anonymous FTP:
Address: **ftp.cs.mcgill.ca**
Path: **/pub/archie/clients/***

Anonymous FTP:
Address: **ftp.cs.widener.edu**
Path: **/pub/archie/***

Cello

A full-featured and highly capable browser for the World Wide Web, gopher servers, and ftp sites. Cello runs under Microsoft Windows and requires a winsock connection to the Internet.

Anonymous FTP:
Address: **ftp.msc.cornell.edu**
Path: **/pub/windows/cello/***

> **Don't worry about technology, just enjoy yourself.**

DOS Internet Kit

A collection of public domain programs that enable Ethernet or serially connected PCs to access Internet services. It is packaged as a relatively easy-to-install kit to help you get started.

World Wide Web:
URL: **http://tbone.biol.scarolina.edu/~dean2/kit/kit.html**

Eudora for Macintosh and Windows

An older, but fully operational version of the popular Eudora mail program from Qualcomm. With Eudora you can keep your correspondence and correspondents straight. Eudora works with TCP/IP networks (including SLIP and dialup PPP accounts) or with a dialup shell account on Unix computers.

Anonymous FTP:
Address: **ftp.qualcomm.com**
Path: **/quest/windows/eudora**

Address: **ftp.qualcomm.com**
Path: **/quest/mac/eudora**

Gopher Clients

A FAQ file with information about how and where to download gopher clients to your own computer. If you have a SLIP or PPP line (or are otherwise on a TCP/IP network) it is much better to run a gopher program on your own computer than to log into an access provider's computer and share their system with hundreds of other people. You can find gopher clients for DOS, Macintosh, Windows, X Window, and many other environments.

Anonymous FTP:
Address: **rtfm.mit.edu**
Path: **/pub/usenet/news.answers/gopher-faq**

Gopher Software

The real thing — direct from the horse's mouth! Get the source code for gopher servers and clients for just about every platform you can imagine from the people who invented the gopher system — the University of Minnesota. The mailing lists are for news and announcements and the Usenet group is for general information and help.

Anonymous FTP:
> Address: **boombox.micro.umn.edu**
> Path: **/pub/gopher/***

Gopher:
> Name: University of Minnesota
> Address: **gopher.micro.umn.edu**
> Choose: **Information About Gopher**

Internet Mailing List:
> List Address:
> **gopher-news@boombox.micro.umn.edu**
> Subscription Address:
> **gopher-news-request@boombox.micro.umn.edu**
>
> List Address:
> **gopher-announce@boombox.micro.umn.edu**
> Subscription Address:
> **gopher-announce-request@boombox.micro.umn.edu**

Usenet:
> Newsgroup: **comp.infosystems.gopher**

Harvest Information Discovery and Access System

Harvest provides a scalable, customizable architecture for indexing and accessing Internet information. You can learn about and experiment with the system through the many hypertext links here, including demonstrations, a technical overview, subsystems, papers, talks, and software details.

World Wide Web:
> URL: **http://rd.cs.colorado.edu/harvest/**

HTML Developer's JumpStation

The HTML Developer's JumpStation is a collection of tools, guides, articles, and techniques used on the Web, organized into categories such as Using Mosaic Forms, HTML Editors, Web Server Software, Web Names and Addresses, HTML Converters, Web Directory Services, Using Mosaic as a Database Client, and others.

World Wide Web:
> URL: **http://oneworld.wa.com/htmldev/devpage/ dev-page.html**

> ## Hungry? Try Food and Drink. Hungry for Love? Try Romance.

HTML Editor for Word for Windows

A Word for Windows template designed to convert Word documents into HTML documents in an easy-to-use environment. The template also allows you to convert any ASCII file to HTML and to edit any existing HTML document.

Anonymous FTP:
> Address: **ftp.einet.net**
> Path: **/einet/pc/ANT_HTML.ZIP**

HTML Mode for emacs

A mode you can add to emacs that makes it easier to write HTML documents for the Web. There is plenty of online help for constructing links, examples, and a completion list with possible input strings.

Anonymous FTP:
> Address: **ftp.reed.edu**
> Path: **/pub/src/html-helper-mode.tar.Z**
>
> Address: **info.cern.ch**
> Path: **/pub/www/contrib/ hm--html-menus-4.1.tar.gz**
>
> Address: **sunsite.unc.edu**
> Path: **/pub/Linux/apps/editors/emacs/ hm--html-menus-4.1.tar.gz**

IRC II Client

IRC II help files and clients for Unix and VMS. If you telnet to the telnet site, the necessary files are downloaded and compiled automagically. You must, however, follow the telnet command with the characters **1 | sh** as shown.

Anonymous FTP:
> Address: **cs.bu.edu**
> Path: **/irc/clients**
>
> Address: **slopoke.mlb.semi.harris.com**
> Path: **/pub/irc/***

Telnet:
> Address: **sci.dixie.edu 1 | sh**

A B C D E F G H I J K L M N O P Q R S T U V W X Y Z

IRC (Internet Relay Chat) is absolutely fantabulous, but to use it you need an IRC client program. If there isn't one already installed on your system, you can download one for yourself.

(Note: Be nice, though, and ask the system manager first. Some managers do not want people using IRC.)

Lynx

Lynx is a non-graphical browser for the World Wide Web that runs under DOS and Unix. If you don't have a Mac, a PC with Windows, or a Unix computer with X Window, you should get one. But in case you just like command-line DOS and command-line Unix, you'll need a non-graphical web browser like Lynx.

Anonymous FTP:
>   Address: **ftp2.cc.ukans.edu**
>   Path: **/pub/lynx/***

MacWAIS

A graphical front end to the Wide Area Information Service for Macintosh computers.

Anonymous FTP:
>   Address: **ftp.einet.net**
>   Path: **/einet/mac/macwais1.29.sea.hqx**

MacWeb

A graphical browser for the World Wide Web for Macintosh computers.

Anonymous FTP:
>   Address: **ftp.einet.net**
>   Path: **/einet/mac/macweb/**
>   **macweb0.98alpha.sea.hqx**

mail2html

This web page offers a Perl program that converts mail messages into HTML format.

World Wide Web:
>   URL: **http://www.uci.edu/indiv/ehood**

Majordomo Mailing List Software

Majordomo is software for an automated mailing on a Unix computer. Majordomo works similarly to listserv software for VM machines and is highly portable between Unix computers because it's just a Perl script. Of course, you do need Perl (see Software and Software: Unix) to use it.

Anonymous FTP:
>   Address: **ftp.greatcircle.com**
>   Path: **/pub/majordomo**

Mosaic for the Mac, Microsoft Windows, and X Window

A great graphical browser for the World Wide Web and gopher system. Mosaic is under constant development at the National Center for Supercomputing Applications (NCSA), and there are versions of Mosaic for the Macintosh, Microsoft Windows, and X Window systems.

Anonymous FTP:
>   Address: **ftp.ncsa.uiuc.edu**
>   Path: **/Mosaic/***
>
>   Address: **info.cern.ch**
>   Path: **/pub/www**

World Wide Web:
>   URL: **http://netmedia.com/ims/IMS_INFO/**
>   **getting_mosaic.html**
>   URL: **http://www.ncsa.uiuc.edu/SDG/Software/**
>   **MacMosaic/MacMosaicHome.**

MOSAIC FOR FREE

No doubt about it: Mosaic (a browser for the World Wide Web) is *the* trendy Internet client program for the mid 1990s. There are a good number of commercial alternatives (including a commercial version of Mosaic itself), but you do not really need to pay for them. Mosaic is available for free on the Net and comes ready to use for the Mac, Microsoft Windows, and in the original X Window flavor. Remember, you need a direct network connection or a SLIP or PPP connection over a phone line in order to use Mosaic. If you are using a regular dial-up (emulate a VT-100) connection, you can use Lynx instead (which is also available for free).

Mosaic Users and Developers List

A forum for communication between the people who use and develop NCSA Mosaic applications. If you use Mosaic or develop applications for it, join **mosaic-l** and get in on the fun.

Listserv Mailing List:
List Address: **mosaic-l@uicvm.uic.edu**
Subscription Address: **listserv@uicvm.uic.edu**

NCSA Web Server for Windows

An HTTPD web server for Windows which offers multi-threaded operations for as many as eight simultaneous connections. The features of this server are similar to that of the HTTPD for Unix.

World Wide Web:
URL: **http://www.alisa.com/win-httpd/**

NUPop

NUPop provides a suite of Internet services in a menu-driven format, including electronic mail, file transfer, remote login, gopher, user lookup, webster, ping and remote password change.

Anonymous FTP:
Address: **ftp.acns.nwu.edu**
Path: **/pub/nupop**

Sunsite Winsock Archive

A web interface to the Sunsite winsock archive at the University of North Carolina (**sunsite.unc.edu**). This page has pointers to the archive's top-level readme file, FAQs, a vendor list, applications, and packages.

World Wide Web:
URL: **http://emwac.ed.ac.uk/html/sunsite/top.html**

TCP/IP

TCP/IP is the glue that holds the Internet together. If you want to have your PC actually be on the Internet, it will have to run some type of TCP/IP software. This newsgroup is for discussion of the zillions and zillions of technical considerations that are unavoidably relevant. A good way to start is by reading the FAQ list, which is posted regularly to the newsgroup and is available from the ftp site. Don't get discouraged: all things come to those who think.

Usenet:
Newsgroup: **comp.protocols.tcp-ip.ibmpc**

Willow

Willow, the Washington Information Looker-upper Layered Over Windows, is a general purpose information retrieval tool. It provides a single, easy-to-use graphical user interface to any number of text-based bibliographic databases. It is fully compatible with web/Mosaic and the Z39.50 database access protocol. Details of how to get Willow, live demos, color screen-shots of the interface, technical description of the architecture, source code, and pre-compiled binaries for DEC/Ultrix, Sun/Solaris, IBM RS6000/AIX, and DEC/Vax-bsd are available here. Information about the development of Wilco, a character-oriented version of Willow that can be run on virtually any system, can also be found here.

World Wide Web:
URL: **http://www.cac.washington.edu/willow/home.html**

Wintalk

Talk to friends around the globe in realtime with this free Microsoft Windows program that implements the Unix **talk** protocol. This web page has information about the program and the author, and a direct link to the ftp site that stores the program.

World Wide Web:
URL: **http://www.elf.com/elf/wintalk.html**

WinWAIS

WinWAIS is a Microsoft Windows client for the Wide Area Information Server (WAIS) system. This package also includes two graphics file viewers for Windows.

Anonymous FTP:
Address: **ftp.einet.net**
Path: **/einet/pc/EWAIS*.***

WinWeb

WinWeb is a great World Wide Web browser for Windows. This page gives details of where to download WinWeb, documentation, installation instructions, developer notes, and license information.

World Wide Web:
URL: **http://galaxy.einet.net/EINet/WinWeb/WinWebHome.html**

A
B
C
D
E
F
G
H
I
J
K
L
M
N
O
P
Q
R
S
T
U
V
W
X
Y
Z

WSGopher

A gopher+ client program for Microsoft Windows and Winsock version 1.1. This program is an executable binary and includes configuration files, announcement files, and help files.

See also: Software: PC

Anonymous FTP:

Address: **boombox.micro.umn.edu**
Path: **/pub/gopher/Windows/***

Address: **dewey.tis.inel.gov**
Path: **/pub/wsgopher/***

Address: **ftp.demon.co.uk**
Path: **/pub/ibmpc/winsock/apps/wsgopher/***

Address: **sunsite.unc.edu**
Path: **/pub/micro/pc-stuff/ms-windows/
   winsock/apps/***

SOFTWARE: MACINTOSH

Applications for the Mac

Discussion about all types of Macintosh applications. The **.apps** newsgroup is for talk about any type of application; **.word** is for word processing; **.comm** is for communications; and **.databases** is for database systems.

Usenet:

Newsgroup: **bit.mailserv.word-mac**
Newsgroup: **comp.sys.mac.apps**
Newsgroup: **comp.sys.mac.comm**
Newsgroup: **comp.sys.mac.databases**

Binaries for the Mac

This moderated newsgroup contains binaries (executable Macintosh programs) ready to download and run.

Usenet:

Newsgroup: **comp.binaries.mac**

Hypercard

Talk about all kinds of issues related to the Macintosh Hypercard: the stack-oriented hypertext system.

Usenet:

Newsgroup: **comp.sys.mac.hypercard**

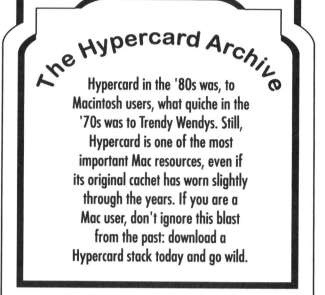

The Hypercard Archive

Hypercard in the '80s was, to Macintosh users, what quiche in the '70s was to Trendy Wendys. Still, Hypercard is one of the most important Mac resources, even if its original cachet has worn slightly through the years. If you are a Mac user, don't ignore this blast from the past: download a Hypercard stack today and go wild.

Hypercard Stack Archive

Hypercard stacks are a fun way of storing information, sounds and pictures. See this selection of creative hypercard stacks on a variety of subjects such as herbs, books, humor, sex, history, and more.

See also: Computers: Macintosh

Gopher:

Name: Lund Institute of Technology
Address: **nic.lth.se**
Choose: **Arkiv**
   | **Lokal ftp**
   | **mac**
   | **info-mac**
   | **info**
   | **NonMacStuff**

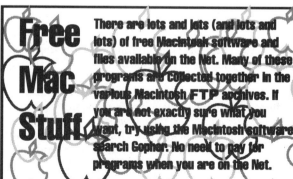

Free Mac Stuff

There are lots and lots (and lots and lots) of free Macintosh software and files available on the Net. Many of these programs are collected together in the various Macintosh FTP archives. If you are not exactly sure what you want, try using the Macintosh software search Gopher. No need to pay for programs when you are on the Net.

Mac FTP List

A large list of anonymous ftp sites that contain many files and programs for the Apple Macintosh. This document also contains information and advice for downloading and running Mac software from the Internet.

Anonymous FTP:
>   Address: **ftp.std.com**
>   Path: **/associations/bmug/help-using-world/**
>   **mac-ftp-list.txt**
>
>   Address: **ftp.sunet.se**
>   Path: **/pub/mac/info-mac/comm/info/mac-ftp-list***
>
>   Address: **ftp.wustl.edu**
>   Path: **/systems/mac/info-mac/Old/report/**
>   **mac-ftp-list***

Archie:
>   Pattern: **mac-ftp-list**

Gopher:
>   Name: Saitama University
>   Address: **gopher.cent.saitama-u.ac.jp**
>   Choose: **FTP**
>   **| mac-ftp-list**

Macintosh Games

What's the point of having a computer without games? Join this discussion group to talk about all aspects of Macintosh games: which ones are best, which ones to avoid, copy protection issues, as well as hints and tricks.

Usenet:
>   Newsgroup: **comp.sys.mac.games**

Macintosh Software Search

Browse, search by keyword, and retrieve Macintosh software from popular ftp archives.

Gopher:
>   Name: Johns Hopkins University
>   Address: **gopher.gdb.org**
>   Choose: **Search and Retrieve Software**
>   **| Search and Retrieve Macintosh Software**

Be cool! Join a mailing list.

MacWeb

MacWeb is a full-featured web browser for the Macintosh. The web page gives details about downloading MacWeb, installation instructions, documentation, developer notes, new additions, and legal restrictions. The ftp site has the actual software.

Anonymous FTP:
>   Address: **ftp.einet.net**
>   Path: **/einet/mac/macweb/***

World Wide Web:
>   URL: **http://galaxy.einet.net/EINet/MacWeb/**
>   **MacWebHome.html**

Object-Oriented Programming

Object-oriented programming is just like regular programming except that you look at everything differently, write your programs differently, maintain them differently, and think with a different part of your temporal lobe. Join the discussion and talk about object-oriented tools, techniques, and problems. The **.misc** newsgroup is for general discussion of Macintosh object-oriented programming. The **.macapp3** group is devoted to Version 3 of the MacApp system. The **.tcl** group is for discussion of the Think Class Libraries.

Usenet:
>   Newsgroup: **comp.sys.mac.oop.macapp3**
>   Newsgroup: **comp.sys.mac.oop.misc**
>   Newsgroup: **comp.sys.mac.oop.tcl**

Programming the Mac

Macintosh programming tips, questions and answers. The **.lisp** newsgroup is for Lisp programming. The **.mac** group is for general discussion about all aspects of programming.

Usenet:
>   Newsgroup: **comp.lang.lisp.mcl**
>   Newsgroup: **comp.sys.mac.programmer**

Software for Macintosh

These ftp sites store volumes of software for the Macintosh. If you can't find what you're looking for at one, try the other.

Anonymous FTP:
>   Address: **ftp.uu.net**
>   Path: **/systems/mac**
>
>   Address: **sumex-aim.stanford.edu**

A
B
C
D
E
F
G
H
I
J
K
L
M
N
O
P
Q
R
S
T
U
V
W
X
Y
Z

System Software

This is the place for discussion about all aspects of the Macintosh system software (such as Finder and Multifinder), as well as working with disks, dealing with viruses, and on and on.

Usenet:
>   Newsgroup: **comp.sys.mac.system**

SOFTWARE: PC

Applications for DOS

Discussion about all types of DOS applications. The **.dbase** newsgroup is for dBase applications; **.wpcorp** is for Wordperfect products; **.word** is for word processing in general; and **.apps** is for any and all PC applications.

Usenet:
>   Newsgroup: **bit.listserv.dbase-l**
>   Newsgroup: **bit.listserv.wpcorp-l**
>   Newsgroup: **bit.mailserv.word-pc**
>   Newsgroup: **comp.os.msdos.apps**

Archives

These Usenet newsgroups contain information about archive sites around the Internet from which you can download programs via anonymous ftp. The **.announce** newsgroup is moderated and contains announcements regarding DOS archives. The **.d** group is for the discussion of related topics. This is a good place to ask where a particular program is available.

Usenet:
>   Newsgroup: **comp.archives.msdos.announce**
>   Newsgroup: **comp.archives.msdos.d**
>   Newsgroup: **comp.binaries.ibm.pc.archives**

Binaries for DOS

These newsgroups contain binaries (executable DOS programs) ready to download and run, and information about binaries. The **.d** newsgroup is for discussion only. The **.wanted** group is the place to ask if anyone has a particular program.

Usenet:
>   Newsgroup: **comp.binaries.ibm.pc**
>   Newsgroup: **comp.binaries.ibm.pc.d**
>   Newsgroup: **comp.binaries.ibm.pc.wanted**

FREE DOS PROGRAMS

PC users, there is lots and lots (and lots) of free software in binary form, as EXE files, all ready to run. Much better to download all your software for free and save your hard-earned money for more important uses. (By the way, Rick's birthday is October 9 and Harley's is December 21.)

Demo Software

A forum devoted to all aspects of creating and using demos: programs that showcase the skills of the programmer and the capabilties of the hardware. As you will see, demo-ing is a well-developed, popular pastime. Sit in with the pros and learn how to show off with flair. (Video programmers: keep an eye out for the Mode X frequently asked question list and learn all about the hidden secrets of VGA programming.)

Usenet:
>   Newsgroup: **comp.sys.ibm.pc.demos**

DOS Archive

There are more goodies for DOS at this site than you will ever have use for in your entire lifetime. Not only do they have techie stuff to make your machine go fast, run smooth, be efficient, but they also have nifty little extras like astronomy and genealogy programs. Bring a shopping cart.

Anonymous FTP:
>   Address: **oak.oakland.edu**
>   Path: **/pub/msdos/***

> ## Anonymous ftp users: try logging in as "ftp".

Games

If God didn't want us to use our PCs for games, he wouldn't have given us so many game discussion groups. The **.games** and **.misc** newsgroups are for general talk about all types of PC games: for DOS, Windows, and OS/2. The **.announce** group is moderated and contains announcements of interest to the PC games community. Look for the "PC Games" frequently asked question list, posted regularly to this group. The FAQ is also available by anonymous ftp. The other groups are for particular types of games (**.rpg** means role-playing games).

See also: Games

Usenet:
> Newsgroup: **comp.sys.ibm.pc.games**
> Newsgroup: **comp.sys.ibm.pc.games.action**
> Newsgroup: **comp.sys.ibm.pc.games.adventure**
> Newsgroup: **comp.sys.ibm.pc.games.announce**
> Newsgroup: **comp.sys.ibm.pc.games.flight-sim**
> Newsgroup: **comp.sys.ibm.pc.games.misc**
> Newsgroup: **comp.sys.ibm.pc.games.rpg**
> Newsgroup: **comp.sys.ibm.pc.games.strategic**

KEEP UP ON THE NEWEST AND COOLEST IN THE PC GAME WORLD. READ THE **comp.sys.ibm.pc.games.**** NEWSGROUPS.

Higher Education National Software Archive

The Higher Education National Software Archive (HENSA) for Microsystems maintains a gopher with connections to large collections of public domain (free) software relating to education.

Gopher:
> Name: Hensa Public Domain Software Archive
> Address: **micros.hensa.ac.uk**

Mail:
> Address: **archive@unix.hensa.ac.uk**
> Body: **help**

This artistic image is called **avn_ati.gif** and is available from Northern Arizona University, Washington University, St. Louis, and the University of Missouri, Kansas City (**ftp.cstp.umkc.edu**).

InfoPop

A hypertext guide to using the Internet in a clever Microsoft Windows help file format. Includes some history, as well as a list of resources.

Anonymous FTP:
> Address: **ftp.gmu.edu**
> Path: **/library/ipwin124.zip**

Archie:
> Pattern: **infopop**

Unix uudecode for Windows

A graphical, Windows-based version of the popular and necessary Unix **uudecode** program.

Anonymous FTP:
> Address: **ftp.cica.indiana.edu**
> Path: **/pub/pc/win3/util**

Waffle BBS Software

A collection of software for use with Waffle BBS, an MS-DOS bulletin board package.

Anonymous FTP:
> Address: **ftp.spies.com**
> Path: **/waffle/***

Learn Unix and walk with the gods.

A B C D E F G H I J K L M N O P Q R S T U V W X Y Z

Windows Shareware Archive

This page is your gateway to a world of free software for Microsoft Windows. The page is organized like an index of categories and each category name is a link. Check out address books, utilities, calendars, scientific tools, educational software, games, graphics, icons, Usenet software, add-ons and utilities for popular application packages and much more. You may never need to buy another program!

World Wide Web:
    URL: **http://coyote.csusm.edu/cwis/winworld/winworld.html**

Windows Utilities

Applications, tips, utilities, drivers, and bitmaps for Windows.

Anonymous FTP:
    Address: **ftp.cica.indiana.edu**
    Path: **/pub/pc/win3/***

    Address: **ftp.wustl.edu**
    Path: **/systems/ibmpc/win3/***

Are you one of those millions of lucky people using Microsoft Windows?

If so, your life is probably so complete that happiness is your constant companion. However, if you become just a tad restless, why not download some of the free Windows Utilities and move yourself just that much closer to heaven on Earth.

Andrew File System Resources

A large collection of pointers to Andrew File System (AFS) resources available on the Net. AFS is the distributed file system that enables cooperating hosts (clients and servers) to efficiently share file system resources across both local area and wide area networks. The resources include FAQs, mailing lists, software, tools, programming interfaces, help files, and much more.

World Wide Web:
    URL: **http://www.cs.cmu.edu:8001/afs/andrew.cmu.edu/usr/db74/www/afs.html**

Calendar of Days

A large list of important days and holidays that can be viewed or used as input for the Unix calendar program.

Anonymous FTP:
    Address: **ftp.spies.com**
    Path: **/Library/Document/calendar.dat**

Gopher:
    Name: Internet Wiretap
    Address: **wiretap.spies.com**
    Choose: **Wiretap Online Library**
        I **Assorted Documents**
        I **Calendar of Days (Holidays, anniv, etc.)**

con

con is a Perl script that facilitates connecting to another site with ftp, mail, telnet, **rlogin/rsh**, **ping**, **traceroute**, **finger**, and **talk**. It was written so users wouldn't have to have a mess of aliases and functions just so they could easily connect to a machine in one of the ways described above. Instead, all this info is contained in one file, and **con** makes intelligent guesses on what you want to do.

Anonymous FTP:
    Address: **athene.uni-paderborn.de**
    Path: **/news/comp.sources.unix/volume26/con**

    Address: **usc.edu**
    Path: **/archive/usenet/sources/comp.sources.unix/volume26/con**

The Built-in Unix Calendar Service

Unix has a built-in utility called **calendar** that provides a useful, easy to manage reminder system. You maintain a file called **calendar** in your home directory. This file contains entries with dates and descriptions. Each day, you can use the **calendar** program to display all the entries for the current day and the following day.

If you are a Unix user, you should definitely learn how to use this service. To display the documentation, use the command **man calendar** to access the online manual. Once you become a **calendar** user, you can download a great file that has a list of many important dates and descriptions that you might want to put in your own personal calendar. (Just in case the file is incomplete, Rick's birthday is October 9, and Harley's birthday is December 21.)

January 19

Sunday	Monday		esda		Fr	day
1	2	3				
8	9		1	12		
15	16	17	18	19	20	21
22	23	24	25	26	27	28
29	30	31				

Elm

The Elm mail program is a popular electronic mail agent used at most major universities and many other sites.

Anonymous FTP:
    Address: **ftp.eu.net**
    Path: **/mail/elm**

    Address: **lth.se**
    Path: **/pub/mail/elm**

Elvis

A clone of vi, the standard Unix editor, available with source for BSD Unix, AT&T SysV Unix, SCO Xenix, Minix, MS-DOS, Atari TOS, and others.

Anonymous FTP:
    Address: **ftp.std.com**
    Path: **/src/editors/elvis-***

    Address: **qiclab.scn.rain.com**
    Path: **/pub/gnu/elvis-***

Archie:
    Pattern: **elvis-***

Emacs Editor

Source code to an excellent text editor. **emacs** is a widely used editor with many nifty features; however, it does consume some disk space.

Anonymous FTP:
    Address: **aeneas.mit.edu**
    Path: **/pub/gnu/emacs-1***

    Address: **prep.ai.mit.edu**
    Path: **/pub/gnu**

    Address: **sol.cs.ruu.nl**
    Path: **/pub/GNU/emacs***

    Address: **sunsite.unc.edu**
    Path: **/pub/gnu/emacs***

Archie:
    Pattern: **emacs-1***

Emacs = Life

Jumping into Emacs is one of the biggest intellectual commitments you will make in your life (and you won't even need a prenuptial agreement). Emacs creates a world of its own from which you can edit text files, write and debug programs, read the Usenet news, and generally live high on the Unix hog. The source for Emacs is readily available, so you can look inside and customize it up the wazoo.

A
B
C
D
E
F
G
H
I
J
K
L
M
N
O
P
Q
R
S
T
U
V
W
X
Y
Z

European X User Group

EXUG is an organization which provides information on the X Window windowing system for European users. Online applications for membership forms are available in addition to upcoming events information.

World Wide Web:
> URL: **http://tommy.informatik.uni-dortmund.de/ EXUG/EXUG.html**

Fax-3 Fax Software

Group 3 fax transmission and reception services for a networked Unix system with faxmodem.

Anonymous FTP:
> Address: **aeneas.mit.edu**
> Path: **/pub/gnu/fax-3***

Archie:
> Pattern: **fax-3**

FlexFAX

Facsimile software source code for Unix systems that allows sending, receiving, and polled retrieval of faxes.

Anonymous FTP:
> Address: **ftp.sgi.com**
> Path: **/sgi/fax/v2.2.src.tar.Z**

gawk

gawk is the GNU version of **awk** with a number of new features. **gawk** programs are often faster and more reliable than comparable **awk** programs.

Anonymous FTP:
> Address: **prep.ai.mit.edu**
> Path: **/pub/gnu/gawk-2.15.2.tar.gz**

> Address: **prep.ai.mit.edu**
> Path: **/pub/gnu/gawk-doc-2.15.2.tar.gz**

Ghostscript

Ghostscript is the GNU PostScript clone. If you need something done in PS, Ghostscript will do it for you.

Anonymous FTP:
> Address: **prep.ai.mit.edu**
> Path: **/pub/gnu/ghostscript-2.6.1.tar.gz**

> Address: **relay.iunet.it**
> Path: **/gnu/ghostscript**

> Address: **sol.cs.ruu.nl**
> Path: **/pub/GNU/ghostscript**

GNU Archives

A large archive of software and source created by the GNU Project.

Anonymous FTP:
> Address: **aeneas.mit.edu**
> Path: **/pub/gnu/***

> Address: **sunsite.unc.edu**
> Path: **/pub/gnu/***

Archie:
> Pattern: **gnu**

GNU C Compiler

A portable optimizing compiler that supports ANSI C, C++ and Objective C languages, and can produce position-independent code for several types of CPUs.

Anonymous FTP:
> Address: **aeneas.mit.edu**
> Path: **/pub/gnu/gcc-2**

> Address: **sunsite.unc.edu**
> Path: **/pub/gnu/development/gcc-2***

Archie:
> Pattern: **gcc-2**

GNU Emacs FAQ

Emacs is not just for gods. Normal people like it, too, although they are the ones that need a little extra help when it comes to actually using Emacs. For a little boost, check out the GNU Emacs FAQ and elevate yourself to the status of guru, wizard or god. This link offers answers to general questions, on-line help as well as other sources of Emacs information.

World Wide Web:
> URL: **http://ancho.ucs.indiana.edu/Emacs/FAQ/**

GNU File Compression Utilities

The GNU compression utility that compresses files to a .Z extension, and the decompression utility that restores files to their original condition.

Anonymous FTP:
> Address: **garbo.uwasa.fi**
> Path: **/pc/unix/gzip124.zip**

GNU Shell Utilities

A collection of Unix commands that are frequently run
from the command line or in shell scripts.

Anonymous FTP:
> Address: **aeneas.mit.edu**
> Path: **/pub/gnu/sh-utils***

> Address: **sunsite.unc.edu**
> Path: **/pub/gnu/utilities/sh-utils***

Archie:
> Pattern: **sh-utils***

GNU Software Search

Search and retrieve software from Project GNU, a large
software project for creating and freely distributing software.

Gopher:
> Name: Johns Hopkins University
> Address: **gopher.gdb.org**
> Choose: **Search and Retrieve Software**
>   **| Search and Retrieve GNU Software**

gnuplot

gnuplot is the GNU plotting/graphics package. Many
university students use this utility.

Anonymous FTP:
> Address: **prep.ai.mit.edu**
> Path: **/pub/gnu/gnuplot3.5.tar.gz**

gzip

A compression program free of any known patents, used
on all archived GNU software, and becoming increasingly
popular on many archive sites. Used to compress and
uncompress **.gz** files.

Anonymous FTP:
> Address: **aeneas.mit.edu**
> Path: **/pub/gnu/gzip***

> Address: **prep.ai.mit.edu**
> Path: **/pub/gnu/gzip-1.2.4.tar.gz**

> Address: **sunsite.unc.edu**
> Path: **/pub/gnu/gzip***

Archie:
> Pattern: **gzip***

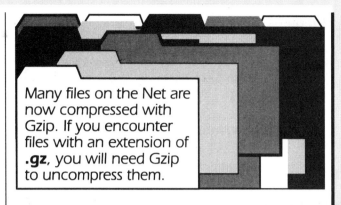

Many files on the Net are now compressed with Gzip. If you encounter files with an extension of **.gz**, you will need Gzip to uncompress them.

Integrated Computer Solutions FAQs

Answers to common technical questions about ICS
products such as Builder Xcessory, ICS Motif, the ICS
Widget Databook widgets, and the Ada Xcessories.

World Wide Web:
> URL: **http://www.ics.com/QandA/**

Internationalized xgopher

A Sun-4 binary package of the internationalized xgopher
client which allows X Window to use Japanese and other
multibyte characters.

Anonymous FTP:
> Address: **ftp.cs.keio.ac.jp**
> Path: **/pub/inet/gopher/JAPANESE/***

joe Editor

joe stands for "Joe's own editor." It is simple to use and is
designed for beginning Unix users.

Anonymous FTP:
> Address: **ftp.germany.eu.net**
> Path: **/pub/applications/textproc/editors**

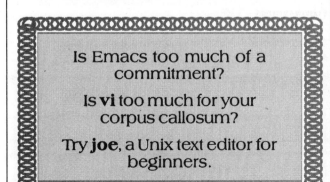

Is Emacs too much of a commitment?

Is **vi** too much for your corpus callosum?

Try **joe**, a Unix text editor for beginners.

Kterm

Kterm is an X.11 terminal emulator that can handle Japanese, Chinese, and Korean text. Kterm comes as C source code for Unix X Window workstations.

Anonymous FTP:
   Address: **bash.cc.keio.ac.jp**
   Path: **/pub/mirror/X11-contrib/R5/kterm***

   Address: **gatekeeper.dec.com**
   Path: **/.b/usenet/comp.sources.x/kterm/***

   Address: **unix.hensa.ac.uk**
   Path: **/pub/uunet/systems/window-sys/X/contrib/R5contrib-fixes/kterm/***

less

less is a paging program similar to the standard Unix **more** program. Named **less** as a play on the name **more**, **less** actually provides more functionality than **more**.

Anonymous FTP:
   Address: **cs.oswego.edu**
   Path: **/pub/Z/less-205.tar.gz**

   Address: **sun.soe.clarkson.edu**
   Path: **/pub/src/less**

Multiverse

X Window-based multiuser graphical environment with sample worlds, complete with source.

Anonymous FTP:
   Address: **ftp.u.washington.edu**
   Path: **/public/virtual-worlds/multiverse/***

nenscript

Format an ASCII file and convert it to PostScript. **nenscript** will beautify your ASCII printouts. This is great for printing source code.

Anonymous FTP:
   Address: **dutepp0.et.tudelft.nl**
   Path: **/pub/Unix/PostScript/nenscript.tar.Z**

   Address: **walton.maths.tcd.ie**
   Path: **/src/misc/enscript**

To dream is human, to telnet is divine.

---

nn

nn, which stands for No News (is good news), is a replacement for the standard Unix newsreader **rn**. **nn** makes the user sift through as little material as possible and is a robust and highly configurable newsreader.

Anonymous FTP:
   Address: **ee.utah.edu**
   Path: **/nn**

   Address: **lth.se**
   Path: **/pub/netnews/sources.unix/volume22/nn6.4**

Oleo

An excellent spreadsheet program for X Window and character-based terminals. Oleo can generate embedded PostScript renditions of spreadsheets.

Anonymous FTP:
   Address: **aeneas.mit.edu**
   Path: **/pub/gnu/oleo***

   Address: **sunsite.unc.edu**
   Path: **/pub/gnu/applications/oleo***

Archie:
   Pattern: **oleo**

Perl

Perl (for Practical Extraction and Report Language) is a very popular replacement for the **awk** and **sed** text formatting languages.

Note: The convex site doesn't store the source code, but does have many scripts and a tutorial on how to use Perl.

Anonymous FTP:
   Address: **convex.com**
   Path: **/pub/perl**

   Address: **prep.ai.mit.edu**
   Path: **/pub/gnu/perl-4.036.tar.gz**

Perl Discussion

A discussion forum for Perl, the Practical Extraction and Report Language.

Internet Relay Chat:
   Channel: **#perl**

```
    Perl: The Ultimate
   Programming Language
         (sort of)
Perl is the holy grail of
programming languages (at least
for a few years) -- powerful
enough to do just about anything
you want; obtuse enough to
collect a cult-like band of
followers; and complex enough to
challenge even the most talented
of hackers. If you like
programming, if you like Unix,
and if you know how to program
the shell, then Perl is for you.

As Socrates once said:

   System managers love Perl.

   Everybody loves system managers.

   Therefore, everybody loves Perl.

Perhaps another way to put it is
that Perl is to the 1990s, what
APL was to the 1970s.
```

Perl Tools Development

A collection of Perl tools and libraries written by Earl Hood and distributed via the GNU General Public License. The Perl tools include a Perl library to allow Perl programs to run as a Unix daemon, a program that generates a HTML document, a program to convert a Mosaic hotlist to a HTML document, a program to automatically generate a table of contents for HTML documents, a program to convert mail messages to HTML, a program to generate a home pages index of all user home pages on a machine, a program to convert Unix man pages to HTML, and other tools dealing with the Web, HTML, and Mosaic.

World Wide Web:
URL: **http://www.uci.edu/indiv/ehood/**

Guess how many items there are in the Trivia section.

Pine

The Pine mailer is a popular mail program for Unix systems.

Anonymous FTP:
Address: **ee.utah.edu**
Path: **/pine**

Address: **ftp.eu.net**
Path: **/mail/pine**

Address: **qiclab.scn.rain.com**
Path: **/pub/mail/pine3.89.tar.Z**

World Wide Web:
URL: **http://www.cac.washington.edu/pine/**

Pine Mailer Demo

Try out an almost full-featured version of the Pine mailer program. This demo package allows the user to send mail messages for demonstration purposes.

Telnet:
Address: **demo.cac.washington.edu**
Login: **pinedemo**

procmail

procmail is a filtering package for incoming and outgoing mail messages. Some mailers have their own packages built in, but you can use **procmail** externally.

Anonymous FTP:
Address: **gatekeeper.dec.com**
Path: **/.b/usenet/comp.sources.misc/volume43/
procmail**

Address: **lth.se**
Path: **/pub/netnews/sources.misc/volume28/
procmail**

pty

pty is a neat program that allows you to run processes on a pseudo-tty (a **pty**). Like **screen**, processes running in a **pty** will continue to run after you log out.

Anonymous FTP:
Address: **archive.cis.ohio-state.edu**
Path: **/pub/comp.sources.unix/Volume23**

Address: **lth.se**
Path: **/pub/netnews/sources.unix/volume25/pty4/***

A
B
C
D
E
F
G
H
I
J
K
L
M
N
O
P
Q
R
S
T
U
V
W
X
Y
Z

Query Interface to the Linux Software Map Broker

This query interface allows you to search the Linux Software Map Broker, which covers more than 500 software distributions available for the Linux operation system. There are several options which you can set from this forms-based interface, including query options and result presentation options. An example query might be to match editors in the Linux software map archives that require XFree to run. There is help documentation for formatting queries. Content summaries, as well as the actual files, mostly in **.tar.gz** format, are available for any results found.

World Wide Web:
> URL: **http://rd.cs.colorado.edu/brokers/lsm/ query.html**

rn/trn

rn (for Read News) and **trn** (for Threaded Read News) are widely used newsreaders on the Internet. **trn** is the threaded version of **rn**.

Anonymous FTP:
> Address: **ee.utah.edu**
> Path: **/rrn/trn-3.0.tar.Z**

> Address: **lth.se**
> Path: **/pub/usenet/source.unix/volume25/trn**

screen

screen is a program that allows Unix users to split a vt100-style terminal screen into multiple sessions and hot-key between them. **screen** works great with dial-up connections and terminal emulation.

Anonymous FTP:
> Address: **aeneas.mit.edu**
> Path: **/pub/gnu/screen-3***

> Address: **faui43.informatik.uni-erlangen.de**
> Path: **/pub/utilities/screen/screen-3.5.2.tar.gz**

> Address: **prep.ai.mit.edu**
> Path: **/pub/gnu/screen-3.5.2.tar.gz**

> Address: **sunsite.unc.edu**
> Path: **/pub/gnu/applications/screen-3***

Archie:
> Pattern: **screen-3***

Shells: bash

The "Bourne again shell" is a great improvement over **sh** and is ideal for interactive work.

Anonymous FTP:
> Address: **prep.ai.mit.edu**
> Path: **/pub/gnu/bash-1.12.tar.gz**

> Address: **unix.hensa.ac.uk**
> Path: **/pub/uunet/pub/shells/bash-1.12/tar.Z**

Shells: pdksh

A public domain version of the popular **ksh**.

Anonymous FTP:
> Address: **qiclab.scn.rain.com**
> Path: **/pub/shells/pdksh-4.1.tar.Z**

> Address: **usc.edu**
> Path: **/archive/usenet/sources/comp.sources.misc/ volume34**

Shells: rc

rc is a simple, elegant shell written for people who want speed and efficiency in their shell scripts without all the interactive glitter.

Anonymous FTP:
> Address: **qiclab.scn.rain.com**
> Path: **/pub/shells**

> Address: **unix.hensa.ac.uk**
> Path: **/pub/uunet/pub/shells/rc**

Shells: tcsh

tcsh is a vast improvement over **csh** for interactive work. It is backwards compatible with the C-Shell, but includes command and filename completion.

Anonymous FTP:
> Address: **midway.uchicago.edu**
> Path: **/pub/unix/tcsh**

> Address: **tesla.ee.cornell.edu**
> Path: **/pub/tcsh**

Shells: zsh

zsh is often regarded as the best interactive Unix shell available.

Anonymous FTP:
> Address: **princeton.edu**
> Path: **/pub/zsh/zsh2.3.1.tar.Z**

> Address: **unix.hensa.ac.uk**
> Path: **/pub/uunet/pub/shells/zsh**

SLaTeX

A package for formatting Scheme source code nicely within a LaTeX document.

Anonymous FTP:
> Address: **cs.rice.edu**
> Path: **/public/slatex.tar.Z**

Smalltalk

The GNU implementation of Smalltalk, the original object-oriented programming language, complete with source code.

Anonymous FTP:
> Address: **aeneas.mit.edu**
> Path: **/pub/gnu/smalltalk***

> Address: **gatekeeper.dec.com**
> Path: **/.9/plan/smalltalk**

> Address: **sunsite.unc.edu**
> Path: **/pub/gnu/development/smalltalk***

Archie:
> Pattern: **smalltalk**

Tgif Image Drawing Software

Tgif is a drawing tool for X Window systems that supports hierarchical construction of drawings.

Anonymous FTP:
> Address: **cs.ucla.edu**
> Path: **/pub/tgif/***

Top

Top is a Unix system administration program that provides continual reports on the state of a system, including a list of the most CPU-intensive processes.

Anonymous FTP:
> Address: **eecs.nwu.edu**
> Path: **/pub/top**

Un-CGI

Un-CGI is a frontend for processing queries and forms from the Web on Unix systems. If you want to process a form without this program, you have to use routines to translate the values of the form fields from URL encoding to whatever your program requires. However, Un-CGI decodes all the form fields for you and places them into environment variables for easy perusal by a shell script, C program, Perl script, or anything else. Details, examples, and the program source in the form of a compressed .shar file can be found here.

World Wide Web:
> URL: **http://www.hyperion.com/~koreth/uncgi.html**

Unix Software Archive

The Higher Education National Software Archive (HENSA) for Unix systems maintains a gopher with connections to large collections of public domain (free) software relating to education.

Gopher:
> Name: Hensa Public Domain Software Archive
> Address: **unix.hensa.ac.uk**

Mail:
> Address: **archive@unix.hensa.ac.uk**
> Body: **help**

World Wide Web:
> URL: **http://www.hensa.ac.uk/hensa.unix.html**

A
B
C
D
E
F
G
H
I
J
K
L
M
N
O
P
Q
R
S
T
U
V
W
X
Y
Z

X Window Image Utilities

These two programs are X Window utilities that allow you to dump and undump an image to a file to be viewed later.

Anonymous FTP:
Address: **ftp.cc.utexas.edu**
Path: **/source/X11R5/mit/clients/xwud/***

Address: **ftp.cs.tut.fi**
Path: **/pub/src/X/X11R5/mit/clients/xwud**

X Window Source Archives

A huge collection of X Window source code and programs.

Anonymous FTP:
Address: **export.lcs.mit.edu**
Path: **/contrib/***

Address: **ftp.uu.net**
Path: **/pub/window-sys/X/contrib/***

Address: **public.x.org**
Path: **/contrib/***

xgrabsc: X Window Utility

xgrabsc allows X Window users to capture rectangular screen images and store them in graphic files.

Anonymous FTP:
Address: **harpo.seas.ucla.edu**
Path: **/pub/xgrabsc***

Address: **unix.hensa.ac.uk**
Path: **/pub/uunet/usenet/comp.sources.x/
    volume18/xgrabsc-2.1**

Address: **usc.edu**
Path: **/archive/usenet/sources/comp.sources.x/
    volume20/xgrabsc/**

XV

This interactive image viewer for X Window will allow you to display and manipulate many different image formats and convert between them.

Anonymous FTP:
Address: **ftp.cis.upenn.edu**
Path: **/pub/xv**

Address: **src.doc.ic.ac.uk**
Path: **/usenet/comp.sources.x/volume10**

ytalk

ytalk is similar to the Unix **talk** and **ntalk** programs, but **ytalk** allows Unix users to talk with more than one person at the same time. It is compatible with both **talk** and **ntalk**, so remote users that you **ytalk** to don't have to have **ytalk** themselves.

Anonymous FTP:
Address: **ftp.cc.utexas.edu**
Path: **/pub/ytalk/***

Address: **sun.soe.clarkson.edu**
Path: **/pub/src/ytalk/***

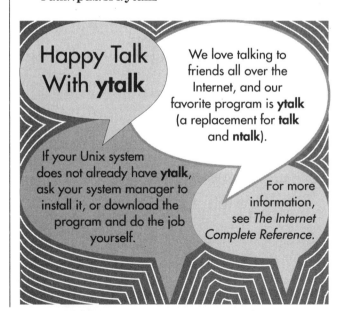

SOFTWARE: UTILITIES

ARJ Utilities

Utilities to un-ARJ those **.ARJ** files, for Unix, VMS, PC, Mac, and Amiga.

Anonymous FTP:
Address: **ftp.tex.ac.uk**
Path: **/pub/archive/tools/unarj/***

ASCII Table

The complete ASCII code table, including control character abbreviations. ASCII stands for the American Standard Code for Information Interchange.

Gopher:
Name: University of Texas at Austin
Address: **gopher.eco.utexas.edu**
Choose: **Index | ascii, character set table**

Automatic Login Executor

The Automatic Login Executor (or ALEX) is a slick C-Shell program that you can run on a Unix system to automate your Internet explorations. This amazing collection of shell scripts was written by a high school student in ten weeks.

Anonymous FTP:
Address: **ftp.gsfc.nasa.gov**
Path: **/pub/alex/csh-alex/***

Benchmark Software

Results and summaries of benchmark programs that have been run on various computers, including Dhrystone 1.1, Towers of Hanoi, the Heapsort algorithm and others.

Anonymous FTP:
Address: **ftp.spies.com**
Path: **/Library/Techdoc/Bench/***

Gopher:
Name: Internet Wiretap
Address: **wiretap.spies.com**
Choose: **Wiretap Online Library**
  | Technical Information
  | Benchmarks

Chimera

Chimera is a World Wide Web browser with an X/Athena graphical interface. Details can be found here about what it offers, support and help files, and where to ftp it from.

World Wide Web:
URL: **http://www.unlv.edu/chimera/index.html**

Chinese telnet

A modified version of the telnet program for the PC. This version uses the eighth bit of every byte to be able to display Chinese characters.

See also: Internet

Anonymous FTP:
Address: **ftp.ccu.edu.tw**
Path: **/pub/ncsa/***

Address: **moers2.edu.tw**
Path: **/chinese-pub/ncsa/***

Chinese Text Viewer

A shareware system for the PC that allows you to view Chinese text and documents.

Anonymous FTP:
Address: **moers2.edu.tw**
Path: **/chinese-pub/chinese-sys/***

Compilers and Interpreters

A catalog of free compilers, interpreters, and compiler building tools available on the Internet. This huge file contains tools for many computer languages, including C and its variants, LISP, Forth, and many other languages and scripting tools you've probably never heard of.

Anonymous FTP:
Address: **wombat.doc.ic.ac.uk**
Path: **/pub/FreeCompilers.gz**

Gopher:
Name: Imperial College
Address: **wombat.doc.ic.ac.uk**
Choose: **Free Compilers list**

Name: University of Toronto
Address: **wave.scar.utoronto.ca**
Choose: **Computing and Instructional Technology**
  | Software
  | Free Compilers list

Displaying Chinese Documents

Instructions for displaying Chinese documents on a PC, Macintosh, or X Window system.

See also: Usenet

Gopher:
> Name: National Chung Cheng University
> Address: **gopher.ccu.edu.tw**
> Choose: **About the Gopher**
> | **About this Gopher**

Displaying Hangul (Korean) Documents

Instructions for displaying Hangul (the Korean language) documents on a PC, Macintosh, or X Window system.

See also: Usenet, Software: Utilities

Anonymous FTP:
> Address: **ftp.kaist.ac.kr**
> Path: **/pub/hangul.FAQ**

Attention All DOS Users

Many of the files that you can snarf for free on the Net are binary files stored in the uuencoded format. It is handy to be able to transfer such files to your PC and then convert them back to their original form. To do so, you will need a DOS version of **uudecode**. No problem. You can download this program for free from many places. (Once you do, you will find that **uudecode** is just the thing to decode all those pictures you need to see in order to carry out your "research" . .)

Displaying Japanese Documents

Instructions for displaying Japanese documents on a PC, Macintosh, or X Window system.

See also: Software: Utilities, Usenet

Gopher:
> Name: Keio University, Science and Technology
> Address: **gopher.st.keio.ac.jp**
> Choose: **Japanese**
> | **How to read Japanese files**

DOS uudecode

A DOS version of the popular Unix **uudecode** program that you can use on your PC.

Anonymous FTP:
> Address: **oak.oakland.edu**
> Path: **/pub/msdos/decode**

Druid

The Druid User Interface Management System is a software development tool that assists the developer in the design and creation of graphical user interfaces (GUIs) for applications using the X11 window system and the OSF/Motif toolkit. The code generated by Druid can be compiled and linked with any C/C++ application. Technical information and details of how to obtain Druid can be found here, or by sending mail to **druid-info@iss.nus.sg**.

See also: Software: Unix

World Wide Web:
> URL: **http://www.iss.nus.sg/public/ISS_OTHER/druid.html**

Eiffel

Eiffel is an advanced object-oriented programming language that emphasizes the design and construction of high-quality and reusable software. Eiffel is not a superset or extension of any other language, though there are interfaces to other languages such as C and C++. Beyond the language aspect, Eiffel may be viewed as a method of software construction. For more on Eiffel, see their server.

Anonymous FTP:
> Address: **ftp.cm.cf.ac.uk**
> Path: **/pub/eiffel**

World Wide Web:
> URL: **ftp://ftp.cm.cf.ac.uk/CLE/**

Hangul (Korean) Software Tools

Emulators, editors, and fonts to read and compose in Hangul, the language of Korea.

Anonymous FTP:
  Address: **ftp.kaist.ac.kr**
  Path: **/pub/hangul/***

Internet Tools List

A large list of tools available on the Internet that are used for network information retrieval (NIR) and Computer-Mediated Communication(CMC), compiled by John December. It gives details and links to many Internet tools, utilities, systems, interfaces, and much, much more. This list is divided into sections for each tool, and is available in a variety of formats, including LaTeX, postscript, HTML, and ASCII by ftp.

Anonymous FTP:
  Address: **ftp.rpi.edu**
  Path: **/pub/communications/**
     internet-tools.readme

World Wide Web:
  URL: **http://www.rpi.edu/Internet/Guides/**
     decemj/itools/top.html

Ispell

An interactive Unix spelling corrector based on the "ITS SPELL" program. The program and its source code are available here.

Anonymous FTP:
  Address: **ftp.cs.ucla.edu**
  Path: **/pub/ispell/***

  Address: **sunsite.unc.edu**
  Path: **/pub/gnu/applications/ispell***

Archie:
  Pattern: **ispell**

Kerberos Resources

A large collection of links to Kerberos resources on the Net. Kerberos is a network authentication system for use on physically insecure networks, based on a key distribution model. It allows entities communicating over networks to prove their identity to each other while preventing eavesdropping or replay attacks. The resources include mailing lists, FAQs, software, patches, and more.

World Wide Web:
  URL: **http://www.cs.cmu.edu:8001/afs/**
     andrew.cmu.edu/usr/db74/www/kerberos.html

OS/2 Utilities

Utility programs for OS/2, including replacements for CMD.EXE, Phil Katz's Pkzip for OS/2, and other useful programs.

Anonymous FTP:
  Address: **ftp-os2.cdrom.com**
  Path: **/.2/os2**

  Address: **ftp-os2.nmsu.edu**
  Path: **/os2**

  Address: **ftp.uni-trier.de**
  Path: **/pub/os2/tools**

PC Archiving Utilities

Pkzip, ARJ, LHA, ZOO, and other less common PC archive programs and their associated utilities for DOS systems.

Anonymous FTP:
  Address: **ftp.ulowell.edu**
  Path: **/msdos/Archivers/***

PC Utilities

Lots of PC utilities and files from *PC Magazine*'s Interactive Reader Service.

Anonymous FTP:
  Address: **ftp.cso.uiuc.edu**
  Path: **/pc/pcmag/***

PC Video Card Drivers

Get the latest version drivers for Diamond Video, ATI, and many other popular video graphics cards.

Anonymous FTP:
  Address: **ftp.cica.indiana.edu**
  Path: **/pub/pc/win3/drivers/video/***

Source Code for Unix Utilities

Source code for Unix and X Window utilities such as **uuencode**, **uudecode**, **xxencode**, **xxdecode**, **whois**, **uucat**, and others.

Anonymous FTP:
  Address: **oak.oakland.edu**
  Path: **/pub/misc/unix**

A
B
C
D
E
F
G
H
I
J
K
L
M
N
O
P
Q
R
S
T
U
V
W
X
Y
Z

See What's Inside

Have you ever wondered how all those famous Unix utilities actually work? Download the source code and take a look for yourself.

**Secrets are for weenies.
Unix is cool.**

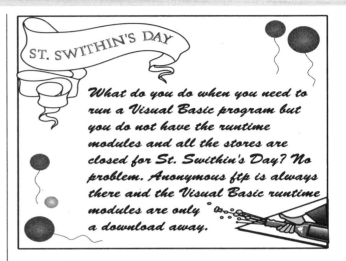

What do you do when you need to run a Visual Basic program but you do not have the runtime modules and all the stores are closed for St. Swithin's Day? No problem. Anonymous ftp is always there and the Visual Basic runtime modules are only a download away.

VESA Driver

A universal VESA driver for industry standard architecture PCs.

Anonymous FTP:
Address: **ftp.wustl.edu**
Path: **/systems/msdos/garbo/graphics/svgakt50.zip**

Visual Basic Runtime Modules

Many newer shareware programs require you to have certain runtime files. Programs written with Microsoft Visual Basic require runtimes called VBRUN100, VBRUN200, or VBRUN300. Here are a few sources for these files.

Note: Substitute the **?** in the paths and Archie pattern below with **1**, **2**, or **3** depending on the runtime version you need.

Anonymous FTP:
Address: **ftp.cdrom.com**
Path: **/.2/cdrom/cdroms/cica/vbrun?00.dll**

Address: **plains.nodak.edu**
Path: **/pub/pc/utils/vbrun?00dll**

Archie:
Pattern: **vbrun?00**

VMS Utilities

A collection of various utilities for VMS, including **diff**, **grep**, **more**, and others.

Anonymous FTP:
Address: **ftp.cs.widener.edu**
Path: **/pub/vms/***

WinPkt

WinPkt is a packet driver interface between Windows 3 Enhanced mode applications and a real packet driver. This is an assembly language program.

Anonymous FTP:
Address: **ftp.cc.utexas.edu**
Path: **/microlib/dos/network/.cap/winpkt.zip**

Address: **oxy.edu**
Path: **/public/msdos_programs/winpkt.zip**

Xtoys

This page offers a directory of cellular automata simulators for X Window. It includes sources and SunOS 4.1.3 executables for a two-dimensional Ising model simulator, Potts model, a totalistic cellular automation simulator, sandpile model, and a simple forest fire automaton. There is also a directory containing similar Amiga programs.

Anonymous FTP:
Address: **penguin.phy.bnl.gov**
Path: **/www/xtoys/***

World Wide Web:
URL: **http://penguin.phy.bnl.gov/www/xtoys/xtoys.html**

SPACE

Aeronautics and Space Acronyms

An acronym list, useful for translating commonly appearing acronyms in the space-related Usenet newsgroups.

Anonymous FTP:
Address: **ftp.spies.com**
Path: **/Library/Article/Aero/space.ac**

Gopher:
Name: Internet Wiretap
Address: **wiretap.spies.com**
Choose: **Wiretap Online Library**
  I **Articles**
  I **Aeronautics and Space**
  I **Astro/Space Frequently Seen Acronyms**

Aeronautics and Space Articles

NASA articles, the space launch list, Japanese aircraft code names, shuttle disaster article, space acronyms, the best fighter pilot, the phenomena on the surface of Venus, and other interesting articles.

Anonymous FTP:
Address: **ftp.spies.com**
Path: **/Library/Article/Aero/***

Gopher:
Name: Internet Wiretap
Address: **wiretap.spies.com**
Choose: **Wiretap Online Library**
  I **Articles**
  I **Aeronautics and Space**

Center for Earth and Planetary Studies

Experience the excitement of outer space. The Center is the home of the Regional Planetary Image Facility, which houses over 300,000 photographs and images of the planets and their satellites. Also available at this server are images and information on the space shuttle.

World Wide Web:
URL: **http://ceps.nasm.edu:2020/homepage.html**

Space images are very popular items. This one is **spacewalk** and it's available in a number of formats, including gif, jpeg and LZH. Often, archive files are stored on Unix computers where long filenames are allowed. If you're looking for files to download to PCs, you may want to look for shorter names. For example, this image exists in many archives as **spacewal.gif** due to DOS's eight character limitation. Using archie to search for **spacewalk** won't find **spacewal**.

Earth Systems Data Directory

The NOAA (National Oceanic and Atmospheric Administration) Earth Systems Data Directory is an information resource for identification, location, and overview descriptions of earth-science data sets (data from satelites).

See also: Weather

Gopher:
Name: National Oceanic and Atmospheric
  Administration
Address: **gopher.esdim.noaa.gov**

Telnet:
Address: **esdim.noaa.gov**
Login: **noaadir**

Address: **esdim1.esdim.noaa.gov**
Login: **noaadir**

World Wide Web:
URL: **http://www.ncdc.noaa.gov/ncdc.html**

EnviroNet

A menu-driven, user-friendly space environment resource with space data as text, graphics, and tables, as well as other interesting documents such as handbooks on spacecraft interactions with the space environment.

See also: Environment

Telnet:
Address: **envnet.gsfc.nasa.gov**
Login: **envnet**
Password: **henniker**

A B C D E F G H I J K L M N O P Q R S T U V W X Y Z

European Space Agency

The Data Dissemination Network of the European Space Agency (ESA). Offers information retrieval services, prototype international directory, and other information and services.

Listserv Mailing List:
　　List Address: **esapress@esoc.bitnet**
　　Subscription Address: **listserv@esoc.bitnet**

Telnet:
　　Address: **esrin.esa.it**

World Wide Web:
　　URL: **http://mesis.esrin.esa.it/html/esis.html**
　　URL: **http://www.esrin.esa.it/**

European Space Information System

ESIS is the Information Systems Division of the European Space Agency (ESA). The ESIS project is a service to the space science community to provide access to scientific data, including catalogs, images, spectra, and time series from ESA/non-ESA space missions. A bibliographic service provides abstracts from a wide range of scientific journals.

World Wide Web:
　　URL: **http://www.esrin.esa.it/htdocs/esis/**
　　esis.html

FIFE Information System

Scientific data from satellites, space flights, and other databases.

Telnet:
　　Address: **pldsg3.gsfc.nasa.gov**
　　Login: **fifeuser**

Galaxy

Space is cool because there is so much of it and it's just waiting to be filled with stuff. Get a closer look at our very own galaxy with all its stars and nebulae and planets. See movies of interacting galaxies and images and light curves of a recent supernova. If you want to impress your special loved one with your knowledge of the stars but the sky happens to be cloudy, this site can be your backup plan.

See also: Astronomy

World Wide Web:
　　URL: **http://zebu.uoregon.edu/galaxy.html**

> ## Isn't this more fun than watching television?

Goddard Space Flight Center

Contains lots of news, images, pictures, information and other resources connected with NASA and the Goddard Space Flight Center.

Gopher:
　　Name: NASA Goddard Space Flight Center
　　Address: **gopher.gsfc.nasa.gov**

Grand Challenge Cosmology Consortium

The questions are a little more complex than "How does the ship get in that glass bottle?" The scale is much more massive, like, "How are galaxies formed?" The Consortium is attempting to answer the latter question by teaming up with astrophysicists, computer experts, and computational scientists to discover the origins of the universe. See current research and publications.

See also: Astronomy, Physics, Science

World Wide Web:
　　URL: **http://zeus.ncsa.uiuc.edu:8080/**
　　GC3_Home_Page.html

Hiraiso Solar Terrestrial Research Center

Space Environment Information Service for the Internet presents a glossary of solar-terrestrial terms, space environment data in realtime, radio spectrograph images, ftp data sites, and data for ionosphere.

Note: Notice the pair of colons in the login name.

Telnet:
　　Address: **hiraiso.crl.go.jp**
　　Login: **crlhir::**

World Wide Web:
　　URL: **http://hiraiso.crl.go.jp/**

> ## Using the Internet won't make you go blind.

Hubble Space Telescope

The Space Telescope Electronic Information System (STEIS) contains information for Hubble Space Telescope proposers and observers. It offers documents, status reports, plans, and weekly summaries. Get the daily update on the scheduled events and the outcome of experiments with the beleaguered Hubble Space Telescope.

Anonymous FTP:
Address: **stsci.edu**
Path: **/stsci/steis/***

Gopher:
Name: Space Telescope Electronic Information System
Address: **stsci.edu**

Telnet:
Address: **stinfo.hq.eso.org**
Login: **stinfo**

Space shuttle images are widely available on the Net. This one is called **shuttlelaunch.gif** and you can find it at Northern Arizona University (**ftp.nau.edu**) in the directory **/graphics/gif/digi**. Don't forget that when you download a file with a long name like this to a PC, the filename will be shortened.

Icarus

Icarus, the International Journal of Solar System Exploration, has a web server which contains information for authors, subscription details, and a listing of papers submitted to the journal. The list of submitted papers is updated every 4-6 weeks.

See also: Magazines

World Wide Web:
URL: **http://astrosun.tn.cornell.edu/Icarus/Icarus.html**

Lunar and Planetary Institute

The Institute is near the NASA Johnson Space Center and includes a computing center, extensive collections of lunar and planetary data, an image processing facility, an extensive library, a publishing facility, and facilities for workshops and conferences. Current topics include the origin and early evolution of the solar system; studies of the moon, meteorites, and the Earth; the outer solar system with emphasis on studies of icy satellites.

Telnet:
Address: **lpi.jsc.nasa.gov**
Login: **lpi**

Manned U.S. Space Flight Images

Images from all manned U.S. space flights and NASA corresponding dates/numbers.

Anonymous FTP:
Address: **images.jsc.nasa.gov**
Path: **PAO**

Mount Wilson Observatory

Much of the initial understanding of our universe came from data acquired at the Mount Wilson Observatory, located just outside Pasadena, California. Their web page offers general and historical information, scientific program details, a special Jupiter page, astronomical services, papers, and tourist information. The tourist information offers a multimedia virtual walking tour of the observatory, including areas not open to the public.

World Wide Web:
URL: **http://www.mtwilson.edu/index.html**

NASA Extragalactic Database (NED)

NED contains extensive cross-identifications for over 200,000 objects — galaxies, quasars, infrared and radio sources, and more. NED provides positions, names, and basic data (e.g., magnitudes, redshifts), as well as bibliographic references, abstracts, and notes.

Telnet:
Address: **ned.ipac.caltech.edu**
Login: **ned**

> ### Before you go on a trip, use the Net to help you plan. Read the Travel section.

NASA News

Up-to-date information on the status of spacecraft currently in space and other NASA happenings. Find out about the new discoveries made with the space-based Hubble telescope and unmanned probes launched towards distant planets and galaxies.

Finger:
Address: **nasanews@space.mit.edu**

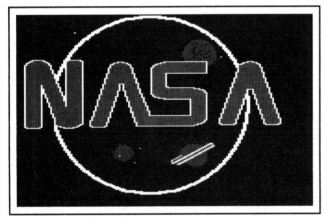

nasalogo is available in gif, HQX and MAC formats from the University of Western Ontario (**ftp.engrg.uwo.ca**) and NASA (**ames.arc.nasa.gov**). At UWO, it's in the directory **/pub/gifpics**. At NASA, it's in **/pub/SPACE/MAGELLAN**.

NASA Research Labs

It's your turn to plan an exciting date for you and the one you love. How about a tour of some of the most famous NASA research labs? After a romantic candle-lit dinner you can go back to your place, fire up the web browser and roam through the Goddard, Dryden, Ames, Langley and Kennedy space centers, to name just a few. In no time, word will be out that you really know how to entertain in style.

World Wide Web:
URL: **http://www.yahoo.com/Government/ Research_Labs/NASA/**

NASA Space Sensors and Instrument Technology Museum

A guide to online exhibits, tours, and details of museums that have an interest in space sensors and instrument technology. Some of the museums include gif images of historic scientific instruments. The guide is a hypertext document with links to the exhibits and museums, including the Museum of the Institute of Physics in Naples, the Astronomical Museum in Bologna, Mount Wilson Observatory in California, the Harvard-Smithsonian Center for Astrophysics, and Poker Flat Research Range.

World Wide Web:
URL: **http://ranier.oact.hq.nasa.gov/Sensors_page/ TechMuseums.html**

NASA Spacelink

History, current events, projects and plans at NASA.

Telnet:
Address: **spacelink.msfc.nasa.gov**

NASA Technological Reports

You're sitting around with your buddies and a heated argument erupts during your chat over Mach 8 crossflow transition experiments. Wagering a round of sarsaparilla, you swear up and down that during a thermal analysis of a 4130 steel skin using turbulent flow conditions, the maximum temperature would not exceed 400 degrees Fahrenheit. Fortunately for you, they didn't read up on their NASA technical reports or they would know you were wrong. Brush up on your NASA technology and you will never have to buy a round again.

See also: Science, Technology

World Wide Web:
URL: **http://techreports.larc.nasa.gov/ cgi-bin/NTRS**

NASDA

The National Space Development Agency of Japan (NASDA) is the Japanese equivalent of NASA.

Telnet:
Address: **nsaeoc.eoc.nasda.go.jp**
Login: **nasdadir**

News About Space

Keep current on the final frontier. Read all the latest news about space, astronomy and spaceflight.

Usenet:
Newsgroup: **clari.tw.space**
Newsgroup: **sci.space.news**

Do you have a favorite item that is not in the catalog? Let us know by sending mail to catalog@rain.org

---

Zines are cool.

Planetary Data System

Take a tour of the planets and other stellar bodies. See information on geoscience, plasma interactions, and a variety of interesting topics that really are out of this world.

See also: Astronomy

World Wide Web:
URL: **http://stardust.jpl.nasa.gov/ pds_home.html**

Excerpt from the Net...

```
Newsgroup: talk.politics.space
Subject: NASA knows about Nazi Moon Base. Important.

                    GERMAN MOON BASE, 1942
        ===================================================

The Germans landed on the Moon in 1942 using larger exo-atmospheric rocket saucers.

The rocket craft was built in diameters of 15 and 50 meters, and the turbine powered
craft was designed as an inter-planetary exploration vehicle.  The craft had a diameter
of 60 meters, had 10 stories of crew compartments, and stood 45 meters high.

Everything NASA has told the world about the Moon is a lie and it was done to keep the
exclusivity of the club from joinings by the third world countries.

In my extensive research of dissident American theories about the physical conditions on
the Moon, I have proven beyond the shadow of a doubt that there is atmosphere, water and
vegetation, and that man does not need a space suit to walk on the Moon.  A pair of
jeans, a pullover and sneakers are just about enough.  All these physical conditions make
it a lot easier to build a Moon base.

Ever since their first day of landing on the Moon, the Germans started boring and
tunneling under the surface, and by the end of the war there was a small Nazi research
base on the Moon.  A free energy tachyon drive craft was used after 1944 to haul people,
material, and the first robots to the construction site on the Moon.

After the end of the war in May 1945, the Germans continued their space effort from their
south polar colony of Neu Schwabenland.  When Russians and Americans secretly landed
jointly on the Moon in the early fifties with their own saucers, they spent their first
night there as guests of the Nazi underground base.

In the sixties a massive Russian/American base had been built on the Moon, and it now has
a population of 40,000 people.  I have discovered a photograph of their underground space
control center there, and I am working to make it available in GIF format.

This is very sensitive information and I am sharing it with you at great risk.  If you
intend to save this information or share it with others, please delete my name and site
location from the headers.
```

A
B
C
D
E
F
G
H
I
J
K
L
M
N
O
P
Q
R
S
T
U
V
W
X
Y
Z

Planetary Image Finders

Detailed maps and high-resolution raw images of some of the planets, including a Mars Atlas and Viking Orbiter image finder, and an image finder for the Voyager flyby.

World Wide Web:
> URL: **http://fi-www.arc.nasa.goV/fia/projects/ bayes-group/Atlas/**

Politics of Space

Do people belong in space? Is all the money worth it? What should we be doing and who should we be doing it with? Discuss nontechnical issues pertaining to space exploration.

Usenet:
> Newsgroup: **sci.space.policy**
> Newsgroup: **talk.politics.space**

SETI

Do you get tired of the same old smart people here on earth? Get a new cultural and intellectual perspective on the Universe by looking in at the SETI Institute. These people spend their time searching for extraterrestrial intelligence and want to share what they have found with you. Their web site has links to science and technology relating to astronomy and planetary sciences as well as biological and cultural evolution. This is the perfect place to start if you are looking for new friends from other planets. Unless of course, you already have your own spaceship.

World Wide Web:
> URL: **http://www.metrolink.com/seti/SETI.html**

Shuttle Payloads

It's a real problem when your shuttle has reached its capacity of 40,000 pounds and you decide that you want to take along your copies of *The Internet Golden Directory* and *The Internet Complete Reference* so you won't get so bored while floating around in outer space. It's difficult to know if the trunion bearings will take the extra weight. Read the NASA information about shuttle payloads and alternative methods to the standard payload such as The Get Away Special and the Hitchhiker carrier systems.

Gopher:
> Name: National Aeronautics and Space
>   Administration
> Address: **sspp.gsfc.nasa.gov**

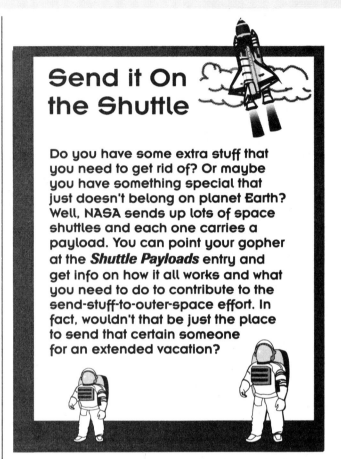

Send it On the Shuttle

Do you have some extra stuff that you need to get rid of? Or maybe you have something special that just doesn't belong on planet Earth? Well, NASA sends up lots of space shuttles and each one carries a payload. You can point your gopher at the *Shuttle Payloads* entry and get info on how it all works and what you need to do to contribute to the send-stuff-to-outer-space effort. In fact, wouldn't that be just the place to send that certain someone for an extended vacation?

Shuttle Snapshots

Snapshots of an astronaut's excursion are going to be much more exciting than Aunt Ethel's pictures of her trip to Haqualoochie, Oklahoma to visit the grandkids. See images of places like Bangkok, Mount St. Helens, Finger Lakes, Alaska, and the Grand Canyon taken from various space shuttle missions.

World Wide Web:
> URL: **http://zebu.uoregon.edu/earth.html**

Smithsonian Astrophysical Observatory

The ASCinfo system is an online bulletin board service that makes a collection of ASC documentation files available to the astronomical community. ASCinfo resides at the Smithsonian Astrophysical Observatory and is accessible to any user over the Internet.

Telnet:
> Address: **asc.harvard.edu**
> Login: **ascinfo**

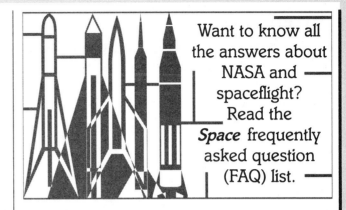

Space Calendar

If you think it's disastrous when you lose your date book, how do you think NASA feels? When you are shooting live human beings into space at high speeds, it's important to keep your scheduling straight. Check here if you want to keep up on what's happening in the cosmos.

Anonymous FTP:
Address: **explorer.arc.nasa.gov**
Path: **/pub/SPACE/FAQ/space.calendar**

World Wide Web:
URL: **file://explorer.arc.nasa.gov/pub/SPACE/FAQ/calendar.html**

Space Digest

The international *Space Digest* archive site.

Anonymous FTP:
Address: **julius.cs.qub.ac.uk**
Path: **/pub/SpaceDigestArchive**

Space Environment Effects Branch

It can be really uncomfortable when you have anomalies in your GEO spacecraft. Especially when you find out that there is a link between the anomalies and electrical discharge phenomena between the spacecraft and the GEO plasma. Check out the web page of the Space Environment Effects Branch and see if they have come up with something in their research of GEO spacecraft design that will help you with your spacecraft.

World Wide Web:
URL: **http://satori2.lerc.nasa.gov/**

Space Frequently Asked Questions

Get answers to the most frequently asked questions (FAQs) regarding NASA, spaceflight, and astrophysics.

Anonymous FTP:
Address: **explorer.arc.nasa.gov**
Path: **/pub/SPACE/FAQ**

Want to know all the answers about NASA and spaceflight? Read the *Space* frequently asked question (FAQ) list.

Space General Discussion

Talk, talk, talk about everything under the sun (and the sun as well). Discuss all manner of space-oriented topics with aficionados around the world.

Usenet:
Newsgroup: **sci.space**
Newsgroup: **sci.space.policy**
Newsgroup: **sci.space.science**
Newsgroup: **sci.space.tech**

Space Missions

Planning to go where no one has gone before? Check out the information on past or present space missions to make sure that nobody has been to your destination before you. You will find links to Apollo missions, the Cassini Mission, Clementine, Magellan and more.

World Wide Web:
URL: **http://www.yahoo.com/Science/Space/Missions/**

Space Movie Archive

Nearly 200 space animations in different formats, including Anim5, Fli, Flc, mpeg, and QuickTime. Offers movies on meteorology, solar eclipses, science fiction, space, Apollo missions, DCX-Y project, lunar probes, and more.

See also: Computers: Graphics

World Wide Web:
URL: **http://www.univ-rennes1.fr/ASTRO/anim-e.html**

Space Newsletter

Selection of newsletters about the final frontier, including *Space News*, *Satscan*, and *Biosphere*.

Anonymous FTP:
  Address: **nigel.msen.com**
  Path: **/pub/newsletters/Space/***

Space Shuttle

Keep up to date on what the space shuttle is doing and what we are doing with the space shuttle.

Usenet:
  Newsgroup: **sci.space.shuttle**

World Wide Web:
  URL: **http://www.ksc.nasa.gov/shuttle/missions/missions.html**

  URL: **http://www.ksc.nasa.gov/shuttle/technology/sts-newsref/stsref-toc.html**

What in heaven's name is going on in the space shuttle?

Read **sci.space.shuttle** and keep up with the only government employees who are paid to get high.

Spacecraft Information

This has text, animations, and images about all spacecraft, including Dante, Voyager, Pioneer, Mariner, Apollo, etc. Also has images of most planets and the moon.

See also: Astronomy

Anonymous FTP:
  Address: **seds.lpl.arizona.edu**
  Path: **/pub/spacecraft**
  Path: **/pub/images**

SpaceNews

A weekly finger report with information on current and upcoming shuttle missions, as well as other current information of interest regarding NASA, space, and space flight.

Finger:
  Address: **magliaco@pilot.njin.net**

Starship Design Home Page

This web page from the Lunar Institute of Technology (est. 2032) offers an interesting collection of information on starship science and engineering. It offers design projects, engineering facts on many rocket and engine types, "Relativity Paradoxes," references, bibliographies, book lists, links to related sites, software, computer simulation contests, online membership forms, and physics FAQs answering such questions as "What is the mass of a photon?". The School of Starship Design is an Internet project attempting to compile as much information as possible on the subject of interstellar travel.

See also: Science

World Wide Web:
  URL:
  http://128.194.15.32/~dml601a/ssd/sdhp.html

Students for the Exploration and Development of Space

SEDS is a student club devoted to the discussion and study of space. Meet people from SEDS chapters around the world. Find out all the latest space news and what SEDS members are up to.

Gopher:
  Name: University of Arizona
  Address: **seds.lpl.arizona.edu**

Telnet:
  Address: **seds.lpl.arizona.edu**

Usenet:
  Newsgroup: **bit.listserv.seds-l**
  Newsgroup: **bit.listserv.sedsnews**

World Wide Web:
  URL: **http://seds.lpl.arizona.edu/**

United Nations Office for Outer Space Affairs

Everyone is anxiously awaiting the news about extraterrestrials joining the United Nations. The U.N. even has an office for Outer Space Affairs which focuses on international cooperation regarding the use of space technology to monitor space activities as well as our terrestrial environment. See the U.N.'s latest activities at their web site.

World Wide Web:
URL: **ftp://ecf.hq.eso.org/pub/un/ un-homepage.html**

SPORTS AND ATHLETICS

.44 Magnum

A variety of recommendations and comments about bullets, powders, and loads for the .44 Magnum.

Anonymous FTP:
Address: **ftp.spies.com**
Path: **/Library/Article/Misc/magnum.44**

Gopher:
Name: Internet Wiretap
Address: **wiretap.spies.com**
Choose: **Wiretap Online Library**
 I **Articles**
 I **Misc**
 I **Magnum .44 Summary**

Aikido Dojos Around the World

A list of hundreds of Aikido dojos worldwide. Dojos in the U.S. are listed first, followed by dojos in other countries. The list covers all styles and affiliations of this popular Japanese martial art.

Anonymous FTP:
Address: **iuvax.cs.indiana.edu**
Path: **/pub/aikido/***

Address: **moose.cs.indiana.edu**
Path: **/pub/aikido/***

THE OLD PERSUADER

If you are like us, you are geniality and diplomacy personified. Still, there are times when tact is not enough and a more powerful, but subtle, form of persuasion becomes necessary. At such times, we find that a .44 Magnum handgun can work wonders. There is something about putting a hole the size of a grapefruit in someone's parietal lobe that makes them become more reasonable and can change even the most difficult situation into a pleasant experience. Just remember, try to use the gun in an area that can be washed immediately afterwards, and always go for a win-win solution.

American Football

Good old summertime. The sun is shining, the birds are singing, the flowers are blooming, and you can work on your tan. The problem is that there is no football. This is something that had to be tolerated until recently. Now you can get your fix during any season. Scores, history, news articles on both college and professional football.

World Wide Web:
URL: **http://www.atm.ch.cam.ac.uk/sports/ gridiron.html**

Aquanaut

Aquanaut is dedicated to the recreational and technical scuba diving community. It offers an archive of the **rec.scuba** newsgroup, mailing list archives, a database of diveable shipwrecks, reviews of dive gear and equipment, details of popular dive destinations, lists of training agencies, clubs, underwater pictures, a catalog of marine fish and invertebrates, classified ads, weather maps, and more.

World Wide Web:
URL: **http://www.opal.com/aquanaut**

ATP Tour Weekly

The ATP Tour Weekly electronic newsletter is your hotline to the best in men's professional tennis each week, with the latest tournament results and draws for the current week's events. It contains the latest IBM/ATP tour rankings, ATP tour news, tournament tidbits, player news, quotes, and more.

Mail:
Address: **rvach@jax.jaxnet.com**
Body: **subscribe ATP**

Australian Rules Football

A summary of the most frequently applied rules in Australian Rules football.

Anonymous FTP:
Address: **ftp.spies.com**
Path: **/Library/Article/Sports/rules.afl**

Gopher:
Name: Internet Wiretap
Address: **wiretap.spies.com**
Choose: **Wiretap Online Library**
  l **Articles**
  l **Sports**
  l **Summary of Rules for Australian Football**

Australian Sporting News

Stay up-to-date with the latest Australian sporting events and results.

Gopher:
Name: MegaGopher
Address: **megasun.bch.umontreal.ca**
Choose: **Australiana - News, sport, FAQs, etc. about Australia**
  l **Australian sports news**

Baseball Archives

What does it say about Americans when their favorite pastime is to sit for hours watching grown men get paid millions of dollars to run around in circles wearing something that closely resembles pajamas? Have a look at the baseball archives and see all the things you might be missing when you aren't actually at the stadium.

Anonymous FTP:
Address: **etext.archive.umich.edu**
Path: **/pub/Sports/Baseball**

World Wide Web:
URL: **http://wuarchive.wustl.edu/pub/baseball/**

Baseball Information Center

The Baseball Information Center is for baseball fans worldwide. In addition to discussion groups, baseball collectible info, stats, rosters, and team reports, there is also a fantasy league.

World Wide Web:
URL: **http://www.gems.com/ibic/**
URL: **http://www.gems.com/ibic/index.html**

Baseball Schedule

Get the day's game schedule for your favorite major league baseball teams. Enter **help** for help. Full season schedules are also available.

Gopher:
Name: University of Colorado Boulder
Address: **gopher.colorado.edu**
Choose: **Professional Sports Schedules**
  l **Major League Baseball Schedule**

Telnet:
Address: **culine.colorado.edu**
Port: **862**

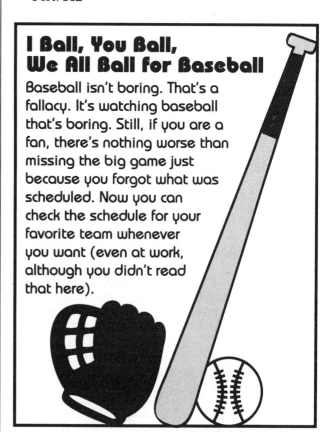

I Ball, You Ball, We All Ball for Baseball

Baseball isn't boring. That's a fallacy. It's watching baseball that's boring. Still, if you are a fan, there's nothing worse than missing the big game just because you forgot what was scheduled. Now you can check the schedule for your favorite team whenever you want (even at work, although you didn't read that here).

Baseball Scores

Get major league baseball scores with the finger command.

Finger:
> Address: **jtchern@ocf.berkeley.edu**
> Address: **robc@xmission.com**

Baseball Server

Articles and coverage from the American and National Leagues, major league standings, season-to-date transactions, statistics, facts, and other statistics and items of interest. This resource is updated on a daily basis.

World Wide Web:
> URL: **http://www.atm.ch.cam.ac.uk/sports/baseball.html**
> URL: **http://www.nando.net/baseball/bbmain.html**

Baseball Strike

An effective means of getting your way is to throw a tantrum and refuse to budge unless people give you what you want. And if you offer a service that is especially interesting or valuable to people, then that gives you an edge. It happens that not only can baseball players get paid lots of money for playing a game that most people play for free, but they can hold an entire nation hostage if they don't get what they want. Find out the latest news on baseball strikes and negotiations.

World Wide Web:
> URL: **http://sfgate.com/examiner/baseballhome.html**
> URL: **http://www.nando.net/newsroom/baseball/strike.html**

Baseball Teams

On those days when it's not enough to watch your favorite team at the stadium or on television, do some reading on their stats, standings and other team information on Usenet and the Web.

Usenet:
> Newsgroup: **rec.sports.baseball.***

World Wide Web:
> URL: **http://www.yahoo.com/Entertainment/Sports/Baseball/Teams/**

> ## No need to get lost in gopher space. Try Veronica.

Basketball FAQs

Earn your reputation as the basketball know-it-all of your neighborhood. Read statistical information about basketball teams, league leaders, team history and playoff standings. This is the best way to impress your friends and loved ones, short of winning a Nobel Prize.

World Wide Web:
> URL: **http://www.mit.edu:8001/services/sis/NBA/html/future.html**

Basketball Server

Having basketball fever doesn't mean that you just sit in front of the television making loud whooping noises. It's much more sophisticated than that. It's a fine balance of gathering statistics, analyzing trends, and making studied observations. Find all you need to become a seasoned basketball fan. Read the *NBA Daily Report*, see scores, hot news, statistics, archives, scheduling, and lists of awards — the perfect blend of information needed to win any heated trivia game.

World Wide Web:
> URL: **http://www.mit.edu:8001/services/sis/NBA/NBA.html**

Basketball Statistics

This ftp site has draft information, playoff schedules and rankings, team records, results, scores, and statistics. The newsgroups cover any topics that relate to basketball.

Anonymous FTP:
> Address: **ftp.wustl.edu**
> Path: **/doc/misc/nbastats/facts**

Usenet:
> Newsgroup: **alt.sports.basketball.nba.***
> Newsgroup: **alt.sports.basketball.pro.***

> ## This is the first book of the rest of your life.

A
B
C
D
E
F
G
H
I
J
K
L
M
N
O
P
Q
R
S
T
U
V
W
X
Y
Z

Bicycle Commuting

Get those legs pumping and the heart racing and save the environment and your bank book at the same time. Forget the hubbub of all those speeding cars trying to jockey for a position on the freeway — travel by bike. This list is mostly for Silicon Valley residents, but discussion centers around bicycle transportation and improving bicycling conditions in city and suburban areas. The web pages give you access to FAQ lists, help you choose routes, coexist with cars, and give you ideas for spiffing up your bike.

Internet Mailing List:
    List Address:
        bikecommute@bike2work.eng.sun.com
    Subscription Address:
        bikecommute-request@bike2work.eng.sun.com

World Wide Web:
    URL: **http://cycling.org/1/reading.room/**
      commuting
    URL: **http://wiretap.spies.com/ceej/bikes.html**

Bicycle Discussion Lists on the Internet

It's not only great exercise, but riding a bicycle is a nice way to save the environment at the same time. Find out all the cycling resources on the Internet, by checking out this Web page.

World Wide Web:
    URL: **http://eksl-www.cs.umass.edu/~westy/**
      cycling/cycling-on-internet.html

Bicycle Mailing List

Local, state, and national bicycling issues, especially for Santa Cruz County, California. Public hearings and government meetings are announced and reported on.

Internet Mailing List:
    List Address: **bikepeople@ce.ucsc.edu**
    Subscription Address:
      bikepeople-request@ce.ucsc.edu

    List Address: **bikepeople@daizu.ucsc.edu**
    Subscription Address:
      bikepeople-request@daizu.ucsc.edu

> ## Using the Internet won't make you go blind.

Bicycles FAQS

It has been said that once you learn to ride a bicycle you never forget how to do it. That doesn't mean you will never have questions about bicycles. When that happens, use your Web browser to look at this lengthy bicycle FAQ and get answers to the Great Bicycle Mysteries of Life.

World Wide Web:
    URL: **http://www.cis.ohio-state.edu/**
      hypertext/faq/usenet/bicycles-faq/top.html

Bicycling

Whether you like to jump ditches and career down steep inclines or if you like to just meander on a bicycle built for two, this forum has something in which you will be interested. Crash helmets are advised, but not mandatory. All cycling topics are covered, but discussion about motorcycling is best taken to another group.

Listserv Mailing List:
    List Address: **bicycle@bitnic.educom.edu**
    Subscription Address: **listserv@bitnic.educom.edu**

Big Eight College Football

College football is great because not only is there plenty of great football, but the cheerleaders are fun to watch, too. Read statistics and information on the Big Eight college teams.

World Wide Web:
    URL: **http://www.cis.ksu.edu/~chiefs/**
      bigeight.html

Bitnet Baseball League

It's sort of like going down to the sports bar — except the noise and smoke are greatly reduced. If you could create the ultimate baseball team, what major league players would be on it? Get together with other fans and go head-to-head trying to create the best team possible. The weekly results are based on player performance and team comparison, so nobody has to pull a hamstring or blacken an eye. It's perfectly safe.

Listserv Mailing List:
    List Address: **statlg-l@ccvm.sunysb.edu**
    Subscription Address: **listserv@ccvm.sunysb.edu**

Boxing

We are not sure, exactly, what the appeal is of watching men hit each other until they are unconscious or exhausted. Imagine the brain cells that could be in full use, but are instead being bashed about like a string of rugs during spring cleaning. But this thought doesn't bother the fans of boxing and they will be found in Usenet talking about the history of boxing as well as the latest knock-down-drag-out.

Usenet:
Newsgroup: **rec.sport.boxing**

Canadian Football League

Football is not just a disease exclusive to America. See how the Canadians play the game. Rules, referee signals, history, schedules and a glossary are available.

See also: Canada

World Wide Web:
URL: **http://www.ee.umanitoba.ca/CFL/CFL.html**

College Football

It must be true if *CNN* and *USA Today* say it is. Read polls from these news sources as well as AP polls and other sources of college football statistics. Links to other football sites are also available.

World Wide Web:
URL: **http://www.math.ufl.edu/~mitgardt/ rsfc.html**

College Hockey

It's exciting to watch a bunch of padded maniacs zip up and down a slab of ice and hit each other with sticks. You can get more involved in collegiate ice hockey by posting or reading scores, team information, and schedules for your favorite teams.

Listserv Mailing List:
List Address: **hockey-l@maine.maine.edu**
Subscription Address: **listserv@maine.maine.edu**

College Hockey Computer Rating

Want to know how your favorite college hockey team ranks? Check out the current ratings and see explanations of how the ratings work.

World Wide Web:
URL: **http://hydra.bgsu.edu/TCHCR/ TCHCR.html**

Commonwealth Games

Information about the Commonwealth Games — an international athletic competition that is held each year. The web page has links to realtime results (while the games are underway), statistics, and related resources.

Gopher:
Name: The Community Learning Network
Address: **cln.etc.bc.ca**
Choose: **CLN Other Partners and Resources | XV Commonwealth Games - Online Information**

World Wide Web:
URL: **http://www.cg94.freenet.victoria.bc.ca/**

Cricket

A mailing list featuring the scoresheets of first class cricket matches and itineraries of the tours. The list is gatewayed to the Usenet newsgroup **rec.sport.cricket.scores**.

Listserv Mailing List:
List Address: **cricket@vm1.nodak.edu**
Subscription Address: **listserv@vm1.nodak.edu**

Usenet:
Newsgroup: **rec.sport.cricket.info**

Cricket Talk

Talk cricket on this channel dedicated to the sport.

Internet Relay Chat:
Channel: **#cricket**

Cricket Web Server

Nobody seems to feel undignified being the fan of a sport that has the same name as an insect — even when that insect is used as a really effective fish bait. Fans of cricket can get information on competitions and players as well as access to Usenet newsgroups.

World Wide Web:
URL: **http://cuda3.me.mtu.edu:8023/home/ maxwell-a.ee/kmushtaq/.mosaic/cricket.html**

If you like trouble, take a look at Mischief.

A
B
C
D
E
F
G
H
I
J
K
L
M
N
O
P
Q
R
S
T
U
V
W
X
Y
Z

Cycling Resources

Oodles of cycling resources are available on the Net. Here is an electronic information desk for cyclists, offering articles, contacts, newsletters, ride calendars, bicycle organization details, public meeting lists, a reading room, technical tips, a FAQ, links to other bicycle resources, and much more.

Anonymous FTP:
> Address: **cycling.org**
> Path: **/pub/gopher/cycling/***

> Address: **draco.acs.uci.edu**
> Path: **/pub/rec.bicycles/***

> Address: **rtfm.mit.edu**
> Path: **/pub/usenet/news.answers/bicycles-faq/***

> Address: **ugle.unit.no**
> Path: **/local/biking/***

Gopher:
> Name: Global Cycling Network
> Address: **cycling.org**

World Wide Web:
> URL: **http://cycling.org/**

Dead Runners Society

Reading about running is much less tiring than actually running, but with these people it doesn't seem to matter. This unmoderated list is swarming with people who love to run not so much for the sport of it, but because it's such a personal experience — the mind expands, the body moves steadily and gracefully, releasing the energy, tension, and knots that build up during the day. Runners of all levels are welcome.

Listserv Mailing List:
> List Address: **drs@dartcms1.dartmouth.edu**
> Subscription Address:
> **listserv@dartcms1.dartmouth.edu**

Disc Sports

FAQs, archives, contact information, rules, championship history, and more for Ultimate, Disc Golf, and other disc-related sports.

Anonymous FTP:
> Address: **ftp.cs.wisc.edu**
> Path: **/pub/ultimate/***

> # The best way to make money is to give something away for free.

Diving Server

The U.K. Diving Resource Server allows scuba divers in the United Kingdom to share information about dive sites, air fill stations, slipways, equipment, news, pictures, trip reports, stolen equipment, and other items of interest.

World Wide Web:
> URL: **http://www.cru.uea.ac.uk/ukdiving/**

East Coast Hockey League

After a while it gets really tiring doing the same old knit and purl. Get a little more physical and follow the teams of the East Coast Hockey League. This discussion list will keep you informed on all the League news.

Internet Mailing List:
> List Address: **echl-news@andrew.cmu.edu**
> Subscription Address:
> **echl-news-request@andrew.cmu.edu**

European Championships in Athletics

When traveling in Europe, don't feel like you are crossing a sports wasteland. Read information on European championships in athletics and get television and radio schedules, live event schedules, results of competitions and news.

World Wide Web:
> URL: **http://helsinki94.eunet.fi/**

Exercise and Sports Psychology

"Mind over matter," "No pain, no gain." You've heard all the motivational clichés designed to inspire you to push that out-of-shape body of yours up the hill, down the hill, and over the finish line. Examine the brain behind the body by participating in the discussion of exercise and sports psychology.

See also: Psychology

Listserv Mailing List:
> List Address: **sportpsy@vm.temple.edu**
> Subscription Address: **listserv@vm.temple.edu**

Fantasy Baseball

It's nice to know that there is an opportunity to achieve greatness even if you are a real klutz in sports. Fantasy baseball is a wonderful way to experience the thrill of the game while never having to leave your seat. Get information on the latest FTP sites, archives, mailing lists, Usenet groups, home pages and FAQs relating to fantasy baseball.

World Wide Web:
URL: **http://www.cm.cf.ac.uk/User/Gwyn.Price/ fantasy_baseball.html**

Fencing

Fencing is more than just making money off stolen goods. It's also a sport that takes speed, grace and finesse. (This is not to say the two are mutually exclusive, though.) This site offers you a glance at the rules, recommends books, and even shows you some art related to fencing.

World Wide Web:
URL: **http://www.ii.uib.no/~arild/fencing.html**

Figure Skating Home Page

A large competitive figure skating FAQ, pictures of skaters, inline skating information, and links to other skating resources and related material on the Net.

World Wide Web:
URL: **http://www.cs.yale.edu/HTML/YALE/CS/ HyPlans/loosemore-sandra/skate.html**

Footbag

If you are fast on your feet or, more accurately, fast *with* your feet, you will love footbag. The object of the game is to keep a small beanbag in the air for as long as possible using only your feet. The execution of this endeavor makes for some interesting gyrations. Join up with other footbag enthusiasts and perfect the sport.

World Wide Web:
URL: **http://gregorio.stanford.edu/footbag/ regionals.html**
URL: **http://gregorio.stanford.edu/www/footbag/ sufc.html**

Planning a picnic? Check the weather using the Net.

Football Resources

Details of college and professional football, updated daily with news, notes, and complete game coverage. Includes sections on the National Football League, the Canadian Football League, Arena Football, and a complete roundup of NCAA Division I football.

Anonymous FTP:
Address: **ftp.vnet.net**
Path: **/pub/football**

Usenet:
Newsgroup: **alt.sports.football.arena**
Newsgroup: **alt.sports.football.pro.***

World Wide Web:
URL: **http://www.awa.com/arena/jackson/**
URL: **http://www.cs.cmu.edu:8001/afs/cs/user/ vernon/www/nfl.html**
URL: **http://www.mit.edu:8001/services/sis/NFL/ NFL.html**
URL: **http://www.nando.net/football/1994/ fbserv.html**

Football Stadiums

A list of U.S. football stadiums, their capacities, and the teams that play in each.

Anonymous FTP:
Address: **ftp.spies.com**
Path: **/Library/Article/Sports/stadium.lis**

Gopher:
Name: Internet Wiretap
Address: **wiretap.spies.com**
Choose: **Wiretap Online Library**
 | **Articles**
 | **Sports**
 | **Stadium Listing**

Formula One Motor Racing

It's not everyday that we all get to hop in the car and burn rubber, leaving everyone else in a cloud of exhaust as well as risking life and limb by careening down a racetrack in a high performance vehicle. If you need a Formula One racing fix, check out this web page which contains updates, history, season results, rules and information on various teams as well as links to other racing sites.

World Wide Web:
URL: **http://www.abekrd.co.uk/Formula1/**

A
B
C
D
E
F
G
H
I
J
K
L
M
N
O
P
Q
R
S
T
U
V
W
X
Y
Z

Goddard Tennis Club

The Goddard Tennis Club offers tennis FAQs, tournament news, some tennis sounds, noises, and pictures, courtside gossip, newsletters, and club reports.

World Wide Web:
URL: **http://epims1.gsfc.nasa.gov/tennis/ GTC_homepage.html**

Golf

You don't have to wear funny pants to play golf, but it helps. What helps even more are secret tips on how to improve your game. We think the real reason Arnold Palmer did so well is because when he wasn't on the green he was hanging out at the golf archives at Princeton.

Anonymous FTP:
Address: **dunkin.Princeton.edu**
Path: **/pub/golf/***

World Wide Web:
URL: **http://www.yahoo.com/Entertainment/ Sports/Golf/**
URL: **http://dallas.nmhu.edu/golf.htm**
URL: **http://www.gdol.com/**

Golfers Mailing List

It's embarrassing when you have been playing golf for years and suddenly you notice that you are hitting your irons off the toe. Have other people noticed and been snickering behind your back? Get help now. Join this discussion group where golfers chat about all forms of golf and all topics relating to golf, including technique, equipment, and tournaments.

Listserv Mailing List:
List Address: **golf-l@ubvm.cc.buffalo.edu**
Subscription Address:
listserv@ubvm.cc.buffalo.edu

No one understands the Internet, so relax and enjoy.

Hockey

Web pages with schedules for the NHL, links to the web pages of various hockey teams, images, a radio list, college hockey computer ratings, and 1993-1994 team statistics. In the newsgroups, you can discuss anything you like relating to hockey and you'll be sure to find hundreds of people eager to talk.

Anonymous FTP:
Address: **andy.bgsu.edu**
Path: **/pub/Hockey/***

Usenet:
Newsgroup: **alt.sports.hockey.echl**
Newsgroup: **alt.sports.hockey.ihl**
Newsgroup: **alt.sports.hockey.nhl.***

World Wide Web:
URL: **ftp://ftp.u.washington.edu/public/hockey/ homepage.html**
URL: **http://maxwell.uhh.hawaii.edu/hockey/ hockey.html**
URL: **http://terrapin.umd.edu/nhl.html**

Hockey Discussion

A meeting place for hockey players and supporters. There is a HockeyBot which can respond to various words and actions sent to the channel, including highsticks, slashes, holds, hooks, and spears.

Internet Relay Chat:
Channel: **#hockey**

Horse Racing Archives

When you are out of money, you can get your racing fix by keeping up with the sport on this web page. Find information on the competitions like the Breeders' Cup and the Kentucky Derby.

World Wide Web:
URL: **http://www.inslab.uky.edu/~stevem/horses/ racing.html**

Human-Powered Vehicles

Save the environment and get healthy at the same time. Human-powered vehicles could be the next trend in transportation. Learn to build and power these unique vehicles.

World Wide Web:
URL: **http://zippy.sonoma.edu:70/1/HPV**

> ## The Internet has lots and lots (and lots) of free software.

Karate

It's a nice feeling to know that if you are walking down the street and someone hassles you, you can simply give them a chop in the neck. Or you can give them a double-whammy, flying-though-the-air, snap kick with a little spin on the end. Of course, for most people, karate is a sport or hobby, but that doesn't mean it's not handy to know. Get to know other people who train in one or more of the traditional Japanese/Okinawan karate styles. Share information and discuss issues that relate to teachers and students of karate.

Listserv Mailing List:
    List Address: **karate@ukanaix.cc.ukans.edu**
    Subscription Address:
        listserv@ukanaix.cc.ukans.edu

Korfball

A Dutch variation on the game of basketball. The main difference is that the team members consist of both men and women. Read about the game, its origins, rules, news and technical articles. What they don't tell you is what the locker room arrangements are.

World Wide Web:
    URL: **http://www.earth.ox.ac.uk/~geoff/**

Major League Baseball Schedules

Get today's, or any day's, baseball schedule, complete with the logo of your favorite team. There is also a facility to set your X Window background display to the team logo of your choice.

World Wide Web:
    URL: **http://tns-www.lcs.mit.edu/cgi-bin/sports/
    mlb/schedule**

> ## Cool words? Look in Quotations.

Martial Arts

These martial arts resources include an archive of aikido-related material including a list of dojos around the world, a mailing list for discussion of martial arts, a web page and even an IRC channel for discussion of karate and other forms.

Anonymous FTP:
    Address: **cs.ucsd.edu**
    Path: **/pub/aikido/***

Internet Relay Chat:
    Channel: **#karate**

Internet Mailing List:
    List Address: **martial-arts@dragon.cso.uiuc.edu**
    Subscription Address:
        martial-arts-request@dragon.cso.uiuc.edu

World Wide Web:
    URL: **http://www.hal.com/~landman/Aikido/**

> ## Send your mother an email note. Right now.

Minor League Baseball

Just because they are called "minor" leagues doesn't mean they are not as much fun as Major League Baseball. Enthusiasts of Minor League Baseball talk about issues affecting leagues, new stadium standards, franchise status and changes, road trips, schedules, team and league status, players and teams, collectibles and anything related to baseball that might make them whoop and holler.

Internet Mailing List:
    List Address: **minors@medraut.apple.com**
    Subscription Address:
        minors-request@medraut.apple.com

Motorsports

Load your Internet shopping cart with this web page which has links to Usenet newsgroups, FAQs and other links to motorsports sites including pictures. This site has lots of resources for people who like to go fast.

World Wide Web:
    URL: **http://barracuda3.me.mtu.edu:8023/
    ~loew/motorsports.html**

A
B
C
D
E
F
G
H
I
J
K
L
M
N
O
P
Q
R
S
T
U
V
W
X
Y
Z

NBA Schedule

Get the day's game schedule for your favorite NBA basketball teams. Enter **help** for help. Full season schedules are also available.

Gopher:
Name: University of Colorado Boulder
Address: **gopher.colorado.edu**
Choose: **Professional Sports Schedules | National Basketball Association Schedule**

Telnet:
Address: **culine.colorado.edu**
Port: **859**

NFL Draft Information

Complete listings of all the draftees and the teams that picked them. The draft picks are presented in order, by round.

World Wide Web:
URL: **http://www.mit.edu:8001/services/sis/NFL/draft/draft_1994.html**

NFL Schedules and Scores

Get the day's game schedule for your favorite NFL football teams. Enter **help** for help. Full season schedules are also available. Use the finger resource for the current standings and statistics as well as the final scores to the weekend's games.

Finger:
Address: **robc@xmission.com**

Gopher:
Name: University of Colorado Boulder
Address: **gopher.colorado.edu**
Choose: **Professional Sports Schedules | National Football League Schedule**

Telnet:
Address: **culine.colorado.edu**
Port: **863**

NFL Server

This collection of web pages offers information and schedules for each of the NFL teams. You start out by choosing either the AFC or the NFC, then you pick your team from its conference. There are game schedules, headline news, and even links to team pages (which are mostly unofficial).

World Wide Web:
URL: **http://www.cis.ksu.edu/~chiefs/nflstat.html**

NFL Talk

After the games and postgame shows have wound it up, if you still haven't had enough football talk, you can always turn on the NFL channel. There are bound to be people here with whom you can strike up a conversation, or an argument.

Internet Relay Chat:
Channel: **#nfl**

NHL Schedule

Get the day's game schedule for your favorite NHL hockey teams. At the telnet site enter **help** for help. Full season schedules are also available.

Gopher:
Name: University of Colorado Boulder
Address: **gopher.colorado.edu**
Choose: **Professional Sports Schedules | National Hockey League Schedule**

Telnet:
Address: **culine.colorado.edu**
Port: **860**

World Wide Web:
URL: **http://www.cs.ubc.ca/nhl**

Olympic Results

Results from the 1994 Winter Olympics at Lillehammer, Norway, as well as links to many great images, the Olympics home page, the Olympics FAQ, and technical information about how Oslonett accomplished their nearly realtime feed to the web.

World Wide Web:
URL: **http://www.sun.com/OL/OL94-mirror.html**

Olympic Winter Games — 1998

The vision for the XVIII Olympic Winter Games in 1998 in Nagano, Japan. This web page includes news and planning information for the games, including events, venues, access to the games, the official mascot, and other items of interest.

World Wide Web:
URL: **http://www.linc.or.jp/Nagano/index.html**

PAC-10 College Football Schedule

Keep up with what your favorite Pacific college team is up to by checking out the PAC-10 college web site. Complete team schedules make it easy for PAC-10 groupies to follow their favorite teams.

World Wide Web:
    URL: **http://www.cs.washington.edu/homes/ ugrads/shoe/uw/info/pac10.html**

Racing Archive

Feed your racing addiction by having a look at this racing archive, which has information on Formula One, Indy Car and NASCAR racing information including schedules and point standings.

World Wide Web:
    URL: **http://www.eng.hawaii.edu/Contribs/ carina/ra.home.page.html**

rec.sport.soccer — The Web Page

FAQs, premier league fixtures, FIFA rules, mailing lists, hints, questions and answers, articles, terminology, computer soccer game details, and links to other soccer resources.

World Wide Web:
    URL: **http://www.atm.ch.cam.ac.uk:80/sports/**

Road Rally

We love adventures. Especially when the adventure involves a road trip of some sort. For those with the spirit of adventure in their blood, read tutorials on road rallying, anecdotes on other rally adventures, information on mailing lists and a sample "Armchair Rally."

World Wide Web:
    URL: **http://www.contrib.andrew.cmu.edu/ usr/ef1c/plug.html**

Rugby

Basic overview of rugby, rules, trivia and FAQs, country-specific information, game schedules, match results, rugby jokes and songs, and video clips and pictures. Find out if the stories about rugby players are true.

World Wide Web:
    URL: **http://rugby.phys.uidaho.edu/rugby.html**

Rugby League

It has been said that in the event of nuclear annihilation, only the cockroaches and rugby players would survive. We don't know if that's true, but we do know that there is a variation on Rugby Union that is more intense, faster-paced, and guaranteed to give you new respect for the human body's ability to withstand punishment. Learn more about this game by reading the rules and the glossary, and by seeing some pictures relating to Rugby League.

World Wide Web:
    URL: **http://www.brad.ac.uk/~cgrussel/**

Running

Besides being good exercise, running is great practice in case you ever encounter a pack of wild dogs or even a pack of wild children. But it's common to encounter other physical problems when running, such as sprains or impact-related pains. Get informed about running in general as well as event schedules for selected local areas.

World Wide Web:
    URL: **http://sunsite.unc.edu/drears/running/ running.html**
    URL: **http://www.furman.edu/drs/drs.html**
    URL: **http://www.recreation.com/running/**

Scuba Diving FTP Sites

Equipment reviews, magazine list, buying guide, huge archives, and lots of related material about scuba diving, snorkeling, dive travel, and other underwater activities.

Anonymous FTP:
    Address: **ames.arc.nasa.gov**
    Path: **/pub/SCUBA/***

    Address: **rtfm.mit.edu**
    Path: **/pub/usenet/rec.answers/scuba-faq**

Immerse yourself in the world of scuba diving: there are some great FTP archives and an informative frequently asked question (FAQ) list just waiting for you.

A B C D E F G H I J K L M N O P Q R S T U V W X Y Z

> ## If you're feeling risque, take a look at the X-Rated Resources.

Scuba Diving Mailing List

People argue about what is the best feature of scuba diving. Some say it's the peace of floating in the water with only your raspy breath in your ears. Some say it's the beauty of the underwater world with its marvelous plant life and colorful fish. Some will say it's the adrenaline rush you get when you are head-butted by a shark. Whichever type of person you are, you will love the scuba list. Scuba and skin-diving fans discuss diving illness, underwater dangers, equipment, diving sites, and the more magical and mysterious aspects of being in the undersea world.

See also: Hobbies

Listserv Mailing List:
List Address: **scuba@cc.itu.edu.tr**
Subscription Address: **listserv@cc.itu.edu.tr**

Scuba Diving Web Pages

A massive collection of hundreds of articles related to scuba diving, including reports, reviews, travel guides, trivia, trip reviews, links to diving software, sounds, video clips, and much, much more about scuba.

World Wide Web:
URL: **http://www.halcyon.com/jong/ scuba/scuba.html**
URL: **http://www.opal.com/aquanaut/pyee.html**
URL: **http://www.scuba.com/scuba/home.html**

Skateboarding

Fun does not have to be complex. Take a plank, slap some wheels on it and suddenly you have a new sport. Skateboard enthusiasts can check out photos, FAQs, and gain access to Usenet newsgroups and links to other skateboarding sites.

World Wide Web:
URL: **http://web.cps.msu.edu/~dunhamda/dw/ dansworld.html**

Skating

Origins, equipment reviews, technique instructions, maintenance advice, FAQs, location lists, and much more for in-line (rollerblading), roller, figure, and speed skating.

Anonymous FTP:
Address: **rtfm.mit.edu**
Path: **/pub/usenet/news.answers/rec-skate-faq/***

Ski Information

If you are planning your ski vacation to Colorado, check the gopher below first. Get daily ski information, distances from various cities to Colorado Springs, resort rates, important phone numbers, and resort information. For other sites, including Utah, Wyoming, and Idaho, check out the ftp site and web page.

See also: Hobbies

Anonymous FTP:
Address: **ski.utah.edu**
Path: **/skiing**

Gopher:
Name: Community News Service
Address: **cscns.com**
Choose: **Enter the CNS Gopher
| Community - Aspen, Colorado
| Ski Information**

World Wide Web:
URL: **http://www.yahoo.com/ Entertainment/Sports/Skiing_Snow/**

Skydiving

FAQs about skydiving, learning to skydive, and the newsgroup **rec.skydiving**.

Anonymous FTP:
Address: **rtfm.mit.edu**
Path: **/pub/usenet/news.answers/skydiving-faq**

Skydiving Archive

"If riding in an airplane is flying, then riding in a boat is swimming. If you want to experience the element, get out of the vehicle." Pictures, skydiving movies, equipment details, relative work manuals, skydiving comics, federal aviation regulations, newsgroup archives, and links to other skydiving resources.

World Wide Web:
URL: **http://www.cis.ufl.edu/skydive/**

Soccer Referees Mailing List

It's hard to say which is more fun — playing soccer or wearing funny clothes and blowing a whistle at high decibels. Soccer referees have their work cut out for them. They have to run up and down the field keeping up with players, and they have to know all the rules and all the changes in the rules and know how to enforce them. (That's what the whistle is for.) This listserv list is designed to help referees keep abreast of the latest developments in the game of soccer and to discuss topics such as rule interpretation, game situations, and referee clinics.

Listserv Mailing List:
   List Address: **socref-l@uriacc.uri.edu**
   Subscription Address: **listserv@uriacc.uri.edu**

Soccer Results

Results from many soccer leagues and countries around the world, including continental tournaments.

World Wide Web:
   URL: **http://www.pitt.edu/~rlpst/ international.html**

Soccer Rules

The rules of the game and a universal guide for referees as authorized by FIFA, the governing body of international soccer.

Anonymous FTP:
   Address: **ftp.spies.com**
   Path: **/Library/Article/Sports/soccer.rul**

Gopher:
   Name: Internet Wiretap
   Address: **wiretap.spies.com**
   Choose: **Wiretap Online Library**
      | **Articles**
      | **Sports**
      | **FIFA Rules of Soccer**

World Wide Web:
   URL: **http://www.di.unipi.it/fos/fos.html**

Want to be relatively happy? Try Genealogy.

Soccer Web Pages

These web pages are your passport to a number of great soccer resources, including the Usenet group **rec.sport.soccer** and the World Cup '94 home page. Access newsgroups, World Cup information, Fantasy Goal Scorers, mailing lists, hints, frequently asked question lists, terminology, and even soccer games for the computer.

World Wide Web:
   URL: **http://haegar.unibe.ch/~ftiwww/Sonstiges/ Tabellen/Eindex.html**
   URL: **http://sotka.cs.tut.fi/riku/soccer.html**
   URL: **http://www.atm.ch.cam.ac.uk/sports/**
   URL: **http://www.atm.ch.cam.ac.uk/sports/ webs.html**
   URL: **http://www.cedar.buffalo.edu/~khoub-s/ WC94.webs.html**

Speed Skating

Who holds the world record in speed skating for the 500 meter race in the women's division? Find out from these lists of speed skating records — men's and women's records from 500 to 10,000 meters, as well as Olympic information.

World Wide Web:
   URL: **http://www.twi.tudelft.nl/Local/sports/ skating.html**

Speedway Home Page

A starting point for speedway fans the world over. Access information about racing and competition events in various European countries. This page also has links to the results of world championship races.

World Wide Web:
   URL: **http://www.amg.gda.pl/speedway/ speedway.html**

Sports Highlights

Browse and watch recent sports highlights using the vssportsbrowser VuSystem application from MIT.

Note: Requires NCSA Mosaic for the X Window System, version 2.0 or higher

World Wide Web:
   URL: **http://tns-www.lcs.mit.edu/vs/ vssportsbrowser.html**

A B C D E F G H I J K L M N O P Q R S T U V W X Y Z

Sports Schedules

Easy access to the professional football, hockey, basketball, and baseball schedules from this single menu.

Gopher:
> Name: Ball State University
> Address: **gopher.bsu.edu**
> Choose: **Professional Sports Schedules**

Sports Servers

Football season, basketball season, baseball season, soccer season. They are starting to overlap, and if you love sports, that's great news. Even better news is that if the television is on the fritz, you can check out all your favorite sports at this web page. News, scores, rules, and history of mainstream sports as well as the more obscure.

World Wide Web:
> URL: **http://www.atm.ch.cam.ac.uk/sports/sports.html**
> URL: **http://www.nando.net/sptsserv.html**

Sports Statistics

Statistics for baseball (MLB), basketball (NBA), football (NFL), and hockey (NHL).

Anonymous FTP:
> Address: **ftp.wustl.edu**
> Path: **/doc/misc/sports/***

Sports Web Page

There is more to sports than just the brawl of physical contact. Sportsters also come in the form of writers and newsmakers. Read articles and news stories about sports of all kinds.

World Wide Web:
> URL: **http://sfgate.com/sports/**

Stadium Sports Articles

If you like stadium sports, check out these resources. There are stadium listings, team rosters, game results, schedules, rules, history, lore, and all kinds of other interesting items about stadiums and stadium sports.

Anonymous FTP:
> Address: **ftp.spies.com**
> Path: **/Library/Article/Sports/***

Gopher:
> Name: Internet Wiretap
> Address: **wiretap.spies.com**
> Choose: **Wiretap Online Library**
> **| Articles | Sports**

Sumo Wrestling

Sumo facts and terms, pictures in gif format of sumo wrestlers, tournament results, news, and links to other Sumo resources on the Net.

World Wide Web:
> URL: **http://akebono.stanford.edu/users/jerry/sumo/**
> URL: **http://www.hal.com/~nathan/Sumo/**

Swimming

Whether you glide through the water like a torpedo or get water up your nose while dog-paddling, this list is for you. When they are not actually splashing about, swimmers of all skill levels talk about swimming. The only bad thing about this list is that you can't post to it while you are in the water.

Listserv Mailing List:
> List Address: **swim-l@uafsysb.uark.edu**
> Subscription Address: **listserv@uafsysb.uark.edu**

Technical Diving

The TechDiver mailing list is a forum for the technical diving community on the Internet. Topics of discussion include safety, wreck penetration diving, cave diving, mixed gases, specialized equipment, technical training facilities, and specialized techniques. TechDiver is both for people new to technical diving and for experienced technical divers.

Internet Mailing List:
> List Address: **techdiver@opal.com**
> Subscription Address:
> **techdiver-request@opal.com**

Tennis Rankings and FAQs

Tennis rankings, FAQs on specific players, including Stefan Edberg, Boris Becker, and Steffi Graf, equipment and rankings FAQs, and links to other tennis resources.

World Wide Web:
> URL: **http://www.cdf.toronto.edu/DCS/FUN/tennis.html**

Tennis Server

Player and equipment tips from the professionals, the rules and codes of tennis, an online tennis shop, competition guides, a FAQ, injury information, and links to several other tennis resources.

World Wide Web:
> URL: **http://arganet.tenagra.com/Racquet_Workshop/Tennis.html**

**Reality is dull.
Try Science Fiction.**

Ultimate Frisbee

Ultimate is a non-contact disc (frisbee) sport played by two seven-player teams. Here you can find the rules to Ultimate, tournament formats, ftp archives, handbooks, and links to other Ultimate and disc sport-related sites.

Internet Mailing List:
List Address: **ultimate-list@doe.carleton.ca**
Subscription Address:
ultimate-list-request@doe.carleton.ca

World Wide Web:
URL: **http://pipkin.lut.ac.uk/~scott/ultimate.html**
URL: **http://raptor.sccs.swarthmore.edu/~dalewis/frisbee.html**
URL: **http://www.cs.rochester.edu/u/ferguson/ultimate/**

Ultrarunning

Not just any old punishment will do. Ultrarunners have to go beyond agony and exhaustion and run until their tennies smoke. Ultrarunning generally refers to anything longer than a marathon or any shorter specialty race like Escarpment, Mount Washington, or the Pikes Peak ascent. For those of you into heavy breathing, join up with other ultra fans to discuss the challenges and excitement of going beyond normal running.

See also: Health

Listserv Mailing List:
List Address: **ultra@dartcms1.dartmouth.edu**
Subscription Address:
listserv@dartcms1.dartmouth.edu

Women's Basketball

This is one sport where there are more women on the court than on the sidelines shaking their pom-poms. Sports enthusiasts check in for daily scores and reports on games as well as to talk about women's basketball around the U.S.

Internet Mailing List:
List Address: **wbball-l@psuvm.psu.edu**
Subscription Address:
wbball-l-request@psuvm.psu.edu

Usenet:
Newsgroup: **rec.sport.basketball.women**

World Skiing

Provides reports on world skiing conditions, both Alpine and Nordic/backcountry. You can add your own report under a specific area, or read the reports of others from ski areas around the world. Many of the reports contain pictures and some travel details.

World Wide Web:
URL: **http://www.cs.colorado.edu/homes/mcbryan/public_html/bb/ski/ski.html**

World Youth Baseball

The World Youth Baseball web server offers scores and standings, schedule information, data on participating teams, the history of the World Youth Baseball Championship, and information about previous stars of World Youth Baseball that now play in the major leagues.

World Wide Web:
URL: **http://www.brandonu.ca/~ennsnr/WYB/**

World Wide Web of Sports

A constant variety of sports information, results, and schedules from around the globe, including major league baseball, tennis, NBA, figure skating, NHL, NFL, soccer, cycling, speed skating, frisbee, rugby, golf, running, rowing, and more. Updated on a regular basis to cover major sporting events around the world.

World Wide Web:
URL: **http://tns-www.lcs.mit.edu/cgi-bin/sports**

Wrestler List

A list of WWF and WCW wrestlers and their managers.

Anonymous FTP:
Address: **ftp.spies.com**
Path: **/Library/Article/Sports/wrestle.wwf**

Gopher:
Name: Internet Wiretap
Address: **wiretap.spies.com**
Choose: **Wiretap Online Library**
| **Articles**
| **Sports**
| **WWF and WCW Names and Managers**

STAR TREK

Animations and Images

A collection of jpeg images and mpeg animations, digitized from the various *Star Trek* movies and TV shows.

World Wide Web:
URL: **http://sherlock.berkeley.edu/docs/info/ star_trek/trek.html**

Conventions and Memorabilia

Dress up funny and romp around with other people dressed up like *Star Trek* characters. Conventions are a great place to really experience Trekker fandom. Discover where to get a replica of that communicator you love or collect the one action figure you are missing from your set.

Usenet:
Newsgroup: **rec.arts.startrek.fandom**

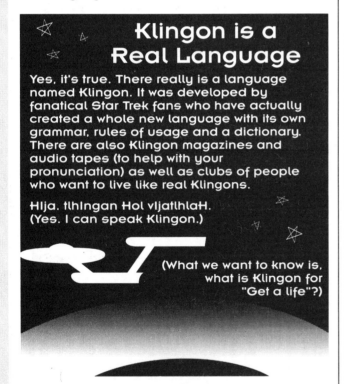

Klingon is a Real Language

Yes, it's true. There really is a language named Klingon. It was developed by fanatical Star Trek fans who have actually created a whole new language with its own grammar, rules of usage and a dictionary. There are also Klingon magazines and audio tapes (to help with your pronunciation) as well as clubs of people who want to live like real Klingons.

HIja. tlhIngan Hol vIjatlhlaH.
(Yes. I can speak Klingon.)

(What we want to know is, what is Klingon for "Get a life"?)

Future Technologists

You look back and laugh at old sci-fi from the '50s. How close are we getting to *Star Trek* technology? Speculate how our technological progress compares with the technology dreamed up in the creative minds of *Star Trek* writers.

Usenet:
Newsgroup: **rec.arts.startrek.tech**

Klingon Shared Reality

Wouldn't it be fun for a little while to pretend you are a Klingon and walk around making lots of gutteral noises and threatening people? Brush up on your Klingon language, don a persona and elbow your way into the crowd for a little Usenet role-playing.

Usenet:
Newsgroup: **alt.shared-reality.startrek.klingon**

Klingons

Ignore the subtitles in the movies: learn to speak Klingon. Explore the culture that devoted fans have worked so hard to develop. Find a variety of interesting topics such as Klingon love poetry, haiku, and thoughts on Kronos as the homeworld.

Usenet:
Newsgroup: **alt.startrek.klingon**

Excerpt from the Net...

(from a message that was sent to us at catalog@rain.org by Mike Lyons)

...I am going to call you on something printed in the first edition on within the Star Trek section, in an ad entitled "Klingon is a Real Language".

You said: "What we want to know is, what is Klingon for 'Get a life'?"

I was given a copy of the Klingon dictionary, and I looked it up.

    yIn'e' yISuq

yIn = life (n)
-'e' = noun prefix indicating topic
yI- = verb prefix (you - [him her it], imperative)
Suq = get (v)

Incidentally, it was a linguist named Marc Okrand who created the Klingon language, based on the few words from the opening scenes in the first movie, which were made up by James "Scotty" Doohan.

Just a little trivia for you.

Resources

Links and pointers to more *Star Trek* resources than there are stars in the galaxy. Newsgroups, pictures, sounds, episode guides, book details, quotes, stories, parodies, and even the Klingon language.

World Wide Web:
>   URL: **http://www.cosy.sbg.ac.at/rec/startrek/ index.html**

Star Trek Archives

Life without *Star Trek* is simply not worth living. You don't have to take our word for it. See the archives that fans have compiled on the old and new *Star Trek* as well as *Deep Space Nine*.

World Wide Web:
>   URL: **http://www.yahoo.com/Entertainment/ Television/Shows/Science_Fiction/Star_Trek/**

Star Trek Fetishes

Sex and *Star Trek*. There's not much more to life than having both of those. Now the ultimate state has been achieved by combining the two. Read stories and commentary about sex, *Star Trek* and other naughty bits.

Usenet:
>   Newsgroup: **alt.sex.fetish.startrek**

Star Trek Games

Don't just watch *Star Trek*, live it! Command your own ship with Xtrek and match wits with the computer or go head to head (or torpedo to torpedo) with others like you on Netrek, the networking version of the game. Both newsgroups cover such topics as tactics, experiences, and troubleshooting software.

Usenet:
>   Newsgroup: **alt.games.xtrek**
>   Newsgroup: **rec.games.netrek**

Star Trek General Discussion

Light and lively debate volleys, occasionally turning warm, then hot as you defend your favorite episode or character. Talk turns to old shows, bloopers, insider information on actors' lives, and burning questions like, "Why is Lt. Worf still only a lieutenant?"

Listserv Mailing List:
>   List Address: **strek-l@pccvm.bitnet**
>   Subscription Address: **listserv@pccvm.bitnet**

Usenet:
>   Newsgroup: **rec.arts.startrek.misc**

Star Trek Information and Trivia

Everything you need to know about *Star Trek*, including Klingon vocabulary, *Deep Space Nine*, the original *Star Trek* and *Next Generation* guides and listings, a spelling list, a timeline, stardates, drinking games, and other important information.

Anonymous FTP:
>   Address: **ftp.spies.com**
>   Path: **/Library/Media/Trek/***

Gopher:
>   Name: Internet Wiretap
>   Address: **wiretap.spies.com**
>   Choose: **Wiretap Online Library | Mass Media | Star Trek**

Star Trek News

Learn what's going on in the world of *Star Trek*. Fans report rumors and facts about new shows, books, and movies. Get the latest word and keep up with the Bones.

Usenet:
>   Newsgroup: **rec.arts.startrek.current**

Star Trek Reviews

Nobody can review *Star Trek* like a Trekkie. Read what fans think about the latest books, movies, and shows (but watch out for spoilers!).

Usenet:
>   Newsgroup: **rec.arts.startrek.reviews**

Star Trek Stories and Parodies

If you can't get enough of *Star Trek* on television or in movies and books, check out this corner of the Internet universe. Creative and witty individuals post stories and parodies related to *Star Trek* in Usenet newsgroups and on ftp sites. Often FAQ lists on submissions are posted containing tips for writing for *Deep Space Nine* and the *Star Trek: Voyager* series, where to send submissions, what to do and what not to do when writing.

Anonymous FTP:
>   Address: **ftp.uu.net**
>   Path: **/doc/literary/obi/Star.Trek.Stories/***

>   Address: **ftp.uu.net**
>   Path: **/doc/literary/obi/Star.Trek.Parodies/***

Usenet:
>   Newsgroup: **alt.startrek.creative**

A B C D E F G H I J K L M N O P Q R S T U V W X Y Z

Star Trek Universe

This moderated group offers in-depth and accurate information on the universe as it relates to *Star Trek*. Read press releases, episode credits, synopses, and factual articles. Since all posts are filtered through a moderator, you can be assured of the reliability of what you read. Queries are best moved to one of the other *Star Trek* groups. All the articles that have been posted to the Usenet newsgroup are available by anonymous ftp.

Anonymous FTP:
Address: **scam.berkeley.edu**
Path: **/pub/misc/trek-info/***

Usenet:
Newsgroup: **rec.arts.startrek.info**

Trekker Discussion

Meet and chat with other Star Trekkers. There are also some clever bots which can lock transporter beams, energize, serve coffee, and do lots of other *Star Trek* things.

Internet Relay Chat:
Channel: **#ds9**
Channel: **#startrek**

Video Clips

Selection of *Star Trek* sequences, including some from the *Star Trek VI* motion picture, *Deep Space Nine*, *Star Trek — The Next Generation*, and *Star Trek* cast members' appearances on talk shows.

World Wide Web:
URL: **http://tns-www.lcs.mit.edu/cgi-bin/vs/ vsbrowser**

SUPPORT GROUPS

30 Plus

If you're over 30, you need support in at least one way! This IRC channel and mailing list are directed at you older Net users. Anyone is welcome, regardless of age, but if you're not mature, do your best to pretend. The IRC online bot has details of the 30 Plus mailing list, real-life get-togethers, and even 30 Plus T-shirts.

Internet Relay Chat:
Channel: **#30libris**
Channel: **#30plus**

Internet Mailing List:
List Address: **30-plus@math.ethz.ch**
Subscription Address: **30-plus-request@math.ethz.ch**

Birthparents of Adoptees

A mailing list provided for communications among and between its primary audience of birthparents of adopted children.

Listserv Mailing List:
List Address: **brthprnt@miamiu.muohio.edu**
Subscription Address:
listserv@miamiu.muohio.edu

Blindness and Family Life

If a loved one of yours is blind, you know of the challenges, trials, and triumphs of leading a normal family life. If you need advice or support, the **blindfam** mailing list is the place to go for discussion of all aspects of family life as they are affected by the blindness of one or more family members.

Listserv Mailing List:
List Address: **blindfam@sjuvm.stjohns.edu**
Subscription Address: **listserv@sjuvm.stjohns.edu**

Transplant Answers

A collection of excerpts and highlights from the **bit.listserv.transplant** newsgroup which deals with issues of interest to transplant patients. The author takes care to point out that this is not a medical forum, but a layperson's support and discussion group.

Anonymous FTP:
Address: **ftp.hmc.edu**
Path: **/pub/science/sci.answers/.mirror.OLD/ transplant-faq**

Usenet Support Groups

It's great to know that when you have a problem there are people who will be supportive of you. All over the world there are people who are willing to take the time to listen to the problems and try to meet the emotional needs of others. Get good information on nearly any subject like medical, emotional or psychological problems.

Usenet:
Newsgroup: **alt.abuse.transcendence**
Newsgroup: **alt.recovery.addiction.sexual**
Newsgroup: **alt.recovery.catholicism**
Newsgroup: **alt.recovery.religion**
Newsgroup: **alt.support.***
Newsgroup: **soc.support.transgendered**

TECHNOLOGY

Artificial Intelligence

Technical papers, journals, and surveys about artificial intelligence, robotics, and neural networks.

Anonymous FTP:
Address: **flash.bellcore.com**
Path: **/pub/ai/***

Address: **ftp.uu.net**
Path: **/pub/ai/***

Address: **solaria.cc.gatech.edu**
Path: **/pub/ai/***

Audio Technology

Mail order surveys, lists, and related information about the art and science of audio recording and playing equipment.

Anonymous FTP:
Address: **ssesco.com**
Path: **/pub/rec.audio/***

Blacksburg Electronic Village

The town of Blacksburg, Virginia, is going digital! The goal of this project is to network the entire town on the Internet. Residents will have electronic mail; the bus schedule will be available online; even the movie schedule at the town theater will be online. This project is a joint effort between the Virginia Polytechnic Institute and State University, Bell Atlantic, and the town of Blacksburg. This page won a PC Week Labs "Cool Web Page" award.

World Wide Web:
URL: **http://crusher.bev.net/index.html**

Canada Department of Communications

CHAT (Conversational Hypertext Access Technology) database system. You can ask questions of this database in plain English. It correctly interprets an amazing number of questions and instantly provides answers about the Canadian Department of Communications. The Canadian DOC manages radio in Canada, participates in high-tech ventures, and promotes Canada's cultural infrastructure through communications.

Telnet:
Address: **debra.dgbt.doc.ca**
Port: **3000**

CAVE Virtual Reality Environment

CAVE is a multiperson, room-sized, high-resolution, 3-D video and audio environment, a virtual reality theater. Background, applications, reports, references, details of the CAVE environment, images and reports about the CAVE can be found here.

World Wide Web:
URL: **http://www.ncsa.uiuc.edu/EVL/docs/cave/cave.html**

Central Virginia's Freenet

A virtual model of a central Virginia community, offering sections on news, art, culture, philosophy, religion, health, fitness, recreation, science, environment, technology, commerce, support and development, politics, and more.

Telnet:
Address: **freenet.vcu.edu**
Login: **guest**
Password: **visitor**

Centre for Research Information Storage Technology

CRIST is a research group in the School of Electronic, Communication, and Electrical Engineering at the University of Plymouth, U.K. They research novel and interesting aspects of recording on optical and magnetic media.

World Wide Web:
URL: **http://crist1.see.plym.ac.uk/**

Compact Disc Formats

A description and history of the various CD formats available, including CD-DA, CD-ROM, CD-ROM/XA, and CD-I.

World Wide Web:
URL: **http://cui_www.unige.ch/OSG/MultimediaInfo/Info/cd.html**

A
B
C
D
E
F
G
H
I
J
K
L
M
N
O
P
Q
R
S
T
U
V
W
X
Y
Z

Conflict Simulation Games

It makes your heart race, your blood pound and your palms get all sweaty. It's not a game, it's almost like life. Conflict simulation games are cool because you can be in the danger zone without actually having to worry about losing any body parts. That's always a plus. An environment has been established in which to discuss historical conflict simulation games as well as recently published games and military history.

Listserv Mailing List:
> List Address: **consim-l@vm.ucs.ualberta.ca**
> Subscription Address: **listserv@vm.ucs.ualberta.ca**

Daresbury Laboratory

The Daresbury Laboratory in Daresbury, England, is a research institution involved in many projects, including synchrotronic radiation, parallel computing and computational science, nuclear physics, RUSTI (Research Unit for Surfaces, Transforms, and Interfaces) and MEIS (Medium Energy Ion Scattering).

World Wide Web:
> URL: **http://www.dl.ac.uk/**

Distribute Interactive Virtual Environment

The Distribute Interactive Virtual Environment (DIVE) is a fully-distributed, heterogeneous VR system where users navigate in 3-D space and may see, meet, and interact with other users and applications in the environment. The DIVE system is available free of charge, and information about the project, software and hardware requirements, instructions on how to obtain DIVE software, DIVE mpeg movies, and online reports are available here.

World Wide Web:
> URL: **http://www.sics.se/dce/dive/dive.html**

Elettra Synchrotron Radiation Facility

Elettra is a third generation synchrotron radiation facility located in Trieste, Italy. Their purpose is the production of extremely brilliant light which is tunable, collimated, and polarized. Elettra's two beamlines are at the disposal of scientists and industrialists from all over the world to investigate the structure of matter. Elettra acts as a very advanced microscope with unique features whose applications range from electronics to biology to the pharmaceutical industry.

World Wide Web:
> URL: **http://waxa.elettra.trieste.it:8080/ ELETTRA.html**

Expert Systems and Vision

Who needs real intelligence when you can have artificial intelligence? You can make it run the way you want, and it's lower in fat and cholesterol than most natural intelligence systems. Vision researchers in artificial intelligence discuss a wide range of vision topics, such as physiological theory, computer vision, machine vision algorithms, industrial applications, robotic eyes, and implemented systems.

Internet Mailing List:
> List Address: **vision-list@ads.com**
> Subscription Address: **vision-list-request@ads.com**

Hitachi

Hitachi offers a web server where you can find information on Hitachi's new product lines, research laboratories, image and media labs and other information about the company.

World Wide Web:
> URL: **http://www.hitachi.co.jp**

Hot Off the Tree

A weekly publication containing excerpts and summaries of information technology articles. Each issue provides article summaries on new and emerging technologies, including virtual reality, neural networks, personal digital assistants, genetic and evolutionary programming, nanotechnology, and many more topics.

Note: For the telnet site, you must type **show hott** after logging in.

Listserv Mailing List:
> List Address: **hott-list@ucsd.edu**
> Subscription Address: **listserv@ucsd.edu**

Telnet:
> Address: **melvyl.ucop.edu**
> Login: *your terminal type*

Become a Know-It-All

Have you ever been to a party and run into one of those people who seems to keep up with all the newest technology?

That in itself is not bad except that, when you talk to such a person, he makes you feel inadequate because he knows all this stuff and you don't, and somehow you feel that you should, even though you don't really have the time and, when you come right down to it, you don't really care but you think that you ought to, because you really haven't thought about anything difficult since you graduated from college.

Well, the good news is you *can* be one of those people. All you have to do is subscribe to the *Hot Off The Tree* mailing list and you, too, will be able to go to parties and intimidate people who are too busy to keep up but too insecure to not care.

Human Communication Research Centre

Information from the University of Edinburgh on their cognitive sciences work groups including grammar processing, dialogue, graphics and language. They also have information about newsletters and periodic seminars.

World Wide Web:
URL: **http://www.cogsci.ed.ac.uk/hcrc/home.html**

Institute for Systems Engineering and Informatics

The Electronics and Sensor Based Application Unit of the Joint Research Center in Ispra, Italy, develops software and hardware systems in the fields of data acquisition, data visualization, surveillance, mobile robotics, and software application development.

World Wide Web:
URL: **http://elec.jrc.it/home.html**

Journal of Artificial Intelligence Research

In a world of artificial coloring, artifical flavoring, and artificial body parts, why not have artificial intelligence? It seems almost natural. Explore the latest breakthroughs in the field of AI research.

World Wide Web:
URL: **http://www.cs.washington.edu/research/jair/home.html**

Knowledge Representation and Reasoning Laboratory

If your Italian is up to the challenge, check out this web page. There are many papers on science and technology as well as pointers to the Natural Language Processing and Communication Laboratory at the same institution.

World Wide Web:
URL: **http://mnemosyne.irst.it:1024/**

Life in the Year 2020

A global, group exploration of life in the year 2020. Based on a weekly column in the *Seattle Times*, this list encourages outrageous yet intellectual ideas that are outside of the typical theories of home shopping and video-on-demand.

Majordomo Mailing List:
List Address: **2020world@seatimes.com**
Subscription Address: **majordomo@seatimes.com**

Los Alamos National Laboratory

The Los Alamos National Laboratory (LANL) server provides information on research projects (by subject and by division), news and events, computing, and more.

World Wide Web:
URL: **http://www.lanl.gov/**

Meta Virtual Environments

Many pointers to different virtual environments or virtual reality home pages on the Net. There is an entry form which allows you to add your own new links.

World Wide Web:
URL: **http://www.cc.gatech.edu/gvu/people/Masters/Rob.Kooper/Meta.VR.html**

A B C D E F G H I J K L M N O P Q R S T U V W X Y Z

Mogul Media

A Norwegian company developing new technologies and media for communications. Mogul Media hopes to provide Internet services, multimedia information systems, and interactive television systems. Check out their technology.

World Wide Web:
URL: **http://www.mogul.no/**

Multicast Backbone FAQ

Frequently asked questions about the Multicast Backbone (MBONE), which is an outgrowth of two "audiocast" experiments in which live audio and video were multicast over the Internet. The idea is to construct a semi-permanent IP multicast testbed to carry transmissions and support continued experimentation. Details of the MBONE topology, multicast tunnels, maps, hardware and software requirements, teleconference events, and much more can be found here.

See also: Internet

World Wide Web:
URL: **http://www.research.att.com/ mbone-faq.html**

Musee des Arts et Metiers

A virtual museum of technology with many documents related to the great technical innovations that have brought technology to where it is today. Many of the texts are in French.

World Wide Web:
URL: **http://web.cnam.fr/museum/**

Museum of Machine-Generated Speech and Singing

This page is divided into sections covering the history of synthesizers, current synthesizers, and current research projects. There are demonstrations, articles, papers, and links to related resources.

World Wide Web:
URL: **http://www.cs.cmu.edu:8001/afs/ cs.cmu.edu/project/nnspeech/WorldWideWeb/ PUBLIC/SpeechMuseum/MainPage.html**

National Institute of Standards and Technology

A gopher server funded and operated by the National Institute of Standards and Technology (NIST). This gopher is primarily for organizations and employees of NIST, but is made available to the entire gopher network and its users. The NIST gopher contains information on applied and computational mathematics at NIST, as well as other information primarily of interest to those involved with NIST.

Gopher:
Name: National Institute of Standards and Technology
Address: **gopher-server.nist.gov**

Neural Network Home Page

This web page offers a brief introduction to artificial neural networks, articles and bibliographic references to specific areas of neural network research and interest, electronic journals, conference information, bibliographic search tools, mailing lists, newsgroups, project details, reports, papers, and much more to do with neural networks and neuro-science.

World Wide Web:
URL: **http://www.emsl.pnl.gov:2080/docs/cie/ neural/neural.homepage.html**

Photonics

Documents, reports, and other information regarding optical computing research and technology.

Gopher:
Name: Colorado State University Optical Computing Lab
Address: **gopher.colostate.edu**

Robotics Video Gallery

A gallery of mpeg movies showing robotics at work. The demonstrations include a hand rolling a can, a hand performing an ordinary household chore, a hand-arm system performing an obstacle-avoiding reach, a clip showing grasping and path planning working together, and a peg-in-hole insertion. There are also papers available on the techniques and development of robots to perform these tasks.

World Wide Web:
URL: **http://piglet.cs.umass.edu:4321/ robotics-mpegs**
URL: **http://piglet.cs.umass.edu:4321/video-gallery**

Sony Research Laboratory

The Sony Research Laboratory (SRL) has a research goal to develop technology enabling the creation of a safe, stable and cohabitating information society. This server contains many documents and project-related papers on their progress toward this goal.

World Wide Web:
URL: **http://www.csl.sony.co.jp**

Technology Board of Trade

Enter the trading floor for reusable software technology. Companies looking for or providing such technology make contacts through this service, which assists software businesses by offering tips and connections.

See also: Business and Finance, Software

World Wide Web:
URL: **http://www.tech-board.com/tbot/home.html**

Technology General Discussion

As technology gets more advanced, we get more new toys to try. Explore the ideas and philosophy of technology as well as the more technical side of applying technology to real life. This newsgroup is good to read while waiting for someone to invent robots that will do all your cooking and cleaning for you.

Usenet:
Newsgroup: **alt.technology.misc**

Technology Marketing Failures

Marketing people are so clever that there is very little they can't get people excited about. Undoubtedly there are inventions that defy all the skills of marketing agents — like a device that washes your car and toasts bread at the same time. Read about technology marketing failures and be sure you don't duplicate someone else's mistakes.

Usenet:
Newsgroup: **alt.technology.mkt-failure**

Technomads

People think of computer users as skinny geeks who sit in cramped rooms with lots of buzzing machinery squeezed in next to them. But there is a new breed of people, a tribe of nomads so technologically advanced that given a cellular phone and a portable computer they can roam the planet and still remain connected. Discussion is not limited to computers.

See also: Cyberpunk, Computers: Culture

Listserv Mailing List:
List Address: **technomads@ucsd.edu**
Subscription Address: **listserv@ucsd.edu**

Video Laserdiscs

Introduction to video laserdisc technology, media quality reports, how-to reports, care, repair, and retail sources — everything you could want to know about this technology.

Telnet:
Address: **panda.uiowa.edu**

Virtual Reality Resources

Here's a great collection of virtual reality resources available on the Net, including web sites, ftp archives, bibliographies, mailing lists, research and academic institutions, newsgroups, FAQs, software, papers, and other material related to virtual worlds and virtual reality. The web page has links to other virtual reality resources, including online papers, research projects, bibliographies, newsgroups, virtual environments, articles, and much more.

Anonymous FTP:
Address: **ftp.u.washington.edu**
Path: **/pub/user-supported/VirtualReality/***

Address: **ftp.u.washington.edu**
Path: **/pub/user-supported/virtual-worlds/***

Listserv Mailing List:
List Address: **virtu-l@uiucvmd.bitnet**
Subscription Address: **listserv@uiucvmd.bitnet**

World Wide Web:
URL: **ftp://140.142.56.2/public/VirtualReality/HITL/ HITLMosaic/onthenet.html**
URL: **http://guinan.gsfc.nasa.gov/WebStars/ VR.html**

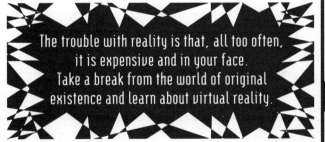

The trouble with reality is that, all too often, it is expensive and in your face. Take a break from the world of original existence and learn about virtual reality.

X-Ray Web Server

The X-Ray Server in Sweden is dedicated to providing information of interest to the XUV and X-ray spectroscopic community. It currently makes available a database of atomic scattering factors and a bibliography and database of molecular core-edge excitation spectra.

World Wide Web:
URL: **http://xray.uu.se**

TELECOMMUNICATIONS

Bell Gopher

As a public service, the Bells have gotten together to provide information on telecommunications and related legislation news.

Gopher:
Name: MJF Task Force Gopher
Address: **bell.com**

Cell-Relay Communications

Here's a discussion group about cell-relay products and technology.

Usenet:
Newsgroup: **comp.dcom.cell-relay**

Data Communications Servers

Selecting and operating data communications servers.

Usenet:
Newsgroup: **comp.dcom.servers**

Distributed Electronic Telecommunications Archive

There is no need for you to be uninformed about the world of telecommunications. Through this web site you can get information on mailing lists, newsgroups and tutorials relating to telecommunications and other forms of data communications.

World Wide Web:
URL: **http://gozer.idbsu.edu/business/nethome.html**

Fax Technology

Fax equipment, including computer hardware and software, and technical specifications and protocols.

Usenet:
Newsgroup: **comp.dcom.fax**

International Telecommunications Union

Information about the global development of telecommunications, including documents, infobases, press releases, news, and other services.

Gopher:
Name: International Telecommunications Union
Address: **info.itu.ch**

Avoiding Despair

Life is hard enough without having to admit to your friends and co-workers that you just don't know what is happening in the world of international telecommunications. Fortunately, the **International Telecommunications Union** has a gopher that you can use 24 hours a day. Never again need you admit to that gorgeous guy (or gal) across the hall that you don't understand the details of the V.34 modem standard. In fact, if you follow our advice, it won't be long before attractive people walk up behind you as you work at your computer and ask if they can hug you while you work.

Internet Business Center Telecommunications Definitions

It's such an embarrassment to be at a cocktail party with a bunch of telecommunications bigwigs and not even know what they are saying when they talk about "activated return capacity," "VSATs," "POTSs" and "SMATVs." If you had read the FAQs and dictionary of terms and acronyms about telecommunications, you wouldn't be in the pickle you are in right now.

World Wide Web:
URL: **http://tig.com/IBC/Telecom.html**

Be cool! Join a mailing list.

Internet Fax Server

This is an experiment in integrating the electronic mail and facsimile communities. Working together, many sites cooperatively provide remote printing access to the international telephone network. This allows people to send faxes via electronic mail. The general purpose Internet mail infrastructure takes care of all the routing and delivering the message to the appropriate remote printer gateway. FAQs and details of how to use this service are available here, complete with a Mosaic form enabling you to send a short fax message to participating areas.

World Wide Web:
    URL: **http://town.hall.org/fax/faxsend-short.html**

Internet Protocol

Discussions of the technical aspects of the Internet Protocol—the IP in TCP/IP and the underlying mechanism for moving data around the Internet.

Usenet: ·
    Newsgroup: **alt.dcom.telecom**

ISDN

Issues and technology relating to ISDN (Integrated Services Digital Network).

Usenet:
    Newsgroup: **comp.dcom.isdn**

National Telecommunications and Information Administration

This BBS contains press releases, public notices and information on international telecommunications activities. Also available are documents from the White House and National Information Infrastruction.

Telnet:
    Address: **ntiabbs.ntia.doc.gov**

OTPAD Gopher

The Office of Telecommunications Policy Analysis and Development is providing telecommunications information and news to the public free of charge. Read the latest news bytes about telecommunications relating to the Internet.

Gopher:
    Name: OTPAD: Office of Telecommunications
        Policy Analysis and Development
    Address: **unix5.nysed.gov**

Pacific Bell Digital Communications Information

Did you know that you might be able to get a high-speed connection to the Internet right in your home? And this is without a modem because it's digital! Point your web browser at the Pacific Bell web page for valuable information about the coming flood of digital communications with ISDN (Integrated Services Digital Network). Also read about CalREN, the California Research Education Network.

See also: Computers: Technology, Technology

World Wide Web:
    URL: **http://www.pacbell.com**

PC Communications and Modems

Serial port specifications, modem technical notes, and answers to telecom FAQs.

Anonymous FTP:
    Address: **ftp.spies.com**
    Path: **/Library/Techdoc/Comm/***

Gopher:
    Name: Internet Wiretap
    Address: **wiretap.spies.com**
    Choose: **Wiretap Online Library**
        | **Technical Information**
        | **Communications and Modems**

Do you have a terrible modem problem that no one else can even understand?

The answer might just be found in the *PC Communications and Modems* archives.

A
B
C
D
E
F
G
H
I
J
K
L
M
N
O
P
Q
R
S
T
U
V
W
X
Y
Z

Privacy and Technology

It used to be you only had to worry about someone picking up on the party line and listening to your conversation. Now people have all sorts of tiny little mechanisms to bug your computer, phone, home, and office. This list is a spinoff of the telecom digest and it sponsors discussion of how technology affects privacy.

See also: Technology, Telephones

Internet Mailing List:
List Address: **telecom-priv@pica.army.mil**
Subscription Address:
telecom-priv-request@pica.army.mil

Telecom Discussions

Discussions about all manner of telecommunications, including the telephone system.

Usenet:
Newsgroup: **alt.dcom.telecom**

Telecommunication Archives

There is more to telecommunications than picking up the phone and dialing a number. Get information on new developments in the phone business as well as other methods of data communications such as electronic mail and the Internet.

Anonymous FTP:
Address: **lcs.mit.edu**
Path: **/telecom-archives**

Telecommunications Digest

A moderated digest containing articles about the phone system and telecommunications.

Usenet:
Newsgroup: **comp.dcom.telecom**

Telecommunications News

Current news about the world of telecom, phones, satellites, and so on.

Usenet:
Newsgroup: **clari.nb.telecom**
Newsgroup: **clari.tw.telecom**

You are what you think.

Telecommunications Organizations

A list providing links to almost 40 telecommunications organizations on the Internet, located around the world.

See also: Organizations

World Wide Web:
URL: **http://www-atp.llnl.gov/atp/telecom-orgs.html**

Telecommunications Page

This web page provides links to telecommunications companies, organizations, programs and projects, standards, and other telecommunication-related resources. The page is supported by the Advanced Telecommunications Program at Lawrence Livermore National Laboratory, and is intended to provide organization for the vast quantity of information available on the emerging global information economy.

World Wide Web:
URL: **http://www-atp.llnl.gov/atp/telecom.html**

TELEPHONES

Cellular Phones

Talk of cellular phones, scanning, plans and modifications, phreaking, and more.

See also: Secret Stuff

Internet Relay Chat:
Channel: **#cellular**

Do you have only a moderate amount of money but an uncontrollable urge to collect something?

Try phone cards.

Phone Cards

Lists of phone card collections, manufacturer lists, and chip diagram pictures of phone cards, those cards you use in public phones instead of coins.

Anonymous FTP:
Address: **ftp.funet.fi**
Path: **/pub/doc/telecom/phonecard/***

Phone Number to Word Translator

Unix C source code to an interesting program that converts phone numbers into words.

Anonymous FTP:
Address: **gatekeeper.dec.com**
Path: **/pub/usenet/comp.sources.misc/volume12/ telewords/***

Your Telephone Number Secrets Unmasked

You know that it is possible to convert your phone number from numbers to letters: 2=A, B or C; 3=D, E or F; and so on. But have you ever taken your personal number and tried all possible combinations to see if they spell anything cool? If so, you will find that there are a lot of combinations. But why should you sweat when you have a computer? Download the phone-number-to-word translating program and let the machine do the work. Maybe you'll get lucky. One person that we know found out that her number spelled out "SEX-YOGA". (You can imagine what this did for her social life.)

Hint: The program is useful for helping to remember any numbers that are entered on a telephone-like keypad, such as your ATM secret code.

Russian Phone Directory

A phone directory of the former Soviet Union. This file contains both a database of phone information and a program to access the data. The file is a self-extracting DOS .EXE file.

See also: World Cultures

Anonymous FTP:
Address: **kekule.osc.edu**
Path: **/pub/russian/phone-directory/ phonedir.exe**

Address: **moose.cs.indiana.edu**
Path: **/pub/central_eastern_europe/phonedir/ phonedir.exe**

Swiss Electronic Telephone Book

Search the Swiss Electronic Telephone Book in either English, German, French, or Italian. Allows you to specify a last name, first name, maiden name, address, and profession for a search.

Telnet:
Address: **etv.switch.ch**
Login: **etv**

Technical Discussion

Next to the Internet, the phone is one of the greatest inventions of humankind. Without the phone, you could never dial the pizza place and have them make you a steaming hot pizza with everything (except black olives) and have it delivered to your door. That's all most of us need to know about the phone, but if you are interested in more than that — like learning what the guts of the telephone look like and how the wires connect, then join up with some telephone tech talk on Usenet.

Usenet:
Newsgroup: **comp.dcom.telecom.tech**

Telefax Country Codes

A list of the international telephone and fax dialing codes for different countries.

Anonymous FTP:
Address: **ftp.funet.fi**
Path: **/pub/doc/telecom/country.codes**

A B C D E F G H I J K L M N O P Q R S T U V W X Y Z

Telephone Information Sites

A collection of links to telephone-related resources on the Internet, including AT&T Bell Labs, Bellcore, Pacific Bell, Cell-relay, telecom archives, EFF, and many more.

World Wide Web:
URL: **http://tig.com/IBC/Telephony.html**

Toll-Free Numbers for Computer Companies

Toll-free (800) phone numbers for many companies in the computer industry, including many computer hardware and software companies.

Anonymous FTP:
Address: **oak.oakland.edu**
Path: **/pub/misc/telephone/tollfree.num**

Toll-Free Numbers for Non-Profit Organizations

A list of toll-free numbers for non-profit organizations and crisis hotlines.

Anonymous FTP:
Address: **oak.oakland.edu**
Path: **/pub/misc/telephone/1800help.inf**

U.S. Telephone Area Code Guides

A guide to U.S. area codes, not only listing the corresponding regions, but also discussing special area codes and the companies involved.

Anonymous FTP:
Address: **ftp.spies.com**
Path: **/Library/Document/areacode.txt**

Gopher:
Name: Internet Wiretap
Address: **wiretap.spies.com**
Choose: **Wiretap Online Library**
  | **Assorted Documents**
  | **Telecom Digest guide to Area Codes**

Name: NASA Goddard Space Flight Center
Address: **gopher.gsfc.nasa.gov**
Choose: **Virtual Reference Shelf**
  | **US telephone areacodes**

The Area Code Blues

WHAT do you do when you wake up in the middle of the night and you just have to know what the area code is for Kokomo, Indiana? Some people would just call the operator and ask, but that is for wimps. No, if you are a reader of this book you are too smart and independent for that.

BETTER to download the **Area Codes Guide** so you can have it available instantly as the need arises. The guide is in the form of a Unix shell script, but even if you don't know Unix and you can't tell a shell script from an entrenching tool, most of the file is just a list of area codes and city names in plain text that is easy to read and search.

U.S. Telephone Area Code Program

A Unix program and area code database for providing area code information gracefully and efficiently. Whether you know the area code and need to find out the location or you know the location and need the area code, this program will provide the answer instantly.

Anonymous FTP:
Address: **lcs.mit.edu**
Path: **/telecom-archives/areacodes**

TELEVISION

Andy Griffith

It would be wonderful if every town sheriff was like Andy Griffith. But then, not every town is like Mayberry. We can't imagine Andy Griffith being sheriff of Los Angeles or New York City. Settle in for discussion of the nostalgia of *The Andy Griffith Show* and *Mayberry RFD*. It's a nice break from the real world.

Listserv Mailing List:
List Address: **mayberry@bolis.sf-bay.org**
Subscription Address: **listserv@bolis.sf-bay.org**

The Andy Griffith Show

Perhaps somewhere there are people who have not watched each of the 249 episodes of *The Andy Griffith Show* and have not immersed themselves in the stories of Andy, Aunt Bee, Opie, Floyd, Gomer, Goober, Helen, Thelma Lou, Otis, and the rest of the inhabitants of Mayberry, North Carolina.

We feel sorry for such people. They probably don't care that Barbara Eden played the manicurist in Floyd's barbershop in episode 48 (January 22, 1962), or that Ron Howard's brother and father had small roles in Episode 102 ("A Black Day for Mayberry", November 11, 1963).

We feel sorry for such people because they are missing out on what is most noble and fine in life: a society in which people most always get along, in which life's problems are well within the capabilities of a small-town sheriff and the homespun wisdom God has seen fit to bestow upon him. Within the show, Andy was sometimes referred to as the "Sheriff without a gun," but he might just as well have been called the "Sheriff who doesn't need a gun."

For at least a few minutes each week (and now, every day in reruns), we could transport ourselves to a small town in which everyday problems were manageable and human dignity was preserved simply as a matter of course. To ask whether there is justice in the world is an elegant but troubling question. To ask whether there is justice in Mayberry is both unnecessary and misleading. One does not watch *The Andy Griffith Show* for anything remotely involving one's higher cortical funtionality. Rather, we worship at the shrine of blessed banality simply because, in a world of discomforting unpredictability and baffling complexity, Mayberry and its inhabitants occupy one of the few safe rest stops available to the typical American spirit in all of us, as it navigates the confusing and oft-times rocky road of life.

Animaniacs

Everything to do with this cartoon series from Steven Spielberg, including FAQs, upcoming episode lists, songs, lyrics, episode summaries, images, sounds, and much more.

World Wide Web:
URL: **http://www.yahoo.com/Entertainment/ Television/Shows/Cartoons/Animaniacs/**

URL: **http://www.cs.cmu.edu:8001/afs/ cs.cmu.edu/user/clamen/misc/tv/Animaniacs/ Animaniacs.html**

Babylon 5 Reviews

Tune in to this electronic forum to read reviews pertaining to the *Babylon 5* television series as well as novels, comic books, games, and parodies. This is not a discussion group for fan chatter — the founders of the list are looking for critical opinion features, so you have to at least pretend that you know what you're talking about.

Listserv Mailing List:
List Address: **b5-review-l@cornell.edu**
Subscription Address: **listserv@cornell.edu**

Battlestar Galactica Home Page

A central repository for resources related to *Battlestar Galactica*, the science fiction television series. It includes a hypertext FAQ, episode guides, articles, rumors, songs, *Galactica*/*Star Trek* crossover stories, and a collection of **.au** audio files.

World Wide Web:
URL: **http://www.carleton.edu/BG/**

BBC TV and Radio

Background information, schedules, services, announcements, transcripts and factsheets, the Caversham Diary, World Service details, and much more to do with the British Broadcasting Corporation.

World Wide Web:
URL: **http://www.bbcnc.org.uk/bbctv/**

Beavis and Butthead

Interviews, ASCII art, episode listings, and quotes for the *Beavis and Butthead* show on MTV. The web page has links to Beavis and Butthead home pages, as well as sound clips and a link to the **alt.tv.beavis-n-butthead** newsgroup.

Anonymous FTP:
Address: **quartz.rutgers.edu**
Path: **/pub/tv+movies/beavis/***

Gopher:
Name: Rutgers University
Address: **quartz.rutgers.edu**
Choose: **Television and Movies | beavis**

World Wide Web:
URL: **http://www.yahoo.com/Entertainment/ Television/Shows/Cartoons/ Beavis_and_Butthead/**

A B C D E F G H I J K L M N O P Q R S T U V W X Y Z

Beverly Hills 90210

Only a city in California would be able to get a television show based on its zip code. Read mailing lists, archives, and see pictures relating to *Beverly Hills 90210* — the show where the only thing that rivals the price of the clothing is the price of the silicone enhancements.

Anonymous FTP:
> Address: **ftp.tcp.com**
> Path: **/pub/90210/***

Majordomo Mailing List:
> List Address: **90210@tcp.com**
> Subscription Address: **majordomo@tcp.com**

The Bold and the Beautiful

The Bold and the Beautiful home page offers daily updates, character information, the cast list, spoilers, and links to other soap home pages.

World Wide Web:
> URL: **ftp://www.digimark.net/wow/bb/**

C-SPAN

The C-SPAN gopher contains schedules and press releases about the live Congress video broadcasts, plus publications, info on ordering transcripts, and a small archive of historic documents such as the Declaration of Independence and the Constitution.

See also: Journalism and Media

Gopher:
> Name: C-Span
> Address: **c-span.org**

Cable Regulation Digest

It was bound to happen. With cables connecting people all over the world, someone had to come up with the idea of regulating them. The name of the bureaucracy game is Complication. Read up on the latest laws, lawsuits, bans, and technology in the cable industry.

See also: Technology, Telecommunications, Telephones

Finger:
> Address: **higgins@dorsai.dorsai.org**

Cable TV

A mailing list for anyone interested in any topic related to cable television programming, technology, or regulation.

Internet Mailing List:
> List Address: **catv@quack.sac.ca.us**
> Subscription Address:
> **catv-request@quack.sac.ca.us**

Cable TV Resources

Cable television is the most widely used drug on planet Earth. And with the exception of some bootleggers, it's even legal. Hook into these cable resources and learn about newsletters, mailing lists, archives, finger sites and newsgroups relating to cable television.

See also: Government, Politics

Gopher:
> Name: InterNIC
> Address: **is.internic.net**
> Choose: **InterNIC Information Services**
> **| About the Internet**
> **| National Information**

Cartoons

Cartoon, comics, and animation-related materials, including a list of Warner Brothers cartoons, a *Simpsons* guide, Asterix annotations, anime articles, and a *Peanuts* bibliography.

Anonymous FTP:
> Address: **ftp.spies.com**
> Path: **/Library/Media/Anime/***

Gopher:
> Name: Internet Wiretap
> Address: **wiretap.spies.com**
> Choose: **Wiretap Online Library**
> **| Mass Media**
> **| Comics and Japanese Anime**

We like cartoons, and we bet that you do too. If so, check out the cartoon archive on the Wiretap Gopher.

Cheers

Episode guides, theme music, Norm sayings, and other trivia from the classic *Cheers* television series.

Anonymous FTP:
> Address: **ftp.funet.fi**
> Path: **/pub/culture/tv+film/Cheers/***
>
> Address: **refuge.colorado.edu**
> Path: **/pub/tv+movies/cheers/***

Gopher:
> Name: Rutgers University
> Address: **quartz.rutgers.edu**
> Choose: **Television and Movies**
>   **| cheers**

Clarissa Explains

Discussion of the Nickelodeon TV show *Clarissa Explains It All*.

Internet Mailing List:
> List Address: **clarissa@ferkel.ucsb.edu**
> Subscription Address:
>   **clarissa-request@ferkel.ucsb.edu**
>
> List Address: **clarissa@tcp.com**
> Subscription Address: **clarissa-request@tcp.com**

Comedies

Get a good laugh by checking out these fun archives of some of your favorite television comedies like *Seinfeld*, *Wings*, *M.A.S.H.* and others.

World Wide Web:
> URL: **http://www.yahoo.com/**
>   **Entertainment/Television/Shows/Comedies/**

Commercials

Some people are really annoyed by commercials, but if you think about it you will realize what a marvelous invention they are. If there were no commercials, you would never have the opportunity to dash to the kitchen for snacks or run to the bathroom for a quick bit of relief. So, pay your homage to the great commercial mecca on Usenet and show how much you appreciate the service that companies are doing for television watchers around the world.

Usenet:
> Newsgroup: **alt.tv.commercials**

Got a web browser?
Got a yen to relive your favorite memories watching TV comedies?
All you need to do is point to the Comedies web site and happiness will mark you for its own.

Dark Shadows

Immerse yourself in the gothic atmosphere of this daily soap opera-style series that was produced in the Sixties and revived in the Eighties. This is not your run-of-the-mill soap. In this show, characters have to worry about witches, vampires, and werewolves. It makes real life seem like a breeze in comparison. **shadows-update** offers synopses of the episodes being shown on cable television. **dark-shadows** is a list for general discussion of the series.

Internet Mailing List:
> List Address: **shadows-update@sunee.uwaterloo.ca**
> Subscription Address:
>   **shadows-update-request@sunee.uwaterloo.ca**
>
> List Address: **dark-shadows@sunee.waterloo.ca**
> Subscription Address:
>   **dark-shadows-request@sunee.waterloo.ca**

David Letterman

How to send mail to Dave, get tickets to the show, and get the Top Ten lists, as well as information about skits, stunts, guests, music and, of course, Dave himself.

Anonymous FTP:
> Address: **quartz.rutgers.edu**
> Path: **/pub/tv+movies/letterman/***
>
> Address: **rtfm.mit.edu**
> Path: **/pub/usenet/news.answers/letterman/faz.Z**

Gopher:
> Name: Rutgers University
> Address: **quartz.rutgers.edu**
> Choose: **Television and Movies**
>   **| letterman**

Usenet:
> Newsgroup: **alt.fan.letterman**

World Wide Web:
> URL: **http://www.yahoo.com/Entertainment/**
>   **Television/Shows/Talk_Shows/**
>   **David_Letterman**
> URL: **http://bingen.cs.csbsju.edu/letterman.html**

A B C D E F G H I J K L M N O P Q R S **T** U V W X Y Z

The David Letterman archives have all kinds of funny material, including Letterman's top ten lists, a summary of the last show and other episodes, the David Letterman songbook, and so on. This image is from NAU (**ftp.nau.edu**) in the file **/graphics/gif/people/lettrman.gif**.

David Letterman Official Song Book

Lyrics to all your favorite songs from the *David Letterman* TV shows, such as the theme song as sung by Bill Murray and Paul Shaffer, the Viewer Mail Theme, and the Strong Guy, the Fat Guy, and the Genius. A hilarious compilation by Keith Rice.

Anonymous FTP:
> Address: **quartz.rutgers.edu**
> Path: **/pub/tv+movies/letterman/songbook.z**

> Address: **rtfm.mit.edu**
> Path: **/pub/usenet/news.answers/letterman/songs/list**

Mail:
> Address: **mail-server@rtfm.mit.edu**
> Body: **send usenet/news.answers/letterman/songs/list**

The Discovery Channel

Prime time program listings for the Discovery Channel divided into days, with a small description for each program. Schedules for several weeks in advance are available.

World Wide Web:
> URL: **gopher://gopher.enews.com:2100/11/collected/destination_discovery/2listing**

Doctor Who

He's wild-haired, strangely dressed, and often chased by hostile robots or aliens. Doctor Who doesn't have to take up jogging because he is almost always running for cover anyway. Join the people who love the excitement and adventure of this futuristic television series.

Listserv Mailing List:
> List Address: **drwho-l@uel.ac.uk**
> Subscription Address: **listserv@uel.ac.uk**

World Wide Web:
> URL: **http://www.phlab.missouri.edu/ccpeace_www/Dr.Who/**

Dr. Quinn, Medicine Woman

This is a woman who would be handy to know on a first-name basis. She is good with a tummyache, broken leg or any number of illnesses that leave you fevered and panting. Fans of *Dr. Quinn, Medicine Woman* post discussion about the television show, which is seen in the U.S., Canada and internationally.

Listserv Mailing List:
> List Address: **dqmw-l@emuvm1.cc.emory.edu**
> Subscription Address:
> **listserv@emuvm1.cc.emory.edu**

Dramas

Don't complicate your life with real drama. Keep the drama within the space of your television or computer. Check out the television drama archives for some of your favorite shows like *NYPD Blue*, *The Prisoner*, and *Quantum Leap*.

World Wide Web:
> URL: **http://akebono.stanford.edu/yahoo/Entertainment/Television/Shows/Dramas/**

European Satellite Information

A collection of channel information, articles, FAQs, magazines, journals, book lists, equipment details, software, contact addresses, and links to other satellite-related resources.

World Wide Web:
> URL: **http://xan.esrin.esa.it:2602/satellite.html**

Game Shows

Game show junkies now have something to do when they are not actually watching the game shows or reading trivia books to improve their game show skills. Read FAQs about popular Canadian and American game shows.

World Wide Web:
URL: **http://www.cis.ohio-state.edu/hypertext/ faq/usenet/tv/game-shows/top.html**

Live Television Images

Realtime live video and audio from U.S. cable and satellite television. This service won a technical award in the WWW Best Pages contest. It is a demonstration of VuSystem applications and VuNet hardware developed by the Telemedia, Networks, and Systems Group at MIT. Now you can watch TV and use the Internet at the same time!

Note: Requires NCSA Mosaic for the X Window System, version 2.0 or higher.

World Wide Web:
URL: **http://tns-www.lcs.mit.edu/cgi-bin/vs/vsdemo**

Married with Children

An archive for the American TV show *Married with Children*. Here you can find a FAQ, episode guides, pictures, photos, mpeg movies, sound samples, quotes, ticket information, merchandise guides, and other items of interest.

World Wide Web:
URL: **http://www.eia.brad.ac.uk/mwc/index.html**

— **Everything we tell you is true.**

— **The above sentence is only partially correct.**

— **Don't believe everything you read.**

Max Headroom

Grab a piece of the '80s with this fun commemoration of *Max Headroom*. Join up with other Max fans who are trying to revive the television series, which originated in Britain. Episode guides, a sound and image library, and a script archive are housed here.

World Wide Web:
URL: **http://net23.com/0/max/main.html**

Melrose Place

Years ago, you would be safe from the soap opera bug as long as you didn't turn the television on in the afternoon hours. Now we are all fair game. Watchers of the show *Melrose Place* are a great example. Not only do they never miss it, but when they aren't watching, they sit around and talk about it. Join in the obsession and check out the pictures and mailing list archives relating to *Melrose Place*.

Anonymous FTP:
Address: **ftp.tcp.com**
Path: **/pub/melrose-place/***

Internet Mailing List:
List Address: **melrose-place@ferkel.ucsb.edu**
Subscription Address:
melrose-place-request@ferkel.ucsb.edu

Muppet Fest

FAQs, many pictures, book guides, links to ftp archives, songs, quotes, some *Sesame Street* pictures, and much more to do with *The Muppets* TV show.

World Wide Web:
URL: **http://www.cs.wustl.edu/~mir/muppets/**

Nielson TV Ratings

The weekly results from the people who rate TV shows.

Gopher:
Name: Imperial College
Address: **gopher.doc.ic.ac.uk**
Choose: **media**
| **tv**
| **collections**
| **tardis**
| **lists**
| **nielsens**
| **current**

A
B
C
D
E
F
G
H
I
J
K
L
M
N
O
P
Q
R
S
T
U
V
W
X
Y
Z

Northern Exposure

Episode guides and summaries, FAQs, music guides, a quotations list, discussions, and other points of interest regarding the *Northern Exposure* television show.

Anonymous FTP:
Address: **jhunix.hcf.jhu.edu**
Path: **/pub/usagi/***

Address: **rtfm.mit.edu**
Path: **/pub/usenet/news.answers/**
northern-exposure-faq

Address: **tmn.com**
Path: **/pub/MetaNet/Nexp/***

Internet Mailing List:
List Address: **trebuchet@noao.edu**
Subscription Address:
trebuchet-request@noao.edu

Usenet:
Newsgroup: **alt.tv.northern-exp**

World Wide Web:
URL: **http://www.yahoo.com/Entertainment/**
Television/Shows/Dramas/Northern_Exposure/

Parker Lewis

All about the *Parker Lewis* television series, including scripts, pictures, sounds, digests, cast lists, and more.

Anonymous FTP:
Address: **ftp.cs.pdx.edu**
Path: **/pub/flamingos/***

Internet Mailing List:
List Address: **flamingo@ddsw1.mcs.com**
Subscription Address:
flamingo-request@ddsw1.mcs.com

List Address: **flamingo@lenny.corp.sgi.com**
Subscription Address:
flamingo-request@lenny.corp.sgi.com

Public Broadcasting Service (PBS)

This contains schedules for public television broadcasting networks, K-12 learning information, and information about adult distance learning satellite feeds.

Gopher:
Name: Public Broadcasting Service
Address: **gopher.pbs.org**

Red Dwarf

The home web page for *Red Dwarf*, the popular British science fiction/comedy series. Read a FAQ, check out *Red Dwarf* images, the script archive, sounds, favorite quotes, and links to other related ftp sites.

World Wide Web:
URL: **http://http2.brunel.ac.uk:8080:/red_dwarf/**
home.html

Ren and Stimpy Show Archives

Fans of Ren and Stimpy can read all about these cartoon characters. The popularity of the *Ren and Stimpy Show* is largely due to its wit and its shameless display of physical functions such as nose-picking and farting. The site has a FAQ, a guide, and an encyclopedia.

Anonymous FTP:
Address: **aug3.augsburg.edu**
Path: **/files/text_files/ren***

World Wide Web:
URL: **http://www.galcit.caltech.edu/~ta/**
renstimpy/rsvote.html

Rush Limbaugh

The rumor is true: Rush is everywhere. Check out the latest information about the man that people love or love to hate. This web page has links to a political report on Rush by a media organization, as well as Rush's response and access to the archives of **alt.fan.rush-limbaugh**.

World Wide Web:
URL: **http://www.yahoo.com/Entertainment/**
Radio/Programs/Rush_Limbaugh/

Satellite TV Images

Imagine holding a remote control in your hand that will show you channels from television stations from around the world. With each click you will get a random picture from satellite television. It's here and it's free. Point your browser to this web site and see random digitized images. For those of you who don't want to use a graphical browser, there is a link to an ftp site.

World Wide Web:
URL: **http://itre.uncecs.edu/misc/images/**
images.html

Satellite TV Page

A web page dedicated to the hobby of satellite television and radio. It offers FAQs, articles, program schedules, the archives of the Satellite Journal, a collection of satellite TV images, and satellite-related lists and charts.

World Wide Web:
   URL: **http://itre.uncecs.edu/misc/sat.html**

Science Fiction TV Shows

Television is a great way to give your brain a break. Fans of Science Fiction television can access information on all their favorite shows like *Babylon 5*, *Doctor Who*, *Star Trek*, *The X-Files*, *The Twilight Zone*, and *Superman*.

World Wide Web:
   URL: **http://www.yahoo.com/Entertainment/ Television/Shows/Science_Fiction/**

> # The best way to make money is to give something away for free.

Seinfeld

The official *Seinfeld* archive and gopher offering quotes, sounds, episode guides, FAQs, and pictures. The web page provides links to dozens of sound samples, jpeg pictures, a newsgroup and an episode guide.

Anonymous FTP:
   Address: **quartz.rutgers.edu**
   Path: **/pub/tv+movies/seinfeld/***

Gopher:
   Name: Rutgers University
   Address: **quartz.rutgers.edu**
   Choose: **Television and Movies | seinfeld**

World Wide Web:
   URL: **http://www.ifi.uio.no/~rubens/seinfeld/**

Series and Sitcoms

Episode guides, lists, FAQs, scripts, and much more to do with films and television series, including *Star Trek*, *Cheers*, *Blade Runner*, *Twin Peaks*, *Monty Python* and many more.

Anonymous FTP:
   Address: **ftp.funet.fi**
   Path: **/pub/culture/tv+film/***

Excerpt from the Net...
(from the television archives at nic.funet.fi)

```
            The Star Trek Prime Directive
            ================================
```

"As the right of each sentient species to live in accordance with its normal cultural evolution is considered sacred, no Star Fleet personnel may interfere with the healthy development of alien life and culture.

"Such interference includes the introduction of superior knowledge, strength, or technology to a world whose society is incapable of handling such advantages wisely.

"Star Fleet personnel may not violate this Prime Directive, even to save their lives and/or their ship, unless they are acting to right an earlier violation or an accidental contamination of said culture.

"This directive takes precedence over any and all other considerations, and carries with it the highest moral obligation."

A
B
C
D
E
F
G
H
I
J
K
L
M
N
O
P
Q
R
S
T
U
V
W
X
Y
Z

The Simpsons

Get the lowdown on the popular animated TV show *The Simpsons*. Bone up on *Simpsons* trivia. This ftp site maintains summaries of each episode, biographies of the characters, and series schedules.

Anonymous FTP:
>Address: **ftp.cs.widener.edu**
>Path: **/pub/simpsons**

World Wide Web:
>URL: **http://www.yahoo.com/Entertainment/ Television/Shows/Cartoons/Simpsons/**
>URL: **http://turtle.ncsa.uiuc.edu/alan/ simpsons.html**

Sitcoms of the U.K.

A complete list of all situation comedies that have ever been made in the U.K. and broadcast on U.K. television.

Gopher:
>Name: Manchester Computing Centre
>Address: **info.mcc.ac.uk**
>Choose: **Miscellaneous items**
>   **| The definitive list of UK sitcoms**

Soap Operas

Links to pages for *Days of Our Lives*, *General Hospital*, *The Bold and the Beautiful*, *The Young and the Restless*, FAQs, and the Usenet newsgroup **rec.arts.tv.soaps**.

World Wide Web:
>URL: **http://www.yahoo.com/Entertainment/ Television/Shows/Soap_Operas/**

Star Trek Archives

Quotes, parodies, episodes, reviews, and more.

Anonymous FTP:
>Address: **ftp.uu.net**
>Path: **/doc/literary/obi/Star.Trek.Stories**

>Address: **ftp.uu.net**
>Path: **/usenet/rec.arts.startrek/***

Star Trek Reviews and Synopses

Synopses and reviews for every episode of *Star Trek: The Next Generation* and *Deep Space Nine*, by Timothy Lynch.

Telnet:
>Address: **panda.uiowa.edu**

Television Guide

This web page offers the ultimate TV list containing links for more than 30 television shows, a list of major TV-related sites, a place to post your favorite links and remove everybody else's boring links, and a TV poll where you can broadcast your opinions to a few hundred people.

World Wide Web:
>URL: **http://www.galcit.caltech.edu:80/~ta/tv/**

Television Industry Discussion

An electronic newsletter about the television industry in the United States. ShopTalk is published weekdays by a San Francisco-based media consulting group, and it covers local station programming as well as the major networks.

World Wide Web:
>URL: **http://www.clark.net/pub/samer/ shoptalk-info.html**

Television News

Catch up on the latest happenings in the television industry by checking out Clarinet news. You will find information on recent television developments, new shows, news about television stars and more.

Usenet:
>Newsgroup: **clari.living.tv**

Television Series Guides and Facts

Material, FAQs, and guides for many television programs and movies, including *Twilight Zone, Tiny Toons, Quantum Leap, M*A*S*H*, and *Ren and Stimpy*.

Anonymous FTP:
>Address: **quartz.rutgers.edu**
>Path: **/pub/tv+movies/***

Gopher:
>Name: Rutgers University
>Address: **quartz.rutgers.edu**
>Choose: **Television and Movies**

Television and the Internet

We know that *you* don't waste your time watching television. Still, you probably have a few friends who do, so why not tip them off to the Internet's TV resources. The Quartz Gopher has a great TV section, as well as pointers to other archive sites. You can spend all day browsing...sorry...we mean your *friends* can spend all day browsing in a cornucopia of TV trivia, episode descriptions, and frequently asked question (FAQ) lists.

Learn how to use anonymous ftp and the world is at your fingertips.

There are only two things worth remembering in life (both of which I forget).

Television Show Discussion

Don't waste your life sitting in front of the computer. Instead, you can waste it in front of another electronic box which gives you a continuous feed of images that will lull you into a hypnotic daze and make you susceptible to the lure of home shopping channels. If you are so hooked that you like to talk about television when you are not actually watching it, check out these newsgroups. The **alt.fan** group is for discussion of characters and actors on television. The **alt.tv** and **rec.arts.tv** are for discussion of specific television shows. The **rec.arts.sf.tv** is for discussion of particular science fiction shows.

Usenet:
    Newsgroup: **alt.fan.***
    Newsgroup: **alt.tv.***
    Newsgroup: **rec.arts.sf.tv.***
    Newsgroup: **rec.arts.tv.***

Excerpt from the Net...

```
Newsgroups: alt.tv.brady-bunch
Subject: Trivia About The Brady Bunch

(1) Name the celebrity that Marcia would stop at nothing to meet.
    [Davy Jones]

(2) What was the name of the detergent the Brady's endorsed?
    [SAFE]

(3) Name the doctors that came to tend the Brady kids when they had measles.
    [Bobby: I like Dr. Cameron, he gives lollipops.
     Cindy: Dr. Porter gives all-day suckers.]

(4) What was the name of Jan's imaginary boyfriend?
    [George Glass]

(5) Why was it imperative that Marcia sneak out of the house,
    out of her window, in the middle of the night?

    (Note from Harley: I have left you question #5 to answer for yourself.)
```

A
B
C
D
E
F
G
H
I
J
K
L
M
N
O
P
Q
R
S
T
U
V
W
X
Y
Z

The Twilight Zone

There is a Twilight Zone within all of us, of course. We live each night in a dream world in which proportion and logic lie dormant like the roots of grass covered by newly fallen snow. And each morning, as we awake and the snow melts, the grass begins to sprout, restoring us to the world of sensation and rational being.

Still, there is much to be said for being able to meld the everyday world into the dark, hidden amorphous shadows of the nighttime and, in recent TV memory, no one has been able to do it as plainly and as effectively as Rod Serling. To say that he was a talented writer and director is to miss the point. The importance of his work is that it is at once entertaining and mystifying. The Twilight Zone episodes are nothing less than modern-day fairy tales cast into the template of 26-minute stories with no repeating cast members and only what basic character development and continuity that the author can create within such a short time.

No doubt the resonance and the attraction of the Twilight Zone will fade as the years pass and the cultural markers lose their meaning. Still, it will be a good long time before Serling and his vignettes lose their power, and there is still much to learn (and much to enjoy) from these unusually powerful shows. To watch *The Twilight Zone* is to visit a strange land inside ourselves that is otherwise inaccessible and forbidden.

Thirtysomething

The episode guide to this popular, but deceased, television series. The guide is available in both ASCII and Postscript formats.

Anonymous FTP:
> Address: **refuge.colorado.edu**
> Path: **/pub/tv+movies/thirtysomething/guide.***

Tiny Toons

Pictures, sound files, guides, cast listings, production credits and numbers, episode title indexes, and commentaries for the *Tiny Toon Adventures* cartoons.

Anonymous FTP:
> Address: **etext.archive.umich.edu**
> Path: **/pub/Quartz/tv+movies/tiny-toon**
>
> Address: **garfield.catt.ncsu.edu**
> Path: **/pub/graphics/images/tinytoons**
>
> Address: **utpapa.ph.utexas.edu**
> Path: **/pub/tta/***

Usenet:
> Newsgroup: **alt.tv.tiny-toon**
> Newsgroup: **alt.tv.tiny-toon.fandom**

Transformers

Life would be very different if all machines were transformers. You could be driving down the highway in your car and when traffic slowed down you could just transform into some behemoth walking robot and trek across land to make it to your 9 o'clock business meeting with enough time left over to pick up coffee and donuts on the way. Until someone manages to make that fantasy a reality, you'll have to settle for *Transformers* on television, in comic books, and on the Internet. Read the FAQ and see links to other *Transformer* archives as well as a MUSH based on the *Transformers*.

See also: Comic Books

World Wide Web:
> URL: **http://www.vt.edu:10021/other/transformers/**

TV Episode Guides

Episode guides for many TV series, including *Alf, Doctor Who, Miami Vice, Twilight Zone, Parker Lewis, Quantum Leap,* and *Twin Peaks*.

Anonymous FTP:
> Address: **ftp.spies.com**
> Path: **/Library/Media/Tv/***

Gopher:
> Name: Internet Wiretap
> Address: **wiretap.spies.com**
> Choose: **Wiretap Online Library**
> **| Mass Media**
> **| Television**

TV Nation

Fans of *TV Nation* should check out this home page. This site lists the history of the shows aired and the corresponding feature stories. Read fan mail and archives for **alt.tv.tv-nation**.

World Wide Web:
> URL: **http://www.teleport.com/~xwinds/ TVNation.html**

TV News Archive

Since 1968, Vanderbilt has been archiving major news broadcasts to make sure they are recorded, preserved and made accessible to researchers. They also keep special news events, like broadcasts of the Gulf War and the USSR coup attempt.

See also: Journalism and Media

Gopher:
> Name: Vanderbilt University, Television News Archive
> Address: **tvnews.vanderbilt.edu**

TV Schedules

Schedules for the Sci-Fi Channel and information on the commercial custom viewer that permits subscribers to receive detailed, personalized TV listing guides via fax or e-mail. The web page has links to BBC-TV and Radio Programme schedules, C-SPAN schedules, late night talk show schedules, *The Discovery Channel* and *The Learning Channel* monthly listings, and upcoming guests on *The Tonight Show*.

Gopher:
> Name: Vortex Technology
> Address: **vortex.com**
> Choose: *** **TV/Film/Video** ***

World Wide Web:
> URL: **http://www.yahoo.com/ Entertainment/Television/Schedules/**

The Twilight Zone

You remember. It's that zone where all the weird stuff happens. You're minding your own business and suddenly everything is out of control (like life isn't difficult enough without this added kink). Rod Serling is the master of the bizarre and unusual, as is evidenced by his creative television series, which aired from 1959 to 1964. Devotees of the show exchange opinions and information.

Internet Mailing List:
> List Address: **t-zone@hustle.rahul.net**
> Subscription Address:
> **t-zone-request@hustle.rahul.net**

Twin Peaks

Fans of the TV show *Twin Peaks* can get information on the cast and characters, read interviews and see an actual road map of Twin Peaks. Also available is the FAQ relating to the show.

World Wide Web:
> URL: **http://pogo.wright.edu/TwinPeaks/ TPHome.html**

Video Files

A collection of video animation sequences, including headline and business news, sports, entertainment, science, and other demonstrations. Uses the vsbrowser VuSystem application for video files developed at the MIT Laboratory for Computer Science.

Note: Requires NCSA Mosaic for the X Window System, version 2.0 or higher

World Wide Web:
> URL: **http://tns-www.lcs.mit.edu/cgi-bin/vs/ vsbrowser**

The X-Files

This web page offers a FAQ, episode guides, and images from the show *The X-Files*. The page also has links to paranormal resources, images of the unexplained, and links to other *X-Files* web pages.

World Wide Web:
> URL: **http://www.rutgers.edu:80/x-files.html**

The Young and the Restless

A web page with daily updates, scoops and spoilers, character information, a cast list, fan club addresses, and other tidbits of interest about this popular American television soap opera. The page also has links to other soaps on the Web.

World Wide Web:
> URL: **http://www.digimark.net/wow/yr**

Web users: if you are in a hurry, use Lynx.

A B C D E F G H I J K L M N O P Q R S T U V W X Y Z

TRAVEL

Alaska

Whether you are planning on taking a trip to Alaska or if you just want to know more about the state, you can get a huge amount of information from the University of Alaska's gopher. Read about sights to see, weather, law, politics, sports and recreation, and even television shows set in Alaska.

Gopher:
Name: University of Alaska
Address: **info.alaska.edu**
Choose: **Information About Alaska**

Amtrak Trains

A comprehensive list of Amtrak trains, including their train numbers, names, originations, destinations, and the days of service for each.

Anonymous FTP:
Address: **ftp.spies.com**
Path: **/Library/Document/amtrak.lis**

Gopher:
Name: Internet Wiretap
Address: **wiretap.spies.com**
Choose: **Wiretap Online Library**
   I Assorted Documents
   I Amtrak Trains

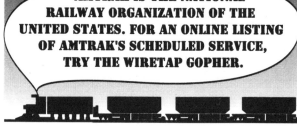

AMTRAK IS THE NATIONAL RAILWAY ORGANIZATION OF THE UNITED STATES. FOR AN ONLINE LISTING OF AMTRAK'S SCHEDULED SERVICE, TRY THE WIRETAP GOPHER.

Arctic Adventours

If you've ever felt the urge to sail to the areas of the Arctic that are inaccessible by any other means, then Arctic Adventours is for you. Arctic snapshots, expedition details, registration forms and large polar bears await you here.

World Wide Web:
URL: **http://www.oslonett.no/html/adv/AA/AA.html**

Atlanta

Guides to Atlanta's restaurants, museums, historic sites, attractions, shopping, entertainment, and much more tourist information.

World Wide Web:
URL: **http://zaphod.cc.ttu.ee/vrainn/ahome.html**

Australian Alpine Information Service

Interactive guide to help you find the right ski resort in the Australian or New Zealand snowfields. It presents a FAQ, news, short stories, club and association information, and some great ski photos.

World Wide Web:
URL: **http://www.adfa.oz.au/aais/**

Austrian Restaurant Guide

This web page is a brief guide to some of the restaurants and cafes in Austria.

World Wide Web:
URL: **http://www.lib.uchicago.edu/keith/austria/restaurants.html**

Baja California

Information on the highways, boat rentals, ferries, whale watches, and general tourism in Baja California.

Anonymous FTP:
Address: **ucrmath.ucr.edu**
Path: **/ftm/baja.california/***

Barbados

Maps, beautiful pictures, articles, and everything you would need to know about Barbados, that chain of Caribbean Islands known to most people as the West Indies.

World Wide Web:
URL: **http://www.cen.uiuc.edu/~rs4184/barbados.html**

Bay Area Places to See

Search a database of almost 150 places to see in the San Francisco Bay Area. Each entry gives contact details, and type and specialty of that sight. You can perform a search by category or location, or view the complete listing.

World Wide Web:
URL: **http://199.171.168.11/IMS/pts/pts.html**

Bay Area Restaurant Guide

This guide contains the names, addresses, and phone numbers of almost 12,000 San Francisco Bay Area restaurants. It is possible to post and read reviews of all the restaurants, view maps, or perform searches by restaurant name, city name, or type of food.

World Wide Web:
    URL: **http://netmedia.com/ims/rest/**
    ba_rest_guide.html

Berlin and Prague

This web page is Philip Greenspun's photo documentary of his epic journey from Berlin down the Elbe river to Prague, in search of traces of Jewish history.

World Wide Web:
    URL: **http://www-swiss.ai.mit.edu/philg/**
    berlin-prague/book-cover.html

Boston Restaurant List

This web page sports a large and complete list of restaurants in the Boston area. It also includes reviews of restaurants, Sunday brunch buffets, and local beers and ciders. You can view the restaurant list alphabetically, by area, by the type of cuisine, or you can search the list by keywords.

World Wide Web:
    URL: **http://www.osf.org:8001/boston-food/**
    boston-food.html

California

A massive collection of information about California. It offers traffic and road-condition reports, maps, pictures, event and attraction guides, museum exhibitions, nude beach lists, details of wine and wineries, government resources, university and school links, yellow pages, and much, much more.

See also: World Cultures

World Wide Web:
    URL: **http://www.research.digital.com/SRC/**
    virtual-tourist/California.html

Cambridge Pub Guide

Your electronic guide to pubs in the city of Cambridge, England. Select an area of the city (New Chesterton, Newtown, Barnwell, etc.) from the map for detailed information about the pubs in that area.

World Wide Web:
    URL: **http://www.cityscape.co.uk:81/bar/**
    pubguide.html

Osborne McGraw-Hill

What do you do when you are vacationing in the San Francisco Bay area and, after having visited the offices of Osborne McGraw-Hill, you have run out of places to go? The Net will come to your rescue. Point your browser to the *Bay Area Places to See* web site and you will have no trouble finding enough activities to occupy your time.

Canary Islands

Las Palmas of Gran Canaria University has information and services relating to the Internet, the university, and tourism, travel, and other cultural information about the Canary Islands.

World Wide Web:
    URL: **http://www.ulpgc.es/**

Caribbean Connection

Travel and tourist guides, newsgroup, gopher, and web links, pictures, reading material, news, current weather conditions, and much more about the Caribbean.

See also: World Cultures

World Wide Web:
    URL: **http://www.cen.uiuc.edu/~rs4184/**
    caribbean.html

A B C D E F G H I J K L M N O P Q R S T U V W X Y Z

Complete Guide to Galway

Detailed information about this town on the west coast of Ireland, including maps, event guides, reviews, articles, tourist guides, shopping information, history, and much more.

World Wide Web:
URL: **http://wombatix.physics.ucg.ie/galway/galway.html**

Currency

Whether you are planning a vacation or making a quick escape from the long arm of the law, be sure you know how much your money is worth in other countries. See a list of conversion rates (which is updated daily) as well as a FAQ on dealing with foreign currencies when you travel.

See also: Business and Finance

World Wide Web:
URL: **http://www.ora.com/cgi-bin/ora/currency**

 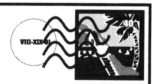

Money and Travel

As you travel, one of the most handy things to have is a bunch of money. The trouble is, each country insists on doing it their way and, if you want to eat and so on, you will most likely need to be able to convert money from one currency to another. For example, what do you do when your hotel bill must be paid in Centigrades and all you have is Fahrenheits? Well, the Net has a currency web site that can help you out in most of the typical conversion quandries, so manipulating your money will be just one less thing to worry about.

Cybertour of the U.S.A.

See the sights and sounds of the U.S.A. in your virtual Chevrolet. You will visit tourist traps, read travel guides, and visit thousands of attractions in many states.

World Wide Web:
URL: **http://www.std.com/NE/usatour.html**

Des Moines

This server contains information about the city of Des Moines, Iowa. It offers a calendar of events, tourist guide, classified ads, pictures, and details of shopping, dining, hotels, sports, leisure, and arts within the city.

World Wide Web:
URL: **http://www.dsmnet.com/**

Dublin Pub Review

Don't head off to Dublin without knowing what pubs to go to when you get there. With this review you will get pricing information as well as a general rating about the atmosphere of many Dublin pubs.

World Wide Web:
URL: **http://www.dsg.cs.tcd.ie/dsg_people/czimmerm/pubs.html**

Explore New York

A travel guide and information center for the Big Apple, including images, with sections on Manhattan, downtown, midtown, the upper west side, upper east side, and uptown.

World Wide Web:
URL: **http://eMall.com/ExploreNY/NY1.html**

Exploring Japan with Maps

Explore Japan by selecting the area or city you wish to visit from this map. You will then be presented with images and descriptions of your destination.

World Wide Web:
URL: **http://www.ntt.jp/japan/explore/index.html**

Gateway to Antarctica

A wealth of information about Antarctica, including tourism and travel, environment, news, science, treaty, and logistical information.

World Wide Web:
URL: **http://icair.iac.org.nz/**

Guide to Australia

A large collection of many information resources about Australia covering geography, environment, communications, travel, culture, government, and history.

World Wide Web:
URL: **http://life.anu.edu.au/education/ australia.html**

Guide to London

An illustrated guide to London, including travel, entertainment, accommodations, and transportation information.

World Wide Web:
URL: **http://web.cs.city.ac.uk/london/guide.html**

Hawaii

Spend your lunch hour taking a grand tour of the Hawaiian Islands. Spread a little sand around the office floor, turn the fans on, crank up your CD of ocean sounds, and fire up the web browser — it will almost seem like you are there. There are many pictures and videos at this site.

World Wide Web:
URL: **http://bookweb.cwis.uci.edu:8042/Books/ Moon/hawaii.html**
URL: **http://www.hcc.hawaii.edu/dinos/hawaii.mpg**
URL: **http://www.mhpcc.edu/tour/Tour.html**

International Travel Health Advice

A guide to vaccinations, immunizations, and illnesses abroad for those traveling to lands afar.

Gopher:
Name: University of Montana Healthline Gopher
Server Address: **selway.umt.edu**
Port: **700**
Choose: **General Health Information
| Health Information for International Travel**

Telnet:
Address: **selway.umt.edu**
Login: **health**

Don't be a Web Potato: participate.

Japan

A travel guide, complete with pictures, to traveling in Japan. It covers planning, airport arrival, the transportation network, accommodations, dining, touring, shopping, and other useful information.

World Wide Web:
URL: **http://www.ntt.jp/japan/TCJ/TC.html**

Jerusalem Mosaic

"Ten measures of beauty were bestowed upon the world; nine were taken by Jerusalem, and one by the rest of the world." Images, exhibits, paintings, maps, views of the Old City of Jerusalem, tours of the New City of Jerusalem, audio sounds and songs, and much more to do with this city with a recorded history of some 4,000 years.

World Wide Web:
URL: **http://shum.cc.huji.ac.il/jeru/jerusalem.html**

Journey North

The Arctic is probably not at the top of many people's lists of summer vacation hot-spots, but it does have its magic. Read "Arctic Bites" — stories and thoughts on the spirit and experience of the Arctic. Track wildlife as it treks across the frozen land. You can pinpoint it on a clickable map that offers you more wildlife and migration information on request.

World Wide Web:
URL: **http://ics.soe.umich.edu/ed712/IAPIntro.html**

Journeys and Destinations

Articles pertaining to journeys and travels, including the amusing "Tourist Traps in the U.S.," life in a virtual community, Arizona and New Mexico travelogues, Cancun tales, a prison saga, and other interesting stories.

Anonymous FTP:
Address: **ftp.spies.com**
Path: **/Library/Article/Journey/***

Gopher:
Name: Internet Wiretap
Address: **wiretap.spies.com**
Choose: **Wiretap Online Library
| Articles
| Journeys and Travels**

On the Internet, you can find images of exotic places and interesting people. This one, entitiled **fijichief.gif** is at Northern Arizona (**ftp.nau.edu**) in the directory **/graphics/gif/people**. Note: When you download this to a PC, the name gets shortened to **fijichie.gif**.

Kenn Nesbitt's Travel Adventures

Like a technoid Indiana Jones, Kenn Nesbitt — Internet columnist and freelance technology writer — totes his laptop like a sidearm as he roams the European countryside. Read his latest travel experiences as he posts them to the Web at each major stop of the journey and watch his progress by following the little red line on his map of Europe. You can even send Kenn mail and tell him to stop in and see your cousin Olga on his way through Puhejarve.

See also: World Cultures

World Wide Web:
    URL: **http://www.thegroup.net/kenn.htm**

Ljubljana

See the sights and scenes of Ljubljana, the capital of Slovenia. There are many jpeg images and descriptions of its castle, the old part of the city, the river, cathedral, fountains, and other views. Also there is a large map of the city in gif format.

World Wide Web:
    URL: **http://www.ijs.si/slo-ljubljana.html**

Madawaska-Victoria

A tourist's guide to Madawaska-Victoria, a land of hospitality at the northwestern tip of New Brunswick. This page offers links to a regional profile, tours of Saint-Jacques, Edmundston, Verret, Saint-Hilaire, Baker Brook, Lac Baker, and Clair, as well as a calendar of events and information about major attractions.

World Wide Web:
    URL: **http://www.cuslm.ca/madvic/emada-vi.htm**

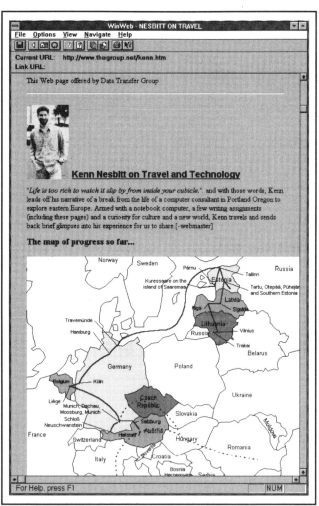

Keep up with Kenn Nesbitt as he makes his way around the continent of Europe. Kenn's progress is indicated by a dark red line marking his trail. You can read all about his adventures by following the links on the page.

Kenn Nesbitt

There are those who compare Kenn Nesbitt to a modern day Mark Twain, a contemporary innocent abroad, stumbling into foreign cultures with the grace and facility of an American pogo stick. There are others who think of Nesbitt as a surrogate explorer, boldly going where everyone else would like to go except that all of us have to stay home and work. And then there are others who simply say, "Kenn who?".

Regardless, there is something appealing about this engaging guy, who quit his job at Microsoft and took off for the unknown in order to soothe a wounded heart and to throw himself into the careless, liberating experience of traveling-by-yourself-with-no-timetable. Use your web browser to check out Kenn's home page and you will be able to read his irregular entries in the Journal of Life. Soon, you too will be traveling with Kenn on his search for meaning, enlightenment, and a free Net connection. What will he encounter in the next town? Will he find true love and for how long? And most important, why is this guy traveling through Europe having a great time when the rest of us have to stay home and work?

Money Abroad FAQ

This hypertext FAQ offers information about dealing with money in almost every country, including cash, traveler's checks and plastic, and how and where to get cash with cards. There is a guide to which form of payment is best for each country, and the black markets are covered for the appropriate countries.

World Wide Web:
  URL: **http://www.cs.cmu.edu:8001/Web/People/ slaveau/money-faq/money-abroad.html**

Net Travel

Travel, any kind of travel, should be well planned, and a good traveler is a prepared traveler. This hypertext guide details how to use the Internet to prepare for a trip to distant lands. It discusses relative newsgroups, IRC, GNN Travel Resource Center, and more.

World Wide Web:
  URL: **http://www.ora.com/gnn/meta/travel/res/ nettravel.html**

New York City Guide

NYC — The Net-Person's Guide to New York City is an extensive guide of sights to see and things to do in New York City, including hotels, restaurants, nightclubs, places to shop, subway guides, and many other invaluable tidbits.

Anonymous FTP:
  Address: **quartz.rutgers.edu**
  Path: **/pub/nyc/***

Gopher:
  Name: Rutgers University
  Address: **quartz.rutgers.edu**
  Choose:
    NYC - The Net-Person's Guide to New York City

Guide to New York

Are you going to visit New York City? There is so much to do and so much to see that you may want to spend some time planning your trip. (For example, the subway system is so large that you can ride for hours and still miss many of the good stations.) Before you leave for your next encounter with the city that never sleeps, check out the Internet's own travel guide to the Big Apple.

Hint from Harley: go to Carnegie Deli (the one in *Broadway Danny Rose*) and order the chicken soup.

A
B
C
D
E
F
G
H
I
J
K
L
M
N
O
P
Q
R
S
T
U
V
W
X
Y
Z

New York City Information

You wouldn't go into the jungle without a map or a guide. Use that same reasoning when going to New York City. If you are planning to travel to the Big Apple or if you just want to know more about the city, check out this outline of history, facts, things to do, transportation, and good eats.

World Wide Web:
URL: **http://www.cs.columbia.edu nyc/**

Oslo Tour

A short sightseeing tour of the beautiful city of Oslo, Norway, with a number of scenic and interesting sights, including Vigeland park, Holmenkollen ski jump, and some proud museums.

World Wide Web:
URL: **http://www.oslonett.no/oslo/oslotour.html**

Promus Hotels

Details of the three Promus Hotel chains, including addresses, telephone numbers, hotel amenities, visual images of the hotels and rooms, maps and more. Promus Hotels include Embassy Suites, Hampton Inn, and Homewood Suites.

World Wide Web:
URL: **http://www.promus.com/**

Railroad Timetables

Timetables for many trains, subways, and metros around the world.

World Wide Web:
URL: **http://www-cse.ucsd.edu/users/bowdidge/railroad/rail-gopher.html**

RailServer

Allows you to find German and other European railway connections by filling in a form with your electronic mail address and travel details. Your query will be returned within six hours.

World Wide Web:
URL: **http://rzstud1.rz.uni-karlsruhe.de/~ule3/info-trn.html**

Recreational Vehicles

We must envy the turtle who carries his home on his back. While he can't run quick like a bunny or leap tall buildings in a single bound, at least he will never be without a nice place to stay as he travels. You can experience this feeling of mobile home comfort by driving around in a recreational vehicle. Talk to adventurous people who motor around the countryside in their home away from home.

Usenet:
Newsgroup: **alt.rv**

Route 66

Details of a drive from Chicago to Santa Monica (Los Angeles) following as much as possible the remains of the historic Route 66, that 2,448-mile stretch of road built in 1926 and crossing eight states. This web page offers a list of Route 66 associations, book references, maps, stories, and some plain advice on traveling Route 66.

World Wide Web:
URL: **http://www.cs.kuleuven.ac.be/~swa/route66/main.html**

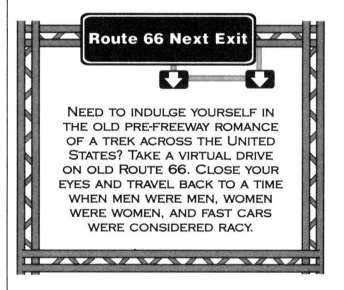

Route 66 Next Exit

NEED TO INDULGE YOURSELF IN THE OLD PRE-FREEWAY ROMANCE OF A TREK ACROSS THE UNITED STATES? TAKE A VIRTUAL DRIVE ON OLD ROUTE 66. CLOSE YOUR EYES AND TRAVEL BACK TO A TIME WHEN MEN WERE MEN, WOMEN WERE WOMEN, AND FAST CARS WERE CONSIDERED RACY.

Russian Travelogue

Travel to Russia without leaving home. This two-week tour comes complete with photographs and illustrations as well as daily writings that will give you the flavor of Russian culture and environment.

World Wide Web:
URL: **http://www.hyperion.com/~koreth/russia/**

Smoky Mountains

A fantastic exhibit that includes maps, a tourguide, information on the park, its history, and a reading list for more information.

World Wide Web:
URL: **http://www.nando.net/smokies/smokies.html**

South Dakota

The *South Dakota — Great Faces, Great Places* home page offers information about South Dakota, including local government, higher education, cities, tourist information, South Dakota Internet resources and more. The tourist information includes sections with images and details of the state capitol, Crazy Horse memorial, Missouri River, wildlife, badlands, hiking, winter sports, and road maps. You can also fill out an online form to request more information from the South Dakota Department of Tourism.

World Wide Web:
URL: **http://www.state.sd.us/**

St. Petersburg Pictures Gallery

Collection of scenic gif pictures of the sights and attractions of St. Petersburg in Russia, including a special section showing St. Petersburg at night.

World Wide Web:
URL: **http://www.spb.su/pictures/index.html**

Staunton, Virginia

The city of Staunton was founded in the 1740s in the central Shenandoah Valley of Virginia along the trail that evolved into the Great Philadelphia Wagon Road. This web page offers a walking tour of Staunton's five historic districts, with photo images, museum details and images, tours of many noteworthy historical buildings, tourist information, recreation guides, and other general details on Staunton and the surrounding area.

See also: History

World Wide Web:
URL: **http://www.elpress.com/staunton/**

Staying Healthy in Asia, Africa and Latin America

Everyone knows not to drink the water, but do you know all the other stuff about not eating peeled fruit and why you shouldn't walk around barefoot? Learn what to do before, during, and after traveling in Asia, Africa and Latin America.

Gopher:
Name: Moon Publications
Address: **gopher.moon.com**
Port: **7000**
Choose: **Travel Health: Staying Healthy in Asia, Africa and Latin America**

Subway Navigator

Find the right route in the subways of several of the world's largest cities, including those in Canada, France, Germany, Italy, Spain, and the U.S. The telnet site is interactive: enter your departure and arrival stations and the guide will suggest a route and provide an estimate of how long it will take you to reach your destination.

Gopher:
Name: Universites P. & M.Curie
Address: **gopher.jussieu.fr**
Choose: **Indicateur des metros | Subway indicator**

Telnet:
Address: **metro.jussieu.fr**
Port: **10000**

Thailand

Experience Thailand through images and travelers' tales of journeys there, including an elephant safari and a trip over the river Kwai. Read articles on travel, Thai history, geography, and climate, as well as interviews and essays on Thailand.

World Wide Web:
URL: **http://nearnet.gnn.com/gnn/meta/travel/mkt/focus/index.html**

A B C D E F G H I J K L M N O P Q R S **T** U V W X Y Z

Tips for Travelers

Don't let your excitement about your big trip get in the way of being organized and careful about planning the details. You may end up stranded in a tiny country known for political unrest and lack of Internet access. Get tips on packing, passports, air travel — and don't forget to send your favorite Internet authors cool postcards from exotic lands.

World Wide Web:
URL: **ftp://netcom7.netcom.com/pub/ducky/docs/ tips/tips.top.html**

Tour de France

Enjoy a tour of the various regions of France through these guides to each area. There are suggested itineraries, pictures, sounds, and details of getting there, climate, dining, accommodations, events, and much more.

World Wide Web:
URL: **http://town.hall.org/travel/france/ france.html**

Tourism Offices

Details on how to get tourist information for a number of destinations, and a directory of tourist information offices worldwide.

Anonymous FTP:
Address: **ftp.cc.umanitoba.ca**
Path: **/pub/rec-travel/tourism-offices.txt**

Address: **quartz.rutgers.edu**
Path: **/pub/misc/tourist-info-offices**

Gopher:
Name: Rutgers University
Address: **quartz.rutgers.edu**
Choose: **Miscellaneous
| tourist-info-offices**

Travel and Tourism Web Pages

There is no sense in keeping yourself closed off from the entire world. Check out all the places that you can travel and start planning your exciting world adventures. Even if you never go, it certainly is fun to dream.

World Wide Web:
URL: **http://www.yahoo.com/Government/ Countries/**

Travel Information

Get travel information and personal accounts about a number of destinations. Travelers post detailed accounts of their vacations, including places to go, places to avoid, where and what to eat, reviews of hotels, and much more.

Anonymous FTP:
Address: **ftp.cc.umanitoba.ca**
Path: **/pub/rec-travel/**

Usenet:
Newsgroup: **rec.travel.***

Travel Marketplace

Upgrades, frequent flyer plans, hotel discounts, travel guides — the longest journey begins with but a single step into Usenet's one-stop travel marketplace. Buy, sell, beg, borrow, steal — then go!

Usenet:
Newsgroup: **rec.travel.marketplace**

Travel Matters Newsletter

A newsletter for people interested in travel — whether for business or pleasure. Read articles on becoming an air courier, contrasting cultures, how to stay healthy during travel, tips on renting a car, travel book reviews and news briefs.

Gopher:
Name: Moon Publications
Address: **gopher.moon.com**
Port: **7000**
Choose: **Travel Matters Newsletter**

Travel Resources

Guides to where to find everything available on the Internet about travel. Consists of a large list of mailing lists, ftp sites, and Listservs of interest to travelers.

Anonymous FTP:
Address: **rtfm.mit.edu**
Path: **/pub/usenet/rec.answers/travel/ftp-archive**

Address: **rtfm.mit.edu**
Path: **/pub/usenet/rec.answers/travel/online-info**

Travelers' Tales

GNN online travel center, with articles on using the Internet to prepare for a trip, travel information for destinations around the world, pointers to other travel resources, and a marketplace.

World Wide Web:
URL: **http://nearnet.gnn.com/gnn/wic/ trav.04.html**

Travels with Samantha

The electronic version of a popular travelogue of North America with many wonderful pictures and links to maps of places mentioned. This won "Best Document Design" in the Best of the Web '94 Awards. It tells the tale of a summer spent seeing North America, meeting North Americans, and trying to figure out how people live. This site features over 500K bytes of text and 250 full-color jpeg photos.

World Wide Web:
URL: **http://www-swiss.ai.mit.edu/samantha/ travels-with-samantha.html**

Trip to Antarctica

Articles written by Peter Amati describing his trip to the joint U.S.-Russian research station, Ice Station Weddell, in Antarctica aboard the research ship Nathaniel B. Palmer in May 1992.

Anonymous FTP:
Address: **ftp.uu.net**
Path: **/doc/literary/obi/Antarctica/***

U.S. State Department Travel Information

Extensive information on current and past travel advisories for those interested in traveling abroad. Each factsheet contains the addresses and phone numbers of American consulates, as well as passport, visa, and government information, and crime data. Files are arranged alphabetically by country name.

Anonymous FTP:
Address: **ftp.uu.net**
Path: **/doc/literary/obi/US.StateDept/Travel/***

Gopher:
Name: St. Olaf College
Address: **gopher.stolaf.edu**
Choose: **Internet Resources**
| **US-State-Department-Travel-Advisories**

Utah's National Parks

You haven't lived if you haven't been to Utah. Take a moment now to visit Utah's famous national parks. See links to over a dozen great places to travel while in Utah and get tips on what to do and what not to do while you're there.

World Wide Web:
URL: **http://sci.dixie.edu/NationalParks/ nationalpark.html**

Virtual Tourist

Connections to tourist guides for many exciting locations, including Europe, the United States, New Zealand, Australia, and Japan. The links are presented on a map of the world, from which you can choose the destination of your dreams.

World Wide Web:
URL: **http://wings.buffalo.edu/world/**

West Virginia

A collection of scenic photos of the sights and landmarks of West Virginia.

World Wide Web:
URL: **http://pcn.proline.com/Sights/views.html**

TRIVIA

Answer Guys

Do you have a nagging question you can't seem to get an answer to? Try the Answer Guys at the *Middlesex News* electronic newspaper.

Gopher:
Name: Software Tool & Die
Address: **gopher.std.com**
Choose: **Periodicals, Magazines, and Journals**
| **Middlesex News**
| **Columns**
| **The Answer Guys**

Coffee Machine

If you spend time wondering if there is coffee in the coffee machine in the computer science department at Cambridge University, wonder no more. Every second a computer snaps a new picture of the coffee machine and places it on this web page.

World Wide Web:
URL: **http://www.cl.cam.ac.uk/coffee/coffee.html**

Coin Toss

Need to toss a coin but don't have one? No problem; gopher here and simulate it.

Gopher:
Name: University of Alabama
Address: **twinbrook.cis.uab.edu**
Choose: **The Continuum**
  I **The Sports Arena**
  I **Coin Toss**

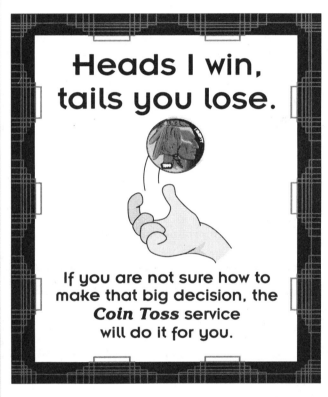

Heads I win, tails you lose.

If you are not sure how to make that big decision, the *Coin Toss* service will do it for you.

Coke Servers

Interesting places to finger for trivial information.

Finger:
Address: **cocacola@columbia.edu**
Address: **coke@cs.cmu.edu**
Address: **coke@cs.wisc.edu**
Address: **coke@xcf.berkeley.edu**
Address: **drink@drink.csh.rit.edu**
Address: **graph@drink.csh.rit.edu**
Address: **info@drink.csh.rit.edu**
Address: **pepsi@columbia.edu**

World Wide Web:
URL: **http://www.cs.cmu.edu:8001/afs/
cs.cmu.edu/user/bsy/www/coke.html**
URL: **http://www.csh.rit.edu/proj/drink.html**

Hot Tub Server

Everybody has fantasies about having a computer environment advanced enough to coordinate launching a space shuttle. And everyone has fantasies about being able to sink into an exquisitely monitored hot tub in which you can bubble your cares away. But who would ever think to put the two together? Someone whose two favorite things are the Internet and his new hot tub. Check out the status of the Paul Haas hot tub and read the documentation on this hot tub project. His hot tub seats eight, so if you know the magic password he might even invite you over.

Finger:
Address: **hottub@hamjudo.com**

Mail:
Address: **hottub@hamjudo.com**

World Wide Web:
URL: **http://hamjudo.com/cgi-bin/hottub**
URL: **http://hamjudo.com/hottub_notes.html**

Internet Index

What better way to break the ice at a party than to start up a little game of trivia? Get this list of factoids and you can ask fun questions like "What percentage of PCs were using TCP/IP in 1993?" and "What is the average number of megabytes of Usenet news per day?" Find out the answers to these questions and more from the Internet Index — a report of interesting statistics relating to net usage.

Internet Mailing List:
List Address: **internet-index@openmarket.com**
Subscription Address:
   internet-index-request@openmarket.com

World Wide Web:
URL: **http://www.openmarket.com/info/
internet-index/**

Talk to a Cat

This web page uses speech synthesis to talk to the author's cat. You type a sentence to the cat, in the form provided, and the author's computer will then say it. If the cat is around, it will hear it. The program is written in arexx and is running on an Amiga. There is also a large list of things people have said to the cat recently. "Woof, Woof, Growl."

See also: Animals and Pets

World Wide Web:
URL: **http://queer.slip.cs.cmu.edu/cgi-bin/
talktocat**

Talk to a Cat

There are lots of things you can do when you are bored, and talking to your cat is one of the most soothing and emotionally satisfying. However, what do you do if you do not have a cat? Well, you can visit Harley or Rick and talk to their cats, or you can point your browser at the *Talk to a Cat* web site and talk to the only cat on the Internet. (Actually, Harley's cat used to be on the Internet, but he kept forgetting his password and so he finally decided it was more fun just to sleep next to the keyboard.)

Today's Date

All sorts of things you didn't know about today's date, based on the book *Numbers: Facts, Figures and Fiction*.

World Wide Web:
URL: **http://acorn.educ.nottingham.ac.uk/ cgi-bin/daynum**

Today's Events in History

Important historical events that happened on today's date in years gone by.

Finger:
Address: **copi@oddjob.uchicago.edu**

Usenet:
Newsgroup: **clari.apbl.today_history**
Newsgroup: **clari.living.history.today**

Trivia Time

Twist your brain with this weekly *Trivia Time* newsletter. These trivia questions cover a variety of topics, so you can choose your favorites or try to answer them all. Send in your answers to Cyndi and if you get them right you could be hailed as one of the weekly winners and see your name in the next newsletter. Fill your head with tons of useless facts and you will always have something to chat about at cocktail parties.

See also: Fun

Finger:
Address: **cyndiw@magnus1.com**

Trivial Questions and Answers

Okay, we all know that Richie Petrie's middle name is Rosebud and that it stands for "Robert Oscar Sam Edward Benjamin Ulysses David." But what was Rob and Laura's address? How about the Ricardos' phone number? Join the pros and test your trivia skill. TV, radio, music, film, Internet books — all the great cultural achievements of mankind are grist for those who pursue the trivial.

Usenet:
Newsgroup: **rec.games.trivia**

A B C D E F G H I J K L M N O P Q R S T U V W X Y Z

Unofficial Smiley Dictionary

This Smiley Dictionary is one of the most complete lists of smileys available on the Internet. Do you feel ;-) or :-(or even just :-I ?

Gopher:

   Name: Universitaet des Saarlandes
   Address: **pfsparc02.phil15.uni-sb.de**
   Choose: **Fun (Spass & Spiel, etc.)**
     | **Cartoons**
     | **Smilies :-)**

Vending Machines

The rage started with being able to check the Coke machine from the Internet. Things got out of control with the invention of CU-SeeMe. Check out coffee machines, temperature gauges, light sensors and a geiger counter without leaving your seat. "Spy cameras" have been set up in offices and pointed out windows so you can even have a view.

World Wide Web:

   URL: **http://www.cs.cmu.edu:8001/afs/
   cs.cmu.edu/user/bsy/www/iam.htm**

Guess how many items there are in the Trivia section.

NOTHING TO DO?

No one to talk to?

Have you read each page of all of Harley's books?

Okay, it's time to check out the Smiley Dictionary.

Smiley Dictionary

Excerpt from the Net...

```
(from fingering copi@oddjob.uchicago.edu)


                      Saturday
                  October 22, 1994
                  11:44:02 PM (CDT)


******************** Birth: Franz Liszt (183 years ago) ********************
****************** Birth: Sarah Bernhardt (150 years ago) ******************
***************** Birth: Joan Fontaine (77 years ago) ******************
****************** Birth: Annette Funicello (52 years ago) *****************
****** Event: Chinese made 1st record of solar eclipse (4129 years ago) *******
* Event: Great Disappointment (Millerites predict 2nd coming) (150 years ago) *
*** Event: Metropolitan Opera House (NY) held grand opening (111 years ago) ***
******* Event: JFK announced USSR missile bases in Cuba (32 years ago) ********
********** Event: US National debt topped $1 TRILLION (13 years ago) **********
***** Event: Harley writes last ad for second edition of this book (today) ****
*******************************************************************************
```

USENET

Anonymous Posting Service

Post messages to Usenet groups anonymously. To find out how, send mail to the address below.

Mail:
Address: **help@anon.penet.fi**

ChooseNews II

You've spent all day slaving over a hot newsreader trying to decide which groups to subscribe to and which to throw out. If only you had known about Scott Yanoff's shell script, you could have saved some time and energy (since he's done all the work for you). ChooseNews II will allow you to choose newsgroups based on your hobbies or interests. Just type in keywords and the script does the rest. Scott's shell script is free.

Anonymous FTP:
Address: **csd4.csd.uwm.edu**
Path: **/pub/choosenews2**

World Wide Web:
URL: **file://csd4.csd.uwm.edu/pub/choosenews2**

Creating Alternative Hierarchy Newsgroups

FAQs and guidelines for creating a new **alt** Usenet newsgroup.

Anonymous FTP:
Address: **rtfm.mit.edu**
Path: **/pub/usenet/news.answers/alt-config-guide**

Creating Standard Newsgroups

Instructions for creating a new mainstream Usenet newsgroup.

Anonymous FTP:
Address: **rtfm.mit.edu**
Path: **/pub/usenet/news.answers/
creating-newsgroups/***

European Usenet

Read European and British Usenet newsgroups through this gopher-based newsreader.

Gopher:
Name: University of Birmingham
Address: **gopher.bham.ac.uk**
Choose: **Usenet News Reader
| European/UK Groups**

Being Anonymous

There are many reasons why you might wish to post Usenet articles anonymously. For example, you might want to contribute personal comments to one of the sex-oriented groups. Or, you might not want your employer or system manager (or significant other) to know the nature of your postings.

In order to protect the right of anyone to say whatever they want without fear of retribution, an anonymous posting service has been set up. Once you register, you will be given a user number and all correspondence will be carried out using that number. Moreover, once you post an article anonymously, people will be able to send you mail commenting on the article, without knowing who you are.

This service is an important one and -- as you can imagine -- there are all sorts of self-righteous zealots who would love to shut it down. Please use your intelligence and do not abuse the system.

FAQs in HTML Format

This list of FAQs is in HTML format, although not each FAQ on the list is in HTML. The ones that are not in HTML format are converted to text so you can easily read them. There are a great deal of FAQs here and they are organized alphabetically so you can skip through to find just the one you want.

World Wide Web:
URL: **http://www.cis.ohio-state.edu/hypertext/
faq/usenet/FAQ-List.ht**

FAQs Searches and Archives

Search and browse some or all of the Usenet FAQs, as posted to the **news.answers** newsgroup, from this easy-access gopher menu.

Gopher:
Name: Johns Hopkins University
Address: **gopher.gdb.org**
Choose: **Usenet News and FAQs
| All FAQs (Frequently Asked Questions)
Searches and Archives**

A B C D E F G H I J K L M N O P Q R S T U V W X Y Z

Frequently Asked Questions Master List

The master list of FAQ lists. Includes cross references to Usenet newsgroups and Internet resources.

Anonymous FTP:
Address: **rtfm.mit.edu**
Path: **/pub/usenet/news.answers/index**

Hangul (Korean) Newsgroups

Read the Hangul Usenet groups from Korea.

Gopher:
Name: Korea Network Information Center
Address: **gopher.nic.nm.kr**
Choose: **USENET Newsgroups
| Hangul News Groups**

Japanese Usenet

Check out Usenet in Japan. It's in Japanese!

Note: Requires a software client to read Japanese text.

See also: Software: Utilities

Gopher:
Name: National Institute for Physiological Sciences
Address: **gopher.nips.ac.jp**
Choose: **A. Netnews**

Periodic Informational Postings List

This multipart list has an entry for informational articles posted to Usenet groups periodically. The list includes FAQs, forms, and other regular postings.

Anonymous FTP:
Address: **rtfm.mit.edu**
Path: **/pub/usenet-by-group/news.answers/
posting-rules/part***

Risks of Posting to Usenet

A story describing how a posting to Usenet resulted in a call from a U.S. Air Force base and an interesting visit from the FBI.

Anonymous FTP:
Address: **ftp.spies.com**
Path: **/Library/Article/Rights/posting.rsk**

Gopher:
Name: Internet Wiretap
Address: **wiretap.spies.com**
Choose: **Wiretap Online Library
| Articles | Civil Rights and Liberties
| Risks of Posting to Usenet**

Want to see how easy it is to get into trouble?

Read **Risks of Posting to Usenet.**

Stanford Netnews Filtering Service

It's going to be an all-day job if you want to check every single Usenet newsgroup for reports of Elvis sightings, so why not let someone do it for you? Subscribe to Stanford's Netnews Filtering Service, and they will send you postings on any keywords or phrases that you choose. So, if you're paranoid and you could just swear people are talking about you, this will be the proof you can finally show your therapist.

World Wide Web:
URL: **http://woodstock.stanford.edu:2000**

Usenet Descriptions

Search Usenet newsgroup descriptions to quickly and easily find newsgroups related to a subject or topic of interest.

Gopher:
Name: Nova Scotia Technology Network
Address: **nstn.ns.ca**
Choose: **Internet Resources
| Search Usenet Newsgroup Descriptions**

Usenet Finger Utility

Lists of FAQ lists, Internet resources, and periodic postings to Usenet newsgroups.

Finger:
> Address: **nichol@stavanger.sgp.slb.com**

Usenet Groups with a Difference

A list of Usenet groups that are connected with interaction, interfaces, and agency, for those of you looking for the real Net News.

Gopher:
> Name: University of Texas at Austin
> Address: **gopher.utexas.edu**
> Choose: **World | USENET News**

Usenet News via Electronic Mail

If, for some reason, you can't post articles to Usenet in the usual way, try posting by mail.

Note: Replace periods in a newsgroup name with hyphens. Example: **alt.bbs** becomes **alt-bbs**.

Mail:
> Address: *newsgroup*@**cs.utexas.edu**

Would you like to post to a Usenet group that is not carried on your system? Do it by mail.

Usenet News via Gopher

Allows you to read Usenet news through gopher.

Gopher:
> Name: Michigan State University
> Address: **gopher.msu.edu**
> Choose: **News & Weather**
>   **| USENET News**
>
> Name: University of Birmingham
> Address: **gopher.bham.ac.uk**
> Choose: **Usenet News Reader**

Usenet Olympics

Parodies of Usenet and its inhabitants, combined into a single file covering each year.

Anonymous FTP:
> Address: **ocf.berkeley.edu**
> Path: **/pub/Usenet_Olympics/***

Usenet Word Statistics

A list of the 1,000 most common words used on Usenet over the period of a year, along with their percentages of occurrence.

Anonymous FTP:
> Address: **ftp.spies.com**
> Path: **/Library/Article/Language/top1000.use**

Gopher:
> Name: Internet Wiretap
> Address: **wiretap.spies.com**
> Choose: **Wiretap Online Library**
>   **| Articles**
>   **| Language**
>   **| Top 1000 Words used on Usenet**

A
B
C
D
E
F
G
H
I
J
K
L
M
N
O
P
Q
R
S
T
U
V
W
X
Y
Z

Worldwide Usenet

Read Usenet newsgroups, including many local and regional newsgroups from around the world, such as Australian, European, South American, and specific U.S. state newsgroups.

Gopher:
>   Name: Johns Hopkins University
>   Address: **gopher.gdb.org**
>   Choose: **Usenet News and FAQs**
>   I **Read USENET News Groups**

USENET CURIOSITIES

Cascades

Every once in a while, someone will reply to a silly one-line message with another silly one-line message. Another person will follow up with a third silly one-line message, and (let the trumpets sound) a *cascade* is born. Cascades have a life and an appeal all their own. If you are one of those lucky persons whose sense of taste is so highly developed as to make you an aficionado of cascades, then you will want to tune into this newsgroup.

Usenet:
>   Newsgroup: **alt.cascade**

Flames

A *flame* may be a complaint, a criticism of a person, or a good old-fashioned tongue-lashing reduced to bits and bytes. Join this group and play with the people who complain for a living.

Usenet:
>   Newsgroup: **alt.flame**

Kibo

Kibo, mythical net-god, is rumored to be omnipresent on the Net. Post any Usenet article with the word "Kibo" to any newsgroup: Kibo will find it and answer. Who exactly is Kibo? That's for us to know and for you to find out. Join in the worship and try to prove (or disprove) Kibo's existence.

Gopher:
>   Name: Wiretap Online Library
>   Address: **wiretap.spies.com**
>   Choose: **Wiretap Online Library**
>   I **Fringes of Reason**
>   I **Very Strange   I Kibology FAQ...**

Usenet:
>   Newsgroup: **alt.religion.kibology**

Net Abuse

Heavy cross-posting, spamming, and annoying commercial advertising are at the top of the list of Ways to Abuse Your Net Privileges. Read about the latest sins against the laws of Net etiquette, thoughts and ideas on the concept of minding our manners and general ranting and raving about people who rant and rave.

Usenet:
>   Newsgroup: **alt.current-events.net-abuse**

Newsgroup Administration

It's bound to happen. When you get thousands of people posting to Usenet, someone is going to decide that things need to get more organized. The **news.admin** groups are a central point for administrative topics relating to Usenet such as the dissemination of information, statement of policies and the relating of technical details about forming and moderating newsgroups.

Usenet:
>   Newsgroup: **news.admin**
>   Newsgroup: **news.admin.misc**
>   Newsgroup: **news.admin.policy**
>   Newsgroup: **news.admin.technical**

Newsgroup Invasion

Sometimes it doesn't matter if you mind your own business. You can be happily posting away in your favorite newsgroup when it eventually erupts into chaos and disorder. And you never saw it coming. That's because the Usenet commandos planned their strategy so keenly. Their plan is to seek out newsgroups and create a stir, cause flame wars and wreak general havoc. This is where they devise their plans.

Usenet:
>   Newsgroup: **alt.syntax.tactical**

Newsgroup Questions

Looking for a newsgroup about Austrian folkdancing or one that will tell you how to make clothes from old beer cans? If you can't find just the one you are looking for, try asking on this newsgroup. Someone might be able to help. People will answer questions not only about specific newsgroups, but about Usenet groups in general. It's a good source of information.

Usenet:
>   Newsgroup: **news.groups.questions**

Shared Realities

Some days you just wake up and think to yourself, "Hey, I think I will be someone else today." It's easy when you participate in some of the shared realities of Usenet. In these groups, people assume a persona and write about their thoughts, feelings and actions as that character. Meet people, form bonds, make friends, entertain and be entertained. Even if you don't want to participate, these newsgroups are fun to read because it's like seeing a story unfold before your eyes.

See also: Role-Playing

Usenet:
    Newsgroup: **alt.dragons-inn**
    Newsgroup: **alt.kalbo**
    Newsgroup: **alt.pub.cloven-shield**
    Newsgroup: **alt.pub.coffeehouse.amethyst**
    Newsgroup: **alt.pub.dragons-inn**
    Newsgroup: **alt.pub.havens-rest**
    Newsgroup: **alt.shared-reality.startrek.klingon**

Usenet Announcements

Stay informed on the latest new groups that are cropping up in Usenet. The **.newgroups** resource is where people post when they want to propose a new group. The **.newusers** group is a place where periodic explanations about Usenet are posted for the benefit of new users.

Usenet:
    Newsgroup: **news.announce.newgroups**
    Newsgroup: **news.announce.newusers**

Usenet Junkies

If something is worth doing, it's worth doing to excess. When Usenet becomes a bit too much and you feel your sanity slipping away, check out this support group for Usenet junkies who can't say no.

Usenet:
    Newsgroup: **alt.usenet.addict**
    Newsgroup: **alt.usenet.recovery**

Instead of watching TV, read about it: take a look at the Television section.

Usenet Kooks

It used to be safe inside your home, but not anymore. The kooks are coming off the street and straight onto the Internet. Collected at this web site is the **alt.usenet.kooks** FAQ, the net.legends archives, information on Kibology, archives of the postings of various Usenet kooks, and the all-important Kook of the Month archive. Check to see if your name is there.

Usenet:
    Newsgroup: **alt.usenet.kooks**

World Wide Web:
    URL: **ftp://ftp.crl.com/users/ro/cd/auk.html**

Usenet Personalities

Just as there are people who gain notoriety in neighborhoods or in the news, there are faceless people who become equally notable in the Internet community and set tongues to wagging around the world. Read about these people and see samples of their posts and join the praise or cursing of them.

Usenet:
    Newsgroup: **alt.net.personalities**

Weird Places to Hang Out on Usenet

Among the thousands of Usenet newsgroups, there are a few strange places to hang out where anything goes. These are newsgroups that were started as a joke, or real newsgroups that have been abandoned by the original settlers. Check out one of these groups and meet the squatters. Sort of the free-trade zone of Usenet commerce. (In fact, there are some newsgroups that are so secret, we can't even tell you about them.)

Usenet:
    Newsgroup: **alt.0d**
    Newsgroup: **alt.1d**
    Newsgroup: **alt.alien.vampire.flonk.flonk.flonk**
    Newsgroup: **alt.alt.alt.alt.alt**
    Newsgroup: **alt.art.theft.scream.scream.scream**
    Newsgroup: **alt.basement.graveyard**
    Newsgroup: **alt.bitch.pork**
    Newsgroup: **alt.bogus.group**
    Newsgroup: **alt.cuddle**
    Newsgroup: **alt.dumpster**
    Newsgroup: **alt.non.sequitur**
    Newsgroup: **alt.religion.monica**
    Newsgroup: **alt.rmgroup**
    Newsgroup: **alt.silly-group.beable**
    Newsgroup: **alt.test.my.new.group**

VICES

Cigar Smoking

Throw away those puny cigarettes and namby-pamby pipes and go for the real manly-man smoking past-time. Light up and meet other cigar smokers on Usenet.

See also: Health, Medicine

Usenet:
Newsgroup: **alt.smokers.cigars**

Excerpt from the Net...

(from the "Gambling and Oddsmaking" directory on the Wiretap Gopher)

The Kelly Criterion [for Blackjack] is a betting heuristic that minimizes your chance of going broke while maximizing your long-run profits. To bet consistently with the Kelly Criterion, you should divide your bankroll into 300-400 units and normally bet 1-4 units on each hand. Your optimal bet on a hand is a percentage of your current bankroll equal to about 0.5*R/D + B, where R is the running count, D is the number of remaining decks (so R/D is the true count), and B is the basic strategy expectation.

Gambling and Oddsmaking

Guides on how to win at Blackjack, optimal wagering, shuffle-tracking, lowball, and other games. These resources also have other helpful gambling information, such as how to test for loaded dice, how to count cards, and so on.

Anonymous FTP:
Address: **ftp.csua.berkeley.edu**
Path: **/pub/rec.gambling/***

Address: **ftp.spies.com**
Path: **/Library/Article/Gaming/***

Gopher:
Name: Internet Wiretap
Address: **wiretap.spies.com**
Choose: **Wiretap Online Library**
| **Articles**
| **Gambling and Oddsmaking**

Usenet:
Newsgroup: **alt.gambling**

No matter who you are or what you believe, somewhere on the Internet, there are people like you.

Hangovers

It's a shame when something that can be fun causes so much misery later. But it's the same with any fun thing — sex, alcohol, excess food or roller coasters. There is always a risk of ensuing nausea or headache afterward. Don't be alone in your misery. Share stories and sure cures for hangovers. Learn from the people who never let the prospect of pain slow them down.

Usenet:
Newsgroup: **alt.hangover**

Horse Racing

And they're off! You can feel the adrenaline rush through your veins and into your fast-beating heart as your pulse quickens and you break out in little beads of perspiration. You clutch the ticket in your fist and hope like heck that your horse comes in first since you bet all of your lunch money on him. If you're addicted, or if you just like the thrill of the race, meet up with other racing fans to discuss the strategies of horse racing and handicapping.

See also: Hobbies

Internet Mailing List:
List Address: **derby@ekrl.com**
Subscription Address: **derby-request@ekrl.com**

**Hungry?
Try Food and Drink.
Hungry for Love?
Try Romance.**

Laszlo's Lengthy List of Luxury Smokes

A huge list that rates different brands of cigarettes, from ordinary to standout to exemplary, and some which are just too bizarre to rate.

Finger:
Address: **laszlo@alpha1.csd.uwm.edu**

World Wide Web:
URL: **gopher://alpha1.csd.uwm.edu:79/0laszlo**

Even if you don't smoke, you should take a moment to look at

Laszlo's Lengthy List of Luxury Smokes.

Here is one of the people who is busy putting the "fan" back into "fanatic."

Lies

In the old days, people used to make telling lies an art form. They would call them "tall tales" or say they were "spinning windies." That made the lying okay, because everyone knew it was for fun. Besides fun, you can tell lies for profit, to get yourself out of trouble or just because you can't help yourself. Think up the biggest whopper you can and post it here. And if you get in trouble for it later you can say, "but Mom, all the other Internet users were doing it..."

Usenet:
Newsgroup: **alt.lies**

Lies, Lies, and More Lies

Hey, listen, it's true. I heard from a guy who knows. Reading *The Internet Golden Directory* will extend your lifespan. Really. They did a study. It was published in this medical journal. I read about it on Usenet, in **alt.lies**.

Pipe Smoking

You know you are addicted when the sweet, rich scent of pipe tobacco makes you all goose-pimply and gives you urges to dress in velvet smoking jackets. Even if you don't like to smoke a pipe, it's fun to go in those tobacco shops with the rich wood paneling and case after case of sweet smelling leaves. This list and newsgroup are for anyone who smokes or collects pipes.

Internet Mailing List:
List Address: **pipes@paul.rutgers.edu**
Subscription Address:
pipes-request@paul.rutgers.edu

Usenet:
Newsgroup: **alt.smokers.pipes**

A
B
C
D
E
F
G
H
I
J
K
L
M
N
O
P
Q
R
S
T
U
V
W
X
Y
Z

Sex Services

Ah, the Modern Age. Overnight mail delivery, faxes, e-mail, pizza in thirty minutes or less, home shopping networks and sex partners on demand. These are the things that make life worth living. Read about the going rates for services and where to find the various objects of your desire.

See also: Sex, X-Rated Resources

Usenet:
Newsgroup: **alt.sex.erotica.marketplace**
Newsgroup: **alt.sex.services**

Smoking Addiction

The phrase "the only way to break a bad habit is to drop it" was invented by someone who never had to quit smoking. It's a habit that is hard to break whether you quit altogether or try to taper off. Find support from other people recovering from their addiction to cigarettes or from people who have already recovered.

See also: Health

Listserv Mailing List:
List Address: **smoke-free@ra.msstate.edu**
Subscription Address: **listserv@ra.msstate.edu**

Usenet:
Newsgroup: **alt.support.non-smokers**
Newsgroup: **alt.support.stop-smoking**

This book is high in fiber.

For advice on using the Internet, read "The Internet Complete Reference."

Smoking News

It used to be that in movies all the cool heroes and heroines smoked. They'd squint their eyes, take a long drag and slowly exhale the smoke in seductive or mysterious ways. These days, smoking is very uncool and is being banned in more places than ever before. Find out the recent laws and news on smoking and tobacco from Clarinet.

Usenet:
Newsgroup: **clari.news.smoking**

Strip Clubs

It's nice when you go to a bar or club and you get the opportunity to see some nice scenery. And it doesn't really have to be anything special like glorious vistas that make you believe there is a God. Just something interesting will do, like a man or woman wearing nothing but strategically placed tassels as they gyrate in the vicinity of your seating area. Fans of strip clubs and exotic dancers discuss the hot clubs, dancers, and places not to go when looking for a good time.

See also: Sex, X-Rated Resources

Usenet:
Newsgroup: **alt.sex.strip-clubs**

Excerpt from the Net...

Newsgroup: alt.sex.strip-clubs
Subject: So, what does your wife think...

> I have been too chicken to go into a strip joint since I got
> married. Then one day, I found lipstick on my wife's blouse where
> some woman had been kissing her through the blouse. I asked about
> it, and she said she paid for a lap dance at a local club...

> I'm looking forward to going as soon as I get some money...

Hmm, if that's the case, run to the strip joint and introduce me
to your wife.

WEATHER

Canadian Weather

Environment Canada provides users with weather forecasts, maps, satellite images, and documentation on Canadian weather.

World Wide Web:
URL: **http://cmits02.dow.on.doe.ca/**

Impress Your Friends

In today's fast-moving culture of MTV, instant celebrity, and quick-paced news from around the world, it's hard to come up with anything compelling and fascinating enough that you are guaranteed to impress your family and friends. But, as a reader of this book, you need never feel wanting for a way to show off your knowledge of the world at large. The next time your friends come over (especially that guy from the next office who always has to show off), simply point your browser at the *Environment Canada* web site and you can proudly demonstrate that, although everyone else may be better looking, dress more effectively, and be more popular with the people who count, *you* know where to get official Canadian weather information whenever you want.

Climate Data Catalog

This is no farmer's almanac. Don't count on the ache in your knees or the singing of crickets to tell you what the weather is going to be like. Get access to three-dimensional oceanic datasets, surface climatologies, air-sea data, global atmospheric circulation statistics, and Navy bathymetry.

World Wide Web:
URL: **http://rainbow.ldgo.columbia.edu/datacatalog.html**

Climate Diagnostics Center

You're leaning on the fence talking to the neighbor about life and the weather when he says "In all my born days, I reckon this is the hottest summer I can ever remember." And when you think about it, you suspect he might have a point. Don't let the mystery of his remark keep you up at night. Use the Climate Diagnostics Center to see exactly how the weather has been — not only for your lifetime — but for the last few centuries. Interesting climatological data is used to track persistant anomalies and see how this affects short term weather.

World Wide Web:
URL: **http://www.cdc.noaa.gov/**

Climatic Research Unit

The server for the Climatic Research Unit at the University of East Anglia, Norwich, England, has information about current weather, online publications about climatic research, and links to other climate research facilities around the world.

World Wide Web:
URL: **http://www.cru.uea.ac.uk/**

Colorado Weather Underground

Detailed weather conditions and forecasts for any location on the planet. Choose a city by its three-letter identifier or navigate a menu system to focus on your area of interest. Includes ski conditions, earthquake reports, severe weather, and marine forecasts and observations.

Gopher:
Name: University of Colorado Boulder
Address: **gopher.colorado.edu**
Choose: **Colorado Weather Underground**

Telnet:
Address: **weather.colorado.edu**
Port: **3000**

Current Weather Maps and Movies

Don't risk leaving the house without knowing if you need your galoshes or not. Check out pictures and movies of the latest satellite weather images, which are updated every hour.

World Wide Web:
URL: **http://rs560.cl.msu.edu/weather/**

DMSP Data Archive Home Page

The Defense Meteorological Satellite Program archives information received from two satellite constellations that can be found hanging out somewhere near the poles. The mission of these sun-synchronous satellites is to monitor the latest happenings relating to the weather, ocean and the earth.

World Wide Web:
URL: **http://web.ngdc.noaa.gov/dmsp/dmsp.html**

Earth Images from Weather Satellites

Display Meteosat satellite images and general interest weather information on your X Window terminal.

Note: The first time, you will be asked to send mail to **meteo-window@csp.it** with the numerical address of your graphics terminal (must be running X Window).

Telnet:
Address: **cspnsv.csp.it**
Port: **5000**

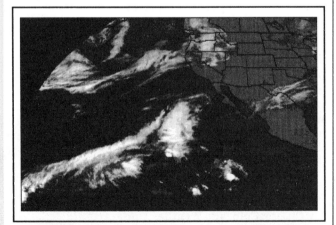

If you use a Unix computer with X Window, you can telnet to port 5000 at **cspnsv.csp.it** to display satellite images on your system. Satellite image files are also widely available from NOAA, NASA, and the National Weather Service.

Flood Damage

Information and pointers on cleaning up after a flood. Good advice from people who have learned the hard way.

Telnet:
Address: **exnet.iastate.edu**
Login: **flood**

Too much water in the wrong place? Look at the **Flood Damage** hints.

Gray's Atlantic Seasonal Hurricane Forecast

Provides 1944-to-date seasonal means and current year forecast for the number of named storms, named storm days, hurricanes, hurricane days, major hurricanes, destruction potential, and so on.

Finger:
Address: **forecast@typhoon.atmos.colostate.edu**

Gopher:
Name: University of Minnesota
Address: **gopher.micro.umn.edu**
Choose: **News**
  | **National Weather Service Forecasts**
  | **Earthquakes, Tropical Storms, Auroral Activity/ Tropical Storm Forecast**

Need help with the morons around you? Try Psychology.

Hourly Auroral Activity Status Report

Get the latest reports on the activities of the Aurora Borealis (northern lights). Reports watches and warnings. This information is updated hourly.

Finger:
Address: **aurora@xi.uleth.ca**

Gopher:
Name: University of Minnesota
Address: **gopher.micro.umn.edu**
Choose: **News**
| **National Weather Service Forecasts**
| **Earthquakes, Tropical Storms, Auroral Activity**
| **Auroral Activity**

Hurricane Images

Images from weather satellites of the hurricanes Emilie and Fernanda.

Anonymous FTP:
Address: **mael.soest.hawaii.edu**
Path: **/pub/spectacular/hurricanes/***

Interactive Weather Browser

It's a real drag when you are the only one in the car wearing a wool suit and everyone else has on deliciously cool and lightweight cotton clothing. If you had checked out the latest weather information from the web, you would be better dressed for success.

World Wide Web:
URL: **http://rs560.cl.msu.edu/weather/ interactive.html**

ATTENTION
ᗡᗡᗡᗡᗡᗡᗡᗡᗡᗡᗡᗡᗡ
Macintosh Users

Now there is an easy way for you to check the weather. The *Interactive Weather Browser* makes obtaining weather information as easy as moving your mouse and clicking. And why waste your effort learning how to pick something from a menu or even (dare we say it?) type a command, when you can point and click? Truly, this is a weather resource for the rest of us.

Japanese Weather

Daily weather reports and satellite images in gif format.

Gopher:
Name: National Institute for Physiological Sciences
Address: **gopher.nips.ac.jp**
Choose: **Weather JAPAN**

Meteorology

Weather buffs no longer have to roam the Internet looking for interesting meteorological information. At this web site you will find links to several meteorological institutes that have resources on the Net.

World Wide Web:
URL: **http://www.yahoo.com/ Environment_and_Nature/Weather/Institutes/**

Meteorology Information

This gopher offers surface maps, satellite images, weather reports, radar images.

Gopher:
Name: University of Nebraska at Lincoln
Address: **kossava.unl.edu**

Monthly Temperature Anomalies

Take control of your own weather information. This web site will allow you to create contour maps or graphs using temperature anomalies from the Global Historic Climate Network and the Monthly Climatic Data of the World. These two items are combined to give you a good overview of monthly temperature anomalies from around the world.

World Wide Web:
URL: **http://www.ncdc.noaa.gov/onlineprod/ ghcnmcdwmonth/form.html**

National Center for Atmospheric Research

National Center for Atmospheric Research (NCAR) is a research center where scientists work to solve fundamental questions that require a mix of specialities and facilities not readily available elsewhere. NCAR conducts research in the areas of atmospheric chemistry, climate, weather, and the sun and upper atmosphere.

World Wide Web:
URL: **http://http.ucar.edu/metapage.html**

A
B
C
D
E
F
G
H
I
J
K
L
M
N
O
P
Q
R
S
T
U
V
W
X
Y
Z

National Weather Service Forecasts

Weather reports for geographical regions as well as reports categorized by type or region (i.e., storm fronts, severe storms, satellite images, Canada, Caribbean, etc.).

Gopher:
Name: University of Illinois
Address: **wx.atmos.uiuc.edu**

Name: University of Minnesota
Address: **gopher.micro.umn.edu**
Choose: **News**
  | National Weather Service Forecasts

NOAA Space Environment Services Center

A database of space environment reports, including solar forecasts and activity reports.

Telnet:
Address: **selvax.sel.bldrdoc.gov**
Login: **sel**

World Wide Web:
URL: **http://www.sel.bldrdoc.gov/today.html**

Solar and Geophysical Reports

Get the latest reports on solar activities. Information is extensive and includes numerous text graphs and tabular data. This information is updated every three hours.

Finger:
Address: **daily@xi.uleth.ca**
Address: **solar@xi.uleth.ca**

Surf Conditions in California

Who needs TV or radio surf reports? You can check out the surf with your Internet connection. Every ten minutes, a camera in California takes a short video clip of the surf, a computer stores the clip digitally and places it under a link on this web page for you to view. The video sequences are Microsoft **.avi** files, and the first person to spot a shark or a dolphin will win a prize.

World Wide Web:
URL: **http://sailfish.peregrine.com/surf/live.html**

Do you feel happy and contented? Good. Now use your browser to look at the pictures of California surf and see what you are missing.

Surface Analysis and Weather Maps

This anonymous ftp site carries current surface analysis and infrared weather maps. The maps are updated often, and the old ones are not archived. Maps are mostly in gif format.

Anonymous FTP:
Address: **vmd.cso.uiuc.edu**
Path: **WX/**

Weather Processor

When the weather is too bad to go outside, you can look at it from inside using your web browser. Connect to this web page and see images and surface maps, data and observations about current weather.

World Wide Web:
URL: **http://thunder.atms.purdue.edu/**

The Internet has lots and lots (and lots) of free software.

Weather Radar

There is a lot more to the weather than licking your finger to see which way the wind is blowing. Nobody knows this better than the MIT Weather Radar Lab. They have a home page containing a gallery of radar images, a FAQ list and glossary of terms, research references, and links to other interesting web pages concerning weather radar. MIT keeps a radar data archive containing 20 years of storm system observation. While the archive is too unwieldy to access through the Net, they do list a contact person if you need information about these files.

World Wide Web:
URL: **http://graupel.mit.edu/Radar_Lab.html**

Weather Reports

Get up-to-date weather reports for any location on the planet. For the telnet site, an easy-to-use interface guides you through the process of selecting a city or location, then you can view the weather report onscreen or download it to your computer.

Telnet:
Address: **downwind.sprl.umich.edu**
Port: **3000**

Usenet:
Newsgroup: **biz.pagesat.weather**
Newsgroup: **clari.apbl.weather**
Newsgroup: **clari.apbl.weather.misc**
Newsgroup: **clari.apbl.weather.storms**
Newsgroup: **clari.apbl.weather.usa**

World Wide Web:
URL: **http://cougarxp.princeton.edu:2112/bpd/webweather.html**

URL: **http://www.mit.edu:8001/weather**

Did you know there are many different books that you can download to your own computer? See Literature for the details.

The Outside World

Living on the Internet is fine, but the outside world has two important advantages: (1) there is pizza, and (2) it's the only place we know of where you can get a computer. However, there are some significant disadvantages, and high on the list is that the outside world has altogether too much weather. Before you actually commit yourself to going outside, use the Internet to check the weather report for your area. Why take a chance when the information is only a few keystrokes away?

Weather Reports for Australia

Current weather, forecasts, recent trends, and future developments, including boating and coastal conditions, river and solar reports for all parts of Australia.

Gopher:
Name: Austin Hospital
Address: **gopher.austin.unimelb.edu.au**
Choose: **General Information and Resources | Australian Weather Forecasts**

Telnet:
Address: **vicbeta.vic.bom.gov.au**
Port: **55555**

Weather Reports for Canada

Weather forecasts and extended forecasts for all areas of Canada.

Gopher:
Name: Nova Scotia Technology Network
Address: **nstn.ns.ca**
Choose: **Canadian Weather Forecasts**

Weather World

The University of Illinois is making itself a veritable mecca of weather information. They provide current satellite and U.S. images, weather maps and animations.

World Wide Web:
URL: **http://www.atmos.uiuc.edu/wxworld/html/general.html**

A B C D E F G H I J K L M N O P Q R S T U V W X Y Z

WOMEN

Abortion

Think you can sway someone's opinion on this issue? If you like to beat your head against a wall, join the heated discussion about abortion.

Internet Relay Chat:
Channel: **#abortion**

Abortion and Reproductive Rights

Whether you are pro-choice or pro-life, this gopher will be of interest to you. Read *Choice Net*, a weekly newsletter that has the latest news on reproductive rights around the world. You will also have access to archives of press releases and other informative files on the legal aspects of abortion.

Gopher:
Name: The Well
Address: **gopher.well.sf.ca.us**
Choose: **Politics**
| **Abortion and Reproductive Rights**

Ada Project

Sponsored by Yale University, the Ada Project acts as a clearinghouse for information and resources relating to women in computing. Find information on fellowships, grants, employment opportunities, statistics, and links to other related resources.

World Wide Web:
URL: **http://www.cs.yale.edu/HTML/YALE/CS/ HyPlans/tap/tap.html**

Attitudes of Women

Wanna know what women really think? Or would you at least like to hear a little bit about what people think that women really think? You will get an earful of both if you check out these newsgroups that discuss women's attitudes.

Usenet:
Newsgroup: **alt.women.attitudes**
Newsgroup: **soc.women**

For Women Only (sort of)

Generalizing about women and their attitudes can be a risky business. Still, there is a place for everything on the Net, and when the time comes and you just have to express your opinion, try **alt.women.attitudes** or **soc.women.**

Warning: before you post your own articles, read what other people have to say for at least a few weeks.

Hint: If you are a C-Shell user, try the command **alias woman man** to provide equal access to the online Unix manual.

Bibliographies of Women's Studies

For anyone doing research in Women's Studies or any topic relating to women, this list will be invaluable. The list of bibliographies is separated by topic, so you can scan the choices and select just the one you need.

World Wide Web:
URL: **http://inform.umd.edu:86/ Educational_Resources/ AcademicResourcesByTopic/WomensStudies/ Bibliographies**

Calls for Papers in Women's Studies

You've been slaving over that paper on feminism and family theory, plus you have the one you wrote last year on lesbian scientists. Don't let those papers just sit around gathering dust. Check here to see if anyone wants them. This list will tell you about calls for papers as well as the deadlines. This could be your big chance.

World Wide Web:
URL: **http://inform.umd.edu:86/ Educational_Resources/ AcademicResourcesByTopic/WomensStudies/ CallsforPapers**

Conferences for Women

Hit the scholarly conference scene by checking out upcoming conferences relating to Women's Studies and gender and sexuality issues. Select links to learn more about a particular conference, including an overview and dates.

World Wide Web:
URL: **http://inform.umd.edu:86/
Educational_Resources/
AcademicResourcesByTopic/
WomensStudies/Conferences**

Electronic Forums for Women

Figure out a way to spend even more hours on the Internet. Get this list of electronic forums relating to women. Some mailing lists are for professionals, some have a specific focus of topics, and many are of general interest to women and a nice gathering place to talk.

World Wide Web:
URL: **http://sunsite.unc.edu/cheryb/women/
elec-forum.html**

> ## The Internet is PEOPLE, not computers.

Feminism

If it weren't for feminists, men wouldn't have anything to grumble about except the President's Address to the Nation interrupting the football game. It's been proven through history that women are good at organizing themselves and getting things done and they've shown it once again in Usenet. Join one or all of these groups and discuss feminism in all its forms.

Usenet:
Newsgroup: **alt.feminism**
Newsgroup: **alt.feminism.individualism**
Newsgroup: **soc.feminism**

Feminism Internationally

Some people say the word with awe and pride in their voice. Some people spit the word out violently between clenched teeth and tight lips. Then there is the group who contemplates feminism and gender from a thoughtful, neutral point of view. Whatever category into which you may fall, you are welcome to join the list, but this is not a battleground to prove whether feminism is inherently good or evil. This is a place for thoughtful folk to share information on feminism, gender, women and international relations, world politics, international political economy or global politics.

Listserv Mailing List:
List Address: **femisa@mach1.wlu.ca**
Subscription Address: **listserv@mach1.wlu.ca**

Excerpt from the Net...

```
Newsgroup: alt.feminism
Subject: Women in Strip Bars

> How is the women perpetuating the patriarchal system by working
> as a stripper?

I'll explain it for you.  First of all, heterosex is bad, because it's
exploitive, and puts the man into an active role, while the woman is
just a passive receptacle.  (Women who enjoy this sort of sex are
obviously brainwashed).  This has been amply demonstrated by Dworkin
and McKinnon, and cannot be questioned.

Any liberated woman knows this, and would only cater to the vile lust
of the depraved members of the patriarchy if forced to do so by sheer
economic necessity.  She is forced into this necessity through evil
machinations of patriarchal lackeys.  Thus she perpetuates the
patriarchal system by reinforcing, through her performance, the image
of women as the worthless slut and temptress...
```

Feminism and Science and Technology

Long gone are the days of women staying home to hand wax the linoleum and punch down bread dough. Women now have lab coats, pocket protectors, geiger counters, microscopes, and a variety of other gadgets and gizmos that they use in science and technology. Join up with brainy women interested in science and technology to discuss critiques of science and to possibly create the science of feminism.

See also: Science, Technology

Internet Mailing List:
   List Address: **fist@hamp.hampshire.edu**
   Subscription Address:
      fist-request@hamp.hampshire.edu

Feminist Theology

Women have never been in the foreground of the traditional church due to some biblical stipulation about showing proper submission. Of course, the Bible was written a long time before anyone knew about feminism, so it's time to take another look at the role of women in religion and feminist theology. The purpose of this list is to have open, stimulating discussion on these topics, and all religions, creeds, and opinions are welcome as long as nobody starts a verbal brawl. You might even find out if God really did create women in Her image.

See also: Religion, Religion: Alternative

Listserv Mailing List:
   List Address: **femrel-l@umcvmb.missouri.edu**
   Subscription Address:
      listserv@umcvmb.missouri.edu

Gender and Computing

For the longest time, computers have been "a guy thing." Why is that? Read articles put up by Computer Professionals for Social Responsibility that cover topics such as women in computer science, feminism, and cross-gender communication.

World Wide Web:
   URL: **http://cpsr.org/cpsr/gender/gender.html**

Ever wonder why most optimizing compilers are written by men? If so, the *Gender and Computing* web site may provide some provocative, challenging, and downright boring answers to questions that no one really cares about anyway.

Gender and Sexuality

There's no escaping it. Gender and sexuality issues run rampant among the population, spurring arguments, thought-provoking discussion, and philosophical meanderings. Read articles and papers about gender and sexuality and explore other feminist resources available at this site.

World Wide Web:
   URL: **http://english-server.hss.cmu.edu/
   Gender.html**

Global Fund for Women

The Global Fund for Women is a nonprofit international grant-making organization whose mission is to begin, strengthen or link groups who work toward the well-being of women and the full participation of women in society. Find out more about their program as well as how to apply for a grant.

World Wide Web:
   URL: **http://www.ai.mit.edu/people/ellens/
   gfw.html**

Health Concerns of Women

Woman have special health concerns — especially when it comes to illnesses like endometriosis and ovarian and breast cancer. Read information on these maladies as well as other topics, such as women and alcohol, breast implants, and AIDS.

World Wide Web:
URL: **http://inform.umd.edu:86/ Educational_Resources/ AcademicResourcesByTopic/ WomensStudies/GenderIssues/WomensHealth**

Issues of Interest to Women

Nobody is on this list to defend the issue of feminism. This is a friendly environment open to men and women to discuss issues and experiences that are of interest to women. Anyone is welcome to join, but to be added to the list, you must provide the moderator with your full name and gender for statistical purposes. They will make no exceptions.

Internet Mailing List:
List Address: **femail@lucerne.eng.sun.com**
Subscription Address:
femail-request@lucerne.eng.sun.com

Liberty and Feminism

Liberty is alive and well on the Internet. Men and women gather to discuss classical concepts of liberty and individual rights in relation to feminist issues such as ideology, politics, culture and gender.

See also: Politics

Internet Mailing List:
List Address: **libfem@math.uio.no**
Subscription Address: **libfem-request@math.uio.no**

Living with a Challenge

This list is open to women only for the discussion of living with a physical handicap. This support group is not just for women in wheelchairs, but is for any woman who experiences physical challenges in her daily environment, whether it's a temporary or permanent condition.

See also: Health

Internet Mailing List:
List Address: **living@qiclab.scn.rain.com**
Subscription Address:
living-request@qiclab.scn.rain.com

> ## Do you like weirdness? Check out Usenet Curiosities.

Menopause

Menopause is a subject of interest for women of all ages, and here is an open forum for all women to gather and share remedies and personal experiences relating to menopause. While the list is geared primarily to women for casual discussion, any interested party is welcome, including members of the medical community.

See also: Health, Medicine, Psychology

Listserv Mailing List:
List Address: **menopaus@psuhmc.maricopa.edu**
Subscription Address:
listserv@psuhmc.maricopa.edu

Midwifery

You just never know when it's going to happen. You'll be stuck in an elevator or on the subway with a pregnant woman in labor. What will you do then? Plan ahead and get some information on midwifery so you will always be prepared. Articles, information on organizations, and links to other resources are a few of the things that are available.

See also: Health, Medicine

World Wide Web:
URL: **http://www.csv.warwick.ac.uk:8000/ midwifery.html**

Notable Women

Everyone has heard of Susan B. Anthony. After all, her picture is on a piece of U.S. currency. Just because nobody happens to use that currency doesn't mean she's not popular. There are many other notable women who are not so famous, like Annie Jump Cannon, Blanche Ames, and Clara Adams-Ender, but they are among the many women who have done something remarkable during their lifetimes. Page through the formatted database or use keywords to find just who you are looking for.

Gopher:
Name: Estrella Mountain Community College
Address: **gopher.emc.maricopa.edu**
Choose: **Information Commons
| Notable Women**

> ## This is the first book of the rest of your life.

Resources for Women

The ambitious task has been undertaken — to make a women's home page and collect as much woman-stuff as possible. It's a remarkable collection not only of resources, but also of writings by or about women. Topics cover professional and academic organizations, Women's Studies resources, and gender and sexuality issues.

World Wide Web:
>
> URL: **http://www.mit.edu:8001/people/sorokin/ women/index.html**

Sexual Assault on Campus

While this list is not exclusively for women, it does concern violence against women on college and university campuses. Learn about anti-rape activist groups and help disseminate information about assaults and methods of reducing sexual assault against women.

Listserv Mailing List:
>
> List Address: **stoprape@brownvm.brown.edu**
> Subscription Address:
> **listserv@brownvm.brown.edu**

Women in Congress

Women have been running homes for years, so they might as well run the House, too. Learn about the women in Congress by reading their online biographies.

Gopher:
>
> Name: University of Maryland
> Address: **info.umd.edu**
> Choose: **Educational Resources**
> **I Academic Resources By Topic**
> **I Women's Studies Resources**
> **I Government and Politics**
> **I Women in Congress**

Women's News

Read the latest news as it relates to women. Clarinet offers you the latest news stories on reproductive issues, sex crimes and laws, harrassment and other issues concerning women.

Usenet:
>
> Newsgroup: **clari.news.group.women**
> Newsgroup: **clari.news.women**

Women's Studies Resources

People have been studying women for years. It's just that now they can get college credit for it. Find out about various Women's Studies programs, women's resources on the Internet, and see a special section on women and literature.

Gopher:
>
> Name: Harvard University
> Address: **gopher.harvard.edu**
> Choose: **VINE (Campus Information - Gopher Version)**
> **I Computer-Related Information**

World Wide Web:
>
> URL: **http://sunsite.unc.edu/cheryb/women/ wsphome.html**

Women's Wire

It's almost like a clubhouse on the Internet and it's just for women. Directories at this gopher cover topics such as women and politics, women's health, women and work, and other interesting items of a more historical nature.

Gopher:
>
> Name: Women's Wire
> Address: **gopher.wwire.net**
> Port: **8101**

Secret Internet Club For Women

Well, sort of. When you get a moment, point your gopher at the Women's Wire (a computer network set up primarily for women) and keep up on whatever is worth keeping up on.

Secret Internet Club For Women

WORLD CULTURES

Aboriginal Studies

A worldwide communications vehicle and central electronic archive for anyone working on or interested in the general study of indigenous Australia.

Majordomo Mailing List:
List Address:
aboriginal-studies-l@coombs.anu.edu.au
Subscription Address:
majordomo@coombs.anu.edu.au

Africa

A channel dedicated to discussing everything about Africa.

Internet Relay Chat:
Channel: **#africa**

African Forum

A mailing list for discussing issues and topics of interest to Africans, both in Africa and elsewhere.

Listserv Mailing List:
List Address: **africa-l@vm1.lcc.ufmg.br**
Subscription Address: **listserv@vm1.lcc.ufmg.br**

African Resource List

A great collection of African resources. Lists Usenet, mailing lists, Clarinet and other news services, online storage sites (ftp, etc.) and dialup BBSs.

Note: For convenience, use a paging command when using this finger site.

Finger:
Address: **mcgee@barney.eecs.nwu.edu**

African Studies

No longer are there any excuses for you to be ill-informed about African history and culture. These web pages offer a huge number of African studies resources including ftp, gopher and telnet sites as well as links to other web sites, bulletin boards and databases.

World Wide Web:
URL: **http://www-penninfo.upenn.edu:1962/ penninfo-srv.upenn.edu/9000**
URL: **http://www.african.upenn.edu/ African_Studies/Home_Page/ Black_African_Resources.html**
URL: **http://www.african.upenn.edu/ African_Studies/Home_Page/WWW_Links.html**

Ignoring this hint may be hazardous to your health.

Arab Press Newsletter

An electronic monthly newsletter of the Arab press. Includes unedited quotes from Arab press members from around the world.

Internet Mailing List:
List Address:
arab-press@jerusalem1.datasrv.co.il
Subscription Address:
arab-press-request@jerusalem1.datasrv.co.il

Argentina

A mailing list and a web server dedicated to Argentina: the food, the culture, and anything else to do with this South American country. The web site has links to many articles, sounds, and images — nearly all of them in Spanish.

Internet Mailing List:
List Address: **argentina@ois.db.toronto.edu**
Subscription Address:
argentina-request@ois.db.toronto.edu

World Wide Web:
URL: **http://arcadia.informatik.uni-muenchen.de/ rec/argentina/argentina.html**

Army Area Handbooks

Army Area Handbooks made available by the University of Missouri, St. Louis are loaded with historical, geographical, cultural and economic information about a number of selected countries including China, Egypt, Indonesia, Israel, Japan, the Philippines, and several other Asian, European, and African countries.

See also: Politics

Gopher:
Name: University of Missouri St. Louis
Address: **umslvma.umsl.edu**
Choose: **The Library**
| **Government Information**
| **Army Area Handbooks**

Army Area Handbooks

You can say what you want about the military: they wear funny clothes, spend a lot of money, and salute the ears of important officers. Still, when it comes to knowledge about the world's trouble spots, the Army keeps up with the best of them. The *Army Area Handbooks* are absolutely great (and you know how hard we are to impress). Spend a few moments looking them over and, when the time comes, you will be glad that you know where to find these jewels of exposition and insight.

Asia Discussion

Talk about Asia, its culture, people, history, and more, with many Asians online.

Internet Relay Chat:
Channel: **#asian**

Asian Studies

Don't limit your knowledge of Asian Studies to perfecting your aim at spearing a piece of raw fish with chopsticks. Broaden your Asian horizons by checking out all the links available at this web site. You'll find servers here for each country in both Asia and the Middle East.

World Wide Web:
URL: **http://coombs.anu.edu.au/ WWWVL-AsianStudies.html**

Australia

The national World Wide Web home page for Australia and other Australian resources. The web page gives you access to Australian Internet resources arranged by access protocol, geographic area, institution, and subject. It also offers a guide to Australia, an interactive map, information about networks in Australia, and more. The gopher has news, sports, FAQs, pictures, radio information, statistics, film guides, and more about Australia. Check out the IRC channels and talk to an Aussie.

Gopher:
Name: Universite de Montreal
Address: **megasun.bch.umontreal.ca**
Choose: **Australiana - News, sports, FAQs, etc. about Australia**

Internet Relay Chat:
Channel: **#aussies**
Channel: **#melbourne**

World Wide Web:
URL: **http://info.anu.edu.au/**

Baltic Republics Discussion List

A mailing list to facilitate communications to, with, and about the Baltic Republics of Lithuania, Latvia, and Estonia.

Listserv Mailing List:
List Address: **balt-l@ubvm.cc.buffalo.edu**
Subscription Address:
listserv@ubvm.cc.buffalo.edu

Batish Institute of Music and Fine Arts

Batish is a well-known family of musicians that passes along cultural knowledge about Indian music through education. This site is home of *RagaNet* magazine — a journal of Indian music and fine art. See artist biographies, Batish archives, and information on concerts.

See also: Art, Music

World Wide Web:
URL: **http://hypatia.ucsc.edu:70/1/RELATED/ Batish**

Berlin

Historical notes, facts and statistics, gif images and descriptions of many famous Berlin sights, and links to universities in Berlin.

See also: Travel

World Wide Web:
URL: **http://www.chemie.fu-berlin.de/adressen/ berlin.html**

Bosnia

A daily mailing list covering news, events, and discussion of Bosnia and Herzcegovina. The list is run by volunteers and submissions in either English or Bosnian are accepted.

Internet Mailing List:
   List Address: **bosnet@math.lsa.umich.edu**
   Subscription Address:
      bosnet-request@math.lsa.umich.edu

Brazil

A mailing list for discussing Brazil. Portuguese is the main language on this mailing list. Or join the Brazilian chat channel where Portuguese is also spoken and lots of Brazilians hang out.

Internet Relay Chat:
   Channel: **#brasil**

Internet Mailing List:
   List Address: **brasil@cs.ucla.edu**
   Subscription Address: **brasil-request@cs.ucla.edu**

Bulgaria

Information about Bulgaria including a hypertexted FAQ, ftp archives, maps, Bulgarian poetry, sounds of Bulgaria, large collection of gif and jpeg images, book references, travel information, articles, and links to Bulgarian resources and sites.

World Wide Web:
   URL: **http://pisa.rockefeller.edu:8080/Bulgaria/**

Cajun Culture

Experience the lure of the sultry and lively environment of Cajun culture. Good food, great music and lively personalities are just a few notables about this culture. Join the discussion of the Cajun history and way of life.

Usenet:
   Newsgroup: **alt.Cajun.info**

California

Gif images of scenic views in California, including Mount Shasta, Death Valley National Monument, Lassen Volcanic National Park, and Yosemite National Park.

World Wide Web:
   URL: **http://www.water.ca.gov/Calif.images.html**

California Photos

Do you feel bad because your life is dull, dreary, and downright boring? Use your web browser to take a look at some of California's fabulous scenery and you'll feel even worse.

Central America Discussion List

A mailing list for students in and from Central American countries, especially Panama and Costa Rica.

Listserv Mailing List:
   List Address: **centam-l@ubvm.cc.buffalo.edu**
   Subscription Address:
      listserv@ubvm.cc.buffalo.edu

Central Asian Studies Mailing Lists

Join in worldwide communications with other people interested in central Asia's history, politics, demography, languages, culture, sociology, economics, religion and philosophy.

Listserv Mailing List:
   List Address: **cenasia@vm1.mcgill.ca**
   Subscription Address: **listserv@vm1.mcgill.ca**

   List Address:
      central-asia-studies-l@coombs.anu.edu.au
   Subscription Address:
      majordomo@coombs.anu.edu.au

Central European Development

A mailing list for issues of relevance to regional development and regional development research in Central Europe, including a wide range of disciplines from regional science to economic geography.

Listserv Mailing List:
   List Address: **cerro-l@aearn.edvz.univie.ac.at**
   Subscription Address:
      listserv@aearn.edvz.univie.ac.at

A B C D E F G H I J K L M N O P Q R S T U V W X Y Z

> ## Lots and lots of music on the Internet: check out the Music category.

Chile

The channel dedicated to Chile, with all discussion in Spanish.

Internet Relay Chat:
Channel: **#chile**

China

This web page provides links to Chinese architecture resources, a Chinese calendar converter, Chinese languages, Chinese literature and music resources, and a link to a Chinese web server. The IRC channel offers discussion about China and the Chinese people.

Internet Relay Chat:
Channel: **#china**
Channel: **#chinese**

World Wide Web:
URL: **http://www.yahoo.com/**
Society_and_Culture/Cultures/Chinese/

Chinese Scenic Pictures

Collection of Chinese scenic pictures in both gif and jpeg formats.

Anonymous FTP:
Address: **cnd.org**
Path: **/pub/InfoBase/scenery/***

For a quick, refreshing break, take a look at some Chinese Scenic Pictures

Chinese Scholars and Students Discussion List

Experience a little cultural exchange between residents of Taiwan and other scholars and students of Chinese studies. The purpose of the list is to develop mutual cultural understanding through open exchange and interaction.

Listserv Mailing List:
List Address: **twuniv-l@twnmoe10.bitnet**
Subscription Address: **listserv@twnmoe10.bitnet**

Country Statistics

Detailed statistical information on nearly every country in the world.

Gopher:
Name: Universite de Montreal
Address: **megasun.bch.umontreal.ca**
Choose: **Australiana - News, sports, FAQs, etc. about Australia**
| Other Countries' Statistics

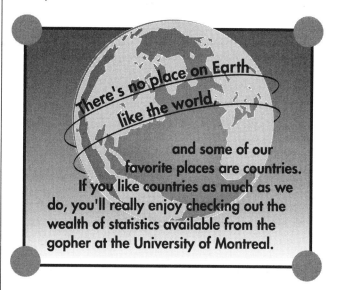

There's no place on Earth like the world,

and some of our favorite places are countries. If you like countries as much as we do, you'll really enjoy checking out the wealth of statistics available from the gopher at the University of Montreal.

Croatian Foreign Press Bureau

The Croatian Information Centre is an independent, cultural and educational, nonprofit, nonpolitical, and nongovernmental institution, with the goal of spreading the truth about Croatia and the Croatian nation throughout the world.

Gopher:
Name: Croatia
Address: **rujan.srce.hr**
Choose: **English Language**
| Information - Subject Tree
| News - Daily..
| Foreign Press Bureau

Diversity Concerns Exchange

Homogeny is boring. Experience the excitement of diversity when people from all cultures get together to discuss their environment. Persons from all backgrounds and genders are welcome.

See also: People

Listserv Mailing List:
List Address: **divers-l@psuvm.psu.edu**
Subscription Address: **listserv@psuvm.psu.edu**

Egypt

Take a guided tour of Egypt without ever having to leave your seat. See pictures and learn a little of the history and culture of the land of the great pyramids. You can even download pictures of some of those great pyramids, the Temple of Osiris and the Nile, and then send them to your friends on the Net, saying, "Having a great time. Wish you were here."

World Wide Web:
URL: **http://www.memphis.edu/egypt/egypt.html**

England

Information about England, including the land, climate, natural resources, plants and animals, population, political divisions, religion, education, culture, libraries and museums, art and archaeology, music, literature, and English law. The IRC channel offers interactive discussion about any of these topics.

Internet Relay Chat:
Channel: **#england**

World Wide Web:
URL: **http://www.abekrd.co.uk/General/England.html**

European Community

Discussions of the European Community and about Europe in general.

Listserv Mailing List:
List Address: **ec@vm.cc.metu.edu.tr**
Subscription Address: **listserv@vm.cc.metu.edu.tr**

List Address: **ec@indycms.bitnet**
Subscription Address: **listserv@indycms.bitnet**

Expatriates

It's scary enough moving across the country. The packing alone is enough to make anyone put down permanent roots. But there are people who will leave the country of their birth and travel thousands of miles in hopes of making better lives for themselves. If you've done this, welcome to the list. There are many other people here who have done the same thing.

Internet Mailing List:
List Address: **expat-l@cis.vutbr.cz**
Subscription Address: **expat-l-request@cis.vutbr.cz**

There's no patriot like an expatriate. Join the **expat-l** mailing list and find out why.

Flags of the World

If you are looking for something unique and colorful with which to decorate your home, try downloading some of these flags of the world. Not only will they look nice hanging in your walls, but your visitors will be convinced that you have culture and good taste.

World Wide Web:
URL: **http://www.adfa.oz.au/CS/flg/**

Fourth World Documentation Project

Organized by the Center for World Indigenous Studies, these documents provide researchers, tribal governments and organizations with essays, position papers, declarations, treaties, speeches and other items relating to the study of indigenous peoples.

World Wide Web:
URL: **http://www.halcyon.com/FWDP/fwdp.html**

France

The French Ministry of Culture has a web page so you can sneak a peek of France without having to suffer the jet lag. Practice your French and experience the culture of France at the same time.

World Wide Web:
URL: **http://web.culture.fr/**

French Chat

En francais, un "Cafe Campus" pour discuter de choses et d'autres. *Causerie* is French for "talk" or "chat," and this list is dedicated to fun conversations in French.

Listserv Mailing List:
   List Address: **causerie@uquebec.ca**
   Subscription Address: **listserv@uquebec.ca**

French Timeline

It's a great feeling of power and liberation to know that any time you want you can find out when Clovis defeated Alaric II in Vouille or when Louis and Alienor were divorced. Make your brain cells jump for joy by reading this timeline on the history of France.

World Wide Web:
   URL: **http://www.cica.fr/France/history.html**

Friends and Partners

Join this information system developed by Russians and Americans in an effort to form a bond between the two countries. There is information on almost anything you would want to know about Russia or the relationship between Russia and America — Cyrillic alphabet, news, history, music, art, medicine, economics, travel and tourism, and culture in general.

Note: Use the telnet site if you do not have a web browser.

Listserv Mailing List:
   List Address: **friends@solar.rtd.utk.edu**
   Subscription Address: **listserv@solar.rtd.utk.edu**

Telnet:
   Address: **april.ibpm.serpukhov.su**
   Login: **friends**

   Address: **solar.rtd.utk.edu**
   Login: **friends**

World Wide Web:
   URL: **http://april.ibpm.serpukhov.su/friends/**
   URL: **http://solar.rtd.utk.edu/friends/home.html**

Germany

Details and information about the geography, people, economy, government, and communications of Germany. There is also a news service in German, a map of Germany, facts and statistics, and a list of all German web servers.

World Wide Web:
   URL: **http://www.chemie.fu-berlin.de/adressen/brd.html**

Hellenic News

The dial of your radio probably doesn't turn as far as it needs to in order to receive the news from Greece. But now available on the Net are audio files of daily news from well-known Greek radio stations. Listen in and give new meaning to the phrase, "It's all Greek to me."

See also: Language, News: World

Gopher:
   Name: Academic and Research Network of Greece
   Address: **alpha.servicenet.ariadne-t.gr**

Hindu Names

A large list of Hindu names and their meanings.

Anonymous FTP:
   Address: **ftp.spies.com**
   Path: **/Library/Article/Language/hindu.nam**

Gopher:
   Name: Internet Wiretap
   Address: **wiretap.spies.com**
   Choose: **Wiretap Online Library**
      I **Articles**
      I **Language**
      I **List of Hindu Names**

Hungary

The Hungarian web page offers an introduction to Hungary, a little of Hungary's history, its geography, the delights of Hungarian cuisine, a tour of the peaceful and bustling city of Budapest with gif images, and a map which provides access to web servers, gophers, and other Internet resources in Hungary.

World Wide Web:
   URL: **http://www.fsz.bme.hu/hungary/homepage.html**

India

This web page has pointers to Internet resources relating to India, including Indian organizations and newsgroups. There is also a FAQ list on Indian culture, a list of Indian restaurants throughout the world, and a list of Indian student associations in North America.

Internet Relay Chat:
   Channel: **#india**

World Wide Web:
   URL: **http://strauss.ce.cmu.edu:2000/mayur/internet.html**

Inter-Tribal Network

A server for Native American interests, including information on taxpayer funds allocated to American Indians, festivals, holidays, and recent policy descriptions.

Gopher:
Name: CNS, Inc.
Address: **cscns.com**
Choose: **SPECIAL: Inter-Tribal Network (ITN)**

Ireland

Meet, chat, and drink with Irish people on these channels dedicated to the discussion of anything Irish or Celtic.

Internet Relay Chat:
Channel: **#celtic**
Channel: **#eire**
Channel: **#ireland**

Irish and Celtic Resources

Many resources relating to Ireland and Irish heritage, including newsgroups, radio programs and sound files, mailing lists, links to ftp sites, back issues of *The Irish Emigrant*, Irish jokes, flags, and much more. The second web page is a list of Ireland-related online resources that exist around the world, including contact information, flags and maps, government, financial, genealogy, university, press, music, mailing list, and other Irish-related resources. Sample a bit of the Emerald Isle.

World Wide Web:
URL: **http://orangutan.cv.nrao.edu/irish.html**
URL: **http://orangutan.cv.nrao.edu/irl_resources.html**

Israel

Resources for Israel and Jewish religious, educational, and social service organizations worldwide. Includes interesting lists, articles, and information on politics, and libraries, as well as extensive information on how to *make aliyah* (go home to Israel), including housing information, military service policies, and what to expect when you get there.

Anonymous FTP:
Address: **israel.nysernet.org**
Path: **/israel/***

Gopher:
Name: Israel Information Service
Address: **israel-info.gov.il**

Name: NYSERNet
Address: **israel.nysernet.org**
Port: **71**

Internet Relay Chat:
Channel: **#israel**

Italy

A map of Europe, maps of Italy, and Italian national statistics on residents by age, sex, education, literacy, employment, and marital status.

Gopher:
Name: CINECA - Interuniversity Computer Center
Address: **vm.cineca.it**
Choose: **Information and Data about Italy**

Japan

Japanese language and culture-related material, including programs and documentation for processing Japanese language documents with computers.

Anonymous FTP:
Address: **ftp.funet.fi**
Path: **/pub/culture/japan/***

The Internet is an excellent resource for artistic drawings of scenery and landscapes that you can use to illustrate or adorn your own work. This image is **mthood.gif** and it's widely available. This copy came from Oakland University (**oak.oakland.edu**) in the directory **/SimTel/msdos/gif**.

Japanese Information

The Japanese information corner of the Web is available in both English and Japanese. Here you can get an audio file of the Japanese national anthem, geography facts, maps and images, details of cultures and customs, multimedia travel tours and guides, government members, Japanese laws and constitution, communication, and links to Japanese Internet sites and resources.

World Wide Web:
URL: **http://www.ntt.jp/japan/index.html**

A
B
C
D
E
F
G
H
I
J
K
L
M
N
O
P
Q
R
S
T
U
V
W
X
Y
Z

Jerusalem One

The Jerusalem One Network is an electronic Jewish library with information about the Jewish people, Jewish organizations, and Jewish art. There are also articles about fighting hate, neo-nazis and holocaust-related articles, a Jewish calendar of events, links to Hebrew software archives, and links to other Jewish resources on the Internet.

Gopher:
> Name: Jerusalem One Network
> Address: **jerusalem1.datasrv.co.il**

Jerusalem Tour

Tour the ancient city of Jerusalem through this novel web page. Mosaic presents its users with a virtual tour of the ancient city of Jerusalem. Learn about the history and events of this city and view pictures of the city and its people.

World Wide Web:
> URL: **http://shum.cc.huju.ac.il/jeru/jerusalem.html**

Jewish Calendar and Events

A 5754 Jewish calendar, the local time in Jerusalem, Jewish community calendars from around the world, and event guides.

Gopher:
> Name: Jerusalem One
> Address: **jerusalem1.datasrv.co.il**
> Choose: **Jewish Calendar & Events**

Jewish Communities

Information about Jewish communities around the world, newsletters, travel guides, and the Kashrut database.

See also: Travel

Gopher:
> Name: Jerusalem One
> Address: **jerusalem1.datasrv.co.il**
> Choose: **Jewish Communities, Travel, and Kashrut Database**

JewishNet

Software resources, libraries and catalogs, reading lists, and other servers and archives of Jewish and Hebrew interest.

Telnet:
> Address: **vms.huji.ac.il**
> Login: **jewishnet**

World Wide Web:
> URL: **http://sleepless.acm.uiuc.edu/signet/JHSI/judaism.html**
> URL: **http://www.huji.ac.il/www_jewishn/www/t01.html**

Korea

A popular channel dedicated to Koreans and Korea, where English is spoken.

Internet Relay Chat:
> Channel: **#korea**

Latin America

This is a clearinghouse of resources relating to the study of Latin America. Find links to ftp, gopher and web sites for topics like job and grant announcements for Latin American Studies, archives for the history of Latin America, information on mailing lists, newsletters and other resources.

World Wide Web:
> URL: **http://history.cc.ukans.edu/history/reading_rooms/latin_america.html**

Lebanon and Levant Cultural Multimedia Server

Experience the culture, scenery and other aspects of life in Lebanon and the Levant. This web page has links to pictures and information covering topics like humor, health, food, language, religion and even cosmetics of these countries.

World Wide Web:
> URL: **http://www.ludvigsen.dhhalden.no/webdoc/levant_servers.html**

Library of Congress Cultural Exhibits

Have some fun exploring a few of the cultural exhibits that have been displayed at the Library of Congress. You'll get to see things like the Dead Sea Scrolls, displays of African-American culture and history, and a few exhibits from the Expo. It's a nice family outing and you don't even have to fight the traffic to get there.

See also: Art, History

World Wide Web:
URL: **http://lcweb.loc.gov/homepage/ exhibits.html**

Little Russia

This web server in San Antonio, Texas, contains various information about the history and culture of Russia. There is a link to the Kizhi Museum of Wooden Architecture, art from the village of Palekh, travel information, articles from various sources about the state of Russia, humor, and links to many other Russian sites.

World Wide Web:
URL: **http://mars.uthscsa.edu/Russia/**

Malaysia

This IRC channel is dedicated to the discussion of the country of Malaysia. If you're planning on traveling to Malaysia, if you live there, or you're just interested, check out **#malaysia**.

Internet Relay Chat:
Channel: **#malaysia**

Malaysia, Singapore, Islam News

A list for news only (no discussions) about Malaysia, Singapore, Islam, and other Asian countries when it is of interest to Malaysians or Singaporeans.

Listserv Mailing List:
List Address: **berita-l@vmd.cso.uiuc.edu**
Subscription Address: **listserv@vmd.cso.uiuc.edu**

> ## Learn how to use anonymous ftp and the world is at your fingertips.

> ## Looking for special fun? Turn to the Vices section.

Mexico

Located in the city of Mexicali, on the Baja California peninsula of Mexico, the Cetys web server provides campus information, university publications, Mexican photographic exhibits, and other items of interest. For chat with Mexicans or about Mexico, connect to the IRC channel below.

Internet Relay Chat:
Channel: **#mexico**

World Wide Web:
URL: **http://infux.mxl.cetys.mx/**

Middle Europe

The first question one must ask when contemplating whether to join a discussion group relating to Middle Europe is: What *is* Middle Europe? It's defined as the countries lying between the Mediterranean/Adriatic and the Baltic Seas and between the German/Austrian borders and the former Soviet Union. That settled, the second question would be: What is the list about? Just about everything. The list is unmoderated, and topics cover history, culture, politics, economics, and current events.

See also: History, News: World, Politics

Listserv Mailing List:
List Address: **mideur-l@ubvm.cc.buffalo.edu**
Subscription Address:
listserv@ubvm.cc.buffalo.edu

Moscow Kremlin Online Excursion

Take a tour of the Kremlin, with this multimedia excursion. See the sights and learn the history of Red Square, Ivan the Great Bell Tower, the residence of the president, Lenin's mausoleum, the Senate building, and more.

World Wide Web:
URL: **http://www.kiae.su/www/wtr/kremlin/ begin.html**

National Flags

The national flags from many countries around the world.

World Wide Web:
URL: **http://155.187.10.12/flags/nation-flags.html**

A B C D E F G H I J K L M N O P Q R S T U V W X Y Z

National Pages

A collection of national web pages for several countries, including Bulgaria, Germany, Hungary, Japan, Netherlands, Poland, Portugal, Slovenia, and Yugoslavia.

World Wide Web:
    URL: **http://info.fuw.edu.pl/national.html**

Native American Mailing Lists

Whether you are Native American or are simply interested in the culture and way of life of the Native Americans, here are several mailing lists that may interest you. The **native-l** and **natchat** are general discussion groups. The **nat-1492** discusses the Columbus quincentenary. The **nat-edu**, **nat-hlth**, and **nat-lang** cover the topics of Native American education, health and language.

Listserv Mailing List:
    List Address: **nat-hlth@tamvm1.tamu.edu**
    Subscription Address: **listserv@tamvm1.tamu.edu**

    List Address: **natchat@tamvm1.tamu.edu**
    Subscription Address: **listserv@tamvm1.tamu.edu**

    List Address: **native-l@tamvm1.tamu.edu**
    Subscription Address: **listserv@tamvm1.tamu.edu**

    List Address: **nat-edu@indycms.iupui.edu**
    Subscription Address: **listserv@indycms.iupui.edu**

    List Address: **nat-lang@tamvm1.tamu.edu**
    Subscription Address: **listserv@tamvm1.tamu.edu**

    List Address: **nat-1492@tamvm1.tamu.edu**
    Subscription Address: **listserv@tamvm1.tamu.edu**

Native Americans

The Oneida Indian Nation of New York web site provides historical and cultural information about the Onyota'a:ka: — the People of the Standing Stone.

World Wide Web:
    URL: **http://nysernet.org:80/oneida/**

NativeNet

This web page is a collection of resources from around the Net which relate to Native Americans. Gain access to mailing list archives as well as information on how to subscribe to various mailing lists that are offered.

World Wide Web:
    URL: **http://kuhttp.cc.ukans.edu/~marc/ native_net.html**

NECTEC Server

The National Electronics and Computer Technology Center (NECTEC) is a research organization operated under the National Science and Technology Development Agency. The server maintains a list of Internet servers (domestic and abroad) that contain information pertaining to Thailand.

World Wide Web:
    URL: **http://www.nectec.or.th/nectec.html**

New Zealand

Everything you could want to know about beautiful New Zealand. Statistics on population, economy, politics, geography, climate, shopping, and other tourist information.

Gopher:
    Name: Wellington City Council
    Address: **gopher.wcc.govt.nz**
    Choose: **New Zealand information**

Norwegian Internet Resources

This graphical map of Norway allows you to click on the site you wish to visit. There are seven different versions of the map which categorize the sites and resources as universities and colleges, research institutes, service providers, commercial services, conferences and festivals, geographical information, or miscellaneous, allowing you to easily locate the necessary site.

World Wide Web:
    URL: **http://www.service.uit.no/homepage-no**

Palo Alto, California

Details of the city life, people, setting, events, climate, commerce, dining and entertainment guides, contact information, natural resources, parks, events, and more to do with Palo Alto.

World Wide Web:
    URL: **http://www.city.palo-alto.ca.us/home.html**

Paris Tours

This resource was the winner of the Best Use of Multiple Media in the Best of Web '94 Awards. It offers multimedia tours of Paris, including trips to the Louvre Pyramide, a walking tour, a historical guided tour, a guide of the Catacombs, and even a view of the Earth from above Paris.

World Wide Web:
    URL: **http://mistral.enst.fr/~pioch/louvre/paris/**

> ## Do you like the "final frontier?" Take a look at Star Trek (or Space).

Poland

Interesting information about Poland and Polish culture, including geographical facts, maps and lists of Polish multimedia servers, newsgroups, Warsaw Stock Exchange quotations, newspapers, journals, information on Polish satellite TV stations, and history articles.

Listserv Mailing List:
List Address: **poland-l@ubvm.cc.buffalo.edu**
Subscription Address:
listserv@ubvm.cc.buffalo.edu

World Wide Web:
URL: **http://info.fuw.edu.pl/pl/PolandHome.html**

Portugal

A home page for Portugal, offering facts and statistics about its geography, people, economy, government, and communications, a text version of the national anthem in Portuguese, postal codes, a Portuguese news journal, list of Internet domains and public BBSs, a bibliography of Portuguese history, many photos in gif format, the song that won the Portuguese Song Contest, travel information, exchange rates, and more.

World Wide Web:
URL: **http://s700.uminho.pt/Portugal/portugal.html**

Russia

There's a wealth of Russian resources on the Internet. Read about the language and culture of Russia. Check out the Russian literature guide, computer-related material, glossaries and word lists, recipes, jokes, lyrics, politics, and translation information.

Anonymous FTP:
Address: **ftp.funet.fi**
Path: **/pub/culture/russian/***

World Wide Web:
URL: **http://sunsite.oit.unc.edu/sergei/Info.html**
URL: **http://www.kiae.su/www/wtr/**
URL: **http://www.pitt.edu/~cjp/rees.html**

San Francisco Bay Area

These newsgroups are focused primarily on the San Francisco Bay Area. The FAQ contains information on publications, Usenet, FAQ archives, gopher, mail, **uucp**, and much more.

Anonymous FTP:
Address: **ftp.spies.com**
Path: **/ba.internet/FAQ**

Usenet:
Newsgroup: **ba.***

Slovakia

Maps, history, statistics, tourist information, pictures, accommodation guides, political information, transportation details, and everything and anything else you could possibly want to know about Slovakia.

See also: Travel

World Wide Web:
URL: **http://www.eunet.sk/slovakia/slovakia.html**

Slovenia

A web page for Slovenia, a young country with an old culture and fantastic scenery. It offers photos and images, travel information, traditional food recipes, a historical overview of science in Slovenia, general facts and statistics, guides to ski resorts, health resorts, spas, Slovene wine, a look at the Karst route and the Upper Carniolan (Alpine) route, a newsgroup, and an interactive map allowing you to obtain details of ski resorts, airports, wine-growing regions, and other locations.

World Wide Web:
URL: **http://www.ijs.si/slo.html**

Southeast Asian Archive

This is a growing archive about Southeast Asia. Get information about the resettlement of refugees and boat people, read newsletters and see pictures which illustrate a little of the Southeast Asian culture.

World Wide Web:
URL: **http://www.lib.uci.edu/sea/seahome.html**

> ## Lonely? Try the Personals.

A
B
C
D
E
F
G
H
I
J
K
L
M
N
O
P
Q
R
S
T
U
V
W
X
Y
Z

Southern U.S. Culture

The culture of the South has a rich diversity, from grand plantations to secluded hills, from the Atlantic coast to the Gulf coast. Read and discuss the history, conversational language, humor, and culture of the South, and maybe get a good recipe for barbequed ribs while you are at it. The web pages also provide links to the Doc Watson Multimedia Exhibit and the University of Mississippi.

See also: History

Listserv Mailing List:
    List Address: **bubba-l@knuth.mtsu.edu**
    Subscription Address: **listserv@knuth.mtsu.edu**

Usenet:
    Newsgroup: **bit.listserv.sthcult**

World Wide Web:
    URL: **http://imp.cssc.olemiss.edu/**
    URL: **http://sunsite.unc.edu/doug_m/pages/
        south/south.html**

Soviet Archives

English translations of newly opened Soviet archives, including documents about the secret police, attacks on intelligentsia, famine, the cold war, and other topics.

Anonymous FTP:
    Address: **ftp.loc.gov**
    Path:
        /pub/exhibit.images/russian.archive.exhibit

Gopher:
    Name: University of Virginia
    Address: **gopher.virginia.edu**
    Choose: **Library Services**
      | **University Library GWIS Collections
        (alpha and subj. organization)**
      | **Alphabetic Organization**
      | **Soviet Archive Exhibit, Library of Congress**

Sweden Channel

The English and Swedish-speaking channel for Swedes and friends.

Internet Relay Chat:
    Channel: **#sweden**

Taiwan

The Taiwan channels with many people from Taiwan online.

Internet Relay Chat:
    Channel: **#taiwan**
    Channel: **#tw**

Thailand

FAQs regarding Thailand, travel information, and economic and demographic data.

Gopher:
    Name: Asian Institute of Technology
    Address: **emailhost.ait.ac.th**
    Choose: **Asian Institute of Technology Campus
        Info**
      | **Information for Faculty and Staff**
      | **Living in Thailand**

Usenet:
    Newsgroup: **soc.culture.thai**

Third World Studies

Academics, government employees, diplomats and culture buffs come together in this electronic forum because they feel the need for improved understanding of Third World peoples, problems, and issues. The discussion group is sponsored by the Association for Third World Studies.

Listserv Mailing List:
    List Address: **thrdwrld@gsuvm1.gsu.edu**
    Subscription Address: **listserv@gsuvm1.gsu.edu**

United Kingdom

The U.K. Guide server presents the user with a map of the U.K. and certain hot spots to investigate. You can find out information on different towns and cities, weather info, and you can also take a guided tour and learn about restaurants, pubs, hotels, museums, and more.

World Wide Web:
    URL: **http://www.cs.ucl.ac.uk/misc/uk/intro.html**

U.S.A. Chat

A popular channel where Americans and others congregate from around the world. Sometimes they even talk about the U.S.A.

Internet Relay Chat:
    Channel: **#usa**

Usenet Cultural Groups

About the languages, culture, people, customs, and many other aspects of countries around the world.

Usenet:
    Newsgroup: **alt.culture.***
    Newsgroup: **soc.culture.***

Venezuela

Pictures of Venezuela, travel tips, links to Venezuelan institutions on the Net, maps, economic data, exchange rates, business practices, export descriptions, local time, and more to do with this South American country.

World Wide Web:
> URL: **http://www.mit.edu:8001/people/serebris/ venezuela.html**

World Constitutions

The constitutions and basic laws for many countries around the world, including Germany, Hong Kong, the United States, Canada, China, Hungary and the Slovak Republic, as well as the texts of the English Bill of Rights, Magna Carta, John at Runnymede, and others.

Anonymous FTP:
> Address: **ftp.spies.com**
> Path: **/Gov/World/***

Gopher:
> Name: Internet Wiretap
> Address: **wiretap.spies.com**
> Choose: **Government Docs (US & World)**
> **| World Constitutions**

World Heritage List

A list of both cultural and natural historic sites, properties, and cities around the world as approved by UNESCO's World Heritage Committee.

Anonymous FTP:
> Address: **ftp.spies.com**
> Path: **/Library/Document/heritage.lis**

Gopher:
> Name: Internet Wiretap
> Address: **wiretap.spies.com**
> Choose: **Wiretap Online Library**
> **| Assorted Documents**
> **| UNESCO's World Heritage List**

Yiddish

If it wasn't for Yiddish, we wouldn't have cool words like *shlemiel* and *shlimazl* (good words useful for a variety of occasions). Even if those are the only two Yiddish words you know, you can still get enjoyment from discussing any topic that involves Yiddish, such as literature, history, news and more.

Listserv Mailing List:
> List Address: **mendele@yalevm.cis.yale.edu**
> Subscription Address: **listserv@yalevm.cis.yale.edu**

Yugoslavian Information

Facts and figures, places to see, people to meet, dishes to taste, and details of Yugoslavia's languages.

See also: Travel

World Wide Web:
> URL: **http://www.umiacs.umd.edu/research/lpv/ YU/HTML/yu.html**

WRITING

Athene, the Online Magazine of Creative Writing

Back issues of *Athene, the Online Magazine of Creative Writing*.

Anonymous FTP:
> Address: **ftp.uu.net**
> Path: **/doc/literary/obi/Athene/***

The Continuum Machine

A collaborative hypertext novel where each chapter ends ambiguously, and readers get ideas and write the next chapter. At any point in the novel, anyone can ask to insert a chapter. The novel is constantly expanding into a hypertext adventure. Guidelines for submission as well as the text of the novel to date and a link to *The Time Machine* by H.G. Wells are there.

World Wide Web:
> URL: **http://www.seas.upenn.edu/~gasser/tcm/ tcm-intro.html**

Create a Story

Have a little fun taking a story that is already in the works and adding your own flair to it. Get the hero into trouble and see if someone else can get him out gracefully and logically. Your browser must support forms for you to participate.

See also: Fun

World Wide Web:
> URL: **http://cybersight.com/cgi-bin/cs/story**

> ## MUDs are real (sort of).

A
B
C
D
E
F
G
H
I
J
K
L
M
N
O
P
Q
R
S
T
U
V
W
X
Y
Z

Creative Writing Pedagogy

Are good writers born or taught? At a college and university level, creative writing is offered as part of the general curriculum. Discuss how and why creative writing is taught, the role it plays in the curriculum, the history of creative writing programs, and the atmosphere of courses and what influence it has on students' lives. This list is for teachers and students.

Listserv Mailing List:
  List Address: **crewrt-l@umcvmb.missouri.edu**
  Subscription Address:
    listserv@umcvmb.missouri.edu

Cyberpunk

Step through a portal to another dimension, a cyberpunk world where darkness, depression, and danger are the norm. Lovers of cyberpunk sling slang around like literary fly-fishing lures. If you love high-tech, heavy metal punk, you will love the virtual reality of cyberpunk.

Usenet:
  Newsgroup: **alt.cyberpunk.chatsubo**

Dr. Who

Who is that odd fellow bedecked in a voluminous overcoat and mile-long neck scarf? Who, that's who. Hop in your tardis and join the Dr. Who following with creative stories based on the adventures of the happy-go-unlucky doctor. (But we thought Who was on first...)

Usenet:
  Newsgroup: **alt.drwho.creative**

Erotica

Stimulate more than your mind. Wrap your brain around sensuously stated sentences and pleasantly playful paragraphs. Slide slowly into the warm depths of the written word. Allow yourself to be swept up in the moment as your fingers press against the keyboard and your screen casts its gentle reflections on your skin.

Usenet:
  Newsgroup: **alt.sex.stories**
  Newsgroup: **alt.sex.stories.d**
  Newsgroup: **rec.arts.erotica**

EROTICA

What a nice word for such an earthy subject. The Internet is full of people who enjoy sex and some of them write stories. You can share those stories in the privacy of your own home just by reading Usenet newsgroups. Be careful though, if you take your computer into the hot tub you might be in for a shocking experience.

Fiction Writers

Just think how much money you can save on reading material if you are a writer. You won't ever have to buy books because you can just write your own. The only person who will probably not like this system is the mystery writer, because the ending would be spoiled for him. If you are interested in writing fiction professionally, you can gain support from a group of peers with whom you can share and discuss writing. Pass around works in progress that you can critique or have critiqued, helping each other find weak spots.

Internet Mailing List:
  List Address:
    fiction-writers%studguppy@lanl.gov
  Subscription Address:
    fiction-writers%studguppy-request@lanl.gov

Star Trek fans:
When the television episodes, videos, movies, books and conventions just aren't enough, turn to Usenet and read original stories based on the *Star Trek* universe.

Manga and Anime

Discover the charm of Japanese animation and storytelling in the form of anime and manga. These two art forms combine words and pictures to create quick and lively stories. You don't have to know Japanese to love these wonderful works of story art.

Usenet:
> Newsgroup: **rec.arts.anime.stories**
> Newsgroup: **rec.arts.manga**

Memoirs, Journals and Correspondence

There is a pleasure in reading the words of those people who are open enough to put their ideas and feelings on paper. This unmoderated list has been created in order that people may discuss and provide references to published first-hand accounts such as memoirs, diaries, journals, travelogues, expedition accounts, and correspondence. Any quality first-person account is acceptable as long as it relates the author's experiences and the prose is of a quality that can be considered enjoyable. Examples of such work are Norman Douglas's *Old Calabria*, Heinrich Schliemann's *Mycenae*, *The Rommel Papers*, and William Howard Russell's *My Diary North and South*.

See also: Literature: Collections

Listserv Mailing List:
> List Address: **memoir-l@latech.bitnet**
> Subscription Address: **listserv@latech.bitnet**

Prose

These bite-sized morsels of prose make the perfect afternoon brain snack. No matter what tickles your fancy, the variety of stories will have something for you. Read or share, it's up to you: just remember, if you don't use it, you'll lose it. The **.prose** newsgroups are for stories and articles. The **.d** newsgroup is for discussion.

Usenet:
> Newsgroup: **alt.prose**
> Newsgroup: **alt.prose.d**
> Newsgroup: **misc.writing**
> Newsgroup: **rec.arts.prose**

Star Trek

Beam aboard for Mr. Spock's wild ride. You will find yourself engaged in raucous laughter at *Star Trek* parodies, so don't read this group while in the library lest you be subjected to some severe ear-twisting by a librarian with a tight bun on her head. Stick to the safer, more suspenseful stories that will keep you at the edge of your seat, while the *Star Trek* crew race through the universe boldly taking you where no one has gone before.

Usenet:
> Newsgroup: **alt.startrek.creative**

Superhero Mailing List

Do you yearn for the taste of heroics? Do you long to rip off that icky necktie and heavy jacket and run into the street clad only in lycra and perhaps a gracefully flowing cape? Unless you have been irradiated by some cosmic chemical, this will probably be the closest you will come to having that sort of experience. Live vicariously through the antics of superheroes by either reading what people have written or by authoring some of your own super stories.

Listserv Mailing List:
> List Address: **superguy@ucf1vm.cc.ucf.edu**
> Subscription Address: **listserv@ucf1vm.cc.ucf.edu**

World Wide Web:
> URL: **http:/www.halcyon.com/superguy/superguy.html**

Trincoll Journal

The *Trincoll Journal* is a student-run multimedia publication at Trinity College in Hartford, Connecticut. All design, programming, contributions, and artwork are created by people from around the world. The *Trincoll Journal* encourages you to write about *anything* — just make sure it is written well!

World Wide Web:
> URL: **http://www.trincoll.edu/tj/trincolljournal.html**

Writers

Being a professional writer is fun because you can work in your pajamas. Professional writers or those who aspire to be writers have established a community on the Net and share thoughts and ideas about writing, critique works in progress and post announcements of workshops, contests, and new publications. Many of the people who have been on this list have been there for a long time, so it has a nice welcoming atmosphere.

See also: Poetry

Listserv Mailing List:
> List Address: **writers@vm1.nodak.edu**
> Subscription Address: **listserv@vm1.nodak.edu**

X-RATED RESOURCES

Bondage, Discipline, Sadism and Masochism Stories

Stories of bondage and discipline, sadism and masochism.

See also: Sex

World Wide Web:
URL: **http://www.iia.org/dcr/bdsm/contents/
stories/stories.html**

Brandy's Babes

The world's first cyber-brothel featuring private dancing and modeling. Brandy's Babes just want to meet new people and exchange erotic mail and pictures. (No big deal, right?) Brandy also says she wants to try new things with computers and sex.

Finger:
Address: **trisha@ramp.com**

Internet Relay Chat:
Channel: **#trisha**

Yes, it's true, clothes do make the man or woman, and they can make you as well. Tune into **alt.sex.fetish.fashion** for a few hints as to what the cognoscenti are doing behind and in front of closed doors.

Clothing

There are people who believe that nudity is highly overrated and that much of the fun in life can be had from fetish clothing like shoes, stockings and other things that you can dress the body in. Whether it's plastic, rubber, leather, silk or another material — this newsgroup is guaranteed to be interesting to people who get excited by dressing up or down.

Usenet:
Newsgroup: **alt.sex.fetish.fashion**

Dirty Talk

Talk dirty to you? Whip me, beat me, hurt me, just don't stop talking dirty to me! It's a hot and popular channel, but you don't even have to get a word in edgewise to get a kick out of this.

Internet Relay Chat:
Channel: **#hotsex**
Channel: **#jack-off**

Dominant Women

Wouldn't it be a big surprise if the demure librarian you've been dating turned out to be a leather-wearing, whip-toting goddess of domination who wanted nothing more than to make you submit to doing somersaults in a vat of lime jello? On this newsgroup you can read about women who dominate and the men who love them.

Usenet:
Newsgroup: **alt.sex.femdom**

Erotic Pictures

There are LOTS and LOTS of X-rated pictures posted to Usenet newsgroups, so you will never have to go without. In order to download the pictures, you will need to be able to use a newsreader program to find and save the appropriate articles. Most pictures are broken into parts and **uuencoded**, each part being posted as a separate article. You must put together the parts and then **uudecode** the resultant file in order to re-create the original picture (which is usually in gif or jpeg format). In order to look at the picture, you will need a gif or jpeg viewer program. If you need help with any of this, buy our book *The Internet Complete Reference* (published by Osborne McGraw-Hill) and read Chapter 18.

Usenet:
Newsgroup: **alt.binaries.pictures.erotica**
Newsgroup: **alt.binaries.pictures.erotica.blondes**
Newsgroup: **alt.binaries.pictures.erotica.female**
Newsgroup: **alt.binaries.pictures.erotica.male**
Newsgroup: **alt.binaries.pictures.erotica.orientals**
Newsgroup: **alt.sex.pictures**
Newsgroup: **alt.sex.pictures.female**
Newsgroup: **alt.sex.pictures.male**

Quiet, Peace, Relaxation

Yes, all of these things are nice but, when life gets just a little too predictable and boring, you can put some zest back into the old red corpuscles by downloading a few auditory stimulators from **alt.sex.sounds**.

Erotic Sounds

If you have a computer that can play sounds, you can download sounds to play with. Not as much fun as making your own, but you can play them over and over, whenever you want.

Usenet:
Newsgroup: **alt.sex.sounds**

Excerpt from the Net...

```
Newsgroup: alt.sex.fetish.feet
Subject: Stereotypes

Although I've enjoyed reading this newsgroup from its beginning, I've never been
comfortable with its name...

I suppose it's a matter of degree. I may like catching glimpses of a woman's bare feet,
someone else may like sucking her toes, and a third likes high heels and painted
toenails, but we're all lumped together as "foot fetishists" with those who cannot get
sexually excited without some contact with feet.

The Net is certainly big enough for all tastes, many of which I may personally find
distasteful, but I agree that the stereotype of the "foot fetishist" as a grovelling
submissive is in large part wrong.

There's got to be a better name for this interest.
```

A B C D E F G H I J K L M N O P Q R S T U V W X Y Z

> ## The only place where Politics comes before Star Trek is in "The Internet Golden Directory."

Fetishes

Don't feel alone just because you have certain... preferences. There are lots of people like you out there and they are ready to share. Even if you don't have a fetish or a strange desire, you may enjoy reading about people who do. Maybe you'll get some new ideas. (By the way, the **.fa** newsgroup is for those who like fat people.)

Usenet:
Newsgroup: **alt.sex.bestiality**
Newsgroup: **alt.sex.bondage**
Newsgroup: **alt.sex.breast**
Newsgroup: **alt.sex.exhibitionism**
Newsgroup: **alt.sex.fetish.amputee**
Newsgroup: **alt.sex.fetish.diapers**
Newsgroup: **alt.sex.fetish.fa**
Newsgroup: **alt.sex.fetish.feet**
Newsgroup: **alt.sex.fetish.hair**
Newsgroup: **alt.sex.fetish.orientals**
Newsgroup: **alt.sex.fetish.watersports**
Newsgroup: **alt.sex.spanking**
Newsgroup: **alt.sex.voyeurism**

Index of Erotic Stories

An ambitious fellow named Ed Stauff maintains an index of the stories posted to **rec.arts.erotica**, **alt.sex** and **alt.sex.stories**. Each listing includes the title of the story, the author's name, the size, and the archive name from **rec.arts.erotica** (if there is one). There is also a brief synopsis or review. This index is posted at irregular intervals to **alt.sex** and **alt.sex.stories**. Note: Ed does not have an archive of all the stories, so don't bother asking him to send one to you. (Also, don't ask him to mail you a copy of the index; wait for it to be posted.)

Usenet:
Newsgroup: **alt.sex**
Newsgroup: **alt.sex.stories**
Newsgroup: **rec.arts.erotica**

World Wide Web:
URL: **http://cad.ucla.edu/repository/library/Cadlab/adult/Adult.html**

The Kama Sutra

Is that special something missing from your relationship? Maybe what you need is a little pick-me-up that goes beyond advice from Dr. Ruth. The Kama Sutra is an ancient text that describes things that have to be seen to be believed. (Unfortunately, you'll probably never see them.) Still, when you're sitting at home bored to distraction, there is probably some solace to be drawn in reading about adventurous techniques that have the potential to make the art of lovemaking even more fun than hanging out at the mall or watching Monday night football.

Kama Sutra

The Kama Sutra is perhaps the most well-known erotic self-help book. See what the ancient commentators have to teach you about mankind's oldest pastime. These teachings describe a wide variety of sex positions and techniques, including the Flag of Cupid, Aphrodite's Delight, and the Monkey.

Anonymous FTP:
Address: **quartz.rutgers.edu**
Path: **/pub/sex/kama.sutra.gz**

Gopher:
Name: Rutgers University
Address: **quartz.rutgers.edu**
Choose: **Sex**
  | **kama.sutra**

Limericks

Probably sometime, somewhere, somebody actually did write a limerick that wasn't dirty. If so, it's not here.

Anonymous FTP:
Address: **quartz.rutgers.edu**
Path: **/pub/humor/limericks.gz**

Gopher:
Name: Rutgers University
Address: **quartz.rutgers.edu**
Choose: **Humor**
  | **limericks**

Magazines

It's important to be cultured and well-read. Not only will you win friends and influence people, but you will undoubtedly find it much easier to get a date. On the other hand, some days it's nice to give yourself a break and look at magazines that are highly prized for their picturesque qualities. Get recommendations on good magazines, where to buy them, information on trading or buying collector's editions, and general discussion about the concepts of sex magazines.

Usenet:
Newsgroup: **alt.sex.magazines**

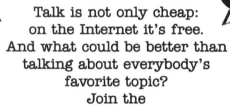

Talk is not only cheap:
on the Internet it's free.
And what could be better than
talking about everybody's
favorite topic?
Join the
General Sex Discussion
on Usenet and experience
the freedom of real talk
about real topics.

Net Sex

You thought you'd done it everywhere. Now try it on the Net, as couples and groups indulge in verbal sex across the world.

Internet Relay Chat:
Channel: **#netsex**

Sex Chat

"Let's talk about sex, baby. Let's talk about you and me." These are the popular channels for hot talkers.

Internet Relay Chat:
Channel: **#sex**
Channel: **#-sex-**
Channel: **#wetsex**

Sex General Discussion

On Usenet, the discussion about sex ranges from serious to XXX-rated. The **alt.sex** group is for just about any topic you want. The **wizards** group is for serious questions, serious sex experts and would-be serious sex experts. (But don't let yourself get too serious.)

Usenet:
Newsgroup: **alt.sex**
Newsgroup: **alt.sex.wizards**

Sex Stories

There comes a time in everyone's life when you get tired of reading Internet books. The next time you are looking for some fresh stimulation, turn to the Usenet newsgroups devoted to sharing erotic stories. (The **rec** newsgroup is moderated.)

Usenet:
Newsgroup: **alt.pantyhose**
Newsgroup: **alt.sex**
Newsgroup: **alt.sex.stories**
Newsgroup: **rec.arts.erotica**

Excerpt from the Net...

(from the Kama Sutra, available via Anonymous FTP and Gopher)

To Enslave a Lover:

Leaves caught as they fall from trees
and powdered with peacock-bone
and fragments of a corpse's winding-sheet
will, when dusted lightly
on the love organ, bewitch any woman living.

A B C D E F G H I J K L M N O P Q R S T U V W X Y Z

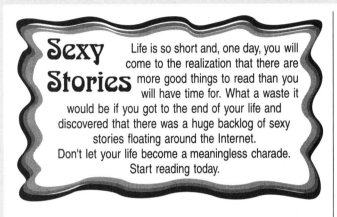

Sexy Stories Life is so short and, one day, you will come to the realization that there are more good things to read than you will have time for. What a waste it would be if you got to the end of your life and discovered that there was a huge backlog of sexy stories floating around the Internet. Don't let your life become a meaningless charade. Start reading today.

Sex Story Archives

Some sex stories from **alt.sex**, **alt.sex.stories** and **rec.arts.erotica** are available via mail. To find out how it all works, send mail to the below. (Note: There is no anonymous ftp service from these sites and none is planned. It would overwhelm the network, so don't even ask them.)

Mail:
> Address: **server@hermes.acm.rpi.edu**
> Body: **help**

Sexual Massage

There is a technique, developed by Eastern know-it-alls, that is pretty good when it comes to one-size-fits-all self-help. Take a look at this article and learn the ins and outs of yoni and lingam massage. (*Yoni* and *lingam* are Sanskrit words. We can't print what they mean in English, so you will have to investigate for yourself.)

Anonymous FTP:
> Address: **ftp.spies.com**
> Path: **/Library/Article/Sex/massage.txt**

Gopher:
> Name: Internet Wiretap
> Address: **wiretap.spies.com**
> Choose: **Wiretap Online Library**
> | **Articles**
> | **Sex**
> | **Yoni Massage How-To**

Need a pick-me-up? Try a new Usenet group.

Slippery When Wet Magazine

Get your fill of erotic poetry, gossip, stories, comics and more from this delightfully naughty zine.

World Wide Web:
> URL: **ftp://ftp.netcom.com/pub/sl/slippery/sww.html**
> URL: **http://www.c2.org/~slippery/sww.html**

Tickling

Oh, the agony and the ecstasy of being tickled. Ticklers and ticklees talk about where and how they like it — on the feet, ribs, back of the knee, inner thigh or places that we can only mention between the hours of midnight and 4 A.M. Read stories, personal experiences and thoughts on tickling as an intimate pasttime.

Usenet:
> Newsgroup: **alt.sex.fetish.tickling**

Wild Sex

Release all your wildest passions and desires.

Internet Relay Chat:
> Channel: **#wildsex**

X-Rated Movies

Who needs gorgeous vistas, great soundtracks and good acting when you have a few naked people gyrating around in front of the camera? Get hard and fast information on X-rated movies, actors and actresses and FAQs from related Usenet newsgroups.

World Wide Web:
> URL: **http://www.yahoo.com/Entertainment/Movies_and_Films/X_rated_Movies**

X-Rated Page

Take a risk. Get racey. Exercise your freedom to do what you want, when you want. Check out the naughty bits of this collection of videos and pictures. This web page is written in Swedish, so if you don't speak that language you will simply have to feel your way around, which is probably more fun anyway.

World Wide Web:
> URL: **http://eru.dd.chalmers.se/home/niky/xrated.html**

Activities for Kids

The kids are getting bored. Quick, think of something for them to do before they start writing on the walls or play "elephant rider" with the family dog. Here are a few things that will keep them busy and you sane.

See also: Families and Parenting

Gopher:
> Name: University of Minnesota
> Address: **tinman.mes.umn.edu**
> Choose: **YFERNet - National Children, Youth...**
> | **Other CYF Information Servers**
> | **Children, Youth and Family Consortium**
> | **Brochures, Newsletters...**
> | **Family Childcare Newsletters 1987 - Current**
> | **Activity Box**

Activities for Kids

It's raining and everyone is bored. The kids have started to look for things to do and you just know that if you don't act soon, it won't be long before your home qualifies for federal disaster aid. The solution? Point your gopher at the *Activity Box* and find something that will occupy the energy of the young ones in a constructive and non-threatening manner.

Planning a picnic? Check the weather using the Net.

Boy Scouts of America

This web page has information on the Cub Scouts and the Boy Scouts, including ranks, activity badges, awards, and a "Guide to Safe Scouting." There is a huge amount of information here and it's all stuff that any good Scout should know.

World Wide Web:
> URL: **http://boyscout.weeg.uiowa.edu/BSA/ BoyScoutHomePage.html**

Christian Youth

Church isn't the only place to meet with other Christian youths. Young people from around the world discuss issues that concern them — not only biblical queries, but thoughts and ideas about society. Topics include sex before marriage, how to get along with people of the same age and how to defend the Christian faith. This group is moderated.

Usenet:
> Newsgroup: **soc.religion.christian.youth-work**

Explorer Posts

For young men and women ages 14-21, the Explorers is a career-oriented part of the Boy Scouts of America that provides a fun atmosphere in which kids can not only have a good time, but also develop skills that will be important later in life. See information on Explorer Post 6398, the first American scouting family to be on the Internet, as well as links to other Explorer and scouting resources.

World Wide Web:
> URL: **http://thoughtport.com/ Boy_Scouts/index.html**

No need to be bored. Try Parties and Entertainment.

A B C D E F G H I J K L M N O P Q R S T U V W X Y Z

Fall Nature Fun

There is a special energy that comes at the changing of the seasons. Kids should get out and experience this. Get ideas about organizing fall nature activities. This article will show you how to make it fun and creative.

See also: Families and Parenting, Fun

Gopher:
Name: University of Minnesota
Address: **tinman.mes.umn.edu**
Choose: **National Extension Children...**
| **Other CYF Information Servers**
| **Children, Youth and Family Consortium**
| **Brochures, Newsletters...**
| **Family Childcare Newsletters 1987 - Current**
| **Activity — Fall Nature Fun**

Fun with Magazines

Get some use out of those old, worn-out magazines that you've read but can't bear to throw out. There are so many fun things kids can do with them. This article will tell you how.

See also: Families and Parenting, Fun, Hobbies

Gopher:
Name: University of Minnesota
Address: **tinman.mes.umn.edu**
Choose: **National Extension Children...**
| **Other CYF Information Servers**
| **Children, Youth and Family Consortium**
| **Brochures, Newsletters...**
| **Family Childcare Newsletters 1987 - Current**
| **Activities — Magazine Fun**

> # The Internet has lots and lots (and lots) of free software.

Gangs

It's safe to assume that very few youths of today join the Mickey Mouse Club. It's much more cool to tattoo your body, pierce yourself in unmentionable places, and see how many times you can come close to being killed without actually dying. And to think kids used to go to sing-alongs when they wanted to have fun. This list is open to gang members, ex-gang members, teachers, family, and anyone interested in gangs and gang-related problems. Join in on discussions with the group or make one-on-one connections with members of the list.

Internet Mailing List:
List Address: **gangtm@dhvx20.csudh.edu**
Subscription Address:
gangtm-request@dhvx20.csudh.edu

Jewish Youth

Jewish youth newsletters and information about Jewish youth groups.

Gopher:
Name: Jerusalem One
Address: **jerusalem1.datasrv.co.il**
Choose: **Jewish Youth: Organizations, Schools and Themselves**

Excerpt from the Net...

```
            (from Activities for Kids)
     ACTIVITY BOXES TO STIMULATE LEARNING

Activity boxes are containers of everyday objects that relate to each
other in some way.  Use the boxes to further children's exploration,
especially when you are busy with household chores.  The boxes provide
an opportunity to touch, compare, sort and manipulate "real things."
Start with good, inexpensive containers and include:

- Objects with a single property in common (all soft, all round, all green)
- Objects that vary in one way (fabrics of different texture)
- Objects with similar functions (all cooking utensils)
- Objects with complementary functions that work together (yarn, needle, cloth)
```

Scouting

What are good fund-raisers and where are the cool summer camps? Find out more about traditions and activities of scouting.

Listserv Mailing List:
List Address: **scouts-l@tcubvm.is.tcu.edu**
Subscription Address: **listserv@tcubvm.is.tcu.edu**

List Address: **e-scouts@tcubvm.is.tcu.edu**
Subscription Address: **listserv@tcubvm.is.tcu.edu**

Usenet:
Newsgroup: **rec.scouting**

Be a good scout.
Read rec.scouting.

Scouting Around the World

No matter where you are in the world, you can find a scouting organization to join. Scouts have taken the concept of exploration one step further by extending their scouting territory to the World Wide Web. This home page offers you international information about the Scouts, as well as links to other scouting pages, mailing lists, and newsgroups and pages in countries like the Netherlands, Germany, Austria, Norway, and the United States.

World Wide Web
URL: **http://www.strw.leidenuniv.nl/
~jansen/scout.html**

No matter who you are
or what you believe,
somewhere on the Internet,
there are people like you.

Teen Date

Looking forward to a big date? Are you stuck on someone who doesn't know you exist? Or are you just lonely and need someone to chat with? Check out the teen dating channel. Hang out here — there's never a curfew.

Internet Relay Chat:
Channel: **#teendate**

Teenagers

A place for teenagers to meet, laugh, and talk.

Internet Relay Chat:
Channel: **#teen**

Young People Talk

Kids, create a safe space for self-discovery, exploring the thoughts and ideas of your peers.

Usenet:
Newsgroup: **alt.kids-talk**

Need a place to talk to young people from all over the world? Try alt.kids-talk.

A
B
C
D
E
F
G
H
I
J
K
L
M
N
O
P
Q
R
S
T
U
V
W
X
Y
Z

ZINES

Albert Hofmann's Strange Mistake

This zine is a hypertext birthday card commemorating the 50th anniversary of the accidental discovery of LSD. Read archives by authorities, and testimonials from CIA agents and random fans of LSD.

See also: Drugs

Anonymous FTP:
Address: **ftp.brown.edu**
Path: **/pub/bobby_rabyd/LSD-51***

Need to know about LSD?
Tune in, turn on, and drop into the
Net. Then take a look at
Albert Hofmann's Strange Mistake.

Arm the Spirit

"Down with imperialism, up with liberation" is the message of *Arm the Spirit*. The writers of this zine advocate armed struggle and militant resistance, offer news of political prisoners in North America and Europe, information on the people of Central and South America, writings from guerrilla groups and hot debates on armed rebellion.

See also: Freedom, Politics

Anonymous FTP:
Address: **ftp.etext.org**
Path: **/pub/Politics/Arm.The.Spirit/***

Gopher:
Name: Whole Earth Lectronic Link
Address: **gopher.well.sf.ca.us**
Choose: **Authors, Books, Periodicals, Zines**
I **Online Zines**
I **Arm the Sp**

Jump into the Net.

Do you like the "Final Frontier?" Take a look at Star Trek (or Space).

Armadillo Culture

Why is it that you never see an armadillo in *Winnie the Pooh*? Probably because nobody wanted to introduce fragile young minds to the armadillo culture, which appears to be fraught with turmoil, energy, and an active imagination that often manifests itself in socially unacceptable ways. The secret of this zine is that there is not an armadillo of the four-legged variety to be found anywhere in its pages. It's guaranteed to be strange, and besides random brain waves and poetic ramblings, there are hip interviews and reviews of the music and Net scene.

See also: Bizarre, Music

Anonymous FTP:
Address: **ftp.etext.org**
Path: **/pub/Zines/Armadillo.Culture**

Gopher:
Name: University of Michigan
Address: **gopher.etext.org**
Choose: **Zines**
I **Armadillo.Culture**

Art Com

Art is by no means dead. Every generation laments the passing of art, thinking there is nothing new to do. *Art Com* is dedicated to the task of uniting art with new forms of technology and communication, opening whole new worlds.

See also: Art

Anonymous FTP:
Address: **ftp.cic.net**
Path: **/pub/e-serials/alphabetic/a/artcom/***

Gopher:
Name: CICNet
Address: **gopher.cic.net**
Choose: **Electronic Serials**
I **Alphabetic List**
I **A**
I **Art Com Magazine**

Usenet:
Newsgroup: **alt.artcom**

Gophers are your friends.

Bad Subjects

Thinking for yourself is Bad. Thinking in ways that are not mainstream or that are radical is Bad. That's why *Bad Subjects* is so good. Check out the zine that promotes the questioning of old ways and tries to show how politics applies to everyday life.

See also: Politics

Gopher:
Name: University of California Berkeley
Address: **gopher-registry.berkeley.edu**
Choose: **University of California at Berkeley Gopher Menu**
  | **Student Information**
  | **Bad Subjects**

Bust

It's fun to be a woman. That's what we hear. And that's what *Bust* says. The women of Generation X are expressing themselves in a wild, free, totally unfettered manner that just demands to be witnessed.

Gopher:
Name: Echo
Address: **echonyc.com**
Choose: **Zines, Publications & Writings**
  | **BUST**

Capacity — The Webzine

A zine available through the Web dedicated to expanding the boundaries of art and culture. It includes poetry, short fiction, political statements/reactions, works of art, cultural critiques, and much more. Back issues are available from here, too.

World Wide Web:
URL: **http://www.wimsey.com:80/Capacity/**

Chaos Control

Get the real story of the electronic music scene through articles and interviews of both mainstream and underground acts.

See also: Music

Anonymous FTP:
Address: **ftp.std.com**
Path: **/obi/Zines/Chaos.Control/***

Cyberspace Vanguard

Sometimes reading science fiction and fantasy isn't enough. Immerse yourself in the culture by getting news and reviews through *Cyberspace Vanguard*. This zine will fill you in on all the details of new books and movies, the latest grit from the television and movie world, and some clever opinion pieces.

See also: Science Fiction

World Wide Web:
URL: **http://www.lysator.liu.se/sf_archive/ sf-texts/Cyberspace_Vanguard/**

Excerpt from the Net...

```
Newsgroup: alt.artcom
Subject: subliminal regression what is it?

> I have been wondering, late at night usually sleepless, about
> subliminal regression in art and how I could find exmples of it that
> would tell me more about it. Is it a stretch to assume that it is
> outside of the realm of thought of most artists? Does Balthus do
> it? Bacon? Freud? DeKooning?

I believe that what you seek rests with you. Just as Freud and others
"tried to figure it out", so must you. As an artist, that is your
challenge. Art is a frontier. It is one that is far behind others.
We must rely on you, on the artists, to tell us. It's a tough job, but
some artist has got to do it. There is no help.
```

A
B
C
D
E
F
G
H
I
J
K
L
M
N
O
P
Q
R
S
T
U
V
W
X
Y
Z

DargonZine

Looking for a story to keep you busy for hours? Check out the archives of *DargonZine* and follow the story of Rien and other characters of the shared world of Dargon.

See also: Science Fiction, Writing

Usenet:
Newsgroup: **rec.mag.dargon**

World Wide Web:
URL: **http://www.lysator.liu.se/sf_archive/sub/dargon.html**

Depth Probe

A hypertext zine containing book, music, and movie reviews mixed with writing on thoughts and dreams.

See also: Writing

World Wide Web:
URL: **http://www.lighthouse.com/~ake/DepthProbe/index/home.html**

E-Zine List

A list of electronic magazines available on the Internet.

Anonymous FTP:
Address: **etext.archive.umich.edu**
Path: **/pub/Zines/e-zine-list.gz**

Electronic Magazines

The Internet has a lot of electronic magazines that you can download whenever you want. No more will you have to put up with all the inconveniences of real magazines, like those subscription forms that fall out when you turn the page, or the perfume ads that smell like one of Zsa Zsa Gabor's bad dreams.

No longer will you have to worry about your name being sold to a mailing list that specializes in junk mail. But the best thing about electronic magazines is that they are free--which makes them ideal for birthday presents.

Empire Times

Calling all hackers, crackers and anarchists. This hip zine is dedicated to organizing the underground Net Mafia and to disseminating knowledge that contributes to subversive activity and political and legal mayhem. And if you don't care about all that stuff, it's just plain fun.

Anonymous FTP:
Address: **ftp.etext.org**
Path: **/pub/Zines/EmpTimes/***

FactSheet Five - Electric

FactSheet Five has gone electric. This clearinghouse for zine information has only been available on paper until now. (How very archaic.) Get information on many of the zines on the market with this thorough guidebook.

Anonymous FTP:
Address: **nigel.msen.com**
Path: **/pub/newsletters/Zine-Reviews/F5-E/***

HyperMedia Zines on the Net

A collection of links to hypertext magazines divided into three categories: independent publishers, academic publishers, and commercial publishers. There are also pages dedicated to other Internet resources about zines and alternative presentation techniques on the Web.

World Wide Web:
URL: **http://www.acns.nwu.edu/ezines/**

Inquisitor

A nice mix of art, technology and culture, the *Inquisitor* offers stories on the Apocalypse, Godzilla, microcontroller projects, global telecommunications, and various sociological observations.

Gopher:
Name: Echo
Address: **echonyc.com**
Choose: **Zines, Publications & Writings**
  | Inquisitor

> ## No one understands the Internet, so relax and enjoy.

International Teletimes

A general interest magazine. Back issues cover these topics: travel, TV and film, history, environment and human rights.

See also: Magazines

World Wide Web:
 URL: **http://www.wimsey.com/teletimes.root/ teletimes_home_page.html**

Journal of Underground Computing

You don't have to be a hard-core computer addict to like this journal. It's loaded with information like the sociolegal aspects of networks of the future, recent legal acts and police actions, new methods of accessing the Internet and thoughts on the cultural aspects of networking. It's meaty, thought-provoking, and it might even include a conspiracy or two.

Anonymous FTP:
 Address: **etext.archive.umich.edu**
 Path: **/pub/Zines/JAUC/***

Mail:
 Address: **sub@fennec.com**

Morpo Review

There are people out on the Net who love to write and want to share their works of literary art with you for free. This bi-monthly zine will offer you some great fiction, non-fiction and poetry.

World Wide Web:
 URL: **http://morpo.creighton.edu/morpo/**

> ## Cool words?
> ## Look in Quotations.

Netsurfer Publishing

A group of netsurfers writing several interesting online periodicals. Back issues of the *Netsurfer Digest*, which offer short reviews and links to fun and useful Net resources, Netsurfer special features, and logos from their way-cool T-shirts can be found here.

Anonymous FTP:
 Address: **ftp.netsurf.com**
 Path: **/pub/nsd/***

World Wide Web:
 URL: **http://www.netsurf.com/nsd/index.html**

The New Sun

Walking past a newsstand, it is easy to be shocked, appalled and discouraged by headlines screaming of death, destruction and scandal. Someone decided it was time to make a happy newspaper, and you can find it on the Net. *The New Sun* prints positive, upbeat and optimistic human interest stories in an attempt to inspire you — or at least bring some cheer to your day.

World Wide Web:
 URL: **http://shebute.com:1440/the_new_sun.html**

OtherRealms

The first 30 or so issues of the science fiction fanzine *OtherRealms*.

Anonymous FTP:
 Address: **ftp.uu.net**
 Path: **/doc/literary/obi/OtherRealms/***

Random Zines

A random collection of popular zines, including *Voices from the Net*, *Soapbox*, and *Zig-Zag*.

Anonymous FTP:
 Address: **ftp.spies.com**
 Path: **/Library/Zines/***

Gopher:
 Name: Internet Wiretap
 Address: **wiretap.spies.com**
 Choose: **Wiretap Online Library**
   | Zines

A
B
C
D
E
F
G
H
I
J
K
L
M
N
O
P
Q
R
S
T
U
V
W
X
Y
Z

ScreamBaby

This zine put the "sub" in sub-culture. Read about literature, art, music, film, television, news and bizarre events. If you don't have a real life, it's a great way to spend a Saturday night.

World Wide Web:
URL: **http://www.ifi.uio.no/~mariusw/futurec/scream/**

Spectra

This is a broad interest zine that is free-form and engaging. The general theme seems to be "Ideas, Expression and Evolution" and the editor believes in allowing the magazine to be shaped by the readers. It's the zen method of publishing.

See also: Literature

Mail:
Address: **plschuerman@ucdavis.edu**

Stream of Consciousness

A zine of poetry and art. You will need a graphical browser to enjoy this zine.

See also: Art, Poetry

World Wide Web:
URL: **http://kzsu.stanford.edu/uwi/soc.html**

Temptation of St. Anthony

A zine based on the temptation of St. Anthony and the seven deadly sins. There are pictures and stories relating to each of the sins, so pick your favorite and settle down for some fun reading. Just don't blame us if you miss confession.

World Wide Web:
URL:
http://www.cis.upenn.edu/~mjd/tsa/tsa.html

Verbiage Magazine

Verbiage puts together a nice collection of short fiction. Read stories from creative writers or submit your own writing to the magazine. All issues, as well as a page containing the submission guidelines, are at this site.

See also: Writing

World Wide Web:
URL: **http://sunsite.unc.edu/boutell/verbiage/index.html**

Virtual Reality Artificial Intelligence Neural Net

The *Virtual Reality Artificial Intelligence Neural Net* web zine offers many collections of web pages with links to an Atlanta travel guide, illustrated audio files, the Whole Internet Scavenger Hunt, advertisements, and other interesting items.

World Wide Web:
URL: **http://zaphod.cc.ttu.ee/vrainn/home.html**

Webster's Weekly

A weekly hypertext web zine with fun regular features like "Ask the Nerd," cartoons from Nick Bruel, and the Horrorscope. They have other features, which change weekly, covering things like movies, men's or women's issues, music, politics, and anything that might be slightly strange in interesting ways.

World Wide Web:
URL: **http://www.awa.com/w2/**

Zines, zines, zines. How we love that word and how it rolls off our tongues like fine port. We believe that zines offer the best way in which to express rugged individualism on the Net. People who would have been cowboys in the last century are publishing electronic zines today. If you would like to jump in or just see what is happening, follow the ongoing discussion and plethora of announcements in alt.zines.

Wimsey's Digital Rag

Read feature articles, information and loads of Net resources from this fun and interesting zine.

World Wide Web:
URL: **http://www.wimsey.com/Digital_Rag/ current/index.html**

Zine Discussion

Zines are cool whether you are in the business of making them or just reading them. Learn about the latest releases, old zines making a comeback or calls for submissions. On this newsgroup, you can also participate in the discussion of publishing or submitting, copyright issues and the production and distribution of electronic or print zines.

Usenet:
Newsgroup: **alt.zines**

Zine Lists

Making your own zine is the rage. In zine-land, no topic is sacred. Zines cover topics as mainstream as education, politics, and philosophy and as bizarre as hyperactive armadillos and free verse about plastic lawn ornaments.

See also: Publications

Gopher:
Name: University of Michigan
Address: **etext.archive.umich.edu**
Choose: **Zines**
 | **e-zine-list**

World Wide Web:
URL: **http://www.3w.com/3W/ezines.html**
URL: **http://www.ora.com:8080/johnl/e-zine-list/**

Zine Reviews

A large collection of reviews from *Factsheet Five - Electric*, covering various and esoteric zines, those opinionated publications with a press run of between 50 and 5,000.

Anonymous FTP:
Address: **nigel.msen.com**
Path: **/pub/newsletters/Zine-Reviews/F5-E**

Gopher:
Name: Whole Earth Lectronic Link
Address: **gopher.well.sf.ca.us**
Choose: **Authors, Books, Periodicals, Zines**
 | **Factsheet Five, Electric**

Zines

A huge collection of zines covering many topics, including art, business, culture, science fiction, computers, short fiction, poetry, and cyberpunk. Check the alphabetical listing for *The Unplastic News*, *Cyberspace Vanguard*, and others.

Gopher:
Name: CICNet
Address: **gopher.cic.net**
Choose: **Electronic Serials**
 | **General Subject Headings**

Name: CICNet
Address: **gopher.cic.net**
Choose: **Electronic Serials**
 | **Alphabetic List**

Zines, the Final Frontier

Zines are small magazine-like thingies that abound on the Net. You can subscribe to a Zine for free and, from time to time, receive a brand new fresh copy in your electronic mailbox. In a world where all too often one size is supposed to fit all, the world of Zines is refreshingly idiosyncratic. Take a look. You are bound to find something that will pique your interest.

ZOOLOGY

Camel Research

A mailing list created by the Camel Research Center at King Faisal University, Saudi Arabia, for the purpose of furthering camel knowledge and awareness.

Listserv Mailing List:
List Address: **camel-l@sakfu00.bitnet**
Subscription Address: **listserv@sakfu00.bitnet**

Census of Australian Vertebrate Species

A database of articles on Australian animals. The articles in the database are categorized, and can be accessed by family, genus, species, common name, scientific name, or the name of the article's author.

Gopher:
> Name: Australian Biological Resources Study
> Address: **kaos.erin.gov.au**
> Choose: **Biodiversity**
>   **| Census of Australian Vertebrate Species**

Electronic Zoo

A compilation of animal-related Net resources: mailing lists, gophers, web sites, newsgroups, archives, databases, commercial online services, and BBSs.

Anonymous FTP:
> Address: **ftp.wustl.edu**
> Path: **/doc/techreports/wustl.edu/compmed/elec_zoo.***

Gopher:
> Name: NETVET Veterinary Resources
> Address: **netvet.wustl.edu**
> Choose: **NETVET Veterinary Resources**
>   **| The Electronic Zoo**

Florida Wildlife

There *is* wildlife in Florida—and not just in Miami, either. Check out the Florida Agricultural Information Retrieval System and learn about problems caused by wildlife, conservation issues, laws to protect Florida wildlife, information about various species and nuisance wildlife that you can add to your "Seek and Destroy" list.

World Wide Web:
> URL: **http://hammock.ifas.ufl.edu/text/uw/wild.html**

Great White Shark

Gif images, facts, and research discussions of this amazing predator and specialized hunter, the great white shark.

World Wide Web:
> URL: **http://ucmp1.berkeley.edu/Doug/shark.html**

Non-Native Fish Information Resources

It's nice to know that wherever you go in the world, you can look up what kind of fish you might encounter. Find data on all sorts of fish organized by state, hydrologic unit or species.

World Wide Web:
> URL: **http://www.nfrcg.gov/noni.fish/**

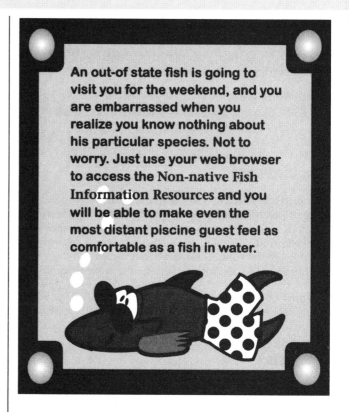

An out-of state fish is going to visit you for the weekend, and you are embarrassed when you realize you know nothing about his particular species. Not to worry. Just use your web browser to access the Non-native Fish Information Resources and you will be able to make even the most distant piscine guest feel as comfortable as a fish in water.

Zoo Atlanta

It's a rainy day and you had promised the kids a trip to the zoo. Not to worry. Tell the kids to stop crying and have them gather around the warm glow of your computer's monitor. Take an electronic tour of the Atlanta zoo as well as other zoo sites around the Net. This site comes complete with wildlife movies and animal sounds and pictures.

World Wide Web:
> URL: **http://www.gatech.edu/zoo/home-page**

Zoological Resources

These days you don't actually have to have an animal to study zoology. All you have to do is connect to the gopher or Web site of choice and immediately you will have access to zoological records, glossaries of zoological terms, links to museums, databases, image galleries and other sites relating to the study of zoology.

Gopher:
> Name: Zoological Record Gopher
> Address: **www.york.biosis.org**

World Wide Web:
> URL: **http://www.cs.fsu.edu/projects/group3/zoo.html**
> URL: **http://www.york.biosis.org/**

Usenet Newsgroups

This section of the book contains a master list of Usenet discussion groups (usually referred to as "newsgroups," although most of them do not have real news). We would like to take a few moments to explain this list and to give you some helpful information. However, if you would like a full explanation of what Usenet is and how it works, or if you need instructions on how to participate in these discussion groups, take a look at our other book, *The Internet Complete Reference*, also published by Osborne McGraw-Hill.

Generally speaking, we can divide Usenet newsgroups into two categories: those that are carried all over the world, and those that are of local or regional interest. This list contains only the worldwide groups that were current at the time we prepared this book.

As you can see, Usenet newsgroup names consist of a number of words or terms, separated by a period. For example:

```
comp.admin.policy
```

The first word is called the *hierarchy*. The name of the hierarchy tells you what type of group you are looking at. For example, all the groups in the **comp** hierarchy have something to do with computers. Altogether, the worldwide newsgroups are divided into 18 different hierarchies.

Of the 18 hierarchies, 7 are *mainstream* and 11 are *alternative*. (These are shown in Tables 1 and 2.) Most Usenet sites carry all the mainstream groups. However, not all sites carry the alternative groups. The reason is that new alternative newsgroups can be created by anyone who knows how to do it. Mainstream groups can only be created after a well-defined, deliberative process. Thus, you will find many more exotic groups in the alternative hierarchy. However, not all system managers will carry them.

What can you do if you see a newsgroup in the list that you can't find on your system? You have two choices. First, you can (politely) ask your system manager if he or she could start carrying the newsgroup. Second, you can get an account on a system that has a better selection.

Hierarchy	Number of Groups
comp	626
misc	56
news	26
rec	381
sci	123
soc	126
talk	22
TOTAL	1360

Table 1. Mainstream Usenet Newsgroup Hierarchies

Hierarchy	Number of Groups
alt	1361
bionet	60
bit	255
biz	41
ddn	2
gnu	28
ieee	12
info	41
k12	36
u3b	5
vmsnet	37
TOTAL	1878

Table 2. Alternative Usenet Newsgroup Hierarchies

So far, all the hierarchies we have mentioned are free to anyone on the Internet. However, there is one hierarchy that costs money. It is called **clari** and it is furnished by a private company called Clarinet.

The **clari** hierarchy contains newsgroups that have real news (like in a newspaper). Clarinet gets their information from a variety of sources, including a live news wire. They edit and repackage the articles into Usenet format and then send them out over the Internet. If your organization subscribes to Clarinet, the **clari** newsgroups will be available to you and you can read them in the same way as you read the regular Usenet newsgroup. Although your organization pays money for this service, there is no special charge for you.

So, how many newsgroups are there?

As you can see from Table 1, there are 1360 mainstream newsgroups. From Table 2, we see that there are 1878 alternative groups. Thus, there are a total of 3238 worldwide newsgroups. (Or rather, there were at the time we wrote this book.) Clarinet has 447 newsgroups. Thus, potentially, there are a grand total of 3685 non-local Usenet newsgroups.

As you might imagine, new newsgroups are added all the time and any list, no matter how comprehensive, will be out of date. As a public service, several master lists of newsgroups are posted to **news.lists** periodically. At any time, you can look for these lists.

```
List of Active Newsgroups, Part I
List of Active Newsgroups, Part II
Alternative Newsgroup Hierarchies, Part I
Alternative Newsgroup Hierarchies, Part II
```

You can also download the lists via anonymous ftp from **rtfm.mit.edu** by using the following paths:

```
/pub/usenet/news.answers/active-newsgroups/part1
/pub/usenet/news.answers/active-newsgroups/part2
/pub/usenet/news.answers/alt-hierarchies/part1
/pub/usenet/news.answers/alt-hierarchies/part2
```

Be aware, however, that these lists are not as good as the list in this book. In order to prepare our list, we carefully checked it against various systems to pick up any newsgroups that were not included. Then, we eliminated the names of such spurious groups that had somehow found their way onto the list. Finally, we rewrote many of the annotations to make sure that the newsgroup descriptions were consistent and informative.

One last point: From time to time you will see various statistics about the Internet that are designed to overwhelm and impress you. Perhaps the most common such statistic is the number of people on the Net. It is common, for example, to hear that the Internet has 10 or even 20 million people on it. You should know that most such numbers are made up and then repeated, over and over (by newspapers, magazines, and so on), until just about everybody believes that they are true.

The plain fact is that nobody actually knows how many people are on the Net and the 10-20 million figure that you hear so often is just plain hooey. We ourselves like to think that the Net is vast beyond imagination because it makes us feel important and because we can impress people who

don't know any better. But, realistically, a figure of 2-3 million is probably a lot closer to the truth.

The reason that we bring this up is that you hear the same sort of exaggerated statistics regarding Usenet and the number of different newsgroups. For example, it is not uncommon to hear that there are 5000-10,000 different groups. In the analysis that you have just read, we explain how there were 3685 different newsgroups, and that's only if you get Clarinet. Without Clarinet, there were only 3238 newsgroups.

We say "were" because those were the numbers when we compiled the list for the second edition of this book. By the time the book went to the printer, there were already more groups, as new ones are being added all the time. Still, the numbers we have given are approximately right and give you a rough idea of the variety of Usenet.

In our list, we have included only those hierarchies of worldwide interest. That is, we have omitted Clarinet, as well as the local groups (such as those for people from Austin, Texas), the regional groups (such as those for staff and students at the University of California at San Diego), and the groups devoted to a particular culture (such as those for people who speak Japanese). There are approximately 3500 such groups so, overall, one could say that there are about 7100 Usenet groups in the world.

However, this would be a highly inflated number. There are really only about 3200 groups (or 3600 with Clarinet) of general interest and there are few sites that carry even all of these groups. Moreover, many of these groups are usually empty.

Still, take a look at the master list. There *are* thousands of different groups, and you would be hard pressed to find something that does not capture your interest. So what we are saying is that there really is no need to exaggerate. The Net is still the largest gathering of people in the history of the world, and Usenet does offer more variety than any system of discussion groups that has ever existed.

We just want you to remember to be more than a little suspicious when you read impressive statistics. It never hurts to say to yourself, "Well, that certainly is an impressive number, but how would anyone ever measure that?"

(By the way, the book you are reading has been translated into 53 different languages and has sold over 5,000,000 copies throughout the world.)

alt

alt.0d	"Zero-dimensional imaging": in reality, bizarre nonsense
alt.1d	"One-dimensional imaging": in reality, bizarre nonsense
alt.2600	*Hackers'* magazine
alt.2600.hope.tech	Leftover group, created for hackers' conference
alt.3d	Three-dimensional imaging
alt.59.79.99	Taco Bell food and advertising
alt.abortion.inequity	Inequity of abortion
alt.abuse-recovery	Helping victims of abuse recover (Moderated)
alt.abuse.offender.recovery	Helping offenders recover
alt.abuse.recovery	Helping victims of abuse recover (Moderated)
alt.abuse.transcendence	Non-standard ways to deal with abuse
alt.activism	Activities for activists
alt.activism.d	A place to discuss issues in alt.activism
alt.activism.death-penalty	Opposition to capital punishment
alt.adjective.noun.verb.verb.verb	Observations on strange newsgroup names
alt.adoption	For those involved with or contemplating adoption
alt.aeffle.und.pferdle	German TV cartoon characters
alt.agriculture.fruit	Fruit farming and agriculture
alt.agriculture.misc	General agricultural and farming topics
alt.alcohol	Alcohol and its problems
alt.aldus.freehand	Aldus Freehand software
alt.aldus.misc	Other Aldus software products
alt.aldus.pagemaker	All about Aldus PageMaker
alt.algebra.help	Assistance with algebra
alt.alien.vampire.flonk.flonk.flonk	Bizarre nonsense, some about vampires
alt.alien.visitors	Space aliens on Earth, abduction, government coverup
alt.alt.alt.alt.alt	Bizarre nonsense
alt.amateur-comp	Amateur computerist
alt.amazon-women.admirers	Worshiping strong, amazon-like women
alt.america.online	America Online, the Internet wannabe
alt.amiga.slip	SLIP connections with Amiga computers
alt.anagrams	Anagrams and other wordplay
alt.angst	Anxiety in the modern world
alt.animals.badgers	Badgers
alt.animals.dolphins	Dolphins
alt.animals.foxes	Foxes
alt.animals.humans	Philosophy of humans as animals
alt.animals.lampreys	Lampreys, eel-like aquatic animals
alt.animation.warner-bros	Warner Brothers cartoons
alt.anonymous	Virtues and benefits of anonymity
alt.answers	Frequently asked questions about the alt groups
alt.aol-sucks	Complaints about America Online and its users
alt.aol.rejects	Complaints about America Online and its users
alt.appalachian	Appalachian regional issues
alt.appalachian.literature	Appalachian literature
alt.aquaria	Aquariums and tropical fish
alt.aquaria.killies	Killifish, members of family cyprinodontidae
alt.archery	Archery
alt.architecture	Building design/construction and related topics
alt.architecture.alternative	Non-traditional building designs
alt.architecture.int-design	Interior design of man-made spaces
alt.art.theft.scream.scream.scream	Bizarre nonsense
alt.artcom	Artistic community, arts, and communication
alt.arts.ballet	Ballet and modern dance
alt.arts.nomad	Nomadic art
alt.ascii-art	Pictures composed of ASCII characters
alt.ascii-art.animation	Animation composed of ASCII characters
alt.asian-movies	Movies from Hong Kong, Taiwan, and China
alt.astrology	Astrology
alt.atari-jaguar.discussion	Atari 64-bit home video game system
alt.atari.2600	Atari 2600 game system
alt.atheism	Atheism
alt.atheism.moderated	Atheism (Moderated)
alt.atheism.satire	Atheism-related humor and satire
alt.authorware	Authorware software
alt.autos.antique	All facets of older automobiles
alt.autos.camaro.firebird	Camaro, Firebird (American sports cars)

USENET NEWSGROUPS

alt.autos.rod-n-custom	Souped-up and customized autos
alt.bacchus	Bacchus organization for lovers of wine
alt.backrubs	Massage and back rubs
alt.baldspot	Treatments for balding
alt.banjo	Banjos
alt.barney.dinosaur.die.die.die	Hate and excoriation of Barney the Dinosaur
alt.basement.graveyard	Bizarre nonsense
alt.bbs	General BBS (bulletin board system) topics
alt.bbs.ads	Ads for various computer BBSs
alt.bbs.allsysop	A forum for BBS system operators (sysops)
alt.bbs.doors	BBSs and external programs (doors)
alt.bbs.first-class	First Class Macintosh GUI BBS
alt.bbs.gigo-gateway	Gigo gateway between Fido and Usenet
alt.bbs.internet	BBS systems accessible via the Internet
alt.bbs.lists	Postings of regional BBS listings
alt.bbs.lists.d	Regional BBS listings
alt.bbs.majorbbs	Major BBS
alt.bbs.metal	METAL telecomm environment
alt.bbs.pcboard	PCBoard BBS
alt.bbs.pcbuucp	UUCP for DOS systems
alt.bbs.renegade	Renegade BBS
alt.bbs.searchlight	Searchlight BBS systems
alt.bbs.unixbbs	Bulletin board systems under Uniclones
alt.bbs.unixbbs.uniboard	Unix Uniboard BBS Systems
alt.bbs.uupcb	UUPCB BBS
alt.bbs.waffle	Waffle BBS
alt.bbs.watergate	WaterGate mail processor
alt.bbs.wildcat	Wildcat BBS
alt.beadworld	Beads
alt.beer	Beer and related beverages
alt.best.of.internet	Reposts of the best articles from other newsgroups
alt.bigfoot	Mythical Bigfoot animal/man/monster
alt.binaries.clip-art	Pictures: DOS, Mac, and Unix clip art
alt.binaries.doom	Pictures: Doom PC game
alt.binaries.misc	Pictures: General images
alt.binaries.multimedia	Sound, text, and graphics data rolled in one
alt.binaries.pictures	Pictures (suitable for displaying on a computer)
alt.binaries.pictures.anime	Pictures: Japanese animation
alt.binaries.pictures.ascii	Pictures: Images composed of ASCII characters
alt.binaries.pictures.cartoons	Pictures: Animated cartoons
alt.binaries.pictures.d	Discussion about pictures
alt.binaries.pictures.dorks	Pictures: Dorks
alt.binaries.pictures.erotica	Pictures: erotic
alt.binaries.pictures.erotica.bestiality	Pictures: Sex with animals
alt.binaries.pictures.erotica.blondes	Pictures: erotic blonds
alt.binaries.pictures.erotica.cartoons	Pictures: Erotic cartoon images
alt.binaries.pictures.erotica.d	Discussion about erotic blond pictures
alt.binaries.pictures.erotica.female	Pictures: erotic women
alt.binaries.pictures.erotica.furry	Pictures: Erotic furry art
alt.binaries.pictures.erotica.male	Pictures: erotic men
alt.binaries.pictures.erotica.orientals	Pictures: erotic Asians
alt.binaries.pictures.fine-art.d	Discussion about fine art pics (Moderated)
alt.binaries.pictures.fine-art.digitized	Pictures: fine art (Moderated)
alt.binaries.pictures.fine-art.graphics	Pictures: graphics (Moderated)
alt.binaries.pictures.fractals	Pictures: fractals
alt.binaries.pictures.furniture	Pictures: Furniture
alt.binaries.pictures.furry	Pictures: Anthropomorphic human/animal art
alt.binaries.pictures.misc	Pictures: miscellaneous
alt.binaries.pictures.supermodels	Pictures: supermodels
alt.binaries.pictures.tasteless	Pictures: tasteless
alt.binaries.pictures.utilities	Programs for scanning and viewing pics
alt.binaries.sounds.d	Discussion about digitized sounds
alt.binaries.sounds.erotica	Sounds: Erotic noise
alt.binaries.sounds.midi	Sounds: MIDI
alt.binaries.sounds.misc	Sounds: all types
alt.binaries.sounds.mods	Sounds: MODs and related formats
alt.binaries.sounds.movies	Sounds: Movies
alt.binaries.sounds.music	Sounds: music

alt.binaries.sounds.tv	Sounds: Television shows
alt.binaries.sounds.utilities	Sounds: Utility programs
alt.bio.hackers	Biological aspects of hacking
alt.bio.minority	Minorities in biology
alt.birthright	Birthright Party propaganda
alt.bitch.pork	Bizarre nonsense
alt.bitterness	Bitterness
alt.bogus.group	Bizarre nonsense
alt.bonsai	Bonsai, growing artificially dwarfed potted trees
alt.books.anne-rice	Anne Rice's books
alt.books.deryni	Katherine Kurtz's books, the Deryni series
alt.books.isaac-asimov	Isaac Asimov's books
alt.books.m-lackey	Mercedes Lackey's books
alt.books.reviews	Reviews of all kinds of books
alt.books.stephen-king	Stephen King's books
alt.books.technical	Technical books
alt.boomerang	Technology and use of the boomerang
alt.brain	Brains and intelligence
alt.brother-jed	Born-again minister touring U.S. campuses
alt.buddha.short.fat.guy	Strange discussion, loosely based on Buddhism
alt.business.import-export	Business aspects of international trade
alt.business.misc	General business and commerce topics
alt.business.multi-level	Multi-level marketing businesses
alt.business.seminars	Business seminars
alt.cable-tv.re-regulate	Regulation of TV networks and cable
alt.cad	Computer aided design
alt.cad.autocad	CAD as practiced by customers of Autodesk
alt.cajun.info	Cajun culture
alt.california	All about California
alt.callahans	Callahan's bar for puns and fellowship
alt.captain.sarcastic	Strangeness inspired by Captain Sarcastic (K. Koller)
alt.cars.Ford-Probe	Ford Probe
alt.cascade	Long, silly followup articles (cascades)
alt.caving	Spelunking (cave exploration)
alt.cd-rom	Optical storage devices (specifically CD-ROM)
alt.cd-rom.reviews	Reviews of CD-ROM products
alt.celebrities	Famous people and their sycophants
alt.cellular-phone-tech	Cellular phones
alt.censorship	Restricting speech and press
alt.cereal	Breakfast cereals
alt.cesium	Trivia relating to the element cesium
alt.chess.ics	Internet chess server
alt.child-support	Child support
alt.chinchilla	Chinchilla farming and cultivation
alt.chinese.computing	Chinese computing
alt.chinese.text	Postings in Chinese; Chinese language software
alt.chinese.text.big5	Posting in Chinese [BIG 5]
alt.christnet	General Christian topics
alt.christnet.atheism	Atheism from a Christian viewpoint
alt.christnet.bible	Bible discussion and research
alt.christnet.dinosaur.barney	Christians who hate Barney the Dinosaur
alt.christnet.evangelical	Evangelism
alt.christnet.hypocrisy	Talk about hypocrisy
alt.christnet.philosophy	Philosophy and Christianity
alt.christnet.second-coming.real-soon-now	Return of Christ and apocalypse
alt.christnet.sex	Sexual issues relating to Christianity
alt.christnet.theology	Christian theology
alt.clearing.technology	Clearing process used by Scientologists
alt.clothing	Clothing
alt.clothing.lingerie	Lingerie
alt.clothing.sneakers	Running shoes
alt.co-evolution	*Whole Earth Review* and associated lifestyles
alt.co-ops	Cooperatives
alt.cobol	Programming in Cobol
alt.coffee	Coffee
alt.collecting.autographs	Autograph collectors and enthusiasts
alt.college.college-bowl	College Bowl competition
alt.college.food	Dining halls, cafeterias, mystery meat, and more
alt.college.fraternities	College fraternities

alt.college.fraternities.sigma-pi	Sigma Pi fraternity
alt.college.fraternities.theta-tau	Theta Tau fraternity
alt.college.sororities	College sororities
alt.college.tunnels	Tunnels on college campuses
alt.college.us	U.S. colleges
alt.colorguard	Marching bands, etc
alt.comedy.british	British humour
alt.comedy.british.blackadder	*Black Adder*, British TV programme
alt.comedy.firesgn-thtre	Firesign Theatre, 1970s comedy/satire group
alt.comedy.slapstick.3-stooges	Three Stooges
alt.comedy.standup	Stand-up comedy
alt.comedy.vaudeville	Vaudeville comedy
alt.comics.alternative	Alternative comics
alt.comics.batman	Batman comics
alt.comics.buffalo-roam	A Postscript comic strip
alt.comics.elfquest	W. and R. Pini's *Elfquest* comics
alt.comics.lnh	Interactive net.madness in the superhero genre
alt.comics.superman	Superman comics
alt.comp.acad-freedom.news	Academic freedom related to computers (Moderated)
alt.comp.acad-freedom.talk	Academic freedom issues related to computers
alt.comp.compression	Computer compression programs
alt.comp.databases.xbase.clipper	Clipper version of xbase programming
alt.comp.fsp	FSP file transport protocol
alt.comp.hardware.homebuilt	Building your own computer hardware
alt.computer.consultants	Computer consultants and contractors
alt.conference-ctr	Announcements about conferences
alt.config	Discussion about alternate newsgroups
alt.consciousness	All about consciousness
alt.consciousness.mysticism	Mysticism
alt.consciousness.near-death-exp	Near-death experiences
alt.conspiracy	Conspiracy theories
alt.conspiracy.abe-lincoln	Conspiracies relating to Abraham Lincoln
alt.conspiracy.jfk	Kennedy assassination
alt.consumers.free-stuff	Free offers
alt.control-theory	Control system theory and practice
alt.cooking-chat	Cooking
alt.cosuard	Council of Sysops, Users Against Rate Discrimination
alt.coupons	Coupons
alt.cows.moo.moo.moo	Cows and related issues
alt.crackers	Saltines and related consumables
alt.creative-cook	Creative cooking
alt.creative-cooking	Creative cooking
alt.cuddle	Hugging, snuggling, and bizarre nonsense
alt.cult-movies	Movies with a cult following
alt.cult-movies.evil-deads	*Evil Dead* movie series
alt.cult-movies.rhps	*Rocky Horror Picture Show*
alt.cult-movies.rocky-horror	*Rocky Horror Picture Show*
alt.culture.alaska	Alaska
alt.culture.argentina	Argentina
alt.culture.austrian	Austria
alt.culture.electric-midget	Midgets
alt.culture.hawaii	Hawaii
alt.culture.indonesia	Indonesia
alt.culture.internet	The Internet
alt.culture.karnataka	Indian state of Karnataka
alt.culture.kerala	People of Keralite origin and the Malayalam language
alt.culture.kuwait	Kuwait
alt.culture.ny-upstate	Upstate New York
alt.culture.ny.upstate	New York State, north of Westchester
alt.culture.oregon	Oregon
alt.culture.somalia	Somalia
alt.culture.southasianet	South Asia
alt.culture.theory	Cultural theory and current practical problems
alt.culture.tuva	Republic of Tannu Tuva
alt.culture.us.1970s	America in the 1970s
alt.culture.us.asian-indian	Asian Indians in the U.S. and Canada
alt.culture.us.southwest	Southwest United States
alt.culture.usenet	Usenet culture
alt.culture.zippies	Zippie culture

alt.current-events.bosnia	Bosnia-Herzegovina
alt.current-events.clinton.whitewater	Clinton Whitewater scandal
alt.current-events.haiti	Haiti
alt.current-events.korean-crisis	North Korea's political upheaval
alt.current-events.la-quake	Earthquakes in Los Angeles
alt.current-events.net-abuse	Usenet spamming and other rude behavior
alt.current-events.russia	Russia
alt.current-events.somalia	Somalia
alt.current-events.ukraine	Ukrainian current events
alt.current-events.usa	United States current events
alt.cyb-sys	Cybernetics and systems
alt.cyberpunk	Computer-mediated high-tech lifestyle
alt.cyberpunk.chatsubo	Literary virtual reality in a cyberpunk hangout
alt.cyberpunk.chatsubo.d	Discussion about Chatsubo stories
alt.cyberpunk.movement	Cybernizing the universe
alt.cyberpunk.tech	Cyberspace and cyberpunk technology
alt.cyberspace	Cyberspace and how it should work
alt.dads-rights	Rights of fathers trying to win custody in court
alt.dcom.catv	Data communications and equipment
alt.dcom.telecom	Telecommunications technology
alt.dcom.telecom.ip	IP (Internet Protocol) telecommunications
alt.dead.porn.stars	Dead (and dying) porno stars
alt.dear.whitehouse	Comments on American White House policy
alt.death-of-superman	Death of Superman (for marketing reasons)
alt.decathena	DEC Athena project
alt.desert-storm	War against Iraq in Kuwait
alt.desert-storm.facts	Factual information on the Gulf War
alt.desert-thekurds	What's happening to the Kurds in Iraq
alt.destroy.the.earth	Fans of destruction
alt.dev.null	Perpetually empty newsgroup (Moderated)
alt.devilbunnies	Real and imaginary bunnies who cause trouble
alt.discordia	Fans of social discord
alt.discrimination	Quotas, affirmative action, bigotry, persecution
alt.divination	Divination techniques (I Ching, Tarot, runes, etc)
alt.dragons-inn	Role-playing/storytelling at the Dragons Inn Pub
alt.dreams	Dreams, what do they mean? and so on
alt.dreams.lucid	Dreams in which you are in control and aware
alt.drinks.kool-aid	Kool Aid drink
alt.drugs	Recreational pharmaceuticals and related flames
alt.drugs.caffeine	Caffeine, the world's most-used stimulant drug
alt.drugs.chemistry	Drug chemistry and synthesis
alt.drugs.culture	Drug culture
alt.drugs.pot	Marijuana
alt.drumcorps	Drum and bugle corps
alt.drunken.bastards	Drunks and their activities
alt.drwho.creative	Stories about Dr. Who
alt.duck.quack.quack.quack	Duck stories
alt.dumpster	Bizarre nonsense
alt.education.bangkok	Education issues in Thailand
alt.education.bangkok.cmc	Education issues in Thailand
alt.education.bangkok.databases	Education issues in Thailand
alt.education.bangkok.planning	Education issues in Thailand
alt.education.bangkok.research	Education issues in Thailand
alt.education.bangkok.student	Education issues in Thailand
alt.education.bangkok.theory	Education issues in Thailand
alt.education.disabled	Learning experiences for the disabled
alt.education.distance	Learning over networks, etc
alt.education.email-project	Email project for teaching English
alt.education.ib	International Baccalaureate diploma program
alt.education.ib.tok	International Baccalaureates in theory of knowledge
alt.education.research	Research into education
alt.elvis.king	Elvis Presley
alt.elvis.sighting	Sightings of Elvis Presley
alt.emulators.ibmpc.apple2	Emulating a PC with an Apple
alt.emusic	Electronic music
alt.energy.renewable	Energy and renewable resources
alt.engr.explosives	Building your own bombs
alt.ensign.wesley.die.die.die	Wesley Crusher character from *Star Trek*
alt.etext	Electronic text

`alt.evil`	Tales from the dark side
`alt.exotic-music`	Exotic and esoteric music
`alt.exploding.kibo`	People who like to blow things up
`alt.extropians`	Extropians, believers in technological immortality
`alt.fairs.renaissance`	Renaissance fairs
`alt.falconry`	Training falcons
`alt.fan.actors`	Actors and actresses
`alt.fan.addams.family`	*Addams Family*
`alt.fan.addams.wednesday`	Wednesday Addams, character from *Addams Family*
`alt.fan.alok.vijayvargia`	Alok Vijayvargia
`alt.fan.amy-fisher`	Amy Fisher and the famous trial
`alt.fan.art-bell`	Art Bell
`alt.fan.asprin`	Robert Lynn Asprin
`alt.fan.barry-manilow`	Barry Manilow
`alt.fan.ben-elton`	Ben Elton, British humourist
`alt.fan.bgcrisis`	Bubble Gum Crisis animation
`alt.fan.bill-gates`	Bill Gates of Microsoft
`alt.fan.blues-brothers`	Blues Brothers band (current and original)
`alt.fan.brie`	Brie cheese
`alt.fan.british-accent`	Talking with a British accent
`alt.fan.bruce-campbell`	Bruce Campbell
`alt.fan.bugtown`	Bugtown/Posts/Savage Henry comics
`alt.fan.cecil-adams`	Cecil Adams (who writes "The Straight Dope")
`alt.fan.ceiling`	Ceiling fans
`alt.fan.chris-elliott`	Chris Elliott
`alt.fan.clarence.thomas`	Clarence Thomas, U.S. Supreme Court Justice
`alt.fan.colin-chapman`	Colin Chapman, creator of Lotus cars
`alt.fan.conan-obrien`	Conan O'Brien, TV talk-show host
`alt.fan.cult-dead-cow`	Cult of the Dead Cow, writing group
`alt.fan.dale-bass`	Dale Bass, baseless refuter of *Scientific American*
`alt.fan.dan-quayle`	Dan Quayle, former U.S. Vice President
`alt.fan.dan-wang`	Dan Wang
`alt.fan.dave_barry`	Dave Barry, humorist
`alt.fan.david-bowie`	David Bowie, singer/actor
`alt.fan.debbie.gibson`	Debbie Gibson, singer
`alt.fan.devo`	Devo, musicians
`alt.fan.dice-man`	Andrew Dice Clay, comedian
`alt.fan.dick-depew`	Dick Depew
`alt.fan.disney.afternoon`	Disney afternoon characters and shows
`alt.fan.don-n-mike`	Don and Mike, radio show hosts
`alt.fan.douglas-adams`	Douglas Adams, writer
`alt.fan.dr-bronner`	Dr. Bronner, maker of esoteric soap products
`alt.fan.dragonlance`	*Dragonlance* fantasy books
`alt.fan.dragons`	General dragon topics and the *Dragonlance* fantasy books
`alt.fan.dune`	Frank Herbert's *Dune* books
`alt.fan.eddings`	David Eddings, writer
`alt.fan.enya`	Enya music
`alt.fan.firesign-theatre`	Firesign Theatre, 1970s comedy/satire group
`alt.fan.frank-zappa`	The late Frank Zappa, bizarre musician
`alt.fan.furry`	Furry animals, anthropomorphized and stuffed
`alt.fan.furry.muck`	MUD-like FurryMUCK, using anthropomorphic characters
`alt.fan.g-gordon-liddy`	G. Gordon Liddy
`alt.fan.gene-scott`	Gene Scott, Christian TV preacher
`alt.fan.goons`	Goon show, radio comedy
`alt.fan.greaseman`	Doug Tracht, disc jockey
`alt.fan.greg-kinnear`	Greg Kinnear, host of *Talk Soup* TV program
`alt.fan.hello-kitty`	Cute little kitty, obnoxiously ubiquitous
`alt.fan.hofstadter`	Douglas Hofstadter, computer scientist and writer
`alt.fan.holmes`	Sherlock Holmes
`alt.fan.howard-stern`	Howard Stern, abrasive radio and TV personality
`alt.fan.hyena`	Hyenas
`alt.fan.itchy-n-scratchy`	Bart Simpson's favorite TV cartoon
`alt.fan.jai-maharaj`	Jai Maharaj, Vedic astrologer
`alt.fan.james-bond`	James Bond
`alt.fan.jello-biafra`	Jello Biafra, Dead Kennedys' lead singer
`alt.fan.jen-coolest`	People who are named Jennifer
`alt.fan.jimmy-buffet`	Jimmy Buffet, singer
`alt.fan.jimmy-buffett`	Jimmy Buffett, country singer
`alt.fan.joel-furr`	Joel Furr

alt.fan.john-palmer	John Palmer
alt.fan.kali.astarte.inanna	Ancient goddesses Kali, Astarte, Inanna
alt.fan.karla-homolka	Karla Homolka, Canadian murderer
alt.fan.kent-montana	Kent Montana book series
alt.fan.kevin-darcy	Kevin Darcy
alt.fan.kroq	Los Angeles radio station KROQ, FM 106.7
alt.fan.laurie.anderson	Laurie Anderson, performance artist
alt.fan.lemurs	Lemur, monkey-like mammal from Madagascar
alt.fan.lemurs.cooked	Weird talk, lemur and non-lemur
alt.fan.letterman	David Letterman, TV personality
alt.fan.lion-king	Disney animated movie *The Lion King*
alt.fan.madonna	Madonna, singer etc
alt.fan.marcia-clark	Marcia Clark, L.A. prosecutor for O.J. Simpson case
alt.fan.mel-brooks	Mel Brooks, filmmaker
alt.fan.michael-bolton	Michael Bolton, singer
alt.fan.mike-jittlov	Mike Jittlov, animator
alt.fan.monty-python	Monty Python, humor group
alt.fan.mr-kfi	Mr. KFI, radio personality
alt.fan.mst3k	*Mystery Science Theater 3000*, TV show
alt.fan.naked-guy	Andrew Martinez, the Naked Guy at U.C. Berkeley
alt.fan.nathan.brazil	Nathan Brazil, hero of a Jack Chalker novel
alt.fan.noam-chomsky	Noam Chomsky, linguist and political dissident
alt.fan.oingo-boingo	Oingo Boingo, pop music group
alt.fan.oj-simpson	O.J. Simpson and his trial
alt.fan.ok-soda	OK Soda, ersatz cola drink marketed to Generation X
alt.fan.penn-n-teller	Magicians Penn (big one) and Teller (quiet one)
alt.fan.pern	Anne McCaffery's science fiction oeuvre
alt.fan.piers-anthony	Piers Anthony, science fiction author
alt.fan.pratchett	Terry Pratchett, science fiction humor writer
alt.fan.q	Qmnipotent Qne
alt.fan.ren-and-stimpy	*Ren and Stimpy*, TV show
alt.fan.robert-jordan	Robert Jordan, writer of fantasy sagas
alt.fan.ronald-reagan	Ronald Reagan, actor and ex-President of U.S.
alt.fan.rumpole	*Rumpole of the Bailey*, British TV show
alt.fan.run-dmc	Run-DMC, rap music group
alt.fan.rush-limbaugh	Rush Limbaugh, conservative talk show host
alt.fan.sam-raimi	Sam Raimi, film director and producer
alt.fan.serdar-argic	Armenia, Turkey, genocide
alt.fan.shostakovich	Shostakovitch, classical music composer
alt.fan.skinny	People who like skinniness
alt.fan.spinal-tap	Spinal Tap, fictitious movie pop music group
alt.fan.sting	Sting, singer/actor
alt.fan.super-big-gulp	Super Big Gulp beverage at American 7-11 stores
alt.fan.surak	Surak, *Star Trek* character
alt.fan.tank-girl	Tank girl
alt.fan.teen.idols	Male teen idols
alt.fan.teen.starlets	Female teen idols
alt.fan.tolkien	J.R.R. Tolkien, fantasy writer
alt.fan.tom-robbins	Tom Robbins, novelist
alt.fan.tom-servo	Tom Servo, *Mystery Science Theater 3000* character
alt.fan.tom_peterson	Tom Peterson from Portland, Oregon
alt.fan.tonya-harding.whack.whack.whack	Tonya Harding, infamous ice skater
alt.fan.u2	U2, Irish pop music group
alt.fan.vic-reeves	Vic Reeves, British entertainer
alt.fan.wal-greenslade	Wal Greenslade, the BBC Home Service
alt.fan.warlord	War Lord of the West Preservation Fan Club
alt.fan.wedge	Wedge, *Star Wars* character
alt.fan.wodehouse	P.G. Wodehouse (pronounced "Woodhouse"), humorist
alt.fan.woody-allen	Woody Allen, filmmaker, writer, comedian
alt.fandom.cons	Conventions, science fiction and others
alt.fandom.misc	General fan-oriented topics
alt.fantasy.conan	*Conan the Barbarian*, films and books
alt.fashion	Fashion industry
alt.fax	Fax hardware, software, and protocols
alt.feminazis	Anti-feminism
alt.feminism	Like soc.feminism, only different
alt.feminism.individualism	Feminism and individualism
alt.filepro	Filepro 4GL database
alt.filesystems.afs	Andrew file system from Carnegie Mellon University

alt.fishing	Fishing as a hobby and sport
alt.flame	Complaints, and complaints about complaints
alt.flame.landlord	Complaints about landlords
alt.flame.roommate	Stories about troublesome roommates
alt.flame.sean-ryan	Detractors of Sean Ryan
alt.flame.spelling	Complaints about spelling
alt.folklore.college	Collegiate humor
alt.folklore.computers	Stories about computers
alt.folklore.gemstones	Stories and myths about gems and minerals
alt.folklore.ghost-stories	Ghost stories
alt.folklore.herbs	Herbs and their uses
alt.folklore.info	Current urban legends and other folklore
alt.folklore.military	Military-oriented urban legends and factoids
alt.folklore.science	Folklore of science (not the science of folklore)
alt.folklore.suburban	Serious discussion of urban legends (Moderated)
alt.folklore.urban	Urban legends, à la Jan Harold Brunvand
alt.food	Food
alt.food.cocacola	Various types of Coca Cola
alt.food.coffee	Coffee
alt.food.fat-free	Fat-free food
alt.food.ice-cream	Ice cream
alt.food.mcdonalds	Food from McDonalds restaurants
alt.food.pancakes	Pancakes
alt.food.sugar-cereals	Sugary breakfast cereals
alt.food.sushi	Sushi (not raw fish, which is sashimi)
alt.food.waffle-house	Waffle House restaurants
alt.food.wine	Wine and general oeneophilic topics
alt.forgery	One place for all forgeries, crossposting encouraged
alt.fractal-design.painter	Creating fractals with Painter software
alt.fractals	Fractals, fractional dimensional pictures
alt.fractals.pictures	Pictures: fractals
alt.fraternity.sorority	Fraternity/sorority life
alt.freaks	Freaks, more figurative than literal
alt.freemasonry	Systems and institutions of Freemasons
alt.freenet	Freenets, free public Internet access
alt.fun.with.luc	Bizarre nonsense related to oddball Luc Theriault
alt.galactic-guide	Entries for actual Hitchhiker's Guide to the Galaxy
alt.gambling	Games of chance and betting
alt.games.air-warrior	Air Warrior game
alt.games.cosmic-wimpout	Cosmic Wimpout, dice game popular among nerds
alt.games.doom	Doom, popular PC computer game
alt.games.doom.announce	Announcements about Doom (Moderated)
alt.games.doom.newplayers	Helping people new to Doom game
alt.games.frp.dnd-util	Utility programs for automated Dungeons and Dragons
alt.games.frp.live-action	Live-action gaming
alt.games.frp.tekumel	Tekumel, role-playing game (Empire of the Petal Throne)
alt.games.gb	Galactic Bloodshed conquest game
alt.games.ibmpc.shadowcaster	Shadowcaster game
alt.games.lynx	Atari Lynx game
alt.games.mk	Mortal Kombat video game
alt.games.mornington.cresent	Fans of Mornington Cresent game
alt.games.mtrek	Multi-Trek, multi-user *Star Trek*-like game
alt.games.netrek.paradise	Paradise version of Netrek
alt.games.omega	Omega computer game
alt.games.sf2	Street Fighter 2 video game
alt.games.tiddlywinks	Game of Tiddlywinks
alt.games.torg	Gateway for TORG mailing list
alt.games.vga-planets	Tim Wisseman's VGA Planets
alt.games.video.classic	From early TV remote controls to Space Invaders, etc
alt.games.whitewolf	Whitewolf storytelling fantasy games
alt.games.xpilot	Xpilot, X Window game
alt.games.xtrek	*Star Trek* game for X Window
alt.gathering.rainbow	Annual Rainbow Gathering
alt.geek	Geeks (nerds who are dull)
alt.genealogy	Genealogy
alt.good.morning	Nice people saying "Good Morning" to one another
alt.good.news	Good news (really!)
alt.gopher	Gopher (menu-driven information)
alt.gorets	Imaginary and not so imaginary silliness

alt.gothic	Gothic movement, things mournful and dark
alt.gourmand	Recipes and cooking information (Moderated)
alt.grad-student.tenured	Grad students who never seem to graduate
alt.grad.skool.sux	Unpleasant aspects of graduate school
alt.graffiti	Graffiti
alt.graphics	Computer graphics
alt.graphics.pixutils	Pixmap utilities
alt.great-lakes	Great Lakes and adjacent places
alt.guitar	Guitar
alt.guitar.bass	Bass guitar
alt.guitar.tab	Music and lyrics (tablature) for guitar fans
alt.hackers	Projects currently under development (Moderated)
alt.hangover	Cures and experiences relating to hangovers
alt.happy.birthday.to.me	Newsgroup to read on your birthday
alt.health.ayurveda	Ayurvedic (East Indian) medicine
alt.health.cfids-action	Chronic Fatigue Syndrome action group (Moderated)
alt.hemp	Marijuana
alt.heraldry.sca	Heraldry in the Society for Creative Anachronism
alt.hi.are.you.cute	Things that are cute
alt.history.living	Hobby of living history
alt.history.what-if	Historical conjecture
alt.home.repair	Home repairs
alt.homosexual	Homosexuality
alt.hoovers	Vacuum cleaners, especially Hoovers
alt.horror	Horror genre
alt.horror.cthulhu	Mythos/role playing based on H.P. Lovecraft's Cthulhu
alt.horror.shub-internet	Fantasy relating to Shub (eternal spirit)
alt.horror.werewolves	Werewolves
alt.hotrod	High-speed automobiles (Moderated)
alt.housing.nontrad	Non-traditional housing concepts
alt.how.to.join.the.mafia	Joining the Mafia
alt.human-brain	Function of the human brain
alt.humor.best-of-usenet	Best of Usenet humor (Moderated)
alt.humor.best-of-usenet.d	Discussion of alt.humor.best-of-usenet
alt.humor.puns	Humorous word play
alt.hurricane.andrew	1992 Florida hurricane disaster
alt.hypertext	Hypertext
alt.hypnosis	Hypnosis
alt.illuminati	Conspirasy, political and financial intrigue
alt.image.medical	Medical imaging
alt.impeach.clinton	Impeaching President Clinton
alt.india.progressive	Progressive politics in India (Moderated)
alt.individualism	Philosophies where individual rights are paramount
alt.industrial	Industrial Computing Society
alt.infertility	Infertility
alt.info-science	Library science
alt.info-theory	Information theory
alt.internet.access.wanted	People looking for Internet access information
alt.internet.media-coverage	Coverage of the Internet by the media
alt.internet.services	Various Internet services
alt.internet.talk.haven	Talk about the Internet
alt.internet.talk.of.the.town	Hot topics about the Internet
alt.internet.talk.radio	Internet Talk Radio, Geek of the Week show
alt.irc	Internet Relay Chat
alt.irc.announce	Announcements about IRC (Internet Relay Chat) (Moderated)
alt.irc.hottub	IRC channel #hottub
alt.irc.ircii	IRC II client program
alt.irc.jeopardy	IRC channel #jeopardy
alt.irc.questions	Questions about IRC
alt.irc.recovery	Recovery from too much IRC
alt.irc.undernet	Undernet IRC servers
alt.japanese.text	Japanese articles and text
alt.journalism	Journalism
alt.journalism.criticism	Criticism of journalists and the media
alt.journalism.gonzo	Gonzo journalism (after Hunter Thompson)
alt.journalism.music	Music journalism
alt.kalbo	Shared reality of imaginary desert dwellers
alt.ketchup	Ketchup and related items
alt.kids-talk	Discussion among children

alt.kill.the.whales	Killing whales and why it is not so bad
alt.krunk	Silliness about a new obscenity
alt.lang.apl	APL programming language
alt.lang.asm	Various types of Assembly languages
alt.lang.awk	Unix language awk scripting language
alt.lang.basic	Basic programming language
alt.lang.ca-realizer	CA-Realizer, GUI programming environment
alt.lang.cfutures	Future of the C programming language
alt.lang.intercal	Intercal programming language
alt.lang.ml	ML and SML symbolic programming languages
alt.lang.teco	TECO editor language
alt.language.urdu.poetry	Poetry in the Indic Urdu language
alt.law-enforcement	Laws of all types, police, and jails
alt.lefthanders	People who are left-handed
alt.lemmings	Lemmings computer game
alt.letzebuerger	Luxembourgish, the traditional language of Luxemburg
alt.lies	Lies of all kinds
alt.life.afterlife	Fantasy talk about life after death
alt.life.internet	The Internet as an institution of human culture
alt.locksmithing	Locksmithing locks, keys, etc
alt.lucid-emacs.bug	Bugs and fixes: Lucid Emacs
alt.lucid-emacs.help	Question and answer forum for Lucid Emacs
alt.lycra	Clothes made of Lycra, Spandex, etc
alt.macedonia.is.greece	Debate about Macedonia and Greece
alt.mag.playboy	Playboy magazine
alt.magic	Stage magic
alt.magick	Supernatural arts
alt.magick.chaos	Magick: chaos
alt.magick.ethics	Magick: ethics
alt.magick.order	Magick: political hierarchy
alt.magick.sex	Magick: pursuing spirituality through sexuality
alt.magick.tyagi	Magick: as revealed by Mordred Nagasiva
alt.make.money.fast	Money-making schemes
alt.management.tech-support	Technical support in management
alt.managing.techsupport	Managing technical support
alt.manga	Non-Western comics
alt.manufacturing.misc	General manufacturing topics
alt.materials.simulation	Computer modeling of materials (Moderated)
alt.math.iams	Internet Amateur Mathematics Society (Moderated)
alt.mcdonalds	Food from McDonalds restaurants
alt.med.allergy	Allergies
alt.med.cfs	Chronic Fatigue Syndrome
alt.med.fibromyalgia	Fibromyalgia
alt.meditation	Meditation
alt.meditation.quanyin	Quan Yin method of meditation
alt.meditation.transcendental	Transcendental meditation
alt.memetics	Memetics, theory that some ideas propagate biologically
alt.messianic	Messianic traditions
alt.military.cadet	Military school cadets
alt.mindcontrol	Mind control (You will buy 10 copies of this book!)
alt.misanthropy	Hatred and distrust toward all
alt.misc	Anything and everything
alt.missing-kids	Locating missing children
alt.models	Model building, design, etc
alt.motd	Messages of the day
alt.motherjones	*Mother Jones* magazine
alt.motorcycles.harley	Harley-Davidson motorcycles
alt.motss.bisexua-l	Homosexuality (members of the same sex)
alt.movies.monster	Monsters in the movies
alt.msdos.programmer	Tips, questions, and answers for DOS programming
alt.mud	Multi-user dimension games
alt.mud.bsx	MUD systems on BSX VR
alt.mud.chupchups	A MUD game called Chupchups
alt.mud.german	For German-speaking MUDers
alt.mud.lp	Help setting up a MUD
alt.mud.tiny	Fans of small MUD sites
alt.music.a-cappella	Unaccompanied singing
alt.music.alternative	Alternative music
alt.music.alternative.female	Alternative music by female artists

alt.music.amy-grant	Amy Grant
alt.music.beastie-boys	Beastie Boys
alt.music.bela-fleck	Bela and the Flecktones
alt.music.big-band	Big Band
alt.music.billy-joel	Billy Joel
alt.music.blues-traveler	Traveling Blues shows
alt.music.brian-eno	Brian Eno
alt.music.canada	Canadian music
alt.music.chapel-hill	Chapel Hill
alt.music.complex-arrang	Complex arrangements
alt.music.danzig	Glenn Danzig
alt.music.deep-purple	Deep Purple
alt.music.dream-theater	Dream Theater
alt.music.ebm	Industrial/electronic body music/cyberculture "music"
alt.music.ecto	Ectophillic female vocalists
alt.music.elo	Electric Light Orchestra
alt.music.enya	Gaelic set to spacey music
alt.music.fates-warning	Fates Warning
alt.music.filk	SciFi/fantasy-related folk music
alt.music.fleetwood-mac	Fleetwood Mac
alt.music.hardcore	Hard core music fans
alt.music.independent	Soloists without major label contracts
alt.music.james-taylor	James Taylor
alt.music.jethro-tull	Jethro Tull
alt.music.jewish	Jewish music
alt.music.jimi.hendrix	Jimi Hendrix
alt.music.kylie-minogue	Kylie Minogue
alt.music.led-zeppelin	Led Zeppelin
alt.music.marillion	Marillion, pop music group
alt.music.misc	General music topics
alt.music.monkees	Monkees
alt.music.moody-blues	Moody Blues
alt.music.nin	Nine Inch Nails, one-person gothic music group
alt.music.nirvana	Nirvana
alt.music.pat-mccurdy	Pat McCurdy
alt.music.paul-simon	Paul Simon
alt.music.pearl-jam	Pearl Jam
alt.music.peter-gabriel	Peter Gabriel
alt.music.pink-floyd	Pink Floyd
alt.music.prince	Prince, pop singer
alt.music.producer	Record production
alt.music.progressive	Music such as Yes, Marillion, Asia, King Crimson
alt.music.queen	Queen, pop music group
alt.music.roger-waters	Roger Waters
alt.music.rush	Rush, pop music group
alt.music.ska	Ska (skank) music, bands, and so on
alt.music.smash-pumpkins	Smashing Pumpkins
alt.music.sonic-youth	Sonic Youth
alt.music.sophie-hawkins	Sophie B. Hawkins
alt.music.swedish-pop	Swedish pop music, like ABBA
alt.music.synthpop	Synthesized pop music
alt.music.techno	Techno music
alt.music.the-doors	Doors
alt.music.the.police	Police
alt.music.tlc	TLC, hip-hop
alt.music.tmbg	They Might Be Giants, pop music group
alt.music.todd-rundgren	Todd Rundgren
alt.music.u2	U2, Irish pop music group
alt.music.ween	Ween
alt.music.weird-al	Weird Al Yankovic
alt.music.world	Music from around the world
alt.music.yes	Yes
alt.my.head.hurts	Thoughts that will make your head hurt
alt.mythology	Mythology
alt.mythology.mythic-animals	Creatures of myth, fantasy, imagination
alt.national.enquirer	*National Enquirer* newspaper
alt.native	Indigenous peoples of the world
alt.necktie	Neckties
alt.net.personalities	Personality and the Net

alt.netgames.bolo	Game of bolo
alt.newbie	Help for people new to the Internet
alt.newbies	Help for people new to the Internet
alt.news-media	News media
alt.news.macedonia	News and current affairs in Macedonia
alt.non.sequitur	Non sequiturs and bizarre nonsense
alt.npractitioners	Nurse practitioners
alt.nuke.the.USA	Negative commentary about the United States
alt.obituaries	Obituaries and talk about dead people
alt.office.management	Managing offices
alt.online-service	Large commercial online services
alt.online-service.america-online	America Online
alt.online-service.compuserve	Compuserve
alt.online-service.delphi	Delphi
alt.online-service.freenet	Freenets (free public Internet access)
alt.online-service.genie	Genie
alt.online-service.portal	Portal
alt.online-service.prodigy	Prodigy
alt.oobe	Out-of-body experiences
alt.org.earth-first	Earth First society
alt.org.pugwash	Technological issues from a social stance
alt.org.toastmasters	Toastmasters International
alt.os.bsdi	BSD (Berkeley) Unix as implemented by BSDI
alt.os.multics	Multics operating system
alt.os.nachos	Nachos, an operating system used for teaching
alt.out-of-body	Out-of-body experiences
alt.overlords	Office of the Omnipotent Overlords of the Omniverse
alt.pagan	Paganism
alt.pantyhose	Pantyhose and related sexual topics
alt.parallel.universes	Parallel universes
alt.paranet.abduct	Stories of abductions by aliens
alt.paranet.metaphysics	Philosophical ontology and cosmology
alt.paranet.paranormal	Paranormal experiences
alt.paranet.psi	Psi phenomena
alt.paranet.science	Theories behind paranormal events
alt.paranet.skeptic	Skeptics explain and refute paranormal stories
alt.paranet.ufo	UFO sightings
alt.paranormal	Phenomena which are not scientifically explicable
alt.paranormal.channeling	Spiritual mediums and channeling
alt.parents-teens	Parent-teenager relationships
alt.party	Parties, celebration, and general debauchery
alt.pave.the.earth	Paving the Earth
alt.pcnews	PCNews software
alt.peace-corps	Peace Corps
alt.peeves	Pet peeves and related topics
alt.periphs.pcmcia	Credit card-sized plug-in peripherals for PCs
alt.personals	Personal ads: general
alt.personals.ads	Personal ads: general
alt.personals.bi	Personal ads: bisexuals
alt.personals.big-folks	Personal ads: big people, not necessarily fat
alt.personals.bondage	Personals ads: bondage
alt.personals.fat	Personal ads: fat people
alt.personals.fetish	Personal ads: fetishes
alt.personals.misc	Personal ads: general
alt.personals.poly	Personal ads: multiple people
alt.personals.spanking	Personal ads: spanking
alt.personals.spanking.punishment	Personal ads: spanking and punishment
alt.pets.chia	Chia pets, small plants in animal shape
alt.pets.rabbits	Pets: rabbits
alt.philosophy.jarf	Jarf philosophy
alt.philosophy.objectivism	Ayn Rand-inspired philosophy of Objectivism
alt.philosophy.zen	Zen philosophy
alt.pinecone	Pinecones
alt.pixar.typestry	Pixar Typestry software
alt.planning.urban	Urban planning
alt.politics.british	Politics: Great Britain
alt.politics.bush	George Bush, former U.S. President
alt.politics.clinton	Bill Clinton, President of the U.S.
alt.politics.correct	Political correctness

alt.politics.datahighway	Politics of global networks
alt.politics.democrats	Democrats
alt.politics.democrats.clinton	Democrats and Bill Clinton
alt.politics.democrats.d	Discussion about Democrats
alt.politics.democrats.governors	Democrats and governors
alt.politics.democrats.house	House of Representatives
alt.politics.democrats.senate	Senate
alt.politics.ec	European Community
alt.politics.economics	Economics
alt.politics.elections	Elections
alt.politics.equality	Political equality
alt.politics.europe.misc	General topics in European politics
alt.politics.greens	Green party politics and activities worldwide
alt.politics.homosexuality	Politics and homosexuality
alt.politics.india.communist	Communism in India
alt.politics.india.progressive	Progressive Indian politics
alt.politics.italy	Politics: Italy
alt.politics.libertarian	Libertarian ideology
alt.politics.media	Politics and the communications media
alt.politics.org.batf	U.S. Bureau of Alcohol, Tobacco, and Firearms
alt.politics.org.cia	U.S. Central Intelligence Agency
alt.politics.org.covert	Covert organizations around the world
alt.politics.org.fbi	U.S. Federal Bureau of Investigation
alt.politics.org.misc	General topics relating to political organizations
alt.politics.org.nsa	U.S. National Security Agency
alt.politics.org.un	Politics at the United Nations
alt.politics.perot	Ross Perot and related issues
alt.politics.radical-left	Radical left
alt.politics.reform	Political reform
alt.politics.sex	Politics and sex
alt.politics.socialism.trotsky	Trotsky and socialism
alt.politics.usa.constitution	U.S. Constitutional politics
alt.politics.usa.misc	General topics relating to U.S. politics
alt.politics.usa.republican	U.S. Republican party
alt.politics.vietnamese	Politics and Vietnam
alt.polyamory	Multiple-love relationships
alt.postmodern	Postmodernism, semiotics, deconstruction, etc
alt.president.clinton	U.S. President Bill Clinton
alt.prisons	Prisons and prison life
alt.privacy	Privacy issues in cyberspace
alt.privacy.anon-server	Anonymous Usenet postings
alt.privacy.clipper	Clipper encoding chip
alt.prophecies.nostradamus	Nostradamus, predictions and score card
alt.prose	Original writings, fiction and otherwise
alt.prose.d	Discussion of alt.prose.d articles
alt.psychoactives	Psychoactive drugs, legal and illegal
alt.psychology.help	Psychological help
alt.psychology.personality	Personality taxonomy, such as Myers-Briggs
alt.psychotic.roommates	Psychotic roommates
alt.pub-ban.homolka	Publication ban on Karla Homolka trial
alt.pub.cloven-shield	Role-playing stories
alt.pub.coffeehouse.amethyst	Coffeehouse atmosphere in which to chat
alt.pub.dragons-inn	A computer fantasy environment
alt.pub.havens-rest	Role-playing stories
alt.pud	Vile, contemptuous, and anti-social topics
alt.pulp	Pulp-genre stories and characters
alt.punk	Punk rock
alt.punk.straight-edge	Straight-edge punk music
alt.ql.creative	*Quantum Leap* TV show and creative thought
alt.quotations	Famous (and not so famous) quotes
alt.radio.digital	Digital radio
alt.radio.networks.npr	U.S. National Public Radio
alt.radio.pirate	Pirate radio stations
alt.radio.scanner	Scanning radio receivers
alt.radio.uk	Radio in the United Kingdom
alt.rap	Rap music
alt.rap-gdead	Grateful Dead and rap (music)
alt.rave	Techno-culture music, dancing, drugs, dancing
alt.rec.camping	Camping

USENET NEWSGROUPS

alt.recovery	Recovery programs (AA, ACA, GA, etc)
alt.recovery.addiction.sexual	Recovering sex addicts
alt.recovery.catholicism	Recovering from Catholicism
alt.recovery.codependency	Codependency
alt.recovery.religion	Recovering from religion
alt.religion.all-worlds	Church of All Worlds from Heinlein's book
alt.religion.amiga	Amiga as a way of life
alt.religion.buddhism.tibetan	Teachings of Buddha as studied in Tibet
alt.religion.christian	Christianity as a way of life
alt.religion.computers	Computing as a Way of Life
alt.religion.eckankar	Eckankar, as founded by Sri Paul Twitchell in 1965
alt.religion.emacs	Emacs as a Way of Life
alt.religion.gnostic	History and philosophies of the Gnostic sects
alt.religion.islam	Islamic faith
alt.religion.kibology	Silliness based on the mythical Kibo
alt.religion.monica	Bizarre nonsense involving Net-Venus Monica
alt.religion.mormon	Mormon (Latter Day Saints) religion
alt.religion.sabaean	Sabaean religious order
alt.religion.santaism	Christmas and Santa Claus
alt.religion.scientology	Scientology and Dianetics
alt.religion.sexuality	Sexuality in religion
alt.religion.shamanism	Shamanism
alt.religion.zoroastrianism	Zoroastrianism
alt.retromod	Retroactive moderation of newsgroups
alt.revenge	Revenge and how to do it
alt.revisionism	Changing interpretations of history
alt.revolution.counter	Counter-revolutionary issues
alt.rhode_island	U.S. state of Rhode Island
alt.rmgroup	Bizarre nonsense for rmgroup/newgroup people
alt.rock-n-roll	General rock and roll
alt.rock-n-roll.acdc	AC/DC, music group
alt.rock-n-roll.aerosmith	Aerosmith
alt.rock-n-roll.classic	Classic rock music
alt.rock-n-roll.hard	Hard rock
alt.rock-n-roll.metal	General metal rock music
alt.rock-n-roll.metal.death	Death metal
alt.rock-n-roll.metal.gnr	Heavy metal rock
alt.rock-n-roll.metal.heavy	More heavy metal rock music
alt.rock-n-roll.metal.ironmaiden	Iron Maiden, music group
alt.rock-n-roll.metal.metallica	Metallica, music group
alt.rock-n-roll.metal.progressive	Progressive metal rock
alt.rock-n-roll.oldies	Rock and roll music from 1950-1970
alt.rock-n-roll.stones	Rolling Stones, music group
alt.rock-n-roll.symphonic	Rock and classical music
alt.rodney-king	L.A. riots and the aftermath
alt.romance	Romantic side of love
alt.romance.chat	Romantic talk
alt.romance.unhappy	Unhappy romances
alt.rush-limbaugh	Rush Limbaugh, conservative talk show host
alt.rv	Recreational vehicles
alt.satanism	Talk about Satan
alt.satannet.barney	Barney the Dinosaur as a Satanic figure
alt.satellite.tv.europe	European satellite TV
alt.satellite.tv.forsale	Satellite TV equipment, wanted and for sale
alt.save.the.earth	Environmentalist causes
alt.sb.programmer	Programming the Sound Blaster card for PCs
alt.school.homework-help	Help with homework
alt.sci.astro.aips	Astronomical Image Processing System
alt.sci.astro.figaro	Figaro data-reduction package
alt.sci.astro.fits	Programming with FITS
alt.sci.physics.acoustics	Acoustics
alt.sci.physics.new-theories	New scientific theories not in journals
alt.sci.physics.plutonium	Strange ideas about science and plutonium
alt.sci.physics.spam	Scientific aspects of Spam
alt.sci.planetary	Planetary science
alt.sci.sociology	Sociology
alt.sci.tech.indonesian	Technology discussed in Indonesian
alt.scientology.scam.scam.scam	Scam aspects of Scientology
alt.scooter	Motor scooters

alt.sect.ahmadiyya	Ahmadiyyat sect of Islam
alt.security	Building and autombile security systems
alt.security.index	Good references to {alt, misc}.security
alt.security.keydist	Exchange of keys for public key encryption systems
alt.security.pgp	Pretty Good Privacy encryption package
alt.security.ripem	A secure electronic mail system
alt.sega.genesis	Genesis video game
alt.self-improve	Self-improvement
alt.sewing	Sewing
alt.sex	General discussion about sex
alt.sex.bestiality	Sex: bestiality
alt.sex.bestiality.barney	Crude comments about Barney the Dinosaur
alt.sex.bondage	Sex: bondage
alt.sex.breast	Sex: female breasts
alt.sex.cthulhu	Sex: sex and Cthulhu
alt.sex.enemas	Sex: enemas
alt.sex.erotica.marketplace	Sex: marketing sex
alt.sex.exhibitionism	Sex: exhibitionism and people who make noise
alt.sex.fat	Sex: fat people
alt.sex.femdom	Sex: female dominant relationships
alt.sex.fetish.amputee	Sex: amputee fetishes
alt.sex.fetish.diapers	Sex: diaper fetishes
alt.sex.fetish.fa	Sex: fat people
alt.sex.fetish.fashion	Sex: rubber, leather, chains, other fetish clothing
alt.sex.fetish.feet	Sex: foot fetishes
alt.sex.fetish.hair	Sex: hair fetishes
alt.sex.fetish.orientals	Sex: oriental people
alt.sex.fetish.startrek	Sex: *Star Trek* fetishes
alt.sex.fetish.tickling	Sex: erotic tickling
alt.sex.fetish.watersports	Sex: enemas and related fetishes
alt.sex.homosexual	Sex: homosexual relations
alt.sex.intergen	Sex: Inter-generational relationships
alt.sex.magazines	Sex: magazines
alt.sex.masturbation	Sex: masturbation
alt.sex.motss	Sex: homosexuality (members of the same sex)
alt.sex.movies	Sex: movies
alt.sex.necrophilia	Sex: necrophilia
alt.sex.pictures	Pictures: erotic
alt.sex.pictures.d	Discussion about erotic pictures
alt.sex.pictures.female	Pictures: erotic women
alt.sex.pictures.male	Pictures: erotic men
alt.sex.services	Sex: sexual services
alt.sex.sounds	Erotic sounds
alt.sex.spanking	Sex: spanking
alt.sex.stories	Sex: stories (no discussion)
alt.sex.stories.d	Discussion about sexual stories
alt.sex.strip-clubs	Sex: strip clubs and erotic dancers
alt.sex.trans	Sex: transsexuals and transvestites
alt.sex.voyeurism	Sex: voyeurism
alt.sex.wanted	Requests for erotica, literary or in the flesh
alt.sex.watersports	Sex: enemas and related fetishes
alt.sex.wizards	Questions for sex experts
alt.sex.woody-allen	Sex: Woody Allen's sex life
alt.sexual.abuse.recovery	Helping others deal with traumatic experiences
alt.sexual.abuse.recovery.d	Recovery from sexual abuse
alt.sexy.bald.captains	Bald captains who are sexy
alt.shared-reality.startrek.klingon	Fantasy using Klingon personas
alt.shenanigans	Practical jokes, pranks, etc
alt.showbiz.gossip	Gossip about the entertainment industry
alt.shrinky.dinks	Shrinky Dink, oven-made synthetic ornaments
alt.shut.the.hell.up.geek	Perfecting the art of telling people to shut up
alt.sigma2.height	Very short or tall people (> 2 standard deviations)
alt.silly-group.beable	Bizarre nonsense
alt.silly-group.lampreys	Silly talk about lampreys
alt.silly.group.names.d	Silliness
alt.skate	Skating
alt.skate-board	Skateboarding

USENET NEWSGROUPS

alt.skinheads	Skinhead culture/anti-culture
alt.skopjea.is.not.macedonia	Debate about Macedonia and Greece
alt.skunks	Skunks
alt.sl9	Shoemaker-Levy comet and Jupiter
alt.slack	Church of the Subgenius
alt.slick.willy.tax.tax.tax	Taxes, U.S. President Bill Clinton, and whining
alt.smokers	Smoking as a pastime
alt.smokers.cigars	Cigar smokers
alt.smokers.pipes	Pipe smokers
alt.snail-mail	Regular postal system mail
alt.snowmobiles	Snowmobiles
alt.soc.ethics	Ethics
alt.society.anarchy	Anarchy
alt.society.ati	*Activist Times* digest (Moderated)
alt.society.civil-disob	Civil disobedience
alt.society.civil-liberties	Individual rights
alt.society.civil-liberty	Civil libertarians
alt.society.conservatism	Social, cultural, and political conservatism
alt.society.foia	U.S. Freedom of Information Act
alt.society.futures	Future of society
alt.society.generation-x	Generation X, those born 1960 to early-1970s
alt.society.neutopia	Gaia and the ultimate society
alt.society.paradigms	Social and cultural patterns
alt.society.resistance	Political talk: resistance
alt.society.revolution	Political talk: revolution
alt.society.sovereign	Political talk: sovereignty
alt.society.underwear	Society and underwear
alt.soft-sys.corel.draw	Corel Draw graphics
alt.soft-sys.corel.misc	General topics about Corel software
alt.soft-sys.tooltalk	ToolTalk
alt.soulmates	Soulmates and the writing of Richard Bach
alt.sources	Free computer programs, unmoderated, caveat emptor
alt.sources.amiga	Technically oriented Amiga PC programs
alt.sources.d	Discussion about programs that have been posted
alt.sources.index	Good references to free programs
alt.sources.mac	Source code for Macintosh computers
alt.sources.patches	Corrections to programs, from non-bugs groups
alt.sources.wanted	Requests for programs
alt.spam	Cooking with Spam, a type of processed meat
alt.sport.bowling	Bowling
alt.sport.bungee	Bungee cord jumping
alt.sport.darts	Darts
alt.sport.falconry	Training falcons
alt.sport.foosball	Table soccer
alt.sport.jet-ski	Jet skis and other personal watercraft
alt.sport.lasertag	Laser tag
alt.sport.officiating	Officiating athletic contests
alt.sport.paintball	Paintball combat game
alt.sport.photon	Photon laser tag game
alt.sport.pool	Pool and billiards
alt.sport.racquetball	Racquetball
alt.sport.squash	Squash
alt.sports.baseball.atlanta-braves	Baseball: Atlanta Braves
alt.sports.baseball.balt-orioles	Baseball: Baltimore Orioles
alt.sports.baseball.bos-redsox	Baseball: Boston Red Sox
alt.sports.baseball.calif-angels	Baseball: California Angels
alt.sports.baseball.chi-whitesox	Baseball: Chicago White Sox
alt.sports.baseball.chicago-cubs	Baseball: Chicago Cubs
alt.sports.baseball.cinci-reds	Baseball: Cincinnati Reds
alt.sports.baseball.cleve-indians	Baseball: Cleveland Indians
alt.sports.baseball.col-rockies	Baseball: Colorado Rockies
alt.sports.baseball.detroit-tigers	Baseball: Detroit Tigers
alt.sports.baseball.fla-marlins	Baseball: Florida Marlins
alt.sports.baseball.houston-astros	Baseball: Houston Astros
alt.sports.baseball.kc-royals	Baseball: Kansas City Royals
alt.sports.baseball.la-dodgers	Baseball: Los Angeles Dodgers
alt.sports.baseball.minor-leagues	Baseball: Minor league
alt.sports.baseball.mke-brewers	Baseball: Milwaukee Brewers
alt.sports.baseball.mn-twins	Baseball: Minnesota Twins

alt.sports.baseball.montreal-expos	Baseball: Montreal Expos
alt.sports.baseball.ny-mets	Baseball: New York Mets
alt.sports.baseball.ny-yankees	Baseball: New York Yankees
alt.sports.baseball.oakland-as	Baseball: Oakland Athletics
alt.sports.baseball.phila-phillies	Baseball: Philadelphia Phillies
alt.sports.baseball.pitt-pirates	Baseball: Pittsburgh Pirates
alt.sports.baseball.sd-padres	Baseball: San Diego Padres
alt.sports.baseball.sea-mariners	Baseball: Seattle Mariners
alt.sports.baseball.sf-giants	Baseball: San Francisco Giants
alt.sports.baseball.stl-cardinals	Baseball: St. Louis Cardinals
alt.sports.baseball.texas-rangers	Baseball: Texas Rangers
alt.sports.baseball.tor-bluejays	Baseball: Toronto Blue Jays
alt.sports.basketball.nba.atlanta-hawks	Basketball: Atlanta Hawks
alt.sports.basketball.nba.char-hornets	Basketball: Charlotte Hornets
alt.sports.basketball.nba.chicago-bulls	Basketball: Chicago Bulls
alt.sports.basketball.nba.hou-rockets	Basketball: Houston Rockets
alt.sports.basketball.nba.la-lakers	Basketball: Los Angeles Lakers
alt.sports.basketball.nba.miami-heat	Basketball: Miami Heat
alt.sports.basketball.nba.mn-wolves	Basketball: Minnesota Timberwolves
alt.sports.basketball.nba.nj-nets	Basketball: New Jersey Nets
alt.sports.basketball.nba.orlando-magic	Basketball: Orlando Magic
alt.sports.basketball.nba.phx-suns	Basketball: Phoenix Suns
alt.sports.basketball.nba.seattle-sonics	Basketball: Seattle Sonics
alt.sports.basketball.nba.utah-jazz	Basketball: Utah Jazz
alt.sports.basketball.nba.wash-bullets	Basketball: Washington Bullets
alt.sports.basketball.pro.ny-knicks	Basketball: New York Knicks
alt.sports.college.ivy-league	Ivy League athletics
alt.sports.darts	Darts
alt.sports.football.arena	Arena football (U.S.-style, not soccer)
alt.sports.football.mn-vikings	Football: Minnesota Vikings
alt.sports.football.pro.atl-falcons	Football: Atlanta Falcons
alt.sports.football.pro.buffalo-bills	Football: Buffalo Bills
alt.sports.football.pro.car-panthers	Football: Carolina Panthers
alt.sports.football.pro.cleve-browns	Football: Cleveland Browns
alt.sports.football.pro.dallas-cowboys	Football: Dallas Cowboys
alt.sports.football.pro.denver-broncos	Football: Denver Broncos
alt.sports.football.pro.detroit-lions	Football: Detroit Lions
alt.sports.football.pro.gb-packers	Football: Green Bay Packers
alt.sports.football.pro.jville-jaguars	Football: Jacksonville Jaguars
alt.sports.football.pro.kc-chiefs	Football: Kansas City Chiefs
alt.sports.football.pro.la-raiders	Football: Los Angeles Raiders
alt.sports.football.pro.miami-dolphins	Football: Miami Dolphins
alt.sports.football.pro.ne-patriots	Football: New England Patriots
alt.sports.football.pro.no-saints	Football: New Orleans Saints
alt.sports.football.pro.ny-giants	Football: New York Giants
alt.sports.football.pro.ny-jets	Football: New York Jets
alt.sports.football.pro.phila-eagles	Football: Philadelphia Eagles
alt.sports.football.pro.phoe-cardinals	Football: Phoenix Cardinals
alt.sports.football.pro.pitt-steelers	Football: Pittsburgh Steelers
alt.sports.football.pro.sd-chargers	Football: San Diego Chargers
alt.sports.football.pro.sea-seahawks	Football: Seattle Seahawks
alt.sports.football.pro.sf-49ers	Football: San Francisco 49ers
alt.sports.football.pro.tampabay-bucs	Football: Tampa Bay Buckaneers
alt.sports.football.pro.wash-redskins	Football: Washington Redskins
alt.sports.hockey.echl	Hockey: East Coast Hockey League
alt.sports.hockey.ihl	Hockey: International Hockey League
alt.sports.hockey.nhl.boston-bruins	Hockey: Boston Bruins
alt.sports.hockey.nhl.buffalo-sabres	Hockey: Buffalo Sabres
alt.sports.hockey.nhl.chi-blackhawks	Hockey: Chicago Blackhawks
alt.sports.hockey.nhl.dallas-stars	Hockey: Dallas Stars
alt.sports.hockey.nhl.hford-whalers	Hockey: Hartford Whalers
alt.sports.hockey.nhl.la-kings	Hockey: Los Angeles Kings
alt.sports.hockey.nhl.mtl-canadiens	Hockey: Montreal Canadiens
alt.sports.hockey.nhl.nj-devils	Hockey: New Jersey Devils
alt.sports.hockey.nhl.ny-islanders	Hockey: New York Islanders
alt.sports.hockey.nhl.ny-rangers	Hockey: New York Rangers
alt.sports.hockey.nhl.pitt-penguins	Hockey: Pittsburgh Penguins
alt.sports.hockey.nhl.que-nordiques	Hockey: Quebec Nordiques
alt.sports.hockey.nhl.sj-sharks	Hockey: San Jose Sharks

USENET NEWSGROUPS

`alt.sports.hockey.nhl.tor-mapleleafs`	Hockey: Toronto Maple Leafs
`alt.sports.hockey.nhl.vanc-canucks`	Hockey: Vancouver Canucks
`alt.sports.hockey.nhl.wash-capitals`	Hockey: Washington Capitals
`alt.sports.hockey.nhl.winnipeg-jets`	Hockey: Winnipeg Jets
`alt.sports.hockey.rhi`	Hockey: Roller Hockey International
`alt.sports.oj-simpson`	O.J. Simpson
`alt.stagecraft`	Technical aspects of the theatre
`alt.starfleet.rpg`	Starfleet role-playing games
`alt.startrek.creative`	Stories and parodies related to *Star Trek*
`alt.startrek.klingon`	Klingons and their language (from *Star Trek*)
`alt.stop.spamming`	Prevention of Net abuse
`alt.stupidity`	Talk about stupid newsgroups
`alt.suburbs`	Suburbs
`alt.suicide.holiday`	Why suicides increase at holidays
`alt.suit.att-bsdi`	The AT&T vs. BSDI lawsuit
`alt.super.nes`	Super Nintendo video game
`alt.supermodels`	Famous and beautiful models
`alt.supermodels.cindy-crawford`	Cindy Crawford, supermodel
`alt.support`	General support group
`alt.support.abuse-partners`	Support group: partners of people who were abused
`alt.support.anxiety-panic`	Support group: panic attacks
`alt.support.arthritis`	Support group: arthritis
`alt.support.asthma`	Support group: asthma
`alt.support.attn-deficit`	Support group: Attention Deficit Disorder
`alt.support.big-folks`	Support group: large people
`alt.support.cancer`	Support group: cancer patients
`alt.support.cerebral-palsy`	Support group: cerebral palsy
`alt.support.crohns-colitis`	Support group: Crohn's disease and colitis
`alt.support.depression`	Support group: depression and mood disorders
`alt.support.diet`	Support group: dieters
`alt.support.divorce`	Support group: divorce
`alt.support.eating-disord`	Support group: eating disorders
`alt.support.epilepsy`	Support group: epilepsy
`alt.support.jock-strap`	Jockstraps
`alt.support.loneliness`	Support group: loneliness
`alt.support.mult-sclerosis`	Support group: multiple sclerosis
`alt.support.non-smokers`	Support group: non-smokers
`alt.support.obesity`	Support group: obesity (Moderated)
`alt.support.shyness`	Support group: shyness
`alt.support.spina-bifida`	Support group: spina bifida
`alt.support.step-parents`	Support group: stepparents
`alt.support.stop-smoking`	Support group: stop smoking
`alt.support.stuttering`	Support group: stuttering
`alt.support.tall`	Support group: tall people
`alt.support.tinnitus`	Support group: tinnitus
`alt.surfing`	Surfing
`alt.surrealism`	Surrealism ideology, transcending reality
`alt.sustainable.agriculture`	Ecologically sound agriculture
`alt.swedish.chef.bork.bork.bork`	Talking with a Swedish accent like the Muppet
`alt.syntax.tactical`	Planning to disrupt other newsgroups
`alt.sys.amiga.demos`	Demo programs for Amiga computers
`alt.sys.amiga.uucp`	UUCP for the Amiga
`alt.sys.amiga.uucp.patches`	Corrections for Amiga UUCP software
`alt.sys.intergraph`	Intergraph computers
`alt.sys.pc-clone.gateway2000`	Gateway 2000 personal computers
`alt.sys.pc-clone.zeos`	Zeos computer systems
`alt.sys.pdp11`	PDP-11 computers
`alt.sys.pdp8`	DEC PDP-8 computers
`alt.sys.perq`	Antique computers
`alt.sys.sun`	Sun computers
`alt.taiwan.republic`	Taiwan
`alt.tarot`	Divination using tarot cards
`alt.tasteless`	Talk about tasteless and disgusting topics
`alt.tasteless.jokes`	Tasteless jokes (offensive to everybody)
`alt.tasteless.penis`	Tasteless comments about male genitalia
`alt.tasteless.pictures`	Pictures: tasteless
`alt.technology.misc`	General technology topics
`alt.technology.mkt-failure`	Technology marketing failures
`alt.technology.obsolete`	Obsolete technology

alt.test	Place to send test articles
alt.test.my.new.group	Bizarre nonsense, mostly test articles
alt.text.dwb	AT&T Documenter's WorkBench
alt.thinking.hurts	Thinking and how it is painful
alt.thrash	Thrash music (an acquired taste)
alt.timewasters	Wasting time
alt.tla	Palindromic fun, Three-Letter-Acronyms
alt.toolkits.xview	X windows XView toolkit
alt.toon-pics	Pictures: cartoons
alt.toys.hi-tech	Toys: High-tech
alt.toys.lego	Toys: Lego
alt.toys.transformers	Toys: transformers
alt.traffic.atlanta	Traffic in Atlanta, Georgia
alt.transgendered	Changing one's sex
alt.travel.road-trip	Traveling by car
alt.true-crime	Famous crimes
alt.tv.animaniacs	*Animaniacs*, TV show
alt.tv.antagonists	*Antagonists*, TV show
alt.tv.babylon-5	*Babylon 5*, TV show
alt.tv.bakersfield-pd	*Bakersfield PD*, TV show
alt.tv.barney	*Barney the Dinosaur*, TV show
alt.tv.beakmans-world	*Beakman's World*, TV show
alt.tv.beavis-n-butthead	*Beavis and Butthead*, MTV cartoon
alt.tv.bh90210	*Beverly Hills 90210*, TV show
alt.tv.brady-bunch	*Brady Bunch*, TV show
alt.tv.brisco-county	*Brisco County*, TV show
alt.tv.comedy-central	Comedy Central, cable TV channel
alt.tv.commercials	Commercials on television
alt.tv.dinosaur.barney.die.die.die	Negative thoughts about Barney the Dinosaur
alt.tv.dinosaurs	Dinosaurs and television
alt.tv.dinosaurs.barney.die.die.die	Hating the *Barney* TV show
alt.tv.duckman	*Duckman*, TV show
alt.tv.eek-the-cat	Eek the Cat, cartoon character
alt.tv.game-shows	TV game shows
alt.tv.hbo	Home Box Office cable movie channel
alt.tv.hermans-head	*Herman's Head*, TV show
alt.tv.highlander	*Highlander*, TV show
alt.tv.infomercials	Infomercials
alt.tv.kids-in-hall	*Kids in the Hall*, TV show
alt.tv.kungfu	*Kung Fu*, TV show
alt.tv.la-law	*L.A. Law*, TV show
alt.tv.liquid-tv	BBC/MTV *Liquid TV* series (weird)
alt.tv.lois-n-clark	*Lois and Clark*, TV show
alt.tv.mad-about-you	*Mad About You*, TV show
alt.tv.mash	*MASH*, TV show
alt.tv.max-headroom	*Max Headroom*, TV show
alt.tv.melrose-place	*Melrose Place*, TV show
alt.tv.mst3k	*Mystery Science Theater 3000*, TV show
alt.tv.muppets	Muppets
alt.tv.mwc	*Married with Children*, TV show
alt.tv.nickelodeon	Nickelodeon, cable TV channel
alt.tv.northern-exp	*Northern Exposure*, TV show
alt.tv.nypd-blue	*NYPD Blue*, TV show
alt.tv.prisoner	*Prisoner*, TV show
alt.tv.real-world	*Real World*, TV show
alt.tv.red-dwarf	*Red Dwarf* (British SciFi/comedy), TV show
alt.tv.ren-n-stimpy	*Ren and Stimpy*, TV show
alt.tv.robocop	*Robocop*, TV show
alt.tv.robotech	*Robotech*, TV show
alt.tv.rockford-files	*Rockford Files*, TV show
alt.tv.roseanne	*Roseanne*, TV show
alt.tv.saved-bell	*Saved by the Bell*, TV Show
alt.tv.seinfeld	*Seinfeld*, TV show
alt.tv.simpsons	*The Simpsons*, TV show
alt.tv.simpsons.itchy-scratchy	*Itchy and Scratchy*, cartoon on *The Simpsons*
alt.tv.snl	*Saturday Night Live*, TV show
alt.tv.talkshows.daytime	Daytime talk shows
alt.tv.talkshows.late	Late night U.S. talk shows
alt.tv.taz-mania	*Tazmania*, cartoon

`alt.tv.time-traxx`	*Time Traxx*, TV show
`alt.tv.tiny-toon`	*Tiny Toons*, TV Show
`alt.tv.tiny-toon.fandom`	*Tiny Toons*, cartoon
`alt.tv.tv-nation`	*TV Nation*, TV show
`alt.tv.twin-peaks`	*Twin Peaks*, TV show
`alt.tv.x-files`	*X-Files*, TV show
`alt.tv.x-files.creative`	Creative writing for *X-Files*
`alt.tv.xuxa`	Xuxa, Brazilian starlet
`alt.unix.wizards.free`	Questions for Unix wizards
`alt.usage.english`	English grammar, word usages, and related topics
`alt.usage.german`	German language usage
`alt.usenet.addict`	Reading Usenet obsessively
`alt.usenet.kooks`	Bizarre Usenet personalities
`alt.usenet.offline-reader`	Reading the news off-line
`alt.usenet.recovery`	Support group for Usenet junkies
`alt.utensils.spork`	Sporks (combination spoon/fork) eating utensils
`alt.uu.announce`	Announcements of Usenet University (UU)
`alt.uu.comp.misc`	Computer department of Usenet University
`alt.uu.comp.os.linux.questions`	UU Linux learning group, questions and answers
`alt.uu.future`	Planning the future of Usenet University
`alt.uu.lang.esperanto.misc`	Usenet University Esperanto
`alt.uu.lang.misc`	Usenet University language department
`alt.uu.lang.russian.misc`	Usenet University Russian
`alt.uu.math.misc`	Usenet University math
`alt.uu.misc.misc`	Usenet University miscellaneous departments
`alt.uu.tools`	Usenet University tools for education
`alt.uu.virtual-worlds.misc`	Usenet University study of virtual worlds
`alt.vampyres`	Vampires
`alt.video.laserdisc`	Laserdisc movies and games
`alt.vigilantes`	Vigilantes
`alt.virtual-adepts`	Studs of the virtual world
`alt.visa.us`	U.S. immigration visas
`alt.wais`	Wais (Wide Area Information Service)
`alt.war`	War
`alt.war.civil.usa`	U.S. Civil War
`alt.war.vietnam`	War in Vietnam
`alt.wedding`	First meetings, dates, romance, weddings, etc
`alt.whine`	Whining and complaining
`alt.whistleblowing`	Uncovering illegal or immoral activity
`alt.windows.cde`	Common Desktop Environment, windowing system
`alt.windows.text`	Text-based (non-graphical) window systems
`alt.winsock`	Socket implementations for Microsoft Windows
`alt.wired`	*Wired* magazine
`alt.wolves`	Wolves and wolf-mix dogs
`alt.women.attitudes`	Attitudes of women
`alt.world.taeis`	Shared-world project
`alt.year.1976`	Topics relating to the year 1976
`alt.zen`	Zen philosophy
`alt.zima`	Zima, a beer-like beverage
`alt.zines`	Small magazines, mostly noncommercial
`alt.znet.aeo`	Atari Explorer Online, electronic magazine
`alt.znet.pc`	PC-oriented electronic magazine

bionet

`bionet.agroforestry`	Agroforestry
`bionet.announce`	Announcements for biologists (Moderated)
`bionet.biology.computational`	Computer and mathematical biology (Moderated)
`bionet.biology.grasses`	Grasses such as cereal, forage, and turf
`bionet.biology.tropical`	Tropical biology
`bionet.biophysics`	Biophysics
`bionet.celegans`	Model organism Caenorhabditis elegans
`bionet.cellbiol`	Cell biology
`bionet.cellbiol.cytonet`	Cytoskeletons, plasma membranes, and cell walls
`bionet.chlamydomonas`	Chlamydomonas, green alga
`bionet.drosophila`	Biology of Drosophila (fruit flies)
`bionet.general`	General forum for the biological sciences
`bionet.genome.arabidopsis`	Arabidopsis project
`bionet.genome.chrom22`	Chromosome 22

bionet.genome.chromosomes	Mapping and sequencing of eucaryote chromosomes
bionet.immunology	Immunology
bionet.info-theory	Biological information theory
bionet.jobs	Job opportunities in biology
bionet.jobs.wanted	Requests for employment in the biological sciences
bionet.journals.contents	Contents of biology journals
bionet.journals.note	Advice on dealing with biology journals
bionet.metabolic-reg	Kinetics and thermodynamics at the cellular level
bionet.microbiology	Microbiology
bionet.molbio.ageing	Cellular and organismal aging
bionet.molbio.bio-matrix	Computer applications to biological databases
bionet.molbio.embldatabank	EMBL nucleic acid database
bionet.molbio.evolution	Evolution of genes and proteins
bionet.molbio.gdb	Messages to and from the GDB database staff
bionet.molbio.genbank	GenBank nucleic acid database
bionet.molbio.genbank.updates	News about GenBank (Moderated)
bionet.molbio.gene-linkage	Genetic linkage analysis
bionet.molbio.gene-org	How genes are organized on chromosomes
bionet.molbio.genome-program	Human Genome Project
bionet.molbio.hiv	Molecular biology of HIV (AIDS virus)
bionet.molbio.methds-reagnts	Requests for information and lab reagents
bionet.molbio.proteins	Proteins and protein databases
bionet.molbio.rapd	Randomly Amplified Polymorphic DNA
bionet.molbio.yeast	Molecular biology and genetics of yeast
bionet.molec-model	Molecular modeling
bionet.mycology	Fungi
bionet.n2-fixation	Nitrogen fixation
bionet.neuroscience	Neuroscience
bionet.organisms.urodeles	Urodele amphibians
bionet.organisms.zebrafish	Model organism Zebrafish (Danio rerio)
bionet.parasitology	Parasitology
bionet.photosynthesis	Photosynthesis
bionet.plants	All aspects of plant biology
bionet.population-bio	Population biology
bionet.prof-society.biophysics	Biophysical Society announcements (Moderated)
bionet.protista	Ciliates and other protists
bionet.sci-resources	Funding agencies, research grants, etc
bionet.software	Software for biology
bionet.software.acedb	Using ACEDB to access genome databases
bionet.software.gcg	GCG software
bionet.software.sources	Free programs relating to biology (Moderated)
bionet.structural-nmr	Exploring the structure of macromolecules using NMR
bionet.users.addresses	Names and addresses in the world of biology
bionet.virology	Virology
bionet.women-in-bio	Women in biology
bionet.xtallography	Protein crystallography

bit

bit.admin	Administrating Bitnet newsgroups
bit.general	General information on Bitnet and Usenet
bit.lang.neder-l	Dutch language and literature (Moderated)
bit.listserv.3com-l	3Com Products
bit.listserv.9370-l	IBM's 9370 and VM/IS operating system
bit.listserv.ada-law	ADA Law
bit.listserv.advanc-l	Geac Advanced Integrated Library System
bit.listserv.advise-l	User services
bit.listserv.aect-l	Educational communication and technology
bit.listserv.aera	American Educational Research Association (Moderated)
bit.listserv.aix-l	IBM's AIX (Unix) operating system
bit.listserv.allmusic	All forms of music
bit.listserv.appc-l	IBM's APPC
bit.listserv.apple2-l	Apple II
bit.listserv.applicat	Applications under Bitnet
bit.listserv.arie-l	RLG Ariel Document Transmission Group
bit.listserv.ashe-l	Higher education policy and research
bit.listserv.asis-l	American Society of Information Science
bit.listserv.asm370	IBM 370 Assembler programming
bit.listserv.authorware	Authorware professional authoring program

`bit.listserv.autism`	Autism and developmental disabilities
`bit.listserv.autocat`	Library cataloging and authorities
`bit.listserv.axslib-l`	Library access for people with disabilities
`bit.listserv.banyan-l`	Banyan Vines network software
`bit.listserv.basque-l`	Basque culture (Moderated)
`bit.listserv.big-lan`	Campus-size local area networks (Moderated)
`bit.listserv.billing`	Chargeback of computer resources
`bit.listserv.biosph-l`	Biosphere, ecology
`bit.listserv.bitnews`	News about Bitnet
`bit.listserv.blindnws`	Blindness (Moderated)
`bit.listserv.blues-l`	Blues music (Moderated)
`bit.listserv.bosnet`	News about Bosnia (Moderated)
`bit.listserv.buslib-l`	Business libraries
`bit.listserv.c+health`	Computer and health
`bit.listserv.c18-l`	18th century interdisciplinary forum
`bit.listserv.c370-l`	IBM's C/370 programming language
`bit.listserv.calc-ti`	Texas Instruments graphics calculators
`bit.listserv.candle-l`	Candle products
`bit.listserv.catala`	Catalan, language of Catalonia, Andorra, Belearic Islands
`bit.listserv.catholic`	Free Catholics
`bit.listserv.cdromlan`	CD-ROM on local area networks
`bit.listserv.cfs.newsletter`	Chronic Fatigue Syndrome newsletter (Moderated)
`bit.listserv.christia`	Practical Christian life
`bit.listserv.cics-l`	IBM's CICS (transaction processing)
`bit.listserv.cinema-l`	Cinema
`bit.listserv.circplus`	Circulation reserve and related library topics
`bit.listserv.cmspip-l`	IBM's VM/SP CMS pipelines
`bit.listserv.coco`	Tandy Color Computers
`bit.listserv.commed`	Communication education
`bit.listserv.csg-l`	Control System Group network
`bit.listserv.cumrec-l`	Computer use, college and university administration
`bit.listserv.cw-email`	Campus-wide electronic mail
`bit.listserv.cwis-l`	Campus-wide information systems
`bit.listserv.cyber-l`	CDC computers
`bit.listserv.dasig`	Database administration
`bit.listserv.db2-l`	IBM's DB2 (relational database)
`bit.listserv.dbase-l`	dBase IV (PC database)
`bit.listserv.deaf-l`	Deafness
`bit.listserv.decnews`	Digital Equipment Corporation news
`bit.listserv.dectei-l`	DECUS Education Software Library
`bit.listserv.devel-l`	Technology transfer in international development
`bit.listserv.devmedia`	Media for development and democracy (Moderated)
`bit.listserv.dipl-l`	Diplomacy game
`bit.listserv.disarm-l`	Disarmament
`bit.listserv.domain-l`	Domain listings
`bit.listserv.down-syn`	Down's syndrome
`bit.listserv.dsshe-l`	Disabled student services in higher education
`bit.listserv.e-europe`	Eastern Europe business network (Moderated)
`bit.listserv.earntech`	EARN technical group
`bit.listserv.easi`	Computer access for people with disabilities
`bit.listserv.ecolog-l`	Ecological Society of America
`bit.listserv.edi-l`	Electronic data interchange
`bit.listserv.edpolyan`	Professionals and students and education
`bit.listserv.edstat-l`	Statistics education
`bit.listserv.edtech`	Educational technology (Moderated)
`bit.listserv.edusig-l`	Education special interest group
`bit.listserv.emusic-l`	Electronic music
`bit.listserv.endnote`	Bibsoft Endnote
`bit.listserv.envbeh-l`	Environment and human behavior
`bit.listserv.erl-l`	Educational research
`bit.listserv.ethics-l`	Ethics in computing
`bit.listserv.ethology`	Ethology
`bit.listserv.euearn-l`	Eastern Europe
`bit.listserv.film-l`	Film making and reviews
`bit.listserv.fnord-l`	New ways of thinking
`bit.listserv.frac-l`	Fractals
`bit.listserv.free-l`	Fathers' rights
`bit.listserv.freemasonry`	Freemasonry (Moderated)
`bit.listserv.games-l`	Computer games

bit.listserv.gaynet	Gaynet (Moderated)
bit.listserv.gddm-1	Graphical Data Display Manager
bit.listserv.geodesic	Buckminster Fuller
bit.listserv.geograph	Geography
bit.listserv.gguide	Bitnic Gguide
bit.listserv.gophern	"Let's Go Gopherin'", learning to use the Internet
bit.listserv.govdoc-1	Government documents
bit.listserv.graph-ti	TI-8x calculators
bit.listserv.gutnberg	Project Gutenberg
bit.listserv.hdesk-1	Running a help desk
bit.listserv.hellas	Hellenic topics (Moderated)
bit.listserv.help-net	Help on Bitnet and the Internet
bit.listserv.hindu-d	Hindu digest (Moderated)
bit.listserv.history	History
bit.listserv.hp3000-1	HP-3000 computers
bit.listserv.humage-1	Humanistic aspects of aging
bit.listserv.hungary	Hungary
bit.listserv.hytel-1	Hytelnet (Moderated)
bit.listserv.i-amiga	Amiga computers
bit.listserv.ibm-hesc	IBM higher education consortium
bit.listserv.ibm-main	IBM mainframe computers
bit.listserv.ibm-nets	IBM mainframes and networking
bit.listserv.ibm7171	IBM's 7171 Protocol Converter
bit.listserv.ibmtcp-1	IBM's TCP/IP products
bit.listserv.idms-1	CA-IDMS
bit.listserv.imagelib	Image databases in libraries
bit.listserv.india-d	India (Moderated)
bit.listserv.info-gcg	GCG genetics software
bit.listserv.infonets	Redistribution from Infonets
bit.listserv.ingrafx	Information graphics
bit.listserv.innopac	Innovative Interface's Online Public Access
bit.listserv.ioob-1	Industrial psychology
bit.listserv.ipct-1	Interpersonal computing and technology (Moderated)
bit.listserv.isn	ISN data switch
bit.listserv.japan	Japanese business and economics network (Moderated)
bit.listserv.jes2-1	IBM's JES2
bit.listserv.jnet-1	Jnet running under VMS
bit.listserv.l-hcap	Handicaps (Moderated)
bit.listserv.l-vmctr	VMCENTER components
bit.listserv.lawsch-1	Law schools
bit.listserv.liaison	Bitnic liaison
bit.listserv.libref-1	Library reference issues (Moderated)
bit.listserv.libres	Library and information science Research
bit.listserv.license	Software licensing
bit.listserv.linkfail	Link failure announcements
bit.listserv.lis-1	Library and information science students
bit.listserv.literary	Literature
bit.listserv.lsoft-announce	Announcements about Listserv (Moderated)
bit.listserv.lstsrv-1	Listserv
bit.listserv.mail-1	Mail
bit.listserv.mailbook	Mail/Mailbook
bit.listserv.mba-1	MBA student curricula
bit.listserv.mbu-1	Megabyte University computers and writing
bit.listserv.mdphd-1	Dual degree programs
bit.listserv.medforum	Medical students (Moderated)
bit.listserv.medlib-1	Medical libraries
bit.listserv.mednews	Mednews Health Info-Com Network Newsletter
bit.listserv.mideur-1	Middle Europe
bit.listserv.mla-1	Music Library Association
bit.listserv.muslims	Islamic news (Moderated)
bit.listserv.netnws-1	Netnews (Usenet)
bit.listserv.nettrain	Network trainers
bit.listserv.new-list	Announcements about new Bitnet lists (Moderated)
bit.listserv.next-1	Next brand computers
bit.listserv.nodmgt-1	Node management
bit.listserv.notabene	Nota Bene
bit.listserv.notis-1	Notis/Dobis
bit.listserv.novell	Novell local area networks
bit.listserv.omrscan	OMR scanners

bit.listserv.opers-1	Mainframe operations
bit.listserv.os2-1	IBM's OS/2 operating system
bit.listserv.ozone	OZONE
bit.listserv.pacs-1	Public access computer systems (Moderated)
bit.listserv.page-1	IBM's 3812/3820
bit.listserv.pagemakr	PageMaker for desktop publishers
bit.listserv.pakistan	Pakistan news (Moderated)
bit.listserv.physhare	Physics
bit.listserv.pmail	Pegasus mail
bit.listserv.pmdf-1	PMDF
bit.listserv.pns-1	Pakistan news (Moderated)
bit.listserv.politics	Politics
bit.listserv.por	Public opinion research
bit.listserv.postcard	Postcard collectors
bit.listserv.power-1	IBM's RS/6000 computers (the Power architecture)
bit.listserv.powerh-1	PowerHouse
bit.listserv.psycgrad	Psychology grad students
bit.listserv.quaker-p	Quaker-oriented peace and social justice (Moderated)
bit.listserv.quality	Total Quality Management in industry (Moderated)
bit.listserv.qualrs-1	Qualitative research of the human sciences
bit.listserv.relusr-1	Relay users
bit.listserv.rhetoric	Rhetoric, social movements, persuasion
bit.listserv.rra-1	Romance Readers Anonymous (Moderated)
bit.listserv.rscs-1	IBM's VM/RSCS
bit.listserv.rscsmods	RSCS modifications
bit.listserv.s-comput	Supercomputers
bit.listserv.sas-1	SAS
bit.listserv.scce-1	Supercomputers for Central Europe
bit.listserv.screen-1	Film and television (Moderated)
bit.listserv.script-1	IBM vs. Waterloo SCRIPT
bit.listserv.scuba-1	Scuba diving
bit.listserv.seasia-1	Southeast Asia
bit.listserv.seds-1	Students for the Exploration and Development of Space
bit.listserv.sedsnews	Space news from SEDS
bit.listserv.sfs-1	IBM's VM Shared File System
bit.listserv.sganet	Student government global mail network
bit.listserv.simula	SIMULA programming (simulation) language
bit.listserv.skeptic	Healthy, intelligent skepticism (Moderated)
bit.listserv.slart-1	SLA research and teaching
bit.listserv.slovak-1	Slovaks
bit.listserv.snamgt-1	IBM's SNA network management
bit.listserv.snurse-1	Student nurses
bit.listserv.sos-data	Social science
bit.listserv.spires-1	Spires conference
bit.listserv.sportpsy	Exercise and sports psychology
bit.listserv.spssx-1	SPSSX
bit.listserv.sqlinfo	IBM's SQL/DS (database language)
bit.listserv.stat-1	Statistical consulting
bit.listserv.sthcult	Southern culture (in the U.S.)
bit.listserv.superguy	Continuing fantasy/superhero stories (Moderated)
bit.listserv.tbi-support	Traumatic Brain Injury support (Moderated)
bit.listserv.tech-1	Bitnic TECH-L mailing list
bit.listserv.techwr-1	Technical writing
bit.listserv.tecmat-1	Technology in secondary mathematics
bit.listserv.tesl-1	Teachers of English as a second language (Moderated)
bit.listserv.test	Place to send test articles
bit.listserv.tex-1	TeX typesetting system
bit.listserv.tn3270-1	tn3270 protocol
bit.listserv.toolb-1	Asymetrix Toolbook
bit.listserv.trans-1	Bitnic TRANS-L mailing list
bit.listserv.transplant	Transplant recipients
bit.listserv.travel-1	Travel and tourism
bit.listserv.tsorexx	IBM's REXX language for TSO
bit.listserv.ucp-1	University Computing Project
bit.listserv.ug-1	Usage guidelines
bit.listserv.uigis-1	User interface for Geographical Info Systems
bit.listserv.urep-1	UREP software
bit.listserv.usrdir-1	User directory
bit.listserv.uus-1	Unitarian-Universalist church

bit.listserv.valert-1	Virus alerts
bit.listserv.vfort-1	IBM's VS/Fortran programming language
bit.listserv.vm-util	IBM's VM utilities
bit.listserv.vmesa-1	IBM's VM/ESA operating system
bit.listserv.vmslsv-1	DEC's VAX/VMS operating system
bit.listserv.vmxa-1	IBM's VM/XA operating system
bit.listserv.vnews-1	VNEWS
bit.listserv.vocnet	Vocational education
bit.listserv.vpiej-1	Electronic publishing
bit.listserv.vse-1	IBM's VSE/ESA mainframe operating system
bit.listserv.wac-1	Writing across the curriculum and writing centers
bit.listserv.win3-1	Microsoft Windows 3.x
bit.listserv.words-1	English language
bit.listserv.wpcorp-1	Wordperfect products
bit.listserv.wpwin-1	Wordperfect for MS Windows
bit.listserv.www-vm	World Wide Web on the IBM VM platform
bit.listserv.wx-talk	Weather
bit.listserv.x400-1	X.400 protocol
bit.listserv.xcult-1	*International Intercultural Newsletter*
bit.listserv.xedit-1	VM system editor
bit.listserv.xerox-1	Xerox products
bit.listserv.xmailer	Crosswell mailer
bit.listserv.xtropy-1	Extopian topics
bit.mailserv.word-mac	Word processing on the Macintosh
bit.mailserv.word-pc	Word processing on PCs
bit.org.peace-corps	Peace Corps and international volunteers
bit.software.international	International software (Moderated)
bit.tech.africana	Information technology and Africa

biz

biz.americast	Americast company
biz.americast.samples	Americast samples
biz.books.technical	Selling and buying books
biz.clarinet	Announcements about Clarinet
biz.clarinet.sample	Free samples from Clarinet newsgroups
biz.comp.hardware	Generic commercial hardware
biz.comp.mcs	MCSNet (Moderated)
biz.comp.services	Generic commercial service
biz.comp.software	Generic commercial software
biz.comp.telebit	Telebit modems
biz.comp.telebit.netblazer	Telebit Netblazer
biz.config	Configuration and administration of biz newsgroups
biz.control	Usenet control information for biz newsgroups
biz.dec	DEC equipment and software
biz.dec.decathena	DEC Athena
biz.dec.decnews	DEC news releases and discussion
biz.dec.ip	IP networking on DEC machines
biz.dec.workstations	DEC workstations
biz.digex.announce	Digex
biz.digital.announce	Announcements from DEC (Moderated)
biz.digital.articles	Newsletter, catalog, and journal from DEC (Moderated)
biz.jobs.offered	Jobs that are available
biz.misc	General commercial postings
biz.next.newprod	New products from the Next Company
biz.oreilly.announce	Announcements from O'Reilly and Associates (Moderated)
biz.pagesat	Pagesat satellite Usenet newsfeed service
biz.pagesat.weather	Weather info, compliments of Pagesat
biz.sco.announce	Santa Cruz Operation (SCO) news (Moderated)
biz.sco.binaries	Programs for SCO Xenix, Unix, or ODT (Open Desktop)
biz.sco.general	General discussion about SCO products
biz.sco.magazine	SCO magazine and its contents
biz.sco.opendesktop	Open Desktop
biz.sco.sources	Free programs to run under an SCO environment
biz.sco.wserver	SCO widget server
biz.stolen	Stolen items
biz.stortek.forum	Storage Technology Corporation
biz.tadpole.sparcbook	Sparcbook portable computer
biz.test	Place to send test articles

biz.univel.misc	Novell's Univel software
biz.zeos.announce	Announcements by Zeos International
biz.zeos.general	General discussion regarding Zeos

comp

comp.admin.policy	Site administration policies
comp.ai	Artificial intelligence
comp.ai.alife	Artificial life
comp.ai.edu	Applications of artificial intelligence to education
comp.ai.fuzzy	Fuzzy set theory, fuzzy logic
comp.ai.genetic	Using artificial intelligence for genetic research
comp.ai.jair.announce	Abstracts from the *Journal of AI Research* (Moderated)
comp.ai.jair.papers	Papers from the *Journal of AI Research* (Moderated)
comp.ai.nat-lang	Natural language processing by computers
comp.ai.neural-nets	All aspects of neural networks
comp.ai.nlang-know-rep	Natural language, knowledge representation (Moderated)
comp.ai.philosophy	Philosophical aspects of artificial intelligence
comp.ai.shells	Artificial intelligence applied to shells
comp.ai.vision	Artificial intelligence vision research (Moderated)
comp.answers	Repository for periodic Usenet articles (Moderated)
comp.apps.spreadsheets	Spreadsheets on various platforms
comp.arch	Computer architecture
comp.arch.arithmetic	Implementing arithmetic on computers and digital systems
comp.arch.bus.vmebus	Hardware and software for VMEbus systems
comp.arch.fpga	Field Programmable Gate Array-based computing systems
comp.arch.storage	Storage system issues, both hardware and software
comp.archives	Descriptions of public access archives (Moderated)
comp.archives.admin	Issues relating to computer archive administration
comp.archives.msdos.announce	Announcements about DOS archives (Moderated)
comp.archives.msdos.d	Discussion of materials available in DOS archives
comp.bbs.misc	General bulletin board systems topics
comp.bbs.tbbs	Bread Board System bulletin board software
comp.bbs.waffle	Waffle BBS and Usenet system on all platforms
comp.benchmarks	Discussion of benchmarking techniques and results
comp.binaries.acorn	Binary-only postings for Acorn machines (Moderated)
comp.binaries.amiga	Encoded public domain programs in binary (Moderated)
comp.binaries.apple2	Binary-only postings for the Apple II computer
comp.binaries.atari.st	Binary-only postings for the Atari ST (Moderated)
comp.binaries.cbm	Binary-only postings for 8-bit Commodore machines
comp.binaries.geos	Binary-only postings for GEOS operating system (Moderated)
comp.binaries.ibm.pc	Binary-only postings for IBM PC/DOS (Moderated)
comp.binaries.ibm.pc.archives	PC archive sites
comp.binaries.ibm.pc.d	Discussions about IBM PC binary postings
comp.binaries.ibm.pc.wanted	Requests for IBM PC and compatible programs
comp.binaries.mac	Encoded Macintosh programs in binary (Moderated)
comp.binaries.ms-windows	Binary programs for Microsoft Windows (Moderated)
comp.binaries.newton	Binary-only postings for the Apple Newton (Moderated)
comp.binaries.os2	Binaries for use under the OS/2 ABI (Moderated)
comp.bugs.2bsd	Bugs and fixes: Unix version 2BSD
comp.bugs.4bsd	Bugs and fixes: Unix version 4BSD
comp.bugs.4bsd.ucb-fixes	Bugs and fixes: BSD Unix (Moderated)
comp.bugs.misc	Bugs and fixes: General Unix (includes V7, UUCP)
comp.bugs.sys5	Bugs and fixes: Unix System V
comp.cad.cadence	Users of Cadence Design Systems products
comp.cad.compass	Compass Design Automation EDA tools
comp.cad.pro-engineer	Parametric Technology's Pro/Engineer design package
comp.cad.synthesis	Logic synthesis
comp.client-server	Topics relating to client/server technology
comp.cog-eng	Cognitive engineering
comp.compilers	Compiler construction, theory, etc (Moderated)
comp.compilers.tools.pccts	Construction of compilers and tools with PCCTS
comp.compression	Data compression algorithms and theory
comp.compression.research	Discussions about data compression research
comp.constraints	Constraint processing and related topics
comp.databases	Database and data management issues and theory
comp.databases.informix	Informix database management software discussions
comp.databases.ingres	Issues relating to Ingres products
comp.databases.ms-access	Microsoft Access, relational database

comp.databases.object	Object-oriented paradigms in databases systems
comp.databases.oracle	SQL database products of the Oracle Corporation
comp.databases.paradox	Borland Paradox, relational database
comp.databases.pick	Pick-like, post-relational database systems
comp.databases.rdb	DEC relational database engine RDB
comp.databases.sybase	Implementations of the SQL Server
comp.databases.theory	Advances in database technology
comp.databases.xbase.fox	Fox Software's xBase system
comp.databases.xbase.misc	General xBase topics
comp.dcom.cabling	Cabling selection, installation and use
comp.dcom.cell-relay	Forum for discussion of cell relay-based products
comp.dcom.fax	Fax hardware, software, and protocols
comp.dcom.isdn	Integrated Services Digital Network (ISDN)
comp.dcom.lans.ethernet	Discussions of the Ethernet/IEEE 802.3 protocols
comp.dcom.lans.fddi	Discussions of the FDDI protocol suite
comp.dcom.lans.hyperchannel	Hyperchannel networks within an IP network
comp.dcom.lans.misc	General local area network topics
comp.dcom.lans.token-ring	Token-ring networks
comp.dcom.modems	Data communications hardware and software
comp.dcom.servers	Selecting and operating data communications servers
comp.dcom.sys.cisco	Info on Cisco routers and bridges
comp.dcom.sys.wellfleet	Wellfleet bridge and router systems
comp.dcom.telecom	Telecommunications digest (Moderated)
comp.dcom.telecom.tech	Technical aspects of telephony
comp.doc	Archived public-domain documentation (Moderated)
comp.doc.techreports	Lists of technical reports (Moderated)
comp.dsp	Digital signal processing using computers
comp.editors	Topics related to computerized text editing
comp.edu	Computer science education
comp.edu.composition	Writing instruction in computer-based classrooms
comp.edu.languages.natural	Computer-assisted languages and instruction
comp.emacs	Emacs editors of different flavors
comp.emulators.announce	Announcements relating to emulators (Moderated)
comp.emulators.apple2	Emulators of Apple II systems
comp.emulators.cbm	Emulators of C-64, C-128, PET, and VIC-20 systems
comp.emulators.misc	Emulators of miscellaneous computer systems
comp.emulators.ms-windows.wine	Wine, a free X-based MS-Windows emulator
comp.fonts	Typefonts design, conversion, use, etc
comp.graphics	Computer graphics, art, animation, image processing
comp.graphics.algorithms	Algorithms used in producing computer graphics
comp.graphics.animation	Technical aspects of computer animation
comp.graphics.avs	Application Visualization System
comp.graphics.data-explorer	IBM's Visualization Data Explorer
comp.graphics.explorer	Explorer Modular Visualization Environment
comp.graphics.gnuplot	Gnuplot interactive function plotter
comp.graphics.opengl	OpenGL 3D application programming interface
comp.graphics.raytracing	Ray-tracing software, tools, and methods
comp.graphics.research	Highly technical computer graphics (Moderated)
comp.graphics.visualization	Info on scientific visualization
comp.groupware	Shared interactive environments
comp.groupware.lotus-notes.misc	Lotus Notes
comp.home.automation	Home automation devices
comp.home.misc	Computers and technology in the home (Moderated)
comp.human-factors	Issues related to human/computer interaction
comp.infosystems	General discussion about information systems
comp.infosystems.announce	Announcements about Internet services (Moderated)
comp.infosystems.gis	Geographic Information Systems
comp.infosystems.gopher	Gopher menu-driven information service
comp.infosystems.interpedia	Project to create an Internet encyclopedia
comp.infosystems.kiosks	Information kiosks (Moderated)
comp.infosystems.wais	Wais full-text search information service
comp.infosystems.www	World Wide Web hypertext-based information service
comp.infosystems.www.misc	World Wide Web: general discussion
comp.infosystems.www.providers	World Wide Web: providers
comp.infosystems.www.users	World Wide Web: users and browsing software
comp.internet.library	Electronic libraries (Moderated)
comp.ivideodisc	Interactive videodiscs uses, potential, etc
comp.lang.ada	Ada programming language
comp.lang.apl	APL programming language

comp.lang.asm370	IBM System/370 Assembler
comp.lang.basic.misc	Basic programming language
comp.lang.basic.visual	MS Visual Basic programming language
comp.lang.c	C programming language
comp.lang.c++	Object-oriented C++ programming language
comp.lang.clos	Common Lisp Object System discussions
comp.lang.clu	CLU language and related topics
comp.lang.dylan	Dylan language
comp.lang.eiffel	Object-oriented Eiffel language
comp.lang.forth	Forth programming language
comp.lang.forth.mac	CSI MacForth programming environment
comp.lang.fortran	Fortran programming language
comp.lang.functional	Functional programming languages
comp.lang.hermes	Hermes language for distributed applications
comp.lang.icon	ICON programming language
comp.lang.idl	IDL (the Interface Description Language)
comp.lang.idl-pvwave	IDL and PV-Wave language discussions
comp.lang.lisp	Lisp programming language
comp.lang.lisp.franz	Franz Lisp programming language
comp.lang.lisp.mcl	Apple's Macintosh Common Lisp
comp.lang.lisp.x	XLISP language system
comp.lang.logo	Logo teaching and learning language
comp.lang.misc	General computer language topics
comp.lang.ml	ML languages ML, CAML, Lazy ML, etc (Moderated)
comp.lang.modula2	Modula-2 programming language
comp.lang.modula3	Modula-3 programming language
comp.lang.mumps	MUMPS programming language
comp.lang.oberon	Oberon language and system
comp.lang.objective-c	Objective-C language and environment
comp.lang.pascal	Pascal programming language
comp.lang.perl	Perl scripting language
comp.lang.pop	Pop11 and the Plug user group
comp.lang.postscript	PostScript Page Description Language
comp.lang.prograph	Prograph, visual object-oriented dataflow language
comp.lang.prolog	Prolog programming language
comp.lang.python	Python programming language
comp.lang.rexx	IBM's REXX command-scripting language
comp.lang.sather	Sather, object-oriented programming language
comp.lang.scheme	Scheme programming language
comp.lang.scheme.c	Scheme language environment
comp.lang.sigplan	Info and announcements from ACM SIGPLAN (Moderated)
comp.lang.smalltalk	Smalltalk 80 programming language
comp.lang.tcl	TCL programming language and related tools
comp.lang.verilog	Verilog and PLI programming languages
comp.lang.vhdl	VHSIC Hardware Description Language, IEEE 1076/87
comp.lang.visual	Visual programming languages
comp.laser-printers	Laser printers, hardware and software (Moderated)
comp.lsi	Large scale integrated circuits
comp.lsi.cad	Computer aided design
comp.lsi.testing	Testing of electronic circuits
comp.mail	General discussions about electronic mail
comp.mail.elm	Elm mail program
comp.mail.headers	Gatewayed from the Internet header-people list
comp.mail.maps	Various maps, including UUCP maps (Moderated)
comp.mail.mh	UCI version of the Rand Message Handling system
comp.mail.mime	Multipurpose Internet Mail Extensions of RFC 1341
comp.mail.misc	General computer mail topics
comp.mail.multi-media	Multimedia mail
comp.mail.mush	Mail User's Shell
comp.mail.pine	Pine mail program
comp.mail.sendmail	Configuring and using the BSD sendmail agent
comp.mail.smail	Smail mail transport system
comp.mail.uucp	Mail in the UUCP network environment
comp.misc	General computer topics
comp.multimedia	Interactive multimedia technologies of all kinds
comp.music	Applications of computers in music research
comp.networks.noctools.announce	Announcements about NOC tools (Moderated)
comp.networks.noctools.bugs	Bug and fixes: NOC tools
comp.networks.noctools.d	Discussion about NOC tools

comp.networks.noctools.submissions	New NOC tools submissions
comp.networks.noctools.tools	Descriptions of available NOC tools (Moderated)
comp.networks.noctools.wanted	Requests for NOC software
comp.newprod	Announcements of new products (Moderated)
comp.object	Object-oriented programming and languages
comp.object.logic	Integrating object-oriented and logic programming
comp.org.acm	Association for Computing Machinery
comp.org.cpsr.announce	Computer Prof. for Social Responsibility (Moderated)
comp.org.cpsr.talk	CPSR, computing and social responsibility
comp.org.decus	Digital Equipment Computer Users' Society
comp.org.eff.news	Electronic Frontiers Foundation (Moderated)
comp.org.eff.talk	Discussion of EFF goals, strategies, etc
comp.org.fidonet	Official digest of Fidonet Association (Moderated)
comp.org.ieee	Issues and announcements about the IEEE
comp.org.isoc.interest	The Internet Society
comp.org.issnnet	International Student Society for Neural Networks
comp.org.lisp-users	Association of Lisp users
comp.org.sug	Sun User's Group
comp.org.usenix	Usenix Association events and announcements
comp.org.usenix.roomshare	Finding lodging during Usenix conferences
comp.os.386bsd.announce	386bsd operating system (Moderated)
comp.os.386bsd.apps	Applications which run under 386bsd
comp.os.386bsd.bugs	Bugs and fixes: 386bsd and its clients
comp.os.386bsd.development	Working on 386bsd internals
comp.os.386bsd.misc	General 386bsd topics
comp.os.386bsd.questions	General questions about 386bsd
comp.os.aos	Data General's AOS/VS
comp.os.chorus	Chorus microkernel
comp.os.coherent	Coherent operating system
comp.os.cpm	CP/M operating system
comp.os.cpm.amethyst	Amethyst, CP/M-80 software package
comp.os.geos	Geoworks' GEOS operating system
comp.os.linux	Linux: free Unix-like operating system
comp.os.linux.admin	Linux: installation and administration
comp.os.linux.announce	Announcements for the Linux community (Moderated)
comp.os.linux.development	Linux: development issues
comp.os.linux.help	Linux: questions and answers
comp.os.linux.misc	Linux: general topics
comp.os.lynx	LynxOS and Lynx real-time systems
comp.os.mach	Mach OS from CMU and other places
comp.os.minix	Discussion of Andy Tanenbaum's Minix system
comp.os.misc	General operating system topics
comp.os.ms-windows.advocacy	Microsoft Windows: debate
comp.os.ms-windows.announce	MS Windows: announcements (Moderated)
comp.os.ms-windows.apps	MS Windows: applications
comp.os.ms-windows.apps.comm	MS Windows: communication applications
comp.os.ms-windows.apps.financial	MS Windows: financial and tax software
comp.os.ms-windows.apps.misc	MS Windows: applications
comp.os.ms-windows.apps.utilities	MS Windows: utilities
comp.os.ms-windows.apps.word-proc	MS Windows: word processing applications
comp.os.ms-windows.misc	MS Windows: general topics
comp.os.ms-windows.networking.misc	MS Windows: general networking
comp.os.ms-windows.networking.tcp-ip	MS Windows: TCP/IP
comp.os.ms-windows.networking.windows	MS Windows: built-in networking
comp.os.ms-windows.nt.misc	Windows NT: general topics
comp.os.ms-windows.nt.setup	Windows NT: configuration and setup
comp.os.ms-windows.programmer	MS Windows: general programming
comp.os.ms-windows.programmer.controls	MS Windows: controls, dialogs, and VBXs
comp.os.ms-windows.programmer.drivers	MS Windows: Win16/Win32 drivers and VxDs
comp.os.ms-windows.programmer.graphics	MS Windows: GDI, graphics, and printing
comp.os.ms-windows.programmer.memory	MS Windows: memory management
comp.os.ms-windows.programmer.misc	MS Windows: general programming topics
comp.os.ms-windows.programmer.multimedia	MS Windows: multimedia programming
comp.os.ms-windows.programmer.networks	MS Windows: network programming
comp.os.ms-windows.programmer.ole	MS Windows: OLE2, COM, and DDE programming
comp.os.ms-windows.programmer.tools	MS Windows: development tools
comp.os.ms-windows.programmer.win32	MS Windows: 32-bit programming interfaces
comp.os.ms-windows.programmer.winhelp	MS Windows: WinHelp development
comp.os.ms-windows.setup	MS Windows: configuration and setup

`comp.os.ms-windows.video`	MS Windows: Video adapters and drivers
`comp.os.msdos.4dos`	DOS: 4DOS command processor
`comp.os.msdos.apps`	DOS: applications
`comp.os.msdos.desqview`	DOS: QuarterDeck's Desqview and related products
`comp.os.msdos.mail-news`	DOS: mail and network news systems
`comp.os.msdos.misc`	DOS: general topics
`comp.os.msdos.pcgeos`	DOS: GeoWorks PC/GEOS
`comp.os.msdos.programmer`	DOS: programming
`comp.os.msdos.programmer.turbovision`	DOS: Borland's Turbovision
`comp.os.os2`	OS/2: general discussion
`comp.os.os2.advocacy`	OS/2: debate
`comp.os.os2.announce`	OS/2: announcements (Moderated)
`comp.os.os2.apps`	OS/2: applications
`comp.os.os2.beta`	OS/2: beta releases
`comp.os.os2.bugs`	OS/2: bugs and fixes
`comp.os.os2.games`	OS/2: games
`comp.os.os2.misc`	OS/2: general topics
`comp.os.os2.multimedia`	OS/2: multimedia
`comp.os.os2.networking`	OS/2: networking
`comp.os.os2.networking.misc`	OS/2: miscellaneous networking issues
`comp.os.os2.networking.tcp-ip`	OS/2: TCP/IP
`comp.os.os2.programmer`	OS/2: programming
`comp.os.os2.programmer.misc`	OS/2: programming
`comp.os.os2.programmer.oop`	Object-oriented programming
`comp.os.os2.programmer.porting`	OS/2: porting software
`comp.os.os2.programmer.tools`	Programming tools
`comp.os.os2.setup`	OS/2: configuration and setup
`comp.os.os2.ver1x`	OS/2: versions 1.0 through 1.3
`comp.os.os9`	Discussions about the OS9 operating system
`comp.os.parix`	Parallel operating system PARIX
`comp.os.qnx`	QNX operating system
`comp.os.research`	Operating systems and related areas (Moderated)
`comp.os.rsts`	PDP-11 RSTS/E operating system
`comp.os.v`	V distributed operating system from Stanford
`comp.os.vms`	DEC's VAX line of computers and VMS operating system
`comp.os.vxworks`	VxWorks real-time operating system
`comp.os.xinu`	XINU operating system from Purdue (Doug Comer)
`comp.parallel`	Massively parallel hardware/software (Moderated)
`comp.parallel.mpi`	Message Passing Interface
`comp.parallel.pvm`	PVM system of multi-computer parallelization
`comp.patents`	Patents of computer technology (Moderated)
`comp.periphs`	Peripheral devices
`comp.periphs.printers`	Printers
`comp.periphs.scsi`	SCSI-based peripheral devices
`comp.programming`	Programming issues that transcend languages and OSs
`comp.programming.literate`	Literate programming
`comp.protocols.appletalk`	Applebus hardware and software
`comp.protocols.dicom`	Digital imaging and communications in medicine
`comp.protocols.ibm`	Networking with IBM mainframes
`comp.protocols.iso`	ISO protocol stack
`comp.protocols.iso.dev-environ`	ISO development environment
`comp.protocols.iso.x400`	X400 mail protocol
`comp.protocols.iso.x400.gateway`	X400 mail gateway (Moderated)
`comp.protocols.kerberos`	Kerberos authentication server
`comp.protocols.kermit`	Kermit communications package (Moderated)
`comp.protocols.misc`	General protocol topics
`comp.protocols.nfs`	Network File System protocol
`comp.protocols.pcnet`	PCNET (a personal computer network)
`comp.protocols.ppp`	Point to Point Protocol
`comp.protocols.snmp`	Simple Network Management Protocol
`comp.protocols.tcp-ip`	TCP and IP network protocols
`comp.protocols.tcp-ip.domains`	Domain-style names
`comp.protocols.tcp-ip.ibmpc`	TCP/IP for IBM-like personal computers
`comp.protocols.time.ntp`	Network Time Protocol
`comp.publish.cdrom.hardware`	Hardware used in publishing with CD-ROM
`comp.publish.cdrom.multimedia`	Software for multimedia authoring and publishing
`comp.publish.cdrom.software`	Software used in publishing with CD-ROM
`comp.publish.prepress`	Electronic prepress
`comp.realtime`	Real-time computing

comp.research.japan	Research in Japan (Moderated)
comp.risks	Risks to public from computers and users (Moderated)
comp.robotics	Robots and their applications
comp.security.announce	Announcements from CERT about security (Moderated)
comp.security.misc	General security topics
comp.security.unix	Unix security
comp.simulation	Simulation methods, problems, uses (Moderated)
comp.society	Impact of technology on society (Moderated)
comp.society.cu-digest	Computer Underground Digest (Moderated)
comp.society.development	Computer technology in developing countries
comp.society.folklore	Computer folklore, past and present (Moderated)
comp.society.futures	Events in technology affecting future computing
comp.society.privacy	Effects of technology on privacy (Moderated)
comp.soft-sys.andrew	Andrew file system from Carnegie Mellon University
comp.soft-sys.khoros	Khoros X11 visualization system
comp.soft-sys.matlab	MathWorks calculation and visualization package
comp.soft-sys.nextstep	Nextstep computing environment
comp.soft-sys.powerbuilder	Application development tools from PowerSoft
comp.soft-sys.ptolemy	Ptolemy simulation/code generation environment
comp.soft-sys.sas	SAS statistics package
comp.soft-sys.shazam	Shazam software
comp.soft-sys.spss	SPSS statistics package
comp.soft-sys.wavefront	Wavefront software products
comp.software-eng	Software engineering and related topics
comp.software.config-mgmt	Configuration management, tools, and procedures
comp.software.international	Non-English software
comp.software.licensing	Software licensing technology
comp.software.testing	Testing computer systems
comp.sources.3b1	Source code-only postings for AT&T 3b1 (Moderated)
comp.sources.acorn	Source code-only postings for Acorn (Moderated)
comp.sources.amiga	Source code-only postings for Amiga (Moderated)
comp.sources.apple2	Source code and discussion for Apple2 (Moderated)
comp.sources.atari.st	Source code-only postings for Atari ST (Moderated)
comp.sources.bugs	Bug and fixes: for posted sources
comp.sources.d	For any discussion of source postings
comp.sources.games	Postings of recreational software (Moderated)
comp.sources.games.bugs	Bug and fixes: for posted game software
comp.sources.hp48	Programs for HP48 and HP28 calculators (Moderated)
comp.sources.mac	Software for Apple Macintosh (Moderated)
comp.sources.misc	General postings of software (Moderated)
comp.sources.postscript	Source code for Postscript programs (Moderated)
comp.sources.reviewed	Source code evaluated by peer review (Moderated)
comp.sources.sun	Software for Sun workstations (Moderated)
comp.sources.testers	Finding people to test software
comp.sources.unix	Complete Unix-oriented sources (Moderated)
comp.sources.wanted	Requests for software and fixes
comp.sources.x	Software for the X Window system (Moderated)
comp.specification	Languages and methodologies for formal specification
comp.specification.z	Discussion about formal specification notation Z
comp.speech	Research/applications in speech science
comp.std.announce	Announcements about standards activities (Moderated)
comp.std.c	C language standards
comp.std.c++	C++ language standards
comp.std.internat	International standards
comp.std.lisp	Lisp standards (Moderated)
comp.std.misc	General standards topics
comp.std.mumps	X11.1 committee on Mumps (Moderated)
comp.std.unix	P1003 committee on Unix (Moderated)
comp.std.wireless	Wireless network technology standards (Moderated)
comp.sw.components	Software components and related technology
comp.sys.3b1	AT&T 7300/3B1/UnixPC
comp.sys.acorn	Acorn and ARM-based computers
comp.sys.acorn.advocacy	Debate about Acorn computers
comp.sys.acorn.announce	Announcements for Acorn and ARM users (Moderated)
comp.sys.acorn.games	Games for Acorn machines
comp.sys.acorn.tech	Technical aspects of Acorn and ARM products
comp.sys.alliant	Alliant computers
comp.sys.amiga.advocacy	Debate about Amiga computers
comp.sys.amiga.announce	Announcements about Amiga (Moderated)

`comp.sys.amiga.applications`	Miscellaneous applications
`comp.sys.amiga.audio`	Music, MIDI, speech synthesis, other sounds
`comp.sys.amiga.cd32`	Commodore Amiga CD32
`comp.sys.amiga.datacomm`	Methods of getting bytes in and out
`comp.sys.amiga.emulations`	Various hardware and software emulators
`comp.sys.amiga.games`	Games for the Commodore Amiga
`comp.sys.amiga.graphics`	Charts, graphs, pictures, etc
`comp.sys.amiga.hardware`	Amiga computer hardware
`comp.sys.amiga.introduction`	Newcomers to Amigas
`comp.sys.amiga.marketplace`	Buying and selling Amigas
`comp.sys.amiga.misc`	General Amiga topics
`comp.sys.amiga.multimedia`	Animations, video, and multimedia
`comp.sys.amiga.networking`	Amiga networking
`comp.sys.amiga.programmer`	Developers and hobbyists
`comp.sys.amiga.reviews`	Reviews of software, hardware (Moderated)
`comp.sys.amiga.telecomm`	Amiga telecom
`comp.sys.amiga.unix`	Amiga Unix systems
`comp.sys.amiga.uucp`	Amiga UUCP packages
`comp.sys.apollo`	Apollo computer systems
`comp.sys.apple2`	Apple II computers
`comp.sys.apple2.comm`	Apple II data communications
`comp.sys.apple2.gno`	Apple IIgs GNO multitasking environment
`comp.sys.apple2.marketplace`	Buying and selling Apple II equipment
`comp.sys.apple2.programmer`	Programming the Apple II
`comp.sys.apple2.usergroups`	Apple II user groups
`comp.sys.atari.8bit`	8-bit Atari micros
`comp.sys.atari.advocacy`	Debate about Atari computers
`comp.sys.atari.announce`	Atari announcements (Moderated)
`comp.sys.atari.st`	16-bit Atari micros
`comp.sys.atari.st.tech`	Technical discussions of Atari ST
`comp.sys.att`	AT&T microcomputers
`comp.sys.cbm`	Commodore computers
`comp.sys.cdc`	Control Data Corporation computers
`comp.sys.concurrent`	Concurrent/Masscomp computers (Moderated)
`comp.sys.convex`	Convex computers
`comp.sys.dec`	DEC computers
`comp.sys.dec.micro`	DEC micros (Rainbow, Professional 350/380)
`comp.sys.encore`	Encore's MultiMax computers
`comp.sys.handhelds`	Handheld computers and programmable calculators
`comp.sys.harris`	Harris computer systems, especially real-time systems
`comp.sys.hp`	Hewlett-Packard equipment
`comp.sys.hp.apps`	Software on all HP platforms
`comp.sys.hp.hardware`	HP hardware
`comp.sys.hp.hpux`	HP-UX and series 9000 computers
`comp.sys.hp.misc`	General HP topics
`comp.sys.hp.mpe`	HP MPE and series 3000 computers
`comp.sys.hp48`	Hewlett-Packard's HP48 and HP28 calculators
`comp.sys.ibm.pc.demos`	PC: demo programs
`comp.sys.ibm.pc.digest`	PC: general digest (Moderated)
`comp.sys.ibm.pc.games`	PC: games
`comp.sys.ibm.pc.games.action`	PC: action games
`comp.sys.ibm.pc.games.adventure`	PC: adventure games
`comp.sys.ibm.pc.games.announce`	PC: announcements relating games (Moderated)
`comp.sys.ibm.pc.games.flight-sim`	PC: flight simulators
`comp.sys.ibm.pc.games.misc`	PC: general game topics
`comp.sys.ibm.pc.games.rpg`	PC: role-playing games
`comp.sys.ibm.pc.games.strategic`	PC: strategy games
`comp.sys.ibm.pc.hardware`	PC: hardware
`comp.sys.ibm.pc.hardware.cd-rom`	PC: CD-ROM drives
`comp.sys.ibm.pc.hardware.chips`	PC: processor, cache, memory chips, and so on
`comp.sys.ibm.pc.hardware.comm`	PC: modems and communication cards
`comp.sys.ibm.pc.hardware.misc`	PC: miscellaneous hardware topics
`comp.sys.ibm.pc.hardware.networking`	PC: network hardware
`comp.sys.ibm.pc.hardware.storage`	PC: hard drives and other storage devices
`comp.sys.ibm.pc.hardware.systems`	PC: entire systems
`comp.sys.ibm.pc.hardware.video`	PC: video cards and monitors
`comp.sys.ibm.pc.misc`	PC: general topics
`comp.sys.ibm.pc.rt`	IBM's obsolete RT computer
`comp.sys.ibm.pc.soundcard`	PC: sound cards

comp.sys.ibm.pc.soundcard.advocacy	PC: debate about soundcards
comp.sys.ibm.pc.soundcard.games	PC: using sound cards with games
comp.sys.ibm.pc.soundcard.gus	PC: Gravis Ultrasound sound card
comp.sys.ibm.pc.soundcard.misc	PC: sound cards in general
comp.sys.ibm.pc.soundcard.music	PC: music and sound cards
comp.sys.ibm.pc.soundcard.tech	PC: technical questions about sound cards
comp.sys.ibm.ps2.hardware	PS/2 and Microchannel hardware, any vendor
comp.sys.intel	Intel systems and parts
comp.sys.intel.ipsc310	Intel 310
comp.sys.isis	ISIS fault-tolerant system, originally from Cornell
comp.sys.laptops	Laptop computers
comp.sys.m6809	6809 processors
comp.sys.m68k	68000 processors
comp.sys.m68k.pc	68000-based computers (Moderated)
comp.sys.m88k	88000-based computers
comp.sys.mac	Macintosh: general discussion
comp.sys.mac.advocacy	Macintosh: debate
comp.sys.mac.announce	Macintosh: announcements (Moderated)
comp.sys.mac.apps	Macintosh: applications
comp.sys.mac.comm	Macintosh: communications
comp.sys.mac.databases	Macintosh: database systems
comp.sys.mac.digest	Macintosh: general digest (Moderated)
comp.sys.mac.games	Macintosh: games
comp.sys.mac.graphics	Macintosh: graphics
comp.sys.mac.hardware	Macintosh: hardware
comp.sys.mac.hypercard	Macintosh: Hypercard
comp.sys.mac.misc	Macintosh: general topics
comp.sys.mac.oop.macapp3	Macintosh: Version 3, MacApp object-oriented system
comp.sys.mac.oop.misc	Macintosh: general object-oriented programming topics
comp.sys.mac.oop.tcl	Macintosh: Think Class Libraries
comp.sys.mac.portables	Macintosh: portable computers
comp.sys.mac.programmer	Macintosh: programming
comp.sys.mac.scitech	Macintosh: scientific and technological work
comp.sys.mac.system	Macintosh: system software
comp.sys.mac.wanted	Macintosh: requests for software and hardware
comp.sys.mentor	Mentor Graphics products and Silicon Compiler System
comp.sys.mips	Systems based on MIPS chips
comp.sys.misc	General computer topics
comp.sys.ncr	NCR computers
comp.sys.newton.announce	Newton announcements (Moderated)
comp.sys.newton.misc	General Newton topics
comp.sys.newton.programmer	Newton software development
comp.sys.next.advocacy	Debate about Next computers
comp.sys.next.announce	Announcements about Next computer system (Moderated)
comp.sys.next.bugs	Bugs and fixes: Next systems
comp.sys.next.hardware	Next computer hardware
comp.sys.next.marketplace	Next hardware, software and jobs
comp.sys.next.misc	General Next topics
comp.sys.next.programmer	Next-related programming issues
comp.sys.next.software	Next computer programs
comp.sys.next.sysadmin	Next system administration
comp.sys.northstar	Northstar microcomputer users
comp.sys.novell	Novell Netware products
comp.sys.nsc.32k	National Semiconductor 32000 series chips
comp.sys.palmtops	Super-powered calculators for the palm of your hand
comp.sys.pen	Interacting with computers through pen gestures
comp.sys.powerpc	PowerPC architecture and products
comp.sys.prime	Prime Computer products
comp.sys.proteon	Proteon gateway products
comp.sys.psion	Psion personal computers and organizers
comp.sys.pyramid	Pyramid 90x computers
comp.sys.ridge	Ridge 32 computers and ROS
comp.sys.sequent	Sequent systems (Balance and Symmetry)
comp.sys.sgi	Silicon Graphics' Iris workstations and software
comp.sys.sgi.admin	Silicon Graphics' Iris system administration
comp.sys.sgi.announce	Announcements for the SGI community (Moderated)
comp.sys.sgi.apps	Iris applications
comp.sys.sgi.audio	Audio on SGI systems
comp.sys.sgi.bugs	Bugs and fixes: IRIX operating system

comp.sys.sgi.graphics	Graphics packages on SGI machines
comp.sys.sgi.hardware	Base systems and peripherals for Iris computers
comp.sys.sgi.misc	General Silicon Graphics topics
comp.sys.sinclair	Sinclair computers: ZX81, Spectrum and QL
comp.sys.stratus	Stratus products (System/88, CPS-32, VOS and FTX)
comp.sys.sun.admin	Sun system administration
comp.sys.sun.announce	Sun announcements and Sunergy mailings (Moderated)
comp.sys.sun.apps	Sun applications
comp.sys.sun.hardware	Sun hardware
comp.sys.sun.misc	General Sun topics
comp.sys.sun.wanted	Requests for Sun products and support
comp.sys.super	Supercomputers
comp.sys.tahoe	CCI 6/32, Harris HCX/7, and Sperry 7000 computers
comp.sys.tandy	Tandy computers new and old
comp.sys.ti	Texas Instruments products
comp.sys.ti.explorer	Texas Instruments Explorer
comp.sys.transputer	Transputer computer and OCCAM language
comp.sys.unisys	Sperry, Burroughs, Convergent and Unisys systems
comp.sys.xerox	Xerox 1100 workstations and protocols
comp.sys.zenith	Heath terminals and related Zenith products
comp.sys.zenith.z100	Zenith Z-100 (Heath H-100) family of computers
comp.terminals	All sorts of terminals
comp.terminals.bitgraph	BB&N BitGraph terminal
comp.terminals.tty5620	AT&T Dot Mapped Display terminals (5620 and BLIT)
comp.text	Text processing issues and methods
comp.text.desktop	Desktop publishing
comp.text.frame	Desktop publishing with FrameMaker
comp.text.interleaf	Interleaf software
comp.text.sgml	ISO 8879 SGML, structured documents, markup language
comp.text.tex	TeX and LaTeX systems and macros
comp.theory	Theoretical computer science
comp.theory.cell-automata	Cellular automata
comp.theory.dynamic-sys	Ergodic theory and dynamic systems
comp.theory.info-retrieval	Information retrieval topics (Moderated)
comp.theory.self-org-sys	Self-organization topics
comp.unix.admin	Administering a Unix-based system
comp.unix.advocacy	Debate about Unix
comp.unix.aix	IBM's version of Unix
comp.unix.amiga	Versions of Unix that run on an Amiga
comp.unix.aux	Unix for Macintosh computers
comp.unix.bsd	Berkeley Software Distribution Unix
comp.unix.cray	Cray computers and their operating systems
comp.unix.dos-under-unix	DOS running under Unix by whatever means
comp.unix.internals	Hacking Unix internals
comp.unix.large	Unix on mainframes and in large networks
comp.unix.misc	General Unix topics
comp.unix.msdos	Unix and DOS
comp.unix.osf.misc	General Open Software Foundation topics
comp.unix.osf.osf1	Open Software Foundation's OSF/1 operating system
comp.unix.pc-clone.16bit	Unix on 16-bit PC architectures
comp.unix.pc-clone.32bit	Unix on 23-bit PC architectures
comp.unix.programmer	Questions regarding Unix programming
comp.unix.questions	Question and answer forum for Unix beginners
comp.unix.shell	Unix shells
comp.unix.solaris	Solaris operating system
comp.unix.sys3	System III Unix
comp.unix.sys5.misc	Versions of System V which predate Release 3
comp.unix.sys5.r3	System V Release 3
comp.unix.sys5.r4	System V Release 4
comp.unix.sysv386	System V on 386-based PCs
comp.unix.ultrix	DEC's Ultrix
comp.unix.unixware	Novell's UnixWare products
comp.unix.user-friendly	Unix user friendliness
comp.unix.wizards	Questions for true Unix wizards only
comp.unix.xenix.misc	Non-SCO Xenix
comp.unix.xenix.sco	Santa Cruz Operation (SCO) Xenix
comp.virus	Computer viruses and security (Moderated)
comp.windows.garnet	Garnet user interface development environment
comp.windows.interviews	InterViews object-oriented windowing system

`comp.windows.misc`	General windowing system topics
`comp.windows.news`	Sun Microsystems' NeWS window system
`comp.windows.open-look`	Discussion about the Open Look GUI
`comp.windows.suit`	SUIT user interface toolkit
`comp.windows.x`	X Window System
`comp.windows.x.announce`	X Consortium announcements (Moderated)
`comp.windows.x.apps`	Getting and using (not programming) X applications
`comp.windows.x.i386unix`	XFree86 window system and others
`comp.windows.x.intrinsics`	X toolkit
`comp.windows.x.motif`	Motif graphical user interface
`comp.windows.x.pex`	PHIGS extension of X Window

ddn

`ddn.mgt-bulletin`	Defense Data Network management bulletin (Moderated)
`ddn.newsletter`	DDN newsletter (Moderated)

gnu

`gnu.announce`	News about the GNU project (Moderated)
`gnu.bash.bug`	Bugs and fixes: Bash (Bourne Again Shell) (Moderated)
`gnu.chess`	GNU chess program
`gnu.emacs.announce`	GNU Emacs (Moderated)
`gnu.emacs.bug`	Bugs and fixes: GNU Emacs (Moderated)
`gnu.emacs.gnews`	News reading under GNU Emacs using Weemba's Gnews
`gnu.emacs.gnus`	News reading under GNU Emacs using GNUS (in English)
`gnu.emacs.help`	Questions and answers about Emacs
`gnu.emacs.sources`	Free C and Lisp programs for GNU Emacs (no talk)
`gnu.emacs.vm.bug`	Bugs and fixes: Emacs VM mail package
`gnu.emacs.vm.info`	Emacs VM mail package
`gnu.emacs.vms`	Port of GNU Emacs to VMS
`gnu.epoch.misc`	Epoch X11 extensions to Emacs
`gnu.g++.announce`	News about g++ (the GNU C++ compiler) (Moderated)
`gnu.g++.bug`	Bugs and fixes: g++ (Moderated)
`gnu.g++.help`	Questions and answers about g++
`gnu.g++.lib.bug`	Bugs and fixes: g++ library (Moderated)
`gnu.gcc.announce`	News about gcc (the GNU C compiler) (Moderated)
`gnu.gcc.bug`	Bugs and fixes: gcc (Moderated)
`gnu.gcc.help`	GNU C Compiler (gcc) user queries and answers
`gnu.gdb.bug`	Bugs and fixes: gcc/g++ debugger (Moderated)
`gnu.ghostscript.bug`	Bugs and fixes: Ghostscript interpreter (Moderated)
`gnu.gnusenet.config`	GNU's Not Usenet administration and configuration
`gnu.gnusenet.test`	Place to send test articles
`gnu.groff.bug`	Bugs and fixes: GNU roff programs (Moderated)
`gnu.misc.discuss`	General GNU (Gnu's Not Unix) topics
`gnu.smalltalk.bug`	Bugs and fixes: GNU Smalltalk (Moderated)
`gnu.utils.bug`	Bugs and fixes: GNU utilities (Moderated)

ieee

`ieee.announce`	News for the IEEE community
`ieee.config`	Managing the `ieee.*` newsgroups
`ieee.general`	IEEE general discussion
`ieee.pcnfs`	Tips on PC-NFS
`ieee.rab.announce`	Regional Activities Board announcements
`ieee.rab.general`	Regional Activities Board general discussion
`ieee.region1`	Region 1 announcements
`ieee.tab.announce`	Technical Activities Board announcements
`ieee.tab.general`	Technical Activities Board general discussion
`ieee.tcos`	TCOS newsletter and discussion (Moderated)
`ieee.usab.announce`	USAB announcements
`ieee.usab.general`	USAB general discussion

info

`info.academic-freedom`	Academic freedom
`info.admin`	Managing the `info.*` newsgroups

info.big-internet	Issues facing a huge Internet
info.bind	Berkeley BIND server (Moderated)
info.brl-cad	BRL's solid modeling CAD system (Moderated)
info.bsdi.users	Users of BSDI's Unix operating system
info.bytecounters	NSstat network analysis
info.convex	Convex computers (Moderated)
info.firearms	Firearms: non-political (Moderated)
info.firearms.politics	Firearms: political
info.gated	Cornell's GATED program
info.grass.programmer	Programming GRASS geographic information system
info.grass.user	Using GRASS geographic information system
info.ietf	Internet Engineering Task Force (IETF)
info.ietf.hosts	IETF host requirements
info.ietf.isoc	The Internet Society
info.ietf.njm	Joint Monitoring Access, Adjacent Nets (Moderated)
info.ietf.smtp	IETF SMTP extension
info.isode	ISO Development environment package
info.jethro-tull	Jethro Tull, pop music group
info.labmgr	Computer lab managers (Moderated)
info.mach	Mach operating system (Moderated)
info.mh.workers	MH development (Moderated)
info.nets	Inter-network connectivity
info.nsf.grants	NSF grants (Moderated)
info.nsfnet.cert	Computer Emergency Response Team
info.nsfnet.status	Status of NSFnet
info.nupop	Northwestern University's POP for PCs
info.nysersnmp	SNMP software distributed by PSI
info.osf	OSF's electronic bulletin (Moderated)
info.pem-dev	IETF privacy enhanced mail (Moderated)
info.ph	Qi, ph, sendmail/phquery
info.rfc	Announcements of newly released RFCs
info.slug	Symbolics Lisp machines
info.snmp	Simple Gateway/Network Monitoring Protocol
info.solbourne	Solbourne computers
info.sun-managers	Sun managers digest (Moderated)
info.sun-nets	Sun Nets digest
info.theorynt	Theory (Moderated)
info.unix-sw	Unix software available via anonymous ftp
info.wisenet	Women In Science and Engineering NETwork

k12

k12.chat.elementary	Elementary students forum, grades K-5
k12.chat.junior	Elementary students forum, grades 6-8
k12.chat.senior	High school students forum
k12.chat.teacher	Teachers forum
k12.ed.art	Art curriculum
k12.ed.business	Business education curriculum
k12.ed.comp.literacy	Computer literacy
k12.ed.health-pe	Health and physical education
k12.ed.life-skills	Home economics and career education
k12.ed.math	Mathematics
k12.ed.music	Music and performing arts
k12.ed.science	Science
k12.ed.soc-studies	Social studies and history
k12.ed.special	Students with handicaps or special needs
k12.ed.tag	Talented and gifted students
k12.ed.tech	Industrial arts and vocational education
k12.lang.art	Language arts
k12.lang.deutsch-eng	German/English practice with native speakers
k12.lang.esp-eng	Spanish/English practice with native speakers
k12.lang.francais	French/English practice with native speakers
k12.lang.russian	Russian/English practice with native speakers
k12.library	Libraries and librarians
k12.sys.channel0	Forum for teachers
k12.sys.channel1	Forum for teachers
k12.sys.channel10	Forum for teachers
k12.sys.channel11	Forum for teachers
k12.sys.channel12	Forum for teachers

k12.sys.channel2	Forum for teachers
k12.sys.channel3	Forum for teachers
k12.sys.channel4	Forum for teachers
k12.sys.channel5	Forum for teachers
k12.sys.channel6	Forum for teachers
k12.sys.channel7	Forum for teachers
k12.sys.channel8	Forum for teachers
k12.sys.channel9	Forum for teachers
k12.sys.projects	Teaching projects

misc

misc.activism.progressive	Progressive activism (Moderated)
misc.answers	FAQ lists and other periodic postings (Moderated)
misc.books.technical	Books about technical topics (including computers)
misc.consumers	Consumer interests, product reviews, etc
misc.consumers.house	Owning and maintaining a house
misc.creativity	Creativity in all human endeavors
misc.education	Education
misc.education.adult	Adult education and literacy
misc.education.home-school.christian	Christian home schooling
misc.education.home-school.misc	General home schooling
misc.education.language.english	Teaching the English language
misc.education.medical	Medical education
misc.education.multimedia	Multimedia in education (Moderated)
misc.education.science	Science education
misc.emerg-services	Paramedics and other first responders
misc.entrepreneurs	Operating your own business
misc.fitness	Physical fitness, exercise
misc.forsale	Short postings about items for sale
misc.forsale.computers	Computers for sale
misc.forsale.computers.d	Discussion of misc.forsale.computers.*
misc.forsale.computers.mac	Macintosh-related computer items
misc.forsale.computers.other	Selling miscellaneous computer stuff
misc.forsale.computers.pc-clone	PC-related computer items
misc.forsale.computers.workstation	Workstation-related computer items
misc.handicap	Issues about the handicapped (Moderated)
misc.headlines	Current events
misc.health.alternative	Alternative health care
misc.health.diabetes	Diabetes
misc.int-property	Intellectual property rights
misc.invest	Investments and the handling of money
misc.invest.canada	Investing in Canadian financial markets
misc.invest.funds	Investments: mutual funds and related topics
misc.invest.real-estate	Property investments
misc.invest.stocks	Investments: stocks and related topics
misc.invest.technical	Highly technical discussion of investment strategy
misc.jobs.contract	Contract labor
misc.jobs.misc	Employment, workplaces, careers
misc.jobs.offered	Announcements of positions available
misc.jobs.offered.entry	Job listings, entry-level positions only
misc.jobs.resumes	Postings of résumés and jobs wanted
misc.kids	Children, their behavior and activities
misc.kids.computer	Computers and children
misc.kids.vacation	Vacationing with children and family
misc.legal	Legalities and the ethics of law
misc.legal.computing	Legal/computing topics
misc.legal.moderated	General discussion of law (Moderated)
misc.misc	Discussions not in any other group
misc.news.east-europe.rferl	Radio Free Europe/Radio Liberty (Moderated)
misc.news.southasia	News from Southeast Asia (Moderated)
misc.rural	Rural living
misc.taxes	Tax laws and advice
misc.test	Place to send test articles
misc.test.moderated	Place for test articles to a moderated group (Moderated)
misc.transport.urban-transit	Urban public transportation systems
misc.wanted	Requests for things (not software)
misc.writing	Discussion of writing in all of its forms

USENET NEWSGROUPS

news

news.admin	Usenet news administration
news.admin.misc	General Usenet news administration topics
news.admin.policy	Policy issues of Usenet
news.admin.technical	Technical aspects of Usenet (Moderated)
news.announce.conferences	Calls for papers and conference notices (Moderated)
news.announce.important	General announcements of interest to all (Moderated)
news.announce.newgroups	Calls for new groups (Moderated)
news.announce.newusers	Explanatory postings for new users (Moderated)
news.answers	Repository for periodic Usenet articles (Moderated)
news.config	Postings of system down times and interruptions
news.future	Future technology of Usenet
news.groups	Discussions and lists of newsgroups
news.groups.questions	Questions as to where to find a particular topic
news.groups.reviews	Reviews of newsgroups and mailing lists (Moderated)
news.lists	Usenet statistics and lists (Moderated)
news.lists.ps-maps	Maps relating to Usenet traffic flows (Moderated)
news.misc	General topics relating to Usenet itself
news.newsites	Postings of new site announcements
news.newusers.questions	Questions and answers for new Usenet users
news.software.anu-news	VMS B-news software from Australian National University
news.software.b	B-news-compatible software
news.software.nn	Discussion about the nn newsreader
news.software.nntp	Network News Transfer Protocol
news.software.notes	Notesfile software from the University of Illinois
news.software.readers	Discussion of Usenet newsreader programs
news.sysadmin	Topics for system administrators

rec

rec.answers	Repository for periodic Usenet articles (Moderated)
rec.antiques	Antiques and vintage items
rec.aquaria	Keeping fish and aquaria as a hobby
rec.arts.animation	Various kinds of animation
rec.arts.anime	Anime: Japanese animation
rec.arts.anime.info	Anime: Japanese animation
rec.arts.anime.marketplace	Anime: buying and selling
rec.arts.anime.stories	Anime: stories
rec.arts.ascii	ASCII art (Moderated)
rec.arts.bodyart	Tattoos and body decoration
rec.arts.bonsai	Minature trees and shrubbery
rec.arts.books	Books of all genres and the publishing industry
rec.arts.books.marketplace	Buying and selling books
rec.arts.books.tolkien	Works of J.R.R. Tolkien
rec.arts.cinema	Cinema (Moderated)
rec.arts.comics.creative	Encouraging good superhero-style writing
rec.arts.comics.info	Reviews, conventions, and other news (Moderated)
rec.arts.comics.marketplace	Buying and selling comics
rec.arts.comics.misc	General comic book and related topics
rec.arts.comics.strips	Comic strips
rec.arts.comics.xbooks	Mutant Universe of Marvel Comics
rec.arts.dance	Aspects of dance not covered in another newsgroup
rec.arts.disney	Any Disney-related subjects
rec.arts.drwho	Dr. Who
rec.arts.erotica	Erotic fiction and verse (Moderated)
rec.arts.fine	Fine arts and artists
rec.arts.int-fiction	Interactive fiction
rec.arts.manga	Manga: Japanese storytelling art form
rec.arts.marching.drumcorps	Drum and bugle corps
rec.arts.marching.misc	Marching-related performance activities
rec.arts.misc	General topics about the arts
rec.arts.movies	Movies and movie making
rec.arts.movies.production	Filmmaking, amateur and professional
rec.arts.movies.reviews	Movie reviews (Moderated)
rec.arts.poems	Poetry
rec.arts.prose	Short works of prose fiction and discussion
rec.arts.sf.announce	Major science fiction announcements (Moderated)

rec.arts.sf.fandom	Science fiction fan activities
rec.arts.sf.marketplace	Buying and selling personal science fiction materials
rec.arts.sf.misc	General science fiction topics
rec.arts.sf.movies	Science fiction movies
rec.arts.sf.reviews	Reviews: science fiction/fantasy/horror (Moderated)
rec.arts.sf.science	Real and speculative aspects of science fiction science
rec.arts.sf.starwars	Discussion of the *Star Wars* universe
rec.arts.sf.tv	Science fiction on television
rec.arts.sf.tv.babylon5	*Babylon 5*, science fiction TV show
rec.arts.sf.tv.quantum-leap	*Quantum Leap*, science fiction TV show
rec.arts.sf.written	Written science fiction and fantasy
rec.arts.sf.written.robert-jordan	Books of Robert Jordan
rec.arts.startrek	General *Star Trek* topics
rec.arts.startrek.current	New *Star Trek* shows, movies, and books
rec.arts.startrek.fandom	*Star Trek* conventions and memorabilia
rec.arts.startrek.info	Universe of *Star Trek* (Moderated)
rec.arts.startrek.misc	General *Star Trek* topics
rec.arts.startrek.reviews	Reviews of *Star Trek* books, shows, films (Moderated)
rec.arts.startrek.tech	*Star Trek*'s depiction of future technologies
rec.arts.theatre	All aspects of stage work and theatre
rec.arts.theatre.misc	General theatre topics
rec.arts.theatre.musicals	Musical theatre
rec.arts.theatre.plays	Dramaturgy and discussion of plays
rec.arts.theatre.stagecraft	Stagecraft and production
rec.arts.tv	Television history, past and current shows
rec.arts.tv.mst3k	*Mystery Science Theater 3000*
rec.arts.tv.soaps	Soap operas
rec.arts.tv.tiny-toon	Tiny Toons, TV show
rec.arts.tv.uk	Telly shows from the U.K.
rec.arts.wobegon	Literary and music esoterica
rec.audio	High fidelity audio
rec.audio.car	Automobile audio systems
rec.audio.high-end	High-end audio systems (Moderated)
rec.audio.marketplace	Buying and selling home audio equipment
rec.audio.misc	General audio topics
rec.audio.opinion	Opinions about home audio
rec.audio.pro	Professional audio recording and studio engineering
rec.audio.tech	Technical aspects of home audio
rec.autos	Automobiles, automotive products, and laws
rec.autos.antique	Automobiles over 25 years old
rec.autos.driving	Driving automobiles
rec.autos.marketplace	Buying and selling cars
rec.autos.misc	General car topics
rec.autos.rod-n-custom	Souped-up and customized autos
rec.autos.simulators	Automotive simulators
rec.autos.sport	Organized, legal auto competitions
rec.autos.sport.info	Auto racing (Moderated)
rec.autos.sport.nascar	NASCAR, professional stock car racing
rec.autos.sport.tech	Technical aspects of auto racing
rec.autos.tech	Technical aspects of automobiles
rec.autos.vw	Volkswagen products
rec.aviation	General aviation topics
rec.aviation.announce	Events for the aviation community (Moderated)
rec.aviation.answers	Questions and answers about aviation (Moderated)
rec.aviation.homebuilt	Selecting, designing, building, restoring aircraft
rec.aviation.ifr	Flying under Instrument Flight Rules
rec.aviation.military	Military aircraft of the past, present, and future
rec.aviation.misc	General aviation topics
rec.aviation.owning	Owning airplanes
rec.aviation.piloting	General discussion for aviators
rec.aviation.products	Products useful to pilots
rec.aviation.questions	Aviation questions and answers (Moderated)
rec.aviation.simulators	Flight simulation on all levels
rec.aviation.soaring	Sailplanes and hang-gliders
rec.aviation.stories	Anecdotes of flight experiences (Moderated)
rec.aviation.student	Learning to fly
rec.backcountry	Outdoor activities
rec.bicycles	General bicycling topics
rec.bicycles.marketplace	Buying and selling cycling equipment

USENET NEWSGROUPS

`rec.bicycles.misc`	General bicycling topics
`rec.bicycles.racing`	Bicycle racing techniques, rules, and results
`rec.bicycles.rides`	Discussions of tours, training, commuting routes
`rec.bicycles.soc`	Societal issues of bicycling
`rec.bicycles.tech`	Cycling product design, construction, maintenance
`rec.birds`	Bird watching
`rec.boats`	Boating
`rec.boats.paddle`	Any boats with oars, paddles, etc
`rec.climbing`	Climbing techniques, announcements, etc
`rec.collecting`	Discussion among collectors of many things
`rec.collecting.cards`	Collecting sport and non-sport cards
`rec.collecting.stamps`	Stamp collecting
`rec.crafts.brewing`	Making beers and meads
`rec.crafts.jewelry`	Jewelry making and lapidary work
`rec.crafts.metalworking`	Working with metal
`rec.crafts.misc`	General topics relating to handiwork arts
`rec.crafts.quilting`	Quilts and similar items
`rec.crafts.textiles`	Sewing, weaving, knitting, and other fiber arts
`rec.crafts.textiles.misc`	Textiles: general topics
`rec.crafts.textiles.needlework`	Textiles: needlework
`rec.crafts.textiles.quilting`	Textiles: quilting
`rec.crafts.textiles.sewing`	Textiles: sewing
`rec.crafts.textiles.yarn`	Textiles: yarn
`rec.crafts.winemaking`	Making wine
`rec.equestrian`	Horses and riding
`rec.folk-dancing`	Folk dances, dancers, and dancing
`rec.food.cooking`	Food, cooking, cookbooks, and recipes
`rec.food.drink`	Wines and spirits
`rec.food.drink.beer`	Beer
`rec.food.drink.coffee`	Coffee
`rec.food.historic`	History of food-making arts
`rec.food.recipes`	Recipes for interesting food and drink (Moderated)
`rec.food.restaurants`	Discussion of dining out
`rec.food.sourdough`	Making and baking with sourdough
`rec.food.veg`	Vegetarians
`rec.food.veg.cooking`	Vegetarian recipes, cooking, nutrition (Moderated)
`rec.gambling`	Games of chance and betting
`rec.games.abstract`	Perfect information, pure strategy games
`rec.games.backgammon`	Backgammon
`rec.games.board`	Discussion and hints on board games
`rec.games.board.ce`	Cosmic Encounter board game
`rec.games.board.marketplace`	Buying and selling board games
`rec.games.bolo`	Networked strategy war game Bolo
`rec.games.bridge`	Bridge card game
`rec.games.chess`	Chess and computer chess
`rec.games.chinese-chess`	Chinese chess (Xiangqi)
`rec.games.corewar`	Core War computer game
`rec.games.deckmaster`	Deckmaster games
`rec.games.deckmaster.marketplace`	Buying and selling Deckmaster paraphernalia
`rec.games.design`	Game design-related issues
`rec.games.diplomacy`	Diplomacy conquest game
`rec.games.empire`	Empire game
`rec.games.frp`	General fantasy role-playing game topics
`rec.games.frp.advocacy`	Debate about various role-playing systems
`rec.games.frp.announce`	Announcements in the role-playing world (Moderated)
`rec.games.frp.archives`	Archivable fantasy stories (Moderated)
`rec.games.frp.cyber`	Cyberpunk related fantasy role-playing games
`rec.games.frp.dnd`	Fantasy role-playing with TSR's Dungeons and Dragons
`rec.games.frp.live-action`	Live-action role-playing games
`rec.games.frp.marketplace`	Role-playing game materials wanted and for sale
`rec.games.frp.misc`	General fantasy role-playing game topics
`rec.games.go`	Go game
`rec.games.hack`	Hack game
`rec.games.int-fiction`	Interactive fiction games
`rec.games.mecha`	Giant robot games
`rec.games.miniatures`	Tabletop wargaming
`rec.games.misc`	Games and computer games
`rec.games.moria`	Moria game
`rec.games.mud.admin`	Adminstrative issues of relating to MUDs

rec.games.mud.announce	Announcements about MUDs (Moderated)
rec.games.mud.diku	Diku MUDs
rec.games.mud.lp	LP MUDs
rec.games.mud.misc	General MUD topics
rec.games.mud.moo	MOOs (object-oriented MUDs)
rec.games.mud.tiny	Tiny MUDs
rec.games.netrek	X Window system game Netrek (XtrekII)
rec.games.pbm	Play-by-mail games
rec.games.pinball	Pinball-related games
rec.games.programmer	Adventure game programming
rec.games.rogue	Rogue game
rec.games.roguelike.angband	Angband, Rogue-like game
rec.games.roguelike.announce	Announcements about Rogue-like games (Moderated)
rec.games.roguelike.misc	Topics relating to Rogue-like games
rec.games.roguelike.moria	Moria
rec.games.roguelike.nethack	Nethack
rec.games.roguelike.rogue	Rogue
rec.games.trivia	Trivia
rec.games.vectrex	Vectrex game system
rec.games.video	Video games
rec.games.video.3do	3DO video game systems
rec.games.video.advocacy	Debate about video game systems
rec.games.video.arcade	Coin-operated video games
rec.games.video.arcade.collecting	Collecting video games
rec.games.video.atari	Atari's video game systems
rec.games.video.cd32	Gaming talk relating to the Amiga CD32
rec.games.video.classic	Older home video entertainment systems
rec.games.video.marketplace	Home video game stuff for sale or trade
rec.games.video.misc	General home video game topics
rec.games.video.nintendo	Nintendo video game systems and software
rec.games.video.sega	Sega video game systems and software
rec.games.xtank.play	Distributed game Xtank
rec.games.xtank.programmer	Coding the Xtank game and its robots
rec.gardens	Gardening
rec.gardens.orchids	Orchids
rec.gardens.roses	Roses
rec.guns	Firearms (Moderated)
rec.heraldry	Coats of arms
rec.humor	Jokes (may be offensive)
rec.humor.d	Discussions on the content of rec.humor articles
rec.humor.funny	Jokes that a moderator thinks are funny (Moderated)
rec.humor.oracle	Sagacious advice from the Usenet Oracle (Moderated)
rec.humor.oracle.d	Comments about the Usenet Oracle's advice
rec.hunting	Hunting (Moderated)
rec.juggling	Juggling techniques, equipment, and events
rec.kites	Kites and kiting
rec.mag	Magazine summaries, tables of contents, etc
rec.mag.fsfnet	Science fiction fanzines (Moderated)
rec.martial-arts	Martial arts
rec.misc	General recreational topics
rec.models.railroad	Model railroads of all scales
rec.models.rc	Radio-controlled models
rec.models.rockets	Model rockets
rec.models.scale	Construction of models
rec.motorcycles	Motorcycles, related products and laws
rec.motorcycles.dirt	Motorcycles and ATVs off-road
rec.motorcycles.harley	Harley-Davidson motorcycles
rec.motorcycles.racing	Racing motorcycles
rec.music.a-cappella	A cappella music, voice with no instruments
rec.music.afro-latin	Music with African and Latin influences
rec.music.beatles	Beatles
rec.music.bluenote	Jazz, blues, and related types of music
rec.music.cd	Music and CDs
rec.music.celtic	Celtic music, traditional and modern
rec.music.christian	Christian music, both contemporary and traditional
rec.music.classical	Classical music
rec.music.classical.guitar	Classical guitar music
rec.music.classical.performing	Performing classical and early music
rec.music.compose	Creating musical and lyrical works

rec.music.country.western	Country and western music
rec.music.dementia	Comedy and novelty music
rec.music.dylan	Music of Bob Dylan
rec.music.early	Pre-classical European music
rec.music.folk	Folk music
rec.music.funky	Funk, rap, hip-hop, house, soul, R&B etc
rec.music.gaffa	Kate Bush and other alternative music (Moderated)
rec.music.gdead	Music of the Grateful Dead
rec.music.indian.classical	Hindustani and Carnatic Indian classical music
rec.music.indian.misc	General topics in Indian music
rec.music.industrial	Industrial-related music styles
rec.music.info	News on musical topics (Moderated)
rec.music.makers	Performers and their discussions
rec.music.makers.bass	Upright bass and bass guitar techniques, equipment
rec.music.makers.builders	Design, building, repair of musical instruments
rec.music.makers.guitar	Electric and acoustic guitar techniques, equipment
rec.music.makers.guitar.acoustic	Acoustic guitar
rec.music.makers.guitar.tablature	Guitar tablature and chords
rec.music.makers.marketplace	Buying and selling music-making equipment
rec.music.makers.percussion	Drum, other percussion techniques and equipment
rec.music.makers.piano	Piano music, performing and composing
rec.music.makers.synth	Synthesizers and computer music
rec.music.marketplace	Records, tapes, and CDs wanted, for sale, etc
rec.music.misc	General music topics
rec.music.movies	Music for movies and television
rec.music.newage	New Age music
rec.music.phish	Phish
rec.music.reggae	Reggae
rec.music.rem	REM, pop music group
rec.music.reviews	Reviews of all types of music (Moderated)
rec.music.synth	Synthesizers and computer music
rec.music.video	Music videos and music video software
rec.nude	Naturist and nudist activities
rec.org.mensa	Mensa high IQ society
rec.org.sca	Society for Creative Anachronism
rec.outdoors.fishing	Sport and commercial fishing
rec.outdoors.fishing.fly	Fly fishing
rec.outdoors.fishing.saltwater	Saltwater fishing
rec.parks.theme	Theme parks
rec.pets	General pet topics
rec.pets.birds	Pets: birds
rec.pets.cats	Pets: cats
rec.pets.dogs	Pets: dogs
rec.pets.herp	Pets: reptiles and amphibians
rec.pets.rabbits	Pets: rabbits
rec.photo	General photography topics
rec.photo.advanced	Advanced photography topics
rec.photo.darkroom	Developing, printing and other darkroom topics
rec.photo.help	Questions and answers about photography
rec.photo.marketplace	Buying and selling of photographic equipment
rec.photo.misc	General photography topics
rec.puzzles	Puzzles, problems, and quizzes
rec.puzzles.crosswords	Making and playing gridded word puzzles
rec.pyrotechnics	Fireworks, rocketry, safety, and other topics
rec.radio.amateur.antenna	Antennas, theory, techniques, and construction
rec.radio.amateur.digital.misc	Packet radio and other digital radio modes
rec.radio.amateur.equipment	Amateur radio equipment
rec.radio.amateur.homebrew	Amateur radio construction and experimentation
rec.radio.amateur.misc	General amateur radio topics
rec.radio.amateur.packet	Packet radio setups
rec.radio.amateur.policy	Radio use and regulation policy
rec.radio.amateur.space	Amateur radio transmissions through space
rec.radio.broadcasting	Local area broadcast radio (Moderated)
rec.radio.cb	Citizen band radio
rec.radio.info	Informative postings related to radio (Moderated)
rec.radio.noncomm	Noncommercial radio
rec.radio.scanner	"Utility" broadcasting traffic above 30 MHz
rec.radio.shortwave	Shortwave radio
rec.radio.swap	Trading and swapping radio equipment

rec.railroad	Real and model trains
rec.roller-coaster	Roller coasters and other amusement park rides
rec.running	Running for enjoyment, sport, exercise, etc
rec.scouting	Scouting youth organizations worldwide
rec.scuba	Scuba diving
rec.skate	Ice skating and roller skating
rec.skiing	General snow skiing topics
rec.skiing.alpine	Downhill skiing
rec.skiing.announce	Announcements about snow skiing (Moderated)
rec.skiing.nordic	Cross-country skiing
rec.skiing.snowboard	Snowboarding
rec.skydiving	Skydiving
rec.sport.baseball	General baseball topics
rec.sport.baseball.analysis	Analysis of baseball (Moderated)
rec.sport.baseball.college	College baseball
rec.sport.baseball.data	Raw baseball data (statistics, birthdays, schedules)
rec.sport.baseball.fantasy	Fantasy baseball
rec.sport.basketball.college	College basketball
rec.sport.basketball.misc	General basketball topics
rec.sport.basketball.pro	Professional basketball
rec.sport.basketball.women	Women's basketball
rec.sport.boxing	Boxing
rec.sport.cricket	Cricket
rec.sport.cricket.info	News, scores and info related to cricket (Moderated)
rec.sport.cricket.scores	Scores from cricket matches (Moderated)
rec.sport.disc	Flying disc-based sports
rec.sport.fencing	All aspects of swordplay
rec.sport.football.australian	Australian (rules) football
rec.sport.football.canadian	Canadian football
rec.sport.football.college	American-style college football
rec.sport.football.fantasy	Fantasy football
rec.sport.football.misc	General American-style football topics
rec.sport.football.pro	American-style professional football
rec.sport.golf	Golf
rec.sport.hockey	Ice hockey
rec.sport.hockey.field	Field hockey
rec.sport.misc	General sport topics
rec.sport.olympics	Olympic Games
rec.sport.paintball	Survival game Paintball
rec.sport.pro-wrestling	Professional wrestling
rec.sport.rowing	Crew for competition or fitness
rec.sport.rugby	Rugby
rec.sport.soccer	Soccer (Association Football)
rec.sport.swimming	Training for and competing in swimming events
rec.sport.table-tennis	Ping-Pong
rec.sport.tennis	Tennis
rec.sport.triathlon	Multi-event sports
rec.sport.volleyball	Volleyball
rec.sport.water-polo	Water polo
rec.sport.waterski	Waterskiing and related boat-towed activities
rec.toys.lego	Lego, Duplo, and compatible toys
rec.toys.misc	General toys topics
rec.travel	Traveling all over the world
rec.travel.air	Airline travel around the world
rec.travel.asia	Travel in Asia
rec.travel.cruises	Travel by cruise ship
rec.travel.europe	Travel in Europe
rec.travel.marketplace	Buying and selling: tickets and accommodations
rec.travel.misc	General travel topics
rec.travel.usa-canada	Travel in the United States and Canada
rec.video	Video and video components
rec.video.cable-tv	Technical and regulatory issues of cable television
rec.video.desktop	Amateur, computer-based video editing and production
rec.video.production	Making professional quality video productions
rec.video.releases	Prerecorded video releases, laserdisc and videotape
rec.video.satellite	Receiving video via satellite
rec.windsurfing	Wind surfing
rec.woodworking	Woodworking

sci

sci.aeronautics	Aeronautics and related technology
sci.aeronautics.airliners	Airliner technology (Moderated)
sci.aeronautics.simulation	Aerospace simulation (Moderated)
sci.agriculture	Farming and agriculture
sci.agriculture.beekeeping	Beekeeping, bee culture, and hive products
sci.answers	Repository for periodic Usenet articles (Moderated)
sci.anthropology	All aspects of studying humankind
sci.anthropology.paleo	Evolution of man and other primates
sci.aquaria	Scientifically oriented postings about aquaria
sci.archaeology	Studying antiquities of the world
sci.archaeology.mesoamerican	Mesoamerican archaeology
sci.astro	Astronomy
sci.astro.fits	Flexible Image Transport System
sci.astro.hubble	Hubble Space Telescope data (Moderated)
sci.astro.planetarium	Planetariums
sci.astro.research	Astronomy and astrophysics research (Moderated)
sci.bio	Biology and related sciences
sci.bio.ecology	Ecological research
sci.bio.ethology	Animal behavior and behavioral ecology
sci.bio.evolution	Evolutionary biology (Moderated)
sci.bio.herp	Amphibians and reptiles
sci.bio.technology	Biotechnology
sci.chaos	Science of chaos
sci.chem	Chemistry and related sciences
sci.chem.electrochem	Electrochemistry
sci.chem.labware	Chemical laboratory equipment
sci.chem.organomet	Organometallic chemistry
sci.classics	Classical history, languages, art, and more
sci.cognitive	Perception, memory, judgment, and reasoning
sci.comp-aided	Computers as tools in scientific research
sci.cryonics	Biostasis, suspended animation, etc
sci.crypt	Data encryption and decryption
sci.data.formats	Modelling and storing scientific data
sci.econ	Economics
sci.econ.research	Economics research (Moderated)
sci.edu	Education
sci.electronics	Circuits, theory, electrons, and discussions
sci.electronics.cad	Computer aided design, schematic drafting, and so on
sci.electronics.repair	Fixing electronic equipment
sci.energy	Energy, science and technology
sci.energy.hydrogen	Hydrogen as an alternative fuel
sci.engr	Technical discussions about engineering tasks
sci.engr.advanced-tv	HDTV/DATV standards, formats, equipment, practices
sci.engr.biomed	Biomedical engineering
sci.engr.chem	Chemical engineering
sci.engr.civil	Civil engineering
sci.engr.control	Engineering of control systems
sci.engr.lighting	Light, vision, color in architecture and media
sci.engr.manufacturing	Manufacturing technology
sci.engr.mech	Mechanical engineering
sci.engr.semiconductors	Semiconductor devices
sci.environment	Environment and ecology
sci.fractals	Objects of non-integral dimension and other chaos
sci.geo.eos	NASA's Earth Observation System
sci.geo.fluids	Geophysical fluid dynamics
sci.geo.geology	Solid earth sciences
sci.geo.hydrology	Surface and groundwater hydrology
sci.geo.meteorology	Meteorology and related topics
sci.geo.satellite-nav	Satellite navigation systems, especially GPS
sci.image.processing	Scientific image processing and analysis
sci.lang	Natural languages, communication, etc
sci.lang.japan	Japanese language, both spoken and written
sci.life-extension	Discussions about living longer
sci.logic	Mathematical logic, philosophical and computational aspects
sci.materials	Materials engineering
sci.math	Mathematics in general
sci.math.num-analysis	Numerical analysis

sci.math.research	Current mathematical research (Moderated)
sci.math.stat	Mathematics from a statistical viewpoint
sci.math.symbolic	Symbolic algebra
sci.mech.fluids	Fluid mechanics
sci.med	Medicine
sci.med.aids	AIDS and HIV virus (Moderated)
sci.med.dentistry	Dentistry and teeth
sci.med.nursing	Nursing
sci.med.nutrition	Physiological aspects of diet and eating
sci.med.occupational	Occupational injuries
sci.med.pharmacy	Pharmacy
sci.med.physics	Physics in medical testing and care
sci.med.psychobiology	Psychiatry and psychobiology
sci.med.radiology	Radiology
sci.med.telemedicine	Clinical consulting through computer networks
sci.military	Science and the military (Moderated)
sci.misc	Short-lived general science topics
sci.nanotech	Self-reproducing molecular-size machines (Moderated)
sci.nonlinear	Chaotic and other nonlinear systems
sci.op-research	Operations research
sci.optics	Optics
sci.philosophy.meta	Metaphilosophy
sci.philosophy.tech	Technical philosophy, math, science, logic, etc
sci.physics	Physics
sci.physics.accelerators	Particle accelerators
sci.physics.computational.fluid-dynamics	Computational fluid dynamics
sci.physics.electromag	Electromagnetic theory and applications
sci.physics.fusion	Fusion
sci.physics.particle	Particle physics
sci.physics.plasma	Plasma science (Moderated)
sci.physics.research	Current physics research (Moderated)
sci.polymers	Polymer science
sci.psychology	Psychology
sci.psychology.digest	*Psycoloquy*, a refereed psychology journal (Moderated)
sci.psychology.research	Research issues in psychology (Moderated)
sci.research	Research methods, funding, and ethics
sci.research.careers	Careers in scientific research
sci.research.postdoc	Post-doctoral studies, including job listings
sci.skeptic	Skeptics discussing pseudo-science
sci.sociology	Scientific approach to sociology
sci.space	Space, space programs and space-related research
sci.space.news	Space-related news items (Moderated)
sci.space.policy	Space policy
sci.space.science	Space and planetary science (Moderated)
sci.space.shuttle	Space shuttle and the STS program
sci.space.tech	Technical issues related to space flight (Moderated)
sci.stat.consult	Statistical consulting
sci.stat.edu	Statistics education
sci.stat.math	Statistics from a mathematical viewpoint
sci.systems	Systems science
sci.techniques.mag-resonance	Magnetic resonance imaging and spectroscopy
sci.techniques.microscopy	Microscopy
sci.techniques.spectroscopy	Spectrum analysis
sci.techniques.xtallography	Crystallography
sci.virtual-worlds	Modelling the universe (Moderated)
sci.virtual-worlds.apps	Virtual worlds technology (Moderated)

SOC

soc.answers	Repository for periodic Usenet articles (Moderated)
soc.bi	Bisexuality
soc.college	College activities
soc.college.grad	Graduate schools
soc.college.gradinfo	Information about graduate schools
soc.college.graduation	College graduation
soc.college.org.aiesec	International Assoc. of Business and Commerce Students
soc.college.teaching-asst	Teaching assistants in colleges and universities
soc.couples	Discussions for couples
soc.couples.intercultural	Intercultural and interracial relationships

USENET NEWSGROUPS

soc.culture.afghanistan	Afghan society
soc.culture.african	Africa and things African
soc.culture.african.american	African-American issues
soc.culture.arabic	Technological and cultural issues (not politics)
soc.culture.argentina	Argentina
soc.culture.asean	Countries of the Association of SE Asian Nations
soc.culture.asian.american	Asian-American issues
soc.culture.australian	Australia
soc.culture.austria	Austria
soc.culture.baltics	Baltic states
soc.culture.bangladesh	Bangladesh
soc.culture.belgium	Belgium
soc.culture.berber	Berber language, history, and culture
soc.culture.bosna-herzgvna	Bosnia and Herzegovina
soc.culture.brazil	Brazil
soc.culture.british	Great Britain
soc.culture.bulgaria	Bulgaria
soc.culture.burma	Burma
soc.culture.canada	Canada
soc.culture.caribbean	Caribbean
soc.culture.celtic	Irish, Scottish, Breton, Cornish, Manx, and Welsh
soc.culture.chile	Chile
soc.culture.china	China and Chinese culture
soc.culture.colombia	Colombia
soc.culture.croatia	Croatia
soc.culture.cuba	Cuba
soc.culture.czecho-slovak	Bohemian, Slovak, Moravian and Silesian life
soc.culture.esperanto	Esperanto, international language
soc.culture.europe	All-European society
soc.culture.filipino	Filipino culture
soc.culture.french	France
soc.culture.german	Germany
soc.culture.greek	Greece
soc.culture.hongkong	Hong Kong
soc.culture.hongkong.entertainment	Entertainment in Hong Kong
soc.culture.indian	India
soc.culture.indian.info	Moderated group about culture of India (Moderated)
soc.culture.indian.telugu	Telugu people of India
soc.culture.indonesia	Indonesia
soc.culture.iranian	Iran and things Persian
soc.culture.israel	Israel
soc.culture.italian	Italy
soc.culture.japan	Everything Japanese, except the Japanese language
soc.culture.jewish	Jewish culture and religion
soc.culture.jewish.holocaust	Holocaust with respect to Jews (Moderated)
soc.culture.korean	Korea
soc.culture.laos	Laos
soc.culture.latin-america	Latin America
soc.culture.lebanon	Lebanon
soc.culture.maghreb	Northwest Africa (Morrocco, Algeria, Tunis)
soc.culture.magyar	Hungary
soc.culture.malaysia	Malaysia
soc.culture.mexican	Mexico
soc.culture.mexican.american	Mexican-American culture
soc.culture.misc	General culture topics
soc.culture.mongolian	Mongolia
soc.culture.native	Aboriginal people around the world
soc.culture.nepal	Nepal
soc.culture.netherlands	Netherlands and Belgium
soc.culture.new-zealand	New Zealand
soc.culture.nordic	Culture up north
soc.culture.pakistan	Pakistan
soc.culture.palestine	Palestinian culture
soc.culture.peru	Peru
soc.culture.polish	Poland
soc.culture.portuguese	Portugal
soc.culture.puerto-rico	Puerto Rico
soc.culture.romanian	Romania and Moldavia people
soc.culture.scientists	Culture and scientists

soc.culture.singapore	Singapore
soc.culture.slovenia	Slovenia
soc.culture.somalia	Somalia
soc.culture.soviet	Russia and Soviet culture
soc.culture.spain	Spain
soc.culture.sri-lanka	Sri Lanka
soc.culture.swiss	Switzerland
soc.culture.taiwan	Taiwan
soc.culture.tamil	Tamil language, history, and culture
soc.culture.thai	Thailand
soc.culture.turkish	Turkey
soc.culture.ukrainian	Ukrainian culture
soc.culture.uruguay	Uruguay
soc.culture.usa	United States of America
soc.culture.venezuela	Venezuela
soc.culture.vietnamese	Vietnam
soc.culture.yugoslavia	Former Yugoslavia
soc.feminism	Feminism and feminist issues (Moderated)
soc.history	History
soc.history.moderated	All aspects of history (Moderated)
soc.history.war.misc	Wars in general
soc.history.war.world-war-ii	World War Two (Moderated)
soc.libraries.talk	Libraries
soc.men	Men, their problems and relationships
soc.misc	General socially oriented topics
soc.motss	Homosexuality (members of the same sex)
soc.net-people	Announcements, requests, about people on the Net
soc.org.nonprofit	Nonprofit organizations
soc.org.service-clubs.misc	Service organizations
soc.penpals	Penpals
soc.politics	Political problems, systems, solutions (Moderated)
soc.politics.arms-d	Arms discussion digest (Moderated)
soc.religion.bahai	Baha'i faith (Moderated)
soc.religion.christian	Christianity and related topics (Moderated)
soc.religion.christian.bible-study	Holy Bible (Moderated)
soc.religion.christian.youth-work	Christians and young people (Moderated)
soc.religion.eastern	Eastern religions (Moderated)
soc.religion.gnosis	Gnosis, esoteric spiritual knowledge (Moderated)
soc.religion.islam	Islamic faith (Moderated)
soc.religion.quaker	Religious Society of Friends (Quakers)
soc.religion.shamanism	Shamanism
soc.rights.human	Human rights and activism
soc.roots	Genealogy, tracing your roots
soc.singles	Single people, their activities, etc
soc.support.transgendered	Transgendered and intersexed people
soc.veterans	Military veterans
soc.women	Women, their problems and relationships

talk

talk.abortion	Discussions and arguments on abortion
talk.answers	Repository for periodic Usenet articles (Moderated)
talk.bizarre	Unusual, bizarre, curious, and often stupid
talk.environment	Environment
talk.origins	Evolution versus creationism
talk.philosophy.misc	General philosophical topics
talk.politics.animals	Use and abuse of animals
talk.politics.china	Politics of China
talk.politics.crypto	Cryptography and government
talk.politics.drugs	Politics of drug issues
talk.politics.guns	Politics of firearm ownership
talk.politics.medicine	Politics of health care
talk.politics.mideast	Politics of the Middle East
talk.politics.misc	General political topics
talk.politics.soviet	Politics of the former Soviet Union
talk.politics.space	Non-technical issues affecting space exploration
talk.politics.theory	Theory of politics and political systems
talk.politics.tibet	Politics of Tibet
talk.rape	Rape (not to be crossposted)

talk.religion.misc	General religious topics
talk.religion.newage	New Age religions and philosophies
talk.rumors	Rumors

u3b

u3b.config	AT&T 3B distribution configuration
u3b.misc	General AT&T 3B computer topics
u3b.sources	Free programs for AT&T 3B systems
u3b.tech	3B technical issues
u3b.test	Place to send test articles

vmsnet

vmsnet.admin	Managing VMS internals, MACRO-32, Bliss, etc
vmsnet.alpha	Alpha AXP architecture, systems, porting, etc
vmsnet.announce	General announcements of interest to all (Moderated)
vmsnet.announce.newusers	Orientation information for new users (Moderated)
vmsnet.databases.rdb	DEC's Rdb relational database
vmsnet.decus.journal	DECUServe Journal (Moderated)
vmsnet.decus.lugs	DECUS local user groups
vmsnet.employment	Jobs sought and offered
vmsnet.epsilon-cd	DEC's free, unsupported OpenVMS AXP CD
vmsnet.groups	Managing the vmsnet.* newsgroups
vmsnet.infosystems.gopher	Gopher software for VMS
vmsnet.infosystems.misc	Infosystem software for VMS (Web, Wais, and so on)
vmsnet.internals	VMS internals, MACRO-32, Bliss, etc
vmsnet.mail.misc	Other electronic mail software
vmsnet.mail.mx	MX email system from RPI
vmsnet.mail.pmdf	PMDF email system
vmsnet.misc	General VMS topics
vmsnet.networks.desktop.misc	Other desktop integration software
vmsnet.networks.desktop.pathworks	DEC Pathworks desktop integration software
vmsnet.networks.management.decmcc	DECmcc and related software
vmsnet.networks.management.misc	Other network management software
vmsnet.networks.misc	General networking topics
vmsnet.networks.tcp-ip.cmu-tek	CMU-TEK TCP/IP package
vmsnet.networks.tcp-ip.misc	Other TCP/IP software for VMS
vmsnet.networks.tcp-ip.multinet	TGV's Multinet TCP/IP
vmsnet.networks.tcp-ip.tcpware	Process Software's TCPWARE TCP/IP software
vmsnet.networks.tcp-ip.ucx	DEC's VMS/Ultrix Connection, TCP/IP for VMS
vmsnet.networks.tcp-ip.wintcp	Wollongong Group's WIN-TCP TCP/IP software
vmsnet.pdp-11	PDP-11 hardware and software
vmsnet.sources	Free programs (no discussion) (Moderated)
vmsnet.sources.d	Discussion about and requests for free programs
vmsnet.sources.games	Recreational software
vmsnet.sysmgt	VMS system management
vmsnet.test	Place to send test articles
vmsnet.tpu	TPU language and applications
vmsnet.uucp	DECUS UUCP software
vmsnet.vms-posix	VMS Posix

Index

*Main subject headings are shown in **bold***

10,000 Maniacs, 490
2020 News & Views, 201
21st Century Constitution, 545
2600, 598
30 Plus, 664
386BSD Unix Supplements for Compaq
    Computers, 110
4AD Eyesore, 464
4DOS Command Processor, 502
40 Tips to Go Green, 201
41 Plus, 530
.44 Magnum, 647
'60s Left Today, 544
911 Gallery, 15

A

A Cappella, 464
A/UX, 514
Aart Gallery, 16
ABC's World News Now, 498
Aboriginal Studies, 717
Aboriginal Studies Archive, 11
Abortion, 210
Abortion and Reproductive Rights, 712
Abuse and Recovery, 607
Academic Advice, 189
Academic Electronic Mail Addresses, 185
Academic Jobs, 361
Academic Magazines, 189
Academic Software Development, 611
Academic Technology, 174
Access Art, 16
Accessing the Internet by Mail, 339
Acid Jazz, 464
Acid Warp, 104
ACLU Reading Room, 228
Acoustic and Electric Bass, 464
Acoustic Guitar Archive, 464
Acoustic Guitar Digest, 464
Acoustic Music Server, 464
Acronym Servers and Archives, 373
Activities for Kids, 737
Actuator MUD, 460
Actuator MUD Gopher, 460
AD&D Discussion, 238
Ada, 133
Ada Project, 712
Adam Curry, 423
Adams, Ansel, 16
Adams, Douglass, 422
Adams, Scott, 422
Addictions, 288
Addventure!, 238
Administrating MUDs, 457
Adult Education and Literacy, 175
Adult Literacy, 175
Adult Movies, 599
Advanced Dungeons and Dragons, 238
Advanced Dungeons and Dragons
    Character Creator, 238
Advanced Nuclear Reactor Technology, 199
Advanced Technology Information
    Network, 1
Adventures of Cyber Cat, 231
Advertising and Marketing, 75
Aegean Palaces, 298
Aeneid, 407
AERA SIG/ENET Discussion, 175
Aerial Combat Simulation, 238
Aeronautics Simulation, 214
Aeronautics and Space Acronyms, 639
Aeronautics and Space Articles, 639
Aerospace Engineering, 37
Aesop's Fables, 407

Africa, 717
African Art, 16
African Forum, 717
African National Congress, 329
African Resource List, 717
African Studies, 717
Afro-Caribbean Music, 464
Afro-Latin, 465
Afterlife, 491
Aging, 47, 315
Agricultural Biotechnology Center, 1
Agricultural, Flood, Food Supply
    Information, 1
Agricultural Genome Resources, 1
Agricultural Mailing List, 1
Agricultural Software, 1
Agriculture, 1-6
Agrippa, 407
Agrippa: A Book of the Dead, 153
Agroforestry, 73
Ahmadiyya, 576
AIDS, 433
AIDS Frequently Asked Questions, 433
AIDS Information, 288
AIDS Information via CHAT Database, 433
AIDS Information Newsletter, 433
AIDS Mailing List, 433
AIDS News, 288
AIDS Statistics, 433
AIDS Treatment News and Facts, 433
Aikido Dojos Around the World, 647
Air Pollution BBS, 201
Air Warrior, 215
Air-Cooled Volkswagens, 31
Aircraft Discussion Forum, 37
Aircraft Group Ownership, 37
Aircraft Images, 37
Airline and Airliner Discussion List, 37
Airline Travel, 37
AirMosaic, 618
Airport Codes, 37
AIX, 514
Al Gore, 423
Aladdin and the Wonderful Lamp, 407
Alan Colmes, 423
Alaska, 686
Albert Einstein, 528
Albert Hofmann's Strange Mistake, 740
Aleister Crowley, 58
AlexMUD, 460
Alfa Romeo Home Page, 31
Alfred Lord Tennyson, 544
Algebra Assistance, 425
Algernon Charles Swinburne, 544
Alice in Unix Land, 113
Alice's Adventures in Wonderland, 407
Alien Cultures, 523
Alien III Script, 591
All About Cryptography, 151
Allen, Woody, 556
Allergies, 434
Allman Brothers, 482
alt.binaries.pictures Image Server, 129
Alternative Approaches to Learning, 175
Alternative Architecture, 13
Alternative Comics, 96
Alternative History, 68
Alternative Institutions, 609
Alternative Medicine, 444
Alternative Medicine Home Page, 444
Amateur Computerist, 114
Amateur Radio, 305, 562
Amateur Radio Information by Mail, 305
Amateur Radio Transmissions, 27
Amazons International, 607
Ambrose Bierce, 399

American Astronomical Society Job
    Register, 361
American/British Lexicon, 373
American Chemical Society, 91
American Football, 647
American Historical Documents, 295
American Indian Work Issues, 361
American Institute of Physics, 537
American Literature Discussion List, 395
American Mathematical Society, 425
American Memory Collection, 298
American Philosophical Association, 532
American Psychological Society, 549
American Risk and Insurance Association,
    75
American Studies, 298
American Type Culture Collection, 47
American/Japanese Economic Relations,
    329
Americans with Disabilities Act, 156
Amiga Archives, 98
Amiga Information Resources, 98
Amiga Mosaic, 98
Amiga Pictures, 98
Amiga Sounds, 98
Amiga Talk, 98
Amiga Telecom, 98
Amiga Unix, 98
Amnesty International, 517
Amos, Tori, 482
Amtrak Trains, 686
Amusing Tests and Quizzies, 317
Anagrams, 231
Ananse—International Trade Law Project,
    383
Anarchist Resources, 6
Anarchy, 6-7
Anarchy 'N' Explosives, 7
Anarchy Discussion List, 6
Anatomy Teaching Modules, 434
Ancient Philosophy, 532
Andrew File System Resources, 626
Andy Griffith, 674
Anecdote, The, 16
Anesthesiology, 434
Anglican Christianity, 565
Anglo-Saxon Mailing List, 298
Anglo-Saxon Tales, 404
Animal Behavior, 47
Animal Defense Network, 545
Animal Resources, 7
Animals in the News, 7
Animals and Pets, 7-11
Animaniacs, 675
Animations and Images, 662
Anime, 86
Anime Video Games, 238
Anne of Green Gables, 408
Annealing, 586
Annotated Scientific Visualization Weblet
    Bibliography, 104
Announcements of Internet Services, 343
Announcements About Microsoft
    Windows, 503
Announcements About OS/2, 507
Announcements About SCO Unix, 508
Annuals, Perennials and Bulbs, 255
Anonymity, 58
Anonymous FTP Site List, 343
Anonymous Posting Service, 699
Ansel Adams, 16
Ansible Newsletter, 592
Answer Guys, 695
Antarctica Resource Guide, 270
Anthropology, 11
Anthropology Mailing List, 586

Anti War-on-Drugs Activist List, 162
Antique Cars, 31
Antique Newspaper Column, 305
Antiques, 305
AOS, 505
Apocalypse, 460
Apogee Games, 238
Apple Computer Higher Education
    Gopher, 185
Apple II Archive, 616
Apple IIgs, 110
Applications for DOS, 624
Applications for the Mac, 622
Applications for Microsoft Windows, 503
Applications for OS/2, 507
April Fools, 451
Aquaculture Discussion List, 586
Aquaculture Information Center, 7
Aquaculture Network Information Center, 2
Aquanaut, 647
Aquaria Mailing List, 7
Aquariums, 7
Aquariums and Tropical Fish, 8
Arab Press Newsletter, 717
Arabic, 373
Arabidopsis Project, 47
Arbor Heights School, 188
Arcade Video Game Tricks, 238
Arcana Arcanorum, 59
Archaeological Computing, 11
Archaeology, 11-13
Archery, 305
Archie, 618
ArchiGopher, 13
Architectural Modeling, 13
Architectural Visualization, 13
Architecture, 13-15
Architecture General Discussion, 13
Architecture of the Tropics, 13
Architronic, 14
Archives, 624
Archives and Archivists List, 389
ArchNet, 11
Arctic Adventours, 686
Argentina, 717
ARJ Utilities, 635
Arm the Spirit, 740
Armadillo, 175
Armadillo Culture, 740
Arms and Disarmament, 329
Army Area Handbooks, 717
Art, 15-26
Art and Images, 17
Art Com, 740
Art Crimes, 16
Art Criticism Forum, 17
Art Educational Materials, 17
Art Exploration, 17
Art Gallery, 17
Art History Server, 17
Art Museums and Exhibits, 17
Art on the Net, 18
Art Network for Integrated Media
    Applications, 17
Art News, 17
Art of Noise, 482
Art Nouveau, 18
Art Papers, 18
Art Projects on the Internet, 18
Art Reviews, 18
Art of Technology Digest, 100
ArthurNet, 298
Articles on Alternative Methods of
    Healing, 444
Articles of Music Composition, 465
Articles on Religion, 565

Artificial Intelligence, 665
Artificial Intelligence Journal, 114
Artificial Intelligence and the Law, 383
Artificial Life, 143
Artistic Expression, 18
Artistic Melange, 18
ArtMetal, 305
Arts and Crafts Information Service, 150
Arts Online, 18
ArtSource, 18
ArtWorld, 19
As a Man Thinketh, 408
ASCII Art Bazaar, 231
ASCII Cartoons, 19
ASCII Table, 635
Asia Discussion, 718
Asia Online, 75
Asia Pacific Business and Marketing Resources, 75
Asian Movies, 453
Asian Studies, 718
Ask Dr. Bean, 317
Ask Joe, 231
ASK Software Information System, 611
AskERIC, 191
Association of American University Presses, 554
Association of Collegiate Schools of Architecture, 14
Association for Computing Machinery, 517
Association for Experiential Education, 176
AsTeR, 140
Astral Projection, 523
Astro FTP List, 27
Astrology, 26-27
Astrology Collection, 26
Astrology Discussion Group, 26
Astrology Resources, 26
Astrometry Science Team, 27
Astronomical Internet Resources, 27
Astronomical Museum, 27
Astronomy, 27-30
Astronomy General Discussion, 27
Astronomy HyperTextbook, 28
Astronomy Programs, 28
Astronomy Servers, 28
Astrophysics Data System, 28
Astrotext, 28
Atari, 616
Atari Archive, 239
Atari Jaguar Game Archive, 239
Atheism, 565
Atheism Satire, 579
Atheist Manifesto, 565
Athene, the Online Magazine of Creative Writing, 729
Atlanta, 686
Atomic Cafe, 239
ATP Tour Weekly, 648
Attention Deficit Disorder Archive, 288
Attitudes of Women, 712
Audi, 31
Audio Experts, 305
Audio Slideshow Guide, 122
Audio Technology, 665
Auggie BBS, 42
Austen, Jane, 399
Austin Fusion Studies, 538
Australia, 718
Australian Alpine Information Service, 686
Australian Environmental Resources Network, 202
Australian Law, 383
Australian National Botanic Gardens, 73
Australian News, 498
Australian Postal Codes, 270
Australian Rules Football, 648
Australian Sporting News, 648
Austrian Beer Guide, 218
Austrian Restaurant Guide, 686
Auto Racing, 31
Automated Library Information Xchange, 389
Automatic Login Executor, 635
Automobile General Discussion Groups, 31

Automotive: Cars, 31-36
Automotive: Motorcycles, 36
Autospamosaurus, 239
Aviation, 37-41
Aviation Archives, 38
Aviation Enthusiast Corner, 38
Aviation General Discussion, 38
Aviation Gopher, 38
Aviation Technology, 38
AwareNet, 491
Awesome List, 343
Ayurvedic Medicine, 445
Aztec Studies, 298

B

Babbage's Best of the Internet, 331
Babies, 210
Babylon 5 Reviews, 675
Backcountry Home Page, 520
Backgammon Server, 239
Bad Subjects, 741
Bagpipes, 465
Baha'i Faith, 576
Baja California, 686
Ballet and Modern Dance, 155
Ballooning, 520
Baltic Republics Discussion List, 718
Banjo Tablature Archive, 465
Banks and Financial Industries News, 76
Banned Computer Material, 229
Baptist Discussion List, 565
Barbados, 686
Barbershop Quartets, 465
Barlow, John Perry, 422
Barney the Dinosaur, 317
Barney's Page, 231
Baseball Archives, 648
Baseball Information Center, 648
Baseball Schedule, 648
Baseball Scores, 649
Baseball Server, 649
Baseball Strike, 649
Baseball Teams, 649
Basic Design in Art and Architecture, 19
Basic Programming Language, 133
Basketball FAQs, 649
Basketball Server, 649
Basketball Statistics, 649
Bassoon and Oboe, 465
Bastard Operator from Hell, 317
Batish Institute of Music and Fine Arts, 718
Battleships, 239
Battlestar Galactica Home Page, 675
Baum, L. Frank, 399
Bay Area Libertarians, 549
Bay Area Places to See, 686
Bay Area Restaurant Guide, 687
BBC TV and Radio, 675
BBS Access via Gopher, 42
BBS Acronyms, 42
BBS General Discussion, 42
BBS Information, 42
BBS Issues, 114
BBS Lists, 42
BBS Programs, 43
BBSs (Bulletin Board Systems), 42-46
BBSs Around the World, 43
Beads, 305
Bear Code, 261
Bears, 261
Bears in Movies, 261
Beastie Boys, 482
Beauty for Ashes, 19
Beavis and Butthead, 675
Beavis and Butthead Quotables, 556
Bee Biology, 2
Beekeeping, 2
Beekeeping Web Page, 3
Beemer List, 31
Beer, 219
Beer Archive, 219
Beer Judging, 219
Beer Page, 219
Beer Ratings, 219

Beginner's Guide to HTML, 339
Bell Gopher, 670
Benchmark Software, 635
Berlin, 718
Berlin and Prague, 687
Best of K12, 191
Best of Usenet, 317
Best of the Web '94 Recipients, 343
Better and Better, 317
Beverly Hills 90210, 676
Bey, Hakim, 533
biancaTroll's Smut Shack, 59
Bible Browser for Unix, 565
Bible Gateway, 566
Bible Online, 566
Bible in Pig Latin, 579
Bible Program, 566
Bible Promises Macintosh Hypercard Stack, 567
Bible Quiz Game, 567
Bible Quotes, 556
Bible Retrieval System for Unix, 567
Bible Search Program, 567
Bible Search Tools, 567
Bible Study, 567
Bible Text, 567
Bible Translations, 567
Bible Verses, 567
Bible Word, Phrase Counts: King James Version, 568
Bible's View of Homosexuality, 261
Biblical Search and Extraction Tool, 568
Biblical Timeline, 568
Bibliographies of Literature, 395
Bibliographies of Science Fiction, 592
Bibliographies of Women's Studies, 712
Bibliography of Internetworking Information, 123
Bibliography of Senate Hearings, 284
Bicycle Commuting, 650
Bicycle Discussion Lists on the Internet, 650
Bicycle Mailing List, 650
Bicycles, 86
Bicycles FAQS, 650
Bicycling, 650
Bierce, Ambrose, 399
Big Band, 466
Big Book of Mischief, 451
Big Drink List, 219
Big Eight College Football, 650
Big Fun Lists, 231
Bigfoot, 59
Bill Clinton, 423
Bill Gates, 423
Billy Barron's Library List, 390
Billy Joel, 486
Binaries for DOS, 624
Binaries for the Mac, 622
Binaries for OS/2, 507
Binaries for SCO Unix, 509
Binaries for Windows, 504
BioBox Wonder World, 47
Biochemistry, 47
Biochemistry Graphics Room at Aberdeen University, 48
BioData Cyberspace Launching Pad, 48
Biodiversity, 48
Bioethics, 48
Bioinformatics Resource Gopher, 48
Biological Databases, 48
Biological Sciences, 361
Biological Sciences Conferences, 48
Biological Scientist's Network Guide, 48
Biologist's Guide to Internet Resources, 49
Biology, 47-58
Biology Announcements, 49
Biology Education, 176
Biology General Discussion, 49
Biology Information Theory, 49
Biology and Information Theory, 49
Biology Job Opportunities, 49
Biology Journals, 49
Biology Newsletter, 50
Biology Resources, 50
Biology Software and Archives, 50

Biology Software Search, 50
Biomechanics, 50
Biomedical Engineering, 434
BioMOO, 51
Biorhythms, 491
Biosphere and Ecology, 51
Biosphere Mailing List and Discussion Group, 202
Biosphere Newsletter, 202
Biotechnology, 51
Bird Keeping, 8
Bird Studies in the Australian National Botanic Gardens, 51
Bird-Watching, 8
Bird-Watching Archives, 8
Bird-Watching Mailing Lists, 8
Birding, 8
Birds, 8
Birthparents of Adoptees, 664
Bisexual Resource List, 261
Bisexuality, 261
Bisexuality and Gender Issues, 261
Bisexuals, 530
Bitnet Baseball League, 650
Bitnet Network, 123
Bizarre, 58-67
Bizarre Board Game, 239
Bizarre General Discussion, 59
Bizarre Literature, 59
Black Holes, 586
Blackjack, 240
Blacksburg Electronic Village, 665
Blade Runner, 453
Blake, William, 542
Blind and Visually Impaired Computer Usage, 157
Blind News Digest, 157
Blindness and Family Life, 664
Blink Magazine, 417
Blotter Art Collection, 162
Bluedog Can Count, 232
Bluegrass Music Discussion List, 466
Blues, 466
Blues Brothers, 453
BMW Information, 32
Board Game Rules and Information, 240
Boat Drinks, 219
Boating Discussion Groups, 67
Boating and Sailing, 67-68
Boating Web Server, 67
Bob Dylan, 483
Boggle, 240
bOING bOING, 417
Bold and the Beautiful, The, 676
Bolo, 240
Bolo Tracker, 240
Bondage, 600
Bondage Talk, 600
Bondage, Discipline, Sadism and Masochism Stories, 732
Bonestell, Chesley, 20
Bonsai, 255
Bonsai Mailing List, 256
Book FAQs and Info, 69
Book of Kells, 19
Book of Mormon, 568
Book and Publishing News, 69
Book Reviews, 69
Book Stacks Unlimited, 69
Books, 68-73
Books General Discussion, 69
Books Online, 69
Books in Zip Format, 405
Bookstore Reviews, 69
Bootleg Music, 87
Bootsie Report, 318
Booze Cookbook, 219
Boredom, 232
Bosnia, 498, 719
Boston Restaurant List, 687
Botanical Gardens at the University of Delaware, 73
Botany, 73-75
Botany Database, 74
Bottom Line Zine, 466

Boxing, 651
Boy Scouts of America, 737
Brain Tumors, 434
Brainwashing, 549
BrainWave Systems Users Group, 611
Brand, Stewart, 422
Brandy's Babes, 732
Brass Musicians, 466
Brazil, 719
Brazilian Tropical Databases, 51
Breast Cancer Information, 434
Brian Eno, 19
Bridge, 241
Bristol Technology, 611
British Cars, 32
British Columbia Regional Information, 88
British Columbia Tourism Information, 88
British Columbian Web Servers, 88
British Comedy, 318
British Economics Research, 168
British Humor, 318
Broadcasting, 366
Brochure on Sexual Orientation, 261
Bromeliaceae, 74
Brontë Sisters, 399
Brother Jed, 576
Brown University Alumni, 185
Bruce, Lenny, 556
Bruce Lavois Shooting, 384
Bruce Springsteen, 490
Bruce Sterling, 592
Bruce Sterling Articles, 153
Bryn Mawr Classical Review, 395
BSD Unix, 514
BSD Unix for PCs, 514
BSDI, 514
BTG, 99
Buckminster Fuller, 528
Buddhism, 568
Buddhism Discussion, 568
Buddhist Studies, 532
Budget of the United States Government, 284
Buffett, Jimmy, 482
Build a Flying Saucer, 199
Building PC Hardware, 128
Bulfinch's Mythology, 216
Bulgaria, 719
Bulgarian Sounds, 467
Bureau of Justice Statistics Documents, 277
Bush, Kate, 482
Business Archives, 76
Business and Commerce, 76
Business Conferences, 76
Business Electronic Mail Addresses, 76
Business and Finance, 75-86
Business and Industry, 76
Business Information Resources, 76
Business Information Server, 76
Business News, 77
Business School Faculty, 191
Business Statistics, 77
Businesses on the Internet, 77
BusinessWeb, 77
Bust, 741
Buying and Selling, 86-87
Buying and Selling Books, 69
Buying and Selling Macs, 120
Buying and Selling Music, 467
Byte Bandit, 100
Byte Magazine, 417

C

C Programs, 133
C++ Frequently Asked Questions, 134
C-SPAN, 676
Cable Regulation Digest, 676
Cable TV, 676
Cable TV Resources, 676
CAD Mailing Lists, 199
Cadence Design Systems, 19
Caffeine, 162
Cajun Culture, 719
Calculator, 425

Calculus Graphics, 426
Calendar of Days, 626
California, 687, 719
California Academy of Sciences, 586
California Emergency Services, 196
California Legal Codes, 384
California Libertarians, 549
California Museum of Photography, 536
California Rivers Assessment, 202
California Yellow Pages, 146
Call of the Wild, The, 408
Callahan's Bar, 59
Calls for Papers in Women's Studies, 712
Camaros and Firebirds, 32
Cambridge Pub Guide, 687
Camel Research, 745
Camelot, 299
Campus Climate, 185
Campus Computing Newsletter Editors, 124
Campus Parking, 185
Campus Radio Disk Jockeys, 562
Campus-Wide Information Systems, 185
Canada, 88-91
Canada Department of Communications, 665
Canadian Airlines International, 38
Canadian Broadcasting Corporation, 562
Canadian Business Information, 88
Canadian Discussion, 88
Canadian Football League, 651
Canadian Forest Service, 202
Canadian Genealogy Resources, 266
Canadian Geographical Web Server, 88
Canadian Government, 277
Canadian Government Documents, 88
Canadian Government Gophers, 89
Canadian History, 89
Canadian Investment, 89
Canadian Issues Forum, 89
Canadian Law, 384
Canadian Music, 89
Canadian News, 89
Canadian Resource Page, 89
Canadian Stock Archives, 89
Canadian Weather, 707
Canadian Web Master Index, 90
Canary Islands, 687
Cancer Mailing List, 288
CancerNet, 434
Canonical Lists, 318
Canterbury Tales, The, 408
Capacity—The Webzine, 741
Car Audio, 32
Car Wars, 241
Cardiff's Movie Database Browser, 453
Career Books, 361
Career Events, 361
CareerMosaic, 361
Caribbean Connection, 687
Carl System, 390
Carlos Museum of Art, 19
Carnegie Mellon School of Computer Science, 344
Carnivorous Plants, 74
Carroll, Lewis, 399
Cartoon Collection, 232
Cartoon Pictures, 129
Cartoons, 676
Cascades, 702
Case of Dr. Jekyll and Mr. Hyde, The, 414
Case Online Information System, 77
Cast Upon the Breakers, 408
Catalan, 373
Catalog of Federal Domestic Assistance, 278
Catalog of Marine Fish and Invertebrates, 51
Cataloging, 390
Catalyst for College Educators, 191
Catholic Christianity, 569
Catholic Doctrine, 569
Catholic Evangelism, 569
Catholicism, 569
Cathouse Archives, 318
Cats, 8
CAVE Virtual Reality Environment, 665

CBC Radio Trial, 495
CCMD Source Code in C, 134
CD-ROM Activities, 191
CDs, 467
Celebrities, 529
Celerity Systems, 99
Cell Biology, 51
Cell-Relay Communications, 670
Cello, 618
Cellular Phones, 672
Celtic Music, 467
Censored Books and News Stories, 229
Censorship and Intellectual Freedom in Canada, 90
Census of Australian Vertebrate Species, 746
Census Data for Massachusetts, 278
Center for Atmospheric Science, 91
Center for Civil Society International, 517
Center for Earth and Planetary Studies, 639
Center for Experimental and Constructive Mathematics, 426
Center for Geometry Analysis Numerics and Graphics, 426
Center for Landscape Research (CLR), 202
Center for Nonlinear Studies, 426
Center for Particle Astrophysics, 538
Center for Research Information Storage Technology, 665
Central America Discussion List, 719
Central Asian Studies Mailing Lists, 719
Central European Development, 719
Central Virginia's Freenet, 665
Ceramic Arts Discussion List, 19
Ceramics Gopher, 20
Cereal, 220
Cesium, 60
Cetys-BBS, 43
Chabad Lubavitch Judaism, 569
Chance Server, 426
Channeling, 523
Chaos Control, 741
Charles Dickens, 400
Charlotte, The Vermont Whale, 299
Charlottetown Agreement, 90
Chat, 232
Cheers, 677
Chemical Engineering, 92
Chemical Engineering List, 92
Chemical Information Sources, 92
Chemical Physics Preprint Database, 92
Chemical Substance Factsheets, 202
Chemistry, 91-95
Chemistry Art Gallery, 92
Chemistry Information, 93
Chemistry in Israel, 92
Chemistry Talk, 93
Chemistry Telementoring, 93
Chernobyl Nuclear Accident, 203
Chesley Bonestell, 20
Chess Archives, 241
Chess Discussion List, 241
Chess Discussion and Play, 241
Chess News, 242
Chess Servers, 242
Chia Pets, 256
Child Support, 210
Childcare Newsletters, 211
Children General Discussion, 211
Children with Special Needs, 288
Children's Discussion, 371
Children's Gardening, 256
Children's Stories, Poems and Pictures, 371
Chile, 720
Chill Horror Role-Playing Game, 579
Chimera, 635
China, 720
China Import/Export News, 77
Chinchilla Farming, 3
Chinese Chess, 242
Chinese Computing and Word Processing, 143
Chinese GIF Collection, 129
Chinese Literature, 405
Chinese News Digest Server, 499

Chinese Poetry, 542
Chinese Scenic Pictures, 720
Chinese Scholars and Students Discussion List, 720
Chinese telnet, 635
Chinese Text Viewer, 635
Chinese Text Viewers, 373
Chips Online, 417
Chit-Chat, 530
Chlamydomonas, 74
ChooseNews II, 699
Christia, 569
Christian Death Home Page, 482
Christian Discussion, 569
Christian Leadership Forum, 569
Christian Music, 467
Christian Resources, 570
Christian Thought and Literature in Late Antiquity, 570
Christian Visions, 570
Christian Youth, 737
Christianity, 570
Christianity and How It Relates to Society, 570
Christianity and Literature, 570
Christmas Carol, A, 408
Chromosome 22, 52
Chronic Fatigue Syndrome, 435
Chronicle of Higher Education, 191
Chronicle of Higher Education—Academe This Week, 361
Chupchups, 460
Church of the SubGenius, 60
CIA World Factbook, 270
Cigar Smoking, 704
Cinema Discussion List, 453
Cinema Talk, 453
Cinema Workers, 362
CinemaSpace, 453
Circuit Analysis Discussion List, 195
Circulation Control, 390
Cisco Information Archive, 124
Citadel, 43
Citizens Band Radio, 562
City of the Sun, 408
Civil Disobedience, 409
Civil Engineering, 199
Civil Rights and Liberties, 229
Civil Society: USA, 517
Civil War, 299
Civilization Editor, 242
Clarinet, 495
Clarinet Players Mailing List, 467
Clarissa Explains, 677
Classic Practical Jokes, 318
Classic Science Fiction and Fantasy Reviews, 592
Classical Architecture of the Mediterranean, 14
Classical Music, 467
Classical Music Mailing List, 468
Classical Studies, 299
Classics, 395
Classics and Mediterranean Archaeology, 11
Clay, Andrew Dice, 556
Clearinghouse for Networked Information Discovery, 344
Clearinghouse for Subject-Oriented Internet Resources, 344
Clemson University Forestry and Agriculture Network, 3
Climate Data Catalog, 707
Climate Diagnostics Center, 707
Climatic Research Unit, 707
Climbing, 520
Climbing Archive, 521
Clinton, Bill, 423
Clinton Jokes, 545
Clinton Watch, 545
Clinton's Cabinet, 285
Clinton's Inaugural Address, 286
Clip Art, 130
Clocks and Watches, 306
Clothes Moths, 213
Clothespins as Toys, 600

Clothing, 732
Coalition for Networked Information, 545
Coalition to Ban Dihydrogen Monoxide, 203
Coastal Management and Resources, 203
Coca-Cola, 220
Coca-Cola World, 220
Cocteau Twins Home Page, 482
Code of the Federal Register, 278
Code of the Geeks, 100
Coffee, 220
Coffee Lover's Resources, 220
Coffee Machine, 695
Cogeneration, 77
Cognition, 315
Cognitive and Psychological Sciences Index, 550
Cognitive Science, 550
Coherent, 514
Coin Toss, 696
Coins and Money, 306
Coke Servers, 696
Cola: Make Your Own, 221
Colibri, 373
Collaborative Clickable Biology, 52
Collected Queer Information, 262
Collecting, 306
Collector's Network, 306
College of Chemistry at Berkeley, 93
College Food, 221
College Football, 651
College Hockey, 651
College Hockey Computer Rating, 651
College Humor, 318
College Libraries, 390
College Slang Dictionary, 373
College and University Teaching Assistants, 192
Colmes, Alan, 423
Color and Vision, 587
Color Perception, 586
Colorado Legislative Information, 549
Colorado Weather Underground, 707
Comedies, 677
Comedy, 319
Comic Book Mailing List, 96
Comic Books, 96-97
Comics, 306
Comics Archives, 96
Comics Marketplace, 96
Comics Newsgroups, 96
Comics Resource Center, 96
Coming Out, 262
Comix, 319
Commerce Business Daily, 77
Commercial Online News Ventures, 495
Commercial Real Estate, 564
Commercial Use of the Internet, 77
Commercials, 677
Commodities, 78
Commodity Market Reports, 3
Commodore 64/128 Archive, 99
Commodore-64 Chat, 99
Common Sense, 532
Commonwealth of Learning, 176
Commonwealth Games, 651
Communicable Diseases, 288
Communist Manifesto, 409
Community Colleges, 186
Community Economic Development, 168
Commutative Algebra, 426
Compact Disc Formats, 665
Compaq Fixes and Patches, 110
Compilers and Interpreters, 635
Complaining, 60
Complete Bibliographies of Major Authors, 592
Complete Guide to Galway, 688
Complete Guide to Guinness Beer, 221
Complex Arrangements, 468
Complex Systems Resources, 143
Composing Good HTML, 339
CompuServe B File Transfer Protocol, 134
Computation and Language E-Print Archive, 374
Computational Chemistry List, 94

Computational Economics, 169
Computer-Aided Design, 195
Computer-Aided Detector Design, 143
Computer Books, 70
Computer Cartoons, 319
Computer and Communication Companies, 146
Computer Emergency Response Team, 114
Computer Fraud and Abuse Act, 384
Computer-Generated Writing, 101
Computer Graphics Bibliography, 104
Computer Graphics Information, 104
Computer Information, 110
Computer Laws, 384
Computer Lore, 143
Computer-Mediated Communication, 344, 417
Computer Nerd Humor, 319
Computer Networking, 176
Computer and Networking Column, 124
Computer-Oriented Humor, 319
Computer Professionals for Social Responsibility, 101
Computer Science Conferences, 143
Computer Science Technical Papers Archive, 115
Computer Science Technical Reports, 115
Computer Security Gopher, 138
Computer Security Sites, 138
Computer Speech, 143
Computer Standards, 143
Computer Underground, 115
Computer Underground Digest, 101
Computer Virus Technical Information, 115
Computer Viruses, 144
Computerized Music, 468
Computers, 87
Computers and Academic Freedom, 102
Computers: Commodore, 98-99
Computers: Companies, 99-100
Computers: Culture, 100-104
Computers in Education, 176
Computers: Graphics, 104-110
Computers: Hardware, 110-113
Computers and Health, 288
Computers and the Law, 138
Computers: Literature, 113-119
Computers: Macintosh, 120-122
Computers and Mathematics, 52
Computers: Multimedia, 122-123
Computers in Music Research, 468
Computers: Networks, 123-127
Computers: PCs, 128-129
Computers: Pictures, 129-133
Computers: Programming, 133-137
Computers: Security and Privacy, 138-140
Computers: Sounds, 140-142
Computers: Technology, 143-146
Computers and Technology in the Home, 144
Computing Across America, 115
Computing Dictionary, 115
Computing Newsletters, 116
con, 626
Conan the Barbarian, 592
Concerning Hackers..., 102
Concert Information, 468
Concrete Blonde, 482
Conferences for Women, 713
Confession Booth, 232
Conflict Simulation Games, 666
Congress Members, 284
Congress of Canadian Engineering Students, 199
Congressional Committee Assignments, 285
Congressional Firsts, 285
Congressional Legislation, 285
Congressional Quarterly, 285
Connect-4, 242
Connecticut Yankee in King Arthur's Court, A, 409
Connecting to the Internet, 357
Conquest, 242
Conrad, Joseph, 400
Consciousness, 550

Conservation Action, 545
Conservation Biology, 52
Conservation OnLine, 203
Conservative Discussion Lists, 545
Conservative Political News, 545
Consortium for Ordinary Differential Equations Experiments, 426
Conspiracies, 359
Constitution in Cyberspace, 384
Constitution of the United States of America, 296
Consumer Information, 146-149
Consumer Information, 146
Consumer Issues, 146
Consumer News, 146
Contemporary Architecture in Hong Kong, 15
Contemporary Humor, 319
Contemporary Russian Fine Arts Gallery, 20
Content Router, 344
Continuum Machine, The, 729
Contract Labor, 362
Controlling Pests, 313
Conventions and Memorabilia, 662
Conversational Hypertext Access Technology, 232
Cookie Recipes, 221
Cooking, 221
Cool Demos, 105
Cool Site of the Day, 232
Cool Things to Try, 371
Coombspapers Social Sciences Data Bank, 316
Cooper, Alice, 483
Cooperative Extension System, 278
Copper Diku, 460
Coptic, 570
Copy Editors Mailing List, 554
Copyright Information, 278
Copyright and Intellectual Property Forum, 384
Core War, 242
Cornell Extension Network, 3
Corporate Finance News, 78
Corvette, 32
Costello, Elvis, 483
Council of Remiremont, 395
Country and Western, 468
Country Statistics, 720
Couples, 583
CP/M, 505
CPM Archives, 616
CPUs and Assembly Language, 134
Crackers, 221
Craft Resources, 150
Craft Suppliers, 150
Crafting on the Internet, 150
Crafts, 150-151
Crafts, 150
Cray, 514
Create a Story, 729
Creating Alternative Hierarchy Newsgroups, 699
Creating Standard Newsgroups, 699
Creative Internet Home Page, 468
Creative Writing Pedagogy, 730
Creativity and Creative Problem Solving, 550
Credit Information, 147
Cribbage, 243
Cricket, 651
Cricket Talk, 651
Cricket Web Server, 651
Criminal Justice Country Profiles, 384
Criminal Justice Discussion Group, 385
Crisis in Rwanda, 329
Croatia, 468
Croatian Christian Information Service, 570
Croatian Foreign Press Bureau, 720
Croatian Medicine, 435
Croatian Ministry of Foreign Affairs, 499
Croatian News, 499
Crohn's Disease and Colitis, 435
Cross-Dressing, 607
Cross-Dressing Chat, 600

Crossfire, 243
Crossword Servers, 243
Crosswords, 233
Crowley, Aleister, 58
Cryonics, 60
Cryonics Frequently Asked Questions, 435
Crypto Glossary, 151
Cryptography, 151-153
Cryptography General Discussion, 151
Cryptography and the Government, 151
Cryptography, PGP, and Your Privacy, 151
Cryptography Sources on the Internet, 151
Csb/Sju BBS, 43
CTHEORY, 417
Cthulhu, 395
CU-LawNet, 385
CU-SeeMe, 331
CU-SeeMe Reflector Sites, 332
CueCosy, 43
Cult Movies, 453
Cult of the Dead Cow, 61
Cultronix, 417
Culture, 90
Culture Magazines, 417
Currency, 688
Currency Converter, 78
Current Affairs Magazines, 495
Current Cites, 390
Current Weather Maps and Movies, 708
Curriculum Materials and Ideas, 176
Curry, Adam, 423
Cyberculture, 154
Cyberkind, 154
Cybermind, 154
CyberMUD Web Game, 243
CyberNet, 233
Cybernet BBS, 43
CyberNet's Art Gallery, 20
Cybernetics, 144
Cyberpunk, 153-154
Cyberpunk, 730
Cyberpunk News, 154
Cyberpunk Reading List, 154
CyberRoots, 267
Cybersight, 233
Cybersmith, 344
Cyberspace, 102
Cyberspace Communications, 124
Cyberspace Quotations, 556
Cyberspace Vanguard, 741
Cybertour of the U.S.A., 688
Cycling Resources, 652
Cypherpunks, 152
Cyrillic Text, 374
Cystic Fibrosis, 435
Czech Slovak, 374

D

D-Day, 299
Daily Newspaper Electronic Mail Addresses, 499
Daily Report Card, 177
Daily Sources of Business and Economic News, 496
Dance, 155-156
Dance Archives and Discussion, 155
Dance General Discussion, 155
Dance Resources on the Internet, 155
Dangerfield, Rodney, 556
Daresbury Laboratory, 666
DargonZine, 742
Dark Shadows, 677
Dark Side of the Net, 61
Dark-Sun, 579
Darkroom Photography, 536
Dartmouth College Library Online System, 553
Data Communications and Networking Links, 124
Data Communications Servers, 670
Data Explorer, 344
Database, 267
Database via finger, 344
Databases via Telnet, 345

Datagram, 124
Datsun Roadsters, 32
Datsun Z Car, 32
David Letterman, 559, 677
David Letterman Official Song Book, 678
Davis, Miles, 483
Dead Runners Society, 652
Dead Sea Scrolls, 12
Dead Teacher's Society, 192
Deaf Magazine, 157
Deaf-Blind Discussion List, 157
Deafness, 157
Death of Rock 'n' Roll, The, 483
Debbie Gibson, 485
Decavitator, 67
Declaration of Arms, 1775, 296
Declaration of Independence, 296
DECUS Library, 616
Deep Thoughts, 319
Deeper Trouble, 460
Defense Conversion Subcommittee, 448
Dell Web Server, 147
Demo Software, 624
Demography and Population Studies, 610
Dental Librarians, 390
Dental Poisoning, 288
Dentistry, 436
Denver Freenet, 345
Department of Commerce, 278
Depeche Mode, 483
Depression Disorders, 550
Depth Probe, 742
Dermatology List, 436
DeRohan, Ceanne, 400
Des Moines, 688
Desktop Publishing, 116
Desqview, 502
Developmentally Disabled and Autism, 157
Devil's Dictionary, 374
Devilbunnies, 61
Diabetes, 289
Diabetic Recipes, 221
Dial-Up Site List, 510
Diaper Fetish, 600
Dick, Philip K., 400
Dickens, Charles, 400
Dictionary of Computing Terms, 375
Dictionary Word Lists, 375
Dietary Information, 289
Dieting, 289
Different Christianities Dialogue, 571
Differential Equations, 426
Digital Art Archives, 20
Digital Audio Broadcasting, 563
Digital Equipment Corporation, 99
Digital Imaging and Communications, 436
Digital Journeys, 20
Digital Movies, 233
Digital Picture Archive on the 17th Floor, 130
DikuMud II, 461
DikuMUDs, 457
Dining Out on the Web, 222
Dinosaur Discussion List, 300
Dinosaur Exhibit, 300
Diplomacy, 243
Diplomacy Discussion List, 243
Dire Straits, 483
Directory of Economists, 169
Directory Servers, 345
Dirt, 461
Dirty Talk, 732
Disabilities, 156-160
Disability Aid, 157
Disability Information, 158
Disability Information Archive, 159
Disabled Computing, 159
Disabled Student Services in Higher Education, 159
Disarmament Discussion List, 448
Disaster Management, 197
Disaster Situation and Status Reports, 197
Disc Sports, 652
Discographies, 469
Discord and Destruction, 61

Discourse on Reason, 409
Discovering Internet Resources, 345
Discovery Channel, The, 678
Discovery Communications Online Listings, 192
Discussion of Sex Stories, 600
Discworld MUD, 461
Discworld MUD Gopher, 461
Diseases Involving the Immune System, 436
Disney, 233, 371
Disney Comics and Cartoons, 453
Disney Talk, 371
Displaying Chinese Documents, 636
Displaying Hangul (Korean) Documents, 636
Displaying Japanese Documents, 636
Distance Learning Resources, 345
Distractions, 233
Distribute Interactive Virtual Environment, 666
Distributed Electronic Telecommunications Archive, 496
Distributed Ocean Data System, 501
Diversity Concerns Exchange, 721
Diversity University, 186
Divine Comedy, The, 409
Diving Server, 521, 652
DMSP Data Archive Home Page, 708
Do Power Lines Cause Cancer?, 437
Do-It Disability Program, 159
Doc Watson, 490
Doctor Fun, 320
Doctor Who, 678, 730
Document Archive, 296
Dodge Stealth/Mitsubishi 3000GT, 33
Dog Resources, 8
Dogs, 9
Dogwood Blossoms, 542
Doll Houses, 306
Domestic Partners, 262
Dominant Women, 733
Don't Ask; Don't Tell, 262
Doom Discussion and Realtime Chat, 243
Doom Information and Files, 244
Doomsday Brunette, 70
DoomWeb Node, 244
Doors, 44
DOS Archive, 624
DOS Internet Kit, 618
DOS News, 502
DOS Under Unix, 510
DOS uudecode, 636
Douglas Adams, 422
Douglass, Frederick, 401
Downtown Anywhere, 147
Doyle, Sir Arthur Conan, 401
Dr. Quinn, Medicine Woman, 678
Dracula, 409
Dragons and Dragonlance Fantasy, 593
Drama, 160-162
Dramas, 678
Dramatic Exchange, 160
Drinking Games, 527
Driving, 33
Driving in California, 33
Driving Schools, 33
Drool, 245
Drosophila, 52
Drug Abuse Education Information and Research, 162
Drug and Alcohol Information, 289
Drug Chemistry and Synthesis, 163
Drug Culture, 163
Drug Information Resources on the Net, 163
Drug News, 163
Drug Talk, 163
Drug Use History, 163
Drug Web Servers, 163
Drugs, 162-166
Drugs Information, 437
Druid, 636
Druid Science Reading Room, 233
Drums and Marching, 306
Drums and Percussion, 469
Drux Electronic Art Gallery, 21

Dryden Photo Archive, 39
DUAT, 39
DUBBS, 44
Dublin Pub Review, 688
Dune Home Page, 593
Dutch, 375
Dutch Literature, 396
Dylan, Bob, 483
Dysfunctional Family Circus, 233

E

E-Math BBS, 427
E-Zine List, 742
E.T. Net, 437
Eagles' Nest BBS, 44
Early Instruments, 538
Early Music, 469
Earnings and Dividend Reports, 78
Earth, 271
Earth Day Bibliography, 203
Earth and Environmental Science, 203
Earth First, 517
Earth Images from Weather Satellites, 708
Earth Negotiations Bulletin, 203
Earth Observation System, 167
Earth Science, 167-168
Earth Science Data Directory, 167
Earth Sciences Resources, 167
Earth and Sky, 587
Earth Systems Data Directory, 639
Earth Views, 28
Earthquake Information, 275
Earthquakes in Alaska, 197
Earthquakes in California, 197
East Coast Hockey League, 652
Easter Eggs, 598
Eastern Europe Trade Leads, 78
Eastern European Business Network, 78
Eastern Orthodox Christianity, 571
Eastern Religions, 571
EBB and Agency Information, 78
Echo Eurodictautom, 375
Eckankar, 576
Ecological Economics, 203
EcoNet, 204
Economic Bulletin Board, 170
Economic Conversion Information Exchange, 278
Economic Development, 170
Economic Indicators, 78
Economic Problems in Less Developed Countries, 170
Economic Resources, 171
Economics, 168-174
Economics Discussion, 171
Economics Gopher, 171
Economics Resources on the Web, 171
Economies of the Caribbean Basin, 171
Economist Resources, 171
Economy, 78
EcoWeb, 204
Ecstasy, 164
Ecuadoran Daily News Summaries, 499
Edgar Allan Poe, 402
EDGAR Mutual Funds, 79
Education, 174-185
Education: Colleges and Universities, 185-188
Education: Elementary, 188
Education Mailing Lists, 177
Education Net, 192
Education Policy, 177
Education-Related Jobs, 362
Education: Students, 189-191
Education: Teachers, 191-195
Educational Administration, 192
Educational K12 Resources, 192
Educational Listserv Lists, 177
Educational Newsgroups, 177
Educational Reform, 178
EDUPAGE, 178
Edward Kennedy, 285, 424
Edwards Aquifer Research and Data Center, 204

EFF's Guide to the Internet, 116
Effectiveness of Teachers, 192
EFFector Online and EFF News, 496
Egypt, 721
Egyptian Artifacts, 12
Eiffel, 636
ElNet Galaxy, 345
ElNet Galaxy Law List, 385
Einstein, Albert, 528
Einstein in 3-D, 538
Eisenhower National Clearinghouse, 178
Elders, 529
Electric Examiner, 496
Electric Gallery, 21
Electric Light Orchestra, 483
Electric Music, 469
Electric Mystic's Guide to the Internet, 571
Electric Vehicles, 33
Electrical Engineering, 200
Electromagnetic Fields and Microwave Electronics, 538
Electromagnetics, 538
Electromagnetics in Medicine, Science and Communication, 587
Electronic Book Discussion, 192
Electronic Books, 405
Electronic Books in ASCII Text, 405
Electronic Books at Wiretap, 70
Electronic Cafe, 345
Electronic and Communications Privacy Act of 1986, 385
Electronic Design and Development, 195
Electronic Forums for Women, 713
Electronic Frontier Foundation, 517
Electronic/Industrial Music Zine List, 470
Electronic Jewish Library, 391
Electronic Journal of Analytic Philosophy, 533
Electronic Journal of Combinatorics, 427
Electronic Journal of Differential Equations, 427
Electronic Journals Project, 417
Electronic Mail Directory of Companies, 147
Electronic Mailing Lists, 262
Electronic Matchmaker, 531
Electronic Membrane Information Library, 204
Electronic Music, 469
Electronic Music and Synthesizers, 469
Electronic Newspapers and Magazines, 418
Electronic Newsstand, 496
Electronic Publishing, 555
Electronic Resources for Art Historians, 21
Electronic Sources for Mathematics, 427
Electronic Text Resources, 396
Electronic Transactions on Numerical Analysis, 427
Electronic Zoo, 746
Electronics, 195-196
Electronics Repair, 196
Elettra Synchrotron Radiation Facility, 666
Elm, 627
Elvis, 627
Elvis Costello, 483
Elvis Presley, 488
Emacs Editor, 627
Emancipation Proclamation, 296
EMBL Nucleic Acid Database, 52
Emergency and Disaster, 196-198
Emergency Medical Services, 197
Emergency Preparedness Information eXchange (EPIX), 198
Empire, 245
Empire Times, 742
Employee Search, 362
Employer Profiles, 362
Employment Opportunities at Microsoft, 362
Employment Statistics, 172
Encheferizer, 320
Encryption Archives, 612
Endangered Australian Flora and Fauna, 74
Endangered Species, 204
Endless Forest BBS, 44
Endometriosis, 437
Energy, 198-199

*Main subject headings are shown in **bold***

Energy and the Environment, 204
Energy Research in Israel, 587
Energy Statistics, 198
Enfolding Perspectives, 21
Engineering, 199-201
Engineering Facilities and Services, 200
Engines for Education, 178
England, 721
English-Chinese Electronics Terms, 196
English-German Dictionary, 376
English Language, 375
English and Modern Language Graduate
    Students, 375
English Server, 396
English-Slovene Dictionary, 376
English is Tough Stuff, 320
Enhanced Feature Supplements, 509
Eno, Brian, 19
*Enquiry Concerning Human
    Understanding, An,* 532
Entering the World Wide Web: Guide to
    Cyberspace, 339
Entertainment Magazines Online, 418
Entomology at Colorado State University, 52
Entrepreneurs, 79
Entrepreneurs on the Web, 79
Entry Level Jobs Offered, 363
EnviroLink Network, 204
EnviroNet, 639
Environment, 201-209
Environmental Education Database, 205
Environmental Engineering, 205
Environmental Factsheets, 205
Environmental Issues, 205
Environmental Protection Agency, 205
Environmental Resource Center, 205
Environmental Scorecard, 205
Environmental Services Data Directory, 205
EnviroWeb, 206
Enya, 483
Epilepsy Information via CHAT Database,
    437
Episcopal Beliefs and Practices, 571
EPROM Models and Manufacturers List, 111
Equestrian, 9
Ernest Hemingway, 401
Erotic Pictures, 733
Erotic Sounds, 733
Erotica, 730
Esperanto, 376
Esperanto-English Dictionary, 376
Esperanto HyperCourse, 376
Esperanto Introduction, 376
Essays in Radical Empiricism, 409
Essiac, 445
Etext Resources, 70
Etheridge, Melissa, 483
Ethics, 102
Ethnomusicology Research Digest, 470
Ethology, 587
Eudora for Macintosh and Windows, 618
Eureka, 391
European Academic Research Network, 124
European Championships in Athletics, 652
European Commission Host Organization,
    79
European Community, 721
European Group for Atomic
    Spectroscopy, 539
European Law Students Association, 385
European Molecular Biology Net, 52
European Network in Language and
    Speech, 376
European Postal Codes, 271
European Satellite Information, 678
European Southern Observatory Bulletin
    Board, 44
European Space Agency, 640
European Space Information System, 640
European Usenet, 699
European X User Group, 628
Evolution of Genes and Proteins, 52
Evolution of Humans and Primates, 11
Executive Branch Information via Gopher,
    286

Executive Branch Resources via the Web,
    286
Exercise, 289
Exercise and Sports Psychology, 652
Exhibitionism, 600
Exotic Cars, 33
Exotic Pets, 9
Expatriates, 721
Experienced Internet User Questions, 357
Expert Systems and Vision, 666
Exploratorium, 189, 463
Explore New York, 688
Explorer, 192
Explorer Posts, 737
Exploring the Internet, 332
Exploring Japan with Maps, 688
Explosions and Blowing Things Up, 61
Expo Exhibit, 21
Export Guide, 79
Exquisite Sonnet Project, 542
Extropians, 533
Eye Care, 290

F

Fabio's Top Ten Pick-Up Lines, 320
Faces Quiz, 262
FactSheet Five—Electric, 742
Fair Credit Reporting Act, 147
Fairy Tales, 410
Falcon 3.0 Archives, 215
Fall Nature Fun, 738
Families and Parenting, 210-212
Family Childcare Newsletter, 211
Family Discussions, 211
Family History Research, 267
Family Life Newsletter, 211
Family News, 211
Family Science, 550
Family Times, 418
Family Times Online, 610
Family Violence, 550
Family Web Page, 211
Fandom, 593
Fanny Hill, 410
Fans of Science Fiction Writers, 593
Fantastic Fantasies, 593
Fantasy Baseball, 653
Fantasy Images, 130
Fantasy Role-Playing, 579
Fantasy Role-Playing Games, 580
Fantasy, Science Fiction, Horror Calendar,
    593
FAQs in HTML Format, 699
FAQs Searches and Archives, 699
Far from the Madding Crowd, 410
Farming and Agriculture, 4
Fascist, 245
Fashion and Clothing, 213-214
Fat Fetish, 600
Fat-Free Food, 222
Fat People, 531
FatherNet, 212
Fathers of Children with Disabilities, 159
Favorite Musicians and Music Groups, 484
Fax Technology, 670
Fax-3 Fax Software, 628
FaxGate, 147
FaxLinq, 147
Faxnet, 148
Feature Stories, 79
Federal Communications Law Journal, 385
Federal Geographic Data Products, 271
Federal Highway, 278
Federal Information Exchange, 80
Federal Information Processing Standards,
    278
Federal Jobs, 363
Federal Register, 279
Federalist Papers, 297
FedWorld, 279
Feminism, 713
Feminism Internationally, 713
Feminism and Liberty, 545
Feminism and Science and Technology, 714

Feminist Theology, 714
Femmes Femmes Femmes, 601
Fencing, 653
Fermilab, 539
Ferrets, 9
Fetishes, 734
Feudal Terms, 300
Fiber Arts, 307
Fiction Therapy Group, 61
Fiction Writers, 730
Field of Clovers, 371
Fields, W.C., 557
FIFE Information System, 640
Fighting Hate, 329
Figlet Fonts, 105
Figure Skating Home Page, 653
File Room, 229
Filk Music, 470
Film Database, 454
Film Mailing List, 454
Film Music, 470
Film, Television, and Popular Culture, 454
Film and TV Studies, 454
Film and Video Resources, 454
Filmmakers, 454
Filmmaking and Reviews, 455
FinanceNet, 80
Financial Executive Journal, 80
Financial Ratios for Manufacturing
    Corporations, 80
Fine Art, 130
Fine Art Forum, 21
Fine Art Forum's Directory of Online
    Resources, 21
Fine Art Pictures, 21
FingerInfo, 346
Fire Safety Tips, 198
FireNet, 206
Firesign Theater, 320
First Century Judaism, 571
First World War, 448
Fish, 9
Fish Cam, 9
Fishing, 521
Flags of the World, 721
Flames, 702
Flashlife, 580
Flat Top, 245
Flatland, 410
Fleas and Ticks, 10
FlexFAX, 628
Flexible Image Transport System (FITS), 28
Flight Planning, 39
Flight Simulator Utilities and Scenery, 215
Flight Simulators, 214-216
Flight Simulators, 216
Flood Damage, 708
Florida Agricultural Information Retrieval
    System, 4
Florida Wildlife, 746
Flower Gardens, 256
Fluid Mechanics, 200
Flying, 39
Flying and Aviation, 39
FM Broadcasting, 563
Folk Dancing, 155
Folk Music Archives, 470
Folk Music Calendar, 470
Folk Music Concerts, 470
Folk Music Digital Tradition, 470
Folk Music Discussion, 470
Folk Music Information, 471
Folk Music Lyrics, 471
Folk and Traditional Dance Mailing List, 155
Folklore and Mythology, 216-218
Food and Beverages, 222
Food and Drink, 218-228
Food and Drug Administration BBS, 290
Food Labeling Information, 290
Food-related Topics, 222
Foot Fetish, 601
Footbag, 653
Football Resources, 653
Football Stadiums, 653
Foothills Multiuser Chat, 44

Ford Mustangs, 33
Foreign Language Dictionaries, 376
Foreign Trade, 172
Forensic Medicine, 437
Forest Science, 206
Forest Tree Genome Mapping Database, 4
Forests, 206
Formula One Motor Racing, 653
FORTHnet, 125
Fortune Cookie Database, 559
Foster, Vince, 548
Fourth World Documentation Project, 721
Fract Int, 105
Fractal Images, 105
Fractal Movie Archive, 105
Fractals, 105, 130
Fractals and Chaos, 105
France, 721
Frank Sinatra, 489
Frankenstein, 410
Frederick Douglass, 401
Free Language Tools, 134
Free Offers, 148
Free Speech, 229
FreeBSD, 515
Freedom, 228-230
Freedom of Information Act, 230
Freenets, 332
Freenets via Gopher, 346
Freethought Web, 405
French, 377
French Chat, 722
French Daily News Transcripts, 499
French Language Press Review, 499
French Literature, 405
French News, 499
French Timeline, 722
Frequently Asked Questions, 230
Frequently Asked Questions Master List, 700
Freud's Occult Studies, 524
Friendly Folk, 531
Friends and Partners, 722
Frog Dissection Kit, 53
Froggy Page, 234
Front, 242, 484
Fruit Growing, 256
FSP, 134
FTP by Mail, 346
FTP Services for Non-FTP Users, 346
Fuller, Buckminster, 528
Fun, 231-237
Fun with Magazines, 738
Fun Reading, 396
Funding and Grants, 53
Fungi, 53
Funk, 471
Funny News, 320
Funny People, 320
Funny Texts, 321
Furry Animals, 62
Furry Stuff, 593
Fusion, 539
Future Culture, 102
Future Culture and Cyberpunks Mailing
    List, 154
Future Culture Digest Archives, 62
Future Technologists, 662

G

G Protein-Coupled Receptor Database, 53
Gabriel, Peter, 484
Gabriel's Horn, 571
Gaelic and Gaelic Culture, 377
Gaelic Mailing List, 377
Galaxy, 640
Gallery of Images from Silicon Graphics,
    106
Gallery of Interactive Online Geometry, 427
Gambling and Oddsmaking, 704
Game Bytes, 245
Game Information Archive, 245
Game of Life, 245
Game Server, 245
Game Shows, 679

Game Solutions, 246
Games, 238-255
Games, 507, 625
Games Domain, 246
Games and Recreation, 246
Games for SCO Unix, 509
Gangs, 738
GAO (General Accounting Office) Reports, 279
Garbo (University of Vaasa, Finland), 616
Garden Encyclopedia, 257
Gardener's Assistant, 257
Gardening, 255-260
Gardening Information, 257
Gardens and Plants, 257
Gate, The, 497
Gates, Bill, 423
Gateway to Antarctica, 688
Gateway to Darkness, 62
gawk, 628
Gay FTP Site, 262
Gay, Lesbian, Bisexual, 260-266
Gay, Lesbian, and Bisexual Resources, 262
Gay, Lesbian, and Bisexual Trivia Game, 263
Gay, Lesbian, and Bisexual White Pages, 263
Gay Public Officials, 263
Gay TV Listings of the Week, 263
Gaye, Marvin, 485
Gays in Russia, 264
Gazeta Wyborcza, 500
Geeks and Nerds, 62
GenBank Database, 53
Gender and Computing, 714
Gender and Sexuality, 714
Gender Collection, 607
Genealogical Smorgasbord, 267
Genealogy, 266-270
Genealogy Handy Tips and How-To's, 268
Genealogy Newsgroups and Mailing Lists, 267
Genealogy Software for the PC, 267
Genealogy Web, 268
General Accounting Office Transitional Reports, 279
General Agreement on Tariffs and Trade (GATT), 172
General Drug Information, 164
General Fashion, 213
Generic Religions and Secret Societies, 576
Genesis, 571
Genetic Linkage, 53
Genetic Movies, 106
Genetic Sequence Data Bank, 438
Genetics Bank, 438
Genetics Resources, 53
Genome Research at Harvard Biological Laboratories, 54
GenomeNet, 54
Geodetic Survey of Canada, 271
Geoffrey Chaucer Mailing List, 400
Geographic Information and Analysis Laboratory, 271
Geographic Information System, 271
Geographic Resources Analysis Support System, 272
Geographische Informationssyteme, 272
Geography, 270-274
Geography Discussion, 272
Geography Education Software, 272
Geography Server, 272
Geological Time Scale, 275
Geology, 275-277
Geometry Center, 427
Geometry Literature Database, 427
Geometry Sender, 106
Geos, 505
Geos Binaries, 505
German, 377
German Cancer Research Center, 438
German-English Dictionary, 377
German Language News Service, 500
German Speakers, 458
Germany, 722

Get Hooked on the Internet, 234
Ghostscript, 628
Gibson, Debbie, 485
GIF Image Files, 130
Gift of the Magi, The, 410
Giggles, 321
Girls, Girls, Girls, 130
Gliding, 39
Global Change and Climate History, 206
Global Christianity Discussion, 571
Global City, 346
Global Electronic Marketing Service, 346
Global Fund for Women, 714
Global Information and Early Warning System, 4
Global Integrated Pest Management Information System, 4
Global Land Information System, 272
Global Network Navigator, 346
Global Ocean Flux Study, 501
Global Positioning System, 587
Global Real Estate Guide, 564
Global Recycling Network, 206
Global Schoolhouse Project, 178
Global Topics, 329
Global Warming, 206
Globe and Mail, 193
Globewide Network Academy, 186
Globin Gene Server, 54
Glossary of Networking Terms, 357
GNA Virtual Library, 179
Gnosticism, 577
GNU, 612
GNU Archives, 628
GNU C Compiler, 628
GNU Chess, 246
GNU Emacs FAQ, 628
GNU File Compression Utilities, 628
GNU Go, 246
GNU for PCs, 612
GNU Plot, 427
GNU Shell Utilities, 629
GNU Software Search, 629
gnuplot, 629
Gnuplot Tutorial, 134
Go, 246
Goddard Space Flight Center, 640
Goddard Tennis Club, 654
Goddess Spirituality and Feminism, 577
Goethe Investment Heimatseite, 80
Golden Retrievers, 10
Goldwyn, Samuel, 559
Golf, 654
Golfers Mailing List, 654
Gonzo Journalism, 366
Good Food, 222
Good Medicine Magazine, 445
Gopher Clients, 618
Gopher Resources, 347
Gopher Software, 619
Gopher and Utilities for VMS, 135
GopherMail, 332
Gore, Al, 423
Gothic Literature Discussion List, 396
Gothic Tales, 405
Gothic Web Pages and Chat, 471
Government, 277-284
Government and Civics Archives, 279
Government Corruption, 279
Government Document Issues, 391
Government Information Sources on the Internet, 280
Government Policy, 280
Government Publications Network, 280
Government-Sponsored Bulletin Boards, 44
Government: U.S. Congress, 284-285
Government: U.S. Executive Branch, 285-287
Graduate Students, 186
Grand Challenge Cosmology Consortium, 640
Grants, Scholarships, and Funding, 179
Grapevine, 222
Graphic Web Analysis Program, 347
Graphical Information Map Tutorial, 332

Graphics, 22
Graphics Software Search, 612
Grateful Dead, 485
Gray's Atlantic Seasonal Hurricane Forecast, 708
Great Beginnings Newsletter, 212
Great Lakes Information Network, 206
Great White Shark, 746
Greek Mythology, 216
Green Manufacturing, 206
GreenDisk Environmental Information, 206
Greenpeace, 207
Gregorian Chants, 471
Gross and Disgusting, 63
Gross State Product Tables, 172
Grotesque in Art, 22
Groucho Marx, 559
Growing Herbs, 257
Growing Vegetables, 257
Grunge, 471
Guess the Animal, 246
Guess the Disease, 247
Guide to Australia, 689
Guide to Lock Picking, 369
Guide to London, 689
Guide to Network Resource Tools, 339
Guide to SLIP and PPP, 339
Guide to System Administrators, 321
Guitar, 472
Guitar Archive, 472
Guitar Chords for Popular Songs, 472
Gulf War Announcement Speech, 297
Guns, 307
gzip, 629

H

H.G. Wells, 404
H.P. Lovecraft, 402
H.P. Lovecraft Image Gallery, 22
Hack Gallery, 451
Hacker Crackdown, 117
Hacker Sites on the Net, 138
Hacker Test, 321
Hacker's Dictionary, 117
Hacker's Technical Journals, 117
Hackers, 103
Hacking, 418
Hair Fetish, 601
Hakim Bey, 533
Halifax Nova Scotia, 90
Hall of Dinosaurs, 300
Ham Radio Archives, 563
Ham Radio Callbooks, 563
Handicap BBS Lists, 159
Handicap Issues, 159
Hang Gliding Server, 39
Hangman, 247
Hangovers, 704
Hangul (Korean) Newsgroups, 700
Hangul (Korean) Software Tools, 637
Hanky Codes, 264
Happy Birthday, 63
Happy People, 234
Hard Bop Cafe, 472
Hard Disk Guide, 111
Hardware Architectures, 111
Hardware Compatibility Handbook, 509
Hardware News, 111
Hardware Technical Material, 111
Harold and Maude, 410
Harpsichord Exercises, 472
Harvest Information Discovery and Access System, 619
Hawaii, 689
Hawaii Legislative Information Service, 385
Hawaiian Glossary, 377
Head to Head Daemon Resources, 247
Headaches, 290
Headline and Business News, 497
Health, 288-295
Health Care Reform Act, 290
Health Concerns of Women, 715
Health General Information, 291
Health Info-Com Network Newsletter, 291

Health Issue Discussion, 291
Health News, 291
Health Newsletters, 291
Health Resources, 291
Health Science Resources, 292
Health Sciences Libraries Consortium, 180, 292
Healthline, 292
HealthNet, 293
HEASARC Astronomical Browser, 28
Heavy Metal, 472
Heavy Thrash Music, 472
Hebrew Quiz, 571
Hebrew Software Archive, 616
Hebrew Users Group, 144
Hellenic News, 722
Hello World!, 135
Hemingway, Ernest, 401
Hendrix, Jimi, 486
HEP Data Archive, 539
Herb Archive, 445
Herb Books and Sources, 446
Herb Hypercard Stack, 446
Herb Information, 258
Herb Mailing List, 258
Herbal Caution, 446
Herbal Medicine, 446
Herbal Variations, 258
Herbs, 222
Herland, 411
Hermann Hesse, 401
Herrick, Robert, 542
Hesse, Hermann, 401
Hewlett-Packard, 99
Hexapawn, 247
High Culture, 559
High Energy Physics Information Center, 539
High Performance Cars, 93
High Performance Computing Gopher, 125
High Times News, 418
High Weirdness, 63
Higher Education National Software Archive, 625
Higher Education Resources and Opportunities, 186
Highly Imaginative Technologies, 593
Hiking, 521
Hindi, 377
Hindu Dharma, 572
Hindu Names, 722
Hinduism, 572
Hints for Marijuana Growers, 164
Hippocratic Oath, 438
Hippocratic Oath and Law, 411
Hiraiso Solar Terrestrial Research Center, 640
Hiroshima, 587
Hiroshima Accounts, 300
Historian's Database and Information Server, 300
Historian's Newsletter, 300
Historic American Speeches, 300
Historical and Celebrity Figures, 264
Historical Costuming, 213
Historical Costuming Discussion, 213
Historical Documents, 295-297
Historical Sounds and Speeches, 301
History, 298-304
History of American Catholicism, 572
History of the Ancient Mediterranean, 301
History Archives, 301
History Discussion, 301
History of Food, 223
History of Languages, 377
History Mailing Lists, 301
History of Medicine Division, 438
History of Philosophy of Science, 518
History of Science and Technology, 587
History and Uses of the Internet, 332
Hitachi, 666
Hitchhiker's Guide to the Internet, 358
Hobbies, 305-313
Hockey, 654
Hockey Discussion, 654
Holdsworth, Allan, 486

*Main subject headings are shown in **bold***

Holistic Healing, 446
Hollyweb Film Guide, 160
Holocaust Discussion, 301
Holst, Ingar, 401
Home Gardening Mailing List, 258
Home Maintenance, 313-315
Home Page Publisher, 347
Home Pages, 347
Home Repairs, 314
Home School Discussion, 180
Home School Resources, 180
Home Test Kits, 438
Home Video Games History, 247
Homebrew Mailing List, 223
Homebrewing, 223
Homebuyer's Fair, 564
Homosexual Assorted Resources, 260
Homosexuality, 264
Homosexuality and the Church, 264
Homosexuality and Gay Rights, 264
Homosexuality in the Middle Ages, 264
Horoscopes by Yul and Doc X, 26
Horror Talk, 455
Horse Fanciers, 10
Horse Racing, 704
Horse Racing Archives, 654
Hot News, 80
Hot Off the Tree, 666
Hot Rods, 34
Hot Tub Server, 696
Hot Wire, 22
Hourly Auroral Activity Status Report, 709
House of the Seven Gables, The, 411
Houses, 148
How Computers Work, 111
How-to Collection, 340
How to Confuse Your Roommate, 321
How to Find a Mail Address, 339
How to Make Movies, 339
How to Make Your Own Booze, 223
How to Recycle Paper, 372
How to Steal Code, 117
How to Use a Condom, 601
Howard Rheingold, 425
Howitzer95, 247
HP Calculator BBS, 196
HPCwire, 117
HTML Developer's JumpStation, 619
HTML Editor for Word for Windows, 619
HTML Mode for emacs, 619
htMUD, 461
Hub Mathematics and Science Center, 427
Hubble Space Telescope, 641
Hubble Telescope, 28
Hugo Awards of 1990, 594
Human Communication Research Centre, 667
Human and Computer Interaction, 144
Human Genome Project, 54
Human-Powered Vehicles, 654
Human Rights, 546
Humanist Mailing List, 316
Humanities, 315-316
Hume Society, 519
Humor, 317-328
Humor Archives, 321
Humor Mailing List, 322
Humorous Quotations, 559
Hungary, 722
HungerWeb, 198
Hunt the Wumpus, 248
Hunting of the Snark, The, 411
Hurricane Images, 709
Hydrogen Bond Calculation Program, 94
Hydroponic Gardening, 258
Hyperactive Molecules, 94
Hyperbolic Movies, 106
Hyperbolic Tiles, 106
Hypercard, 622
Hypercard Stack Archive, 622
HyperDiscordia, 63
HyperDoc, 438
Hypermedia Star, 234
HyperMedia Zines on the Net, 742
Hypertext Fiction, 405

Hypertext Markup Language, 340
Hytelnet, 391

I

I Ching, 533
"I Have a Dream," 302
IBM Kiosk for Education, 180
IBM News, 128
IBM Songbook, 103
IBM Whois Server, 347
Icarus, 641
Ice Cream, 223
Iceland, 378
Icelandic Fisheries Laboratories, 501
Icon Browser, 106
Icons, 130
IEEE Gopher, 196
IFR Flight Simulator, 216
Illegal Recreational Drug Information, 164
Illinois Mathematics and Science Academy, 428
Illuminati Online, 580
Illuminati Online Games, 248
Illustrated Audio Slide Show Technology, 122
Image and Audio File Formats, 107
Image Databases, 391
Image and Movie Archives, 131
Image Processing with Live Video Sources, 122
Images of Architecture and Sculpture in Turkey, 15
Images of Renaissance and Baroque Architecture, 15
Immanuel Kant, 533
Immunology, 54
Impeaching Clinton, 286
Impulse, 473
Incident Response Teams, 138
Income Taxation Information, 80
Incomplete Guide to the Internet, 180
Index of Abstracts, 539
Index of Erotic Stories, 734
Index to Literature Servers, 397
Index of Sounds, 140
Index to Web Servers, 501
India, 722
Indian Classical Music, 473
Indiana University School of Law Web Server, 385
Indigenous Peoples, 180
Indigo Girls, 486
Indoor Plants, 259
Industry Statistics, 80
Infertility, 439
Infinite Illusions Home Page, 149
Infinity City, 594
Info und Softserver, 612
InfoMatch, 347
InfoPop, 625
Information on Authors, 397
Information Law Papers, 385
Information Resources Management Division, 4
Information Technology Laboratory, 80
Initgame, 248
Inquisitor, 742
Institute for Global Communications, 519
Institute of High Energy Physics, 539
Institute for Molecular Science, 94
Institute for Remote Sensing Applications, 501
Institute for Systems Engineering and Informatics, 667
Institutes of Astronomy, 28
Institutional Communications Network, 180
Institutions of Music, 473
Instrument Flight Rules, 39
Integrated Computer Solutions FAQs, 629
Interactive Astrology Chart, 27
Interactive Employment Network, 363
Interactive Fiction, 248
Interactive Fiction Game Programming, 135

Interactive Natural History Museum, 302, 463
Interactive Weather Browser, 709
Interactive Web Games, 248
Intergenerational Relationships, 601
International Arctic Buoy Program, 207
International Association of Gay Square Dance Clubs, 264
International Background Information, 272
International Business Practices Guide, 81
International Internet ChainArt Project, 22
International Market Insight Reports, 81
International Organization of Paleobotany, 74
International Politics, 329-331
International System of Units, 588
International Telecommunications Union, 670
International Teletimes, 743
International Travel Health Advice, 689
Internationalized xgopher, 629
Internaut, 418
Internet, 331-338
Internet Access Providers List, 340
Internet with Attitude, 418
Internet Better Business Bureau, 81
Internet Bibliography, 117
Internet Book Information Center, 70
Internet Books, 71
Internet Books List, 71
Internet Business Center, 81
Internet Business Center Telecommunications Definitions, 670
Internet Business Journal, 418
Internet Candy Dish, 234
Internet Classroom, 340
Internet Computer Index, 118, 347
Internet Conference Calendar, 332
Internet Connectivity for PCs, 505
Internet Consultants Directory, 149
Internet Drafts, 333
Internet by E-Mail, 347
Internet Engineering, 333
Internet Fax Server, 348, 671
Internet Font Browser, 107
Internet General Discussion, 333
Internet Growth Statistics, 333
Internet: Help, 339-343
Internet Help, 340
Internet Hunt, 234
Internet Index, 696
Internet Information, 341
Internet Macintosh Resources, 120
Internet Mailing Lists, 348
Internet Mall, 149
Internet Market Place, 348
Internet Modem Players Listing, 248
Internet Newbies, 341
Internet Overview, 118
Internet Poetry Archive, 542
Internet Protocol, 671
Internet Resource Guides, 348
Internet: Resources, 343-357
Internet Resources Metamap, 348
Internet: RFCs, 357-358
Internet Security Firewalls, 138
Internet Services, 348
Internet Services Directory, 149
Internet Services List, 348
Internet Services and Resources, 349
Internet Society Gopher, 333
Internet Talk Radio, 419
Internet Talk Radio Traveling Circus, 333
Internet Timeline, 302, 333
Internet Tools List, 349, 637
Internet University, 335
Internet Users' Glossary, 358
Internet Worm, 335
Inter-Network Mail Guide, 125
InterNIC Directory of Directories, 349
InterNIC InfoGuide, 349
InterNIC Information Services, 335
InterNIC Web Picks, 349
InterScape, 349
InterText Magazine, 335, 406

Inter-Tribal Network, 723
Intimate Violence, 550
Intrigue, 359-360
Introduction to HTML, 118
Investments, 81
Invisible Man, The, 411
Iowa Political Stock Market, 549
Iowa State University Scholar System, 4
IP Address Resolver, 335
IRC (Internet Relay Chat), 336
IRC Bar, 234
IRC channel #WWW, 336
IRC Help, 341
IRC Questions, 230
IRC Thesis, 118
IRC II Client, 619
Ireland, 723
Irish and Celtic Resources, 723
Irish Politics, 329
ISCA BBS, 45
ISDN, 671
Islam, 572
Islam Discussion, 572
Islamic News, 500
Island, 461
Island Internet, 350
Ispell, 637
Israel, 723
Israeli News, 500
Israeli Politics, 329
Issues of Interest to Women, 715
Issues in Religion, 572
Italian Lessons, 378
Italian Literature, 406
Italy, 723

J

J. Krishnamurti, 533
J.R.R. Tolkien, 403
J.R.R. Tolkien Discussions, 403
Jabberwocky, 411
Jackson Laboratory, 54
Jackson, Steve Games, 388
Jainism, 572
James Woods, 425
Jane Austen, 399
JANET Network, 181
Japan, 689, 723
Japan Animal Genome Database, 54
Japan That Can Say No, 411
Japanese, 378
Japanese Animation, 22
Japanese Animation Images, 131
Japanese Business Studies, 81
Japanese Food and Culture, 223
Japanese Information, 723
Japanese Popular Music, 473
Japanese Prime Minister's Official Residence, 281
Japanese Research, 144
Japanese Usenet, 700
Japanese Weather, 709
Jargon File, 341
Jarre, Jean-Michel, 486
Jazz/Blues/Rock and Roll Images, 473
Jazz Clubs Around the World, 473
Jazz Performers, 486
Jazz Photography, 473
Jazz Server, 473
Jeopardy, 248
Jerry's Guide to Law, 386
Jerusalem Mosaic, 689
Jerusalem One, 724
Jerusalem Tour, 724
Jesuits and the Sciences, 302
Jewelry, 150
Jewish Calendar and Events, 724
Jewish Communities, 724
Jewish Culture and Religion, 572
Jewish Law, 572
Jewish Literature, 397
Jewish Mailing List, 268, 573
Jewish Music, 474
Jewish Organizations, 519

Jewish Recipes, 223
Jewish Religious Institutions, 573
Jewish Software, 613
Jewish Youth, 738
JewishNet, 724
JFK Conspiracy, 359
JFK Conspiracy Documents, 297
Jihad to Destroy Barney on the Web, 63
Jim Warren Gopher, 549
Jimi Hendrix, 486
Jimmy Buffett, 482
Jittlov, Mike, 423
Jive Server, 322
Job Search, 363
Job Seeking, 363
Jobnet, 363
Jobs, 361-366
Jobs General Discussion, 364
Jobs Offered, 364
joe Editor, 629
Joe's Adventure, 235
Joel, Billy, 486
John December's Internet Web Text, 341
John Greenleaf Whittier, 544
John Keats, 542
John Lennon, 487
John Milton, 402
John Muir Exhibit, 529
Joist Span Calculator, 314
Joke Collections, 322
Jokes, 322
Jokes and Fun Archive, 323
Jokes, Moderated, 323
Jokes and Stories, 324
Joseph Conrad, 400
Joshua Tree National Monument, 207
Josip Broz Tito, 330
Journal of Artificial Intelligence Research, 667
Journal of Underground Computing, 743
Journalism, 366, 553
Journalism Criticism, 366
Journalism Discussions, 366
Journalism and Media, 366-368
Journals with a Difference, 553
Journey North, 689
Journeys and Destinations, 689
JPEG File Viewer for Macintosh, 107
JPEG File Viewer for Windows, 107
JPEG Files, 131
Judaica Collection, 573
Juggling, 235, 307
Juggling Archives, 307
JumpStation, 350
Jungle Book, The, 411
Just David, 412

K

K12 Internet School Sites, 181
K12 Resources, 181
K-Sculpt Music Software, 613
K-theory Preprint Archives, 428
Kaleidospace, 22
Kama Sutra, 734
Kandinsky Image Archive, 131
Kant, Immanuel, 533
Kapor, Mitch, 424
Karate, 655
Kate Bush, 482
Katherine Mansfield, 402
Kayaking, 521
Keats, John, 542
Keepsake Stories, The, 412
Kenn Nesbitt's Travel Adventures, 690
Kennedy, Edward, 285, 424
Kerberos Resources, 637
Kermit Manual, 118
Ketchup, 223
Keys and Locks, 369-371
Kibo, 702
KidArt, 372
Kidcafe, 188
Kidlink, 188, 372
Kids, 371-372

Kids and Computers, 372
Kid's Internet Delight, 372
Kids Mailing List, 372
Kidsphere, 193
Kierkegaard, Soren, 533
Kindergarten to Grade 6 Corner, 193
Kinetics and Thermodynamics, 54
Kinsey Questions and Answers, 607
Kiss, 486
Kit Cars, 34
Kites and Kiting Resources, 307
Kitten Page, 10
Klingon Shared Reality, 662
Klingons, 662
Knowbot Information Service, 350
Knowledge Representation and Reasoning
    Laboratory, 667
Kool-Aid, 224
Koran (or Qur'an), 573
Korea, 724
Korfball, 655
Krannert Art Museum, 22
Krishnamurti, J., 533
Kriya Yoga, 577
Kterm, 630
Kurtz, Katherine, 401
KVI Research Network, 540

L

L. Frank Baum, 399
Labor, 82
Lacemaking, 307
Laetrile and Vitamin B17, 446
LambdaMOO, 461
LAN Management, 118
Lancia, 34
Landscaping and Lawns, 259
Language, 373-382
Language Articles, 378
Language FAQs, 135
Language IRC Channels, 378
Language List, 135
Languages of the World, 378
Large People, 531
Laszlo's Lengthy List of Luxury Smokes, 705
Late Night Talk Show Monologues, 324
Latin America, 724
Latin Language Textbook, 181
Latin Study Guides, 378
Launchpad, 392
Launchpad BBS, 45
Lavois Shooting, Bruce, 384
Law, 383-389
Law Discussion, 386
Law Resources, 386
Law Schools, 386
Law Schools and Law Firms on the Web,
    386
Law Server, 386
LawTalk, 386
Le Louvre, 23
League of Conservation Voters, 207
League for Programming Freedom, 387
League for Programming Freedom/Free
    Software Foundation, 103
Learn Spanish in South America!, 378
Learning to Fly, 39
Leasing a Web Server, 82
Lebanon and Levant Cultural Multimedia
    Server, 724
Legal and Criminal Articles, 387
Legal Domain Network, 387
Legal News, 82, 387
Legend of Sleepy Hollow, The, 412
Legislative Branch Resources, 285
Lego, 308
Lemurs, 63
Lennon, John, 487
Lenny Bruce, 556
Lesbian Lexicon, 265
Lesbian Love, 265
Lesbian Mothers, 265
Lesbian, Gay, and Bisexual Mailing Lists,
    265

less, 630
Lesson Plans, 193
Lessons in Spanish, 379
Let's Go Gopherin' Now, 341
Letterman, David, 559, 667
Letterman, David, Official Song Book, 678
Lewis Carroll, 399
Lexia, 23
Libertarian Manifestos, 546
Libertarian Student Network, 546
Libertarians, 546
Liberty and Feminism, 715
Liberty Network, 546
Liberty Web, 230
Libraries, 389-394
Libraries, 82
Library Catalogs and Databases, 392
Library Catalogs via telnet, 392
Library of Congress, 392
Library of Congress Cultural Exhibits, 725
Library Humor, 324
Library and Information Science, 393
Library Newsletters, 393
Library Policy Archive, 393
Library Resources, 393
Library Resources on the Internet, 393
Library Topic Lists, 393
Lichtenstein, Roy, Pre-Pop 1948-1960, 25
Lies, 705
Life-Threatening Medical Emergencies, 439
Life in the Year 2020, 667
LifeLines Database, 268
Lightful Images, 524
Lighthouses, 131
Lighthouses in the Eastern U.S., 15
Limbaugh, Rush, 424, 680
Limbaugh, Rush Archives, 547
Limbaugh, Rush Political Discussion, 548
Limerick Server, 324
Limericks, 734
Lincoln Conspiracies, 360
Linear Programming Answers, 135
Lingerie, 213
Linguist List, 379
Linguistics, 379
Linux, 515
Linux Chat and Support, 515
Lips, 63
Listserv Information Home Page, 342
Listserv User Guide, 350
Literature, 395-399
Literature: Authors, 399-404
Literature: Collections, 404-407
Literature Discussions, 397
Literature General Discussion, 397
Literature: Titles, 407-416
Little Russia, 725
Live Television Images, 679
Live-Action Role-Playing, 580
Living History, 308
Living with a Challenge, 715
Ljubljana, 690
Local Times Around the World, 273
Lock Picking, 369
Lock Talk, 369
Locksmithing Archives, 371
Logic, 428
Logintaka, 118
Lojban, 379
Loopback Service, 336
loQtus, 559
Lore, 216
Los Alamos National Laboratory, 667
Love, 583
Lovecraft, H.P., 402
Lovecraft, H.P. Image Gallery, 22
Lowfat Vegetarianism, 224
LPMUDs, 458
LSD: My Problem Child, 164
Lucid Dreams, 491
Ludvigsen Residence—A Family Server, 63
Lunar and Planetary Institute, 641
Lunch Servers, 64
Lute, 474
LYCOS Web Searcher, 351

Lynx, 505, 620
Lynx, The, 421
Lynx Cheats, 248
Lyrics Archive, 474
Lyrics from Musicals, 474

M

MaasInfo Files, 351
Mac FTP List, 623
Mac Hardware, 120
Mac Shrodinger's Cat, 412
Mach, 505
MacinTalk, 120
Macintosh Announcements, 121
Macintosh Archives, 616
Macintosh Games, 623
Macintosh General Discussion, 121
Macintosh Graphics, 107
Macintosh Index, 121
Macintosh News, 121
Macintosh Resources, 121
Macintosh in Science and Technology, 121
Macintosh Secret Tricks List, 598
Macintosh Software Search, 623
Macintosh Sounds, 140
Macintosh User's Group, 121
Macintosh User's Group at Arkansas
    College, 121
Macintosh User's Group at Johns Hopkins,
    121
MacWAIS, 620
MacWeb, 620, 623
Madawaska-Victoria, 690
Madlibs, 235
Magazine, 128
Magazine Summaries, 419
Magazines, 417-421
Magazines, 735
Mage's Guide to the Internet, 577
Magic, 308
Magic: The Gathering, 248
Magic Square Puzzle, 248
Magick, 492
Magick Galore, 492
Mail Addresses of Ukraine Businesses, 82
Mail to Famous People, 422-425
Mail Gateway Guide, 125
Mail Robot, 336
Mail and Usenet News, 503
mail2html, 620
Mailbase Gopher, 351
Mailing List Search, 351
Mainframes and Large Networks, 510
Maize Genome Database Project, 4
Major League Baseball Schedules, 655
Major Resource Kit, 364
Majordomo Mailing List Software, 620
Malaysia, 725
Malaysia, Singapore, Islam News, 725
Malt Whiskey Tour, 224
Mammal Database, 74
Mammoth Records Internet Center, 474
Man and the Biosphere, 207
Managing Networked Information, 125
Mandelbrot Explorer, 107
Mandelbrot Images, 132
Manga and Anime, 731
Manly Men's Ten Commandments, 324
Manned U.S. Space Flight Images, 641
Mansfield, Katherine, 402
Map Related Web Sites, 273
MapMaker, 351
Mapping Chromosomes, 54
Maps, 273
Marching Bands, 474
Mardi Gras, 527
Maricopa Center for Learning and
    Instruction (MCLI), 186
Marijuana Discussion, 164
Marijuana Fiction, 164
Marijuana Usage, 165
Marine Signal Flags, 68
Maritimes Web Servers, 90
Mark Twain, 403

Mark Twain Discussions, 403
Mark Twain, quotations, 561
MarketBase Online Catalog, 87
Marketing, 172
Marketplace, Buy and Sell, 87
Married with Children, 679
Mars Atlas, 29
Marshmallow Peanut Circus Home Page, 235
Martial Arts, 655
Marvin Gaye, 485
Marvin Minsky, 424
Marx, Groucho, 559
Marx and Engels' Writings, 302
Mass Media, 367
Massage, 293
Master Gardener, 259
Masters, Extraterrestrials and Archangels, 492
Masturbation, 601
Masturbation Index, 601
Material Safety Data Sheets, 293
Math Archives Gopher, 428
Math Articles, 428
Math and Calculus Programs, 428
Math Gophers, 428
Math Information Server, 181
Math and Philosophy, 429
Math Problem-Solving Skills, 189
Math Programs for the Mac, 429
Mathematical Association of America, 429
Mathematical Publications List, 429
Mathematical Research, 429
Mathematical Sciences Server, 429
Mathematical Topics at the Center for Scientific Computing, 430
Mathematics, 425-433
Mathematics City, 430
Mathematics General Discussion, 430
Mathematics Resource Pointers, 430
Mathematics Servers, 430
MathWorks, 430
Matrix News, 125
Max Headroom, 679
Maximizing Life's Choices, 533
MayaQuest, 372
McCartney, Paul, 487
McCartney, Paul, Death Rumor, 487
McDonald's, 225
McDonnell Douglas Aerospace, 40
McEntire, Reba, 487
McGraw-Hill Internet Resource Area, 555
McGuinn, Roger, 424
Mead Maker's Resources, 225
Mechanical Engineering, 200
MEDCAL, 439
Media Coverage, 336
Media in Education, 181
Media List, 367
Media Magazines, 367
Medianet OnLine Public Catalog Access, 393
Medical Education Information Center, 439
Medical and Health Information, 439
Medical Information About Marijuana, 165
Medical Libraries, 439
Medical Physics, 439
Medical Resources, 439
Medical Software, 439
Medical Software and Data, 440
Medical Students, 440
Medical Students Forum, 440
Medicine, 433-444
Medicine: Alternative, 444-447
Medicine General Discussion, 440
Medieval History, 302
Meditation, 493
Mednews, 440
MedSearch America, 364
Meeting People, 531
Melrose Place, 679
Memetics, 534
Memoirs, Journals and Correspondence, 731
Men and Women, 583

Men's Issues, 610
Mennonites, 573
Menopause, 715
Mensa, 519
Mentally Retarded Deaf, 159
Mergers and Acquisitions, 82
Merit Network Information Center, 342
Meta, 419
Meta Virtual Environments, 667
Metalworking, 308
Metaphysics, 534
Metaverse, 475
Meteorology, 709
Meteorology Information, 709
Methods and Reagents, 54
Mexico, 725
Michael Tucker, 324, 425
Microbiology at the Technical University of Denmark, 55
MicroMUSE Learning Community , 181
Microprocessor Instruction Set Cards, 111
Microsoft Archives, 99
Microsoft Flight Simulator, 216
Microsoft Gopher Server, 99
Microsoft Research, 99
Microsoft Web Server, 504
Microsoft Windows 3.1 Book List, 71
Microsoft Windows Developer Information, 504
Microsoft Windows Networking Environment, 125
Middle English, 379
Middle Europe, 725
Middlesex News, 497
MIDI Archives, 140
MIDI Home Page, 475
Midwifery, 715
Migraine Headaches, 293
Miles Davis, 483
Military, 448-451
Military Aircraft, 40
Military Collections, 448
Milton, John, 402
Milwaukee Frozen Custard, 225
Mind, The, 588
Mini-Journal of Irreproducible Results, 588
Miniatures, 581
Mining the Internet, 342
Ministry of Education in Singapore, 181
Minix, 506
Minor League Baseball, 655
Minority College and University Information, 186
Minsky, Marvin, 424
Miscellaneous DOS Topics, 503
Miscellaneous Pictures, 132
Miscellaneous Sounds, 141
Mischief, 451-452
Miss Netters' Advice Column, 325
Missing Children, 212
Missing Children Database, 212
Missing and Stolen Clearinghouse, 463
Missouri Botanical Garden, 74
MIT Soaring Association, 40
Mkzdk, 64
Mnemonics, 380
Moby Dick, 412
Models, 308
Modem Doomer's Hangout, 249
Modems, 112
Modern British and Irish Literature, 397
Mogul Media, 668
Molecular Biology Laboratory, 55
Molecular Biology Network, 55
Molecular Biology of HIV, 55
Molecular Modeling, 55
Mona Lisa, The 23
Monetary Statistics, 172
Money Abroad FAQ, 691
Monitor Radio, 563
Monochrome, 45
Monster Movies, 455
Monthly Temperature Anomalies, 709
Monty Python's Flying Circus, 325
Mood Disorders Server, 440

Moorish Orthodox Church, 573
Morbidity and Mortality Weekly Report, 293
More Comics, 96
Mormon, 574
Morningstar Spotlight, 173
Morpo Review, 743
Mortgage Calculator, 82
Mosaic Gizmos, 108
Mosaic for the Mac, Microsoft Windows, and X Window, 620
Mosaic Mail Gateway, 336
Mosaic Users and Developers List, 621
Moscow Kremlin Online Excursion, 725
Moscow News, 500
Mother Jones, 419
Mother-of-All BBSs, 351
MotherCity Coffee—A Guide to Seattle Coffee, 225
Motif BioInformatics Server, 55
Motorcycle Archive, 36
Motorcycle Design, 36
Motorcycle Racing, 36
Motorcycle Reviews, 36
Motorcycles, 36
Motorsports, 655
Mount Wilson Observatory, 641
Mountain Biking, 521
Mountain Biking Areas, 521
Mouse Biology, 55
Movie Database Request Server, 455
Movie and Film Festivals, 455
Movie Folklore, 455
Movie Information, 456
Movie List, 456
Movie Reviews, 456
Movie of the Week, 235
Movies, 453-457
Movies Archives, 456
Movies and Filmmaking, 456
Movies News, 456
Movies and Television, 141
MPEG Animation Shows, 122
MPEG Movie Archive, 123
MPEG Movies, 123
MPEG Movies from JRC, 123
MUD Access via Gopher, 462
MUD Announcements, 458
MUD Documents, 458
MUD Information, 459
MUD List, 459
MUD Usenet Discussion Groups, 459
MUD as a Psychological Model, 459
MUDs: General Information, 457-460
MUDs: Specific Types, 460-463
MUDWHO Server, 459
Muir, John, Exhibit, 529
Multi-Trek, 249
Multicast Backbone FAQ, 668
Multics, 506
Multilevel Marketing, 83
Multilingual Classrooms, 181
Multimedia in Education, 123
Multimedia OS/2, 507
Multimedia Textbooks, 440
Multiple Choice Quiz, 235
Multiuser Games, 249
Multiverse, 630
Muppet Fest, 679
Musee des Arts et Metiers, 668
Museum of Machine-Generated Speech and Singing, 668
Museum of New Zealand, 23
Museums, 463-464
Museums, Exhibits and Special Collections, 463
Museums on the Web, 463
MUSH Documents, 459
Music, 464-481
Music, 141
Music Archives, 475
Music and Behavior, 475
Music Chat, 475
Music Composition, 475
Music Database, 475

Music Discussion, 476
Music Facts, 476
Music FAQs, 476
Music Festival Information, 476
Music Journalism, 367
Music Kitchen, 476
Music Library Association, 476
Music List of Lists, 476
Music News, 476
Music Performance, 476
Music: Performers, 482-490
Music Resources, 477
Music Reviews, 477
Music Samples, 477
Music Server, 477
Music and Sound Files, 477
Music Underground Archive, 477
Music Videos, 477
Musical Instrument Construction, 478
Musicals, 160
Mutual Fund Market Manager, 173
Mutual Fund Price Movement Chart, 83
Mutual Fund Quotations, 173
Mutual Funds Phone Numbers, 173
Mysteries, 397
Mystery Genre, 398
Mystery Science Theater 3000, 594
Mysticism, 493
Mysticism Discussion, 574
Mythical Animals, 217

N

Nachos, 506
Nails, 462
Naked Guy, 64
Name Guide, 380
Names in Genealogy, 270
Nancy Drew, 398
NandO.net (North Carolina Web Server), 351
NASA Aviation Server, 40
NASA Extragalactic Database (NED), 641
NASA Hot Topics, 497
NASA News, 642
NASA Research Labs, 642
NASA Space Sensors and Instrument Technology Museum, 642
NASA Spacelink, 642
NASA Technological Reports, 642
NASA's Computer Software Management and Information Center, 613
NASDA, 642
National Archaeological Database, 12
National Archives and Records Administration, 269, 281
National Cancer Center, 440
National Cancer Center Database (Japan), 441
National Center for Atmospheric Research, 709
National Center for Supercomputing Applications, 144
National Child Rights Alliance, 519
National Cooperative Extension Service, 5
National Education BBS, 182
National Environmental Data Referral Service, 207
National Flags, 725
National Genetic Resources Program, 5
National Geophysical Data Center, 275
National Income and Products Accounts, 173
National Information Infrastructure Agenda, 126
National Institute of Allergy and Infectious Disease, 293
National Institute of Health, 293
National Institute of Health Projects, 588
National Institute of Standards and Technology, 519, 668
National Library of Medicine, 441
National Library of Medicine Locator, 441
National News Stories, 497

National Nuclear Data Center Online Service, 540
National Optical Astronomy Observatories, 29
National Pages, 726
National Performance Review, 286
National Performance Review Web Site, 281
National Press Club Luncheon Addresses, 529
National Referral Center Master File, 182
National Renewable Energy Laboratory (NREL), 198
National Research and Education Network Bill, 546
National Science Foundation Publications, 588
National Telecommunications and Information Administration, 671
National Trade Data Bank, 83
National Weather Service Forecasts, 710
National Wetlands Inventory, 207
National Wildlife Refuges, 208
Native American Literature, 398
Native American Mailing Lists, 726
Native Americans, 726
NativeNet, 726
NATO, 330
NATO Handbook, 330
NATO Press Releases, 330
NATODATA, 330
Natural Childbirth Anecdotes, 447
Natural Environment Research Council, 208
Natural History Museum, London, 463
Naval Fighting Ships, 448
Navy News Service , 449
Navy Policy Book, 449
NavyOnLine, 449
NBA Schedule, 656
NCSA Digital Gallery CD-ROM Science Theater, 589
NCSA Telnet, 613
NCSA Web Server for Windows, 621
NCTU CIS BBS, 45
Near-Death Experiences, 524
Neat Educational Tricks, 193
Neat Tricks, 372
NEC, 100
Necromicon, 64
Necronomicon, 524
NECTEC Server, 726
Needlework, 150
Negative Emotions, 64
nenscript, 630
Nerd Club, 529
Nerd Humor, 325
Nerd Page, 103
Nesbitt, Kenn, Travel Adventures, 690
Net Abuse, 702
Net Happenings, 336, 352
Net Law, 388
Net Legends, 217
Net Sex, 735
Net Travel, 691
NetBoy, 235
Nethack, 249
NetLib Software Server, 431
NetPages, 352
Netrek, 249
NetResults, 281
Netsurfer Publishing, 743
NetVet—Veterinary Resource Line, 5
Netweaver, 419
Netwit Mailing List, 325
Network Bibliography, 119
Network and Computer Security Reference Index, 139
Network Hardware Suppliers List, 126
Network Information Services, 336
Network Maps, 126
Network Newsletters, 119
Network Politics, 126
Networking, 504
Networking Articles, 127
Networking Computers, 119

Networks and Community, 336
NETworth, 83
Neural Network Home Page, 668
NeuroNet, 127
Neuropharmacological Anarchy, 165
Neuroscience, 55
New Age, 491-495
New Age Music, 478
New Age Talk, 493
New Atlantis, The, 412
New Gophers, 352
New Internet User Questions, 358
New Music, 478
New Patterns in Education, 182
New Products and Services, 83
New Religious Movements, 577
New Republic, The, 546
New Sites, 352
New South Polar Times, The, 273
New Sun, The, 743
New and Trendy Protocols, 144
New telnet Sites, 353
New Wais Sources, 353
New Ways of Thinking, 534
New York City Guide, 691
New York City Information, 692
New York Journal of Mathematics, 431
New York State Department of Health, 293
New York State Statistics, 273
New Zealand, 726
Newbie Newz, 182
Newcastle Earthquake, 198
News & Observer, The, 497
News About the Aviation and Aerospace Industries, 40
News on Children, 212
News About Drugs, 165
News on the Family, 212
News Media, 367
News About Space, 643
News About Unix, 510
News: U.S., 495-498
News: World, 498-500
Newsgroup Administration, 702
Newsgroup Invasion, 702
Newsgroup Questions, 702
Newsgroups, 230
Newsletters, Electronic Journals, Zines, 554
Newsletters and Journals Available via Gopher, 497
Newspapers and Journalism Schools, 497
Newton, 182
NeXT Sounds, 141
Nexus, 23
NFL Draft Information, 656
NFL Schedules and Scores, 656
NFL Server, 656
NFL Talk, 656
NHL Schedule, 656
Nicecafe, 235
NICOL, 353
Nielson TV Ratings, 679
Nightfall MUD, 462
Nightfall MUD Information, 462
Nightmare MUD, 462
Nine Inch Nails, 487
Nitrogen Fixation, 55
Nitrous Oxide FAQ, 165
Nitrous Oxide Synthesis, 165
Nixpub List, 337
nn, 630
No Treason—The Constitution of No Authority, 546
NOAA Space Environment Services Center, 710
Nobel Prize, 316
Nomad, 353
Non-DOS Software, 269
Non-English Software, 613
Nonlinear Dynamics, 431
Nonlinear Programming Facts, 135
Non-Native Fish Information Resources, 746
Nonprofit Organizations, 83, 519

Nootropics (Intelligence-Enhancing Drugs), 165
Norm Peterson from *Cheers,* 560
North America, 302
North American Free Trade Agreement, 282
Northern Exposure, 680
Northridge Earthquake Simulation, 208
Norwegian Internet Resources, 726
Not Just Cows, 5
Notable Women, 715
Nottingham Arabidopsis Stock Centre, 5
NSFNET Traffic Analysis, 337
Nuclear Engineering, 200
Nude Beaches, 235
Nudity, 308
Number Synthesizer, 141
Numerical Analysis, 431
NUPop, 621
Nurses, 441
Nursing, 441
Nursing Web, 441
Nutrition, 294
Nutritional Healing, 447
Nutshell Code, 613

O

O Pioneers!, 412
O'Connor, Sinead, 487
O'Reilly & Associates, 71
O'Reilly Book Samples, 71
Oak Ridge National Laboratory, 199
Obfuscated C Code, 135
Obituary Page, 530
Object-Oriented Programming, 623
Object-Oriented Programming Using C++, 136
Objectivism, 534
Objectivism Mailing List, 534
Observatories, 29
Occult Archives, 524
Occult and Magick Talk, 493
Occult Mailing List, 493
Occult and Mysticism Network, 524
Occult and Paranormal, 524
Occultist Temple of Set, 525
Occupational Medicine, 441
Oceania, 535
Oceanic (The Ocean Network Information Center), 501
Oceanography, 501-502
Oceanography Information, 501
Oedipus Trilogy, The, 413
Off the Wall Gallery, 24
Office Automation, 83
Official Touring Guide to New Brunswick, 91
Offroad Driving, 34
Oklahoma Geological Survey Observatory, 275
Oleo, 630
Ollie the Ostrich, 325
Olympic Results, 656
Olympic Winter Games—1998, 656
On Liberty, 413
Oncology, 442
Online Art References, 24
Online Book Initiative, 71
Online Bookstore, 72
Online Career Center, 364
Online Job Services, 364
Online Journal of Education and Communication, 182
Online Newspapers, 368
Online Publications, 554
Online Services, 353
Open Desktop, 509
Open Software Foundation, 510
Open Systems Today, 419
Opera Schedule Server, 161
Operating Systems: DOS, 502-503
Operating Systems General Discussion, 503
Operating Systems: General Topics, 503
Operating Systems: Microsoft Windows, 503-505

Operating Systems: Miscellaneous Systems, 505-507
Operating Systems: OS/2, 507-508
Operating Systems: SCO, 508-510
Operating Systems: Unix in General, 510-513
Operating Systems: Unix Systems, 514-516
Operating Systems: Windows NT, 516
Optical Engineering, 200
OpticsNet, 540
Oracle, 326
Oral Tradition, 218
Orange Room Toy Box, 235
Organ Transplant, 442
Organizations, 517-520
Organometallic Chemistry, 94
Oriental Fetish, 601
Orienteering and Rogaining, 521
Origami, 309
Origin of the Universe, 589
Orthodox Christianity, 574
Orvotron Newsletter, 525
OS/2 Archive, 613
OS/2 Beta Releases, 507
OS/2 Bugs and Fixes, 507
OS/2 Chat, 508
OS/2 General Discussion, 508
OS/2 Home Page, 508
OS/2 Information, 508
OS/2 Networking, 508
OS/2 Networking Environment, 127
OS/2 Programming, 136
OS/2 Setup, 508
OS/2 Utilities, 637
OS/2 Versions 1.x, 508
OS9, 506
Oscar Wilde, quotations, 561
OSF/1, 516
Oslo Tour, 692
OSU Art Gallery, 24
Othello Home Page, 249
OtherRealms, 743
OTIS Project, 24
OTPAD Gopher, 671
Ottawa, 91
OuluBox, 45
Our Mr. Wrenn, 413
Out List, The, 265
Out-of-Body Experiences, 525
Outburst, 249
Outdoor Activities, 520-522
Outdoors Discussion Group, 522
Overview of the Internet and World Wide Web, 337
Owning Airplanes, 40
Oxygen and Ozone Therapy, 447
Ozone Depletion, 208

P

P.G. Wodehouse, 404
PAC-10 College Football Schedule, 657
Pacific Bell Digital Communications Information, 671
Paddling, 522
Paddling Web Server, 68
Pagan Religion and Philosophy, 577
Pagan Yule Customs, 578
Paganism, 493
Paint Estimator, 314
Paintball Server, 250
Pakistan, 500
Palace of Diocletian, 302
Paleoenvironmental Records of Past Climate Change, 208
Palindromes, 380
Palo Alto, California, 726
Pancakes, 225
Panic Disorders, 551
Pantyhose, 64
Pantyhose and Stockings, 601
Paradigms, 610
Paradise Lost, 413
Parallel Computing Archive, 112
Parallel Programming Laboratory, 136

Paramedics, 442
Paranormal, 523-527
Paranormal Phenomena General
    Discussion, 525
Parapsychology, 525
Parent Trap, 212
Parents and Teens, 212
Paris Tours, 726
Parix, 506
Parker Lewis, 680
Parler au Quotidien, 380
Parnassus on Wheels, 413
Particles, 540
Parties and Entertainment, 527-528
Partnerships Against Violence, 519
Party Ideas, 528
Party Time, 528
Pascal to C Translator, 136
Patchwork Electronic Literature, 398
Patent Office Reform Panel Report, 282
Pathfinder Land Data Sets, 273
Pathology and Histology Server, 442
Paul McCartney, 487
Paul McCartney Death Rumor, 487
Paving the Earth, 64
Pawn Shop, 235
PC Archives, 617
PC Archiving Utilities, 637
PC Catalog, 128
PC Clones, 128
PC Communications and Modems, 671
PC Downloading, 119
PC Game Archives, 617
PC Games Frequently Asked Question List,
    250
PC General Discussion, 128
PC Hardware, 112, 128
PC Hardware Introduction, 129
PC Index, 129
PC Lube and Tune, 129
PC and Macintosh Guides, 112, 511
PC Magazine, 420
PC Software Search, 614
PC Sounds, 141
PC Utilities, 637
PC Video Card Drivers, 637
PC Week Labs, 420
PC/MS-DOS: The Essentials, 119
Peace Corps, 519
Peace Watch, 520
Pediatric Oncology Group, 442
Penn and Teller, 236
Penn World Trade Tables, 84
Pennsylvania Census, Housing
    Information, 282
PENpages, 5
Penpals, 584
People, 528-530
People on the Internet, 337
Percussion, 478
Percy Bysshe Shelley, 543
Performance Database Server, 112
Performing Classical Music, 478
Period Calendar, 574
Periodic Informational Postings List, 700
Periodic Table of the Elements, 94
Periodic Table of the Elements (Online), 94
Periodic Table in Hypertext Format, 95
Perkins Vocational and Applied
    Technology Education, 182
Perl, 630
Perl Archives, 614
Perl Discussion, 630
Perl Scripts, 614
Perl Tools Development, 631
Pern Role-Playing, 581
PernMush, 462
Persistence of Vision, 108
Personal Finance, 84
Personal Idealogies, 535
Personal Investing and Finance News, 84
Personalities, 282
Personals, 530-532
Pest Management, 259
Pests, Diseases and Weeds, 259

PET Scan Image Database, 442
Peter Gabriel, 484
Peter Pan, 413
Pets General Discussion, 10
PGP Encryption/Decryption Program, 152
PGP Keyservers, 139
PGPShell, 152
Pharmacological Cornucopia, 166
Pharmacy, 442
Philip K. Dick, 400
Philippine Literature, 406
Philosophical Discussions, 535
Philosophy, 532-536
Philosophy of the Middle Ages, 535
Philosophy at the University of Bologna, 535
Phone Cards, 673
Phone Number to Word Translator, 673
Photo Database, 536
Photography, 536-537
Photography Archives, 537
Photography General Discussion, 537
Photography Mailing List, 537
Photography Questions and Answers, 537
Photonics, 668
Photosynthesis, 75
Phrack, 420
Phreaking, 599
Physical Sciences Conferences, 294
Physics, 537-542
Physics Discussion Groups, 540
Physics Gopher, 540
Physics Information Service, 541
Physics Mailing Lists, 541
Physics on the Net, 541
Physics Student Discussion List, 541
Physics Teachers, 193
pi Page, 431
pi to 1 Million Digits, 431
pi to 1.25 Million Digits, 431
Pick-Up Lines, 602
Picture Viewing Software, 132
Picture-Related Files FTP Site List, 132
PiHKAL, 166
Piloting, 40
Pinball Pasture, 250
Pinball and Video Game Machine
    Auctions, 87
Pine, 631
Pine Mailer Demo, 631
Pinhole Camera, 537
Pink Floyd, 487
Pipe Organ, 478
Pipe Smoking, 705
Piss List, 230
Pit and the Pendulum, The, 413
Pixel Pushers, 25
Pixel-Planes Graphics Machine, 108
Pizza Server, 236
Planet Earth Home Page, 353
Planet Earth Images and Movies, 167
Planetariums, 29
Planetary Data System, 643
Planetary Image Finders, 644
Planetary Tour Guide, 29
Planets, 29
Planets and the Solar System, 29
Plant Biology, 75
Plant Factsheets, 260
Plato, 535
Play-by-Mail Archives, 250
Play-by-Play Sportscasters, 368
Play Scripts, 161
Playboy, 602
Playboy Centerfolds, 602
Playground Gallery, 25
Plugged In, 188
Poe, Edgar Allan, 402
Poems, 543
Poems and Prose, 543
Poet's Cafe, 543
Poeticus, 236
Poetry, 542-544
Poetry About Life, 406
Poetry Archives, 543
Poetry Assortments, 406

Poetry Index, 543
Poetry Workshop, 543
Pogues, The, 488
Poker, 250
Poland, 727
Polar Research, 167
Police, The, 488
Political Discussions, 547
Political Forum, 547
Political Humor, 326
Political Implications of the Internet, 337
Political Party Platform Statements, 547
Politically Correct Primer, 326
Politics of Contraband, 166
Politics and Drugs, 166
Politics and Homosexuality, 265
Politics and Medicine, 442
Politics: National (U.S.), 544-548
Politics and the Network Community, 547
Politics and Sex, 265
Politics of Space, 644
Politics: State and Local (U.S.), 549
Pollution and Groundwater Recharge, 208
Pollution Research Group, 208
Polyamory, 531, 585, 602
Polyfidelity, 608
Polymer Science and Technology, 95
Ponder Lab Web Server, 95
Popular FTP Archives, 353
Population Biology, 55
Pornographic Pictures, 602
Porsche, 34
Porschephiles Home Page, 34
Portable Computer Information, 112
Porter List, 65
Portugal, 727
Position Papers of Senator Harkin, 547
Positive Emotions, 65
Post-Polio Syndrome, 443
Postcards, 309
Postmodern Culture, 493
Power Tips and Tricks for Photoshop, 537
Powerful Computer List, 113
PowerPC News, 129
Powertech BBS, 45
Practical Christian Life, 574
Practical Jokes, 452
Practical Psychology Magazine, 551
Prairie Dog Hunt for Windows, 250
Praser Maze, 250
Pratchett, Terry, 402, 424
Prehistoric Flying Creatures, 303
President's Daily Schedule, 286
President's Economic Plan, 286
Presidential Documents, 287
Presley, Elvis, 488
Press Photographers, 368
Press Releases from U.S. Trade
    Representative, 173
Price and Productivity Statistics, 173
Price and Volume Charts, 84
Primates, 56
Prince, 489
Prince Edward Island, 91
Principia Cybernetica Web, 535
Principia Discordia, 326
Print Media, 368
Prints Database, 25
Prism Hotel BBS, 46
Privacy and Anonymity Issues, 139
Privacy Forum Digest, 139
Privacy and Technology, 672
procmail, 631
Products for Pilots, 40
Profanity and Insult Server, 65
Professional Career Organizations, 364
Programming, 504, 511
Programming in Ada, 136
Programming Examples, 136
Programming General Discussion, 136
Programming Language Material, 137
Programming Languages, 137
Programming the Mac, 623
Programming for Microsoft Windows, 136
Programming in OS/2, 508

Progressive, 478
Project Galactic Guide, 326
Project Gutenberg, 406
Project Kaleidoscope, 182
Promus Hotels, 692
Pronunciation, 380
Propaganda, 7
Proposed Idea Exchange, 316
Prose, 731
Prostitute Prices, 602
Protein, 56
Protein Crystallography, 56
Protein Databases, 56
Psi Phenomena, 525
Psychoactive Drugs, 166
Psychological Help, 552
Psychology, 549-553
Psychology Graduate Student Journal, 552
Psycoloquy, 552
pty, 631
Public Access Catalogs, 393
Public Broadcasting Service (PBS), 680
Public Health Information Guide, 294
Public Internet Encyclopedia, 353
Public Key Exchange, 153
Publications, 553-554
Publisher's Catalogs, 554, 555
Publishing, 554-555
Pulp Fiction, 72
Punk Rock, 478
Puns, 326
Purity Tests, 603
Puzzles, 236, 309
Pyramix, 236

Q

Q & A About Aviation, 41
QNX, 506
Quadralay Cryptography Archive, 153
Quality of Education, 182
Quanta, 420
QuarkWeb, 236
Quartz BBS, 46
Queer Resources Directory, 266
Queer Zines, 266
Queers 'R' Us, 266
Query Interface to the Linux Software Map
    Broker, 632
Questionables, 599
Questions and Answers About Unix, 511
Quick and Dirty Guide to Japanese, 380
QuickTime Movies, 123
Quilting, 309
Quotation Reference Books, 560
Quotations, 556-561
Quotations Archive, 560
QuoteCom, 84
Quotes About Religion, 560

R

Rabbits, 10
Racing, 34
Racing Archive, 657
Radford University Computer Science Club
    BBS, 46
Radiance, 108
Radio, 562-564
Radio and TV Networks Electronic Mail
    Addresses, 424
Radio Broadcasting, 563
Radio-Controlled Models, 309
Radio Free Europe/Liberty Research
    Institute, 330
Radiocarbon and Radioisotopes Mailing
    List, 589
Radiocarbon Gopher, 589
Radiology, 443
Railroad, 309
Railroad Databases, 310
Railroad Maps, 310
Railroad Modeling, 310
Railroad Timetables, 692
Railroad-Related Internet Resources, 310

*Main subject headings are shown in **bold***

RailServer, 692
Random Portrait Gallery, 530
Random Quotes, 560
Random Zines, 743
Randomly Amplified Polymorphic DNA, 56
Rap, 478
Rare Books, 72
Rare Groove, 478
Rasta Dictionary, 381
Rave, 479
Rave Discussion, 479
Ravel, 137
Rayshade, 109
Raytrace Graphics, 108
REACH, 316
Reading Disabilities, 160
Reading Room, 194
Real Estate, 564-565
Real Estate Brokers, 564
Real Estate Discussion Group, 564
Real Estate News, 565
Real-Life on the Internet, 342
Reba McEntire, 487
rec.sport.soccer—The Web Page, 657
Recipe Archives, 225
Recipe Assortments, 226
Recipes, 226
Recipes from Slovakia, 226
Record Production, 479
Recreational Arts, 236
Recreational Drugs, 166
Recreational Vehicles, 692
Red Dwarf, 594, 680
Regenesis, 462
Reggae, 479
Regional Economic Statistics, 173
Related Sciences, 56
Relativity, 541
ReliefNet, 198
Religion, 565-576
Religion: Alternative, 576-578
Religion: Humor, 579
Religious Denominations, 574
Religious Humor, 579
Religious News, 574
Religious Studies Publications, 575
Ren and Stimpy, 561
Ren and Stimpy Show Archives, 680
Renaissance, 303
Renaissance Instruments, 479
Renewable Energy, 199
Repairs, 314
Repetitive Motion Injuries, 443
Repetitive Stress Injuries, 443
Report on Waco, 368
Research and Advanced Study: Canada, Italy, 187
Research into Artifacts Center for Engineering, 12
Research and Data, 565
Research Methods, 589
Research on Operating Systems, 503
Resource Guides to the Humanities, 316
Resource Guides to Science, 589
Resources, 663
Resources for Apple Users, 121
Resources for Women, 716
Responsibilities of Host and Network Managers, 358
Restaurant Le Cordon Bleu, 226
Restaurants, 226
Restaurants on the Web, 226
Résumé Database, 364
Résumé Server, 365
Résumé, 365
Revelations of Awareness, 493
Revenge, 452
Reviews of Children's Books, 72
RFC Archive, 357
RFC Lists, 358
Rheingold, Howard, 425
RiceGenes, 6
Right Side of the Web, 547
RIPEM Resources, 139
Risk, 251

Risks of Posting to Usenet, 700
RISKWeb, 84
River and Rowing Museum, 68
rn/trn, 632
Road Rally, 657
Roadkill R Us, 65
Rob's Multimedia Lab, 109
Robert Herrick, 542
RoboGopher, 25
Robotics, 201
Robotics Video Gallery, 668
Rock and Classical Music, 479
Rock Collection, 310
Rock and Roll, 479
Rocker Group Web Pages, 489
Rockwell Network Systems, 127
Rodney Dangerfield, 556
Roger McGuinn, 424
Roget's Thesaurus, 381
Role-Playing, 579-583
Role-Playing, 581
Role-Playing Archives, 581
Role-Playing Famous Last Words, 582
Role-Playing Games, 582
Roller Coasters, 236, 310
Rolling Stones, 489
Romance, 583-585
Romance, 585
Romance Readers Anonymous, 585
Romantic Whisperings, 585
Rome Reborn, 25
Roommates from Hell, 65
Root Chatline, 503
Rosen Sculpture Exhibition, 25
Roswell Electronic Computer Bookstore, 72
Route 66, 692
RoverWeb, 35
Rowing, 522
Roy Lichtenstein Pre-Pop 1948-1960, 25
Rplay, 141
RSA Data Security, Inc., 139
RSTS, 506
RTD Web Server, 354
RTE Radio News, 500
Rubik's Cube, 236, 251
Rubik's Revenge, 236
Rugby, 657
Rugby League, 657
Rumors, 65
RuneQuest, 582
Running, 657
Rush, 489
Rush Limbaugh, 424, 680
Rush Limbaugh Archives, 547
Rush Limbaugh Political Discussion, 548
Russia, 727
Russian and East European Studies, 381
Russian Economics, 174
Russian Phone Directory, 673
Russian Swear Words, 381
Russian Talk, 381
Russian Travelogue, 692

S

Sabaean Religious Order, 578
Safe Sex, 604
SAIDIE: The Intellectual Disability Network, 160
Sailing, 68
Sailing Laser Boats, 68
Sailing Mailing List, 68
Sailing Page, 68
Saki, 402
Salk Institute for Biological Studies, 56
Samuel Goldwyn, 559
San Francisco Bay Area, 727
San Francisco Bay Area Concerts, 479
San Francisco Examiner News Wires Page, 497
Santa Claus, 65
Santa Cruz Operation, 100
Sardinia, 303
Satanism, 578

Satellite Communications for Learning Associated, 194
Satellite Images of Europe, 132
Satellite TV Equipment, 87
Satellite TV Images, 680
Satellite TV Page, 681
Saturn, 35
Savage Archive, 84
Scandals of the Clinton Administration, 548
Scarlet Letter, The, 413
Scarlet Pimpernel, The, 414
Scavenger Hunt, 190
Schizophrenia, 553
Schizophrenia Nervosa, 65
Scholarly Conferences, 183
School Humor, 190
School Nurse Network, 183
Schoolnet, 183
Schoolnet Resource Manual, 183
Schoolnet's News Flash, 183
Schools on the Internet, 183
Sci-Fi Books, 594
Sci-Fi Lovers, 594
Sci-Fi Publishers Newsletters, 555
Science, 586-591
Science Beat, 589
Science Education, 183
Science Fiction, 591-598
Science Fiction, 87
Science Fiction Announcements, 595
Science Fiction and Fantasy, 595
Science Fiction and Fantasy Archive, 595
Science Fiction, Fantasy, and Horror, 407
Science Fiction Forum, 595
Science Fiction Marketplace, 595
Science Fiction Movies, 457, 596
Science Fiction Resource Guide, 596
Science Fiction Reviews, 72, 596
Science Fiction Television, 596
Science Fiction TV Series Guides, 597
Science Fiction TV Shows, 681
Science Fiction Writing, 597
Science Fraud, 590
Science Magazines, 590
Science and Science Fiction, 595
Science and Technology Information System, 590
Scientific Articles, 590
Scientific Ponderings, 590
Scientific Research, 365
Scientific Secrets, 1861, 414
Scientific Skepticism, 591
Scientific Theories behind Paranormal Events, 525
Scientific Urban Legends, 218
Scientist, The, 591
Scientist's Workbench, 591
Scientology, 578
SCO General Discussion, 509
SCO Magazine, 509
SCO Unix Files for Compaq Computers, 509
SCO Unix Supplements: Compaq Computers, 509
SCO World Magazine, 420
Scott Adams, 422
Scottish Dancing, 156
Scottish Style Drumming, 480
Scout Report, 354
Scouting, 522, 739
Scouting Around the World, 739
Scouting Meets, 310
ScreamBaby, 744
screen, 632
Scripps Institute of Oceanography, 502
Scuba Diving, 310
Scuba Diving FTP Sites, 657
Scuba Diving Mailing List, 658
Scuba Diving Web Pages, 658
SEA Gopher, 520
Sea Level Increase, 208
Search Engines, 337
Searching for Software, 614
Searching the Internet, 354
SeaWiFS Project, 502
Secret Stuff, 598-599

Secular Web, 578
Securities and Exchange Commission's Database, 174
Security, 511
Security APL Quote Server, 84
Security Resources, 139
Security Web, 140
Seed, The, 7
Sega Game Secrets, 251
Sega Hardware, 251
Seinfeld, 681
Seinfeld Quotes, 561
Seismic Information, 276
Selected Cartoons, 326
Selling on IRC, 87
Seminars for Men, 326
Serbian, 381
Series and Sitcoms, 681
Service Organizations, 520
SETI, 644
Severed Heads, 489
Sewing, 311
Sewing Archives, 311
Sewing Discussions, 214
Sex, 599-607
Sex Addiction Recovery, 608
Sex, Censorship, and the Internet, 604
Sex Chat, 735
Sex Experts, 604
Sex General Discussion, 735
Sex and Magick, 494
Sex in the News, 608
Sex Pictures, 132
Sex Questions and Answers, 604
Sex-Related Articles, 604
Sex-Related Humor, 604
Sex Services, 706
Sex Sounds, 141, 605
Sex Stories, 735
Sex Story Archives, 736
Sex Talk, 605
Sex Wanted, 605
Sexual Assault and Sex Abuse Recovery, 608
Sexual Assault on Campus, 716
Sexual and Gender Identity Glossary, 608
Sexual Health Topics, 294
Sexual Identity and Gender Glossary, 605
Sexual Massage, 736
Sexuality, 607-609
Sexuality and Religion, 575
SFI BBS, 144
ShadowRun, 582
ShadowRun on the Web, 582
Shadowy Science Projects, 184
Shakers, 575
Shakespeare Discussion, 161
Shakespeare Glossary, 161
Shakespeare, William, 402
Shakespearean Insults, 326
Shamanism, 578
Shared Realities, 703
Sheet Music Collection, 480
Shelley, Percy Bysshe, 543
Shells, 511
Shells: bash, 632
Shells: pdksh, 632
Shells: rc, 632
Shells: tcsh, 633
Shells: zsh, 633
Sherlock Holmes Novels, 414
Shiki Internet Haiku Salon, 543
Shoemaker-Levy Comet, 29
Shogi, 251
Short Stories, 407
Short-Lived Reactive Pollutants, 95
Shorter Oxford Dictionary, 381
Shortwave Radio, 563
Shuttle and Satellite Images, 133
Shuttle Payloads, 644
Shuttle Snapshots, 644
Siamese Fighting Fish, 10
Sid Vicious, 490
Siege Warfare, 450
Silicon Graphics Gallery, 109

*Main subject headings are shown in **bold***

Silicon Graphics Silicon Surf, 109
Silicon Sister's Java Hut, 237
Simpsons, The, 682
SIMTEL Software Archives, 614
Simultaneous Projects, 184
Sinatra, Frank, 489
Sinclair Archive, 617
Sinclair ZX-Spectrum Web server, 113
Sinead O'Connor, 487
Singles, 585
Sir Arthur Conan Doyle, 401
Sisters of Mercy, 490
Sitcoms of the U.K., 682
Skateboarding, 311, 658
Skating, 311, 658
Skeptic, 420
Skepticism, 525
Ski Information, 658
Skydiving, 658
Skydiving Archive, 658
Skynet BBS, 46
Slang Dictionary, 381
SLaTeX, 633
Sleeping Dog, 25
Sleeping Problems, 294
Slippery When Wet Magazine, 736
Sloan Digital Sky Survey (SDSS), 30
Slovakia, 727
Slovenia, 727
Small Business Administration, 84
Smalltalk, 633
Smithsonian Astrophysical Observatory, 644
Smithsonian Botany Gopher, 75
Smithsonian Gem & Mineral Collection, 276
Smithsonian Natural History Gopher, 168
Smithsonian Photographs, 133
Smithsonian Vertebrate Zoology Gopher, 75
Smoking Addiction, 706
Smoking News, 706
Smoky Mountains, 693
Snackman, 252
Snakebites, 294
Snapple on the Net, 227
Snowmobiles, 522
Soap Operas, 682
Soapbox, 420
Soccer Referees Mailing List, 659
Soccer Results, 659
Soccer Rules, 659
Soccer Web Pages, 659
Social Deviants, 66
Social Organization of Computer
    Underground, 103
Social Science Gateway, 610
Social Science Information Gateway, 610
Social Sciences Resource Guides, 610
Social Security Administration, 282
Social Security Administration
    Information, 282
Social Security Administration Online, 283
Society for Creative Anachronism, 311
Society of Friends, 575
Society for Industrial and Applied Math, 432
Society for Neuroscience, 56
Society for the Preservation of Film Music,
    457
Society and Underwear, 610
Socio-Legal Preprint Archive, 388
Sociological Issues, 611
Sociology, 609-611
Sociology and Science, 611
Sockets for Microsoft Windows, 504
Software, 57
Software, 611-615
Software: Archives, 616-618
Software Archives, 614
Software Engineering, 201
Software and Information for the
    Handicapped, 160
Software: Internet, 618-622
Software: Macintosh, 622-624
Software for Macintosh, 623
Software: PC, 624-626
Software Sites, 614
Software: Unix, 626-634

Software: Utilities, 635-638
Softwords COSY, 46
Soka Gakkai International, 575
Sokoban, 252
Solar and Geophysical Reports, 710
Solar Cars, 35
Solar Vehicles at the University of
    Michigan, 35
Solar Vehicles at UC Berkeley, 35
Solaris, 516
Somerville Stories, 66
Song, 543
Song of Hiawatha, The, 414
Song Lyrics, 480
Song and TV Show Parodies, 327
Sonic, 480
Sony Research Laboratory, 669
Soren Kierkegaard, 533
Soulmates, 585
Sound Archives, 142
Sound Cards, 142
Sound Site Newsletter, 421
Sound Tools, 142
Sound Utility Programs, 142
Sounds from Chaos, 541
Source Code for Macintosh, 122
Source Code to Omega, 252
Source Code for Programs for SCO, 510
Source Code to Unix Programs, 511
Source Code for Unix Utilities, 637
Source Documents on the Holocaust, 297
Sourdough, 227
South African Environmental Information
    Gateway, 209
South Dakota, 693
Southeast Asian Archive, 727
Southern Rock Music, 480
Southern U.S. Culture, 728
Soviet Archives, 728
Space, 639-647
Space Calendar, 645
Space Digest, 645
Space Environment Effects Branch, 645
Space Frequently Asked Questions, 645
Space General Discussion, 645
Space Missions, 645
Space Movie Archive, 645
Space Newsletter, 646
Space Shuttle, 646
Space Telescope Science Institute, 30
Spacecraft Information, 646
SpaceNews, 646
Spaceships, 526
Spam, 227
Spanish and Portuguese History, 303
Spanking, 531, 606
Spanky Fractal Database, 432
Special Education, 194
Specific Domestic Pets, 11
Spectra, 744
Spectrum, 25
Speculative Fiction Clearing House, 597
Speech by Philip Agee, 330
Speech Generator, 145
Speed Skating, 659
Speedway Home Page, 659
Spelunking, 522
SPIE Employment Service, 365
Spills and Stains, 315
Spirit Web, 494
Spiritual Grab Bag, 494
Spiritual Healing, 494
Spoonerisms, 382
Sporks, 227
Sports and Athletics, 647-661
Sports Highlights, 659
Sports Schedules, 660
Sports Servers, 660
Sports Statistics, 660
Sports Web Page, 660
Springsteen, Bruce, 490
Spunk Press, 7
Square Root of 2, 432
St. Petersburg Pictures Gallery, 693
Stadium Sports Articles, 660

Stagecraft, 161
Stalking the Wily Hacker, 140
Stamp Collecting, 312
Standard Disclaimer, 327
Standard & Poors 500 Index, 84
Standards, 511
Stanford Linear Accelerator Center, 541
Stanford Netnews Filtering Service, 700
Star Trek, 662-664
Star Trek, 561, 731
Star Trek Archives, 663, 682
Star Trek Fetishes, 663
Star Trek Games, 663
Star Trek General Discussion, 663
Star Trek Information and Trivia, 663
Star Trek News, 663
Star Trek Reviews, 663
Star Trek Role-Playing, 582
Star Trek Sounds, 142
Star Trek Stories and Parodies, 663
Star Trek Universe, 664
Star Wars, 462, 597
Star Wars Archive, 597
Star*s Family, 30
Starbuilders, 526
Starlink, 30
Starship Design Home Page, 646
State by State, 269
State News, 498
Statistics, 432
Statistics Canada Daily Reports, 91
Statistics and Operations Research, 432
StatLib Archives, 432
StatLib Gopher Server, 432
Staunton, Virginia, 693
Staying Healthy in Asia, Africa and Latin
    America, 693
Steam Engines, 312
Stego, 153
Stereograms and 3-D Images, 537
Sterling, Bruce, 592
Sterling, Bruce, Articles, 153
Steve Jackson Games, 388
Steven Wright, 561
Steven Wright Quote Server, 327
Stewart Brand, 422
Stock Market, 85
Stock Market Data, 85
Stock Market Discussion Groups, 85
Stock Market Report, 85
Stock Market Simulations, 85
Stonewall Images, 266
Stonewall Riot, 266
Stories, Sex, 606
Stories About Children, 372
Stories About Flying, 41
Stories by RICHH, 66
Strange Interactions, 26
Strange Rantings, 66
Strange Sounds, 480
Strange Tales, 66
Strasbourg Astronomical Data Center, 30
StrategyWeb, 85
Stream of Consciousness, 744
Strip Clubs, 706
Strip Joint Reviews, 606
Student Financial Aid Administration, 187
Student Governments, 191
Students for the Exploration and
    Development of Space, 646
Stuttering, 553
Subject Trees, 354
Submitting News via the Internet, 498
Subway, 354
Subway Navigator, 693
Sugar Cereals, 227
Suicide Prevention, 553
Sumeria Web Page, 494
Summaries of Current Economic
    Conditions, 174
Sumo Wrestling, 660
Sun Microsystems, 100
Sun Sound Files, 142
Sunset BBS, 46
SunSITE, 354

SunSITE Classic, 354
Sunsite Winsock Archive, 621
Sunspots, 30
Supercomputer Documentation, 113
Superhero Comic Writing, 97
Superhero Mailing List, 731
Supermodels, 133
Support Groups, 664
Support Level Supplements, 510
Supreme Court Rulings, 388
Surf Conditions in California, 710
Surface Analysis and Weather Maps, 710
Surfers Web, 355
Surfing the Internet, 342
Surfing Tutorial, 522
SurfNet, 312
Surgeon General's Warning on AIDS, 294
Susan Lenox: Her Rise and Fall, 415
Sushi, 227
Sustainable Agriculture, 6
Sustainable Agriculture Information, 6
Sweden Channel, 728
Swedish Chef, 66
Swifties, 327
Swimming, 660
Swinburne, Algernon Charles, 544
Swiss Academic and Research Network,
    355
Swiss Electronic Telephone Book, 673
Symbolic Algebra, 432
Symbolic Mathematical Computation
    Information Center, 432
Sysop Information, 46
System Software, 615, 624
System V, 516

T

Tag Lines Galore, 327
Taiwan, 728
Talented and Gifted, 184
Talk to a Cat, 696
Talk.Bizarre Web Page Thing, 67
Tango, 156
Tao of Programming, 119
Tapestry, 67
Tarot, 494
Tarot Reading, 494
Tasteless (and Dirty) Jokes, 327
Tasteless Pictures, 133
Tasteless Tales, 67
Tasteless Topics, 67
Tattoo, 450
Taxacom FTP Server, 57
Taxacom Listserv Lists, 57
Taxing Times, 85
Taylorology, 360
TCP/IP, 621
TCP/IP Development Tools, 137
TCP/IP Introduction, 127
Teaching: Elementary and High Schools,
    432
Teaching English as a Second Language,
    194
Teaching Health and Physical Education,
    195
Teaching and Learning with the Web, 184
Team.Net Automotive Information
    Archives, 35
Tech, The, 421
Techne, 145
Technet, 184
Technical Aspects, 86
Technical Automotive Discussion, 35
Technical Books, 73
Technical Discussion, 673
Technical Diving, 660
Technical Japanese Program, 382
Technical Library Supplements, 510
Technical Report Index, 355
Technical Reports Online, 119
Technology, 665-669
Technology Board of Trade, 669
Technology in the Classroom, 184
Technology General Discussion, 669

Technology and Information Education Services, 184
Technology Insertion, 450
Technology Magazines, 145
Technology Marketing Failures, 669
Technomads, 669
Techno/Rave Gopher, 480
Teen Date, 739
Teenagers, 739
Tekumel, 583
Telecom Discussions, 672
Telecommunication Archives, 672
Telecommunications, 670-672
Telecommunications Digest, 672
Telecommunications News, 672
Telecommunications Organizations, 672
Telecommunications Page, 672
Telefax Country Codes, 673
Telemedicine, 443
Telephone Information Sites, 674
Telephones, 672-674
Television, 674-685
Television Guide, 682
Television Industry Discussion, 682
Television News, 682
Television News Archive, 368
Television Series Guides and Facts, 682
Television Show Discussion, 683
Temptation of St. Anthony, 744
Ten Commandments for C Programmers, 328
Ten Commandments for C Programmers (Annotated), 328
Tennis Rankings and FAQs, 660
Tennis Server, 660
Tennyson, Alfred Lord, 544
"Terance, This Is Stupid Stuff," 544
Termcap and Terminfo Updates, 510
Terrorist's Handbook, 452
TeX Archive, 617
TeX Text Typesetter, 615
Texas Cancer Data Center, 443
Text-based Animation, 109
Text Formatter, 512
Textiles Discussion Groups, 214
Textiles Mailing List, 214
Textiles Reference Material, 214
Textiles and Sewing Archives, 214
Tgif Image Drawing Software, 633
Thailand, 693, 728
Thant's Animations Index, 109
Theater, 161
Theater Home Page, 162
Theater Plays and Musicals, 162
Theoretical Physics Pre-print List, 541
Theosophy, 578
There's Gold in them thar Networks!, 358
Thesaurus Construction Program, 615
Theta Xi Fraternity, 187
Third World Studies, 728
Thirtysomething, 684
Thoughts on Economics, 174
Thousand Points of Sites, 355
Three Kingdoms MUD, 463
Three-Letter Acronyms, 67
Through the Looking-Glass, 415
Tic Tac Toe, 252
Tickling, 736
TidBITS, 122
Tiddlywinks, 252
Time Machine, The, 415
Time Wasting, 237
Tintin, 328
Tiny MUDs, 460
Tiny Toons, 684
Tips for Travelers, 694
Tipsheet, 119
Tito, Josip Broz, 330
"To His Coy Mistress," 544
Toastmasters, 520
Toasts, 528
Today's Date, 697
Today's Events in History, 697
Today's Internet Highlights, 355
Tolkien, J.R.R., 403

Tolkien, J.R.R., Discussions, 403
Toll-Free Numbers for Computer Companies, 674
Toll-Free Numbers for Non-Profit Organizations, 674
Tom Sawyer, 415
Tomservo Raytraced Images, 109
Top, 633
Top 10 Signs Your Web Homepage is Not Cool, 328
Top 100 PC Games, 252
Top (and Bottom) 100 Lists, 480
Top News, 86
Topics In Primary Care, 443
Tor Books, 555
Torg, 583
Tori Amos, 482
Tour Canada Without Leaving Your Desk, 91
Tour de France, 694
Tourism Offices, 694
Toxic Custard Workshop Network, 328
Toyota, 35
Toys, 237
Trade Law Library, 389
Trademark Act of 1946, 86
Trademarks, 86
TradeWars Discussion, 252
Trading Cards, 312
Trains and Railways, 313
Transformations, 597
Transformers, 684
Transgender, 609
Transplant Answers, 664
Transputer Archive, 113
Travel, 686-695
Travel Information, 694
Travel Marketplace, 149, 694
Travel Matters Newsletter, 694
Travel Resources, 694
Travel and Tourism Web Pages, 694
Traveler Memories, 355
Traveler's Japanese, 382
Travelers' Tales, 695
Traveller, 583
Travels with Samantha, 73, 695
Treaties, 331
Treatment of Animals, 11
Trees, 260
Trekker Discussion, 664
TrekMuse, 463
TrekMUSE Gateway, 252
Trickle Server Documentation, 355
Trincoll Journal, 731
Trip to Antarctica, 695
Trivia, 695-698
Trivia Time, 697
Trivial Questions and Answers, 697
Tropical Biology, 57
Troubleshooting Your PC, 113
Truth or Dare, 252
Tucker, Michael, 324, 425
Turbo Vision, 137
Tutorial for PC Users, 342
TV Episode Guides, 684
TV Nation, 685
TV News Archive, 685
TV Schedules, 685
Twain, Mark, 403
Twain, Mark, Discussions, 403
Twain, Mark, quotations, 561
Twilight Zone, The, 685
Twin Peaks, 685
Twink Code, 266
Twisted Code, 137
Two-Year Colleges, 187
Typing Injuries, 295

U
U.C. Berkeley Museum of Paleontology, 276, 464
U.K. BDSM Scene, 606
U.N. Resolutions on Desert Storm, 297
U.S. Census Information for 1990, 283

U.S. Census Information Server, 283
U.S. Code of Military Justice, 450
U.S. Colleges, 187
U.S. Department of Education, 184
U.S. Department of Health and Human Services, 295
U.S. Department of Housing and Urban Development, 283
U.S. Department of Justice Job Listings, 365
U.S. Economic Statistics, 174
U.S. Environmental Protection Agency, 209
U.S. Federal Government Information, 283
U.S. Geographic Name Server, 274
U.S. Geological Survey Gopher, 276
U.S. Government BBS List, 284
U.S. Government Gophers, 284
U.S. Government Reports, 287
U.S. Government Today, 284
U.S. History, 303
U.S. Military News, 450
U.S. National K12 Gopher, 185
U.S. Patent Database, 389
U.S. Snow Cover Maps, 274
U.S. State Department Travel Information, 695
U.S. Telephone Area Code Guides, 674
U.S. Telephone Area Code Program, 674
U.S.A. Chat, 728
U.S.A. Statistics, 274
U.S.D.A. Economics and Statistics Gopher, 6
U.S.D.A. Extension Service, 6
U.S.G.S. Seismology Reports, 276
UFOs—Discussion Groups, 527
UFOs—Incident in Roswell, 527
UFOs—Mysterious Abductions, 527
UK-Dance, 156
ULS Report, 209
Ultimate Frisbee, 661
Ultralab—Learning Technology Research Center, 188
Ultralight Flying, 41
Ultrarunning, 661
Ultrasound, 113
Ultrix, 516
Umney's Last Case, 415
Un-CGI, 633
Underground Music Archive, 481
UNESCO World Heritage List, 209
Unhappy Romances, 585
Unicycling, 313
Uniform Resource Identifiers, 338
Unitarianism, 578
United Kingdom, 269, 728
United Nations Declaration of Human Rights, 416
United Nations Gopher, 331
United Nations Office for Outer Space Affairs, 647
United Nations Resolutions, 331
United We Stand, 416
Universe of Discourse, 237
University and College Education, 188
University of Chicago Philosophy Project, 535
University of Maryland Information Database, 394
University of Minnesota Medical School, 57
University of Southampton Department of Archaeology, 13
Unix Administration, 512
Unix and BBSs, 46
Unix Book Lists, 73
Unix C Archive, 618
Unix Chat and Help, 512
Unix General Discussion, 512
Unix Information Server, 512
Unix Internals, 512
Unix Manual, 512
Unix on PC Architectures, 512
Unix Security, 140
Unix Security Tutorial, 140
Unix Software and Source Code, 513
Unix Software Archive, 633
Unix uudecode for Windows, 625
Unix World, 421

Unofficial Internet Book List, 73
Unofficial Smiley Dictionary, 698
Unplastic News, 67
Unusual Foods of the World, 227
Up from Slavery, 416
Upcoming Aviation Events, 41
Upcoming Events in the Computer Industry, 145
Update Electronic Music Newsletter, 481
Urantia Book, 495
Urban Folklore, 218
Urban Legends, 218
Urban Sex Legends, 606
Urdu Dictionary, 382
URouLette, 237
USA Today, 498
Usenet, 699-702
Usenet Announcements, 703
Usenet Cultural Groups, 728
Usenet Curiosities, 702-703
Usenet Descriptions, 700
Usenet FAQ List Archive, 230
Usenet Finger Utility, 701
Usenet Groups with a Difference, 701
Usenet Hobby Groups, 313
Usenet Junkies, 703
Usenet Kooks, 703
Usenet News via Electronic Mail, 701
Usenet News via Gopher, 701
Usenet Olympics, 701
Usenet Personalities, 703
Usenet Support Groups, 664
Usenet University, 188
Usenet Word Statistics, 701
User-Friendliness, 513
Using Internet Libraries, 394
Utah's National Parks, 695
UTBBS, 46
Utopia, 536
uucp for DOS, 503

V
V, 506
Vacationing with Children, 212
Vacuum Cleaners, 315
Vampire, 583
Vampire Chat Channel, 67
Vangelis, 490
Vatican Exhibit, 303
VAX/VMS Software List, 615
Vaxbook, 113
Vectrex Arcade System, 252
Vedic Civilization, 575
Vegans, 227
Vegetable and Herb Growing, 260
Vegetarian Archives, 227
Vegetarianism, 228
Venable Attorneys at Law, 389
Vending Machines, 698
Venezuela, 729
Ventana Press Internet Resource Area, 555
Verbiage Magazine, 744
VESA Driver, 638
Veterinary Medicine, 443
vi Reference Card, 513
vi Tutorial, 513
Vibe Magazine, 481
Vibe Recording Studio, 481
Vices, 704-706
Vicious, Sid, 490
Victorian Institute for Forensic Pathology, 443
Video, 504
Video Clips, 664
Video Files, 685
Video Game Archive, 252
Video Game Collecting, 253
Video Game Database Browser, 254
Video Game Debates, 254
Video Game Discussions, 254
Video Game List, 254
Video Game Systems, 254
Video Games, 87

Video Games Frequently Asked Questions, 254
Video Laserdiscs, 669
Video Puzzle with Live Video Sources, 254
Video Webalog, 123
VIDIMED Project Image Gallery, 443
Vienna Stock Exchange, 86
Vietnam War Information, 303
Vietnam War Mailing List, 304
Views of the Solar System, 30
Vigilantes, 360
Vikings, 304
Vince Foster, 548
Vintage Clothing and Costume Jewelry, 214
Violin and Bow Makers, 481
Virgil, 404
Virology, 57
Virtual Art Gallery , 26
Virtual Genome Center, 57
Virtual Hospital, 444
Virtual Law Library, 389
Virtual Library of Chemistry, 95
Virtual Library of Electronic Journals, 421
Virtual Library of Employment Opportunities, 365
Virtual Library of Engineering, 201
Virtual Library of Math, 433
Virtual Library of Medicine, 444
Virtual MeetMarket, 532
Virtual Online University, 188
Virtual Pub & Beer Emporium, 228
Virtual Radio, 481
Virtual Reality, 145
Virtual Reality Artificial Intelligence Neural Net, 744
Virtual Reality Markup Language, 110
Virtual Reality Resources, 669
Virtual School of Natural Sciences, 591
Virtual Tourist, 695
Visions of Jesus and Mary, 495
Visual Basic Runtime Modules, 638
Vital Records in New York State, 269
VMS, 506
VMS Jobs, 365
VMS Utilities, 638
Vnet Outdial Servers, 127
Vocational Education, 185
Voice of America, 564
Voices from the Net, 421
Void, 237
Volcanoes, 276
Volcanology, 276
Volkswagen, 36
Volkswagen Names, 36
Vote Smart, 548
Voyage of the Beagle, 416
Voyeurism, 606
VSE/ESA Mainframe, 507
VuSystem, 110
VuSystem and VuNet Demonstrations, 145
VxWorks, 507

W

W.C. Fields, 557
Waffle BBS Software, 625
Wais Gateways, 355
Walking Man, 237
Walkthroughs, 254
Wall O'Shame, 328
Wanderers, Robots, and Spiders, 146
War, 304
War History, 451
War of the Worlds, The, 416
Warez, 599
Washburn School of Law, 389
Washington, D.C., 133

Washington and Lee University Law Library, 389
Washington Post, 498
Washington University Services, 394
Waste Reduction, 209
Watersports, 607
Watson, Doc, 490
Weather, 707-711
Weather Processor, 710
Weather Radar, 711
Weather Reports, 711
Weather Reports for Australia, 711
Weather Reports for Canada, 711
Weather World, 711
Web Addict's Pop-Culture Scavenger Hunt, 237
Web BBS List, 46
Web Collaboration Projects, 338
Web fingerinfo, 355
Web Introduction, 343
Web Mailing List for Librarians, 394
Web Mailing Lists, 338
Web Page Graphics and Icons, 110
Web Power Index, 356
Web Search Engines, 356
Web Servers in Quebec, 91
Web Tutorial Slides, 338
Web Wide World of Music, 481
Web of Wonder, 356
WebCrawler, The, 338
WebCrawler Top 25, 356
WebElements, 95
webNews, 356
WebOOGL Home Page, 110
WebStars: Astrophysics in Cyberspace, 30
WebStars: Astrophysics on the Web, 542
Webster's Weekly, 744
WebWisdom, 561
WebWorld, 103, 338
Weddings, 585
Weights and Measures, 433
Weird Movie List, 457
Weird Places to Hang Out on Usenet, 703
Weird Politics and Conspiracy, 548
Wellness Mailing List, 295
Wells, H.G., 404
West Virginia, 695
Western Square Dancing, 156
What the Welsh and Chinese Have in Common, 544
What's New with NCSA Mosaic and the Web, 356
"When Lilacs Last in the Dooryard Bloom'd," 544
White House, 287
White House Archives, 287
White House News, 287
White House Papers, 287
White House Press Releases, 287
White House Press Releases: Daily, 287
Whitewater Scandal, 548
Whittier, John Greenleaf, 544
Who's Who in Biology, 58
Who's Who Online, 338 ·
Who's Who in Russia, 530
Whole Earth Review Articles, 554
Whole Frog Project, 58
Whole Internet Catalog, 356
Whole Internet Scavenger Hunt, 237
Why Are Internet Resources Free?, 343
Why?, 328
Wicca, 495
Widget Server, 510
Wild Sex, 736
Wilde, Oscar, quotations, 561
Wilderness Society, 209
William Blake, 542
William Butler Yeats, 404
William Shakespeare, 402

William Wordsworth, 544
Willow, 621
Wimsey's Digital Rag, 745
Windows General Discussion, 504
Windows News, 505
Windows NT General Discussion, 516
Windows NT News, 516
Windows NT Setup, 516
Windows Setup, 505
Windows Shareware Archive, 626
Windows Utilities, 626
Windsurfing, 522
Wine, 228
Wine Page, 228
WinPkt, 638
Wintalk, 621
WinWAIS, 621
WinWeb, 621
Wired, 421
Wiretap Online Library, 394
WIT Interactive Talk Forum, 356
Wodehouse, P.G., 404
WOMAD—World of Music, Arts, and Dance, 481
Wombat Dictionaries, 146
Women, 712-716
Women in Biology, 58
Women and Computer Science, 104
Women in Congress, 716
Women and Literature, 407
Women in Science and Engineering, 365
Women in Science Hypercard Project, 591
Women's Basketball, 661
Women's Book List, 398
Women's News, 716
Women's Studies, 366
Women's Studies Resources, 716
Women's Wire, 716
Wonderful Wizard of Oz, The, 416
Woods, James, 425
Woodstock '94 Multimedia Center, 481
Woodworking, 313
Woodworking Archives, 313
Woody Allen, 556
Woody Plants, 260
Word-a-Day, 382
Word Lists, 382
WordPerfect, 505
Wordsworth, William, 544
Working Paper Archive, 174
Workshop on Electronic Texts, 398
World Association of Theoretical Organic Chemists, 95
World Bank, 86
World City Maps, 274
World Constitutions, 729
World Cultures, 717-729
World Health Organization, 295
World Heritage List, 729
World Map Collection, 274
World Music, 481
World News, 500
World of Coca-Cola, 86
World Organizations, 520
World Paleomagnetic Database, 277
World Skiing, 661
World War I Poetry, 544
World War II, 304
World War II Documents, 304
World Wide Web Access Point, 356
World Wide Web by Electronic Mail, 357
World Wide Web Home, 357
World Wide Web of Sports, 661
World Wide Web Worm, 357
World Youth Baseball, 661
Worldwide Education Net, 195
Worldwide Usenet, 702
Wrestler List, 661
Wright, Steven, 561

Wright, Steven, Quote Server, 327
Writer Resource Guide, 399
Writers, 731
Writing, 729-731
WSGopher, 622
Wuthering Heights, 416
WWPing, 127

X

X-10 Protocol, 615
X-Files, The, 685
X-Men, 97
X-Rated Movies, 736
X-Rated Page, 736
X-Rated Resources, 732-736
X-Ray Web Server, 669
X Window Image Utilities, 634
X Window Software Index, 137
X Window Source Archives, 634
x4war, 255
x4war Players, 255
Xanth Series, 598
xearth Graphics Software, 168
Xenix, 510, 516
Xerox Corporation, 149
Xerox Map Viewer, 274
xgrabsc: X Window Utility, 634
Xinu, 507
Xpilot Game, 41
xsokoban, 255
XTC, 490
Xtoys, 638
Xtoys Gallery, 146
xv, 634

Y

Yale Peabody Museum of Natural History, 58
Yarn, 151
Yarn Server, 338
Yeast, 58
Yeats, William Butler, 404
Yiddish, 729
Yoga, 295
Young and the Restless, The, 685
Young People Talk, 739
Your Complete Guide to Credit, 149
YourMom, 328
Youth, 737-739
ytalk, 634
Yugoslavian Information, 729

Z

Z39.50 Resources, 127
Zarf's List of Interactive Games on the Web, 255
Zebrafish Information Server, 58
Zen, 463, 536
Zen and the Art of the Internet, 119
Zen Buddhist Texts, 575
ZIB Electronic Library, 615
Zine Discussion, 745
Zine Lists, 745
Zine Reviews, 745
Zines, 745
Zines, 740-745
Zip Codes of the U.S., 274
Zmodem, 615
Zoo Atlanta, 746
Zoological Resources, 746
Zoology, 745-746
Zoroastrianism, 576